EDUCATION AND SOCIOLOGY
AN ENCYCLOPEDIA

ADVISORY BOARD

EDUCATION AND SOCIOLOGY AN ENCYCLOPEDIA

DAVID L. LEVINSON

General Editor

Bergen Community College

Peter W. Cookson, Jr.

Co-editor

Teachers College
Columbia University

Alan R. Sadovnik

Co-editor

Rutgers University

ROUTLEDGEFALMER

NEW YORK LONDON

Published in 2002 by
RoutledgeFalmer
29 West 35th Street
New York, NY 10001

Published in Great Britain by
RoutledgeFalmer
11 New Fetter Lane
London EC4P 4EE

RoutledgeFalmer is an imprint of the Taylor & Francis Group

10 9 8 7 6 5 4 3 2 1

Library of Congress Cataloging-in-Publication Data

Education and sociology : an encyclopedia / editors, David L. Levinson, Peter W. Cookson, Jr., Alan R. Sadovnik.
     p.   cm.
   Includes bibliographical references and index.
   ISBN 0-815-31615-1 (alk. paper)
   1. Educational sociology—Encyclopedias.   1. Levinson, David L.   II. Cookson, Jr., Peter W.
III. Sadovnik, Alan R.

LC189.95.E38 2001
306.43—dc21   00-066486

CONTENTS

ACKNOWLEDGMENTS   xiii

PREFACE   xv

LIST OF CONTRIBUTORS   xvii

EDUCATION AND SOCIOLOGY: AN INTRODUCTION   1
David L. Levinson and Alan R. Sadovnik

ADOLESCENCE AND SCHOOLS   17
Nancy Lesko, Roberta Jentes-Mason, and Jolanda Westerhof-Shultz

ADULT EDUCATION   23
Peter Katopes

AFFIRMATIVE ACTION IN EDUCATION   29
Roslyn Arlin Mickelson

AFRICAN-AMERICAN ACHIEVEMENT MOTIVATION   43
Margaret Hunter and Walter R. Allen

AT-RISK STUDENTS   49
Gary Natriello

BILINGUAL EDUCATION   55
Virginia Vogel Zanger

BROWN V. BOARD OF EDUCATION   67
Jennifer L. Hochschild

CATHOLIC SCHOOLS   75
Helen M. Marks

CLASSROOM PROCESSES   83
Elizabeth G. Cohen

CODE THEORY, PEDAGOGIC DISCOURSE, AND SYMBOLIC CONTROL   89
Alan R. Sadovnik

COMMUNITY COLLEGES   99
Kevin J. Dougherty

CONFLICT THEORY   111
Christopher J. Hurn

COOPERATIVE LEARNING IN ELEMENTARY AND SECONDARY SCHOOLS   115
Robert E. Slavin

CULTURAL CAPITAL   121
Timothy J. Madigan

CURRICULUM   125
Adam Gamoran

CURRICULUM HISTORY   133
Ivor F. Goodson

DESEGREGATION   141
Stephen Samuel Smith

DESEGREGATION OF HIGHER EDUCATION   151
Faith G. Paul

ECONOMICS OF EDUCATION   169
Ivar Berg

EDUCATIONAL ACHIEVEMENT AND ATTAINMENT
IN THE UNITED STATES   181
Thomas M. Smith

EDUCATIONAL ASSESSMENT   191
Leslie C. Soodak

EDUCATIONAL ATTITUDES: ABSTRACT AND CONCRETE   199
Roslyn Arlin Mickelson

EDUCATIONAL PRODUCTIVITY   203
Mark Berends

EDUCATIONAL REFORM AND SOCIOLOGY IN ENGLAND AND WALES   211
Geoffrey Walford

EDUCATIONAL REFORM IN THE UNITED STATES: 1980s AND 1990s   221
Alan R. Sadovnik, Peter W. Cookson, Jr., Susan F. Semel, and David L. Levinson

ELITES AND EDUCATIONAL REFORM   235
Peter W. Cookson, Jr. and Brenda Donly

EQUALITY IN EDUCATION   241
Maureen T. Hallinan

ETHNICITY   247
Edith W. King

ETHNOGRAPHY   255
Peter McLaren and Amanda Datnow

EXTRACURRICULAR ACTIVITIES   261
Pamela Anne Quiroz

FUNCTIONALIST THEORIES OF EDUCATION   267
Peter W. Cookson, Jr. and Alan R. Sadovnik

GENDER AND EDUCATION   273
Sara Delamont

GENDER AND MATH EDUCATION   281
Karen Karp

GENDER INEQUALITY   289
Linda Grant and Xue Lan Rong

GENDER INEQUALITY IN EDUCATION: INTERNATIONAL COMPARISONS   295
Karen Bradley

GENDER SOCIALIZATION AND EDUCATION:
WHERE WE'VE BEEN AND WHERE WE MIGHT GO   301
Joan Z. Spade

GLOBALIZATION   307
John Boli

HIGH SCHOOL DROPOUTS   315
Aaron M. Pallas

HIGHER EDUCATION   321
Floyd M. Hammack

HIGHER EDUCATION: INTERNATIONAL   329
James C. Hearn and Jan Sandor

HIGHER EDUCATION AND SOCIAL EQUALITY   335
Sophia Catsambis

HIGHER EDUCATION IN THE UNITED STATES: ACCESS TO BY MINORITIES   343
Thomas M. Smith

HIGHER EDUCATION IN THE UNITED STATES: LATINOS   353
Susan Moreno and Chandra Muller

HISTORICALLY BLACK COLLEGES   359
Joseph O. Jewell and Walter R. Allen

HOME SCHOOLING: CONTEMPORARY   365
Maralee Mayberry

HOMELESS CHILDREN AND YOUTH   371
Roslyn Arlin Mickelson

HUMAN CAPITAL THEORY   377
David L. Levinson

IDEOLOGY AND CURRICULUM   381
Yoshiko Nozaki and Michael W. Apple

IMPERIALISM AND EDUCATION   387
Mark B. Ginsburg and Thomas Clayton

INTERNATIONAL COMPETITION AND EDUCATION CRISES:
CROSS-NATIONAL STUDIES OF SCHOOL OUTCOMES   393
David P. Baker

IQ   399
Christopher J. Hurn

LONGITUDINAL STUDIES: AN INTRODUCTION: OPENING THE BLACK BOX   403
Kathryn S. Schiller

LONGITUDINAL STUDIES DATA COLLECTION PROGRAM   409
Carl Schmidt

MAGNET SCHOOLS IN URBAN EDUCATION   421
Rolf K. Blank

MASS SCHOOLING   429
Francisco O. Ramirez

MERITOCRACY   435
Thomas B. Hoffer

MULTICULTURALISM   443
Patricia Gandara

POLITICS OF EDUCATION   451
Kevin J. Dougherty

PROGRESSIVE EDUCATION   463
Susan F. Semel

QUASI-MARKETS IN EDUCATION   473
Geoff Whitty

RACE AND EDUCATION   485
Roslyn Arlin Mickelson

RESTRUCTURING   495
Peter M. Hall and Patrick J. W. McGinty

SCHOOL-BASED MANAGEMENT: WHAT IT IS AND DOES IT MAKE A DIFFERENCE   501
Priscilla Wohlstetter, Kerri L. Briggs, and Amy Van Kirk

SCHOOL CHOICE   507
Amy Stuart Wells

SCHOOL EFFECTS   519
Roger C. Shouse

SCHOOL, FAMILY, AND COMMUNITY PARTNERSHIPS   525
Joyce L. Epstein and Mavis G. Sanders

SCHOOL TEXTBOOKS AND CULTURAL AUTHORITY   533
Sandra L. Wong

SINGLE-SEX EDUCATION AND COEDUCATION   539
Helen M. Marks

SOCIAL CAPITAL: A UBIQUITOUS EMERGING CONCEPTION   545
Barbara Schneider

SOCIAL REPRODUCTION   551
David Swartz

SOCIOLOGY OF EDUCATION AS CRITICAL THEORY   559
Michael Young

SOCIOLOGY OF EDUCATION: FEMINIST PERSPECTIVES: CONTINUITY AND
CONTESTATION IN THE FIELD   571
Jo-Anne Dillabough and Madeleine Arnot

SOCIOLOGY OF EDUCATION: MARXIST THEORIES   587
Fred L. Pincus

SOCIOLOGY OF EDUCATION: NEW   593
Philip Wexler

SOCIOLOGY OF EDUCATION: OPEN SYSTEMS APPROACH   599
Jeanne H. Ballantine

SOCIOLOGY OF EDUCATION: POSTMODERNISM   605
Alan R. Sadovnik

SOCIOLOGY OF EDUCATION: THEORETICAL APPROACHES   613
Jeanne H. Ballantine

SPECIAL EDUCATION   619
Hugh Mehan, Jane R. Mercer, and Robert Rueda

SPORT AND SCHOOLING   625
C. Roger Rees

STRUCTURALISM   633
Paul Atkinson

STUDENT CULTURES AND ACADEMIC ACHIEVEMENT   639
Sandra L. Wong

SUMMER LEARNING   645
Barbara Heyns

TEACHER ASSESSMENT AND EVALUATION   651
Richard M. Ingersoll

TEACHER BURNOUT   659
A. Gary Dworkin

TEACHER UNIONS, OLD AND NEW   665
Ronald Henderson

TEACHERS AND TEACHING   681
Bruce J. Biddle and Thomas L. Good

TRACKING   687
Amanda Datnow and Robert Cooper

URBAN SCHOOLS   693
Julia Gwynne

VOCATIONAL EDUCATION   705
James E. Rosenbaum

WORKING PARENTS   711
Chandra Muller

INDEX   717

*For the students, faculty, and staff
of Bergen Community College*

ACKNOWLEDGMENTS

The gestation of this book spanned many more years than could have possibly been imagined when it commenced in the spring of 1993. Marie Ellen Larcada, our original editor at Garland Publishing, launched this project. It was Marie Ellen's enthusiasm, zeal, and belief in its importance that sustained the book through the new millennium.

Our contributors stood with us through what for many (including us) seemed like an eternity! Throughout this toil, they provided a relentless bastion of support and goodwill. Our advisory board played a critical role in defining the scope of this project and offered invaluable suggestions along the way.

Karita dos Santos, Andrew Bailis, and Joe Miranda at RoutledgeFalmer provided a much needed boost at the end. Through her organizational prowess, Robin Harvison meticulously assembled all eighteen hundred–plus manuscript pages and was instrumental getting the book into publishable form.

David wishes to especially thank Shana, Emily, and his dear wife, Evan, for putting up with the trials and tribulations of this project. Hopefully the next one will be easier!

PREFACE

According to the *Oxford English Dictionary*, the word encyclopedia connotes a "circle of learning; a general course of instruction."[1] It is in this spirit that this encyclopedia was developed. Rather than offering an array of simplistic definitions from A to Z, this volume provides the reader with provocative treatments on topics that make up a vibrant sociology of education. As such we make no claim that this text will completely cover the vast amount of subject matter that constitutes the writings of educational sociologists. Rather we thought that it would be more appropriate to take stock of what we consider to be key topics in the sociology of education.

The reader will find a provocative treatment of topics ranging from adolescence and schools to working parents. Authors range from established scholars in the sociology of education to researchers who are just beginning their careers. What they all share is a passion for the sociology of education, which we are sure will be infectious upon reading this volume. Enjoy!

---

[1] *The Compact Oxford English Dictionary*, p. 153. My thanks to Carolyn Prager for enlightening my understanding of what is meant by "encyclopedia." D. L. L.

LIST OF CONTRIBUTORS

Walter R. Allen
University of California, Los Angeles

Michael W. Apple
University of Wisconsin at Madison

Madeleine Arnot
University of Cambridge, England

Paul Atkinson
University of Wales, Cardiff

David P. Baker
Pennsylvania State University

Jeanne H. Ballantine
Wright State University
Dayton, Ohio

Mark Berends
Rand Corporation

Ivar Berg
University of Pennsylvania

Bruce J. Biddle
University of Missouri

Rolf K. Blank
Council of Chief State School Officers
Washington, D.C.

John Boli
Emory University

Karen Bradley
Western Washington University

Kerri L. Briggs
University of Southern California

Sophia Catsambis
Queens College, City University of New York

Thomas Clayton
University of Kentucky

Elizabeth G. Cohen
Stanford University

Peter W. Cookson, Jr.
Teachers College, Columbia University

Robert Cooper
Johns Hopkins University

Amanda Datnow
Ontario Institute for Studies in Education
University of Toronto

Sara Delamont
University of Wales, Cardiff

Jo-Anne Dillabough
Ontario Institute for Studies in Education
University of Toronto

Brenda Donly
Georgetown University

Kevin J. Dougherty
Teachers College, Columbia University

A. Gary Dworkin
University of Houston

Joyce L. Epstein
Johns Hopkins University

Adam Gamoran
University of Wisconsin, Madison

Patricia Gandara
University of California, Davis

Mark B. Ginsburg
University of Pittsburgh

Thomas L. Good
University of Missouri

Ivor F. Goodson
University of British Columbia

Linda Grant
University of Georgia

Julia Gwynne
University of Chicago

Peter M. Hall
University of Missouri-Columbia

Maureen T. Hallinan
University of Notre Dame

Floyd M. Hammack
New York University

James C. Hearn
University of Minnesota

Ronald Henderson
National Education Association

Barbara Heyns
New York University

Jennifer L. Hochschild
Princeton University

Thomas B. Hoffer
National Opinion Research Center
University of Chicago

Margaret Hunter
University of California, Los Angeles

Christopher J. Hurn
University of Massachusetts/Amherst

Richard M. Ingersoll
University of Georgia

Roberta Jentes-Mason
Indiana University at Bloomington

Joseph O. Jewell
University of California, Los Angeles

Karen Karp
University of Louisville

Peter Katopes
Adelphi University

Edith W. King
University of Denver

Nancy Lesko
Indiana University at Bloomington

David L. Levinson
Bergen Community College
New Jersey

Timothy J. Madigan
Shippensburg University
Pennsylvania

Helen M. Marks
The Ohio State University

Maralee Mayberry
University of Nevada
Las Vegas

Patrick J. W. McGinty
University of Missouri-Columbia

Peter McLaren
University of California, Los Angeles

Hugh Mehan
University of California, San Diego

Jane R. Mercer
University of California, Riverside

Roslyn Arlin Mickelson
University of North Carolina at Charlotte

Susan Moreno
University of Texas at Austin

Chandra Muller
University of Texas at Austin

Gary Natriello
Teachers College, Columbia University

Yoshiko Nozaki
University of Wisconsin at Madison

Aaron M. Pallas
Teachers College, Columbia University

Faith G. Paul
The Public Policy Research Consortium

Fred L. Pincus
University of Maryland Baltimore County

Pamela Anne Quiroz
University of Illinois, Chicago

Francisco O. Ramirez
Stanford University

C. Roger Rees
Adelphi University

Xue Lan Rong
University of North Carolina

James E. Rosenbaum
Northwestern University

Robert Rueda
University of Southern California

Alan R. Sadovnik
Rutgers University-Newark

Mavis G. Sanders
Johns Hopkins University

Jan Sandor
University of Minnesota

Kathryn S. Schiller
State University of New York at Albany

Carl Schmidt
The National Center for Education Statistics

Barbara Schneider
The University of Chicago

Susan F. Semel
City College of New York

Roger C. Shouse
The Pennsylvania State University

Robert E. Slavin
Johns Hopkins University

Thomas M. Smith
Peabody College, Vanderbilt University

Stephen Samuel Smith
Winthrop University
South Carolina

Leslie C. Soodak
Rutgers University

Joan Z. Spade
State University of New York at Brockport

David Swartz
Boston University

Amy Van Kirk
University of Southern California

Geoffrey Walford
University of Oxford

Amy Stuart Wells
University of California, Los Angeles

Jolanda Westergof-Shultz
Indiana University, Bloomington

Philip Wexler
University of Rochester

Geoff Whitty
University of London

Priscilla Wohlstetter
University of Southern California

Sandra L. Wong
Wesleyan University
Connecticut

Michael Young
University of London

Virginia Vogel Zanger
The Boston Children's Museum

EDUCATION AND SOCIOLOGY

AN INTRODUCTION

David L. Levinson
Bergen Community College

Alan R. Sadovnik
Rutgers University

The recurring effort to improve the school despite the massive evidence that reforms generally do not change the schools very much or make them more effective in achieving their goals reveals the enormous faith in schooling that characterizes modern society. (Boli, 1989:49)

Political leaders habitually turn to the school as the institutional antidote for a variety of social ills and as a stage upon which Western ideals and moral commitments can be debated and ritualistically enacted. (Fuller and Rubinson, 1992:3)

Over the past two decades, educational policymakers in the United States and other industrialized countries have instituted a variety of reforms aimed at increasing academic achievement. The debates over these reforms have often revolved around the impact of increased standards on equality of opportunity and social justice. Unfortunately, many of these debates occur in the absence of a careful consideration of empirical evidence; or the ideological interpretation of such evidence is so politicized that educational policies often have far reaching consequences for groups of children, particularly those from lower socioeconomic backgrounds. Although sociologists of education have been tangentially part of the policymaking process, for the most part educational policy has not benefited from the insights and findings of sociological research on education, despite the rich array of studies conducted over the past 30 years. Often dismissed as irrelevant or written in academic jargon (Cookson, 1987), sociological research on education has too often been overlooked. The purpose of this volume is to demonstrate the value of theory and research in the sociology of education for understanding complex issues facing educational systems, as well as to indicate that the relationship between society and schooling is far more complex than educational policymakers often assume. Most importantly, the articles in this volume support the principal tenet of the sociology of educa-

tion: that schools must be understood in the larger context of the society and social relations of the society in which they exist and that school reforms aimed at schools alone will be insufficient to produce significant change. Although sociologists of education do not suggest that school-based reforms are thus doomed to failure, they do suggest that school reform is a necessary but not sufficient condition for significant school improvement, especially for children from low socioeconomic backgrounds.

At the dawning of a new millennium, there is compelling evidence of growing social inequality throughout Organization for Economic Development (OECD) countries.[1] Within many there has been a significant decline in manufacturing employment (Alderson, 1997), an overall pattern of deindustrialization (Bluestone and Harrison, 1982), and high rates of unemployment (Sen, 1997). The liberalization of trade has been closely linked to growing economic inequality (Power, 1997) as poverty increases in many countries where a low-wage workforce fuels global development (Human Development Report, 1997; Kapstein, 1996). The new realities of globalization, warns the International Monetary Fund (IMF), signal a need to abandon

---

[1] A total of 29 nations currently belong to OECD. See the OECD Homepage http://www.oecd.org for additional information about member nations and OECD as an organization.

policies designed to promote social equality (International Monetary Fund, 1997:55).

In the United States, there are numerous signs that inequality is expanding (Burtless, 1996a; Danzinger and Gottschalk, 1993; Gottschalk and Joyce, 1995). Recent studies of the distribution of income and wealth in the United States support the adage that the "rich are getting richer and the poor are getting poorer" (Mishel et al., 1997; Levy, 1988; Wolff, 1995). The literal disappearance of work for the disadvantaged (Wilson, 1996) and what may portend as a fundamental restructuring of work in a technologically intensive world (Aronowitz and DiFazio, 1994; Rifkin, 1995) represent a plethora of social conditions that increasingly stratify citizens.

Schools are a pandora's box for visualizing a number of conundrums currently facing liberal democratic societies. While open access and inclusion are increasingly the operative norm for primary, secondary, and higher education, inequitable student achievement is pervasive. Although schools play a prominent role as ubiquitous gateways for attaining cultural and cognitive prerequisites for citizenship, schools engage in elaborate selection and sorting processes that reflect and reproduce social inequality. Despite espousing an ideological adherence to meritocratic standards of assessment, evaluation practices continue to be shaped by larger systemic needs for social differentiation and control (Broadfoot, 1996).

To a large extent, these contradictions emanate from the oppositional qualities of liberalism and democracy. Whereas liberalism promotes the realization of individual self-interest via a free market, democracy, states Alan Wolfe, is anticapitalistic for "it stands for participation and equality" (Wolfe, 1977, 3).[2] Bringing this contradiction to bear upon education, Broadfoot states: "this Tocquevillean dilemma, this tension between liberalism and democracy, between the democratic demand for leveling and the continuing existence of inequalities, tends to generate expectations and needs which the educational system is necessarily unable to meet" (1996:222).

Schools embody many of the tensions and contradictions found in contemporary liberal democratic societies. Although through compulsory schooling nation states mandate education as a social right of citizenship, there is no guarantee that the outcome of educational processes will be equitable. In the United States, educational appropriations vary widely and impact negatively on the poor (U.S. Government Accounting Office, 1996; Kozol, 1991; Parrish, 1996; Swan, 1995). Although schools offer the promise of being inclusive and meritocratic (Hoffer,[3] p. 435) schools often sort and track students in ways that reproduce and exacerbate social inequality (Datnow and Cooper, this volume, p. 687; Foster et al., 1996; Oakes, 1985).

Sociologists of education in the United States (Dreeben, 1994) and United Kingdom (Bernstein, 1996; Foster et al., 1996) have historically been concerned with issues pertaining to stratification and inequality. However, the conceptualization of this problem has vacillated between institutional and individual explanations. As Bidwell and Friedkin (1988:450) state: "Although the concern for relationships between education and social stratification persists, attention has shifted from institutional topics to an individual-centered analysis of the sources of educational attainments and of the contribution of these attainments to status inheritance and social mobility." While structural dimensions of inequality have been the subject of much contemporary sociological analysis of educational processes (Bowles and Gintis, 1976; Collins, 1979), there are vestiges of individualism in recent formulations of human capital theory that often center on individual determinants of upward social mobility (Fagerlind and Saha, 1989). To some extent this parallels the status attainment research of the 1960s where a father's occupational status was viewed as key for the upward mobility of sons (Blau and Duncan, 1967).

In this volume, Hallinan reviews (p. 241) the different ways in which sociologists have conceptualized educational inequality. Cookson and Sadovnik (this volume, p. 267) discuss how the functionalism of Emile Durkheim influenced the formulation of approaches, such as status attainment research, for studying in-

---

[2] Lindblom (1977) expressed this as the tension between politics and markets, a construct used effectively by David Labaree (1988) in his analysis of the tensions between learning and occupational preparation in the history of American education.

---

[3] Reference to an author solely by name and page number refers to an article in this volume.

equality.[4] Conflict theory also has a long lineage in the sociology of education (Hurn, 1993) and has manifested itself in diverse forms such as Samuel Bowles and Herbert Gintis' *Schooling in Capitalist America* (1976) and Randall Collins' *The Credential Society* (1979). Hurn (1993; this volume, p. 111) reviews how conflict theory offers a view of educational inequality that is in opposition to functionalism. Given the growing inequalities at the century's end, the sociology of education can make important contributions to understanding and perhaps ameliorating such conditions. However, it is imperative to first have an understanding of what we mean by the sociology of education.

Defining the Sociology of Education

Defining the sociology of education is not an easy task. Varying theoretical frameworks and methodologies comprise what has been a centenary enterprise. Initially steeped in a larger disciplinary problematic of social control and social order, sociologists of education have studied numerous aspects of educational processes. Similar to its parent discipline, the sociology of education is not a cauldron of theoretical, methodological, or empirical uniformity. In fact, some assert that the absence of a unifying perspective and a willingness to transcend disciplinary boundaries (Apple, 1996) provide the sociology of education with its intellectual "promise" (Mills, 1959). Pink and Noblit (1995) assert that the discipline's five concurrent analytical perspectives—empirical, applied, interpretive, critical, and postmodern—give the sociology of education its vitality.

As with any body of knowledge, the sociology of education is in a constant state of flux as a growing ensemble of empirical and theoretical research continually modifies its contours. Witness how the "new sociology of education" brought the social construction of knowledge to the forefront of curriculum studies (Wexler, p. 593). Similarly, the new institutionalism in organizational analysis (DiMaggio and Powell, 1991) has enlarged our understanding of organizational nuances, institutional resilience, and legitimacy by

focusing on the importance of cultural and ideological factors (Crowson et al., 1996).

Authors of recent texts in the sociology of education find that the "3 Ds"—divergence, disagreement, and difference—typify the subfield. Whether it be the *limits and possibilities* of schooling (Hurn, 1993), the paradox of *equality and achievement* (Riordan, 1997), the *continuities and contradiction* found in the sociology of education (Pink and Noblit, 1995), or the dichotomy of *freedom and constraint* (Mulkey, 1993), a multiplicity of perspectives and foci are viewed as evidence of analytical gusto (Ballantine, 1997).

What a given body of knowledge "looks like" also depends on the observer's vantage point. The assessment and evaluation of any collection of work are themselves a social construct and must be judged within the particular temporal and spatial context of the analyst. *Education and Sociology* appears during a time of tremendous interest in educational reform. The ascendance of human capital theory and the new skill requirements engendered by a high tech economy require an understanding of how schools will prepare students for the changing nature of work. Although much educational policy is based on the assumption that all students need high level thinking and technological skills for the new economy, policymakers too often accept a functionalist, human capital approach uncritically. For example, the fact that the number of high skilled jobs produced will be less than the unskilled jobs they replace may lead to significant disjunctions between what schools teach and what the economy may require from large groups of workers.

Robert Dreeben notes the following paradox in tracing the development of the sociology of education in the United States:

> in the early years, when those who wrote about sociology and education addressed matters of educational practice and policy, their influence was negligible. Later, when they ceased being direct and hortative about such matters and their interests turned in a more scholarly direction, the temper of the times had changed and their work became drawn into the public arena. (Dreeben, 1994:7–8)

Although there is an extensive body of research on many facets of education, relatively little filters into the

---

[4] It is also interesting to note how Durkheim's work continues to influence educational research as seen in Phillip W. Jackson, Robert E. Boostrom, and David Hansen's *The Moral Life of Schools*. San Francisco: Jossey-Bass, 1993.

U.S. policy arena.[5] While there are a number of insightful analyses about this problem (Cookson, 1987; Epstein, 2000), along with recent efforts to unite scholarship and practice,[6] educational reforms in the United States continue to suffer from this lacuna.[7] Yet schools are typically depicted as forlorn institutions, devoid of effective educational practices. What accounts for this? Isn't it ironic, though at the same time laudable, that the theme of the 1997 American Educational Research Association (AERA) Annual meeting was "Talking Together in Educational Research and Practice?"

What has prevented this from occurring? If the sociology of education is to influence policy formation, it must do a better job of communicating with the practitioner, legislator, parent, and student. It is ironic, given the Latin root of the word, education is *educere* —to lead forth—that sociologists of education play second fiddle to pundits whose reform proposals are often devoid of empirical research and theoretical understanding. Part of the problem is the way in which educational problems have been defined in the public arena over the past two decades.

Education for a High-Skilled Workforce

Although the "symbolic analysts" (Reich, 1991) increasingly prosper, there is a danger that swelling structural barriers will prevent many from accessing the cognitive skills needed to prosper in a knowledge-intensive, information-based economy.

There is much ado about nations producing the human capital required for competing in an increasingly technologically intensive global economy. Psacharopoulos (1995) argues that increasing investment in human capital by nations throughout the world will produce a higher standard of living, decrease poverty levels, and promote overall economic growth. Marc Tucker, president of the National Center on Education

and the Economy, is even more emphatic when he states that

> Knowledge—and the capacity to put knowledge to good use—is now the only dependable source of wealth all over the world. The people, organizations and nations that succeed will be those that make the most of the human desire and capacity for never-ending learning.[8]

A recent OECD (1997) report asserts that an insufficiently educated workforce threatens economic expansion in advanced capitalistic societies. The World Bank (1997:89) contends that investing in education, especially in the primary level, "is an important determinant of subsequent growth." Studies such as the Commission on the Skills of the American Workforce's *America's Choice: High School or Low Wages!* (1990), the Hudson Institute's *Workforce 2000* (1987), and the sequel *Workforce 2020* (1997) underscore the centrality of an educated workforce for an increasingly high-skilled economy. Numerous reports from organizations such as the *Business-Higher Education Forum* and *Committee for Economic Development* underscore the need for closer intertwined partnerships between educational institutions and corporations in order to facilitate school-to-work transitions (Rosenbaum, p. 705). Similarly, many contend that instruction in the "new basic skills" (Murnane and Levy, 1996) is direly needed for a high-tech society.

One of the defining moments of contemporary civilization is the global provision of mass schooling (Ramirez, this volume). Increasingly provided as a right of citizenship (Ramirez and Ventresca, 1992), nation states have steadily expanded the public provision of education throughout the nineteenth and twentieth centuries. Although it appears that national prosperity and individual social mobility will increasingly hinge on education throughout the next century, many advanced nations are beginning to question whether they can afford to provide universal access to what is an increasing costly social resource—education. A burgeoning "fiscal crisis of the state" (O'Connor, 1973) has lead to a litany of quasi-market solutions (Whitty, p. 473) to this growing problem.

---

[5] The influence of sociology on policy formation varies by national context. See the *British Journal of Sociology of Education,* Special Number (7): International Perspectives on the Sociology of Education, Volume 17, Number 2, June 1996.

[6] For example, see *Sociology of Education* extra 1996 issue and Borman et al. (1996).

[7] This vexing problem was at the heart of the 1997 American Educational Research Association (AERA) Annual Meeting theme "Talking Together in Educational Research and Practice."

---

[8] National Center on Education and the Economy Web Page http://www.ncee.org/WhoWeAre/whoPage.html, December 1997.

The apocalyptic vision offered by Michael Young in *The Rise of the Meritocracy* (1958) some 40 years ago is proving to be partly true (Bluestone, 1995). Fictitiously set in the years 1870–2033, Young predicts that a society based solely on technical competence and merit (Hoffer, p. 435) and devoid of racism and "sponsored mobility" (Turner, 1960) would increasingly produce inequitable outcomes. Departing from Young's prophecy, racism continues to subvert upward mobility for blacks (Oliver and Shapiro, 1995) and class advantage continues to reproduce privilege (Cookson and Persell, 1985).

Beyond social class inequities, racial and gender differentials remain omnipotent. Beginning with *Brown v. Board of Education* (Hochschild, p. 67), there have been numerous judicial rulings and legislative attempts to mitigate racial segregation (Mickelson, p. 485; Paul, p. 151; Smith, p. 141) and promote affirmative action (Mickelson, p. 29) in the United States. However, recent studies indicate that segregation is on the rise (Orfield, 1996), affirmative action is being attacked, and the persistence of racial inequality shows few signs of abating (Oliver and Shapiro, 1995). Incessant conflict over bilingual education (Zanger, p. 55) and ceaseless debates over multiculturalism (Gandara, p. 443) speak to the unresolved tensions surrounding ethnic and racial pluralism. Although wage differentials between men and women in the United States are somewhat abating (Mishel et al. 1997:147–148), women continue to face formidable barriers in the workplace (Federal Glass Ceiling Commission, 1995; Rhode, 1997).

Organizations such as the OECD (1997) and the World Bank (1997) continue to maintain that educational spending can promote equity, especially in terms of how an educated, skilled workforce can enhance gross domestic production (GDP) and improve a nation's ability to compete in an increasingly global marketplace. Growing wage inequities in advanced economies, asserts the International Monetary Fund (1997), reflect a bifurcation of skill levels that can be corrected by viable educational programs.

But is this a viable strategy? Does it reflect an ideological rather than pragmatic truism? Can schools make a difference (Shouse, p. 512)? Hanushek et al. (1994), for example, argue that spending is not necessarily the answer; rather, accountability and performance-based rewards are what matters (Burtless, 1996b; Ladd, 1996). Whose interests are served in the proliferation of school–corporate partnerships (Shea et al., 1989)? These remain fertile issues for the sociology of education.

Sociologists of education have introduced a number of conceptual domains such as cultural capital (Madigan, p. 121) and social capital (Coleman, 1988; Schneider, p. 545) that have enhanced the study of stratification. Farkas (1996) presents an innovative matrix of these formulations in his study of ethnicity and poverty in an urban school district. Borjas (1992) asserts that ethnic capital is an important variable to consider with respect to how "skills and earnings are transmitted across generations" (124). Borjas concludes:

> Ethnicity acts as an externality in the production function for human capital. In particular, the quality of the ethnic environment in which a person is raised, which I call ethnic capital, influences the skills and labor market outcomes of the children. This human capital externality, similar to those that motivate much of the new economic growth literature and also similar to the concept of 'social capital in the sociology literature, indicates that differences in skills and labor market outcomes among ethnic groups may persist across generations, and need never converge.' (p. 148)

Borjas refers to Coleman's concept of "social capital" where "the culture in which the individual is raised, which can be thought of as a form of human capital common to all members of that group, alters his opportunity set, and has significant effects of behavior, human capital formation, and labor market outcomes" (pp. 126–127).

Roslyn Mickelson's formulation of abstract/concrete attitudes (Mickelson, p. 199) provides an important conceptual apparatus for uniting a number of seemingly disparate dimensions in the study of stratification. Basil Bernstein's work on linguistic codes also provides an avenue for bridging all too often unfortunate bifurcated accounts of micro- and macro-social processes (Sadovnik, 1995b; this volume, p. 605).

Enmeshed in the debate over school effects (Shouse, p. 519) is whether and how schools matter. Sociologists have made important contributions to this debate by recognizing social and cultural factors that rest outside of schools.

What is often missing from the educational reform literature is recognition of the importance of social capital for social mobility (Schneider, p. 545; Farkas, 1996). This is especially evident upon seeing that individualistic, market-based educational reforms (Whitty, p. 473) continue to grow in popularity despite widespread concern about the erosion of civic life and community (Bellah et al., 1985, 1991; Etzioni, 1993; Lesko, 1988; Putnam, 2000). The dominance of markets over politics, a tension whose analytical prowess was effectively used to explain the rise of secondary schools (Labaree, 1988), aptly describes much of contemporary educational reform. Comments Robert Kuttner about the remains of the welfare state at the end of the twentieth century: "Unfettered markets are deemed both the essence of human liberty, and the most expedient route to prosperity" (Kuttner, 1996:3). Articulating one of the central dilemmas of modern liberalism, John Hall asks: "How can social cohesion . . . be created and maintained if actors are dedicated to only enhancing their self interests?" (Hall, 1987:57).

Similar concerns were raised in the aftermath of the ancien régime in the late eighteenth century. Addressing the problem of "How is social order possible?" in the context of mammoth social change, social theorists advanced explanations that coalesced on issues that have become central problems in the sociology of education: social mobility, social reproduction, and the social construction of knowledge. A scientifically engineered meritocracy where "idlers would be punished and people would be paid according to the wealth they produce" (Martindale, 1981:75) was advanced by Henri de Saint-Simon as the raison d'état for a new social order. Positivism, argued Auguste Comte, not only provided a construct for knowledge in the "Age of Reason" but provided the working class with moral sustenance equivalent to the teachings of the Catholic Church during medieval times (Lenzer, 1975). Schools, asserted Emile Durkheim, were primary sites of moral education where children learned "discipline, attachment, and autonomy" (Cladis, 1992:198) for they provided a social environment where children learn the normative expectations of the *conscience collective* (Durkheim, 1956, 1961).

The issue of citizenship was at the heart of these discussions, as it is at the center of the politics of education (Dougherty, p. 451; Gutmann, 1987). Schools have historically played an important role in creating citizenship in liberal democratic societies. As John Boli states: "schooling is the major initiation ceremony, or rite of passage, of modern society" (Boli, 1989:49). Citizenship can be defined as "the set of social practices which define social membership in a society which is highly differentiated both in its culture and social institutions, and where social solidarity can only be based upon general and universalistic standards" (Turner, 1993:5). The creation of citizenship requires an ideological apparatus that transcends the particularistic qualities of liberalism, such as self-interest and individualistic acquisitive actions. It involves the creation of obligatory demands and a social sense of interdependence, or what Dauenhauer (1996) defines as "complex citizenship," which involves a "recognition of political responsibilities to all . . . and the making of citizen competency an explicit issue."

Citizenship was of central concern to antebellum education reformers in the United States. Horace Mann, the first secretary of the Massachusetts Board of Education, argued that schooling "would lay the foundation for the responsible exercise of citizenship in a free society" (Cremin, 1980:137). The proliferation of common schools in the United States brought the hope of a "thoroughly American curriculum" that "would help unify the language and culture of the new nation and wean America away from a corrupt Europe" (Kaestle, 1983:7). During the nineteenth century public education was viewed as important for creating a virtuous moral character, not to enhance skills or positively impact on occupational attainment (Vinovskis, 1995:78).

According to T. H. Marshall, there are three dimensions of citizenship, each associated with particular historical periods in England: civil rights—eighteenth century, political rights—nineteenth century, and social rights—twentieth century (Kymlicka and Norman, 1994: 354).[9] The educational revolution, for Talcott Parsons and Gerald Platt (Parsons and Platt, 1973), produces a fourth dimension of citizenship—cultural citizenship (Turner, 1993:7; Turner, 1997:13). Pakulski (1997) extends the concept of cultural citizenship to include the following: "Full cultural citizenship is seen primarily as not a matter of legal, po-

---

[9] In a similar fashion, this typology can be applied to the development of citizenship in the United States (Parsons, 1971:21–22).

litical and socioeconomic location, but as a matter of symbolic representation, cultural-status recognition and cultural promotion" (Pakulski, 1997:80). "Throughout the history of American educational reform," states Michael Katz, "one theme has remained constant: the grandiose and unrealistic expectations that schools can solve America's social, economic, cultural, political, and moral problems" (Katz, 1987:124). If this is indeed the case, what accounts for the incessant interest in reforming education?

The discourse of reform has been ubiquitous since the 1980s. In 1983, the National Commission on Excellence in Education released *A Nation At Risk* in the United States and implementation of the 1988 Education Reform Act in the United Kingdom (Walford, p. 211) occurred. These reports, and the hundreds that followed (Ginsberg and Plank, 1995), have spurred a massive assessment of schools that has touched on items such as standards, testing, and assessment (Soodak, p. 191) and heightened interest in international comparisons of educational attainment (Baker, p. 393). The professionalization (Abbott, 1988; Larson, 1987) of reform is certainly a factor that must be considered. The tacit monopolization of knowledge on the part of professionals, the emergence of expertise as a commodity in much demand, and the cultural context for such activity (Bledstein, 1976, Brint, 1994) are deserving of further sociological analysis.

Sociologists of education have demonstrated that much of what passes for fact emerges as fiction when subject to empirical analysis (Berliner and Biddle, 1995). Reforms heralded as new and different often are little more than reincarnations of the past (Ravitch and Vinovskis, 1995; Semel, p. 463; Tyack and Cuban, 1995). A thorough, empirical analysis of educational outcomes (Smith, 1996) yields a more dynamic picture than what is typically conveyed in the popular press. Even the practice of *assessment*, often viewed as benign and value neutral, is in desperate need of sociological scrutiny (Broadfoot, 1996). Much of what passes for education reform would benefit from a sociological consideration of the process of fad and fashion (Sperber, 1990).

Educational change is a political process (Cookson and Daly, p. 235), resulting from the complex convergence of activities by policy planners, educational "experts," practitioners, and political officials (Fullan,

1991). Understanding the role of key organizational players such as foundations (Lagemann, 1983, 1989), think tanks (Peschek, 1987; Smith, 1991), and teacher unions (Murphy, 1990; Henderson, p. 665) is essential. The recent creation of "Division L—Educational Policy and Politics" as part of the American Educational Research Association (AERA) is further proof of the salience of this analytical dimension.

Organizational analysis continues to be a mainstay in the sociology of education (Meyer and Scott, 1992). The alleged severity of the current crisis in education has led many to proclaim that the organizational structure of schools needs to be radically reshaped (Cookson and Sadovnik, p. 267; Semel, p. 463; Levinson, p. 377; Walford, p. 211). Metaphors such as *reengineering*, *reinventing*, and *restructuring* (Hall and McGinty, p. 495) have become a discursive mainstay in educational policy. Works like Louis Gerstner's *Reinventing Education: Entrepreneurship in America's Public Schools* (1994), Paul Hill's *Reinventing Public Education* (1995), and Hill et al.'s *Reinventing Public Education: How Contracting Can Transform America's Schools* (1997) call for an infusion of market forces to reform education (Whitty, p. 473). Companies such as Education Alternatives, Inc. and the Edison Project attempt to profit from this line of reasoning, though their financial and service-delivery records are mixed as the twentieth century comes to a close.

Numerous alternative education-delivery schemas have been implemented such as magnet schools (Blank, p. 421), school choice (Wells, p. 507), and school-based management (Wohlstetter et al., p. 501). There has also been a reexamination of alternative educational practices such as home schooling (Mayberry, p. 365).

Educational sociologists have also explored organizational features of "successful" institutions such as Catholic schools (Coleman et al., 1982; Bryk et al., 1993). The communal orientation of these institutions, coupled with a tacit agreement on their principles and purpose by participants, largely accounts for their success (Marks, p. 75). Whether public institutions can replicate these remains to be seen. Certainly successful reform efforts, such as the Yale School Development Program, have demonstrated the importance of moral cohesion of "buy-ins" by all constituents (Comer et al., 1996). Financial constraints, open access, along with concerns over what constitutes the "common good" for a diverse, multicultural student body make it difficult for public schools to replicate the features of Catholic institutions.

Education Reform and Organizational Analysis

Race and Ethnicity

Brown v. Board of Education was a major turning point in the history of race relations and the sociology of education. As Hochschild demonstrates, this momentous U.S. Supreme Court decision not only paved the way for entirely new policy initiatives but gave rise to a rich sociological research tradition in the study of desegregation (Paul, p. 151; Smith, p. 141) and race (Mickelson, p. 405).

African-American achievement motivation is a complex phenomenon (Hunter and Allen, p. 43). Mickelson's differentiation of abstract and concrete educational attitudes (this volume, p. 199) provides a unique conceptual apparatus for understanding the linkages between achievement, self-esteem, social aspirations, and material social conditions. Tom Smith's discussion of minority groups' college aspirations and educational attainment provides an important contribution to the field.

Roslyn Mickelson's article on affirmative action (this volume, p. 29) bridges the study of school segregation, race, employment, and ethnicity (King, p. 247). Multiculturalism as discussed by Gandara (this volume, p. 443) subsumes a number of areas important for the sociology of education such as the study of immigration, assimilation, and bilingual education (Zanger, p. 55).

Gender

It is only lately that sociologists of education have paid much attention to the issue of gender (Delamont, p. 273). As discussed by Smith (this volume, p. 181), women have made considerable progress with respect to educational achievement. However, when it comes to mathematics considerable differences in proficiency remain with overall low levels of proficiency for males and females (Karp, p. 281). As Bradley (this volume, p. 295) points out, even with some of the barriers removed, women continue to select programs of study that result in lower status and lower paid occupations than men. What is especially interesting in Bradley's

article is that this occurs universally, although educational systems vary significantly across nations.

Noticeable inequities endure as sociologists of education continue to test a number of competing explanations (Grant and Rong, p. 289). Spade's analysis of gender socialization points to the perseverance of inequitable treatment in the classroom (Spade, p. 301; Maher and Tetreault, 1994) and Bradley discusses how women still congregate into programs of study that lead to relatively lower paid, lower status positions compared with their male counterparts. What is especially interesting here is how this holds true universally, although nation states vary with respect to the structure of their educational system. Dillabough and Arnot (this volume, p. 571) provide a sweeping review of existing feminist work in the sociology of education and conclude by suggesting that feminism needs to expand its account of globalization, poverty, and privatization.

Higher Education

As Hammack (this volume, p. 321) notes, sociological interest in the study of U.S. higher education dates back to Thorstein Veblen's *Higher Learning In America* (1918), which was noteworthy for its criticisms of business involvement in higher education. The tremendous expansion of higher education throughout the twentieth century has been the subject of a number of foundational works in the sociology of education such as Christopher Jencks and David Riesman's *The Academic Revolution* (1968) and Talcott Parsons and Gerald Platt's *The American University* (1973), which discussed higher education's importance for producing "cognitive competence."

Hearn and Sandor (this volume, p. 335) traces the study of higher education to the work of classical social theorists such as Max Weber and Emile Durkheim and provides fascinating conjectures about how recent developments in Eastern Europe will impact the study of higher education. Dougherty (this volume, p. 99) presents a cogent analysis of community colleges and Katopes (this volume, p. 23) considers adult students.

Curriculum

The concept of curriculum has a multitude of dimensions in the sociology of education. As Gamoran (this volume, p. 125) states, sociologists use this concept to denote everything from formal to informal processes; the key is the connection between curriculum and achievement. Gamoran makes an important point: the need for curriculum studies to bridge macro- and micro-processes. This point is also highlighted in Ballantine's discussion of learning environments (this volume, p. 613). Goodson (this volume, p. 133) makes the important point of considering this from a historical perspective, thus showing how the curriculum represents various constructs of knowledge that are indicative of a particular time.

The ideological aspects of curriculum are highlighted by Nozaki and Apple (this volume, p. 381). They show how the specific social historical material reality is important for appreciating the meaning of curriculum. Wong (this volume, p. 533) illustrates that textbooks are a major way that curriculum as ideology is transmitted.

In addition to the ideological aspects of curriculum, sociologists have examined the ways in which the formal and informal curriculum affects socialization and achievement. For example, Quiroz (this volume, p. 261) makes an important point about the extracurricula, which represent an important additional dimension of study for the sociology of education. Additionally, summer learning (Heyns, p. 645) and sports (Rees, p. 625) are two additional dimensions that are relevant for discussions on curriculum.

Teachers/Students

An important issue in the sociology of education is teachers, a concern raised by the 1986 Carnegie Commission Report, the work of the Holmes Group (Labaree, 1996), and the recent report by the National Commission on Teaching and America's Future (1996). Henderson's (this volume, p. 665) article on unionization and Dworkin's article on teacher burn-out illustrate the importance of sociological research on teachers and teaching, which examines the ways in which roles are affected by political, social, economic, and organizational forces.

Students

After the tragic school violence in Littleton, Colorado, Americans were asking why two middle class students

opened fire on their classmates and teachers, killing 13 of them. Sociologists of education have provided significant research on students and students' lives, linking the social psychology of adolescence to popular culture and school organization and processes. Lesko et al.'s article, p. 17, on adolescence, Natriello's article, p. 49, on at-risk students, Pallas's article, p. 315, on dropouts, and Katopes's article, p. 23, on adult students all provide important sociological insights into student culture and behavior.

Conclusion: The Sociology of the Sociology of Education

Analyzing the concerns of sociologists of education in the early and late twentieth century, it is striking how many themes raised in the past resonate in the present. Emile Durkheim's lectures on morality at the Sorbonne in the early 1900s (Durkheim, 1961) are embodied in Amatai Etzioni's discussion of the "communitarian school" (Etzioni, 1993:89–115). Willard Waller's analysis of schools as distinct social systems (Waller, 1965) implicitly can be found in the localized practice of educational reform by the Coalition of Essential Schools, which places the locus of change in the student–teacher relationship. Pitirim Sorokin's analysis of education, social mobility, and the role that schools play in reproducing inequality (Sorokin, 1959) is reflected in a number of critical analyses (Bowles and Gintis, 1976).

Since publication of John G. Richardson's *Handbook of Theory and Research for the Sociology of Education* (1986) much has occurred in the sociology of education. Advances on a number of theoretical,[10] methodological,[11] and empirical fronts,[12] characterize the field. Controversial studies on topics such as intelligence (Herrnstein and Murray, 1994; Hurn, p. 399), educational finance (Hanushek et al., 1994), and market competition (Chubb and Moe, 1990) have generated a

---

[10] See in this volume Atkinson on structuralism, p. 633, Hurn on conflict theory, p. 111, Pincus on Marxist theories of education, p. 587, Sadovnik on postmodernism, p. 605, Swartz on reproduction theory, p. 551, Young on critical theory, p. 559, and Wexler on the new sociology of education, p. 593.

[11] See McLaren and Datnow (this volume, p. 255) on ethnography.

[12] See in this volume Schmitt, p. 409, on High School and Beyond and Schiller, p. 403, on Longitudinal Studies.

vociferous response on the part of educational research-ers. Debates on issues such as tracking (Hallinan, 1994; Oakes, 1994; Datnow and Cooper, p. 687) and com-parative measures of educational attainment (Westbury, 1992; Baker, 1993; this volume, p. 393) have raged in educational journals.

There are a number of recent studies that illustrate how sociological studies of educational processes can point to the possibility of increasingly equitable insti-tutional arrangements. Lavin and Hyllegard (1996) demonstrate in their study of the open admissions pro-cess at the City University of New York (CUNY) that the economic prosperity of students admitted under this program overshadows concerns that open admis-sions was tantamount to an abandonment of standards. Analyzing a secondary school detracking experiment in San Diego, Mehan et al. (1996) offer a similar endorse-ment to access and equity when they find that *It is not that dumb kids are placed in slow groups or low tracks; it is that kids are made dumb by being placed into slow groups or low tracks"* (Mehan et al., 1996; emphasis in original).

Just as sociology offered the promise of a better un-derstanding of the social world at the last millennium, it provides the same opportunity as we move into the next century. Whereas at the end of the nineteenth cen-tury, Durkheim argued for the scientific understanding of society as social as an antidote to the overly individ-ualistic perspective of psychology and the overly ra-tionalistic perspective of economics, sociology today faces the increased domination of postmodernism and cultural studies (Sadovnik, 1995a; this volume, p. 605) as explanatory systems. The discipline of sociology rests on the analytical possibility of discovering patterns of social interaction that account for the construction of social life. Unlike much of postmodernism and cultural studies, it relies on empirical evidence to support its claims about society and its institutions. Hopefully, the sociology of education will continue to provide an un-derstanding of the ways in which schools and other educational institutions reproduce social stratification, as well as their potential for reducing it. Finally, socio-logical research on schools must discover the nuances of successful reform efforts (Meier, 1995; Comer, 1993b) so that all can benefit from their universal ap-plicability in what has become an increasingly polar-ized world. We hope that the articles in this volume provide the beginnings of such endeavors.

REFERENCES

Abbott, Andrew. 1988. *The System of Professions. An Essay on the Division of Expert Labor*. Chicago: University of Chicago Press.

Alderson, Arthur S. 1997. "Globalization and Deindustrial-ization: Direct Investment and the Decline of Manufac-turing Employment in 17 OECD Nations." *Journal of World-Systems Research* 3:1–34.

Apple, Michael. 1996. "Power, Meaning and Identity: Criti-cal Sociology of Education in the United States." *British Journal of Sociology of Education* 17(2):125–144.

Baker, David. 1993. "Compared to Japan, the U.S. Is a Low Achiever . . . Really." *Educational Researcher* 22 (April): 18–20.

Ballantine, Jeanne H. 1997. *The Sociology of Education: A Systematic Analysis,* 4th ed. Englewood Cliffs, NJ: Prentice-Hall.

Bennett, William J. 1988. *Our Children and Our Country. Improving America's Schools and Affirming the Common Culture.* New York: Simon & Schuster.

Bellah, Robert N., Richard Madsen, William M. Sullivan, et al. 1985. *Habits of the Heart.* Berkeley: University of California Press.

Bellah, Robert N., Richard Madsen, William M. Sullivan, et al. 1991. *The Good Society.* New York: Alfred A. Knopf.

Berger, Peter L., and Richard John Neuhaus. 1977. *To Em-power People: The Role Of Mediating Structures in Public Policy.* Washington, DC: American Enterprise Institute.

Berliner, David C., and Bruce J. Biddle. 1995. *The Manu-factured Crisis: Myths, Frauds, and the Attack on America's Public Schools.* Reading, MA: Addison-Wesley.

Bernstein, Basil. 1996. *Pedagogy, Symbolic Control and Iden-tity: Theory, Research, and Critique.* London: Taylor & Francis.

Berryman, Sue E., and Thomas R. Bailey. 1992. *The Double Helix of Education and the Economy.* Teachers College/ Columbia University: Institute on Education and the Economy.

Bidwell, Charles E., and Noah E. Friedkin. 1988. "The So-ciology of Education." In Neil J. Smelser (ed.), *Handbook of Sociology*, pp. 449–472. Newbury Park, CA: Sage.

Blau, Peter M., and Otis D. Duncan. 1967. *The American Occupational Structure.* New York: Wiley.

Bledstein, Burton J. 1976. *The Culture of Professionalism. The Middle Class and the Development of Higher Educa-tion in America.* New York. W. W. Norton.

Bloom, Allan. 1987. *The Closing of the American Mind: How Higher Education Has Failed Democracy and Impoverished the Souls of Today's Students.* New York: Simon & Schuster.

Bluestone, Barry. 1995. "The Inequality Express," *The Amer-ican Prospect* No. 20(Winter):81–93.

Bluestone, Barry, and Bennett Harrison. 1982. *The De-industrialization of America: Plant Closings, Community Abandonment, and the Dismantling of Basic Industry.* New York: Basic Books.

————. 1988. *The Great U-Turn: Corporate Restructuring and the Polarization of America*. New York: Basic Books.

Boli, John. 1989. *New Citizens for a New Society. The Institutional Origins of Mass Schooling in Sweden*. Oxford: Pergamon Press.

Borjas, George J. 1992. "Ethnic Capital and Intergenerational Mobility." *The Quarterly Journal of Economics*, 107(1).

Borman, Kathryn, Peter W. Cookson, Jr., Alan Sadovnik, and Joan Spade. 1996. *Implementing Educational Reform: Sociological Perspectives on Educational Policy*. Westport, CT: Ablex.

Bowles, Samuel, and Herbert Gintis. 1976. *Schooling in Capitalist America*. New York: Basic Books.

Brint, Steven. 1994. *In An Age of Experts*. Princeton, NJ: Princeton University Press.

Broadfoot, Patricia M. 1996. *Education, Assessment and Society*. Buckingham: Open University Press.

Burtless, Gary 1996a. Worsening American Income Inequality: Is World Trade to Blame? *The Brookings Review* 14(2):26–31.

————. (ed). 1996b. *Does Money Matter? The Link between Schools, Student Achievement, and Adult Success*. Washington, DC: The Brookings Institution.

Byrk, Anthony S., Valerie E. Lee, and Peter B. Holland. 1993. *Catholic Schools and the Common Good*. Cambridge, MA: Harvard University Press.

Chubb, John E., and Eric A. Hanushek. 1990. "Reforming Educational Reform." In Henry J. Aaron (ed.), *Setting National Priorities. Policy for the Nineties*. Washington, DC: The Brookings Institution.

Chubb, John E., and Terry M. Moe. 1990. *Politics, Markets, and America's Schools*. Washington, DC: The Brookings Institution.

Cladis, Mark S. 1992. *A Communitarian Defense of Liberalism: Emile Durkheim and Contemporary Social Theory*. Stanford, CA: Stanford University Press.

Cole, Mike (ed.) 1988. *Bowles and Gintis Revisited: Correspondence and Contradiction in Educational Theory*. London: Falmer Press.

Coleman, James. 1988. "Social Capital, Human Capital, and Schools." *Independent School*, 48(1).

Coleman, James, Tom Hoffer, and Sally Kilgore. 1982. *High School Achievement*. New York: Basic Books.

Collins, Randall. 1979. *The Credential Society*. New York: Academic Press.

Comer, James P. 1993a. *School Power: Implications of an Intervention Project*. New York: The Free Press.

————. 1993b. "Inner City Education: A Theoretical and Intervention Model." In William J. Wilson (ed.), *Sociology and the Public Agenda*. American Sociological Association Presidential Series. Newbury Park, CA: Sage.

Comer, James P., Norris M. Haynes, Edward T. Joyner and Michael Ben-Avie (eds.). 1996. *Rallying the Whole Village: The Comer Process for Reforming Education*. New York: Teachers College Press.

Commission on the Skills of the American Workforce. 1990. *America's Choice: High Skills or Low Wages!* Rochester, NY: National Center on Education and the Economy.

Cookson, Peter. W. 1987. "Closing the Rift between Education and Scholarship: The Need to Revitalize Educational Research." *Educational Policy* 1(3):321–331.

Cookson, Peter W. Jr., and Caroline Hodges Persell. 1985. *Preparing for Power: America's Elite Boarding Schools*. New York: Basic Books.

Cremin, Lawrence A. 1980. *American Education: The National Experience, 1783–1876*. New York: Harper & Row.

Crowson, Robert L., William Lowe Boyd, and Hanne B. Mawhinney. 1996. *The Politics of Education and the New Institutionalism: Reinventing the American School*. Washington, DC: The Falmer Press.

Culpitt, Ian. 1992. *Welfare and Citizenship: Beyond the Crisis of the Welfare State?* London: Sage.

Danziger, Sheldon, and Peter Gottschalk. 1993. *Uneven Tides: Rising Inequality in America*. New York: Russell Sage Foundation.

Dauenhauer, Bernard P. 1996. *Citizenship in a Fragile World*. Lanham, MD: Rowman and Littlefield.

Davidson, Alastair. 1997. "Regional Politics: The European Union and Citizenship." *Citizenship Studies* 1(1):33–56.

DiMaggio, Paul J., and Walter W. Powell. 1991. *The New Institutionalism in Organizational Analysis*. Chicago: University of Chicago Press.

Donahue, John. 1989. *The Privatization Decision: Public Ends, Private Means*. New York: Basic Books.

Dreeben, Robert. 1994. "The Sociology of Education: Its Development in the United States." In Aaron M. Pallas (ed.), *Research in Sociology of Education and Socialization, Vol. 10*, pp. 7–52. Greenwich, CT: JAI Press.

Durkheim, Emile. 1956. *Education and Sociology*. Glencoe, IL: The Free Press.

————. 1961. *Moral Education: A Study in the Theory and Application of the Sociology of Education*. New York: The Free Press.

Ginsberg, Rick, and David N. Plank. 1977a. On Education and Society. In Jerome Karabel and A. H. Halsey (eds.), *Power and Ideology in Education*. New York: Oxford University Press.

————. 1977b. *The Evolution of Educational Thought*. London: Routledge, Kegan Paul.

————. 1995. *Commissions, Reports, Reforms, and Educational Policy*. Westport, CT: Praeger.

Ehrenreich, Barbara. 1989. *Fear of Falling. The Inner Life of the Middle Class*. New York: HarperCollins.

Epstein, Joyce. 2000. *Schools and Family Partnerships: Preparing Educators and Improving Schools*. Boulder, Colorado: Westview Press.

Etzioni, Amatai. 1993. *The Spirit of Community: Rights, Responsibilities, and the Communitarian Agenda*. New York: Crown.

Fagerlind, Ingemar, and Lawrence Saha. 1989. *Education and*

National Development: A Comparative Perspective, 2nd ed. New York: Pergamon.

Farkas, George. 1996. *Human Capital or Cultural Capital? Ethnicity and Poverty Groups in an Urban School District.* Hawthorne, NY: Aldine de Gruyter.

Federal Glass Ceiling Commission. 1995. *A Solid Investment: Making Full Use of the Nation's Human Capital.* Washington, DC: Superintendent of Documents.

Fosler, R. Scott. 1988. *The New Economic Role of American States. Strategies in a Competitive World Economy.* New York: Oxford University Press.

Foster, Peter, Roger Gomm, and Martyn Hammersley. 1996. *Constructing Educational Inequality: An Assessment of Research on Social Processes.* London: Falmer Press.

Fullan, Michael. 1991. *The New Meaning of Educational Change.* New York: Teachers College Press.

Fuller, Bruce, and Richard Rubinson. 1992. *The Political Construction of Education. The State, School Expansion, and Economic Change.* New York: Praeger.

Fuller, Bruce, Richard F. Elmore, and Gary Orfield. 1996. *Who Chooses? Who Loses?: Culture, Institutions, and the Unequal Effects of School Choice.* New York: Teachers College Press.

Gerstner, Louis V. 1994. *Reinventing Education: Entrepreneurship in America's Public Schools.* New York: Penguin.

Giddens, Anthony. 1982. "Class Division, Class Conflict, and Citizenship Rights." In Anthony Giddens (ed.), *Profiles and Critiques in Social Theory,* pp. 164–180. Berkeley: University of California Press.

Ginsberg, Rick, and David N. Plank. 1995. *Commissions, Reports, Reforms, and Educational Policy.* Westport, CT: Praeger.

Giroux, Henry. 1997. *Pedagogy and the Politics of Hope: Theory, Culture and Schooling. A Critical Reader.* Boulder, Colorado: Westview Press.

Glouchevitch, Philip. 1992. *Juggernaut: The German Way of Business: Why It Is Transforming Europe and the World.* New York: Simon & Schuster.

Gordon, David M., Richard Edwards, and Michael Reich. 1982. *Segmented Work, Divided Workers. The Historical Transformation of Labor in the United States.* London: Cambridge University Press.

Gottschalk, Peter, and Mary Joyce. 1995. "The Impact of Technological Change, Deindustrialization, and Internationalization of Trade on Earnings Inequality: An International Perspective." In Katherine McFate, Roger Lawson, and William Julius Wilson (eds.), *Poverty, Inequality and the Future of Social Policy: Western States in the New World Order.* New York: Russell Sage Foundation.

Gross, Beatrice, and Ronald Gross. 1985. *The Great School Debate: Which Way for American Education?* New York: Simon & Schuster.

Gutmann, Amy. 1987. *Democratic Education.* Princeton: Princeton University Press.

Hall, John A. 1987. *Politics, Ideology and the Market.* Chapel Hill: University of North Carolina Press.

Hallinan, Maureen. 1994. "Tracking: From Theory to Practice." *Sociology of Education* 67:79–84, 89–91.

Hanushek, Eric, et al. 1994. *Making Schools Work: Improving Performance and Controlling Costs.* Washington, DC: The Brookings Institution.

Hill, Paul T. 1995. *Reinventing Public Education.* Santa Monica, CA: The Rand Corporation.

Hill, Paul T., Lawrence C. Pierce, and James W. Guthrie. 1997. *Reinventing Public Education: How Contracting Can Transform America's Schools.* Chicago: The University of Chicago Press.

Hirsch, E.D., Jr. 1988. *Cultural Literacy: What Every American Needs to Know.* New York: Vintage Books.

Hornbeck, David W., and Lester M. Salamon (eds). 1991. *Human Capital and America's Future.* Baltimore: The Johns Hopkins University Press.

Hudson Institute. 1987. *Workforce 2000: Work and Workers for the 21st Century.* Washington, DC: U.S. Government Printing Office.

———.1997. *Workforce 2020: Work and Workers in the 21st Century.* Indianapolis, IN.

Human Development Report, 1997. Cary, NC: Oxford University Press.

Hurn, Christopher. 1993. *The Limits and Possibility of Schooling.* Boston: Allyn & Bacon.

International Monetary Fund. 1997. *World Economic Outlook: Globalization Opportunities and Challenges.* Washington, DC.

Jencks, Christopher, and David Riesman. 1968. *The Academic Revolution.* New York: Doubleday.

Jencks, Christopher, Marshall Smith, Henry Acland, Mary Jo Bane, David Cohen, Herbert Gintis, Barbara Heyns, and Stephan Michelson. 1972. *Inequality: A Reassessment of the Effect of Family and Schooling in America.* New York: Basic Books.

Jones, Byrd L., and Robert W. Maloy. 1996. *Schools for an Information Age: Reconstructing Foundations for Teaching and Learning.* Westport, CT: Praeger.

Kaestle, Carl F. 1983. *Pillars of the Republic: Common Schools and American Society, 1780–1860.* New York: Hill and Wang.

Kapstein, Ethan B. 1996. "Workers and the World Economy: Breaking the Postwar Bargain." *Foreign Affairs* 75(3): 16–38.

Karabel, Jerome, and A. H. Halsey. 1977. *Power and Ideology in Education.* New York: Oxford University Press.

Katz, Michael. 1987. *Reconstructing American Education.* Cambridge, MA: Harvard University Press.

Kelley, E.W. 1987. *Policy and Politics in the United States: The Limits of Localism.* Philadelphia, PA: Temple University Press.

Kliebard, Herbert M. 1992. *Forging the American Curriculum. Essays in Curriculum History and Theory.* New York: Routledge.

Kozol, Jonathan. 1991. *Savage Inequalities: Children in America's Schools.* New York: Crown Publishers.

Kupferberg, Feiwel. 1996. "The Reality of Teaching: Bringing Disorder Back into Social Theory and the Sociology of Education." *British Journal of Sociology of Education.* 17(2):227–PAGES?.

Kuttner, Robert. 1996. *Everything for Sale: The Limits and Virtues of Markets.* New York: Alfred A. Knopf.

Kymlicka, Will. 1996. *Multicultural Citizenship.* New York: Oxford University Press.

Kymlicka, Will, and Wayne Norman. 1994. "Return of the Citizen: A Survey of Recent Work on Citizenship Theory." *Ethics* 104(January):257–289.

Labaree, David F. 1988. *The Making of an American High School: The Credentials Market and the Central High School of Philadelphia, 1838–1939.* New Haven, CT: Yale University Press.

———. 1996. "A Disabling Vision: Rhetoric and Reality in Tomorrow's Schools of Education. *Teachers College Record* 97(2):166–205.

———. 1997. *How to Succeed in School without Really Learning: The Credential Race in American Education.* New Haven, CT: Yale University Press.

Ladd, Helen F. (ed). 1996. *Holding Schools Accountable: Performance-Based Reform in Education.* Washington, DC: The Brookings Institution.

Lagemann, Ellen Condliffe. 1983. *Private Power for the Public Good. A History of the Carnegie Foundation for the Advancement of Teaching.* Middletown, CT: Wesleyan University Press.

———. 1989. *The Politics of Knowledge. The Carnegie Corporation, Philanthropy, and Public Policy.* Chicago, IL: University of Chicago Press.

Larson, Magalli Safatti. 1987. *The Rise of Professionalism: A Sociological Analysis.* Berkeley: University of California Press.

Lavin, David E., and David Hyllegard. 1996. *Changing the Odds: Open Admissions and the Life Chances of the Disadvantaged.* New Haven, CT: Yale University Press.

Lenzer, Gertrud. 1975. *Auguste Comte and Positivism.* New York, Harper & Row.

Lesko, Nancy. 1988. *Symbolizing Society: Stories, Rites and Structure in a Catholic High School.* New York: The Falmer Press.

Levy, Frank. 1988. *Dollars and Dreams: The Changing American Income Distribution.* New York: W. W. Norton.

Lindblom, Charles E. 1977. *Politics and Markets; The World's Political-Economic Systems.* New York: Basic Books.

Lowi, Theodore J. 1969. *The End of Liberalism.* Second Edition (1979). New York: W. W. Norton.

———. 1995. *The End of the Republican Era.* Norman, OK: University of Oklahoma Press.

Lukes, Steven. 1973. *Emile Durkheim: His Life and Work.* New York: Harper & Row.

Maher, Frances A., and Mary Kay Thompson Tetreault. 1994. *The Feminist Classroom.* New York: Basic Books.

Marshall, Gordon. 1994. *The Concise Oxford Dictionary of Sociology.* Oxford: Oxford University Press.

Marshall, T.H. 1965. *Class, Citizenship, and Social Development.* New York: Anchor Books.

Martindale, Don. 1981. *The Nature and Types of Sociological Theory.* New York: Harper & Row.

Mehan, Hugh, Irene Villanueva, Lea Hubbard, and Angela Lintz. 1996. *Constructing School Success: The Consequences of Untracking Low-Achieving Students.* Cambridge: Cambridge University Press.

Meier, Deborah. 1995. *The Power of Their Ideas: Lessons for America from a Small School in Harlem.* Boston: Beacon Press.

Meyer, John W., and W. Richard Scott. 1992. *Organizational Environments: Ritual and Rationality.* Newbury Park, CA: Sage.

Mills, C. Wright. 1959. *The Sociological Imagination.* London: Oxford University Press.

Mishel, Lawrence, Jared Bernstein, and John Schmitt. 1997. *The State of Working America.* New York: M.E. Sharpe.

Mulkey, Lynn. 1993. *Sociology of Education: Theoretical and Empirical Investigations.* New York: Harcourt, Brace Jovanovich.

Murnane, Richard, and Frank Levy. 1996. *Teaching the New Basic Skills: Principles for Educating Children to Thrive in a Changing Economy.* New York: Martin Kessler Books, The Free Press.

Murphy, Marjorie. 1990. *Blackboard Unions: The AFT and the NEA 1900–1980.* Ithaca, NY: Cornell University Press.

National Commission on Teaching and America's Future. (1996). *What Matters Most: Teaching for America's Future.* New York: National Commission on Teaching and America's Future.

Oakes, Jeannie. 1985. *Keeping Track: How Schools Structure Inequality.* New Haven, CT: Yale University Press.

——— 1994. "More Than Misapplied Technology: A Normative and Political Response to Hallinan on Tracking." *Sociology of Education* 67:84–89, 91.

O'Connor, James. 1973. *The Fiscal Crisis of the State.* New York: St. Martin's Press.

Oliver, Melvin L., and Thomas M. Shapiro. 1995. *Black Wealth/White Wealth: A New Perspective on Racial Inequality.* New York: Routledge.

Orfield, Gary. 1996. *The Growth of Segregation: African Americans, Latinos, and Unequal Education in Dismantling Desegregation: The Quiet Reversal of Brown v. Board of Education.* New York: New Press.

Organization of Economic Coop. 1997. *Industrial Competitiveness. Benchmarking Business Environments in the Global Economy, April.*

Organization for Economic Cooperation and Development. 1997. *Education and Equity in OECD Countries.* Washington, DC.

Pakulski, Jan. 1997. "Cultural Citizenship." *Citizenship Studies* I(1):73–86.

Pallas, Aaron. 1997. What is the Sociology of Education?

American Sociological Association Sociology of Education Homepage website (www.asanet.org/soe) November.

Parrish, Thomas. 1996. *Do Rich and Poor Districts Spend Alike? Issue Brief.* NCES.

Parsons, Talcott. 1971. *The System of Modern Societies.* Englewood Cliffs, NJ: Prentice-Hall.

Parsons, Talcott, and Gerald M. Platt. 1973. *The American University.* Cambridge: Harvard University Press.

Persell, Carolyn Hodges. 1977. *Education and Inequality. A Theoretical and Empirical Synthesis.* New York: The Free Press.

Peschek, Joseph G. 1987. *Policy-Planning Organizations. Elite Agendas and America's Rightward Turn.* Philadelphia, PA: Temple University Press.

Pink, William T., and George W. Noblit. 1995. *Continuity and Contradiction: The Futures of the Sociology of Education.* New York: Hampton Press.

Powell, Arthur, Eleanor Farrar, and David Cohen. 1985. *The Shopping Mall High School.* Boston: Houghton Mifflin.

Power, Jonathan. 1997. "The World's Income Distribution Is Worsening, Thanks to Globalization and Liberalization." In *Transnational Foundation for Peace and Future Research* (www.transnational.org/forum/power/1997/pow1997.html) September.

President's Commission on Privatization. 1988. *Privatization: Toward More Effective Government.* Washington, DC: U.S. Government Printing Office.

Psacharopoulos, George. 1995. *Building Human Capital for Better Lives.* Washington, DC: The World Bank.

Putnam, Robert. 2000. *Bowling Alone: The Collapse and Revival of American Community.* New York: Simon and Schuster.

Ramirez, Francisco O., and Marc J. Ventresca. 1992. "Building the Institution of Mass Schooling: Isomorphism in the Modern World." In Bruce Fuller and Richard Rubinson (eds.), *The Political Construction of Education. The State, School Expansion, and Economic Change,* pp. 47–59. New York: Praeger.

Ravitch, Diane, and Maris A. Vinovksis (eds). 1995. *Learning from the Past: What History Teaches Us about School Reform.* Baltimore: Johns Hopkins University Press.

Reich, Robert B. 1991. *The Work of Nations: Preparing Ourselves for 21st Century Capitalism.* New York: Alfred A. Knopf.

Rhode, Deborah. 1997. *Speaking of Sex: The Denial of Gender Inequality.* Cambridge, MA: Harvard University Press.

Richards, Craig E., Rima Shore, and Max B. Sawicky. 1996. *Risky Business: Private Management of Public Schools.* Washington, DC: Economic Policy Institute.

Rifkin, Jeremy. 1995. *The End of Work: The Decline of the Global Labor Force and the Dawn of the Post-Market Era.* New York: G. P. Putnam's Sons.

Riordan, Cornelius. 1997. *Equality and Achievement: An Introduction to the Sociology of Education.* New York: Longman.

Rueschemeyer, Dietrich, and Theda Skocpol. 1996. *States, Social Knowledge and the Modern Origins of State Policies.* Princeton, NJ: Princeton University Press, The Russell Sage Foundation.

Sadovnik, Alan R. 1995a. "Postmodernism and the Sociology of Education: Closing the Gap between Theory, Research and Practice." In William Pink and George Noblit (eds.), *Continuity and Contradiction: The Futures of the Sociology of Education,* pp. 309–326. Creskill, NJ: Hampton Press.

———. 1995b. *Knowledge and Pedagogy: The Sociology of Basil Bernstein.* New York: Ablex.

Scott, John. 1995. *Sociological Theory: Contemporary Debates.* Cheltenham, UK: Edward Elgar Publishing Limited.

Sen, Amartya. 1997. "Inequality, Unemployment and Contemporary Europe." *International Labour Review* 136(2): 155–172.

Shea, Christine M., Ernest Kahane, and Peter Sola (eds.). 1989. *The New Servants of Power: A Critique of the 1980s School Reform Movement.* New York: Greenwood Press.

Shor, Ira. 1986. *Culture Wars: School and Society in the Conservative Restoration, 1969–1984.* Boston: Routledge and Kegan Paul.

Slaugher, Sheila. 1990. *The Higher Learning and High Technology: Dynamics of Higher Education Policy Formation.* New York: SUNY Press.

Smart, Barry. 1993. *Postmodernity.* London: Routledge.

Smith, James A. 1991. *The Idea Brokers: Think Tanks and the Rise of the New Policy Elite.* New York: The Free Press.

Smith, Thomas. 1996. *The Condition of Education.* U.S. Department of Education, National Center for Education Statistics. Washington, DC: U.S. Government Printing Office.

Sorokin, Pitirim. 1959. *Social and Cultural Mobility.* Glencoe, IL: Free Press.

Sperber, Irwin. 1990. *Fashions in Science.* Minneapolis: University of Minnesota Press.

Swan, Edward T. 1995. "Equitable Access to Funding. The Equal Funding Struggle." *Contemporary Education* 66(4): 202–204.

Swartz, David. 1997. *Culture and Power: The Sociology of Pierre Bourdieu.* Chicago: University of Chicago Press.

Turkle, Sherry. 1997. *Life on Screen: Identity in the Age of the Internet.* New York: Touchstone Books.

Thurow, Lester. 1992. *Head to Head: The Coming Economic Battle among Japan, Europe, and America.* New York: William Morrow.

Turner, Ralph. 1960. "Sponsored and Contest Mobility." *American Sociological Review* 25:855–867.

Turner, Bryan S. 1993. "Contemporary Problems in the Theory of Citizenship." In Bryan S. Turner (ed.), *Citizenship and Social Theory,* pp. 1–18. London: Sage.

———. 1997. "Citizenship Studies: A General Theory." *Citizenship Studies* 1(1):5–18.

Turner, John D. (ed.). 1996. *The State and the School: An International Perspective.* London: Falmer Press.

Tyack, David, and Larry Cuban. 1995. *Tinkering toward Uto-*

pia: A Century of Public School Reform. Cambridge, MA: Harvard University Press.

Vinovskis, Maris A. 1995. *Education, Society, and Economic Opportunity: A Historical Perspective on Persistent Issues.* New Haven, CT: Yale University Press.

Waller, Willard. 1965. *The Sociology of Teaching.* New York: Wiley.

Wells, Amy Stuart, and Robert Crain. 1997. *Stepping Over the Color Line: African-American Students in White Suburban Schools.* New Haven, CT: Yale University Press.

Wesselingh, Anton. 1996. "The Dutch Sociology of Education: Its Origins, Significance, and Future." *British Journal of Sociology of Education* 17(2):213–226.

Westbury, Ian. 1992. "Comparing American and Japanese Achievement: Is the United States Really a Low Achiever?" *Educational Research* 21(June–July):18–24.

Wexler, Philip. 1987. *Social Analysis of Education: After the New Sociology.* New York: Routledge.

Wolfe, Alan. 1977. *The Limits of Legitimacy.* New York: Basic Books.

Wolff, Edward N. 1995. *Top Heavy: A Study of the Increasing Inequality of Wealth in America.* New York: The Twentieth Century Fund Press.

World Bank. 1997. *World Economic Outlook: Globalization Opportunities and Changes.* Washington, DC.

Young, Beth Aronstramm, and Thomas M. Smith. 1997. "The Social Context of Education." In U.S. Department of Education, National Center for Education Statistics, *The Condition of Education 1997*, pp. 2–21. NCES 97–388, by Thomas M. Smith, Beth Aronstramm Young, Yupin Bae, Susan P. Choy, and Nabeel Alsalam. Washington, DC: U.S. Government Printing Office.

Young, Michael. 1958. *The Rise of the Meritocracy, 1870–2033: An Essay on Education and Equality.* London: Thames and Hudson.

ADOLESCENCE AND SCHOOLS

Nancy Lesko, Roberta Jentes-Mason, and Jolanda Westerhof-Shultz
Indiana University—Bloomington

What is taught and what is learned by youth in secondary schools? What do adolescents learn in the planned curriculum and in the whole of their school experiences? Any attempt to determine what is taught and learned by youth in schools is dependent upon a prior question: How are schools related to other social institutions, such as families, the economy, higher education, and the welfare state? This review begins to answer these questions with a look at several foundational studies, which exemplify different views of the relationships between schools and society. The review then moves to research on both the formal and informal curricula of secondary schools. The final area of focus is current scholarship on the concept of adolescence itself. This review is a selective introduction to important scholarship on adolescence and schools of the last four decades as seen through the prism of the authors' interests and perspectives.

Schools in Society: What Are the Relations?

The direct linking of schools and adolescents in sociological studies began with *Elmtown's Youth* (Hollingshead, 1949), which showed how inequalities in the surrounding community pervade the interactions of youth in school. This topic of youth and schools came of age with the publication of Coleman's *The Adolescent Society* (1961). Coleman trumpeted the "problem" of adolescence and schools: teenagers were more interested in being popular than in being educated; Cusick (1973) found that high school students considered it worse to sit alone at lunch than to fail a test. The adolescent "society" later became the "subculture," but adult-centered examinations of youth continued to find their

peer relations often pushed youth toward nonproductive, deviant, even criminal activity, with the gang portrayed as the archetypal antisocial unit.

Undoubtedly the broader social environment of the 1960s with its student and antiwar movements, placed youth prominently in the media and in the cultural consciousness in the United States and in the West overall. This youth consciousness infected the sociology of education and studies of youth multiplied. Another milestone study, this one ethnographic in method, was Willis's *Learning to Labor: How Working Class Kids Get Working Class Jobs* (1977). Before Willis, researchers had viewed the school and students from the adult expectations of equality of opportunity in schools or the belief that schools were primarily places for learning the formal curriculum. Willis focused upon students' understandings of differentiated school lives in a stratified society; his "lads" saw through the sham of unequal schooling and mocked it, but were nevertheless trapped in blue collar jobs.

Elmtown's Youth, The Adolescent Society, and *Learning to Labor* (among others) established an emphasis on the impact of community social class relations on adolescents' school experiences, the development of a semiautonomous peer society, and the connection between schooling experiences and waged work. These topics continue to be actively pursued in sociology of education. Both quantitative and qualitative methods are used, though ethnographic explorations have become more popular.

These studies also illustrate the applications of functionalist and conflict views of secondary schools. The sociology of education has been dominated by questions stemming from a liberal-progressive perspective, i.e., schools were assumed to be neutral social sites that al-

lowed the individualistic competition and upward mobility of the "winners" (Wexler, 1976). Terms such as
achievement, merit, opportunity, and *deprivation* became
commonsense terms of educational description and
analysis as certain questions dominated research:
Which students were achieving and which were not?
Were schools really meritocracies? How did culturally
deprived students fare in schools? What reforms could
make schools truly meritocratic institutions? The work
of Coleman, Hollingshead, Cusick and many others operated from the schools-as-neutral-sites (or functionalist) perspective.

Scholars critical of the universalistic, neutral view of
schools as reward-granting agencies that function beyond politics examined schools as contested arenas,
where social inequalities helped create notions of "real
school" and were not just the result of schools tainted
by social class. Willis' *Learning to Labor* quickly became a classic of this conflict view of youth and school.

In the last decades, "intermediate" theoretical positions between the extremes of the functionalist and
conflict perspectives have developed and provided fresh
interpretations of what youths learn in school. For example, Lesko's (1988) study of a Catholic high school
emphasized the symbolic and ritual dimensions of
school life and the ways those dimensions of curriculum
mediated between the school's emphasis of both radical
individualism and communitarianism. Page's (1991)
study of lower-track classrooms emphasized their ser-
endipitous and ironic dimensions. Unlike studies of
tracking that portray it as always oppressive and the
result of a conspiracy against kids from poor and historically marginalized groups, Page portrayed school as
"games of chance," but with serious consequences.
Wexler (1992) wove a theoretical position between a
strict conflict view and apolitical symbolic studies of
school; he argued that the serious work of youth is that
of creating identities. Because of the emptiness of
school knowledge and of social relations, teenagers'
identities are constructed as negative. For Wexler, the
work of school is primarily identity-labor, becoming
somebody (rather than becoming a worker), and in the
1980s this occurred in schools that provided few raw
materials for a positive school-based self regardless of
social class.

These "intermediate" theoretical positions are postmodern perspectives on schooling, in their avoidance
of grand theories and in their attention to ironic and

conflicting patterns of school life. They also address the
limits of rationalistic analyses. These studies also powerfully portray the alienating absurdities of adolescents'
school lives, both in social relations, and as the next
section discusses, in the formal school curriculum.

Formal Curriculum

Historically secondary school curriculum has been fragmented into separate subject matter classes taught by
math, English, or science specialists. Because the subject matters' domains are seen as discrete entities, "their
boundaries are virtually etched in stone by schedules,
teacher loyalties, and organizational structures like
departments" (Beane, 1995:4). Therefore, teachers
have usually focused on the "bits and pieces" of their
subject area and ignored the connections across the
knowledge domains. Lacking these connections, the
"curriculum is likely to be little more than a smorgas-
bord of superficial abstract, irrelevant, and easily forgotten pieces" (Beane, 1995:4). Consequently, adolescents' learning experiences resemble endurance tests, or
rites of passage to adulthood, rather than meaningful
or coherent learning.

With the student protests and antiwar movement of
the 1960s, the irrelevance of the traditional curriculum
was criticized. By the early 1970s, this concern for relevance, spurred by the crisis in student apathy, precipitated a move to more elective courses within the
subject areas. These often became even smaller disas-
sembled "bits and pieces" of a knowledge domain, but
students did have choices in their curriculum. However, dropping SAT scores in the broader context of
economic slowdowns and social fragmentation fueled
the fires of the back-to-basics movement. The *Report
of a Nation at Risk* (National Commission on Excellence, 1983) became the statement of conservative
groups who wanted schools to return to traditional curriculum and tracking practices and to prepare youth
(differentially) for economic slots.

The *Shopping Mall High School* (Powell et al., 1985)
further detailed adolescents' lack of engagement in
school knowledge and contributed to the debate about
appropriate curriculum. Ethnographic studies of high
schools offered additional dimensions of the formal curriculum. McNeil's (1986) study of social studies curriculum in four high schools demonstrated that control
over students was the teachers' highest priority and bits

and pieces of subject matter helped maintain orderly, quiet, and passive students. Newmann (1988) demonstrated that teachers feel the need to "cover" all the material in the textbook and therefore teach superficially.

Curricular Innovations

In *Horace's Compromise* (1984), Sizer articulated the curricular problems of incoherence, subject matter-centered coursework, and credit-based schooling. He argued for the integration of the knowledge domains to encourage students to make connections across the curriculum domains. "Less is more," Sizer proposed. The parts of a "coherent" curriculum are unified and connected to a sense of the whole (Beane, 1995). Sizer also supported the idea that graduation requirements not be based upon time spent in classrooms but upon the demonstrated capacity to accomplish certain kinds of tasks.

Sizer (1984) recognized that teachers must stop envisioning themselves as expert lecturers who transmit information and see themselves as coaches supporting students' learning. This new view of teachers' role perceives learning and teaching as transactive rather than transmissive. In a transmissive view of curriculum, students are seen as empty and passive vessels into which knowledge (isolatable skills, facts) is to be poured; the school knowledge is typically isolated from action or meaning-making in the world beyond school. In the transactive view of curriculum, students are seen as already knowing and thinking and the curriculum is intended to engage and extend their abilities and knowledge. In a transactive curriculum, adolescents are active rather than passive learners as they make connections to their lived reality (Weaver, 1994). Furthermore, assessment of student learning must also change. Exhibitions and portfolios are now favored to replace accumulated seat time as the basis for a high school diploma; students must demonstrate understanding of topics in several forms of expression.

A *Wall Street Journal* (December 28, 1994) review of assessments of schools implementing Sizer's plans found difficulties: "Five research studies—based on visits, interviews and questionnaires at more than two dozen coalition schools—describe schools traumatized by political infighting between teachers divided over the change efforts, ambiguity over the coalition's guiding principles . . . among other problems" (p. A1).

Another issue in this debate about curriculum is the tendency to separate reason from emotion by severing the mind from the body or thinking from acting. This dichotomy is represented in the view that students who are good with their hands are talented but not necessarily intelligent. The belief that "[t]hose who are emotive, sensitive, or imaginative might have aptitudes for the arts, but the 'really bright' go into mathematics or the sciences" is pervasive (Eisner, 1994:23). Apple sees this dichotomy between the arts and sciences in sociopolitical terms. In his view, many efforts to restructure curriculum such as Sizer's fail to acknowledge the larger social and political circumstances that mitigate against change. There is a growing realization that schools in advanced industrial societies like the United States maintain certain social class inequities and high and low status knowledges. Scientific and technical knowledge has discrete, identifiable content, stable structure, and is both teachable and easily tested. "The socially acceptable definitions of high status knowledge preclude the consideration of nontechnical knowledge" (Apple, 1990:38) such as the arts and humanities. Because they are not easy to teach or test with objective criteria, the arts and humanities are "not seen as *macroeconomically* beneficial; that is, the long run benefits to the most powerful classes in society" are not clear (Apple, 1990:38).

The problems of curriculum—incoherence, irrelevance, and high status knowledges limited to sciences and math—have a "sense of urgency" for "[i]ncreasingly, our students are questioning the purpose and the meaning of the things we ask them to do. Their lives in school have been deadened by the litany of disconnected facts and skills they face every day" (Beane, 1995:2). Adolescents who want to feel powerful in the face of the social–political realities of their lives frequently turn to popular cultural icons such as Dirty Harry and Terminator Man. Ironically, many adolescents develop a "disdain for books. They see literacy as an enemy, something used to control them by those in positions of power" (Sanders, 1994:137).

The Hidden Curriculum

Vallance (1977:592) defines the hidden curriculum as "Those nonacademic but emotionally significant consequences of schooling that occur systematically but are not made explicit at any level of the public rationales for education." And she explains that it is "a device for identifying those systematic side effects of schooling that we sense but which cannot be adequately accounted for by reference to the explicit curriculum" (1977:592). This overview of the hidden curricula includes findings on gender, race, and class.

The Hidden Curriculum of Gender

Since the 1972 landmark federal Title IX legislation prohibiting sex discrimination in education, researchers have attempted to identify both the obvious barriers to gender equity in schools (e.g., sex differences in course enrollments) and the subtle obstacles to achieving academic parity between female and male students (e.g., pressure to conform to stereotyped expectations). Twenty years after Title IX was passed into law, gender equity in education remains an elusive goal. Sadker and Sadker (1994) provide extensive evidence of how girls are systematically denied opportunities in the classroom where boys are encouraged to excel (often by well-intentioned teachers). Whereas girls in the primary grades routinely outperform boys on standardized tests, by the time girls graduate from high school, they lag far behind the boys. The researchers also found that teachers were more likely to call on boys, to provide more encouragement and guidance when boys were answering questions, and to allow them to call out in class (Sadker and Sadker, 1994).

Other research documents how adolescent girls retreat from a sense of their own opinions and perspectives on the world and adopt beliefs about how "nice girls" relate to others (Brown and Gilligan, 1992). Another contributing factor in adolescent girls' schooling experience is the presence of sexual harassment, especially from peers (Stein, 1993). The combination of less academic attention from teachers, norms for good girls, and sexual harassment in schools clearly impacts the schooling experiences and learning of teenage girls.

Although there is less research on boys and the construction of masculinity, Weis (1993) and Connell (1993) document a range of masculinities, but the existence of a dominant masculinity in each school. In a city with declining economic opportunities for white males, Weis documents the aggression and hatred of these young men toward women and people of color who are perceived as benefiting from their losses.

Sexuality is intertwined with conceptions of masculinity and femininity and a major learning of the informal curriculum. Researchers suggest that schools largely ignore and perpetuate conceptions of young women as inferior to boys, as sexualized objects, and as delimited by boys' constructions of female sexuality (Eder, 1995). Researchers of gay and lesbian youth document the difficult experiences these teenagers have in secondary schools characterized by male dominance and compulsory heterosexuality (Rofes, 1989). As long as adolescence continues to be defined as the time of hormonally charged and sexually maturing bodies, sexuality will remain a primary, though largely muffled, curriculum of secondary schools.

Race/Ethnicity in the Hidden Curriculum

Jonathan Kozol (1991) updated the fallacy of schools as meritocratic institutions. He attributes widening differences in academic achievement among white, black, and Hispanic students in U.S. schools to variations in school finance, and he is convinced that the U.S. policy of funding schools through local property taxes guarantees the failure of any genuine fiscal reform effort. If all students are to have an equal chance at achieving academic success and realizing economic equality, schools must be financed equitably.

Hispanics have the highest dropout rate in the United States. "In 1983, only 50.3 percent of Hispanics 18–19 years old had graduated from the nation's high schools, as compared to 75.6 percent of non-Hispanic whites and 59.1 percent of blacks" (Velez, 1989:381). Velez believes one reason for their disproportionate dropout rate may be the confrontational relationship that Hispanic students often have with school. The sanctions imposed against nonconforming Hispanic students keep them out of school for extended periods of time and frequently lead to termination. Velez does not excuse delinquent Hispanic students, but argues that educators need to take the "hostile student subculture" into account.

John Ogbu's (1992) anthropological work illuminates how schools alienate African-American youth. Ogbu has examined black youths' expressive and instrumental alienation from schools, where school success appears to be at the cost of remaining with their black friends, culture, and language and where few future employment opportunities are seen. Thus, the "cost" of staying in school is culturally steep and the economic payoffs are risky, at best.

Research on native Americans' school experiences

also document cultural and social class differences that alienate the students. Experiences include outright racism and hostility to beliefs about intellectual abilities and inferior family life (Deyhle and LeCompte, 1994).

The Hidden Curriculum of Social Class

Conflict theorists argue that the elite sector of society depends on an economic underclass willing to accept dehumanizing chores. According to some researchers, low academic achievement among certain populations is economically necessary, and a high dropout rate is a convenient way to induct unsuspecting adolescents into low-paying or dangerous jobs. Bowles and Gintis argue that schools function to reproduce "inequality by justifying privilege and attributing poverty to personal failure" (1976:309).

Ellen Brantlinger's study (1993) of low-income students in the midwest found that they accepted their poor status in the school hierarchy as something for which they were personally responsible. And they felt their high-income peers were deserving of the better treatment they received by teachers and administrators. Low-income students "defined themselves as guilty, were apologetic, excused teachers for penalizing them . . . [and] most adhered to a code that endorsed a passive, cooperative approach and delegitimated anger and aggression" (p. 5). Although schools are often viewed as "emotionally neutral or as therapeutic environments" wrote Brantlinger, "school is a source of stress" for low-income students even though it is typically "a source of strength and contentment for high-income students" (p. 1).

Sizer (1984) noted how the security of one group of youth compared to the toughness of another. The secure, he wrote, "can afford to pay attention to the abstractions of school because they have little concern about their safety, health, or futures. They believe that they truly will live happily ever after" (1984:36). In contrast, Sizer's low-income "tough" students were "watchful, and rank low those school routines which seem relatively unconnected with their immediate predicament" (1984:36). The concern of the "tough" students for basic needs such as food, safety, and shelter was more pressing than academics.

Their differential treatment by teachers and administrators may lead low-income students to be suspicious of the functionalist promise of the universal opportunities afforded by an education. And when their basic needs are not being met at home, or if they must contend with extreme and dangerous conditions in the greater community, it is difficult to understand why students would devote their attention to such secondary concerns as math or history.

Research on the hidden curriculum of schools points out the significant lessons that youth acquire outside of the formal curriculum of subject matter areas. This research finds that conflicting lessons permeate schools: official rhetoric of universal achievement stumbles on the strongly differentiated experiences of girls and boys of different racial, ethnic, and class backgrounds.

Areas of Future Research

Numerous scholars locate the appearance of the modern idea of "adolescence," as universal and in psychological terms, at the same time period as the beginning of mass public schooling. And like schooling, adolescence is not a neutral entity. The social position that Western societies have marked as "adolescent" is a contested one, a site of struggles over meanings and power. The struggles over the meaning and control of youth are visible in battles over sex education, citizenship education, responses to teenage pregnancy, and whose knowledge grounds the formal curriculum.

Sociological examinations of the idea of adolescence must confront the historical roots of contemporary views and the way concepts of *development* and *socialization* constrain research on youth. Scholarship on childhood (James and Prout, 1990) emphasizes that age, time, and temporality are central to constructions of youth. However, time and age remain elusive in sociological analyses and require both theoretical and empirical scholarship.

The reliance on a few concepts in the conceptualization and empirical study of adolescents has impoverished the field of sociology, and failed to demythologize youth and the adult-centered views ensconced in science and in school practices.

REFERENCES

Apple, M. 1990. *Ideology and Curriculum,* 2nd ed. New York: Routledge.

Beane, J. 1995. "Introduction: What Is a Coherent Curriculum?" In J. Beane, (ed.), *Toward a Coherent Curriculum,* pp. 1–14. Alexandria, VA: ASCD.

Bowles, Samuel, and Herbert Gintis. 1976. *Schooling in Capitalist America*. New York: Basic Books.

Brantlinger, Ellen. 1993. "Adolescents' Interpretation of Social Class Influences on Schooling." *Journal of Classroom Interaction* 28(1):1–12.

Brown, Lyn Mikel, and Carol Gilligan. 1992. *Meeting at the Crossroads: Women's Psychology and Girls' Development*. Cambridge: Harvard University Press.

Coleman, James S., et al. 1966. *Equality of Educational Opportunity*. Washington, DC: U.S. Office of Education.

Connell, R. W. 1993. "Disruptions: Improper Masculinities and Schooling." In Lois Weis and Michelle Fine (eds.), *Beyond Silenced Voices*, pp. 191–208. Albany: State University of New York Press.

Cusick, Philip. 1973. *Inside High School*. New York: Holt, Rinehart & Winston.

Deyhle, Donna, and Margaret LeCompte. 1994. "Cultural Differences in Child Development: Navaho Adolescents in Middle Schools." *Theory into Practice* 33(3): 156–166.

Eder, Donna. 1995. *School Talk*. New Brunswick, NJ: Rutgers University Press.

Eisner, E. W. 1994. *Cognition and Curriculum Reconsidered*, 2nd ed. New York: Teachers College Press.

Hollingshead, August B. 1949. *Elmtown's Youth: The Impact of Social Classes on Adolescents*. New York: Wiley.

James, Allison, and Alan Prout, eds. 1990. *Constructing and Reconstructing Childhood*. London: Falmer Press.

Kozol, Jonathan. 1991. *Savage Inequalities*. New York: Crown.

Lesko, Nancy. 1988. *Symbolizing Society: Stories, Rites, and Structure in a Catholic High School*. London: Falmer Press.

McNeil, Linda M. 1986. *Contradictions of Control: School Structure and School Knowledge*. New York: Routledge.

National Commission on Excellence. 1983. *Report of a Nation at Risk*. Washington, DC.

Newmann, Fred. M. 1988. "Can Depth Replace Coverage in the High School Curriculum?" *Phi Delta Kappan* 69:345–348.

Ogbu, John U (with M. A. Gibson). 1992. *Minority Status and Schooling: A Comparative Study of Immigrants and Involuntary Minorities*. New York: Garland.

Page, Reba Neukom. 1991. *Lower-Track Classrooms: A Curricular and Cultural Perspective*. New York Teachers College Press.

Powell, A. G., E. Farrar, and D. K. Cohen. 1985. *The Shopping Mall High School: Winners and Losers in the Educational Marketplace*. Boston: Houghton Mifflin.

Rofes, Eric. 1989. "Opening Up the Classroom Closet: Responding to the Educational Needs of Gay and Lesbian Youth." *Harvard Educational Review* 59:444–452.

Sadker, Myra, and David Sadker. 1994. *Failing at Fairness: How America's Schools Cheat Girls*. New York: Charles Scribner's Sons.

Sanders, B. 1994. *A is for Ox: Violence, Electronic Media, and the Silencing of the Written Word*. New York: Pantheon Books.

Sizer, Theodore R. 1984. *Horace's Compromise: The Dilemma of the American High School*. Boston: Houghton Mifflin.

———. 1992. *Horace's School: Redesigning the American High School*. Boston: Houghton Mifflin.

Stein, Nan. 1993. "It Happens Here, too: Sexual Harassment and Child Sexual Abuse in Elementary and Secondary Schools." In S. K. Biklen and D. Pollard (eds.), *Gender and Education*, Chicago: National Society for the Study of Education.

Valance, Elizabeth. 1977. "Hiding the Hidden Curriculum: An Interpretation of the Language of Justification in Nineteenth-Century Educational Reform." In Arno A. Bellack and Herbert M. Kleibard (eds.), *Curriculum and Evaluation*. Berkeley, CA: McCutchan.

Velez, William. 1989. "Why Hispanic Students Fail: Factors Affecting Attrition in High Schools." In Jeanne H. Ballantine (ed.), *Schools and Society: A Unified Reader*, 2nd ed. Palo Alto, CA: Mayfield.

Weaver, C. 1994. *Reading Process and Practice: From Sociopsycholinguistics to Whole Language*, 2nd ed. Portsmouth, NH: Heinemann.

Weis, Lois. 1993. "White Male Working-Class Youth: An Exploration of Relative Privilege and Loss." In Lois Weis and Michelle Fine (eds.), *Beyond Silenced Voices*, pp. 237–258. Albany: State University of New York Press.

Wexler, Philip. 1976. *The Sociology of Education: Beyond Equality*. Indianapolis: Bobbs-Merrill.

———. 1992. *Becoming Somebody*. London: Falmer Press.

Willis, Paul. 1977. *Learning to Labor: How Working Class Kids Get Working Class Jobs*. New York: Columbia University Press.

ADULT EDUCATION

Peter Katopes
University College, Adelphi University

The growing presence of adult learners on campuses across the nation is a much-heralded fact. The demographics of the nation indicate that it will be some years into the twenty-first century before numbers of traditionally aged freshmen begin to grow significantly. In the meantime, adult learners will comprise some 50% of all college students. What is adult education and who is the adult learner? Although definitions of adult education remain ambiguous, it may be worthwhile to simply state that adult education is that which, especially at the postsecondary level, recognizes that adults bring to the educational process an experiential foundation radically different from their more traditionally aged counterparts—that is, more grounded in the "real worlds" of business and family and their attendant demands and responsibilities—and so, because the constituency is more rooted in its ideologies and beliefs, may ultimately be more profoundly transformative than the traditional educational process.

Further, while of course sharing some characteristics with their younger counterparts, adult learners, besides in fact being somewhat older (although often marginally so) than their more traditional counterpart, are themselves unique in at least two ways. They are nontraditional in terms of how they consume education. They bring to the classroom a broad experiential base and as a consequence are often capable of greater sophistication in thought than their more traditional younger colleagues. And adult students often consume courses in a sporadic manner. The pressures of family and work often impose periods of relative inactivity on these students with the consequence that they do not proceed neatly through their studies in tight cohorts. Further, these same external pressures often create a small window of opportunity for students to enter the classroom. Adult students have tight schedules and so are often unable to pursue their education through traditional means. Also, much adult education, although of course not all, is quasivocational. The majority of adult students pursue courses of study that will enable them to advance in their current careers or that train them for new careers. As a result, adult students tend to be relentlessly goal oriented.

Although adult education in some form has existed in the United States since colonial times, manifesting itself in various forms—apprenticeships, community-oriented and sponsored programs, labor union-backed training, Chautaqua-style enrichment and improvement programs, it did not emerge as a sociologically significant issue until perhaps sometime after the Second World War, when for the first time large numbers of returning soldiers, encouraged by the relative largesse of the GI Bill, availed themselves of the opportunity to pursue education—particularly college and vocational education—in a manner perhaps unprecedented in American society. In other words, for perhaps the first time in the history of American education, postsecondary schooling was made available to the working and middle classes. This opportunity, of course, radically altered the face of American education by transforming both the educational process and the educational environment from what had been selective and exclusive to what soon became relatively more democratic and inclusive.

Since that time, adult students and adult education, although definitionally often categorized as "nontraditional," are becoming more traditional all the time. According to a study by the National Center for Education Statistics, approximately 43% of all college students today are older than 25 years, compared with

39% in 1981. The majority of these students, according to the College Board, are white, female, 25–34 years old, married, and working full time. This "graying" of the traditional college student population is a national trend that appears unlikely to change much for the foreseeable future.

In spite of this, however, institutions of higher learning, often rendered inert by tradition and precedent, have not always adapted themselves to meet the academic and professional needs of this growing population. In fact, often universities and colleges have statistically lumped adult students together with other so-called "nontraditional students" (minorities, educationally disadvantaged, or disabled students, for example) and by so doing have historically, until very recently, failed to make appropriate distinctions between adult students and others. For instance, there are relatively few baccalaureate programs designed exclusively for adults nor do many colleges and universities provide separate and distinct support services for these students. However, because these students are often by definition vastly more experienced and well informed than their younger counterparts, curricula and individual course syllabi must be designed with this sophistication in mind. Further, adult students, perhaps because many inhabit the aggressive everyday world of business, tend to be "active learners" in the sense that they rarely are content to passively endure lectures by their professors. Although deeply appreciative of the contributions higher education can make to their lives (after all, they want their children to go to college!) they demand engagement and a clear demonstration of the relevance and purpose of the subjects they undertake to study. In many cases, for example, and unlike their younger, more traditional colleagues, these students have been participants in the very events and occurrences that they may be studying. It is not unusual, for instance, for veterans of World War II, Korea, and Vietnam to be taking classes in modern American history, or for fiftyish females to have been participants in the very women's movement they may be studying in Women's Studies courses. Educators who ignore the impact of these students on the dynamics of the traditional classroom do so at their own peril.

Also, because adult students typically pursue their studies on a part-time basis, frequently "stop out" for a semester or two due to the demands of work, home,

and finances, and, in addition, must often struggle on a semester-to-semester basis to create a personal schedule that will permit them to attend class, they require an approach to college study that offers them a degree of flexibility perhaps not necessary for more traditional undergraduates. This translates, of course, into weekend and evening classes, as well as more imaginative scheduling of semesters.

Although education in general has long been a fertile ground for sociological study, adult education, perhaps surprisingly given its somewhat rapid growth during the latter part of the twentieth century, has not been accorded a separate and distinct category for study. As a consequence, attempts to introduce sociological considerations into this field have been spotty and erratic. One of the earliest sociological treatments of adult education was Lindemans's study (1945) of adult education as a social and collective phenomenon. By the 1960s, however, perhaps in keeping with the general mood of the times and the movement away from the more consensual society of the prewar era, researchers had begun to focus on the practice of adult education with particular attention paid to the individual. More recently, however, as more and more adults have become involved in the educational process and the impact of their experiences has contributed more significantly to the shaping of their immediate culture, the trend has been toward the study of the societal aspects of adult education. According to Rubenson (1989), this surge of interest can be attributed to three factors: the increasing significance of adult education within all forms of society, the state of adult education in developing nations, and the perspectival changes that have occurred in the social sciences, and in sociology in particular, with regard to the study of education in general.

Although there may be several conceptual perspectives relevant to the sociological study of adult education, the two primary ones are the consensus paradigm and the conflict paradigm. Although the consensus approach has been the most popular for many years, interest in the conflict paradigm has steadily increased over the past quarter century.

The consensus paradigm rests on the assumption that societies cannot survive unless their members share at least some perceptions, attitudes, and values in common. Because the consensus paradigm insists upon common beliefs and values, conflict must of necessity occupy an inferior position. According to the consensus model, the needs of society as a whole result, somewhat paradoxically, in a society in which inequalities not only exist but are in fact inevitable. The particular interests of specific individuals or groups, although of course important to consider, are not significant in terms of overall societal development. Thus, in the consensus model, inequality is a necessary condition because the individual's well being must be defined in terms of the well being of the larger society to which he or she may belong. This model clearly supports an educational environment that is highly selective and exclusive regarding higher and specialized education and accepts as a necessary reality that not all members of a society will have access to the educational process at every level. This model is at odds with the current social trend that emphasizes multiculturalism and cultural relativism precisely because it insists upon a somewhat homogeneous cultural matrix.

The consensus model was challenged by Merritt and Coombs (1977), among others, on the basis that since the consensus model rejected the idea that education reform was significantly influenced by politics and social structure, adherence to this paradigm interfered with an understanding of the essential nature of adult education. They urged social scientists to reevaluate both their theoretical frameworks and their conceptualizations of adult education. Said another way, sociologists had to recognize that the importance of conflict and ideology had been underestimated in their consensus paradigms. The result for the sociology of education led to the introduction of several alternative paradigms on the relationship between education and society. The most significant of these is the conflict paradigm.

Basing their study on the work of Marx and Engels, adherents of the conflict paradigm approach questions of social change, inequality, mobility, and stratification, and of course adult education as it reflects these issues, from the standpoint of the various individuals and interest groups within society. Social inequality is considered as a manifestation of the conflict among various factions for power, privileges, and goods and services that are in short supply. Conflict theorists, basing their theories on the framework provided by Marx and Engels, of course pay particular attention to the elements of domination, exploitation, and coercion. The conflict model, of course, views the current debates over bilingual education, multiculturalism, and the needs of particular special interest groups (homosexuals, for instance) to have input into curricula at all levels, as an expression of the struggle of previously disenfranchised or excluded groups to confront the extant power structure.

Without question, the consensus and conflict models present quite different views on the social function of education. Parsons (1964), for example, one of the leading proponents of consensus theory, sees schools as selection instruments that operate as agencies of socialization whose primary role is to apportion manpower to appropriate positions. Socialization is further determined according to commitment to the broad values of society and commitment to the performance of a specific type of role in that society.

Because it presents education as a coherent and unified mechanism existing in a consensual world, this view has been criticized by the conflict theorists. The criticism is of the implicit assumption made by consensus theorists that the pedagogic actions of families from different social classes, as well as the actions of the schools, work together in a harmonious way to transmit a cultural heritage that is considered the property of the whole society. Therefore, the conclusion is that the educational system promotes mobility in a fair and equitable way. Again, one may view the ongoing debates about bilingual and multicultural education as expressions of the dissatisfaction with the consensus model.

The conflict theorists, on the other hand, argue that educational institutions are controlled by the dominant culture that determines not only the structure of the symbols of education but also of the knowledge that the institutions are empowered to impart. Therefore, for the conflict theorists, educational institutions and systems neither function nor exist as fair and impartial entities but rather as instruments for control and domination that simply perpetuate the inequalities already inherent in society.

When analyzing adult education and its role as both a cause and as a result of social change, it is not only vital to consider these two contrasting paradigms, but also to consider the more specific issues concerning the extent to which the end of adult education is directed toward either the collective or the individual good, to realize that organized adult education, as well as self-education, can be of a collective or individual nature, and to question the extent to which the educational activities are connected to a broader social and political struggle.

One might contend that because adult education has a lesser role to play in the development of values and attitudes (because supposedly adults have already internalized these) than does preadult education, that its study is perhaps less relevant. Yet, given the growing existence of adult education, its role must be considered. Employing a consensus paradigm, for example, an important use of adult education is to provide the knowledge and capability necessary to maintain an efficient performance of one's allocated adult role for the good of society at large. Thus, a clear social function of adult education is to maintain and upgrade the human capital necessary for the competitive and efficient economy to work for society's good. Said another way, one objective of adult education is to create and maintain a steady and reliable labor pool that will contribute to the maintenance and growth of the larger economy, therefore generally providing a higher standard of living and greater social stability.

The need to facilitate change in a dynamic society derives from the desire of adults to remain current in the wake of rapid change and an increasing pool of knowledge. This purpose, however, has two dimensions: one is social and the other is material.

On the social dimension, as values, attitudes, and beliefs change, so do social role expectations. And as role expectations change so must the behavior of adults. (Consider the significant increase of women in the labor force and the concomitant alteration of social perspective concerning gender roles and responsibilities.) This need to change and to respond to change has been a factor not only in continuing professional education programs in law, medicine, nursing, and other fields, but has also led many adults to pursue undergraduate degrees in order to remain competitive in the job market.

Rapid change in a material sense pertains to the rapid change in knowledge needed to perform specialized tasks, especially in the scientific and technical occupations in which there has been a tremendous amount of growth over the past 50 years. As knowledge has increased, larger fields break down into more spe-

cialized ones and work becomes organized into specialized functions. One glaring example of this is, of course, the increasingly specialized field of computer technology and related areas. Specialization dramatically increases the need for communication and coordination among specialized units and results in a demand for more efficient management and management training. This, in turn, increases the demand not only for "in-house" adult education conducted by professional institutions and businesses, but also for more specialized degree and certificate offerings by educational institutions.

As stated earlier, the number of adult students has been steadily increasing since the end of World War II. This increase may be attributed to a rapidly changing economy and a concomitant requirement that people become continually more competitive in the labor market. In addition, the entry of large numbers of women into the labor force and of necessity into credit-bearing adult programs has had a significant impact on the nature of adult education.

In the early 1960s, approximately 36% of adult students participated in courses sponsored by community organizations while only about 21% were enrolled in college and university courses. Since then, the role of community organizations has diminished and that of formal educational institutions, especially colleges and universities, has increased. Currently, over 43% of college students are over the age of 25 while only about 20% of college students are full time, in residence, and under 22 years of age. Due to developments linked to the information economy, as well as rapid developments in technology, the economic function of adult education is becoming increasingly important.

Regarding the social functions of adult education, we must consider participation patterns and what these patterns suggest about mobility and the use of adult education as a form of leisure consumption. Adult education, with rare exceptions, is governed by self-selection; that is, unlike their younger, traditionally aged counterparts, although they may be under economic compulsion to do so, adults are under no legal compulsion to attend school. Therefore, the issue of participation is significant regarding an understanding of the social functions of adult education.

Rubenson (1980) has argued that there is a correlation between socioeconomic status of participants and the extent to which "education pays off in terms of income, status, occupation, political efficacy, cultural competence, and similar matters."

Participation must be understood in relation to the processes that foster the social construction of attitudes toward adult education and in relation to the social functions that adult education is allocated in society. Any system of adult education that either openly or implicitly assumes that the adult is a conscious, self-directed individual capable of exploiting the available possibilities for adult education—a system that relies on self-selection to recruit the participants—will inevitably widen the educational and cultural gaps in society.

This widening gap is of course viewed as inevitable and acceptable by the consensus point of view as long as there has been prior equality of opportunity and as long as the selection is based upon achievement. One purpose of adult education traditionally has been to support and maintain the good social order. True democracy requires not only a citizenry capable of critical thinking, but also one that is willing and able to participate. This view, incidentally, because it assumes shared societal values, ideals, and goals, may be considered as part of the foundation for the current attack on programs such as affirmative action and bilingualism, which implicitly assert that "prior equality of opportunity" has been denied certain groups within the society.

Of course, the notion of "equality" is challenged by proponents of the conflict perspective, who allege that the subsequent stress on achievement serves only to legitimate inequality. Citing the cycle of substandard childhood conditions, to include inadequate and short-term formal education, menial employment, and limited access to political participation, conflict theorists assert that factual opportunities to participate are far from equal.

An important point concerning the social functions of education and inequality is the connection between supply of and demand for adult education—the processes that govern who gets what kind of adult education. As local economies in many parts of the country worsen or remain stagnant, and as companies lay off their workers or reduce benefits—including tuition remission—while all the time the cost of higher education continues to increase, it becomes increasingly

more difficult for the adult, who is often sending his or her own children to college, to afford to be educated. This economic factor, therefore, may have as a result a potential inequality of opportunity regarding the availability of education.

Yet adult education still seeks to promote productivity on both the societal and the organizational level. On the organizational level, there is a desire to increase efficiency through the enhancement of employee competence. This, among other reasons, is why employers often provide tuition reimbursement of some kind as a part of their benefits package. That is, they expect to get back something in return—a better-trained, more highly competent employee. On the societal level, the belief that human skills and knowledge are vital to economic growth fosters the belief in an on-going educational endeavor.

Another general purpose of adult education is to facilitate personal growth. The early twentieth-century ideal of the development of the "whole person" was transformed in the 1950s and 1960s by the humanist school of psychology led by Maslow and Rogers. For these humanists, the object of adult education is to assist learners in exercising the quality that separates humans from other animals—the ability to choose; or said another way, the ability to become even more human. Given this, adult education becomes highly learner centered, and the adult educator functions primarily as a facilitator rather than as the more traditional teacher or professor. This has had a direct impact on the curricular thinking and development of many adult education programs as planners and faculty constantly seek out ways to provide their adult students with opportunities to participate in curriculum development and to tailor programs to their specific needs and interests.

The field of adult education remains a fertile one for research. As adult learners increasingly become more visible in educational institutions and as these institutions, suffering from declining numbers of available traditionally aged freshmen, compete more and more intensely for these adult students, certain questions and issues will certainly arise. For example, one might well consider the nature of curriculum for these students, given not only a dynamic and rapidly changing technological society, but also the acknowledgment that they bring to the classroom a wealth of experiential knowledge far in advance of their younger counterparts. (And in some cases, especially in highly technical areas, more expertise than their instructors!) Or how will the on-going multiculturization of educational institutions impact upon curriculum and the delivery of educational services? And what will be the social consequences of these changes? What is the impact, considering not only the time required but also the possibility of personal enlightenment and fulfillment, of adult education on marriage and family life? Finally, in what way will the broadening of educational opportunities to include an ever-increasing number of adults affect the political and institutional structures of the larger society?

REFERENCES

Cassara, Beverly Benner, ed. 1990. *Adult Education in a Multicultural Society*. London: Routledge.

Grattan, Hartley C. 1959. *American Ideas About Adult Education, 1710–1951*. New York: Columbia University Press.

Lindeman, E.C. 1945. "The Sociology of Adult Education." *Journal of Educational Sociology* 19:4–13.

Merriam, Sharan B., and Phyllis M. Cunningham, eds. 1989. *Handbook of Adult and Continuing Education*. San Francisco: Jossey Bass.

Merritt, R., and F. Coombs. 1977. "Politics and Educational Reform." *Comparative Education Review* 21:247–273.

Parsons, Talcott. 1964. *The Social System*. New York: Free Press.

Rubenson, Kjell. 1980. "Background and Theoretical Context." In R. Hoeghielm and Kjell Rubenson (eds.), *Adult Education for Social Change*. Lund, Sweden: Liber.

———. 1989. "The Sociology of Adult Education." In Sharan B. Merriam and Phyllis M. Cunningham (eds.), *Handbook of Adult and Continuing Education*, pp. 51–69. San Francisco: Jossey-Bass.

AFFIRMATIVE ACTION IN EDUCATION

Roslyn Arlin Mickelson
Department of Sociology, University of North Carolina at Charlotte

Affirmative action in education refers to policies and programs designed to advance equality of educational opportunity for individuals from groups that have suffered systematic historical discrimination. Affirmative action practices employed by educational institutions include (1) those that seek out candidates from underrepresented groups and recruit them to apply for admission, for faculty positions, and for scholarships; (2) those that, given a pool of candidates with comparable credentials, hire, admit, or award scholarships to individuals from underrepresented groups; and (3) those that, utilizing separate performance standards or criteria, hire, admit, and award scholarships to individuals from underrepresented groups. Individuals who may receive affirmative action benefits include members of certain ethnic, racial, and gender groups, social classes, veterans, and people with physical disabilities. Actual affirmative action policies and programs and ways they are implemented vary by state, locality, and educational institution. The focus of this chapter will be higher education, although affirmative action in secondary schools will be discussed briefly.

Affirmative action in education is related to, but distinct from, affirmative action in employment. Because of the crucial linkages between formal educational credentials and entry into most professional and top managerial occupations, affirmative action in education has implications for affirmative action in the occupational structure as well. This is most directly true with respect to graduate and professional school admissions because the flow of candidates through the academic pipeline supplies the pool of candidates for the professoriate and the professions. Unless the numbers of people from underrepresented groups in the academic labor pool are sufficiently large, affirmative action in faculty employment is extremely difficult. It is in this way that affirmative action in undergraduate, graduate, and professional school admissions has a direct affect on affirmative action in the occupational structure of the academy and the professions, and an indirect affect on the larger occupational structure.

Affirmative Action and School Desegregation

For the past 30 years, race, ethnic, and gender inequality of educational opportunity at secondary and tertiary levels has been addressed through the twin policies of desegregation and affirmative action. In many cases, affirmative action policies are implemented as part of court-ordered desegregation efforts. Local school districts that were found guilty of segregation were required to take race into account when assigning students, teachers, and other staff members to schools. State university systems found guilty of segregation were required to employ, among other remedies, affirmative action in admissions and hiring. As evidence that it does not intend to segregate, a desegregating district can build into its plan certain procedures for using race-conscious policies for hiring and promoting minorities and women. Pending legislation and litigation in a number of states will seriously curtail affirmative action policies and practices in elementary and secondary schools, including the use of magnets that take race into consideration as tools for desegregation.

Race-conscious practices have been utilized to de-segregate selective public secondary schools such as Lowell High School in San Francisco, Bronx School of Science in New York, and Boston's Latin School. Lowell High School was an excellent illustration of the inter-section of race-conscious policies and desegregation at the secondary level. Admission to this school is by ex-amination and all students must meet minimum re-quirements. But because it is a public school and part of the San Francisco school district, Lowell was required to comply with the court-ordered desegregation plan. For San Francisco's nine primary racial/ethnic groups to be represented in each school, no student body of any San Francisco school was to exceed 40% of a single ethnic group. Although eligibility criteria varied by ethnic group, all those admitted to Lowell met the minimum. To maintain court-mandated diversity, Chinese-American youth were required to meet more stringent requirements than whites and other Asian-American students; Latino and black students meet less stringent requirements. Without the differential scor-ing system, Lowell's student body could become over-whelmingly Chinese American.

Although the intent of using disparate criteria was to keep Lowell integrated, critics claimed this arrange-ment worked as a preferential admissions program for all non-Chinese students [see Takagi (1993) for a nu-anced treatment of the complexity of affirmative action and Asian Americans in California]. Lowell High School continued to consider race in its admissions de-cisions until 1998 when, as a result of the settlement of a lawsuit brought by Asian-American parents, the San Francisco school district agreed to end race-conscious desegregation and admission policies.

The status of affirmative action in secondary school admissions is ambiguous. In 1998, a federal judge up-held the Boston school system's use of race for admit-ting students to the prestigious Boston Latin School because the policy advanced the goal of diversity, an objective the judge considered a legitimate state inter-est. The school reserved 35% of its seats for black and Latino students. Citing the absence of evidence for the educational value of diversity for Boston Latin students, the court of appeals reversed the lower court's decision. But the appellate court went to considerable length to uphold the principle of diversity as a possible justifi-cation for affirmative action (White, 1999).

A Brief History of Affirmative Action in Higher Education

Although a number of universities have sought diverse student bodies (typically on geographic and religious dimensions) through some form of preferential admis-sions for a very long time (Bowen and Bok, 1998; Ru-denstine, 1996), what is commonly understood as af-firmative action in higher education is rooted in the 1964 Civil Rights Act that bars discrimination based on race. In 1965 President Lyndon Johnson specifically outlined the rationale underlying racial preferences in education during a speech at Howard University: "You do not take a person who for years has been hobbled by chains, and liberate him, bring him up to the start-ing line, and then say, You are free to compete with all the others" (cited in Hacker, 1995:124).

Table 1 presents an overview of the key events re-garding affirmative action in higher education over the past 35 years. In the decades following President John-son's initiatives, many public and private universities developed affirmative action plans, eventually expand-ing them to faculty recruitment as well. Overall, these initiatives were responses to the changing social cli-mate, the political pressure from the civil rights and student movements, and legislative actions and judicial rulings requiring diversification of student bodies and faculties. Several key court cases refined the scope and limits of affirmative action policies in higher education.

Adams

This decision is directed at the integration of public university student bodies primarily, but not exclusively in the South. In the past 24 years, however, the many rulings in the case have alluded to faculty integration as a necessary component of the institutional changes that will facilitate and solidify the integration of stu-dent bodies. Such rulings illustrate the integral nature of affirmative action's relationship to desegregation of higher education. *Adams v. Califano* was first heard in 1971 and dismissed in 1987. Many states, nevertheless, continued to operate under its provisions voluntarily. The federal courts revived the *Adams* case in 1989 and expanded it to 18 states. Scholars generally agree that *Adams* was successful in desegregating undergraduate student bodies at public universities, but less successful in opening access to greater numbers of minority youth (Trent, 1991). Enrollment patterns suggest that mi-

TABLE 1. Key Events Regarding Affirmative Action in Higher Education

YEAR	EVENT
1964	Congress passes the Civil Rights Act that bars discrimination based on race.
1965	Congress passes the Higher Education Act that will later be extended to include most federal student-aid programs.
1965	President Johnson delivers speech at Howard University in which he outlines many of the ideas underlying policies of affirmative action. Executive Order 11246 issued by President Lyndon B. Johnson in 1965 lays the policy groundwork for affirmative action in higher education.
1967	Texas Supreme Court rejects a legal challenge to Rice University's decision to change its charter and admit students of all races.
1967	President Johnson issued Executive Order 11375 that adds sex to race as illegitimate bases for discrimination.
1969	City University of New York adopts an open-admissions policy for 1970.
1970	NAACP Legal Defense and Education Fund sues the United States charging that it has failed to order the desegregation of public colleges in 10 Southern and border states.
1971	Harvard University adopts an affirmative action program for the hiring of women and members of minority groups.
1972	Williams College adopts a policy of affirmative action in faculty recruitment and hiring.
1972	Congress creates Basic Education Opportunity Grants (Pell Grants) that are the primary government grant to low-income students.
1973	American Association of University Professors endorses the use of affirmative action in faculty hiring.
1973	In the *Adams* case, the judge rules that the federal government must seek desegregation plans from the 10 states found operating segregated systems of higher education.
1974	California Assembly passes a resolution that promotes minority representation at the University of California proportionate to the racial composition of the state's high schools, setting the stage for various affirmative action policies and programs for greater recruitment and enrollment of minority students.
1978	Supreme Court rules in *University of California v. Bakke* that colleges may use race as a factor in admissions decisions, but may not set aside a specific proportion of seats for minority students.
1978	Congress passes the Tribally Controlled Community College Assistance Act providing federal funds to colleges run by American Indian tribes.
1980	President Carter issues the first executive order on black colleges that directs federal agencies to give greater consideration to them when awarding grants and contracts.
1983	Supreme Court rules that Bob Jones University cannot receive nonprofit tax exempt status because of its racially discriminatory policies.
1985	College Board reports that gains made by black students in the 1960s and early 1970s have eroded during the previous 10 years and trends are threatening to reverse the movement toward equality.
1987	A federal judge dismisses the *Adams* case.
1987	A study by the University of California at Berkeley rejects the charge that its admissions policies have been discriminatory toward Asian Americans.
1987	University of Michigan unveils a plan to increase the number of minority faculty and students.
1988	University of Wisconsin unveils a plan to increase the number of minority faculty and students.
1988	Duke University unveils a plan to increase the number of minority faculty.
1988	American Council on Education declares that the future prosperity of the United States is at risk unless the nation recommits to the advancement of minority group members.
1989	Federal court of appeals revives the *Adams* case, expanding it to 18 states.
1990	Head of the Education Department in the U.S. Office for Civil Rights declares race-based scholarships to be illegal.
1992	Supreme Court rules that Mississippi has not sufficiently dismantled segregation in its universities and the state responds by closing and merging several historically black colleges.
1994	Education Department upholds the legality of minority scholarships created by colleges in order to promote diversity or to remedy past discrimination.
1995	President Clinton orders a review of all federal laws involving affirmative action.
1995	Supreme Court declares unconstitutional race-based scholarships in *Poderesky v. Maryland*.
1995	Supreme Court declares unconstitutional minority set-asides in granting of contracts in *Adarand Construction v. Pena*.
1995	University of California regents prohibit any admission, contract, or employment policy that permits gender or racial preferences.

(Continued on next page)

TABLE 1. *(continued)*

Year	Event
1995	*U.S. v. Louisiana* and *U.S. v. Fordice* permit Louisiana and Mississippi to use racial considerations in admissions in order to integrate universities in compliance with court mandated desegregation.
1996	Proposition 209, which eliminates race, gender, or ethnic preferences in any state governmental institution or action, is approved by California voters.
1996	5th U.S. Circuit Court of Appeals rules in *Hopwood v. Texas* that the University of Texas law school may not justify affirmative action programs based on the benefits of a diverse student body to the school's learning environment and that the law school violated the law by using affirmative action programs that used race in its admission criteria. The U.S. Supreme Court declines to review the lower court's ruling.
1997	Texas state law requires the university to admit the top 10% of seniors from each of the state's high school graduating classes. Due to *de facto* segregation of Texas high schools, large numbers of Latino and black students are eligible for admission to the University of Texas despite *Hopwood*.
1997	In *Taxman v. Board of Education of the Township of Piscataway* the court of appeals reversed a lower court's decision and, citing *Hopwood*, declared that while the goal of a racially diverse faculty was laudable, an employer is not permitted to advance that goal through the use of discriminatory measures such as the school board's race-based exceptions to seniority protected layoffs.
1998	William G. Bowen, former President of Princeton, and Derek Bok, former President of Harvard, publish a defense of affirmative action in higher education, *The Shape of the River*.
1998	U.S. Supreme Court declines to hear an appeal of a Nevada Supreme Court decision in *Farmer v. University and Community College System of Nevada*. The Nevada Supreme Court upheld the use of affirmative action in faculty hiring because the University of Nevada demonstrated a compelling interest in fostering an ethnically and culturally diverse faculty.
1998	In *Wessman v. Gittens,* a lower court upheld the Boston school system's use of race to foster diversity in admitting students to Boston Latin. However, the court of appeals ruled that the admission procedure was insufficiently narrowly crafted and thus discriminated against white applicants.
1999	In *Wooden v. Board of Regents of the University System of Georgia*, a trial judge invalidated the university's already replaced affirmative action plan. The same judge dismissed on technical grounds a later challenge to the revised affirmative action plan.
1999	The President of the University of Georgia, Michael Adams, announced that the admissions office would continue to use race as a factor in admissions.
2001	Regents of the University of California unanimously rescind their ban on affirmative action because of its devastating effects on minority enrollment, which plummeted since the 1995 ban, and its companion constitutional amendment, Prop. 209.

Sources: Chronicle of Higher Education (1995–2001) and White (1999).

nority students have shifted from historically black colleges to historically white ones.

Bakke

In 1978, Alan Bakke, a white male, contended that when the University of California at Davis Medical School set aside 16 of 100 seats for underrepresented minorities, it lowered its standards for admission, restricted white peoples' access to the medical school, and had denied him admission on the basis of his race. A divided U.S. Supreme Court ruled in *Regents of the University of California v. Bakke* that (1) unless evidence of specific discrimination by an institution is established, race cannot be used as a remedy; (2) a person's race cannot be used as a sole criterion for an admissions decision; and (3) race and ethnicity along with other

criteria can be used in admissions in order to meet criteria that advance an institution's priorities.

Poderesky

In 1995, a Hispanic student denied a Benjamin Banneker scholarship to the University of Maryland because he was not black sued the state of Maryland for racial discrimination. The Supreme Court ruled in *Podersky v. Maryland* that race-based scholarships were unconstitutional. Critics of race-based scholarships claim they are unfair and often are unnecessary because many of the minorities receiving them could afford to attend any university. This ruling has greater symbolic than substantive significance. Approximately 2% of all financial aid available to college students is money geared for minority scholarships and less than 3% of minority students receive race-specific scholarships (Jaschik, 1991).

Hopwood

In March 1996 a federal appeals court upheld a lower court ruling in *Hopwood v. Texas* that the University of Texas law school's affirmative action policy designed to diversify the student body was unconstitutional, although one that employs affirmative action to remedy past discrimination is not. *Hopwood*'s ban on race-conscious policies applies to higher education in Texas, Louisiana, and Mississippi. This ruling directly challenges the *Bakke* precedent. In the wake of this decision, the Texas legislature revised the laws governing undergraduate admission criteria to the University of Texas. Now, the University of Texas is required to admit the top 10% of seniors in each high school class across the entire state. Because of *de facto* segregation, significant numbers of black and Latino students who attend segregated high schools are eligible for admission without the use of the affirmative action banned by *Hopwood*.

Proposition 209

In 1995, the Regents of the University of California voted to end the university system's use of gender or racial preferences in admissions, contracts, or employment. This action began a contentious public debate over affirmative action in the state of California that culminated in the 1996 passage of Proposition 209, also called the California Civil Rights Initiative. Proposition 209 bans the use of race, ethnic, or gender preferences in any state government institution or action. The initiative's constitutionality was upheld by the federal appellate court in 1997.

Farmer v. University and Community College System of Nevada

The Nevada Supreme Court upheld the use of affirmative action in faculty hiring because the University of Nevada demonstrated a compelling interest in fostering an ethnically and culturally diverse faculty. In 1998, the U.S. Supreme Court declined to hear an appeal of *Farmer v. University and Community College System of Nevada*. The plaintiff's attorneys argued that her case was similar to that of a white high school teacher in Piscataway, New Jersey who was laid off so

that an equally qualified black teacher could diversify the otherwise all white business education department. In *Taxman v. Board of Education of the Township of Piscataway*, the federal court agreed with the white teacher that the school administration had discriminated against her. The school board settled the race discrimination case just months before the U.S. Supreme Court was to hear the Piscataway case on appeal.

Results of Affirmative Action Efforts over the Past 25 Years

The long-term results of 25 years of affirmative action are mixed. They neither have confirmed critics' worst fears of gross unfairness to white males and psychological damage to minorities, or realized advocates' dreams of equalizing educational opportunities. Studies indicate that modest progress in desegregating or diversifying formerly racially exclusive student bodies has been made during the past several decades (Trent, 1991). Some progress toward race and gender parity has occurred at the undergraduate level, and to a lesser extent at the graduate level. Professional school enrollment has been affected the most by affirmative action. Underrepresented groups, especially white women, made notable inroads into the ranks of university faculties. But the gains have been in selective fields and at the lower ranks.

Student Enrollment

A comparison of enrollments in institutions of higher education by level of study, gender, and race in 1976 and 1996 appears in Table 2. At the undergraduate level, the proportion of black and white males enrolled has dropped while that of all other race and gender groups has increased. In 1976, white males comprised 43.7% of undergraduates and 33.7% in 1993. Black and white women experienced modest gains. The largest gains have been among Hispanic and Asian men, and especially women who have tripled their proportions of undergraduate seats. Racial and gender shifts in enrollment at the professional school level are the most striking. In 1976, 71.5% of all professional school students were white males and 19.7% were white females, leaving 8.8% of seats to be filled by members of other racial groups. By 1993, white males comprised 48% and white females represented 31.1% of profes-

TABLE 2. Enrollment in Institutions of Higher Education by Level of Study, Gender, and Race/Ethnicity, 1976 and 1993

	1976			1993		
LEVEL OF STUDY	ALL (%)	MALE (%)	FEMALE (%)	ALL (%)	MALE (%)	FEMALE (%)
Undergraduates						
Number		9,419,000			12,324,000	
White (non-Hispanic)	83.4	43.7	39.8	75.5	33.7	41.8
Black	9.9	4.6	5.5	10.7	4.1	6.5
Hispanic	3.8	2.1	1.7	7.6	3.4	4.2
Asian/Pacific Islander	1.8	1.0	0.8	5.3	2.6	2.7
American Indian/Alaskan	0.8	0.3	0.4	0.9	0.4	0.5
	100			100		
Graduates						
Number		1,322,500			1,689,300	
White (non-Hispanic)	89.2	47.1	42.1	84.6	36.6	48.0
Black	6.3	2.6	3.7	6.7	2.3	4.4
Hispanic	2.1	1.2	0.9	3.9	1.7	2.2
Asian/Pacific Islander	2.0	1.2	0.8	4.3	2.3	2.0
American Indian/Alaskan	0.4	0.2	0.2	0.5	0.2	0.3
	100			100		
Professionals						
Number		244,000			292,400	
White (non-Hispanic)	91.3	71.5	19.7	79.1	48	31.1
Black	4.6	3.0	1.6	7.1	3.1	4.0
Hispanic	1.9	1.5	0.4	4.4	2.5	1.9
Asian/Pacific Islander	1.7	1.2	0.5	8.6	4.9	3.9
American Indian/Alaskan	0.5	0.4	0.1	0.6	0.3	0.3
	100			100		

Source: National Center for Educational Statistics (1995).

sional school students. The largest absolute gains in enrollment have been enjoyed by white women, but Asian, Hispanic, black, and American-Indian women have also garnered greater shares of seats in professional schools.

During the past century, historically black institutions of higher education began to meet the demand for higher education for students excluded from other universities because of their race. Today, there are 99 historically black schools, almost all in southern and border states. Their enrollments remain overwhelmingly black largely because of voluntary decisions by students. Nevertheless, there are almost twice as many students who are not black at historically black colleges as there are minority students at historically white campuses. Today ethnic and racial minority students largely attend integrated schools, but typically, the student

bodies of historically white campuses are less than 15% minority. White graduate student enrollment at a number of historically black universities, particularly in professional programs in the most selective schools, sometimes approaches 50%. Overall gender and race segregation between and within colleges has diminished over the past 25 years, but continues to be significant on many dimensions such as enrollment in engineering programs (Jacobs, 1996a).

It would be inaccurate to attribute these demographic shifts to affirmative action alone. Although there is little doubt that affirmative action policies were responsible to some degree for these changes, at the same time, cultural norms have changed and many legal and structural barriers have eased. The weakening of the structural barriers that historically blocked women and people of color from pursuing higher education has operated in conjunction with affirmative action policies to effect the enrollment changes reflected in Table 2.

Higher Education Faculty

One measure of affirmative action's accomplishments is the degree to which the teaching ranks of the academy have been diversified over the past 25 years. Today, 32.5% of all professors and 42.5% of assistant professors are women. In 1995 racial and ethnic minorities constituted 13.2% of professors; in 1969, only 3.7% were racial and ethnic minorities. Among assistant professors today, 16.5% are minorities. Black academics constitute 5.8% of the professoriate, up from 2.2% in 1969 (see Table 3). However, minority faculty are disproportionately found at the less prestigious institutions and at lesser ranked institutions. Attempts by prestigious universities to hire more minority faculty have resulted in greater occupational mobility for "superstars," but have not expanded the overall number of minority faculty or equalized their distribution across the academy.

It is well documented that minorities were prohibited from acquiring the education and training necessary to become academics prior to 1960. Until then, for example, only 2% of professors were African Americans and most were faculty in historically black colleges (Jackson, 1991). Since the 1960s, the factors contributing to the underrepresentation of minority faculty have become more complex than merely outright exclusionary practices. They include the limited supply of minorities with terminal degrees in fields other than education, the continued use of exclusionary practices, and the subtle racism of the search and recruitment, screening processes (Mickelson and Oliver, 1991).

The difficulties of women in the academy are somewhat different. Today, there is no overall shortage of women Ph.D.s, although their distribution across disciplines tends to reflect traditional gender differences. Women are found disproportionately in the lower rungs of the academy and are less likely to be promoted and tenured. Jacobs (1996b) concludes that the notion of cumulative disadvantage reasonably summarizes the underrepresentation of women in faculty positions.

Although affirmative action has brought limited and uneven gender diversity to faculties, there are still large discrepancies between university faculties, the aca-

demic labor pool, and minority demographics. The number of racial and ethnic minorities exiting the academic pipeline continues to be a mere trickle. In 1993, only 3.25% of doctoral degrees were awarded to blacks and 41% of these degrees were in education (thereby limiting the number of potential candidates for academic positions in other disciplines). Asians received 3.7% of doctorates, most of which were in the physical sciences or engineering. The number of doctorates awarded to Hispanics and American-Indian students remains minuscule. Table 4 presents the percent of doctoral degrees awarded by race and gender in 1993.

The creation of a faculty relies on a three-stage process: (1) the production of Ph.D.s, (2) the search and hiring process, and (3) tenure and promotion practices. Affirmative action pertains most directly to the process of academic searches. Although search processes are formally designed to utilize neutral, objective, and universalistic criteria, an established literature demonstrates that the search process is riddled by precisely the opposite tendencies. Search committees charged with securing a new colleague often rely on so-called proven categories of evaluation to assess potential candidates, namely the ranking of a candidate's graduate department and the recommendations of prestigious, influential, and well-known scholars. In this initial screening, the candidate is not the issue; the school and the referee's reputation serve as proxies for the applicant's own merit. The process by which faculty candidates are identified, screened, and selected, although guided by a set of ostensibly meritocratic norms, actually works against the selection and hiring of minorities because so few are graduates of leading institutions and have renowned scholars as mentors. Most minorities, then, never make the "short list" where affirmative action hiring policies are put into practice (Mickelson and Oliver, 1991).

Current Controversy

Affirmative action policies in public education, particularly at the tertiary level, were at the center of many heated debates across the United States in the 1990s. The conflict over affirmative action is a part of a struggle over the uses of education, a struggle that has intensified as the effects of economic restructuring widen.

TABLE 3. Percent Distribution of Full Time Faculty by Gender and Race/Ethnicity, 1969 and 1992; Assistant Professors, 1992

	1969	1992		
	TOTAL (%)	TOTAL (%)	MALE (%)	FEMALE (%)
All Faculty				
White, non-Hispanic	96.3	86.8	58.9	27.8
Black	2.2	4.9	2.6	2.3
Hispanic	n.a.	2.5	1.7	0.8
Asian/Pacific Islander	1.3	5.3	4.0	1.3
American Indian/Alaskan Native	n.a.	0.5	0.3	0.2
	100	100		
Assistant Professors				
White, non-Hispanic		83.5	47.5	36.0
Black		5.8	2.8	3.0
Hispanic		3.2	2.0	1.2
Asian/Pacific Islander		7.1	5.0	2.1
American Indian/Alaskan Native		0.4	0.2	0.2
		100		

Source: National Center for Educational Statistics (1976, 1995).

Formerly secure middle-class Americans have become more anxious about their own and their children's economic future (Mickelson and Ray, 1994). The importance adults attach to education for status attainment and maintenance has sharpened. Parents' fears of their children's potential downward mobility have heightened the perceived importance of children getting into a *good* college.

At the same time that families see the American Dream fading for their children, many of the better institutions of higher education are becoming more competitive. This is especially true for the most selective colleges and universities that receive far more applications than they have seats. With competition for college admission growing stiffer and college degrees becoming an increasingly necessary credential for movement into or maintenance of middle-class status, any perceived unearned advantages in the college admission process, like affirmative action, have become intolerable to many people.

The debate over affirmative action is also a manifestation of racial politics (Takagi, 1993). Part of the difficulty in analyzing the controversy is that it is extremely difficult to disentangle the racial, gender, and class politics of education from larger ideological struggles over race, immigration, and class conflict. In the 1990s, many people saw affirmative action as one ele-

ment in an array of special services and programs, including bilingual and multicultural education, that disadvantaged white students and their families while privileging immigrants and minority youngsters. At the higher education level, critics often link affirmative action to attempts to expand the canon. In their view, the former gives unearned advantages to minorities and the latter attacks white cultural traditions as it weakens standards of excellence in education.

Traditional Preferential Admissions Policies

Ethnic, racial, and religious struggles over admission to top universities are not new. Race or group conscious (nonmeritocratic) criteria have been used to admit or exclude students from institutions of higher education throughout the twentieth century. Until 30 years ago, women and minority students were regularly denied admission solely on the basis of their gender and race. As Jews began to outscore many white Anglo-Saxon Protestants on college entrance exams during the early part of the twentieth century, student bodies of Ivy League schools experienced an increase of Jewish students. In response to this encroachment on white Anglo-Saxon Protestant privileged access, Ivy League schools began to utilize nonacademic criteria like char-

TABLE 4. Percent Doctoral Degrees Awarded by Race/Ethnicity and Gender, 1993

	TOTAL (%)	MALE (%)	FEMALE (%)
White, non-Hispanic	63.7	34.7	28.0
Black	3.25	1.5	1.75
Hispanic	1.9	1.0	0.9
Asian/Pacific Islander	3.5	1.7	1.8
American Indian/ Alaskan Native	0.7	0.35	0.35
Nonresident	27		
	100		

Source: National Center for Educational Statistics (1995).

acter and lineage for admissions. Later, many Ivy League colleges established quotas limiting the number of Jews who could be admitted in a given class.

Today, minority students are far from the only groups that receive special or preferential treatment in college admissions. Often overlooked in the affirmative action debate are the other categories of preferential admission that include students from elite preparatory schools, veterans, musicians, artists, students from rural areas, children of faculty, of powerful state legislators, and, in the case of California, the children of members of the board of regents of the university itself.

The practice of admitting children of alumni— legacies—is widespread throughout higher education, especially at selective public and private colleges and universities. This form of preferential admissions primarily benefits the offspring of affluent, white male alumni. It results in the admission of students who tend to score significantly lower on college entrance exams and who have high school grades lower than non-legacies. Legacies, who comprise the largest segment of the preferential admissions population at most campuses, displace applicants with higher grades and test scores, yet they are twice as likely to be admitted than a black or Hispanic student admitted by affirmative action. With the exception of athletes, nonlegacies who are admitted score better than legacies in almost all areas of comparison (Larew, 1991).

Admissions Based on Merit?

A common argument against affirmative action in college admissions is the claim that such programs violate the precept of fair competition based on individual merit. Opponents advocate that admissions decisions be made primarily on the basis of objective indicators of merit (some argue for only merit-based admissions). Such calls are based on two assumptions: (1) that current educational outcomes (test scores and grades) are no longer tied to historical conditions that created huge gaps in opportunities to learn, and (2) there are simple, valid, quantifiable, and objective techniques to assess merit. In fact, the indicators most often used—standardized entrance exams and high school grades—are as likely to reflect class, race, and gender privilege as they are to indicate academic qualifications for college.

Opportunities to Learn in Secondary Schools

High school grades and ranks are questionable objective indicators of merit. The quality and rigor of secondary institutions vary widely and must be considered in any meaningful evaluation of high school grades. Levels of secondary school segregation remain extremely high in urban areas where most minority youngsters live. A wealth of scholarship points to the strikingly different educational experiences experienced by inner city, rural, and suburban youth. For example, California urban high schools with large minority populations offer relatively fewer Advanced Placement courses than suburban schools. These variations in opportunities to learn are reflected in high school grade point averages and test scores.

College Entrance Exams

A great deal of literature has been written about the validity and reliability of grades and college board scores for predicting college success. Even test manufacturers caution against overreliance on test scores to indicate the probability of college persistence. First, the tests are only predictive of the likely academic performance of students during the first 2 years of college. Second, scores can be improved through coaching, tutoring, and practice test-taking. Students from certain social groups are more likely to have access to the cultural and financial capital that provide these score-enhancing opportunities. Scores may reflect class and cultural differences rather than aptitude. For example, some Asian Americans are less likely to score well on verbal sections than individuals from similar social classes in other ethnic groups. Third, the likelihood of the tests predicting college performance varies by sub-groups. They are notoriously uneven predictors for African Americans.

Given the widely understood purpose of these tests as the prediction of university retention and graduation, it is strikingly ironic that scores do not increase a college's ability to make more accurate decisions to admit over high school records alone (Crouse and Trusheim, 1988). This may be due to the tests' inability to assess crucial qualities such as creativity, self-discipline, or perseverance that undoubtedly contribute to college success. Despite years of research with hundreds of bias consultants, no tests have been devised that are race, culture, gender, or class neutral.

Arguments in Favor of Affirmative Action

A careful evaluation of the standard indicators of merit upon which college admissions decisions are made suggests they are far from objective. In conjunction with the long-term and widespread use in admissions decisions of nonmeritocratic criteria such as athletic prowess or academic lineage, it is problematic to call for a *return* to meritocratic procedures in the name of fairness. One could argue that fairness requires affirmative action as a countervailing force against the practices and procedures described in the previous sections.

Three pillars undergird the argument in support of affirmative action. The first is that affirmative action is a necessary legal and moral remedy for past discrimination. The current debate glosses over or ignores the facts that created the need for the preferential policies in the first place. Few critics acknowledge that until about 40 years ago, the state (both federal and state levels) sanctioned and enforced segregation in employment, housing, and education at virtually all levels. Until about 50 years ago, almost all colleges were formally segregated. A critique of this position holds that those from whom the preferential admissions debt is exacted are not necessarily responsible for the past discrimination. Immigrants and their children, for example, are not culpable for slavery and its sequela. Numerous white ethnic groups—Jews, Poles, and Irish—experienced overt discrimination this century. Walter Feinberg (1996) makes a moral case for backward-looking race- and gender-affirmative action in university admissions despite these concerns.

The second argument maintains that affirmative action is a protection or a prophylactic necessary to deal with the persistent race and gender barriers to equal educational opportunities. The United States still does not offer equal education to its citizens. The absence of an equal start stands at the heart of the continuing educational discrimination that affirmative action seeks to remedy. Membership in certain racial, ethnic, gender, and class groups is likely to deny some while it enables other people to enjoy educational advantages. Affirmative action practices intervene in ways that compensate for the disadvantages of unequal opportunities to learn that accumulate over 13 years.

The third argument is that affirmative action can be transformative because inclusivity and diversity in higher education strengthen and democratize institutions and the people who attend them and, ultimately, society. The diversity that students bring to campus makes for a more dynamic intellectual environment and a richer undergraduate experience. However in March 1996 the 5th U.S. Circuit Court of Appeals in *Hopwood v. University of Texas* struck down a law school admissions policy premised upon this logic. The U.S. Supreme Court declined to review the circuit court's decision, thus allowing the ruling to become the law in the southwestern portion of the nation (Texas, Louisiana, and Mississippi).

Affirmative action policies also can be transformative when they contribute to the credentialing of more minority and women teachers, police, physicists, physicians, and managers who provide effective service to society and also serve as role models for children of all races. Once minorities and women are in decision-making positions, they can enforce greater fairness. Affirmative action practices can be transformative because they allow majority group members to interact with diverse students in situations of mutuality, cooperation, and equal status—conditions that make possible reductions in racism and sexism.

One difficulty with this argument is that the empirical record does not suggest that affirmative action has enjoyed remarkable success in transforming American society along these lines. Although enrollment levels of women and minority students have improved, and university faculty are more diverse than 25 years ago, clearly there are limitations to this approach to social change.

Arguments against Affirmative Action

The first argument against affirmative action is that it is damaging to minorities. Justice Clarence Thomas, himself a beneficiary of preferential admissions policies at Holy Cross where he received his undergraduate degree and Yale University where he attended law school, has argued that affirmative action is a type of racial paternalism that implies minorities cannot compete without whites' indulgence. Other minority critics (Carter, 1991; Steele, 1991) claim that the very quality that earns minorities preferences is an implied inferiority. Racial preferences place minorities in the realm of debilitating self-doubt and others do not hold them to the same level of performance as white students, thus compromising the education minority students receive.

But there is little evidence that blacks and other recipients of these actions have self-doubts and misgivings because of the preferential admissions, although some whites may assume that any minority is *ipso facto* an affirmative action candidate and therefore less qualified (Hochschild, 1995). Andrew Hacker (1995) observes that feelings of unworthiness seldom plague white Americans who profit from traditional forms of preference.

A second line of criticism holds that affirmative action is ultimately unfair and unethical because it violates the basic principles of equality of opportunity when it privileges group rights over individuals. Yet, as W.E.B. Dubois noted, the history of the world has been the history of groups, not individuals. Similarly, critics charge affirmative action violates legal and constitutional prescriptions for racial and gender neutrality by the state. The neoconservative civil rights agenda, for example, is simply a policy of race and gender neutrality that necessitates the elimination of all forms of racial and gender discrimination by public officials and institutions. Calls for every person to be treated as an individual without reference to any group membership assume that once legislation enshrines equal treatment under the law, individuals and institutions will cease to discriminate against some while favoring others. Sadly, history and contemporary events suggest otherwise.

Third, critics believe that affirmative action unfairly displaces more qualified applicants with less qualified members of protected groups. It is, however, difficult to demonstrate that this is true because those with better test scores may have been displaced by legacies, children of faculty, artists, athletes, and so on. Moreover, this argument presumes that tests and grades are the only valid measures of "qualifications." Students typically admitted under race and gender preferential policies are qualified under the broad terms of a university's requirements. For example, the University of California considers those students UC-qualified who graduated in the top 12.5% of their high school class and have passed the requisite high school courses. This creates a large pool of eligible youths with a very broad range of grade point averages. Moreover, the two most selective UC campuses, Berkeley and Los Angeles, receive thousands of applications from students with grade point averages (GPAs) above 4.0. Students with 3.8 GPAs are officially UC eligible, but they must compete with others who have higher GPAs. Simply ranking students as more or less qualified by scores alone does not consider whether a 3.8 GPA from an inner city high school pupil represents greater achievement, persistence, and determination than a 4.4 GPA earned by a student from a suburban school that offered more Advanced Placement courses.

The fourth argument holds that affirmative action is ineffective in advancing overall equality of opportunity because it does not benefit poor minorities in whose interests the policies were ostensibly created and women no longer need affirmative action because they already have advanced so far based on their accomplishments. Other critics reason that race-specific programs have benefited mainly the best prepared and least disadvantaged minorities and have alienated whites from the Democratic Party coalition that then hurts minorities more than affirmative action has helped them. Instead, some progressive critics advocate for race-neutral social programs and policies based on economic disadvantage.

The trouble with using class in lieu of race is that there are so many low-income and poor whites, that most available seats for preferential admissions will be utilized by whites, edging out minorities and defeating one of the purposes of preferential admissions—increasing minority presence in higher education. Moreover, as Dana Takagi (1993) argues, class is not a proxy for race. Although they intersect, the two are independent sources of discrimination. Walter Feinberg (1996) suggests that class-based affirmative action ignores the moral imperative for affirmative action. He calls for policies that fold economic need into ethical considerations based on historic debts to people of color.

Conclusions and Policy Considerations

The legacies of *Hopwood* and Proposition 209 are ambiguous. Anti-affirmative action legislation and litigation continue in many states. For example, the University of Michigan faces two lawsuits aimed at ending affirmative action in admissions (*Gratz et al. v. Bollinger et al.,* and *Grutter et al. v. Bollinger et al.*). Many state university systems are consciously seeking ways to ensure public higher education is available to all citizens without affirmative action. The University of Texas's undergraduate admission rates for racial and ethnic minority students remains comparable to pre-*Hopwood* numbers. Because of the 1997 Texas law requiring admission for the top 10% of each high class, in the fall of 1998, only 6% fewer black undergraduates and 2% fewer Latino students are admitted to the University of Texas (Sandham and Johnston, 1998). And although *Hopwood* applies to the states of Texas, Louisiana, and Mississippi, the effects of the ruling vary across the three states. *U.S. v. Louisiana* and *U.S. v. Fordice* require desegregation of public universities, so Mississippi and Louisiana continue to consider race in admissions and financial aid decisions. Due to the heated public struggles in the wake of *Hopwood* and Proposition 209, several state legislatures have failed to pass measures banning the use of racial preferences in education. Some university leaders, like the University of Georgia's President Michael Adams, have announced their intention to continue to use affirmative action in university admissions.

To a significant degree, the fundamental reasons that affirmative action programs were first introduced still exist. Access to higher education has improved for women, and to a lesser degree, for minority students. But race and gender stratification between and within institutions persists. If all preferential admissions and hiring practices are eliminated, it is likely that these race, ethnic, and gender disparities will grow. Such patterns are likely, especially in states with large ethnic and racial minority populations. The effects of ending affirmative action in graduate and professional programs will be even stronger. The most prestigious professional schools are likely to become almost overwhelmingly white and Asian.

There is widespread societal agreement that inequality in educational opportunity is unseemly and undesirable, even dangerous, in a democratic society. There is little controversy surrounding affirmative action programs that merely recruit candidates from underrepresented groups to apply for admission or positions; there is some controversy over programs that, given a pool of comparably credentialed candidates, hire or admit women and minorities in order to increase their representation on a campus. The most contentious and divisive policies are those that employ separate performance standards or criteria for hiring, promoting, and admitting women and people of color.

Any evaluation of the role of affirmative action in advancing equality of educational opportunity must acknowledge the linkages between this array of policies and systemic inequality throughout society. The need for affirmative action policies is rooted in the race, class, gender, and ethnic disparities in opportunities to learn in secondary schools, past and present. To the extent that affirmative action enhances the opportunities of one generation to acquire educational credentials and employment, it lays the groundwork for the next one. Yet it is difficult to expand opportunities in one institution without commensurate changes in the others. This interconnectedness suggests the limits and possibilities of affirmative action in education for advancing equality of educational opportunities. Given the limitations of affirmative action, the difficult legal and moral issues it raises, and the political passions it stirs, one could easily say of affirmative action in education what Winston Churchill said about democracy: "It is the worst possible system until you consider the alternatives."

REFERENCES

Bowen, William G., and Derek Bok. 1998. *The Shape of the River: Long-Term Consequences of Considering Race in College and University Admissions.* Princeton, NJ: Princeton University Press.

Carter, Stephen. 1991. *Reflections of an Affirmative Action Baby.* New York: Basic Books.

Crouse, James, and Dale Trusheim. 1988. *The Case Against the SAT.* Chicago: University of Chicago Press.

Feinberg, Walter. 1996. "Affirmative Action and Beyond: A Case for a Backward-Looking Gender- and Race-Based Policy." *Teachers College Record* 97:362–399.

Hacker, Andrew. 1995. *Two Nations.* New York: Ballantine.

Hendrie, Caroline. 1998. "U.S. Judge Upholds Race-Based Plan For Prestigious Boston High School." *Education Week* June 3:7.

Hochschild, Jennifer. 1995. *Facing up to the American Dream. Race, Class and the Soul of the Nation*. Princeton, NJ: Princeton University Press.

Jackson, Kenneth W. 1991. "Black Faculty in Academia." In Philip G. Altbach and Kofi Lomotey (eds.), *The Racial Crisis in American Higher Education,* pp. 135–148. Albany, NY: SUNY Press.

Jacobs, Jerry A. 1996a. "Gender Inequality and Higher Education." *Annual Review of Sociology* 22:153–185.

———. 1996b. "Gender and Race Segregation between and within Colleges." Paper presented at the Eastern Sociological Society, Boston, Massachusetts, April.

Jaschik, Scott. 1991. "Minority Scholarships." *Chronicle of Higher Education* June 5:A15.

Johnston, Robert C. 1998. "Minority Admissions Drop Sharply at California Universities." *Education Week* April 8:12.

Larew, John. 1991. "Who's the Real Affirmative Action Profiteer?" *Washington Monthly* June:10–14.

Mickelson, Roslyn Arlin, and Melvin L. Oliver. 1991. "Making the Short List: Black Candidates and the Faculty Recruitment Process." In Philip G. Altbach and Kofi Lomotey (eds.), *The Racial Crisis in American Higher Education,* pp. 149–166. Albany, NY: SUNY Press.

Mickelson, Roslyn Arlin, and Carol Axtell Ray. 1994. "Fear of Falling from Grace: The Middle Class, Downward Mobility, and School Desegregation." *Research in Sociology of Education and Socialization* (10):207–238.

National Center for Education Statistics. 1976. *Digest of Education Statistics*. U.S. Department of Education, Office of Educational Research and Improvement. Washington, DC: U.S. Government Printing Office.

———. 1995. *Digest of Education Statistics*. U.S. Department of Education, Office of Educational Research and Improvement. Washington, DC: U.S. Government Printing Office.

Rudenstine, Neil L. 1996. "The Uses of Diversity." *Harvard Magazine* March–April:48–63.

Sandham, Jessica L., and Robert C. Johnston. 1998. "Colleges Retool Outreach Efforts as Affirmative Action Changes." *Education Week* March 19:1–???.

Steele, Shelby. 1991. *The Content of Our Character*. New York: Basic Books.

Takagi, Dana Y. 1993. *The Retreat from Race. Asian-American Admissions and Racial Politics*. New Brunswick, NJ: Rutgers University Press.

Trent, William T. 1991. "Student Affirmative Action in Higher Education: Addressing Under-representation." In Philip G. Altbach and Kofi (eds.), *The Racial Crisis in American Higher Education,* pp. 107–134. Albany, NY: SUNY Press.

White, Lawrence. 1999. Address to the Conference on Diversity, American Council on Education, October 29, Albuquerque, NM.

AFRICAN-AMERICAN ACHIEVEMENT MOTIVATION

Margaret Hunter and Walter R. Allen
Department of Sociology, UCLA

The motivation of African-American students is a key concept in the national debate about the education of African-American children. Though an often studied topic in the 1960s and 1970s, much of the research in this area has shed little light on the enduring questions about African-American student achievement, self-concept, and motivation. This chapter attempts to highlight the major areas of research on African-American student motivation and their respective theoretical bases and empirical findings. Three primary areas of research in studies of black student motivation emerge: (1) the achievement motive model, (2) the locus of control studies, and (3) the self-concept and its relationship to motivation.

During the 1950s and 1960s, the United States enjoyed unprecedented economic prosperity due to the postwar boom. However, Jim Crow segregation in the South and persistent discrimination nationally continued to deny African Americans full access to the fruits of prosperity. Social scientists turned to the studies of achievement motivation in desperate attempts to understand the paradox of black failure and exclusion in the midst of widespread success and affluence in America.

Basing most of their work on Henry Murray's 1938 creation of the "need for achievement" concept, researchers such as McClelland and others brought this tool into something of a "Golden Age" during the 1950s and 1960s. The need for achievement motive is a social psychological tool used to understand individual motivation. Murray believed that an individual's "need for achievement" would be the primary impetus for his or her motivation. Whether or not one possessed this need for achievement was seen as a personality trait that would predict eventual success. The need for achievement motive, often referred to as nAch, became the standard bearer in motivation research throughout the 1950s and 1960s.

An underlying assumption of the approach is that motivation is an individual phenomenon that can be measured devoid of social context. This means that one can test for this trait in any individual by administering standardized questions that would measure the extent to which an individual possessed the personality traits associated with the "need for achievement." One of the tests most commonly used to test for nAch was the Thematic Apperception Test (TAT).

McClelland, Atkinson, Clark, and Lowell wrote a landmark piece of research on the nAch in 1953 entitled *The Achievement Motive*. At this time, however, these studies were still monoracial, usually focusing on white students. The first racially comparative study on the achievement motive was done by Mussen in 1953. From research done on elementary school boys, Mussen reported that white boys had greater motive strength than African-American boys. This finding came to represent what many of the subsequent researchers on the topic also found: white students have higher measured levels of "need for achievement" than do African-American students.[1]

Critiques reveal many limitations associated with the need for achievement motive model. First, racial comparisons are greatly limited by the confounding factors of race and socioeconomic status (SES). It seems

---

[1] Though many studies did find that white students continue to have greater motive strength than do black students, there is a current debate on how to interpret the vast number of studies done on the topic. For further information on this debate see Graham (1994), and Cooper and Dorr (1995).

quite plausible that one's "need for achievement" might well be affected by the resources available to that person, resources such as social class, background, opportunity structure, and quality of schooling. With this in mind, it seems problematic to draw conclusions from this model without controlling for socioeconomic class and background. Because African-American students are disproportionately low-income students, some findings attributed to race may in fact be more correctly seen as resulting from SES differences.

In McClelland's later work, he theorized that differences in need for achievement were derived from different childrearing patterns among families. As cultural explanations were becoming more and more popular as ways to explain racial group differences, the idea of childrearing differences between the races was often in the public debate. Though not confirmed by the data, McClelland's proposition that family socialization is the root of motivational differences among children set the agenda for further "cultural" research.

The second primary area of research on African-American student motivation is represented by the locus of control literature. These studies examine how students attribute personal successes and failures. Students who believe that factors such as luck or difficulty of a task are responsible for their successes and failures are said to have external loci of control. Often referred to as "externals" these students do not attribute successes or failures to their own behavior. They usually feel that powerful "higher-ups" or things beyond their control are responsible for outcomes. The opposite orientation, an internal locus of control, is characterized by feelings that attribute success or failure to personal competence or effort. These students tend to see themselves as completely responsible for their own behavior and outcomes. "Internals" usually blame themselves for failures and accept praise for successes.

This dichotomy of external and internal clearly has a Western, masculine bias that values self-efficacy over faith, individualism over social structure, and rationalism over emotion. This theory is limited in that it sees motivation and achievement only through a Western lens. Manifestations of such motivation or achievement must occur within a limited framework of socially approved, class-related individual behaviors and successes. Because it is culturally specific to only a subset of the children in the United States, the locus of control dichotomy can measure only one limited type of student motivation or achievement.

These concepts emphasize individual or psychological explanations of student motivation. Several researchers have identified the internal locus of control as a characteristic of highly motivated and achieving people. Many locus of control studies conclude that African-American students are more likely to exhibit an external locus of control and are therefore more likely to be lower achievers. Graham (1994) reports that 44% of the studies done on locus of control show that whites are more internal than blacks. In the remaining 56% of the studies, either mixed results or inconclusive results were reported. Though it is true that many studies do not confirm the hypothesis that blacks are more external than whites, clearly there is a significant proportion of the literature that has reached such a conclusion.

One of the major research endeavors on this topic was the Equality of Educational Opportunity Study done by James Coleman and a team of researchers in 1966. The Coleman Report, which came out of this study, was a major statement about student motivation, locus of control, and academic performance. Coleman and his team studied African-American students' "perceived control" over their behavior and outcomes in response to a growing national debate about school funding and equity. They found that perceived control accounted for more of the variance in African-American student achievement than family background characteristics. This publication drew the attention of many educational researchers and further popularized the association between locus of control and student motivation. Further, Coleman's conclusions fueled the debate about educational social policy. Many interpreted his findings to support the view that schools could not hope to erase the achievement gap between blacks and whites. Instead responsibility for this persistent gap was seen as evidence of poor socialization by black families and negative black cultural values.

Such theorization about African Americans came to be known in the 1970s as the Culture of Poverty perspective. Culture of Poverty theorists purport that even though racism is dead (or greatly diminished), poor black people have internalized negative beliefs and values that discourage them from working hard and competing in what they perceive as an inalterably unfair system of opportunities (i.e., the external locus of control). In turn these ghetto residents, or members of the "underclass," are said to "wrongly" believe that racism is an insurmountable obstacle, leaving them inevitably stuck in dead-end jobs and in extreme poverty. This failure to achieve is attributed to internal shortcomings and not to the continuing barriers of historic and contemporary discrimination.

The Coleman Report joins this category of research because it concludes that the main cause of African-American students' underachievement is their attitude or value system. More specifically, Coleman states that it is the attitude of black students to feel little control over their own outcomes and to feel less self-effective in surmounting the obstacles that they face. These findings and their interpretation fall well in line with the Culture of Poverty theorists who consistently underestimate the staying power of institutional racism and grossly overstate the feelings of helplessness and hopelessness in the African-American community. The Culture of Poverty perspective differs from the need for achievement model in its focus on cultural factors. However, with both perspectives, individual explanations ultimately loom large; inappropriate values rather than structural barriers are proposed to explain black underachievement. The effect is to mute attempts to examine the role of racial and class discrimination (both historical and contemporary) in explaining the disproportionate location of African Americans at the bottom reaches of the social hierarchy.

The role of institutional racism in the formation of an external locus of control is an important point overlooked by many researchers. Institutional racism encompasses a set of social structural relationships that circumscribes the lives of African Americans. This is a key concept for understanding the development of an external locus of control. As the forces of prejudices and discrimination limit African Americans' self-effacy in life choice (i.e., employment, housing, schools), these constraints affect whether one locates locus of control internally or externally. In other words, because the lives of many African Americans are constrained by external forces of racial discrimination and economic deprivation over which they have little or no control, African-American students may develop external loci of control. It is also important to note that even where these students develop internal loci of control, the ul-

timate determinant of success will be whether they are given sufficient opportunity to express and to act on these beliefs.

Though locus of control studies have been extremely popular in educational research, the actual empirical connection between locus of control and motivation has been sorely underresearched. Many researchers have relied on the yet-to-be-established premise that motivation is positively associated with internality and that, therefore, students with external loci of control are not motivated or achieving. This association, imperative to the theoretical cohesion of the locus of control literature, has yet to be sufficiently investigated in the empirical sociological literature.

The third primary area of research in African-American student motivation concerns self-concept. Many social scientists believe that because black students tend to have external loci of control, they will also hold negative self-concepts. The general hypothesis of the area is that extreme poverty and poor school achievement have taken their toll on the psyches of young African Americans and have led them to possess poor self-concepts and to have low self-esteem. In line with the famous "doll studies" of the *Brown vs. Board of Education* decision to end legal segregation in American public schools, the focus on African-American self-esteem and self-concept, including the presumption that black students have a poor self-concept, still persists.[2]

One of the main theoretical presuppositions in this research area is that self-appraisals are associated with high motivation and achievement. The more students accept praise for a job well done, assuming that they have an internal locus of control and believe that they are responsible for the job being done well, the more

---

[2] The "doll studies" of the Brown case refer to studies done by Kenneth and Mamie Clark that attempted to show that black students favored white skin and thought that white children were smarter and better people than black children were, as African-American students chose white dolls over black dolls when asked questions like, "which doll is the smarter one?" These studies were used to exemplify a poor self-concept among black students and consequential glorification of whiteness. Racial segregation was presented as a practice that would further damage the psyches and self-esteem of the African-American students. The theme of protecting the self-image and self-concepts of black children is one with a long history that persists into the present day.

likely they are to be motivated and to achieve. In other words, students must first believe that they successfully completed a task because of their own competence and effort. Then, students must accept praise and praise themselves for their success. This self-appraisal is thought to be the impetus for motivation and achievement. The causal properties of this relationship are very important; that is, self-appraisal causes motivation and achievement. This is the theorized causal ordering of events, but empirically this theory has mixed results.

When the ideas of self-concept and motivation/ achievement are studied empirically, a seeming contradiction develops in the case of African-American students. Throughout the 1970s and 1980s social scientists showed that black students consistently maintain positive self-concepts equal to and often greater than those of white students. This is true even when African-American students are not as academically successful as their white counterparts. Researchers have overwhelmingly found that even in the face of failure, African-American students maintain positive self-concepts. This persistent optimism does not seem to vary by social class, unlike some of the other measures of black motivation.

In response to these findings, many scholars have developed explanations for the seeming contradiction between African-American student motivation and self-concept. One of the most common explanations is based on a methodological critique of the research. This theory states that the response styles of the students are reflected in the differences in self-concept measurements. Another explanation is based on the social comparison process that states that African-American students compare themselves to other students like themselves and not the members of the privileged class, thus deriving a more positive self-concept. The third primary explanation is called the self-protection mechanism, which predicts that subordinate minority groups will have external loci of control and make in-group rather than out-group comparisons in order to protect their self-esteem and self-concept.

Sandra Graham writes that "the problem with all of these explanations is that they assume that self-concept of African Americans would (or should) be lower than that of whites" (1994:99). Graham critiques the presumed causal relationship between self-concept and motivation/achievement. The presupposition that self-appraisal causes student motivation and achievement is not established and in light of the evidence seriously called into question. Instead of theorizing about why the African-American students are an exception to the rule of self-appraisal and motivation, we should question the premise itself as an explanatory tool in understanding student motivation.

Ultimately, the dilemma of how best to interpret research on African-American achievement motivation reduces to a commentary on the fundamental character of race and race relations in this society. Gunnar Myrdal spoke of *An American Dilemma* rooted in the inherent contradiction between the exclusion/degradation of the country's black citizens and a national ethic of equality/ opportunity for all. In his view, white Americans felt the tension between the deplorable conditions under which blacks were forced to live as second-class citizens and the American Creed, which promised them equality. By implication and assertion, he saw white Americans as committed to resolving this dilemma and eventually consenting to admit black Americans to full citizenship. A less generous view than Myrdal's would restate the American Dilemma as the challenge of how to reconcile the reality of permanent black exclusion/ discrimination within a rhetoric of equal opportunity (Allen and Jewell, 1995). Interpreted from this view, a scientific literature that attributes black underachievement to failures of individual effort, preparation, and motivation serves a vital function. In the end, attention is shifted from societal discrimination to the pathology of black people and black culture. The country is thereby released from its responsibility to confront racism and racial discrimination as well as the persistence of a system of racial, gender, and class inequality that prevents motivated, qualified, hardworking people from the wrong backgrounds opportunity to improve their status.

In the final analysis, one must conclude that African-American student motivation continues to be a misunderstood phenomenon. Though much work has been done on the topic, much of it has been based on premises that are yet causally or theoretically established in the sociological or educational literature. More research is needed to ascertain the content, sources, and consequences of high motivation to achieve in this population. Certainly, achievement motivation is the result of a combination of factors—both individual and institutional—although this interaction has been often overlooked. Equally certain is the fact that motivation cannot be fully comprehended apart from the historical, cultural, political, socioeconomic, and epistemological context within which an individual is located.

REFERENCES

Allen, Walter R., and Joseph O. Jewell. 1995. "African American Education Since an American Dilemma." *Daedalus* 124:77–100.

Borgatta, Edgar, and William Lambert. 1968. *Handbook of Personality Theory and Research*. Chicago, IL: Rand McNally.

Coleman, James S. 1966. *Equality of Educational Opportunity*. Washington, DC: U.S. Dept. of Health, Education, and Welfare, Office of Education.

Cooper, Harris, and Nancy Dorr. 1995. "Race Comparisons on Need for Achievement: A Meta Analytic Alternative to Graham's Narrative Review." *Review of Educational Research* 65:483–508.

Graham, Sandra. 1994. "Motivation in African Americans." *Review of Educational Research* 64:55–117.

Jones, Reginald L. 1991. *Black Psychology*. Berkeley, CA: Cobb and Henry.

McClelland, D., J. Atkinson, R. Clark, and E. Lowell. 1953. *The Achievement Motive*. New York: Appleton-Century-Crofts.

Mussen, P. H. 1953. "Differences between the TAT Responses of Negro and White Boys." *Journal of Consulting Psychology* 17:373–376.

Rosenberg, Morris, and Ralph Turner. 1981. *Social Psychology: Sociological Perspectives*. New York: Basic Books.

AT-RISK STUDENTS

Gary Natriello
Teachers College, Columbia University

At-risk students is the identifying term applied to those students who have a greater than average chance of not succeeding in school and graduating. Natriello et al. (1990) note that the term "at risk" became widely used in the 1980s to refer to students who face some disadvantage in achieving school success. The term carries a future orientation, referring to students who may be more likely to experience problems at some point in the future. This emphasis is typically related to efforts to identify such students before the problems become fully manifest. The implication is that at-risk students have certain characteristics that make it possible to identify them, but that these characteristics become problematic only in conjunction with events and conditions that have yet to unfold.

Conceptions of At Risk

As an identifying term applied to students having difficulty with their education, the conceptual basis of the word has been the subject of some dispute. Use of the term in the early and mid-1980s was linked to attempts to avoid blaming students for their difficulties achieving school success. Advocates of use of the term instead of educationally disadvantaged or deprived sought to employ it to avoid the personal negative connotations of those earlier labels. Indeed, at risk implies that school failure is traceable to a combination of individual and environmental characteristics and that being at risk involves a differential susceptibility in which the environment becomes unnegotiable for certain individuals. Frost (1994) notes that the concept has its roots in epidemiology in which physicians use statistical techniques to identify populations at risk of contracting diseases and then inoculate groups against the disease when the inconvenience and danger of the vaccination is thought to be less than the increased level of protection it affords against the disease.

Despite attempts to use at risk to avoid assigning blame to individual students for their lack of success in school, the use of the term has become problematic. Notwithstanding the implication that being at risk involves a differential susceptibility to environmental conditions, the term is regularly used to designate students who possess certain characteristics without attention to the environmental conditions that might pose problems for them. Margonis (1992) explains that although the term at risk was first used by critics of the excellence movement who sought to shift the thinking of policymakers and practitioners away from the notion that school failure was primarily a result of lack of individual effort, the term was coopted and used as a label to identify students and their problems.

Frost (1994) reports that the majority of states have incorporated the term at risk as a label for students in education legislation and provides the actual definitions contained in the legislation of 31 states. As Frost notes, most of the definitions used in legislation involve environmental factors in combination with individual characteristics. This legislation is usually directed at providing special programs or resources for the targeted group of students to improve their educational outcomes.

The early identification of students as being at risk might lead to the assignment of students to appropriate programs designed to help them achieve school success or it might lead to the pejorative labeling of students and the self-fulfilling prophecy that consigns such students to exposure to lower teacher expectations for their entire school careers. Moreover, unlike earlier terms that identified students based on current problems, at risk suggests an ability to predict how students might turn out in the future, which could lead to problems for students who otherwise would not have experienced them, particularly in light of our limited ability to predict future school performance, especially with young students (Natriello et al., 1990; Frost, 1994).

In reaction to the continuing use of the term at risk to label students without acknowledging the environmental and structural factors that contribute to the risk, there have been efforts to recast the term and the dialog around such students. The naming of the federal research and development center for at-risk students as the Center for Research on the Education of Students Placed at Risk (Johns Hopkins University and Howard University, 1994) is an attempt once again to call attention to the fact that the poor chances for school success associated with certain groups of students result from things done to them or not done for them by the major institutions in their lives, the family, the community, the school.

Even more challenging for the at-risk concept is the position of Swadener and Lubeck (1995). Beginning with the assumption that the use of "at risk" as a label is implicitly racist, classist, sexist, and ableist in locating problems in certain individuals, families, and communities, they argue that it would be far more productive to view all children and their families as facing great challenges and yet being "at promise" and then to mobilize efforts to help realize that promise.

Indicators of At-Risk Status

As the discussion above indicates, the very definition of at-risk students is a matter of social and political contention. Thus the specification of particular indicators of at-risk status is itself not without controversy. Nonetheless, educators, policymakers, and researchers have identified a set of factors that seems to portend greater chance of school failure. These include racial and ethnic minority status, poverty, single-parent families, poorly educated mothers, limited English proficiency, health problems, poor community conditions, high mobility, and poor school resources.

Race and Ethnicity

Historically, members of minority groups in the United States have failed to succeed in school at the same levels as the majority of white children. There is substantial evidence documenting the lower participation and performance of black and Hispanic children in schools relative to white children. These differences are apparent at all levels of the system.

Although in the mid-1970s black and white enrollment rates in prekindergarten programs were similar, by 1991 average white enrollment in prekindergarten programs was 40.1% while the average enrollment rates for black and Hispanic children were 30.8% and 21.0%, respectively (U.S. Department of Education, 1994:26). In terms of measured performance while in school black and Hispanic students lag behind white students in reading, writing, mathematics, and science proficiency, although the performance gap between white students and black and Hispanic students has been closing in recent years (U.S. Department of Education, 1994:50–57). Dropout rates also show a disadvantage for black, Hispanic, and native American students who are more likely to leave school prior to graduation than white and Asian students (U.S. Department of Education, 1994: 34–35).

Poverty

Household poverty is a commonly recognized factor for placing students at greater risk of school failure. Since 1981 the percentage of children living in poverty in the United States has ranged from 19 to 21% (U.S. Department of Education, 1994:132). Poor students have less access to school resources and perform less well in school than their wealthier counterparts. In 1992 52.0% of children from high-income families were enrolled in prekindergarten education while 30.5% of those from middle-income families and only 23.9% of those from low-income families were enrolled (U.S. Department of Education, 1994:26).

Children living in families with incomes below the poverty line are nearly twice as likely to be retained in a grade as children in nonpoverty-stricken families (Bianchi, 1984). In terms of persistence in high school those students from higher income families also enjoy an advantage. In 1992 98.3% of students in the tenth through twelfth grades from high-income families continued their enrollment while 95.6% of students from middle-income families and only 89.1% of students from low-income families continued in school (U.S. Department of Education, 1994:32).

Single-Parent Families

Family structure is related to educational outcomes (Milne et al., 1986). Nationally, about 13.5 million children (about 21%) lived in households with just a mother present in 1988. About 1.8 million or slightly less than 3% lived in households with just a father present, and about the same number lived in households with neither parent present.

Children living in single-parent families have been found to score lower on standardized tests and receive lower grades in school, and to be more likely to drop out of high school.

Family status or composition is an important indicator of the level of familial support a child is likely to receive. Despite the fact that there are many examples of single-parent households that provide substantial social, emotional, and economic support to children, the national data are quite clear in indicating that children in single-parent families are likely to fare less well in school than their peers in two-parent families (Natriello et al., 1990). Children in single-parent families are almost twice as likely to drop out of high school as children from two-parent families. Stedman et al. (1988), using the High School and Beyond data describing 1980 high school sophomores, found that 22.4% of children from single-parent families dropped out of school, compared to 12.0% of those children from two-parent families.

Family structure is closely linked to poverty. Ellwood (1988) showed that long-term poverty is characteristic of single-parent households. His analysis indicates that, among children who grew up in the 1970s, nearly three-quarters of those who spent at least some time in a single-parent family lived in poverty at least part of the time. In contrast, children living continuously in a two-parent, male-headed family have but a 20% chance of living in poverty at least 1 year in their first decade, and only a 2% change of being poor continuously from birth to age 10. Family structure is also correlated with racial/ethnic origin. Minority children are much more likely to live in a single-parent family than are white children (U.S. Bureau of the Census, 1989).

Poorly Educated Mothers

The importance of the educational attainment of parents, particularly of mothers, becomes apparent when education is viewed as a process that occurs not only in schools, but also in families and communities. Mothers who are more highly educated themselves have more knowledge of their children's schooling, have more social contact with school personnel, and are better managers of their children's academic careers (Baker and Stevenson, 1986; Stevenson and Baker, 1987). Children of highly educated mothers do better in school, and stay in school longer, than children whose parents have not completed high school (Natriello et al., 1990).

About one in every five children under the age of 18 in 1987 lived with mothers who had not completed high school, representing a total of 12.7 million children. These children were disproportionately African American and Latino. Among African-American youth living in families where the mother was present, nearly 30% had mothers who had not finished high school. And among Latino children living in families with mothers present, over 50% had mothers who were not high school graduates. The educational attainments of white mothers are much higher. Approximately 87% of the white children living in families with the mother present had mothers who had at least completed high school (U.S. Bureau of the Census, 1988).

Limited English Proficiency

Students whose primary language is not English, or who have limited English proficiency, face serious obstacles to success in school. There is little agreement on how to define limited English proficiency or how to measure the size of the population with limited English proficiency. The Bilingual Education Act of 1984 defined an individual as "limited English proficient" (LEP) if that individual comes from a home environment where a language other than English is the one most relied upon for communication and if he or she has sufficient difficulty in understanding, speaking, reading, and writing English to deny the individual the opportunity to learn successfully in all-English classrooms. In 1990 6.3 million students between the ages of 5 and 17 spoke a language other than English, and nearly 2.4 million spoke English with difficulty (U.S. Department of Education, 1994).

Regardless of how limited English proficiency is assessed, by most criteria students defined as limited English proficient are at a substantial disadvantage in U.S. classrooms. Nor is this shortfall limited to verbal skills, as succeeding even in science and mathematics courses may require the ability to communicate well in English. In addition to performance differences in school, there is some evidence that children from minority-language backgrounds are more likely to drop out of high school than children from homes where English is spoken exclusively. Salganik and Celebuski (1987) reported that among sophomores in the High School and Beyond study, those from homes where only a non-English language was spoken were more than twice as likely to drop out of high school as students from homes where English was the sole or primary language spoken.

This indicator of educational disadvantage also highlights the importance of family and community factors, as well as school influences. Parents who do not speak English may be severely hampered in their ability to help their children with schoolwork or in their ability to manage their children's school careers.

Health and Nutrition

There has long been a concern with the health and well-being of mothers and children in the United States. There is striking evidence for the link between the health of expectant mothers and infants and long-term physical and intellectual well being. Edwards and Grossman (1979) and Wolfe (1985) have reported on the positive relationship between health and cognitive development in children. Children who begin life with problems such as low birthweight may have low IQs throughout their lives. Moreover, health problems in childhood are likely to interfere with school attendance and, ultimately, with school performance.

A particular difficulty in the area of maternal and infant health is the large number of births to teenage mothers in the United States. The limited evidence available suggests that male children born to teenage parents are at a developmental disadvantage in preschool and elementary school, compared to children born to older mothers. These developmental deficits increase over time, so that by adolescence, children of teen mothers are more than twice as likely as children of older mothers to have repeated a grade and twice as likely to misbehave in school (Furstenberg and Brooks-Gunn, 1985). Poverty may compound these risks mak-

ing children especially vulnerable to the effects of health problems (Montgomery and Rossi, 1994).

Community Conditions

Poor communities characterized by high levels of crime and violence may present special risks for children. Students may face danger walking to and from school and may be unable to play outside for fear of threats to their personal safety. Montgomery and Rossi (1994) point out that students in poor urban and poor rural communities may have fewer opportunities and a narrower range of activities to participate in than their counterparts in communities with stronger economic bases.

The income level of one's community is also related to educational performance. Data from the 1986 NAEP reading proficiency tests show that the average 13 year old in a disadvantaged urban community scored only about a quarter of a standard deviation higher than the average 9 year old in an advantaged urban community. Moreover, 17 year olds in a disadvantaged urban setting scored at about the same level as a typical 13 year old residing in an advantaged urban area (Applebee et al., 1988; Natriello et al., 1990).

Mobile Students

Students who are highly mobile may have special problems in pursuing their education. In many cases the schools they attend lack adequate support services, both administrative and instructional, to assess their needs and marshall the appropriate school resources to meet them. Migrant children may suffer from the lack of articulation and communication among schools. Homeless children may bring special problems to which schools may be unable to respond. Immigrant children not only bring cultural differences with them but also may enter school districts with limited experience with the English language and with schooling itself.

Limited School Resources

There are well-documented disparities in available resources among school districts and schools. Montgomery and Rossi (1994) note that despite the failure to find strong correlations between school expenditures and student learning outcomes, resource disparities translate into disparities in things such as staff quality, which should be related to student achievement. In light of the special needs of at-risk students, limited school resources may be particularly detrimental to their educational progress.

Size of the At-Risk Population

Given the diversity of the definitions and indicators used to identify students at risk of educational failure, it is not surprising that estimates of the size of the at-risk population vary widely. Natriello et al. (1990) note that on any one of the major indicators of at-risk status from one-fifth to one-fourth of children under 18 may be classified as at risk of not completing high school. When they consider the multiple indicators of at-risk status together and allow for the presence of multiple indicators for many students, Natriello et al. conclude that a conservative estimate would place at least 40% of children in the at-risk category. This estimate, based on indicators of background status, is consistent with results on the reading tests of the National Assessment of Educational Progress, which show that about 35–40% of students are at risk of educational failure.

Efforts to Address the Needs of At-Risk Students

With the increased attention to the educational needs of at-risk students in recent years there has been a range of programs and approaches advanced as appropriate for meeting those needs (Natriello et al., 1990). Among the most often mentioned strategies are those that involve early intervention into the developmental and educational processes that affect all children. Such efforts attempt to take advantage of the early identification of students likely to experience difficulty in making academic progress. These include increasing attention to maternal and child health services, increasing the availability of preschools, and enhancing the learning environments of kindergartens. In addition, there have been efforts to ensure the effectiveness of the early elementary years with programs designed specifically to ensure the academic progress of all students.

Other approaches have involved changes that impact the entire school career. These include attempts to modify the school curriculum so that it reflects the multiple cultures of the children who comprise growing proportions of the student population, efforts to integrate academic and vocational skills and to embody

more real-world learning within the school, and efforts to make greater use of technology in instruction. Some strategies have sought to alter the organization of schools to make them more conducive to the education of at-risk youth. Such strategies include increasing the availability of role models of the same race or sex either on the staff or as adult mentors from the community, creating smaller school environments either through the establishment of new schools or the division of existing schools into separate houses, making greater use of peers in tutoring or social support roles, incorporating new forms of assessment that recognize the multiple and diverse talents of students, and establishing closer connections between schools and colleges and the workplace to give students a clear sense of the impact of their efforts on school work on their later lives.

The most appropriate instructional approach for at-risk students has been the subject of some contention. Although some have advocated the use of the less directive strategies generally associated with progressive education, others have suggested that when such strategies are followed to the exclusion of more skill-oriented approaches the learning of at-risk students is impeded (Delpit, 1995). Following a review of the systematic evaluations of various instructional programs, Natriello et al. (1990) concluded that the programs most effective for enhancing the learning of at-risk students were those that adjusted instruction to the needs of individual students while maximizing academically focused, teacher-directed activities involving sequenced and structured approaches.

REFERENCES

Applebee, A.N., J.A. Langer, and I.V.S. Mullis. 1988. *Who Reads Best? Factors Related to Reading Achievement in Grades 3, 7, and 11.* Princeton, NJ: Educational Testing Service.

Baker, D.P., and D.L. Stevenson. 1986. "Mothers' Strategies for Children's School Achievement: Managing the Transition to High School." *Sociology of Education* 59:156–166.

Bianchi, S.M. 1984. "Children's Progress Through School: A Research Note." *Sociology of Education* 57:184–192.

Delpit, Lisa. 1995. *Other People's Children: Cultural Conflict in the Classroom.* New York: Free Press.

Edwards, L.N., and M. Grossman. 1979. "The Relationship Between Children's Health and Intellectual Development." In. S. Mushkin (ed.), *Health: What Is It Worth?*, pp. 84–103. Elmsford, NY: Pergamon Press.

Ellwood, R. F. 1988. *Poor Support: Poverty in the American Family*. New York: Basic Books.

Frost, Lynda E. 1994. "At-Risk Statutes: Defining Deviance and Suppressing Difference in Public Schools." *Journal of Law and Education* 23:123–165.

Furstenberg, F.F, Jr., and J. Brooks-Gunn. 1985. "Teenage Childbearing: Causes, Consequences and Remedies." In L.H. Aiken and D. Mechanic (eds.), *Applications of Social Science to Clinical Medicine and Health Policy*, pp. 307–334. New Brunswick, NJ: Rutgers University Press.

Johns Hopkins University and Howard University. 1994. *Technical Application: Center for Research on the Education of Students Placed At Risk*. Johns Hopkins University and Howard University.

Margonis, Frank. 1992. "The Cooptation of 'At Risk': Paradoxes of Policy Criticism." *Teachers College Record* 94:343–364.

Milne, A.M., D.E. Myers, A.S. Rosenthal, and A. Ginsberg. 1986. "Single Parents, Working Mothers, and the Educational Achievement of School Children." *Sociology of Education* 59:125–139.

Montgomery, A.F., and R.J. Rossi. 1994. "Becoming At Risk of Failure in America's Schools." In R.J. Rossi (ed.), *Schools and Students at Risk: Context and Framework for Positive Change*, pp. 3–22. New York: Teachers College Press.

Natriello, Gary, Edward L. McDill, and Aaron M. Pallas.

1990. *Schooling Disadvantaged Children: Racing Against Catastrophe*. New York: Teachers College Press.

Saiganik, L., and C. Celebuski. 1987. *Educational Attainment Study: Preliminary Tables*. Washington, DC: Pelavin Associates.

Stedman, L.C., L.H. Salganik, and C.A. Celebuski. 1988. *Dropping Out: The Educational Vulnerability of At-Risk Youth*. Washington, DC: Congressional Research Service.

Stevenson, D.L., and D.P. Baker. 1987. "The Family-School Relation and the Child's School Performance." *Child Development* 58:1348–1357.

Swadener, Beth Blue, and Sally Lubeck, eds. 1995. *Children and Families "At Promise": Deconstructing the Discourse of Risk*. Albany, NY: State University of New York Press.

U.S. Bureau of the Census. 1988. *Household and Family Characteristics: March 1987* (Current Population Reports, Series P-20, Nov. 424). Washington, DC: U.S. Government Printing Office.

————. 1989. *Marital Status and Living Arrangements: March 1988* (Current Population Reports, Series P-20, No. 433). Washington, DC: U.S. Government Printing Office.

U.S. Department of Education, National Center for Education Statistics. 1994. *The Condition of Education 1994*. Washington, DC: U.S. Government Printing Office.

Wolfe, B.L. 1985. "The Influence of Health on School Outcomes." *Medical Care* 23:1127–1138.

BILINGUAL EDUCATION

Virginia Vogel Zanger
The Boston Children's Museum

Definitions

Bilingual education, also known as dual-language curriculum, is an instructional approach that offers academic content in two languages and instruction in a second language. The bilingual instructional approach is used to some extent in almost every country in the world. This chapter will refer to the research on bilingual education programs in public schools within the United States, serving a student population that is preponderantly the children of non-English-speaking immigrants and other marginalized groups. In 1991, there were approximately 40 million public and private school students enrolled in K–12 in the United States; of these, 2.2 million were limited English speakers (LEPs), and 250,000 of this subset were enrolled in bilingual education programs funded by the federal government (Cisneros and Leone, 1995). No statistics are available to tell us how many additional students, limited English-speaking or otherwise, participate in bilingual education programs funded by other sources: local, state, or private.

The three aims of bilingual education programs, defined by Ovando and Collier (1985), are the continued development of the student's first language (L1), the acquisition of the second language (L2), and academic achievement in content areas such as math and science, in which various combinations of L1 and L2 are utilized as media of instruction. The various bilingual education program models reflect differing emphases on one or another of these goals. In the United States, the most common forms of bilingual programs are transitional, maintenance, and two-way (Nieto, 1992). Transitional models, which are often early-exit programs of 1 or 2 years duration, utilize the native language only insofar as it is useful in promoting the primary goal of the program: proficiency in the second language (English, in the United States). The other two program types, which are far less common, are also known as developmental or enrichment because they stress the development of native language proficiency and academic achievement in addition to learning the second language. The first of these models, known as two-way on the East Coast or immersion in the West, involves students from L1 and L2 backgrounds learning together in both languages. In contrast, the transitional bilingual program model segregates participants from native English speakers for all or part of the school day. The maintenance model, a developmental model that encourages proficiency on both languages, also isolates students from their English-speaking peers. All program models in the United States contain an English as a Second Language (ESL) component to promote the acquisition of English.

Language education reflects the sociocultural context of the society in which schooling takes place. The right of elites around the world to choose to educate their children bilingually is rarely questioned. However, it has become a highly controversial topic in recent years in the United States, arguably because it has served a different population of students: the children of immigrants and of other marginalized language groups—Native Americans, Puerto Ricans in the continental United States, and the descendants of Spanish settlers in the Southwest. Within this sociocultural context, bilingual education is often viewed by its sup-

55

porters as a civil rights issue (Nieto, 1992), a response to educational inequalities and underachievement experienced by language minority students. As language minority communities have struggled for access to educational equity through the establishment of bilingual education programs, the research on bilingual education has drawn upon work in linguistics, cognitive psychology, anthropology, and sociology of education to explain why bilingual schooling may be helpful in reversing traditional educational underachievement by language minority students. Highlights from this work are summarized in the next section.

Few educational programs have engendered the amount of public controversy in recent years as bilingual education (Crawford, 1992). Despite the research evidence, the debate rages on. The second part of this chapter explores the sociopolitical context in which the bilingual education controversy has emerged and explores the demographic and economic changes that have contributed to the emergence of the English-only movement. This review suggests that the politics of bilingual education have largely overshadowed the research in the public debate.

Research on Bilingual Education

Research evidence supporting the effectiveness of bilingual education is largely drawn from the literature on second language acquisition. Collier and Thomas (1989) have established that it takes students who are schooled entirely in a second language 7 to 10 years to achieve academic parity with their native English-speaking peers. Before then, most students fail to achieve as well as their English-speaking peers on standardized tests of academic performance in English because they lack sufficient fluency in the language in which academic instruction and academic assessment are provided. Bilingual education programs, it is argued, shorten the time that it takes to catch up to 4 to 7 years, because they provide instruction in the English language (through ESL) while students continue to develop academic skills in their native tongue. After they develop proficiency in English, the research suggests, their academic skills transfer into their new language and are reflected on standardized tests in English.

According to Collier's synthesis of the research, "Many, many studies have found that cognitive and academic development in first language has an ex-

tremely important and positive effect on second language schooling" (Collier, 1995:12). She cites research by Cummins (1991), Diaz and Klingler (1991), Freeman and Freeman (1992), E. Garcia (1993, 1994), Genesee (1987), Hakuta (1986), Lessow-Hurley (1990), Lindholm (1991), McLaughlin (1992), Snow (1990), Tinajero and Ada (1993), Wong Fillmore and Valadez (1986), as well as her own studies (Collier, 1989, 1992). This finding may help explain why students who immigrate between the ages of 8 and 11 are able to catch up with their English-speaking peers on achievement tests in English faster than language minority students who immigrated at a younger age or were born in the United States, because the former had the opportunity for cognitive development in L1 (Collier, 1989). These studies not only demonstrate how academic skills, including literacy, transfer from one language into the other, but indicate the difficulties faced by students who have not reached a certain threshold of literacy development in the first language. Other research is cited that supports the conclusion that "During the initial years of exposure to English, continuing cognitive and academic development in first language is considered to be a key variable for academic success in second language achievement" (Collier, 1995:15).

In addition to focusing on the question "Does it work?," much research on bilingual education has sought to identify which program models are most effective. Program success in these studies is generally defined as academic achievement in English; rarely is native language proficiency cited. One of the largest studies was commissioned by the U.S. Department of Education to determine the program effectiveness of three kinds of programs: immersion programs, in which students received only informal native language support; early-exit bilingual programs, in which only 30 to 60 minutes of native language instruction was used daily, and students were placed in mainstream programs in less than 3 years; and late-exit programs, in which students received 40% of instruction in their first language and remained in the program even after developing proficiency in English (Ramirez, 1991). The federal government, under President Reagan, sought to suppress the results of the Ramirez study because the superiority of academic achievement of the late-exit bilinguals did not coincide with the English-only philosophy of the administration.

Cummins (1979, 1981, 1986, 1989, 1991) developed a theoretical model to explain the findings that L1 learning promotes L2 achievement. He differentiates between two kinds of language proficiency, social language, or basic interpersonal communicative skills (BICS) and academic language, or cognitive academic language proficiency skills (CALPS). BICS is context embedded, the kind of fluency evidenced in face-to-face conversation, and generally takes 2 years to attain. CALPS is context reduced and cognitively demands proficiency, the kind of language skill necessary for academic success in school where so many tasks take place in context-reduced linguistic situations. CALPS takes far longer to develop, and is largely dependent on cognitive development in L1. Students whose oral fluency in English suggests that they are capable of performing academically in English may fail because they have not yet achieved the necessary CALPS. Cummins also argues for the existence of a common underlying proficiency hypothesis, whereby subject matter and cognitive development in L1 are automatically transferred into L2.

Linguistic and cognitive barriers may not be the most serious obstacles to academic achievement by language minority students, according to researchers who have looked at sociocultural issues in schooling (for a summary, see Zanger, 1991). Bilingual/bicultural educational programs are designed to serve as a buffer to some of these barriers. The extent to which they succeed is difficult to measure, since the isolation of linguistic, cultural, educational, and social variables is problematic. Following is a review of some of the sociocultural research that is relevant to bilingual education.

Beginning in the early 1970s, anthropological research methods have been used with increasing frequency to learn more about the hidden obstacles that face students whose cultural backgrounds differ from that of the dominant culture. These ethnographic and microethnographic studies have given rise to the cultural mismatch paradigm, the central thesis of which is that the communication process is disrupted when students and school personnel come from backgrounds that have vastly different conventions governing appropriate behaviors, values, and nonverbal styles (Erickson, 1987). One focus of the research has been to investigate ways in which language is used, the unspoken rules that govern discourse (Wong Fillmore, 1983;

Cazden et al., 1972). For example, Philips' (1972) study at the Warm Springs Indian Reservation compared the conditions for speech use in the Native-American community and in the government school. She identified basic distinctions in participant structures, which are the rules that govern who speaks when. One example of the way in which this cultural discrepancy was found to cause "sociolinguistic interference" in the classroom was the reluctance of Native-American students to speak up when called upon in class. Philips contrasted the students' lack of verbal responsiveness in teacher-directed situations to their participation in peer-learning situations, which are more culturally congruent to their lives outside of school. In a similar vein, Boggs (1972) identified the reluctance of native Hawaiian children to respond to direct questioning by teachers.

Other sources of discontinuity between the home and school that have been studied extensively are the areas of nonverbal communication (Nine Curt, 1984) and cultural values. Sindell (1988), for example, painted a searing portrait of the cross-cultural conflicts between the traditional values in which Cree children were raised and the values of the dominant Canadian culture, enforced in governmental residential schools, centering on the extent to which dependence/independence in children was encouraged. Yet another area is the degree to which competition or independence is stressed (Delgado-Gaitan, 1987; Jordan, 1977). The damaging effects of teachers acting as unwitting enforcers of the dominant culture's values have been documented by Sindell (1988), Ortiz (1988), and Heath (1983). The breakdown in student–teacher trust is one element of the marginalization experienced by Hispanic high school students identified in a study of Hispanic literacy issues from a Vygotskian perspective (Zanger, 1994).

Proponents of bilingual education argue that it can mitigate against culture shock, largely through the dynamic of bicultural personnel who function as cross-cultural guides for their students. For example, Macias (1987) described the hidden curriculum of native Papago preschool teachers, who introduced their students to classroom behaviors that they knew would be expected in white schools, at the same time taking care not to compromise key Papago values, such as individual autonomy. Montero-Sieburth and Perez (1987) analyzed the techniques employed by a Puerto Rican bilingual teacher who capitalized on her knowledge of the students' cultures and their circumstances, defining her goal as a teacher as the reduction of students' *ena-jenacion* (alienation). Abi-Nader's analysis of an Anglo bilingual teacher's use of students' cultural values to raise student achievement suggests that bicultural skills are not restricted to native speakers of students L1 (Abi-Nader, 1990).

Sociolinguistics has yielded findings suggestive of the importance of sociocultural factors such as intergroup dynamics in second language learning. Gardner and Lambert summarized 12 years of research on foreign language learning with this conclusion about the importance of attitudes: "The learner's ethnocentric tendencies and his attitudes toward the members of the other group are believed to determine how successful he will be, relatively, in learning the new language" (1972:3). In explaining differences between native speakers' learning foreign languages and immigrants learning the language of their adopted country, Lambert (1975) distinguished between the "additive" context of the former and the "subtractive" context of the latter. The subtractive context leads to language shift (Veltman, 1983), which may engender certain resistant attitudes in learners loyal to their native language and culture. Schumann (1978) proposed that second language learning is most likely to take place in contexts where the target language and the native language have equal status and that there is minimal social distance between the two groups. His proposed Acculturation Model of second language learning identifies key social variables that define relations between the language learner group and the target language group: dominance/nondominance, subordination, assimilation/acculturation/preservation, enclosure, cohesiveness, size, congruence, attitude, and intended length of residence. Gardner (1979) developed a theoretical model of second language acquisition that includes yet another social factor: cultural beliefs about language learning. Clemant (1980), another Canadian researcher, described the psychosocial variables operative in determining motivation: the interplay between integrativeness and fear of assimilation.

Although these findings strongly suggest the influence that psychosocial, sociocultural, and sociopolitical factors might play in influencing learning in bilingual education programs, there has been surprisingly few studies that examine these factors within the context of bilingual education programs. One study did explore the negative impact of the stigmatization experienced by Hispanic and Vietnamese high school students in bilingual programs on their learning of English and their academic achievement (Zanger, 1987). Cummins (1986) also raised the potential significance of intergroup dynamics in bilingual education, despite the fact that most of his research uses a linguistic model. He points out that research findings that support the positive correlation between high student achievement and bilingual programs are based on the assumption that language of instruction is the crucial variable responsible. He raises an alternative explanation: given the disabling educational effects of the devaluation of students' native culture and language by the larger school environment, bilingual education may in fact owe its success to the identity reinforcement it provides through incorporating native language and culture into the education experience of language minority students, thus increasing motivation, a major component of academic success.

Sociocultural factors such as intergroup dynamics are an understudied issue in bilingual education research, which has tended to focus instead on linguistic and instructional variables. However, they may be responsible for both some of the success as well as the limitations of bilingual programs.

The Sociopolitical Context of the Bilingual Education Debate

Whereas the education research community has focused on bilingual education largely as an issue of pedagogical effectiveness, the immigrant community has viewed it as fundamentally a question of civil rights (Nieto, 1992). And indeed, federal law has placed bilingual education within a civil rights context, beginning with the Civil Rights Act of 1964, which prohibits discrimination on the basis of national origin. The 1974 Supreme Court ruling in the area of language rights in schools, *Lau v. Nichols,* further refined the definition of equality of educational opportunity, established under the Civil Rights Act, as it applied to limited English-speaking students in U.S. schools. It forced the educational establishment to recognize that "equal opportunity demanded more than equal treatment" (Crawford, 1989:1). The original case was a class action suit in San Francisco brought by the Lau family and 1,789 other Chinese parents, who claimed that their children were denied equal educational opportunities because they could not understand the language of instruction. In supporting the plaintiffs, Supreme Court Justice Douglas wrote that "There is no equality of treatment merely by providing students with the same facilities, teachers, and curriculum; for students who do not understand English are effectively foreclosed from any meaningful education" (quoted in Crawford, 1989:36).

Historical Context

Although Chinese-American parents brought the first successful lawsuit that laid the legal basis for bilingual education (*Lau v. Nichols*, 1974), the vast majority of students in bilingual programs are Hispanic. The impetus for bilingual education in Latino communities may be viewed partly as a response to centuries of repressive policies toward Spanish speakers by representatives of both local and federal Anglo authorities. Historically, language policies in schools have been embedded in the broader political context of the struggle for political and cultural hegemony by the Spanish-speaking citizens whose lands the United States acquired. The history of Puerto Rico and of the American Southwest reveals the extent to which political domination has included deliberate attempts to eradicate the Spanish language. In both contexts, the schools have been the battlegrounds on which the primary assault on native languages has been launched. The brief summary that follows suggests the extent to which bilingual education may be understood as a sociopolitical struggle by both sides in the current era.

Puerto Rico achieved national sovereignty in 1897 under the Charter of Autonomy granted by Spain; however, the following year Spain lost the Spanish-American War and ceded the island to the United States as compensation for war losses (EPICA Task Force, 1976). "From the beginning of North American occupation of Puerto Rico, the goal of the colonial power to culturally assimilate Puerto Ricans and to make 'good North Americans' of them was clear" (Maldonado-Denis, 1972). The schools were crucial to achieving this goal, and from 1900 until 1948, every strategy was tried in an explicit attempt to replace Spanish with English as the vernacular on the island. English was mandated as the only language of instruction in most or all grades, according to policies that

varied slightly every few years. As soon as the United States took over in 1898, it immediately established Spanish as the only language of instruction permitted in the schools; by 1900, Spanish was permitted in the elementary grades, but this policy was rescinded in 1905, reverting to an English-only policy, despite the fact that there were few teachers on the island who were fluent in English (Waggenheim, 1975). Once Puerto Ricans were permitted to elect their own governors, in 1948, Spanish was finally restored as the medium of instruction, with English a mandatory subject. However, in the ongoing struggle to define the island's political relationship to the United States, "language instruction continues to be viewed as a political tool by all sides" (Waggenheim, 1975:104).

Language policies in the schools of the American Southwest have also mirrored a broader political agenda. Following the defeat of Mexico and the purchase of the Southwest in 1848, the United States acquired territories occupied by inhabitants who were Spanish speakers. In 1855, however, English-only instruction was mandated in the schools, both private and public (Crawford, 1992). By 1918, "Texas enacted criminal penalties for teachers speaking anything else in the classroom, except to teach foreign languages in the upper grades" (Crawford, 1992:72); it remained a crime until 1973. The U.S. government's insistence on the "civilizing influence" of English in relation to native American students reflected a similarly contemptuous regard for their languages, or "barbarous dialects" in the word of one federal Indian commissioner (Crawford, 1989:25). In 1879, the federal government began a policy of forcibly removing Indian children from their families and educating them at boarding schools, where they were prohibited from using their native languages. The official repression of native languages was rescinded in 1934, though English remained the language of instruction in classrooms.

The United States federal government's English-only language policies in the schooling of these subjugated citizens contrast sharply with the tolerant attitudes it showed toward native language use in the public schooling of Northern European immigrant children during the nineteenth century. European settlers established schools in their native languages for their children, both private and public, and throughout the nineteenth century bilingual education proliferated in many states, tolerated by a laissez-faire policy at the federal level (Crawford, 1989). By 1900, 600,000 students were enrolled in bilingual German programs in U.S. schools, approximately 4% of the national elementary school population (Kloss, 1977). These figures reflect a significantly higher percentage of students in bilingual education programs than are enrolled today, a hundred years later. Yet within a few years bilingual schools had all but disappeared as a result of a combination of political, rather than educational, forces: anti-immigrant and anti-Catholic nativist movement, following the huge waves of Southern and Eastern European immigration, and the xenophobia that accompanied World War I. "After the United States entered the war in April 1917, anti-German feeling crested in an unprecedented wave of language restrictionism. Several states passed laws and emergency decrees banning German speech in the classroom, on the street, in church . . . even on the telephone" (Crawford, 1989:23). A "fervor of Anglo-conformity" followed, and in 1919, 15 states legislated English as the basic language of instruction. Language loyalty became identified as the litmus test of patriotic loyalty, and bilingualism as an instructional alternative virtually disappeared until 40 years later, when it was reinstituted by a group whose patriotic loyalties were unquestioned: the first wave of the anti-Castro Cuban émigré community of Dade County, Florida. The success of their Coral Way School's bilingual education model, begun in 1963, coincided with the civil rights movement, which focused national attention on the inadequate educational opportunities available to black children. Latino activists incorporated the demand for bilingual education, and in 1968 the Bilingual Education Act was passed at the federal level.

Current Sociopolitical Context

"Paradoxically, political support was stronger in 1968, when the concept of bilingual education was virtually untested, than in 1988, when research is increasingly documenting its benefits" (Crawford, 1989:12). The current political attacks on bilingual education, organized by the English-only movement, have roots in the massive demographic changes and economic insecurities that have fueled the conservative movement in American politics of the 1980s and 1990s. The backlash against bilingual education programs are often thinly veiled attacks against immigrants themselves;

"bilingual education is arousing passions about issues of political power and social status that are far removed from the classroom" (Crawford, 1989:13). Indeed, Nieto (1992) suggests that the hidden controversy over bilingual education is not so much that it does not succeed in educating language minority children, but that it does: "Bilingual education is a political issue because both its proponents and opponents have long recognized its potential for empowering . . . traditionally powerless groups" (Nieto, 1992:160).

The rapidly changing demographic shifts in U.S. society may well contribute to the public's interest in pedagogical techniques that might otherwise go unnoticed. California, it is claimed, is currently "ethnically, racially, and culturally the most diverse society that has ever existed—a historically unprecedented experiment. This diversity poses whole new challenges to all public institutions, but particularly to the schools: immigrants, primarily a young population, arrive in California from all over the world in prime childbearing years" (Olsen and Dowell, 1989:5). Not only are the numbers of limited English speakers in the public schools significant (one-fifth of all California public school students by the mid-1990s were born outside the United States), but the change has been rapid. The number of students who speak languages other than English has tripled from the mid-1980s to the mid-1990s, and there has been a 41% increase of English language learners in the past 4 years (Wink, 1995). It can be argued that one impact of these changes has been the arousal of anxiety and hostility among native-born citizens, which has resulted in scapegoating of immigrant students and bilingual education programs. The 1995 passage of Proposition 187, which sought to deny admission to public schools to the children of undocumented immigrants, was just one example of the hostility that the conservative political trends directed toward immigrant students.

The projected ethnic composition of the United States mirrors the changes currently experienced in California. One projection estimates that by 2040, it is expected that the number of residents who speak languages other than English will triple, reaching 96.1 million (Cisneros and Leone, 1996), a number that refers to foreign-born immigrants and their native-born children in homes where a language other than English is spoken. Studies of the linguistic behaviors of immigrant groups to the United States suggest that language shift will occur in that second generation, however, linguistic assimilation, or Anglicization, has characterized the immigration experience over two generations of every immigrant group to the United States, although Hispanics tend to retain a bilingual orientation slightly lower (Veltman, 1983).

The extent to which hostility toward the new arrivals is racially motivated is difficult to gauge, but race is often pointed to as a factor. By far the largest numbers of immigrants come from Asian and Latin American countries; most new immigrants are nonwhites who have been traditionally considered the "nonmeltable" ethnics (Crawford, 1989). Just as the late nineteenth-century criticisms of German schools were veiled attacks on the Catholicism of German immigrants, it has been argued that language politics have become a "convenient surrogate for racial politics" (Crawford, 1989:14).

The new surge in nativism, fueled by the dramatic increases in immigration at the same time that changing tax codes and the globalization of the economy created economic insecurities in the workplace, gave birth to the English-only movement. English only has as its goal to make English the official language of the United States; it also seeks to make English the only medium of instruction in the schools. English-only campaigns have been orchestrated by the well-funded conservative organization U.S. English. As of 1995, some 21 states had passed official language bills (Walsh, 1996).

Public controversy over bilingual education has had a direct and indirect impact on the educational opportunities open to language minority students and on bilingual education programs. Certainly one effect is the denial of bilingual instructional services, even where it is the legally established right of students. In a case study of Lowell, Massachusetts, where the Cambodian population swelled from 604 to 11,493 in a 10-year period, Kiang (1990) documents the city's passage of an English-only referendum, and the struggle that Asian and Latino parents launched in order to overcome attempts to segregate Asian and Hispanic students in substandard facilities, led by an antiimmigrant School Committee member. The harsh antiimmigrant political campaigns in California and the political powerlessness of Hispanics there have led to a rollback in bilingual education programs in the state (Navarro, 1985), including the "sunsetting" of the bilingual edu-

cation law. In reviewing the many studies on bilingual program effectiveness, Freeman and Freeman found: "What all these studies have found is that students who receive sustained first language support develop both English proficiency and academic competence. The research results seem quite clear, but negative attitudes toward bilinguals and bilingual education have prevented many schools from adopting the most effective practices" (Freeman and Freeman, 1994:213).

A second effect of the negative sociopolitical context surrounding bilingual education is in the implementation of such programs. "At times it is difficult to assess the influence that particular bilingual education programs have on the schooling of a particular group of students, because bilingual programs vary widely in their implementation and administrative support" (Cisneros and Leone, 1996:359).

Ortiz (1988:69) found that "school personnel's status within the school is determined by the group of students they teach, that is, whether they teach Hispanic or non-Hispanic." This status differential largely accounted for the differences in materials and equipment Ortiz found in 97 bilingual and "traditional" classrooms she studied. Another difference was the remedial orientation of the bilingual classrooms, marked by low expectations, a preponderance of worksheets, and lack of materials corresponding to the district's testing program. (It should be noted that within the educationally superior "traditional" programs studied by Ortiz, Hispanic students experienced discriminatory attitudes by teachers.) The financial and administrative support given or withheld from individual bilingual programs is often subject to political pressures in a school district, and these are directly affected by the larger sociopolitical context, including organized movements such as English only. One critic of bilingual education programs asserts in a recent study that although transitional bilingual education appears to be the dominant approach to teaching limited English-speaking students, in fact very little native language instruction actually occurs in transitional classrooms, especially among non-Spanish language programs (Rossell and Baker, 1996).

Finally, the pressures on programs to be remedial, compensatory, transitional, and short term, a direct result of the political climate, often severely undercut their effectiveness. By their very nature, students and programs under the transitional model are caught in a

Catch-22: programs are judged effective by how quickly students are moved out of them; yet a large body of research, cited earlier, suggests that it is unrealistic to expect a 1-, 2-, or even 3-year program to adequately prepare students to successfully compete academically in the mainstream. When bilingual program graduates fail because they are inadequately prepared, bilingual education is then blamed. Some suggest that transitional bilingual education is in fact a deliberate strategy to underprepare language minorities for higher paying jobs: "The attacks on transitional bilingual education are not consistent with the available research evidence on bilingualism, but they can be seen as consistent with trends toward the further lowering of the job ceiling for immigrants in the United States" (Spener, 1988).

The sociopolitical difficulties inherent in the transitional model of bilingual education, which isolates low-status students from their peers, are not as evident in the two-way model, also known as developmental enrichment, or immersion. Two-way programs, which integrate language minority and language majority students in the same classroom, studying the same bilingual curriculum, seem to produce better prepared language minority students and to generate an entirely different sociopolitical response. In a large-scale study that analyzed the records of 42,000 language minority students in school systems with a variety of well-supported program models, Collier (1995) found that,

> For students who are schooled in the U.S. from kindergarten on, the elementary school program with the most success in language minority students' long-term academic achievement, as measured by standardized tests across all the subject areas, is two-way developmental bilingual education. As a group, students in this program maintain grade-level skills in their first language at least through sixth grade and reach the fiftieth percentile of NCE in their second language generally after 4–5 years of school. (p. 34)

The two-way model incorporates the following predictors of schools most likely to produce academically successful language minority students:

> Changes in the sociocultural context of schooling, e.g. integration with English speakers, in a supporting, affirming context for all; an additive bilingual context, in which bilingual education is perceived as the gifted and talented program for all students; and the transformation of majority and minority relations in school to a positive school climate for all students, in a safe school environment. (Collier, 1995:33)

One reason for the popularity of two-way programs, many of which have long waiting lists of language majority students, is the growing recognition that bilingualism is an asset in the global economy of the twenty-first century—*for language majority children*. Massachusetts state education reform, for example, sets as a goal for all students oral and written proficiency in two languages (including English) by the time of high school graduation. Two-way programs are an obvious means to achieving this goal; the perception that they are enrichment programs that also benefit language majority students seems to assuage the hostility that transitional and maintenance bilingual programs tend to engender.

Conclusion

The bulk of research in the United States on bilingual education following the passage of the 1968 Bilingual Education Act has focused on linguistic and, to a lesser extent, cognitive aspects of learning among language minority students. There is a need to look at bilingual schooling within the broader sociopolitical context, as the above review clearly suggests. Several questions need further investigation. How do sociopolitical factors impact policy and implementation of bilingual programs? What factors successfully change the sociopolitical context so as to promote enrichment rather than remedial program models? Within these broader questions, it may be useful to explore the dynamics of majority–minority relations as they relate to teachers, students, and administrators in schools with bilingual programs. Finally, there is a need for research linking education reform with the research on successful bilingual education models.

REFERENCES

Abi-Nader, J. 1990. "A House for My Mother: Motivating Hispanic High School Students." *Anthropology and Education Quarterly* 21(1):41–58.

Boggs, S. T. (1972). "The Meaning of Questions and Narratives to Hawaiian Children." In C. Cazden, V. John, and D. Hymes (eds.), *Functions of Language in the Classroom*. New York: Teachers College Press.

Cazden, C., V. John, and D. Hymes, (eds.). 1972. *Functions of Language in the Classroom*. New York: Teachers College Press.

Cisneros, R., and B. Leone. 1995. "Introduction: Critical Descriptions of Classrooms and Programs." *Bilingual Research Journal*. 19(3&4):353–368.

Clemant, R. 1980. "Ethnicity, Contact, and Communicative Competence in a Second Language." In H. Giles and W. Robinson (eds.), *Language*. Oxford: Pergamon Press.

Collier, V. P. 1987. "Age and Rate of Acquisition of Second Language for Academic Purposes." *TESOL Quarterly* 21:617–641.

———. 1989. "How Long? A Synthesis of Research on Academic Achievement in Second Language. *TESOL Quarterly* 509–531.

———. 1992. "A Synthesis of Studies Examining Long-Term Language Minority Student Data on Academic Achievement." *Bilingual Research Journal* 16(1–2):187–212.

———. 1995. *Promoting Academic Success for ESL Students: Understanding Second Language Acquisition for School*. Trenton, NJ: NJTESOL-BE.

Collier, V. P., and W. P. Thomas. 1989. "How Quickly Can Immigrants Become Proficient in School English?" *Journal of Educational Issues of Language Minority Students* 5:26–38.

Crawford, J. 1989. *Bilingual Education: History, Politics, Theory, and Practice*. Trenton, NJ: Crane.

———. 1992. *Hold Your Tongue: Bilingualism and the Politics of "English Only."* Reading, MA: Addison-Wesley.

Cummins, J. 1979. "Cognitive/Academic Language Proficiency, Linguistic Interdependence, the Optimal Age Question, and Some Other Matters." *Working Papers on Bilingualism* 19:197–205.

———. 1981. "The Role of Primary Language Development in Promoting Educational Success for Language Minority Students." In *Schooling and Language Minority Students*, pp. 2–49. Sacramento, CA: California Department of Education.

———. 1986. "Language Proficiency and Academic Achievement." In J. Cummins and M. Swain, (eds.), *Bilingualism in Education*, pp. 138–161. New York: Longman.

———. 1989. *Empowering Minority Students*. Sacramento, CA: California Association of Bilingual Education.

———. 1991. "Interdependence of First- and Second-Language Proficiency in Bilingual Children." In E. Bialystok (ed.), *Language Processing in Bilingual Children*, pp. 70–89. Cambridge: Cambridge University Press.

Delgado-Gaiten, C. 1987. "Traditions and Transitions in the Learning Process of Mexican Children: An Ethnographic View." In G. Spindler, and L. Spindler (eds.), *Interpretive Ethnography of Education: At Home and Abroad*. Hillsdale, NJ: Lawrence Erlbaum Associates.

Diaz, R. M., and C. Klinger, 1991. "Towards an Explanatory Model of the Interaction between Bilingualism and Cognitive Development." In E. Bialystok (ed.), *Language Processing in Bilingual Children*, pp. 70–89. Cambridge: Cambridge University Press.

EPICA Task Force. 1976. *Puerto Rico: A People Challenging Colonialism*. Washington, DC: EPICA Task Force.

Erickson, F. 1987. "Transformation and School Success: The Politics and Culture of Educational Achievement." *Anthropology and Education Quarterly* 18(4):335–356.

Freeman, D. E., and Y. S. Freeman. 1992. *Whole Language for Second Language Learners*. Portsmouth, NH: Heinemann.

———. 1994. *Between Worlds: Access to Second Language Acquisition*. Portsmouth, NH: Heinemann.

Garcia, E. 1993. "Language, Culture, and Education." In L. Darling-Hammong (ed.), *Review of Research in Education*, Vol. 19, pp. 51–98. Washington, DC: American Educational Research Association.

———. 1994. *Understanding and Meeting the Challenge of Student Cultural Diversity*. Boston: Houghton Mifflin.

Gardner, R. 1979. "Social Psychological Aspects of Second Language Acquisition." In H. Giles and R. St. Clair (eds.), *Language and Social Psychology*. Baltimore: University Park Press.

Gardner, R., and W. Lambert. 1972. *Attitudes and Motivation in Second Language Learning*. Rowley, MA: Newbury House.

Genesee, F. 1987. *Learning Through Two Languages: Studies of Immersion and Bilingual Education*. Cambridge, MA: Newbury House.

Hakuta, K. 1986. *Mirror of Language: The Debate on Bilingualism*. New York: Basic Books.

Heath, S. B. 1983. *Ways with Words*. Cambridge: Cambridge University Press.

Jordan, K. 1977. *Maternal Teaching, Peer Teaching, and School Adaptation in an Urban Hawaiian Population*. Technical Report No. 67. Honolulu: Kamehameha Schools, Kamehameha Early Education Program.

Kiang, P. N. 1990. "Southeast Asian Parent Empowerment: The Challenge of Changing Demographics in Lowell, Massachusetts." In C.E. Walsh (ed.), *Education Reform and Social Change*. Mahwah, NJ: Lawrence Erlbaum Associates.

Kloss, H. 1977. *The American Bilingual Tradition.* Rowley, MA: Newbury House.

Lambert, W. 1975. "Culture and Language as Factors in Learning and Education." In A. Wolfgang (ed.), *Education of Immigrant Students.* Toronto: O.I.S.E.

Lessow-Hurley, J. 1990. *The Foundations of Dual Language Instruction.* New York: Longman.

Lindholm, K. J. 1991. "Theoretical Assumptions and Empirical Evidence for Academic Achievement in Two Languages." *Hispanic Journal of Behavioral Sciences* 13:3–17.

Macias, J. 1987. "The Hidden Curriculum of Papago Teachers: American Indian Strategies for Mitigating Cultural Discontinuity in Early Schooling." In G. Spindler and L. Spindler (eds.), *Interpretive Ethnography of Education: At Home and Abroad.* Hillsdale, NJ: Lawrence Erlbaum Associates.

Maldonado-Denis, M. 1972. Puerto Rico: *A Socio-historic Interpretation.* New York: Random House.

McLaughlin, B. 1992. *Myths and Misconceptions about Second Language Learning: What Every Teacher Needs to Unlearn.* Santa Cruz, CA: National Center for Research on Cultural Diversity and Second Language Learning.

Montero-Sieburth, M., and M. Perez. 1987. " 'Echar pa'lante,' Moving Onward: The Dilemmas and Strategies of a Bilingual Teacher.*" Anthropology and Education Quarterly* 18:180–189.

Navarro, R. 1985. "The Problems of Language Education and Society: Who Decides?" In E. Garcia and R. V. Padilla (eds.), *Advances in Bilingual Education Research,* pp. 289–312. Tucson: University of Arizona Press.

Nieto, S. 1992. *Affirming Diversity: The Sociopolitical Context of Multicultural Education.* White Plains, NY: Longman.

Nine Curt, C. J. 1984. *Nonverbal Communication.* Fall River, MA: Bilingual Evaluation, Dissemination and Assessment Center.

Olsen, L., and C. Dowell. 1989. *Bridges: Promising Practices for the Education of Immigrant Children.* San Francisco, CA: California Tomorrow.

Ortiz, F. I. 1988. "Hispanic-American Children's Experiences in Classrooms: A Comparison between Hispanic and Non-Hispanic Children." In L. Weis (ed.), *Class, Race and Gender in American Education.* Albany, NY: State University of New York Press.

Ovando, C. J., and V. Collier. 1985. *Bilingual and ESL Classrooms: Teaching in Multicultural Contexts.* New York: McGraw-Hill.

Philips, S. 1972. "Participant Structures and Communicative Competence: Warm Springs Children in Community and Classroom." In C. Cazden, V. John, and D. Hymes (eds.), *Functions of Language in the Classroom.* New York: Teachers College Press.

Ramirez, J. David. 1991. *Final Report: Longitudinal Study of Structured English Immersion Strategy, Early-Exit and Late-Exit Bilingual Education Programs.* U.S. Department of Education. NTIS, 300–87–0156.

Rossell, C. H., and K. Baker. 1996. *Bilingual Education in Massachusetts: The Emperor Has No Clothes.* Boston, MA: The Pioneer Institute for Public Policy Research.

Schumann, J. H. 1978. "The Pidginization Hypothesis." In E. Hatch (ed.), *Second Language Acquisition,* pp. 256–271. Rowley, MA: Newbury House.

Sindell, P. 1988. "Some Discontinuities in the Enculturation of Mistassini Cree Children." In J. Wurzel (ed.), *Toward Multiculturalism: A Reader in Multicultural Education.* Yarmouth, ME: Intercultural Press.

Snow, C. E. 1990. "Rationales for Native Language Instruction: Evidence from Research." In A.M. Padilla, H.H. Fairchild, and C.M. Valadez (eds.), *Bilingual Education: Issues and Strategies.* Newbury Park, CA: Sage.

Spener, D. 1988. "Transitional Bilingual Education and the Socialization of Immigrants." *Harvard Educational Review* 58(2):133–154.

Tinajero, J. V., and A. F. Ada. (eds.). 1993. *The Power of Two Languages: Literacy and Biliteracy for Spanish-Speaking Students.* New York: Macmillan/McGraw-Hill.

Veltman, C. 1983. *Language Shift in the United States.* New York: Mouton.

Waggenheim, K. 1975. "Puerto Rico: A Profile." In F. Cordasco and E. Bucchioni (eds.), *The Puerto Rican Experience: A Sociological Sourcebook.* Totowa, NJ: Littlefield, Adams.

Walsh, C. E. 1996. "Making a Difference: Social Vision, Pedagogy, and Real Life." In C.E. Walsh (ed.), *Education Reform and Social Change.* Mahwah, NJ: Lawrence Erlbaum Associates.

Wink, J. (and collaborators). 1995. "California: A picture of Diverse Language Groups and ESL Programs." *Bilingual Research Journal* 19(3&4):641–660.

Wong Fillmore, L. 1983. "The Language Learner as an Individual: Implications of Research on Individual Differences for the ESL Teacher." In M.A. Clarke and J. Handscombe (eds.), *On TESOL '82: Pacific Perspectives on Language Learning and Teaching.* Washington, DC: TESOL.

Wong Fillmore, L., and C. Valadez. 1986. "Teaching Bilingual Learners." In M.C. Wittrock (ed.), *Handbook of Research on Teaching,* 3rd ed. New York: Macmillan.

Zanger, V. V. 1987. "The Social Context of Second Language Learning: An Examination of Barriers to Integration in Five Case Studies." Unpublished doctoral dissertation. Boston University.

———. 1991. "Social and Cultural Dimensions of the Education of Language Minority Students." In A. Ambert (ed.), *Bilingual Education and English as a Second Language: A Research Handbook 1988–1990.* New York: Garland Publishing.

———. 1994. " 'Not Joined in:' The Social Context of English Literacy Development for Hispanic Youth." In B.M. Ferdman, R-M .Weber, and A.G. Ramirez (eds.), *Literacy Across Languages and Cultures.* Albany, NY: State University of New York Press.

BROWN V. BOARD OF EDUCATION

Jennifer L. Hochschild
Princeton University

Brown v. Board of Education was one of the most important decisions ever made by the United States Supreme Court. It has been criticized for going too far or not far enough, for saying too much or too little, for being too moralistic or too much based in factual claims. Despite those and other criticisms, it stands out for a simple but essential reason: Until it was handed down, it was permissible and even advantageous for public servants and politicians to endorse racial segregation. Twenty years later, the political mainstream did not permit open support for segregation. Furthermore, *Brown* committed the federal government to ending legal racial segregation, a task that took several decades and eventually involved all branches of government but was eventually accomplished. Those were extraordinary, if insufficient, changes in the United States' shameful racial history, and *Brown v. Board of Education* was partly responsible for them.

The Antecedents of *Brown v. Board of Education*

One must begin with the Thirteenth and Fourteenth Amendments to the U.S. Constitution and with the history of those amendments over the succeeding century really to understand the import of *Brown*. The Thirteenth Amendment of 1865 abolished slavery and "involuntary servitude . . . within the United States, or any place subject to their jurisdiction." The Fourteenth Amendment followed in 1868, requiring that no state "abridge the privileges . . . of citizens of the United States." "It thus ensured that the Thirteenth Amendment (among others) applied within as well as across states. It also (as in the Fifth Amendment) promised "due process of law" and required that states guarantee "equal protection of the laws" to all of their citizens.

Over the next quarter century, the Supreme Court narrowed the scope and import of these amendments (along with the Fifteenth, which provided suffrage for male ex-slaves). But it was not until the 1896 decision in *Plessy v. Ferguson* that the vision of racial equality apparently endorsed by the Civil War amendments was definitively squelched. In its decision on the *Civil Rights Cases* and the *Slaughterhouse Cases* in the previous decade, the Court had implicitly allowed private racial discrimination by explicitly forbidding discriminatory acts by state and local governments. In *Plessy*, the Court removed all but the last barrier to the reinstatement of slavery—the right to buy and sell individuals—by allowing state and local governments to pass whatever laws or ordinances they wished to reinstate white supremacy.

Specifically, the Supreme Court found in *Plessy* that blacks could legitimately be given "equal but separate accommodations" in railroad cars, restaurants, schools, and other public places. *Plessy* justified this decision by declaring it a "fallacy" to assume "that the enforced separation of the two races stamps the colored race with a badge of inferiority." The authors of the 7–1 decision further declared that they could "not accept [the] proposition[s] . . . that social prejudices may be overcome by legislation, and that equal rights cannot be secured to the negro except by an enforced commingling of the two races."

Brown v. Board of Education and its successors eventually overturned, in fact if not in name, the basic holding and all three of the defending propositions of *Plessy*, but not until severe damage had been inflicted on the nation. In the decade before *Plessy*, blacks' rights to vote, hold office, attain an education, buy land, and move had all been eroded since the high point of Reconstruction. But *Plessy* legitimated and hastened the institutionalization of Jim Crow laws. For example, in 1870, 10% of "Negro and other races" were enrolled in school; by 1880 that percentage had risen dramatically, to 33 percent. Twenty years later, the proportion of blacks enrolled in school had declined slightly, to 31%. (The proportion of whites enrolled in school declined even more dramatically between 1880 and 1900, from 62 to 54%—suggesting that Jim Crow was just as harmful to the apparent "winners" as to the obvious losers.) Between 1882 (the first year for which data are available) and 1890, an average of "only" 69 blacks were lynched each year. Between 1891 and 1900—the *Plessy* decade—that average jumped to 113 per year. (The average number of whites who were lynched declined, from 76 per year in the first decade to 43 per year in the second.[1]) The number of blacks registered to vote in, for example, Louisiana declined from 130,300 in 1896 (the year that *Plessy* was decided) to 1,300 in 1904. Other southern states followed suit in prohibiting black suffrage.[2] In short, the half century after *Plessy* demonstrated a level of white supremacy, exploitation, and terrorism very little different from the period of enslavement before the Civil War.

In 1910, W.E.B. DuBois and others solidified the nascent National Association for the Advancement of Colored People (NAACP), thus beginning the long legal effort to overturn *Plessy* and undo Jim Crow. The NAACP's Legal Defense Fund began in the 1930s to litigate a series of cases, the decisions on which would eventually allow, or even impel, the Supreme Court to reject the doctrine of "separate but equal." Critical decisions in the decade before *Brown*, such as *Sweatt v. Painter*, began to require that if educational accommodations were to be kept separate, they at least had to be made more equal—and if equality was impossible, then separation was not permissible. The NAACP itself was internally divided on the issue of whether to pursue truly equal, separate schools instead of desegregation. Most arguments for separate equality were strategic; it was a demand whose gratification seemed more likely than a reversal of the 60-year-old precedent of *Plessy*. But a few argued for the virtues of respectful separation; Herbert Wechsler, a law professor at Columbia University asked Thurgood Marshall, who was leading the NAACP campaign to overturn *Plessy*, if it "was so plain . . . that a Negro child attending a segregated school was worse off than a Negro child attending a non-segregated school where he might feel the full brunt of white prejudice? Could it not reason-

ably be argued that . . . [the latter child] would be doubly frustrated by the limited economic and social opportunity that would later confront him in a world where *de facto* segregation prevailed?" (Kluger, 1975: 2:671). Such a view was then unusual in civil rights circles, but it was an eerie harbinger of sentiments and situations that would be much more prevalent several decades later.

Several factors other than the brilliant legal campaign against *Plessy* led to the decision in *Brown v. Board of Education*. Some were idiosyncratic; President Eisenhower happened to appoint as Chief Justice the Republican Californian politician Earl Warren, whom he reasonably but mistakenly expected to be a centrist conservative. Other factors were broadly structural. Black southern farm workers and their families were moving to cities and to the north, and beginning to demand education, civil rights, decent jobs, and political power. Black soldiers were returning from World War II, full of pride at their achievements, inspired by the relative freedom they had enjoyed abroad, and angry at restrictions that remained at home. Whites were chastened by the Nazis' example of what racism could produce. Politicians were starting to fight the Cold War, and found it difficult to claim with a straight face that the United States, in contrast with the Soviet Union, was the land of freedom and equality for all. The revelation of their hypocrisy was hastened by accusations from African leaders whom American diplomats were trying to woo. Most generally, the south was emerging from its post–Civil War poverty, isolation, and intransigence, and both southerners and northerners were beginning to realize just how much Jim Crow dragged down all facets of American society.

The *Brown* Decisions

For whatever combination of reasons, the Supreme Court unanimously declared in May 1954 that "separate educational facilities are inherently unequal"—thus overruling the central finding of *Plessy*. The Court went on to reject *Plessy*'s three supporting contentions. First and most straightforwardly, it repudiated the "fallacy" claim by declaring that "to separate [children in schools] from others of a similar age and qualifications solely because of their race generates a feeling of inferiority as to their status in the community that may affect their hearts and minds in a way unlikely ever to

[1] Education figures are from U.S. Bureau of the Census, *Historical Statistics of the United States, Part 1*, table H 443–441; the lynching data are derived from table H 1168–1170.
[2] C. Vann Woodward, *Origins of the New South, 1877–1913* (Louisiana State University Press, 1951), pp. 342–343.

be undone." Second, the implementation decision a year later, *Brown II*, itemized possible local school problems and found that "the primary responsibility for elucidating, assessing, and solving these problems" lay with school authorities, backed (or prodded) by "the {federal district} courts which originally heard these cases." Although many criticized *Brown II* for its caveat about proceeding "with all deliberate speed," this decision implicitly refuted *Plessy*'s claim that legislation cannot "overcome . . . social prejudices." It could, and it would—through a combination of educational administration, local court decisions, legislation, and Supreme Court rulings.

The Supreme Court, and Americans in general, are still debating the third *Plessy* contention, "that equal rights cannot be secured . . . except by an enforced commingling of the two races." Before turning to that debate, it is worth noting two additional features of the *Brown* decision. First, the holding apparently rested as much on empirical findings by psychologists as on constitutional or moral principles. The crucial finding that separate is *inherently* unequal, regardless of the luxury of the accommodations, rested on experiments by Kenneth and Mamie Clark showing that black children chose light rather than dark dolls when asked to choose the nicest, prettiest, best, or otherwise most preferable doll. These experimental results have been replicated, contradicted, and discussed voluminously since 1954; perhaps their greatest contribution beyond the findings of the case itself has been to legitimize (at least in the eyes of some) the use of empirical social science in making constitutional decisions. At lawyers' behest, sociologists, political scientists, educators and others have rushed into the space created by footnote 11. It is unclear what effect their sometimes confusing and contradictory results have had on the development of law, but social scientists' participation in legal battles has had an enormous impact on the discipline of sociology itself.

The second point to note about *Brown* is the controversy it generated about its objects and requirements. Its stated object is clear: *de jure* segregation in public schools. Some of the language of *Brown* suggests that schools are its only object, since it is at pains to distinguish education from other public functions (e.g., "Today, education is perhaps the most important public function of state and local governments. . . . It is the very foundation of good citizenship.") Subsequent

Supreme Court decisions extended the principles of *Brown* beyond public schools, but the question of whether its holding reached as far as private acts of discrimination or racist sentiments remains controversial.

Similarly, *Brown*'s stated requirement is clear: the abolition of state-mandated segregation. But some subsequent Supreme Court decisions and legislation have defined the abolition of segregation to require positive action to desegregate, to compensate victims of prior segregation, or even to seek an end to the American racial hierarchy. The question of what actions the state must take fully to overcome segregation remains deeply controversial. Do *Brown* and its successors require affirmative action to keep schools integrated, once previous segregatory practices have been dismantled? Does the principle of integration reach as far as *de facto* segregation? Is there even a meaningful distinction between state-imposed and "accidental" segregation, given that the latter necessarily developed in the context of and often under the protection of the former? What if the victims of prior mandatory segregation prefer voluntary separation to grudging integration? These and other questions about the extent and depth of *Brown* have exercised political activists, lawyers, and academic analysts alike in the decades since it was handed down.

The Subsequent History of School Desegregation

Those debates, however, lay in the future in May 1954. The immediate response to *Brown* "was predictable: all hell broke loose" (Spaeth, 1977:2). Southern politicians, editors, and school administrators fulminated; white citizens' councils sprang up or were revivified; northern whites mostly watched placidly in the comfortable assurance that the ruling did not affect them. Some Americans were overjoyed. The *Cincinatti Enquirer* editorialized that the Court "simply . . . act[ed] as the conscience of the American nation." Thurgood Marshall predicted "up to five years" for all schools to be integrated, and nine for all of American society (Hochschild, 1984:15).

Supporters of segregation and opponents of change were somewhat reassured by *Brown II*'s promise that local officials would deal with specific local problems, and that the dealing would occur "with all deliberate speed." And as innumerable wags have since pointed out, the next decade saw at best much more deliberation than speed in the field of school desegregation.

Officials in one county in Virginia closed the public school system; Governor Faubus used state troops to prevent the desegregation of schools in Little Rock, Arkansas; other southern states devised simple or ingenious laws and practices to avoid desegregation. A decade after the *Brown* decision, only 2% of black children in the south attended school with white children.

The Supreme Court finally lost its patience, declaring in 1965 that "delays in desegregation of school systems are no longer tolerable," and in 1969 that "every school district is to terminate dual school systems at once and to operate now and hereafter only unitary schools." A federal district court charged New Rochelle, New York—a northern school district—with deliberate segregation in 1964, and the courts at all levels began pushing districts to take affirmative steps to desegregate their schools even across traditional neighborhood boundaries.

At the same time, the civil rights movement was reaching its peak of legislative, political, and moral power. The 1964 Civil Rights Act forbade the use of federal funds in segregated institutions. The 1965 Elementary and Secondary Education Act put teeth into that provision by suddenly making considerable federal aid available to compliant districts. The Justice Department, Department of Health, Education, and Welfare, and Congress in later regulations, law suits, and appropriations all joined the effort to turn the law of desegregation into a reality. Thus began a decade of action to desegregate schools across the country. Resisters of "forced busing" rioted in Boston, Pontiac (Michigan), and other cities, and many children of all races suffered from the accumulated hatreds of their parents. But schools slowly were desegregated; by 1976, 45% of black students in the south attended schools in which a majority of students were white. Levels of desegregation remained lower in other regions; nevertheless, racial isolation slowly diminished. In addition, black students' years of schooling and achievement levels rose at a faster rate than whites', thus beginning to close the educational gap between the races.

By 1974, the political opposition to school desegregation became so great, and the comparatively easy districts to desegregate became so sparse, that the drive to desegregate schools almost halted. The most telling blow was *Milliken v. Bradley* (1974), in which a split Supreme Court ruled that courts could not order busing across school district lines unless all of the affected districts were found guilty of *de jure* segregation. Such a finding is possible but extremely difficult legally and politically, and *Milliken* demoralized civil rights litigators.

The history of school desegregation since 1974 can be told briefly—there have been very few new efforts. School districts have mostly concentrated on various measures to improve the quality of education for whatever children are already in the district. Educators who have focused on issues of racial balance have mostly turned to magnet schools and other voluntary methods to lure white students back into the public education system. A few districts (notably Kansas City and St. Louis) won court cases against their state boards of education, requiring the state to fund extensive capital and programmatic expenditures. (In June 1995, however, the Supreme Court found that the district court in the Kansas City case had overstepped its authority, so it is unclear if the strategy of bringing states in as defendants in a school desegregation case has any future.) By 1988, the percentage of black children in predominantly white schools had declined in the northeast and south from the high point of a decade earlier, and that proportion remained static in the rest of the country.

Citizens' Evaluations of *Brown* and Its Consequences

Whites have always been split in their views on desegregation. Support for the abstract principle of school desegregation and other forms of racial integration and equality has risen steadily since 1954, reaching a large majority by the late 1970s. That result suggests that the *Plessy* Court was at least partly wrong in declaring that legislation could not change views. But support for the implementation of those principles, especially if implementation involved mandatory school desegregation, has always been much lower. A huge majority of whites always opposed "forced busing" (although support among college freshmen has risen every year since the question was first asked in 1972, and now reaches about two-thirds), and most whites have always been at least skeptical about other means of mandatory desegregation.

White political activists have mirrored the split in public views. Some white parents stoned buses carrying black children into their own child's school; other white parents put their children and themselves on those buses. Few elected politicians spoke out strongly in favor of mandatory school desegregation, and most who did quickly ceased to be elected politicians. Some explicitly opposed mandatory desegregation, whether out of conviction or calculation is hard to say. Most sought to avoid the issue.

African Americans have had a more complicated set of views on *Brown* and its consequences. Polls show that throughout the 1950s and 1960s, most strongly supported integration and sought improved education for their children. In pursuit of those goals they were willing to have their children bused out of newly closed neighborhood schools into white schools. By the 1970s, however, many African Americans became disillusioned. They perceived that whites did not welcome them, that the black community bore most of the risks and burdens of desegregation, that their children suffered from second-generation discrimination once inside the formerly white schools, that black teachers and principals were losing precious jobs, and that their children were losing a sense of history and community that segregated schools had sometimes fostered. Some opposed school desegregation on normative as well as pragmatic grounds, valuing the maintenance of a tight-knit black community over even the possible virtues of a well-integrated society.

At present, the black community is split. Some African Americans retain their faith in school desegregation, pointing out that desegregated black children do better in college and jobs and arguing that our nation must pursue the moral goal of racial integration. Others take the pragmatic view (first and best espoused by W.E.B. Du Bois, 1935) that what black children most need—and what *Brown* really called for, in this interpretation—is excellent education regardless of racial balance. Thus they turn their efforts to improving schools in which their children are already enrolled. A third group argue that black children are better off in all-black schools with fewer tensions and distractions, with more black role models, and with a distinctively African-oriented curriculum. A few even ask, "was the decision [in *Brown*] beneficial for the African American community?"—and answering "no," claim that the

principle of equal but separate accommodations should guide educational policy in the future.[3]

Sociologists' Evaluations of *Brown* and Its Consequences

Sociologists have been extensively involved in evaluating the process and outcomes of school desegregation, and they have played an important role in legal decisions and public judgments. Their focus has ranged from general principles for attaining effective desegregation to detailed case studies of the process to quantitative analyses of the results. Gordon Allport (1954) enunciated the principles of successful social contact that set the standards for many desegregators in the decades after 1954. Since then, studies of school desegregation have fallen into three major camps, defined more by judgments of the legitimacy of, or evaluations of the success of, school desegregation than by any methodological or disciplinary distinction.

The first camp can be defined roughly as enthusiasts. Thomas Pettigrew, Robert Crain, Gary Orfield, and Willis Hawley (the latter two are political scientists) are among the best known and most prolific supporters of mandatory desegregation. Robert Crain led the way toward studying the long-term consequences for desegregated students in higher education, job attainment, and residential choices. He finds through elegant analyses of natural experiments that in general students from desegregated schools do better later in life. Thomas Pettigrew has used a wide array of empirical means, generally deriving from social psychological models, to demonstrate that school desegregation does not cause extensive white flight, benefits both black and white participants, and is essential for a democratic society. Gary Orfield has provided some of the most detailed studies both of the federal government's processes for developing desegregation policy and of local governments' mechanisms for implementing specific desegregation plans. Willis Hawley has specialized in studying techniques to desegregate schools more effectively, ranging from assignment patterns to community involvement to changes in curriculum to reorganizing the teaching and administrative staff. Other sociolo-

---

[3] Jawanza Kunjufu, quoted in Mary-Christine Phillip. 1994. "*Brown* at 40." *Black Issues in Higher Education* Jan. 13:9–14.

gists, especially including Jeffrey Raffel, Janet Schofeld, and Mary Metz, wrote insightful case studies of desegregated schools in Wilmington (Delaware), Pittsburgh, and Oakland (California) respectively. Their tone is probing but sympathetic, seeking to understand both why school desegregation is so difficult to achieve and how to do it better.

The second camp can be defined roughly as skeptics. It includes notably David Armor, Norman Miller, Eleanor Wolf, Donald Horowitz (a law professor), D. Garth Taylor, Gerald Rosenberg, and Robert Meier (the latter three are political scientists). These authors, among others, endorse the basic principles of school desegregation but doubt that the means used to create it can lead to any good end. David Armor (1995) has written extensively on the likelihood of white flight, and more generally on the need for citizens voluntarily to choose desegregation in order for it to have good educational or social results. Norman Miller, from the perspective of a social psychologist, argues that many desegregated schools have no impact, or even harmful effects, on their students. Eleanor Wolf's detailed case study of desegregation in Detroit, like Horowitz's study of Washington, D.C., demonstrate how poorly equipped courts are to engage in educational policymaking and how little help ostensibly "expert" social scientists really give them. D. Garth Taylor emphasizes how undemocratic court-ordered bussing is, and Robert Meier and his colleagues document the more subtle but equally harmful nature of second generation discrimination. Gerald Rosenberg (1991) is perhaps the most profound skeptic, arguing that the *Brown* decision had very little impact, either positive *or* negative, on the succeeding few decades of civil rights activism and desegregation.

An interesting group of scholars has switched from enthusiasm to skepticism. Prominent among them are Christine Rossell (a political scientist), Robert Carter, and Derrick Bell (both law professors). Rossell used to produce detailed methodological demonstrations that white flight was not as extensive in mandatory plans as Armor and others argued; eventually she determined that white flight was in fact extensive, and now argues for voluntary plans on the grounds that they will produce more interracial contact. Bell and Carter were prominently involved in the first decade of litigation over school desegregation; they eventually came to believe that desegregation policy as implemented benefited no one, or benefited only a few select (relatively wealthy) blacks, or even benefited whites at the expense of blacks. They ended by opposing further efforts to desegregate schools and supporting strong black-run educational institutions.

A final group are normative opponents. They include Daniel Monti, Lino Graglia (a law professor), Asa Hilliard, and Molefi Asante. Monti endorses the broad goals of school desegregation but sees even the most extensive efforts as superficial covers for deeply rooted racial and class supremacy that supposed reformers are unwilling to challenge. Abandoning the pretense of systematic change would at least make this hypocrisy more visible, in his view. Graglia focuses on the illegitimacy of courts seeking to dictate to citizens of a purportedly free nation what they may do in an arena as important and intimate as their children's education. Hilliard and Asante endorse Afrocentric education, in which black children are taught African-oriented history, culture, and moral stances. In their view, such teaching is not possible in desegregated schools, in which African-American children are second-class citizens trained to absorb a culture fundamentally hostile to them.

It is probably safe to conclude that none of these studies offers definitive findings (beyond a few generalities) or profound normative judgments on which all reputable sociologists concur. That unsatisfactory conclusion obtains for several reasons. Consider the empirical issues first: To begin with, schools keep poor records and almost never had baseline data from which one could reliably measure change. Second, methodological disputes within the profession of sociology (over, for example, how to measure changes in student achievement or in enrollment patterns by race) further complicate data gathering, analysis, and evaluation. Third, school desegregation occurred at the same time as a wide array of other complex social, political, and economic changes—typically lumped together as "the 60s"—and the separate effects of the many changes cannot be distinguished. Fourth, school desegregation was not a single event, or even a single process; it happened differently in different years, school districts, schools, and even classrooms, and "it" was really a large set of changes happening simultaneously and interactively. Patterns can be discerned from this melange, but not easily and not without caveats and dispute (see Hochschild, 1984). Fifth, the effects of school desegregation may be subtle and played out over decades— features that make it very difficult for researchers to identify and trace them. Finally, sociologists are as susceptible to political convictions and moral judgments as are parents and politicians, and their own views inevitably color their investigations and findings. Especially, but not only, those who became involved in the legal process as expert witnesses were identified with one side or another in school desegregation battles, and they found it hard to maintain a neutral stance even in their purely academic research.

The reasons for normative disagreement are as deep as the problem of race in America. Few if any sociologists will argue in favor of racial domination—a profound result, in itself, of the *Brown* decision—but beyond that basic concurrence lie deep disagreements of principle. When, if ever, should the value of equality override that of liberty? What should be the proper role of unelected courts and bureaucrats in a democracy, or of the national government in a federal system of locally based schools? What, if any, compensation do blacks deserve from whites for a history of racial slavery and subordination in which no living person participated? And so on. Sociologists are not disciplinarily trained to resolve such questions (and political philosophers, who are, cannot answer them in any case). But one's answers to these questions inevitably color anyone's evaluation of *Brown* and its aftermath.

In the end, the profession of sociology gained at least as much from the American experience with school de-segregation as it contributed to it. Methodological developments in aggregate data analysis, case study and ethnographic techniques, meta-analysis, and the integration of legal with sociological thinking all emerged from work on school desegregation. So did substantive understandings of interracial contact, the educational process, the long-term consequences of schooling, and the nature of policy implementation in complex social settings. Although the United States has largely abandoned the effort to desegregate more school districts, the profession of sociology will not abandon what it has learned along the way.

REFERENCES

Allport, Gordon. 1979. *The Nature of Prejudice.* Reading, MA: Addison-Wesley, reprinted.

Armor, David. 1995. *Forced Justice: School Desegregation and the Law.* New York: Oxford University Press.

Du Bois, W. E. B. 1935. "Does the Negro Need Separate Schools." *Journal of Negro Education* 4:328–335.

Hochschild, Jennifer. 1984. *The New American Dilemma: Liberal Democracy and School Desegregation.* New Haven, CT: Yale University Press.

Kluger, Richard. 1975. *Simple Justice.* New York: Vintage.

Rosenberg, Gerald. 1991. *The Hollow Hope: Can Courts Bring About Social Change?* Chicago IL: University of Chicago Press.

Spaeth, Harold. 1977. *Classic and Current Decisions of the United States Supreme Court—Plessy v. Ferguson, Brown v. Board of Education, and Milliken v. Bradley.* San Francisco, CA: W.H. Freeman.

CATHOLIC SCHOOLS

Helen M. Marks
The Ohio State University

Catholic schools, among the oldest educational institutions in the United States, trace their origins to colonial times. Although few in number during the seventeenth and eighteenth centuries, the Catholic schools of the era—college seminaries for boys and academies for girls—generally educated the Catholic elite. Religious orders of women dispensed tuition revenues from the girls' academies in major cities to fund free schools for children of the poor. The first parish primary schools emerged in these cities late in the eighteenth century.

Not until well into the nineteenth century, with the founding of many new churches to serve the immigrant population, did parochial (i.e., Catholic parish) schools begin to multiply. For the immigrants, these schools functioned as bridging institutions (Bryk et al., 1993). While nurturing the Catholic values and ethnic identities of the immigrants, Catholic schools assisted their assimilation into the mainstream of American life.

Continuing to proliferate into the latter half of the twentieth century, Catholic schools numbered close to 13,000 in the early 1960s, educating 5.3 million students or 12% of the school-age population. As a result of many factors—including the opening of Catholicism to secular culture following Vatican Council II and the financial burden of operating parish schools with the diminishing supply of unpaid teachers (i.e., members of religious orders of women)—Catholic schools began to close. By 1990, staffed mainly by lay teachers, Catholic schools represented 10% of the elementary and secondary schools in the United States and they enrolled about 7.5% of the country's school-age children. The decline in the number of Catholic schools has continued, with fewer than 2.5 million students enrolled during 1993–1994, less than half the number enrolled three decades earlier.

Demographic Characteristics of Catholic Schools

Within the universe of private schools, an educational sector constituting about one-fourth of all U.S. elementary and secondary schools, Catholic schools represent the largest segment, 36%, enrolling 60% of all private school students. Although some private schools have traditionally drawn their clientele from a socioeconomic elite, Catholic schools enroll a population that is socioeconomically representative of the nation. Since the early 1970s, the minority population in Catholic schools has risen substantially—from 5% African American in 1970–1971 to 9% in 1987–1988. During the same period, the proportion of Hispanic students doubled, increasing from 5% to 10%; and the proportion of Asians, while still small, tripled from 1 to 3%.

Typically smaller than U.S. public schools but larger than other private schools, Catholic schools in the mid-1980s averaged an enrollment of 363 students. During that same period, the student–teacher ratio in Catholic schools was somewhat larger than in public schools (21:1 vs. 18:1) and considerably larger than in other religious and nonsectarian private schools (21:1 vs. 15:1 and 10:1, respectively).

Most Catholic schools are elementary schools and parish controlled. Only one-fourth of Catholic high schools are parochial (including interparish high schools); the remaining high schools are conducted under private or diocesan auspices. Of these high schools, about 9% are single sex (4% boys schools, 5% girls schools).

Parochial School: The First Sociological Study of Catholic Schools

Capturing their culture in the late 1950s, on the brink of the transformation wrought by Vatican Council II, Joseph Fichter, a Harvard-trained sociologist and Jesuit priest, conducted the first "thorough-going and scientific examination" of the Catholic school. At the time of the study, religious teaching orders largely staffed Catholic schools and parishes generally charged no tuition for students to enroll.

Focus of the Research

Unlike later researchers who would study the Catholic high school and investigate the academic and social outcomes of Catholic schooling, Fichter examined the daily workings of the parish elementary school as a social system. Two research questions were central to this early study: How did Catholic schools inspire such confidence as to elicit their total financial support from the voluntary contributions of Church members? and, How did these schools simultaneously socialize new generations into both a religious and an American culture?

As part of a larger research project—a comprehensive investigation of the Catholic parish in America—Fichter's study of Catholic schools focused primarily on their patterns of socialization, social structures, agencies of control, and the social correlates of membership. Over the course of a single year, Fichter and his research team collected observational, interview, and survey data in a single representative Catholic elementary school located in a small midwestern city. For comparative analytic purposes, the team also collected test and questionnaire data from students in grades six through eight in a neighboring public school.

Distinctive Features of Catholic Schools

Comparing Catholic and public schools structurally, Fichter identified four fundamentally differentiating features—the local autonomy of Catholic schools, the voluntary participation of the clientele, the discretionary authority of Catholic school administrators and staff, and the personalistic, familial atmosphere pervading the school organization.

The institutions of education, religion, and family were seamlessly interwoven in the operation of the Catholic school, Fichter concluded. Within the context of the American Catholic Church, the parish school provided the "locus of social solidarity, cohesion and integration at the adult as well as the child level of parishioners" (Fichter, 1958:433).

Vatican Council II and Its Impact on U.S. Catholic Schools

Between 1962 and 1965, the 2,500 bishops of the Catholic church convened in Rome for the intermittent sessions of Vatican Council II, an ecumenical council called by Pope John XXIII for the renewal of Catholicism in response to the changing social conditions of the modern era. Revolutionary in its impact, Vatican Council II affected virtually every aspect of Catholic life. Deviating from precedent, the council defined the church in nontriumphal terms as the "people of God" —a pilgrim people journeying through time, charged with pursuing peace and justice.

Catholic Schools at a Crossroads

The revitalization of the social mission of the Catholic church had profound implications for American Catholic schools. With the election of a Catholic, John F. Kennedy, as President of the United States and the movement of vast numbers of Catholics into the middle class, American Catholicism during the 1960s cast off its identity as a ghetto church. Faced with the issue of new institutional priorities in a changing society, Catholics questioned the future of their schools. If the church had fulfilled its traditional mission of assisting immigrant Catholics to take their place in the mainstream of American society, was it necessary, useful, or even justifiable to maintain a separate school system? The issue of the identity and future of Catholic schools became the subject of heated debate within the church for the next two decades.

To underscore the importance of Catholic schools within the church and society, Vatican Council II issued *The Declaration on Christian Education*, stressing the vital role of Catholic schools in religious socialization and calling on them to be the "leaven of the human community." The council further directed national conferences of Catholic bishops to discern the implications of Vatican II teachings for the renewal of Catholic schools. In 1972 the National Council of Catholic Bishops issued a pastoral statement on Catholic schools, *To*

Teach as Jesus Did. Urging them to embody the gospel message of social justice, the statement delineated a three-fold mission for Catholic schools—to teach a message of hope, to build community, and to serve all people.

Catholic Schools and Social Justice

The call to social justice required American Catholics to examine their institutions critically in order to root out unjust structures and practices. Confronting the issue of systemic racism, the American Catholic church acknowledged past complacency on segregation. But the issue of race was challenging the church in new ways. Because of the *de facto* segregation in urban areas and the movement toward forced busing to achieve racial balance, ethnic whites seeking to evade integrated public education sought to enroll in Catholic schools. Increasingly dependent on student tuition, many Catholic schools facing serious financial problems would have welcomed new students to boost their enrollments.

Under strong episcopal leadership that decried the schools ever becoming "havens for separatists and racists," Catholic schools ultimately resisted racially motivated enrollments. Taking a proactive stand on behalf of social justice, the church strengthened its commitment to maintaining Catholic schools in urban areas where the population was becoming increasingly non-Catholic as well as nonwhite. Although many inner-city Catholic schools did close during the 1970s, Catholic dioceses and religious orders allocated a disproportionate share of their human and fiscal resources to keeping urban schools open.

Within the policy context of the late 1970s and early 1980s, Catholic schools, along with private schools generally, gained increased visibility. Nonpublic schools attracted interest because of their organizational design. Organization by religious identity or educational philosophy distinguished most private schools from public schools, typically organized by geographic area (Coleman et al., 1981). Organizational differences such as these could have vital consequences for student achievement and other valued outcomes of schooling.

Would such marked school organizational differences also increase social stratification? Would they benefit some students more than others? Since improving achievement—especially of minority and eco-

nomically disadvantaged students—had become an issue of public concern, researchers and policymakers began to question the relative efficacy of public and private schools.

Comparing the Effectiveness of Public and Catholic High Schools

Amid a swirl of issues surrounding educational equity, school effectiveness, and educational finance, researchers in the early 1980s undertook comparative studies of public and private schools. Did they differ in how equitably, effectively, and efficiently they educated their students? While proponents viewed private schools as a social and educational resource, critics regarded them as stratifying and divisive. Meanwhile, escalating costs and demographic change threatened the survival of many private schools, raising a new consideration: Should the economic viability of private schools be a matter of public concern?

Comparisons of academic achievement between students in public and private schools had the potential to evoke considerable scrutiny and controversy. If private schools demonstrated higher levels of student achievement—particularly for disadvantaged students, for example—policymakers might seek to extend the benefit to more students by expanding access to these schools, employing such means as tuition tax credits or a system of tuition vouchers. Identifying the mechanisms that account for the success of these schools could be a catalyst for producing change in schools where achievement is low.

Valid comparisons between public and private schools require representative data, reliable measures, an adequate study design, and appropriate statistical methods. Most critically, to evaluate achievement differences, researchers must attend to the issue of selection bias: Do higher standardized test scores among private school students reflect a more effective schooling process or do these successful schools simply enroll more capable students?

To investigate public and private school comparisons empirically, educational researchers employed the *High School and Beyond* (HS&B) database. In 1980, the U.S. National Center for Educational Statistics had undertaken HS&B, a nationally representative longitudinal survey of a sample of U.S. secondary schools and their students. Drawn as a two-stage probability sample, the study first selected 1,015 secondary schools, with Catholic schools and schools with high proportions of minorities deliberately oversampled. The second-stage sampling drew 58,000 students—36 sophomores and 36 seniors from each sampled school. HS&B contains extensive data on the schools and their students, including student backgrounds, attitudes, and behaviors. Tests developed by the Educational Testing Service assessed achievement in reading, vocabulary, mathematics, writing, civics, and science.

High School and Beyond Base Year Findings

Following the publication of two early studies by Coleman et al. (1981, 1982) using HS&B data, a national debate ensued arguing the relative effectiveness of public and private schools. Although Coleman and colleagues initially sought to compare public schools with both Catholic and non-Catholic private schools, they focused primarily on Catholic schools because the sample of non-Catholic private schools in HS&B was too small and highly diverse to yield useful information.

Catholic Schools and Potential Selection Bias

Because Catholic school students, on average, attained higher scores on the HS&B measures of achievement, the researchers announced an effectiveness edge for the private sector. Critics objected to the study on the grounds of selection bias, seizing on the inherent limitations of the cross-sectional first wave of HS&B data —the lack of a pretest, posttest structure to support a valid comparative evaluation. Selection bias would occur if public and Catholic schools enrolled different types of students, critics asserted, thus violating the assumption of initially equivalent groups.

To compensate for these limitations, Coleman and colleagues took two steps: (1) They incorporated into their multivariate analyses statistical adjustments for student differences in socioeconomic status, race, ethnicity, and family structure, and (2) they used the results of the test scores of a matched group of sophomores to impute senior pretest scores. Finding that the relationship of background characteristics to achievement differed for students in each sector, the authors also examined public and Catholic school effects in separate regression analyses.

In multiple comparative analyses, the researchers found a consistent and statistically significant advantage for Catholic schools on the reading, vocabulary, and mathematics tests. With score differences translated into years, Catholic schools accounted for an additional year of high school achievement. Minorities and students from lower social class backgrounds did particularly well in Catholic schools (see also Greeley, 1982). These researchers claimed that school policies in such areas as homework and discipline were largely responsible for the Catholic school advantage.

Curricular Track Placement in Catholic Schools

Critics also faulted Coleman and colleagues for ignoring the effect of curricular track on senior year achievement. Since pre-high school factors influence track choice, the critics reasoned, controlling for track would help correct for selectivity bias. In addition, an adjustment for track would equalize the effect of sector mission, since Catholic schools can be more exclusively academic than public schools, which must educate all students (Williams, 1983). Arguing that taking track into account would overadjust for selection effects, Coleman and his colleagues refuted their critics.

Track placement policy, they pointed out, differentiates the sectors and strongly contributes to the success of Catholic schools. For the same students, moreover, the probability of being in the academic track is higher in Catholic schools (Kilgore, 1983). While the debate following upon the initial studies by the Coleman team was heated, a final verdict on the controversy had to wait for the first HS&B follow-up data in 1982. By then, the original sophomore cohort had become seniors and pre- and postmeasures of their achievement were available for analysis.

High School and Beyond First Follow-up Study

Upon the release of the second wave of HS&B data in 1983, two members of the original Coleman team (Coleman and Hoffer) together with Andrew Greeley undertook a new analysis. Reporting their effects in grade-level equivalents, they continued to find Catholic sector advantages of about one grade level for reading, vocabulary, mathematics, and writing achievement. Catholic schools sustained their particular effectiveness for black, Hispanic, and lower socioeconomic status students.

The "Common School" Hypothesis and Its Critics

Because Catholic schools succeeded in minimizing the effect of social origins on achievement, the researchers held that Catholic schools reflected the "common school" ideal of American schools in the nineteenth century (Coleman et al., 1981, 1982; Greeley, 1982). Other researchers objected to the common school hypothesis. Despite finding positive Catholic school effects in almost all the achievement areas, in comparing background effects on achievement for Catholic and public school students, Alexander and Pallas (1983) found little evidence to support the common school hypothesis. Questioning the lack of Catholic school effects in some curriculum-specific areas, Willms (1983) characterized the sector difference as trivial and also dismissed the claim that Catholic schools provide a "common school experience."

Defending the Catholic School Advantage

Although the differences favoring Catholic schools are small, both Haertel (1987) and Jencks (1985) agreed that they were systematic. In accounting for the Catholic school advantage, Haertel supported the early interpretations of the original Coleman team, citing the effectiveness of course-taking patterns, amount of homework, curricular track placement, and school standards for discipline. Concluding that comparisons of schools on gross differences mask more than they reveal, Alexander (1987) recommended that future research focus on potentially more instructive studies on the "internal workings" of schools.

Internal Workings: Public vs. Catholic Schools

Attempting to account for *why* the sectors differed in their effects on students, some researchers undertook field-based studies to examine day-to-day activity in Catholic schools—patterns of relationships, governing values, the curriculum, teaching, and learning (Bryk et al., 1984; Lesko, 1988). Other researchers, using HS&B data, conducted quantitative analyses to investigate differences in the social organization of public and private schools. Some of these studies applied a newly devel-

oped statistical technique, Hierarchical Linear Modeling, to the public versus Catholic school question (Lee and Bryk, 1989; Raudenbusch and Bryk, 1986). Employing this methodological advance, researchers revisited the "common school" controversy and resolved some lingering dilemmas (Lee and Bryk, 1989).

Communal School Organization

Research in the late 1980s compared the organizational forms of Catholic and public high schools. Catholic school organization tends to be communal, as contrasted with the bureaucratic form typifying large urban and suburban public schools. Communally organized schools—characterized by shared values, a common agenda, and caring relationships—engender high levels of teacher commitment, student engagement, and student achievement (Bryk and Driscoll, 1988; Bryk et al., 1993).

Coleman and Hoffer (1987) took a different perspective on communal organization. Attempting to account for the demonstrated efficacy of Catholic schools, they emphasized the functional character of the community—that is, the unifying religious education mission of Catholic schools. Functional communities are relatively circumscribed, situating students and their families within a social network that reinforces positive norms and produces social capital. The significance of social capital, according to Coleman and Hoffer, is its function in promoting human capital, including academic achievement.

Revisiting the Common School Hypothesis

Pursuing the common school hypothesis, an unresolved theme from the first rounds of the public vs. private schools debate, Lee and Bryk (1988, 1989) investigated the academic experiences of students in Catholic and public schools. They found support for the common school hypothesis. Track placement and academic course-taking link student background with senior-year mathematics achievement, but in Catholic schools both these experiences are less dependent on family background or prior achievement.

Regardless of students' family background or academic preparation, Catholic schools tend to place most students in the academic track. Following a general or vocational program in a Catholic school also entails a solid core of academic courses. Lee and Bryk (1989) explained Catholic–public differences in achievement, including its more equitable distribution in Catholic schools, by taking into account sector differences in the academic organization and the normative environment of these schools.

Catholic Schools and the Common Good

Catholic Schools and the Common Good (Bryk et al., 1993) combined extensive fieldwork in seven Catholic high schools (four coeducational schools, two girls' schools, and a boys' school) and statistical analyses (based on data from HS&B) to probe the operation of Catholic schools. The researchers sought to investigate how school organization affects the relationship between students' social background and their development over the course of high school. Why, for example, is the achievement gap for minority students smaller by sophomore year in Catholic high schools compared to public schools? Why does that gap narrow even further during students' last 2 years in Catholic school, while expanding during the same period for minorities in public school?

The researchers drew on observational data (collected during 1982–1983) to establish their central findings explaining the effectiveness of Catholic schools—the power of a focused *academic structure* embedded in a *communal organization* that is supported by *decentralized governance* and infused with an *inspirational ideology*.

Core Components of Catholic School Organization

The communal organizational form typically found in Catholic schools derives its strength from several school features, the researchers concluded—multiple school activities, events, and rituals where teachers and students can interact face to face, an extended role for teachers enabling them to work and relate with students as advisors or mentors in other than instructional settings, shared beliefs and values focusing on norms for student learning and instruction, the nurturance of caring relationships based on a conception of personal worth and human dignity, and a commitment to openness and dialogue. Small school size and a sense of trust and respect among the faculty contribute to the smooth functioning of the communally organized school.

The Future of Catholic Schools

When they initiated their study in the early 1980s, Bryk and colleagues noted the time as relatively stable for Catholic schools after dramatic changes in the preceding two decades: Fewer schools had closed, enrollments held steady, and the remaining religious faculty appeared committed to staying. Nonetheless, follow-up data a decade later portrayed most of the seven studied schools struggling to survive. Continually increasing operational costs kept tuitions rising in all the schools. But the well-supported suburban schools—serving relatively affluent populations—had grown stronger and thrived; while the economically less viable urban schools—serving poor populations in changing neighborhoods—dwindled in size, grew weaker, and, in one instance, ceased to exist.

Among Catholic schools nationally, 1991 saw 10% fewer Catholic schools than when Bryk and colleagues began their study in 1983. Inner-city Catholic schools have closed in Washington, D.C. (1989), Detroit (1990), Boston (1991), and Philadelphia (1992). Although church officials justified the decisions to close these schools pragmatically—the consolidation of less viable schools into a single and stronger entity, the relatively small numbers of Catholic compared to non-Catholic students enrolled, and the need to support other vital urban ministries, critics contended that the church was abandoning its historical mission to educate the urban poor.

REFERENCES

Alexander, Karl L. 1987. "Cross-Sectional Comparisons of Public and Private School Effectiveness: A Review of Evidence and Issues." In Edward H. Haertel, Thomas James, and Henry M. Levin. (eds.), *Comparing Public and Private Schools. Vol. 2: School Achievement,* pp. 33–65. New York: Falmer Press.

Alexander, Karl L., and Aaron M. Pallas. 1983. "Private Schools and Public Policy: New Evidence on Cognitive Achievement in Public and Private Schools." *Sociology of Education* 56:170–182.

Bryk, Anthony S., and Mary E. Driscoll. 1988. *The School as Community: Theoretical Foundation, Contextual Influences, and Consequences for Students and Teachers.* Madison, WI: National Center for Effective Secondary Schools, University of Wisconsin.

Bryk, Anthony S., Peter B. Holland, Valerie E. Lee, and Rueben A. Carriedo. 1984. *Effective Catholic Schools: An Exploration.* Washington, DC: National Catholic Education Association.

Bryk, Anthony S., Valerie E. Lee, and Peter B. Holland. 1993. *The Catholic School and the Common Good.* Cambridge: Harvard University Press.

Coleman, James S., and Thomas Hoffer. 1987. *Public and Private High Schools: The Impact of Communities.* New York: Basic Books.

Coleman, James S., Thomas Hoffer, and Sally Kilgore. 1981. *Public and Private Schools. An Analysis of High School and Beyond: A National Longitudinal Study for the 1980s.* Final Report to the National Center for Educational Statistics, Contract No. 300–78–0208. Chicago: National Opinion Research Center.

———. 1982. *High School Achievement: Public, Catholic, and Private Schools Compared.* New York: Basic Books.

Fichter, Joseph H. 1958. *Parochial School: A Sociological Study.* Notre Dame: Notre Dame University Press.

Greeley, Andrew M. 1982. *Catholic High Schools and Minority Students.* New Brunswick, NJ: Transaction Books.

Haertel, Edward H. 1987. "Comparing Public and Private Schools Using Longitudinal Data from the HSB Study." In Edward H. Haertel, Thomas James, and Henry M. Levin (eds.), *Comparing Public and Private Schools, Vol. 2, School Achievement,* pp. 9–27. New York: Falmer Press.

Hoffer, Thomas, Andrew M. Greeley, and James S. Coleman. 1987. "Catholic High School Effects on Achievement Growth." In Edward H. Haertel, Thomas James, and Henry M. Levin (eds.), *Comparing Public and Private Schools, Vol. 2, School Achievement,* pp. 67–88. New York: Falmer Press.

Jencks, Christopher. 1985. "How Much Do High School Students Learn?" *Sociology of Education* 58:128–135.

Kilgore, Sally B. 1983. "Statistical Evidence, Selectivity Effects and Program Placement: Response to Alexander and Pallas." *Sociology of Education,* 56:182–186.

Lee, Valerie E., and Anthony S. Bryk. 1988. "Curriculum Tracking as Mediating the Social Distribution of High School Achievement." *Sociology of Education* 61:78–94.

———. 1989. "A Multilevel Model of the Social Distribution of High School Achievement." *Sociology of Education,* 62:172–192.

Lesko, Nancy. 1988. *Symbolizing Society: Stories, Rites, and Structure in a Catholic High School.* New York: Falmer Press.

National Center for Education Statistics. 1991. *Private Schools in the United States: A Statistical Profile with Comparisons to Public Schools.* Washington, DC: U.S. Department of Education.

———. 1995. *A Digest of Education Statistics 1995.* Washington, DC: U.S. Department of Education.

Raudenbush, Stephen W., and Anthony S. Bryk. 1986. "A Hierarchical Model for Studying School Effects." *Sociology of Education* 59:1–17.

Willms, J. Douglas. 1983. "Do Private Schools Produce Higher Levels of Academic Achievement? New Evidence for the Tuition Tax Credit Debate." In Thomas James and Henry M. Levin (eds.), *Public Dollars for Private Schools: The Case of Tuition Tax Credits,* pp. 223–231. Philadelphia: Temple University Press.

CLASSROOM PROCESSES

Elizabeth G. Cohen
School of Education, Stanford University

Classroom processes do not occur in a vacuum. Both the context of the society and the organizational roles of the teacher and student shape what happens in the classroom. In addition to these forces affecting classroom processes, there is an intricate social system inside the classroom that affects relationships between students and relationships between students and teachers. This chapter will sketch what sociologists of education have learned about four aspects of classroom processes: (1) the teacher as an authority figure, (2) changes in the role of the teacher in response to changes in methods of teaching, (3) the origin and consequences of status hierarchies that develop among the students, and (4) interpersonal relationships between students and their interconnections with work arrangements in the classroom.

Sociologists of education have come to these topics by traveling different intellectual roads. For example, in the case of the studies of teacher's authority and role, they have applied to the classroom concepts and propositions from other areas of sociology such as organizational theory. In other cases, they start, not from sociology, but from more general educational research such as the effects of ability grouping and ask the more sociological question: What is the mechanism by which ability groups take their effect? In still other cases, the origin of their interest lies in earlier work in sociology of education such as the effects of social class and race on schooling; they want to know how the processes of social stratification work inside classrooms. The origins of the research on each topic will be briefly described.

The Teacher as an Authority Figure

Much of what happens in a classroom flows from the simple fact that the teacher occupies a position of authority in the formal organization of the school. The teacher is responsible for maintaining order. To carry out this task, he or she can offer praise and rewards (positive sanctions) or criticism and punishment (negative sanctions). The teacher assigns work to the students and determines how the work will proceed. Most important, the teacher has the right and duty to evaluate the performance of students.

Classrooms typically have only two roles and the role of the teacher is far more powerful than that of the student. According to Bidwell (1970), classrooms are based on a dichotomous age-stratified power structure and on an acknowledged division between professional and clients. Teachers have the legal, organizational, and cultural recognition to rule over classroom teaching and their organizational authority is rarely challenged. Students learn in their earliest schooling what is the conduct expected of pupils and the bulk of behavior one observes in a classroom is in conformity to that role.

The effects of the outside society on this relationship only occasionally become visible. When the status of teaching declines sharply, and when the power and standing of youth in the society at large increases equally sharply, one can see the teacher's authority in the classroom decline as a consequence. This was observed in schools run by the Israeli authorities in the recent period in East Jerusalem during the Palestinian youthful uprising known as *intifada* (Yair and Katab, 1995). Students attacked teachers physically. Youth on local strike committees gave out answers to examinations and forced the teachers to assign good grades. This extreme case permits us to understand how the teacher's authority rests not only on a position in the school hierarchy, but on the acknowledgment and support of that authority and of the subordinate status of youth in the society at large.

In many ways, the teacher's method of evaluation is the jugular of the classroom social system. The way the teacher evaluates students has powerful consequences for the individual's expectations for academic competence, for the sense of his or her own intellectual ability, and even for the effort the individual exerts toward accomplishing classroom goals.

Much of the sociological research on classroom evaluation arose from an application of the theory of evaluation and authority by Scott and Dornbusch to classrooms. In this research, students reported their perceptions of the soundness of the teacher's evaluation on questionnaires. According to Natriello and Dornbusch (1984), students do not see classroom evaluations as very soundly based, but they still consider evaluations they receive to be important. They continue to devote effort to those tasks they consider important whether or not they perceive evaluation as soundly based.

This generalization does not hold universally. Under some conditions, student effort will depend on the perceived soundness of the teacher's evaluations. College students of average academic competence reported putting out more effort if they received detailed and specific feedback on their written work and if they perceived those evaluations as soundly based (Cohen, 1986). In contrast, students who reported higher levels of competence put out great effort regardless of the evaluation system.

Students may experience incompatible evaluation systems in which they perceive that evaluation is uncontrollable, unpredictable, and unattainable such as when there are inappropriately high standards. Under these conditions, students are more likely to report being disengaged from their work (Natriello and Dornbusch, 1984).

The Changing Technology of Teaching and Teacher's Role

The years from 1970 to 1980 were years of profound innovation in the elementary classroom and to a lesser extent in the secondary school. This was the heyday of individualized instruction, which called for many different tasks to be carried out simultaneously, and open classrooms, wherein students were allowed to choose which of the many tasks they would do. Instead of every child doing the same task, the rule in conventional classrooms, different children were doing different tasks. Instead of children working individually, they were working interdependently. To sociologists this was a grand natural experiment in which they could study what would happen if the technology or task structure of the classroom were radically changed. (In sociology, the technology refers to all the ways in which the organization does its work, not just to machines.) Since 1985, the rapid development and adoption of techniques of cooperative learning have furthered this trend toward multiple tasks in simultaneous operation and have highlighted peer interaction processes in the classroom.

As in other organizations, when the technology or methods of doing work change and become more complex and uncertain, the role of the supervisor must change as well. When all the students are working on the same task, the most efficient and effective role for the teacher is one of direct supervision. She or he tells the students what to do and how to do it, directly monitoring both procedure and products. Obviously when students are working interdependently in small groups, the teacher's role changes. He or she cannot be everywhere at once telling people what to do. Whenever the teacher tries to tell the class something directly, the interaction in the small groups comes to an abrupt halt. When individual students or groups of students are working on different tasks that have no single right answer and are uncertain, it becomes important for the teacher to delegate authority to the students. The students then use each other as resources to answer the many questions generated by the uncertain tasks. Although the teachers hold students accountable for the final product, they allow them to make mistakes on their own and to decide on procedures. The sociologist predicts that teachers who fail to make these changes in response to newer technologies of instruction will be far less effective than those teachers who do delegate authority to lateral relations among the students.

Using systematic observation, sociologists of education have been able to gather evidence on this relationship of the methods of instruction to the teacher's role and to student interaction. The earliest finding was the observational study of Bossert (1979), who showed that when there were multiple tasks in operation, teachers were much less likely to discipline the students than when there was a single task for all students.

Since 1979, Cohen and her colleagues have systematically observed classrooms using an approach called complex instruction, where multiple groups are working on different tasks that are very challenging and uncertain (Cohen, 1994:7–8). When students are working on such uncertain and challenging group tasks, the higher the percentage of students talking and working together, the higher are the average learning gains for the class as a whole. It is also true that the more that individuals talk and work together, the more they learn. Of the teachers trained in complex instruction, some were unable or unwilling to delegate authority —that is, to let go and to allow students to solve problems for themselves. If teachers tried to keep students under direct supervision, there were fewer small groups in operation, the percentage of students talking and working together was lower, and, as a consequence, the average learning gains were lower. It was also the case that if teachers tried to instruct students directly or to discipline students when they were working in small groups, it similarly cut down on the interaction and the learning. However, these very same behaviors can be very effective in increasing student engagement when the teacher is working with the whole class (Cohen, 1994:29).

Status Hierarchies among Students

Sociologists of education, from the beginning of their field of study, have emphasized the effects of race, ethnicity, and social class on what happens to students as a result of schooling. Reasoning from this large body of evidence, it was first assumed that teachers were biased in favor of more middle-class, white students and responded differently according to the student's social background in such a way as to produce educational disadvantage and advantage. Study of classroom processes reveals that the relationship is much less direct.

Teachers respond primarily to achievement behaviors and to conformity to classroom rules. Thus teachers have high expectations for performance for those minority students or students from backgrounds of poverty who show promise of achievement and who present no behavior problems. On the other hand, lower social class students as well as African-American and Latino students are more likely to experience difficulties with the conventional academic program and are more likely to show behavior problems. It is in response to these latter characteristics that teachers develop lower expectations for performance. As a result of this linkage between social stratification and academic performance and behavior, nonwhite, low socioeconomic status (SES) students are much more likely to be in lower ability groups within the classroom, and are more often the target of criticism for their behavior. The outcome of lower educational attainment for students from low SES and minority backgrounds is partly the product of classroom processes. Nonetheless, academic performance and the teacher's response to the student's achievement and behavioral conformity affect outcomes more directly than the student's class or race.

A major status hierarchy among students in the classroom is a perceived rank order based on academic ability. Some students are perceived to be generally competent at important school tasks while other students are seen as generally incompetent at those same tasks. For younger students, the ability to read is the most central indicator of academic status and of intelligence. The strength of this perceived social ranking in a classroom has been measured by the degree of agreement between students in rank ordering their classmates on reading ability. Rosenholtz and Simpson (1984) identified the following key conditions in classrooms that lead to strong agreement between classmates on where each person stands on the rank order: Everyone does the same task so that it is easy to make social comparisons, students have very little choice of what task to carry out; the teacher works with the whole class so that each person's performance is visible to all, and finally, the teacher emphasizes competitive grading and marking as the main form of feedback to students. This kind of classroom leads students to form clear, unidimensional conceptions of their own ability and that of their peers.

Also very important to students are status hierarchies based on popularity and attractiveness—peer status. In elementary schools the same children who are seen as good in reading are highly chosen as friends. By the time the students reach middle school, popular students may or may not be seen as good students—one basis for status may have nothing to do with the other.

There are observable consequences of such status distinctions among classmates. According to status characteristic theory, once a strong status order has emerged among students, it will have an effect on how students interact with each other (Cohen, 1986). Those students who are high on academic and peer status will be expected to be more competent than those who are low on the rankings. These different expectations for competence turn into different rates of participation and influence in small groups of students. Students who are higher on academic status and peer status are more active and influential within cooperative learning groups than students who are lower on academic status and peer status (Cohen, 1994:23–25). Teachers can change the expectations for competence that produce these inequalities in interaction, influence, and learning.

Another status distinction between children in elementary classrooms stems from membership in ability groups; one's ability group is an obvious clue for judging reading ability or academic ranking. Ability groups are not a clear reflection of differences in test scores. Researchers have already found that the number of ability groups in a classroom and the placement of students in first grade groups are not closely related to the achievement characteristics of the class or to individual test scores.

Sociologists of education have entered the research debate about the wisdom of using ability groups. They want to discover the mechanism whereby ability groups appear to increase inequalities in the classroom. Studies that have followed the same students over time show that among students who start out with the same initial achievement score, being in a low ability group has a negative effect on test scores in the long run. There are three major possible explanations for this effect: differences in instruction according to ability group, differences in student motivation as a consequence of being labeled "high" or "low" ability, and differences in expectations for the student's performance held by teachers and parents as a result of membership in different ability groups.

There is already a fair amount of evidence that differences in instruction do play a part in increasing inequality. Students in low ability groups receive instruction that is more basic and less sophisticated than that offered to high ability groups. The challenge for future research will be to test the power of one of these three explanations against the others.

Interpersonal Relationships between Students

The study of friendship relations between classmates has a 60 year history, starting with the work of Jacob Moreno in the 1930s. Moreno was an early action researcher who wanted to improve social relations and to bring about classroom democracy. He developed the technique of sociometry in which students select the names of their classmates who are their friends on a questionnaire. Study of a diagram of who chooses whom reveals clusters of choices. Some students are highly chosen by others—sociometric stars; and others receive few or no choices—social isolates. Early researchers in the sociometric tradition found evidence that social isolates do not achieve up to their potential, indicating the consequences for learning of low peer status.

Sociometric techniques used by modern sociologists such as Maureen Hallinan assess student friendship choices repeatedly over time. Sophisticated computer and statistical techniques are now used to analyze the data. Cliques are well-defined, densely connected networks of peers who are tied to each other by positive sentiment (Hallinan, 1989). Cliques tend to form within the boundaries of a grade or classroom where opportunities to interact are greatest. Clique members are likely to work and play together. Students not in cliques interact less frequently with their classmates or interact with fewer peers than clique members.

Peer influences may facilitate or hinder the learning process. Frequent interactions that take place among clique members promote peer influences through which students shape each other's attitudes and affect each other's behavior. For example, some cliques have a negative view of school and school authorities. As a result of the power of cliques to establish rules for behavior, they can undermine a student's willingness to attend class and do homework. Alternatively, cliques can foster positive attitudes toward schoolwork and college attendance.

Gender, race, and ethnicity are more similar within friendship pairs and groups than between groups. At the elementary school level, boys and girls almost invariably select members of their own sex as friends. Self-segregation extends to work groups in the classroom and to play groups in the schoolyard. This almost universal tendency has been observed as early as kindergarten. In multiracial classrooms, there is a tendency for friendship groups to be of the same race. The frequency of cross-racial, cross-ethnic friendships is a common measure of social integration.

Just as with the development of status hierarchies, work arrangements of the classroom and the teacher's methods of evaluation strongly influence the development of friendship ties. The more a teacher emphasizes grades and test scores, the more cliques are likely to be homogeneous with respect to achievement. Classrooms with a high proportion of recitation and common worksheet assignments have clear sociometric stars who interact with only a small group of peers—mostly from their own high-performing reading group.

A remarkable number of independent studies all attest to one powerful generalization: Increased opportunities for students to interact with one another while they do tasks in the classroom will increase friendliness. This may occur through cooperative learning, in open classrooms, or even through grouping for instruction. One of the best documented findings concerning cooperative learning is the increase in friendliness, including the increase in interracial friendship that results from this technique.

Conclusion

Classroom processes have powerful effects on individual students, on how they feel about themselves, on how they relate to other students, and on how well they achieve in school. The outside society and the organization of the school set the stage for what happens in the classroom. Students arrive from different places in the stratification system with different amounts of preparation to succeed in the conventional curriculum. The organizational role of teacher and student strongly influences the classroom social system. Yet even within these constraints, teachers have important choices as to how they enact their role. They typically choose the technology of instruction as well as the way in which they will provide feedback and evaluation to individual students.

As this chapter has shown, these decisions have major consequences for both students and for the role of the teacher. The nature of classroom tasks and the evaluation system have consequences for the way the students evaluate themselves and each other, for the ways in which they interact with each other, and for the way the teacher relates to students. Both status hierarchies among the students and friendship relations depend partly on these work arrangements the teacher has chosen. These important relationships in turn have consequences for participation and learning on the part of students.

Classroom processes can be a faithful reflection of the social stratification system of the society. Teachers can unwittingly build strong status hierarchies among the students that resemble status orders of the society as a whole. Those students on the bottom of the hierarchy may often be disengaged from their work, may put out little effort on academic tasks, and may withdraw from participation in group tasks with their classmates. Alternatively, because of the power of the social system of the classroom, teachers can select methods of instruction, patterns of grouping, and systems of feedback and evaluation that discourage the growth of such status hierarchies, promote interracial friendship, and provide access for all students to successful educational experiences.

REFERENCES

Bidwell, Charles E. 1970. "Students and Schools: Some Observations on Client-Serving Organizations." In W. R. Rosengren and M. Lefton (eds.), *Organizations and Clients: Essays in the Sociology of Service*, pp. 37–70. Columbus, OH: Charles E. Merrill.

Bossert, Steven T. 1979. *Tasks and Social Relationships in Classrooms*. London: Cambridge University Press.

Cohen, Elizabeth G. 1986. "On the Sociology of the Classroom." In J. Hannaway and M.E. Lockheed (eds.), *The Contributions of the Social Sciences to Educational Policy and Practice: 1965–1985*, pp. 127–162. Berkeley, CA: McCutchan.

———. 1994. "Restructuring the Classroom: Conditions for Productive Small Groups." *Review of Educational Research* 64:1–35.

Hallinan, Maureen T., and Stevens S. Smith. 1989. "Classroom Characteristics and Student Friendship Cliques." *Social Forces* 67:898–919.

Natriello, Gary, and Sanford Dornbusch. 1984. *Teacher Evaluative Standards and Student Effort*. New York: Longmann.

Rosenholtz, Susan J., and Carl Simpson. 1984. "The Formation of Ability Conceptions: Developmental Trend or Social Construction." *Review of Educational Research* 54:31–63.

Yair, Gad, and Nabil Khatab. 1995. "Changing of the Guards: Teacher-Student Interaction in the Intifada." *Sociology of Education* 68:99–115.

CODE THEORY, PEDAGOGIC DISCOURSE, AND SYMBOLIC CONTROL[1]

Alan R. Sadovnik
Rutgers University

Code theory, pedagogic discourse, and symbolic control are components of the theoretical and empirical project of the late British sociologist Basil Bernstein (1924–2000). For over four decades, Bernstein was a centrally important and controversial sociologist, whose work influenced a generation of sociologists of education and linguists. From his early works on language, communication codes, and schooling, to his later works on pedagogic discourse, practice, and educational transmissions, Bernstein attempted to produce a theory of social and educational codes and their effect on social reproduction. Although structuralist in its approach, Bernstein's sociology drew on the essential theoretical orientations in the field, Durkheimian, Weberian, Marxist, and interactionist, and provides the possibility of an important synthesis.

Karabel and Halsey (1977:62), in their review of the literature on the sociology of education, called Bernstein's work the "harbinger of a new synthesis." Bernstein's early work on code theory was highly controversial, as it discussed social class differences in language, that some labeled a deficit theory, but it nonetheless raised crucial questions about the relationships among the social division of labor, the family, and the school, and explored how these relationships affected differences in learning among the social classes. His work in the 1970s (Bernstein, 1977a) began the difficult project of connecting macropower and class relations to the microeducational processes of the

school. Whereas class reproduction theorists, such as Bowles and Gintis (1976), offered an overtly deterministic view of schools without describing or explaining what goes on in schools, Bernstein's work promised to connect the societal, institutional, interactional, and intrapsychic levels of sociological analysis. In doing so, it presented an opportunity to synthesize the classical theoretical traditions of the discipline: Marxist, Weberian, and Durkheimian.

Over the years, Bernstein's work has often been viewed as too theoretical and lacking sufficient empirical evidence to test and support his theories (Sadovnik, 1991). Bernstein responded to this criticism by citing a body of empirical research over the past three decades (Bernstein, 1995, 1996). Studies conducted by his doctoral students at the University of London's Institute of Education and others have contributed to our knowledge of the relationships among the division of labor, the family, and schooling through research on specific aspects of Bernstein's work. Although a good deal of this work is not easily accessible to U.S. sociologists and educational researchers, it nonetheless provides an important application of Bernstein's theories. In a detailed and comprehensive chapter in his last book, *Pedagogy, Symbolic Control and Identity* (1996), Bernstein provided a historical discussion of code theory and outlined some of the empirical work to test it. Throughout this chapter, I will give examples of these empirical studies.

Bernstein (1996) noted that his body of work has evolved over the past 35 years as it moved back and forth between the theoretical and the empirical. According to Bernstein, the theoretical always preceded the empirical, and often by the time the research had been conducted, the original theory had been modified

[1] This article is adapted from Alan R. Sadovnik. 1991. "Basil Bernstein's Theory of Pedagogic Practice: A Structuralist Approach." *Sociology of Education* 64(1):48–63; and Alan R. Sadovnik (ed.). 1995. *Knowledge and Pedagogy: The Sociology of Basil Bernstein,* pp. 3–35. New York: Ablex, with permission.

and clarified. As the research was often conducted by Bernstein's Ph.D. students as their dissertation research, the Sociological Research Unit (SRU) at the Institute of Education became a primary testing ground for Bernstein's theories. The core of Bernstein's early work was to develop a code theory that examined the interrelationships among social class, family, and school.

Bernstein's early work on language (1958, 1960, 1961a, 1961b) examined the relationship between public language, authority, and shared meanings (Danzig, 1995:146–147). By 1962, Bernstein began the development of code theory through the introduction of the concepts of restricted and elaborated codes (1962a, 1962b). In *Class, Codes, and Control, Volume 1* (1973a), Bernstein's sociolinguistic code theory was developed into a social theory examining the relationships among social class, family, and the reproduction of meaning systems (code refers to the principles regulating meaning systems). For Bernstein, there are social class differences in the communication codes of working class and middle class children that reflect the class and power relations in the social division of labor, family, and schools. Based upon empirical research, Bernstein distinguished between the restricted code of the working class and the elaborated code of the middle class. Restricted codes are context dependent and particularistic, whereas elaborated codes are context independent and universalistic. For example, working class boys when asked to tell a story describing a series of pictures used many pronouns and their story could be understood only by looking at the pictures. Middle class boys, on the other hand, generated descriptions rich in nouns and their story could be understood without the benefit of the pictures (Bernstein, 1970). Although Bernstein's critics (see Danzig, 1995) argued that his sociolinguistic theory represented an example of deficit theory, as they alleged that he was arguing that working class language was deficient, Bernstein has consistently rejected this interpretation (see Bernstein, 1996:147–156). Bernstein has argued that restricted codes are not deficient, but rather are functionally related to the social division of labor, where context-dependent language is necessary in the context of production. Likewise, the elaborated code of the middle classes represents functional changes necessitated by changes in the division of labor and the middle classes new position in reproduction, rather than pro-

duction. That schools require an elaborated code for success means that working class children are disadvantaged by the dominant code of schooling, not deficient. For Bernstein, difference becomes deficit in the context of macropower relations.

The funded research in the middle 1960s and early 1970s "was concerned to study the social origins of codes in the family, their sociolinguistic realisations in children between 5 years and 7 years, and the influence of the primary school on the initial codings lower working class children brought to the school" (Bernstein, 1996:95). Although Bernstein did not develop his theory of positional versus personal family types in published form until 1971 in an article entitled "A Sociolinguistic Approach to Socialisation with Reference to Educability" (Bernstein, 1971), from 1963 on there was considerable empirical research on the subject. By 1971, Bernstein developed an Index of Communication and Control to measure different family types and to relate them to social class differences. As the original index, according to Bernstein (1996:96) was crude and indirect, Bernstein sought to develop a more direct and sensitive measure. Based upon empirical research, Bernstein and Jenny Cook-Gumperz developed "complex principles of descriptions of the speech of parents and children" (Bernstein and Cook-Gumperz, 1973). Cook-Gumperz (1973:48–73) provided an in-depth description of these principles in her own work.

By the third volume of *Class, Codes, and Control* (1977a), Bernstein developed code theory from its sociolinguistic roots to examine the connection between communication codes and pedagogic discourse and practice. In this respect, code theory became concerned with the processes of schooling and how they related to social class reproduction. Bernstein's quest for understanding the microprocesses of schooling led him to continue to pursue the fruitful avenue of inquiry developed in his article "Class and Pedagogies: Visible and Invisible" (1977b). In that article, Bernstein analyzed the significant differences between two generic forms of educational transmission and suggested that the differences in the classification and framing rules of each pedagogic practice (VP = visible = strong classification and strong framing; IP = invisible = weak classification and weak framing) relate to the social-class position and assumptions of the families served by the schools. Classification refers to relations between categories regarding the social division of labor and is related to the distribution of power. Framing refers to the location of control over the rules of communication. (For a detailed analysis of this aspect of Bernstein's work, see Atkinson, 1985; Atkinson, et al., 1995; Sadovnik, 1991, 1995.) The article clearly demonstrated that sociologists of education had to do the difficult empirical work of looking into the world of schools and of linking educational practices to the larger institutional, societal, and historical factors of which they are a part.

Over the past 30 years, Bernstein developed this approach into a systematic analysis of pedagogic discourse and practices. First, he outlined a theory of pedagogic rules that examines the "intrinsic features which constitute and distinguish the specialized form of communication realized by the pedagogic discourse of education" (Bernstein, 1986/1990d:165). Second (Bernstein, 1990b), he related his theory of pedagogic discourse to a social-class base and applied it to the ongoing development of different educational practices.

Classification, Framing, and Code

The concept of code is central to Bernstein's structural sociology. From the outset of its use in his work on language (restricted and elaborated codes), code refers to a "regulative principle which underlies various message systems, especially curriculum and pedagogy" (Atkinson, 1985:136). Curriculum and pedagogy are considered message systems, and with a third system, evaluation, they constitute the structure and processes of school knowledge, transmission, and practice. As Bernstein (1973b:85) noted: "Curriculum defines what counts as valid knowledge, pedagogy defines what counts as valid transmission of knowledge, and evaluation defines what counts as a valid realization of the knowledge on the part of the taught." Thus, his theory of curriculum must be understood in terms of the concepts of classification, framing, and evaluation, and their relationship to the structural aspects of his sociological project.

Bernstein's major earlier work on curriculum is contained in two important articles, "On the Classification and Framing of Educational Knowledge" (Bernstein, 1971/1973b) and "Class and Pedagogies: Visible and Invisible" (1977b). The first article outlined the concepts of classification and framing and related them to an overall structuralist theory of curriculum and ped-

agogic practice. The second extended this analysis by applying it to the evolution of organic solidarity and to changes in the dynamics of production and social-class reproduction. It is this latter article of which Bernstein's later work on pedagogic practice is an extension. To understand the evolution of his work, it is necessary to begin with the first article and the concepts of classification and framing.

The concept of classification is at the heart of Bernstein's theory of curriculum. Classification refers to "the degree of boundary maintenance between contents" (Bernstein 1971/1973a:205; 1971/1973b:88) and is concerned with the insulation or boundaries between curricular categories (areas of knowledge and subjects). Strong classification refers to a curriculum that is highly differentiated and separated into traditional subjects; weak classification refers to a curriculum that is integrated and in which the boundaries between subjects are fragile.

Using the concept of classification, Bernstein outlined two types of curriculum codes: collection and integrated codes. The first refers to a strongly classified curriculum; the latter, to a weakly classified curriculum. In keeping with his Durkheimian project, Bernstein analyzed the way in which the shift from collection to integrated curriculum codes represents the evolution from mechanical to organic solidarity, with curricular change marking the movement from the sacred to the profane.

Whereas classification is concerned with the organization of knowledge into curriculum, framing is related to the transmission of knowledge through pedagogic practices. Framing refers to the location of control over the rules of communication and, according to Bernstein (1990c:100) "if classification regulates the voice of a category then framing regulates the form of its legitimate message." Furthermore, "frame refers to the degree of control teacher and pupil possess over the selection, organization, pacing and timing of the knowledge transmitted and received in the pedagogical relationship" (1971/1973b:88). Therefore, strong framing refers to a limited degree of options between teacher and students; weak framing implies more freedom.

In keeping with the Durkheimian project, Bernstein's inquiry into the organization (curriculum) and transmission of knowledge (pedagogy) sought to relate shifts in classification and framing to the evolution of the social division of labor. In "Class and Pedagogies: Visible and Invisible" (1977b), he demonstrated how the move to an integrated code with weak classification and weak framing represents conflicts between the positioning of the old and new middle classes in the social division of labor and provides an illuminating examination of how pedagogic discourse and practice are structurally related to shifts in social structure. Moreover although Bernstein is not a Marxist, he incorporated class and power relations into an overall structural theory, as he does in all his work.

A number of empirical studies examined these concepts. Neves (1991) studied the relationship between the pedagogic codes of families and schools and provided empirical support for Bernstein's thesis. Ana Marie Morais and her colleagues (Morais, et al., 1991a, 1991b) demonstrated that it was possible to design different pedagogic practices and to evaluate their outcomes. She designed three different pedagogic practices in terms of varying degrees of classification and framing and trained a teacher to teach the same subject to four different classes using different pedagogic practices. Based upon her research the complex relationship between the pedagogic code of the family and the school, social class differences in families, the educational development of the child, and the educational achievement and behavior of the child was more fully understood.

Bernstein's analysis of the relationship between social class and pedagogic practice resulted in his distinction between visible and invisible pedagogy. Bernstein's thesis that these pedagogic practices represented differences between the old and the new middle classes and their different placement in the division of labor is confirmed by Jenkins' research (1990) on the social class basis of progressive education in Britain. Through an analysis of articles in the *Journal of the New Education Fellowship* between 1920 and 1950, she supported Bernstein's central thesis about the social class basis of invisible pedagogy, which Jenkins argued was precisely what the progressives were talking about. Semel (1995) further supports this thesis as applied to independent progressive schools in the United States from 1914 to 1935.

The relationship between the fields of symbolic control and production and gender classification was explored by Holland (1986). Her study concluded that socialization processes differ in classification and fram-

ing in relation to the place of families in the division of labor. Families in the field of symbolic control have weaker classification in their modeling of domestic and economic divisions of labor than families in the field of production. Holland's work provides important empirical evidence to support Bernstein's thesis that classification and framing are social class related and related to the fields of production and symbolic control. Further, this study broadened the emphasis away from class reproduction to the related and equally significant area of gender role reproduction.

Following this earlier work on curriculum and pedagogic practice the ways in which codes are transmitted became a central concern of Bernstein. In "On Pedagogic Discourse" (1986/1990d), Bernstein explored the nature of the pedagogic device and discourse. He distinguished three different rules, which make up the pedagogic device: distributive rules, which make different forms of knowledge available to different groups; recontextualizing rules, which make up official knowledge; and evaluative rules, which make up pedagogic practices as they define what is to be transmitted (Bernstein, 1996:116–117).

Thus, Bernstein's work on pedagogic discourse was concerned with the production, distribution, and reproduction of official knowledge and how this knowledge is related to structurally determined power relations. What is critical is that Bernstein was concerned with more than the description of the production and transmission of knowledge; he was concerned with its consequences for different groups. Whereas his work on pedagogic discourse was concerned more with the classification rules of the pedagogic device (that is, in the production and reproduction of knowledge), his work on pedagogic practice returned to framing rules and there he is directly interested in the transmission of knowledge. Once again, Bernstein returned to the manner in which social class and power relations affect pedagogic practice.

The work of Diaz (1984, 1990) and Cox Donosa (1986) examined Bernstein's theory of pedagogic discourse. Diaz's research explored the institutionalizing of primary education as a form of pedagogic discourse. Cox Danosa's work on state education in Chile, according to Bernstein, "drew together the model of pedagogic discourse and its relation to the field of symbolic control" (Bernstein, 1996). Cox Danosa's research compared the educational policies of the Christian

Democratic Party and Allende's Popular Unity Party. Through an analysis of the relationship between pedagogic discourses and each party's relationship to the symbolic and economic fields, Cox Danosa provided a concrete sociological and historical testing of Bernstein's theory.

Theory of Pedagogic Practice

Bernstein's analysis of pedagogic practice began with the distinction between a "pedagogic practice as a cultural relay and a pedagogic practice in terms of what it relays" (1990b:63). That is, Bernstein looked at the process and content of what occurs inside schools in terms of the "how" and the "what." The theory of pedagogic practice examined a series of rules that define its inner logic and considers both how these rules affect the content to be transmitted and, perhaps more important, how they "act selectively on those who can successfully acquire it" (1990b:63).

From a detailed analysis of these rules, Bernstein examined "the social class assumptions and consequences of forms of pedagogic practice" (1990b:63). Finally, he applied this theory first to oppositional forms of pedagogic practice (conservative/traditional versus progressive/child centered) and, second, to oppositional types within the conservative/traditional form. He differentiated between a pedagogic practice that is dependent on the economic market—that emphasizes vocational education—and another that is independent and autonomous of the market—that is legitimated by the autonomy of knowledge. Through a detailed analysis of these two competing traditional ideological forms, Bernstein concluded that both forms, despite their claims to the contrary, will not eliminate the reproduction of class inequalities. Thus, through a careful and logical consideration of the inner workings of the dominant forms of educational practice, Bernstein contributed to a greater understanding of how the schools (especially in the United States) reproduce what they are ideologically committed to eradicating—social-class advantages in schooling and society.

Bernstein's analysis of the social-class assumptions of pedagogic practice is the foundation for linking microeducational processes to the macrosociological levels of social structure and class and power relations. His basic thesis was that there are significant differences in the social-class assumptions of VPs and IPs and despite these differences between what he termed "opposing modalities of control" (1990b:73), there may indeed be similar outcomes, especially in the reproduction of power and symbolic control.

King (1976, 1981) tested Bernstein's early model of pedagogic practice but did not find strong evidence in his research to support this model; however, Tyler (1984) argues that King's statistical methods were severely flawed. More recently, researchers (see Sadovnik, 1995, Parts IV and V) have provided empirical evidence to support the social class basis of pedagogic practice. However, as I have pointed out elsewhere (Sadovnik, 1991, 1995), more systematic empirical research is needed. Toward this end, a recent volume presents empirical studies testing Bernstein's theories (Morais, Neves, Daniels, and Davies, 2001).

Toward a Structuralist Theory

Much of the criticism of Bernstein's early work revolved around issues of deficit and difference. It is important to note here that Bernstein rejected the view that his work was based on either a deficit or a difference approach. Rather, he argued that his code theory attempted to connect the macrolevels of family and educational structures and processes and to provide an explanation for unequal educational performance. He stated (Bernstein, 1990c:118–119):

> The code theory asserts that there is a social class regulated unequal distribution of privileging principles of communication . . . and that social class, indirectly, effects the classification and framing of the elaborated code transmitted by the school so as to facilitate and perpetuate its unequal acquisition. Thus the code theory accepts neither a deficit nor a difference position but draws attention to the relations between macro power relations and micro practices of transmission, acquisition and evaluation and the positioning and oppositioning to which these practices give rise.

Thus, from his early work on code theory to the more recent works on pedagogic discourse (Bernstein, 1986/1990d) and pedagogic practices (Bernstein, 1990b), Bernstein's project sought to link microprocesses (language, transmission, and pedagogy) to macroforms—

to how cultural and educational codes and the content and process of education are related to social class and power relations.

Karabel and Halsey (1977:71) stated that one of the most unresolved problems of Bernstein's work was how "power relationships penetrate the organization, distribution and evaluation of knowledge through the social context" (Bernstein, 1970:347). Over the past 20 years, Bernstein continued to search for answers to this question and developed an increasingly sophisticated model for understanding how the classification and framing rules of the official pedagogic field affect the transmission, the distribution, and, perhaps, the transformation of consciousness, and how these processes are indirectly related to the economic field of production. His positing of an indirect relation of education to production and his emphasis on the manner in which the realm of symbolic control does not directly correspond to the economic field will not answer his neo-Marxist critics. However, this work does continue his attempt to demonstrate the interrelationships between the economy, the family, and the school, and how educational practices reflect complex tensions in these relationships.

As a theoretical model, Bernstein's work presented, in painstaking detail, the rules of pedagogic discourse and practices and a comprehensive picture of both the "what" (classification rules) and the "how" (framing rules) of educational systems. Furthermore, his work on pedagogic practice (Bernstein, 1990b) attempting to link these micro and institutional processes to educational change opened an exciting but as yet undeveloped avenue of inquiry. Bernstein conceded that those who seek answers to difficult educational questions often prefer a top-down approach—one that begins with the large policy questions and builds down to an analysis of how the schools work to provide solutions or to constrain their formulation. He admitted, however, that the nature of his project was to build from the bottom to the top—an approach that sought to write the rules of educational process, then to link them to larger structural conditions, and, finally, to place this analysis in the context of the larger educational and policy questions of educators (Bernstein, 1990b).

Bernstein's project, then, from his early work on language, to the development of code theory, to the work on curriculum and pedagogic practice, was to develop a systematic structuralist theory that provided an analytic description of the way in which the educational system is related to the social division of labor. Because his work deals with so many of the themes central to the development of sociological theory, he is often portrayed as a neo-Marxist, a functionalist, a Weberian conflict theorist, or a interactionist new sociologist of education. Code theory, taken as a whole, however, has at its core the goal of his entire project: to develop a Durkheimian structuralist theory that analyzes the way in which changes in the division of labor create different meaning systems and codes, that provides analytic classifications of these systems, and that incorporates a conflict model of unequal power relations into its structural approach.

Atkinson (1981, 1985) argued that the evolution of Bernstein's sociology must be understood as the movement from its early Durkheimian roots to a later convergence with European structuralist thought, especially French social theory. In the United States, however, because the Durkheimian tradition was appropriated both by Parsonian structural functionalism and by positivism, Bernstein's work was rarely linked to Durkheim and structuralism or was criticized for being linked to Durkheim. For example, Karabel and Halsey's (1977) treatment of Bernstein as the "harbinger of a new synthesis" speaks of his need to link his Durkheimian perspective more explicitly to neo-Marxist categories. Although his work on pedagogic practice clearly does link the two, Bernstein has never moved out of a Durkheimian–structuralist position; rather, he has incorporated the neo-Marxist and Weberian categories of class and power relations into his overall theory. It is necessary to remove the consensus aspects of functionalism that are associated with structural functionalism to understand Bernstein's sociology. Although his work has been concerned with how communication, cultural, and educational codes function in relation to particular social structures, Bernstein is concerned not with the way in which such functioning leads to consensus but with how it forms the basis of privilege and domination.

It is with respect to the relationship with privilege and domination that Bernstein's work, while remaining consistent with a Durkheimian and structuralist foundation, has systematically integrated Marxism and Weberian categories and has provided the possibilities for the synthesis that Karabel and Halsey called for. Bernstein's later work continued to be Durkheimian because, as Atkinson (1985:36) pointed out, an essential activity has been the exploration of changes from mechanical to organic solidarity through an analysis of the division of labor, boundary maintenance, social roles, the ritual-expressive order, cultural categories, social control, and types of messages. It attempted to look at modes of cultural transmission through the analysis of codes. In addition, this work continued to link classification and framing codes to the unequal distribution of resources in capitalist societies. Whereas the original article on class and pedagogy was clearly more Durkheimian in its analysis of changes in organic solidarity, his later work (Bernstein, 1990a, 1990b; 1996) was more interested in the consequences of different pedagogic practices for different social classes and, most important, returns to the very questions of education and inequality that were the original bases of the project over 30 years ago.

Thus, Bernstein's work on pedagogic discourses and practice accomplished a number of related and important things. First, it provided a theory of school knowledge and transmission and demonstrates how the what of education is transmitted. Second, it linked the sociolinguistic aspects of his early work to the analysis of the codes of schooling. Third, in relating the process and content of transmission to differences in social class and in calling for an analysis of the consequences of those differences in curriculum and pedagogy, Bernstein provided a tentative integration of structuralist and conflict approaches within sociology.

Conclusion

Over the past three decades, Bernstein's work was the subject of considerable criticism and controversy. Bernstein (1990c) classified a typology of different types of criticism and argued that much of his work had been taken out of context or recontextualized incorrectly. Much of the criticism has not been based on a close reading of his work, but rather on secondary interpretations. The major criticism of his early sociolinguistic work as "cultural deficit" theory has diverted attention from his larger body of work. Thus, Danzig (1995) correctly points out, Bernstein is often viewed narrowly in the context of sociolinguistics. The important point is that the early work on social class and language was part of a larger, ongoing sociological project. From the outset, Bernstein was concerned with connecting the levels of sociological analysis: societal, institutional, in-

teractional, and intrapsychic (see Persell, 1977) and understanding the ways in which meanings are transmitted to individuals, from the division of labor, through the family and the schools. Code theory is then an overarching sociological approach to understanding how consciousness is dialectically related to the division of labor, especially in terms of differences between the fields of production (economic), symbolic control (culture), and institutions (family and school), and how meaning systems are relayed, transmitted, and acquired. Most importantly, Bernstein's sociology places power squarely in the equation. Although the emphasis of Bernstein's work, especially since the 1970s, was on schooling, his project always proceeded from a theoretical base. His theoretical approach has been labeled Durkheimian, neo-Marxist, structuralist, and interactionist, as well as being part of the "new sociology." Bernstein (1996) states that these have been the labels of others and that they have often been too exclusive, often simplifying the theoretical complexity of his model. He acknowledged that Durkheim has always been at the heart of his sociological theory, in part as a corrective to the conservative interpretation of Durkheim's work, especially in the United States; in part as a consequence of Parson's structural-functional interpretation of Durkheim. Additionally, although he acknowledged the structuralist interpretations of his work by Atkinson (1985) and Sadovnik (1991), he did not see his work as exclusively structuralist. He rejected the view that he was part of the "new sociology," as he believed that his work was "old" sociology, particularly in terms of its roots in classical sociological theory. Finally, he suggested that the idea that it was his project to connect disparate sociological theories was not his but was suggested by others, particularly Karabel and Halsey (1977). Although their labeling of his work as the "harbinger of a new synthesis" was complimentary, it also raised an expectation of a kind of synthesis that had not been explicitly part of his project. Rather than working from one sociological theory, or attempting to synthesize a number of theories, Bernstein attempted to develop and refine a model that is capable of describing the complex interrelationships between different aspects of society.

In response to the criticism that his work lacks empirical testing, Bernstein stated that in addition to research on his theory produced by his own Ph.D. students, there have been numerous other empirical studies using his work. He reported 15 articles in the *British Journal of the Sociology of Education* based on the theory (as well as the new volume edited by Morais, et al.). Although much of the research reported here has not been readily available to U.S. sociologists, this does not detract from the enormous size of both the theoretical and the empirical project. What is clear is that over a 40-year period, Bernstein developed a systematic code theory, which has been constantly refined and developed and which, through his students, has been empirically researched. Moreover, Bernstein's theories have undergone revision and clarification in light of this research. What comes through in his reflection on his sociological project is how theory and research have been crucially related to each other (Bernstein, 1996).

Despite the criticisms in his work, it is undeniable that Bernstein's work represents one of the most sustained and powerful attempts to investigate significant issues in the sociology of education. Forty years ago, Bernstein began with a simple but overwhelming issue: how to find ways to "prevent the wastage of working-class educational potential" (1961b:308). The problem of educability led to the development of code theory. Code theory, while a powerful and controversial perspective on educational inequality, did not sufficiently provide an understanding of what goes on inside the schools and how these practices are systematically related to social-class advantages and disadvantages. In an attempt to connect the macro and the micro further, Bernstein's work since the 1970s centered on a model of pedagogic discourse and practices, beginning with the concepts of classification and framing and continuing to a more systematic outline of the "what" and the "how" of education. Taken as a whole, Bernstein's work provides a systematic analysis of codes, pedagogic discourse and practice, and their relationship to symbolic control and identity.

REFERENCES

Atkinson, P. 1981. "Bernstein's structuralism." *Educational Analysis* 3:85–96.

———. 1985. *Language, Structure and Reproduction: An Introduction to the Sociology of Basil Bernstein.* London: Methuen.

Atkinson, P., B. Davies, and S. Delamont. 1995. *Discourse and Reproduction: Essays in Honor of Basil Bernstein.* Cresskill, NJ: Hampton Press.

Bernstein, B. 1958. "Some Sociological Determinants of Perception: An Enquiry into Subcultural Differences." *British Journal of Sociology* 9:159–174.

———. 1960. "Language and Social Class: A Research Note." *British Journal of Sociology* 11:271–276.

———. 1961a. "Social Structure, Language, and Learning." *Educational Research* 3:163–176.

———. 1961b. "Social Class and Linguistic Development: A Theory of Social Learning." In A. H. Halsey, J. Floud, and C. A. Anderson (eds.), *Education, Economy and Society,* pp. 288–314. New York: Free Press.

———. 1962a. "Linguistic Codes, Hesitation Phenomena and Intelligence." *Language and Speech* 5:31–46.

———. 1962b. "Social Class, Linguistic Codes and Grammatical Elements." *Language and Speech* 5:221–240.

———. 1970. "Education Cannot Compensate for Society." *New Society* 387:344–347.

———. 1971. "A Sociolinguistic Approach to Socialisation with Reference to Educability." In D. Hymes and J. Gumperz (eds.), *Directions in Sociolinguistics.* New York: Holt, Rinehart & Winston. (Reprinted in B. Bernstein, 1973a.)

———. 1973a. *Class, Codes and Control: Vol. 1.* London: Routledge & Kegan Paul. (Original published in 1971.)

———. 1973b. *Class, Codes and Control: Vol. 2.* London: Routledge & Kegan Paul. (Original published in 1971.)

———. 1973c. "On the Classification and Framing of Educational Knowledge." In B. Bernstein (ed.), *Class, Codes, and Control: Vol. 1,* pp. 202–230, and *Class, Codes, and Control: Vol. 2,* pp. 85–115. London: Routledge & Kegan Paul. (Original published in M. F. D. Young (ed.), *Knowledge and Control: New Directions for the Sociology of Education.* London: Collier-Macmillan.)

———. 1977a. *Class, Codes and Control: Vol. 3.* London: Routledge & Kegan Paul. (Original published in 1975.)

———. 1977b. "Class and Pedagogies: Visible and Invisible" (rev ed.). In B. Bernstein (ed.), *Class, Codes and Control: Vol. 3,* pp. 116–156. London: Routledge & Kegan Paul.

———. 1986. "On Pedagogic Discourse." In J. G. Richardson (ed.), *Handbook for Theory and Research in the Sociology of Education,* pp. 205–240. New York: Greenwood. (Revised and reprinted in Bernstein, 1990d:165–218.)

———. 1990a. *Class, Codes and Control: Vol. 4. The Structuring of Pedagogic Discourse.* London: Routledge.

———. 1990b. "Social Class and Pedagogic Practice." In B. Bernstein (ed.), *Class, Codes and Control: Vol. 4. The Structuring of Pedagogic Discourse,* pp. 63–93. London: Routledge.

———. 1990c. "Elaborated and Restricted Codes: Overview and Criticisms." In B. Bernstein (ed.), *Class, Codes and Control: Vol. 4. The Structuring of Pedagogic Discourse,* pp. 94–130. London: Routledge.

———. 1990d. "The Social Construction of Pedagogic Discourse." In B. Bernstein (ed.), *Class, Codes and Control: Vol. 4. The Structuring of Pedagogic Discourse,* pp. 165–218. London: Routledge.

———. 1995. "A Response." In A. R. Sadovnik (ed.), *Knowledge and Pedagogy: The Sociology of Basil Bernstein,* pp. 385–424. Norwood, NJ: Ablex.

———. 1996. *Pedagogy, Symbolic Control and Identity: Theory, Research, Critique*. London: Taylor & Francis.

Bernstein, B., and J. Cook-Gumperz. 1973. "The Coding Grid, Theory and Operations." In J. Cook-Gumperz (ed.), *Social Control and Socialization: A Study of Social Class Differences in the Language of Maternal Control,* pp. 48–72. London: Routledge & Kegan Paul.

Bourdieu, P., and J. C. Passeron. 1977. *Reproduction in Education, Society and Culture*. London: Sage.

Bowles, S., and H. Gintis. 1976. *Schooling in Capitalist America*. New York: Basic Books.

Cox Donoso, C. 1986. "Continuity, Conflict and Change in State Education in Chile: A Study of the Pedagogic Projects of the Christian Democratic and the Popular Unity Governments." *C.O.R.E.* 10(2), University of London, Institute of Education.

Danzig, A. 1995. "Applications and Distortions of Basil Bernstein's Code Theory." In A. R. Sadovnik (ed.) *Knowledge and Pedagogy: The Sociology of Basil Bernstein,* pp. 145–170. Norwood, NJ: Ablex.

Diaz, M. 1984. "A Model of Pedagogic Discourse with Special Application to Colombian Primary Education." Unpublished doctoral dissertation, University of London.

———. (ed.) 1990. *La Construccion Social Del Discurso Pedagogica*. Valle, Colombia: Prodic-EI Griot.

Holland, J. 1986. "Social Class Differences in Adolescents' Conception of the Domestic and Industrial Division of Labor." *C.O.R.E.* 10(1), University of London, Institute of Education.

Jenkins, C. 1990. "The Professional Middle Class and the Origins of Progressivism: A Case Study of the New Educational Fellowship, 1920–1950." *C.O.R.E.* 14(1). University of London, Institute of Education.

Karabel, J., and A. H. Halsey. 1977. *Power and Ideology in Education*. New York: Oxford University Press.

King, R. 1976. "Bernstein's Sociology of the School: Some Propositions Tested." *British Journal of Sociology* 27: 430–443.

———. 1981. "Bernstein's Sociology of the School: A Further Testing." *British Journal of Sociology* 32:259–265.

Morais, A. M., D. Peneda, and A. Madeiros. 1991a. "The Recontextualizing of Pedagogic Discourse: Influence of Differential Pedagogic Practices on Students' Achievements as Mediated by Class, Gender, and Race." Paper given at the International Sociology of Education Conference, University of Birmingham, UK. Also available from the Department of Education, Faculty of Sciences, University of Lisbon.

Morais, A. M., D. Peneda, A. Madeiros, F. Fontinhas, and I. Neves. 1991b. "Recognition and Realisation Rules in Acquiring School Science: The Contribution of Pedagogy and Social Background of Pupils." Paper given at the annual meeting of the National Association for Researching Science Teaching, University of Wisconsin. Also available from the Department of Education, Faculty of Sciences, University of Lisbon.

Neves, I. P. 1991. *Practicas Pedagogicas Difereuciaia n Faulia e Suas no (in) Sucesso En Ciencias*. Lisbon: University of Lisbon.

Persell, C. H. 1977. *Education and Inequality*. New York: Free Press.

Sadovnik, A. R. 1991. "Basil Bernstein's Theory of Pedagogic Practice: A Structuralist Approach." *Sociology of Education* 64(1):48–63.

———. (ed.) 1995. *Knowledge and Pedagogy: The Sociology of Basil Bernstein*. Norwood, NJ: Ablex.

Semel, S. F. 1995. "Basil Bernstein's Theory of Pedagogic Practice and the History of American Progressive Education: Three Case Studies." In A. R. Sadovnik (ed.), *Knowledge and Pedagogy: The Sociology of Basil Bernstein,* pp. 337–358. Norwood, NJ: Ablex.

Tyler, W. 1984. "Organizational Structure, Factors and Code: A Methodological Inquiry into Bernstein's Theory of Educational Transmissions." Unpublished doctoral dissertation, University of Kent.

COMMUNITY COLLEGES[1]

Kevin J. Dougherty
Teachers College, Columbia University

Community colleges are one of the most important sectors of U.S. higher education. These public 2-year colleges (excluding branches of state 4-year colleges) comprise over one-quarter of all higher educational institutions in the United States, numbering 949 in 1996 (American Association of Community Colleges, 1997:9). They enroll 36% of all college students (some 5.3 million in fall 1996) and 44% of all first-time freshmen.[2] This enrollment share is even greater for less advantaged students, for whom community colleges are the single widest point of entry into higher education. Community colleges enroll 44% of all minority college students, 44% of all students age 25 and older, and 54% of all part-time students (American Association of Community Colleges, 1997: 9, 26–35; United States National Center for Education Statistics, 1999:197, 200, 206, 228).[3]

Though some community colleges are largely vocational, most are comprehensive institutions, managing diverse portfolios of programs. Still, in most community colleges, a majority of students are enrolled in occupational education programs, and these programs graduate a large proportion of our nation's nurses, com-

puter operators, and auto mechanics. Although baccalaureate preparation is no longer dominant, baccalaureate aspirants still account for 20 to 30% of community college students, and transfers from community colleges make up a sizable portion of 4-year college students, especially in California and Florida. In addition, community colleges provide remedial education, nonvocational or leisure courses, contract training for employers, advice and assistance to small businesses, and entertainment and other programs for the general community (Cohen and Brawer, 1996:Chapters 8–12).

The governance and finance of community colleges are just as complex as their functions. Depending on the state, community colleges may be governed by local districts, state agencies, or the state university. They receive funds from student tuitions, local taxes or appropriations, state appropriations and grants, federal grants, corporate fees, and private donations (Cohen and Brawer, 1996:Chapters 4–5).

Despite their educational importance and complex nature, community colleges have received surprisingly little systematic empirical scrutiny. Most research on the community college has tended to have a rather anecdotal, even hortatory quality. However, sociologists have contributed mightily to the small body of systematic research. What I aim to do in this chapter is to demarcate the general boundaries of community college scholarship, describe the sociological intervention, and sketch out where further research is needed. Sociological research on the community college has focused on how and why it hinders the educational attainment of baccalaureate aspirants. I will summarize this body of research and then identify various holes that merit plugging. At the same time, I also identify other re-

---

[1] I would like to thank the following for comments on this article: Thomas Bailey, Floyd Hammack, Margaret Terry Orr, and Dolores Perin.

[2] Degree credit enrollments are not total enrollments. They do not include nondegree credit enrollments, which are common at community colleges, especially in remedial education, adult education, or contract training. I estimate total enrollments to be 1.5 times credit enrollments, based on the unweighted average of the ratio of total enrollments to credit enrollments for the states of California, Illinois, Maryland, New York, and Washington for fall 1993.

[3] Women enroll at community colleges at a slightly higher rate than do men.

search topics—involving the community college's role in economic development and community services—that deserve much greater attention than they have received thus far.

Community College Scholarship Generally

Several journals and many books are devoted exclusively to the community college. But the bulk of this literature is of relatively low analytic scope and rigor. Written largely by community college administrators and teachers and their university mentors, commentary on the community college tends to be anecdotally descriptive and hortatory rather than systematically evaluative and critical. It focuses on describing how the institution operates, what social functions it purportedly meets now and could meet in the future, and the best strategies to advance the community college's position, prestige, and resources. When there is empirical analysis of the community college's social impact and of the forces that gave birth to it and will shape its future, this analysis is often based on single-institution case studies. The implicit analytic framework is an often unconscious functionalism in which the community college is seen as shaped by the consensual needs of "the community," whether for job preparation, educational opportunity, or community building.

Despite the above, islands of critical analysis do stand out within the main drift of commentary on the community college. Community college officials and scholars such as L. Steven Zwerling (1976), Arthur Cohen and Florence Brawer (1996), and Judith Eaton (1988) have written illuminating analyses of the institution's social role. Nonetheless, these isolated efforts have left a large deficit of critical scholarship that has been substantially filled by a small group of sociologists and other social scientists. In what follows, I will sketch this sociological contribution and note areas needing further research.

The Sociological Intervention

The relatively few sociologists who have studied the community college have had a weighty impact, which community college "locals" have noticed, often in dismay but sometimes with appreciation. The central concern of this sociological intervention has been whether community colleges inhibit or advance equality of educational opportunity.

Key Early Statements

The sociological analysis of the community college began with Burton Clark's *The Open Door College* (1960), which astutely analyzed the organizational implications of the community college's open door admissions policy, diffuse social mission, allegiance more to secondary school than the university, and dependence on other educational institutions. Clark posited that the community college is profoundly shaped by its unselective admissions policy, which floods it with students with baccalaureate ambitions but subbaccalaureate abilities. To preserve its academic status, the community college responds by "cooling out" weak but ambitious students by diverting them toward terminal subbaccalaureate degrees. Clark saw this task as a necessary but dirty job: necessary because universities' selectivity must be preserved in order to meet society's need for expertise, but dirty because cooling out must be done behind students' backs in order to be effective (Clark, 1960: 162–163).

Clark's attention to the community college's cooling out function and how the college is shaped by its relation to other kinds of educational organizations powerfully shaped subsequent sociological commentary.

In 1972, Jerome Karabel issued a stirring manifesto for subsequent sociology of the community college by picking up Burton Clark's cooling out concept and grounding it in a conflict, rather than functionalist, theory of education. Whereas Clark saw the community college's role as a painful but necessary resolution of the contradiction between the American values of educational opportunity and educational excellence, Karabel (1972) instead saw the community college as a weapon deployed by the capitalist class against the working class in the class struggle over life chances. He noted that those cooled out were largely working class and nonwhite while those upholding the putative value of educational quality were the privileged classes. For Karabel, the community college's emphasis on vocational education arises from a class-stratified capitalist society. In this society, the demand for good jobs outstrips the supply, requiring the elite to find ways of defusing this politically explosive contradiction. In addition, capitalist elites—centered in business, the selective universities, and prestigious foundations—support the vocationalized community college because it provides business with publicly subsidized employee training and selective universities with a covert means of deflecting the enrollment demands of less desirable students. Community college leaders have acquiesced to these capitalist imperatives, according to Karabel (1972), because vocationalization affords their institution a unique identity: that of a "community" college that is no longer "junior" to the university. However, community college students, particularly minority students, have resisted vocationalization just as workers have resisted capitalist work demands.

Karabel (1972) backed up his argument by citing evidence that community colleges and their vocational programs disproportionately enroll working class students, that very few community college aspirants to a baccalaureate degree ever receive one, and that a key basis of this result is that community college students are pressured to enroll in vocational courses (a process that Karabel termed "cooling out," following Burton Clark). Karabel's argument about the capitalist origins of the community college is more cursory, relying on general comments by business people, foundations, and scholars rather than detailed studies of the founding and later vocationalization of specific community colleges.

Karabel's (1972) arresting argument—which was joined by Fred Pincus (1974)—broke sharply with the celebratory commentary of community college "locals" and Burton Clark's fatalistic belief in the inescapability of social contradictions. As New Left ideas diffused through sociological scholarship, Karabel's position set the terms for most subsequent sociological research on the community college. This research has strongly buttressed most of Karabel's statements about the community college's *effects,* while calling into question the instrumentalist Marxist analysis of the community college's *origins* that he propounded then (but not in his later work, which will be discussed below).

Recent Research on the Effects of Community Colleges

Since Karabel's (1972) ground-breaking article, sociologists of the community college have focused on its impact on students' life chances: namely, college access, eventual educational attainment, and economic attainment. At the same time, other scholars—often not sociologists—have shed light on whether the community college really diverts students away from the universities and effectively meets employers' demand for "middle level" workers.

Student Outcomes. Many different studies converge to impressively validate Karabel's (1972) argument that the mere fact of entering a community college has a significantly inhibitory impact on students' eventual educational and economic attainment. Primarily using national longitudinal surveys, sociologists David Lavin, William Velez, Kristine Anderson, Elizabeth Monk-Turner, and Fred Pincus, economists David Breneman, Susan Nelson, Charlene Nunley, and W. Norton Grubb, and the higher educational researchers Alexander Astin and Ernest Pascarella have found that even controlling for differences in family background, academic aptitude, high school record, and educational and occupational aspirations, community college entrants on average receive 0.12 to 0.25 fewer years of education, 11 to 19% fewer baccalaureate degrees, and significantly less prestigious and remunerative jobs than similar students entering 4-year colleges and universities (for more on these findings, see Dougherty, 1994:52–61; Pascarella and Terenzini, 1991:372–373, 506–507).

However, a few studies also suggest that defenders of the community college are correct that community colleges are more helpful than 4-year colleges to students with low educational ambitions and disadvantaged backgrounds (Dougherty, 1994:56; Pascarella et al., 1995:90; 1996:38–39; Whitaker and Pascarella, 1994:204). In addition, W. Norton Grubb and Leland Medsker and James Trent have found that areas rich in community colleges have higher college-going rates than areas rich instead in 4-year colleges (see Dougherty, 1994:50–52).

Dougherty (1994:Chapters 3–4) critically synthesizes the evidence on the community college's impact on students and advances a theory of how it produces lower rates of baccalaureate attainment than does the 4-year college. This theory focuses on the *institutional* causes of three critical events for community college entrants: attrition during the first 2 years of college, failure to transfer to 4-year colleges, and attrition after transfer. To explain how community colleges contribute to their students' higher dropout rate, over and above the handicaps students bring with them, Dougherty documents community colleges' lesser ability to socially and academically integrate their students through such influential devices as campus residence and an academically oriented student and faculty culture. To explain why community college students have a low rate of transfer to 4-year colleges, Dougherty examines such institutional factors as inadequate financial aid, weak encouragement of transfer (largely due to community colleges' emphasis on occupational education), and 4-year colleges' preference for freshmen over transfer students. And to explain why community college transfers less often attain a bachelor's degree than do 4-year college juniors, Dougherty shows the impact of loss of academic credits in transfer, difficulty in securing financial aid, poorer preparation for the academic demands of upper-division courses, and inadequate efforts by universities to socially integrate community college transfers.[4]

Diverting Students from the Universities. Various studies document Jerome Karabel's (1972) argument that community colleges do not simply attract students to higher education but also entice them away from universities. W. Norton Grubb, Gary Orfield, and Faith Paul have found that the more extensive a state's community college system the fewer the number going on to 4-year colleges. Moreover, Grubb and others find that the lower tuitions charged by community colleges pull students away from 4-year colleges (see Dougherty, 1994:47–49).

---

[4] Pascarella et al. (1995, 1996) question whether community colleges provide inferior academic preparation. They find that with controls for social background and precollege ability and aspirations, community college students perform just as well as 4-year college students on tests of reading comprehension, mathematics, and critical thinking (at the end of the first year) and writing and science reasoning (at the end of the second year). These findings are quite heartening, but three caveats are in order. The community college sample is drawn from only five colleges (yielding 280 students the first year and 147 the second year) and six 4-year colleges. Also, the study controls for the average precollege academic ability of first-year students at each college and whether the students resided on campus or not. This has the effect of controlling for two potent devices by which colleges affect student achievement: exposure to high ability students and provision of campus residence. Finally, it is not clear how well the tests administered measure the skills needed to succeed in a 4-year college (Pascarella et al., 1995:87; 1996:37).

Meeting Labor Market Demands. As both critics and defenders of the community college claim, the community college is indeed a central supplier of trained workers for "middle level" or "semiprofessional" occupations such as registered nurses and engineering technicians. But Fred Pincus (1980) and W. Norton Grubb (1996), among others, find that its response to the labor market's call is more clumsy than acknowledged by both its defenders and critics. The community college often under- and overshoots the demands of the labor market: sometimes training far more people than the labor market can absorb and other times producing fewer workers than business would like (see Dougherty, 1994:44–46).

Recent Research on the Origins of Community Colleges

Sociologists coming after Karabel (1972) and Pincus (1974) significantly shifted the terms of the debate over why community college arose and later moved in a sharply vocational direction. The main element was to recast business influence more in terms of indirect constraint rather than direct intervention and to highlight the important role as well of other actors.

Analyzing national-level data and the history of the community college system in Massachusetts, Steven Brint and Jerome Karabel (1989) substantially reorient Karabel's (1972) analysis of why the community college was vocationalized and bring it closer to Burton Clark's (1960) organizationally oriented argument. In contrast to Karabel (1972), Brint and Karabel (1989) find much less evidence of a direct business role in the rise and vocationalization of the community college; instead business's influence had been mostly indirect, based on its control of jobs that community colleges seek to fill. Moreover, Brint and Karabel argue that the internal dynamics of the field of higher education—particularly entrepreneurial activity by community colleges—played an even greater role than Karabel suggested in 1972. Drawing on institutional theory within organizational sociology, Brint and Karabel portray higher education as an "organizational field" composed of colleges competing for prestige and resources. Within this Darwinian universe, universities are at the top of the food chain, securing the best students, the most revenues, and the greatest prestige. Their chief concern has been to protect their academic and social exclusivity and thus the exchange value of their credentials in the face of the clamor for admissions by less privileged but ambitious students. To avoid throwing their doors open to the teeming masses, the universities supported the expansion of an alternative, the vocationalized community college.

Community colleges, in the meantime, collaborated with this university thrust, according to Brint and Karabel (1989). Seeing that the universities and 4-year colleges had snapped up the best occupational-training markets, community colleges began many years ago to carve out a market of their own, supplying middle level or semiprofessional occupations. Beginning in the 1920s, the American Association of Community Colleges (AACC) conceived of and then militantly proselytized for a vocationalized community college. And in time, this vision persuaded not only AACC members but also external supporters such as state university heads, government officials, business, and foundations (Brint and Karabel 1989:16–17, 34–46, 54–66, 77–78, 96–100, 107–108, 124–126, 208–210).

Kevin Dougherty's (1994) examination of the origins and vocationalization of the community college—based on an examination of community college politics at the national level and at the state and local level in five states (California, Washington, Illinois, Indiana, and New York)—both converges with and diverges from Brint and Karabel's. Although they advance a largely organizational explanation, Dougherty's analysis is grounded more in political sociology. The crux of Dougherty's argument is that government officials took the lead in establishing and vocationalizing the community college, but they did so within the constraints set by a democratic polity and a capitalist economy. Like Brint and Karabel (1989), Dougherty (1994) concludes that direct student or business demand is insufficient to explain the rise and vocationalization of the community college. However, contrary to Brint and Karabel, Dougherty finds that governmental initiative went well beyond the actions of state university and community college officials. A wide variety of government officials supported the establishment and vocationalization of community colleges in part out of a sincere belief in educational opportunity but also out of more self-interested reasons. At the local level, school superintendents and high school principals instigated local drives to found community colleges in good part

because this would bring them prestige as educational innovators and the opportunity to become college presidents. At the state level, governors, state legislators, and state education departments joined state universities in pushing for state aid for community colleges because, among other things, they saw the community college as a cheap way to meet the demand for college access and to stimulate politically popular economic growth through publicly subsidized training for business. And at the national level, Presidents and Congress members supported federal aid for the community college for much the same reasons as their state counterparts.

But if business's direct role in establishing and vocationalizing community colleges was only secondary, Dougherty (1994) finds that its *indirect* role—based on its economic and ideological hegemony—has been quite strong. Dougherty agrees with Brint and Karabel (1989) that one aspect of this indirect influence has been the fact that business controls jobs that community college officials seek to fill. But Dougherty also argues that business's power to constrain governmental initiative goes further. Business also controls capital for investment and thus the pace and distribution of economic growth. Realizing that capital investment is the key to economic growth and therefore their own political prospects, public officials have taken the initiative to offer business publicly subsidized vocational education in order to secure business investment in their jurisdictions. Furthermore, business has constrained government initiative not only economically but also ideologically. Government officials subscribe to values and beliefs—such as the importance of economic growth and that this growth must come through an expansion of jobs in the private rather than public sector—that have made them ready to serve business interests with little prompting (Dougherty, 1994:125).

For Dougherty (1994), an awareness of the community college's complex origins allows us to see how the community college could powerfully, and yet largely unintentionally, hinder the baccalaureate opportunities of its students. The fact that community colleges lack dormitories contributes to their higher dropout rate, but the reason they lack dormitories is because this made community colleges cheaper to operate, a potent consideration in the minds of the local educators founding them and the state officials financing them. The fact that community colleges are heavily vocational lessens their students' desire to transfer, but they are so strongly vocational not in order to track students but to meet business's need for trained employees and government officials' desire for an attractive incentive to secure business's political support and economic investment. The fact that community colleges are 2-year schools discourages students from pursuing a baccalaureate degree, because they have to transfer to separate 4-year institutions with different academic standards. But the reason community colleges are 2-year schools is largely because university heads did not want the competition of many more 4-year schools, state officials did not want the financial burden of a myriad of 4-year colleges, and local educators believed it would be easier to establish 2-year rather than 4-year colleges. The precipitate of these varying desires is an institutional structure that, unfortunately and largely unintentionally, often subverts to the educational ambitions of baccalaureate aspirants entering community college, even as it opens up opportunities for students with nonbaccalaureate ambitions.

Further Research Needed on the Community College

Although sociologists have powerfully illuminated the community college's effects and origins, there is a need for much more research. Some of this involves refining the findings extant. But there is a need as well for research that explores territories largely neglected by sociologists of the community college, particularly, the community college's role in economic development, remedial education, community building, and education for citizenship and public participation.

Refining the Research on Students' Educational and Occupational Attainment

As noted above, a wide variety of excellent studies show that community college students on average secure less education and poorer jobs than comparable students (in background, high school achievement, and ambitions) entering 4-year colleges. And compared to similar students entering public or private vocational schools, community college entrants do better educationally but, economically, fare no better and sometimes worse

(Dougherty, 1994:52–66; Pascarella and Terenzini, 1991:372–373, 506–507).

Despite the strength of this research, there are four areas in which further research is much needed.

More Recent Data. The research extant is based primarily on students who entered college in the 1960s and 1970s, which raises the question of whether the community college's impacts on students have since changed. Because of a heavily reliance on the National Longitudinal Survey of the High School Class of 1972, most of the best national research on the impact of community colleges has been restricted to analyzing students who entered college in the early 1970s. But in comparison to the early 1970s, community colleges today enroll a much greater number of nontraditional students, provide much more extensive vocational and remedial programs, have sharply raised tuitions in order to make up for sharp cutbacks in government appropriations, etc. These changes raise the question of whether the impact of community colleges on their students' educational and economic attainment has changed considerably.

Luckily, the U.S. National Center for Education Statistics has sponsored three excellent national longitudinal studies examining students who entered college in the 1980s and even 1990s: the High School and Beyond Survey of high school sophomores and seniors in 1980; the National Educational Longitudinal Study of the 8th grade in 1988 (some of these students started entering college by 1993); and best yet, the Beginning Postsecondary Student Longitudinal Study (which began with 7000 respondents in 1989–1990).

Economic Attainment. Sociologists have focused far more on the impact of community colleges on educational attainment (particularly baccalaureate acquisition) than on economic attainment. To be sure, economists such as W. Norton Grubb (1996, 1998) have been doing excellent research in this area, but it is still one that sociologists need to pay attention to. There are too few studies that rigorously compare the economic returns to attending a community college to the returns for other 2-year institutions such as proprietary schools, public vocational schools, etc. And there are no studies that I am aware of that compare community colleges with nonschool training providers such as employers, the armed services, distance education services using the Internet, etc.

Variations in Community College Effects. The research extant has focused on main effects, yet there is suggestive evidence that community college effects may vary considerably depending on students' traits and community colleges' characteristics. On the student side, students' aspirations and social background shape what impact community colleges have on their academic, educational, and economic attainment. White, middle class, and female students seemingly experience greater cognitive growth and attain more education if they attend 4-year colleges rather than community colleges, but the reverse appears to be true for nonwhite, working class, and male students (Dougherty, 1994:56; Pascarella et al., 1995:90; 1996:38–39). Similarly, students with high educational or occupational aspirations attain significantly more educationally or occupationally if they enter 4-year colleges rather than community colleges, but those with low aspirations seemingly do as well or better attending community colleges (Dougherty, 1994: 56; Whitaker and Pascarella, 1994:204). Finally, among community college graduates, men graduating with vocational associates' degrees secure higher status occupations and higher hourly wages than do women, but women get higher hourly wages than men among those graduating with vocational certificates (Dougherty, 1994:75–76). Given this suggestive evidence, we need to examine rigorously how community college effects vary by students' social background (social class, race, sex), age, educational and occupational aspirations, etc. using large national samples with extended follow-ups.

Community college effects vary greatly not only according to student characteristics but what they study. As in 4-year colleges, different fields of studies bring very different returns. Academic programs are more likely to lead to transfer but they also pay off less well than vocational programs if students do not transfer. And among vocational programs, payoffs vary greatly, with the returns being particularly high for engineering and computers and for women, health and business (Grubb, 1996:95; Grubb, 1998:36–37).

On the institutional side, we know that community colleges vary greatly among themselves in their de-

clared missions, degree of support for college transfer, financial resources, etc. And again we have suggestive evidence that variations in the characteristics of community colleges produce variations in their students' educational and occupational attainment. For example, the more vocational a community college is the lower its transfer rate (Dougherty, 1994:94). Again, this suggests the need to disaggregate community colleges and examine whether different types produce different results for their students.

More Data on How Baccalaureate Aspirants are Hindered. Though Dougherty (1994:Chapter 4) and others have provided detailed explanations of why baccalaureate aspirants entering community colleges less often acquire bachelor's degrees than their peers entering 4-year colleges, we still could learn more about how this differential effect is produced. The finding that community college entrants suffer higher rates of attrition in the lower division than do comparable 4-year college entrants is based on but a few studies, only two of which control for differences in background, ability, etc. between the two kinds of students. And both of these studies involve students who entered college in the late 1960s and early 1970s (see Dougherty, 1994: 85–92).

Similarly, the finding that community college students have a higher rate of failure to continue on to the upper division than do comparable students who first entered 4-year colleges is based on studies that do not control for a wide range of possible differences between these two kinds of students (see Dougherty, 1994:92–97). Hence, there is a need for careful multivariate studies in order to conclusively establish that there is a significant *institutional* contribution to the lower transfer rate of community college entrants.

Finally, a disagreement has cropped up over whether community college transfers more often drop out of the university than do similar 4-year college juniors. Based on studies done by several states, Dougherty (1994:97–105) argued that community college transfers suffered a higher rate of dropout than did comparable students who started at 4-year colleges. However, based on a multivariate analysis of data from High School and Beyond, Lee et al. (1993) argued that there was no difference in baccalaureate attainment between community college transfers and 4-year college natives. However, there is reason to doubt whether the Lee et al. study settles the question.[5]

It would be very useful if we could have studies that examine the impacts all at once of all the career contingencies (lower-division attrition, failure to transfer, and attrition in the upper division) facing B.A. aspirants. By examining them all within one data set, rather than having to paste together several different pieces of data, we can determine the relative weights of the career contingencies.

Beyond refining our estimates of the impacts of the career contingencies faced by baccalaureate aspirants, it would be good if we better understood *how* precisely these contingencies operated. Here qualitative research would be useful, but sociologists have done it all too rarely. The major exception is the work of Howard London and Kathleen Shaw (London, 1978; Shaw and London, 1998).

Exploring Sociologically Uncharted Dimensions of the Community College

Students' educational and economic attainment are not the only community college impacts of note, but they are the ones that have gotten the lion's share of sociological attention, because they fit nicely with the status-attainment focus of the sociology of education and of social stratification. Yet community colleges have other important goals besides shaping students' life chances, and unfortunately the content and effectiveness of these other goals have been little studied. We need to investigate vast territories of the community college that we have largely left unexplored by sociologists: namely, the community college's role in economic development, remedial education, community building, and education for civic responsibility. Furthermore, given the community college's complexity of function, governance, and finance, we need to

explore its nature as an organization that is quite different from either 4-year colleges or high schools. And as this complex institution comes under massive and conflicting social, economic, and political pressures, we need to forecast its likely and/or desirable future trajectory.

The Community College's Role in Economic Development. In the past two decades, community colleges have taken on a key role as engines for local economic development, but this role is only beginning to be studied in any major way. Community colleges have diversified their economic development role beyond the training of technicians and other "middle level" workers to include such things as contract training for employers, helping small businesses get started and then prosper, and participating in local economic development planning. Only a few studies of the origins, dimensions, and impacts of this new role have appeared (Brint and Karabel, 1989:192–202; Dougherty and Bakia, 2000; Grubb et al., 1997; Pincus, 1989), and far more are needed. We need to investigate the factors leading to the development of this new economic role, how that role varies across different kinds of community colleges, how effectively community colleges have discharged this economic development role, and what impact it has had both on society and on the community college itself. In studying the community college's effectiveness, we need to examine its contribution not just to meeting the needs of firms but also the larger needs of the community for economic stimulus and economic planning. And on the question of the impact on the community college of its new economic role, we need to analyze how a major commitment to working closely with employers on their training needs affects the community college's willingness and ability to meet its other functions, such as baccalaureate preparation, remedial education, and community building and civic education. As it is, research by Dougherty and Bakia (2000) finds that closer connections to employers do appear to benefit community colleges by attracting new funds, enrollments, and political support and bringing the vocational curriculum into closer connection with cutting edge changes in the labor process. At the same time, the new economic role may also undermine other functions of the community college by pulling away necessary resources. For example, the organizational energy and imagination necessary to

---

[5] Lee et al. (1993) do not seem to control for how many credits the students have accumulated, as a result the comparison becomes one between the persistence rate of 4-year college natives over 4 years as versus that for community college transfers only over the years after transfer. As it happens, studies by the states of California, Florida, and Illinois found that 5 years after transfer about 39% of community college transfers had dropped out, but the figure for 4-year native *juniors* (roughly comparable to the transfers in number of credits attained) was only about 24% (Dougherty, 1994:97–99).

construct and maintain transfer and articulation arrangements with 4-year colleges may instead be poured into forging stronger connections to employers because these promise new funds, enrollments, and political support (Dougherty and Bakia, 2000).

Remedial Education. As portals into higher education for students that 4-year colleges would turn away as unprepared, community colleges have long provided remedial education to many students (Cohen and Brawer, 1996:Chapter 9). In 1995, 41% of freshmen in public 2-year colleges were enrolled in remedial courses either in reading, writing, or arithmetic, as compared to 29% of college students generally (United States National Center for Education Statistics, 1997: 102). And this role promises to become even larger, as state legislators and 4-year college boards continue to push to have remedial education reduced or even eliminated at 4-year colleges and instead relegated to community colleges (Shaw, 1997). We need to know more about the forces behind this redefinition of institutional responsibilities for remedial education, what impact it will have on students and their colleges (both 2-year and 4-year), and how well community colleges actually do remediate. For example, what proportion of remedial students ever escape from remedial education programs in the community college and go on to graduate? What role does unsuccessful remediation have in the poorer educational attainment of working-class and minority students?

Education for Civic Participation. Under the rubric of general education, the community college has long been committed to the nonvocational education of its students for citizenship and social participation (Cohen and Brawer, 1996:Chapter 12). But we have few rigorous data on how effective it is in this role. For example, how much general education do students in vocational majors get and how much impact does it have? We also do not know how the community college's contribution to civic education is being affected by its growing role in workforce preparation and economic development.

Community Building. Community colleges are an important means of generating a vibrant "civil society," by providing a place for citizens of diverse backgrounds to come together in noncredit evening and weekend classes, public affairs events, arts presentations, etc. (Cohen and Brawer, 1996:Chapter 10). Yet, this community-building function, though much described and celebrated by community college observers, has not been systematically studied except in recent research by Kathleen Shaw and Howard London (1998). We need to investigate the degree to which these community-building efforts do enhance civic consciousness and social solidarity in the community and how the community college contribution compares to that of churches, volunteer groups, clubs, etc.

Multicultural Education. The community college has been unique among colleges in its willingness to enroll students of quite different backgrounds. However, we have little information on how successful the community college has been in aiding this diverse clientele to foster understanding and forge friendships across class, racial, and ethnic divisions.

Analyzing the Community College as an Organization. The preceding remarks about the community college's multiple roles—baccalaureate preparation, occupational training, economic development, remedial education, civic education, community building, and multicultural education—indicate how complicated its functions are. Add to this its diversity of governance and finance (Cohen and Brawer, 1996:Chapters 4–5) and its multiple linkages to a host of other educational institutions including high schools, 4-year colleges, postsecondary vocational schools, and employment training organizations. This complexity makes the community college a unique institution, one quite different from either the 4-year college or the high school. Yet it has received far too little *organizational* analysis except by Burton Clark (1960) and Brint and Karabel (1989). Both the community college and the sociology of educational organizations would benefit greatly from sociological analysis of the structure, culture, internal processes, and external relations and linkages of this complex and unique institution.

Research on the Community College's Future. The community college will not remain static. It will continue to change, perhaps sharply, due to its diffuse institutional mission and high responsiveness to its economic, social, and political environment (Brint and Karabel, 1989; Clark, 1960; Dougherty, 1994). As it is, this environment is changing rapidly and rather chaotically. Economically, as our economy further globalizes, the occupational composition, class distribution, and employment stability of the U.S. population are being transformed. Semiskilled jobs in factories and offices are being killed or moved abroad, and class inequality is increasing. Hence, community colleges, both out of internal volition and external pressure, are stepping up their efforts at job preparation and economic development. Meanwhile, high immigration is bringing increasing numbers of people who require acculturation and preparation for high-skill jobs. But at the same time, recent changes in immigration law pull immigrant students out of the community college because they are denied access to social-welfare programs that allow them to afford going to community college. Similarly, the drive to reform welfare by moving people rapidly into jobs is bringing the community college students needing short-term job training but also depriving it of others who have to leave college to take jobs either to make up for the loss of welfare benefits or to meet work requirements in order to retain them. Finally, the community college faces a more hostile political environment, with government becoming more stingy in its appropriations, demanding greater accountability, and more frequently denouncing remedial education in the community college (Dougherty, 1998).

Beyond affecting the number and kind of students the community college gets, these same external pressures are also affecting its programmatic composition. Occupational and remedial education are rising, but transfer education—despite brave holding efforts—will probably continue to decline. Teaching may change dramatically with the wholesale introduction of distance education designed to keep down instructional costs (Dougherty, 1998).

It is important that sociologists chart how the community college *is* responding to, and being changed by, these environmental pressures. Will the net effect be expansion or contraction of the community college? Will the growth of workforce preparation and economic development dangerously undercut the commitment to baccalaureate preparation, civic preparation, and community building? Because of these dangers, sociologists perhaps should also envisage how the community college *could* respond to environmental changes and yet protect a commitment to equality of opportunity and democratic socialization.

Summary

Sociology of education has given the community college sector far less attention than it deserves, given its large size and key role in education and the economy. Despite this, the small band of sociologists who have studied the institution have made an impressive contribution to understanding its historical origins and its impact on students' educational and economic attainment. But much remains to be done, both in refining the research that has been conducted and in exploring vast areas that have been left untouched. In terms of refining and extending our research on students' educational and economic attainment, we need to use more recent data sets, more deeply examine how community college effects vary by students' backgrounds, fields of study, and college characteristics, and further uncover the institutional mechanisms hindering the educational attainment of baccalaureate aspirants. But sociologists need to go beyond plugging holes in existing research. We must also investigate vast areas of the community college that we have largely left unexplored: the community college's role in economic development, remedial education, community building, and education for civic responsibility. We also need studies of the community college as an organization that is highly complex and quite different both from high schools and 4-year colleges. And rounding all this out, we need to investigate the community college's likely and possible future trajectories: how it will be reshaped by the many and conflicting demographic, economic, and political forces now impinging on the community college and by its own efforts to proactively control its changing environment.

REFERENCES

American Association of Community Colleges. 1997. *National Profile of Community Colleges: Trends and Statistics, 1997–1998*. Washington, DC: Author.

Brint, Steven G., and Jerome B. Karabel. 1989. *The Diverted Dream*. New York: Oxford University Press.

Clark, Burton. 1960. *The Open Door College*. New York: McGraw Hill.

Cohen, Arthur C., and Florence B. Brawer. 1996. *The American Community College,* 3d ed. San Francisco: Jossey-Bass.

Dougherty, Kevin J. 1994. *The Contradictory College: The Conflicting Origins, Impacts, and Futures of the Community College.* Albany: State University of New York Press.

————. 1998. *Community College Scenarios: Prospects and Perils.* New York: Community College Research Center, Teachers College, Columbia University.

Dougherty, Kevin J., and Marianne F. Bakia. 2000. "Community Colleges and Contract Training: Content, Origins, and Impacts." *Teachers College Record* 102(1):197–243.

Eaton, Judith. ed. 1988. *Colleges of Choice: The Enabling Impact of the Community College.* New York: American Council on Education and Macmillan.

Grubb, W. Norton. 1996. *Working in the Middle: Strengthening Education and Training for the Mid-Skilled Labor Force.* San Francisco: Jossey-Bass.

————. 1998. *Learning and Earning in the Middle: The Economic Benefits of Sub-Baccalaureate Education.* New York: Community College Research Center, Teachers College, Columbia University.

Grubb, W. Norton, Norena Badway, Denise Bell, Debra Bragg, and Maxine Russman. 1997. *Workforce, Economic, and Community Development: The Changing Landscape of the 'Entrepreneurial' Community College.* Mission Viejo, CA: League for Innovation in the Community College.

Karabel, Jerome. 1972. "Community Colleges and Social Stratification." *Harvard Educational Review* 42:521–562.

Lee, Valerie E., Christopher Mackie-Lewis, and Helen M. Marks. 1993. "Persistence to the Baccalaureate Degree for Students Who Transfer from Community College." *American Journal of Education* 102:80–114.

London, Howard B. 1978. *The Culture of a Community College.* New York: Praeger.

Pascarella, Ernest T., and Patrick T. Terenzini. 1991. *How College Affects Students.* San Francisco: Jossey-Bass.

Pascarella, Ernest T., and Louise Bohr, Amaury Nora, and Patrick Terenzini. 1995. "Cognitive Effects of 2-Year and 4-Year Colleges: New Evidence." *Educational Evaluation and Policy Analysis* 17:83–96.

Pascarella, Ernest T., and Marcia Edison, Amaury Nora, Linda Hagedorn, and Patrick Terenzini. 1996. "Cognitive Effects of Attending Community Colleges." *Community College Journal* Dec.–Jan.:35–39.

Pincus, Fred L. 1974. "Tracking in Community Colleges." *Insurgent Sociologist* 4:17–35.

————. 1980. "The False Promises of Community Colleges: Class Conflict and Vocational Education." *Harvard Educational Review* 50:332–361.

————. 1989. "Contradictory Effects of Customized Contract Training in Community Colleges." *Critical Sociology* 6:77–93.

Shaw, Kathleen M. 1997. "Remedial Education as Ideological Battleground: Emerging Remedial Education Policies in the Community College." *Educational Evaluation and Policy Analysis* 19:284–296.

Shaw, Kathleen M., and Howard B. London. 1998. "The Interplay between Ideology, Culture, and Educational Mobility: A Typology of Urban Community Colleges with High Transfer Rates." AERA presentation. Philadelphia, PA: Temple University, School of Education.

United States National Center for Education Statistics. 1997. *The Condition of Education, 1997.* Washington, DC: U.S. Government Printing Office.

————. 1999. *Digest of Education Statistics, 1998.* NCES 99–036. Washington, DC: U.S. Government Printing Office.

Whitaker, David G., and Ernest L. Pascarella. 1994. "Two-Year College Attendance and Socioeconomic Attainment." *Journal of Higher Education* 65:194–210.

Zwerling, L. Steven. 1976. *Second Best: The Crisis of the Junior College.* New York: McGraw-Hill.

CONFLICT THEORY

Christopher J. Hurn
University of Massachusetts–Amherst

Are human societies generally characterized by harmony and order or marked by continual conflict? And if both order and conflict are present virtually everywhere, which is the best starting point for further analysis? Does the appearance of conflict usually conceal a deeper agreement on the basic rules of the game, as when chess players, enemies on either side of the board, nonetheless freely subscribe to a set of binding rules about appropriate play. Or is it order and harmony that are superficial? Do we obey laws, or accept less than our equal share of valuable resources, not because we accept the fairness of the social order, but because we fear the consequences of our disobedience or rebellion. Are revolutions relatively rare in human society because most people regard the status quo, perhaps not as entirely just, but as a taken for granted reality, or is it the case that most are cowed by the threat of force or intimidated by the superior organization of their rulers?

If questions of this kind have preoccupied thinkers since Greek times, systematic answers date back only to the nineteenth century, particularly to the work of the founding giants of sociology: Marx, Weber, and Durkheim. The lives of these men roughly coincided, or followed shortly after, an unprecedented transformation of human society: the development of an industrial society powered by the rapid expansion of capitalism, and the disappearance, at least in the West, of the last remnants of feudal society: the rule of kings and aristocrats, and strong convictions that those who ruled had a God given right to power. None of them doubted that this transformation brought with it increased, or at least more overt conflict, both in the form of political rebellion and increased clashes between social classes. The crucial issue, however, was whether

these conflicts were, as Durkheim believed, part of a relatively short transitional phase toward a truly modern industrial order, or a permanent feature of modern society. For Durkheim, and for his contemporary followers, the bitter class conflicts of the nineteenth century flowed from the incomplete evolution of a new basis for justifying inequality and political authority: the replacement of hereditary justification by the principle of equality of opportunity, and a belief in "natural" inequality by a belief in the people's right to rule themselves through democratic elections. Durkheim believed that industrialization and specialization would soon reduce systematic conflict, particularly on class lines, as new rules regulating relationships between managers and workers evolved and new opportunities were created by the spread of mass education (Durkheim, 1933). Durkheim was no utopian thinker: he argued that one of the major costs of that transformation was the loss of meaning and purpose in individual lives because of the weakening of traditional religious injunctions and increasing mobility. But he did not envisage increasing conflict as a long-term characteristic of the contemporary social order.

Marx's argument was radically different. Not only did he believe that class conflict would steadily increase to the point that capitalism itself would be overthrown, he projected his theory of class conflict backward through history. Virtually all historians, he argued, had misperceived (in part because they themselves were members of the privileged groups) the fundamental conflicts between classes that had occurred throughout history, whether they were conflicts between slaves and free men in ancient Rome, clashes between peasants and feudal lords in the Middle Ages, or class conflicts between factory workers and owners in the mid-nineteenth century. The difference between the present and the past, Marx argued, was that whereas today increasing numbers of individuals correctly perceived their exploitation at the hands of capitalists, in the past "false consciousness" almost universally prevailed: beliefs in the divine right of kings and the natural superiority of aristocrats, for example, were effective in preventing massive rebellion. False consciousness was still important, Marx believed, but both his own theory, which debunked the reigning ideology, and the increasing misery of the masses would make conflict ever more intense until the final collapse of capitalism (Marx, 1946).

Weber's argument owed little to Durkheim, but was nonetheless fundamentally different and more pessimistic than Marx's theory. Agreeing with Marx that historians had greatly overestimated the degree of order and consensus in human societies, and conceding that economic inequalities were crucial to understanding that conflict, Weber argued that the abolition of capitalism would do little to reduce its incidence. The basic and stark inequalities of power and prestige, as well as income, would, Weber believed, remain a source of conflict in any future noncapitalist society. Every large-scale society contained groups who were struggling with one another for greater power and other, not necessarily identical groups, competing for honor and esteem. Even nominally democratic societies ultimately rested on the elite's monopoly of force; to the extent that order prevailed it was the result not of consensus on norms of appropriate behavior and ultimate values, but on the ultimate threat of violence (Weber, 1947).

It is not entirely true that the conflict theory of education was a product of the 1960s and 1970s. Willard Waller's classic book *The Sociology of Teaching,* published in 1932 (Waller, 1961), debunked conventional pieties about the identity of interest between teachers and students. Characterizing the classroom as a scene of almost continuous conflicts, Waller's skepticism about the possibility of attainment of progressive educational goals was hardly less cynical and pessimistic in its implications than Weber's analysis of the prospects for capitalist or socialist societies. As an antidote to the naiveté of much contemporary thought about what takes place in schools, Waller's work is hardly less valuable today than when it was published.

But although Waller's work anticipates some themes

of modern conflict theory, contemporary conflict theories of education were essentially shaped during the late 1960s and 1970s—an era in which almost all previous orthodoxies were challenged. The best way to grasp the main thrust of these ideas is to see them as an attack on two assumptions that still underlie much contemporary orthodox thought about education.

The first assumption is that schools are, in principle if not always in practice, meritocratic institutions. Of course, talented young students from less prestigious backgrounds do not always do well in school and go on to careers in professional occupations, anymore than the untalented children of the more privileged always experience downward mobility. But a society in which jobs are increasingly allocated on the basis of educational credentials is nonetheless inherently more meritocratic than a society where status is assigned primarily on the basis of heredity. Thus schools do not reinforce inequality; to a limited degree, they can compensate for the handicaps of low-status origins. The second assumption is that what schools teach is a combination of knowledge, skills, and values that is in a broad sense ideologically neutral (Clark, 1961). Modern societies, this argument goes, require high levels of general cognitive skills among the population, they also require, as Durkheim maintained at the beginning of the century, a consensus on broadly defined goals and means for achieving them. What schools teach reflects that consensus, and they also reinforce it.

Conflict theorists reject the meritocratic argument. Schools, they argue, reinforce, or as Bowles and Gintis put it, "reproduce" inequality (Bowles and Gintis, 1976). Indeed they are, with the possible exception of families, the major mechanism by which this takes place. The very large differences in the outcomes of schooling for students from different social origins do not arise from differences in ability, nor, for the most part, from the impact of childhood environments on the development of intelligence in the first few years of life. Schools, rather, systematically reinforce and add to initial inequalities because, ultimately, they serve the interest of those who hold the greatest power and wealth.

The simplest version of this argument goes as follows: inequalities in outcomes are the result of differential resources allocated to different kinds of schools. Privileged children attend schools with smaller classes and better teachers; these inequalities, in turn, are a product of school financing practices (local school financing), which reflect the vested interest of high-status groups. What makes this view too simple, however, is that a great deal of research concludes that relationships between student performance and school expenditures are quite weak. Class size, teacher salaries, the overall expenditure per pupil: none of these bears a close relationship to measures of student learning (Coleman et al., 1966).

A second line of argument focuses on processes within schools as the major mechanism through which unequal outcomes are produced. Here the interest shifts first, to the differential expectations that teachers have of students from different social origins—expectations that are often formed on the basis of appearance and manners rather than measurable competence in school work. Teachers may not be consciously biased against students from low-status origins; they frequently assume, however, that deportment, dress, and demeanor are likely indicators of academic potential. And this interpretation is closely linked to work on streaming and tracking within schools. Once decisions on reading groups in elementary schools, or assignment to academic or vocational tracks in high schools are made, the performance of students further diverges. Low-status students assigned to slow reading groups receive less opportunities to practice reading, whereas those assigned to the non-college preparatory curriculum receive less instruction in academic subjects. Thus initial differences between students, which may be quite small, are magnified by these practices: students in different tracks or streams come to be defined, and to some extent define themselves, as "able" or "slow," "college material" or potential "drop-outs." Schools, as one theorist argued, are engaged in Making Inequality (Rosenbaum, 1976).

Some conflict theorists push this argument further. Grades, rather than being assigned on the basis of objective performance, are closely linked to styles of self-presentation and behavior, which are associated with class or ethnic origins. Tests of ability [see Hurn (I.Q.), in this volume] do not measure "intelligence" in some pure cross-cultural sense, but merely the aptitudes associated with success in school. Indeed widely held beliefs that grades and IQ scores represent objective indicators of school performance and general intellectual

ability work to obscure the true character of educational selection: that schools work to reproduce inequalities from generation to generation rather than creating opportunities for talented but low-status children. Schools, and the educational system in general, help create what Marx called "false consciousness": in this case, the myth of a meritocratic society where all have an equal chance (Willis, 1981).

If the arguments I have described fit more closely with Marx's wing of conflict theory—though it should be recognized that an emphasis upon the inequalities produced by tracking are not necessarily indicative of Marx's influence—Weber's work provides the main inspiration for conflict theories, which attack conventional views of the relationship between educational qualifications and jobs, and, in particular, the assumption that the complexity of work in modern society requires ever increasing levels of schooling. Early in the twentieth century Weber described what he characterized as the growing "tyranny" of educational credentials as a prerequisite for high-status positions. Randall Collins, one of the more prominent of modern conflict theorists, elaborates this idea into a full scale critique of what he calls The Credential Society (Collins, 1979). Collins argues that educational qualifications have expanded far more rapidly in the past few decades than the number of jobs that can reasonably be said to require complex skills. The result is "credential inflation": a process whereby rapidly increasing levels of educational qualifications are required for any given occupation, including many whose skills can be learned in a few months. Collins is skeptical of claims that most jobs in modern society require complex cognitive skills for their effective performance; he is even more skeptical that the schools' primary effect is to teach these skills. Much of what is learned in schools, Collins argues, is quickly forgotten; it is also of dubious relevance to the effective performance of most jobs. What schools do provide, he argues, is membership in a particular status culture: distinctive styles of self-presentation, manners, and even tastes and interests. Thus high-status occupations—Wall Street law firms for example—hire Harvard law students not because they are either more able or know more law than graduates from lesser schools, but because the graduates of the most prestigious schools share the same status culture as the members of the firm. The nonmeritocratic nature of this recruitment is concealed by official rhetoric, particularly on ceremonial occasions, stressing that "ability" and "motivation" or "character" are the crucial elements in the exceptional success of graduates of high-status institutions.

The inflation of educational credentials, Collins believes, is driven by powerful vested interests. On the one hand, employers have interests in enhancing their power and prestige by raising educational entry requirements for the jobs under their control. Thus funeral directors, for example, can claim more professional status and, perhaps, justify higher fees, by recruiting entrants who are graduates of funeral science programs. At the same time educational institutions benefit by increased enrollments and corporate support, whether for new programs in "Hotel, Restaurant or Travel Administration," or in "Sports Management." This credential inflation can then be "sold" to the public as a necessary response to the increasing complexity of work in these fields.

If the expansion of education is driven by status competition rather than the increasing complexity of work, it is, of course, by no means a vehicle for increasing upward mobility. In the contest for educational credentials low-status groups face substantial handicaps. They lack what Bourdieu (1977) calls "cultural capital": styles of self-presentation and tastes that high-status groups employ to impress others. They also may suffer from the illusion that a particular level of educational qualifications can give them entry to the same occupation today that it provided in the previous generation. But does the fact that, for example, rates of high school graduation among low-status students are now only slightly below those of middle class students not mean that their opportunities for upward mobility

have improved? The same occupation that used to require only high school graduation now may require 2 years of college; many jobs formerly opened to college graduates now require a masters degree. Thus the increasing linkage between educational qualifications and jobs, and what appear to be expanding educational opportunities, does little or nothing to diminish the importance of inherited inequalities. Schools remain today what they have been in the past (and to a large extent must be in modern society), institutions that help to legitimize the existing highly unequal social order. Not only do they reproduce inequality, they are perhaps the most important way of justifying that inequality and thus concealing its true character.

REFERENCES

Bourdieu, Pierre. 1977. *Reproduction*. Beverly Hills, CA: Sage.

Bowles, Samuel, and Herbert Gintis.1976. *Schooling in Capitalist America*. New York: Basic Books.

Clark, Burton. 1961. *Educating the Expert Society*. San Francisco: Chandler.

Coleman, James, et al. 1966. *Equality of Educational Opportunity*. Washington, DC: U.S. Government.

Collins, Randall. 1979. *The Credential Society*. New York: Academic Press.

Durkheim, Emile. 1933. *Capital*. New York: Modern Library.

Marx, Karl. 1946. *The Division of Labor in Society*. New York: Macmillan.

Rosenbaum, James E. 1976. *Making Inequality*. New York: Wiley.

Waller, Willard. 1961. *The Sociology of Teaching*. New York: Wiley.

Weber, Max. 1947. *The Theory of Social and Economic Organization*. New York: Free Press.

Willis, Paul. 1981. *Learning to Labor*. New York: Columbia University Press.

Cooperative Learning in Elementary and Secondary Schools[1]

Robert E. Slavin
Johns Hopkins University

Cooperative learning methods are instructional techniques in which students work in small groups to help one another master academic content or carry out group projects. The use of cooperative learning is based on motivational as well as cognitive theories (see Slavin, 1995a, 1996). Motivational theories emphasize the idea that in groups working toward a common goal, students support one another's academic efforts, because each group member's success helps the group to succeed. Cognitive theories emphasize opportunities for collaborating students to model higher order solutions for one another, and to provide immediate, context-appropriate explanations and feedback to one another.

Cooperative learning methods are becoming very widely used in elementary and secondary schools. A recent national survey (Puma et al., 1993) found that 79% of elementary teachers and 62% of middle school teachers reported making some sustained use of cooperative learning.

There are many quite different forms of cooperative learning that have been studied in classroom experiments. This chapter describes the cooperative learning programs that have been most extensively studied in elementary and secondary schools and summarizes the outcomes of these studies.

Student Team Learning

Student Team Learning methods are cooperative learning techniques developed and researched at Johns Hopkins University. More than half of all experimental studies of practical cooperative learning methods involve Student Team Learning methods.

All cooperative learning methods share the idea that students work together to learn and are responsible for one another's learning as well as their own. In addition to the idea of cooperative work, Student Team Learning methods emphasize the use of team goals and team success, which can be achieved only if all members of the team learn the objectives being taught. That is, in Student Team Learning the students' tasks are not to *do* something as a team but to *learn* something as a team.

Three concepts are central to all Student Team Learning methods: *team rewards, individual accountability, and equal opportunities for success*. In these techniques, teams may earn certificates or other *team rewards* if they achieve above a designated criterion. Grades are not given based on team performance, but in senior high schools students may sometimes qualify for as many as five bonus points (on a hundred-point scale) if their teams meet a high criterion of excellence. The teams are not in competition to earn scarce rewards; all (or none) of the teams may achieve the criterion in a given week. *Individual accountability* means that the team's success depends on the individual learning of all team members. This focuses the activity of the team members on tutoring one another and making sure that everyone on the team is ready for a quiz or other assessment that students will take without teammate help. *Equal opportunities for success* means

[1] This article was written under funding from the Office of Educational Research and Improvement, U.S. Department of Education (No. OERI-R-117–40005). However, any opinions expressed are those of the author and do not necessarily represent OERI positions or policies.

that students contribute to their teams by improving over their own past performance. This ensures that high, average, and low achievers are equally challenged to do their best, and the contributions of all team members will be valued.

Research on cooperative learning methods (summarized below) has indicated that team rewards and individual accountability are essential elements for producing basic skills achievement (Slavin, 1995a). It is not enough to simply tell students to work together. They must have a reason to take one another's achievement seriously. Further, research indicates that if students are rewarded for doing better than they have in the past, they will be more motivated to achieve than if they are rewarded based on their performance in comparison to others, because rewards for improvement make success neither too difficult nor to easy for students to achieve.

Three principal Student Team Learning methods have been extensively developed and researched: Student Teams—Achievement Divisions, or STAD, and Teams-Games-Tournament, or TGT, and Cooperative Integrated Reading and Composition (CIRC), which is used in reading and writing instruction in grades 3–7.

Student Teams—Achievement Divisions (STAD)

In STAD (Slavin, 1994), students are assigned to four-member learning teams that are mixed in performance level, sex, and ethnicity. The teacher presents a lesson, and then students work within their teams to make sure that all team members have mastered the lesson. Finally, all students take individual quizzes on the material, at which time they may not help one another.

Students' quiz scores are compared to their own past averages, and points are awarded based on the degree to which students can meet or exceed their own earlier performance. These points are then summed to form team scores, and teams that meet certain criteria may earn certificates or other recognition. The whole cycle of activities, from teacher presentation to team practice to quiz, usually takes three to five class periods.

STAD has been used in a wide variety of subjects, from mathematics to language arts to social studies, and has been used from grade two through college. It is most appropriate for teaching well-defined objectives with single right answers, such as mathematical computations and applications, language usage and mechanics, geography and map skills, and science facts and concepts.

Teams-Games-Tournament (TGT)

Teams-Games-Tournament (DeVries and Slavin, 1978; Slavin, 1994) was the first of the Johns Hopkins cooperative learning methods. It uses the same teacher presentations and team work as in STAD, but replaces the quizzes with weekly tournaments, in which students compete with members of other teams to contribute points to their team scores. Students compete at three-person "tournament tables" against others with similar past records in mathematics. A "bumping" procedure keeps the competition fair. The winner at each tournament table brings the same number of points to his or her team, regardless of which table it is; this means that low achievers (competing with other low achievers) and high achievers (competing with other high achievers) have equal opportunities for success. As in STAD, high-performing teams earn certificates or other forms of team recognition.

Cooperative Integrated Reading and Composition (CIRC)

CIRC is a comprehensive program for teaching reading and writing in the upper elementary and middle grades (Stevens et al., 1987). In CIRC, students are assigned to teams composed of pairs of students from different reading groups. While the teacher is working with one reading group, students in the other groups are working in their pairs on a series of cognitively engaging activities, including reading to one another, making predictions about how narrative stories will come out, summarizing stories to one another, writing responses to stories, and practicing spelling, decoding, and vocabulary. If the reading class is not divided into homogeneous reading groups, all students in the teams work with one another. Students work as a total team to master main idea and other comprehension skills. During language arts periods, students engage in writing drafts, revising and editing one another's work, and preparing for "publication" of team books.

In most CIRC activities, students follow a sequence of teacher instruction, team practice, team preassessments, and quizzes. That is, students do not take the quiz until their teammates have determined that they are ready. Certificates are given to teams based on the average performance of all team members on all reading and writing activities.

CIRC is mostly used in elementary schools, but is

often used in the early middle grades and has been studied at that level by Stevens and Durkin (1992).

Jigsaw

Jigsaw was originally designed by Elliot Aronson and his colleagues (Aronson et al., 1978). In Aronson's Jigsaw method, students are assigned to six-member teams to work on academic material that has been broken down into sections. For example, a biography might be divided into early life, first accomplishments, major setbacks, later life, and impact on history. Each team member reads his or her section. Next, members of different teams who have studied the same sections meet in "expert groups" to discuss their sections. Then the students return to their teams and take turns teaching their teammates about their sections. Since the only way students can learn sections other than their own is to listen carefully to their teammates, they are motivated to support and show interest in one another's work.

Slavin (1994) developed a modification of Jigsaw and incorporated it in the Student Team Learning program. In this method, called Jigsaw II, students work in four- or five-member teams as in TGT and STAD. Instead of each student being assigned a unique section, all students read a common narrative, such as a book chapter, a short story, or a biography. However, each student receives a topic on which to become an expert. Students with the same topics meet in expert groups to discuss them, after which they return to their teams to teach what they have learned to their teammates. Then students take individual quizzes, which result in team scores based on the improvement score system of STAD. Teams that meet preset standards may earn certificates.

Learning Together

David and Roger Johnson at the University of Minnesota developed the Learning Together model of cooperative learning (Johnson and Johnson, 1994). The methods they have researched involve students working in four- or five-member heterogeneous groups on assignment sheets. The groups hand in a single sheet, and receive praise and rewards based on the group product. Their methods emphasize teambuilding activities before students begin working together and regular discussions within groups about how well they are working together.

Group Investigation

Group Investigation, developed by Shlomo Sharan at the University of Tel-Aviv (Sharan and Sharan, 1992), is a general classroom organization plan in which students work in small groups using cooperative inquiry, group discussion, and cooperative planning and projects. In this method, students form their own two- to six-member groups. After choosing subtopics from a unit being studied by the entire class, the groups further break their subtopics into individual tasks, and carry out the activities necessary to prepare group reports. Each group then makes a presentation or display to communicate its findings to the entire class.

Research on Cooperative Learning

A recent review of research on cooperative learning (Slavin, 1995a) identified 99 studies conducted over periods of at least 4 weeks in regular elementary and secondary schools that have measured effects on student achievement. These studies all compared effects of cooperative learning to those of traditionally taught control groups on measures of the same objectives pursued in all classes. Teachers and classes were either randomly assigned to cooperative or control conditions, or they were matched on pretest achievement level and other factors.

Academic Achievement

Overall, of 99 studies of the achievement effects of cooperative learning, 63 have found significantly greater achievement in cooperative than in control classes. Thirty-one found no differences, and in only five studies did a control group significantly outperform the experimental group. However, the effects of cooperative learning vary considerably according to the particular methods used. As noted earlier, two elements must be present if cooperative learning is to be effective: *group goals* and *individual accountability* (Slavin, 1983a, 1983b, 1995a). That is, groups must be working to achieve some goal or earn rewards or recognition, and the success of the group must depend on the individual learning of every group member. In studies of methods of this kind (e.g., STAD, TGT, CIRC), effects on achievement have been consistently positive; 50 out of 64 such studies (78%) found significantly positive achievement effects. In contrast, only 13 out of 35 studies (37%) of cooperative methods lacking group goals and individual accountability found positive effects on student achievement, and five found higher scores in control groups.

Cooperative learning methods generally work equally well for all types of students. Although occasional studies find particular advantages for high or low achievers, boys or girls, and so on, the great majority find equal benefits for all types of students. Sometimes a concern is expressed that cooperative learning will hold back high achievers. The research provides absolutely no support for this claim; high achievers gain from cooperative learning (relative to high achievers in traditional classes) just as much as do low and average achievers (Slavin, 1991).

Intergroup Relations

Social scientists have long advocated interethnic cooperation as a means of ensuring positive intergroup relations in desegregated settings. Contact theory (Allport, 1954), the dominant theory of intergroup relations for many years, predicted that positive intergroup relations would rise from school desegregation if and only if students were involved in cooperative, equal-status interaction sanctioned by the school. Research on cooperative learning methods has borne out the predictions of contact theory. These techniques emphasize cooperative, equal-status interaction between students of different ethnic backgrounds sanctioned by the school (Slavin, 1995b). In most of the research on intergroup relations, students were asked to list their best friends at the beginning of the study and again at the end. The number of friendship choices students made outside their own ethnic groups was the measure of intergroup relations. Positive effects on intergroup relations in secondary schools have been found for STAD, TGT, Jigsaw, Learning Together, and Group Investigation models (Slavin, 1995a, 1995b).

Two of these studies, one on STAD (Slavin, 1979) and one on Jigsaw II (Ziegler, 1981), included followups of intergroup friendships several months after the end of the studies. Both found that students who had been in cooperative learning classes still named significantly more friends outside their own ethnic groups than did students who had been in control classes. Two studies of Group Investigation (Sharan et al., 1984; Sharan and Shachar, 1988) found that students' improved attitudes and behaviors toward classmates of different ethnic backgrounds extended to classmates who had never been in the same groups.

Self-Esteem

Students in cooperative learning classes have been found to have more positive feelings about themselves than do students in traditional classes. These improvements in self-esteem have been found for TGT and STAD (Slavin, 1995a), for Jigsaw (Blaney et al., 1977), and for the three methods combined (Slavin and Karweit, 1981).

Other Outcomes

In addition to effects on achievement, positive intergroup relations, greater acceptance of mainstreamed students, and self-esteem, effects of cooperative learning have been found on a variety of other important educational outcomes. These include liking of school, development of peer norms in favor of doing well academically, feelings of individual control over the student's own fate in school, and cooperativeness and altruism (see Slavin, 1995a). TGT (DeVries and Slavin, 1978) and STAD (Slavin, 1995a; Janke, 1978) have been found to have positive effects on students' time on-task. A study in the Kansas City (Missouri) schools found that lower socioeconomic-status students at risk of becoming delinquent who worked in cooperative groups in sixth grade had better attendance, fewer contacts with the police, and higher behavioral ratings by teachers in seventh through eleventh grades than did control students (Hartley, 1976). A year-long study of TGT and STAD in middle schools by Hawkins et al. (1988) found that low achievers who experienced cooperative learning had fewer suspensions and expulsions than did control students, and gained more in educational aspirations and attitudes toward school.

Conclusion

Research on cooperative learning methods in elementary and secondary schools supports the usefulness of these strategies for improving such diverse outcomes as student achievement at a variety of grade levels and in many subjects, intergroup relations, and student self-esteem. Cooperative learning, especially when groups are rewarded based on the individual learning of all group members, gives students a degree of independence and authority within their groups, and sets up a situation in which progress of each group member contributes to the success of his or her peers, thereby creating peer norms favoring academic excellence. Cooperative learning is not a panacea for all of the problems of education, but it can provide a means of harnessing students' peer-oriented energies for prosocial activities, and helping all students to gain access to the best thinking of their peers. With appropriate training and supports, cooperative methods can be used in any instructional context and should be a part of every teacher's repertoire.

REFERENCES

Allport, G. 1954. *The Nature of Prejudice.* Cambridge, MA: Addison-Wesley.

Aronson, E., N. Blaney, C. Stephan, J. Sikes, and M. Snapp. 1978. *The Jigsaw Classroom.* Beverly Hills, CA: Sage.

Blaney, N.T., S. Stephan, D. Rosenfeld, E. Aronson, and J. Sikes. 1977. "Interdependence in the Classroom: A Field Study." *Journal of Educational Psychology* 69:121–128.

Cooper, L., D.W. Johnson, R. Johnson, and F. Wilderson. 1980. "Effects of Cooperative, Competitive and Individualistic Experiences on Interpersonal Attraction Among Heterogeneous Peers." *Journal of Social Psychology* 111: 243–252.

DeVries, D. L., and R. E. Slavin. 1978. "Teams-Games-Tournament (TGT): Review of Ten Classroom Experiments." *Journal of Research and Development in Education* 12:28–38.

Hartley, W. 1976. "Prevention Outcomes of Small Group Education with School Children: An Epidemiologic Follow-up of the Kansas City School Behavior Project." Unpublished manuscript, University of Kansas Medical Center.

Hawkins, J. D., H. J. Doueck, and D. M. Lishner. 1988. "Changing Teacher Practices in Mainstream Classrooms to Improve Bonding and Behavior of Low Achievers." *American Educational Research Journal* 25:31–50.

Janke, R. 1978. "The Teams-Games-Tournament (TGT) Method and the Behavioral Adjustment and Academic Achievement of Emotionally Impaired Adolescents." Paper presented at the annual convention of the American Educational Research Association, Toronto, April.

Johnson, D. W., and R. T. Johnson. 1994. *Learning Together and Alone,* 4th ed. Boston: Allyn & Bacon.

Puma, M. J., C. C. Jones, D. Rock, and R. Fernandez. 1993. *Prospects: The Congressionally Mandated Study of Educational Growth and Opportunity*. Interim Report. Bethesda, MD: Abt Associates.

Sharan, S., and C. Shachar. 1988. *Language and Learning in the Cooperative Classroom*. New York: Springer.

Sharan, Y., and S. Sharan. 1992. *Group Investigation: Expanding Cooperative Learning*. New York: Teacher's College Press.

Sharan, S., P. Kussell, R. Hertz-Lazarowitz, Y. Bejarano, S. Raviv, and Y. Sharan. 1984. *Cooperative Learning in the Classroom: Research in Desegregated Schools*. Hillsdale, NJ: Erlbaum.

Slavin, R. E. 1979. "Effects of Biracial Learning Teams on Cross-Racial Friendships. *Journal of Educational Psychology* 71:381–387.

———. 1983a. *Cooperative Learning*. New York: Longman.

———. 1983b. "When Does Cooperative Learning Increase Student Achievement?" *Psychological Bulletin* 94:429–445.

———. 1991. "Are Cooperative Learning and Untracking Harmful to the Gifted?" *Educational Leadership* 48(6):68–71.

———. 1994. *Using Student Team Learning*, 4th ed. Baltimore: Johns Hopkins University, Center for Social Organization of Schools.

———. 1995a. *Cooperative Learning: Theory, Research, and Practice,* 2nd ed. Boston: Allyn & Bacon.

———. 1995b. "Cooperative Learning and Intergroup Relations." In J. Banks (ed.), *Handbook of Research on Multicultural Education* pp. 628–634. New York: Macmillan.

———. 1996. "Research on Cooperative Learning and Achievement: What We Know, What We Need to Know." *Contemporary Educational Psychology* 21(1):43–69.

Slavin, R. E., and N. Karweit. 1981. Cognitive and Affective Outcomes of an Intensive Student Team Learning Experience. *Journal of Experimental Education* 50:29–35.

Stevens, R. J., and S. Durkin. 1992. *Using Student Team Reading and Student Team Writing in Middle Schools: Two Evaluations.* (Tech. Rep. No. 36). Baltimore: Johns Hopkins University, Center for Research on Effective Schooling for Disadvantaged Students.

Stevens, R. J., N. A. Madden, R. E. Slavin, and A. M. Farnish. 1987. "Cooperative Integrated Reading and Composition: Two Field Experiments." *Reading Research Quarterly* 22:433–454.

Ziegler, S. 1981. "The Effectiveness of Cooperative Learning Teams for Increasing Cross-Ethnic Friendship: Additional Evidence." *Human Organization* 40:264–268.

CULTURAL CAPITAL

Timothy J. Madigan
Shippensburg University

The French social theorist and researcher Pierre Bourdieu is interested in how capitalist class society reproduces itself and has been spanning theoretical traditions in his exploration of this issue. He has written extensively about how, in more general terms, systems of power maintain themselves through the transmission of culture. The concept of cultural capital occupies a critical position in his work.

What is Cultural Capital?

Various forms of capital, or accumulated labor, exist in society. They have in common the potential capacity to produce profits and to reproduce the system of social hierarchies. In economics, human capital is traditionally thought of as investments a person makes in his or herself that can be translated into profits in the market. In sociology, social capital is described by Bourdieu as investments a person makes through forming and maintaining networks with other people that when called upon provide information, advice, access, etc. More broadly, cultural capital is seen by Bourdieu as cultural practices or dispositions a person acquires often through disguised or hidden ways that realize profits in the economic field primarily through ensuring academic success.

In its embodied state, cultural capital can be represented by "highbrow" cultural dispositions, knowledge, and practices such as familiarity with classical artists or regular patronage of museums or the theater. Cultural capital can also be represented by the ability to identify composers and pieces of classical music or to play a "noble" instrument such as the piano. People who possess a substantial amount of cultural capital are more likely to evidence these dispositions or knowledge, or in other words, to display exceptional taste.

In its objectified state, cultural capital can be represented by a person's collection of paintings, classical books, monuments, instruments, etc. The value of cultural capital in this state goes beyond the actual monetary value of the item(s) itself. Bourdieu argues that its very existence provides an educational element to the environment by inculcating schemes of perception and appreciation. It also allows a display of mastery over a realm of the social world since the act of collecting cultural capital requires appropriate (rare) dispositions and competencies. Cultural capital in this form represents objectified evidence of conspicuous spending and personal taste.

Cultural capital can be objectified in the form of academic qualifications. Bourdieu calls this form institutionalized cultural capital. High educational credentials are usually a good indicator that a person's dispositions and knowledge match those of the dominant class. Certificates, educational qualifications, and recruitment exams have power in that they impose collective recognition of hierarchy. Institutional recognition also ensures that cultural capital can be converted into economic capital.

Where and How Is Cultural Capital Obtained?

A child in the dominant class learns or acquires highbrow interests mainly through socialization in his or her family. This form of cultural capital can be acquired unconsciously or without explicit inculcation through repeated and prolonged contact with cultured people and cultural works. Over time, cultural capital is turned into a habitus, or durable schemes of perception and action (permanent dispositions). For example, particular pronunciations learned in the family such as Oxford or Paris accents separate and distinguish one person from another.

Why are children in the dominant class more likely to acquire cultural capital? Families in the dominant class are more likely to be free from economic necessity. This freedom allows its members to explore and organize diversities in many practices, to mount a stylization of life. Thus, children from such families are predisposed toward symbolic mastery of operations, whether it is the decoding of a work of art or of a mathematical function. In contrast, children from working class families lead a life dominated by meeting everyday urgencies, and as a result, do not develop comparable competencies.

For children whose social origins and, as a consequence, dispositions are not of the dominant class, schools contribute to inculcating values and dispositions in line with the dominant culture. Hence, correlations can be found, according to Bourdieu, between competence in music or painting and academic capital. Schools help students acquire more "classical" and safer cultural capital, types that are not on the fringe of interest and exploration by the bourgeois. Bourdieu argues that primary and secondary teachers from working class or middle class backgrounds owe most of their cultural capital to the educational system.

The acquisition of cultural capital in the family or school takes time, effort, sacrifice, and ingenuity. Unlike economic capital, it is not something that can be given to someone in a moment's notice or in a day's time. When the possessor of cultural capital passes away, his or her cultural capital cannot be given to someone else. It goes with them to the grave.

How Does Cultural Capital Tie in with the Idea of Social Reproduction?

Recurrent throughout the writings of Bourdieu are themes of power, dominance, and struggle. Within every social field people struggle to create social distinctions, to separate themselves from that which is easy, general, or popular. Out of the ordinary, everyday, social world evolves sacred objects and distinctive ways of thinking and behaving. People aligned with this ex-

traordinary system of representing social reality possess power because their frame of representation survives the competition, rises above others, and shapes how people internalize the structure of social space. Ultimately, their system of classification shapes how people structure their lives. To maintain this power, people possessing alternative or contradictory ways of thinking (systems of meanings) are weeded out, passed over, attacked softly through symbolic violence, while those with matching ways are acknowledged and rewarded. This sorting and selecting is performed by a detached entity, or third party, according to Bourdieu, to help conceal the power relations that underlie the structure of social hierarchy.

The success of a person's struggle for access to the dominant class depends on their accumulated capital —cultural, economic, social, or symbolic. In particular, the extent to which their family background provided them with cultural capital shapes their likelihood of being selected to become inheritors of the positions of dominance. The profits a person receives for accumulating cultural capital are reaped when the social system reproduces itself and they become the dominant group.

The degree to which schools are successful in their attempts to educate a child depends on how much cultural capital was directly transmitted to the child by his or her family and how early the transmission occurred. Schools demand, more or less, what students from families high in cultural capital possess. Through administering degrees, therefore, the educational system regulates the conversion of cultural capital acquired in the family of origin into educational capital (which eventually produces economic capital). Educational capital guarantees cultural capital. School personnel reproduce social hierarchies, Bourdieu argues, while maintaining the appearance that they are certifying technical competencies or abilities.

What Are Some Examples of the Use of the Concept of Cultural Capital in Education Research?

Bourdieu found in his research that students in Paris who spoke with a Parisian accent were more likely to be selected for advanced educational opportunities. In his book, *Distinction*, Bourdieu (1984) identified doctors, lawyers, and private sector executives—occupations requiring a high level of education—as possessing the most economic and cultural capital. Secondary and higher education teachers had low amounts of economic capital and high amounts of cultural capital. Craftsmen, shopkeepers, farmers, and semi- or unskilled workers—those with lowest amounts of education—had the lowest amount of economic and cultural capital.

Research on status attainment in the United States has moved beyond treating parental job status and education as primary explanatory variables to focusing on the behaviors and dispositions of students. DiMaggio (1982, 1985) found cultural capital to positively predict grades, college enrollment, and degree completion of U.S. high school students. Cultural capital was represented by common variation among student responses to questionnaire items concerning reading of literature, attendance at arts events, acting or performing, interest in symphony concerts, and a cultivated self-image.

Moving away from high culture characteristics of students, Lareau (1987) looked at class-based tendencies of parents to participate in education of their offspring and interpreted it as a form of cultural capital. Although parents from both working and upper middle class backgrounds were involved in the schooling of their children, the latter parents had more information on schooling and were more likely to build social networks among other parents. These actions impacted on the educational experience of offspring (were turned into profit) by bringing parents and teachers into contact and by creating orientations to learning in and outside of school that were in line with the expectations held by the school.

Finally, McLaren (1989) interpreted his efforts to teach inner-city children in a reproduction framework. He vividly described instances of physical violence that required quick action and hostile parents who often made his job more difficult. He felt that his difficulties to communicate and motivate the disadvantaged students from minority groups, public housing, and broken families were due to his dissimilar white, middle class background. Although not admitting to being imbued in high culture, differences in cultural backgrounds led him to feel less comfortable with them, spend less instructional time with them, and encourage them less often to work in an independent manner compared to other students. Moreover, this cultural chasm did not occur while he worked in a suburban school at an earlier point in time.

What Are Some Critiques of the Cultural Capital Concept?

Collins (1979) argues that Bourdieu's reproduction argument does not disprove the technomeritocratic or biological inheritance interpretation of education. Indeed, DiMaggio encountered some difficulty in estimating the effect of cultural capital on grades of students because his measure of cultural "information" had too high a correlation with vocabulary test performance. Acquiring cultural information and performing well on vocabulary tests, he argued, may require the same aptitudes, skills, and dispositions.

Collins also argues that Bourdieu does not provide an historical explanation of the emergence of education, especially across societies. More recent work by Bourdieu, however, touches on this issue by noting the absence of cultural capital in simple, undifferentiated societies and by discussing the growth in proportions of French people who possess educational capital.

After reviewing the descriptions of cultural capital across a number of Bourdieu's works and finding various shades of meaning, LaMont and Lareau (1988) criticized the concept for being ambiguous. This ambiguity is partly responsible, they argue, for the contradictory findings of research on cultural capital. In addition to pointing out how shifty definitions lead to confusing research results, they question whether cultural capital can be useful for explaining social mobility in a society where a highly cultured elite does not seem as prevalent as in Paris, the home front of the cultural capital concept.

Summary

The concept of cultural capital is increasingly being used as a tool for investigating and explaining why students from the upper strata segments of U.S. society typically obtain more education than others. Its attractiveness is due in part to its encompassing applicability: it covers many educational processes in the home and at school, addresses the macro–micro issue in sociology, and incorporates themes from various theoretical perspectives ranging from microinteractionist to structuralist. In addition, because it is not described in exact, specific terms, perhaps more scholars are inclined to use it. Cultural capital may also derive a degree of popularity from being nested in a larger theoretical model that turns the traditional meritocratic explanation of social stratification upside down. The assets of a wide applicability and a unique, atypical approach to explaining social phenomena are also liabilities as some theorists misclassify or criticize his work and others apply the concept in ways contrary to how Bourdieu envisioned. The overall strength and utility of cultural capital at explaining educational stratification in the United States await deeper and more rigorous exploration and debate.

REFERENCES

Bourdieu, Pierre. 1973. "Cultural Reproduction and Social Reproduction." In R. Brown (ed.), *Knowledge and Change*. London: Tavistock.

———. 1977. *Outline of a Theory of Practice*. Cambridge: Cambridge University Press.

———. 1984. *Distinction*. Cambridge: Harvard University Press.

———. 1985. "Symbolic Violence and Cultural Capital." In Randal Collins (ed.), *Three Sociological Traditions*. New York: Oxford University Press.

———. 1988a. "The Forms of Capital." In J. G. Richardson (ed.), *Handbook of Theory and Research for the Sociology of Education*. Cambridge: Harvard University Press.

———. 1988b. "Social Space and Symbolic Power." *Sociological Theory* 7(1):14–25.

———. 1991. *Language and Symbolic Power*. Cambridge: Harvard University Press.

———. 1993. *Sociology in Question*. Beverly Hills, CA: Sage.

Bourdieu, Pierre, and Jean-Claude Passeron. 1977. *Reproduction in Education, Society, and Culture*. London: Sage.

Collins, Randal. 1979. *The Credential Society*. New York: Academic Press.

DiMaggio, Paul. 1982. "Cultural Capital and School Success: The Impact of Status Culture Participation on the Grades of U.S. High School Students." *American Sociological Review* 47:189–201.

DiMaggio, Paul, and J. Mohr. 1985. "Cultural Capital, Educational Attainment, and Marital Selection." *American Journal of Sociology* 90:1231–1261.

LaMont, Michele, and Annette Lareau. 1988. "Cultural Capital: Allusions, Gaps, and Glissandos in Recent Theoretical Developments." *Sociological Theory* 6:153–168.

Lareau, Annette. 1987. "Social Class Differences in Family-School Relationships: The Importance of Cultural Capital." *Sociology of Education* 60:73–85.

McLaren, Peter. 1989. *Life in Schools*. New York: Longman.

CURRICULUM

Adam Gamoran
University of Wisconsin–Madison

In conventional usage "curriculum" refers to a formal course of study, but many writers broaden the term to refer to the totality of a learner's experiences in an educational setting (see Jackson, 1992, for a full discussion of definitional issues). Among sociologists, curriculum has been a relatively neglected field of study, whether narrowly or broadly defined. Until recently, most sociologists avoided what was obvious about curriculum—such as subject matter content and the materials of instruction—despite the importance of these conditions for other aspects of education that are of sociological interest, including the organization and outcomes of schooling. Instead, sociological studies of curriculum initially focused on the latent or "hidden" aspects of curriculum that were communicated to students beneath the surface of the more obvious course of study. Beginning in the 1980s and increasingly in the 1990s, sociologists have discovered the importance of the overt or manifest curriculum, and the field appears to be expanding rapidly.

From the Hidden to the Overt Curriculum

A variety of researchers have examined the underlying meanings and messages that students encounter in their experiences in schools and classrooms. Dreeben (1968), for example, maintained that the structure of schools and classrooms helps socialize students to four norms: achievement (students are evaluated on the basis of performance); independence (the importance of working on one's own); universalism (the same rules apply to all); and specificity (the student–teacher relationship is specific to the classroom, and does not encompass the full range of a student's interests, activities, and personality). A very different approach was offered by Young (1971; Whitty and Young, 1976) and his colleagues, who argued that the materials and processes of classroom instruction socialize students toward conformity, obedience to authority, and competition, in support of the prevailing class system of society. According to this view, the ordinary activities in which teachers and students engage, such as reading, responding to questions, and taking tests, push students toward accepting their positions in the larger social order.

Despite theoretical and political differences, these two lines of work have important similarities. First, both recognize that the hidden curriculum of schooling provides socialization for the transition from the home and family to the world of work and the wider society. Second, both perspectives view the school as a mediator for prevailing norms. Third, both include individual effort and competitiveness as well as respect for authority figures as key attitudes in the home-to-work transition, although for Dreeben this socialization is politically neutral, whereas for Young and his colleagues it supports the prevailing political and economic system. Fourth, both arguments were originally put forth on conceptual grounds, with little systematic empirical corroboration. Following Young's approach, a few empirical case studies have supported and elaborated the theoretical formulation. Observing a comprehensive secondary school in Britain, Keddie (1971) showed that teachers' views of students in different ability levels, or "streams," affected the way they interacted with students and the extent to which students' ideas were legitimated in the classroom. Questions posed by A-stream students typically fit within the conceptual framework of the lesson, and they were treated as legitimate inquiries by teachers. In contrast, questions from C-stream students often challenged the assumptions of the lesson, and teachers dismissed them as irrelevant. Thus, students who rank higher in the school's hierarchy (typically, students from higher status origins) find their concerns and interests validated, while lower ranking students are left out.

Whereas Keddie revealed differences within schools in the impact of the hidden curriculum, Anyon (1981) found that the way knowledge is used also differs among schools located in varied social contexts. Exploring fifth-grade social studies classes in four schools, Anyon showed that knowledge presented in schools attended by working-class students was typically fragmented, "basic" facts and information, whereas students in a more affluent neighborhood school more often encountered activities that emphasized creativity and independent thought. Both Keddie's and Anyon's studies emphasize the role of curriculum in identifying and maintaining class differences. Similarly, Bowles and Gintis (1976) argued that the emphasis on conformity and obedience in high schools, which prepares young people for the capitalist workforce, contrasts with greater independence and creativity encouraged in college, where managers are trained. Apple (1983) has further maintained that the form of curriculum—the way ideas and knowledge are presented—serves the capitalist economic system by fragmenting and "deskilling" the knowledge and activities of teachers and students. Subsequent work in this tradition has upheld Young's (1971) formulation, mainly through new analyses of individual cases along the lines of those studied by Keddie and Anyon (e.g., Ball, 1981; Everhart, 1983; McNeil, 1983; Labaree, 1986).

Although these studies focused on the relation between the curriculum and socialization for life outside schools, sociologists interested in student achievement began to notice the central role of curriculum in the academic learning process. Dreeben (Barr and Dreeben, 1983) was one of the first to place the connection between curriculum and achievement in a sociological framework.

In light of his earlier conclusion that "what is learned in school" consists of socialization for adult life, it is interesting to note Dreeben's recognition that concrete information and skills—e.g., how to read and write—are also learned in school. Just as the hidden curriculum plays an important role in socialization, the overt or manifest curriculum, consisting of textbooks, lesson plans, exercises, content coverage, and so on, is crucial for establishing the conditions under which content learning occurs. Whereas educational researchers had earlier recognized the connection between curricular content and learning (e.g., Barr, 1975; Walker and Shaffarzick, 1974), Barr and Dreeben (1983) placed this relation in the context of classroom and school organization. Content coverage—that is, the coverage of curricular materials—is responsive to the composition of the class, instructional materials that are available to the teacher, time available for instruction, and the teacher's preferences and skills (Barr and Dreeben, 1983; Gamoran and Dreeben, 1986). In turn, content coverage is a key predictor of student learning (Barr and Dreeben, 1983; Rowan and Miracle, 1983; Dreeben and Gamoran, 1986).

In their study of first grade reading, Barr and Dreeben (1983) noted that students did not all have access to the same reading curriculum. In particular, students assigned to different reading groups—which were created on the basis of students' varied reading "readiness" at the beginning of first grade—differed in the pace at which new words were introduced. These differences in curricular exposure accounted for differences among students in their reading skills at the end of the year, after taking account of variation in reading readiness at the beginning of the year. Thus, differential access to curriculum explained varied outcomes among students within classes. These findings addressed a topic of longstanding sociological interest: curriculum differentiation.

Curriculum Differentiation

It is well established that students enrolled in different high school curricular programs such as the academic, vocational, and general tracks differ in the amount of schooling they obtain. Students in academic tracks are more likely to attend college and, overall, obtain more years of schooling, even among those with similar grades and test scores at the end of high school (see Gamoran and Berends, 1987, for a review). Because track assignment is correlated with socioeconomic background, tracking tends to magnify inequality of educational attainment by social origins (Heyns, 1974;

Gamoran and Mare, 1989). High school tracking also reinforces achievement differences that students bring with them to school (see Gamoran and Berends, 1987, and Oakes et al., 1992, for reviews).

Survey studies of curriculum tracking grew out of the larger literature on status transmission (e.g., Blau and Duncan, 1967), and they received a major boost from the discovery that differences within schools (rather than among schools) were the predominant source of variation in achievement (Coleman et al., 1966). Researchers such as Heyns (1974) and Alexander and McDill (1976; Alexander et al., 1978) showed that divisions among students into varied curricular programs helped explain within-school differences in achievement, over and above differences that were attributable to students' academic and social backgrounds. These findings have made the study of curricular tracking one of the most popular lines of research within the sociology of education.

Ironically, at least as seen from the late 1990s, these studies of curriculum differentiation had little to say about curriculum. For survey researchers, the curriculum was a structural device that sorted students into different positions and oriented them toward varied futures, not a technological tool for producing learning. Differences in the courses of study that students encountered in different tracks, which might yield variation in learning, received little empirical attention and no conceptual focus. Even when Alexander and Cook (1982) incorporated courses taken in different tracks into their model of tracking and achievement, they did so without a conceptual framework that specified which courses were likely to be found in which tracks. At that time, survey research on curriculum differentiation consisted of structural analysis of status attainment, not organizational research on the production of learning. The same can be said of most research on elementary school ability grouping and achievement (e.g., Yates, 1966): researchers were concerned with students' positions in the hierarchy and with the association of positions and outcomes, but not with students' curricular experiences within their varied classes and groups. Thus, research on curriculum differentiation was mainly about differentiation, not about curriculum.

In the 1980s, researchers studying curriculum differentiation began to examine the nature of the curriculum itself. Oakes' (1985) landmark study of tracking

in secondary schools built on earlier case studies (e.g., Rosenbaum, 1976) but gave much closer attention to the subject matter content to which students were exposed in different tracks. Interviews with students revealed substantial differences across tracks in the types of knowledge that students encountered. For example, asked about the most important thing they learned in class, high-track science students gave answers such as "We have learned the basics of the laws of relativity, and basics in electronics. The teacher applies these lessons to practical situations" (p. 69). In contrast, a low-track response was, "I can distinguish one type of rock from another" (p. 71). Similarly, a high-track English student reported learning "How to read a classic novel and be able to pull out details and write a complete and accurate report" (p. 69), whereas a low-track response was "To spell words you don't know, to fill out things where you get a job" (p. 71). Oakes corroborated these student reports by examining course materials such as texts and lesson plans, finding more high-status content and problem-solving activities in high-track classes and more fragmented and simplified content in low-track classes.

Subsequent observers have largely confirmed the pattern of differentiated content and experiences reported by Oakes. Page (1991), for example, viewed low-track classes as "caricatures" of high-track classes, because the purported academic content was trivialized through games and worksheets that deflected attention away from subject matter knowledge in favor of conforming to the procedures of schoolwork. However, not all low tracks are caricatures; some classes even attempt to engage students in serious academic work (Valli, 1990; Camarena, 1990; Gamoran, 1993). Taken as a whole, work in this field shows that typically, curriculum differentiation results in more extensive and rigorous coverage of academic material in higher status tracks, but within this generalization, variability exists (Hanson, 1990; Camarena, 1990; Gamoran, 1993). For example, a persistent finding is that noncollege tracks in Catholic schools tend to be more demanding academically than noncollege tracks in public schools (Valli, 1990; Camarena, 1990; Bryk et al., 1993).

For Oakes (1985), the importance of these findings is in their implications for unequal access to high-status knowledge (echoing Keddie, 1971) and for class reproduction (echoing Bowles and Gintis, 1976). The results of Oakes's and other observational studies also have implications for student achievement: Unequal access to academic content and pedagogy is a likely source of the gap between tracks in student learning that survey researchers uncovered. Gamoran et al. (1995) found support for this view in a study of eighth- and ninth-grade English classes. In this study, differences in student engagement and in the quality of classroom discourse accounted for part of the variation in achievement across honors, regular, and basic English classes. More important than the way teachers and students talked, however, was what they talked about: In honors classes, open-ended (or "authentic") questions focused on the literature students were reading, whereas in basic classes, authentic questions still occurred, but rarely about literature. Apparently for this reason, authentic questions contributed positively to literature achievement in honors classes, but detracted from literature achievement in basic classes. Thus, the overt curriculum that students encountered (what they read and talked about in class) affected what they learned.

Research on curriculum differentiation has moved toward a microsocial analysis of the curriculum as experienced by the learner. Survey research, which originally looked only at positions and outcomes, now takes into account students' varied experiences in schools (e.g., Gamoran, 1987; Hoffer and Gamoran, 1993), and recent observational studies emphasize content, instruction, and learning as much or more than class reproduction (see Page and Valli, 1990). At the same time, macrosocial research on curriculum has moved in other directions, with renewed interest in comparative work both across and within nations.

Educational Systems and Curriculum Change

In his classic analysis of changes in educational theory in France, Durkheim (1977 [1938]) placed the historical study of curriculum development in a sociological context. Durkheim discovered two principles in his investigation: first, that educational change responds to and is reflective of changes in the wider society; and second, that an educational system has its own internal momentum, so new features of an educational system reflect in part the features of the same system in earlier time periods. These themes persist in recent work, although they are expressed in new ways.

Cross-National Comparisons

The sociological analysis of curriculum change was largely dormant following Durkheim's contribution until it was revived by Meyer and his colleagues (e.g., Meyer et al., 1991). Meyer et al. (1991) presented three theoretical positions about the development of contemporary school curricula. First was Durkheim's "functionalist" approach. According to Meyer et al., Durkheim's perspective predicted that modern curricula (i.e., curricula that include modern subjects such as the physical, natural, and social sciences) would emerge in countries undergoing modernization, as indicated by increasing urbanization, technological and economic development, and expanded communication and transportation. A second view was identified as "historicist" and taken from writers such as Young (1971) and Bowles and Gintis (1976). This perspective, according to Meyer et al., would predict variation in curriculum development across nations, corresponding to differences in conflicts between classes or between elite and mass interest groups. The third perspective, the "world system" view, came from Meyer's earlier work (e.g., Meyer et al., 1977). According to this view, widely shared norms about what constitutes a legitimate education system would lead to cross-national similarities in curriculum development, irrespective of differences in modernization and in class conflict.

Evidence on the official primary school curricula of a wide variety of countries supports the world-system view (Meyer et al., 1992). The subject matter of primary schools generally developed in similar ways across countries during the twentieth century, and indicators of modernization made little difference in this process. These findings are not as divergent from Durkheim's views as they may initially appear to be. Durkheim's first principle, that educational change reflects broader social change, is upheld, but only if one understands that social change in the twentieth century occurred in a global context. The second principle, that an educational system has its own momentum, is reflected in the finding that national departments of education tended to adopt what they perceived as legitimate curricula even when those curricula were largely unrelated to national social and economic conditions.

The most recent work in the world-system approach indicates that curriculum development in secondary education has not followed a single common model to the same degree as occurred at the primary level (Kamens et al., 1996). Analyses of official secondary curricula revealed cross-national differences in the extent to which classical curricula were replaced by comprehensive programs, on the one hand, or by specialized programs such as mathematics/sciences or humanities curricular emphases on the other. These differences are not related to variation in national economic development, but they are linked to differences across countries in the degree to which secondary education has been used as mass preparation or as a mechanism for selecting and sponsoring the elite.

Comparisons within Countries

In addition to studies of curricular similarities and differences across countries, sociologists have recently begun to explore differences within countries, focusing especially on equality of access to curricula that promote academic learning. For the United States, Wilson and Rossman (1993) examined high schools' responses to state-mandated changes in curricula. During the 1980s, they reported, schools increased the number of academic courses offered, and students tended to enroll in more academic courses than in the previous decade. Consequently, high school graduates at the end of the 1980s had stronger academic preparation than did those at the beginning. However, the greatest increase in academic courses often occurred at the lowest levels of academic subjects. For example, many schools offered more low-level general math courses. Hence, expanded availability of courses in academic subjects did relatively little to reduce inequality of access to high-status, college-preparatory curricular material. Secondary curricula also appear to vary by public and private sector within the United States. Culminating a series of studies on the differences between public and Catholic high schools, Bryk et al. (1993) showed that the more rigorous and tightly focused academic curriculum of Catholic schools promotes higher achievement, especially for students from disadvantaged backgrounds.

Ayalon (1994) explored differences in high school curricula across communities in Israel. Like Wilson and Rossman in the United States, Ayalon uncovered substantial inequality in access to high-status courses. Communities with larger proportions of students from Asian and African origins (the disadvantaged ethnic group among Israeli Jews) were less likely to offer ad-

vanced courses in the most prestigious subjects, such as mathematics, sciences, French, and art. Moreover, Ayalon and Yogev (1997) argued that scientific courses are becoming increasingly dominant over the humanities in Israeli secondary education, and more able students, males, and members of the privileged ethnic group tend to specialize in the sciences.

Within the sciences, Ayalon (1995) observed that physics and biology are sex typed, with males tending to enroll in physics and females in biology. Croxford (1997) reported the same pattern for Scotland. This gender inequality within the subject area of science may have subverted the larger trend in Scotland toward gender parity in the study of science overall (Croxford, 1994), and one suspects that the same phenomenon has occurred in Israel and in the United States. That is, girls and boys have become more equal in the probability of studying science, but they do not study the same science fields. Evidence from Scotland for a decline in socioeconomic inequality in curricular access is more secure. Croxford (1994) noted that expanded access to academic studies in Scottish secondary schools helped to narrow the gap in academic coursework between students from lower and higher status origins. Gamoran (1996, 1997) showed that these reforms resulted in a decline in achievement inequality for students from different social backgrounds during the 1980s.

Promising Directions for Future Research

In recent years, sociologists have paid increasing attention to curriculum, focusing particularly on the overt curriculum, that is, the subject matter content that provides the context for the work of teaching and learning. Researchers have been concerned with accounting for the particular content that American and other school systems tend to emphasize, and with understanding differences in curriculum content both across and within countries. In addition, sociologists have recognized the important consequences of curriculum for students' opportunities and achievement.

The research agenda thus far has contained separate studies at the macrosocial level (e.g., cross-national comparisons of official curricula) and at the microsocial level (e.g., analyses of unequal access to curriculum within schools). As research on curriculum develops, sociologists may find ways to bridge the gap between macrosocial and microsocial analyses. For example, whereas we now know much about cross-national similarities in official curricula, we know far less about similarities and differences in how these curricula are implemented in schools and experienced by students. What national and local conditions affect the implementation of official curricula? Are the same limiting conditions important in a wide variety of countries? How does inequality in the wider society affect inequality in the implementation of curriculum, in light of the broad similarity of official curricula across nations? From research on curriculum differentiation, we know that unequal access to high-status knowledge contributes to unequal learning. In the future, sociologists may ask how teachers can deliver a common academic curriculum to an increasingly diverse student body. Moving outward toward the macrosocial level, sociologists may consider whether increased standardization in the curriculum may help reduce inequality of knowledge in the wider society. At the same time, however, pressures for a more diverse curriculum may prevent such standardization. Indeed, broader participation for racial and ethnic minority groups in defining what constitutes a legitimate curriculum is increasingly seen as an aspect of equal opportunity (Olneck, 1993).

Scholars who study the hidden curriculum have long been concerned with the transition from school to work. In the future, research on the overt curriculum may also address this concern. For example, what blend of academic and vocational curricula offers the best preparation for the high-performance workplace? Does workplace preparation in schools invariably reproduce social inequality, or can it serve as a mechanism for improving economic opportunities? These questions are fundamental to the design of secondary and post-secondary education.

REFERENCES

Alexander, Karl L., and Martha A. Cook. 1982. "Curricula and Coursework: A Surprise Ending to a Familiar Story." *American Sociological Review* 47:626–640.

Alexander, Karl L., and Edward L. McDill. 1976. "Selection and Allocation within Schools: Some Causes and Consequences of Curriculum Placement." *American Sociological Review* 41:963–980.

Alexander, Karl L., Martha A. Cook, and Edward L. McDill. 1978. "Curriculum Tracking and Educational Stratification." *American Sociological Review* 43:47–66.

Anyon, Jean. 1981. "Elementary Schooling and Distinctions of Social Class." *Interchange* 12:118–132.

Apple, Michael W. 1983. "Curricular Form and the Logic of Technical Control." In Michael W. Apple and Lois Weis (eds.), *Ideology and Practice in Schooling,* pp. 143–165. Philadelphia: Temple University Press.

Ayalon, Hanna. 1994. "Monopolizing Knowledge? The Ethnic Composition and Curriculum of Israeli High Schools." *Sociology of Education* 67:264–278.

———. 1995. "Math as a Gatekeeper: Ethnic and Gender Inequality in Course Taking of the Sciences in Israel." *American Journal of Education* 104:34–56.

Ayalon, Hanna, and Abraham Yogev. 1997. "Students, Schools, and Enrollment in Science and Humanity Courses in Israeli Secondary Education." *Educational Evaluation and Policy Analysis* 19:339–353.

Ball, Stephen J. 1981. *Beachside Comprehensive.* Cambridge, MA: Cambridge University Press.

Barr, Rebecca. 1975. "The Effect of Instruction on Pupil Reading Strategies." *Reading Research Quarterly* 10:555–582.

Barr, Rebecca, and Robert Dreeben. 1983. *How Schools Work.* Chicago: University of Chicago Press.

Blau, Peter M., and Otis Dudley Duncan. 1967. *The American Occupational Structure.* New York: Wiley.

Bowles, Samuel, and Herbert Gintis. 1976. *Schooling in Capitalist America.* New York: Basic Books.

Bryk, Anthony S., Valerie E. Lee, and Peter B. Holland. 1993. *Catholic Schools and the Common Good.* Cambridge, MA: Harvard University Press.

Camarena, Margaret. 1990. "Following the Right Track: A Comparison of Tracking Practices in Public And Catholic Schools." In Reba Page and Linda Valli (eds.), *Curriculum Differentiation: Interpretive Studies in U.S. Secondary Schools,* pp. 159–182. Albany, NY: State University of New York Press.

Coleman, James S., Ernest Q. Campbell, C. Hobson, J. McPartland, A. Mood, F. Weinfield, and R. York. 1966. *Equality of Educational Opportunity.* Washington, DC: U.S. Government Printing Office.

Croxford, Linda. 1994. "Equal Opportunities in the Secondary School Curriculum in Scotland, 1971–91." *British Educational Research Journal* 20:371–391.

———. 1997. "Participation in Science Subjects: The Effect of the Scottish Curriculum Framework." *Research Papers in Education* 12:69–89.

Dreeben, Robert. 1968. *On What is Learned in School.* Reading, MA: Addison-Wesley.

Dreeben, Robert, and Adam Gamoran. 1986. "Race, Instruction, and Learning." *American Sociological Review* 51:660–669.

Durkheim, Emile. 1977 [1938]. *The Evolution of Educational Thought.* London: Routledge and Kegan Paul.

Everhart, Robert B. 1983. *Reading, Writing, and Resistance: Adolescence and Labor in a Junior High School.* London: Routledge and Kegan Paul.

Gamoran, Adam. 1987. "The Stratification of High School

Learning Opportunities." *Sociology of Education* 60:135–155.

———. 1993. "Alternative Uses of Ability Grouping in Secondary Schools: Can We Bring High-Quality Instruction to Low-Ability Classes?" *American Journal of Education* 101:1–22.

———. 1996. "Curriculum Standardization and Equality of Opportunity in Scottish Secondary Education, 1984–1990." *Sociology of Education* 29:1–21.

———. 1997. "Curriculum Change as a Reform Strategy: Lessons from the United States and Scotland." *Teachers College Record* 98:608–628.

Gamoran, Adam, and Mark Berends. 1987. "The Effects of Stratification in Secondary Schools: Synthesis of Survey and Ethnographic Research." *Review of Educational Research* 57:415–435.

Gamoran, Adam, and Robert Dreeben. 1986. "Coupling and Control in Educational Organizations." *Administrative Science Quarterly* 31:612–632.

Gamoran, Adam, and Robert D. Mare. 1989. "Secondary School Tracking and Educational Inequality: Reinforcement, Compensation, or Neutrality?" *American Journal of Sociology* 94:1146–1183.

Gamoran, Adam, Martin Nystrand, Mark Berends, and Paul C. LePore. 1995. "An Organizational Analysis of the Effects of Ability Grouping." *American Educational Research Journal* 32:687–715.

Hanson, Susan. 1990. "The College-Preparatory Curriculum Across Schools: Access to Similar Knowledge?" In Reba Page and Linda Valli (eds.), *Curriculum Differentiation: Interpretive Studies in U.S. Secondary Schools,* pp. 67–89. Albany, NY: State University of New York Press.

Heyns, Barbara. 1974. "Social Selection and Stratification within Schools." *American Journal of Sociology* 79:1434–1451.

Hoffer, Thomas, and Adam Gamoran. 1993. "Effects of Instructional Differences among Ability Groups on Student Achievement in Middle-School Science and Mathematics." Paper presented at the annual meeting of the American Sociological Association, Miami, August.

Jackson, Philip W. 1992. "Conceptions of Curriculum and Curriculum Specialists." In Philip W. Jackson (ed.), *Handbook of Research on Curriculum,* pp. 3–40. New York: Macmillan.

Kamens, David, John W. Meyer, and Aaron Benavot. 1996. "Worldwide Patterns in Academic Secondary Education Curricula, 1920–1990." *Comparative Education Review* 40:377–403.

Keddie, Nell. 1971. "Classroom Knowledge." In Michael F. D. Young (ed.), *Knowledge and Control,* pp. 133–160. London: Collier-Macmillan.

Labaree, David. 1986. "Curriculum, Credentials, and the Middle Class: A Case Study of a Nineteenth-Century High School." *Sociology of Education* 59:42–57.

McNeil, Linda. 1983. "Defensive Teaching and Classroom Control." In Michael W. Apple and Lois Weis (eds.), *Ideology and Practice in Schooling,* pp. 143–165. Philadelphia: Temple University Press.

Meyer, John W., Francisco O. Ramirez, Richard Rubinson, and John Boli-Bennet. 1977. "The World Educational Revolution." *Sociology of Education* 50:242–258.

Meyer, John W., David H. Kamens, and Aaron Benavot. 1992. *School Knowledge for the Masses.* Washington, DC: Falmer Press.

Oakes, Jeannie. 1985. *Keeping Track: How Schools Structure Inequality.* New Haven, CT: Yale University Press.

Oakes, Jeannie, Adam Gamoran, and Reba N. Page. 1992. "Curriculum Differentiation: Opportunities, Outcomes, and Meanings." In Philip W. Jackson (ed.), *Handbook of Research on Curriculum,* pp. 570–608. New York: Macmillan.

Olneck, Michael R. 1993. "Terms of Inclusion: Has Multiculturalism Redefined Equality in American Education?" *American Journal of Education* 101:234–260.

Page, Reba N. 1991. *Lower Track Classrooms: A Curricular and Cultural Perspective.* New York: Teachers College Press.

Page, Reba N., and Linda Valli, eds. 1990. *Curriculum Differentiation: Interpretive Studies in U. S. Secondary Schools.* Albany, NY: State University of New York Press.

Rosenbaum, James E. 1976. *Making Inequality: The Hidden Curriculum of High School Tracking.* New York: Wiley.

Rowan, Brian, and Andrew W. Miracle, Jr. 1983. "Systems of Ability Grouping and the Stratification of Achievement in Elementary Schools." *Sociology of Education* 56:133–144.

Valli, Linda. 1990. "A Curriculum of Effort: Tracking Students in a Catholic High School." In Reba Page and Linda Valli (eds.), *Curriculum Differentiation: Interpretive Studies in U.S. Secondary Schools,* pp. 45–65. Albany, NY: State University of New York Press.

Walker, Decker, and Jon Schaffarzick. 1974. "Comparing Curricula." *Review of Educational Research* 44:83–111.

Whitty, Geoff, and Michael F. D. Young, eds. 1976. *Explorations in the Politics of School Knowledge.* Driffield, England: Studies in Education Ltd.

Wilson, Bruce L., and Gretchen B. Rossman. 1993. *Mandating Academic Excellence.* New York: Teachers College Press.

Yates, Alfred, ed. 1966. *Grouping in Education.* A report sponsored by the UNESCO Institute for Education. New York: Wiley.

Young, Michael F. D., ed. 1971. *Knowledge and Control.* London: Collier-Macmillan.

CURRICULUM HISTORY

Ivor F. Goodson
University of East Anglia

The need for curriculum history arises from the view that recent modes of curriculum reform and curriculum study commonly share interlocking inadequacies. Both modes tend to share an obsessive contemporality allied with a belief that past curriculum traditions could, given conviction and resources, be transcended. One reason for the antipathetic relationship between curriculum reform strategies, curriculum studies, and history (whether as a mode of study, as artifact, as tradition, or as legacy) relates to the historical period of growth.

The great period of expansion both for curriculum reform initiatives and curriculum studies as a discipline ran from 1960 to around 1975 (Rubinstein and Simon, 1973:108). This was a period of economic expansion and social optimism, of rapid reorganization into comprehensive schools, and increasing public expenditure on schooling and universities. A period in short where previous traditions and legacies were subject to major challenge, where a common assumption was that a new world of schooling (and curriculum) was about to be constructed.

The documents and statements of the curriculum reform movement inaugurated in the 1960s reveal a messianic yet widespread belief that there could be a more or less complete break with past tradition. A belief that history in general and curriculum history in particular could somehow be *transcended*. Besides the all-pervasive term "innovation," there was common reference to "radical change in education," "revolutionizing classroom practice," and "redrawing the map of learning." For instance, writing in 1968 Professor Kerr asserted that "at the practical and organizational levels, the new curricula promise to revolutionize English education" (Kerr, 1971:180). Retrospectively, there

may seem something admirable, however misconceived, about such belief in contemporary possibility that history seemed of little relevance.

So at a time when traditional curriculum practice was thought to be on the point of being overthrown it was perhaps not surprising that so many reforms paid scant attention to the evolution and establishment of traditional practice. In any event radical change did not occur. Curriculum study now requires strategies that allow us to examine the emergence and survival of the "traditional" as well as the failure to generalize, institutionalize, and sustain the "innovative."

The *transcendent view* of curriculum change infected many of those involved in researching schools and curriculum. The irony is supreme but for the best of reasons. Particularly "infected" were those researchers involved in evaluation and case study work. Reflecting the participants' perceptions, their transcendent bias is therefore partly explained by an historical climate of opinion where curriculum change was considered the order of the day.

Yet, if many of those employing qualitative methods in evaluation and case study took a transcendent view of history they were not alone. By a peculiar convergence many contemporary interactionist and ethnographic studies were similarly ahistorical.

The experimental model of sociological investigation with its emphasis on single studies to test preselected hypotheses, while for long dominant, neglected participant perspectives and interactional processes. Paradoxically, the interactionist and ethnographic models that were conceived in reaction to this model have often focused on situation and occasion with the result that biography and historical background have continued to be neglected. Interactionist studies have focused on the perspectives and definitions emerging through interaction and have stressed situation rather than background and history. In this work, the backcloth to action is often presented as a somewhat monolithic "structural" or "cultural" legacy that constrains, in a rather disconnected manner, the actors' potentialities. But in overreacting to more deterministic models, interactionists may be in danger of failing to present any clear connection with historical process. Of course, "this danger can be best evidenced in those interactionist studies of micropolitical action (particularly in those studies which focus on 'resistance') where the actor is often invested with notions of autonomy and free agency, which plainly fly in the face of the historical circumstances in which those actions are embedded." (Goodson, 1998, p. 14.)

In studying the relationship between proscribed curriculum content and practice, the dangers of such an approach have been clearly evidenced in the past two decades. Classroom practice, a crucial and often neglected area, can be interactionist overreaction, be presented as the exclusive and essential context wherein patterns of curriculum knowledge are defined. One unfortunate side-effect of this focus is that when attempts to reform classroom practice fail, the teacher, who is the immediate visible agency of that failure, may be presented as exclusively culpable. We need a strategy that is curative of the classroom myopia exhibited in such accounts and that develops a historical perspective on the constraints beyond the classroom.

In much of their work on curriculum, philosophers have taken the curriculum as a given. Hence the historical environment in which knowledge is socially produced has been ignored. This ahistorical aspect of philosophy has defused its capacity to act as an antidote to the transcendence and immersed immediacy we have noted above.

Hirst (1967), for example, has talked about school subjects "which are indisputably logically cohesive disciplines" (p. 44). In fact such a philosophical perspective is rooted in particular and rather contestable educational convictions. Most notable is the assertion that "no matter what the ability of the child may be, the heart of all his development as a rational being, I am saying, intellectual" (Hirst, 1976). In accordance with these convictions Hirst and Peters (1970) have argued that "the central objectives of education are developments of mind" (pp. 63–64). These objectives are best pursued by "the definition of forms of knowledge"

(later broadened to include "fields of knowledge"). These forms and fields of knowledge then provide "the logically cohesive disciplines" on which school subjects are based.

The philosophy of Hirst and Peters, therefore, provides an explanatory basis for the school curriculum as trying to promote the intellectual development of its pupils. In their model of school subject definition it is often implied that the intellectual discipline is created by a community of scholars, normally working in a university, and is then translated for use as a school subject. Phenix (1964) defines the intellectual discipline base in this way:

> The general test for discipline is that it should be the characteristic activity of an identifiable organized tradition of men of knowledge, that is of persons who are skilled in certain specified functions that they are able to justify by a set of intelligible standards. (p. 317)

Once a discipline has established a university base it is persuasively self-fulfilling to argue that here is a field of knowledge from which an "academic" school subject can receive inputs and general direction. The problem is that this version of events by virtue of its ahistoricality simply celebrates a *fait accompli* in the evolution of a discipline and associated school subjects. What is, therefore, left unexplained are the stages of evolution toward this culminating pattern and forces that push aspiring "academic" subjects to follow similar routes. To understand the progression along the route to academic status it is necessary to examine the social histories of school subjects and to analyze the strategies employed in their construction and promotion.

Of course the manner in which philosophical studies offer justification for the academic subject-based curriculum has been noted by sociologists. A major development in sociological studies, the sociology of knowledge, has sought to elucidate more fundamental patterns. Knowledge is seen as evolving in response to the promotional and presentational agency of particular subject groups that act to defend and expand their "interests." Similarly, knowledge patterns are viewed as reflecting the status hierarchies of each society through the activities of the dominant groups. Very often, however, such work has not presented the evolutionary, historical process at work. Studies have developed horizontally, working out from theories of social structure and social order to evidence of their application. Such an approach inevitably obscures, rather than clarifies, those historical situations in which "gaps," discrepancies, and ambiguities are created within which individuals can maneuvre. More worrying where history has been considered it has often been "raided," in Silver's (1977) elegant phrase, to prove a contemporary point (p. 17). I have evidenced elsewhere a "raid" on David Layton's (1973) study *Science for the People* and the use of his work to prove a contemporary political point about school science. In this case a disembodied historical snapshot is used in an attempt to further our understanding of certain basic assumptions about contemporary school science. I argued that without direct parallels and with no evidence produced of continuities it is difficult to move to *any* understanding of the basic assumptions of contemporary school science from the specific historical evidence presented from Layton's work. Clearly the danger of "raiding" history is that such moves can span centuries of change at all levels of content and context. A more systematic *evolutionary* understanding of how the curriculum is negotiated is therefore needed (Goodson, 1983).

As we have noted, historians of education have provided an important antidote to the ahistoricality of much curriculum study yet paradoxically a refined awareness of some of the problems cited above has led to an often overreactive posture to the sociological abuse of "raiding" for contemporary theoretical purposes.

Writing of the work of curriculum specialists with respect to historical perspective, Marsden (1979) judges that they "have often been deficient and can roughly be divided into those which are *a-historical and unhistorical*, in so far as the categories can be isolated from one another." He defines an ahistorical approach as

> one which disregards the historical perspective, the writer perceiving it to be irrelevant and/or uninteresting. . . . Thus work proceeds, almost naively, in a temporal vacuum. (p. 81)

An unhistorical approach is characterized

> as one inconsistent both in gross and in refined terms with the accepted canons of historical scholarship, purveying inaccurate, over-simplified and otherwise distorted impressions of the past. At-

tention is drawn to the past, not for its own sake but as a means of sharpening a particular contemporary axe. (p. 82)

Alongside this "misuse" of history Marsden places those curriculum studies "in which the past is scanned for support of some broad socio-political interpretation or theory" (p. 82).

Historians have rightly reacted to the misuse of history for "sharpening contemporary axes" or "supporting broad socio-political interpretations or theories." In my view that reaction has gone too far (understandable though it is if placed in historical context). The result is that the history of education has often become rigidly "periodized"; it has often pursued a policy of "splendid isolation" from the messy and unresolved contemporary situation. This is to limit both its aspiration and its importance. The history of education should clearly obviate any concern with "sharpening contemporary axes." But such a correct reaction should not be taken as disbarring concern with contemporary events. By my view the history of education should set as an important criteria a concern, where possible, to elucidate the precedents, antecedents, and constraints surrounding contemporary curriculum and practice. Likewise, the reaction to theoretical enterprises should be conquered. Historical study has a valuable role to play in challenging, informing, and sometimes generating theory. This role should not be emasculated through a fear of theoretical misuse by others.

Beyond the ambivalence to contemporary situations and theoretical enterprises much history of education shares a further characteristic that argues for a growing dialogue between historians and curriculum specialists. In many ways the history of education has taken an "external" view of curriculum focusing on political and administrative contexts and on general movements in education and schooling. Partly this is a reflection of the documents available, which often relate to central regulations, edicts, or commissions on education and curriculum. This is a long way from curriculum as enacted, transacted, realized, and received. Rudolph (1977) has warned that

> The best way to misread or misunderstand curriculum is from a catalogue. It is such a lifeless thing. So disembodied, so unconnected, sometimes even intentionally misleading. Because the curriculum

is a social artifact, the society itself is a more reliable source of curricular information. (p. 6)

If an understanding of curriculum and curriculum change is given priority then a mode of study that focuses on and analyzes "internal" issues is of paramount importance. Partly the crucial nature of internal factors results from the way education and schooling are structured and relate to the broader economy and society. As Webster (1976) has pointed out: "Educational institutions are not as directly nor as essentially concerned with the economic and social welfare of the community as, say, factories or hospitals. They are, therefore, particularly well equipped to weather any crisis that may be going on around them" (pp. 206–207). This relative autonomy explains the peculiar force of historical traditions and legacies in curriculum change. As a result as Waring reminds us "it is hardly surprising that originality always works within the framework of tradition and that a totally new tradition is 'one of the most improbable of events.' " Hence developing a sense of history will modify our view of curriculum. Instead of the transcendent expectation of basic change we look for alteration followed by regression, for change attempted and aborted in one place to emerge unexpectedly elsewhere. Through history we develop a longer view and with it a different time scale of expectations and, presumably, range of strategies.

Studying the Social History of School Subjects

The important work by sociologists of curriculum in defining research programs for studies of school knowledge led on then to an acknowledgment by some of them that historical study might complement and extend their project and that school subjects should provide a focus for study. Initial work in the early twentieth century has provided some important precursors to our work; the sociologists of knowledge have subsequently played a vital role in rescuing and reasserting the validity of this intellectual project; in the process, however, some of the necessary focus on historical and empirical circumstances has been lost. The task now being undertaken is to reexamine the role of historical methods in the study of curriculum and to rearticulate a mode of study for carrying further our understanding of the social history of the school curriculum and, in this work, particularly school subjects.

In *School Subjects and Curriculum Change*, first published in 1983, I looked at the history of three subjects: geography, biology, and environmental studies (Goodson, 1993). Each of the subjects followed a similar evolutionary profile and this initial work allowed a series of hypothesis to be developed about the way that status and resources, the structuration of school subjects, push school subject knowledge in particular directions: toward the embrace of what I call the "academic tradition." Following this work is a new series, *Studies in Curriculum History,* was launched. In the first volume, *Social Histories of the Secondary Curriculum* (Goodson, 1985), work is collected together on a wide range of subjects: classics (Stray, 1985, English) or science (Waring, 1985, who had written an earlier seminal study on Nuffield science), domestic subjects (Purvis, 1985), religious education (Bell, 1985), social studies (Franklin, 1985; Whitty, 1985), and modern languages (Radford, 1985). These studies reflect a growing interest in the history of curriculum and besides elucidating a symbolic drift of school knowledge toward the academic tradition, raise central questions about past and current explanations of school subjects, whether they be sociological or philosophical. Other work in the series *Studies in Curriculum History* has looked in detail at particular subjects; in 1985 McCulloch, Layton, and Jenkins produced *Technological Revolution?* (McCulloch et al., 1985). This book examines the politics of school science and technology curriculum in England and Wales since World War II. Subsequent work by Brian Woolnough (1988) has looked at the history of physics teaching in schools in the period 1960 to 1985. Another area of emerging work is the history of school mathematics: Cooper's book *Renegotiating Secondary School Mathematics* (1985) looks at the fate of a number of traditions within mathematics and articulates a model for the redefinition of school subject knowledge; Bob Moon's (1986) book *The 'New Maths' Curriculum Controversy* meanwhile looks at the relationship between mathematics in England and America and has some very interesting work on the dissemination of textbooks.

Scholarly work in America has also begun to focus on the evolution of the school curriculum studied in an historical manner. H.M. Kliebard's (1986) seminal

The Struggle for the American Curriculum 1893–1958 discerns a number of the dominant traditions within the school curriculum. The book also comes to the intriguing conclusion that by the end of the period covered the traditional school subject remained "an impregnable fortress." But Kliebard's work does not take us into the detail of school life. In this respect Barry Franklin's (1986) book, *Building the American Community*, provides us with some valuable insights in a case study of Minneapolis. Here we see the vital negotiation from curriculum ideas, the terrain of Kliebard's work, toward implementation as school practice. In addition a collection of papers put together by Tom Popkewitz (1987) looks at the historical aspects of a range of subjects: early education (Bloch, 1987), art (Freedman, 1987), reading and writing (Monagha and Saul, 1987), biology (Rosenthal and Bybee, 1987), mathematics (Stanic, 1987), social studies (Lybarger, 1987), special education (Franklin, 1987; Sleeter, 1987), socialist curriculum (Teitelbaum, 1987), and a study of Rugg's textbook by Kliebard and Wegner (1987).

Canadian curriculum history has been launched as a field most notably by George Tomkins' (1986) pioneering work *A Common Countenance*. This studies the patterns of curriculum stability and change in a range of school subjects over the past two centuries throughout Canada. The book has stimulated a wide range of important new work of curriculum history. For instance, Rowell and Gaskell's (1988) very generative study of the history of school physics. The Rowell and Gaskell piece provides one important case study in a new book *International Perspectives in Curriculum History* (Goodson, 1988), which seeks to bring together some of the more important work emerging in different countries on curriculum history. Besides some of the work already noted by Stanic, Moon, Franklin, McCulloch, Ball, Rowell and Gaskell, there are important articles on Victorian school science by Hodson (1988), on science education by Louis Smith (1988), on English on the Norwegian common school by Gundem (1988), and on the development of senior school geography in West Australia by Marsh (1988).

Importantly, new work has begun to look beyond traditional school subjects to focus on broader topics. For example, Peter Cunningham's (1988) book looks at the curriculum change in the primary school in Brit-

ain since 1945. P.W. Musgrave's (1988) book, *Whose Knowledge?*, is a case study of the Victoria University Examinations Board from 1964 to 1979. Here historical work begins to elucidate the change from curriculum content to examinable content, which is such an important part of understanding the way that status and resources are apportioned within the school.

Recent work has begun to explore gender patterns in curriculum history. Jane Bernard Powers' (1992) excellent study *The Girl Question in Education* is a pioneering work in this regard. Likewise, work is beginning on the modernist construction of curriculum as a world movement. The work of John Meyer et al. (1992), *School Knowledge for the Masses*, provides a path-breaking study of national primary curricula categories in the twentieth century throughout the world.

New directions for the study of school subjects and curriculum will require a broadened approach. In particular this work will have to move into examining the relationship between school subject content and form, and issues of school practice and process. It is now vital in England and Wales to also redirect this work to an exploration and critique of the National Curriculum, for the resonances, certainly at the level of class, to previous patterns are overwhelming. The comparison between Bernstein's (1971, 1975) work on the curriculum and the current state of the art of curriculum analysis in the United Kingdom is a salutary reminder of the changes in political climate and responses within the academy. There could be no clearer indicator of the general climate of withdrawal and deference within the academy. For the National Curriculum cries out for the kind of social analysis epitomized by Bernstein and first called for by Foster Watson (1909). To paraphrase, "It is high time that the historical facts with regard to the National Curriculum were known, and known in connection with the social forces which brought them into the educational curriculum."

In terms of what I have called social constructionist study of the curriculum (Goodson, 1990a) this lacuna in studying the National Curriculum is little short of astounding. As I have detailed, work on the history of school subjects has been sustained, particularly in Britain itself, for over a decade of intensive scholarship. We now know a great deal about the class, gender, and racial biases of school subjects. Yet in recent years, scholars close to these developments, with a few dignified exceptions, have virtually ignored this legacy in their work on the National Curriculum. The effect is to conspire with the Thatcherite view that the National Curriculum is a new and compelling revolution in educational provision. In fact, curriculum history indicates that nothing could be further from the truth. As I have argued elsewhere (Goodson, 1994), government policy and pronouncements have encouraged this amnesia (and a failure to present academic challenges has the same effect):

> The obsessive presentism of many of the current government initiatives has successfully obscured this deeply-embedded connectedness which is of course relevant to the present and future of the UK as a class society. (Goodson, 1990b:231)

Curriculum histories then should provide a systematic analysis of these ongoing social constructions and selections that form the school curriculum, pointing up continuities and discontinuities of social purpose over time. It is important to note that the prevailing paradigm of curriculum study focusing on implementation is devoid of such sociohistorical perspective, but more importantly so to is the more "radical" focus on curriculum that studies school-based "resistance" to new national directives. Not only is such work without sociohistorical range but it focuses only on the reaction. To quote Fredric Jameson (1992), "The violence of the riposte says little about the terms of the engagement." So it is with school resistance to the National Curriculum. The social construction of the National Curriculum sets the terms of the engagement and does so in ways that link to a history of social purposes.

Curriculum histories can elucidate and analyze this ongoing process of the social construction of curriculum. Such histories provide a new terrain of study where the school subject might again be employed as an entry point for the social analysis of education.

REFERENCES

Bell, A. 1985. "Agreed Syllabuses of Religious Education Since 1944." In I. F. Goodson (ed.), *Social Histories of the Secondary Curriculum,* pp. 177–201. London: Falmer Press.

Bernard Powers, Jane. 1992. *The Girl Question in Education: Vocational Education for Young Women in the Progressive Era.* London: Falmer Press.

Bernstein, B. 1971. "On the Classification and Framing of Educational Knowledge." In M. F. D. Young (ed.), *Knowledge and Control.* London: Collier-Macmillan.

———. 1975. *Class, Codes and Control, Volume 3, Towards a Theory of Educational Transmissions,* 2nd ed. London: Routledge and Kegan Paul.

Bloch, M. N. 1987. "Becoming Scientific and Professional: An Historical Perspective on the Aims and Effects of Early Education." In T. S. Popkewitz (ed.), *The Formation of School Subjects: The Struggle for Creating an American Institution.* London: Falmer Press.

Cooper, B. 1985. *Renegotiating Secondary School Mathematics.* London: Falmer Press.

Cunningham, P. 1988. *Curriculum Change in the Primary School Since 1945.* London: Falmer Press.

Franklin, B. M. 1985. "The Social Efficiency Movement and Curriculum Change 1939–1976." In I. F. Goodson (ed.), *Social Histories of the Secondary Curriculum,* pp. 239–268. London: Falmer Press.

———. 1986. *Building the American Community.* London: Falmer Press.

———. 1987. "The First Crusade for Learning Disabilities: The Movement for the Education of Backward Children." In T. S. Popkewitz (ed.), *The Formation of School Subjects: The Struggle for Creating an American Institution.* London: Falmer Press.

Freedman, K. 1987. "Art Education as Social Production: Culture, Society and Politics in the Formation of Curriculum." In T. S. Popkewitz, (ed.), *The Formation of School Subjects: The Struggle for Creating an American Institution.* London: Falmer Press.

Goodson, I. F. 1983. "Subjects for Study: Aspects of a Social History of Curriculum." *Journal of Curriculum Studies* 15(4):391–408.

———, ed. 1985. *Social Histories of the Secondary Curriculum.* London: Falmer Press.

———, ed. 1988. *International Perspectives in Curriculum History,* 2nd ed. London: Routledge.

———. 1990a. "Studying Curriculum: Towards a Social Constructionist Perspective." *Journal of Curriculum Studies* 22(4):299–312.

———. 1990b. "'Nations at Risk' and 'National Curriculum': Ideology and Identity." *Politics of Education Association Yearbook 1990,* 219–232.

———. 1993. *School Subjects and Curriculum Change,* 3rd ed. London: Falmer Press.

———. 1994. *Studying Curriculum: Cases and Methods.* Buckingham: Open University Press/New York: Teachers College Press/Toronto: OISE Press.

Goodson, I. F. with C. J. Anstead and J. M. Mangan. 1998. *Subject Knowledge: Readings for the Study of School Subjects.* London and Washington, DC: Falmer Press.

Gundem. B. B. 1988. "The Emergence and Redefining of English for the Common School 1889–1984." In I. F.

Goodson (ed.), *International Perspectives in Curriculum History*. London: Routledge.

Hirst, P. M. 1967. "The Logical and Psychological Aspects of Teaching a Subject." In R. S. Peters (ed.), *The Concept of Education*. London: Routledge and Kegan Paul.

———. 1976. "The Educational Implications of Social and Economic Change." In *Schools Council Working Paper No. 12*. London: HMSO.

Hirst, P. M., and R. S. Peters. 1970. *The Logic of Education*. London: Routledge and Kegan Paul.

Hodson, D. 1988. "Science Curriculum Change in Victorian England: A Case Study of the Science of Common Things." In I. F. Goodson (ed.), *International Perspectives in Curriculum History*. London: Routledge.

Jameson, F. 1992. Conversation, University of Western Ontario, Feb. 18, 1992. See especially Jameson, F. 1992. *Postmodernism or, the Cultural Logic of Late Capitalism*. Durham: Duke University Press.

Kerr, J. 1971. "The Problem of Curriculum Reform." In R. Hooper (ed.), *The Curriculum Context, Design and Development*. Edinburgh: Oliver and Boyd.

Kliebard, H. 1986. *The Struggle for the American Curriculum 1893–1953*. London: Routledge and Kegan Paul.

Kliebard, H., and G. Wegner. 1987. "Harold Rugg and the Reconstruction of the Social Studies Curriculum: The Treatment of the *Great War* in his Textbook Series." In T. S. Popkewitz (ed.), *The Formation of School Subjects: The Struggle for Creating an American Institution*. London: Falmer Press.

Layton, D. 1973. *Science for the People*. London: George Allen and Unwin.

Lybarger, M. B. 1987. "Need as Ideology: Social Workers, Social Settlements, and the Social Studies." In T. S. Popkewitz (ed.), *The Formation of School Subjects: The Struggle for Creating an American Institution*. London: Falmer Press.

Marsden, W. E. 1979. "Historical Approaches to Curricular Studies." In W. E. Marsden (ed.), *Postwar Curriculum Development: An Historical Appraisal*. History of Education Society Conference Papers.

Marsh, C. J. 1988. "The Development of a Senior School Geography Curriculum in Western Australia 1964–84." In I. F. Goodson (ed.), *International Perspectives in Curriculum History*. London: Routledge.

McCulloch, G., E. Jenkins, and D. Layton. 1985. *Technological Revolution?* London: Falmer Press.

Meyer, J. W., D. H. Kamens, A. Benavot, with Y. K. Cha, and S. Y. Wong. 1992. *School Knowledge for the Masses*. London: Falmer Press.

Monagha, J., and W. Saul. 1987. "The Reader, the Scribe, the Thinker: A Critical Look at Reading and Writing Instruction." In T. S. Popkewitz (ed.), *The Formation of School Subjects: The Struggle for Creating an American Institution*. London: Falmer Press.

Moon, B. 1986. *The 'New Maths' Curriculum Controversy*. London: Falmer Press.

Musgrave, P. W. 1988. *Whose Knowledge?* London: Falmer Press.

Phenix, P. M. 1964. *The Realms of Meaning*. New York: McGraw-Hill.

Popkewitz, T. S., ed. 1987. *The Formation of School Subjects: The Struggle for Creating an American Institution*. London: Falmer Press.

Purvis, J. 1985. "Domestic Subjects Since 1870." In I. F. Goodson (ed.), *Social Histories of the Secondary Curriculum*. London: Falmer Press.

Radford, H. 1985. "Modern Languages and the Curriculum in English Secondary Schools." In I. F. Goodson (ed.), *Social Histories of the Secondary Curriculum*. London: Falmer Press.

Rosenthal, D. B., and R. W. Bybee. 1987. "Emergence of the Biology Curriculum: A Science of Life or Science of Living." In T. S. Popkewitz (ed.), *The Formation of School Subjects: The Struggle for Creating an American Institution*. London: Falmer Press.

Rowell, P. M., and P. J. Gaskell. 1988. "Tensions and Realignments: School Physics in British Columbia 1955–80." In I. F. Goodson (ed.), *International Perspectives in Curriculum History*. London: Routledge.

Rubinstein, D., and R. Simon. 1973. *The Evolution of the Comprehensive School 1926–1972*. London: Routledge and Kegan Paul.

Rudolph, F. 1977. *A History of the American Undergraduate Course of Study Since 1636*. San Francisco: Jossey Bass.

Silver, H. 1977. "Nothing But the Past, or Nothing But the Present?" *Times Higher Education Supplement* 1.

Sleeter, C. E. 1987. "Why Is There Learning Disabilities? A Critical Analysis of the Birth of the Field in Its Social Context." In T. S. Popkewitz (ed.), *The Formation of School Subjects: The Struggle for Creating an American Institution*. London: Falmer Press.

Smith, L. M. 1988. "Process of Curriculum Change: An Historical Sketch of Science Education in the Alte Schools." In I. F. Goodson (ed.), *International Perspectives in Curriculum History*. London: Routledge.

Stanic, G. M. A. 1987. "Mathematics Education in the United States at the Beginning of the Twentieth Century." In T. S. Popkewitz (ed.), *The Formation of School Subjects: The Struggle for Creating an American Institution*. London: Falmer Press.

Stray, C. A. 1985. "From Monopoly to Marginality: Classics in English Education Since 1800." In I. F. Goodson (ed.), *Social Histories of the Secondary Curriculum*. London: Falmer Press.

Teitelbaum, K. 1987. "Outside the Selective Tradition: Socialist Curriculum for Children in the United States, 1900–1920." In T. S. Popkewitz (ed.), *The Formation of School Subjects: The Struggle for Creating an American Institution*. London: Falmer Press.

Tomkins, G. S. 1986. *A Common Countenance: Stability and Change in the Canadian Curriculum*. Scarborough: Prentice-Hall.

Waring, M. 1985. " 'To Make the Mind Strong, Rather Than to Make It Full': Elementary School Science Teaching in London 1870–1904." In I. F. Goodson (ed.), *Social Histories of the Secondary Curriculum*. London: Falmer Press.

Watson, F. 1909. *The Beginning of the Teaching of Modern Subjects in England*. London: Pitman.

Webster, J. R. 1976. "Curriculum Change and 'Crisis'." *British Journal of Educational Studies* 24(3).

Whitty, G. 1985. "Social Studies and Political Education in England since 1945." In I. F. Goodson (ed.), *Social Histories of the Secondary Curriculum*. London: Falmer Press.

Woolnough, B. E. 1988. *Physics Teaching in Schools 1960–85: Of People, Policy and Power*. London: Falmer Press.

DESEGREGATION

Stephen Samuel Smith
Political Science Department, Winthrop University

Few issues in education have aroused as much controversy as desegregation, the differences in opinion sometimes even extending to the meaning of the term itself. Often used synonymously with *integration* in casual discourse, *desegregation* more precisely "refers to the removal of both legal and social practices" that separate pupils of differing ethnicities and race, as well as to the physical presence of these pupils in the same schools. Integration, on the other hand, "occurs only if there then develops joint participation and mutual acceptance in all activities normally associated with school attendance, from classroom to extracurricular activities" (Jaynes and Williams, 1989:81). Among other things, the definitions indicate that segregation and integration can be considered ends of a continuum, one position on which might be the attendance of blacks and whites in the same school, but their systematic enrollment in different classes [see Datnow and Cooper (*Tracking*), this volume, p. 687].

Another important issue in the conceptualization of desegregation involves the groups to whom it pertains. Given the historical importance of *Brown v. Board of Education,* segregation has most frequently been used with reference to blacks and whites, and only later with reference to other peoples of color and whites. In some localities, however, the desegregation/integration experience of various peoples of color vis-à-vis each other may be extremely important, but this topic has received considerably less attention from scholars and policymakers.

History

More important than either of these or many other conceptual and measurement issues is the opposition, political and otherwise, that school desegregation has frequently faced. Whereas the Supreme Court's landmark school desegregation decision *Brown v. Board of Education* is often credited with helping birth the civil rights movement, the movement's most clear-cut and lasting accomplishments were in other areas, e.g., the desegregation of public accommodations and the enfranchisement of African Americans. As often noted, the first 10 years after *Brown* saw little desegregation, as the Court's acceptance of "all deliberate speed" allowed southern politicians and school boards to engage in massive and protracted resistance and evasion. Significant amounts of school desegregation took place only after the political insurgencies of the early 1960s —most notably the civil rights movement—helped bring forth the Civil Rights Act of 1964, the Elementary and Secondary Education Act of 1965, and a leadership in the Department of Health, Education, and Welfare (HEW) willing to develop and enforce tougher desegregation guidelines. These new guidelines contributed, in turn, to the legal reasoning that would undergird three of the Supreme Court's most important school desegregation decisions since *Brown: Green v. County School Board* (1968), *Swann v. Charlotte-Mecklenburg* (1971), and *Keyes v. School District No. 1, Denver* (1973). *Green* was the first decision in which the court stated that it was not enough for a school district to eliminate laws mandating racial separation. Rather, it had an affirmative duty to desegregate and develop a plan "which promises realistically to convert promptly to a system without a 'white' school and a 'Negro' school, but just schools." In *Swann*, the Court upheld intradistrict busing and the limited use of mathematical ratios of black to white students as remedies for segregation. In *Keyes,* the first decision involving a major city outside the South, the Court drew on *Swann* to allow district-wide reassignment of students in Denver.

However, at a time when these judicial decisions were opening the door to additional school desegregation, the executive branch, whose guidelines had buttressed *Green, Swann, and Keyes,* was now, in several important ways, trying to shut it. A new president, Richard Nixon, sought political advantage by appealing to, if not mobilizing, antibusing sentiment. His Solicitor General argued against the district federal court's busing order when *Swann* reached the Supreme Court, and during the 1972 campaign Nixon called for a ban on court-ordered busing. By 1974, the year of his resignation, the Supreme Court was also sharply limiting desegregation remedies. The key case, *Milliken v. Bradley,* arose in Detroit whose public schools were over 70% African American. Because that high percentage of blacks precluded meaningful desegregation within Detroit, a federal district court ordered busing between Detroit and its predominantly white suburbs. By a 5-4 vote—four members of the majority being Nixon appointees—the Supreme Court rejected that remedy on the basis that these suburban schools were not in the same district that the Detroit schools were in. That ruling has served to prohibit interdistrict busing for desegregation except under circumstances whose existence has been very difficult to prove. In the many areas where demographic patterns resemble Detroit's, but a school district boundary separates a central city from its suburbs, *Milliken v. Bradley* has thus posed very high barriers to the mandatory metropolitan-wide busing plans that some desegregation proponents view as the ones most likely to be successful. Because critics of desegregation have often claimed that the Court drew too heavily on social science's understanding of the *consequences* of segregation in *Brown,* it seems appropriate to note that the decisive fifth vote in *Milliken I* indicated an even greater *un*willingness to draw upon social science's understanding of the *causes* of segregation in a Northern city such as Detroit. That vote was cast by Justice Stewart who, commenting on the demographic patterns precluding intradistrict desegregation, said "this essential fact of a predominantly Negro school population in Detroit," was caused by "unknown and perhaps unknowable factors."

Its interdistrict busing remedy for segregation having been rejected by the Supreme Court, the federal district court then approved the implementation of a broad range of additional and special education programs for students in Detroit. Often called *Milliken II* remedies after the 1977 Supreme Court decision approving their use, these programs attempt to deal with the noxious consequences of school segregation through various compensatory education programs rather than through desegregation. *Milliken II* programs have been used in a wide range of districts as the demographic patterns that characterized the Detroit area in 1974 have since become an even more prominent feature of the nation's metropolitan landscape. At the same time that *Milliken II* programs have become an important aspect of metropolitan education, so too have various voluntary programs, especially magnet schools that seek to promote desegregation by offering a range of specialized programs that are typically designed to draw whites to schools in nonwhite neighborhoods. The extent to which the growing emphasis on voluntary desegregation programs facilitates desegregation and improves educational outcomes remains an important research question (Orfield et al., 1996; Rossell, 1995; Wells and Crain, 1997). Also affecting desegregation have been three Supreme Court decisions handed down between 1991 and 1995. In *School Board of Oklahoma City v. Dowell* (1991), *Freeman v. Pitts* (1992), and *Missouri v. Jenkins* (1995), the Court's rulings served to make it easier for districts to dismantle desegregation plans. These decisions added credence to claims that the country was giving up on school desegregation 40 years after *Brown.* But proponents of desegregation often emphasize the accomplishments of those 40 years, especially because it was only from the mid-1960s until *Milliken I* that the federal government was vigorously seeking desegregation, and even in that period, its various branches and agencies were often not in sync.

Desegregation in Higher Education

The political and legal history of the struggle for desegregated primary and secondary education in America is intimately connected to a similar struggle at the tertiary level. The protracted legal campaign of the National Association for the Advancement of Colored People (NAACP) against Jim Crow education included many courtroom challenges to segregated public systems of higher education because the absence of many professional and graduate programs in such systems was an especially stark challenge to the "separate-but-equal" sham. Important legal precedents for *Brown* were laid in a series of judicial decisions that forced states either to provide programs where none had existed, or to admit African Americans to the programs available for whites.

Opportunities for African Americans to attain higher education were minimal until the second half of the nineteenth century. The movement to establish private historically black colleges had arisen to fill this void. The first historically black colleges—Wilberforce University in Ohio and Cheyney State and Lincoln University in Pennsylvania—were founded in the years before the Civil War. During Reconstruction and throughout the latter part of the nineteenth century, northern philanthropy supported the creation of many more private colleges for blacks (Anderson, 1988). Only a handful of private historically white colleges—Oberlin being among the first—opened their doors to blacks prior to 1900. A dual system of higher education was further institutionalized in the first half of the twentieth century with the establishment of additional institutions, both public and private, for black students.

The enrollment of Latinos in higher education is a relatively recent phenomenon. Even in the West and Southwest, where large populations of Latinos have lived for centuries, access to higher education was limited by a host of economic, educational, linguistic, and legal obstacles. According to Gándara (1995), the G.I. Bill provided returning World War II veterans with unprecedented opportunities for higher education. The civil rights movement of the 1960s provided additional opportunities. Although prior to the development of this movement, few efforts had been made to identify and count Latinos in higher education, it is clear that until the 1970s, even campuses in heavily Latino communities sometimes enrolled very few Latino students. Today, Latinos remain the least educated race/ethnic group in the United States [see Mickelson (*Affirmative Action* and *Race and Education*), this volume, p. 29].

Significant impetus for the dismantling of dual systems in public higher education came from *Adams v. Richardson* (1973), which called for the submission of acceptable desegregation plans from states found to be operating segregated systems. Compliance with *Adams* has been uneven. North Carolina has been more successful than many other southern states in dismantling its dual system. Initially, the North Carolina system of higher education had 5 institutions for African Americans, 10 for whites, and 1 for Native Americans [now University of North Carolina (UNC) Pembroke]. UNC Greensboro was formerly the women's college. As Table 1 indicates, at present no institution is exclusively one race or the other, but student bodies are still racially identifiable. Of the historically white campuses, the larger ones are the more racially diverse. However, overall, the percentage black enrollment at the historically white campuses is less than the percentage white enrollment at the historically black campuses.

Today, the vast majority of colleges and universities are racially desegregated to various degrees. However, several southern states in which compliance with *Adams* has been weakest have been involved in additional litigation. The litigation involving Mississippi has been especially controversial because the state's desegregation plan called for the merging and closing of some black colleges.

Publicly supported institutions of higher education are desegregated by gender as well. Historically, a southern state typically had one or more institutions reserved for the education of women, but women were excluded from other schools, including, usually, the flagship institution. Most publicly supported institutions of higher education became coeducational several decades ago. However, Virginia and South Carolina continued to reserve their state-supported military academies for men. As a result of litigation, South Carolina's Citadel admitted its first female cadets in 1996, and the Virginia Military Institute did the same in 1997.

The interrelationship among affirmative action, desegregation, and increased educational opportunities for underrepresented peoples of color is especially apparent in higher education. As both courts and legislatures revisit earlier affirmative action and desegregation decisions, much of the increase in access to higher education that these groups have won in the past 40 years is likely to be threatened [see Mickelson (*Affirmative Action*) and Paul (*Desegregation of Higher Education*), this volume, p. 151].

Trends in Desegregation

Any discussion of desegregation trends quickly encounters controversy over their measurement (Armor, 1995;

TABLE 1. Enrollment by Race, Institutions of the University of North Carolina (UNC) System of Higher Education, Fall 1998[a]

Historically Black Campuses	White (%)	Historically White Campuses	Black (%)
Elizabeth City	23	UNC Charlotte	17
Fayetteville	22	UNC Greensboro	15
Winston-Salem	16	East Carolina	12
North Carolina Central	13	UNC Chapel Hill	9.9
North Carolina A&T	7.3	North Carolina State	9.8
		North Carolina School of the Arts	7.4
		UNC Wilmington	5.5
		Western Carolina	4.7
		UNC Asheville	3.4
		Appalachian	2.9

Source: University of North Carolina, 1999.

[a]The state of North Carolina is approximately 22% black. Enrollment at UNC Pembroke, at one time Pembroke State College for Indians, is 16% black, 57% white, and 23% Native American.

Rivkin, 1994; Rossell, 1990). Furthermore, such methodological differences often coincide with those between what Hochschild has called enthusiasts and skeptics [see Hochschild (*Brown v. Board of Education*), this volume, p. 67]. These differences notwithstanding, there is general consensus on overall trends: nationwide, the segregation of black students decreased significantly between 1968 and 1972, but progress slowed in subsequent years. Furthermore, some measures indicate considerable *re*segregation of black students in the late 1980s and 1990s. Among Latinos segregation has increased since 1968 (see Table 2).

Historically, desegregation enforcement efforts were concentrated in the South. This emphasis is reflected in Table 3, which indicates that for blacks, segregation is less in that region than in the Northeast or Midwest. Furthermore, for both blacks and Latinos, the Northeast has the highest level of intensely segregated schools.

Desegregation Outcomes

A combination of empirical, methodological, historical, and normative considerations has made it difficult for scholars to reach broad consensus on two especially important issues: the extent to which desegregation induces white flight and the extent to which desegregation benefits students. White flight refers to the tendency of white students to leave a desegregating school district for one that is not desegregating, or to attend a private school. The literature on this topic is suffi-ciently voluminous, technical, and contentious to allow only several summary remarks: Declining white enrollments have a range of causes including differential birth rates and growing suburbanization. White enrollment has dropped in districts that have desegregated as well as those that have not, thus lending support to the conclusion that "other factors had a much larger impact on [declining white enrollments] than did the implementation of school desegregation programs" (Rivkin, 1994:290).

Although there is also scholarly disagreement about the benefits of a desegregated education, a fuller summary of this topic can be provided. Most assessments of outcomes for students of color focus upon short-term effects: equalizing access to quality educational programs, resources, and other indicators of opportunities to learn; closing the racial achievement and attainment gaps; and reducing psychologically destructive self-concepts and oppressive racial stereotypes. Other assessments look at levels of tolerance, racial prejudice, racial tension, and appreciation of human diversity. Over time, the general thrust of the accumulated evidence suggests that some small but significant academic gains accrue to students of color (mainly African American) if the desegregation programs are designed carefully, conducted well, enroll children at an early age, and continue over many years. There is also substantial evidence from these studies of short-term issues that white children are not harmed by, and can often benefit from, programs that are designed well and implemented thoughtfully (Social Scientists, 1991).

TABLE 2. Percentage of U.S. Black and Latino Students in Predominantly Minority and 90 to 100% Minority Schools, 1968–1996

YEARS	50–100% MINORITY		90–100% MINORITY	
	BLACKS	LATINOS	BLACK	LATINOS
1968–69	76.6	54.8	64.3	23.1
1972–73	63.6	56.6	38.7	23.3
1980–81	62.9	68.1	33.2	28.8
1986–87	63.3	71.5	32.5	32.2
1991–92	66.0	73.4	33.9	34.0
1996–97	68.8	74.8	35.0	35.4

Source: Orfield and Yun (1999).

However, the strongest and least ambiguous evidence on the outcomes of desegregated schooling involves its long-term effects on African Americans (there is relatively little research on the long-term effects of desegregation on Latinos and other people of color). Wells and Crain (1994) reviewed 21 of the most important studies of the long-term effects of school desegregation and concluded that a measurable, tangible advantage accrues to black students who attend desegregated schools. Those who attend desegregated schools are more likely to experience upward social mobility, are less likely to live and work in segregated settings, are more likely to have higher yet realistic educational and occupational aspirations and attainment, are more likely to work in higher status jobs, and are more likely to have desegregated social and professional networks in later life than those who attend segregated schools.

Wells and Crain developed a micro–macro theory that explains how desegregated education appears to break the cycle of racially stratified and segregated lives that typically characterize individuals' work, recreational, religious, and educational careers. They draw upon Braddock and McPartland's seminal work on perpetuation theory and upon Granovetter's notion of the strengths of weak ties to explain how desegregation breaks the intergenerational cycle of segregation by allowing nonwhite students access to high-status institutions and the powerful social networks within them. According to perpetuation theory, when individuals live segregated lives, segregation tends to repeat itself across the stages of the life cycle and across institutions. Braddock's work supplements the corpus of research that demonstrates the continuing effects of structural

barriers to equal opportunity by showing how individuals who choose to maintain physically segregated lives do so in part because, as children, they never tested their racial beliefs in integrated situations (Braddock, 1980; Braddock and McPartland, 1982). Granovetter's (1986) network analysis research demonstrates how the structure of segregation is expressed at the microlevel because African Americans and Latinos lack access to informal interpersonal networks that provide information about, and entrance into, desegregated institutions and employment. Desegregated schools provide sites where weak ties between students of different races can be established. These weak ties to more knowledgeable and privileged students—who are typically white and middle class—furnish others with information about, and access to, college and employment.

This micro–macro theory, then, accounts for the findings that black students who attend desegregated schools have improved long-term life chances relative to those who remain in racially isolated schools. To desegregation enthusiasts, these long-term effects are especially important because they substantiate *Brown*'s most basic premise: a desegregated education would provide a gateway to mainstream institutions and to at least some of the benefits that such access typically confers.

Conditions for Desegregation

Forty years of scholarship since *Brown* have illuminated many of the conditions that facilitate effective desegregation. As the history of desegregation efforts indicates, the first condition is a political one: no significant school desegregation would have taken place "absent

TABLE 3. Segregation by Region, 1996–1997 School Year

	PERCENTAGE OF LATINO STUDENTS IN REGION IN SCHOOLS		PERCENTAGE OF BLACK STUDENTS IN REGION IN SCHOOLS	
REGION	50–100% MINORITY	90–100% MINORITY	50–100% MINORITY	90–100% MINORITY
South	75.9	38.3	65.3	27.9
Border	43.5	12.6	63.2	37.3
Northeast	78.2	46.0	77.3	50.5
Midwest	54.0	22.3	72.0	43.4
West	77.1	33.0	73.5	27.5
U.S. Total	74.8	35.4	68.8	35.0

Source: Orfield and Yun (1999).

authoritative imposition from an agent outside and 'above' the school districts themselves" (Hochschild, 1997). In most instances, the courts have been the source of this authoritative imposition, but in some cases it was HEW or state boards of education.

The conditions within schools that generally facilitate effective desegregation include the involvement of parents in education activities; recruitment of a significant proportion of teachers, administrators, and support staff of color; support by teachers, administrators, and support staff for the desegregation plan; the development of multicultural curricula and bilingual educational programs; appreciation of, and sensitivity to, cultural differences among students, especially those pertaining to learning styles and possible disciplinary issues; the establishment of safe schools with fair and consistent discipline policies; minimal use (or complete elimination) of ability grouping and tracking; structured cooperative learning strategies; and the development of extracurricular activities that maximize opportunities for cooperative interaction among students of different racial and ethnic groups.

At the district and community level, these conditions generally include desegregating over a large area to increase socioeconomic as well as racial/ethnic diversity; assuring a critical mass of students of each racial/ethnic group at each desegregated school; desegregating as many grades as feasible at the same time, emphasizing the early grades; continuing desegregation throughout both primary and secondary school; developing stability in pupil assignment plans as quickly as possible; and persisting in the plan's implementation despite opposition.

Busing, Magnets, and Desegregation's Uncertain Future

The wide range of desegregation experiences among the nation's school districts cannot fully be captured by one, or perhaps many, case studies. But the experience of North Carolina's Charlotte-Mecklenburg district (CMS) is especially significant because it illustrates the political conditions facilitating successful desegregation, the evolution of desegregation strategies, and the problematic future of desegregation as the twenty-first century begins.

Charlotte's desegregation accomplishments are especially noteworthy because, as the district that gave rise to the *Swann* case, much of its success involved mandatory busing, typically the most controversial desegregation strategy. Historically, busing has long been part of United States education. Buses were often used to maintain segregation as well as to provide access to schooling for upper income whites from suburbs whose population density was too low to support neighborhood schools. By 1969–1970, a year before the Supreme Court's *Swann* decision, approximately 40% of the nation's students were bused to school with minimal controversy (Orfield, 1978:128). It is only busing for desegregation that has provoked such frequently intense opposition. In fact, public opinion polls show that a large majority of respondents support the concept of school desegregation so long as the questions do not contain the words "forced busing" (Hochschild, 1997).

Political struggle over desegregation continued in Charlotte-Mecklenburg for several years after the Supreme Court's decision in *Swann* in 1971. By 1974–

1975, however, CMS adopted a mandatory busing plan that would be considered one of the nation's most successful and that would allow civic boosters and industry recruiters to tout Charlotte as "The City That Made it Work." In Charlotte, as elsewhere, the perseverance of the African-American community was the *sine qua non* of whatever success the city could claim for its desegregation accomplishments, but other factors were also crucial. Some involved the persistence and vision of the federal district judge overseeing the desegregation case in Charlotte-Mecklenburg. Other factors involved the district's size and racial composition. As the name suggests, CMS is a consolidated district covering all of Mecklenburg county, not just the city of Charlotte. The county-wide district's large size—530 square miles— made white flight difficult (Douglas, 1995). The presence of many rural and suburban white students in the district made desegregation easier than would have been the case had the district's boundaries been coterminous with the city's, rather than the county's. Furthermore, blacks never constituted more than 40% of the district's students during the busing plan's existence, which made desegregation easier than if that percentage were larger. In addition, the school board, under intense political pressure from middle-class whites, agreed to bus students from the city's most affluent white neighborhood to an historically black high school, thus assuring that, with only a few exceptions, all CMS students would be bused for desegregation during some portion of their education. Finally, Charlotte's business elite saw racial tranquility and school desegregation as furthering its economic and political interests.

Even at its high point, the early 1980s, CMS's busing plan had various shortcomings and inequities; in particular, blacks bore a disproportionately large share of whatever inconveniences and hardships busing entailed. Nonetheless, busing flourished for over a decade until the economic boom that it helped facilitate also proved its undoing. The boom brought to Charlotte-Mecklenburg middle-class whites from all over the country, especially the North, who were accustomed to suburban, predominantly white school districts and who lacked the pride that many more established Charlotteans took in CMS' desegregation accomplishments (Mickelson et al., 1994). The vocal objections of newcomers—both individual and institutional—to CMS' busing plan in the late 1980s resonated with much broader political currents, among which were the putative crisis in U.S. education, the merits of choice as a school-improvement strategy, and middle-class families' anxieties about their children's future in a restructured economy. In this economic context, many middle-class whites were increasingly concerned, not about desegregation per se, but with the class aspects of it. In particular, these white families worried that busing jeopardized their children's education—and hence life chances—by putting them in the same classroom with what they considered to be ill-prepared, unmotivated, and undisciplined black students from disadvantaged economic backgrounds. Although support for busing remained much higher among blacks, there was also increasing dissatisfaction with the inequities of the busing plan and the quality of education that African-American students were getting. Finally, fearing that the increasing dissatisfaction with the school system would jeopardize future economic growth, Charlotte's business elite threw its considerable political weight behind a large turnover in school board membership and the recruitment of a new superintendent. In March 1992 the school board, on the recommendation of its new superintendent, voted to dismantle most of CMS' mandatory busing plan and replace it with other desegregation strategies of which a system of magnet schools received the most resources and attention. Although CMS continued to envision itself as the "premier urban, integrated public school system in the nation," desegregation "declined modestly" in the first few years of the magnet plan's operation (Morantz, 1996:203). The district's commitment to desegregation continued to generate intense controversy and eventually resulted in the reactivation of the *Swann* case and a 2 month trial in 1999 that exemplified the terms of much of the debate about school desegregation in the late 1990s.

The white plaintiffs, whose lawsuit triggered the new litigation, argued that whatever racial imbalance existed in 1999 could not be attributed to the state-mandated segregation thirty the Jim Crow era since CMS had been pursuing desegregative remedies for almost 30 years. Therefore, the white plaintiffs continued, CMS had met its legal obligations under *Swann* and was no longer legally required to pursue such remedies. Both CMS and the black families involved in the case claimed the reverse, asserting that CMS had yet to comply adequately with the original *Swann* court orders. Therefore, they countered, the ongoing and large black/white differences in student assignment, opportunities to learn, and academic achievement had their roots in the deliberatively segregative policies that CMS had pursued for many years prior to the original *Swann* decision. Thus, in their view, CMS was still legally obliged to pursue policies aimed at alleviating these differences.

The similarity in 1999 between the positions of CMS and the black plaintiffs was one of the major differences between this trial and the one 30 years earlier in which, of course, CMS had vigorously resisted black desegregation demands. A second major difference involved the judicial system itself. In addition to taking place in an environment in which the Supreme Court's decisions earlier in the decade had imposed many legal barriers to the continuation of desegregation policies, the 1999 case was heard by a different federal district court judge, a Reagan appointee who, as a private citizen in the 1960s, had been active in Charlotte's anti-busing movement.

The judge's decision was a sweeping victory for the white plaintiffs. His opinion credited their expert witnesses' testimony that current racial imbalances in pupil assignment and academic achievement resulted from factors over which CMS had no control such as demographic changes and the socioeconomic characteristics of students, rather than vestiges of state-mandated segregation. His order prohibited CMS from considering race in student assignment or the allocation of educational benefits and opportunities. At this time (October 1999), there is no way of knowing whether this decision will be sustained by the higher courts to which both CMS and the black plaintiffs have appealed. But there is little doubt that, if not reversed, the decision will increase resegregation in CMS. For a federal court's decision to have such consequences in CMS, a district that exemplifies the promise of *Brown,* would provide still more evidence that the United States was giving up on school desegregation at the end of the twentieth century.

The Desegregation Dilemma

Whatever the eventual outcome of the reactivated *Swann* case, the experience of other districts that have dismantled mandatory desegregation plans is quite cautionary. Especially relevant in this regard is Norfolk, the first city to stop busing for desegregation with federal court approval. The end of busing in 1986 drew far fewer white students back to the Norfolk schools than the school board had predicted; it did, however, markedly increase the segregation of black students (Armor, 1991; Carr, 1991; Carr and Zeigler, 1990). The Norfolk experience together with the legacy of *Milliken v. Bradley* highlights the fundamental dilemmas of desegregation policy in contemporary metropolitan areas: the combination of political fragmentation and residential segregation poses extremely high barriers to the desegregation of education. However, it is a desegregated education that, according to research on its long-term effects, can offer nonwhites an important gateway to mainstream institutions and some of the benefits that accompany such access. Hence desegregation is one way of breaking the intergenerational cycle of segregation and its consequences to which perpetuation theory calls attention. The need to strengthen approaches other than desegregation that can also break this cycle may of necessity become an increasingly urgent research question given the experience exemplified by Norfolk, the reactivated *Swann* litigation, Supreme Court decisions in the early 1990s, and the normative opposition by some blacks to desegregation [see Hochschild (*Brown v. Board of Education*), this volume]. However, given the heavy concentration of poor people of color in central cities (and in some older suburbs as well), proponents of desegregation can legitimately ask: Just what conditions would make "separate" public education any more "equal" in the twenty-first century than it was in the twentieth? Unless the trends of the 1990s are reversed, there may be ample opportunity for citizens, scholars, and policymakers to grope for an answer to that question in the years to come.

REFERENCES

Anderson, James D. 1988. *The Education of Blacks in the South, 1860–1935.* Chapel Hill: University of North Carolina Press.

Armor, David J. 1991. "Response to Carr and Zeigler's 'White Flight and White Return in Norfolk.'" *Sociology of Education* 64:134–139.

———. 1995. *Forced Justice: School Desegregation and the Law.* New York: Oxford University Press.

Braddock, Jomills. H., II. 1980. "The Perpetuation of Segregation Across Levels of Education: A Behavioral Assessment of the Contact-Hypothesis." *Sociology of Education* 53:178–186.

Braddock, Jomills, H., II, and James M. McPartland. 1982. "Assessing School Desegregation Effects: New Directions in Research." *Research in the Sociology of Education and Socialization* 3:259–282.

Carr, Leslie G. 1991. "Reply to Armor." *Sociology of Education* 64:223–228.

Carr, Leslie G., and Donald J. Zeigler. 1990. "White Flight and White Return in Norfolk: A Test of Predictions." *Sociology of Education* 63:272–282.

Douglas, Davison M. 1995. *Reading, Writing, & Race: The Desegregation of the Charlotte Schools.* Chapel Hill, NC: University of North Carolina Press.

Gándara, Patricia. 1995. *Over the Ivy Walls: The Educational Mobility of Low Income Chicanos.* Albany, NY: SUNY Press.

Granovetter, Mark. 1986. "The Micro-structure of School Desegregation." In Jeffrey Prager, Douglas Longshore, and Melvin Seeman (eds.), *School Desegregation Research: New Directions in Situational Analysis,* pp. 81–110. New York: Plenum Press.

Green v. County School Board. 1968. 391 U.S. 430.

Hochschild, Jennifer. 1997. "Is School Desegregation Still a Viable Policy Option?" *PS: Political Science and Politics* 30:458–466.

Jaynes, Gerald David, and Robin M. Williams, Jr. 1989. *A Common Destiny: Blacks and American Society.* Washington, DC: National Academy Press.

Keyes v. School District No. 1, Denver. 1973. 413 U.S. 189.

Mickelson, Roslyn A., Carol Ray, and Stephen Samuel Smith. 1994. "The Growth Machine and Politics of Urban Educational Reform: The Case of Charlotte, North Carolina." In Nelly Stromquist (ed.) *Education in Urban Areas: Cross National Dimensions,* pp. 169–195. Westport, CT: Praeger.

Milliken v. Bradley (Milliken I). 1974. 418 U.S. 717.

Morantz, Alison D. 1996. "Desegregation at Risk: Threat

and Reaffirmation in Charlotte." In Gary Orfield, Susan Eaton, and the Harvard Project on School Desegregation (eds.), *Dismantling Desegregation: The Quiet Reversal of Brown v. Board of Education,* pp. 179–206. New York: The New Press.

Orfield, Gary. 1978. *Must We Bus? Segregated Schools and National Policy.* Washington, DC: Brookings.

Orfield, Gary, and John Yun. 1999. *Resegregation in American Schools.* Cambridge: Harvard University Civil Rights Project.

Orfield, Gary, Susan Eaton, and the Harvard Project on School Desegregation. 1996. *Dismantling Desegregation: The Quiet Reversal of Brown v. Board of Education.* New York: The New Press.

Rivkin, Steven G. 1994. "Residential Segregation and School Integration." *Sociology of Education* 67:279–292.

Rossell, Christine H. 1990. *The Carrot or the Stick for School Desegregation Policy: Magnet Schools or Forced Busing.* Philadelphia: Temple University Press.

————. 1995. "Controlled-Choice Desegregation Plans: Not Enough Choice, Too Much Control?" *Urban Affairs Review* 31:43–76.

Social Scientists. 1991. "School Desegregation: A Social Science Statement," in brief of the NAACP et al., as amicus curiae in *Freeman v. Pitts,* signed by 52 social scientists.

Swann v. Charlotte-Mecklenburg Board of Education. 1971. 402 U.S. 1.

University of North Carolina. 1999. *Statistical Abstract of Higher Education in North Carolina, 1998–99.* Chapel Hill, NC: University of North Carolina General Administration Program Assessment and Public Service Division.

Wells, Amy Stuart, and Robert L. Crain. 1994. "Perpetuation Theory and the Long-Term Effects of School Desegregation." *Review of Educational Research* 64:531–555.

————. 1997. *Stepping over the Color Line: African American Students in White Suburban Schools.* New Haven, CT: Yale University Press.

DESEGREGATION OF HIGHER EDUCATION

Faith G. Paul
The Public Policy Research Consortium

The desegregation of higher education in America was not a product of moral leadership by an enlightened institution setting an example for a nation paralyzed by race. It was imposed on a higher education enterprise deeply rooted in a culture of contentment, peacefully reflecting the larger social mores of society. It was compelled by litigation, by protests, by violence and fear, and the strong arm of the law, to address a major inequity in higher education and society.

Once compelled, the campuses began to discover an advantage in diversity, so long as it could be made to fit within the overall paradigms of higher education. But the process of change violated important elements of those paradigms, particularly where meritocratic standards and affirmative action collided, ensuring contended ground between liberty and equality, between the goals of social justice and the institutional imperative.

The task was daunting because David had to bring down Goliath. Goliath's progeny were equally difficult. Deeply held beliefs about race have freer play in the decentralized and professional environment of higher education. Autonomous higher education systems can blame poor preparation at the elementary and secondary level for a limited and unacceptable pool of black students. No constituency existed to unite lower and higher education in one seamless web, or to build voluntary partnerships across domains.

The circumstances impelling change were irrefutable. No black student was admissible at any white higher education campus in the South. Programs and resources at the separate black campuses, public and private, were rich in purposeful endeavor, but poor in depth and breadth of program, in supporting libraries and laboratories. There were no black graduate and professional programs in the public sector before World War II, and, with the exception of Howard University, few on the private black campuses. Black students seeking a broader education had to go North. Here too, options were limited, for few, if any, blacks from the North or the South were enrolled on many of these northern campuses.

As black leaders forged a strategy to challenge the legal bulwark of separate education in the South—*Plessy v. Ferguson* 163 US 537 (1896)—in the years just prior to, and immediately following World War II, a key element of the strategy was to open a beachhead at the level of graduate education, where integration would involve adults rather than young children, to minimize the resistance that would follow.

The first real success came in Missouri in 1938, in *ex rel. Gaines v. Canada* (305 U.S. 337, 59 S.Ct. 232, 83 L.Ed. 208, 1938), when the court held that if separate education was maintained it had to be equal at both the undergraduate and graduate levels. The Alabama response was typical. The legislature and governor hastened to increase funding for the two historically black campuses, so they could qualify for accreditation, and satisfy the Court's criteria for separate but equal education.

After the war, as black veterans returned and tried to enter the white campuses in the South, they were peremptorily refused on the basis of race. The NAACP-Legal Defense Fund (LDF) continued to press. In *Sipuel v. Board of Regents* in 1948, in *Sweatt v. Painter* in 1950, and in *McLauren v. Oklahoma State Regents* in 1950, they forced the Southern states and courts to come to grips with the prohibitively high costs associated with a separate but equal system of higher education.

That point made, LDF organized to strike the final blow, using a compulsory elementary and secondary education case. The result was *Brown v. Board of Education* 347 US 483, 495 (1954), the decision that declared segregated education unconstitutional under the Equal Protection Clause of the Fourteenth Amendment. Two principles were enunciated: that separation of persons by race creates inherently unequal systems of education, and that black citizens have a right to obtain an education equal to that of white citizens (*Brown-Scott*, 1994). Though the cases before the Court pertained to elementary and secondary education, the Court addressed public education in its decision, with the implication that it was addressing higher education as well as elementary and secondary education.

When the Court based its decision on the Equal Protection Clause of the Fourteenth Amendment, it grounded it in equity guarantees inherent in the fundamental fabric of American democracy, and provided the lower courts with a broad equity base for applying the law to erase a persistent and ubiquitous inequity in American history. In fashioning remedy, however, in the elementary and secondary education cases that preceded litigation in higher education, the lower courts turned to tort law, and to a particular branch of that law to carry out their work.

Tort law derives from the common law morality that one who hurts another should compensate him. Its purpose is to end the evil act, eliminate the injury, and restore the victim's losses, rather than to punish the perpetrator. The purpose of remedy is to compensate for losses, not to redistribute resources. The concern of the court is with proportionality between the violation's effects and the remedy, rather than between the violation itself and the remedy.

Under tort law it is the obligation of the plaintiff to demonstrate how the defendant's action caused the plaintiff's injury, and that a particular defendant bears responsibility for that conduct. The lower courts therefore placed the burden of proof on the plaintiffs with the requirement that plaintiffs prove intentional discrimination.

At the higher education level plaintiffs would have to prove intent to discriminate in admissions, faculty and staff hiring, finances, program duplication, facilities, membership on governing boards, and any other area they perceived segregation. At the elementary and secondary level the burden was to prove public officials' intentional assignment of African-American students to racially identifiable schools.

Intent represents only one branch of tort law, however. The courts also had available other criteria such as reckless and negligent infliction of harm, or infliction of harm itself. But just as the district courts preferred tort law over the broader equity grounds of the Fourteenth Amendment, so did they hold strictly to intent, rather than embrace the broader criteria of reckless and negligent infliction of harm, or infliction of harm itself.

Reflecting constituencies determined to resist, but obligated by law to respond to decisions of the Supreme Court, the district courts narrowed the scope of remedy and placed burden squarely on the back of the plaintiffs.

In the *Brown* decision, the Court narrowly tailored its finding to state-imposed (*de jure*) separation, without establishing a concomitant legal obligation to address *de facto* segregation. It also limited its ruling to the broad principles of the case, without offering guidelines for implementation. Insofar as those principles framed the remedy and legal ideology of implementation, it was to require that black students be provided the same quality and level of public education afforded white students, by educating both in integrated public schools.

In this remedy the Court did not have a solid block of plaintiffs as its friends and defendants as its enemies. The broader constituency plaintiffs and defendants represented was divided about the advisability of desegregation. Gunnar Myrdal framed the issue well when he wrote,

> The situation is complicated by the fact that both whites and Negroes are divided in their own minds. . . . In the North the official opinion among whites is that segregation is not compatible with equality, but, . . . much segregation is actually in effect as a consequence of residential segregation . . .
>
> In the South direct segregation in schools is a necessary means of keeping up the tremendous financial discrimination against Negro schools . . . (and) as a precaution against social equality . . .

[For the Negroes] [I]n so far as segregation means discrimination and is a badge of Negro inferiority, [Negroes] are against it. . . . Some Negroes, however, prefer the segregated school . . . when the mixed school involves humiliation for Negro students and discrimination against Negro teachers. . . . Other Negroes prefer the mixed schools at any cost, since for them it is a matter of principle or since they believe that it is a means of improving race relations. (Myrdal, 1944)

The issue was contentious in the black community as early as 1935, when black leaders initiated serious discussion of how to provide equal education for black students, and W.E.B. Du Bois and Charles Thompson of Howard University argued in public in Thompson's *Journal*. In a provocative piece entitled "Does the Negro Need Separate Schools?" DuBois wrote,

I know that this article will forthwith be interpreted . . . as a plea for segregated Negro schools and colleges. It is not. . . . It is saying in plain English: that a separate Negro school, where children are treated like human beings, trained by teachers of their own race, who know what it means to be black . . . is infinitely better than making our boys and girls doormats to be spit and tramped upon and lied to by ignorant social climbers. (Quoted in Kluger, 1977:170–172)

And Charles Thompson responded,

Those who argue that the separate school with equal facilities is superior to the mixed school with prejudice should know that the separate school, or separate anything, with equal facilities is a fiction. (Quoted in Kluger, 1977:170–172)

The disagreement in the black community revolved around three substantive issues. Would integration require or inevitably lead to cultural assimilation? What effect would hostility have on the personal efficacy and academic resilience of black students in desegregated colleges or schools? Would desegregation destroy the public black campuses? The latter was particularly contentious. The black campuses had been indispensable agents of education for generations of African Ameri-

cans, and were a primary institutional pillar in the African-American community, second only to the black church.

Under a unitary system those campuses could be merged with nearby white campuses. Or they could remain separate but lose their identity through extensive white enrollment and control on boards of trustees. Or they could remain primarily black, but become so attenuated in their enrollment, as black students opted for white campuses, that they would no longer be viable black institutions. The ultimate irony for large segments of the black community would be for desegregation to destroy the very institution that had fostered their education and sustained black culture.

The immediate question, however, was whether *Brown* applied to higher education at all. The courts clarified the issue in two cases in 1955 and 1956. In *Florida ex rel. Hawkins v. Board of Control* [350 U.S. 413 (1956)] the court found segregation unconstitutional in graduate schools. And in *Frasier v. Board of Trustees of the University of North Carolina,* 134 F.Supp. 589, 592–93 (M.D.N.C. 1955), aff'd per curiam, 350 U.S. 979 (1956) the court ruled that a state must ensure a racially nondiscriminatory admissions policy at its public higher education campuses. But the campuses by and large ignored the decision, preferring to believe that their distinctive characteristics as higher education institutions made them immune to *Brown* in any substantive sense. It was not until the civil rights movement and student protests of the 1960s changed the political and social dynamic on the campuses, and in the country, and forced the issue, that desegregation was initiated on the campuses.

Those protests began when four black students from North Carolina Agricultural and Technical College staged a sit-in at a segregated lunch counter in Greensboro, North Carolina in February 1960, and roused the conscience of a nation. The protests of the civil rights movement quickly became an integral part of a larger student protest spreading across the country aimed at ending persistent racial injustice, the Vietnam War, the plight of the poor, the materialism of society, the indifference of higher education to the social problems of society, and to the needs of its own students.

Three elements of the movement shaped the desegregation of higher education. As protesters on campuses across the North forced university administrators to negotiate their demands, they compelled the campuses to address their civil rights concerns. This initiated desegregation in the North.

When the Civil Rights movement captured the conscience of the nation, and Congress passed the Civil Rights Act of 1964, the mandate to desegregate broadened to include both *de facto* and *de jure* segregation. Title VI of the Civil Rights Act provided that no institution receiving federal financial assistance could discriminate on the basis of race, color, or national origin. Because virtually every campus in the country was receiving some form of federal financial assistance, and the scope of federal financial assistance would expand greatly in 1965, when Congress passed the Higher Education Act a year later, the Civil Rights Act ended the debate about whether *Brown* applied to higher education, whether remedy should extend to *de jure* segregation alone, and whether private campuses were exempted, and widened the scope to include all campuses that accepted federal funds.

Third, when states in the South continued to operate dual systems of higher education, Title VI was invoked. The cases were heard in the context of the principles of *Brown* 1 and *Brown* 2, the applications of tort law developed in earlier elementary and secondary education desegregation cases, and Title VI. These higher education cases shaped desegregation throughout the South.

Desegregation in the North

The Civil Rights movement that began in the South in 1960 had a profound effect on black and white students on the northern campuses. For black students it was an affirmation of their dignity and value as human beings and as American citizens; and from the mid-1960s onward a catalyst for rediscovering and affirming their rich African and American cultural heritage. The reform agenda they espoused began with demands to admit more black students, and widened over the course of a decade to include a broad range of issues pertaining to students, faculty and staff, the curriculum, dormitories, and social programs.

Issues of access focused on admitting substantially more black students at the undergraduate and graduate levels, in large enough numbers to constitute a critical mass.

The pool of students was to include at-risk as well as better prepared students, with increased financial aid

for all black students, and academic support programs for at-risk students. There were calls for open admission for all minority students and more prudent requests for campuses to work with high schools in their feeder areas to identify potential students, and work with them through their high school years, to shape preparation for college.

Transforming all white, or virtually all white, faculty, administration, and staff was a second target. The issue was both cognitive and psychological, seeking understanding of the black experience and role models. Students pressed for more black faculty, for a black dean of students and other administrators, and for black staff in admissions, financial aid, and counseling. They demanded improved working conditions for black employees on campus, and more opportunities for blacks to find employment on their campuses.

Curriculum issues were even more contentious. Demands for the inclusion of black history and culture in the on-going curriculum grew to include demands for black studies courses and programs, and for those programs to be autonomous, taught only by black faculty, and, on some campuses open only to black students. Where there were large numbers of Mexican students, the demands included similar courses and programs in Mexican-American culture, and for Mexican-American centers.

Demands for separate black dormitories, black student unions, and black social programs followed demands to eliminate segregation in student unions, the library, and in sororities and fraternities. These requests, however, brought strong warnings from the NAACP and the Office for Civil Rights that separate courses, programs, or dormitories, black or white, would place the campuses in violation of Title VI.

From 1960 until the demonstrations at Berkeley in 1964, protests on and off the campuses were peaceful, civil, and addressed primarily to increasing black enrollment and adding black faculty, administrators, and staff, seeking change within the existing system. These demonstrations raised the level of social consciousness, but were unable to generate desegregation.

Then, within the scope of a few months, the tenor and impact of the protest movement changed. Passage of the Civil Rights Act created an expectation of rapid change. But a divisive confrontation at Berkeley that brought police on campus, and resulted in mass arrests, punctured that expectation, and transformed the protest movement from peaceful demonstrations to confrontations that were forceful, ugly, and violent. At Brandeis in 1968, 65 black students occupied the university communications center, to press a set of demands that included more recruitment of black students and faculty, an autonomous African-American studies program, and a center for black students. They remained 11 days, and were granted most of their requests.[1]

Similar demands at San Francisco State, including a program in Mexican-American studies, resulted in clashes between students and police, when administrators accepted the two academic programs but refused the students' other demands. At the University of Wisconsin at Oshkosh angry black students tore up administrative offices causing $12,000 worth of damage, after the President of the campus refused to sign an agreement to meet their similar demands.[2]

At Swarthmore, 25 black students staged an 8-day sit-in at the Admissions Office to compel the President and faculty to act on their demands. They left only after the President suffered a fatal heart attack while preparing for a faculty committee meeting to discuss the students demands.[3] At Wittenberg University, 38 of the 45 black students on campus boycotted to press demands for a 12% black enrollment, and a curriculum that would "reflect the contribution of the black man in western world culture."[4] They received a Center with an African-American library, and programs in black music and art.

Confrontation and intimidation were achieving what no amount of civil protest had been able to achieve. A measure of the change that was taking place as a result can be gained from reading the December 23, 1968 issue of *The Chronicle of Higher Education*. It reported that after a major confrontation, Brown University agreed to spend more than $1 million over the next 3 years to increase Negro enrollment and to develop programs for Negro students. The university pledged "to reflect in each entering . . . class, the black representation in the general populace which is about 11 per cent." It was also taking steps to enlarge its

admission and counseling staffs, and use other factors, in addition to standard national norms, to determine admission and amounts of scholarships.

In the same issue, the *Chronicle* reported that Yale was planning to introduce an undergraduate major leading to a bachelor's degree in Afro-American studies in September 1969, making it one of the first in the country to offer a program leading to the bachelors degree. The Yale committee report was quoted as saying "the experience of black people in the world is not merely a suitable object for serious academic study and teaching, but one too relevant, vital, important, and rich in content to ignore." The *Chronicle* then quoted Robert A. Dahl, the political science professor who chaired the committee that designed the program, saying, "It is hard to say which is the more appalling, the ignorance of whites about black people or the ignorance of Afro-Americans about their own experience."[5]

On January 27, 1969, the *Chronicle* noted that Harvard University had recommended majors in Afro-American studies, an African-American studies center, a social center for Negro students, and a major recruitment effort for graduate students. "Whether out of conscience, fear, or conviction," the December 23 article said, "many colleges and universities have been rushing to accommodate . . . demands."[6] In 1971, Harvard went on to create an office of minority affairs, and adopted an affirmative action program for hiring women and members of minority groups. In 1972 Williams College adopted a policy of affirmative action in faculty recruitment and hiring. In 1973 the American Association of University Professors endorsed the use of affirmative action in faculty hiring.

The other side of the coin involved problems campuses faced implementing the goals they agreed to, and disputes about the extent to which those problems were real or convenient. The issue is well illustrated by the University of Michigan, one of approximately 15 highly selective campuses that met in May 1973 at a 2-day conference on minority admissions sponsored by The College Entrance Examination Board. Michigan had a very specific plan to meet its diversity goals, as a consequence of a student strike in the 1969–1970 academic year. One of those goals was a black enrollment of 10% and a substantial increase in the enroll-

[1] *The Chronicle of Higher Education*, January 27, 1969, p. 6.
[2] *The Chronicle of Higher Education*, December 9, 1968, pp. 1, 3.
[3] *The Chronicle of Higher Education*, January 27, 1969, pp. 1, 6.
[4] *Ibid.*

[5] *The Chronicle of Higher Education*, December 23, 1968.
[6] *Ibid.*

ment of other minority groups by 1973–1974. Approximately 3.5% of Michigan's undergraduate and graduate students were black in 1969 when the strike took place. By the following fall it was 5%. In fall 1992 it was 6.8%, and in fall 1973 it was expected to rise to 8.6%. But the 10% goal would not be reached by 1973–1974. Competition from other campuses that could offer more attractive financial aid packages to minority students, and difficulty in identifying students who can succeed in a highly competitive environment, were cited as primary reasons for the delay.

Among the larger group of highly selective campuses at the 2-day meeting on minority admissions, most had increased the proportion of minority students on their campuses from essentially zero to 5 or 10%. But many said their institutions' commitment to further increases, and to support for minority students after they are admitted, was slackening.

Another example comes from the University of Maryland at College Park, which had only a general goal to increase minority enrollment prior to the fall of 1972, and a minority enrollment in 1972 of 4% overall, and 10% in the freshman class. Subjected to intense pressure from black faculty and staff, the Board of Regents voted in 1972 to establish specific goals for minority enrollment, and to seek to admit each year a cohort of minority students equal to the proportion graduating from high school, which was 15% in 1972. The director of minority affairs predicted a substantial decline in the number of minority students that would be admitted in fall 1973, however, because not enough money was allocated to conduct an adequate recruiting program.[7]

From the perspective of the demonstrators, and the larger constituency supporting desegregation, these were transparent excuses to slow down or halt the process. They were also indicative of progress—competition among the campuses for the best prepared black students—of flashpoints, where the requirements of desegregation and the paradigms of higher education conflicted, and of what was happening in important context areas.

If race had been the only issue, and all other variables were equalized, such as preparation, number of spaces in high demand programs, and funding, the problems

of desegregation would have been difficult enough. When they were not, the requirements of desegregation came into conflict with the basic paradigms of higher education, and created a need to redistribute scarce resources from the majority to the minority.

Within the paradigm, institutional identity and integrity are defined at the intersection of role and mission and selectivity of admissions. To lower admissions is to violate the identity and integrity of the campus, and transform higher education from a privilege to a right. In a speech at Howard University in 1965, Lyndon Johnson had offered the counterrationale, the justification for affirmative action, when he said, "You do not take a person who, for years, has been hobbled by chains and liberate him, bring him up to the starting line of a race, and then say, 'You are free to compete with all the others,' and still justly believe that you have been completely fair."[8] Only the City University of New York was willing to go so far as to adopt an open-admissions policy, which it did in 1969, effective in 1970. The rest of the campuses insisted on maintaining their selectivity, and agreed, only reluctantly, to limited and carefully tailored affirmative action programs that would make exceptions for a limited few. The institutional paradigm and imperative would bend slightly, but not change.

When the demand to desegregate was not accompanied by funds for student recruitment, for additional black faculty, administrators, and staff, change became a zero sum game, redistributing resources from the majority to the minority. Pressed to provide additional financial aid to black students, campuses had to either raise the money from foundations and donors, convince states to provide more money, or take money previously used for other programs and students. When Congress created the Basic Educational Opportunity Grants in 1972, there was some help, but need always exceeded supply. The issue was one of finite resources, multiple constituencies, and conflicting pressures, as well as willingness to desegregate.

Allocating space in high demand programs was the most contentious issue. It received national attention in two cases, *Odegaard v. DeFunis*, 94 S.Ct. 1704, and *Regents of the University of California v. Bakke*, 438 U.S. 265, which set a national standard. Denied admission

---

[7] *The Chronicle of Higher Education*, May, 21, 1972, p. 5.

[8] *The Chronicle of Higher Education*, April 28, 1995, p. A16.

to the medical school at the University of California at Davis, when minority students with lower scores were admitted, Allan Bakke sued. In 1978 the Supreme Court ruled in *Regents of the University of California v. Bakke* that colleges may use race as one factor in admissions decisions, but cannot set aside a specific proportion of their entering class for minority students.

In their decision, the Court reflected a larger social, economic, and political environment across the country that had become increasingly resistant to busing and affirmative action. The heightened social consciousness of 1964 had ebbed in the early 1970s as attention turned to the business at hand and economic conditions tightened. Though charged with implementing Title VI, the Nixon administration took a determined stand to limit its enforcement, and curtailed, even halted, the role of executive agencies charged with monitoring compliance. Liberty, rather than equality, was dominating the civic agenda, and the President and the Court responded in kind.

A number of contextual variables within education were also factors. At the elementary and secondary level, studies repeatedly showed minority students in larger proportions in general studies and vocational tracks than their majority peers. And a larger proportion of black high school graduates were attending community colleges than their white peers, with very low transfer rates for both. Schools and counselors were accused of steering minority students into these programs. Others pointed to issues of poor preparation in large, inner-city urban elementary and secondary school districts that could not be ignored, and conditions in the ghettos. As the climate of opinion changed in the 1970s and 1980s, many campuses turned to issues of quality, and began to raise admissions standards. Changes in financial aid also worked to the detriment of low-income and minority students. The gap between black and white college enrollment that was closing in the middle and late 1970s, widened once again, and did not improve substantially until the 1990s.

At the two historically black campuses in the North created before the Civil War, Central State in Ohio and Cheyney State in Pennsylvania, patterns were similar. Early efforts to bring more white students on campus slowed in the ensuing years, so that by 1994, Central State had only 10% nonblack enrollment and Cheyney State 5% nonblack enrollment.

Desegregation in the South

In February 1956, Autherine Lucy enrolled at the University of Alabama as the first black student. Three days later an angry group of students yelling "nigger whore" hurled rocks and food at her. State police forced her to leave the campus. The next day she was suspended by the university "for her own safety" and subsequently expelled.[9]

In 1959, two black high school seniors, Hamilton Holmes and Charlayne Hunter, applied to the University of Georgia for admission. No black student had been admitted in its 176 years of existence. Both were turned down in spite of superior academic credentials. In 1960 they applied again as transfer students. Once again they were refused admission. After a 4-month court battle they were ordered admitted, and enrolled on January 9, 1961. Two days later an antiblack riot erupted on campus enveloping the two in an atmosphere of extreme hostility. Holmes said later there were times when he would go for days without anyone saying a word to him. Both graduated 2 years later.[10]

In 1962, James Meredith applied to the University of Mississippi and was accepted, but Governor Ross Barnett blocked his admission. A federal court order, and two dozen United States marshals with guns drawn, were required before Meredith was allowed to register. Riots broke out. Two bystanders were killed and 150 federal marshals were injured, some from gunfire. Three thousand federal troops, ordered by President Kennedy, were required to end the disturbance. Federal troops remained on campus until August 1963 when Meredith graduated.[11]

The case that captured the attention of the nation most fully, however, took place a year later. In June 1963, when Vivian Malone and James Hood prepared to enter the University of Alabama under court order, Governor George Wallace was standing at the entrance to Foster Auditorium to bar their admission. Malone and Hood were accompanied by Assistant Attorney General Nicholas Katzenback, General Weaver, and a caravan of marshals. Robert Kennedy and the President were carefully watching.

[9] *The Journal of Blacks in Higher Education*, Vol. 13, Autumn 1996, p. 75.
[10] *Ibid.*, p. 77.
[11] *Ibid.*, p. 80.

Katzenback proceeded up the steps, and asked for the Governor's unequivocal assurance that he would allow the two students to register. When Wallace refused, Katzenback phoned Robert Kennedy, who asked the White House for permission to federalize the National Guard. The President gave his immediate assent. The Alabama National Guard was federalized under General Graham, who ordered 100 Guardsmen to the campus, and marched a platoon to the Auditorium. On arrival, General Graham saluted the Governor, and asked him to step aside, on order of the President of the United States. Unwilling to defy the President of the United States, Wallace withdrew, and Vivian Malone and James Hood registered (Culpepper, 1993:225–231).

Segregation in education was the law of the land throughout the South in 1954, when the *Brown* decision was rendered, and as these experiences indicate, dual systems of higher education were the practical reality throughout the South in 1964, when the Civil Rights Act was passed, and for as many years thereafter as possible. Only the action of the courts, and the pressure of a sturdy few, procured change.[12]

When the passage of the Civil Rights Act made it clear that higher education was not exempt from desegregation, the policy debate in the South turned to how best to resist; or, if forced to comply, what the terms of desegregation were. Was the legal obligation satisfied by dismantling the constitutional and legal provisions establishing segregation, or was there a further affirmative duty? If the latter, was affirmative action essentially a question of opening admissions to students of all races, or did it extend to desegregating faculty and staff, to degree completion, and other tangible and less tangible elements of educational opportunity?

Were the historically black campuses vestiges of segregation, or positive choices for black and white college students seeking educational opportunity? Was the goal unitary systems of public higher education, or equal educational opportunity with a diverse set of campuses? Were good faith efforts, or measured results, to constitute the standard?

The first answer that the states had an affirmative duty to desegregate came in a Tennessee case, originating as *Sanderv v. Ellington* in 1968, and cited more recently as *Geier v. Sundquist*. Rita Sanders, later Rita Geier, a young black woman, charged that expansion of a University of Tennessee center in Nashville would perpetuate segregation at Tennessee Agricultural and Technical State University, a nearby historically black campus, and ensure the continued existence of a dual system of public higher education in the state.

U.S. District Court Judge Frank Gray, Jr., denied plaintiffs' request for an injunction against the construction project in August 1968, but ruled that the state had maintained a racially segregated system of higher education and that it had an affirmative duty to devise and implement a comprehensive program of desegregation at all of its public colleges and universities in order to dismantle it.

After lengthy proceedings to secure voluntary desegregation, and little progress, the Judge concluded in February 1977 that the parties were not going to produce a constitutionally satisfactory plan on their own, and ordered the merger of historically black Tennessee State and the University of Tennessee branch in Nashville, under the governing authority of historically black Tennessee State. Gray's 1968 ruling was the first court order requiring a state to disestablish its racially separate higher education systems, and his 1977 order was the first, and only, court order to merge a black and white campus.[13]

Federal enforcement of desegregation under Title VI was assigned to the Department of Health, Education, and Welfare (DHEW). Its Office of Civil Rights (OCR) focused on elementary and secondary education first, and turned to higher education only in 1968. Then it initiated some 200 compliance reviews across the country, including an intensive investigation in 10 southern states. As expected, it found the higher education systems in all 10 states operating in violation of Title VI.

Letters were sent to the governors of Arkansas, Florida, Georgia, Louisiana, Maryland, Mississippi, North Carolina, Oklahoma, Pennsylvania, and Virginia, informing them that their state's dual system of public higher education was in violation of Title VI, and that their campuses were in danger of losing federal funding.

---

[12] West Virginia State College and Bluefield State College in West Virginia, both historically black campuses, integrated voluntarily in 1954, and became predominantly white campuses.

---

[13] *The Chronicle of Higher Education*, April 4, 1977, pp. 6–7.

Title VI required DHEW to attempt to secure voluntary compliance first. If that failed, there was an opportunity for a quasi-judicial administrative hearing. If the institution under investigation failed to make its case, DHEW could terminate or refuse to grant federal financial assistance. Or DHEW could refer the matter to the Department of Justice to file suit in the federal district court. When none of the 10 states complied, five for failure to submit a plan and the other five for providing inadequate ones, OCR did not initiate enforcement proceedings.

As a result of this, and other failures to enforce Title VI, the NAACP Legal Defense and Education Fund, Inc. (LDF), filed a class action suit in 1970, *Adams v. Richardson*, 356 F.Supp. 92, initiating the *Adams* case that was to continue through most of the 1980s. At the same time the National Association for Equal Opportunity in Higher Education (NAFEO), representing black colleges, filed an *amicus curiae* brief requesting that the suit be dropped, because it feared the demise of black colleges and universities.

The larger social context was an important variable. The case was initiated in 1970, in the middle of Nixon's first term as President. The national mood was turning against affirmative action. The Nixon administration understood the importance of this shift, and the value of Southern support, and severely curtailed the efforts of all Federal agencies charged with Title VI compliance.

As a consequence, the plaintiffs were forced to return to Court repeatedly to force the federal government to fulfill its obligations, as well as to get states, campuses, and schools to comply with desegregation requirements. The problems of executing public policy when both the agent of the plaintiff, one part of the plaintiffs, and the defendants are either opposed or reluctant to move forward are illustrated in *Adams v. Richardson*.

The plaintiffs had four goals. They wanted to force HEW officials to (1) respond to the desegregation plans that had been submitted several years previously, (2) initiate enforcement procedures where needed, (3) monitor compliance and progress, and (4) conduct compliance reviews in the seven other states that had practiced *de jure* segregation in higher education.

The process was painstakingly slow. It was February 1971 before the District Court ruled that DHEW had to begin enforcement proceedings against the 10 states, and that it had to do so within 60 days. DHEW ap-

pealed and was turned down, gaining only 10 months of additional time. In 1973, Judge Pratt ordered DHEW to either obtain acceptable corrective plans or begin compliance procedures within 120 days. DHEW again appealed the decision but the U.S. Court of Appeals for the District of Columbia upheld the District Court, modifying the District Court's order only to allow an additional 180 days after the submission of the state's higher education desegregation plan.

Compelled by the Appeals Court, DHEW notified all 10 of the states to submit new desegregation plans. By June 1974, 8 of the 10 states submitted new plans and gained approval from DHEW. Louisiana refused once again to submit a plan, and Mississippi's plan was found unacceptable.

The plaintiffs then reviewed the accepted plans, together with progress reports submitted in 1975. Finding the plans inadequate, and progress negligible, they returned to Court. Judge Pratt found in their favor, and ordered DHEW to draw up specific criteria for developing a desegregation plan, an initiative that should have taken place at least 6 years earlier. DHEW was also instructed to once again require 6 of the 10 states to submit new desegregation plans, based on the Criteria, with specific standards for accomplishment.[14]

DHEW issued its preliminary guidelines, its *Criteria*, in July 1977 and obtained the approval of the Court in February 1978. These Criteria established the policies of desegregation. Four basic principles defined their scope and intent. First, every campus had an affirmative duty to eliminate segregation wherever it existed in the higher education enterprise. Second, there must be a statewide approach. Actions by individual campuses had to be coordinated for their overall effect. Third, realistic goals capable of overcoming the effects of past discrimination, numerical objectives, and timetables would measure compliance, not verbal intentions. Fourth, the unique role of the traditionally black colleges in meeting the educational needs of black students was to be acknowledged and supported.

The transition to a unitary system was not to be accomplished by placing a disproportionate burden on black students, faculty, or institutions, or by reducing the educational opportunities currently available to them. Therefore, the state and the campuses were obligated to specify exactly how the black campuses

---

[14]*Adams v. Califano*, 430 F. Supp. 118, 121 (D.D.C. 1977).

would be enhanced to ensure their viability to black and white students.

Under the terms of the Criteria, states, and campuses, were required to develop 5-year plans to achieve targeted desegregation outcomes. Mission, academic program, student enrollment, and the racial composition of faculty, administrative staff, nonacademic personnel, and governing boards were to be constrained, subject to desegregation policies and priorities.

Mission was targeted to separate mission from race, and to give the black campuses a viable role attractive to white as well as black students. Academic program was to be constrained to end the pervasive practice of placing courses on white campuses, branches, or outreach centers, proximal to black campuses, that duplicated what was offered on the black campuses, giving white students no reason to attend the black campuses, and to give the black campuses a set of unduplicated programs sought after by all students. To this end, the state would have to commit to give priority consideration to placing any new undergraduate, graduate, or professional degree programs, or courses of study, at traditionally black campuses consistent with their missions.

Access goals were specific. Across the state as a whole, the proportion of black high school graduates going on to college was to be brought to parity with white high school graduates. The proportion of black students attending the traditionally white 2-year and 4-year campuses was to increase annually on each campus and across the state, and produce at least a 50% reduction in disparity at the conclusion of the 5-year plan. Baccalaureate graduation rates were to be equalized at the end of the 5-year period. The proportion of black and white college graduates going on to graduate school was also to be equalized by the end of the 5 years, with separate goals and totals for each major field of study and professional field. Specific goals were also to be set to increase the proportion of white students attending traditionally black campuses. All goals were to be numerical, and timetables were required.

Hiring of faculty, selection of administrators and their staffs, recruitment of nonacademic personnel, and selection to governing boards were to be similarly directed by desegregation policy, goals, and measured outcomes. Where a doctoral degree was required, the proportion of blacks hired was to equal the proportion

of black individuals with the credentials required for the position, in the relevant labor market area. Where a doctoral degree was not required, the proportion was to be equivalent to the proportion of black students graduating with a masters degree, in the appropriate discipline, from institutions within the state system, or in the relevant labor market area.

Desegregation policy would reshape higher education by purposively constraining mission and academic program and by affirmatively directing student enrollment, faculty and administrative hiring, and representation on higher education boards to achieve proportional representation. States as well as campuses were to be held accountable, and compliance would be measured by performance (Williams, 1988:9–10).

Arkansas, Florida, Georgia, Oklahoma, Virginia, and North Carolina submitted new plans to DHEW. After revision and renegotiation, all of the plans but North Carolina's were accepted for the 1978–1979 school year. When negotiations with North Carolina broke down, DHEW initiated compliance proceedings. It also notified six more states of *de jure* violations in January 1981, and asked them to assemble plans based on the Criteria. They included Alabama, Delaware, Kentucky, Missouri, South Carolina, Ohio, Texas, and West Virginia (Williams, 1988:11).

With the exception of five states, North Carolina, Alabama, Mississippi, Louisiana, and Ohio, states and campuses reacted cooperatively, but passively. They drew up plans, hired affirmative action officers, made a number of genuine efforts, but did far less than was necessary to accomplish desegregation goals.

They were able to operate in this limited response mode because DHEW, and its successor, the Department of Education, did little to push the states and campuses to more rigorous levels of compliance, cooperating in effect with their strategies of limited compliance. When the plaintiffs' returned to court to protest plans accepted by DHEW and ED that did not approach meeting the state's own goals, the court agreed with the plaintiffs.[15]

On March 25, 1987, *The Chronicle of Higher Education* featured an article on how few goals had been

---

[15] *Adams v. Weinberger*, 391 F. Supp. 269 (D.D.C. 1975); *Adams v. Califano*, 1977; *Adams v. Bell*, 1983 D.C. Civil Action No. 70-3095, March 24, 1982.

met. After reviewing data submitted to the Department of Education, the *Chronicle* concluded that "few of the goals for predominantly white institutions have been met." It cited Arkansas, for example, where the state set a goal of 16% black enrollment, but its black enrollment in 1986 was 10.7%, slightly *less* than it had been in 1978–1979 when the plan was drawn up. In Florida, where no numerical goal was established, black enrollment *dropped* from 7.1 to 6.4%. It noted that states with increases had only moderate ones, and cited Georgia, with a 26% black population, where black enrollment at all levels increased from 10.5 to 10.9% between 1977–1979 and 1985–1986, although the goal had been 16.9% by 1982.[16]

It noted that the campuses had been more successful at recruiting black administrators than faculty, and in hiring for positions requiring a masters degree than a doctorate. Virginia was a case in point. In 1985–1986, blacks occupied 6.7% of the administrative positions requiring a Ph.D, and 10.8% of those requiring a masters degree, but only 2.5% of the faculty positions requiring a doctorate. In Georgia, five campuses had only one black faculty member, and in Arkansas, six campuses had two or fewer.[17]

For the plaintiffs, and the broad constituency supporting desegregation, a combination of persistent racism and indifference was responsible for such poor efforts. From the standpoint of the states and the campuses it was circumstances beyond their control, such as a decline in the pool of high school graduates, lack of financial aid, and very few black Ph.D.s.

The issue, in fact, was not whether the contextual circumstances existed, but rather how much of an obstacle they posed. Civil rights leaders argued vigorously that they were not insuperable obstacles. "It's a little artificial, NAACP spokesmen said, "for the states to talk as if they could only deal with higher education. They knew all along that there were things they needed to do in the public schools to get more students, but they just didn't do it."[18] Mary Francis Barry, then a former member of the U.S. Commission on Civil Rights, was even more pointed. "In recruiting faculty, the state efforts have been outrageous. The states have

had years to work with the graduate schools, the colleges, and the public schools, and they just haven't done enough. When it comes to . . . football teams, they manage to find a way to recruit blacks"[19]

Where there was slow but steady progress in most states was in white enrollment on the black campuses. Between 1978–1979 and 1985–1986, white enrollment rose from 3.5 to 7.5% in Virginia, from 7.7 to 13.9% in Georgia, and from less than 1 to 33.4% at Langston University in Oklahoma. But it was frequently concentrated in one or two programs, at an off-campus location, or on one small part of the campus, and did not necessarily constitute an integrated enrollment.[20]

The election of Ronald Reagan in 1980 brought federal compliance efforts to a standstill. Angered by affirmative action, and mandates of the *Adams* court directing the way the Department of Education had to respond to desegregation issues, the Reagan administration went to court to have the *Adams* case dismissed. They argued in the Circuit Court of Appeals that the plaintiffs lacked standing, that the court's detailed time frames were a violation of separation of powers, and that the remedy sought could not cure the problem.

The Court of Appeals ordered Judge Pratt to consider the Government's case in light of the Supreme Court decision in *Allen v. Wright* 468 U.S. 737 (1984), where the Court questioned if, in the absence of actual present, or immediately threatening injury resulting from unlawful government action, it was appropriate for federal courts to act as "virtually continuing monitors of the wisdom and soundness of Executive action."[21]

Upon review, Judge Pratt ruled to dismiss the case. The plaintiffs, he wrote, had clearly shown that they had suffered discrimination. But they had not shown that the discrimination suffered was fairly traceable to the government's action or inaction, or that the discrimination would be redressed by a cut-off of federal funds. Through the detailed imposition of time frames, governing every step in the administrative process, the *Adams* court had sought to control the way the Executive Branch was to carry out its responsibilities, and this was a violation of separation of powers.

---

[16] *The Chronicle of Higher Education*, March 25, 1987, p. 22.
[17] *Ibid*.
[18] *Ibid*.

[19] *Ibid*.
[20] *Ibid*.
[21] *Allan v. Wright*, 1984.

Pratt's decision to dismiss the case was appealed, and in July 1989 a three judge panel of the U.S. Court of Appeals for the District of Columbia Circuit revived the case. The decision, written by Judge Ruth Bader Ginsburg, affirmed that the plaintiffs still had legal standing, that a direct relationship existed between federal enforcement of antibias laws and state decisions, and that it was appropriate for the courts to supervise antibias enforcement if federal agencies were not fulfilling their obligations. But additional hearings were necessary to resolve some other questions.

After hearings on those issues, the Court of Appeals reversed itself, upheld the District Court, and dismissed the *Adams* case. In a unanimous decision, they found that the plaintiffs could not sue the federal government to force it to take steps against states and colleges that might be breaking the law. Instead suits should be filed directly against the states and colleges.[22] The implications were staggering. The Executive Department could no longer be held accountable for its behavior in enforcing Title VI. And every higher education desegregation case would have to be litigated individually, in the most costly and time-consuming manner.

The three states that had offered the most resistance to *Adams*, Alabama, Louisiana, and Mississippi, were already in individual litigation at the choice of private plaintiffs. The resolution of those cases, and further challenges to affirmative action, would shape the desegregation of higher education in the 1990s.

The fundamental common denominator in the Alabama, Louisiana, and Mississippi cases was the conviction that if segregation had to be eliminated in their higher education systems, then removing the offending statutes and opening access through race-neutral policies fulfilled the legal requirements of desegregation. There was no further obligation.

The Mississippi case, initiated in 1969, did not move forward until 1992, when the Supreme Court heard the case, and established the standard for desegregation in *U.S. v. Fordice*, 112 S.Ct. 2727 (1992). Justice White wrote,

> If the State perpetuates policies and practices traceable to its prior system that continue to have segregative effects—whether by influencing student enrollment decisions or by fostering segregation in other facets of the university system—and such policies are without sound educational justification and can be practically eliminated, the State has not satisfied its burden of proving that it has dismantled its prior system.[23]

The standard of the Court in *Fordice* established the legal parameters for the District Court to rehear the Mississippi case, and for all further desegregation cases, including ongoing litigation in Louisiana and Alabama. In all three cases, plaintiffs provided extensive evidence of traceable effects in mission, academic program, composition of the faculty, in administration and staff, in facilities, and funding. The cases, however, were decided on the narrowest grounds, providing minimum relief.

Upgrading the public black campuses was particularly contentious. In its *Fordice* ruling the Court addressed the issue when it said,

> If we understand private petitioners to press us to order the upgrading of Jackson State, Alcorn State, and Mississippi Valley *solely* so that they may be publicly financed, exclusively black enclaves by private choice, we reject that request. The State provides these facilities for *all* its citizens and it has not met its burden under *Brown* to take affirmative steps to dismantle its prior *de jure* system when it perpetuates a separate, but 'more equal' one. Whether such an increase in funding is necessary to achieve a full dismantlement under the standards we have outlined, however, is a different question, and one that must be addressed on remand.

Noting the difficulty of the issue, Justice Thomas wrote, "It would be ironic, to say the least, if the institutions that sustained blacks during segregation were themselves destroyed in an effort to combat its vestiges."[24]

The narrow scope of the desegregation decisions in Mississippi, Louisiana, and Alabama left important vestiges unresolved in mission, duplication of program, composition of the faculty, administration, and staff, in

[22] *The Chronicle of Higher Education*, July 5, 1990, pp. 1, A22.

[23] *U.S. v. Fordice*, 112 S.Ct. 2727 (1992).
[24] *Ibid.*, p. 2746, Justice Thomas concurring.

facilities and funding. As a result, the missions of the historically black campuses continue to reflect their past. There is extensive program duplication on proximal white campuses, and few high demand, non-duplicated programs on the historically black campuses. The distribution of land-grant funds between the white and black land-grant campuses continues to favor the white campuses in overwhelming proportions.

Fundamental student and faculty disparities continue. Increased black enrollment on the traditionally white campuses has been confined largely to the less selective campuses, and black faculty and students on those campuses have great difficulty initiating courses in black history and culture in the same proportion as on campuses in the upper South or across the country, and no Alabama campus offers a major in African-American studies. White enrollment on the traditionally black campuses has proceeded slowly, and been more effective in selected graduate programs, on evening or week-end hours, and in off-campus locations.

In Mississippi, a uniform set of admissions standards has been imposed on all the 4-year campuses that would theoretically make it easier for the best prepared black students to access the white campuses, but will have the practical effect of reducing, by as much as 50%, the access of less prepared black high school graduates to the historically black campuses, because they will no longer meet admissions requirements for those campuses.

National Trends in the 1990s

The tension between individual liberty and equity in the American experience has, with only brief respites, been resolved in favor of individual liberty. The respite that allowed the Civil Rights movement of the 1960s was brief, and began to unravel in the early 1970s, particularly where issues of affirmative action interfered with individual liberty, and has been unraveling with renewed vigor in the 1990s.

The issue has been particularly contentious over admissions decisions at the highly selective campuses, and the use of race-based scholarships, with two recent decisions in the fourth and fifth circuits challenging whether race can be taken into consideration at all in admissions decisions or scholarships.

The *Podberesky* case (46 F. 3rd, 5), challenged the use of race-targeted scholarships. At issue was a chal-

lenge by Daniel J. *Podberesky*, a Hispanic student, who applied for admission to the University of Maryland, and a Benjamin Banneker Scholarship in 1988–1989. The scholarships had been created to increase black enrollment on the campus, and to overcome a long standing reputation for discrimination in admissions, racial hostility on the campus, and low graduation rates, that had made the University of Maryland an unfavorable choice within the black community. When *Podberesky* was denied a scholarship he sued the University of Maryland.

The federal district court upheld the Maryland program in 1991 as a substantive effort to overcome a long history of *de jure* segregation. But a three-judge panel of the U.S. Court of Appeals for the Fourth Circuit ruled unanimously in 1994 that the University of Maryland at College Park had no right to use race in allocating scholarships. The Supreme Court refused to hear the case on appeal, leaving stand the appeals court decision.[25]

The second case, the *Hopwood* admissions case (95 F. 3rd, 53), has challenged the use of race as even one factor among many in admissions decisions and has had profound implications. In July 1996 the Supreme Court let stand a ruling of the U.S. Court of Appeals for the Fifth Circuit that barred the law school at the University of Texas from considering race in admissions. That fifth circuit decision in effect repudiated *Regents of the University of California v. Bakke*, the 1978 Supreme Court decision that allowed race to be taken into account as one of several factors in admissions decisions.

Controversy immediately ensued over what the ruling meant. In a rare written statement about why the Supreme Court declined to review a case, Justice Ginsberg said the Supreme Court did not need to hear the case, because the University of Texas law school had already abandoned the particular methods of the challenged admission program. Others argued that the decision had the tacit consent of the Supreme Court, and prohibited all public colleges in Texas, Mississippi, and Louisiana from taking race into account when they admit students.

The strength of the latter interpretation can be seen in the rapidity with which the Attorney General of

---

[25] *The Chronicle of Higher Education*, November 2, 1994, p. A52.

Texas who had appealed the Fifth Circuit ruling issued legal counsel to all colleges and universities in the state, advising them to discontinue using race in admissions or financial aid decisions. His request was immediately heeded by most of the public campuses, including the University of Texas and Texas A&M. Many of the private campuses, including Southern Methodist and Rice, said they too would comply, although the opinion applied only to public higher education.[26]

The complexity of the situation is illustrated by the fact that the *Hopwood* decision is in conflict with other federal court orders to use race as a factor to remove vestiges of segregation in the Alabama, Mississippi, and Louisiana higher education systems. This places the campuses in the fifth circuit between two opposing court orders. In the immediate term, officials at both the University of Mississippi and Louisiana State University say they will follow their court-ordered desegregation mandates for admissions, financial aid, and scholarship policies.

Though the *Hopwood* and *Podberesky* decisions apply only in their respective Circuits, the practical effect of both decisions has been to offer cover for those eager to dismantle affirmative action. An excellent example comes from Georgia, where the Attorney General has informed each public campus that he will not defend either a campus, or a campus program, that takes race into account, although Georgia has not been sued, and is not in the Fifth Circuit.

The national scope of the retreat from affirmative action is best illustrated by the California Civil Rights Initiative, Proposition 209, which prohibits taking race, gender, or ethnicity into account in education, public employment, or in contracts. Last year legislation was introduced in 26 states and in Congress to limit or roll back affirmative action programs.[27] This year Pennsylvania and Arizona are endeavoring to pass laws outlawing affirmative action. In South Carolina, efforts are underway to obtain signatures for a ballot initiative, and in Colorado the governing board for postsecondary education has limited affirmative action.[28]

The complexity of the issue is illustrated by the way it is divisive in both the majority and minority communities. Within the minority community, concerns about the stigma that can attach to any special attention mingle with a fundamental awareness of how doors have had to be forced open. In the majority community three agendas interweave. For some, the issue is fairness to compete in an unfettered environment, versus assurances of an equal opportunity to compete. Others cover neoracism with meritocratic criteria. Still others manipulate racial issues for political opportunism.

It is of more than passing interest to note that as originally conceived, affirmative action did not imply quotas or set-asides. It meant finding innovative ways to locate the students who could profit from higher education, broadening definitions of potential, finding new and different yardsticks, rather than utilizing different standards, or setting specific numerical goals. Separate standards and racial quotas emerged when campuses declined the challenge to broaden their horizons, plaintiffs pressed for compliance, and resistance necessitated purposeful goals and accountability for actions.

The imperative need now is to find new ways to achieve diversity within a framework acceptable to the broad public. The difficulty is that virtually any marker other than race will favor whites, who are greater in number and have a larger number of poor families. In a recent computation of the probable effects of *Hopwood* on the admission of black students to the most selective universities, the conclusion was that it would eliminate 75% of the African Americans who now qualify for admission at those campuses.[29]

The strength of the movement to end affirmative action should not be underestimated. It is well funded, and guided by conservatives at key policy institutes such as the Institute for Justice, the Center for Individual Rights, and the Pacific Legal Foundation. It has strong Congressional advocates, including 8 Senators and 92 members of the House of Representatives in 1996. This includes Representative Charles Canady, Republican of Florida, who is co-sponsor with former Senator Robert Dole of a bill that, if enacted, will outlaw all racial preferences in employment, contracting, and other federal programs. This bill, the Equal Op-

[26] *The Chronicle of Higher Education*, July 12, 1996, pp. A25, A29.

[27] *The New York Times*, November 10, 1996, p. 1.

[28] *The Journal of Blacks in Higher Education*, Vol. 11, Spring, 1996, p. 68.

[29] *Ibid.*, p. 67.

portunity Act of 1996, has passed out of subcommittee and is slated for further action.

The challenge to devise proposals that will further diversity without incurring the disfavor of affirmative action is difficult. Among the proposals beginning to surface are two with quite different approaches and costs. The first is to pay more attention to rank in class, which is approximately as predictive as the SAT score, and is situational, retaining the high level of competition for selective admissions. The other is to provide more selective campuses, giving a larger proportion of well-prepared students the opportunity to have an excellent education, a less costly option than repeated visits to court, now that this issue must be litigated campus by campus, or state by state.

What Has Been Accomplished?

Important progress has taken place in reducing the black–white disparity in higher education. In 1970, black enrollment was only 57% of white enrollment. In 1996 it was 71%. In the decade from 1984 to 1994, black enrollments rose from 8 to 10.1% of the higher education enrollment in the United States. Black enrollment at 4-year campuses outpaced enrollment at 2-year campuses over this same period, with a current distribution of 57% at the 4-year campuses and 43% at the 2-year campuses. Graduate school enrollments rose 66% from a decade ago, and from 5% of all graduate students in 1984 to 6.4% in 1994. Black professional school enrollment rose from 13,000 in 1984 to 21,000 in 1994.[30]

Degree attainment has also increased at all levels. Between 1985 and 1993 the proportion of blacks receiving bachelor degrees increased 35.5%, masters degrees 42%, and professional degrees 35%. At the doctoral level there has been a 56.2% increase between 1986 and 1995, and a large part of this increase has been in the sciences and engineering. The number of blacks earning doctoral degrees in the biological sciences has more than doubled over the past decade, and the number of doctorates in engineering has increased 286% from its minute number in 1986.

There has also been progress in eliminating differences in the rate of black and white degree attainment, though substantial problems remain. At the flagship state universities where blacks make up at least 3% of the state population, the disparity rate has closed to 7% at the University of South Carolina and 8% at the University of Virginia; but it is 37% at Indiana University at Bloomington, 29% at the University of Massachusetts, 28% at the University of Kentucky, and 22% at the University of North Carolina at Chapel Hill. The greatest progress has been made at some of the most elite campuses where the difference is only 2% at Harvard, 4% at Princeton, 6% at Brown, 10% at Duke, Northwestern, and Stanford, but 18% at the University of Pennsylvania, and 20% at the University of Michigan.[31]

There has also been progress in attracting white students to the historically black colleges and universities. Ten formerly all black campuses now have student bodies at least 20% white. Three have white enrollments of approximately 25%, the University of Maryland at Eastern Shore, Bowie State, and Delaware State. Two are approaching a third, Tennessee State, and Fayetteville State. Kentucky State has a fifty–fifty enrollment, while Lincoln University in Missouri is 70% white.[32]

The percentage of black faculty on the white campuses has also increased, though more slowly. As a percentage of tenured faculty at the state flagship campuses, African-American faculty are now 5% of the tenured faculty at Rutgers, the high point, but only 1.4% at the University of Nevada at Las Vegas and the University of Oklahoma. The only campuses other than Rutgers where black faculty constitute more than 3% of the tenured faculty are the University of Michigan, where they are 3.7%, and the University of Maryland at College Park, where they are 4.7%. At another 12 campuses they are between 2.0 and 2.9%. And at the remaining 12 campuses that have at least 3% black population in the state, they are between 1.4 and 1.9% of the tenured faculty. As a percentage of total faculty, black academics are 6.6% of the faculty at the University of Maryland and at the University of Mississippi, the high, and 1.8% at the University of Wisconsin, which is the low.

[30] *The Journal of Blacks in Higher Education*, Volumes 11, 12, 13, 1996.

[31] *Ibid.*, Vol. 13, pp. 22, 68–69.
[32] *Ibid.*, p. 27.

Is Desegregation Still an Issue?

Although important progress has been made, very serious problems remain. They begin with the need to raise the parity in black–white participation in higher education from 71 to 100%. For those enrolled on the 4-year campuses, there is an imperative need to facilitate access to the broad range of major fields and adult roles. An important example comes from Alabama where a larger proportion of black students are now attending the predominantly white campuses than the historically black ones, but they are concentrated on the regional campuses with a narrow selection of major fields.

A comparison of the distribution of enrollment with the distribution of academic program illustrates the need at both the undergraduate and graduate levels. The two flagship campuses have an average of 114 undergraduate majors, 116 masters level programs, 3 professional programs, and 83 doctoral degree programs. Thirty-eight percent of white undergraduates are enrolled on these campuses and 13% of black students. At the graduate level, the comparable figures are 34% for white students and 13% for black students (Paul, 1995).

National data from the U.S. Department of Education on bachelor degree recipients by field in 1993–1994 give the broad picture. Utilizing an aggregation of 30 categories, the data show that over a third of all degrees earned by black students were in business management, the social sciences, and history. Education, psychology, and the health sciences accounted for another 20%. There were many fewer degrees in architecture, engineering, mathematics, the biological and physical sciences, and the visual and performing arts. The distribution of academic program by campus is an intervening variable. As long as black students are overrepresented at the regional comprehensive campuses, that have few or minimal programs in these areas, and underrepresented at the doctoral-granting and flagship campuses, where these programs are well represented, the disparity will remain.[33]

Large disparities in graduate and professional degree attainment also remain. A long look, from 1978 to 1994, shows that there has actually been a decline in doctoral recipients from 3.3% in 1978 to 2.7% in

1994. The distribution of black doctorates by discipline is also highly concentrated, with 41% in education, 18.3% in the social sciences, 10.6% in the life sciences, 4.8% in the physical sciences, 4% in engineering, and 8.8% dispersed in a range of other areas. There were at least 18 fields in 1994 where National Research Council data show blacks received no doctorates at all, including astronomy and astrophysics, nuclear physics, meteorology, oceanography, marine sciences, bioengineering, engineering mechanics, biophysics, zoology, and archaeology.[34]

Affirmative action programs in admissions, scholarships, financial aid, and supporting services have been essential elements in progress achieved. How that progress can be sustained, and carried forward, in the absence of those programs is the critical issue in desegregation today.

Pressing Social Science Issues in the Desegregation of Education

A number of theories have been put forth to explain desegregation from a social science perspective. They include the equal opportunity theory, the integration theory, the correction theory, the prohibition theory, the prophylaxis theory, and a reformative theory, among others (Liebman, 1990). Although providing important insights, none has yet to come to grips with the full dimensions of desegregation in education, or to take account of issues in the 1990s. Important theoretical work has yet to be taken up.

There is a great sparsity of analytical studies at the campus, state, or national level. Most of the work has been descriptive, and does not proceed from theoretical frameworks. It falls largely in the domain of action or advocacy research, and seeks to capture at discrete or comparative points in time what has happened, and what remains to be done.

Important second-generation work needs to be done utilizing theory, and a range of theoretical and scholarly perspectives, that will look prospectively as well as retrospectively at desegregation needs in light of key national, state, and campus variables. Some of these variables, and the research questions that need to be addressed, are suggested below. They conclude this discussion of desegregation in higher education by sug-

---

[33] *The Journal of Blacks in Higher Education*, Vol. 13, p. 22.

[34] *Ibid.*, Vol. 10, 1995–96, pp. 49–50.

gesting a path for second-generation research that will contextualize the past, and offer theoretical and analytical perspectives to guide the present and future.

I begin with an overarching question. To what extent can our current approaches to political, economic, and organizational sociology, to gender, to formal and informal social control, and to macrosocial effects on prejudice and discrimination bring analytical and theoretical clarity to the social change process we have been discussing, and to the need to continue the process?

At the state level these approaches need to be utilized to understand the relationship between the broad political agendas of the governor and legislature as they relate to higher education, the politics of fiscal support, the larger set of policies of state coordinating or governing boards for higher education, the influence of strategic individuals and groups, and what takes place at the level of policy and practice. How have these contextual factors facilitated and constrained desegregation efforts? How are they doing so now? To what extent are other foci, or specific attitudes toward diversity, driving these agendas?

At the campus level, we need to understand how the larger mission and strategic plans of campuses shape different responses to diversity. We need to follow changing admission and financial aid policies and their effects on self-selection of campus, on recruitment, and on desegregation outcomes. We need to understand how variations in resource commitment have affected outcomes, and the extent to which resource allocation has been a significant factor in outcomes, or an excuse for delaying or avoiding the desegregation process. There is little substantive research on the role of campus leadership, including that of the President or Chancellor, Board of Trustees, Faculty Senate, and student leaders, relating patterns of leadership to diversity outcomes. Nor are there studies of accountability of faculty search, promotion and tenure committees, and desegregation outcomes.

At the level of the campus recruitment area, there are few systematic studies of the proportion of minority high school graduates, their preparation, and recruitment patterns, initiatives, and outcomes. Nor are there

systematic studies of how different preparation can be, on campuses at different levels of selectivity, and academic outcomes through affirmative action.

At the national level, there is an important need to trace federal policies on financial aid and the ability of campuses to increase their proportion of minority students. We know very little about the role of accreditation agencies in facilitating and constraining diversity at campuses with different missions. Nor has there been a systematic analysis of the effects of foundation support and of the work of such external, but highly connected groups, as the College Entrance Examination Board in fostering or inhibiting desegregation.

Most important of all we need to understand the key variables at the national, state, and campus level that are facilitating or inhibit diversity today, and address them from our best theoretical and policy frameworks. The progress we have achieved is noteworthy, and serves to highlight the distance that remains, before we can say American higher education is truly desegregated. The challenge to affirmative action is greater than it has ever been, and shows strong evidence of succeeding. Our ability to persist and continue the desegregation process will depend, to an important extent, on our knowledge of how to intervene in light of the social forces at work.

REFERENCES

Culpepper, Clark E. 1993. *The Schoolhouse Door: Segregation's Last Stand at the University of Alabama*. New York: Oxford University Press.

Kluger, Richard. 1977. *Simple Justice: The History of Brown v. Board of Education and Black America's Struggle for Equality*. New York: Vintage Books.

Liebman, G. 1990. *Columbia Law Review* 1463–1664.

Myrdal, Gunnar. 1944. *An American Dilemna*. New York: Harper and Bros. (McGraw-Hill Paperback, 1964.)

Paul, Faith G. 1995. "The Distribution of Educational Opportunity Through Role and Mission and Its Segregative Effects." Report prepared by *Knight v. Alabama*, CV 83-M-1676 (N.D. Ala.), August 3.

Williams, John B. III, ed. 1988. *Desegregating America's Colleges and Universities: Title VI Regulation of Higher Education*. New York: Teachers College Press.

ECONOMICS OF EDUCATION

Ivar Berg
University of Pennsylvania

Our concerns in this chapter are (1) with sociological treatments of the two basic ways in which investments in education are treated by economists, and to comment on the intellectual and social forces that contribute to these approaches; and (2) a comparison between these approaches and those among sociologists—very few of them—who treat similar issues.

A brief review of these matters is rewarded by the finding that Keynes was almost completely right in his observation about the long run, so dear to critics of economic neoorthodoxy: it sometimes lasts as long as most person's lifetimes. A more helpful version is that the "long run" that economists have in mind is a succession of a great many short runs, which is simply to say that the long run measured in years is a continuous variable, but an economy's "years" are not spaced at equal intervals. There are secular trends, fairly regular shorter cycles, but there are also "periods" that are irregularly punctuated by the beginnings and endings of eventful trusts, "ups," turns and "downs."

The mainline economic theory of education of the post-World War II period began with what were substantially gratuitous assumptions in the early 1960s. The basic conclusion, one-third of a century later, is that these assumptions may now be granted, as a result of unfolding socioeconomic events, and that the theory currently meets relevant tests fairly well, as we shall see as we review the "human capital" schools' offerings.

One of the earliest treatments was by Adam Smith. He theorized, in *The Wealth of Nations*, that the higher earnings of professionals and artisans reflected, at once, the costs (including "opportunity costs") of preparation for their occupations and the "honorableness" imputed to their callings by their grateful fellow citizens.

Smith's formulation became a principle of sociology, outside the Marxist tradition, in line with Durkheim's "functionalist" approach, later, and urged, with more moralistic fervor, by Herbert Spencer, and then William Graham Sumner, in the nineteenth century.

One subset of modern sociology's functionalists—that observable social arrangements emerge as they do because they contribute, in manifest or latent fashion, to social systems' well being—won a renewed vote of confidence among admirers of an article by the late Kingsley Davis and Wilbert Moore (1945), who argued that income was distributed unequally in developed societies because higher rewards needed to be accorded to those who performed a society's most important functions lest the functions be neglected. The excess of physicians' earnings over those paid to those who build and maintain urban sewage systems reflects social assessments of "need," however greater the later group's work may count for public health. Their version of income distribution and, more generally, of stratification, became one important part of the functional approach, nowadays, including analyses of sociologists in one of the subsets of the status attainment school of social stratification.

Functionalism's critics argued that by combining popular perceptions of status, gauged from surveys, with income returns to different occupations, into an index, while positing the significant role of "social necessity" in generating incentives, the authors were reifying the status quo. As critics see it many functionalists leave too little room for the *power* of a minority to constrict reward systems through social, economic (market), and political controls over occupations. For the critics these controls include those over the means of production, for example, and those that are given by the high costs of entry into established universities, tuition charges, licensing fees, institutionalized discriminatory preferences, one-sided labor contracts, and through industry structures, especially those that are oligopolistic, that temper or severely contain price competitive forces. The larger of the two schools of the economics of education similarly lives comfortably, if implicitly, with its own functionalist "human capital" approach according to which inequalities in income distribution result from market forces—collectively, the "invisible hand" of natural law thought during the Enlightenment—that rationally reward economic efficiency in the service of the "greatest good for the greatest number."

Kiker reviews "The Historical Roots of the Concept of Human Capital" in an edited volume (1971) that affords interested readers a splendid and detailed introduction to and overview of "human capital theory" (Becker, 1964) as we know it today. A cottage industry in the 1960s, this theory has since spawned one of contemporary economics' sprawling enterprises (Becker, 1993:1–8). Becker's and others' theoretical apparatus derived, in intellectual terms, from the emergence of economic growth and development as principal objects of economic policy, in 1946 and beyond, following upon the earlier focus, from 1929 to 1942, by the profession on unemployment (Arndt, 1978).

Changes in economic theories thus tend to reflect changes in central socioeconomic circumstances; perceived necessity thus gives birth to inventive intellectual direction. Economists' theories since the 1890s have been notably influenced by changing social circumstances, as the problems they have pursued have reflected the partisans of one or another side of emerging versions of political, social, and squarely ideological positions. These partisans do intellectual battle over the appropriateness of diagnoses of and prescriptions for solving pervasive and different problems occurring at different points in time. The *science* of the partisans, i.e., economics' rigorous methods, is an appendage to their evolving predilections, which are informed by judgments about the roles of ever-changing social, political, and cultural forces that contribute to the shaping of markets' operations in succeeding periods not, as some economists appear to believe, by the specifications in their science per se. To put it crisply, Marxists' economic determinism "was not all wrong," but specifically *what* in an economy is determined—in-

cluding ideas—will reflect different circumstances in a given economy's evolution; the possibly inflationary consequences of growth were a far lower level concern in the 1940s and 1950s than they are in present day America.

The human capital enterprise continued to expand beyond 1965 (Becker, 1993:xix), however, i.e., even after the growth concept was called into question by ("liberal") environmentalists, among other critics. In Spring 1998 it was possible to test modern human capital theory more fully as the ranks of the environmentalist critics of robust economic growth had been swollen by most large investors, particularly among speculative bond marketers, whose dread of inflation, blamed largely on tight labor markets, generates ever-larger appetites for growth-slowing public policies, including interest rate increases. These potent investors, in competition with a substantial shift, thanks to global competition, from oligopolistic to price-and-quantity competition (1980–1995), forced employers to cross economists' "marginal cost" with "marginal revenue" curves far more assiduously than in the period 1945–1975. The single most obvious result has been the relentless "restructuring" of industries and business enterprises, the most visible manifestation of which has, in turn, been "downsizing," of which more below.

The absence of acute price competition coupled with the generally sanguine attitudes toward inflation in the period 1945–1975, as we will see below, contributed to the generation of sufficient market imperfections in the "core" economy that the returns to college graduates approximated windfall gains as much—or more—than they did returns to college attendance per se, as postulated by the first major modern human capital writers. About all that college students truly and consistently have in common by the time they convene for their graduation exercises, meantime, is that they have all aged by 4 years, and have roughly equal accesses to a colleges' placement office, facts that make college attendance's actual income correlates problematical, given the considerable differences among colleges in their selection criteria, the differences in maturation of the members of a given student body, and the differences in accesses to better and less rewarded jobs for students from different social backgrounds and courses of study.

Two of the three architects of the (larger) affirmative side of the debate over "capitalizing" men and women's educations, T. Schultz and G. Becker, have since won Nobel memorial Medals in Economics, akin to Nobel Prizes, many years after their initial reports; the awards reflect the high esteem in which disciplinarians have held the seminal work of the human capital concept's modern architects.

T. Schultz started building the modern era's version of a formal model for the analysis of the "Human Capital Concept Applied to Man" (1959) upon an article by John R. Walsh (1935), and upon the works of Frank Knight in 1944, M. Friedman and S. Kuznets in 1945, and J. Mincer in 1958. Schultz was closely followed by Burton Weisbrod and by Schultz's own student, G. Becker, who, after articles staking out his intellectual domain in the early 1960s, offered one of the most conceptually elegant, best argued, and influential books (1964) on any post-World War II subject in economics. Schultz, Becker, and others, given to the notion that we can treat investments in education in ways similar to investments in other forms of capital (that is, by measuring the costs of and returns to social and personal educational expenditures), attracted many economists as well as many of their colleagues in other social science departments.

Dissenting economists, taking their cues from Alfred Marshall's work in the 1920s, argued that education's production role was a distinctly residual one; expenditures on education, with its enormously varied program contents, they argued, were, in most instances, for consumption. Marshall urged that it was neither appropriate nor practical to apply the concept of capital to persons. In one of the most trenchant critiques of the human capital concept, H. G. Shaffer (1961) argued (1) that education is indeed undertaken for consumption purposes, not as a decision resulting from rational calculations of monetary benefits; (2) that even if one could distinguish an investment in a person from an expenditure for a consumption good, it would not be possible to allocate a specific return to a specific investment in a given person; and finally (3) that it would be inadvisable, in any event, to structure public policies, as they very well might be around the investment construct, because education would become vulnerable to misuse by policymakers, under the guise of economists' implicit blessings, as a cure for problems caused by other forces. Shaffer's apprehensions were fully realized in Democrats' "war against poverty," during the Johnson administration, in which education was figured as the heavy weapon in the policy arsenal, and in which skirmishes were accordingly organized against the poor for their insufficient "human capital."

Sociologists, meanwhile, have been more given to studies of Shaffer's other forces in matters of income distribution, including parental "inputs," opportunity structures, the sorting of pupils and students into "tracks," the selections, by youths, of their peer groups, the effects of families' residential patterns, and the roles of third parties—"sponsors"—who help locate jobs and place a great many employable people. Sociologists of education are also interested in the shifting balances of power and influence among groups who shape markets, particularly labor markets, employer tastes and preferences, and speculations by investors, regulators, lenders, and key decision makers, about the economy that impact upon the policies of firms concerning the mobilization and utilization of human resources.

The critics, in the tradition of the Wisconsin School, heirs of the so-called "institutionalists" in the late nineteenth and early twentieth centuries, thus locate economic transactions in far less abstract terms than those who focus, more narrowly, on markets with supposedly rampant price competition. They locate commercial transactions in social relationships and social networks, occurring in markets that are often far from being perfectly competitive, and that take place among persons with different combinations of urges and demiurges as well as with differential knowledge about occupational structures.

On the latter point, economists live comfortably with the problematical proposition that the knowledge about labor markets of new entrants, for example, is normally extensive; sociologists are more comfortable with the proposition that most workers have flawed knowledge about these markets, a proposition that is supported by the high turnover in jobs of younger workers, during tight labor market periods especially, who "shop" extensively for successions of jobs during their early years in the labor force. Parents, school officials, and teachers, meanwhile—as other chapters in this volume will amply document—have a great deal to say about exactly what particular groups of pupils and students will be able to bring with them to labor markets, by way of accomplishments, aspirations, expectations, self-discipline, self-esteem, dispositions toward risks, capacities for deferring gratifications, and social backgrounds and sponsors. We may note, in passing, that most mothers discouraged women graduates from a national (U.S.) probability sample of the high school class of 1972, who later actually earned graduate degrees, from ever even attending college! Discriminatory practices, untainted by malice of subtle and not so subtle natures, like charity, can thus begin at home. There were few parents, in this author's (older) generation, who did not urge their daughters to undertake courses in nursing and teaching, careers whose modest income returns were arguably offset by cycle-proof employment and valuable reentry prospects, thus allowing for "family formations."

Beyond Walsh and Shaffer, human capital's leading critics among economists have included K. Boulding, R.S. Eckhaus, N. Chamberlain, J. Dunlop, E. Ginzberg, M. Reder, A. Reese, and, jointly, S. Bowles and H. Gintis. All have written in the tradition of the institutionalists, with the latter two in the neo-Marxian school of the 1970s.

Human capital writers agree that there are indeed consumption or "cultural" benefits from education, but that many Americans simultaneously pursue occupational and income goals. All pupils and students, moreover, are affected by public and private expenditures that make it both relevant, prudent, and perhaps obligatory for political analysts, parents, and youths to borrow from economists' measure of education's "income effects." These borrowing practices, in the aggregate, fit human capital theory very well.

These writers also remind human capital's critics that all consumption interests are essentially converted from desires into "effective demand" by parents' and students' earnings, and by significant portions of local, state, and federal taxes on individuals' earnings that are expended on schools and educational loans. And banks, for example, specifically reckon loan applicants' educational achievements in their mortgage decisions about real estate, the purchases of which represented, until 1996, i.e., "before mutual funds," the largest portions of most Americans' net worth. One's short-term appetites for poetry, art history, or studies of "gender roles," and for the "examined life," meantime, may readily coexist, as human capital aver, with yearnings for future creature comforts and intergenerational mobility.

Sociologists, by now, would agree with this defense of the human capital construct, though many of them continue to be significantly discomfited by the *essen-*

tially cavalier isolation of and emphasis on formal education from other, more social and political factors in income distribution, including the roles of third parties in sponsoring job candidates in whom these bonding agents invest confidence and on whose behalf they intervene with employers. As a commencement speaker quipped at the end of his speech in May 1996: It isn't "who you know, but whom you know," as status groups, more or less consciously, satisfy their own tastes for kindred spirits but, sociologists must acknowledge some savings, in the information costs related to on-the-job screening, to employers who screen job applicants by use of educational histories.

The defenders of econometric analyses of income returns to education did allow, meantime, that they had rested their case entirely on circumstantial evidence (Becker, 1975:10); their faith was not all shaken by Henry David Thoreau's dictum, given fears that his purveyor watered his milk, that "Some circumstantial evidence is very strong, as when you find a trout in the milk." Indeed their faith, with only a few exceptions, grew when Edward Dennison (1962) reported that differential investments in human resources (education and health) accounted for more of the differences in the rates of developed nations' economic growth (and thus their statuses as modern systems) in an international comparison than did differences in their respective investments in physical capital, this at a time when growth was still a key issue in economics.

What was controversial in the 1960s thereafter became the sapient orthodoxy among most economists as well as among antipoverty warriors in the 1960s. The idea that human capital could be "mobilized" was, of course, also both cheering and useful to college presidents seeking funds from Congress, state legislators, foundations, and private benefactors. Educators and public officials could argue forcefully that public support for veterans' educations by the so-called G.I. Bill, in the 1940s and 1950s, and for the National Defense Education Act in the 1960s, for example, was far, far more than just balanced by the taxes on the incomes earned, later, by those who served during World War II and during the war with Korea and China, whose putatively college-built productivity contributed simultaneously to economic growth. Jokes about muddle-headed professors continued in "sitcoms" of course, but interestingly, were focused increasingly upon academicians in the Northeast, while higher education, particularly public higher education, grew rapidly around the country. "Sputnik" had already added a Cold War coefficient to this growth in the late 1950s. We have only discovered later that the college craze, unfortunately, turned attention away from primary and secondary education.

For sociologists it was of critical interest that human capital writers emphatically, if only implicitly, offered three politically conservative and thus valuable rationalizations for inequalities in income distribution in the United States: (1) a great many low-income earners could essentially blame themselves for not seizing educational opportunities even as many Americans had demonstrably blamed themselves for their miseries during the Great Depression; (2) it is far easier, in a nominally egalitarian social and political system, to argue that a preference for better educated job applicants is at least *objective* if we can *measure* desirable and putatively valuable human attributes than if we are driven to choices entirely uninformed by "empirical" criteria like diplomas and degrees with their (equal interval) incremental years and grades and their *apparent* evidence of "merit"; for the economist, as I have noted, an equal interval continuous interval variable is to be preferred to alternative data that can be processed only in accord with the restrictions on interpretations inherent in "nonparametric techniques." And finally, (3) it has been difficult, until after two decades of "downsizing" among white collar workers, for most Americans (including economists) to imagine that managers would hire increasingly better educated people if they did not *actually* need them. As a pair of distinguished labor economists put it: "if education is *not* a good signal for productivity, firms should essentially find this out and stop using formal schooling as a screening device! (The argument that education will survive as a signal for productivity only if it is an indicator should not suggest, however, that firms will learn about signaling errors immediately.)" (Ehrenberg and Smith, 1991:352, emphasis in the original).

As we see it, it *is* indeed clear that many employers did not estimate or even look for signs of such a possible error until after nearly a third of a century. A voluminous human capital literature was thus produced by a large cadre of economists whose faith in the dispositive conclusions that may be inferred from circumstantial evidence remained unshakable (Becker, 1975:1–8).

The basic article of this faith can be reduced to what logicians call a tautology, and what sociologists call an ecological fallacy: better educated people earn more than their less educated fellow citizens because they are more productive, and we know that they are more productive because they earn more.

The major premise is that earnings are essentially valid proxies for direct measures of productivity. The minor premise is that employers are driven by price competition to minimize their costs and would not otherwise, in accord with the theory Ehrenberg and Smith just urged, pay more for either diplomas and degrees or for more years of schooling than was repaid by productivity; the social sciences are notoriously longer on theorems than on axioms. The theory here and as it has been augmented in more recent literature, in sociology only a little less than in economics, is that of "rational expectations," inspired by the Chicago School of economics from whence human capital theory also came.

A few sociologists, S. M. Miller (whose graduate degree from Princeton was in economics) especially, in a Ford Foundation occasional paper, questioned, in 1964, whether Becker's and others' indirect approach to productivity, using earnings as a proxy for productivity, was at all reasonable in orthodox economic terms, at the time many high school graduates' jobs had already been significantly upgraded to jobs for college graduates, as was shown in virtually all studies of occupations in 1955–1965.

In justice to the human capital school, it must be frankly and fully conceded that *direct* measures of American's productivity are, indeed, scarce, and that economic theorists have not undeservedly prospered from their intellectual investment in price theory, from their imputations of economic rationality to the parties in labor markets, and from their elastic test that holds that if employers err in purchasing more "units" of human capital than are truly needed, they will eventually be punished by competitors for their sins. The economists' "long run," meantime, leaves space for sociologists to study the forces that permit employers to indulge "tastes" for education, for protracted periods, for reasons that are not so evidently rational in the economists' sense of the reasonable adoption of means to desirable ends.

One sociologist sought to explore the productivity–education nexus directly during a period in which many college graduates, in many work settings, worked side by side with less educated peers (Berg, 1970), a large body of circumstances in the 1950s and 1960s that would be exceedingly hard to find, nowadays. First he interviewed human resources executives in 20 of the so-called Fortune 500 companies; only one offered any evidence, whatever, that his company had ever collected any data on the subject. The other 19 executives speculated that, *eventually*, they would likely promote the better educated workers in their high school-level jobs to more demanding positions, in which case their educational requirements would *eventually* make sense, thus begging the question, as we will see.

Next, the investigator exploited a collaborative study by employers and Labor Department job analysts of the General Education Requirements (G.E.D.s) for 40,000 occupational titles (80% plus of the workforce). In their studies they made rough estimates of the number of years of schooling that would afford students the cognitive and related skills needed in each of the 40,000 jobs. He reported that the application even of an extreme version of "matchups," a version that was totally friendly to employers' "upgrading" practices, revealed that, by the most conservative estimate, about 15% of American college graduates in 1960 were already at work in occupations well performed by high school graduates only 10 years earlier. This portion of the study has recently been meticulously replicated by Livingstone (1998) using American and Canadian data; he confirms that the "gap" between employers' needs and job holders' educational achievements has widened very significantly.

We should note, in this context, that in *1940* only 4% of all Americans 25 and older had completed 4 or more years of college; by 1994 the figure was 25%. American employers thus produced the very important economic side of the victory in World War II with a workforce, over age 25, in which, moreover, only *24.5%* even had 4 years of *high school;* this, in an economy, 1940–1945, that became increasingly "higher tech" by the week.

Sociologists refer to such an analysis as a "critical" or "natural experiment" regarding, in this event, the actual needs of employers for formal education, because prices and wages were essentially controlled by Uncle Sam while "preferences" were overshadowed by the imperatives of a wartime draft of nearly 13 million youths. American employers could and, indeed, did "make do" during the war years; it was the highest point, in American employers' entire history, to date, of adept personnel management. The only possible exception was the rapid industrialization of the republic, 1870 and beyond, with an even less educated workforce, and the production of a well-disciplined workforce only a few of whose members actually remonstrated against the "barons" who ruled over them prior to the 1930s.

Finally, the investigator looked at employers' rewards, 1965–68, to differentially educated blue and white collar workers at New York Bell; the Prudential Insurance Co; a leotard manufactory and a pantyhose manufactory, in Mississippi; all the technicians at St. Regis Paper Co; N.Y. City Teachers; skilled and semi-skilled auto workers at GMs Tarrytown, N.Y. plant; editorial office workers at Time Magazine; tellers in New York City's Chemical Bank; and 110 scientists and engineers in America's six largest manufacturers of heavy electrical equipment. He also reviewed records of all the tower controllers in the FAA (then almost all high school grads); all the grades and scores of all the students in service schools, many "high tech", in the Marine Corps, Army, Navy and Air Force; and the careers of a 5% sample, from grades G4 through G13, of all the civil servants in the U.S. Government. Berg (1970)

After reviewing the correlations between education and performance as determined by job evaluations, rewards, promotions, prizes, and bonuses, i.e., *employer's* acknowledged measures of productivity, he reported no differences in employee performance, *as judged directly*, for emphasis here, by employers, that related to individuals' academic credentials.

Why, one will ask, would the direct relationship between performance and rewards be so indifferent in the 1950s and 1960s and become apparently more negligent in the 1990s, in Livingstone's very recent study? One explanation did emerge from the earlier data sets: a great many better educated persons left their less challenging employers in quest of better paying jobs; they did not wait for promotions and moved to more demanding jobs while their less educated former co-workers inherited the promotion opportunities.

Another, and more important answer is that employers in the high employment "core" economy were simply not pressed by economic circumstances to deal energetically with their costs; the costs of the widespread preference for college grads could be passed on to a rapidly expanding middle class of avid consumers, another of oligopolies' munificent if selectively awarded social dividends. Circumstantial evidence, as Thoreau sarcastically urged, may well be dispositive.

Berg concluded (1970) that the case for the human capital paradigm should be accorded the Scottish verdict, "not proved"; comparisons of the dollar differences between the incomes of better and less educated Americans in the early post-World War II era took no account of the socioeconomic context. Sociologists have been more inclined to look at top corporate leaders as decision makers who *will* be literally *driven* by cost consciousness and the crossing of marginal cost with marginal revenue curves essentially *only when price competition is pervasive* rather than when it is confined to the smaller enterprises that make up the so-called peripheral economy. Under alternative conditions, termed "managed competition" by economists, they can hire and promote in accord with socially given values, preferences, tastes, and, of course, plain old prejudices. Employers' human resource practices did not truly fit human capital theory because the theory was "price driven" whereas the practices were not.

The overridingly preponderant influences of "managed competition"—price leadership by networks of leaders and followers among the largest producers, coupled with popular interests in brand labels assiduously promoted by costly advertising, the unexploited capacity to initiate "cut throat" competition, favored by very low breakeven points (and virtually no foreign competition) in our large employers' basic industries, and the high cost of entry to would be industry entrants— made it possible, for a very long time, for employers to look away from textbook pressures for more education. The reports we read from economists who had studied industry structures, starting with Schumpeter (an institutionalist par excellence), through the Temporary National Economic Committee in the 1940s, and beyond, and studies of competition by a commission to study the structure of the American Economy (1940s), through the 1980s, reported unremittingly, almost numbingly, of the gains and losses of "oligopolistic" or managed competition.

The gain was spared vigorous price competition; large corporations could follow "price leaders" (in steel, glass, rubber, autos, aluminum, petroleum, and the "big tag" consumer durables), pass on large portions of

costs, including those of union agreements, socially valuable "R.&D.," and the costs of college hires to consumers. Prices were set in product markets in definable if not measurable parts by leaders of key markets' "corporate hierarchies," and by price setters in nonconspiratorial business networks (Collins, 1995), and by pricing conspirators, as in the heavy electrical equipment industry, wherein competitive bids were "rigged" from 1935 to 1959.

As we have noted there were other "upsides" to oligopoly: an expansion of middle income earners, an impressive decline in socioeconomic inequality, and continuing technological virtuosity from R.&D. The costs were growing inflation and, gradually, sluggish growth, coupled with what self-righteous corporate raiders in the investment community, later, in the 1980s, called the "hidebound bureaucracies" that would later "downsize"; Michael Milkin made far bigger dents in the reputations of Big Business than American (or other) neo-Marxists could have ever dreamed of. On their way to what became their moments of truth in the 1970s, the biggest hierarchies and most extensive networks did well enough: by 1954 16 of the nations largest companies shipped *83%* of the products of *120* industries. Unaccustomed to thinking about the complexities of market structures, many sociologists, a few functionalists especially, overlooked the extraordinary sociological significance—to job opportunities, job formation, income distribution, and technological changes—of long periods of what once were regarded as commonplace market structures in a great many industries.

Readers know well that we are no longer the world's cornucopia; competition from Germany and Japan began to cut into the markets of General Motors, for example, by the early 1970s. Protected by low breakeven points (the utilization of as little as 48% capacity at GM in 1963 would still yield large profits) our large employers long enjoyed a protective cover that became more and more frayed by the continuing discipline of the Japanese and Germans (who have only very recently begun a very limited substitution of education for training) and by the emergence of Pacific Rim nations, including the (currently wounded) "Asian Tigers" and, now, China, Mexico, and several Latin American countries.

It is entirely apposite to note that corporations are *appreciably* closer in the 1990s than they were in the

1950s to the type of market competition postulated in the larger theory underlying human capital analyses in the 1960s. If a few of us pronounced the "Scottish verdict" on the human capital tautology in 1970 we must now, that conditions do approximately match the human capital writers' earlier suppositions, revisit the issue and commend the application *today* of human capital theory, even if the grossly inegalitarian results of price competition, and of managerial methods for dealing with it, are upsetting to many thoughtful observers, including conservative political strategists like K. Phillips (1992).

A revisit reveals that the returns on investments in males' college education in constant dollars (as currently measured, i.e., pre-Boskin Commission and other agencies' revelations in 1996–1997) have, on the average, dropped several points below the rate of inflation, and that the number of college graduates in high school-level jobs has climbed, in conservative estimates by the Bureau of Labor Statistics, to 30%; according to a national survey by job placement experts at Northwestern University, in 1992, entry level pay to graduates of liberal arts programs averaged $27,700 per annum, or $800 less than this group's inflation-adjusted entry earnings in 1968! Rugged price competition, when we have it, appears either (1) to chasten easy spending employers, (2) enable employers to play a growing surfeit of college males against each other, (3) encourage employers to be far less admiring, now, of the capacities of professors' and teachers' prowesses, overall, or, most likely, (4) all of the above.

Employers, quite evidently, are counting their human resources dollars far more scrupulously than in what Becker, writing about 1955–1965, called the human capital's "salad days" (Becker, 1975:8). Fine times they were indeed, for colleges, for markets for teachers, for better educated workers, and for the ticket takers in Bursars' offices, but the *model* commends itself far better as good *theory* now, with competition rife, than it did in the halcyon days.

The favorable news *now* is not that returns to college education are so much higher than those to high school graduates, as indeed they are, but that while white male graduates are experiencing a decline in living standards, they are *losing far less*, in constant dollars, than are high school diplomates, even as (or partly because) so many college graduates displace these high school-

ers. This gap, however, is presently stabilizing, and may quite likely not grow larger in the future.

The Bureau of Labor Statistics estimated in 1993, meantime, that by Spring 2010—the college graduation date for those who are now about to enter eighth grade—college graduates will, on average, have 5 chances in 10 of entering into jobs that do not require a college diploma as traditionally conceived.

The story for woman college graduates, under conditions of heightened competition and in constant dollar terms, is considerably cheerier: these women, on average, are earning salaries in excess of inflation; according to the Bureau of Labor Statistics in 1995, a male college graduate would need two additional years of schooling to match their female peers' rising rates of return, a development to which we will return below.

As noted, a few paragraphs back, future outcomes of current debates about our use of the standard (BLS) measure of inflation may require recalculations of some relevant earnings and productivity data in the near future.

In accord with human capital theory one might conclude, first, that male college graduates, now paid less (in constant dollars) by cost conscious employers than they were in bygone days, *are sufficiently more productive than high school graduates* to be *rational* choices for employers, especially given, first, that these graduates' real earnings have dropped, and, second, that even lower level jobs have become more demanding than they were in the period 1945–1970, computers and all that. It is also fairly well known that both primary and secondary education, in many heavily populated precincts, have been victimized by what sociologists term white flight, i.e., as better off white families leave heavily populated urban precincts, the public educational system's quality in these precincts has declined to the disadvantage of diploma winners' earnings.

One may also conclude that if human capital writers are more on target, now that their controlling assumptions about competition have been finally realized, it is presently the case that the *most* productive workers among college graduates, the women who will receive higher rewards, cannot be reasonably viewed as beneficiaries, simply, of "affirmative action dividends." College women, on average, are, *by human capital theory's lights*, more productive than college males, or they would not have been paid more. Affirmative action may well have opened doors, but price competition is, at the very least, as potent a cause of the rewards that productive women are now reaping.

The result, in stratification terms, is that investments in higher education by women, on the average, are presently investments in an *offensive* occupational weapon; for college males, these investments are, on the average, a *defensive* weapon, in their mobility struggles, against the more "free fall" quality of returns plaguing high schoolers, a gap between college males and high schoolers that, as noted, has recently stabilized. The high return for males, discounted over a lifetime (11%), reported by Becker and others in the 1960s and 1970s, finally, was apparently inflated by the difference between the far, far lower real returns to them, over the past 20 years, compared with the enviable— and inflated—returns accorded these males in the earlier period.

The biggest overlaps between economists' and sociologists' studies of income distribution are in their joint concerns with parents' contributions, through their complex roles as "socializers," to their children's educational achievements, and their mutual interests in the relative roles of talent and ability, holding educational achievements constant, in generating occupational successes. Both groups generally compare the earnings of youth from different income backgrounds. Sociologists, meanwhile, generally look beyond parents' socioeconomic status, as an omnibus-type independent variable, to observe childrearing practices, parental expectations, and parental contributions to "learning effects," and some sociologists also go beyond households to consider neighborhoods', peer groups', and communities' effects, as well as the continuing effects of discrimination against minorities whose educational achievements match those of majoritarian competitors.

Sociologists, including most of those who have contributed to this volume, however, also go on to look at social networks, school systems, classroom experiences, "tracking" policies, school governance, and personality traits, among many other factors' roles, in our fellow Americans' efforts to get ahead; Jencks et al. (1979) showed the way.

Sociologists also look at the different judgments teachers make about students from different socioeconomic backgrounds when they have commerce with students in classrooms. The most comprehensive treatments are by Blau and Duncan (1967), Jencks et al. (1979), and Brieger (1990), who part company with other functionalists among those belonging to the "status attainment school" noted earlier. These scholars report that the early and significant effects of educational achievements impact upon an individuals "life chances," which are further shaped by the passing of time—maturation—and by the effects of either more or less valuable and cumulative work-relevant experiences. The "educational effects" on individuals, favored by economists, are more conspicuous in Americans' early career experiences than they are later. The more institutionalist sociologists, meantime, are also well represented in works by Collins (1979), Carnoy and Levin (1985), and recently, as noted, by Livingstone (1998), who focus on power, influence, network access, and competition among status groups, in shaping income distribution and the parameters of poverty. The specific reliance on status group preferences, i.e., arbitrary, essentially capricious predilections as more low-income offspring attend college, has been significantly attenuated by the ways in which some racial issues are joined in congressional actions, Presidential Executive Orders, and, subsequently, by the Supreme Court in connection with civil rights.

A clear difference in the interests alluded to in the immediately preceding paragraphs, between economists and sociologists, in brief, is that one group focuses on markets and prices while the other focuses on social structures, social roles, social norms, and social rewards and sanctions. As price competition has set in the results obtained by these researchers are not inconsistent with those of human capital-inspired studies of earnings.

A few economists continue to contest human capital concepts' "production" view of education's contributions to individuals and social welfare. But polls and surveys indicate that nearly all Americans, by the 1970s, came to appreciate education's "screening" or "signaling" functions. And as the sluice gate functions of educators have favored college graduates over the victims of primary and secondary education's short falls, whatever doubts human capital critics may have about the powers of educational achievements to influence work performance have been attenuated. Colleges offer highly sophisticated "career planning centers," with abundant amenities for employers' representatives, even an enormous proliferation of tutorial programs, and course advising systems. Many colleges afford abundant numbers of remediation programs, even in "elite" collegiate programs, to those whose lips become tired when they read; these services have also helped admissions officers to augment the prestige appeal in their degree with reassurance about job opportunities.

It should be noted, though, that the United States Supreme Court explicitly and unanimously disallowed the equivalent human capital writers' theoretical dependence on circumstantial evidence in screening employees, in *Griggs v. Duke Power Co.* (1971), one of three landmark civil rights cases. In a decision, informed by the study detailed above (Berg, 1970), the Court held that it was unconstitutional to use educational requirements (or test results) for hiring or promoting individuals if the results were discriminatory against "protected groups," *unless the employer can demonstrate a business necessity for the requirement.* If an employer cannot demonstrate that better educated persons are, in fact, more productive in given jobs than less educated candidates, the educational requirements fail a *constitutional* test. The court's decision, favoring direct evidence, was transformed into statutory federal law in the so-called Civil Rights Act of 1991, complete with new possibilities, for successful plaintiffs, to collect damages. The widely perceived decline in public education's quality could, indeed probably will, lead some judges, however, to view "upgraded" requirements benignly.

Public policy positions like *Griggs* and the 1991 Act are of signal sociological significance; circumstantial evidence showing aggregated correlates of education with income will certainly continue to be used in defense of public expenditures on education and financial aid, and many will approve.

There is a considerable problem with both the *Griggs* case and the Civil Rights Act of 1961, however, and it is the same problem that led human capitalists to use aggregated income and education data to measure education's productivity "pay off" back in the 1960s: not many of us have jobs requiring behavior that can be directly linked to one or more units of production or service in an uncontroversial way. Even my own direct data, above, reluctantly accepted employers' evaluation

practices as more revealing of performance than income returns, even though employers' evaluations may be far less than incontestable versions of reality; most readers who have evaluated the performance of colleagues, as employers struggle to evaluate their workers, realize that we are often sculpturing fog. On the other end of the human capitalists' tautology, their measures of earnings to college graduates, from census data, do not include the billions of dollars of the stock options that a minority of them earn, as top corporate officers, *whether or not* their firms prosper; indeed some are paid off in stock shares even when they prove to have failed and must be "pink slipped."

In social policy terms the Court, the Congress, and the President must attend explicitly to *direct* measures of individual workers' productivity, vis-à-vis differentially educated aggregates of workers, however problematic such evaluations may be. Relevant laws are accordingly enforced not on the basis of the functionalist view of the *putative* social importance or "social necessity" of an occupational activity but on the basis of evidentiary *proof* of an employers' own actual "business needs" for differentially educated candidates. These firm-specific needs may be filled virtually any old way, however, *so long as they are not* discriminatory against protected groups.

If indirect "human capital"–style measures of productivity can support only a tautology, direct measures of "real" job requirements will be available for relatively few work positions, a pair of problems sociologists can clarify but about which they cannot offer answers except to suggest that judgments will be *socially* defined in accord with increasingly *socially* acceptable conclusions that college graduates *are* "better"—and now cheaper— than they were. College degree holders will continue to proliferate and primary and secondary education will continue to remain a puzzlingly questionable means to work place success.

One evolving test of the validity of job requirements will be in health services, as "health provider" managers set terms for doctors about doctors' treatments, diagnostic tests, hospital admissions, and for nurses who will clearly inherit a growing number of doctoral tasks, and so on. Cost-conscious deans are increasingly interested in their faculties' enrollments, meanwhile, an invitation, perhaps, for teachers to be more "user friendly" toward students, with who knows what consequences. Meaningful, i.e., entirely valid measures of performance, apart from those in sports (with their endless performance measures), piecework jobs, and certain sales jobs, are hard to come by. The pride that academics takes in "peer reviews" is generally tempered by recollections of intradepartmental debates over candidacies that produce both winners and losers, as newly minted tenured faculty all too often "meltdown."

CEOs' salaries, meantime, are a genre unto themselves; a new breed of "relationship investors" has emerged, with these CEOs' salaries high among their concerns. Among the issues these investors, principally pension fund money managers, seek to join with eyes to their portfolios, are the logics for supporting the tremendous increases in CEOs' reward packages. It could well happen, as "investor relationships" deepen, that all reward systems will come up for review as yet another constituency attentive to price competition emerges on the nation's institutional landscape.

In the meantime, Michael Jordan's income, as a member of a professional sports team, has raised the average rate of return on his Chapel Hill's college class (from which he dropped out) by a *very* substantial margin, a "social fact" that is not as likely to be recorded in a college economics text, with "average earnings," as in the Guiness Book of Records!

REFERENCES

Arndt, H. W. 1978. *The Rise and Fall of Economic Growth*. Chicago: University of Chicago Press.

Becker, Gary. 1964. *Human Capital: A Theoretical and Empirical Analysis*. New York: National Bureau of Economic Research.

Becker, Gary. 1993. *Human Capital* (3d ed.). Chicago: University of Chicago Press.

———. 1975. *Human Capital: A Theoretical Analysis, with Special Reference to Education*, 2nd ed. Chicago: University of Chicago Press.

Berg, Ivar. 1970. *Education and Jobs: The Great Training Robbery*. New York: Praeger.

Blau, Peter, and Otis Dudley Duncan. 1967. *The American Occupational Structure*. New York: Wiley.

Brieger, Ronald, (ed.). 1990. *Social Mobility and Social Structure*. New York: Cambridge University Press.

Carnoy, Martin, and Henry M. Lewin. 1985. *Schooling and Work in the Democratic State*. Stanford, CA: Stanford University Press.

Collins, Randall. 1975. *The Credentials Society*. New York: Academic Press.

———. 1995. "The Handbook of Economic Sociology." *Contemporary Sociology*. 24 (3):300–304.

Davis, Kingsley, and Wilbert Moore. 1945. "Some Principles of Stratification." *American Sociological Review* X (2): 242–249.

Dennison, Edward. 1962. *Sources of Economic Growth in the United States*. Washington, DC: Committee for Economic Development.

Ehrenberg, Ronald G., and Robert S. Smith. 1991. *Modern Labor Economics: Theory and Public Policy*. New York: Harper Collins.

Jencks, Christopher, et al. 1979. *Who Gets Ahead?* New York: Basic Books.

Kiker, B. F. 1971. "The Historical Roots of the Concept of Human Capital." B. F. Kiker (ed.), *Investment in Human Capital*, pp. 51–77. Columbia, SC: University of South Carolina Press.

Livingstone, D. 1998. *The Education and Jobs Gap: Underemployment of Economic Democracy*. Boulder, CO: Westview Press.

Phillips, Kevin. 1993. *Boiling Point*. New York: Random House.

Schultz, T. W. 1959. "Investment in Man: An Economist's View." *Social Service Review* 33: 109–117.

Shaffer, Harry G. 1961. "Investment in Human Capital: Comment." *American Economic Review* December: 11026–11034.

Walsh, John R. 1935. "Capital Concept Applied to Man." *Quarterly Journal of Economics* XLIX:255–285.

EDUCATIONAL ACHIEVEMENT AND ATTAINMENT IN THE UNITED STATES

Thomas M. Smith
Peabody College, Vanderbilt University

Over the past two decades, U.S. women have made substantial educational progress. The large gaps between the education levels of women and men that were evident in the early 1970s have essentially disappeared for the younger generation. Gaps in mathematics and science achievement have also narrowed, although the one in science remains significant. High school females on average outperform males in reading and writing, and take more credits in academic subjects. In addition, females are more likely than males to attend college after high school, and are more likely to graduate with a postsecondary degree. Although female freshman are as interested in studying mathematics and science as their male counterparts, they are more likely to switch to other fields before graduation.

It remains to be seen, however, how these gains in educational attainment will be rewarded in the marketplace. In 1997, the average earnings of female high school graduates aged 25–34 were more than one-third lower than those of male graduates of the same age. Similarly, female college graduates earn, on average, salaries that are less than 80% of what their male counterparts receive. Although some of these differences can be explained by differences in field of study, a gender gap in wages persists across fields among recent college graduates. Differences in academic achievement, progression rates, types of courses taken, level of effort, and field of study all affect the labor market opportunities of women relative to men. This chapter summarizes educational differences between females and males that research has shown to be related to labor market outcomes.

Do Females and Males Progress at Similar Rates through School?

Females are generally younger than males in first grade and are less likely to fall behind. In 1993, a smaller percentage of females than males in first grade were aged 7 or older (17 and 22%, respectively) (U.S. Department of Education, 1993:20). Females are also less likely than males to repeat a grade. In 1995, girls aged 5–12 were less likely than boys of this age group to have repeated a grade since starting school (U.S. Department of Education, 2000d:40). Boys and girls in this age group were both more likely to repeat kindergarten or first grade than they were to repeat a grade between second and sixth grade. In a research study on elementary classrooms, however, Sadker and Sadker (1994) found that teachers were more likely to do things for girls while showing boys how to do things. This may be just the start of a differential pattern of treatment of boys and girls in school.

Are Females More or Less Likely Than Males to Be Labeled as Disabled or Placed in Special Education Programs?

Males in grades 1–12 were far more likely to be identified by their parents as having a disabling condition than were females in 1995 (10 vs. 6%). Boys were more than twice as likely than girls to have learning disabilities, speech impediments, and emotional disturbances, whereas instances of visual impairments, mental retardation, and orthopedic impairments were similar (U.S. Department of Education, 2000d:32). Among those whose parents identified them as having a disabling condition, boys were more likely to receive special services for their disabilities in school (50 vs. 39%), while similar proportion of both groups received services from a doctor or other sources. Females were also far less likely than males to be enrolled in special education programs: in 1990, less than one-third of students in special education were female (U.S. Department of Education, 1995:347).

Do the Achievement Levels of Females and Males Differ in the Early Grades?

Differences in the academic performance of female and male students appear as early as age 9, and persist through age 17. Although girls have consistently outperformed boys in reading and writing, gender gaps in mathematics and science performance in the early grades have been much narrower and have varied over time. In 1999, 9-year-old girls had higher average reading scores on the National Assessment of Educational Progress (NAEP) than did boys, although this gap has narrowed since 1971 (U.S. Department of Education, 2000c:45). In mathematics, scores favoring girls in the 1970s shifted to scores favoring boys in the 1990s. In 1999, however the slight gender gap favoring boys was not statistically significant. In science, boys have tended to perform better than girls at age 9, although as in mathematics, the small gap evident in 1999 was not statistically significant (Table 1).

Cross-nationally, more countries have a gender gap favoring boys in science than in mathematics in the early grades. The United States was one of 22 out of 26 countries participating in the Third International Mathematics and Science Study (TIMSS) in which there was no significant gender gap in fourth-grade mathematics achievement in 1995. In the science overall score, the United States is one of 10 countries in which a gender gap exists. Examining boys' and girls' scores in the various science content areas, U.S. boys significantly outperform U.S. girls in the content areas of earth science and physical science. There was no significant difference between U.S. boys' and girls' scores in life science and in environmental issues and the nature of science (U.S. Department of Education, 1997).

Do The Differences That We See in the Achievement of Females and Males Age 13 Persist into High School?

Female–male achievement differences remain nearly unchanged at age 13. For example, in 1999, the average reading proficiency score for a 13-year-old female was 12 scale points higher than for a 13-year-old male, while females scored at about the same level in math and 6 scale points lower in science (U.S. Department of Education, 2000c:45). When 17 year olds are assessed near the end of high school, female–male differences persist. For example, in 1999, average reading proficiency for 17-year-old females was 13 scale points higher than for males of the same age. This corresponds to about 45% of the difference between the average scores of 13 and 17 year olds in 1999. In other words, the gap in reading proficiency between females and males at age 17 is roughly equivalent to between 1.5 and 2 years of schooling.

In mathematics and science, scores tend to favor men, although the gap is narrower. At age 17, a gender gap favoring males in mathematics narrowed from 8 points in 1973 to a statistically insignificant 3 points in 1999. The gender gap at this age in science has narrowed from 16 points in 1973 to 10 points in 1999 (about a year's worth of science). Hanson (1996) reports consistent patterns in her analysis of three nationally representative longitudinal data sets, finding that young women fall behind in science before they fall behind in math—women score lower on standardized science exams by seventh grade and on math exams by tenth grade.

Can These Differences in Achievement Be Explained by Differences in Course Taking?

Both female and male students are following a more rigorous curriculum than they were two decades ago. Comparisons of the transcripts of high school graduates indicate that female and male students have similar course-taking patterns. Between 1982 and 1998, the percentage of high school graduates earning the 4 units of English and the 3 units each of science, social studies, and mathematics recommended for all high school graduates in *A Nation At Risk* increased sharply, from 14 to 55% (U.S. Department of Education, 2000b:156).

TABLE 1. Average Proficiency Scores on the National Assessment of Educational Progress (NAEP)

SUBJECT AND YEAR	FEMALE			MALE		
	AGE 9	AGE 13	AGE 17	AGE 9	AGE 13	AGE 17
Reading						
1975	216	262	291	204	250	280
1984	214	262	294	208	253	284
1992	215	265	296	206	254	284
1999	215	265	295	209	254	282
Mathematics						
1973	220	267	301	218	265	309
1986	222	268	299	222	270	305
1992	228	272	305	231	274	309
1999	231	275	307	233	277	310
Science						
1970[a]	223	253	297	228	257	314
1986	221	247	282	227	256	295
1992	227	256	289	235	260	299
1999	228	253	291	231	259	300

[a]At age 17, the first science assessment was administered in 1969.
Source: U.S. Department of Education (2000c:112–114).

Although course taking increased for both genders through 1998, female graduates were more likely than males to complete this "core" curriculum (58 vs. 53%) (Table 2).

Female students are as likely as males to take advanced math and science courses, and are more likely to study a foreign language. Between 1982 and 1992, the percentage of both female and male graduates who took advanced mathematics and science courses in high school increased, although for many subjects gender parity had been attained by 1982. In the class of 1998, females were less likely than males to take remedial mathematics in high school, and at least as likely as their male peers to take upper level mathematics courses such as algebra II, trigonometry, precalculus, and calculus. With respect to science, females were more likely than males to take biology and chemistry. Females have continued, however, to be less likely than males to take physics (U.S. Department of Education, 2000b:156). Other research has shown that once women get into science courses, they are taught similar amounts of science and receive grades similar (or better than) those of their male counterparts (Hanson et al., 1996; Baker and Jones, 1993; DeBoer, 1984).

How Early Do Women Develop Negative Attitudes toward Mathematics and Science?

Findings are mixed concerning when boys' and girls' attitudes about mathematics and science diverge. Hanson (1996) found few differences between girls and boys in their attitudes about science in the early secondary school years. For example, she found that in seventh and eighth grade, girls are no more anxious than boys about math or science and are just as likely to believe that math knowledge is necessary for a good job. These findings contrast with those who have found that girls' attitudes are more negative even in the early years (Linn and Hyde, 1989; Dossey et al., 1988).

Data on student attitudes toward mathematics and science from NAEP show similarities among girls and boys in fourth grade, but by twelfth grade males are more likely than females to state that they like mathematics, they are good at mathematics, and they understand mathematics most of the time (U.S. Department of Education, 2000d:54). Although equal percentages of boys and girls reported that science was a hard subject in both fourth and eighth grades, the

TABLE 2. Percentage of High School Graduates Taking Selected Mathematics and Science Courses

MATHEMATICS AND SCIENCE COURSES	1982		1998	
	FEMALE	MALE	FEMALE	MALE
Mathematics				
Geometry	47.0	47.2	77.3	73.7
Algebra II	39.0	40.8	63.7	59.8
Trigonometry	7.0	9.2	9.7	8.2
Precalculus	5.9	6.5	22.9	23.0
Calculus	4.4	5.7	10.6	11.2
Science				
Biology	78.8	75.8	94.1	91.4
AP/honors biology	10.6	9.4	18.6	14.5
Chemistry	30.9	33.5	63.5	57.1
Physics	10.5	20.2	26.2	31.7
Engineering	0.8	1.7	6.5	7.1

Source: U.S. Department of Education (2000d:24).

percentage of males who reported that science was a hard subject in twelfth grade increased by 7 percentage points, whereas the percentage of females who reported this perception increased by 18 percentage points.

Do Teachers Treat Female and Male Students Differently in the Classroom?

There is some evidence that teachers give more attention to boys than to girls (AAUW, 1992; Sadker and Sadker, 1986), invest more cognitive time with boys than with girls in mathematics (Brophy and Good, 1974) and science classes (Morse and Hadley, 1985), and hold higher expectations of mathematics achievement for boys than for girls even before actual differences in achievement appear (Becker, 1981; Hallinan and Sorensen, 1987). Although teachers may treat students differently on the basis of gender, they appear to be unaware of this differential treatment (Sadker and Sadker, 1986).

Some also argue that certain cultural norms influence females' perceptions of their abilities. For example, a number of studies show that students' achievement in mathematics depends on its perceived usefulness to their future careers (Armstrong, 1985; Fennema and Sherman, 1977; Hilton and Berglund, 1974). This implies that relatively low scores in mathematics among women may be due to their implicit understanding

that math skills will not be useful to them in their future family and work roles (Fox et al., 1985; Sherman, 1983). Baker and Jones (1993) find that cross-national variation in gender stratification of higher education and the labor market was associated with cross-national gender differences in eighth-grade academic mathematics performance in the early 1980s. There are also parallel associations between future opportunity structure and cross-national gender differences in parental encouragement to learn mathematics (Baker and Jones, 1993; Jones, 1989). These studies highlight the inherent endogeneity between attitudes, achievement, and the opportunity structure in the labor force, although increasing labor market opportunities for women may forecast continued improvement in the attitudes and performance of girls in mathematics and science.

How Do Female and Male Students Differ with Regard to Their Parents' Involvement in Their Education?

Parents may be able to improve the academic performance of their children by becoming more involved in their school life. In general, female students are no less likely than male students to have their parents involved in their education. In 1988, eighth-grade females were more likely than their male peers to report talking to their parents about selecting courses, about their school activities, and about their class studies. Males and females were equally likely to have their parents review their homework, limit their television watching, limit their going out with friends, and visit their classes. Females were less likely than males to have had their parents speak with their teacher or guidance counselor. However, it is difficult to interpret this last finding without more specific information about the reasons for these contacts (U.S. Department of Education, 1994:124). There is evidence, however, that parents encourage mathematical achievement more in boys than girls (Eccles and Jacobs, 1986) and accept lower mathematics achievement in girls than boys (Maccoby and Jacklin, 1974). These data are becoming quite dated, however, and it is not clear how parental attitudes toward their children's mathematics and science achievement have changed over time.

Do Men and Women Differ with Respect to Attending College Immediately after High School Graduation?

Females are slightly more likely than males to make an immediate transition from high school to college. Between 1972 and 1998, immediate enrollment rates of female high school graduates increased faster than those of males. Much of the increase in enrollment rates between 1984 and 1998 was due to increases in female enrollment rates at 4-year colleges. In 1997, the enrollment rate for women at 4-year institutions was 45%, compared to 38% for men. That year, women were about as likely as men to enroll in 2-year institutions after high school graduation (24% respectively) (U.S. Department of Education, 2000a:151).

How Have Increasing College Enrollment Rates Raised the Proportion of Degrees Earned by Women at Different Levels?

Although the women now make up the majority of undergraduate students, they have made even greater gains at the graduate level. In 1970, women made up 42% of undergraduate students and 39% of graduate students, but by 1996, 56% of graduate students were women, the same proportion as at the undergraduate level (U.S. Department of Education, 2000a:151). The

majority of first-professional students are still men, although women have made significant gains since 1970, increasing their share from 9 to 40%. In 1970, 5% of law degrees, 8% of medical degrees, and 1% of dentistry degrees were awarded to women; in 1996, the corresponding percentages were 44, 41, and 36% (U.S. Department of Education, 2000d:72)

To What Degree Do Women and Men Study Different Fields in College?

Women and men continue to study different fields in college, although differences have narrowed for undergraduates and in many fields for graduates. At the bachelor's level, women were more than twice as likely as men to graduate with degrees in education in 1996–1997, although this represents a decline from 1971. Women were also more likely than men to major in English, psychology, and the health sciences (Table 3).

Although the differences between men and women are decreasing in the biological/life sciences and business, women are still less likely than men to major in these fields. Moreover, women continue to be less likely than men to major in mathematics, engineering, the physical sciences, computer sciences, and social sciences (U.S. Department of Education, 2000d:70) (Table 4).

These gender differences are a result of choices of major made as freshmen, as opposed to major switching during college. For example, the UCLA study of freshmen norms (Astin et al., 1994) found that women of all racial/ethnic groups were less likely than men to choose to study science and engineering (S&E). A number of studies have shown that gender differences in S&E major selection and persistence are closely related to women's self-perceived ability to learn math and science (e.g., Seymour and Hewitt, 1997). Huang et al. (2000) found, however, that female students who do enter science and engineering programs as freshmen tend to have slightly higher completion rates in these fields than do their male counterparts. Among women who do switch out of science, Seymour and Hewitt (1997) report that declining self-confidence in math-related subjects is associated with a switch from S&E to other fields. Adelman (1998), however, found a 20% gap in engineering program completion rates between men and women, a field where women tend to face the toughest institutional and cultural barriers.

At the graduate level, the tendency of women and

TABLE 3. Percentage of Bachelor's Degrees Conferred to Women in Selected Fields of Study: School Years Ending 1970–1997

	1970	1975	1980	1985	1990	1995	1996	1997
Architecture and related programs	5	17	28	35	39	34	36	36
Biological/life sciences	30	33	42	48	51	52	53	54
Business	9	16	34	45	47	48	49	49
Communications[a]	35	40	52	59	61	58	59	59
Computer and information sciences[a]	14	19	30	37	30	28	28	27
Education	75	73	74	76	78	76	75	75
Engineering and engineering-related technologies	1	2	9	13	14	16	16	17
English language and literature	67	62	65	66	67	66	66	66
Modern foreign languages and literatures	75	77	76	74	74	70	71	71
Health professions and related sciences[a]	77	78	82	85	84	82	82	81
Mathematics	37	41	41	46	46	47	46	46
Physical sciences	14	18	24	28	31	35	36	37
Psychology	43	53	63	68	72	73	73	74
Social sciences and history[a]	37	37	44	44	44	47	48	49

[a]Data for this field in 1970 are from the school year 1970–1971.
Source: U.S. Department of Education (2000c:323–333).

men to choose different fields of study has declined in many major fields. For example, the share of master's degrees awarded to women increased from 3.6% to nearly 38% in business, from 9.3% to 27% in computer and information sciences, from 1% to 17% in engineering, and from 14% to 32% in physical sciences and science technology. Gains have been even larger at the doctoral level, albeit from a smaller base. Large gaps remain in some fields of study, however. For instance, at the master's degree level, women were almost three times as likely as men to earn graduate degrees in education and the health professions, but only about one-fifth as likely to earn degrees in engineering.

How Do These Field Differences Among Women in the United States Compare to Those of Women in Other Countries?

Among 26 countries with highly developed economies, patterns of field concentration among women are generally similar to those in the United States. Women earn the majority of bachelor's and master's level qualifications in most countries—Germany, Korea, Japan, Switzerland, and Turkey are notable exceptions. Women are far more likely to earn degrees in humanities, arts, and education than in mathematics/computer science or engineering (OECD, 2000:176). In a cross-national study of seven countries Hanson et

al. (1996) show that young women's participation in science education decreases with increasing levels of schooling, but there is considerable cross-national variation in the extent of gender stratification in science. They also find greater gender stratification in science occupations across countries than in science education, suggesting factors other than education help maintain inequality in high-status science occupations. Bradley (2000) found that gender differentiation by field has declined little cross-nationally between 1960 and 1990, although the number of women in different fields has risen as access to higher education has expanded. As earnings opportunities are strongly affected by field of study, the persistent gender gaps in some fields of study are a barrier to economic and occupational gender desegregation.

To What Extent Has the Increasing Education Levels of Women Affected Their Labor Market Outcomes?

Employment and earnings rates rise with educational attainment for both women and men, but earnings remain lower for women with the same level of education than their male counterparts. The gap between the employment rates for women and men narrows, however, with increasing levels of educational attainment. For example, between 1971 and 1997, the difference between the employment rates of 25- to 34-year-old fe-

TABLE 4. Percentage of Master's, First-Professional, and Doctor's Degrees Conferred to Women in Selected Fields of Study: School Years Ending 1970–1996

	1970	1975	1980	1985	1990	1994	1995	1996
Master's degrees	40	45	49	50	53	55	55	56
Business management	4	9	22	31	34	37	37	38
Computer and information sciences	9	15	21	29	28	26	26	27
Education	55	62	70	73	76	77	77	76
Engineering	1	2	7	11	14	16	16	17
Health professions and related sciences	52	62	72	76	78	79	78	79
Physical sciences and science technologies	14	14	19	23	26	29	30	32
Psychology	42	46	59	65	69	72	72	72
Social sciences and history	28	30	36	38	41	44	45	46
First-professional degrees[a]	5	12	25	33	38	41	41	42
Dentistry	1	3	13	21	31	39	36	36
Medicine	8	13	23	30	34	38	39	41
Law	5	15	30	39	42	43	43	44
Doctor's degrees	13	21	30	34	36	39	39	40
Business management	2	4	15	17	25	28	27	29
Biological sciences/life sciences	14	22	26	33	38	41	40	42
Computer and information sciences	2	7	11	10	15	15	18	15
Education	20	30	44	52	57	61	62	62
Engineering	1	2	4	6	9	11	12	13
Physical sciences and science technologies	5	8	12	16	19	22	24	23
Health professions and related sciences	16	29	45	53	54	59	58	57
Psychology	23	32	43	50	59	62	63	66
Social sciences and history	13	21	27	32	33	36	38	38

[a]First professional degrees are degrees awarded in the fields of dentistry (D.D.S. or D.M.D.), medicine (M.D.), optometry (O.D.), osteopathic medicine (D.O.), pharmacy (D.Phar.), podiatric medicine (D.P.M.), veterinary medicine (D.V.M.), chiropractic medicine (D.C. or D.C.M.), law (J.D.) and the theological professions (M.Div. or M.H.L.).
Source: U.S. Department of Education (2000d:72).

males and males narrowed from 51 to 16 percentage points for high school graduates and from 36 to 10 percentage points for college graduates (U.S. Department of Education, 2000d:82).

The gender gap in earnings among young women has also narrowed. Although female 4-year college graduates aged 25 to 34 earned less on average than male college graduates of the same age in 1997 ($25,558 and $32,875, respectively), the gap has narrowed considerably in the 1970s and 1980s. In 1971, young women earned only 57% of their male counterparts while by 1990 the percentage had climbed to 76%. Between 1990 and 1997, however, this gap remained stable (U.S. Department of Education, 2000d:86). About half of the difference in the overall median starting salaries between males and females is attributable to gender differences in choice of college major (U.S. Department of Education, 2000d:86).

As with field choice in education, there continues to be strong gender segregation by occupation. Although women make up almost one-half of the American labor market, they made up only 23% of the science and engineering labor force (that is, those who are either employed or seeking work) in 1997 (National Science Foundation, 2000: Table 5–2). Women constitute higher percentages of some science and engineering occupations than of others. For example, more than half of all psychologists (63%) and sociologists (55%) were women, compared with 10% of physicists and 9% of engineers.

Full-time employed female scientists and engineers generally earn less than men, but these salary differences are due primarily to differences in age, occupation, and highest degree attained. Female scientists and engineers are younger, on average, than men and are less likely than men to be in computer science or engineering—occupations that command higher salaries. The 1997 overall median salary for full-time female scientists and engineers was $47,000; this was much lower than that for men ($58,000), but within occupations and within younger age categories, the median salaries of men and women were more alike. With increasing age, however, the gap in salaries between male and female scientists widens in both the education and business sectors. On the other hand, for engineers employed in business or industry, men's and women's salaries keep pace with increasing age through age 40 (National Science Foundation, 2000:Appendix table 5–24)

Although early labor market research suggested positive consequences of development for women's status in the labor market, their is some evidence that structural aspects of advanced economies, including the incorporation of women's work into a large service sector and the development of highly bureaucratic employers (with little self-employment), lead to gender-segregated labor markets. Expanded formal labor markets often pull newcomers (usually women) into lower level jobs and sectors (Charles, 1992).

In summary, women have made important advances in education over the past few decades, closing the gender gap in educational attainment among younger women that existed 20 years ago. In high school, females read and write better than males, perform about as well in math, and slightly worse in science. The mathematics and science courses that females and males take in high school are similar, with the exception that females are less likely than males to study physics. Moreover, females are more likely than males to go to college immediately after high school and are more likely to earn degrees. Although females tend to major in different subjects than males in college, many of these differences have narrowed over time. And despite large gains in educational attainment and labor force participation, significant differences in earnings persist between females and males, even at similar levels of education and within certain fields of study. The hard sciences remain an area where the gender gap remains large, having an impact on both occupational and economic opportunities.

REFERENCES

Adelman, C. 1998. *Women and Men of the Engineering Path: A Model for Analyses of Undergraduate Careers.* PLLI 98–8055. U.S. Department of Education, Office of Educational Research and Improvement. Washington, DC: U.S. Government Printing Office.

American Association of University Women (AAUW). 1992. *How Schools Short-Change Girls.* Washington, DC: American Association of University Women Educational Foundation.

Armstrong, J. M. 1985. "A National Assessment of Participation and Achievement of Women in Mathematics." In S. F. Chipman, L. R. Brush, and D. M. Wilson (eds.), *Women and Mathematics: Balancing the Equation*, pp. 59–94. Hillsdale, NJ: Lawrence Erlbaum.

Astin, A. W., W. S. Korn, L. J. Sax, and K. M. Mahoney. 1994. *Survey of the American Freshman: National Norms.* Los Angeles, CA: Higher Education Research Institute, UCLA.

Baker, D. P., and D. P. Jones. 1993. "Creating Gender Equality: Cross-National Gender Stratification and Mathematical Performance." *Sociology of Education* 66:91–103.

Becker, J. R. 1981. "Differential Treatment of Females and Males in Mathematics Classes." *Journal of Research in Mathematics Education* 12:40–53.

Bradley, K. 2000. "The Incorporation of Women into Higher Education: Paradoxical Outcomes?" *Sociology of Education* 73:1–18.

Brophy, J., and T. Good. 1974. *Teacher-Student Relationships.* New York: Holt, Rinehart & Winston.

Charles, M. 1992. "Cross-National Variation in Occupational Sex Segregation." *American Sociological Review* 57:483–502.

DeBoer, G. 1984. "A Study of Gender Effects in the Science and Mathematics Course-Taking Behavior of a Group of Students Who Graduated from College in the Late 1970s." *Journal of Research in Science Teaching* 21:95–103.

Dossey, J. A., I. V. S. Mullis, M. M. Lindquist, and D. L. Chambers. 1988. *The Mathematics Report Card: Are We Measuring Up?* Princeton, NJ: Educational Testing Service.

Eccles, J. S., and J. E. Jacobs. 1986. "Social Forces Shape Math Attitudes and Performances." *Signs: Journal of Women in Culture and Society* 11:367–380.

Fennema, E., and J. A. Sherman. 1977. "Sex-Related Differences in Mathematics Achievement, Spatial Visualization, and Affective Factors." *American Educational Research Journal* 14:51–71.

Fox, L. H., L. Grody, and D. Tobin. 1985. "The Impact of Early Intervention Programs Upon Course-Taking and Attitudes in High School." In S. F. Chipman, L. R. Brush, and D. M. Wilson (eds.), *Women and Mathematics: Balancing the Equation,* pp. 249–274. Hillsdale, NJ: Lawrence Erlbaum.

Hallinan, M. T., and A. B. Sorenson. 1987. "Ability Grouping and Sex Differences in Mathematics Achievement." *Sociology of Education* 60:63–72.

Hanson, Sandra L. 1996. *Lost Talent: Women in the Sciences.* Philadelphia: Temple University Press.

Hanson, S. L., M. Schaub, and D. P. Baker. 1996. "Gender Stratification in the Science Pipeline: A Comparative

Analysis of Seven Countries." *Gender and Society* 10(3): 271–290.

Hilton, T. L., and G. W. Berglund. 1974. "Sex Differences in Mathematical Achievement: A Longitudinal Study." *Journal of Educational Research* 67:231–237.

Huang, G., N. Taddese, and E. Walter. 2000. *Entry and Persistence of Women and Minorities in College Science and Engineering Education*. NCES 2000–601. U.S. Department of Education, National Center for Education Statistics. Washington, DC: U.S. Government Printing Office.

Jones, D. 1989. "Gender differences in mathematics achievement: A cross-national analysis." Unpublished doctoral dissertation, Catholic University of America, Washington, DC.

Linn, M., and J. Hyde. 1989. "Gender, Mathematics, and Science." *Educational Researcher* 18:17–19, 22–27.

Maccoby, E., and C. Jacklin. 1974. *The Psychology of Sex Differences*. Stanford, CA: Stanford University Press.

Morse, L., and H. Hadley. 1985. "Listening to Adolescents: Differences in Science Classroom Interaction," In L. Wilkinson and C. Marrett (eds.), *Gender Influences in Classroom Interaction*, pp. 37–56. Orlando, FL: Academic Press.

National Science Foundation. 2000. *Women, Minorities and Persons with Disabilities in Science and Engineering: 2000*. Arlington, VA. NSF 00–327.

Organisation for Economic Co-operation and Development (OECD). 2000. Education at a Glance: OECD Indicators 2000, Paris: Author.

Sadker, M., and D. Sadker. 1986. "Sexism in the Classroom from Grade School to Graduate School." *Phi Delta Kappan* 68:512.

———. 1994. *Failing at Fairness: How Our Schools Cheat Girls*. New York: Simon & Schuster.

Seymour, E., and N. M. Hewitt. 1997. *Talk about Leaving: Why Undergraduates Leave the Sciences*. Boulder, CO: Westview Press.

Sherman, J. A. 1983. "Girls Talk about Mathematics and Their Future." *Psychology of Woman Quarterly* 7:338–342.

U.S. Department of Education, National Center for Education Statistics. 1993. *The Condition of Education 1993*, by Nabeel Alsalam et al. NCES 93–290, Washington, DC: U.S. Government Printing Office.

———. 1994. *The Condition of Education 1994*, by Thomas M. Smith et al. NCES 94–149. Washington, DC: U.S. Government Printing Office.

———. 1995. *The Condition of Education 1995*, by Thomas M. Smith et al. NCES 95–273, Washington, DC: U.S. Government Printing Office.

———. 1996. *The Condition of Education 1996*, by Thomas M. Smith et al. NCES 96–304. Washington, DC: U.S. Government Printing Office.

———. 1997. *Pursuing Excellence: A Study of U.S. Fourth-Grade Mathematics and Science Achievement in International Context*, NCES 97–255. Washington, DC: U.S. Government Printing Office.

———. 2000a. *The Condition of Education 2000*, by John Wirt et al. NCES 00–062. Washington, DC: U.S. Government Printing Office.

———. 2000b. *The Digest of Education Statistics 1999*, by Thomas D. Snyder (ed.). NCES 00–031. Washington, DC: U.S. Government Printing Office.

———. 2000c. *NAEP 1999 Trends in Academic Progress: Three Decades of Student Performance*, by J. R. Campbell, C. M. Hombo, and J. Mazzeo. NCES 2000–469. Washington, DC: U.S. Government Printing Office.

———. 2000d. *Trends in Educational Equity of Girls & Women*, by Yupin Bae et al. NCES 2000–030. Washington, DC: U.S. Government Printing Office.

EDUCATIONAL ASSESSMENT

Leslie C. Soodak
Rutgers University

Assessment is an integral part of American education, reflecting society's desire to substantiate its decisions about students and schools with precise and objective data. The rise of the testing movement in this country, beginning with the introduction of the intelligence test almost a century ago, is a testament to society's need to evaluate and quantify performance. Dramatic increases in the use of tests in educational decision making and in the consequences of the decisions based on test scores during the past three decades suggest that society's fascination with tests is in no way abating.

The growth in the testing movement has not occurred without controversy and debate. Sociological research conducted within the past several decades indicates that assessment practices may have far reaching effects on learning. Therefore, reforms in assessment policies and practices must be considered within a larger framework, i.e., the goals of education as defined by its various stakeholders. The purpose of this chapter is to explore current controversies in the field of educational assessment and to demonstrate the complexities involved in establishing an appropriate direction for the field. Although there has been much debate as to the *purposes* of testing since the 1970s, questions regarding the *type* of tests used have been raised only in recent years. Until recently, standardized tests have been employed almost exclusively regardless of testing purpose. However, educational reform initiatives aimed at enhancing academic standards and ensuring equity of educational opportunity have served to highlight the limitations of this prevailing assessment practice. In response to growing criticism of standardized tests, current inquiry in educational assessment has focused on exploring alternative approaches to the assessment of student learning. This shift in focus raises new questions about the role of assessment in educational reform. Do traditional approaches to student assessment facilitate accurate decisions and promote equity in educational opportunities? How do assessment practices affect learning? Can alternative measures of performance be employed to assess student learning fairly and accurately?

While advocates of assessment reform and those seeking to continue the use of traditional measures argue the merits of each approach, there is general agreement that the appropriateness of a specific type of test cannot be determined without considering how the test data will be used. Historically, test data have served a number of functions. First, they are used to inform instructional decisions. For example, information regarding the degree of knowledge a student has acquired can be used to plan subsequent instruction or to determine within-class grouping. There are many types of tests that are used for this purpose, although informal, non-standardized, teacher-made tests are most commonly used for decisions pertaining to classroom practices.

Second, assessment data are used to determine a student's educational placement. Most notably, tests are used, in part, to determine a student's classification, i.e., disability category, and eligibility for special education. Evaluations to determine eligibility for special education predominantly rely on standardized tests. Standardized tests are also used in decisions regarding graduation, promotion, retention, and class assignment.

The third purpose of assessment is to provide accountability. Since the 1970s there has been a dramatic rise in the use of tests to hold schools and teachers accountable for student achievement with the initiation of numerous statewide testing programs. Standardized tests are used almost invariably in these testing programs. Accountability decisions based on tests of student achievement often hold high stakes, such as the allocation of school funds.

Although there is little debate that educational testing serves multiple functions, several educators have expressed concern as to whether the importance of the accountability and eligibility functions of testing have superseded the other purposes of testing, and in doing so promoted the use of objective, standardized tests as the preferred approach to student assessment (e.g., Madaus, 1988; Resnick and Resnick, 1991). In addition to general skepticism with the notion that one type of test is able to serve multiple purposes with equal effectiveness, these educators are concerned about the appropriateness of the most widely used test format, i.e., standardized, norm-referenced tests.

Standardized tests can be either norm referenced or criterion referenced. Criterion-referenced tests are tied to specific objectives; interpretation of scores is based on the degree to which the performance demonstrates achievement of the objectives. Criterion-referenced tests have been linked to specific instructional practices such as mastery learning, in which absolute standards or competencies can be identified. In contrast to criterion-referenced tests, interpretation of scores on norm-referenced tests is based on one's ranking relative to the performance of others. Norm-referenced tests are used with exceedingly greater frequency than criterion-referenced tests, particularly when testing is conducted for the purpose of student selection or program accountability.

Norm-referenced tests are based on psychometric theory, which maintains that all humans differ from one another on various traits that can be accurately measured. Because it is assumed that variability on any given trait occurs in a known, i.e., normal or bell-shaped pattern, traditional test theory maintains that it is meaningful to report an individual's standing on a particular trait relative to a distribution of measures of that trait for others. In other words, it is not the absolute degree of mastery of a standard, but rather the individual's standing relative to others that is interpreted. For example, a score obtained from a standardized reading or math achievement test takes on meaning only when it is compared to the scores of others who have taken the same test under similar conditions. It is assumed in this form of testing that the scores of

the comparison, or norm, group are representative of the distribution of scores within the general population.

Why are standardized tests, particularly those that are norm referenced, preferred when the purposes of testing involve program accountability and student placement? Standardized tests attempt to ensure objectivity, which is perceived as being extremely important when the results of testing will have a powerful, direct, and long-lasting effect on students, teachers, and schools. Standardized tests ensure objectivity by controlling the test content and format and by providing explicit directions for test administration and scoring. Teacher or examiner judgment is minimized throughout the testing process so that, theoretically, a "pure" and "culturally neutral" measure of achievement is obtained. Norm-referenced, standardized tests are used extensively in program evaluation and placement decisions because they permit comparisons among individuals, classes, and schools. Because all scores are evaluated with reference to the performance of others, rankings among individuals emerge. These rankings provide the basis for determining which students or programs are strongest and which are weakest in the measured area. Thus, the use of norm-referenced, standardized tests has proliferated in high-stakes decisions because they provide objective measures of student achievement that permit comparisons among individuals.

As use of standardized tests of student performance has increased, so has criticism of this practice. Sociological research on the effects of prevailing testing practices suggests that the use of traditional, norm-referenced tests may be incompatible with current efforts to increase standards, facilitate higher level thinking among learners, and promote educational equity. The research upon which these arguments are based has focused on the unintended outcomes of traditional assessment practices, and in doing so has raised questions regarding the assumptions underlying traditional test theory as well as the role of assessment in educational reform.

One of the major concerns in using standardized tests pertains to the effects these tests have on curriculum and instruction. In an effort to control test content, reduce scoring errors, and neutralize contextual effects, standardized tests rely heavily on simple and highly controlled formats, such as multiple-choice items. Multiple-choice items address subject matter in an unambiguous, direct, and simple manner. However, Resnick and Resnick (1991) argue that two erroneous assumptions underlie standardized, multiple-choice tests, which they term the decomposability and the decontextualization assumptions. Decomposability refers to the assumption that knowledge can be deconstructed into its component parts, so that assessment need only sample fragments of information. Decontextualization assumes that components of complex skills and concepts are fixed and students will respond to them in similar ways regardless of form or context. Both assumptions have been challenged by research in cognitive psychology, which maintains that knowledge is not limited to or demonstrated by recall of isolated facts, but rather knowledge involves the organization and use of complex rules and principles that are very much influenced by context. For example, it has been demonstrated that in reading, the processes of decoding and analysis are interrelated and occur simultaneously, suggesting that these processes cannot be neatly separated, as is often done in widely used standardized tests. Furthermore, context and background knowledge have been found to be critical factors in reading comprehension so that the content and form of testing reading achievement will affect performance. Based on an analysis of various standardized achievement tests that were found to focus on rote, isolated, and decontextualized skills, Resnick and Resnick concluded that current testing practices are contrary to the goals of a curriculum that focuses on problem solving and higher order thinking.

The tension between traditional assessment practices and curriculum goals is particularly problematic given the influence of testing on teaching and learning. Madaus (1988) cogently argues that tests drive instruction because teachers will teach only the material necessary for their students to perform well on tests perceived to be important, such as high-stakes, accountability tests. He further argues that instruction will imitate test format and style as well as test content, such that testing rote recall will encourage the teaching of memorized facts. Thus, tests that focus on low-level knowledge and isolated skills not only fail to measure higher order thinking, but use of these tests ultimately forces the curriculum to conform to the tests. Based on the premise that tests define curriculum, Madaus argues that tests have been used by administrators and legislatures to ensure compliance among teachers and students. In this vein, the effort to expand national testing may be more accurately characterized as an attempt to impose a national curriculum than as an effort to streamline comparisons among students.

However, not all educators agree with the notion that assessment should be ancillary to curriculum and instruction. Proponents of measurement-driven instruction, such as Airasian (1988) and Popham (1987), maintain that the power of tests to drive curriculum is a positive quality that should be used to help focus instruction, unify standards, and facilitate accountability. The assumption is that once critical skills and outcomes are identified and measured on tests, the tendency to "teach to the test" will ensure that the identified curriculum goals are addressed. The proposal to enhance test validity by changing the curriculum, rather than the test (as in the use of alternative assessment), has fueled several heated debates among those interested in assessment reform. Referring to measurement-driven instruction as "psychometric imperialism," Madaus (1988:84), maintains that using tests as the basis for curriculum restricts the curriculum and stifles the creativity of teachers and students. He further contends that this approach to setting educational standards will undermine the professional judgment and status of teachers. Shepard (1989) argues that because tests are developed outside of schools, the objectives of testing and curriculum will be externally imposed and, therefore, may not reflect a school's unique curriculum or the needs of its students.

Assessment practices affect students in ways other than through the curriculum. To be educationally justifiable, tests must motivate students so that they are able to demonstrate their knowledge and abilities. However, a study of nearly 1,000 students conducted by Paris and his colleagues (1991) demonstrated that standardized tests can have debilitating effects on many students. They found that as they got older, students became more suspicious of the validity of test scores and less motivated to excel on tests, and perceived themselves to be less prepared to take tests. Test anxiety was found to increase with age but did not differ by ability; both high and low achievers grew more apprehensive. Based on these findings, the researchers concluded that the negative effects of testing on student morale, motivation, and achievement warrant changes in testing policies and practices.

Thus, it has been argued that standardized testing compromises educational excellence through its powerful and deleterious influence on curriculum, instruction, and learning. In addition, those arguing for the reform of assessment practices claim that the proliferation of standardized testing has thwarted efforts to achieve equity and access to educational opportunity. The predominant use of tests for the purpose of sorting and selecting students into and out of particular placements is seen by many as a means of limiting students' life choices.

The sorting and selecting function of tests can be traced back to the beginning of the early part of the twentieth century with the introduction of intelligence testing in this country. The test developed by Binet and Simon in 1905 for the purpose of identifying educationally deficient children in France was introduced to America in 1908 and immediately put to use in similar selections. Most notable is the work of Goddard (1912), who examined the legitimate and illegitimate line of descendants of a man who had children both with his wife, a "worthy" Quakeress, and with a "feebleminded" woman. Goddard's study of the Kallikaks was used to support the notion that feeblemindedness was prevalent among immigrants and the poor. Although his research was later disproved, beliefs regarding the inherent nature of group differences and the fixed and immutable structure of intelligence persist to this day.

Tests continue to be used to promote social class stratification by supporting decisions that differentially appropriate educational placements. Oakes' (1985) seminal work on tracking indicated that students from low-income families and those from minority backgrounds are significantly overrepresented in tracks for low-ability or non-college-bound students and underrepresented in programs serving gifted and talented children. Oakes also documented evidence of curricular differences in programs based on track, whereby students in lower tracks are exposed to a more limited curriculum than those in untracked or academic programs. As might be expected when encountering an inferior curriculum, students placed in lower or nonacademic tracks achieve less than their peers who are placed in classes offering a more rigorous curriculum. Thus, students who are from minority backgrounds and those of lower socioeconomic status are not given the same educational opportunities as other students.

In recent years, the issues involved in tracking students have been replicated in the field of special education. Provisions for educating students with disabilities were mandated nationally in 1975. Included in the legislation were procedures to ensure accuracy and equity in eligibility decisions. Despite the inclusion of these procedures, almost all children referred for evaluation are eventually identified as disabled and placed in special education, leading to what has been called an "overidentification phenomenon" (Ysseldyke and Algozzine, 1982). Furthermore, as these researchers point out, children of color, those from low socioeconomic groups, and students for whom English is not a primary language are dramatically overrepresented in special education. The ease with which students enter special education is particularly troubling given that few children are declassified and returned to the mainstream.

The use of standardized tests in eligibility decisions contributes to the overrerepresentation of children from minority and low-income backgrounds in special education and lower or nonacademic tracks. Potential sources of bias in student assessment have been discussed by several educators (e.g., Darling-Hammond, 1994; Ysseldyke and Algozzine, 1982). Although standardized tests are assumed to be objective and culturally neutral, the selection of test items and acceptable responses necessarily favors certain knowledge and experiences over others. In addition to biases inherent in test content, the format of standardized tests gives preference to those able to demonstrate their knowledge within the parameters of the test requirements; standardized procedures do not recognize alternate ways of knowing. Furthermore, administration procedures may exacerbate the existing biases toward certain learners due to an insensitivity to social, cultural, and linguistic differences on the part of the examiners. Perhaps the most apparent source of bias in standardized tests lies in the underrepresentation of some cultural groups in the norming samples to whom all future test takers are compared. Testing students on unfamiliar content in a manner to which they may be unaccustomed will likely result in depressed performance. To make judgments about the quality of a student's performance relative to others who are better prepared to take the test, by virtue of personal background and educational experience, serves to exacerbate differences and perpetuate inequities in educational opportunities. Darling-Hammond

(1994) points out that the practice of tracking students out of the mainstream is reinforced by the manner in which schools are held accountable for meeting externally imposed standards. Typically, rewards and sanctions are dispensed to schools based on the judgments of performance derived from aggregated test data. Therefore, in an effort to ensure the highest possible score for the school overall, administrators are encouraged to prevent the scores from low-achieving students from being considered. Placing students in segregated programs, such as special education, provides an efficient means to this end.

Criticism of the use of standardized tests in educational assessment centers on two key elements: excellence and equity. It is argued that if schools are to help students meet the standards necessary for this country to maintain its world class standing and do so in a way that ensures that all students have access to opportunities that would allow them to meet the same standards, then new forms of assessment must be implemented. Proponents of assessment reform maintain that the country's longstanding fascination with efficiency and objectivity in testing and its emphasis on sorting and selecting students stand in the way of meaningful educational reform.

The movement for the reform of educational assessment has gained momentum since the end of the 1980s. Linn (1994) identified three distinctive features of the current movement that differentiates it from earlier measurement-based reform efforts. First, there have been a number of federal initiatives for states to develop new assessments, including The Goals 2000 Educate America Act of 1994. Second, there is a strong emphasis on the formulation of standards of excellence, including clearly defined levels of performance that would indicate whether content standards had been adequately met. And lastly, national and state level efforts reflect a growing interest in new forms of assessment, which would serve as an alternative to standardized, multiple-choice tests. In the past few years, an increasing number of states and local school districts have begun to assess student learning through portfolios, exhibitions, projects, and observations in an effort to obtain a more valid measure of student performance. Collectively, such measures are referred to as alternative assessments.

The terms "authentic assessment" and "performance assessment" are both forms or subsets of alternative as-

sessment. Authentic assessment refers to measures that reflect both the processes underlying knowledge and the conditions under which the achievement normally occurs. Performance assessment requires the student to demonstrate skills and competencies related to agreed upon standards of performance; however, the instructional tasks used for evaluation may or may not be authentic. Meyer (1992) distinguishes between authentic assessment and performance assessment by the degree to which the assessment reflects tasks that are encountered in real life and are valued in their own right.

There have been several criteria for authenticity offered, most of which are based largely on Wiggins' (1989) discussion of authentic assessment or "the assessment of *performance of exemplary tasks*" (p. 712). Authentic tests are characterized by being curriculum embedded rather than independent of classroom instruction. They look at changes over time on tasks that require students to use higher order, complex skills involved in formulating questions, solving problems, and reasoning. As such, authentic tests rely on open-ended tasks rather than forced-choice test items. In fact, flexibility in test design, administration, and response format is permitted and students and teachers may be given a choice of tasks. Unlike standardized tests, authentic tests allow for collaboration among students and teachers; for example, students may work together to complete a project or teachers may collaboratively examine and discuss standards of excellence as they develop scoring procedures for an assignment. In authentic assessment the quality of a student's work is judged relative to an explicit standard of performance and not relative to others. Furthermore, the student is involved in the design, implementation, and scoring of exemplary work; in this way self-assessment is made as an integral part of the assessment process.

The reform of educational assessment is predicated on the notion that authentic assessments will provide a measure of student abilities and knowledge that is an accurate and fair reflection of capabilities (Wiggins, 1989) that will ultimately broaden the focus of the curriculum (Resnick and Resnick, 1991). Support for these assumptions is derived from descriptions of classroom-based initiatives that suggest that students are motivated to engage in authentic assessments and are enriched by the metacognitive process of self-reflection (Gordon and Bonilla-Bowman, 1996). However, unresolved issues in the use of performance assessments may hinder realization of the potential benefits of these new assessments.

First, controversy regarding the technical adequacy of performance assessments persists. The most critical concern focuses on the validity of the new measures, i.e, whether performance assessments provide an accurate characterization of student achievement. Several researchers and psychometricians have called for an expanded view of validity to encompass the broader goals of the newer assessment formats. Central to many of the recent conceptions of validity is the notion of consequential validity, which Messick (1989) defines as the social consequences stemming from the uses and interpretations of the assessment. Linn et al. (1991) propose that judgments of validity also include consideration of fairness, cognitive complexity, content quality, content coverage, meaningfulness, cost, and efficiency. The criteria traditionally employed to assess validity, i.e., transfer and generalizability, are also considered within new conceptions of the construct. However, application of these criteria of validity to performance assessments indicates limitations in the generalizability of performance across tasks (Shavelson et al., 1992). Linn and Baker (1996) maintain that ultimately there will be trade-offs in reaching judgments regarding the overall validity of performance assessments. For example, establishing more explicit standards for defining tasks or rating performance may be necessary to enhance validity, although doing so may limit the authenticity or flexibility of the newer assessments.

A second area of concern regarding performance assessments involves the issue of equity, i.e., whether performance assessment enables broader access to educational opportunities for culturally and linguistically diverse students. Darling-Hammond (1994) maintains that authentic assessments are not inherently equitable, but rather use of assessment data determines whether an assessment method is fair to all students. She further contends that use of performance assessments for ranking students and schools, as is presently done with externally mandated accountability tests, may highlight differences in student abilities and detract from the teachers' use of these tests to inform instruction. Gordon and Bonilla-Bowman (1996) discuss the importance of demonstrating success on "gatekeeper" type assessments for African-American and poor students and suggest that if performance assessments do not reflect valued skills and success on these tests will not serve as an "admission ticket" to real opportunities, then they are of little value to these students. Furthermore, they maintain that performance assessments pose a potential difficulty for language minority students due to increased demands on the production of language required in many tasks and the introduction of bias in the scoring of performance assessments.

Taylor (1994) maintains that a particular approach to testing is not inherently correct or unbiased, rather it is the appropriateness of a test in relation to its intended use that is of importance. Therefore, modifications in testing format will be insufficient for meaningful reform in educational assessment without concomitant changes in assumptions regarding the purposes of schools, the nature of learning, and functions of testing. America's schools have not yet abandoned the need to rank students and to hold school's accountable based on the relative ranking of their students. To do otherwise challenges school personnel and other stakeholders to make explicit their standards for performance, and more importantly, to provide opportunities for all students to meet the standards.

REFERENCES

Airasian, Peter W. 1986. "Measurement Driven Instruction: A Closer Look." *Educational Measurement: Issues and Practice* 7:6–11.

Darling-Hammond, Linda. 1994. "Performance-Based Assessment and Educational Equity." *Harvard Educational Review* 64:5–30.

Goddard, Henry H. 1912. *The Kallikak Family: A Study in the Heredity of Feeblemindedness.* New York: Macmillan.

Gordon, Edmund W., and Carol Bonilla-Bowman. 1996. "Can Performance-Based Assessments Contribute to the Achievement of Educational Equity?" In *Performance-Based Student Assessment: Challenges and Possibilities. Ninety-fifth Yearbook of the Society for the Study of Education,* pp. 32–51. Chicago: University of Chicago Press.

Linn, Robert L. 1994. "Performance Assessment: Policy, Promises, and Technical Measurement Standards." *Educational Researcher* 23:4–14.

Linn, Robert L., and Eva L. Baker. 1996. "Can Performance-Based Student Assessments Be Psychometrically Sound?" In *Performance-Based Student Assessment: Challenges and Possibilities. Ninety-fifth Yearbook of the Society for the Study of Education,* pp. 84–103. Chicago: University of Chicago Press.

Linn, Robert L., Eva L. Baker, and Stephen B. Dunbar. 1991. "Complex Performance-Based Assessment: Expectations and Validation Criteria." *Educational Researcher* 20:15–21.

Madaus, George F. 1988. "The Influence of Testing on the Curriculum. In L. N. Tanner (ed.), *Critical Issues in Cur-*

riculum: Eighty-seventh Yearbook of the National Society for the Study of Education, pp. 83–121. Chicago: University of Chicago Press.

Messick, Samuel. 1989. "Validity." In Robert L. Linn (ed.), Educational Measurement, 3rd ed., pp. 13–103. New York: Macmillan.

Meyer, Carol A. 1992. "What's the Difference between Authentic and Performance Assessment?" Educational Leadership 49:39–40.

Oakes, Jeannie. 1985. Keeping Track: How Schools Structure Inequality. New Haven, CT: Yale University Press.

Paris, Scott G., Theresa A. Lawton, Julianne C. Turner, and Jodie L. Roth. 1991. "A Developmental Perspective on Standardized Achievement Testing." Educational Researcher 20:12–20.

Popham, W. James. 1987. "The Merits of Measurement-Driven Instruction." Phi Delta Kappan 68:679–682.

Resnick, Lauren B., and Daniel P. Resnick. 1991. "Assessing the Thinking Curriculum: New Tools for Educational Re-

form." In Bernard R. Gifford and Mary C. O'Connor (eds.), Changing Assessments: Alternative Views of Aptitude, Achievement, and Instruction, pp. 37–75. Boston: Kluwer.

Shavelson, Richard J., Gail P. Baxter, and Jerry Pine. 1992. "Performance Assessments: Political Rhetoric and Measurement Reality." Educational Researcher 21:22–27.

Shepard, Lorrie A. 1989. "Why We Need Better Assessments." Educational Leadership 46:4–9.

Taylor, Catherine. 1994. "Assessment for Measurement or Standards: The Peril and Promise of Large-Scale Assessment Reform." American Educational Research Journal 31:231–262.

Wiggins, Grant. 1989. "A True Test: Toward More Authentic and Equitable Assessment." Phi Delta Kappan, 79:703–713.

Ysseldyke, James E., and Bob Algozzine. 1982. Critical Issues in Special and Remedial Education. Boston: Houghton Mifflin.

EDUCATIONAL ATTITUDES

ABSTRACT AND CONCRETE

Roslyn Arlin Mickelson
Department of Sociology, University of North Carolina at Charlotte

Educational outcomes generally reflect a society's pattern of racial, ethnic, and social class stratification. In the United States, students from African-American, Hispanic, and Native-American groups are less likely to do as well in school as their white or Asian-American counterparts of similar social class backgrounds. Similarly, poor and working-class youth tend to perform worse and leave school earlier than those from more prosperous families. This pattern is especially perplexing because minority and working-class youth, parents, and their cultural, religious, and political leaders universally stress the importance of education for individual and group betterment. The concept of dual educational attitudes, composed of abstract and concrete aspects, offers insights for understanding both the phenomenon of poorer educational outcomes and the inconsistency between stated attitudes toward education and academic achievement.

The concept of dual educational attitudes approaches the disjuncture between attitudes and behavior by conceptualizing people's beliefs about education as multidimensional. Mickelson (1990) demonstrated that adolescents' attitudes toward education take two forms. The first, abstract attitudes, is based on the dominant American ideology that holds that education is the solution to most individual and social problems. Education unlocks the door to social mobility and is the remedy for poverty and unemployment. Furthermore, according to this view, one's educational credentials are evaluated by the larger society according to merit. Abstract attitudes are ideologically based and essentially reflect the belief that opportunity through education exists for everyone. Because there is widespread ideological consensus, abstract attitudes toward education do not vary widely.

The second belief system, concrete attitudes, treats the relationship between education and opportunity with greater skepticism. Concrete attitudes are influenced by race, ethnicity, and class forces that shape individual and group experiences in the opportunity structure. The beliefs that comprise concrete attitudes are grounded in the different material realities that people experience. Concrete attitudes differ from abstract ones in that they reflect neither adherence to ideological shibboleths nor hopes for the future. Instead they reflect essential material realities in which education may or may not lead to status maintenance or upward mobility. Concrete attitudes are derived from a person's familial and community experiences. Adolescents' concrete attitudes, then, are expressions of their lived cultures—cultures produced in ongoing interactions with other societal institutions on terrains wherein class, race, and gender meanings and conflicts are lived out. Unlike abstract attitudes, concrete attitudes vary widely. They can be identical to or quite different from the dominant belief system that is expressed in an individual's abstract attitudes.

Concrete attitudes reveal students' perceptions of their probable returns on education from the opportunity structure. Because concrete attitudes reflect the material world in which adolescents live, students' educational performance is informed much more by this set of beliefs than by their abstract attitudes. Concrete attitudes, therefore, are crucial for understanding how family background and race influence school outcomes. They offer insights into the ways that race, ethnic, and social class forces influence people's opportunities and how, in turn, these realities influence adolescents' perceptions of the relationships between education and opportunity for people like them.

Related Work

Previous research on the relationship between educational attitudes and school performance largely ignored the fine but necessary distinction between people's abstract and concrete attitudes. However, other sociologists have drawn this kind of distinction with respect to broader, more general societal values. Parkin (1976) distinguished between dominant and subordinate value systems found in industrial societies. The first reflects society's abstract norms while the subordinate value system is situationally specific to people's lives. Parkin notes that most social science surveys of attitudes tap primarily abstract beliefs that often do not lie at the heart of people's behavior. This is because in situational contexts of choice and action, the subordinate value system tends to provide the moral frame of reference. Rodman (1963) proposed a "lower-class value stretch," described as a subordinate belief system formed by the realities of working-class life. He theorized that it was actually a negotiated version of the dominant system.

Empirical Evidence

Mickelson's research with racially diverse Los Angeles area adolescents first demonstrated the existence of abstract and concrete educational attitudes and their relationship to educational achievement (Mickelson, 1989, 1990; Mickelson et al., 1995). She surveyed 1893 high school seniors from two counties in southern California and found that all students simultaneously held abstract and concrete attitudes, and that abstract attitudes were uniformly positive about education and opportunity while students' concrete attitudes varied with students' social class and race/ethnicity. Only concrete attitudes predicted their achievement. Significant social class differences existed within all ethnic groups in students' concrete attitudes. Whereas African-American and Asian-American youth held significantly more pessimistic concrete attitudes than white students, Asian-American students' achievement was more similar to that of whites than to African Americans.

Over a decade of further research by other social scientists utilizing surveys and qualitative methodologies with racially and ethnically diverse populations have confirmed the existence of dual educational attitudes and the utility of these constructs for understanding class and ethnic differences in educational attitudes and school performance.

Ogbu (1995) conducted a large scale survey ($N = 2245$) of community forces and educational strategies among African-American, Chinese, and Hispanic youth and their families in Oakland, California. Triangulating his survey data with ethnographies of families in his sample, Ogbu found the widespread existence of dual educational attitudes among the adults and children in all the groups he studied. He reported students and parents from all three ethnic groups espoused favorable abstract attitudes toward education and opportunity. Furthermore, Ogbu found divergent concrete attitudes and educational strategies among African American, Hispanic, and Chinese students.

Hochschild (1995) systematically reviewed the social science and public opinion literature regarding education and the American Dream. She found widespread adherence across racial and class lines to the dominant ideology's account of opportunity through education. She reports that, at the same time, African-American adolescents "dream with only one part of themselves" and are much more discouraged at their own prospects for the future.

Gender and Attitudes

Given the social structural dynamic that underlies the conceptualization of abstract and concrete attitudes' relationship to achievement, one might expect that gender differences would parallel racial and class ones. In particular, well-known gender disparities in wages, promotions, and career ladders lead one to expect that the concrete attitudes and academic achievement of women compared to men would reveal a pattern similar to that of minorities compared to whites or working-class compared to middle-class youth.

But this is not the case. Among whites, Hispanics, and African Americans, the academic achievement and attainment of women continue to match and frequently surpass those of men of comparable ethnic and class backgrounds. No gender differences appear among Asian Americans in either attitudes or grades. Mickelson (1989) suggested that while women perceive a weakened link between their education and opportunity, it is likely that they evaluate it differently than do men.

This explanation is consistent with a feminist paradigm that challenges the traditional dichotomy between public and private spheres. Specifically, this approach suggests the boundaries between the two domains are less clearly demarcated for women than for men. Consequently, women are likely to evaluate their returns to education in terms not only of income, status, and careers, but through familial and community roles and relationships as well. Although this feminist approach supplements the structural analysis upon which multidimensional educational attitudes are founded, the anomaly of women's continued achievement and attainment remains unexplained.

Solving the Paradox of Positive Attitudes and Poor Achievement

The reverential support of education, particularly among subordinate people in American society, appears paradoxical in light of the wide variation in their educational achievement and attainment. This is especially apparent among African Americans and Hispanic Americans who rhetorically embrace education, yet all too frequently underachieve. The paradox rests upon both a conceptual and measurement problem in attitude–behavior research. As noted earlier, people's beliefs about education can be accurately conceptualized as complex and multidimensional. This is consistent with other social research that indicates people simultaneously hold multilayered values about society; at one level these are drawn from the putative dominant ideology and at another level they are drawn from practical or concrete levels of experience. The measurement of attitudes must take into consideration the dual nature of people's beliefs in order to predict their behavior. If concrete attitudes toward education, rather than abstract beliefs, are examined in conjunction with achievement behavior, a relationship can be demonstrated to exist between what youths say about education and what they do in school.

Summary and Policy Implications

Abstract and concrete educational attitudes advance an understanding of a number of important topics in the sociology of education. First, the enduring findings of social science regarding the relationship between family background and academic outcomes infrequently reveal *how* a person's race, ethnicity, or social class influences his or her achievement in school. The substantive meaning of concrete attitudes and the ways they influence school performance sheds light on the process by which the structure of opportunity shapes academic achievement among adolescents in high school.

Second, that adolescents simultaneously hold both abstract and concrete attitudes toward education suggests that although people may share a pervasive value system grounded in the hegemonic ideology of the dominant group, they also possess a subordinate value system based on the exigencies and experiences of day-to-day life. The existence of dual educational attitudes supports the arguments that Western industrialized societies are characterized by class- and race-differentiated rather than unitary value systems.

Third, abstract and concrete educational attitudes offer a methodological refinement in the measurement of attitudes and prediction of behavior. The oft-reported poor match between what people say and what they do likely is an artifact of the abstract, decontextualized, and general nature of the questions posed. If more situationally specific, concrete questions are examined in conjunction with behavior, a better fit between attitudes and action will be found.

Fourth, this approach readily accounts for the paradox of virtually universal positive attitudes toward education among certain working-class and minority youth who either underachieve or fail in school. Most research on attitudes toward education tap idealistic notions of the role of education and opportunity. Because everyone agrees at this level of abstraction, there is little variation. An attitude that does not vary cannot predict a behavior that does. People's concrete attitudes, which vary by race, ethnicity, and social class, predict their achievement. The paradox disappears.

Finally, the notions of abstract and concrete educational attitudes have important policy implications. Many reformers approach school improvement as if educational institutions exist in a social vacuum. They assume that if standards are raised, measurement is refined and better linked to improved curricula, and pedagogy is elevated, then students will *ipso facto* learn more, achieve better, stay in school, and attain higher levels of education. Although arguably useful reforms, they are unlikely to be sufficient for improving the educational outcomes for many working-class and minority youth.

The key policy implication suggested by the relationship between concrete attitudes and academic achievement is that without a fundamental transformation of the larger opportunity and reward structures, the underachievement of certain minority and working-class youth is likely to persist even in the face of the best designed and most lavishly funded educational reforms. This is because persistence and achievement make sense only if there is a fairly close match between the promise and the reality of opportunity through education.

REFERENCES

Hochschild, Jennifer L. 1995. *Facing Up to the American Dream. Race, Class, and the Soul of the Nation.* Princeton, NJ: Princeton University Press.

Mickelson, Roslyn Arlin. 1989. "Why Does Jane Read and Write So Well? The Anomaly of Women's Achievement." *Sociology of Education* 62:47–63.

———. 1990. "The Attitude-Achievement Paradox Among Black Adolescents." *Sociology of Education* 63:46–61.

Mickelson, Roslyn Arlin, Sumie Okazaki, and Dunchen Zheng. 1995. "Reading Reality More Closely Than Books: The Opportunity Structure and Minority Achievement." In Barbara Schneider and Peter Cookson (eds.), *Transforming Schools*, pp. 81–105. New York: Garland.

Ogbu, John U. 1995. *Community Forces and Minority Educational Strategies: A Comparative Study*. Final Report #1 to the Russell Sage Foundation. Department of Anthropology, University of California, Berkeley.

Parkin, Frank. 1976. *Class Inequality and Political Order*. New York: Praeger.

Rodman, Hyman. 1963. "The Lower Class Value Stretch." *Social Forces* 43:205–215.

Rotter, Julian B. 1975. "Some Problems and Misconceptions Related to the Construction of Internal Versus External Control of Reinforcements." *Journal of Consulting and Clinical Psychology* 43:56–67.

EDUCATIONAL PRODUCTIVITY

Mark Berends
Rand Corporation

As part of the learning process, educational productivity refers to whether the average level of some educational "output" (e.g., standardized test scores) increases or decreases according to some "input" (e.g., per-pupil expenditures). Researchers in this area face great challenges because the learning process is complex, so it is difficult to be exact about how social and economic factors are related to achievement. Still, sociologists have made substantial progress in understanding the social conditions that contribute to student achievement. What follows is a further definition of educational productivity, why it has been important, what the trends have been in indicators measuring it, and how families, schools, and communities contribute to it.

Educational Productivity and Economic Crises

Educational productivity is a term rooted in economics, which by definition is concerned with the production and distribution of goods and services. Economists link educational productivity to the development of human capital—the acquired skills, knowledge, and abilities of human beings. The notion underlying this connection is that the development of skills and knowledge increases human productivity, thereby justifying the costs incurred in the process. That is, investing in human capital is worthwhile because greater human productivity benefits society (Schultz, 1961, 1981; Becker, 1964).

These concepts are by no means new. Over two centuries ago, Adam Smith in the *Wealth of Nations* pointed out that a critical part of a nation's wealth is people. However, this insight was largely ignored until after World War II when several productivity crises put

the American education system in the spotlight: Sputnik, civil rights, and the U.S. slump in international competition.

Before the late 1950s, economists tended to focus more on land, capital, and labor as the important determinants of economic growth—not the quality of human beings' inputs. Then came the Soviet launch of Sputnik in 1957. Suddenly, the United States was scrambling to reclaim its place as a technological leader. One step toward this recovery was a strong commitment to investing in the public education system. If human capital was to promote productivity and thereby advance our struggle against communism, where was the acquisition of knowledge and skills generated? According to economists, the answer was in school.

At about the same time, the civil rights movement drew sociologists into studies of social inequality. There were questions to answer about the quality of education provided to minority and poor children compared to that provided to white middle-class children. There was a wide gap in their academic achievement scores, drop out rates, educational attainment levels, and the schooling conditions, so the importance of individual background characteristics versus educational experiences and accomplishments became the primary focus of sociologists.

An aim of sociological analyses of inequality was to understand how the social relationships within and among societal institutions contributed to differences in educational outcomes among social groups—i.e., the social organization of learning. However, some of the economists ideas about educational productivity and human capital (e.g., the logic of examining the direct relationships between inputs and outputs) influenced sociologists. Thus, in studies of the 1960s and

203

1970s, sociological analyses of the social organization of learning meant understanding how school characteristics (e.g., the inputs of per-pupil expenditures and school minority or socioeconomic composition) and student achievement (output) were related (Coleman et al., 1966; Jencks et al., 1972, 1979).

Despite the input–output studies by economists and sociologists and the social policies that resulted from them, the United States did not fully address its educational productivity problems during the 1960s and 1970s. Then, a third crisis emerged: the United States was falling behind in the international economic competition. In 1983, the National Commission on Excellence in Education's report *A Nation at Risk* placed much of the blame for this on the educational system when it stated that "our once unchallenged preeminence in commerce, industry, science, and technological innovation is being taken over by competitors throughout the world. . . . If an unfriendly power had attempted to impose on America the mediocre educational performance that exists today, we might have viewed it as an act of war."

Of course, Sputnik, the civil rights movement, and *A Nation at Risk* were not the only indications of productivity crises. However, they were key events that put the educational system on the defensive and the question of "what produces learning?" at the forefront.

Trends in Student Achievement

To understand productivity and the implications for inequality, it is important to understand where we are and where we have been. In monitoring the learning of the nation's students, perhaps no other indicators have received more attention than standardized test scores in subject areas such as mathematics and reading. Although such attention to test scores may be myopic if it lessens attention to other important educational outcomes, national test scores for all students and selected racial-ethnic groups are used here to illustrate trends in student learning.

How do today's students compare to those of 20 years ago? Students, especially minority students, are scoring higher on mathematics and reading tests today than they were 20 years ago. Figures 1 and 2 show these trends for 17-year-old students between the early 1970s and 1992 on the National Assessment of Educational Progress (NAEP) mathematics and reading tests. [The

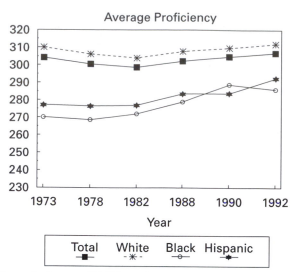

Figure 1. *Average NAEP mathematics proficiency for 17 year olds by race–ethnicity.*
Source for Figures 1 and 2: U.S. Department of Education, National Center for Education Statistics, National Assessment of Educational Progress, *Trends in Academic Progress: Achievement of U.S. Students in Science, 1969 to 1992; Mathematics, 1973 to 1992; Reading, 1971 to 1992; and Writing, 1984 to 1992,* 1994. (Data available for Latinos only back to 1975 in reading.)

NAEP is the best information available on the test score trends of nationally representative groups of students at various age and grade levels (e.g., grades, 4, 8 and 12).] Overall, the U.S. student population today is scoring slightly higher in both mathematics and reading than 20 years ago (on average, roughly three percentile points).

These overall trends mask significant progress made among certain groups. For instance, over the past 20 years, minority students made substantial progress toward closing the minority–nonminority test score gap in both mathematics and reading. In 1992, African-American students scored 16 points higher on the NAEP mathematics test and about 22 points higher in reading than those in the early 1970s. These gains translate into about 17 percentile points on both tests. Similarly, Latinos made large improvements in achievement. Between 1973 and 1992, Latinos gained 16 points on the NAEP mathematics test and 19 points in reading. These improvements mean that Latino students in 1992 scored about 15 percentile points higher than their counterparts in 1973.

In recent years, as the minority trend lines in Figures

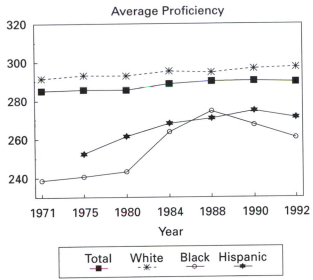

Figure 2. Average NAEP reading proficiency for 17 year olds by race–ethnicity.

1 and 2 show, African-American gains in mathematics and especially reading have been reversed, and Latino reading trends have leveled off. However, minority students are still performing markedly higher than those of 20 years ago.

Despite these statistics, public rhetoric and reform efforts would have us conclude that educational productivity is worse today than 20 years ago. It is not. If students do not know anything now, they did not know anything 20 years ago. However, adding to current public concerns are the international comparisons of test scores. Recent evidence shows that the academic achievement of American students, especially in mathematics and science, is below that of students in other industrialized countries. This presents serious challenges as the United States attempts to develop international markets and its global competitiveness. Thus, although educational productivity today is no worse than 20 years ago when examining domestic test score trends, the public sense is that it could be much improved when students in the United States are compared to other industrialized nations.

The Social Organization of Learning

When examining what contributes to educational productivity, sociologists have not limited their attention to schools. Because a significant amount of learning occurs outside of schools, they have also studied factors such as families and communities. What follows is a brief review of what sociologists currently know about school, family, and community influences on student learning.

School and Schooling Effects

A substantial amount of research in sociology has examined the effects of *schools—organizations* that conduct instruction—on student achievement. There have been much fewer studies on the effects of *schooling—* the *process* through which instruction occurs—on achievement (Bidwell and Kasarda, 1980). Schools' structural characteristics (e.g., socioeconomic or racial–ethnic mix, size, sector) have been shown to have a weaker influence on student achievement than students' individual background characteristics, so sociologists have recently attempted to address schooling processes more directly by focusing on the way students and teachers interact.

Socioeconomic and Racial-Ethnic Composition

One school characteristic related to achievement is its socioeconomic (SES) composition. Schools with more students from high SES backgrounds tend to have higher achievement levels. This has been known for some time (Coleman et al., 1966; Jencks et al., 1972). However, the interesting question is, what is causing those higher achievement levels. Is it the student's higher SES background? Or is it the more nurturing school environment as reflected in the higher SES composition? This topic has received considerable attention over the past 30 years. Generally, research by James Coleman and others shows that the net effect of school SES on achievement is not as strong as the student's SES background.

Research has also shown that the achievement of minority students is higher in racially integrated schools, but the net effect of school minority composition on achievement is not as strong as the student's race–ethnicity. Long-term effects of school desegregation also show generally positive results for minority students (Wells, 1995). Sociologists have recently raised interesting questions concerning the implementation of desegregation and the various school processes that contribute to or detract from successful desegregation policies (Armor, 1995).

Size

Several studies have shown that students learn more in smaller schools than in larger ones, but not all the evidence points in this direction. For instance, larger schools may offer more learning opportunities for students because they offer more courses and activities allowing students to find a niche that meets their needs. The downside of large schools is that they may be bureaucratic and impersonal, leading to students feeling isolated and alienated.

Some research has revealed that school size influences achievement through other schooling processes. For example, students may learn more in smaller schools because these kinds of schools are more communal. That is, smaller schools tend to have shared values about the educational mission, a less diversified curriculum for students, a teaching staff that is committed and collegial, and teachers who go beyond their defined roles to help students learn and adjust socially (Bryk et al., 1990).

Others have reported that the effects of size differ by socioeconomic conditions of schools. Higher achievement has been shown to occur in larger, high-SES schools, but larger size is related to lower achievement among low-SES schools (Friedkin and Necochea, 1988). A reason for this pattern is that bigger schools offer more opportunities, but also more constraints. In high-SES schools the opportunities outweigh the constraints, but the opposite holds in low-SES schools. Wealthier schools have certain advantages in acquiring more local funding and thus improving services provided to students. However, poorer schools have a difficult time obtaining the resources directed toward student learning because resources are allocated to address the greater frequency of nutritional and delinquency problems that larger size typically brings.

Sector

It is generally accepted that Catholic schools outperform public schools, though how much more is uncertain (Coleman and Hoffer, 1987). The implications of these uncertain effects of Catholic schools are often the center of heated debate. The uncertainty is likely to remain since it is very difficult to address the fact that certain types of students are inclined to attend Catholic schools (despite innovative statistical methods).

Some research also shows that Catholic schools benefit educationally disadvantaged students (Coleman and Hoffer, 1987). To understand why, a growing number of studies have compared the organization of Catholic to public schools in terms of ability grouping and tracking, social relationships between teachers and students, parent involvement, and the normative order of the school. Many of the positive effects of the Catholic schools on disadvantaged students are explained by these organizational factors.

Resources

One of the landmark sociological studies that followed the input–output human capital logic of economic educational productivity models was the *Equality of Educational Opportunity* report by Coleman et al. (1966). This was a response to the Civil Rights Act of 1964 and directed the U.S. Commissioner of Education to "conduct a survey and make a report to the President and the Congress . . . concerning the lack of availability of equal educational opportunities for individuals by reason of race, color, religion, or national origin in public educational institutions at all levels" (p. iii). Its original purpose was to investigate the lack of equal opportunity for individuals. Examining the effects of school resources (size, location, per-pupil expenditures, library books, science laboratories, and guidance counselors), many anticipated that these measures of school quality would explain the differential achievement between lower class and middle class, and African-American and white students. Contrary to these expectations, Coleman et al. found that differences between schools in terms of these resources had little effect on students' academic achievement once student background characteristics were taken into account.

There continues to be a contentious debate about whether school expenditures are related to student learning (Hanushek, 1994; Hedges et al., 1994). In the last three decades per-pupil expenditures have roughly doubled. Has this massive increase in spending led to higher student achievement? The results are mixed, but there is recent evidence that student achievement is related to school funding levels. Larry Hedges and colleagues (1994) have calculated that if a typical school district wisely increased its annual per-pupil expenditure by $500, students in that district would gain an average of 24 percentile points on academic achievement tests.

From these findings spring questions about how the

money has been used by districts and schools and whether this use relates to student learning activities. For instance, a significant proportion of the increases in school spending has gone toward transportation costs and special education. Although, important, these expenditures certainly would not be expected to raise the average achievement levels of the nation's students.

Grouping

There are a growing number of studies that examine schooling processes—those social factors inside schools that may contribute to learning (Barr and Dreeben, 1983; Gamoran et al., 1995). This body of research has attempted to explain another finding of the Coleman report: that test score differences among students are much greater *within* schools than *between* schools.

One organizational factor thought to be especially important is high school tracking, the placement of students into different curricular programs purportedly based on student interest and ability. Does this separation of students within schools contribute to educational productivity (Gamoran and Mare, 1989)? Sociological research to date suggests that tracking puts students in the low groups at a disadvantage, and students in the high groups at an advantage, so the overall effect appears to be zero (Oakes et al., 1992). But because not all the educational research in this area provides similar results, policy implications are unclear.

Classroom Instruction

Some sociologists have argued that the missing link in understanding how tracking contributes to educational productivity is the interaction within classrooms between teachers and students (Barr and Dreeben, 1983; Oakes et al., 1992; Gamoran et al., 1995). After all, the argument goes, these experiences give students immediate socialization experiences. The problem with examining teacher–student interaction, though, is that it is ambiguous and thus not easily measured, and when it is measured, it is too narrowly defined.

Family Effects

Of course, schools are not the only place where learning occurs. In fact, variation in educational outcomes is more closely linked to students' families than to their schools. For example, in a recent longitudinal study, Doris Entwisle and Karl Alexander (1992) found that

economically advantaged and disadvantaged students began kindergarten with similar levels of cognitive skills, and parallel growth occurred during the school year. A learning gap emerged during the summer before first grade. The authors argue that this is primarily because higher SES families are able to provide a more positive learning environment during the summer than low SES families. This study suggests that differing levels of educational productivity should be attributed not only to schools, but to experiences outside of school. Rather than creating differences in productivity among various groups of students, schools appear to prevent such differences from becoming even larger (see also Heyns, 1978).

Just as it criticizes schools, conventional wisdom often attributes the *presumed* declines in student performance to the deteriorating American family. Families have changed dramatically over the past 20 years, but contrary to popular opinion, family changes have actually contributed to educational productivity, especially for African Americans and Latinos.

For instance, a RAND study examines the relationships between structural characteristics of families (i.e., parents' education, family income, number of siblings, mother's employment status, age of mother at birth of child, and single-parent households) and student achievement (Grissmer et al., 1994). Based on its analysis of national data, the study found that characteristics such as parent education, income, small family size, and mother's age at child's birth were positively related to student achievement. Factors such as single-parent families and mother's work status did not have a significant relationship to achievement once other family factors were taken into account.

Using these results, RAND found that students in 1990 would be predicted to score higher, not lower, on achievement tests than youth in families in 1970. Why? The main reasons are that parent education has increased markedly over the past 20 years, family size has decreased substantially, and family income has remained relatively stable, so families in the 1990s have more family resources to devote to their children than families of the 1970s. These analyses point to the importance of looking at changes in several family characteristics simultaneously rather than one at a time.

When comparing actual NAEP test score trends to these predicted test score changes due to family characteristics, the RAND report shows that changes in family characteristics accounted for most of the white gains, but only about one-third of the dramatic gains for African Americans and Latinos. This latter finding suggests the importance of nonfamily factors affecting the achievement growth of minority students (e.g., impact of changes in schooling opportunities and public investment in youth).

In addition to these structural characteristics of families, sociologists have examined how parents influence their child's learning through family processes, such as setting normative standards and becoming directly involved in their child's school and schooling activities. In their extensive review of this literature, Anthony Bryk and colleagues (1990) report several findings. First, parent involvement in learning activities within the home is related to socioeconomic status (especially parent education levels). Second, even though parents remain concerned about their child's schooling throughout secondary school, their direct involvement in school becomes less frequent. Third, the degree to which parents become involved is directly related to whether they feel informed and able to contribute to their child's learning. Fourth, parents of engaged, high-achieving students are more involved in homework and school career decisions than parents of disengaged, low-achieving students.

Although sociologists have examined these parent involvement activities, few have studied how involvement varies for different racial and ethnic groups. Moreover, much of the work to date analyzes data that are ill-suited to making causal inferences. That is, much of the work is correlational, so it is difficult to assess whether parent involvement produces higher student achievement, or whether achievement leads parents to become more involved. Although these issues have yet to be resolved, the attention to both structure and processes within families is an encouraging development that will provide critical information about student learning and educational productivity.

Neighborhood and Community Effects

Sociologists have considered the local neighborhood context an important contributor to student learning. For example, lower quality neighborhoods (e.g., high proportions of single-parent households, high unemployment rates, overcrowding) have been found to negatively affect student achievement. Findings about neighborhood effects on test scores, however, are mainly speculative at this point because it is difficult to conduct analyses that take into account all three main contexts that influence student learning: families, schools, and communities. Typically, there are rich data in two of these three contexts, but little in all three.

In a review of this area, Susan Mayer and Christopher Jencks (1989) cite several processes that may explain neighborhood effects on students: (1) *contagion theories* suggesting that once peer influence passes a certain threshold, significant effects on schooling outcomes result; (2) *collective socialization* theories hypothesizing that neighborhood role models and monitoring are important for child development; (3) *competition theories* postulating that neighbors compete for scarce resources within the neighborhood; and (4) theories of *relative deprivation* hypothesizing that people evaluate their situation or relative standing by comparing themselves to their neighbors. The first two theories predict positive outcomes for children if the neighbors are affluent; competition or deprivation theories predict that affluent neighbors may contribute to negative outcomes. The evidence for or against any one of these theories is far from clear due to the scarcity of data.

Conclusions

Although sociologists have expanded the input–output studies rooted in economics to include both structural aspects and processes within schools, families, and communities, this wide casting of the net has its advantages and disadvantages. On the one hand, understanding the social relationships within and between these social contexts provides a rich understanding of the complex learning process and educational productivity. Such understanding has profound implications for social policies. With knowledge about how families, schools, and communities contribute to student learning, public investment decisions can be better targeted.

On the other hand, such a complex picture seldom results in information that can tell policymakers that if they invest "x" amount of public funds in "y" program, they will get "z" benefit in achievement gains. Seldom does the social world present such simplistic answers. Still, sociologists have made great strides in describing and explaining the complex relationships between social context and educational productivity so that public policy decisions can be made with the best information possible.

In future research, sociologists need to be better attuned to how social context relates to productivity, not just inequality. Typical in most studies of student achievement is an emphasis on inequalities in student outcomes. Although this is no doubt critical to assess in a democratic society, a dual focus on both inequality (e.g., the dispersion of achievement among groups) and productivity (i.e., the average increase in achievement) would paint a more elegant portrait of the social organization of learning. It is possible to have an equitable system that is not productive, and vice versa. It is also possible to have a productive system that is equitable. Although this is a daunting challenge, it is the goal of recent federal legislation concerning education. Worthy aims, indeed. However, a more sophisticated understanding about the social conditions that contribute to both educational productivity and inequality will provide critical information to guide educators and policymakers as they make decisions affecting these goals.

REFERENCES

Armor, David J. 1995. *Forced Justice: School Desegregation and the Law*. New York: Oxford University Press.

Barr, Rebecca, and Robert Dreeben. 1983. *How Schools Work*. Chicago, IL: The University of Chicago Press.

Becker, Gary S. 1964. *Human Capital*. New York: National Bureau of Economic Research.

Bidwell, Charles E., and John D. Kasarda. 1980. "Conceptualizing and Measuring the Effects of School and Schooling." *American Journal of Education* 88:401–430.

Bryk, Anthony S., Valerie Lee, and Julia B. Smith. 1990. "High School Organization and Its Effects on Teachers and Students: An Interpretative Summary of the Research." In William H. Clune and John F. Witte (eds.), *Choice and Control in American Education, Vol. 1*, p. 136–226. New York: Falmer Press.

Coleman, James S., and Thomas B. Hoffer. 1987. *Public and Private High Schools: The Impact of Communities*. New York: Basic Books.

Coleman, James S., Ernest Campbell, Carol Hobson, James McPartland, Alexander M. Mood, Frederic Weinfield, and Robert York. 1966. *Equality of Educational Opportunity*. Washington, DC: U.S. Government Printing Office.

Entwisle, Doris R., and Karl L. Alexander. 1992. "Summer Setback: Race, Poverty, School Composition, and Mathematics Achievement in the First Two Years of School." *American Sociological Review* 57:72–84.

Friedkin, Noah, and J. Necochea. 1988. "School System Size and Performance: A Contingency Perspective." *Educational Evaluation and Policy Analysis* 10:237–249.

Gamoran, Adam, and Robert D. Mare. 1989. "Secondary School Tracking and Educational Inequality: Reinforcement, Compensation, or Neutrality?" *American Journal of Sociology* 94:1146–1183.

Gamoran, Adam, Martin Nystand, Mark Berends, and Paul LePore. 1995. "An Organizational Analysis of the Effects of Ability Grouping." *American Educational Research Journal* 32:59–87.

Grissmer, David W., Sheila Nataraj Kirby, Mark Berends, and Stephanie Williamson. 1994. *Student Achievement and the Changing American Family*. Santa Monica, CA: RAND.

Hanushek, Eric A. 1994. *Making Schools Work: Improving Performance and Controlling Costs*. Washington, DC: The Brookings Institution.

Hedges, Larry V., Richard D. Laine, and Rob Greenwald. 1994. "Does Money Matter? A Meta-Analysis of Studies of the Effects of Differential School Inputs on Student Outcomes." *Educational Researcher* 23:5–14.

Heyns, Barbara. 1978. *Summer Learning and the Effects of Schooling*. New York: Academic Press.

Jencks, Christopher S., Marshall Smith, Henry Acland, Mary Jo Bane, David Cohen, Herbert Gintis, Barbara Heyns, and Stephan Michelson. 1972. *Inequality: A Reassessment of the Effect of Family and Schooling in America*. New York: Basic Books.

Jencks, Christopher S., Susan Bartlett, Mary Corcoran, James Crouse, David Eaglesfield, Gregory Jackson, Kent McClelland, Peter Mueser, Michael Olneck, Joseph Schwartz, Sherry Ward, and Jill Williams. 1979. *Who Gets Ahead? The Determinants of Economic Success in America*. New York: Basic Books.

Mayer, Susan, and Christopher Jencks. 1989. "Growing Up in Poor Neighborhoods: How Much Does It Matter?" *Science* 17:1441–1445.

Oakes, Jeannie, Adam Gamoran, and Reba N. Page. 1992. "Curriculum Differentiation: Opportunities, Outcomes, and Meanings." In P. W. Jackson (ed.), *Handbook of Research on Curriculum*, pp. 570–608. New York: Macmillan.

Schultz, Theodore W. 1961. "Investment in Human Capital." *American Economic Review* 51:1–17.

———. 1981. *Investing in People: The Economics of Population Quality*. Berkeley, CA: University of California Press.

Wells, Amy Stuart. 1995. "Reexamining Social Science Research on School Desegregation: Long- Versus Short-Term Effects." *Teachers College Record* 96:691–706.

EDUCATIONAL REFORM AND SOCIOLOGY IN ENGLAND AND WALES

Geoffrey Walford
University of Oxford

The 1988 Educational Reform Act for England and Wales was designed to bring about dramatic change throughout the educational system. This Act fundamentally restructured the organization and content of education in schools, colleges, and universities and was seen as the culmination of a series of smaller Education Acts throughout the 1980s. In practice, although it must be seen as a milestone in the history of English and Welsh education, further legislation followed that of 1988—in part designed to deal with inadequacies in the 1988 and earlier Acts. Sociologists of education have been active during the 1980s and early 1990s in their critique and appraisal of these policy changes. Sociologists have contributed to the intense debate and controversy that surrounded almost all of the policy changes, and have now conducted extensive research on the policy implementation process, the nature of the changes, and their effects on minority or underprivileged groups.

English and Welsh Schooling before 1980

Throughout most of its development, education in England and Wales has reflected and perpetuated inequalities of gender, class, and ethnic group (Walford, 1992). From the start of state support for schooling in 1833, through the beginnings of a national system in 1870, to the major 1944 Act, inequalities of class and gender in particular were unquestioningly reinforced.

The 1944 Act controlled education in England and Wales for nearly half a century. It established a national education system that was locally administered, and that was part of an integrated public service welfare state. It provided free education for all children and made secondary education a distinct stage for all children. Church schools were integrated into the state-maintained system through a system of voluntary aided or voluntary controlled schools leaving, by 1951, an elite 9% of the school-age population in private schools. The 1944 Act stated that provision for older children was to be made according to "age, ability and aptitude," but did not stipulate whether this was to be in comprehensive schools or in separate schools that selected according to ability and achievement. In practice, different local education authorities (LEAs) chose their own scheme, but most initially made separate provision for three types of pupil in grammar, technical, and secondary modern schools.

The only element of the curriculum to be made compulsory in all state-maintained schools was religious education, which was explicitly included in the 1944 Act as part of the compromise with the churches. The three different types of schools that made up the tripartite system did, however, develop their own curricular emphases, with greater "practical" teaching in the secondary modern and technical schools while the grammar schools retained their academic curriculum designed for university entry. There were also major differences between the curriculum for boys and girls. Girls in secondary modern schools, for example, were prepared for their role as wives and mothers, whereas girls in grammar schools had little comparable instruction.

The tripartite system did not last long. In most areas there were never more than a few technical schools, so selection at 10 became a contest where those who "passed" went to grammar schools and those who "failed" ended up in the secondary moderns. However, as the 1950s and 1960s progressed, the sociologists of education of the day gradually gained evidence showing that there was considerable class bias in the way in which children were selected (Floud et al., 1956). The tests themselves came under severe criticism, and there was growing concern about the social effects of selection and differentiation at an early age (Hargreaves, 1967; Lacey, 1970). In 1955 the Labour Party became firmly committed to the abolition of selection and the introduction of comprehensive schools. It strongly encouraged LEAs to change to comprehensive schools during its term of government from 1964 to 1970— a period that coincided with close links between several eminent sociologists and Government policymakers and a widely held public desire for greater equality of educational provision. In 1960 the majority of LEAs had a selective system of schools, but by 1979 practically all LEAs had changed to comprehensive schools.

Concern about the relationship between education and employment was projected into the public arena by James Callaghan (then Labour Prime Minister) in his speech in 1976, which launched what he called the "Great Debate" on education. He cast doubts on the benefits of progressive education and suggested that schools had perhaps overemphasized their social role and underplayed their duty to prepare children for the world of work. The Great Debate that followed the speech occurred too near the next general election for much to change as a result, but the incoming Conservative government of 1979 clearly had the political will to bring about radical change.

The newly elected Conservative government quickly overturned Labour's 1976 Education Act, which had made moves toward comprehensive education obligatory for all LEAs, and encouraged those few LEAs that still had grammar schools to retain them. It perceived that greater harmony between employment and education was likely to be brought about through greater differentiation between schools and the reintroduction of selection, such that children could be taught the skills and knowledge appropriate to their probable future position in society.

The government further signaled its desire for greater differentiation through the introduction of the Assisted Places Scheme (APS) in the 1980 Education Act. This scheme supported the private sector of schooling (and encouraged the idea that maintained schools were not able to provide adequately for all children) by giving means-tested assistance with fees to selected children who wished to attend named private

schools. The scheme has been the focus of several sociological studies, all of which have shown that it has increased inequity of provision. Edwards et al., (1989) show that the scheme has been a major financial and ideological support for private schools, and that there is bias against girls in who receives a place. They also show that although Government intended the places to support children from homes that would otherwise not be able to pay for private schooling, the reality is that far from all the parents receiving help with their fees can be considered to have genuine financial need.

This theme of greater parental choice was also central to the second main part of the 1980 Education Act for England and Wales, which gave parents a right to express a preference between maintained schools for their children rather than being automatically allocated a neighborhood school, or a church school if applicable. The Act obliged schools to publish information on examination performance, facilities, philosophy, curriculum, and so on, so that parents could have more information on which to base their preference. In turn, the LEAs were obliged to take this preference into account in allocating children to schools, but the Act also allowed the LEAs to retain powers to manage falling school rolls and to plan the overall provision in their areas in an efficient and effective way. This was a particularly important provision given that the number of secondary school children was set to fall by about a third in the years from 1978 to 1990. Stillman and Maychell (1986) have shown that the effect of this legislation was extremely variable, as some LEAs tried to encourage parental choice and others endeavored to restrict it. Those offering minimal choice justified their behavior mainly in terms of catchment area schools fostering better links with the local community, and that this ensured that the LEA could engage in long-term planning.

The next major legislative change came with the 1986 Education Act, which greatly increased the powers of school governing bodies. The governing bodies established in the 1944 Education Act had previously played a trivial role in the everyday management of schools. Many schools shared their governing body with other nearby schools, and in a few LEAs all schools were served by a single committee. The 1986 Education Act revitalized governing bodies, by ensuring that each school had its own committee and by giving it real powers and responsibilities over appointments, the curriculum, and the management of the school. The Act also reconstituted the membership of governing bodies such that local politicians and their nominees were no longer in the majority. The aim was that they were to be largely replaced by members of the local community (in particular, people in business and commerce), and parents of children in the school. The changes were justified in terms of increasing local accountability and fostering stronger links between schools and the world of work, but they can also be seen as encouraging differentiation and generating competition between schools. Such a reorganization and strengthening of the powers of governing bodies were also necessary prerequisites for the greater role that they have later been asked to play in the local management of schools, where they have come to control the overall budget of their school.

The 1988 Education Reform Act

The 1988 Education Reform Act led to many radical changes within education. First, a national curriculum was to be established, with attainment targets and associated testing of performance at around age 7, 11, 14, and 16 years. Second, governing bodies of all secondary schools and many primary schools were to be given control over their own budgets. Third, parental choice was to be strengthened by ensuring that pupil numbers in state-maintained schools could not be restricted by LEAs to less than the number the building could actually hold. Fourth, a network of City Technology Colleges (CTCs) was to be established. Fifth, state schools were to be given the right to opt out of local education authority control and become grant-maintained schools, directly funded by the Department for Education. The main thrust of this complex Act is best seen as an attempt to introduce greater diversity between schools and to develop a form of quasi-market competition. Schools were intended to compete with each other for pupils and teachers and to be run as separate nonprofit organizations rather than being part of a wider educational and social service to the whole community.

Conservative policy toward education has never been completely consistent over time or even within this one Act. A variety of sociologists have examined the contradictions within Conservative policy (see, for example, Bash and Coulby, 1989; Chitty, 1992; Flude and

Hammer, 1990; Lawton, 1994), and pointed to the inconsistencies between various government policies. Perhaps the most stark illogicality is that the powers that governing bodies were given to control the curriculum in the 1986 Act were taken away again by the 1988 Act through the imposition of a national curriculum! Sociologists have also examined the strong attack on LEAs that is such a prominent feature of the 1988 Act. Several have argued that this can be seen as a reaction to firm egalitarian stands taken by some Labour-controlled councils, particularly in the implementation of antiracist and antisexist policies (Troyna, 1993; Measor and Sikes, 1992). Some LEAs also attempted to implement antiheterosexist initiatives that, in the moral panic surrounding AIDS, provoked some extreme reactions. Labour LEAs taking all of these issues seriously were frequently labeled as "looney left" by popular newspapers and by various Conservative Members of Parliament, and regarded as profligate. In particular, it galled many Conservative Members of Parliament that the Inner London Education Authority was Labour controlled and invested heavily in equal opportunities policy. To solve this perceived problem, the Act simply abolished the ILEA, and devolved the responsibility for education down to the constituent local councils within the inner London area.

The National Curriculum

The 1944 Education Act was unconcerned with the content of education, and ceded power over the curriculum to teachers, who were constrained only by the demands of a range of external academic examinations at postcompulsory school age. Technically, only religious education was compulsory, and that was the very subject that was omitted in many schools. With an increasingly geographically mobile population, the need for greater similarity in what was taught in various schools was evident, and there was little direct controversy about the principle of a national curriculum. Nevertheless, there was considerable debate about exactly what the national curriculum should entail and even more over the nature of the associated testing of attainment.

In outline, the idea was simple. After a phasing-in period, all maintained schools were to follow a "broad and balanced curriculum" that would consist of the core subjects of mathematics, English, and science, and the foundation subjects of history, geography, technology, music, art, physical education, and, at the secondary level, a modern language. Religious education is also a compulsory part of the curriculum and Welsh is "core" in Welsh-speaking Wales and "foundation" elsewhere in Wales. Separate Councils were established to develop the detailed programs of study for each subject and to develop examinations and assessments covering the whole age range from 5 to 16. All children were to be tested at around ages 7, 11, 14, and 16 as well as having regular assessments of their levels of attainment on a 10-point scale for each subject.

In practice, this meant that from 1989 onward schools were inundated with booklets, leaflets, circulars, and ring binders, and teachers found their work loads escalated. Assessment trials in primary schools during early 1990 showed that the burden of extra work required to give standardized tests to all children would severely prejudice good teaching. Both the tests and the curriculum itself had been developed too quickly and with little consultation. The tasks were time consuming, unwieldy, and largely confirmed what teachers already knew about pupils' abilities. Teachers were overwhelmed by the task and children put under undue stress. Teachers, headteachers, and unions protested strongly and, to some surprise, the government announced that testing at 7 and 11 would be conducted only for the three core subjects—mathematics, English, and science—rather than for all subjects. It was further announced that the curriculum and assessments for the foundation subjects were to be more flexible and allow greater scope for choice by teachers and pupils. However, most teachers remained unimpressed, and were still concerned about the nature of the tests and the use to which test scores would be put in producing tables that would rank schools according to results. Most teachers simply refused to test or, if they did, they refused to pass the results on to the local education authorities.

Meanwhile, secondary teachers were facing a "quart into a pint pot" problem with their part of the National Curriculum. As they began to prepare for the new system, it gradually became evident that there was simply not enough time to cover all they were expected to do. The first break from the original plan came in science, when it was announced that not all students would have to follow the same program of study, but that they

could choose to follow a more restricted program if they wished. By July 1990 it had been announced that students would be able to drop some whole subject areas, and that history, geography, music, art, and physical education were effectively being downgraded by being made more optional after age 14. Secondary teachers also boycotted testing, and some refused to implement parts of the National Curriculum. The result of the continued protest and disarray in schools was that further legislation was introduced (the 1993 Education Act) that combined the previous Councils into a single National Curriculum and Assessment Authority. The new Chairman, Sir Ron Dearing, was instructed to radically slim the National Curriculum and testing arrangement. His final report proposed a reduced curriculum and greatly simplified testing, and was accepted by Government in early 1994.

The revised National Curriculum and associated testing mark a considerable victory for teachers and educationists, but far from all of sociologists' concerns about the National Curriculum have been dealt with. The content of any curriculum is a selection based upon the particular political and moral values of those with the power to select (Apple, 1993). With the English and Welsh National Curriculum this political nature of the selection of contents became clear as protagonists fought for their particular view of what should be included in each subject. Thus within music the debate was about the extent to which classical or popular music should be included. In geography, it was whether the focus should be on Great Britain and Europe or World geography. In history, it was on the balance between "British" history and world history, and on where "history" ended and sociology and politics (both not included in the National Curriculum) began. In many cases the neoconservative political New Right achieved a great deal of success, and many sociologists argue that the contents of each of the National Curriculum subjects are heavily biased against particular ethnicity minority pupils, and frequently favor white, middle-class, males.

There are particular problems about ethnic minorities, for it has been argued that the nature of the National Curriculum is fundamentally based on an ideology of assimilationism, which takes no account of cultural differences (Whitty and Menter, 1989). For example, it was originally intended that only European

Union working languages would be included as options within the modern foreign languages part of the National Curriculum. Intense political pressure led to a change in policy, but this still led to a two-tiered system whereby ethnic minority languages such as Urdu, Punjabi, and Gujerati can be included as long as the school also offers at least one of the European Union languages. This compromise still retains implications of "second-class" languages, but does actually enhance the status of the ethnic minority languages compared with their previous position. Young pupils are now also able to be assessed in the language of their home for their math and science tests of attainment. However, major inequalities remain in the content of several subjects and in the form of collective worship and religious education introduced by the 1988 Education Reform Act, and strengthened by the 1992 Education (Schools) Act. Prior to 1988, religious education had often been taught within integrated humanities courses and had become multifaith and multicultural. To counteract this type of religious education teaching, amendments were passed that ensured a place for religious education in the basic curriculum, and reaffirmed the need for a compulsory act of school worship each day. Crucially, for the first time, the legislation stated that (with a few exceptions) both of these must be wholly or mainly of a broadly Christian character. Multicultural and antiracist education are clearly under attack (Troyna, 1993; Tomlinson and Craft, 1995).

The hope that greater equality between the sexes might be encouraged through the National Curriculum has also turned out to be false. Since 1976 all curriculum subjects offered at a school have had to be open to both boys and girls, but there were still gender biases in the subjects chosen for options at age 13 or 14. The National Curriculum as originally proposed would have ensured that all pupils take all subjects up to age 16, which might have encouraged, for example, more girls to enter scientific and technological work. The revisions allowing pupils to drop certain subjects, and to choose a restricted science program, mean that this possibility has been lost. The compulsory technology subject (which combined a broad range of interests including art, textiles, design, manufacture, and food science) has also proved to be less gender positive than expected as sex stereotyping is still evident in the choices that boys and girls make within the subject.

Two New Types of Schools

Two completely new types of schools were introduced since in the late 1980s—City Technology Colleges (CTCs) (announced in 1986) and grant-maintained schools (as part of the 1988 Education Reform Act). City Technology Colleges are schools for 11–18 year olds, established outside the LEA system. They are officially private schools, run by educational trusts closely linked to industry but directly government funded in line with per capita expenditure for schools in similar areas. The colleges charge no fees, but sponsors are expected to cover the extra costs involved in providing a highly technological curriculum and should make substantial contributions to both capital and current expenditure. But, as is explained more fully elsewhere (Walford, 1990), although the desire to increase technological education is a major feature of the plan, the CTCs are also about reintroducing selection, destroying the comprehensive system, and reducing the powers of the LEAs.

It was intended that the colleges would be established in urban areas, especially the "disadvantaged" inner cities. They were to admit pupils spanning the full range of ability, but selection was a major feature of the plan, not according to ability, but based on general aptitude, readiness to take advantage of the type of education offered, and on the parents' commitment to the college and to full-time education or training up to age 18. Selection was thus to be based not only on the motivation of the child but also that of its parents.

The reality of the CTCs did not match the rhetoric. The Government found it difficult to find industrial and commercial sponsors prepared to donate funding on the scale anticipated, the costs of establishing the colleges were far greater than expected, and the aim to site the colleges in inner city areas brought the scheme in direct conflict with Labour-controlled local councils who fiercely oppose it (Whitty et al., 1993). The first CTC at Solihull in the West Midlands has been investigated in depth (Walford and Miller, 1991), and it was shown that although the college is giving advantage to the children it accepts, it is not acting as a catalyst for raising the quality of education in the schools in the nearby area. In fact, it is doing the reverse, and taking from those schools the very children and parents who might otherwise have fought for those schools and encouraged teachers and other pupils.

The fate of the CTCs is, therefore, far from the optimistic future presented in 1986. In practice, the College at Solihull, which opened in 1988, was followed by two more in 1989, and just four more in 1990. The original scheme has now been abandoned with just 15 CTCs in operation, and a far cheaper Technology College scheme was launched in 1993. Nevertheless, the significance of the CTCs is far greater than the number of pupils involved would signify. Fundamentally, the CTC idea made it clear that the government wished to develop an educational system based on inequality of provision and on selection of children for specific schools with better facilities, funding, and support than are available for the majority. Further, the CTCs made it clear that new types of school were possible, and that the government wished to see a greater diversity of schools and a decline in LEA power.

The grant-maintained schools that developed following the 1988 Act were the next step in developing this diversity. Grant-maintained schools are owned and managed by their governing bodies rather than their local education authority. They are not allowed to charge fees and are funded by the Department for Education, which recoups the costs from the relevant LEA's revenue support grant. Following recent changes all county or voluntary secondary, middle, and primary schools may now apply for grant-maintained status. Parents or governors can initiate the process, but the crucial vote is by parents. Additionally, since the 1993 Education Act, it has been possible for existing private schools to become grant maintained and for independent sponsors to apply for grant maintained status for a planned school. In all cases, after consultation, the Secretary of State for Education makes the final decision.

The rise in the number of grant-maintained schools has been slower than Government expected. The first 18 grant-maintained schools opened in September 1989, and by March 1995 there were still only just over 1000 out of a total of more than 30,000. To encourage the policy, additional transitional capital and recurrent funding were made available in comparison to LEA schools, and legislation was introduced to make the ballot process easier. The 1993 Education Act also established a Funding Agency for Schools to distribute funding and to plan the provision of school places. Where more than 15% of children are in grant-maintained schools, this planning function is shared between the

Funding Agency for Schools and the relevant LEA, but the FAS takes full responsibility after 70%.

Sociological research evidence (Fitz et al., 1993; Bush et al., 1993) indicates that grant-maintained schools are popular with the parents associated with these schools, but this popularity is largely due to many grant-maintained schools being selective or single sex. Headteachers in grant-maintained schools are also generally highly favorable as it gives them greater control, independence, and (usually) a higher salary. In contrast to Government expectations, more grant-maintained schools are in Conservative-controlled LEAs than Labour LEAs, for it is the Conservative-controlled LEAs that have traditionally spent less on education than Labour LEAs. The move to grant-maintained status was often made in the hope of receiving additional funding.

The sociological research studies have also found many other negative features of the policy. Fitz et al. (1993) indicate that the opt-out process has often caused great disruption within schools and between schools. Several LEAs have had their plans for reorganization of schooling inhibited or frustrated by schools designated for closure being allowed to opt-out. Additionally, it has been found that most grant-maintained schools have not developed significant innovative features, and that they do not represent a distinct new type of school as Government hoped. This means that parental choice has not been widened in any real sense, and, in contrast, some nominally comprehensive grant-maintained schools have started to select. Schools thus choose students and parents rather than parents and students choosing schools.

Overall, both of the new types of school that have been introduced have been less important to the educational restructuring process than had been expected. In practice, the changes in open enrollment and local financial management of schools have together wrought greater changes throughout the maintained sector.

Local Management of Schools and Open Enrollment

The increased power given to school governing bodies was a precursor to delegating greater local management and financial decision making to individual schools. For many years heads have been given the freedom to spend a small proportion of the budget as they feel best suits their school, but the 1988 Education Reform Act gave schools autonomy over practically all of their spending including, most importantly, staff salaries. All schools now have delegated budgets, and governing bodies are responsible for expenditure on all manual, technical, secretarial, and teaching staff, books and equipment, heat and light, and cleaning and rates (local property taxes). The school's share of LEA funding is calculated on a formula basis that depends mainly on the number and age of pupils in the school, but also includes allowances for some special circumstances of the school. The school's budget is thus dependent upon the number of pupils it can attract, and schools are expected to compete for pupils in a quasi-market.

Although heads now have a higher workload, delegated budgets have generally been popular with heads and teachers. However, when coupled with the open enrollment legislation that obliges schools to take all applicants up to the maximum the buildings could hold, there is very little difference between maintained schools under the new regulations and grant-maintained schools. All schools are now under the management of a powerful governing body, and the pupil number-based formula funding encourages them to compete with each other in the market for pupils (Wallace, 1993). Popular schools take in more pupils than the less popular ones, with the result that these schools either compete more fully for pupils or enter a downward spiral of decay with fewer pupils leading to fewer teachers and eventual closure.

The move toward individually competitive self-managed schools is also unlikely to favor ethnic minority pupils, or any wider social aims for interethnic understanding. Many LEAs targeted equal opportunities and antiracism as areas where additional support and training were given, but schools controlling their own budgets may well place these vital issues low on their list of priorities. Indeed, this is the government's expectation, as the attack on LEAs was often explicitly in terms of their "profligacy" in funding antiracist, antisexist, and antiheterosexist programs. The fear is that a school will see it as wasteful to use money on multicultural or antiracist education when it has few black or Asian pupils.

Greater parental choice also often may not act in the best interests of all children or the wider society. There have already been several cases of parents choosing to move their child from a school on the basis of its ethnic mix, and the government has admitted that parental choice could lead to some schools becoming all black, but that this was the "price that had to be paid" for greater choice.

In a similar way, it is likely that local management of schools will lead to less emphasis on gender equality and antisexism. Formal policies will undoubtedly remain, but monitoring and implementing a program of antisexism may well cost more than the school is prepared to spend.

New Forms of Selection

Several sociologists have argued that the 1988 Education Reform Act and subsequent legislation is concerned with increasing inequalities rather than reducing them. The overall policy is seen as a return to the discredited selective system of the 1950s and is designed to bring into existence a continuum of different types of schools with unequal provision, into which various children will be fitted through a process of mutual selection closely linked to social class, gender, and ethnic group. There will be a shift toward greater inegalitarianism within a more self-consciously stratified society. There will be increased vocationalism, with schools having links with particular types of industrial or commercial organizations. This will lead to growing differentiation between groups, as children are more clearly channeled into "appropriate" occupational positions.

The 1988 Education Reform Act and the 1993 Education Act encouraged a shift away from comprehensive schooling by promoting new types of schools, locally managed schools, and increased choice between schools. Although these changes were promoted in terms of increasing choice for parents and children, at oversubscribed schools, it has become clear that "choice of school" often means that the schools are able to select the children they wish. Selection has become more overt and the criteria on which pupils are selected have become more varied and confused than ever before. The research evidence on grant-maintained schools is mixed. Fitz et al. (1993) argued that (at the time of their research) there was little evidence for a widespread return of a selective system. In contrast, the second study by Bush et al. (1993) showed that 30% of the supposedly comprehensive schools in their grant-maintained sample were using covert selection and one had introduced a selection examination. These authors argued that the grant-maintained policy was leading to the development of a two-tier system. Many sociologists of education fear that reintroducing selection will result in the return of the inequities in provision and results identified by their colleagues in the 1960s.

Since these studies of grant-maintained schools were conducted, a small number of comprehensive grant-maintained schools have successfully applied for a "change in character" to become fully academically selective grammar schools, while several others have been granted permission to select up to 50% of their intake. Changes in the admissions criteria that involve this degree of selection require Department for Education (DFE) authorization following a full consultation process, but in mid-1993 new DFE guidelines on admissions announced that all schools were to be allowed to specialize and to select up to 10% of their intake on the basis of abilities in areas such as music, art, sports, and technology without any need for official approval. The Government argued that specialization need not lead to selection, but once there are more applications than places, selection must inevitably increase.

Differentiation and selection were also further encouraged through the 1993 Education Act. Grant-maintained schools and voluntary aided schools were encouraged to appoint sponsor governors from business and become Technology Colleges specializing in science, technology, and mathematics. So far, 50 schools have been able to find at least £100,000 from sponsors, and in return the schools have received more than matching extra resources from the DFE. Such extra resources to a limited number of schools can lead to substantial differences between the learning environments of neighboring schools. Although overt selection is not necessarily introduced, self-selection will operate in a way similar to the original City Technology Colleges. Those parents with little interest in education simply will not apply for places in what are likely to be the most popular schools. As already indicated, a further development as a result of the 1993 Education Act is that existing private schools or groups sponsoring a proposed new school have been able to apply to establish their own grant-maintained schools. Thus, for example, Sikh, Muslim, or evangelical Christian groups can establish faith-based grant-maintained schools that

have parents' and children's expressed and demonstrated values and beliefs as explicit criteria for selection.

There have now been several English research studies that have indicated social class inequalities in the workings of the new "market" for schools, and a process of self-selection occurring in addition to actual selection by schools. It has been shown that some groups are far more able to "play the market" (Ball et al., 1994, 1995) than others and that hierarchies of schools are developing in various local areas. It would appear that the children of well-motivated, educated, or wealthy families are more likely to make applications to the popular schools. These oversubscribed schools then select children on a diverse and unclear range of criteria, but in a way likely to be heavily skewed toward children from families already highly valuing education. These popular schools will thus improve further through the financial and cultural support of the parents and children selected. In contrast, children from families that do not value education highly will probably find themselves in schools at the bottom of the hierarchy with low levels of financial and parental support. Any preexisting differences between schools will widen.

Conclusion

The introduction of more "choice and diversity" was presented by Government as a means of giving more power and responsibility to parents. Throughout the 1980s and early 1990s very many sociologists of education have questioned these policies in terms of their possible deleterious effects on minority and disempowered groups and have subsequently undertaken research into these areas. They argue that rather than all parents entering a free market on an equal basis, they enter with different financial and cultural capital and that a mutual choice process between parents and schools cannot fail to be discriminatory. If it is the parents who must apply to CTCs, popular grant-maintained or LEA schools, and for Assisted Places on behalf of their children, and if they must be prepared to be interviewed and supportive of the education provided, then there are bound to be inequities (Walford, 1994). Obviously, some working-class and ethnic minority parents will seize the chance to take advantage of the better facilities, staff, and teaching that will probably be available in the schools at the top of any hierarchy, but it still remains true that working-class and ethnic minority parents are likely to have had a poorer education and to be less knowledgeable about education than their white middle-class competitors. Even if they apply on behalf of their children, they are less likely to be able to negotiate educational bureaucracies or to present themselves as "supportive" parents in interviews with head teachers or other selectors, who are themselves mostly white and middle class.

In summary, the educational reforms of the last decade have been designed to widen differences between the educational experiences of various children, and to link them more closely to their most probable occupational destinations. The result is that schooling is likely to become more closely linked to social class, gender, ethnic group, and geographic regional differences. Rather than aiming to increase equity, these reforms are likely to confirm and reinforce the preexisting social order of wealth and privilege.

REFERENCES

Apple, Michael W. 1993. *Official Knowledge.* New York: Routledge.

Ball, Stephen J., Richard Bowe, and Sharon Gewirtz. 1994. "Market Forces and Parental Choice." In Sally Tomlinson (ed.), *Educational Reform and its Consequences.* London: IPPR/Rivers Oram.

———. 1995. "Circuits of Schooling: A Sociological Exploration of Parental Choice in Social Class Contexts." *Sociological Review* 43(1):52.

Bash, Leslie, and David Coulby, eds. 1989. *The Education Reform Act: Competition and Reform.* London: Cassell.

Bush, Tony, Marianne Coleman, and Derek Glover. 1993. *Managing Autonomous Schools. The Grant-maintained Experience.* London: Paul Chapman.

Chitty, Clyde. 1992. *The Education System Transformed.* Manchester: Baseline Books.

Edwards, Tony, John Fitz, and Geoff Whitty. 1989. *The State and Private Education: An Evaluation of the Assisted Places Scheme.* London: Falmer.

Fitz, John, David Halpin, and Sally Power. 1993. *Grant Maintained Schools. Education in the Market-place.* London: Kogan Page.

Floud, J., A. H. Halsey, and F. M. Martin. 1956. *Social Class and Educational Opportunity.* London: Heinemann.

Flude, M., and Merril Hammer, eds. 1990. *The Education Reform Act, 1988. Its Origins and Implications.* London: Falmer.

Hargreaves, David. 1967. *Social Relations in the Secondary School.* London: Routledge & Kegan Paul.

Lacey, Colin. 1970. *Hightown Grammar.* Manchester: Manchester University Press.

Lawton, Denis. 1994. *The Tory Mind on Education 1979–94.* London: Falmer.

Measor, Lynda, and Patricia Sikes. 1992. *Gender and Schools.* London: Cassell.

Stillman, Alan, and Karen Maychell. 1986. *Changing Schools: Parents, LEAs and the 1980 Education Act.* Windsor: NFER-Nelson.

Tomlinson, Sally, and Maurice Craft, eds. 1995. *Ethnic Relations and Schooling.* London: Athlone.

Troyna, Barry. 1993. *Racism and Education.* Buckingham: Open University Press.

Walford, Geoffrey. 1990. *Privatization and Privilege in Education.* London: Routledge.

———. 1992 "Great Britain." In Peter W. Cookson, Jr., Alan R. Sadovnik, and Susan F. Semel (eds.). *International Handbook of Educational Reform.* New York: Greenwood Press.

———. 1994. *Choice and Equity in Education.* London: Cassell.

Walford, Geoffrey, and Henry Miller. 1991. *City Technology College.* Buckingham: Open University Press.

Wallace, Gwen, ed. 1993. *Local Management, Central Control: Schools in the Market Place.* Bournemouth: Hyde Publications.

Whitty, Geoff, Tony Edwards, and Sharon Gewirtz. 1993. *Specialisation and Choice in Urban Education. The City Technology College Experiment.* London: Routledge.

Whitty, Geoff, and Ian Menter. 1989. "Lessons of Thatcherism: Education Policy in England and Wales." *Journal of Law and Society* 16(1):42–64.

Educational Reform in the United States: 1980s and 1990s[1]

Alan R. Sadovnik
Rutgers University

Peter W. Cookson, Jr.
Teachers College, Columbia University

Susan F. Semel
City College of New York (CUNY)

David L. Levinson
Bergen Community College

The 1980s and 1990s were decades of significant debate and reform in U.S. education. Beginning in 1983, with the National Commission on Educational Excellence's report *A Nation at Risk*, government leaders, educational reformers, teacher organizations, administrators, and various other interest groups attempted to improve the quality of U.S. schools. Although the decades included two specific waves of reform, the first beginning in 1983, and the second beginning in 1985 and continuing through the end of the 1990s, the period must be understood as a conservative response to the progressive reforms of the 1960s and 1970s, if not the entire progressive agenda of the twentieth century.

In the 1980s the major reform actors shifted from the federal to the state to the local levels. In the 1990s, the federal government through President Clinton's *Goals 2000*, placed the federal government back at the forefront of educational policy. From the outset, the federal government through the Department of Education attempted to balance its ideological belief that education is not a federal governmental matter with its commitment to providing the impetus for change. First, through its influential report *A Nation at Risk* written during the tenure of Secretary Terrell Bell, and second, through his successor William Bennett's use of his office as a "bully pulpit," the U.S. Department of

Education played a significant role in keeping the pressure on states and localities to improve educational outcomes, which for Secretary Bennett defined the goals of educational reform.

The first wave of reforms involved the states becoming the primary level of educational reform. Through the setting of tougher standards and the implementation of new standardized testing procedures, educational reform became centralized to the state level (Honig, 1990; Passow, 1989). As many critics began to point out the problematic and, at times, contradictory nature of these rational-bureaucratic processes, the second wave of reforms began to target the local and school levels as the appropriate venues for improvement, and administrators, teachers, and parents as the appropriate actors.

The educational reforms of the 1980s and 1990s consisted of two waves of reform (Bacharach, 1990; Passow, 1989). The first wave, marked by the reports of the early and mid-1980s and the educational initiatives directly responding to them, was concerned primarily with the issues of accountability and achievement (Dougherty, 1990:3). Responding to the call for increased academic achievement, many states increased graduation requirements, toughened curriculum mandates, and increased the use of standardized test scores to measure student achievement.

By the mid to late 1980s, however, it became increasingly clear that such top-down reform would be ineffective in dealing with the schools' myriad problems. Although raising achievement standards for students, and implementing accountability measures for

---

[1] This chapter is a revised version of "United States." In Peter W. Cookson, Jr., Alan R. Sadovnik, and Susan F. Semel (eds.), 1992. *International Handbook of Educational Reform*, pp. 443–472. Westport, CT: Greenwood Press. Adapted with permission of Greenwood Press.

evaluating teachers had some positive effects, many, including the National Governors Association (which took a leading role in reform), believed that educational reform had to do more than provide changes in evaluation procedures. The second wave of reform, which has continued through the 1990s, was targeted at the structure and processes of the schools themselves, placing far more control in the hands of local schools, teachers, and communities. Whereas the first wave was highly centralized at the state level, the second wave was more decentralized to the local and school levels. What they had in common, however, was what the Governors Conference emphasized as the "triple theme of achievement, assessment, and accountability" (Alexander, 1986; Bacharach, 1990:8). By the mid-1990s, however, the first and second waves began to overlap, with top-down federal and state mandates defining the goals and standards of education, but leaving it to local districts to implement them.

Despite the second wave's insistence that locally based reforms were central to success, many critics, including teacher organizations and unions, argued that the reforms were highly bureaucratic and aimed primarily at assessment procedures. Significant reforms, they suggested, had to emphasize both changes within schools and changes that involved teachers, students, and parents, as part of the reform process, not merely as objects of it. From the latter part of the 1980s through the end of the 1990s reforms that emphasized teacher empowerment, school-based management, and school choice, charter schools and tuition vouchers became the most important ones under consideration.

During both waves of educational reform, there were a number of programs and initiatives that received considerable attention. Among these were school choice, charter schools and tuition vouchers, school-based management, school–business partnerships, the effective school movement, and reform of teacher education.

School Choice, Charter Schools, and Tuition Vouchers

During the 1980s and 1990s, many educational researchers and policy analysts indicated that most public schools were failing in terms of student achievement, discipline, and morality. At the same period, some researchers were investigating private schools and concluding that they were more effective learning environments than public schools. Private schools were reputed to be accountable, efficient, and safe. Moreover, the work of Coleman et al. (1982) seemed to prove that private school students learned more than their public school counterparts. Other research on "magnet" schools (schools with special curricula and student bodies) seemed to indicate that public schools that operated independently of the public school bureaucracy were happier, healthier, and more academically productive than zone schools where students were required to attend based on their residence.

As the decade came to a close, some researchers reasoned that magnet schools and private schools were superior to neighborhood public schools because schools of choice reflected the desires and needs of their constituents and were, thus, sensitive to change. For several decades, the idea of school choice had been on the fringes of the educational policy world in the form of voucher proposals. Essentially, voucher proponents argued that if families, rather than schools, were funded, it would allow for greater parental choice and participation. Moreover, by voting with their dollars, parents would reward good schools and punish bad schools. A voucher system, in effect, would deregulate the public school system. That a voucher system might also privatize the public school system was a muted issue.

By the late 1980s, however, public school choice was at the forefront of the educational reform movement. Presidents Reagan and Bush supported choice and one influential White House report enumerated a number of reasons why choice was the right reform for the times (Paulu, 1989). In essence, choice was a panacea that was nonbureaucratic, inexpensive, and fundamentally egalitarian because it allowed market forces to shape school policy, rather than subjecting educators to the heavy hand of the educational bureaucracy. A very influential book by John E. Chubb and Terry M. Moe, *Politics, Markets and America's Schools* (1990), seemed to provide empirical evidence that unregulated school choice policies, in and of themselves, would produce a structural reform in American education. Congressional support for greater school choice had been expressed in a bill that was passed by the House of Representatives in the summer of 1990 that, among other things, provided direct federal support for open enrollment experiments. Needless to say, all this political activity stirred up a great deal of controversy and confusion. Choice is controversial because it is deeply political and rests on a set of assumptions about educational marketplaces and private schools that is questionable. It is confusing because choice is a rubric that covers a wide variety of policies that are quite different, except that they include an element of student and parental choice. (See Cookson, 1991, 1993, for a complete discussion.)

Throughout the 1990s, public school choice, tuition vouchers for private schools, and charter schools (schools that are publicly funded by state charters, but independent of many school district mandates) have been key educational reforms. Powers and Cookson (1999) summarize the available evidence on school choice and conclude that (1) market-driven choice programs increase stratification within school districts; (2) choice programs increase the educational opportunities for minority students, who, without these programs, would be limited to their neighborhood public schools; (3) choice parents tend to be more involved in their children's education; (4) choice parents tend to be more satisfied with their children's education; and (5) there is disagreement among researchers about the effect of choice on student achievement. For example, using the same data on Milwaukee Parental Choice Program (MPCP), Witte et al. (1994, 1995; Witte, 1996, 1997) argue that the effect of choice has been inconsistent; Greene and Peterson (1996) argue that MPCP has resulted in significant achievement gains; and Rouse's (1998) findings are in the middle.

The choice movement resulted in the development of charter schools and tuition vouchers for private schools. Whereas conservatives became the major proponents of tuition vouchers, advocates of charter schools often came from all sides of the political spectrum. Wells et al. (1998) summarize the claims by charter school advocates: (1) charter schools are more accountable for student outcomes; (2) charter schools have greater autonomy and thus are empowered to better serve their students; (3) charter schools are more efficient; (4) charter schools provide greater choice to more families; (5) charter schools create a competitive market and will force public schools to change; and (6) charter schools are more innovative.

The UCLA Charter School Study of 10 California school districts (Wells et al., 1998) reported the following findings:

1. California charter schools (CCS) are most often

not held accountable yet for increased student achievement.
2. School boards are ambivalent about monitoring CCS.
3. CCS are accountable to multiple constituencies.
4. CCS vary greatly in their autonomy.
5. CCS funding widely varies between and within districts.
6. Private resources are needed for CCS to survive.
7. CCS differ greatly in their ability to raise private funds.
8. CCS depend on strong leadership.
9. CCS have significant control over the types of students they admit.
10. The requirement that CCS reflect the racial/ethnic makeup of their districts has not been enforced.
11. Teachers in CCS welcome their freedom, small class size, and collegiality, but note their heavy workloads.
12. Although it is not required, most CCS have state credentialed teachers.
13. Teachers in schools converted to CCS continue to belong to unions, but teachers in new CCS do not.
14. There is little formal way for public schools and CCS to learn from each other.
15. Public school educators believe that CCS have an unfair advantage that limits competition.

The UCLA study indicates that charter schools in California have not fulfilled many of their advocates claims and suggest that charter schools may continue to advantage already advantaged families. However, because the study did not include an empirical investigation of achievement outcomes, it is still premature to reach any overall conclusions about the efficacy of charter schools, particularly for children from lower socioeconomic backgrounds.

Clearly, it is too early to tell whether school choice will lead to the revitalization of public education in the United States. It may well be that choice is a method of school improvement, but cannot by itself resolve many of the fundamental problems associated with public education. Moreover, choice plans usually involve complex and volatile issues of constitutionality, equity, and feasibility. In sum, there is evidence that school choice can lead to improvement in individual schools, but there is little convincing evidence that choice will result in the overall improvement of American education.

School–Business Partnerships

During the 1980s, business leaders became increasingly concerned that the nation's schools were not producing the kinds of graduates necessary for a revitalization of the American economy. Several school–business partnerships were formed, the most notable of which was the Boston Compact begun in 1982. These partnerships have been formed in other cities; for instance, in 1991 the Committee to Support Philadelphia Public Schools pledged management assistance and training to the Philadelphia School District to restructure and implement a site-based management plan. In return, the city promised that by 1995 it would raise the test scores of its graduates and improve grade promotion rates. Other school–business partnerships include scholarships for poor students to attend college and programs where businesses "adopt" a school.

Despite, however, the considerable publicity that surrounds these partnerships, the fact is that in the 1980s only 1.5% of corporate giving was to public primary and secondary public schools (Reich, 1991:43). In fact, corporate and business support for public schools has fallen dramatically since the 1970s. School–business partnerships have attracted considerable media attention, but there is little convincing evidence that they have significantly improved schools or that, as a means of reform, school–business partnerships will address the fundamental problems facing American education.

School-to-Work Programs

In the 1990s, school–business partnerships became incorporated into school-to-work programs. Their intent was to extend what had been a vocational emphasis to non-college-bound students regarding skills necessary for successful employment and stressed the importance of work-based learning (Wieler and Bailey, 1997).

On May 4, 1994 President Bill Clinton signed the School-to-Work Opportunities Act of 1994. This law provided seed money to states and local partnerships of business, labor, government, education, and commu-

nity organizations to develop school-to-work systems. This law did not create a new program, but allowed states and their partners to bring together efforts at education reform, worker preparation, and economic development to create a system to prepare youth for the high-wage, high-skill careers of today's and tomorrow's global economy.

Using federal seed money, states and their partnerships were encouraged to design the school-to-work system that made the most sense for them. Although these systems were different from state to state, each was supposed to provide every American student with the following:

- Relevant education, allowing students to explore different careers and see what skills are required in their working environment;
- Skills, obtained from structured training and work-based learning experiences, including necessary skills of a particular career as demonstrated in a working environment; and
- Valued credentials, establishing industry-standard benchmarks and developing education and training standards that ensure that proper education is received for each career.

Every state and locally created school-to-work system had to contain three core elements: (1) school-based learning—classroom instruction based on high academic and business-defined occupational skill standards; (2) work-based learning—career exploration, work experience, structured training, and mentoring at job sites; and (3) connecting activities—courses integrating classroom and on-the-job instruction, matching students with participating employers, training of mentors, and the building of other bridges between school and work.

Although the school-to-work programs were well intentioned, researchers (Charner, 1996; Mortimer, 1996) suggest that these programs often failed to fulfill their promise. The U.S. system of vocational education remains a "second-class" educational track, which often does not equip students with a sound liberal arts foundation and is not adequately connected to career opportunities. Unlike other nations such as Japan and Germany, U.S. students who do not wish to go on to postsecondary education are not given adequate career paths.

School-Based Management and Teacher Empowerment

In part, the history of education in the United States can be characterized as a struggle between the rivaling traditions of decentralization and centralization. Generally, the educational system, as a whole, is decentralized, because the ultimate authority for educational policy rests with the individual states and not with the federal government. Yet, within states and school districts, there has been a long-term tendency to centralize decision making in state agencies, elected and appointed school boards, and superintendents' offices. Throughout the 1980s there were repeated calls for the exercise of local and community authority in educational decision making.

Major school-based management reforms have been put in place in places such as New York City; Dade County, Florida; San Diego, California; Rochester, New York; Louisville, Kentucky; and Chicago, Illinois. Perhaps the most dramatic of these reforms has been in Chicago, where locally elected councils—composed of six parents, two community residents, two teachers, and the principal—have been put in charge of each of the city's 541 public schools. Although all of the legal issues surrounding this reform have not been settled, there is little doubt that school-based management reforms will continue to enjoy support among many policymakers, some teachers, and local communities. The notion that local decision making, however, will automatically make schools better learning environments and more collegial may ignore some of the problems implicit in extreme decentralization. For example, how can the tension between providing teachers with more decision-making authority, while simultaneously providing for administrative action and initiative, be resolved? There is considerable research that suggests that principals play a key role in creating effective schools. Moreover, some actions that may be required to make schools more effective may run counter to teachers' desires or self-perceived interests. If teachers and parents are to successfully formulate and implement policy, they need to be given training and related technical assistance and unless teachers are given substantial amounts of time to plan, implement, monitor, and change their initiatives, there is little reason to expect that school-based reforms will be successful.

This issue is becoming more acute in states where budgetary short-falls have resulted in teacher layoffs and increased teaching work loads. Finally, school-based management requires that some rules and regulations be waived by federal, state, and local authorities as well as teachers' unions. To some extent, these negotiations may mean that school-based reforms may be slowly and partially implemented and, thus, their effectiveness may be diminished. Evidence from the Chicago school reform suggests that school-based management by parents and teachers has not been particularly effective in reforming urban education or significantly raising achievement levels (Bryk et al., 1993).

The Effective School Movement

In response to *A Nation at Risk* and other reports criticizing the effectiveness of American public schools the school effectiveness movement emerged and suggested that there were characteristics in good schools that could be used as models for improving educational effectiveness. The late Ron Edmunds, one of the early leaders of this movement, argued that educational reform and improvement must consider problems of both equity and quality. Based upon Edmonds' work on effective schools for disadvantaged students (Edmonds, 1979), research on school effectiveness sought to identify the characteristics of effective schools (Brookhover et al., 1979, 1982). The school effectiveness research points out five key factors that define successful schools: (1) high expectations for all students, and staff acceptance of responsibility for student learning; (2) instructional leadership on the part of the principal; (3) a safe and orderly environment conducive to learning; (4) a clear and focused mission concerning instructional goals shared by the staff; and (5) frequent monitoring of student progress (Gartner and Lipset, 1987:389).

Based on these principles, school effectiveness researchers and reformers focused their attention on both the content and process of education. First, some critics of present educational practices argued that American schools paid too little attention to the traditional curriculum and that students learned very little subject matter. From Powell et al.'s *Shopping Mall High School* (1985) to Ravitch and Finn's *What Do Our Seventeen Year Olds Know?* (1987), the American schools were portrayed as having lost their sense of what knowledge is important and, therefore, left students with very little sense of the value of knowledge. Popular critiques, including E.D. Hirsch's *Cultural Literacy* (1987) and Allan Bloom's *The Closing of the American Mind* (1987), although the subject of passionate criticism, also portrayed a school system that, in their view, had failed to teach a systematic common body of culturally valuable knowledge. The debate over the usefulness of such knowledge, the Eurocentric and Western bias of the authors, and other criticisms, although important, are not central to this chapter. What is, however, is that such criticisms resulted in an increasing emphasis both on what should be taught and how it should be taught. Thus, much of the school effectiveness movement places a primary emphasis on teaching, teacher effectiveness, and learning, not in terms of the process of learning, but in terms of the outcomes of learning.

According to Larry Cuban (1984), the school effectiveness movement recommendations on teaching, teacher effectiveness, and learning are based on research findings concerning factors that correlate favorably with student test scores on standardized tests in reading and math, such as teachers focusing on academic goals and closely monitoring student progress toward institutional objectives. Based upon these findings, the school effectiveness movement sought to develop scientific models for ensuring better teaching and the supervision of teachers to ensure increased student achievement.

Although there is some merit to the attempt to rationalize educational practice based upon research findings, the bureaucratic-rational model that underlies this science of teaching is often misguided and distorted by its becoming an end, rather than a means to and end. Most importantly, this model ignores important realities of teaching and learning, as well as the relationship between schools and other external institutional and societal forces. In the 1990s, in response to these criticisms, some reformers attempted to integrate some of the effective school findings into a more comprehensive school restructuring approach. The work of Sizer (1985, 1992, 1996) and his *Coalition of Essential Schools* and the *National Center for the Restructuring of Education, Schools, and Teaching* at Teachers College, Columbia University, founded by Linda Darling-Hammond and Anne Lieberman, reflected this view.

Teacher Education

The emergence and development of teacher education as an educational problem were responses to the initial debates concerning the failure of the schools (Labaree, 1992a, 1992b, 1995). If the schools were not working properly, then teachers and teaching, perhaps the most important piece in the puzzle, had to be looked at critically. In addition, teacher organizations such as NEA and AFT, fearing the scapegoating of their members, took an active role in raising the debate as the opportunity to both recognize and improve the problematic conditions under which, from their perspective, most of their members work. Finally, if teachers and teaching were indeed part of the problem, then perhaps the education and training of teachers were good starting points for analysis. Thus, teacher education and schools and colleges of Education, long the object of critical scrutiny within universities, became the subject of intensive national investigation. By 1986, at least five major reports, by the National Commission on Excellence in Teacher Education, The California Commission on the Teaching Profession, The Holmes Group, The Southern Regional Education Board, and the Carnegie Report of the Task Force on Teaching as a Profession, all outlined major problems in teacher education and the professional lives of teachers and proposed a large-scale overhaul of the system that prepares teachers. Although the reports differed in some respects, there was widespread agreement about the nature of the problem.

The debate revolved around three major points: (1) the perceived lack of rigor and intellectual demands in teacher education programs; (2) the need to attract and retain competent teacher candidates; and (3) the necessity to reorganize the academic and professional components of teacher education programs at both the baccalaureate and postbaccalaureate levels (Teacher Education Project, 1986).

Although all five reports contributed to the ongoing discussions, the Carnegie and Holmes reports, perhaps because they represented two of the major interest groups in teacher education (in the case of Carnegie, major political and educational leaders and for Holmes, the Deans of Education from the major research universities), attracted the most public response, and became symbolic of the teacher education reform movement.

The Carnegie Report, entitled *A Nation Prepared:*

Teachers for the 21st Century (1986) and prepared by its Task Force on Teaching as a Profession (including representatives from corporations, the NEA and AFT, school writers and administrators, legislators, the Governor of New Jersey, and a Dean of Education of a major research university), focused on the necessity of educational quality for a competitive U.S. economy, and the value of education in a democratic political system. Building upon the critique offered by *A Nation at Risk*, the Carnegie Report suggested that improvements in teacher education were necessary preconditions for improvements in education. Finally, in addition to this the underlying democratic–liberal model of education, the report argued that the decline in traditional low-wage jobs in the U.S. economy and the corresponding increase in high-technology and service positions would require the schools to better prepare its students for this "new" economic reality. In this regard, also, the Carnegie Report stressed the centrality of better prepared teachers to meet the challenges of the twenty-first century.

To accomplish these democratic–liberal goals, the Carnegie Report (1986:3) calls for "sweeping changes in educational policy," which would include the restructuring of schools and the teaching profession, the elimination of the undergraduate education major, the recruitment of minorities into the teaching profession, and the increase of standards in teacher education and in teaching.

The Holmes Group, on the other hand, avoided explicit political–economic goals, but also focused on the relationship between university-based teacher education, the professional lives of teachers, and the structure of the schools themselves. Arguing that their role as teacher educators gave a unique and also perhaps subjective perception of these issues, the Holmes Report, entitled *Tomorrow's Teachers* (1986), outlined a set of five goals and proposals for the improvement of teacher education. The goals of the report included raising the intellectual soundness of teacher education, creating career ladders for teachers, developing entry level requirements into the profession, linking schools of education at the university level to schools, and improving schools for students and teachers. In two subsequent reports, *Tomorrow's Teachers* (1990) and *Tomorrow's Schools of Education* (1995), the Holmes Group advocated systemic changes in professional development and radi-

cally altering schools of education with an emphasis on school–university partnerships and professional development schools (PDS). Critics of the Holmes Group (Labaree, 1992a, 1992b, 1995) argued that its proposals represented a "disabling vision" for schools of education as they limit their roles to teacher education only, while deemphasizing their other important roles in research and education in broader societal and psychological contexts.

Despite differences in tone and some minor differences in emphasis, both the Carnegie and Holmes Reports focused on the same general concerns.

1. They agreed that overall problems in education cannot be solved without corresponding changes in teacher education.
2. Teacher education programs must be upgraded in terms of their intellectual rigor and focus, their need to emphasize the liberal arts, their need to eliminate undergraduate teacher education programs, and, like other professions (i.e., psychology, social work, law, medicine), move professional training and certification to the graduate level.
3. It was necessary to implement rigorous standards of entry into the profession and to develop systematic examinations to monitor such entry.
4. University teacher education programs and schools must be connected in a more systematic and cooperative manner.
5. Career ladders for teachers must be created that recognize differences in knowledge, skill, and commitment.
6. Necessary changes must be made in the schools and the professional lives of teachers to attract and retain the most competent candidates for the profession.

John Goodlad, in *Teachers for Our Nation's Schools* (1990), proposed a radical transformation of the way we prepare teachers requiring an overhaul of university-based teacher preparation. Echoing many of the recommendations of the Carnegie Commission and the Holmes Group on school–university cooperation, Goodlad stressed the importance of rewarding teacher-educators for their work, rather than relegating them, as is currently the case, to the bottom rung of the university status hierarchy.

In the 1990s, teacher education and professionalization continued to be significant issues. Talbert (1996) argued that both teacher education and professional development programs have been inadequate for equipping prospective teachers and existing teachers with the ability to fulfill their myriad responsibilities. Most teachers receive one shot professional development workshops that have little effect on their performance. She argued that long-term systemic professional development is needed.

As head of the National Commission on Teaching and America's Future, Linda Darling-Hammond has been one of the leaders of the teacher education reform movement in the 1990s. The commission report (1996) indicated that the criticisms presented by the Carnegie and Holmes reports in the 1980s had not been adequately addressed. Therefore, the Commission recommended the following:

1. Get serious about standards, for both students and teachers.
2. Reinvent teacher preparation and professional development.
3. Fix teacher recruitment and put qualified teachers in every classroom.
4. Encourage and reward teacher knowledge and skill.
5. Create schools that are organized for student and teacher success. (National Commission on Teaching and America's Future, 1996, pp. vi–vii.)

Representative of the second wave of educational reforms, both the effective school movement's recommendations, and those of the Carnegie and Holmes reports, emphasized the processes of teaching and learning, the school environment, and especially the need to improve the professional lives and status of teachers.

Education Reform in the 1990s

In 1990, President Bush with the support of the National Governor's Association announced six national goals for American education:

- Goal 1: By the year 2000, all children will start school ready to learn.

- Goal 2: By the year 2000, the high school graduation rate will increase to at least 90%.
- Goal 3: By the year 2000, American students will leave grades 4, 8, and 12 having demonstrated competency in challenging subject matter, including English, mathematics, science, history, and geography, and every school in America will ensure that all students learn to use their minds well, so they may be prepared for responsible citizenship, further learning, and productive employment in our modern economy.
- Goal 4: By the year 2000, U.S. students will be first in the world in mathematics and science achievement.
- Goal 5: By the year 2000, every adult American will be literate and will possess the skills necessary to compete in a global economy and exercise the rights and responsibilities of citizenship.
- Goal 6: By the year 2000, every school in America will be free of drugs and violence and will offer a disciplined environment conducive to learning (*Education Week*, 1990:16–17).

Goals 2000: Building on a Decade of Reform

Goals 2000 was a direct outgrowth of the state-led education reform agenda of the 1980s, which included increasing high school graduation requirements, particularly in math and science, instituting statewide testing programs, offering more advanced placement courses, promoting the use of technology in the classroom, and instituting new teacher evaluation programs.

Unlike the piecemeal approach favored during the Reagan–Bush years, the systemic approach to educational reform was comprehensive and focuses on coordinating state policy with restructured governance. The objective of systemic reform was to create coherent educational policy (Fuhrman and Massell, 1992).

Systemic reform gave the Clinton educational agenda a set of organizing principles that was unique in American educational history. Supporters of systemic reform like to describe it as "top-down support for bottom-up reform." By creating a coherent plan for reform, the Clinton administration had been unusually successful in winning bipartisan support prior to the November 1994 elections. This support resulted in the passage of several bills including Direct Government Student Loans, National Service, the Safe Schools Act, the reauthorization of the Office of Educational Research and Improvement, the School-to-Work Opportunities Act of 1994, the Improving America's Schools Act of 1993, and the overall reauthorization of the Elementary and Secondary Education Act.

The key intellectual element of the administration's effort was Goals 2000. This law provides the framework of reform that shaped the educational ethos of the Clinton administration. Title I codified the original six National Education Goals concerning school readiness, school completion, student academic achievement, leadership in math and science, adult literacy, and safe and drug-free schools, and added two new goals related to parental participation and professional development. Title II established the National Education Goals Panel, which built public support for the goals, reports on the nation's progress on meeting the goals, and reviews the voluntary national content, student performance, and voluntary learning standards. Title III provided a state grant program to support, accelerate, and sustain state and local education improvement efforts. Title IV established a new program to create parent information and resource centers. Title V created a National Skills Board to serve as a catalyst in stimulating the development and adoption of a voluntary national system of occupational skills standards. Rather than seeing the federal government as an educational safety net, the authors of Goals 2000 saw the federal government, despite the rhetoric of volunteerism, as crafting, shaping, and, to some degree, controlling education throughout the 50 states. There can be little doubt that issues of school autonomy and authority have been dramatically altered by the passage of the bill.

Borman et al. (1996) provide a comprehensive sociological analysis of Goals 2000 in the following areas: (1) systemic reform, (2) national standards for content and performance, (3) opportunity-to-learn standards, (4) school-to-work programs, (5) school, parent, and community support, (6) professional development, (7) safe, disciplined, and drug-free schools, and (8) implications of the Goals 2000 legislation. They indicate that although there have been some significant gains in each of the areas, Goals 2000 is insufficient to provide significant systemic reform of U.S. schools. As sociologists of education, the authors conclude that sys-

temic reform requires significant reforms outside of the educational context, which federal legislation has not required.

Educational Reform in the 1980s and 1990s: Major Themes

Bacharach (1990) outlined the major themes of reform in the 1980s. These reforms are still useful in categorizing the 1990s as well.

Reconceptualizing the Role of the Teacher

The first wave of reform in the 1980s attempted to reduce uncertainty in the classroom and thus sought to increase bureaucratic controls on teacher behavior. The standardization of teaching through tightened bureaucratic control, it was thought, would result in increased student achievement. As it became increasingly clear that these efforts often were counterproductive, as they lead to the deskilling of the teaching profession and teachers mindlessly teaching to tests, the second wave of reforms sought to redefine the role of teachers as professionals. The Holmes (1986, 1990, 1995) and Carnegie (1986) Reports both proposed radical reforms in teacher education and the professional lives of teachers. Stressing career ladders, a national board for professional standards, and cooperation between universities and schools, among other things, these reports sought to professionalize rather than deskill teachers. Other reforms of this period, including teacher empowerment and school-based management, sought to make teachers essential actors in the reform process.

As the decade drew to a close, the conflict between two differing models of school administration, the bureaucratic and the professional (Bacharach, 1990:427) was still unresolved. The former dominated the first wave of reformers and the latter dominated the second wave. As the 1990s unfolded, this conflict remained as central to ongoing reform efforts. In the 1990s, they coexisted tenuously, with federal and state mandates requiring local compliance, especially with regard to student achievement and learning standards, but with local districts receiving autonomy with respect to how to meet these standards and to increase student achievement.

The 1980s and 1990s were decades of momentous debate about education and considerable debate about education and considerable efforts at school improvement. As Passow (1989:37) pointed out, the fact that educational issues became so fundamental to the nation, and that the emphasis in the second wave was on pedagogy, curriculum, teachers as professionals, school organization, and school improvement, was reason for some optimism. However, as many of the best criticisms of American education such as Boyer's (1983) on high schools, Sizer's (1985, 1990, 1996) on school structure and process, and McNeil's (1988) on the contradictions of reform, pointed out, educational improvement requires more than ideological rhetoric; it will require fundamental school restructuring. So far, despite some efforts such as Sizer's imaginative *Coalition of Essential Schools*, a nationally implemented school restructuring effort, and the action research of the *National Center for Restructuring Education, Schools and Teaching* (NCREST), the nation's schools appear resistant to structural change. This should not come as a surprise, as Sarason (1982) has suggested the culture of the school has always been difficult to alter. Perhaps, more importantly, school improvement cannot occur without societal reforms as well. Nonetheless, at the very least the 1980s and 1990s represented a period of national soul searching about complex educational problems.

Excellence and Equity

From the outset of the reforms of the 1980s the tensions between excellence and equity have been a central concern. Although, as Passow points out (1989:16), "excellence became a shibboleth of the reform movement," many writers were equally concerned with how the new tougher standards would affect students already disadvantaged because of unequal educational opportunities (Borman et al., 1996; Boyer, 1990; Apple, 1990; Cuban, 1990). Whereas the first wave of reforms was explicitly tied to the excellence side of the equation, the second wave of reforms was more often concerned with the need to balance the objectives of equity as well. Many of the reform proposals of this period, including magnet schools, the effective school movement, public school choice, charter schools, and school restructuring, all, at least in part, addressed the need to create schools that work for all students. Although many critics of proposals such as school choice asserted they would increase not decrease inequality, nonethe-

less during the second wave equity issues began to emerge as vitally important.

At the core of the discussion about these issues are fundamentally differing views of the goals of education. On the one hand, the conservatives, as exemplified by the Heritage Foundation (see Pincus, 1985), stressed the role of schools from a functionalist perspective. From this perspective, the role of the schools is to provide a sorting mechanism to select and educate the "best and the brightest" to fill the functionally essential positions in our society. To do this effectively requires that educational funding be geared to programs that ensure high standards. On the other hand, liberals and others to the political left stress the importance of serving the educational needs of all students, and have warned of the deleterious effects on the already disadvantaged of raising standards. Although there have been no easy answers to these complicated questions, it is safe to say that the reforms of the 1980s and 1990s, at least ideologically, were concerned with balancing excellence and equity. In practice, however, this balance has been far from a reality.

Redefining Good Education

As in previous periods of U.S. educational reform the 1980s and 1990s were concerned with the definition of what constitutes a good education. Just as in the progressive era of the first part of the twentieth century, educational reformers debated the question of whether all children should receive the same education, or should the schools provide different types of education for different students? Additionally, the question of what constitutes the type of education necessary for the increasing technological demands of the twenty-first century became a critical issue of the decade.

Interestingly, it was centrist conservatives such as E.D. Hirsch (1987), and Ravitch and Finn (1987) who seized the offensive in these debates. Arguing that the progressive reforms of the twentieth century had resulted in the decline of traditional knowledge (defined as Western), they called for a return to a liberal arts curriculum for all students. By inserting the concern for equity into the call for action, they seized the left's own platform; additionally, by criticizing progressive education, they sought to combine the dual demands for excellence and equity. Although the left would criticize this centrist conservative position for its ethnocentric Western bias (and call for a more multicultural curriculum), the centrist conservatives effectively dominated the curriculum discourse by taking what they saw as the "moral high ground."

Whereas these curriculum debates were essentially about what should be taught to students within the liberal arts tradition, another aspect of the debates concerned the role of education in preparing students for life and the world of work. Although a major theme of many of the reports concerned the relationship between education and economic competitiveness, it was not clear throughout the decades exactly what constituted the proper role of the school toward the end. Many business leaders, including David Kearns of Xerox Corporation, called for closer linkages between school and corporations. Others, such as Robert Reich (1990), pointed out that fundamental changes in the global economy would necessitate workers who can be creative, imaginative, and flexible and that schools would have to change accordingly. Still others, such as Michael Apple (1990), suggested that the new global economy would reduce the number of jobs requiring such intellectual and analytical dispositions, and that the contradiction of the reforms of the 1980s and 1990s was the increased emphasis on critical and analytical thinking in a world where the largest number of new jobs would not require them. Finally, others, such as Futrell (1990) and Ravitch (1985), returned to the notion that education had to prepare students for civic responsibility, and in Futrell's (1990:423) words "[an education] that prepares them not only for a life of work but for a life of worth."

Clearly, the debate about what constitutes a good education for the twenty-first century, although a central philosophical concern of the 1980s, is nowhere close to resolution. Perhaps, as Diane Ravitch (1985) pointed out, because Americans have had little consensus about the goals of education, they have been unable to create an educational system with a unified set of objectives.

Conclusion

Educational reform in the United States in the 1980s and 1990s has emphasized the excellence side of the excellence and equity equation. Although federal, state, and local reforms have resulted in some improvement in achievement, critics (Berliner and Biddle, 1996) have pointed out that the U.S. educational system was never as problematic as its conservative critics suggested. They suggest that the real problem in American education has been, and continues to be, that it works exceptionally well for children from higher socioeconomic backgrounds and exceptionally poorly for those from lower socioeconomic backgrounds. Despite the efforts of school choice and charter school programs to address these inequalities, particularly those in urban schools, the available evidence does not overwhelmingly support the claims of their advocates for a reduction in educational inequality. As we move into the next millennium, educational equity needs to be put back on the front burner of educational reform.

REFERENCES

Alexandar, Lamar. 1986. "Chairman's Summary." In *Time for Results: The Governor's Report on Education*. National Governor's Association Center for Policy Research and Analysis. Washington, DC: National Governor's Association.

Apple, Michael. 1990. "What Reform Talk Does: Creating New Inequalities." In Samuel Bacharach (ed.), *Educational Reform: Making Sense of It All*, pp. 155–164. Needham Heights, MA: Allyn & Bacon.

Bacharach, Samuel. 1990. *Educational Reform: Making Sense of It All*. Needham Heights, MA: Allyn & Bacon.

Berliner, David, and Bruce Biddle. 1996. *The Manufactured Crisis*. New York: Longman.

Bloom, Allan. 1987. *The Closing of the American Mind*. New York: Simon & Schuster.

Borman, Kathryn, Peter W. Cookson, Jr., Alan R. Sadovnik, and Joan Z. Spade. 1996. *Implementing Educational Reform: Sociological Perspectives on Educational Policy*. Westport, CT: Ablex.

Boyer, Ernest. 1983. *High School*. New York: Harper & Row.

———. 1990. "The New Agenda for the Nation's Schools." In Samuel Bacharach (ed.), *Education Reform: Making Sense of It All*, pp. 30–38. Needham Heights, MA: Allyn & Bacon.

Brookover, Wilbur, et al. 1979. *School Social Systems and Student Achievement: Schools Can Make a Difference*. New York: Praeger.

———. 1982. *Creating Effective Schools: An Inservice Program for Enhancing School Learning Climate and Achievement*. Holmes Beach, FL: Learning Publications.

Bryk, Anthony et al. 1993. *A View from the Elementary Schools: The State of Reform in Chicago*. Chicago: Consortium for Chicago School Research.

Carnegie Task Force on Teaching as a Profession. 1986. *A Nation Prepared: Teachers for the 21st Century*. Washington, DC: Carnegie Forum on Education and the Economy.

Charner, Ivan. 1996. "School-to-Work Opportunities: Prospects and Challenges." In Kathryn Borman, Peter W.

Cookson, Jr., Alan R. Sadovnik, and Joan Z. Spade (eds.), *Implementing Educational Reform: Sociological Perspectives on Educational Policy*, pp. 139–170. Westport, CT: Ablex.

Chubb, John E., and Terry M. Moe. 1990. *Politics, Markets, and America's Schools*. Washington, DC: Brookings Institution.

Coleman, James, Thomas Hoffer, and Sally Kilgore. 1982. *High School Achievement*. New York: Basic Books.

Cookson, Peter W., Jr. 1991. "Politics, Markets, and America's Schools: A Review." *Teacher College Record* 93:156–160.

———. 1993. *School Choice: The Struggle for the Soul of American Education*. New Haven, CT: Yale University Press.

Cuban, Larry. 1984. *How Teachers Taught: Constancy and Change in American Classrooms, 1890–1980*. New York: Longman.

———. 1990. "Cycles of History: Why Do Some Reforms Persist." In Samuel Bacharach (ed.), *Education Reform: Making Sense of It All,* pp. 135–140. Needham Heights, MA: Allyn & Bacon.

Dougherty, Kevin. 1990. "Quality, Equality, and Politics: The Political Sources of the Current School Reform Wave." Paper presented at the Annual Meeting of the American Sociological Association.

Edmonds, Ronald. 1979. "Effective Schools for the Urban Poor." *Educational Leadership* 37(1):5–24.

Education Week. 1990. "Text of Statement of Goals Adopted by the Governors." *Education Week* 9:16–17.

Fuhrman, S. H., Massell, D., and Associates. 1992. *Issues and Strategies in Systemic Reform*. New Brunswick, NJ: Consortium for Policy Research in Education.

Futrell, Mary Hatwood. 1990. "Redefining National Security: New Directions for Education Reform." In Samuel Bacharach (ed.), *Education Reform: Making Sense of It All*, pp. 259–268. Needham Heights, MA: Allyn & Bacon.

Gartner, Alan, and Dorothy Kerzner Lipsky. 1987. "Beyond Special Education: Toward a Quality System for All Students." *Harvard Educational Review* 57:367–395.

Goodlad, John. 1990. *Teachers for Our Nation's Schools*. San Francisco: Jossey-Bass.

Greene, Jay, and Paul Peterson. 1996. Methodological Issues in Evaluation Research: The Milwaukee School Choice Program." Occasional Paper 96–4. Cambridge, MA: Harvard University Program in Educational Policy and Governance.

Hirsch, E. D. 1987. *Cultural Literacy*. Boston: Houghton Mifflin.

Holmes Group. 1986. *Tomorrow's Teachers*. East Lansing, MI: Holmes Group.

———. 1990. *Tomorrow's Teachers*. East Lansing, MI: Holmes Group.

———. 1995. *Tomorrow's Schools of Education*. East Lansing, MI: Holmes Group.

Honig, Bill. 1990. "The Key to Reform: Sustaining and Expanding Upon Initial Success." In Samuel Bacharach (ed.), *Education Reform: Making Sense of It All*, pp. 52–56. Needham Heights, MA: Allyn and Bacon.

Labaree, David F. 1992a. "Doing Good, Doing Science: The Holmes Group Reports and the Rhetorics of Educational Reform." *Teachers College Record* 93(4):628–640.

———. 1992b. "Power, Knowledge, and the Rationalization of Teaching: A Genealogy of the Movement to Professionalize Teaching." *Harvard Educational Review* 62(2):123–155.

———. 1995. "A Disabling Vision: Rhetoric and Reality in *Tomorrow's Schools of Education*." *Teachers College Record* 97(2):166–205.

Laird, Susan. 1989. "Reforming 'Women's True Profession': A Case for 'Feminist Pedagogy' in Teacher Education?" *Harvard Educational Review* 58(4):449–463.

McNeil, Linda M. 1988. *Contradictions of Control: School Structure and School Knowledge*. New York: Routledge, Chapman and Hall.

Mortimer, Jeylan T. 1996. "A Sociological Perspective on School-to-Work Opportunities: Response and Rejoinder." In Kathryn Borman, Peter W. Cookson, Jr., Alan R. Sadovnik, and Joan Z. Spade (eds.), *Implementing Educational Reform: Sociological Perspectives on Educational Policy*, pp. 171–184. Westport, CT: Ablex.

National Commission on Excellence in Education. 1983. *A Nation at Risk*. Washington, DC: U.S. Government Printing Office.

National Commission on Teaching and America's Future. 1996. *What Matters Most: Teaching for America's Future*. New York: author.

Passow, A. Harry. 1989. "Present and Future Directions in School Reform." In Thomas Sergiovanni and John Moore (eds.), *Schooling for Tomorrow*, pp. 13–39. Needham Heights, MA: Allyn & Bacon.

Paulu, Nancy. 1989. "Improving Schools and Empowering Parents: Choice in American Education." Washington, DC: U.S. Government Printing Office.

Pincus, Fred L. 1985. "From Equity to Excellence: The Rebirth of Educational Conservatism." In Beatrice Gross and Ronald Gross (eds.), *The Great School Debate*, pp. 329–344. New York: Simon & Schuster.

Powell, Arthur, David Cohen, and Elizabeth Ferrar. 1985. *The Shopping Mall High School*. Boston: Houghton Mifflin.

Powers, Jeanne M., and Peter W. Cookson, Jr. 1999. "School Choice as a Political Movement." *Educational Policy* 13(1,2):104–122.

Ravitch, Diane. 1985. *The Schools We Deserve*. New York: Basic Books.

Ravitch, Diane, and Chester E. Finn. 1987. *What Do Our Seventeen Year Olds Know?* New York: Basic Books.

Reich, Robert B. 1990. "Education and the Next Economy." In Samuel Bacharach (ed.), *Education Reform: Making Sense of It All*, pp. 194–212. Needham Heights, MA: Allyn & Bacon.

———. 1991. "Succession of the Successful." *The New York Times Magazine*, (January 20):42–45.

Rouse, Cecilia. 1998. "Private Vouchers and Student Achievement: An Evaluation of the Milwaukee Parental Choice Program." *Quarterly Journal of Economics* 113(2): 553–602.

Sarason, Seymour B. 1982. *The Culture of the School and the Problem of Change*. Boston: Allyn & Bacon.

Sizer, Theodore R. 1985. *Horace's Compromise*. Boston: Houghton Mifflin.

———. 1992. *Horace's School*. Boston: Houghton Mifflin.

———. 1996. *Horace's Hope*. Boston: Houghton Mifflin.

Skinner, B. F. 1971. *Beyond Freedom and Dignity*. New York: Bantam.

Talbert, Joan. 1996. "Primacy and Promise of Professional Development in the Nation's Education Reform Agenda: Sociological Views." K. Borman, et al. (1996), pp. 283–311.

Teacher Education Project. 1986. "A Compilation of the Major Recommendations of Teacher Education."

Time Magazine. 1991. "Do Poor Kids Deserve Poor Schools." *Time Magazine* (October 14):60–61.

U.S. Government. 1991. *America 2000*. Washington, DC: The White House.

Wells, Amy, L. Artiles, S. Carnochan, C. Cooper, C. Grutzik, J. Holme, A. Lopez, J. Scott, J. Slayton, and A. Vasuveda. 1998. *Beyond the Rhetoric of Charter School Reform: A Study of Ten California Districts*. Los Angeles, CA: UCLA.

Witte, John. 1996. "Who Benefits from the Milwaukee Choice Program." In B. Fuller, R. F. Elmore, and G. Orfield (eds.), *Who Chooses? Who Loses? Culture Institutions and the Unequal Effects of School Choice,* pp. 118–137. New York: Teachers College Press.

Witte, John, C. A. Thorn, K. M. Pritchard, and M. Claiborn. 1994. *Fourth-Year Report: Milwaukee Parental Choice Program*. Department of Political Science and the Robert LaFollette Institute of Public Affairs, University of Wisconsin—Madison.

Witte, John, T. D. Sterr, and C. A. Thorn. 1995. *Fifth-Year Report: Milwaukee Parental Choice Program*. Department of Political Science and the Robert LaFollette Institute of Public Affairs, University of Wisconsin—Madison.

ELITES AND EDUCATIONAL REFORM

Peter W. Cookson, Jr.
Teachers College, Columbia University

Brenda Donly
Georgetown University

Is There an American Elite?

Historically, most Americans have viewed the class system as relatively flat. It is generally believed that there is considerable occupational mobility and, through hard work, individuals can achieve economic security and social status. Great wealth and great poverty are viewed, respectively, with admiration and contempt. In this view, power is distributed among competing groups, creating a pluralistic power structure that is kept relatively democratic by a system of checks and balances. This picture of American society is quite inaccurate. The class system is well entrenched and few individuals are upwardly mobile. There is concentrated power at the apex of the economic pyramid; the top 10% of American households own 98% of the tax-exempt state and local bonds, 94% of business assets, and 95% of the value of all trusts. The richest 1% own 60% of all corporate stock and 60% of all business assets. Ninety percent of American families have little or no net assets (Parenti, 1995:9). The gap between the rich and the poor in the United States is the largest of any industrialized country.

This concentration of wealth is the foundation of a highly stratified society. The maintenance of concentrated wealth, especially in the face of the democratic norm of equality, requires the active participation of a power elite that controls and coordinates the major centers of institutional power. Although scholars vary in their assessments of who comprises the power elite (Mills, 1959; Domhoff, 1967; Useem, 1984), there is general agreement that at the apex of the power structure, highly placed business executives, politicians, and other leaders of the "Establishment" share information, often coordinate their activities, and direct the public

agenda. They are successful in this agenda-setting behavior because, through the media, publishing, education, and other cultural institutions, they are able to shape public perception and construct consensus around those issues of most interest to them.

This review examines the impact of elites on educational policymaking. To what degree do elites shape the public debate concerning educational reform? How are the interests of these elites expressed? What are the consequences of elites managing the reform process? Scholars have examined the influence of elite decision making at the local, state, national, and international levels. There can be little doubt that local and state elites have a significant impact on educational policy. Local elites often dominate school boards; in large cities, their influence can be felt through the control of public interest lobbying groups. State elites can influence educational policy through the media, the courts, and the legislature. In some ways, it is at the state level that economic and political elites may have a significant impact because education is the responsibility of state governments, and not the federal government. In the past 20 years, however, the federal government and other national organizations have begun to play an increasingly important role in educational policymaking. Kaestle and Smith (1982) refer to this group as "cosmopolitan centralists." In this review the power of these cosmopolitan centralists will be assessed in terms of their ability to shape the national debate on educational reform. It is argued that this influence can be direct or indirect. An example of direct effect is the ability of the elites to define educational problems, to set the national agenda for reform, and to keep alternative reforms from attracting attention or a following. An example of an indirect effect is the ability of elites to remove their children from public schools and public colleges and to maintain a separate exclusive system of private schools and colleges. Roughly 12% of American children attend private schools. Only 1–2% attend schools that are supported by the power elite. These private schools play a critical role in the maintenance of the class structure (Cookson and Persell, 1985).

Theories of Elite Influence

Most mainstream educational researchers ignore the effects of class on the structure and processes of American education; these researchers implicitly or explicitly argue that improving education will result in greater equity. From the beginning of the Industrial Revolution, however, critical thinkers and conflict theorists have argued that education, despite its overt function of providing equal opportunity, covertly reproduces society and the inequalities upon which society is built. Recent theorists, such as Pierre Bourdieu and Jean-Claude Passeron (1977) in France and Henry Giroux (1988) in the United States, have explored how the educational system reproduces society by rewarding the cultural values and knowledge of the dominant classes and by creating school systems that effectively track students according to their class backgrounds.

There are three related but distinctive theories as to how schools reproduce society. Marxists and neo-Marxists, such as the political economists Samuel Bowles and Herbert Gintis (1976), argue that there is a correspondence between the school system and the class system. Students from the economically dominant classes receive educations that promote the active use of the mind and develop mentalities compatible with understanding larger political, economic, and cultural arrangements. Children from the subordinate classes, on the other hand, receive educations where abstract thinking is not rewarded and where there is little opportunity for students to think critically about the world in which they live. Sociologists such as Basil Bernstein (1977) and Jay Macloud (1987) have described and analyzed how differences in educational opportunities result in working-class children having few opportunities to express themselves in linguistic codes suitable to elaborated and sophisticated thought.

Sociologist Max Weber, who was active in the late nineteenth and early twentieth century, was influenced by Marx but believed that economic determinism could not entirely explain how groups and individuals achieved their social statuses. Groups, especially elite groups, distinguish themselves from others through a variety of noneconomic credentials, including family origin, military prowess, and cultural achievement. This Weberian perspective has been most actively developed by the sociologist Randall Collins (1975), who considers education to be little more than a credentializing process; the content of education pales in significance compared to the social power a school's degree can confer on its graduates. Thus, elites credentialize themselves as intellectually superior by graduating from and ensuring that their children graduate from high schools, colleges, and universities that are publicly recognized as producing "the best and the brightest." Sociologist John Meyer (1977) calls a school's power to symbolically socially define its graduates its "charter."

A third explanation of elite influence emphasizes the institutional arrangements of an advanced industrial technological society. This explanation, promoted by economists such as John Kenneth Galbraith and the former Secretary of Labor Robert Reich, argues that the basis of power is knowledge. Knowledge is the currency of the expert society. They believe that a technical and intellectual elite is increasingly directing and managing the American economy and society and that these elite knowledge managers are replacing those leaders whose power base rests on class and status. This new cognitive elite gains its authority and power from its ability to generate new ideas and create the new knowledge required in a rapidly changing economy.

Each of these theories shares the concept of power. Dennis Wrong (1995) has distinguished the "power to" from the "power over"; that is, power can be used to create constructive social action or power can be used to control other human beings for little purpose other than the satisfactions related to privilege. Power is the dynamic energy that drives change. A comprehensive theory of the power base of elites would undoubtedly weave together class, status, and expertise. In the United States, the power elite uses all three of these social "platforms" to maintain its dominant role, particularly in the economy and politics, but also in culture and education. The inner circle draws its membership primarily from those that share the same class background, but is also receptive to new members who may have become wealthy through the development of new products and ideas.

As Raymond Callahan (1962) and others have demonstrated, American education has always closely
aligned itself with the interests of the business community. Business elites have sought to influence public
education from its inception. In general, however, public education for the first three-quarters of the twentieth century was not an object of continuous interest to
national economic and political elites. Public education, like other public institutions, was seen as providing limited opportunities for the subordinate classes,
while at the same time instilling in the children of the
working and middle classes a sense of patriotism and a
reverence for the institutions of government. Beginning in the mid-1970s, however, business elites and
the policy foundations, and think tanks they sponsor,
began to actively criticize the performance of public
education. Elite leaders in the business community and
in politics became extremely active in setting the
agenda for the reform of public education.

The Elites Take Charge of Reform

If President Dwight Eisenhower in the 1950s had suggested that public schools be deregulated and that the
government should support private education, it is
probably safe to say that most Americans would have
been shocked, even scandalized. But this is the position
that another Republican President, George Bush, took
in 1992 when he advocated a voucher program that
would use public funds to support private schools.
What had happened in the years between Eisenhower
and Bush to make the unthinkable possible, even desirable in the eyes of many policymakers and an increasing number of Americans? There is considerable
evidence that the actual quality of American public
education, with the exception of education in the inner-
cities, had actually improved in the years separating
Eisenhower and Bush (Berliner and Biddle, 1995). Yet,
most Americans are convinced that public education,
in general, is a failure. Interestingly, public opinion
polls repeatedly demonstrate that the majority of
Americans are satisfied with their childrens' public
schools, but consider public schools, in general, to be
of poor quality. How do people come to this contradictory belief?

When Ronald Reagan was campaigning for the pres-
idency in 1980, he suggested that if he were elected,
he would close the Department of Education, which
had been established by President Jimmy Carter in the
late 1970s. For Ronald Reagan and other conservatives,
the expanding role of the federal government in education was a dangerous intrusion on local control.
When he was elected President, however, Reagan did
not abolish the Department of Education, but appointed a series of Secretaries of Education who attacked public education as inefficient and as jeopard-
izing the economic well being of the country. Most
prominent among these Secretaries was William Bennett, who portrayed public schools as valueless institutions responsible for the mediocrity in student
achievement.

This assault on public education was given great
support by the publication of the National Commission
on Excellence's *A Nation at Risk* (1983). That report
claimed that the quality of public education was so low
that foreign competitors, particularly the Japanese,
were about to overtake the United States economically.
The Report stated, "Our concern, however, goes well
beyond matters such as industry and commerce. It also
includes the intellectual, moral, and spiritual strengths
of our people which knit together the very fabric of our
society" (1983:1). This alarm prompted other elite
groups to issue other alarming reports. These included
the Business-Higher Education Forum (1983), the Carnegie Task Force on Teaching as a Profession (1986),
the Twentieth Century Fund (1983), the College Board
(1983), and the National Governor's Association
(1986). Sociologist Kevin Dougherty (1992) suggests
that the reforms in the 1980s were dominated by what
he terms "centrist conservatism." In contrast to the new
right's call for a complete reversal of the liberal reforms
of the 1960s and 1970s, and the left's belief that educational problems reflect the inherent dilemmas of
capitalism, centrist conservatives believe that "education is crucial to the basic interests of society, whether
economic competitiveness, military preparedness, or
cultural transmission" (1992 1:3).

This centrist conservatism was echoed by other significant members of the educational power elite, including representatives of conservative foundations and
think tanks, such as the Heritage Foundation in Washington, D.C. and the Manhattan Institute in New York
City and from representatives from the business community such as David Kearns, CEO of IBM, who later
became an Assistant Secretary of Education in the De-

partment of Education. Joining this centrist conservative coalition was Albert Shanker of the American Federation of Teachers who used the power of the AFT to argue that the American educational system ought to look a lot like the educational systems in continental Europe. An emerging spokesperson for this position was Chester Finn of Vanderbilt University and the Hudson Institute (a conservative think tank), who became George Bush's closest educational advisor.

The criticisms leveled against public education were reinforced by an academic elite that published a series of reports and books that argued that private education was academically superior and better managed than public education. Foremost among these elite researchers was James Coleman and his associates at the University of Chicago. Based on the "High School and Beyond" data set, Coleman et al. (1982) argued that private school students, even when accounting for their family backgrounds, were far better prepared than public school students. Coleman's work was widely cited by other elites as evidence that competition produced better schools than state-managed systems. Coleman's work was extended by political scientists John Chubb and Terry Moe in their book *Politics, Markets, and America's Schools* (1990). Published by the Brookings Institution and supported in part by two conservative foundations (The Lynde and Harry Bradley Foundation and the John M. Olin Foundation), Chubb and Moe's work argued for the deregulation of public education. Their work was widely cited and supported by a variety of private school advocates who believe that school choice and the privatization of public education will solve the perceived failures of public schools.

As an example of how educational elites have been influential in setting the reform agenda during the 1980s and 1990s, one can point to the educational reform career of the former governor of Tennessee, Lamar Alexander. As governor he was instrumental in publishing the report, *Time for Results: the Governor's 1991 Report on Education*. This report called for school choice and greater accountability. Governor Alexander became Secretary of Education under George Bush after William Bennett resigned. Alexander is a colleague of Chris Whittle who is the chairman and founder of Whittle Communications. This media company developed Channel 1, which puts televisions in classrooms on the condition that advertisements can be run in each program. Alexander was on the Whittle advisory board

that guided Channel 1 and worked for Whittle after leaving the governorship of Tennessee. His compensation was $125,000 and the opportunity to buy shares in Whittle Communications. After becoming Secretary of Education, Alexander conferred with Whittle and sold his house in Knoxville, Tennessee for a profit to a top executive of Whittle Communications. This executive received a mortgage of over $750,000 from the First Tennessee Bank where Alexander was on the board of the holding company (Berliner and Biddle, 1995). These details are significant because they underline the close relationship that elite members maintain with each other and emphasize that in the world of educational policymaking, ideas and personal relationships become entangled and have repercussions that influence public policy. Elites form networks that include some players who are closely linked to each other and some that are weakly linked to each other. At the center of a network, the linkages are strongest and most powerful. In educational policymaking there are certain individuals and groups that form the policy elite. Most of these elite members come from the important committees of the United States Congress, business, major think tanks and foundations, media, prestigious universities, and include a small number of individuals who have achieved national recognition as educational reformers. Very often these groups and individuals meet for seminars, colloquia, and informal discussions. These meetings are generally funded by foundations and as a consequence of these meetings, certain policies are advanced and sometimes endorsed. When the policy elite speaks, the media listens and thus the influence of the elite is magnified and shapes public perception. An example of how an issue can become part of the public policy agenda through the efforts of a policy elite is school choice.

Although the choice movement has some grassroots support, its general acceptance by the public is primarily the result of the efforts of key politicians and foundations in promoting choice. Choice has been placed on the legislative calendar by governors and other legislators in many states and advocates of choice have conducted a major publicity campaign announcing the academic and social virtues of school choice. This political movement has been documented by Henig (1994) and Cookson (1994). Both of these authors conclude that the school choice movement is a coalition of religious fundamentalists, market advocates, libertarians, and the Roman Catholic church. In the early 1990s these groups were successful in establishing a center for school choice within the U.S. Department of Education. Regional meetings were conducted throughout the country on choice and "exemplary" choice districts were touted as the wave of the future. At the same time, there was virtually no evidence that school choice was related to greater student achievement (Henig, 1994; Cookson, 1994). Thus, in this case, the policy elite was successful in promoting a reform policy as a solution to the country's educational problems without any substantial investigation concerning the claims' basis in fact.

The primary agenda of this coalition has been to promote private school choice through the use of vouchers. As mentioned earlier, President Bush advocated a national system of vouchers and since that time numerous conservative politicians, businessmen, and their allies have argued for the deregulation of public education. These include Bret Schundler, Mayor of Jersey City, New Jersey and the Speaker of the House, Newt Gingrich. The issue of how to finance private education, including religious education, through the use of public funds is likely to continue for the foreseeable future. To this extent the centrist conservative educational reform elite has been extremely successful in setting the reform agenda and possibly restructuring public education according to market principles; over 30 educational management organizations (EMOs) are now publicly traded on the New York Stock Exchange.

Power and Educational Policymaking

It appears that the governance of American education has increasingly moved from local autonomy to centralized control. Ironically, the elites who call for school choice do so as leaders of a national movement, located primarily in the nation's capital. What the new educational policymaking elite has accomplished is attributable to the power that it has brought to bear on public perception and on the public reform agenda. Very often, educators and sociologists view education from a technical point of view, acting and thinking as though education was not highly politicized or susceptible to control by those who are ideologically driven. This chapter draws attention to the role that power plays in

shaping educational reform and how power is generally concentrated in the hands of a business and political elite whose members are primarily drawn from the upper and upper-middle classes. This power elite uses techniques of persuasion to influence public opinion and the media. To that degree, they are able to "distort" educational reform so that it complements their personal and institutional interests. This raises fundamental questions about the role of education in promoting democracy and educating children to be critical and independent thinkers. There is much research that needs to be done concerning the role of elites in educational reform if we are to get a comprehensive picture of how school change is socially managed and politically orchestrated.

REFERENCES

Berliner, David C., and Bruce J. Biddle. 1995. *The Manufactured Crisis: Myths, Fraud and Attack on America's Public Schools*. Reading, MA: Addison-Wesley.

Bernstein, Basil. 1977. *Class, Codes and Control, Vol. 3, Towards a Theory of Educational Transmissions*, rev. ed. London: Routledge and Kegan Paul.

Bourdieu, Pierre, and Jean-Claude Passeron. 1977. *Reproduction: In Education, Society and Culture*. Beverly Hills, CA: Sage.

Bowles, Samuel, and Herbert Gintis. 1976. *Schooling in Capitalist America*. New York: Basic Books.

Business/Higher Education Forum. 1983. *America's Competitive Challenge*. Washington, DC: American Council on Education.

Callahan, Raymond E. 1962. *Education and the Cult of Efficiency*. Chicago: The University of Chicago Press.

Carnegie Task Force on Teaching as a Profession. 1986. *A Nation Prepared: Teachers for the 21st Century*. Washington, DC: Carnegie Forum on Education and the Economy.

Chubb, John E., and Terry M. Moe. 1990. *Politics, Markets and America's Schools*. Washington, DC: The Brookings Institution.

Coleman, James, Thomas Hoffer, and Sally Kilgore. 1982. *High School Achievement: Public, Catholic and Private Schools Compared*. New York: Basic Books.

Collins, Randell. 1975. *Conflict Sociology: Toward an Explanatory Science*. New York: Academic Press.

College Board. 1983. *Academic Preparation for College*. New York: College Board.

Cookson, Peter W., Jr. 1994. *School Choice: The Struggle for the Soul of American Education*. New Haven, CT: Yale University Press.

Cookson, Peter W., Jr., and Caroline Hodges Persell. 1985. *Preparing for Power: America's Elite Boarding Schools*. New York: Basic Books.

Dougherty, Kevin J. 1992. *Schools to the Rescue: The Politics of the Educational Excellence Movement.* (Report to the Spencer Foundation.) New York: Manhattan College.

Dumhoff, G. William. 1967. *Who Rules America?* Englewood Cliffs, NJ: Prentice-Hall.

Giroux, Henry A. 1988. *Teachers as Intellectuals.* Granby, MA: Bergin and Garvey.

Henig, Jeffrey R. 1994. *Rethinking School Choice: Limits of the Market Metaphor.* Princeton, NJ: Princeton University Press.

Kaestle, Carl F., and Marshall S. Smith. 1982. "The Federal Role in Elementary and Secondary Education, 1940–1980." *Harvard Educational Review* 52(4):384–408.

Macleod, Jay. 1987. *Ain't No Making It: Leveled Aspirations in a Low-Income Neighborhood.* Boulder, CO: Westview Press.

Meyer, John. 1977. "Education as an Institution." *American Journal of Sociology* 83(July):55–77.

Mills, D. Wright. 1959. *The Power Elite.* London: Oxford University Press.

National Governor's Association. 1986. *A Time for Results.* Washington, DC: National Governor's Association.

Parenti, Michael. 1995. *Democracy for the Few.* New York: St. Martin's Press.

Twentieth Century Fund, Task Force on Elementary and Secondary Education Policy. 1983. *Making the Grade.* New York: Twentieth Century Fund.

Useem, Michael. 1984. *The Inner Circle: Large Corporations and the Rise of Business Political Activity in the U.S. and U.K.* New York: Oxford University Press.

Wrong, Dennis. 1995. *Power: Its Forms, Bases and Uses.* New Brunswick, NJ: Transaction.

EQUALITY IN EDUCATION

Maureen T. Hallinan
University of Notre Dame

The term "equality" has several referents in education. Researchers and educators consider equality with respect to school finances, expenditures, resources, access to the curriculum, distribution of students for instruction, academic and social mobility, classroom processes, and educational policies. Each of these issues is one dimension of the broader relationship between schooling and social inequality. Jencks (1972) argues that the most important research by sociologists of education in the past 50 years has examined how schools maintain or diminish social inequality.

Concern about equality in education is related to the widespread belief that equity should govern access to society's resources. A large majority of Americans are committed to establishing a meritocratic society. To ensure a meritocracy, all persons must have equal opportunities to compete for those resources that produce success. In particular, they must have equal access to processes that provide educational and occupational mobility. Social background and other ascribed characteristics are not factors in the attainment process in a true meritocracy; achieved characteristics, and in particular cognitive ability, determine educational outcomes. One reason several highly regarded social scientists criticize *The Bell Curve* (Hernstein and Murray, 1994) so severely is that the study seemingly justifies limiting the access of blacks to societal resources based on their alleged inferior cognitive abilities. Not only have scientists raised serious questions about the quality of the empirical research reported in the book, they strongly objected to the premise that blacks or any demographic group should be denied equal access to societal resources.

A large body of research examines the role of the school in influencing social inequality. Status attainment research examines in depth the relationship between background characteristics and social stratification and mobility. A major component of this research is an investigation of how schools modify the effects of socioeconomic status on academic achievement and educational attainment. An important review of the earlier studies in this tradition is found in Campbell (1983). Status attainment research demonstrates that schools can indeed mitigate the negative effects of social origins on status attainment by increasing educational and occupational aspirations, academic achievement, and income.

Critics of status attainment research question the ability of schools to facilitate the attainment of social equality. The most radical critics argue that schools ensure the continuation of the social stratification found in American society through the particular educational processes, practices, and policies that characterize contemporary schools (see Bowles and Gintes, 1976; Katz, 1971; Illich, 1983). This viewpoint is reflected in recent studies of the hidden curriculum, tracking, the informal organization of the school, and the effects of gender and race on classroom processes.

A second tradition in studies of educational inequality was initiated by the landmark Coleman Report (1966) and has grown through subsequent reanalyses, replications, critiques, and extensions of this work. The Coleman Report examines school effects on academic achievement, with the aim of determining how segregated schools affect the educational opportunities of students. Although the results show that school characteristics explain less of the variance in student achievement than does family background, they also demonstrate that black students attain higher achievement in majority white schools than in segregated black schools. This finding led to the widely practiced policy of busing students to attain racially integrated schools. This policy later fell into disrepute because it resulted in white flight from integrated urban schools and neighborhoods to private schools and segregated suburbs.

Both the status attainment research and the school effects studies led to a clearer conceptualization of the notion of equality of educational opportunity. As outlined in Coleman (1990), educational equality has five distinctive meanings that are reflected in the research. Initially, educational inequality referred to unequal inputs to schools, as measured by such school characteristics as per-pupil expenditures, teacher–student ratios, number of library books, laboratory facilities, and teacher qualifications.

A second meaning of educational inequality pertains to school outcomes, and in particular, to academic achievement. Schools are viewed as providing unequal opportunities to students when pupils with the same abilities and family resources attain different achievement levels. If the students attend different schools, the unequal outcomes may be due to between-school differences in resources or climate. If the students attend the same school, it may be attributed to unequal access to resources within the school. A third interpretation of educational inequality appears when schools are expected to play a compensatory role in producing equal educational outcomes. Schools are expected to raise the academic achievement of disadvantaged students to the same level as that of their more advantaged peers.

A fourth way of viewing equality of educational opportunity emerged after *Brown v. Board of Education* was argued before the Supreme Court in 1954. Prior to this case, segregated schools were believed to be capable of providing the same quality of education as desegregated schools. After the ruling, segregated schools were seen as disadvantaging black students. Equality of opportunity came to mean access to desegregated schools for all students.

A fifth conceptualization of equal educational opportunity is related to school climate. Research demonstrates that a school with a strong academic climate has a positive effect on student aspirations and achievement. Climate typically is measured by the socioeconomic status of the student body, by mean achievement, by teacher characteristics and expectations, and by student culture.

Interestingly, the conceptualization of equality of educational opportunity occurred only after a significant number of empirical research studies on educational equity had accumulated. The progression from empirical research to theory is not unusual in a discipline that has the potential for numerous and immediate applications. Often an educational problem or crisis leads researchers to examine an issue empirically and then to develop related concepts and theoretical explanations when they have studied the data. What is unusual in the case of the concept of educational equality is the systematic nature of the empirical work that accumulated in the absence of a guiding theoretical framework. Also somewhat unique is the power of the theoretical ideas that emerged from the empirical research and the ease with which these ideas were linked to central concepts and theories in sociology. A likely reason for this success is the high quality of the empirical research on school equity issues, which was based on large, cross-sectional and longitudinal surveys and which employed rigorous statistical models. These early studies dominated the field of sociology of education for years and produced a unifying conceptual framework that had considerable heuristic value in the subsequent study of equality of educational opportunity.

The remainder of this chapter will focus on two aspects of equality of educational opportunity that relate to current school policy and practice: equality of access to the curriculum, and the effects of background characteristics on classroom processes. These two aspects of schooling are amenable to change by school administrators and teachers, and thus are among the topics currently receiving special attention by advocates of school reform.

Inequality and Access to the Curriculum

In examining equality of educational opportunity, a natural focus is the formal organization of the school. A major dimension of school organization is the arrangement of students for instruction. Students typically are divided into grades and assigned to classes within grades. The bases for the assignments are pupils' ascribed and achieved characteristics. Hence, students may be assigned to groups by age, language proficiency, gender, and educational and vocational aspirations. Other than age, the most common basis for grouping students is academic ability. Tracks and within-class ability groups are commonplace in American schools. The issue of concern here is how ability grouping affects students' access to the curriculum. The reason for the concern is the belief that unequal access produces differences in future educational opportunities, and in occupational prestige, income, and social mobility. Consequently, researchers ask whether tracking is a mechanism through which unequal educational opportunities are channeled to students.

Advocates of tracking claim that the practice of assigning students to ability groups facilitates the instructional process by permitting teachers to gear their lessons to the ability level of the students. Content and pace of instruction can be adapted to meet the learning needs of the pupils. Critics of tracking argue that tracking creates unequal opportunities for students to learn. They assert that the quantity and quality of instruction are superior in the higher tracks and that the climate is more conducive to learning.

A large, systematic body of empirical research has emerged on the determinants of track assignment and on the effects of tracking on academic achievement. Research on track assignment leads to several conclusions. First, in practice, track assignment is determined both by ability and by nonacademic factors. Ability is measured by standardized test scores, grades, teachers' and counselors' recommendations, and previous course history. Nonacademic factors include scheduling considerations, student choice, work demands, class size restrictions, teacher availability and resources, and extracurricular participation. Hence ability groups tend to be less homogeneous than if ability were the only basis for assignment.

Empirical studies also demonstrate that the criteria on which track assignments are based vary across schools, making a high track assignment more likely in one school than another. Moreover, minority and low-income students are disproportionately assigned to lower tracks, due primarily to their lower achievement scores. However, even when achievement is controlled, race and gender have small effects on the track level to which a student is assigned. Finally, student social status is related to track level; high-track students have higher social status than those assigned to lower tracks.

Research on the effects of track level on academic achievement reveals the following relationships. First, students in higher tracks learn more and at a faster pace than those in lower tracks. Second, the gap between the achievement of high- and low-track students increases over high school. Third, track level has an independent effect on achievement, controlling for ability and prior achievement. Fourth, tracking has no main effect on achievement; that is, the mean achievement of students in tracked and untracked schools is the same, other factors being controlled. Finally, tracking has no effect on students in the middle tracks, only on those in the high and low tracks.

These results point to significant inequities in the practice of tracking as it currently exists in American schools. Tracking favors higher ability students, providing them with greater opportunities to learn through access to a superior curriculum. Tracking disadvantages low achieving students by significantly limiting their opportunities to learn. Moreover, since low ability is related to demographic characteristics, particularly race or ethnicity and social class, tracking has a segregative effect, resulting in proportionately more middle- and upper-income white students in the high tracks and more lower income and nonwhite students in the low tracks. Finally, tracking disadvantages low-track students socially, by creating labels that are associated with lower social status.

Given the inequities related to tracking, many educators advocate detracking schools by assigning students to instructional groups that are heterogeneous with respect to ability. However, detracked schools have not been shown to be more effective in promoting student learning than tracked schools. Moreover, many teachers favor tracking because they believe it facilitates the instructional process. Consequently, researchers recently have been recommending that tracking be modified, rather than abandoned, in order to reduce or remove its inequitable features while retaining its pedagogical benefits.

Four negative consequences of tracking can be reduced by modifying educational policy and practice. First, the tendency of tracking to segregate students by race and, in some courses, by gender, can be countered by ensuring that students are integrated in all their untracked courses, and in every other event in their school day. Moreover, the achievements of minority students and girls can be given public recognition to help dispel the perceived relationship between race and gender and ability.

Second, track assignments can be made flexible so

that students who are capable of learning faster than their peers in an assigned track can move to a higher track to increase their learning opportunities. Similarly, students who are assigned to a track that is too challenging can be reassigned to a lower track to avoid discouragement and failure. Track flexibility increases the potential for tracking to provide appropriate opportunities for all students to learn according to their capability.

Third, school policy should ensure that the pedagogical inadequacies found in lower tracks are removed. Considerable attention must be paid to the curriculum and instruction provided to students in the low tracks and the qualifications and expertise of teachers assigned to instruct low-ability students. Further, school administrators must confront negative assumptions about the learning potential of low-ability students and draw on current research on learning styles and multiple modes of intelligence to increase teachers' expectations for low-achieving students.

Finally, although students typically benefit from attending a school with a strong academic climate, low-ability students must be protected from influences that would negatively affect their self-image. The academic reward system can be designed to reward effort and improvement as well as level of accomplishment. Honors assemblies can include recognition for numerous kinds of achievement, in order to reward the efforts of students who cannot compete academically. Teachers can increase their demands on low-track students and communicate confidence that the students can achieve at a higher level. Efforts to enhance the social status and self-image of low-ability students could reduce or eliminate one of the major sources of inequity associated with tracking.

Recently, a number of countries have altered their traditional school structures in order to create greater access for all students to a curriculum that maximizes the opportunities of students for educational and occupational attainment. Preliminary research on these new educational structures indicate that they are effective in reducing the effects of background on achievement. Studies of curriculum changes in Scotland, England, and Israel suggest that the effects of socioeconomic status on achievement has decreased in those schools that have created greater access to college-bound courses. If tracking practices in the United States and elsewhere permit and encourage student ac-

cess to the highest level courses of which they are capable, rather than limiting access in various ways, then this common practice can avoid many of the inequities that presently characterize it. Further, if a concerted effort is made to improve instruction in the lower tracks and to avoid the stigma attached to low-track assignment through school policy and practice, then tracking will no longer act as a mechanism that provides unequal learning opportunities to students.

Efforts to reduce inequality in access to the curriculum also are evident in gifted and talented programs and in special education. Critics of gifted and talented programs argue that they are separatist, elitist, and deny access to many talented students. In response to these charges, educators have modified these programs in a number of ways. These modifications include broadening the criteria for admission to the programs, integrating them into the normal school curriculum, replacing them with supplementary programs that are conducted after school or during the summer, and requiring that the students in these programs act as peer tutors to lower ability peers. Similarly, special education has increased educational opportunities for disabled students. In accordance with recent federal and state legislation, special education students are now mainstreamed whenever possible, to ensure that they are instructed in the least restrictive environment. This change has increased the access of special education students to the general curriculum. These efforts to reduce inequality have improved students' opportunities for educational attainment and, eventually, for social mobility.

Inequality and Classroom Processes

Several processes occur within the classroom that channel educational opportunities to students. Cognitive, instructional, social-psychological, and interaction processes affect students' attitudes and behaviors. These processes can differentially affect students' opportunities to learn.

The traditional school curriculum was developed on the assumption that intelligence is unidimensional. Educators stressed only one kind of cognitive ability, that which involved logic, inference, deduction, and memory skills. Standardized tests were designed to measure this kind of intelligence. More recently, researchers have identified several different kinds of intelligence (Gardner, 1993), including creativity, sensitivity, artistic ability, and motor skills. Moreover, they have distinguished different learning styles, such as auditory, visual, and kinetic. These major breakthroughs in how individuals experience the world and how they best learn can lead to significant changes in the curriculum and in pedagogical practices.

A recent change in schools that is consistent with a broader definition of intelligence is the creation of magnet schools that permit students to specialize in an area of interest or talent, such as communication and drama, science, or literature. In traditional schools, the curriculum has been expanded to include chorus and other musical activities, journalism, certain athletics, independent research, and even social service activities. Teacher education programs now include courses on learning styles. Many teachers try to identify the way individual students learn and to adapt their instructional methods to students' learning needs.

Until recently, instructional processes in most classrooms were teacher centered. Teachers acted as information sources and communicated information to students in lectures. In the past decade, classrooms have become more student centered. Instructional techniques now include the formation of student groups that work together on assigned tasks. Teachers use both cooperative and competitive student groups to motivate learning. Peer tutoring is common. Individual research is encouraged. Students work on long-term projects, and submit portfolios of their work for evaluation. These changes in the instructional process provide greater opportunities for students with different learning styles to interact with the curriculum.

Two important social-psychological processes that affect students' opportunities to learn involve teacher expectations and students' status characteristics. A significant body of research examines the basis for teacher expectations and how they affect student behavior (e.g., Rosenthal and Jacobsen, 1968; Rist, 1970; Brophy and Good, 1974). Some studies show that students' ascribed characteristics affect a teacher's perception of their ability. They report that teachers hold lower expectations for the performance of students who are in a racial or ethnic minority, for low-income students, and for females. Other studies show no evidence of an effect of student origins on teachers. Research on the effects of teacher expectations on student achievement are somewhat more conclusive. The studies show that students

who teachers believe have high ability tend to have higher achievement. Examining the linkages between teacher expectations and student achievement reveals that teachers interact with and praise students more often when they believe they are high achievers. Teacher expectations, then, remain a potential source of instructional inequity in the classroom.

Status expectations research (Berger et al., 1992) examines how status characteristics affect participation in group discussion. Empirical research focuses on how race or ethnicity and gender affect task-related interactions in the classroom. Studies show that low status contributes to low levels of participation. However, using various techniques to raise a student's status overcomes the disadvantages of low status and leads to more equal participation rates and to greater self-esteem for the lower status students. The duration of these effects is a concern since it is difficult to maintain the positive effects of intervention, especially when students are low achievers. Nevertheless, this body of research both identifies a source of inequality in classroom dynamics and suggests ways to overcome it, at least in the short run.

Finally, inequalities emerge in teacher–student and peer interactions in the classroom. Research on race and gender effects on teacher–student interactions (see Wilkinson and Marrett, 1985, for a review) shows that teachers provide less feedback and praise to female and minority students, and that teacher interaction patterns reflect sex stereotypes found outside the classroom. Studies of peer interactions show that the more black students in an integrated classroom, the more likely both blacks and whites are to have cross-race friendships. Moreover, the creation of integrated task-related groups, and especially cooperative learning groups, increases interracial sociability. Because teachers can influence the proximity of students through organizational structures, they have the ability to affect the incidence of interracial interactions and friendships. Greater interracial sociability is likely to lessen segregative behavior and to create an environment that is more conducive to learning for all students.

In short, the cognitive, instructional, social-psychological, and interactional processes that occur in the classroom play an important role in students' ability to learn. The research shows that when students are treated as equals by teachers and peers, their attitudes and behaviors are more positive. As a result, they are more involved in the learning process and, ultimately, more successful. Inequities exist in all of these processes. Identifying these inequities and making efforts to reduce or eliminate them should produce more positive attitudes and behaviors among students and remove barriers to their opportunities to learn.

Conclusions

Education has a major impact on social inequality in American society. Through the roles of transmission of knowledge and culture, socialization, and occupational preparation, schools can determine to what extent social origins or ability and effort affect student achievement and social mobility. Schools play a strategic role in creating either a classed society or a meritocracy.

Two major ways that schools affect social inequality are through the social organization of students for instruction and through classroom processes. Careful evaluation and monitoring of these aspects of schooling can ensure that student background does not limit student access to educational opportunities and that students can advance in school and beyond to the level that their abilities permit.

Schools cannot be expected to compensate for social inequalities in the larger society, or to transform society and eliminate these inequalities. At the same time, the social impact of schooling is difficult to overestimate. Schools do have the ability to lessen the influence of race, ethnicity, gender, and class on academic achievement and educational attainment. They also can create opportunities for students to utilize their cognitive abilities and talents to become upwardly mobile. By commitment to these goals and by systematic analysis and effort on the part of researchers and educators to ensure equality of educational opportunity, considerable progress can be made toward increasing social equality.

REFERENCES

Berger, J., B. Cohen, and M. Zelditch, Jr. 1972. "Status Characteristics and Social Interaction." *American Sociological Review* 37:241–255.

Bowles, Samuel, and Herbert Gintis. 1976. *Schooling in Capitalist America*. New York: Basic Books.

Brophy, Jere, and Thomas Good. 1974. *Teacher-Student Relationships*. New York: Holt, Rinehart & Winston.

Campbell, R. T. 1983. "Status Attainment Research: End of the Beginning or Beginning of the End?" *Sociology of Education* 56:47–62.

Coleman, James. 1990. *Equality and Achievement in Education*. Boulder, CO: Westview Press.

Coleman, James S., E. Q. Campbell, C. J. Hobson, J. McPartland, A. M. Mood, F. D. Weinfeld, and R. L. York. 1966. *Equality of Educational Opportunity*. Washington, DC: U.S. Printing Office.

Gardner, Alan. 1993. *Multiple Intelligences: The Theory in Practice*. New York: Basic Books.

Hernstein, Richard, and Charles Murray. 1994. *The Bell Curve*. New York: The Free Press.

Illich, I. 1983. *Deschooling Society*. New York: Harper Colophon.

Jencks, Christopher. 1972. *Inequality*. New York: Basic Books.

Katz, Michael. 1971. *Class, Bureaucracy, and Schools*. New York: Praeger.

Rist, Ray. 1970. "Social Class and Teacher Expectations: The Self-Fulfilling Prophecy in Ghetto Education." *Harvard Education Review* 40:411–451.

Rosenthal, Richard, and Lenore Jacobsen. 1968. *Pygmalion in the Classroom*. New York: Holt, Rinehart & Winston.

Wilkinson, L., and C. Marrett, eds. 1985. *Gender Influences in Classroom Interaction*. Orlando, FL: Academic Press.

ETHNICITY

Edith W. King
College of Education, University of Denver

Significant Term

What is ethnicity? In recent years ethnicity has come to play an important role in everyday living. It impacts almost everyone. It affects our behavior in the social spheres of our lives. Consider that ethnicity can affect how we spend our money, how we vote, even where we live or where we go out to dine. We use ethnicity as a filter for forming our identities, opinions, and attitudes toward others. Sociologists acknowledge that ethnicity is central to many peoples' images and concepts of self-identity. Furthermore, sociologists recognize that individuals function on a continuum of ethnic affiliations ranging from nonrecognition of one's ethnicity in daily life to an almost complete identification with an ethnic group in all activities, choices, and designations in daily actions.

Since the rise to prominence of this concept in the 1960s, ethnicity has been defined by numerous social scientists as

a sense of peoplehood and commonality derived from kinship patterns, a shared historical past, common experiences, religious affiliations, language or linguistic commonalities, shared values, attitudes, perceptions, modes of expression and identity.

Other terms are frequently cited by sociologists in connection with the concept of ethnicity:

Ethnic Identity—defined as the personal dimension of ethnicity or how one identifies oneself.
Ethnic Group—a group of people within the larger society that has a common ancestry and history, may speak a language other than English, and practice customs and traditions that reflect their ancestry.
Ethnic Minority Group—an ethnic group that has unique physical characteristics that make its members easily identifiable and may subject them to discrimination in the broader society.
Social Construction of Ethnic Identity—how a person views social reality and interprets the meanings of actions and experiences by filtering these experiences through one's ethnicity or ethnic identification.
Ethnocentrism—the attitude that one's traditions, customs, language, and values are the only way of doing things and that all other's ways (including language) are inadequate or wrong.
Socialization and Enculturation—the dynamic processes of internalizing the values, the folkways, and the language of one's group of people. Socialization is a lifelong process.
Acculturation—the subtle process of taking on new cultural traits and folkways when interacting with new and different groups of people.
Assimilation—also referred to as "the melting pot theory," the absorption of a subgroup of people or a person into the major group of the society. The giving up of unique and particular folkways and mores to practice the ways of the majority.

Some Important Issues That Sociologists Have Addressed about Ethnicity

Why has ethnicity arisen as an important issue in our daily lives? The persistence of ethnicity and one's ethnic identification in contemporary, highly diverse societies is due to both negative and positive factors. When the primary reason for group affiliation is hostility from the majority group, it is inevitable that ethnicity seems more to confine and constrict the individual than to provide opportunities and enhance the quality of life. But people are usually drawn to ethnic identification because of the advantages it offers. The ethnic group can be a buffer between the individual and the broader society; individuals use ethnicity as a filter for forming their opinions, tastes, values, and habit patterns. Ethnic affiliations also help organize social, economic, political, and religious interaction, both among individuals and among groups.

The Social Construction of Ethnicity

In exploring the concept of ethnicity or one's ethnic identity, we inevitably encounter questions about the "reality" of the social world in which the individual exists. It seems appropriate here to cite the theory of the social construction of reality and to apply it to the meaning of ethnicity and ethnic identity. The leading theorists on the topic of the social construction of reality are Peter Berger and Thomas Luckmann, whose ideas and insights help clarify the significance of the social construction of ethnicity and ethnic identity.

Berger and Luckmann contend that the reality of everyday life presents itself to us as a world we share with others. We share a common sense about what is reality and, therefore, our everyday life is characterized by a taken-for-granted reality. But human beings are unique among living creatures, for they can experience and exist in several provinces of meaning or taken-for-granted realities. These can be enclaves within the paramount reality. The theater provides an excellent metaphor for coexisting realities. To this point Berger and Luckmann tell us that the transition between realities is marked by the rising and falling of the curtain. As the curtain rises, the spectator is "transported into another world" with its own meanings and an order that may or may not have much to do with the order of everyday life. As the curtain falls, the spectator "returns to reality" (Berger and Luckmann, 1966:25)

So it is with ethnicity and an individual's ethnic identity. Within the ethnic group, the taken-for-granted world calls for conduct, use of language, referents, and mutual affinities and antipathies that are implicit and unspoken. These ways are shared with others of the same ethnic and racial affiliations. The same individual functions within the majority society in the taken-for-granted reality of the supermarket, the street traffic, or the daily newspaper. Common habit patterns take over to guide conduct. A person pays the price posted and does not bargain with the cashier at the supermarket; goes on the green light and halts on the red light, not chancing the traffic just because no cars are apparent; and comprehends the news story on the front page about rising food prices. We accept and function within cultural continuities even from childhood. Our view of reality and of the world helps us to make sense of our experiences. We interpret social events in light of the social meanings we attach to them. Here our ethnicity or our ethnic identification and ethnic affiliation come forth to interpret the meaning of everyday occurrences.

Often, growing up in the ethnic enclave, ghetto, or barrio socializes children into the belief that all the world is Mexican American or Jewish or Italian or Puerto Rican. It is useful to realize that children hold these conceptions quite naturally and logically. Biographies and personal histories reveal how the chance factors of everyday life can affect people's conceptions of the ethnic and social world that surrounds them. Examples of the type of socialization that lulls a child into believing that most of the existing society that she or he will ever encounter is made of people of the same ethnicity or race as the child are revealed in these statements compiled from experienced teachers' accounts of their childhood socialization. Following are some excerpts from adults recalling childhood impressions and remembrances of experiences that influenced their attitudes toward various ethnic groups (King et al., 1994:106–107):

As a young child I had limited contact with people of color. I knew that they existed because I would see them on the busses, or at the shopping malls, or at the movies when I would go. I never really thought too much about them though, because I never met a person of color, nor did I ever have an opportunity to speak with one.

An ethnic experience that I remember was when we went out to eat once at a Chinese restaurant. I was totally amazed to see a room full of Chinese people. The food was totally weird to me, and watching the people using chop-sticks, kept me mesmerized during the entire meal.

I am a product of the South. In the 1950s my town was a racially segregated city. It was two cities in one. The blacks lived in an area referred to as "colored" town and rarely mingled with the white population except when catching the bus. In "colored" town were churches, schools, small stores—all the essentials to keep the blacks from mingling with the whites. On Saturdays on Main Street there were no blacks doing their weekly shopping only crowds of white people. Blacks did not buy their shoes at Thompson's or ice cream at the Dairy Queen. Although my neighborhood was only three blocks from "colored" town, I never visited that area of town nor did any of my friends. It was off limits to us. Sometimes our parents would drive blacks home from their jobs cleaning our houses or yards, but we were never invited to ride along.

These comments demonstrate the power of the social construction of ethnicity on an individual's attitudes, opinions, and actions.

The Aspects of Ethnicity

Ethnicity is a complex concept that is intricately bound to other concepts such as acculturation and assimilation described previously. To better understand the dynamics and the variables involved in issues of ethnicity, social scientists have attempted to scrutinize the question of what comprises one's ethnicity. Many sociologists have rejected the idea of assimilation, that immigrants and foreigners permanently living in the United States should absorb the "American Way of Life" recognizing that there is more than one way to be an American. Rather, Americans become acculturated as they pass from generation to generation, leaving their immigrant experience behind. Acculturation influences people to change and reshape customs and patterns of behavior to incorporate new and different folkways. Interesting and colorful customs blending traditions and cultures are created through the process of acculturation and cultural diffusion. Acculturation is occurring in America today. It leads us toward an ethnically diverse or culturally pluralistic society, a so-

ciety that values the traditions and practices that are uniquely Polish American, Italian American, Jewish American, Mexican American, etc. American ethnic groups with ties to nations around the globe are still uniquely American, though their families originated far from the United States. The process of acculturation, the subtle changing of ways and traditions, is also experienced by ethnic groups with origins in the United States—our American Indians.

With this background in mind let us examine another meaningful perspective on ethnicity—*the aspects of ethnicity*. The aspects of ethnicity, first detailed by Longstreet (1978) and later elaborated by King (1990; King et al., 1994), are predicated on the social science disciplines of history, geography, sociology and sociolinguistics, psychology, economics, political science, international relations, and philosophy. They are as follows:

- the *historical* aspects of cultures and heritage;
- the *geographic* aspects of cultures, nationalities, and ethnic enclaves;
- the *linguistic* variations between peoples and cross-language groups;
- the *religious* aspects that include the customs, ceremonies, and traditions associated with different belief systems;
- the *social class* aspects and their economic implications;
- the *political* aspects including international or transnational ties;
- the *moral* aspects of stereotyping, prejudice, and racism—the negative aspects of ethnicity.

A brief discussion of each of these aspects of ethnicity will illuminate their meaning more fully. The *historical* aspect or component of ethnicity is the most obvious aspect. It comes immediately into recognition as we examine the phenomenon of ethnicity. It is the sharing of a heritage, often ancient and revered, that brings people together in an ethnic group identification. For example, museums and historical societies everywhere are filled with exhibits of artifacts and relics of many peoples who comprise the nationalities and ethnic groups of the society. When discussing and considering the attributes of an ethnic group one must take up its historical development, whether in the recent past or going back generations and even centuries to recount the origin of its traditions, myths, and legends. An historical perspective of an ethnic group increases understanding of the particular group of people, their art, music, drama, and literature.

Allied to the historical is the *geographic* aspect of ethnicity, an essential component in the formation of ethnic groups. We are continually aware of how people left their native homelands in the "Old World" to journey to the new land and found colonies and settlements in geographic locations similar to their native lands. Literature often includes large and carefully detailed maps of migration patterns, initial settlements, and areas of habitation and populations. These maps and displays clearly indicate to the readers why people moved, as well as where they settled in various locations, how natural forces influenced the settlements, and where the mingling of ethnic groups occurred.

Language is inherent in the ability to communicate and is critical to group identity and affiliation. The *linguistic* aspect of ethnicity is an essential component with which all social scientists must deal. Sociolinguists continually point out that ethnicity is one of the inevitable attributes of social life. They remind us that new ethnicities arise, old ones alter, and others disappear, but people cannot exist without their language that is deeply tied to their ethnicity (Fishman, 1976). Language is the medium through which the individual makes sense of the everyday world. Therefore, one's language is intricately entwined in ethnicity and self-identity.

Religion, too, plays a central role in the life of ethnic groups. The *religious* aspects of ethnicity are embodied in religious ceremonies, rituals, and festivals often entailing the use of elaborate artifacts, sacred objects, icons, and special items. Religious ceremonies are carried out in magnificent buildings like the great cathedrals of Europe, or in more humble settings like rural churches and mosques. But the impact of religion on ethnicity cannot be understated. For some ethnic groups religious identity and observances fill every waking hour and almost every mundane act. Religious practice is not, nor ever has been, limited to national boundaries or secular states.

Intimately tied to geographic and religious aspects of ethnicity are the *social class* and *economic* affiliations of groups. Sociologists cannot examine the lives of people without touching on the social class structure of the group or subgroup. Economic wherewithal is tied to

accumulations of material goods and the amassing of treasured arts as wealth. What is valued comes from the worth imbued to the material good, such as precious metals and jewels, through a cultural definition of what is valuable. Further, accumulation of wealth and status means power and superiority over other groups. Social and economic status tends to give one group power over another and leads to attitudes that one ethnic or racial group is inherently better than another because it is richer and holds a higher social status.

Material wealth not only endows an individual or group with greater social status, often it is accompanied by wider political power. *Political* aspects are reflected in ethnic group affiliation. Electing officials to public office or influencing the passage of particular laws can be effected by ethnic power blocs. Treaties and agreements between nations also can be influenced by ethnic affiliations, alliances or antipathies—all political aspects of ethnicity.

The recognition of the political and economic components leads to the negative aspects of ethnicity—the stereotyping, prejudice, and racism that are labeled the *moral* aspects of ethnicity. These, too, are part of human nature. Racism can be formal, institutionalized, and written into the laws of the land, or racism can be informal, personal subtle acts of exclusion and rejection. These negative aspects of ethnicity are part of history and often are evident in our attitudes and in our customs. Accounts of discrimination and prejudice can be obvious and blatant, such as treatment of Native Americans in the United States during the nineteenth and twentieth centuries when their lands and settlements were summarily appropriated. Sometimes discrimination is evidenced more indirectly, as in the inability of ethnic artists and women artists to have their work accepted and valued by the majority culture.

To summarize, the historical, geographic, linguistic, religious, social class, economic, political, and moral aspects of ethnicity intertwine in dynamic relationships to define an individual's or group's heritage, roots, and identity. Delineating the aspects of ethnicity is essential in recognizing the complexity of the concept of ethnicity.

A Typology of the Stages of Ethnicity

Another effort to come to better understandings of the dynamics of ethnicity and ethnic identity in our widely diverse society has been the work of James Banks of the University of Washington in the development of a typology on the stages of ethnicity. This highly regarded and well-known ethnic scholar has been researching, writing, and teaching in the field of ethnic education and educational sociology for over two decades. This typology describes stages in the life of a person in our American society. The typology is an ideal-type construct in the Weberian sense and constitutes a set of hypotheses based on previous theoretical development and Banks' extensive research in the fields of sociology, anthropology, social psychology, and education. These stages should be seen as dynamic and multidimensional with the characteristics of each stage forming a continuum. An overview of the typology of the stages of ethnicity is as follows:

Stage 1: Ethnic Psychological Captivity. The individual internalizes the negative and deleterious images of the affiliated group that causes self-rejection and low self-esteem. The individual is ashamed of the group and of identification with this group.

Stage 2: Ethnic Encapsulation. The individual opts for ethnic exclusiveness even to the point of voluntary separatism. During ethnic encapsulation individuals associate primarily with those of the same ethnic groups and believe that their group is superior. Individuals such as Anglo-Americans, have internalized the dominant society's myths about the superiority of their ethnic or racial group and the innate inferiority of other ethnic groups. They often choose to live in highly ethnocentric and encapsulated communities.

Stage 3: Ethnic Identity Clarification. The individual is able to clarify personal attitudes and ethnic identity and to develop more positive attitudes toward his or her ethnic group. The individual is now able to accept and understand both the positive and negative attributes of his or her ethnic group. The individual's pride in the ethnic group is not based on the hate or fear of outside groups.

Stage 4: Biethnicity. A sense of ethnic identity and the skills needed to participate in both the mainstream culture and the individual's subculture evolve, so that the person can function successfully at work, while still holding to one's ethnic ways of life at home.

Stage 5: Multiethnicity and Reflective Nationalism. The individual has a commitment to the affiliated ethnic group while holding empathy and concern for other groups and a broader allegiance to the nation state including idealized values of human rights. Individuals at this stage have cross-cultural competency within their own nation, but not a global perspective.

Stage 6: Globalism and Global Competency. The individual has achieved the ideal delicate balance of ethnic, national, and global identification, commitments, literacy, and behaviors. The individual has internalized the universalistic ethical values and principles of humankind and has the skills and competencies for commitment to a worldwide society (Banks, 1994: 223–228).

Banks, his colleagues, and associates at the Center for Multicultural Education, at the University of Washington, Seattle have researched and written extensively on the implications of the typology of stages in ethnicity and its applications to teaching and education at all levels. These investigations into the nature of ethnicity and other topics in the field have been published in *The Handbook on Research on Multicultural Education* (Banks and Banks, 1995) and are ongoing.

Ethnic Groups, Multiculturalism, and Educational Issues

Drawing from the section that specifically focuses on the education of Native Americans, African Americans, Mexican Americans, Puerto Ricans, and Asian Pacific Americans, as these ethnic groups have been categorized in the *Handbook on Research on Multicultural Education*, certain key issues come into prominence. In the *Handbook* leading educational authorities representing these ethnic groups discuss important concerns embedded not only in American society, but also in the ever-widening worldwide culture. These educational policy issues and their implications reflect the typology of the stages of ethnicity, moving from the stage of ethnic encapsulation to globalism and global competency.

Each ethnic scholar gives an overview of the *historical aspects* that have impacted the directions of research on their particular ethnic group. The *linguistic aspects* and the centrality of the group's language that are distinctly different from English are emphasized, especially for the Native Americans, the Mexican Americans, and the Puerto Ricans. As is to be expected the ramifications for the *socioeconomic and political aspects* of ethnic affiliation as they impact research are covered in these chapters. The recurring theme of the wide diversity within each American ethnic group, the Native Americans, the Mexican Americans, the African Americans, the Asian Pacific Americans, and even among the Puerto Ricans, who might be assumed to be the most monoethnic, is threaded throughout each of the essays. Each piece helps researchers to recognize how these American ethnic groups are increasingly characterized by wide differences in social class, hues of skin color, gender, and sexual orientation, and recency of immigration to the United States that impacts the degree of assimilation of individuals, families, and whole communities into the broader American society. Additionally, ethnic "minority" groups such as Mexican Americans, African Americans, and Puerto Ricans have been traditionally viewed as if all members are poor, of lower socioeconomic origins, marginal, and oppressed; the authors of these essays stress that these conditions are changing and should be acknowledged by educators and researchers.

Some specific points and issues presented by the essays bring attention to the fact that in recent years research and educational strategies for teaching these "minority" children have moved away from models that characterized deficit thinking and the need for efforts to make up for so-called cultural disadvantagement. Rather researchers, educators, and curriculum developers now are seeking to examine and promote the characteristics of successful students and the implications of the strengths and support they draw from their ethnic identity for teaching and learning. In the 1960s those who conceived and implemented programs such as Project Head Start mistakenly believed that groups of parents such as African Americans and the home environment they engendered were responsible for the inadequate start in school their children displayed. Now in the 1990s these attitudes have changed to incorporate multicultural guidelines, as well as developmentally appropriate practices in the early childhood curriculum.

Another major policy issue impacting ethnic groups such as Mexican Americans and Puerto Ricans, as well as some Native Americans, is the use of a first language other than English in the home and community. Educational authorities in language learning emphasize the utility of proficiency in more than one language, especially in contemporary worldwide culture. Trends in education and research are now moving toward recognition for the need of more years and more flexibility toward fluency in learning to use all aspects of a language including English. Specialists now emphasize how deeply linguistic skills are embedded in the culture of the language community.

The authors of the essays in the *Handbook* reiterate that schools, teachers, and administrators need to look into their own practices, policies, and procedures rather than continuing to focus on students and their families as the problems in education. Parental support for education and schooling has been a core value for many ethnic groups, especially Asian Americans. The ethnic authority, Ooka Pang, points out that this typical American value has been characteristic of a wide array of groups in our multicultural society. She also notes that research and study of the widely diverse group of Asian and Southeast Asian Americans has mainly involved high school or adult students. Little investigation of the school experiences of children from Asian American ethnic groups has been carried out, yet many generalizations have characterized educational practice with this widely diverse ethnic population.

The editors of the *Handbook of Research on Multicultural Education* astutely conclude their volume with a section on international perspectives on multicultural education underscoring the global circumstances of multiculturalism. Additionally, throughout the *Handbook* contributors provide coverage about the waves of ethnic groups who have historically immigrated to America from various sectors of the globe. They make us aware of how this constant movement of individuals, families, and even whole communities is changing the processes of socialization and enculturation, acculturation, assimilation, and ethnic identity.

Ethnicity and Further Sociological Inquiry

In recent years the concept of ethnicity has spawned consideration of, as well as research into, the nature of biethnicity of children of biracial marriages or cross-racial adoptions. Initial conceptual research viewed the condition of biracial or biethnic identity development as placing the individual at risk for developing a variety of social and psychological problems. However a qualitative research study carried out in the early 1990s on the racial identity of biethnic children, adolescents, and adults demonstrated positive aspects of belonging to two ethnic groups (black and white) (Kerwin et al., 1993). Of the children and adolescents that participated in the study none perceived themselves as marginal in two cultures and their parents displayed a secure sense of their own ethnic identity, as well. Now studies are needed to learn how individuals sustain multiethnic affiliations and a sense of global identity.

As the previous discussion of the concept and issues surrounding ethnicity has indicated, research strategies and methods used to study the phenomenon have been mainly qualitative, naturalistic, ethnographic approaches. As techniques and research designs that combine both quantitative and qualitative research methods become available, enhanced by the use of computer analyses, more elaborated and layered designs to investigate issues of ethnicity and ethnic affiliations are possible. This may open the way for creative and insightful studies on the implications of ethnicity in American life and in international and cross-cultural perspectives.

REFERENCES

Allport, Gordon. 1954. *The Nature of Prejudice*. Garden City, NJ: Doubleday Anchor Books.

Banks, James A. 1994. *Multiethnic Education: Theory and Practice*. Needham Heights, MA: Allyn & Bacon.

Banks, James A., and Cherry Banks, eds. 1995. *Handbook of Research on Multicultural Education*. New York: Macmillan.

Barth, Frederick, ed. 1969. *Ethnic Groups and Boundaries*. Boston: Little, Brown.

Berger, Peter, and Thomas Luckmann. 1966. *The Social Construction of Reality*. New York: Anchor Books.

Fishman, Joshua. 1976. *Bilingual Education: An International Sociological Perspective*. Rowley, MA: Newbury House.

Glazer, Nathan, and Daniel P. Moynihan, eds. 1975. *Ethnicity, Theory, and Experience*. Cambridge, MA: Harvard University Press.

Gordon, Milton. 1964. *Assimilation in American Life*. New York: Oxford University Press.

Kerwin, Christine, et al. 1993. "Racial Identity in Biracial Children: A Qualitative Investigation." *Journal of Counseling Psychology* 20(2):221–231.

King, Edith. 1990. *Teaching Ethnic and Gender Awareness*, 2nd ed. Dubuque, IA: Kendall/Hunt.

King, Edith W., Marilyn Chipman, and Marta Cruz-Janzen. 1994. *Educating Young Children in a Diverse Society*. Needham Heights, MA: Allyn & Bacon.

Longstreet, Wilma. 1978. *The Aspects of Ethnicity*. New York: Teachers College Press.

ETHNOGRAPHY

Peter McLaren
UCLA Graduate School of Education and Information Studies

Amanda Datnow
Ontario Institute for Studies in Education
University of Toronto

At one time ethnography referred to the field methods of anthropologists in studying "exotic" cultures. It is now used by sociologists, educational researchers, cultural anthropologists, and other social science researchers to study any bounded group of people in virtually any context, urban or rural, global or local. Although some still prefer to think of ethnography as a research method grounded in anthropological concepts (Wolcott, 1987), others have argued for differentiating ethnography so as to reflect the multiple disciplines associated with it. Hence the terms "socioethnography" and "anthroethnography" (Spindler, 1982). Most agree, however, that ethnography is transdisciplinary; it critically appropriates elements from various theoretical traditions and is utilized by researchers across the social sciences in answering a variety of different research questions.

There are several common features of ethnography: (1) the researcher spends an extended time with the group under study through participant observation; (2) notes on observations and interactions are the major data source; (3) research is done within the real life context in which it occurs; it is naturalistic and the researcher has no control over events; (4) the focus is on how individuals make meaning of events and actions; (5) the ethnographer attempts to build contextualized view of life in the group; and (6) ethnographic accounts blend "thick" description with a theoretical point of view. In sum, it is a field-based inquiry process guided by prior knowledge (Goetz and LeCompte, 1984).

Ethnography is both a process and a product (Wolcott, 1987). Ethnographers look at everyday events and groups as if they were exceptional and unique. In doing so, the ethnographer can offer productively complex analyses of the seemingly mundane features of everyday life that characterize that group or process. Ethnographers provide richly textured, accessible accounts of social life of a group of people, whether in a classroom, a school, or a village. A focus on the culture of that group, as lived by the individuals within in it, is the subject of ethnography. Geertz (1973) aptly defines ethnography as "thick description," which constitutes untangling the webs of meaning in a culture.

Ethnographic methods in sociology are often allied with the interpretive theoretical traditions of symbolic interactionism and ethnomethodology. These theories share the assumption that people construct meaning through interaction and operate under the premise that social fact is social action. Because these meanings are embedded in people's actions, the only way to access meanings is to observe interaction among people in the setting under study. Individuals and the contexts in which they interact are seen as intertwined, and behavior is explained within a sociocultural context. In sum, ethnographers are concerned with how people make meaning of actions and events in their lives. The task of the ethnographer is to illuminate the subjects' world by translating for the informed reader the meanings and transactions that occur in the subjects' own lived context.

Ethnographic studies have had a major impact in the field of sociology of education, arguably changing the way we view schools and the individuals within them (Louis, 1992). We no longer look at schools and classrooms as monolithic entities or artifacts to be explained but rather as lived cultures to be processually engaged. We see teachers and students as active agents negotiating interaction. Evaluations of school programs often now include narrative accounts and case studies based on intensive observations (Fetterman, 1984). Moreover, ethnographic studies in the interpretive tradition have made contributions to theories that attempt to account for social inequality by introducing cultural elements and human agency into these theories and by revealing the reflexive relationship between institutional practices and students' lives in schools (Mehan, 1992).

The Origins of Ethnography

Many view Malinowski's (1922) anthropological account, *Argonauts of the Western Pacific*, as the first example of ethnographic work. Several features made Malinowski's study of the Trobriand Islands distinct: First, his account attempted to characterize meaning from the actor's point of view. Second, he also tied his account to the larger body of social science theory. And third, Malinowski was the first to systematically, although not thoroughly, attempt to describe methods of fieldwork. Not surprisingly, Malinowski's example became the paradigm for a generation of ethnographers, both in anthropology and in sociology (Erickson, 1984).

Around the time that Malinowski's ethnography was published, sociologists, including Robert Park, Everett Hughes, and Louis Wirth of the University of Chicago, began to use field work methods much like Malinowski's to study life in urban communities in the United States. However, as sociologists, they spoke of society and socialization. Later, anthropologists Whyte and Gans studied ethnic enclaves in American society through participant observation and long-term residence in communities. This marked a convergence of the issues studied by anthropologists and sociologists. Sociologists were increasingly becoming more interested in finding out the answers to questions that only small-scale, in-depth studies could address.

Sociological field studies in the area of education also began to emerge, offering rich, context-bound descriptions of participants and activities in classrooms and schools. Early studies, such as Waller's *The Sociology of Teaching*, were few and far between, largely descriptive, and small scale. Sociologists of education were still focused primarily on secondary analysis of quantitative data. In the late 1960s, however, the questions that sociologists of education asked began to change: They wanted to know not just what was happening in the

classroom or the school, but whether processes and outcomes were occurring as predicted (Goetz and LeCompte, 1984).

With theoretical groundwork in mind, sociologists of education began to conduct in-depth, ethnographic studies of classrooms, the teaching profession, and schools as a social organization. They began to analyze interactions among students and between teachers and students. However, many of these studies were based on a structural–functional view of schooling and society. Only later did sociologists of education use ethnography to explore the complex questions of why there are differences in the educational experiences of students from different social or ethnic backgrounds, and how school and society are related.

However, one of the major challenges still facing ethnographers today is how to relate microstudies of interaction to macrosocietal level forces. Ethnographers tend to be criticized for overemphasizing the effects of individual agency at the microlevel, ignoring macrostructural constraints. Still, others who have tried to overcome that criticism have fallen into the trap of blatantly linking microlevel interaction to macrolevel forces without demonstrating how in fact this linkage takes place. More promising have been constitutive ethnographies, which show how social facts are constructed in interaction, and more recent critical ethnographies, which treat culture as a product of competing discourses, ideologies, or rituals (Willis, 1977; Oakes, 1985; McLaren, 1993).

Conducting an Ethnographic Study

Although traditional ethnography consists of a researcher spending an extended length of time (i.e., a year or more) with the group under study, the enthusiasm for ethnography as a research method has led to the proliferation of what some call "quasi-ethnographies," which may adopt some but not all of the methods characteristic of traditional ethnography. There are also examples of what is called "blitzkrieg" ethnography, which relies upon several days of intensive fieldwork, rather than extensive time in the field. These researchers are not conducting ethnography per se, but rather are utilizing ethnographic methods or techniques for collecting data. Purists eschew these hybrid approaches. In this section, we will discuss some of the methods and issues in traditional ethnography, including gaining access to and trust of the group under study and triangulating data from a variety of sources.

Because the ethnographer often spends an intensive, lengthy time in the field, he or she must establish the trust of the group under study. This is one of the most difficult aspects of ethnographic research. Being of a different ethnicity, culture, and/or social class often constitutes a barrier to ethnographers' gaining trust or acceptance by a group. Some ethnographers establish a relationship with one member of the group first, who then serves as an entree into the rest of the group. Others offer services or help in exchange for access. Ethnographers must consider the process of gaining access carefully, for this can be an arena where problematic power relations between the researcher and the researched can come into rigorous play (Emerson, 1988).

Producing a strong ethnographic account relies upon the triangulation of data from a variety of sources in the field. Participant observation is the cornerstone of ethnographic research methods. However, the act of participant observation takes on a variety of meanings in different field settings. In some settings, the ethnographer participates in everyday life with the group under study. In other settings, such as a school classroom, when the ethnographer does not take on the role of teacher or student, the ethnographer may be more of an observer than a participant (Wolcott, 1988). However, there are cases when the ethnographer initially becomes a student or a teacher, and then over time becomes more of a participant than an observer.

Because the data collected in participant observation vary in depth and scope, ethnographers often use a variety of other techniques to augment their knowledge of the group or culture under study. One widely used technique is interviewing. Interviews may be formal or informal. They may occur repeatedly with someone who is considered a key informant, or they may occur with a broad range of subjects. Because of their extended length of time in the field, ethnographers often find informal interviewing on an ongoing basis to be an important source of data.

Ethnographers often make use of archival data sources, including primary documents, such as letters or memoirs, or secondary documents, such as meeting minutes or reports written by participants for another purpose. Ethnographers are also likely to take photographs, collect maps, or tap into any other such source that may help them understand the setting. Whereas many participant observers take copious notes of what they observe, others may choose to do a more in-depth analysis of interactions among individuals by audiotaping or videotaping what they see and systematically analyzing the tapes later.

Ethnographic research can pose challenges to an ethnographer's own identity and to his or her role as a researcher. Conducting an ethnography can be a transformative, life changing experience for the ethnographer. In the course of participant observation, ethnographers may be asked to take a more activist role within the community they are studying or they may choose to do so on their own. Some ethnographers have written about how their field experience caused them to question their own social position.

Ethnographers struggle with the question of whether to report the findings of their study back to the members in the field. Classical ethnographic approaches assumed ethnocentrically that the subjects under study could not understand their own social reality as well as the ethnographer. However, the emergence of phenomenological approaches in sociology and anthropology—not to mention the emergence of postcolonial ethnography (developed to address the Eurocentrism of most Western anthropological accounts)—pointed toward the significance of subjects' versions of their own reality. As a result, ethnographers began to propose that the real test of the validity of the study's findings was to have the account judged by the group under study. The members' responses can be integrated into the ethnography itself. However, reporting back to the field often poses a set of dilemmas in itself, as the encounter often reveals points of contrast, ambiguity, and uncertainty (Emerson and Pollner, 1992).

Writing the Ethnographic Account

Ethnographers often spend as much time analyzing data and writing their ethnographic accounts as they do conducting fieldwork, oftentimes more. Seasoned ethnographers advise that the writing task be coupled with ongoing data collection in the field (Wolcott, 1988). This allows the ethnographer to identify areas or issues that require further investigation in the field and also helps the ethnographer iteratively work with both theory and data.

Ethnography is an inquiry process in which the researcher has one foot in the field and the other in anthropological or sociological literature (Erickson, 1984). The ethnographer brings to the field a set of questions, implicit or explicit, and a theoretical point of view, often based in anthropology or sociology. This is as much a cornerstone of ethnography as is the participant observation research techniques that are used, and is especially salient in the writing of ethnographic accounts.

Good ethnographic accounts can give the reader the feeling of being in the setting and sharing the emotions of the participants. Ethnographers must depend on textual conventions in order to achieve their status as factual. The use of rhetorical practices serves to convince the reader of the authenticity and plausibility of the ethnographer's work. For example, ethnographers create a "reality effect" through the use of a highly graphic passage that depicts a scene from the field in a gripping manner (Atkinson, 1990). In this regard, writing an ethnographic account is similar to creative storytelling.

Ethnographers must strike a balance between over-identifying with the participants, on the one hand, and superficially portraying them on the other. In their accounts, ethnographers must display passionate involvement in the field, but yet maintain a level of objectivity. This is the greatest challenge for the ethnographer—walking the fine line of participant/observer. Because ethnographers become very involved in the lives of their subjects, often becoming a participating member of the group themselves, they must make ethical choices that are not required in more "hands off" research approaches. Because ethnographic researchers often encounter such dilemmas in the field, there is an extensive body of literature on how ethnographers have dealt with these issues, and in general about ethnographers' field research experiences. Critical ethnography (discussed later) has a different perspective on this aspect of field research.

The ethnographer must be careful to avoid privileging his or her own agency and subjectivity as the reference point by which to judge the subjects under study (McLaren, 1992). Additionally, he or she must be wary of the categories that are being imposed on the data. Not only does being of a different ethnicity, culture, and/or social class constitute a barrier to gaining acceptance by a group under study, but it can also mean that the researcher uses a subjective lens in making

sense of the phenomena under study. This is unavoidable, and it is recommended that the ethnographer be aware of and self-conscious about his or her subjectivity in analyzing the data and writing the ethnographic account (Peshkin, 1988).

Fleeting Forward: Critical Ethnography

Ethnography is part of a larger paradigm shift in social sciences, the move toward poststructuralism and transdisciplinary fusion. Within this shift, there exists the need for a more critical form of ethnography that recognizes that ethnographers undertake their projects not just within a field site, but within a field of competing discourses. Critical ethnography recognizes the contestatory character of the discursive field. For instance, critical poststructuralist ethnography calls for a reconceptualization of culture as a field of discourse that is implicated in relations of power and constituted by normative understandings. Critical ethnographers take into account the fact that ethnographic researchers actively construct and are constructed by the discourses they embody and the metaphors they enact. Critical ethnography emphasizes the need to connect data to the discourses that produce them and at the same time produce the subjects under study (McLaren and Giarelli, 1995).

Critical ethnography relies on qualitative methodologies that can be described as both interpretive and analytic, structural and interactional. It is both a theory of experience and a theory of social structure. It follows the idea that while individuals as active agents constitute the social order, they do so in order to reproduce and transform existing asymmetrical relations of power and privilege.

When ethnographers attempt to adduce information from the examination of social texts, their interpretations and accounts of social life often appear authorless. Consequently, critical ethnographers examine their own interpretive accounts by investigating how meaning is produced by a system of signs, by examining the specific meanings produced within particular sign systems, and by analyzing how such sign systems are read differently across different contexts. Critical ethnographers begin with the premise that the ethnography's diegesis—the plane of rhetoric supporting the ethnographer's exposition of events—frequently occludes the signs of its own construction, its own rhetoricity. Therefore, in their work critical ethnographers attempt to read social and cultural texts symptomatically, that is, they attempt to identify where and how ideological masking takes place, and to tease out what a so-called natural or authentic event seeks to conceal. From the standpoint of the critical ethnographer, there exists no natural or authentic events if by that one means that events speak for themselves or exist unsullied or untainted by ideology or interest. In fact, some ethnographers such as Clough (1992) have traced traditional ethnographic accounts to the narrative structure and authoritative stance of the nineteenth-century realist novel. From a criticalist position, traditional ethnographic criticism and the empirical sciences in general are seen as grounded in unconscious (and often male forms of) desire and the narrative production of scientific concepts. As such, traditional ethnographic literature needs to be decanonized through a sustained development of critical approaches to textuality (Clough, 1992).

Ethnography undertaken critically necessitates recognizing the complexity of social relations and the researcher's own socially determined position within the reality that one is attempting to describe. Critical ethnographers must ask the fundamental question: What social effects do you want your evaluations and understanding to have? Only in answering this question can ethnographers be self-conscious and self-reflective.

A significant challenge for critical ethnographers is to rethink the categories that are used to shape the problematics of research. The questions being asked must be decentered and reexamined in light of voices from the margins (groups marginalized by ethnicity, class, sexual orientation, age, religion, etc.). Moreover, one of the most important tasks in which a field researcher can engage is understanding and transforming the various ways in which his or her own subjective formation privileges certain discourses that constructs subjects as the "other."

Where critical ethnography is fleeting forward is in its argument that ethnographers need to locate their work in a transformative praxis that leads to the overcoming of oppression. Critical ethnography seeks to analyze the possibilities for the resistance and transformation of social life, both individuated and collective, personal and macropolitial. It engages in such an analysis by attempting to understand how wider relations

of power are played out in the agential spaces of social and cultural sites and also by attempting to investigate how wider structures of mediation at the level of the economy are able to "take root" in the everyday lives of individuals and groups who operate at the level of common sense actions. In this way, critical ethnography links texuality to materiality. That is, it makes connections between the texts that we read (cultural artifacts) and those that read us (the realm of language and discursive structures). Critical ethnography advocates sharing with the subjects under investigation (often refigured as coparticipants) the discourses at work that are shaping the field site analysis, and how the researcher's subjectivity is contributing to the analytic process. As such, critical ethnography can help produce those forms of agency necessary for the transformation of historical forces and the structures of oppression.

Critical ethnography can be separated into reflexive or interpretive ethnography and deconstructive ethnography. According to Visweswaran (1994:78), reflexive ethnography, like mainstream or normative ethnography, develops from the "declarative mode" (imparting knowledge to the reader whose position is stabilized by an embeddedness in an identifiable community of discourse) while deconstructive ethnography is built upon an interrogative mode [a self-conscious refusal to explain through a practice of deferral, a discouragement of identification with the object of analysis, a disruption of the identity of the reader with a unified (usually a Euro-American male subject of enunciation), or an exposition of the limits of existing "facts"]. According to Bourdieu and Wacquant (1992), critical reflexivity is aimed at overcoming the nihilistic relativism of some forms of deconstruction and the scientistic absolutism of modern rationalism. By examining the historically constructed structures of the scientific field, self-reflexive ethnography refers to "uncovering the social at the heart of the individual, the impersonal beneath the intimate, the universal buried deep within the most particular" (Bourdieu and Wacquant, 1994:44). Mainstream ethnography, for the most part, is impertinent to this form of reflexivity.

Critical ethnography also operates in the subjunctive mode of "as if" in the sense that it attempts—often through forms of "action research" or "participant research"—to challenge and to transform within the communities under study what is determined to be existing forms of exploitation and oppression.

REFERENCES

Atkinson, P. 1990. *The Ethnographic Imagination: Textual Constructions of Reality*. London: Routledge.

Bourdieu, Pierre, and J. D. Wacquant. 1992. *An Invitation to Reflexive Sociology*. Chicago, IL: The University of Chicago Press.

Clough, P. T. 1992. *The Ends of Ethnography: From Realism to Social Criticism*. Newbury Park and London.

Emerson, R. M. 1988. *Contemporary Field Research: A Collection of Readings*. Prospect Heights, IL: Waveland.

Emerson, R. M., and M. Pollner. 1992. "Difference and Dialogue: Members' Readings of Ethnographic Texts." *Perspectives on Social Problems* 3:79–98.

Erickson, F. 1984. "What Makes School Ethnography 'Ethnographic'?" *Anthropology & Education Quarterly* 15:51–66.

Fetterman, David M. 1984. *Ethnography in Educational Evaluation*. Beverly Hills, CA: Sage.

Geertz, C. 1973. *The Interpretation of Cultures*. New York: Basic Books.

Goetz, J. P., and M. D. LeCompte. 1984. *Ethnography and Qualitative Design in Educational Research*. Orlando, FL: Academic Press.

Malinowski, B. 1922. *Argonauts of the Western Pacific*. New York: E. P. Dutton.

McLaren, P. 1992. "Collisions with Otherness: 'Traveling' Theory, Post-Colonial Criticism, and the Politics of Ethnographic Practice—The Mission of the Wounded Ethnographer." *Qualitative Studies in Education* 5(1):77–92.

———. 1993. *Schooling as a Ritual Performance: Towards a Political Economy of Educational Symbols and Gestures*, 2nd ed. London: Routledge.

McLaren, P., and J. Giarelli. 1995. *Critical Theory and Educational Research*. Albany, NY: State University of New York Press.

Mehan, H. 1992. "Understanding Inequality in Schools: The Contribution of Interpretive Studies." *Sociology of Education* 65:1–20.

Oakes, J. 1985. *Keeping Track: How Schools Structure Inequality*. New Haven, CT: Yale University Press.

Peshkin, A. 1988. "In Search of Subjectivity—One's Own." *Educational Researcher* 17(3):17–21.

Smith, L. 1992. "Ethnography." *Encyclopedia of Educational Research*, 6th ed. New York: Macmillan.

Spindler, G. 1981. *Doing the Ethnography of Schooling: Educational Anthropology in Action*. New York: Holt, Rinehart & Winston.

Visweswaran, Kamala. 1994. *Fictions of Feminist Ethnography*. Minneapolis: University of Minnesota Press.

Willis, P. 1977. *Learning to Labor: How Working Class Kids Get Working Class Jobs*. Farnborough: Saxon House.

Wolcott, H. F. 1988. "Ethnographic Research in Education." In R. M. Jaeger (ed.), *Complementary Methods for Research in Education*. Washington, DC: American Educational Research Association.

EXTRACURRICULAR ACTIVITIES

Pamela Anne Quiroz
University of Illinois, Chicago

Philosopher and educational reformer John Dewey viewed the school as the microcosm in which children could be taught self-direction and social skills, thus preparing them for their appropriate places in the modern adult world (Dewey, 1915). To accomplish these goals Dewey recommended a different style of learning along with incorporating activities in the curriculum that would instill these qualities in children.

Origins of the Extracurriculum

Industrialization brought with it the emergence of large-scale corporations and factories along with increasing technological improvements. As self-employment such as family farms and businesses disappeared, the early part of the twentieth century saw increases in high school enrollments as the high school diploma became more valuable in securing work. Consequently, the rapid expansion of the educational system, particularly high schools, necessitated consideration of how these schools should be organized. Added to this was an increased focus on what was newly defined as the "adolescent problem." The adolescent problem was located in social class and was seen as the problem of those who lacked supervision and a commitment to the moral order, namely the children of immigrants and poor urban youth whose different cultures and lifestyles threatened the established social order (Nasaw, 1979:93–100). As a consequence of increased high school enrollments and the changing demographics of urban areas, businessmen, social reformers, and educators began to reexamine the mission of education and propose solutions to the perceived social problems. One proposed solution found its support in the *social effi-*

ciency movement, which came to dominate these discussions and, ultimately, educational policy. Proponents of social efficiency argued that the school should function to differentiate students into their respective niches or roles in society. Their solution was to use the school to prepare children for adult life in an industrialized society. A well-designed academic curriculum combined with activities directed at the socialization of children would accomplish these goals. Academic subjects were evaluated and reorganized with regard to how each contributed to the social welfare of children, hence of the nation. In addition, schools began the formal implementation of extracurricular programs. Thus, the extracurriculum was to be one of the two major organizational mechanisms for implementing policies grounded in social efficiency (Spring, 1994:220–223).

In 1918, the Commission of the Reorganization of Secondary Education articulated the three main objectives for high schools in its *Cardinal Principals of Secondary Education* (National Education Association, 1918): (1) the differentiation of the curriculum, (2) specialization by students, and (3) the socialization of students to become enthusiastic participants in a democratic society. This report provided the framework for the modern comprehensive high school elevating the extracurriculum to a central status within it.

During the first two decades of the twentieth century extracurricular activities expanded exponentially within U.S. public high schools. Stimulated by the doctrine of social efficiency and now officially sanctioned, these activities were to serve multiple functions: to teach students self-direction in social, athletic, and academic responsibilities; to integrate and assimilate heterogeneous populations of students; to foster both cooperation and competition; and to instill a commitment to the concept of equality of opportunity and participation in democracy (Krug, 1969). With the stratification of students through differentiation of the curriculum and implementation of standardized testing, extracurricular activities were idealized as the main venue of equality of opportunity for students:

> The one place where democratic ideals and objectives may function in a natural matrix is in the conduct of the extra-curricular activities. Whether a student is notably dull, studious, clever, rich, poor, handsome, or ugly he should have an equal opportunity to be a member of a school organization which ought under all circumstances to be organized upon a basis of democratic society. (Fass, 1989:76)

In addition to these elevated goals, extracurricular activities were also supposed to assist the school in maintaining discipline and in retaining students. Student government, assemblies, and athletics were ranked first in the hierarchy of activities, with any other activity that could be justified as contributing to the goals established by the *Cardinal Principals* included in extracurricular programs (e.g., newspaper, debating, drama).

By the 1930s most high school extracurricular programs contained an assortment of academic, social, and special interest clubs. Powell and associates write that the extracurriculum had such a profound impact on the curriculum that many schools were even giving students academic credit for their participation in activities. By the 1930s and 1940s extracurricular activities were a significant component of the high school experience.

Contemporary Views and Research of the Extracurriculum

What does the current literature say about the extracurriculum? The extracurriculum has been addressed in several ways; for the most part, it is seen as having positive influences on adolescent development. However, school-sponsored activities have also been regarded as having a potentially negative impact on students' academic performance or their social status. By the time extracurricular programs became fashionable in the 1930s sociologist Willard Waller was already cautioning about the detrimental effects these activities

could have for students and sponsors; that is, diverting attention from the real purpose of schooling, academics (Waller, 1965). In his classic study, the *Adolescent Society,* James S. Coleman argued that our society had generated a separate society, one of adolescents, whose goals, values, and extracurricular activities share only perfunctory commonalities with adult society. According to Coleman, distinctive subcultures that emerge within the high school can be seen as extensions of activity participation that pervade the lives of teenagers and attenuate connections between teenagers and their academic investments in education.

The principal foci of research on extracurricular participation shifts our attention from one of the purpose or function of the extracurriculum to an examination of implicit causal relations between participation and individual student outcomes such as academic achievement, social development (e.g., self-esteem, status), political involvement, and student retention. Most of this research utilizes self-reports, surveys, and individual level data (e.g., grade point average) to demonstrate relationships between these variables.

Less emphasis has been devoted to the relationship between student participation and the organizational features of the school. For example, Barker and Gump (1965) found significant correlations between school size and students' opportunities to participate in activities. However, with few exceptions little attention has been given to how the school organizes the extracurriculum and how this organization impacts student involvement (see Morgan and Alwin, 1980; Quiroz et al., 1996). In addition to the structural characteristics of the school such as size, are exogenous characteristics such as the social class of a student's family, which has been found to have a significant positive relationship with student participation (Otto, 1976).

Nevertheless, Holland and Andre (1987) describe the research on participation in extracurricular activities as typically atheoretical, lacking specification of the processes involved in participation and how participation influences adolescent development. One explanation for this problem is that inferences are drawn largely from survey data, and are thus limited in their utility for illuminating the social processes involved in participation.

More recent work has focused on the processes involved in student activity participation and the construction of identity. In combining data from separately conducted ethnographies on the same high school, Quiroz et al. (1996) found formal and informal constraints operating in the high school that limit student participation in activities (i.e., participation criteria, teacher recruitment). Arguing that the processes involved in activity participation interact with the school's tracking system to recruit and reward students already demonstrating comparatively greater success with schooling, this work delineates some of the processes involved in activity participation. David Kinney's (1993) examination of the construction of adolescent identity via activity participation in high school also reveals how extracurricular activities and peer culture coalesce to shape adolescent values and behavior.

Other examinations of the extracurriculum focus on the processes involved in the reproduction of inequality. Although most of this research has focused predominantly on participation in athletic activities (Coleman, 1961; Eitzen, 1975; Otto, 1982; Braddock, 1982; Braddock et al., 1991; Spreitzer and Pugh, 1973), comparatively little attention has been given to the impact of female participation in athletics. Theoretically, with the passage of Title IX, girls and women were provided equal opportunity for participation in athletics. As a consequence, female participation in athletics rose from approximately 4% in 1972 to 26% by 1987. Nonetheless, male participation in athletics remains almost twice that of females. Moreover, among females, ethnic minority girls and women demonstrate consistently lower participation rates across activities (AAUW Report, 1995).

Insights into these figures are given in Eder and Parker's (1987) study of middle school students illustrating how participation in certain extracurricular activities reproduces gender differences. Eder and Parker argue that students learn different values through participation in various activities. These values align with gender and are reinforced within peer cultures, thus reproducing *gender* cultures.

Following the early lead of James S. Coleman, other researchers have examined the consequences of activity participation for student social development, frequently interpreting the extracurriculum as facilitating the social reproduction of inequality. Activities are ranked in terms of the status and influence they afford their individual members, with certain activities contributing to the reproduction of particular peer cultures. Added to this is the fact that schools utilize various criteria for participation in activities (e.g., grade point average, competition, skills, popularity), thus limiting access to activities for many students.

Nevertheless, the dominant view of the extracurriculum is as a positive source of development for students. It is assumed that through participation students learn to identify with the school and to increase their academic investments in education (Haensly et al., 1986; Otto, 1982). The extracurriculum is also observed as an opportunity for increasing and improving interracial interactions (Slavin and Madden, 1979; Crain, 1981; Crain et al., 1982; Thornton, 1982), a means of achieving social status and enhancing self-esteem (Coleman, 1961; Cusick, 1973; Grabe, 1981; Eckert, 1989), and a mechanism that keeps kids in school (Powell et al., 1985). As an incentive structure offering respite from academic pursuits, the extracurriculum provides both a break from the evaluative character of classroom work and an alternative route to achievement for students who are academically weak (Dreeben, 1968; Murtaugh, 1988; Finn, 1989; Snyder and Spreitzer, 1992). Indeed, McNeal (1995) found that those students participating in extracurricular activities are less likely to drop out of high school.

Thus, the modern characterization of the extracurriculum is of an incentive system, dependent upon voluntary student participation, and one of the more enjoyable aspects of student life that contributes to the social and academic development of students. In fact, Powell and colleagues argue "There is nothing *extra* about the extracurriculum. . . . It is as integral to high schools as food service and celebrity appearances are integral to shopping malls" (1985:29).

Summary

To what degree do contemporary extracurricular programs fulfill the original goals set forth in the early twentieth century? We can infer from the current research that at least some of the goals of the early reformers have been realized by a segment of participants. For example, the socializing function of the extracurriculum can be seen in such activities as student government, where members are taught the rules of parliamentary procedure as well as the rudimentary skills of participation in a democratic system (e.g., the actual working of different branches of government). Such organizations actually create constitutions, maintain elections, and introduce the entire student body to the democratic political process. Junior Achievement and other business clubs teach their participants such things as entrepreneurship, individual responsibility, the problematic nature of making a profit, and private ownership, all essential characteristics of the capitalistic enterprise.

In addition to the socialization of participants, the extracurriculum complements the academic curriculum through the fostering of competition. Perhaps the best illustration of this is the sports program of a school. Other examples include music, dramatics, and a variety of other activities in which students must compete both interscholastically and within the school as well. Many extracurricular activities maintain selection criteria for participation such as grade point average, tryouts, popularity, etc. Of course a basic lesson of all competition is the within-group cooperation that is required in these programs. Athletic competition must be expressed as "team" cooperation just as musical competition must be expressed as "ensemble" music. Thus, in all competition *between* groups, there is the element of cooperation *within* the group.

Another goal of early reformers focused on student retention. Through both quantitative and qualitative efforts, researchers have found a positive relationship between extracurricular participation and student retention. Despite these positive correlations, we still do not know whether participation in activities influences students to remain in school, or whether students who are secure in the educational process form the population that participates in the extracurriculum. There has even been some evidence to suggest that through formal and informal mechanisms, the school assists in disproportionately sorting (through recruitment and participation criteria) into activities those students who have already demonstrated comparatively greater academic success. Indeed, if this mechanism does contribute to the retention of students then it compels us to address the following questions: *Which students are most likely to become involved in activities?* and *How does this process occur?*

Analogous to the issue of student retention, the verdict is still out on the extracurriculum's capacity to integrate populations of students. In fact, what little attention has been given to this issue indicates that although opportunities for interracial and cross-gender

interaction are enhanced through participation in the extracurriculum, the extent to which this actually occurs in multiethnic and coeducational environments remains undocumented. Questions as such, *Do the rates of participation for students from different ethnic groups vary in multiethnic schools? Which groups participate and in which activities? What are the differing effects of participation for these distributions across types of activities? How does this hold for different social class or gendered groups of students?* have yet to be adequately addressed.

What are the net benefits of extracurricular participation on social or academic development? How does this occur? Are these benefits locused in the student and in the school or do these benefits get translated in postsecondary work or education? In what ways have extracurricular programs changed over time? These are perhaps the most important questions for those interested in school organization, student identity, educational reform, and public policy. Unless we are able to specify both the causal and substantive relationships of extracurricular participation and the consequences for student participation, this feature of the school structure will either remain a means of filling up time for a fraction of the student population, a political football in times of school fiscal crises, or simply an untapped source of potential curricular innovation. Moreover, the methods we use in examining these potential relationships also merit further attention. We need to reevaluate whether survey information on students, currently our dominant source of data, is the optimal way to obtain insights into this aspect of schooling.

The extracurriculum has become a major addition to the American high school, providing students with experiences as valuable as those found in the academic curriculum. However, more research is needed to answer questions raised about both the goals of the extracurriculum and its actual functions in the high school. Considering the many ways in which the extracurriculum has grown, perhaps its continued popularity with students, teachers, and parents best alerts us to its success as a permanent facet of American education.

REFERENCES

AAUW Report. 1995. *How Schools Shortchange Girls.* New York: Marlowe & Company.

Barker, R. G., and P. V. Gump. 1964. *Big School, Small School: High School Size and Student Behavior.* Stanford, CA: Stanford University Press.

Braddock, J. 1988. "Academics and Athletics in American High Schools: Some Future Considerations of the Adolescent Subculture Hypothesis." *Journal of Social and Behavioral Sciences* 28(4):88–94.

Braddock, J., D. A. Royster, L. F. Winfield, and R. Hawkins. 1991. "Bouncing Back: Sports and Academic Resilience among African-American Males." *Education and Urban Society* 24(1):113–131.

Coleman, J. S. 1961. *The Adolescent Society*. New York: Free Press.

Crain, R. L. 1981. "Making Desegregation Work: Extracurricular Activities." *The Urban Review* 13(2):121–127.

Crain, R. L., R. E. Mahard, and R. E. Narot. 1982. *Making Desegregation Work: How Schools Create Social Climates*. Cambridge, MA: Ballinger.

Cusick, P. 1973. *Inside High School*. New York: Holt, Rinehart & Winston.

Dreeben, R. 1968. *On What Is Learned in School*. Reading, MA: Addison-Wesley.

Eckert, P. 1989. *Jocks and Burnouts: Social Categories and Identity in the High School*. New York: Teachers College Press.

Eder, D., and S. Parker. 1987. "The Cultural Reproduction of Gender: The Effect of Extracurricular Activities on Peer-Group Culture." *Sociology of Education* 60:200–213.

Eitzen, D. S. 1975. "Athletics in the Status System of Male Adolescents: A Replication of Coleman's *The Adolescent Society*." *Adolescence* 10(38):267–276.

Fass, P. S. 1989. *Outside In: Minorities and the Transformation of American Education*. Oxford: Oxford University Press.

Finn, J. D. 1989. "Withdrawing from School." *Review of Educational Research* 59(2):117–142.

Grabe, M. 1981. "School Size and The Importance of School Activities." *Adolescence* 61:21–31.

Gutowski, T. W. 1988. "Student Initiative and the Origins of the High School Extracurriculum: Chicago, 1880–1915." *History of Education Quarterly* 28(1):49–72.

Haensly, P. A., A. E. Lupkowski, and E. P. Edlind. 1986. "The Role of Extracurricular Activities in Education." In *The High School Journal*, pp. 110–119. Raleigh, NC: The University of North Carolina Press.

Holland, A., and T. Andre. 1987. "Participation in Extracurricular Activities in Secondary School: What Is Known, What Needs to Be Known?" *Review of Educational Research* 57(4):437–466.

Kinney, D. 1993. "From Nerds to Normals: The Recovery of Identity among Adolescents from Middle School to High School." *Sociology of Education* 66:21–40.

Krug, E. A. 1969. *The Shaping of the American High School: 1880–1941*. Madison: University of Wisconsin Press.

McNeal, R. B., Jr. 1995. "Extracurricular Activities and High School Dropouts." *Sociology of Education* 68:62–81.

Murtaugh, M. 1988. "Achievement Outside the Classroom: The Role of Non Academic Activities in the Lives of High School Students." *Anthropology & Education Quarterly* 19:382–395.

Nasaw, D. 1979. *Schooled to Order: A Social History of Public Schooling in the United States*. Oxford: Oxford University Press.

National Education Association. 1918. *Cardinal Principles of Secondary Education*. Bureau of Education Bulletin. Washington, DC: U.S. Government Printing Office.

Otto, L. B. 1976. "Extracurricular Activities and Aspirations in the Status Attainment Process." *Rural Sociology* 41:217–233.

———. 1982. "Extracurricular Activities." In H. J. Walberg (ed.), *Improving Educational Standards and Productivity*, pp. 217–227. Berkeley, CA: McCutchan.

Powell, A. G., E. Farrar, and D. K. Cohen. 1985. *The Shopping Mall High School*. Boston: Houghton Mifflin.

Quiroz, P. A., N. Gonzalez, and K. A. Frank. 1996. In A. M. Pallas (ed.), *Research in Sociology of Education and Socialization*. Greenwich, CT: JAI Press.

Slavin, R. E., and N. A. Madden. 1979. "School Practices That Improve Race Relations." *American Educational Research Journal* 16:169–180.

Snyder, E. E., and E. Spritzer. 1992. "Social Psychological Concomitants of Adolescents' Role Identities as Scholars and Athletes: A Longitudinal Analysis." *Youth and Society* 23(4):507–522.

Spreitzer, E., and M. Pugh. 1973. "Interscholastic Athletics and Educational Expectations." *Sociology of Education* 46:171–182.

Spring, J. 1994. *The American School 1642–1993*. New York: Longman.

Thornton, C. H. 1982. "School Desegregation, Athletics and Educational Achievement." *Journal of Social and Behavioral Sciences* 28(4):104–112.

Trent, W., and J. Braddock. 1995. "Extracurricular Activities in Secondary Schools." *Encyclopedia of Education*.

Waller, W. 1965. *The Sociology of Teaching*. New York: Wiley.

FUNCTIONALIST THEORIES OF EDUCATION

Peter W. Cookson, Jr.
Teachers College, Columbia University

Alan R. Sadovnik
Rutgers University

Overview

For almost two decades Americans have been told that their schools are failing to produce graduates that were capable of competing in the international marketplace. Academics, government and nongovernment organizations, and lobbying groups have produced research results that claim that the declining literacy and numeracy of American youth are responsible for the substantial economic dislocations that have occurred since the 1960s. Although these studies vary in their methodologies, samples, and results, they share certain basic assumptions about the relationship between school and society. Like most Americans these researchers assume that (1) schools and democracies are organized on the basis of merit and (2) there is a close fit between schools and society. They presume a "functional" relationship between school and society that guides the research questions that are asked, the data that are collected, and the results that are reported. This research paradigm dominates educational and sociological research, with the exception of those sociologists working in the conflict tradition [see Hurn (*Conflict Theory*), this volume]. In this chapter, we examine the functionalist world view, the application of functionalism to the study of education and to research, and offer a brief critique.

The Functionalist World View

Functionalist sociologists begin with a picture of society that stresses the interdependence of the social system; these researchers are apt to examine how well the parts are integrated with each other. Functionalists view society as a kind of machine, where one part articulates with another to produce the dynamic energy required to make society work. Most importantly, functionalism stresses the processes that maintain the social order by emphasizing consensus and agreement. Although functionalists understand that change is inevitable, they underscore the evolutionary nature of change. Further, although they acknowledge that conflict between groups exist, functionalists argue that there must be a common bond to unite groups or society will disintegrate. Thus, functionalists examine the social processes necessary to the establishment and maintenance of social order.

Functionalist theories of schools and society trace their origins to Durkheim's general sociology theory. Durkheim's sociology (1893/1947, 1915/1954) was at its center concerned with the effects of the decline of traditional rituals and community during the transition from traditional to modern societies. Durkheim's analysis of the differences between mechanical and organic solidarity in the *Division of Labor* (1893/1947), and his concept of anomie in *Suicide* (1897/1951), examined the need for societies to create rituals and institutions to provide social cohesion and meaning. Like Ferdinand Tonnies' (1887/1957) analysis of gemeinschaft and gesellschaft, Durkheim provided a sociological analysis of the effects of modernity on community. For Durkheim, the processes of industrialization, urbanization, and modernization resulted in the breakdown of traditional rituals and methods of social control. In *Suicide* (1897/1951), he demonstrated empirically how the breakdown in traditional community resulted in the decline of collective conscience and the rise of individualism. Such a breakdown led to what Durkheim called *anomie*, the condition of normlessness in individuals and society. As the bonds that connected individuals to each other and to society became un-hinged, modern societies faced disintegration from within. Durkheim, however, was not a reactionary; he did not believe that the solution to social disintegration was a return to the past, with its strict forms of social control and regulation. Rather, he believed that modern societies had to develop new forms of social control and cohesion that would allow for the newly developed individualism of modernity to exist within a cohesive society. Such a society, what Durkheim called organic solidarity, would allow for a balance between individualism and community.

The Application of Functional Theory to Education

Durkheim was the first sociologist to apply sociological theory to education. His major works on education include *Moral Education* (1962), *The Evolution of Educational Thought* (1977), and *Education and Sociology* (1956). Although Durkheim recognized that education has taken different forms at different times and places, he believed that education, in virtually all societies, was of critical importance in creating the moral unity necessary for social cohesion and harmony.

Durkheim's emphasis on values and cohesion set the tone for how present day functionalists approach the study of education. Functionalists tend to assume that consensus is the normal state in society and that conflict represents a breakdown of shared values. In a highly integrated, well-functioning society, schools socialize students into the appropriate values and sort and select students according to their abilities. Education reform, then, from a functional point of view, is supposed to create structures, programs, and curricula that are technically advanced, rational, and encourage social unity. Whereas conflict theory (see Hurn, this volume) argues that schools function in the interests of the dominant groups in a society, functionalism sees schools as operating in the interests of the majority of citizens. Functionalists identify four particular purposes of schooling: intellectual, political, social, and economic (Bennett and LeCompte, 1990:5–21).

- The intellectual purposes of schooling include teaching basic cognitive skills such as reading, writing, and mathematics; transmitting specific knowledge, for example, literature, history, and science; and helping students acquire higher order thinking skills such as analysis, synthesis, and evaluation.

- The political purposes of schooling include inculcating allegiance to the existing political order; preparing citizens to participate in this political order; helping assimilate diverse cultural groups into a common political order; and teaching children the basic laws of the society.

- The social purposes of schooling include socializing children into the various roles, behaviors, and values of society. This process, referred to by sociologists as socialization, is a key ingredient to the stability of any society. If children are not socialized into the social order, they will not be able to work in the society's social institutions, will not maintain social relationships, and will not ensure the continuance of the social order.

- The economic purposes of education include preparing students for their later occupational roles and to select, train, and allocate individuals into the division of labor. Whereas the degree to which schools directly prepare students for work varies from society to society, most schools have at least an indirect role in this process. In modern industrial and technological societies, the economic purposes of education are particularly important because there is an inherent tension between the division of labor and the norm of social allocation by merit.

Modern functionalist theories of education have their origin in the work of Talcott Parsons (1937). Parsons believed that education is a vital part of a modern society, a society that differed considerably from all previous societies. From this perspective, schooling performs important functions in the development and maintenance of a modern, democratic society, especially with regard to equality of opportunity for all citizens. Functionalists such as Davis and Moore (1945) argued that inequality was necessary in all societies, as it ensured that the most talented individuals would fill the most important positions. Schools play a critical role in the functionalist social scenario because achievement and advancement are based on merit rather than privilege. This democratic–liberal perspective views education as a vital institution in capitalist society (Hurn, 1993:44–47). Although considerable inequality remains, this society is characterized by the evolutionary movement from ascription to achievement with equal educational opportunity being the crucial component of a fair and meritocratic order. According to this perspective, the historical pattern of academic failure by minority and working class students was a blemish on the principles of justice and equality of opportunity. This educational pattern necessitated the formulation of reform programs to ensure equality of opportunity. Although functionalist theorists disagree on the causes of academic failure, they vigorously believe that the solutions to both educational and social problems are possible within the capitalist social structure. As researcher Diane Ravitch argues:

It is indisputable that full equality has not been achieved, but equally indisputable in the light of the evidence is the conclusion that a democratic society can bring about effective social change, if there is both the leadership and the political commitment to do so. To argue, against the evidence, that meaningful change is not possible is to sap the political will that is necessary to effect changes. (1977:114–115)

Parson's work initiated an American tradition of functionalism; his best known disciple and critic was Robert Merton. One of Merton's contributions to functionalist theory was his critique of Parson's all-encompassing system of concepts; Merton argued for theories of middle range. A theory of middle range differs from grand theory because it is couched at a lower level of abstraction and is expressed in operationalized concepts that are testable through measurement. In effect, the work of Merton set the tone for a great deal of sociological research. He believed that sociologists had to create an interlocking set of middle range testable theories. The sociological enterprise became increasingly empirically oriented and this trend directly affected the research of sociologists of education.

The Application of Functional Theory to Research

Building on the work of Durkheim, Parsons, and Merton, researchers such as Robert Dreeben began to study schools from a functionalist perspective. Dreeben's 1968 study, *On What Is Learned in School*, is a classic analysis on the social organization of schools from a

functionalist perspective. At the same time as Dreeben and others were describing schools in functionalist terms, James Coleman and his colleagues began to conduct large-scale quantitative studies of American education. Virtually all of Coleman's work assumes a functional relationship between school and society. His fundamental research model is to compare student inputs (i.e., social class background, race, academic ability) with student outputs (generally scores on standardized tests) and to draw inferences about the organization of schooling from the variation in achievement. This research strategy implies that there is a close connection between the values of the school and the values of society. In his later work (1982, 1987), Coleman, with his colleagues, was quite explicit about the necessity of schools to be value cultures. Much of this functionalist perspective is embedded in the research methodology and on certain unquestioned assumptions about the social order. For Coleman and other functionalist researchers, society is more or less a given. The role of education is to create consensus and economic productivity.

The work of Dreeben, Coleman, and others permeates and shapes most of mainline sociology of education. An example of this tradition is the status attainment school of research (Blau and Duncan, 1967; Sewell et al., 1969). This research examines the degree of variation in a dependent variable (i.e., occupational status) that can be explained by individual's characteristics and the amount of schooling they have attained. This research strategy has many variations but its underlying assumptions about the nature of sociological inquiry and the relation of school and society are quintessentially functional. The status attainment literature indicates that educational attainment is a key variable in occupational mobility; the higher the educational attainment, the greater the likelihood of occupational mobility. This model, however, questions neither the nature of the occupational order nor the internal relationship between number of years of education completed and actual preparation for an occupation. This research, which is highly quantitative, set the standard for most sociological research.

This style of inquiry has affected research in related areas. When, for example, the National Commission on Excellence issued its report, *A Nation at Risk*, in 1983, it was assumed that public schools were responsible for America's relative economic decline. There was no suggestion in the report that education might not have the power to overcome deep social and economic problems without changing other aspects of American life. Virtually every report since *A Nation at Risk* has assumed a functionalist perspective without a great deal of regard for the empirical findings that demonstrate that the American educational system is far from meritocratic and that there are major pressures within the system to keep it that way. American education reproduces the social order with surprising exactitude and this may be because its latent function is to reward privilege rather than merit.

Critiques of Functionalist Theory

Conflict theorists question many of the assumptions of functionalist theorists. Whereas functionalists view society as based on value consensus, conflict theorists tend to see the social order as a product of coercion and ideological manipulation. There are two variations of conflict theory: Marxist and Weberian. In the mid-1970s, Marxist economists Samuel Bowles and Herbert Gintis published a controversial book, *Schooling in Capitalist America* (1976). In this work, they argue that there was a correspondence between schooling and the class system; that is, upper class students receive an education that prepares them for college and the world of management, whereas working class students receive an education that prepares them for manual labor and occupations that required very little intellectual attainment. The Marxist critique of functionalism is not that there is no relationship between school and society, but that this relationship is based on inequality and maintained by social power.

In some ways, the Weberian critique is even more radical. In the early 1970s sociologist Randall Collins published an article, "Functional and Conflict Theories in Educational Stratification" (1971). What does an educational credential mean? Do employers really care what graduates study in school? Or are credentials social shorthand for desirable status? In his work, Collins discovered that, contrary to the functionalist perspective, most employers look for educational credentials as an indicator of social status and class background. Since his early work, Collins has continued to argue that education works to preserve the social order of inequality by providing credentials that appear to be based on merit, but are primarily based on privilege.

It is difficult to argue, for instance, that students who attend the most elite secondary schools in the country find their way into Ivy League colleges simply based on their academic abilities (Cookson and Persell, 1985). Sociologists such as Hopper (1971) point out that functionalists generally fail to distinguish between educational route and educational amount. Two people may have the same amount of education, but the route by which they achieve that amount may be substantially different and result in differential educational and occupational opportunities. It is equally difficult to argue that students from the lower-middle class, the working class, and the impoverished class experience school failure at an extremely high rate simply because they fail to make an effort (MacLoud, 1987). Numerous sociologists have argued that non-middle-class, non-white students either are systematically discriminated against in schools and/or develop styles of resistance that reject education. Qualitative and ethnographic studies seldom give comfort to functionalists because in studying individuals and small groups, the effects of class and race on mobility become apparent. In fact, since the 1960s, functionalist theories within the academic world have become increasingly subject to empirical and theoretical criticism. The future of functionalism, as a theoretical approach, is in some doubt because much of the evidence indicates that differences within schools (tracking) and differences between schools (private vs. public, suburban vs. urban), account for more of the variation in student achievement and mobility than functional arguments can credibly endure.

REFERENCES

Bennett, K. P., and M. D. LeCompte. 1990. *How Schools Work*. New York: Largimcer.

Blau, P., and O. D. Duncan. 1967. *The American Occupational Structure*. New York: Wiley.

Bowles, S., and H. Gintis. 1976. *Schooling in Capitalist America*. New York: Basic Books.

Coleman, J. S., and T. Hoffer. 1987. *Public and Private High Schools: The Impact of Communities*. New York: Basic Books.

Coleman, J. S., T. Hoffer, and S. Kilgore. 1982. *High School Achievement: Public, Catholic, and Private Schools Compared*. New York: Basic Books.

Collins, R. 1971. "Functional and Conflict Theories of Educational Stratification," *American Sociological Review* 36:1002–1019.

Cookson, P., and C. Persell. 1985. *Preparing for Power: America's Elite Boarding Schools*. New York: Basic Books.

Davis, K., W. E. Moore. 1945. "Some Principles of Stratification." *American Sociological Review* 10(2):242–249.

Dreeban, R. 1968. *On What Is Learned in School*. Reading, MA: Addison-Wesley.

Durkheim, E. 1947. *The Division of Labor in Society*. Glencoe, IL: Free Press. (Original work published in 1893.)

———. 1951. *Suicide*. Glencoe, IL: Free Press. (Original work published in 1897.)

———. 1954. *The Elementary Forms of Religious Life*. Glencoe, IL: Free Press. (Original work published in 1915.)

——— 1956. *Education and Sociology*. New York: The Free Press.

———. 1962. *Moral Education*. New York: The Free Press.

——— 1977. *The Evolution of Educational Thought*. (P. Collins, Trans.). London: Routledge and Kegan Paul.

Hopper, E. 1971. "Stratification, Education and Mobility In Industrial Societies," In E. Hopper (ed.), *Readings in the Theory of Educational Systems*. London: Hutchinson.

Hurn, C. 1993. *The Limits and Possibilities of Schooling*. Needham Heights, MA: Allyn & Bacon.

MacLoud, J. 1987. *Ain't No Making It: Learned Aspirations in a Low-Income Neighborhood*. Boulder, CO: Westview.

Parsons, T. 1937. *The Structure of Social Action*. New York: McGraw-Hill.

Sewell, W. H., A. O. Haller, and A. Portes. 1969. "The Educational and Early Occupational Attainment Process." *American Sociological Review*. 34:82–92.

Tonnies, F. 1957. *Community and Society*. New York: Harper. (Original work published in 1887.)

GENDER AND EDUCATION

Sara Delamont
University of Wales

Sociologists of education paid little attention to gender until the 1970s. During the growth in the sociological study of education from 1945 onward many studies were conducted on male-only samples, and the sexual division of labor in industrialized societies was taken for granted, not treated as a topic for investigation or for theoretically informed debate. This is demonstrated (with a content analysis of major journals) for the United Kingdom by Acker (1981, 1994), who reviewed educational research in Britain from the 1950s to the 1970s. She found that gender issues were frequently ignored, and that female experiences and the outcomes of education for women were regularly left unresearched. Many highly respected studies were based on male-only samples. The 1972 social mobility study of England and Wales (Halsey et al., 1980), for example, was based on a sample of 10,000 men. Lightfoot (1975) reached a similar conclusion about American research. The third edition of the textbook by Havighurst and Neugarten (1967) devoted more space to feral children (reared as or by wild animals) than to gender divisions in the United States. Cordasco (1970) gave more space to Inuit education than to gender.

The rise of the feminist movement in the 1970s produced educational researchers who wanted to examine sex differences in the outcomes of schooling and higher education (such as exam results), to explore how females experienced learning, and to conduct action research to try and change both the experiences and the outcomes (see, for example, Gutentag and Bray, 1976). This development had an impact on the sociology of education so that the fourth edition of Havighurst and Neugarten (1975) differs from the third because it includes material on gender.

The central questions addressed by sociologists of education concerning gender have been both macrolevel (i.e., at the level of the whole society) and microlevel (i.e., focused on patterns of classroom interaction and the lives of individuals). Questions have been asked about equality of opportunity (Are both sexes given an equal opportunity to learn physics or enter law school?), equality of outcome (Which sex gets the best high school results?), about experiences in education (What is it like to be a third-grade girl in America?), the content of education (Does the history textbook mention Jane Addams?), and the opinions of pupils and teachers (Do third-grade girls think women can be dentists? Do male high school football coaches believe boys should learn ballet?). In the United States gender issues cannot be disentangled from class and ethnicity: the achievement, experiences, and opinions of a tenth-grade girl from a professional home, of Japanese-American ancestry, in a Californian city are very different from those of a tenth-grade boy from an African-American blue-collar home in the rural Carolinas, and many of the differences have nothing to do with gender, and everything to do with other sociological variables such as class, ethnicity, and urban or rural residence. Compare the small town high school studied by Peshkin (1978) with the large city center and suburban high schools portrayed by Lightfoot (1983).

Sociologists of education have used a wide range of methods to gather data on gender and education. These include individual interviews (designed to gather life and oral history, or narratives, or current experience and opinion), focus groups and group interviews, diaries, open-ended writing, direct observation with or without prespecified coding schedules, surveys, and the experiment and the quasi-experiment. Whatever method is chosen, sociologists interested in gender and education at school level must face the ethical issues that surround gathering data from children (see Fine and Sandstrom, 1990; Denscombe and Aubrook, 1992). Also, because sex, gender, sexuality, and sexual identity are private, hidden areas of many people's lives, data collection is difficult. The "hidden curriculum" of beliefs about sex, gender, sexuality, and sexual identity is sympathetically described by Raphaela Best (1983). She followed a cohort of pupils from childhood into adolescence, learning about their culture and simultaneously confronting them with illogicalities in their sex role stereotypes. Her central argument is that schools teach children three curricula, one overt and two hidden. The academic curriculum and the official school rules are manifest, but behind them, and largely invisible to adults, are the rules of appropriate male and female behavior learned from peers and enforced by them. Concealed behind that first "hidden" curriculum was a third, even more secret children's culture, where sexuality and obscenity were crucial. The third area was the most carefully hidden from adults, because, as Bauman (1982:178) explains:

> The free peer group activity of children is by its very nature a privileged realm in which adults are alien intruders, especially so insofar as much of the children's folklore repertoire violates what children understand to be adult standards of decorum.

Pupils' feelings about gender are frequently in this "privileged realm." It is both practically difficult and ethically problematic to gather data on the two hidden curricula. See Fine (1987:238–240), Canaan (1986), Measor (1989), Measor and Woods (1984), Delamont (1991), and Delamont and Atkinson (1995:145–168). Researchers can gradually gain access if, like Best, they reveal themselves to be unshockable and trustworthy. Such things as sexual harassment in schools (Mahoney, 1985; Herbert, 1989), accusations about young women being sexually immoral (Canaan, 1986), and peer pressures on boys to act tough, and display *machismo* (Best, 1983; Fine, 1987), flourish in this privileged realm. Such topics are easier for sociologists to study among students in higher education (e.g., Moffat, 1989; Holland and Eisenhart, 1990).

Cutting across the literature on research methods is a set of arguments about how gender issues should be researched. Since the 1970s there has been a philosophical debate about the nature of "scientific" enquiry in Western capitalist societies (see Harding, 1986) and whether its whole basis was actually contaminated by *unexamined* assumptions about masculinity versus femininity, male versus female, objectivity versus subjectivity, mind versus body, and reason versus emotions. These debates are acutely relevant to studies of gender, because there is no neutral ground from which a scholar can investigate males and females (see Haste, 1994). Such concerns led to developing feminist research methods (Maynard and Purvis, 1994). Maynard (1994) presents the interrelated arguments over qualitative *versus* quantitative methods and whether feminist research must use the former to be true to the experiences of women. Sociologists of education and gender issues need to be familiar with debates on feminist methods and epistemologies.

Two qualitative methods are currently fashionable for research on gender and education: collecting life histories and narratives.

Sociologists have done life histories of teachers (both men and women) to explore how gender impacts on teaching (Weiler, 1988) and educational administration (Shakeshaft, 1989). Peterson (1964) is a classic piece of life history, done on women teachers in the United States. Sikes et al. (1985) and Connell (1985) carried out life history work on men and women teachers in England and Australia, respectively. In the 1990s the collection and analysis of stories, especially teachers' stories, have become a major research activity. Cortazzi (1993) is an excellent methods book on narrative, and Cortazzi (1991) is a useful example of the data produced. Feminist researchers have been particularly enthusiastic about the collection of narratives from women teachers and girl pupils: see Witherall and Noddings (1991) and Fine (1988).

Good research on gender and education can be done using any method or combination of methods. The important thing is *not* to treat gender as something known and familiar, but as an issue for the research (Delamont and Atkinson, 1995). So a well-designed survey that investigates whether both girls and boys can be good at math or take leadership roles is "better" than a qualitative study that assumes that only boys can do math or be leaders.

Good researchers need to do several things. First, collect and report data on gender in the field setting;

second, pay equal attention to all the informants in the setting, whether they are male or female (see Smith, 1978); third, collect data on how the actors in a field setting understand and view gender; fourth, gather data on how those beliefs are enacted (e.g., in speech, or in nonverbal behavior); fifth, examine the relation between gender and power in the field setting; *and* all the time the researcher needs to make his or her *own* beliefs about gender problematic (Delamont and Atkinson, 1995:Chapter 9).

Central Research Questions and Findings

Kessler et al. (1985:131) argue that "There is abundant evidence that inequality between women and men is a very general feature of Western educational systems."

Sociologists of education in the United States, Canada, Australia, New Zealand, the United Kingdom, and Western Europe have discovered inequalities between men and women at all levels of the education system from the nursery class to the graduate school (Wrigley, 1992; Arnot and Weiler, 1993). Among faculty males hold positions of power over women, among students male perspectives and demands are privileged over female, and women are more frequently steered into avenues that lead to low paid work. Organizational structures, adult prejudices, peer pressures, curricula content, and parental conservatism frequently combine to make educational institutions places where sex role stereotyping is strong.

There are three main approaches to the sociology of education: research on the macrolevel, which focuses on structures and inequalities, research on face-to-face interaction and the everyday lives of individuals, and studies of the sociology of educational knowledge.

All three approaches can usefully be adapted to feminist perspectives and to focus on gender: equally all three approaches can be used to question the gender balance of the subdiscipline of sociology of education itself. So, just as a researcher can ask whether young women have equal access to high school sports, experience sexual harassment, or read U.S. history textbooks that fail to mention Carey Thomas, Jane Addams, or Prudence Crandall, while giving 10 pages to Davy Crockett, one can ask whether women sociologists of education have equal access to the top jobs at Stanford and Columbia, experience sexual harassment, or find their publications lie uncited and ignored by publishers, reviewers, and male scholars.

Research findings at the societal level are consistent across the capitalist industrialized world: for example, there are very few women entering engineering in any country, and although the proportion of women entering professional courses in higher education (e.g., law) has been rising (Granfield, 1992), the physical sciences, especially at the top level, have stayed resolutely male. However, at the microlevel, there is controversy about the findings.

Projects looking for sex differences in classroom interaction have produced contradictory findings. Some authors (e.g., Spender 1982) have claimed that in mixed classrooms, boys take two-thirds or more of the discourse, and react violently if this proportion is reduced. Other authors (e.g., French and French, 1984) have found teachers focusing a disproportionate amount of their attention on boys because boys receive disciplinary interactions more than girls. (See Hammersley, 1990, for a critique of this research.) Such findings have been reported for both male and female teachers. However Bossert (1982), Brophy (1985), and Lindow et al. (1985) reviewing American literature have concluded that this pattern is *not* universally found, and when it is discovered, it is not clear that there are measurable or specific consequences. One of the biggest projects done on classroom interaction patterns in the United Kingdom (Galton et al., 1980) failed to find a major bias in teacher attention toward boys, only a slight tendency (p. 66). Kelly (1988) in a meta-analysis of 81 published studies on this topic concluded that "teachers consistently interact more with boys than with girls" (p. 13). She concludes that if a student's school career is 15,000 hours, a typical boy gets 1,800 hours more teacher attention than a typical girl. However, classrooms differ widely on this variable, for reasons that are not clear. Kelly also highlights one bias in the research: most of it has been done in elementary classrooms (see Croll and Moses, 1990), not at secondary level. The impact of such differences on achievement and attitudes is also unknown. Where boys do receive more disciplinary comment from teachers, they routinely perceive it as unfair, believing teachers are biased against them and erroneously blame males for all trouble, whether it originates with girls or boys.

Researchers have concentrated on patterns of talk in

coeducational classrooms: looking to see whether boys and girls contribute differently and whether teachers treat male and female pupils alike (e.g., Shuy, 1986). We lack studies of all-male or all-female classrooms to compare with those of the coeducational ones. The arguments advanced by Hammersley (1990, 1993) could only be addressed by such comprehensive research.

The same pattern—research concentrated in co-educational classrooms rather than comparing co-educational and single-sex ones—is replicated in the studies of students' educational experience at school and college level. This means we are often unable to determine whether findings are due to the dynamics of schooling *sui generis* or the presence of males and females in the same rooms. The same criticism can be leveled at sociological research on the interactions of ethnicity and gender. Frequently researchers have produced insightful studies of an ethnic group that do not disentangle gender issues, or focused on gender to the neglect of ethnicity. Where the researcher *does* focus on gender and ethnicity, as in Gibson's (1988) work on Punjabis in California or Mac an Ghaill's (1988) on Afro-Caribbean and Asian students in England, the interactions between the two turn out to be complex and important for educational achievement.

Contemporary feminist sociologists have also focused on how the subdiscipline is itself gendered. It is not sufficient that research is done on both sexes without stereotyped biases, it also has to be published, read, cited, and accepted as part of the canon for the subdiscipline to rid itself of sexism. In the United Kingdom there has been a gender inequality in the public availability of data on adolescent boys done by men compared to data on adolescent girls done by women. Work on adolescent boys is much more likely to be funded, and to be published. There has also been an inequality in publication outlets. Research on male adolescents is being published in monographs, whereas equivalent data on young women have been available only in journal articles or research reports, which have lesser impact (see Delamont, 1989:Appendix 1). For example, Hargreaves (1967) and Lacey (1970) are frequently described as pioneers of British school ethnography, whereas Lambert (1977, 1982), their female contemporary, is ignored, because their work was published in books, whereas her study of the girls in the same cities was not. Similarly the research of Furlong (1976) and Fuller (1980) on Afro-Caribbean girls is less well known than parallel studies of young men (e.g., Willis, 1977).

The subdiscipline has made enormous efforts to remove sexist bias from sociology of education, and make gender the focus of high quality work. However there is still an agenda of topics that has yet to be addressed.

The Agenda for Future Research

One of the biggest gaps in our knowledge is why indeed Anglo-Saxon culture is so scared of "sissies" (see Connell, 1987). When students hold stereotyped views about male and female behavior, then the school teachers' reinforcement of them makes classrooms uncomfortable places for the pupil who diverges from the stereotype. Wolpe (1977) and Abraham (1989a,1989b) have both reported secondary teachers' repulsion when faced with boys they saw as "effeminate" (see also Mac an Ghaill, 1991, 1994). Clarricoates (1987) reports similar distaste for a sissy at the elementary school level. She studied a boy—Michael—who really worried both his teacher, Miss Mackeson, and his classmates. When Clarricoates asked why Michael was despised by his classmates, another pupil reported: "When Miss Mackeson asked him what he wanted to be when he grew up he said he wanted to be a butterfly. He's just a great big sissy" (p. 61).

Such distastes for boys who do not measure up is routinely reported by sociologists, but we do not know why schools are so intolerant of sensitivity and imagination in males.

This gap is part of a general shortage of research on masculinity in educational settings. Mac an Ghaill (1994) is the first monograph to treat the area seriously, and there is scope for a great deal more research in all sectors of education. Moffat (1989) touches on masculinity in college culture, as do Adler and Adler (1992) in their work on college athletes, but the topic has been totally neglected in the United Kingdom or Australia.

There is a chronic shortage of research on men as teachers in schools, further or higher education. Connell (1985) stands alone in his attempt to show how masculine identity and working as a schoolteacher interact. The experiences of straight and gay men in all spheres of teaching need documenting along the lines taken by Skelton (1993) and Sparkes (1994).

Despite the research done in the past 20 years there are many areas of female students' experiences that are not yet properly investigated. The school experiences of females in fee-paying schools, both single sex and coeducational, need studying. Many of the initiatives designed to change women's experience of education have not been evaluated by researchers (see Delamont: 1990:114–115). There is a shortage of research on women in vocational programs (Valli, 1986) and higher education (Holland and Eisenhart, 1990; Thomas, 1990). The gender balance of universities has changed markedly over the past 20 years, and the proportion of women reading medicine, law, accountancy, and other "professional" subjects has increased rapidly, but the sociology of higher education has fallen behind (Greed, 1991).

There is a body of research on women in school teaching (Weiler, 1988; Spencer, 1996) and school administration (Shakeshaft, 1989) but less on women college faculty. The factual position of the latter can be gleaned from Lie et al. (1994), but the experiential side is represented by only a few journal articles (e.g., Bagihole, 1993) and occasional books such as Sutherland (1985) and Aisenberg and Harrington (1988).

Most serious, however, is the lack of a large, reliable database on classroom interaction patterns across the whole age range in all subjects, which compares males' and females' experiences of classroom interaction in mixed and single-sex classes. It is a matter of urgency to discover whether girls are routinely receiving less teacher attention, and/or teacher attention of different kinds of boys, and how their learning experiences are different when only girls are in the room. Only when we have this large body of data can we really claim to know what the male and female pupils' experiences of schooling are.

There is also urgent need to design effective ways to incorporate feminist insights into teachers' occupational culture, so that schools change as a result of existing research. Observations in the South East of England in reception classes at two schools (Lloyd, 1989; Lloyd and Duveen, 1992) and data on playgroup workers (Hilton, 1991) show teachers of young children in the United Kingdom reinforcing the behaviors in girls that they dislike. Serbin's (1978) research showed nursery school teachers objecting to girls "clinging" and keeping close to them. Yet, when observed, it became clear that girls could get teachers' attention and re-

sponse only when physically close. Girls beyond touching distance were ignored, unlike boys who received teacher attention wherever they were in the nursery. Other studies of teachers (see Delamont, 1990) and of recruits to the occupation (e.g., Sikes, 1991) reveal an occupational group largely unaware of feminist perspectives, ignorant that gender is socially constructed, and unconscious of the school's role in reinforcing conservative messages about sex roles. Feminism has not penetrated teachers' occupational culture nor has it changed classroom behavior (Acker, 1994). Despite the currency of feminist ideas in recent years, the apparent resistance to them in many educational settings highlights the resilience of occupational and institutional cultures, a central concern for sociologists of education.

REFERENCES

Abraham, J. 1989a. "Teacher Ideology and Sex Roles in Curriculum Texts." *British Journal of Sociology of Education* 10:33–52.

——— 1989b. "Gender Differences and Anti-school Boys." *Sociological Review* 37(1):65–88.

Acker, S. 1981. "No Woman's Land." *Sociological Review* 29(1):65–88.

———. 1994. "No Woman's Land." In S. Acker (ed.), *Gendered Education*, pp. 27–42. Philadelphia: The Open University Press.

Adler, P., and P. Adler. 1992. *Backboards and Blackboards*. New York: Columbia University Press.

Aisenberg, N., and M. Harrington. 1988. *Women of Academe*. Amherst: University of Massachusetts Press.

Arnot, M., and K. Weiler, eds. 1993. *Feminism and Social Justice in Education*. London: Falmer.

Bagihole, B. 1993. "How to Keep a Good Woman Down." *British Journal of Sociology of Education* 14(3):261–274.

Bauman, R. 1982. "Ethnography of Children's Folklore." In P. Gilmore and A. A. Glatthorn (eds.), *Children in and out of School*, pp. 172–186. Washington DC: Center for Applied Linguistics.

Best, Raphaela. 1983. *We've All Got Scars*. Bloomington: Indiana University Press.

Bossert, S. 1982. "Understanding Sex Differences in Children's Classroom Experiences." In W. Doyle and T. L. Good (eds.), *Focus on Teaching*, pp. 170–181. Chicago: The University of Chicago Press.

Brophy, J. 1985. "Interactions of Male and Female Students with Male and Female Teachers." In L. C. Wilkinson and C. Marrett (eds.), *Gender Influences in Classroom Interaction*, Orlando, FL: Academic Press.

Canaan, J. 1986. "Why a 'Slut' Is a Slut." In H. Varenne (ed.), *Symbolizing America*, pp. 385–408. Lincoln, NE: University of Nebraska Press.

Clarricoates, K. 1987. "Child Culture at School." In A. Pollard (ed.), *Children and their Primary Schools*, pp. 188–206. London: Falmer.

Connell, R.W. 1985. *Teachers Work*. Sydney: Allen & Unwin.

———. 1987. *Gender and Power*. Oxford: Polity Press.

Cordasco, F., ed. 1970. *The School and the Social Order*. Scranton, PA: Intext.

Cortazzi, M. 1991. *Primary Teaching: How It Is*. London: David Fulton.

———. 1993. *Narrative Analysis*. London: Falmer.

Croll, P., and D. Moses. 1990. "Sex Roles in the Primary Classroom." In C. Rogers and P. Kutnick (eds.), *The Social Psychology of the Primary School*, pp. 131–152. London: Routledge.

Delamont, S. 1983. *Interaction in the Classroom*. London: Routledge.

———. 1989. *Knowledgeable Women*. London: Routledge.

———. 1990. *Sex Roles and the School*. 2nd ed. London: Routledge.

———. 1991. "The Hit List and Other Horror Stories." *Sociological Review* 39(2):238–259.

Delamont, S., and Paul A. Atkinson. 1995. *Fighting Familiarity*. Cresskill, NJ: Hampton Press.

Denscombe, M., and L. Aubrook. 1992. "It's Just Another Piece of Schoolwork: The Ethics of Questionnaire Research on Pupils in Schools." *British Educational Research Journal* 18(2):11–132.

Fine, G. A. 1987. *With the Boys*. Chicago: The Chicago University Press.

Fine, G. A., and K. Sandstrom. 1990. *Knowing Children*. Newbury Park, CA: Sage.

Fine, Michelle. 1988. "Sexuality, Schooling and Adolescent Females." *Harvard Educational Review* 58(1):29–53.

French, J., and P. French. 1984. "Gender Imbalances in the Primary Classroom: An Interactional Account." *Educational Research* 26(2):127–136. Reprinted in P. Woods and M. Hammersley (eds.), *Gender and Ethnicity in Schools*, pp. 95–112.

Fuller, M. 1980. "Black Girls in a London Comprehensive School." In R. Deem (ed.), *Schooling for Women's Work*, pp. 52–65. London: Routledge.

Furlong, V. J. 1976. "Interaction Sets in the Classroom." In M. Stubbs and S. Delamont (eds.), *Explorations in Classroom Observation*, pp. 23–44. New York: Wiley.

Galton, M., B. Simon, and C. Croll. 1980. *Inside the Primary Classroom*. London: Routledge.

Gibson, M. 1988. *Accommodation without Assimilation*. Ithaca, NY: Cornell University Press.

Granfield, R. 1992. *Making Elite Lawyers*. New York: Routledge.

Greed, C. 1991. *Surveying Sisters*. London: Routledge.

Guttentag, M., and H. Bray, eds. 1976. *Undoing Sex Stereotypes*. New York: McGraw-Hill.

Halsey, A. H., A. Heath, and J. M. Ridge. 1980. *Origins and Destinations*. Oxford: Clarendon.

Hammersley, M. 1990. "An Evaluation of a Study of Gender Imbalance in Primary Classrooms." *British Educational Research Journal* 11(2):125–143.

———. 1993. "An Evaluation of a Study of Gender Imbalance in Primary Classrooms." In P. Woods and M. Hammersley (eds.), *Gender and Ethnicity in Schools*, pp. 113–126. London: Routledge.

Harding, S. 1986. *The Science Question in Feminism*. Milton Keynes: The Open University Press.

Hargreaves, D. 1967. *Social Relations in a Secondary School*. London: Routledge.

Haste, Helen. 1994. *The Sexual Metaphor*. Cambridge, MA: Harvard University Press.

Havighurst, R. J., and B. Neugarten. 1967. *Society and Education*, 3rd ed. Boston: Allyn & Bacon.

———. 1975. *Society and Education*, 4th ed. Boston: Allyn & Bacon.

Herbert, C. 1989. *Talking of Silence*. London: Falmer.

Hilton, G. L. S. 1991. "Boys will be Boys—Won't They?" *Gender and Education* 3(3):311–314.

Holland, D. C., and M. A. Eisenhart. 1990. *Educated in Romance*. Chicago: Chicago University Press.

Kelly, A. 1988. "Gender Differences in Teacher-pupil Interaction: A Meta-analytical Review." *Research in Education*.

Kessler, S., D. J. Ashenden, R. W. Connell, and G. W. Dowsett. 1985. "Gender Relations in Secondary Schooling." *Sociology of Education* 58:34–48.

Lacey, C. 1970. *Hightown Grammar*. Manchester: Manchester University Press.

Lambert, A. 1977. "The Sisterhood." In M. Hammersley and P. Woods (eds.), *The Process of Schooling*, pp. 152–159. London: Routledge.

———. 1982. "Expulsion in Context." In R. Frankenberg (ed.), *Custom and Conflict in British Society*, pp. 188–208. Manchester: Manchester University Press.

Lie, S. S., L. Malik, and D. Harris, eds. 1994. *The Gender Gap in Higher Education*. Philadelphia: Kogan Page.

Lightfoot, S. L. 1975. "Sociology of Education: Perspectives on Women." In M. Millman and R. M. Kanter (eds.), *Another Voice*, pp. 106–145. New York: Doubleday.

———. 1983. *The Good High School*. New York: Basic Books.

Lindow, J., C. Marrett, and L. Wilkinson. 1985. "Overview." In L. C. Wilkinson and C. Marrett (eds.), *Gender Influences in Classroom Interaction*, pp. 1–15. Orlando, FL: Academic Press.

Lloyd, B. 1989. "Rules of the Gender Game." *New Scientist* (December 2):66–70.

Lloyd, B., and G. Duveen. 1992. *Gender Identities and Education*. London: Harvester Wheatsheaf.

Mac an Ghaill. 1988. *Young, Gifted and Black*. Milton Keynes: The Open University Press.

———. 1991. "Schooling, Sexuality and Male Power." *Gender and Education* 3(3):291–310.

———. 1994. *The Making of Men*. Philadelphia: The Open University Press.

Mahoney, P. 1985. *Schools for the Boys*. London: Hutchinson.

Maynard, M. 1994. "Methods, Practice and Epistemology." In M. Maynard and J. Purvis (eds.), *Researching Women's Lives from a Feminist Perspective.* London: Taylor & Francis.

Maynard, M., and J. Purvis, eds. 1994. *Researching Women's Lives from a Feminist Perspective.* London: Taylor & Francis.

Measor, L. 1989. "Are You Coming to See Some Dirty Films Today?" In L. Holly (ed.), *Girls and Sexuality,* pp. 38–51. Milton Keynes: Open University Press.

Measor, L., and P. Woods. 1984. *Changing Schools.* Milton Keynes: Open University Press.

Moffat, M. 1989. *Coming of Age in New Jersey.* New Brunswick, NJ: Rutgers University Press.

Peshkin, A. 1978. *Growing Up American.* Chicago: Chicago University Press.

Peterson, W. 1964. "Age, Teachers Role and the Institutional Setting." In B. J. Biddle and W. Elena (eds.), *Contemporary Research on Teacher Effectiveness,* pp. 264–315. New York: Holt, Rinehart & Winston.

Serbin, L. 1978. "Teachers, Peers and Play References." In B. Sprun, (ed.), *Perspectives in Non-Sexist Early Childhood Education,* pp. 79–93. New York: Teachers College Press.

Shakeshaft, C. 1989. *Women in Educational Administration,* revised. Newbury Park, CA: Sage.

Shuy, R. 1986. "Secretary Bennett's Teaching." *Teaching and Teacher Education,* 2(4):315–324.

Sikes, P. J. 1991. "Nature Took Its Course?" *Gender and Education* 3(2):145–162.

Sikes, P., L. Measor, and P. Woods. 1985. *Teachers' Lives and Careers.* Milton Keynes: The Open University Press.

Skelton, A. 1993. "On Becoming a Male Physical Education Teacher: The Informal Culture of Students and the Construction of Hegemonic Masculinity." *Gender and Education* 5(3):289–304.

Smith, L. S. 1978. "Sexist Assumptions and Female Delinquency." In C. Smart and B. Smart (eds.), *Women, Sexuality and Social Control,* pp. 74–86. London: Routledge.

Sparkes, A. 1994. "Self, Silence and Invisibility as a Beginning Teacher." *British Journal of Sociology of Education* 15(1):93–118.

Spencer, D. A. 1996. "Gender and the Teachers Work." In B. J. Biddle, T. L. Good and I. Goodson (eds.), *Encyclopedia.* Dordrecht, The Netherlands: Kluwer.

Spender, D. 1982. *Invisible Women.* London: Writers and Readers Publishing Cooperative.

Sutherland, M. 1985. *Women Who Teach in Universities.* Trentham: Trentham Books.

Thomas, K. 1990. *Gender and the Subject in Higher Education.* London: Society for Research in Higher Education.

Valli, L. 1986. *Becoming Clerical Workers.* New York: Routledge.

Weiler, K. 1988. *Women Teaching for Change.* New York: Bergin and Garvey.

Willis, P. 1977. *Learning to Labour.* Farnborough: Gower.

Witherall, K., and N. Noddings, eds. 1991. *Narrative and Dialogue in Education.* New York: Teachers College Press.

Wolpe, A. M. 1977. *Some Processes in Sexist Education.* London: Women's Rights and Resources Centre.

Wrigley, J., ed. 1992. *Education and Gender Equality.* London: Falmer.

Gender and Math Education

Karen Karp
University of Louisville

In 1972, Title IX legislation declared that discrimination on the basis of sex in federally funded educational programs was illegal. Schools were charged with eliminating sex bias, creating equal opportunities, and encouraging females to enter male-dominated careers with the expectancy that a reduction of pay differential would follow. The funding to support these activities was distributed to individual school systems as they began to enact piecemeal remedies. However, the initial promise anticipated by these actions fell short of expectations. Recent data reveal that 70% of all females in vocational high schools study traditionally female fields, thereby avoiding careers that involve mathematics, science, and technology (National Commission on Working Women, 1989); females are still outscored by an average of approximately 40 points on the mathematics component of the SAT (College Board, 1997); and females in the workforce earn only a fraction of the salaries of males (U.S. Department of Education, 1997), unless they have earned eight or more mathematics credits in college (Adelman, 1991).

Although these disheartening statistics raise issues about school practices in general, more importantly they stimulate particular inquiries as to why the improvement of females' mathematics performance has proceeded at such an uneven pace. In our ever increasingly technological society, mathematical literacy and competency are keys to the future. We can no longer afford to allow any student to navigate around mathematics.

Mathematics is often called the "critical filter" (Sells, 1978). For example, when students enter college with less than the full complement of high school mathematics classes they often miss essential prerequisites and can suffer the de facto elimination of 82 potential career paths (Toronto Board of Education, 1989). This fact is especially compelling when linked with the recognition that we live in a time when a rank ordering of the best jobs in America for the twenty-first century results in most of the top 10 occupations relating directly to mathematics (Krantz, 1995). Yet, over three times as many males as females who have taken physics and calculus select college majors relating to mathematics and science (Dick and Rallis, 1991). When these data are correlated with the reality that males comprise more than 90% of the employment force in professions relating to mathematics and science, the results are no longer surprising. In actuality, many females are still confined to a range of professions that is, in general, poorly paid.

The impact this narrow range of choices has on females' economic status is discouraging. For example, the average male college graduate earns approximately $13,215 more per year than the average female college graduate (U.S. Department of Education, 1997). Further examination of the data reveal that female college graduates' salaries fall in the range between males who have only graduated from high school (the females are only $2500 higher) and males with some college but no degree. Therefore it is obvious that the career paths chosen by males and females lead to different life-styles. Over a lifetime this wage gap yields lower social security and retirement benefits for women, which result in a woman receiving an average of half the pension that a man collects (Brunner, 1998). Careers involving mathematics, science, and technology are frequently the high paying occupations of the future. A person's foundation in mathematics has lifelong consequences.

Another barrier in the complex intersection of schooling and future career goals is the SAT:

In a world where test scores translate into scholarships and admission to college, and college in turn leads to high-paying jobs, the failure of high school girls to score as well as boys on college-entrance examinations has led to widespread concern. (Goleman, 1987:42)

Although research indicates gender differences in areas such as spatial and mathematical ability are nearly eliminated, the differential performance on the mathematics portion of the SAT between males and females lingers as a painful exception (Linn and Hyde, 1989). In the period between 1987 and 1997, females scored an average of 43 points less than males on the SAT mathematics section (SAT-M). For example, in 1994, males outscored females by 501 to 460 on the SAT-M (College Board, 1995). When headlines reported that this was the smallest difference between the scores in 20 years, articles that followed suggested that the gender gap for the SAT-Mathematics was closing. In fact, a test fairness group reported, "At the current pace, it will take another twenty-five years to eliminate the SAT gender gap" (FairTest, 1994). Additionally, in the population of students designated as "high scorers" (having scores between 750 and 800) the male:female ratio as reported in the College Board's 1995 profile is approximately 3:1. That ratio translates into 11,618 males as compared to 4,294 females, clearly a compelling statistic.

Such differences in SAT scores translate into serious consequences for females. Girls are at risk of losing out academically, through rejection from competitive post-secondary institutions; psychologically, as they are more apt than males to deem the SAT as an accurate assessment of their intelligence, leaving them without the confidence to apply to colleges requesting higher test scores; and financially, through scholarships that are bound directly or indirectly to the SAT-M score. Several years ago, New York State's granting of Regents and Empire State Scholarships, which were awarded solely on the basis of SAT scores, was ruled unconstitutional. Up to that time, males captured 72% of the awards. A similar case based on the gender discrepancies resulting from the allocation of National Merit Scholarships, which were based on the related PSAT exam, also yielded changes in the scholarship selection process (FairTest, 1996).

In contrast to SAT-M results, the grades high school

females earn in class are comparable to, or in some cases higher than, those of males (Gross, 1988). This dichotomy between classroom performance and the results of summative testing has enormous impact on female students as well as the public mind, for the results of national testing, not student report cards, are what is shared in public forums. This situation continues to reinforce images of females with inadequate mathematics performance.

Despite outstanding academic records, fewer females are admitted to the most prestigious colleges and universities as a result of SAT-M scores. This situation continues to exist despite an awareness that some testing materials may be patently unfair to females. Certain common testing practices such as biased problem contexts and sexist language are so often and so consistently shown to discriminate against females that knowledge of them is public; however, many of these patterns still exist. Although the authors of the SAT, Educational Testing Service, report that they are vigilant in attempting to eliminate overt and subtle biases in their testing instruments, researchers questioning the types of items seem to suggest otherwise (e.g., Kelly-Benjamin, 1990).

Regardless of changes in testing materials, males may have an advantage over females in their speed of response. Test preparation courses commonly claim to boost overall scores by teaching students to make rapid assessments of problems and then produce quick guesses rather than employ lengthy computations. Indeed, if males are more confident in their mathematics ability (Hyde et al., 1990), then they may be more inclined to trust intuitive thinking and holistic examinations of problems. On the other hand, females, who frequently find themselves rewarded for rule compliance behavior, might be less likely to employ swift inspections of problems and revert to lengthy but reliable formulas.

The tendency is for males to exhibit more confidence in their mathematics abilities than females, even when both groups perform equally well (Linn and Hyde, 1989). By the time females enter institutions of higher education there is no correlation between their confidence in their ability to do mathematics and their actual ability (Singer and Stake, 1986). This confidence gap is one possible explanation commonly used to account for females' performance in mathematics. The following sections examine other possible factors and discuss means for fostering improved mathematics performance in female students.

Biological Variables

In 1980, Benbow and Stanley conducted what initially seemed to be critical research supporting the genetic inferiority of females in terms of mathematics ability. In an effort to control for concerns about previous research that did not consider differential course taking behaviors of males and females, the researchers administered the SAT mathematics component to gifted seventh and eighth graders presumably at a point where they all had taken the same mathematics courses. The resulting scores on the SAT-M suggested "huge and significant differences" favoring males over females. According to the study, at the seventh grade there are approximately 13 male math geniuses for every female. The researchers concluded that males have superior innate mathematics ability and that it is this ability that naturally guides the selection of advanced mathematics courses. They suggested that females were not as capable of understanding mathematics and, as a consequence, Camilla Benbow stated, "Women would be better off accepting the differences" (1980:1235). Unfortunately, only after this study received tremendous publicity and media attention did other researchers move to the forefront with questions and serious concerns regarding the methods and conclusions of the investigation (Alexander and Pallas, 1983; Egelman et al., 1981). These critics demanded more details as to how Benbow and Stanley equated SAT-M performance with innate mathematics ability (no biological data were collected), how they reconciled the inherent bias against females in the testing instrument, what impact the overwhelmingly large percentage of males in the sample had on the results, how the socioeconomic status of the students may have skewed outcomes (most came from families where financial support for a summer program for gifted students was possible), how the findings of research with a highly select sample could be generalized to an entire population, and whether the schooling experience up to that point had in reality been the same for males and females. The answers raised serious and substantial doubts. Although the Benbow and Stanley study originally heralded the belief that there were causative biological factors, the early support this hypothesis garnered has disappeared. Unfortunately misguided authors still report the conclusions of the study as statements of fact in articles and textbooks for readers ranging from parents to college students (Brandt, 1989; Christen, 1995).

Diminishing differences between male and female performance in both mathematics and spatial skills suggest that a biological causation is not probable (Halpern, 1989). In the words of Rosenthal and Rubin (1982:71), such changes in gender differences are happening "faster than the gene can travel." Few researchers today would posit that biogenetic theories provide a worthwhile explanation for discrepancies in mathematics achievement. Instead, most would concur with the premise that gender expectations and differential performance remain enmeshed in environmental and cultural variables.

School Variables

Researchers overwhelmingly report that mathematics learning is largely a function of mathematics teaching (Fennema, 1990; Karp, 1991). Although mathematical terms may be used outside school, the classroom remains the central site for instruction. Yet, school is clearly a place of uneven opportunities for females. A comprehensive report undertaken by the American Association for University Women Foundation (1992) states that research findings debunk "another myth— that boys and girls receive equal education. The wealth of statistical evidence must convince even the most skeptical that gender bias in our schools is shortchanging girls—and compromising our country" (McKee, 1992:A1). Over the years, researchers have identified that the "shortchanging" females experience unfolds in various forms.

Sadker and Sadker found that "at all grade levels, in all communities (urban, suburban and rural) and in all subject areas, boys dominated classroom communication. Boys participated in more interactions than girls did, this participation becoming greater as the year went on" (1985:54). Males receive more verbal contact with teachers, both positive and negative (Spender, 1982). They are called on more frequently, asked more complex and open-ended questions, and are more often engaged in inquiries that involve abstract reasoning (Jones, 1989). Conversely, interactions between teachers and female students often include rewards for following rules, conformity, neatness, silence, and appearance (Sadker and Sadker, 1994). For instance, in a nursery school classroom in England, Walden and Walkerdine (1985) observed two students approach the teacher with a drawing. One was told, "Well done, John, that's a good drawing"; the other, "You do look pretty today, Alice." Females are asked more basic recall questions and are often given correct answers when they cannot produce them. Teachers also encourage learned helplessness by performing a task for a female student who is having difficulty but will give males eight times more information on how to solve the problem themselves (Serbin and O'Leary, 1975). Thus, the crux of the problem regarding disparities between treatment of males and females in classroom discourse lies in the content of student–teacher interactions rather than the quantity.

Both in composition and in organization, curriculum explicitly and implicitly reflects culture. Critical sociologists (e.g., Apple, 1979) considered the "hidden curriculum" of schools as including the nonacademic but significant outcomes of schooling that are rarely explicitly expressed. These are often assumptions that underlie what is taught and frequently result in the replication of culture, class, and gender expectations. Although linkages between the school's culture and society are expected, critical sociologists ask why access to educational experiences differs for some groups and why some individuals are able to resist such forces? For example, in many classrooms the methodology frequently incorporates debate, argument, and challenge, all of which center around the drive to win and are not aligned with females' learning styles (Belenky et al., 1986; Lewis, 1991; Tannen, 1992). Yet, initially through informal groupings and now more formally through structuring by teachers, the ever increasing incorporation of cooperative learning in mathematics sends messages contrary to the usual competitive model. Cooperative learning attempts to balance members' contributions while increasing the focus on group dynamics and encouraging cohesiveness. Females consistently respond more favorably, through measured increases in academic performance, to the use of cooperative groupings (as compared to competitive) (Isaacson, 1990). Perhaps this propensity to function well in groupings that combine academic growth with the nurturing of relationships relates to the development of the "ethic of care" (Noddings, 1992), which may be

a passive form of resistance to traditional mathematics lessons.

Home Variables

Consistent with stereotypical expectations from the past, parents of males hold more positive beliefs regarding their child's mathematics performance and more frequently identify the need for their child to continue in upper level mathematics than parents of females (Eccles et al., 1987). Upon closer examination of the sample, this finding becomes more surprising as the female students were matched with the males precisely for equivalent performance on both formal mathematics tests and in classroom grades. Parents of a subset of the females in the study rated their daughters' abilities in language arts as higher than their mathematics abilities, even though their daughters had identical grades in both subjects. In contrast, parents of males with identical grades in these subjects gave a higher rating to their sons' mathematical abilities. Parental influence is a more potent factor in impacting mathematics performance than originally thought (Campbell and Mandel, 1990). Therefore, it seems likely that males and females can be swayed by their parents' expectations and the way their parents reinforce some achievements over others. Subtle messages sent by parents to children may be an element in the trend for females to lose confidence in their performance in mathematics and for them to opt out of advanced mathematics and mathematically oriented careers.

Societal Variables

Factors impacting on gender role socialization encompass a variety of behaviors, feelings, attitudes, and interests designated by society as appropriate for females or males. They are learned through interactions with parents, peers, teachers, books, toys, and the media. In addition, participation in social events and encounters with social institutions shape each child's reality. Sometimes, pressures for children to conform to social definitions of suitable behavior for their sex are great. Even from the moment after a baby's birth where "Is the baby a boy or girl?" is the most commonly asked question (Inton-Peterson and Reddel, 1984), patterns for orchestrating the world around the child as male oriented or female oriented begin. When given an opportunity to play with a baby, adults engage in different activities depending on whether they are told the infant is a male or a female (Will et al., 1976). Similarly, the first playthings purchased often reflect societal beliefs. Males are frequently supplied with objects that encourage moving, building, and taking things apart and putting them back together. They are apt to be taught at a very young age how to catch a ball and keep score. In contrast, females are inclined to be given toys that involve relationships with people. Therefore, when males and females first enter school, socialization patterns previously established in the home promote the continuation of play with items and settings that are familiar. In this way, through what is described as the "practice component," children avoid classroom activities about which they are unfamiliar or less confident (Greenberg, 1985). Hence, the sex roles established in the home environment take on increased potency. After exposure to conventional societal expectations, males tend to "judge themselves by what they are able to do," and females "portray their worth in terms of their physical appearance" (Harris and Pickle, 1992:12). This culture-bound, systematic conditioning of humans into patterns of performance is referred to as the "social construction of gender." Undoubtedly, these are the most complex variables to consider as well as the most difficult to unravel. Yet, change in this domain has the potential to generate the greatest effects.

Conclusion

Schools remain sources of cultural reproduction, therefore, an awareness of students' developing roles and values is critical. By tolerating an environment of gender bias, females and males are exposed to behaviors and attitudes that corrupt their overall growth. Educators need to consider the following actions:

- Consider the elimination of tracking and instead work toward class groupings that encourage more cooperative experiences than competitive situations.
- Provide access to mathematical concepts and relevant real world applications through hands-on experiences.

- Move away from dependence on traditional standardized, timed tests to authentic models that better link learning and assessment.
- Create support groups using mentors and role models to nurture females' confidence.
- Conduct ongoing, formal assessments of gender equity in schools that include the examination of basic statistics on course enrollments and participation in extracurricular activities.
- Provide information about the teaching patterns that promote equity so that classroom instruction can avoid biases in areas such as classroom interactions and curriculum.
- Create a formal structure that encourages females to continue taking mathematics coursework after it becomes optional, in the process building in the connection among mathematics courses, careers, and salaries.
- Educate parents through specialized programs that inform them of the importance of mathematics for every child's future.
- Encourage guidance counselors to interpret aptitude/career testing with caution as many tests were based on biased samples that will consistently link females to a narrow range of careers.
- Encourage counselors to seek career materials that use nonsexist pronouns, that include examples of women in diverse occupational settings, and that specifically encourage females to pursue mathematically related careers.

Males who excel over females in mathematics still constitute a small percentage. Not enough students of either gender attain the high levels of mathematics thinking realized by students in other nations. Fortunately there is not a zero-sum relationship to the nurturing of females' mathematics abilities. Classroom strategies that create an environment in which females can be successful do not disadvantage males and in many instances have been beneficial to them. Gender inequities do not just harm females: they impact on everyone.

The answers we seek in creating an environment that encourages females to welcome mathematical experiences and consider possible careers in the discipline are still being generated. In fact, we may need to think of other questions. The key may lie in the more subtle or complex constructs we have not yet investigated.

REFERENCES

Adelman, Clifford. 1991. *Women at Thirtysomething: Paradoxes of Attainment*. Washington, DC: U.S. Department of Education.

Alexander, Karl, and Aaron Pallas. 1983. "Reply to Benbow and Stanley." *American Educational Research Journal* 20:475–477.

American Association of University Women. 1992. *How Schools Shortchange Girls*. Washington, DC: AAUW Educational Foundation and National Education Association.

Apple, Michael. 1979. *Ideology and Curriculum*. London: Routledge & Kegan Paul.

Belenky, Mary Field, Blythe McVicker Clinchy, Nancy Rule Goldberger, and Jill Mattuck Tarule. 1986. *Women's Ways of Knowing: The Development of Self, Voice, and Mind*. New York: Basic Books.

Benbow, Camilla. 1980. "Math and Sex: Are Girls Born with Less Ability?" Science 210:1234–1235.

Benbow, Camilla, and Julian Stanley. 1980. "Sex Differences in Mathematical Ability: Fact or Artifact?" *Science* 210:1262–1264.

Brant, Anthony. 1989. "Sex and the Facts of Math." *Parenting* (December/January):122–124, 127.

Brunner, Borgna. 1998. *Information Please Almanac*. Boston, MA: Information Please LLC.

Campbell, James Reed, and Francine Mandel. 1990. *Sexism is Alive and Well in Japan*. Paper presented at the Annual Meeting of the American Educational Research Association, San Francisco.

Christen, Yves. 1995. "Brain Structure Explains Male/Female Differences. In David Bender and Bruno Leone (eds.), *Male/Female Roles: Opposing Viewpoints,* pp. 48–56. San Diego, CA: Greenhaven Press.

College Board. 1994, 1995, 1997. *1994–5 Profile of SAT and Achievement Test Takers*. Princeton, NJ: College Entrance Examination Board.

Dick, Thomas. P., and Sharon F. Rallis. 1991. Factors and Influences on High School Students' Career Choices. *Journal for Research in Mathematics Education* 22:281–292.

Eccles, Jacquelynne, Connie Flanagan, Rena Goldsmith, Jan Jacobs, Toby Jayaratne, Allan Wigfield, and Doris Yee. 1987. *Parents as Socializers of Achievement Attitudes*. Paper presented at the Society for Research in Child Development, Baltimore, MD.

Egelman, Edward, Joseph Alper, Lila Leibowitz, Jonathan Beckwith, Regina Levine, and Anthony Leeds. 1981. Letter to the editor. *Science* 212:116.

FairTest. 1994. "SAT/ACT Gender Gaps Narrow." *FairTest Examiner* (Fall):2–3.

———. 1996. "FairTest Complaint Will Lead to Millions More for Girls." *FairTest Examiner* (Fall):1–3.

Fennema, Elizabeth. 1990. "Justice, Equity, and Mathematics Education." In Elizabeth Fennema and Gilah Leder (eds.), *Mathematics and Gender*, pp. 1–9. New York: Teachers College Press.

Goleman, Daniel. 1987. "Girls and Math: Is Biology Really Destiny?" *New York Times: Educational Supplement* (August 2):42–46.

Greenberg, Selma. 1985. "Educational Equity in Early Childhood Environments." In Susan Klein (ed.), *Handbook for Achieving Sex Equity Through Education*, pp. 457–469. Baltimore: The Johns Hopkins University Press.

Gross, Susan. 1988. *Participation and Performance of Women and Minorities in Mathematics (E–4)*. Rockville, MD: Department of Educational Accountability.

Halpern, Diane F. 1989. "The Disappearance of Cognitive Gender Differences: What You See Depends on Where You Live." *American Psychologist* 44:1156–1157.

Harris, Mary McDonnell, and Judy Gebhardt Pickle. 1992. "Creating an Equitable Environment: Gender Equity in Lincoln, Nebraska." *The Educational Forum* 57:12–17.

Hyde, Janet, Elizabeth Fennema, Marilyn Ryan, Laurie Frost, and Carolyn Hopp. 1990. "Gender Comparisons of Mathematics Attitudes and Affect: A Meta-Analysis." *Psychology of Women Quarterly* 14:299–324.

Intons-Peterson, Margaret, and Michele Reddel. 1984. "What Do People Ask About a Neonate?" *Developmental Psychology* 20:358–359.

Isaacson, Zelda. 1990. "They Look at You in Absolute Horror": Women Writing and Talking about Mathematicians. In Leone Burton (ed.), *Gender and Mathematics: An International Perspective*, pp. 20–28. New York: Cassell Education.

Jones, Gail. 1989. "Gender Bias in Classroom Interactions." *Contemporary Education* 60:216–222.

Karp, Karen. 1991. "Elementary School Teachers' Attitudes Toward Mathematics: The Impact on Students' Autonomous Learning Skills." *School Science and Mathematics* 91(6):265–270.

Kelly-Benjamin, Kathleen. 1990. *The Young Women's Guide to Better SAT Scores: Fighting the Gender Gap*. New York: Bantam.

Krantz, Les. 1995. *The Jobs Rated Almanac*. New York: Ballantine Books.

Lewis, Anne. 1991. "Taking Women Seriously." *Phi Delta Kappan* 73(4):268–269.

Linn, Marcia, and Janet Shibley Hyde. "Gender Mathematics, and Science." *Educational Researcher* 12:17–19, 22–27.

McKee, Alice. 1992. "Bias Against Girls Is Found Rife in Schools, with Lasting Damage." authored by Susan Chira, *New York Times* (February 12):A1, A23.

National Commission on Working Women. 1989. *Women, Work and the Future*. Washington, DC: Wider Opportunities for Women.

Noddings, Nel. 1992. "The Gender Issue." *Educational Leadership* 49(4):65–70.

Rosenthal, Robert, and Donald B. Rubin. 1982. "Further Meta-Analytic Procedures for Assessing Cognitive Gender Differences." *Journal of Educational Psychology* 74:708–712.

Sadker, Myra, and David Sadker. 1985. "Sexism in the Schoolroom of the '80s." *Psychology Today* (March):54–57.

———. 1994. *Failing at Fairness: How Our Schools Cheat Girls*. New York: Simon & Schuster.

Sells, Lucy. 1978. "Mathematics—A Critical Filter." *The Science Teacher* 45:28–29.

Serbin, Lisa, and K. Daniel O'Leary. 1975. "How Nursery Schools Teach Girls to Shut Up." *Psychology Today* (December):55.

Singer, Joan M., and Jayne Stake. 1986. "Mathematics and Self Esteem: Implications for Women's Career Choice." *Psychology of Women Quarterly* 10:339–352.

Spender, Dale. 1982. *Invisible Women: The Schooling Scandal*. London: Writers and Readers.

Tannen, Deborah. 1991. "How Men and Women Use Language Differently in Their Lives and in the Classroom." *Education Digest* 57(6):3–4.

Toronto Board of Education. 1989. *Dropping Math? Say Good-Bye to 82 Jobs*. Toronto, Canada: Board of Education for the City of Toronto.

U.S. Department of Education. 1997. *Digest of Education Statistics*. Washington, DC: Office of Educational Research and Improvement.

Walden, Rosie, and Valerie Walkerdine. 1985. *Girls and Mathematics: From Primary to Secondary Schooling* (Bedford Way Papers, No. 24.). London: Institute of Education, London University.

Will, Jerrie Ann, Patricia Self, and Nancy Datan. 1976. "Maternal Behavior and Perceived Sex of Infant." *American Journal of Orthopsychiatry* 46(1):135–139.

GENDER INEQUALITY

Linda Grant
Department of Sociology and Institute for Behavioral Research,
University of Georgia

Xue Lan Rong
University of North Carolina

Decades of feminist activism, legal reforms, and change-oriented policies such as affirmative action have failed to eradicate gender inequality in American society. In the labor force, women of all ages, races, and educational level still earn lower salaries than male counterparts. Women workers face a "glass ceiling" that limits upward mobility in jobs, and few advance to top leadership positions. Women have been underrepresented in medical research, and hence much less is known about their health status relative to men's. Women remain woefully underrepresented in public life and politics, especially in the highest posts.

In households, women retain most of the responsibility for domestic labor and child care, regardless of their duties outside the home (Hochschild, 1989). A substantial number of women face violence at home and in intimate relationships. The Center for Disease Control and Prevention in Atlanta estimates that nearly one in five hospitalizations of women in the United States result from physical violence suffered in an intimate relationship.

Compared to many other sectors of social life, girls and women have made great strides toward equity in education. U.S. women now obtain, on the average, more schooling each year than male counterparts (U.S. Department of Education, 1995). Although a female education advantage for African Americans is a long-standing pattern, higher levels of educational attainment for women from other ethnic groups was first observed in the late 1980s. Women now earn more high school diplomas and bachelor's and master's degrees compared to men. Nevertheless, men continue to earn more doctorates and first professional degrees in fields such as law or medicine (U.S. Department of Education, 1995). And as an increasing body of literature documents, educational institutions are themselves male-dominated domains with nonsupportive or even hostile climates that keep women from reaching their full potential (AAUW, 1992; Sadker and Sadker, 1994).

These trends raise several puzzling questions. How do we explain persistent gender inequality in the United States? And what role does education play in perpetuating or reducing gender inequality? In the sections that follow we discuss three types of explanations used to explain gender inequality: gender socialization theories, dual-labor market theories, and socialist feminist theories. We also consider what each approach has to say, explicitly or implicitly, about the role of education in the maintenance and transformation of gender inequality in society.

Gender Socialization Theories

Gender socialization theories are the most prevalent explanation of how gender inequality is perpetuated in American society. Although there are many variations of socialization theories, some stressing psychological characteristics of individuals and others stressing social structural arrangements [see Spade (*Gender Socialization and Education*), this volume], all see inequality as stemming from attitudes and values that people learn throughout life, but especially in early childhood. This learning takes place in formal settings such as schools but also informal settings, such as family life or playground activities, where boys and girls learn what types of behaviors and outlooks are considered to be appropriate for their gender. Gender roles become incorporated as part of individual identity, so that "acting like a boy" or "acting like a girl" becomes a validating act, rewarded by others.

Once gender-differentiated socialization has begun, girls and boys tend to make choices consistent with traditional roles. These choices usually also are reinforced by influential adults, such as parents, teachers, guidance counselors, and religious leaders. Girls may choose cheerleading over soccer, for example, because cheerleading conforms with traditional images of "what a girl should be like" and because girls are rewarded by others for engaging in these activities. Boys may avoid feminine-stereotyped activities, such as cooking or ballet, for similar reasons, even when they have interest and talent in these areas. In fact, some scholars have argued that as children, girls have more leeway to engage in stereotypical male activities than the reverse. Female tomboys are tolerated more than boys who display effeminate characteristics or interests associated with girls.

Socialization theorists recognize that what is regarded as "masculine" or "feminine" can vary over time and place. For example, although high attainment in mathematics may not be expected for Anglo white high school girls, Asian and Asian-American parents often expect this of their daughters. Whereas art and music once were seen as the domains of male achievement, they often are viewed as feminine activities in contemporary high schools.

Socialization theorists typically envision education as playing an important causal role in the creation and transformation of gender inequality. Formal education (in-classroom learning via formally prepared curriculum materials), informal aspects of school life (patterns of gender relationships among school staff that are visible to students), and extracurricular and nonschool activities affect what students learn about gender roles, and the subsequent choices they make about their lives. School curricula that overlook or trivialize contributions of women in American life, sexist relationships among school staff, sharp divisions of labor between players and cheerleaders on athletic fields, and observations of gender-inequitable relationships in out-of-school settings such as family, community, and media all can contribute to a reproduction of gender inequality—even when the professed goals of the educational institution are to transform them.

All of these forces, in combination, can lead women and men to choose gender-traditional roles in adult life

and to expect other women and men to conform to such roles. Women choose to be full-time homemakers rather than paid workers, or, if in the labor market, to do more housework and child care than their male partners. As workers, most women select jobs that are female dominated and consistent with feminine values. Nursing embodies skills and values thought stereotypically feminine (nurturance, caring, sensitivity), while engineering does not. Men shy away from female-stereotyped roles such as homemaker or nurse, because they have learned that these are "inappropriate" roles for men and that others might criticize them for such choices or question their masculinity.

Whereas gender socialization theories envision education as important in maintaining gender inequality, these perspectives also regard education as a point for intervention to create more equitable gender relations. As a centralized cultural agency, schools can be influential in presenting gender role models that challenge traditional forms.

Structural Inequality Theories

Structural inequality theories propose that gender is a major base of social stratification in American society. All social institutions (including education) reflect gender inequality, and all are actively involved in its maintenance. One version of structural theory, usually termed the dual-labor market perspective, places particular emphasis on differences in women's and men's access to the jobs and occupations, and the division of labor maintained between men's jobs and women's jobs. Another version, called socialist feminist theory, examines the division of labor existing between women and men in the household as well as in the labor market, and the interconnections between inequality in work and personal life. Both versions of structural theory analyze how industrialization in the United States and other developed nations has affected patterns of gender inequality.

In structural theories, education is viewed as one of many gendered social institutions, where traditional gender relationships are socialized, reinforced, and reproduced. As workplaces themselves, educational institutions usually reflect gender hierarchies in which men in top positions (e.g., principals and superintendents) direct the work of women in subordinate ones (e.g., teachers and lunchroom staff). Everyday practices of schools, intentionally or not, typically reinforce traditional gender roles, and curriculum and "hidden curriculum" (or the everyday practices of schools that teach students lessons about social relations) legitimate a gender-inequitable society as normal and acceptable. Gender inequality becomes a taken-for-granted, background characteristic of schools and of social life.

Gender Inequality and the Process of Industrialization

Although male dominance (termed patriarchy in some versions of these theories) existed prior to industrialization, the separation of the workplace from the home that occurred during industrialization furthered gender inequality. Prior to industrialization, women, men, and often also children, worked at home to produce goods and services that were consumed mostly within the household. Both parents shared in childrearing and the maintenance of the home. Although families sometimes traded goods and services with others in their communities, neither women nor men were much involved in a cash economy that produced surplus value, or profits.

With industrialization, labor moved out of the home into factories. Workers (mostly male) toiled for cash wages. Men were paid a family wage, or a sum sufficient to support a wife and family. Employers assumed that men's subsistence needs (for food, emotional nurturance, etc.) would be fulfilled in the home and would no longer be the responsibility of the employer.

Women remained in the home, bearing the major responsibility for childrearing and domestic labor. Women sometimes engaged in piece work, such as sewing or handicrafts, or other home-based economic activities (laundering, taking in boarders), but their access to cash wages was much less than men's. In periods of economic needs, women—especially working class women—were brought into paid labor, but usually at wages lower than men's. Women could also be excluded from the labor market when their services were not needed. Because women had less stable employment records than men, lower wages for them and greater responsibility for domestic labor could be justified (Andersen, 1993). These developments created a sharper division of activities by gender than in the preindustrial era. Only men's work yielded cash wages, and only paid labor was regarded as real work. In a society increasingly influenced by cash economies, men's power over women was magnified.

Single women, widows, women of color, and women with low-waged spouses worked for pay, despite popular images that a nonworking wife was the American tradition (Coontz, 1992). They typically were confined to low-waged jobs reserved for women, or they worked in the informal economy, the unregulated portion of the economy that includes both legal and illegal activity, bartering, and informal cash exchanges that do not figure into calculations of economic production. Domestic service, the occupation of many poor and working-class white and nonwhite women in the nineteenth and early twentieth century, was an example of such work. Domestic workers typically worked for less than minimum wage, without benefits such as health insurance, vacations, or pensions (Rollins, 1985).[1]

Dual-Labor Market Theories

Changes occurring during industrialization laid the groundwork for the development of the dual-labor market. Nowadays most workers are in jobs where the majority of co-workers of their same status are of a single gender. Men's jobs usually are located in the *primary sector*. These jobs tend to be highly paid and stable. They also offer good fringe benefits and long job ladders, or opportunities for promotion in rank. Executive, professional managerial jobs are in this sector, along with skilled blue-collar positions.

Jobs occupied by women usually are in the *secondary sector*, where jobs are poorly paid and less often provide benefits. Most secondary sector jobs have short job ladders, with few chances of promotion (for example, waitressing, hairdressing, or retail sales). These jobs are easy to reenter after time out of paid labor for family duties, but they offer few opportunities for promotion and virtually no access to primary sector jobs. They also are unstable and more subject to cutbacks during economic downturns.

An important feature of dual-labor market theories

---

[1] Recent "Nannygate" controversies show that such practices still exist, with women who are recent immigrants most likely to be employed in domestic service positions in which employers fail to pay social security taxes or otherwise comply with federal regulations regarding wages, working conditions, and pensions.

is that experience in the secondary sector is not valued or rewarded as creditable work in the primary sector. A secretary may do complex managerial work on behalf of her boss, but this work is not credited if she applies for a managerial job in the primary sector.

Where women gain access to the primary sector, through education, union advocacy, or court action, they often face *secondary discrimination* by men workers who do not like competition from women. Secondary discrimination can include formal and informal exclusion from career-enhancing networks, denial of opportunities for advanced training, and even sexual harassment. These actions limit women's opportunities in primary sector jobs, or drive them out of that sector altogether.

Even when women work in white-collar jobs in large organizations, they tend to be clustered in staff jobs, or those devoted more to the maintenance of the organization (personnel, public relations) than in line jobs, or those devoted to direct production of the organization's primary goods or services. Line jobs are better protected in economic downturns and are more likely to lead to top leadership posts. Manufacturing organizations may make substantial use of women's labor, and even move plants overseas in search of inexpensive female labor, but top management usually stays in the United States and remains dominated by white men.

Education can contribute to the maintenance of dual-labor markets in several ways. Curriculum reflecting traditional occupational roles for boys and girls, counseling that differentially steers boys and girls to preparatory courses, and components of the hidden curriculum, such as more teacher attention to boys than girls, reinforce expectations of a male-dominated society. But even progressive education offering less gender-stereotyped options is not sufficient to eliminate gender inequality. Girls may be encouraged via education to aspire for nontraditional occupational roles, but structural barriers in the labor market may nevertheless block their access to such jobs.

Socialist Feminist Theories

Although some sociologists who study gender-segregated labor markets concentrate solely on the workplace, others argue that we must also look at patterns of domestic relations that affect the availability of women and men for paid labor (Hochschild, 1989;

Sokoloff, 1980). These theories build upon dual-labor market perspectives, but find these approaches incomplete because they ignore the gendered division of domestic labor. Women's greater responsibility for housework and child care, relative to men's, is well documented. Even when both adult partners in a family work for pay, women usually put in a "double day" of paid and unpaid labor. Hochschild (1989) finds that when both paid and unpaid domestic labor are taken into account, women in dual-career couples work an average of one month more a year than men (or 30 8-hour days more per year).

Because women as a group are seen as having greater family responsibilities than men, employers see them as poorer candidates for promotion or training. Sokoloff contends working women are seen as mothers—actual, potential, and former—and women's supposed home responsibilities are used as a justification for paying them less and promoting them less frequently. Additionally, women in the labor force may be expected to perform *motherwork*. Motherwork consists of domestic-like duties that are not seen as requiring particular skills but are presumed to reflect the "natural" attributes of women. This includes occupying jobs in the paid labor force that parallel the activities typically performed by women in preindustrial societies (nursing, elementary-level teaching, child care, for example), and also the domestic-like activities performed by women workers for male bosses. Entertaining visitors, presenting the boss in a favorable light, resolving squabbles among office workers—all tasks apt to be performed by an executive secretary—closely parallel women's roles in private life. Because these activities are seen as drawing upon natural attributes presumed to be present in all women, they are not recognized or rewarded as valued experts, performing work that has real economic value.

Rather than considering the public sphere of work and the private sphere of domestic life to be separate, socialist feminists view them as tightly linked. Women's status in one domain is directly connected to their status in the other. Because women have less earning power than men, which gives women larger shares of housework, child care and interrupts their careers rather than men's, children or other family members then become (economically) rational decision for families.

Because women do often make these choices, they (and all women) become less valued as workers and can be paid lower wages in comparison to men. Women's devalued status as workers reinforces their disadvantaged status in the domestic division of labor, which in turn further disadvantages them as workers. What often are viewed as individual choices of women and men are in fact affected by structural patterns well established in both homes and workplaces. Women who lack opportunities to support themselves with wage labor have less power within the family to influence interpersonal relationships, and less ability to leave unsatisfying relationships.

In socialist feminist theories, education is one of a number of social institutions, along with media, religion, and politics, for example, that legitimate patriarchal relationships in private and public. Patriarchal relationships are reproduced, intentionally and unintentionally, in educational settings. For example, Eder and Parker (1986) argue that middle-school extracurricular activities reinforce not only a gender division of activities (boys are football players, girls are cheerleaders), but also signal to students that boys' activities take center stage and girls' are peripheral. Similarly, Holland and Eisenhart (1990) find that talented college women with skills in mathematics and science are within college peer networks to place involvement in heterosexual romance above academic attainment in male-dominated fields. (Hierarchical relationships based on other criteria such as race, social class, and sexual orientation are reproduced in similar ways.)

In socialist feminist approaches, the role of education is complex and multifaceted. Although education can provide women with training that helps them challenge gender inequality, educational institutions also play roles in reproducing and legitimating conventional gender relations more often than transforming them (see Grant et al., 1994). Institutions of higher education, in particular, credential the experts and cultural leaders who dominate in many social arenas (for example, law, science, medicine, politics, religion, the arts), and thus, intentionally or not, usually reproduce male dominance. However, education—particularly higher education—can also be the site of resistance and revisioning of a society where gender relationships are more equitable.

REFERENCES

American Association of University Women (AAUW). 1991. *How Schools Shortchange Girls.* Washington, DC: AAUW.

Andersen, Margaret A. 1993. *Thinking about Women: Sociological Perspectives on Sex and Gender,* 3rd ed. New York: Macmillan.

Coontz, Stephanie. 1992. *The Way We Never Were: The American Family and the Nostalgia Trap.* New York: Basic Books.

Eder, Donna J., and Stephen Parker. 1987. "The Cultural Production and Reproduction of Gender." *Sociology of Education* 60(3):200–213.

Grant, Linda, Patrick M. Horan, and Betty Watts-Warren. 1994. "Theoretical Diversity in the Analysis of Gender and Education." *Research in Socialization of Education and Socialization* 10:71–110.

Hochschild, Arlie R. 1989. *The Second Shift: Working Parents and the Revolution at Home.* New York: Viking.

Holland, Dorothy A., and Margaret Eisenhart. 1990. *Educated in Romance: Women Achievement, and College Culture.* Chicago: University of Chicago Press.

Rollins, Judith. 1985. *Between Women: Domestic Workers and Their Employers.* New Brunswick, NJ: Rutgers University Press.

Sadker, Myra, and David Sadker. 1994. *Failing at Fairness: How America's Schools Treat Girls.* New York: Scribner's.

Sokoloff, Natalie J. 1980. *Between Money and Love: The Dialectics of Women's Home and Market Work.* New York: Praeger.

U.S. Department of Education. 1995. *The Condition of Education, 1995.* Washington, DC.

GENDER INEQUALITY IN EDUCATION

INTERNATIONAL COMPARISONS

Karen Bradley
Western Washington University

Gender inequality in education has received considerable attention during recent decades from researchers, educators, activists, and policy analysts. Concern about women and education is not itself a new issue. Historically, debates surrounding women's education have focused on what has been characterized as the competing demands of the private sphere of the family and the public sphere of paid labor. The education of women has been variously categorized as supportive of family interests (by making women better mothers) and as detrimental to family interests (by enabling women to work for pay outside the home). Perhaps not surprisingly, the social construction of the private sphere as "woman's domain" and the public as "man's domain" continues to influence the nature of women's and men's participation in formal schooling today.

This chapter examines issues surrounding educational access and attainment, and the nature of the participation of boys/men and girls/women in schools, colleges, and universities throughout the world. Most of the research in this area consists of descriptive case studies focusing on individual countries or geopolitical regions. These studies have provided important insights regarding the gendered nature of education in particular settings. Unfortunately, the dearth of research using a cross-national research design limits our ability to distinguish between factors that are unique to individual societies and those that are representative of broader phenomena. Suggestions for such cross-national research are included in this chapter.

Getting in the Door: The Problem of Educational Access

Heightened interest in gender inequality in schools coincided with extensive international activity regarding the status of women. During the International Decade for Women (1975–1985) in particular, the United Nations and affiliated international governmental and nongovernmental organizations devoted considerable resources to projects to elevate the status of women worldwide. This attention to women's status unfolded during an era of significant expansion of educational systems in countries throughout the world. The number of schools, colleges, universities, and technical institutes increased dramatically as states attempted to transform educational systems from elite to mass institutions. New kinds of educational institutions were created, especially at the level of higher education. In addition, significant curricular changes took place at all levels, with the introduction of new fields of study and the reclassification of some fields, such as teacher training, from the secondary level to higher education.

With the global expansion of enrollment and educational facilities, access to education has improved considerably for persons who were previously limited on the basis of gender, race, and socioeconomic class. The enrollment of girls and women has increased in countries where there have been policies to promote women's enrollment, and in countries without explicit policies (Kelly, 1992:548–549). In countries with varying levels of economic development, political organization, and religious customs, the trend has been toward gender parity in enrollment rates. During this period of overall enrollment growth, the enrollment of women in higher education grew at a faster rate than that of men (Bradley and Ramirez, 1996).

Explaining this global phenomenon of increased gender equality in educational access necessitates examining factors that are supranational, or beyond national-level characteristics. For example, international organizations such as UNESCO and the World Bank directed and funded projects to improve women's participation in schooling, particularly during the 1970s and 1980s. International agencies, organizations, and educational experts have disseminated the message that modern nations should work toward gender parity in enrollments both to improve their national economic development and to improve the status of women as a goal in and of itself. To this end, international organizations have loaned money to less economically developed countries for the building of schools and provided advisors to governments on how to set up and manage educational systems in the "modern" way. Various United Nations and World Bank publications continually stress that "modern" systems include girls and women as students.

The UNESCO Convention against Discrimination in Education (1960), the United Nations Convention on the Elimination of All Forms of Discrimination against Women (1979), and the 1975 EEC Directive on Equality of Treatment between Men and Women Workers also have been credited for influencing governments to promote gender equality in education and training (Grimm, 1994:113–125; Wilson, 1991). These international agreements establish normative guidelines for states constructing educational policies. By ratifying these conventions, states agree to work toward the goal of eliminating gender discrimination in access and unequal conditions within the schools. States also agree to submit periodic progress reports to international organizations for widespread publication and cross-national comparison.

State policies that address gender equality in schools include legal restrictions on discriminatory admission practices, allocation of funds for adequate facilities, and policies promoting equivalent curricula. Although the state plays a major role in educational planning cross-nationally, there have been few studies that directly examine the effects of state policies on gender equality

using a cross-national research design. Stromquist (1990) makes a strong argument for research attention to the role of the state, noting that there are few women at the state level of decision making. As a result, women are the objects of educational policies rather than active agents in their construction. It is also unclear which forms of state action exert an effect independent of global economic, political, and cultural factors. In one cross-national study, Bradley and Ramirez (1996) found a positive relationship between the degree of state constitutional authority and women's share of higher education from 1965 through 1985, controlling for economic dependency effects. Those states with more authority over more domains of life were more likely to increase women's share of higher education. It has yet to be determined empirically whether the presence of women makes a difference either in the types of policies passed or their effects on gender inequality.

Despite the overall trend of increased gender parity in enrollments, some gender differences in educational access remain. In countries throughout the world, the higher the level of education, the fewer the number or proportion of women students compared to men (Moore, 1987:24). This is true regardless of the proportion of girls enrolled in lower levels of schooling, and regardless of the relative academic performance of girls and boys at the secondary level of schooling. In rural areas in less economically developed countries, girls and women are much less likely to attend and complete schooling than girls/women in urban areas, and in comparison to boys/men in rural areas (Bourque, 1993; Cammish, 1993). Socioeconomic class is more often a factor in the educational attainment of women than it is for men (Stromquist, 1990; Bourque, 1993).

Whereas growth in the enrollment rate of girls and women can be attributed to the dual effects of educational expansion interacting with global attention to women's status, explanations of gender difference in education tend to focus on more proximate causes. The factors mentioned most frequently in the literature are family attitudes and resources, organizational structure of the schools, religious and local cultural practices, state policies, and labor market characteristics. Each of these areas is briefly discussed in the following.

The preference of "families" to educate sons rather than daughters, particularly in the instance of limited resources, is usually attributed to rational decision making by parents. The rational parents compare the future earning differential of sons and daughters and opt to educate sons, since sons are expected to earn more than daughters and thus provide greater future support for the aging parents (Brinton 1988; Tsai, et al., 1994). Particularly in less economically developed countries, as daughters' domestic responsibilities increase with age, parents are more likely to withdraw their daughters from school, resulting in higher attrition rates for girls as compared to boys (Cammish, 1993; Stromquist, 1992). In some cultures, wives are expected to be less educated than their husbands, discouraging families from financing their daughters' education while encouraging them to educate their sons to enhance the marriage prospects of both (Fujimura-Fanselow, 1989; Tsai et al., 1994).

In addition to describing the differences among parental decisions vis-à-vis sons and daughters, it is important to uncover the conditions under which boys are given preference over girls. Much of the family-decision explanation rests on a notion of a rational, economic calculus on the part of parents. This seemingly economic decision only appears to be rational, however, within the context of a set of interrelated cultural assumptions about the roles of women and men in society. These cultural assumptions continue to reflect the historical association of women with the "private" sphere of family responsibilities and men with the "public" sphere of paid labor force and political participation.

A cross-national research design that allows for comparison among the factors expected to contribute to parental preference would allow for testing of hypotheses explicitly. For example, if the primary motivating factor of family decisions concerning education is economic, does the presence of state-provided financial assistance affect the family's decision-making behavior? The educational attainment of men and women in countries with such funding available could be compared to those in countries without such funding to test the extent to which economic considerations alone dictate such behavior.

The influence of mothers on the education of sons and daughters typically has not been considered in status-attainment studies, however, the increased educational attainment of women during recent decades suggests that mothers' as well as fathers' educational status may affect the educational attainment of their children. The findings of Tsai et al. (1994) are suggestive of this trend. They analyzed boys' and girls' probability of progressing from one level of schooling to another in Taiwan, using logistic models. In their study, fathers' educational attainment had an effect on both sons' and daughters' educational attainment at all points of transition, however, mothers' educational attainment had an independent, positive effect on their daughters' attainment of post-high school education. One might also predict that the increased presence of mother-headed families might affect the decision-making process regarding the relative educational attainment of sons and daughters.

One organizational characteristic of schools, coeducation, has mixed meaning and mixed impact, depending on its cultural interpretation. In most instances (particularly in Western cultures), coeducation is the modern liberal expression of gender equality in the schools—girls and boys should have access to the same kind, quality, and status education. In some societies, however, coeducation is a hindrance to the enrollment of girls. When religious or cultural customs forbid the intermingling of boys and girls in public spaces beyond a certain age, families may refuse to send their daughters to coeducational schools (Bourque, 1993).

There is considerable variation in the organization of educational systems, providing fertile ground for examining structural effects on gender inequality. Comparisons of the effects of the timing and nature of qualifying examinations and the organization of curriculum on gender equality in enrollment, educational attainment, and field of study may provide insight into the ways in which the structure of educational systems influence outcomes that previously had been examined solely as an individual-level or family-level decision-making process. Evidence from some European countries that girls academically perform better than boys in secondary schools suggests that when secondary grades are criteria for entry to higher education, girls might have an advantage over boys (Sutherland, 1988; Polydorides, 1985). When states raised the age of compulsory education, more girls completed the secondary level of schooling. Thus, the state can short-circuit parental preference to educate sons as compared to daughters.

As an outgrowth of the expansion of educational systems throughout the world, the enrollment of women increased at all levels. Recent research has indicated, however, that the incorporation of women into education has taken place in a gender-differentiated manner.

Once Inside the Door

Throughout the world, women and men are clustered in different fields of study at the level of higher education and vocational/technical training (Moore, 1987; Kelly, 1992). The fields that are dominated by men—engineering, law, medicine, natural science, and math—tend to require additional education beyond the undergraduate level and lead to higher status occupations. The fields that are dominated by women—teaching, nursing, social service, and the humanities—tend to be linked to lower status occupational areas and require less postgraduate training.

This cross-national trend is surprising, given the diversity in economic, political, organizational, and religious characteristics of countries. Since the legal barriers to enrollment in particular fields of study or institutions have been removed almost unilaterally in recent decades, the task for researchers is to account for why women throughout the world choose fields that lead to lower status occupations. Several studies have found that when schools allow students to make curriculum choices, the greatest degree of gender difference in enrollments is found (Plateau, 1991; Kontagiannopolou-Polydorides, 1991). Research has shown that women academically perform as well as men at the secondary level, so lack of ability among women as a whole compared to men as a whole does not seem to be a reasonable explanation for this cross-national phenomenon (Wilson, 1991). Instead, it is necessary to examine women's (and men's) educational participation within the context of the social institutions in which education is embedded—the family, the labor market, the state, and religion.

The notion of "choice" needs to be understood within the framework of social factors that shape the "decisions" of boys/men and girls/women. There are both direct and indirect ways to influence choice. Schools may channel students directly through tracking, curriculum requirements, and quotas. Cultural ideas concerning gender relations and the roles of women and men in society also influence the behavior of students, teachers, parents, educational administrators, and employers.

The lower enrollment of women in men-dominated fields is often attributed to the occupational gender segregation that women observe in countries throughout the world. One study found that women were less likely to take out loans to finance their education than men (Ve and Fjelde, 1991). The suggested explanation was a rational calculation of expected labor force participation and wages versus the costs of the educational loans. Because women expect to earn less than men, women are less willing to undertake loan debts for further education (even when this additional education would lead to better paying jobs). Following this reasoning, until the labor market is less gendered, education will remain gender segregated. An alternative explanation is the "pipeline" argument—until there are more women in the fields of study that are currently dominated by men, there will not be qualified women to fill the positions. This chicken-and-egg conundrum has yet to be disentangled empirically.

The expansion of systems of higher education in recent decades resulted in status differentiation among the 2-year and 4-year colleges, universities, and technical institutes. In some countries, women and men are enrolled in different types of institutions, with women more often found in lower status institutions. In Japan, women predominate in the 2-year college sector and are scarce in the elite universities (Fujimura-Fanselow, 1989; Brinton, 1988). In France, men are found disproportionately in the grandes écoles (the elite sector of French higher education) while women are more likely to be enrolled in the lower status universities, despite the high academic performance of girls at the secondary level (Charles, 1991:84). These distributional differences among different kinds of institutions may have significant effects on the future life trajectories of women and men. Elite institutions and historically male-dominated academic programs have been found to provide more opportunities for utilizing social networks that facilitate the conversion of educational capital into economic capital (Useem and Karabel, 1986; Lee and Brinton, 1996). The relationship between gender and educational structure is an area of research waiting to be explored comparatively.

Given the characteristics of educational participation just described, does the skewed gender distribution in enrollment by program of study represent a form of gender inequality or of gender "difference"? Concern about the low proportion of women in high-status, men-dominated fields of study has led to local and global programs to increase the enrollment of women in science, engineering, and math. This approach represents the liberal feminist view of inequality—as citizens equivalent in reasoning capability to men, women have the right to participate in public sphere activities to the same extent as men. Therefore, it is expected that the state should take steps to ensure that women are given access to the same opportunities as men, an approach that has been labeled the "female deficit model" (Foster, 1992:61).

Alternatively, one could argue that a major reason that women are being strongly encouraged worldwide to enter men-dominated fields is that they lead to higher paying, higher status occupations than women-dominated fields. After all, if gender "equality" in some pure liberal form were the goal, there would be equally large-scale efforts to draw men into preschool teaching, nursing, and other women-dominated fields. A more radical feminist challenge to the "problem" of gender imbalance within education is to confront the culturally constructed hierarchy that results in higher rewards for men-dominated fields than women-dominated fields. This is evident at the level of curriculum organization itself. Men-dominated math and science are the main instruments of selection among program options, so if students fail at math, their options to "succeed" are limited. This hierarchy is so strongly institutionalized that it is no longer questioned as to whether these areas are the valid and necessary discriminators (Plateau, 1991:15–40).

Theorizing about Gender Inequality in Education

The picture of gender inequality that emerges from the research is paradoxical—educational systems are characterized by gender equality along some dimensions and gender difference along other dimensions. To understand this puzzle, analysis of gender inequality in education is shifting from considering gender as a demographic variable (do the same factors have the same effect on girls as compared to boys) to considering gender a culturally constructed, integral component of education as a social institution.

Social reproduction theorists are extending Bourdieu's class-based analysis to examine the ways in which educational policies and the behavior of persons reflect prevailing cultural norms concerning gender roles and relations. The more radical of these approaches criticizes the liberal feminist view of schools for failing to consider the effects of the gender power imbalance found in society on the social construction of the educational process. The liberal perspective considers the school an impartial mediator of the status attainment process of autonomous individuals. In contrast, the social reproduction literature argues that the school is a microcosm of the broader pattern of asymmetric gender relations institutionalized in society (MacDonald, 1980; Arnot, 1984). These and other "gender-centered" approaches challenge sociological theories and empirical generalizations derived from analyses of boys' and men's experiences. In response, some have placed girls' and women's experiences at the center of sociological inquiry (see, for example Luttrell, 1989). Researchers have also examined the situations in which gender becomes salient in social interactions and in the organization of social institutions such as education, recognizing that "gender" is a variable rather than a constant (Thorne, 1994; Grant et al., 1994).

The taken-for-granted association between women/private sphere and men/public sphere is made apparent in the different "choices" made by boys/men and girls/women in the educational process. Women disproportionately prioritize family considerations over other forms of activities, particularly at the advanced levels of education. It has been observed in several ethnographies that some girls internalize attitudes suggesting that "girls do not really need to go to school" (Cammish, 1993:99) and that it is more appropriate for girls to choose "female"-identified areas of study (Plateau, 1991:15–40). No overt mechanism is needed to maintain gender boundaries within educational systems beyond the strong cultural myths establishing the "real" alternatives among the seemingly open array of options presented to gendered students throughout the world. The onus is upon sociologists of education to explain both the content of these cultural myths and the ways in which they are socially constructed and transmitted.

REFERENCES

Arnot, Madeline. 1984. "A Feminist Perspective on the Relationship Between Family Life and School Life." *Journal of Education* 166:5–24.

Bourque, Susan, and Jill Ker Conway. 1993. *The Politics of Women's Education*. Ann Arbor: The University of Michigan Press.

Bradley, Karen, and Francisco O. Ramirez. 1996. "World Polity and Gender Parity: Women's Share of Higher Education, 1965–1985." *Research in Sociology of Education and Socialization* 10:63–91.

Brinton, Mary C. 1988. "The Social-Institutional Bases of Gender Stratification: Japan as an Illustrative Case." *American Journal of Sociology* 94:300–334.

Cammish, Nadine K. 1993. "Sons and Daughters: Attitudes and Issues Affecting Girls' Education in Developing Countries." *Oxford Studies in Comparative Education* 3:87–107.

Charles, Frederic. 1991. "France." In Maggie Wilson (ed.), *Girls and Young Women in Education: A European Perspective*, pp. 67–89. New York: Pergamon Press.

Foster, V. 1992. "Different But Equal? Dilemmas in the Reform of Girls' Education." *Australian Journal of Education* 36:53–67.

Fujimura-Fanselow, K. 1985. "Women's Participation in Higher Education in Japan." *Comparative Education Review* 29:471–489.

Grant, Linda, Patrick M. Horan, and Betty Watts-Warren. 1994. "Theoretical Diversity in the Analysis of Gender and Education." *Research in Sociology of Education and Socialization* 10:71–109.

Grimm, S. 1994. "The Promotion of Women at Institutions of Higher Education in Western Europe." *International Sociology* 9(1):113–125.

Kelly, Gail P. 1992. "Women and Higher Education Reforms: Expansion without Equality." In J. Peter Cookson, Alan R. Sadovnik, and Susan F. Semel (eds.), *International Handbook of Educational Reform*, pp. 545–559. Westport, CT: Greenwood Press.

Kontogiannopoulou-Polydorides, G. 1991. "Greece." In Maggie Wilson (ed.), *Girls and Young Women in Education: A European Perspective*, pp. 91–113. New York: Pergamon Press.

Lee, Sunhwa, and Mary C. Brinton. 1996. "Elite Education and Social Capital: The Case of South Korea." *Sociology of Education* 69(3):177–192.

Luttrell, Wendy. 1989. "Working-Class Women's Ways of Knowing: Effects of Gender, Race and Class." *Sociology of Education* 62:33–46.

MacDonald, Madeline. 1980. "Socio-Cultural Reproduction and Women's Education." In Rosemary Deem (ed.), *Schooling for Women's Work*. Boston: Routledge and Kegan Paul.

Moore, Kathryn. 1987. "Women's Access and Opportunity in Higher Education: Toward the Twenty-first Century." *Comparative Education* 23:23–34.

Plateau, Nadine. 1991. "French-Speaking Belgium." In Maggie Wilson (ed.), *Girls and Young Women in Education: A European Perspective*, pp. 15–40. New York: Pergamon.

Polydorides, G. 1985. "Women's Participation in the Greek Educational System." *Comparative Education* 21:229–240.

Stromquist, Nelly P. 1990. "Gender Inequality in Education: Accounting for Women's Subordination." *British Journal of Education* 11:137–153.

———. ed. 1992. *Women and Education in Latin America*. Boulder, CO: Lynne Rienner Publishers.

Sutherland, Margaret. 1988. "Women in Higher Education: Effects of Crises and Change." *Higher Education* 17:479–490.

Thorne, Barrie. 1994. *Gender Play: Girls and Boys in School*. New Brunswick, NJ: Rutgers University Press.

Tsai, Shu-Ling, Hill Gates, and Hei-Yuan Chiu. 1994. "Schooling Taiwan's Women: Educational Attainment in the Mid-20th Century." *Sociology of Education* 67:243–263.

Useem, Michael, and Jerome Karabel. 1986. "Pathways to Top Corporate Management." *American Sociological Review* 51:184–200.

Ve, Hildur, and Nina Fjelde. 1991. "Public-Private Tendencies within Higher Education in Norway from a Women's Perspective." In Gail P. Kelly and Sheila Slaughter (eds.), *Women's Higher Education in Comparative Perspective*. Dordrecht, The Netherlands: Kluwer.

Wilson, Maggie. 1991. *Girls and Young Women in Education: A European Perspective*. New York: Pergamon.

GENDER SOCIALIZATION AND EDUCATION

WHERE WE'VE BEEN AND WHERE WE MIGHT GO

Joan Z. Spade
State University of New York at Brockport

The topic of gender socialization and education can be approached from several different angles. Research addressing this issue developed historically across disciplines to create diverse literatures on socialization and gender. I draw from these diverse literatures with the intention of exploring their meaning for research and practice in education, asking what insights this research adds to our understanding of the ways in which boys and girls are socialized in schools. In general, I conclude that the process of gender socialization is not as simple as earlier studies suggest. Instead of a monolithic model of gender socialization, sensitivity to variations across race and class is necessary when examining gender socialization and education. In addition, attention should focus on both those contexts in which gender socialization takes place in school as well as the interpersonal interactions that create gender.

The meaning of socialization is ambiguous. Socialization typically refers to an open-ended concept that describes how humans learn the way of life around them. Sociologists see socialization as the vehicle through which individuals learn the values and norms of their society. To be effective, socialization must be consistent in all institutions (i.e., family, schools) within society. Sociological studies regard socialization as something that is pervasive, both throughout the life cycle and across all institutions in one's life.

Gender socialization, as a subset of socialization studies, focuses on how society socializes boys and girls into appropriate behaviors. Although families are seen as the primary source for socialization in society, schools also are viewed as an important vehicle for socializing youth. The socialization that occurs within schools reinforces gender-appropriate behaviors learned in other social institutions. A natural consequence of research on gender and socialization is the study of how norms defining gender are constructed and maintained in schools, including analyses of textbooks and teachers' behaviors. Researchers also examine the social organization of education to see how structures create and maintain differential treatment for girls and boys.

Children are socialized into gender-appropriate behavior long before they enter school, therefore studies of gender that examine differences in the ways boys and girls are reared are linked to behavior in schools. Beginning in the delivery room, boys are handled and spoken to more roughly than newborn girls (Tavris and Wade, 1984). Toys children play with, books they read, as well as the games they play reinforce gender-appropriate behavior (Tavris and Wade, 1984). These gender socialization practices teach boys and girls the gender-appropriate behaviors that will shape interactions in schools.

Throughout the process of socialization, girls, more so than boys, are taught to focus on feelings, connections to others, and attention to their appearance (Eder, 1995; Thorne, 1993; Tavris and Wade, 1984). Brown and Gilligan (1992) examine the relational aspects of girls' development and note that in the process of teaching girls to be "nice" we also teach girls to suppress their individual voices in relationships. The socialization of girls creates almost perfect students who sit quietly and listen, wanting to please their teachers. However, Bell (1989) argues that the way we socialize girls thwarts the academic achievement of intelligent young girls. In the typically competitive school environment, girls are less likely to be competitive, to want to excel at the expense of others (Best, 1989). In competitive situations, girls often end up feeling less than adequate because, in general, girls have not been taught that "winning is everything." Bell (1989) finds that girls who do win are less willing than male peers to brag about their accomplishments. Girls tend to remain silent about their accomplishments rather than accept success at the expense of others. Instead, the literature suggests that girls are more likely to attribute success to external factors, including luck, rather than their own ability (Bell, 1989).

Horner (1972), based upon her research on college students, argues that women have learned to "fear success." That is, in her laboratory study Horner found that femininity and achievement are mutually exclusive, which results in women avoiding success. Other researchers, however, question the likelihood that women are motivated to avoid success (Paludi, 1984; Levine and Crumrine, 1975). Whatever the process that is occurring, it is safe to assume that, in general, the socialization of young girls does not prepare them for a school atmosphere that is typically competitive.

Boys, on the other hand, are socialized to be aggressive, assertive, and dominant. Studies find that young boys are socialized into a dominant role in society, and given little leeway in deviating from this definition of traditional masculinity (Eder, 1995; Best, 1989). As such, boys face a double bind in school. While the socialization of young boys prepares them for the typically competitive environment of schools, it does not support a docile role in the classroom. The traditional authority patterns in education are such that teachers are dominant and students are passive and submissive. Thus, expectations for masculinity do not fit the model of a "good student," who is expected to be quiet, to listen, and not be disruptive in the classroom (Connell, 1989). In elementary and junior high school, boys who are good students are likely to have their masculinity questioned and are in danger of being ridiculed by their peers (Kinney, 1993; Best, 1989). Furthermore, teachers and adults often expect and reinforce masculine behavior in boys and are alarmed when boys are quiet and attentive (Sadker and Sadker, 1994).

The gender differences found in classrooms also are supported in the context of play groups, as boys and girls develop different patterns for joining and separating. Boys join together to play games that are segregated from girls and vice versa. These same-sex play groups reinforce gender-appropriate behavior for boys and girls through the patterning of play. Girls' groups tend to be less hierarchical, and conversation focuses around issues of physical appearance and relationships. Even in the lunchroom and on school grounds, these separate patterns of play prevail (American Association of University Women, 1995; Best, 1989). Thorne (1993) finds that the few exceptions to separate gender play groups are gender-neutral games such as dodge ball, often supervised by school staff.

It is clear that teachers reinforce the gender differences students bring to schools. Sadker and Sadker (1994) provide considerable documentation of teachers' participation in gender socialization in classrooms. In addition to segregating students into separate lines for boys and girls (Sadker and Sadker, 1994; Thorne, 1993; Best, 1989), teachers communicate both formally and informally how boys and girls should behave. Within the dialog of the classroom, the Sadkers find that although boys are not seen as ideal students, they are more likely than girls to get their teachers' attention, including being called on more often and receiving more criticism and help such as praise and correction. In addition, teachers wait longer for boys to respond to questions, allowing them to think through their responses. The attention boys receive in the classroom is likely to foster student achievement, support that girls do not typically receive (American Association of University Women, 1995).

Instead, teachers are more likely to comment on girls' clothing and appearance (Sadker and Sadker, 1994). This emphasis by teachers only reinforces the sociocultural focus on appearance for women that young girls already have incorporated into their self-image based upon earlier socialization and pressure from peers (Eder, 1995; Bell, 1989). Unfortunately, overemphasis on appearance is linked to dieting, with 50% of high school women admitting to having dieted at some time in their life, with concerns about body weight beginning in the elementary school (Moreno and Thelen, 1995). This emphasis on appearance for girls can result in life threatening situations, when dieting gets out of hand for young women.

Teachers also bring sexism into the classroom in terms of spacial arrangements. Sadker and Sadker (1994) studied the "gender geography" of 100 elementary school classrooms throughout the United States and found that in over half of the classrooms, desks and work/play areas were sex segregated, with boys and girls assigned to separate areas. They found more interaction across race than between boys and girls, a sad commentary on gender relations in schools. The Sadkers argue that "gender segregation is a major contributor to female invisibility in schools" (p. 65).

Sexist curricula add to the gender socialization processes inherent in classrooms. Sadker and Sadker (1994) were stunned when they considered how little students in 16 fourth-, fifth-, and sixth-grade classrooms knew about women in history. When asked to name women in history, most of the children they studied could list the names of only a couple women and several listed no women. Their responses are not surprising given the gender bias found in the history books these children read in elementary school. Sadker and Sadker found that there were four times as many men as women pictured in one history textbook published in 1989 and in a 1992 history book for sixth graders "only eleven female names were mentioned, and not a single American adult woman was included" (p. 72). The Sadkers concluded:

> women were left out of the curriculum, the students knew nothing about them. Even worse, without real knowledge, the children filled in the gaps with stereotypes and distortions. The result was a twisted view of half the people and their history. (Sadker and Sadker, 1994:73)

Studies of course taking and achievement point to the important role schools play in reinforcing gender. Elementary school boys and girls are relatively similar in their interest and ability in mathematics and science (American Association of University Women, 1995). However, as children grow up, the gender gap in both interest and ability in these two subjects increases. Even the small initial advantage that girls hold in reading seems to disappear as girls and boys enter high school (American Association of University Women, 1995).

The gender gap in ability shows up on most standardized tests students take. Bias in the standardized tests used to determine college entrance, scholarships and loans, and entrance into professions is particularly problematic (American Association of University Women, 1995; Sadker and Sadker, 1994). For example, on the Preliminary Scholastic Aptitude Test, boys outscore girls on both the verbal and math sections, even though girls have higher grade averages in high school (American Association of University Women, 1995; Sadker and Sadker, 1994). In response to possible bias, the testing company doubles verbal scores on the PSAT;

however, there are far fewer girls who score in the top categories of both verbal and math sections (Sadker and Sadker, 1994). Thus, the bias in testing becomes a problem of discrimination against girls when PSAT scores are used to determine National Merit Scholarships and many other state and college scholarships.

The end result of bias in the classroom and on college entrance exams is that by the time young women enter college, they feel like second-class citizens. Experiences in schools inevitably contribute to segregating girls into particular academic specialties in college, a pattern that is reflected in gender distribution that continues today (American Association of University Women, 1995; Jacobs, 1995). For example, the percentage of women graduating with a Bachelor's Degree in engineering increased only from 9.3% in 1980 to 13.8% in 1990 and in physical sciences from 23.7 to 31.2%. Although some progress has been made, with women making up approximately 50% of the Bachelor's Degree recipients in life sciences and law, women are disproportionately represented in areas such as education (78% in 1990), health professions (84%), and home economics (90%) (Jacobs, 1995).

Earlier gender socialization comes through in college, with women more likely to see themselves as having less ability than their male peers, despite having higher grade point averages (Spade and Reese, 1991; Hawks and Spade, 1996). These lowered perceptions of ability affect not only performance in college, but also choice of major and plans for careers. Even those women who overcame the influence of socialization and chose traditionally male fields are likely to be influenced by earlier gender socialization as they prepare to enter their careers. As women anticipate their futures, they are more likely than men to take future family responsibilities into account as they plan their careers, a factor that may inhibit their ambitions in college (Spade and Reese, 1991; Hawks and Spade, 1996).

These studies of socialization recognize clear differences in the process for boys and girls; however, these differences are portrayed only in terms of a dichotomy in which all boys and all girls experience socialization similarly. Recent models of socialization focus more on context and children's backgrounds and experiences, as well as the influence of peers in the socialization process.

In alerting us to the importance of context, Thorne (1993) argues against dichotomous models of gender.

She disagrees with arguments that boys and girls naturally form separate cultures, and believes that institutional frameworks can and do facilitate the development of separate cultures for boys and girls. Because schools bring together children in large, homogeneous age groups, schools, in particular, provide a vehicle for boys and girls to separate and join peer groups based on gender (Goodwin, 1990). Outside of these institutional settings, such as at home or in neighborhoods, where children play together in smaller, heterogeneous groups, separate groups of boys and girls are less likely to form.

Yet, even within nonschool playgroups, expectations of the larger society influence context and behavior. For example, when observing heterogeneous playgroups, Goodwin (1990) finds that girls, who are more likely to be given child-care responsibilities, are more likely than boys to form mixed-age and mixed-sex playgroups. Girls also are more likely than boys to engage in noncompetitive play, such as school, which is more conducive to mixed-age and mixed-sex playgroups. As a consequence of the play activities, girls are socialized into a more supportive role and are likely to assume the mother role in play and other interactions in school (Best, 1989).

Evidence of race and class differences in socialization also calls for expansion of previous views of socialization (Grant and Sleeter, 1988). Race is an important component to be considered when examining gender socialization in classrooms. Teachers respond to black girls based upon both race and gender and are more likely to reward them for custodial or clerical tasks than to challenge them academically (Grant, 1984). Minority girls receive the least amount of attention of all students and are called upon less often by teachers than other students (Sadker and Sadker, 1994). The response of students to this differential treatment of teachers varies by race and gender as well. Bell finds that black girls are more likely to react aggressively to dismissive treatment by teachers whereas white and Hispanic girls are more likely to be passive or silent (see also American Association of University Women, 1995; Eder, 1995). Passive, silent girls miss out on academic enrichment; however, teachers' responses to the aggressive behavior of young girls were likely to be punitive and hostile (Bell, 1989).

Social class also provides a context that shapes socialization and gender identity. Although socioeconomic class is the strongest predictor of achievement in schools, race and gender intersect to shape the educational experiences of boys and girls (American Association of University Women, 1995). According to Goodwin (1990), most studies done on middle-class children reflect a setting in which physical distance creates barriers to "relaxed, extended social interaction [which] prevented girls and boys from exploring mutual interests which would lay the foundation for a friendship" (p. 49). In her studies of inner-city children, Goodwin (1990) found that proximity was not an issue for the lower class children, who played together on a regular basis. For preadolescents, who are increasingly aware of their own sexuality, the physical distance that separates middle-class boys and girls creates an uncomfortableness with their own budding sexuality. The lower class boys and girls Goodwin studied entered preadolescence much more comfortable with their own sexuality given the pattern of frequent interactions in heterosexual play groups. Thus, gender socialization in adolescence is framed by the context of social class and neighborhood settings in establishing contacts in mixed-sex play groups.

These differences by race and class challenge approaches that dichotomize gender in previous socialization studies. It is time to shift focus and recognize that gender socialization is a complex process in which race, ethnicity, and social class frame the experiences of boys and girls in school and elsewhere.

One final issue to be addressed in this chapter is that of the processes by which gender is created in schools. Sociologists are less likely than psychologists or social psychologists to consider how gender is transmitted and interpreted by individuals, however, this dimension of gender socialization is equally important in schools. West and Zimmerman (1987) describe the process of "doing gender," in which gender is created in the context of everyday interactions.

In classrooms, teachers hold an inordinate amount of power in interpersonal interactions. Teachers, however, are often not conscious of the role they play in gender socialization and how their presentation of curriculum to students reinforces traditional gender roles. Many teachers, when confronted with sexist patterns in their classrooms, were totally unaware of their practices (Sadker and Sadker, 1994). For meaningful change to occur in our classrooms, attention to both content and process is necessary.

In conclusion, it is worthwhile to reflect on the themes presented throughout this chapter and consider directions for research and practice. First, in terms of context, we need continued research to identify those aspects of school that segregate girls from boys in terms of both space and activities. The work of Thorne (1993), on playgrounds, needs to be extended to classrooms and counseling settings to identify why it is young women are less likely to take mathematics and science classes and why young women feel they are less able than their male counterparts. As researchers further examine the role of context in socializing boys and girls in schools, they must be sensitive to the divergent experiences of boys and girls of different racial/ethnic and social class backgrounds. Research is only beginning to address the intersection of race, class, and gender; much more needs to be done to understand the interplay of these three factors on the education of our young people.

Lastly, following the work of Sadker and Sadker (1994), we need to attend to the interpersonal interactions that sustain gender in our schools. Further work is needed to understand the complex interplay of sexist curriculum along with unconscious and often unintended sexism on the part of teachers. Teachers need to be aware of the ways in which they create and recreate gender in our classrooms. There are many excellent suggestions for making classrooms and schools less sexist (cf. American Association of University Women, 1995). Sensitivity to the often unconscious interpersonal dimensions by which we "do gender" is particularly important if teachers wish to create gender-neutral classrooms. Principals and school administrators need to be aware that gender is created in the social organization of schools, by placing students in particular classes or play groups; in the curriculum of schools, by maintaining and reinforcing gender stereotypes or ignoring nonstereotypical gender behavior; by the treats and rewards that students reap on each other as they banter in formal and informal conversations; and by teachers and school staff in the way they deliver curriculum and school business.

The difficulty in understanding gender socialization in education is that it represents the "normal" life of schools or typical behavior of boys and girls and their teachers. There is danger in dichotomizing behavior for males and females. Instead, researchers and teachers need to be sensitive to the complex nature of socialization and the danger of focusing on simple differences between boys and girls.

REFERENCES

American Association of University Women. 1995. *How Schools Shortchange Girls: The AAUW Report*. New York: Marlow.

Bell, L. A. 1995. "Something's Wrong Here and It's Not Me: Challenging the Dilemmas that Block Girls' Success." *Journal for the Education of the Gifted* 12:118–130.

Best, Raphaela. 1989. *We've All Got Scars: What Boys and Girls Learn in Elementary School*. Bloomington, IN: Bloomington University Press.

Brown, L. M., and C. Gilligan. 1992. *Meeting at the Crossroads: Women's Psychology and Girls' Development*. Cambridge, MA: Harvard University Press.

Connell, R. W. 1989. "Cool Guys, Swots and Wimps: The Interplay of Masculinity and Education." *Oxford Review of Education* 15:291–303.

Eccles, J. S. 1986. "Gender-Roles and Women's Achievement." *Educational Researcher* (June/July):15–19.

Eder, D. 1995. *School Talk: Gender and Adolescent Culture*. New Brunswick, NJ: Rutgers University Press.

Gilligan, C. 1977. "In a Different Voice: Women's Conceptions of Self and of Morality." *Harvard Educational Review* 47:481–517.

Goodwin, M. H. 1990. *He-Said-She-Said: Talk as Social Organization among Black Children*. Bloomington, IN: Indiana University Press.

Grant, C. A., and C. E. Sleeter. 1988. "Race, Class, and Gender and Abandoned Dreams." *Teachers College Record* 90:19–24.

Hawks, B. K., and J. Z. Spade. 1996. "Carrying a Full Load: Perceptions of Women and Men Engineering Students." Unpublished manuscript.

Horner, M. S. 1972. "Toward an Understanding of Achievement-Related Conflicts in Women." *Journal of Social Issues* 28:157–176.

Jacobs, J. A. 1995. "Gender and Academic Specialties: Trends Among Recipients of College Degrees in the 1980s." *Sociology of Education* 68:81–98.

Kinney, David A. 1993. "From Nerds to Normals: The Recovery of Identity Among Adolescents from Middle School to High School." *Sociology of Education* 66:21–40.

Levine, A., and J. Crumrine. 1975. "Women and the Fear of Success: A Problem in Replication." *American Sociological Journal* 80:964–973.

Moreno, A. B., and M. H. Thelen. 1995. "Eating Behavior in Junior High School Females." *Journal of Adolesence* 30:170–175.

Paludi, M. A. 1984. "Psychometric Properties and Underlying Assumptions of Four Objective Measures of Fear of Success." *Sex Roles* 9/10:765–781.

Sadker, M., and D. Sadker. 1994. *Failing at Fairness: How Our Schools Cheat Girls.* New York: Simon & Schuster.

Spade, J. Z., and C. A. Reese. 1991. "We've Come a Long Way, Maybe: College Students' Plans for Work and Family." *Sex Roles* 24:309–321.

Tavris, C., and C. Wade. 1984. *The Longest War: Sex Differences in Perspective.* San Diego, CA: Harcourt, Brace Jovanovich.

Thorne, B. 1993. *Gender Play: Girls and Boys in School.* New Brunswick, NJ: Rutgers University Press.

West, C., and D. H. Zimmerman. 1987. "Doing Gender." *Gender & Society* 2:125–151.

GLOBALIZATION

John Boli
Emory University

The globalization of education and schooling (terms that will be used interchangeably here) has four major dimensions. It began in medieval times, particularly from the eleventh century onward, with (1) the revitalization and bureaucratization of the Western Church and the accompanying establishment of a decentralized European "system" of education for the production of clergy and secular officials. That dimension will be treated only briefly in favor of more recent developments. In the nineteenth century we find (2) international comparisons and rivalries between countries involved in the initial construction of mass schooling, a process of mutual imitation that gave schooling a largely uniform structure among these competing countries. In the twentieth century, educational globalization intensified with (3) the spread of the state as the dominant political form everywhere in the world, with the consequence that the construction of national educational systems became a ubiquitous endeavor, along with the establishment and growth of transnational or global organizations concerned with education. These organizations, especially UNESCO and the many nongovernmental bodies associated with UNESCO, came to constitute a normatively authoritative "global center" for the discussion and implementation of educational ideas and organizational models. Hand in hand with the latter two dimensions we find (4) growing social scientific interest in education, producing analyses of the history and operations of schooling in many countries and studies of the effects of schooling on phenomena such as economic growth, stratification, and political behavior. In recent decades much of the social scientific research has been incorporated into the work of global educational organiza-

tions and thereby has become part of the globalization process itself.

Transnational and National Education in Premodern Europe

The expansion and bureaucratization of the Roman Catholic Church was predicated on the production of literate clerics. The Church directly promoted the founding and expansion of cathedral schools and universities; religious orders devoted at least partly to education, including the Augustinians and Dominicans, flourished from the thirteenth century onward. Teaching principally in Latin and concentrating on abstract knowledge and skills, these institutions constituted a transnational community of scholars and students equally at home in Dublin, Aachen, or Bologna.

The universalism of the system was complicated by the emerging system of competing states, which gradually fashioned bureaucratic administrations based on the model provided by the Church. Monarchs relied heavily on Church men to staff their administrations; this interpenetration of secular and spiritual authority formed the organizational basis for the centuries-long struggle between Church and state. One result was recurring state attempts to wrest control of education from the hands of the Church, particularly through the establishment of independent universities.

The increasing nationalization of formal education, which would remain an elite activity producing clerics, lawyers, and administrators through the eighteenth century, is indicated by the introduction of vernacular languages and the founding of regional universities designed to promote a common national culture. Lund

University, for example, was established in 1668 to promote the Swedification of Scania, which the Swedes had taken from Denmark 10 years earlier. Yet the curriculum of the universities retained its abstract philosophical/theological character well into the modern era, focusing on forms of knowledge that transcended considerations of national identity, and educated elites continued to constitute an essentially transnational community as well. Seventeenth-century monarchs in post-Reformation Europe may have founded academies of science, language, and the arts for the purpose of national aggrandizement, but the scholars, artists, and clergymen supported by those academies saw themselves as engaged in universally applicable discourse, expression, analysis, and spiritual meditation.

Nineteenth-Century Nationalism and Internationalism

By the nineteenth century, the thoroughgoing cultural transformation of the West produced an entirely new social logic regarding education. The spread of capitalist exchange, technological development, bureaucratic political administration, and individualistic concern for liberty and self-development made exclusively elite schooling seem inadequate for the problems of the day. The masses, too, needed schooling.

Precursors of the notion that mass schooling was both necessary and useful had surfaced as early as the sixteenth century, when the Reformation shifted the focus of religiosity from rituals conducted by the clerical elite on behalf of their flocks to direct participation and faith on the part of individual parishioners. Both Protestants and Counter-Reformation Catholics, especially the Jesuits, turned to schooling as a means of winning souls. Compulsory schooling laws formalized this notion as early as 1619 in Lutheran Weimar and 1642 in Puritan Massachusetts. Two centuries later, the necessity of schooling had become conventional wisdom throughout the European-centered world system. Schooling was needed to teach the lower classes better agricultural methods and new skills required for factory work. Schooling would instill the virtues of sobriety, discipline, and respect for authority. Schooling would foster patriotism and a willingness to sacrifice for the national good. Schooling would, in short, transform the "lower classes" into model individuals who would create strong, efficient, progressive societies.

This view of schooling as functionally imperative was not without its critics. Schooling for the masses was a dangerous business, they claimed; it would give the lower classes ideas and capabilities unsuited to their station, and encourage rebellious attitudes to boot. But the infectious optimism of the nineteenth century produced a remarkably common outcome of the schooling debate: everywhere in Europe, and in most independent countries that had once been European colonies, states built school systems in which most children spent a fair proportion of their childhood days. The transnational character of this process is evident in the sheer fact of its simultaneity: In 1800 not a single mass schooling system was in operation, but by 1900 such systems were commonplace.

Nineteenth-century educational development was, however, more international than global. The "educated person" ideal to be pursued via mass schooling was certainly a transnationally shared image, but national systems were the means to be used in the pursuit. The internationalism of the process became clear as elites and educators looked to one another in designing and constructing school systems: What was under construction was not distinctly French, Australian, Bavarian, or Canadian systems, but a range of variants on a common basic model. American educators like Alexander Dallas Bache (1839), Horace Mann (1844), and Henry Barnard (1835–1837) toured the continent to study structure and methods with an eye to school reform at home. Victor Cousin visited Holland and Germany on France's behalf; Swedish educators experimented with the English monitorial method of instruction; Pestalozzi and Herbart became international figures of great regard. Prussian education quickly established itself as a favorite model, with its strict discipline, close ties to the expansive Prussian military machine, and obvious effectiveness (the French were wont to attribute their loss of the war with Prussia in 1870 to the "Prussian schoolmaster"). The U.S. Office of Education, established after the American Civil War and initially led by Barnard, became the most prominent source of statistics and in-depth reports on European systems through the end of the century.

This "age of nationalism" was also, then, an age of systematic mutual surveillance and learning in which state administrators and educators searched for optimal models and methods. Parliamentary debaters in places as diverse as England, Sweden, the Netherlands, Argentina, and Mexico routinely made reference to developments in other countries as arguments for or against proposals in their own countries. The ideas and mechanisms to be used for education were seen as transnationally valid, despite much disagreement about matters such as the desirability of maintaining two-track systems to keep children of different classes apart.

Internationalism was institutionalized in an unexpected way in the work of statisticians who strove to standardize the compilation of vital and educational statistics. Leading the way was the International Statistical Congress (ISC), under the leadership of Adolphe Quetelet, which met nine times between 1853 and 1876 to coordinate the activities of official representatives from a large number of states. Eventually undermined by Bismarck's refusal to allow Prussian officials to participate, the ISC gave way to nongovernmental bodies in which many of the same participants acted as private members. Chief among these were the International Demographic Congress, first held in 1878, and the International Statistical Institute, founded in 1885.

These developments sharply improved the basis for country-to-country comparisons, thereby facilitating more intense international competition regarding education. In addition, reform groups within countries increasingly turned to statistical sources to buttress their concerns about the relatively advanced state of schooling in other countries and, therefore, the necessity of improvements at home.

The Spread of Statehood and Global Organization

The transformation of colonies and dependencies into politically independent countries following the collapse of the Ottoman, Austro-Hungarian, British, and French empires led to an unprecedented wave of state formation and nation building in the twentieth century. By this time, it was taken for granted that every state should establish and vigorously support a national educational system. Compulsory mass schooling laws and rapidly growing school systems sprang into being almost everywhere, enrolling most children in some semblance of a school despite a frequent dearth of trained teachers, up-to-date textbooks, school buildings, or competent administrators. Schooling became a major national project in all countries as this "world educational revolution" (Meyer et al., 1977) proceeded.

Table 1 shows some of the remarkable trends in educational enrollments in the postwar period. For the world as a whole, the primary enrollment ratio (primary school enrollments as a proportion of the relevant age group of the population) rose from about 58% in 1950 to 84% in 1970 and 98% in 1992.

For secondary schooling, the corresponding ratio rose from about 13% in 1950 to 53% in 1992, and for higher education from 1.4% to about 14%. Most of the increase in primary enrollment ratios is due to expansion in the less developed world, since the richer countries already had virtually universal elementary schooling by 1950. The increases in secondary and tertiary education reflect across-the-board change, the general pattern being higher absolute ratios in the richer countries but more rapid expansion among poorer countries. This expansive process is all the more remarkable in light of the fact that so many new countries with relatively weak states and few resources achieved independence in this period.

In counterpoint to the extraordinary expansion of national systems, the global organization of education also rose sharply. Prior to 1900, only a handful of education-oriented transnational organizations had emerged, such as the World ORT Union of 1880 (for the education of Jews in manual labor occupations), the International Society of Study, Correspondence and Exchange of 1895, and the International Society for the Development of Commercial Education of 1897. As Figure 1 shows, however, after World War I these non-

TABLE 1. World Educational Enrollment Ratios, 1950–1992[a]

Year	Primary Schooling (%)	Secondary Schooling (%)	Tertiary (University) (%)
1950[b]	58	13	1.4
1960	77	27	6.0
1970	84	36	11
1980	96	45	11
1992	98	53	14

[a]Figures are total schooling enrollments in the world divided by the number of children or youth in the relevant age groups. All data are from the UNESCO *Statistical Yearbook*, as follows: for 1950, the 1970–1971 volume; for 1960 and 1970, the 1984 volume; for 1992, the 1992 volume. Retrospective figures are not entirely consistent in the various editions.
[b]Values are mean figures for national enrollment ratios of independent countries, rather than total world ratios.

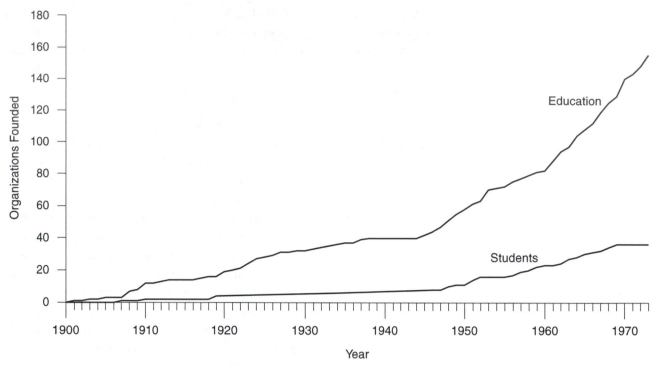

Figure 1. International nongovernment organizations in education cumulative foundings, 1900–1973. Note: Founding dates unknown for 32 educational and 5 student organizations.
Source: *Yearbook of International Organizations* (1985, 1988)

governmental educational organizations became quite numerous, and after 1945 they proliferated rapidly. These bodies include professional teacher associations, associations of schools, societies for the promotion of teaching techniques (everything from audio-visual instruction to the Montessori method), and groups devoted explicitly to global educational development (for example, the International Reading Association, the International Council on Education for Teaching, and the World Association for Educational Research).

Alongside them, and to some extent following the lead of the nongovernmental organizations, intergovernmental bodies have become increasingly important global actors; the first of these was the International Bureau of Education, founded in 1925.

For 50 years now, the single most important organization in the globalization of education has been UNESCO. Its programmatic efforts help states organize teacher training facilities, prepare curricular programs, establish systems for textbook preparation and procurement, and much more. UNESCO's statistics-gathering system, which has become increasingly comprehensive and standardized through the years, itself

has significant effects: many countries have restructured their national systems to match the model suggested by the statistics-gathering form, including the sequence of 6 years of primary school followed by 3 years each of intermediate and secondary schooling.

By these and other means, including the many global conferences on education that it sponsors, UNESCO has shaped the educational system-building process by promoting a largely uniform model of schooling, and it has become more effective in doing so as more non-Western administrators and staff have joined its ranks. No longer perceived, as in the early days, as a body dominated by the West, UNESCO is now heard readily by state officials in the less developed world. Thus, UNESCO has become a primary instructor of and aid to states in the educational realm.

In relationships that range from easy harmony to rather tense coexistence, the intergovernmental and nongovernmental organizations that structure the global field engage in intense interaction. Some 900 nongovernmental organizations have consultative status with UNESCO, more by far than with any other UN agency. Because education is considered crucial to many aspects of development, from economic growth to environmental protection to social equality, a wide range of nongovernmental organizations can reasonably claim to have concerns relevant to schooling. For this reason, bodies as diverse as the Arab Industrial Development Organization, the International Council on Women, and the Latin American Peace Research Council work actively with UNESCO, in addition to such directly educational organizations as the World Organization for Early Childhood Education and the International Association of Universities.

The globalization of education since World War II has encompassed a good deal more than structure, methods, and transnational organizations. Increasingly, a common educational ideology has been adopted and, in good measure, implemented in the world's national school systems. Statements of national educational purpose show rising emphasis on both national development and individual growth and advancement for all citizens, at the expense of elite training and the strengthening of local communities. National constitutions almost without exception define schooling as both a right and a duty of citizens, and as an obligation on the part of the state to ensure that the right to education is implemented. Studies of the curricula of national systems reveal impressive uniformity in the subjects taught and the amount of time allocated to each subject. They also show widespread trends over time, such as increasing emphasis on modern foreign languages and integrated social studies programs at the expense of classic languages (Latin, Greek) and history and geography. Another curricular impact is the rise of self-styled global education, designed to help students see issues in transnational terms and understand the significance of global interdependence. Meanwhile, longitudinal analyses of secondary education show that vocational training has declined sharply in favor of comprehensive schooling. Everywhere in the world, educators have come to put the "whole student" more at the center of the enterprise, reserving the narrower education entailed in occupational preparation for the tertiary level.

One striking aspect of education's ideological development is a marked increase in sexual equality in schooling over the past several decades. Female enrollment rates have risen to match or approach those for males not only at the compulsory schooling level, where enrollment equality is bound to occur as mass schooling becomes universal, but also at the secondary and tertiary levels. By 1992, women accounted for 46% of all primary school enrollments in the world and 45% of all secondary enrollments. These figures are not so different from the 1950 figures, which were 43% for both levels. In higher education, though, the change is dramatic: from 32% in 1950 to 37% in 1970 and 45% in 1992. Even in regions with what are considered highly patriarchal cultures, such as the Middle East, women's share of tertiary schooling has risen rapidly (from 21% in 1955 to 42% in 1985). The entry of women into once male-dominated areas of advanced study, such as law, medicine, and engineering, is also a worldwide phenomenon. Such growing sexual parity in education obviously cannot be attributed to the action of educators and administrators alone, but it is equally clear that school officials have by and large been enthusiastic promoters of this aspect of the worldwide drive for sexual equality.

Finally, some effort has been made to create a uniform set of standards for educational credentials so that diplomas obtained in one country will be valid in others. The leading organization in this effort is the International Baccalaureate Office, created by the International Schools Association in 1968 in cooperation with UNESCO. UNESCO itself has also established a goal of producing a universal system for the mutual recognition of credentials. To this point, the success of these efforts is limited. The International Baccalaureate is generally recognized only in Europe, and relatively few students apply for it. Despite the halting progress of such formal efforts toward credentialing comparability, the propensity of students to study abroad has increased rapidly throughout the world, with the United States being the greatest magnet for foreign students.

What is most striking about the trends in schooling structure, purposes, curricular content, and enrollments is their very general character. The trends apply to African, Asian, Latin American, European, and Middle Eastern school systems. They apply to the most developed and the least developed countries. They are found in countries with strong democratic traditions and countries subject to long periods of authoritarian or one-party rule. In short, they are very nearly universal. Education has become a central sector of every national society and the primary means whereby children receive formal preparation for adult life. Given the great diversity among countries in terms of wealth, power, technology, cultural traditions, and history, the uniform character of schooling cannot be accounted for by national-level causal mechanisms. The main conclusion of all these detailed studies of education in the postwar world is, then, that education has become a global social process that both reflects and helps create the global society that is under formation.

The Intellectualization of Education as a Global Enterprise

Well into the nineteenth century, most writing about education was moral-philosophical, concerned with prescriptions for the "proper" aims and methods of education rather than analyses of educational institutions' origins and actual operations. When analysis began to supplement prescription, internationally oriented work quickly settled on the comparative study as the favored model. Still common today, this model is usually atheoretical, concerned mainly with describing similarities and differences in the educational systems of two or a few countries and treating only speculatively issues such as the relative effectiveness of different systems or methods. In early comparative work, schooling success essentially meant schooling expansion: Successful systems enrolled large proportions of children, and the best systems reached all children.

In the 1950s and 1960s, analyses of education became more theoretical. The working assumption, rarely stated explicitly, was that schooling operates in accordance with general principles that apply in all societies. Economists began to incorporate education into their models via the concept of "human capital," first as a convenient residual category to account for economic growth not explained by conventional factors of production, and later as a variable measured by school completion rates. On the sociological side, theories of the origins and effects of schooling received formal statement. Functionalist theory described schooling as a product of urbanization and industrialization in nineteenth-century Europe; for less developed countries, schooling was supposed to be an engine for modernization, reversing the original causal relationship. Schooling's effects were presumed to operate through the changes they wrought in individual students, and these changes were seen as beneficial both to the students themselves (empowering them as modern eco-

nomic and political actors) and to the societies that schooled them.

These were the ideas that came to dominate in transnational and intergovernmental educational organizations, particularly UNESCO and the host of nongovernmental bodies associated with it. They are strikingly apparent in the highly influential *World Survey of Education* conducted by UNESCO in the 1950s and 1960s, which became a landmark document in the globalization of education. The intellectualization process crystallized into what can best be described as an unoffical but authoritative world ideology regarding education, a received wisdom that national schooling systems sought to implement as fully as possible. Consultants, advisers, and experts from global organizations became active agents of this ideology, teaching national school officials how to construct their systems in accordance with it.

Challenges to the received wisdom appeared in several guises from the late 1960s onward. Scholars reacting against the generally harmonious tone of functionalism emphasized the stratifying effects of schooling, developing theories of education as elite social control or as status competition among ethnic, religious, and class-based groups. Careful historical studies overturned the presumed connection between modernization and schooling, showing that schooling often preceded urbanization and industrialization and that education's effects on economic and political development were often small, sometimes negative, and at best ambiguous. Meanwhile, John Meyer and his colleagues developed the institutional perspective on schooling that downplays schooling's effects on individuals, focusing instead on the broad implications for societies of the rise of formal education as a major axis of social organization.

As comprehensive cross-national statistical data banks began appearing in the 1970s, the ground was thus prepared for systematic studies evaluating these general theories of the causes and effects of educational growth. A host of studies appeared, almost all of them making the global assumption that politically independent countries were wholly comparable cases subject to a common set of causal processes. In counterpoint, studies of the comparative effectiveness of schooling systems became a minor industry, led by the International Evaluation of Educational Achievement (initiated in 1959) and related programs. The latter studies provided a new set of metrics for comparing national systems of schooling—mean country scores on tests of mathematics, natural science, geography, foreign language ability, and so on. As such, they provided new dimensions of national competition and concern, leading to widespread reform efforts in many parts of the world to "catch up with the Japanese" or "meet the challenges of the twenty-first century."

In the 1980s, the mounting body of evidence regarding the largely unexpected homogenization of schooling throughout the world led researchers to recognize the world-systemic character of educational development. Institutional theory in particular developed explanations based on the globalization of educational principles and models and the promotion of those ideas by global organizations. Deeper immersion in historical materials, both for the period of mass schooling (since the early nineteenth century) and reaching back to the origins of formal schooling in Europe, has both expanded the reach of these analyses and uncovered new puzzles to be solved.

The global institutionalization view of schooling calls into question both functionalist and conflict theories of schooling, particularly at the primary and secondary levels. Above all, it has led to the view that education is better conceptualized as the symbolic transformation of individuals in line with idealized models of the good citizen than as a mechanism for the transmission of directly useful skills, attitudes, and self-concepts. So far, however, this and the other challenges to functionalist thinking on education have made little headway in the global education sector. The view that education is indispensable to economic growth, political modernization, and individual development remains the bedrock of educational policy almost everywhere.

Still only two decades old, global analysis has so far neglected several major issues in world educational development. First, traditional educational institutions in numerous societies (especially in Asia and the Arab world) have been ignored. Even though contemporary models of mass schooling derive mainly from the European experience, the interplay between traditional and contemporary models must enter the analysis. Second, much of the evidence regarding globalization is purely formal. Researchers use readily available data on matters such as policy statements, official enrollments, and curricular plans for the allocation of teaching time, rather than the much less accessible information about actual administrator behavior, student attendance, or teacher use of classroom time. The links between formal structure and everyday action must receive greater attention. Third, globalization study too often assumes the absence of alternative and competing models of educational systems in world culture. Islamic, Asian, and African models coexist to varying degrees with Western models, and they have the potential to pose challenges to Western-derived systems. In this respect, globalization study would benefit by bringing the methods of in-depth comparative research into its more highly theorized approach to global educational analysis.

REFERENCES

Arnove, Robert F., Philip G. Altbach, and Gail P. Kelly, eds. 1992. *Emergent Issues in Education: Comparative Perspectives.* Albany: State University of New York Press.

Boli, John, and Francisco O. Ramirez. 1986. "World Culture and the Institutional Development of Mass Education." In John G. Richardson (ed.), *Handbook of Theory and Research in the Sociology of Education,* pp. 65–90. Westport, CT: Greenwood Press.

Comparative Education Review. 1977. "Special Double Issue on the State of the Art." 21 (June–October).

Fuller, Bruce, and Richard Rubinson, eds. 1992. *The Political Construction of Education: The State, School Expansion, and Economic Change.* New York: Praeger.

Meyer, John W., and Michael T. Hannan, eds. 1979. *National Development and the World System: Educational, Economic, and Political Change, 1950–1970.* Chicago: University of Chicago Press.

Meyer, John W., Francisco Ramirez, Richard Rubinson, and John Boli[-Bennett]. 1977. "The World Educational Revolution, 1950–1970." *Sociology of Education* 50:242–258.

Meyer, John W., David Kamens, Aaron Benavot, Yun-Kyung Cha, and Suk-Ying Wong. 1992. *School Knowledge for the Masses: World Models and National Primary Curriculum Categories in the Twentieth Century.* London: Falmer.

UNESCO. 1950–94. *Statistical Yearbook.* Paris: UNESCO.

UNESCO. 1955–71. *World Survey of Education.* Five volumes. Geneva: UNESCO.

HIGH SCHOOL DROPOUTS

Aaron M. Pallas
Teachers College, Columbia University

In societies that are deeply stratified by how far one goes through school, early school-leaving is a critical marker distinguishing the haves from the have-nots. Over the past three decades, there has been recurring attention to the problem of dropping out of high school, as there is a widespread belief that most of today's jobs, and nearly all of those in the future, require the skills and competencies that a high school diploma is intended to represent. In the United States and many other Western societies, dropping out of secondary school before completion is viewed as both a social and an educational problem.

Yet the interests of sociologists of education in the problem of school dropouts extend beyond the education and training needs of society and concerns for individual and collective well-being. Dropping out of school can be understood through the theoretical lenses that sociologists apply to social phenomena. A sociological understanding of the dropout problem may promote sensible strategies for addressing the problem. In particular, sociological approaches to the study of school dropouts emphasize the importance of the contexts in which dropping out takes place.

For example, whether dropping out is viewed as a problem depends on the local context. In developing countries, relatively few young people complete secondary schooling, and thus dropping out of high school may be both normative and typical. Most industrialized societies, however, have laws specifying the ages at which schooling is compulsory, and dropping out of school before the legally sanctioned age is typically viewed as problematic. Even within a given society there may be differences in local norms regarding dropping out that are associated with the geographic concentration of various racial and ethnic groups.

Defining Dropping Out

There is no consensus on how to define a school dropout. Although we might define a school dropout as someone who leaves school before completion, such a definition masks the complexity of the phenomenon, particularly in a highly differentiated and open schooling system, where leaving school does not preclude a return at some later date. Moreover, different administrative agencies and jurisdictions may use different definitions of who is a dropout, and these definitions may differ from those used by social scientists in large-scale social surveys and other forms of research (Morrow, 1987; Pallas, 1989). In fact, dropping out can be viewed as a socially constructed category, thereby allowing for the possibility that students and their families may have a different perception of when, or even if, a student dropped out of school than the school staff as noted in administrative records.

There is a great deal of interest in the calculation of dropout rates, which are often used as an indicator of the success of the educational system. Such rates depend on the definition of a dropout, the population thought to be at risk of dropping out, and the time frame over which the rate is to be calculated (Morrow, 1987; Pallas, 1989). There are three common types of dropout rates reported: the event dropout rate, the status dropout rate, and the cohort dropout rate (Frase, 1989).

The event rate indicates the proportion of students at risk of dropping out that leaves school before completion in a particular time period, typically a single year. Event rates are frequently used to make comparisons over time. In 1993, 4.5% of 15 to 24 year olds in grades 10 through 12 dropped out of school, a figure

315

that has declined slowly over the preceding 15 years (National Center for Education Statistics, 1994).

The status rate indicates the proportion of a population or subpopulation that has not completed high school and is not enrolled in school at a particular point in time, regardless of when they dropped out. The status rate suggests the magnitude of dropping out as a social and educational problem for a society at a particular time. The status rate usually is much higher than the event rate, as it represents the cumulative status of individuals over many years. In 1993, the status dropout rate of persons aged 16 to 24 was 11%, which also represented a moderate decline from the status dropout rates of the 1970s.

The cohort rate refers to the rate of dropping out within an age or grade cohort over a specified period of time. Cohort rates describe the experience of a particular cohort of young people over time. They are useful for studying the movement of individuals into and out of the schooling system because they characterize the longitudinal experiences of individuals. Whereas event and status dropout rates provide a snapshot of the enrollment histories of youth, cohort rates portray a moving picture of those histories. Although in many respects cohort dropout rates are the most useful of the common dropout statistics, they are also the most difficult to gather, as they demand longitudinal data on individual students.

Dropout rates and graduation rates are not complementary. This is because some graduates have dropped out during their school careers (sometimes referred to as "stopouts"), and some students who are currently enrolled in school (and therefore not counted as dropouts) will not eventually graduate. Thus, although the status dropout rate in the United States for 16 to 24 year olds was 11% in 1993, the proportion of young people completing high school by ages 21 and 22 was 86%, not the 89% that might have been expected if these calculations truly were complementary.

Social Background and Dropping Out

High school dropouts have different social background characteristics than youth who complete high school. They are disproportionately from racial and ethnic minorities, are less likely to be proficient in English, and are more likely to have grown up in poverty or a household with low socioeconomic status (Smith et al., 1994; Steinberg et al., 1984). Youth growing up in urban areas are more likely to drop out than those in suburban or rural areas, and there are regional differences in dropping out as well, with higher rates in the South and West than in the Northeast and Midwest regions of the United States (Smith et al., 1994). Children growing up in single-parent families or stepfamilies are more likely to drop out of school than children residing in families with both parents present, but there are different explanations for the effects of these two family configurations. Single-parent families have lower incomes than two-parent families, and there is frequently less parental supervision and support (Astone and McLanahan, 1994). In contrast, stepfamilies have high rates of residential mobility, which may weaken children's bonds with the school and contribute to disengagement and dropping out (Astone and McLanahan, 1994).

Poverty may well be at the root of many of these correlations between social background and dropping out. Racial and ethnic minority children and children from non-English language backgrounds are considerably more likely to live in poverty than majority English-speaking children. Moreover, children in single-parent families or stepfamilies are at much greater risk of growing up in poverty than children in intact two-parent families. Astone and McLanahan (1994) estimate that one-half of the effect of living in a single-parent family on the risk of dropping out is due to poverty, and this explanation may apply to several other risk factors described above.

Students' school experiences are a powerful determinant of who drops out of school and who persists to graduation. Dropouts have lower grades and test scores than graduates, and are more likely to have patterns of absenteeism and misbehavior in school that foreshadow dropping out (Rumberger, 1995). Dropouts also are more likely to have been retained in grade than graduates (Grissom and Shepard, 1988; Roderick, 1995; Rumberger, 1995), although there is some evidence that retention in later grades is more consequential than retention in earlier grades (Roderick, 1995; Rumberger, 1995). In spite of these associations between academic performance and dropping out, it is striking that many dropouts appear to be sufficiently capable academically of completing high school. Only a small proportion, for example, have a "D" grade average or below.

The Consequences of Dropping Out

There is an abundance of evidence that dropouts encounter various cognitive, social, and economic disadvantages that their peers who graduate from high school do not. It is difficult, however, to determine whether dropping out is properly viewed as a cause of these disadvantages or merely a correlate. In many instances, the cognitive, social, and economic problems that dropouts experience are presaged by the characteristics and experiences of these youth prior to the actual date of dropping out. In such cases, dropping out may be a symptom of other underlying problems, rather than a problem in its own right (Bachman et al., 1971). Nevertheless, recent research attempting to take account of the characteristics and experiences of dropouts before they leave school suggests that dropping out frequently does have an independent impact on subsequent life chances.

For example, dropouts are more likely to be unemployed, and on average earn less money than high school graduates (Smith, 1986; Catterall, 1988). But a substantial part of the association between dropping out and subsequent economic success is due to the fact that dropouts are more likely to be from disadvantaged social origins and to have poor records of academic performance, two factors that lower the likelihood of economic success regardless of whether an individual has dropped out of school (McDill et al., 1986).

High school dropouts also do less well on cognitive tests than graduates, even when the fact that dropouts have less successful earlier school careers than graduates is taken into account (Alexander et al., 1985). Thus, dropping out of school slightly widens the achievement gap between youth who are doing well in school and those who are not. Dropping out of school has other measurable consequences. Dropouts are more likely to be involved in delinquent behavior than graduates, even when their prior histories of delinquent activity are taken into account (Jarjoura, 1993). High school dropouts also are more likely to become parents out of wedlock than comparable graduates (Yamaguchi and Kandel, 1987).

Overall, the social and economic costs to society of the dropout problem are substantial. Levin (1972) and Catterall (1988) have estimated these costs, noting that the lessened economic and life chances of individuals translate into less aggregate economic productivity for American society, fewer tax revenues, and greater needs for costly public services such as welfare, publicly subsidized health care, and an expanded criminal justice system. McDill et al. (1986) and others have argued that the economic costs of the dropout problem greatly exceed the estimated cost of dropout prevention efforts, and that investing further in the education of prospective dropouts may be cost effective in the long run.

Competing/Alternative Explanations of the Dropout Phenomenon

There are a number of explanations of the dropout phenomenon that have been developed over the past few decades. Two of the most important perspectives have differed substantially in where they have focused attention. One perspective has viewed dropping out primarily as an individual attainment process, placing the individual in the foreground, and the social and institutional context in the background. Another perspective has viewed dropping out as a social and institutional process, placing the social and institutional context in the foreground, and the individual in the background. An emerging perspective tries to bring these two perspectives together, viewing dropping out from a life-course perspective that attends both to the individual and to the social and institutional context.

Dropping Out as an Individual Attainment Process

Historically, dropping out has been characterized as a manifestation of an individual's personal characteristics. Some of the earliest writings on dropping out viewed dropouts as unmotivated, lazy, and low achieving youths who possessed various personality disorders and bad habits (see, e.g., Wehlage et al., 1909; Lichter et al., 1962). Since the problem was defined in terms of the youth's personal characteristics, the solution was largely seen as transforming those characteristics, perhaps through psychological counseling or other socialization processes.

The image of dropping out as an individual attainment process is consistent with the influential status attainment literature in sociology. The formulations of Otis Dudley Duncan (Blau and Duncan, 1967; Duncan et al., 1972) and of the "Wisconsin Model" developed by William Sewell and his colleagues at the University of Wisconsin (Sewell et al., 1969, 1970; Sewell and Hauser, 1975) viewed educational attainment as the key mediating variable in the process of transforming social origins into adult attainments, and the individual's aspirations and expectations, formed through social interaction with parents, teachers, and peers, were central determinants of educational attainment. This perspective viewed how far a youth went through school as a matter of achievement socialization, and paid little attention to opportunity structures in schools that might facilitate or constrain attainments (Kerckhoff, 1976).

Another manifestation of this view of dropping out was the popular image of the dropout as a social misfit, alienated from self and society. School dropouts are more likely than their peers to use drugs (Kaplan and Liu, 1994; Mensch and Kandel, 1988; Newcomb and Bentler, 1986), to become adolescent parents (Forste and Tienda, 1992), to engage in delinquent and criminal activity (Jarjoura, 1993), and to pursue other high-risk behaviors, although it is often difficult to discern the causal ordering of these events.

The view of dropping out as an individual attainment process also has been reflected in attempts to identify at an early age those children and youth who are at risk of dropping out of school. Because school performance and personality traits have been viewed as relatively fixed attributes of individuals, some researchers have attempted to predict the risk of dropping out of school on the basis of school records and/or teacher ratings in the elementary years (e.g., Stroup and Robins, 1972; Ensminger and Slusarcick, 1992; Lloyd, 1978; Barrington and Hendricks, 1989). For some youth, early problems with academic performance or behavior do presage subsequent dropping out. But for many others, the process of disengagement from school begins in the middle grades and gradually intensifies over time (Roderick, 1993). Thus, a program of early intervention that showers students identified as being at risk of dropping out with resources may be successful with those students, but have little effect on the larger number of students who are difficult to identify early on as potential dropouts.

Dropping Out as a Social and Institutional Process

More recently, dropping out has increasingly been viewed as a social and institutional process, where the root causes of the problem are located in society at large and in the ways schools are organized. As Wehlage et al. (1989) point out, this perspective is faintly apparent in early writings on the topic such as Ayers (1909), but it has become much more salient in the past two decades, concurrent with the proliferation of research on school organization and school effectiveness.

Recent writings have emphasized the structural features of schools and the ways in which those features facilitate engagement and achievement or present barriers to school success. For example, Bryk and Thum (1989) documented that school organizational factors such as school size and the presence of curricular tracking are associated with the risk of dropping out, even when students' background characteristics are taken into account. Similarly, Bryk et al. (1993) showed that dropout rates are lower in Catholic high schools than in public high schools, at least in part due to the strong social communities that Catholic high schools form and the common expectations and standards held for all students who attend them. Whereas Bryk and his colleagues have emphasized the structural features of schools that can contribute to student engagement and persistence, Fine's (1991) case study of a New York City high school drew attention to the ways in which comprehensive high schools serving poor and/or minority students can silence and exclude such youth through their curricula, attitudes, and expectations.

Dropping out has also been viewed as an institutional process, a perspective that acknowledges that the status of dropout is a socially constructed category. For example, Riehl (1993) found that there are school-to-school differences in the likelihood of a student being discharged as a dropout, and that these differences among schools are associated with school-level environmental characteristics. Riehl (1993) and Fine (1991) also describe the discharge process in urban high schools serving poor and minority youth, documenting the discretion that school administrators have in classifying students who do not attend school on a regular basis. These studies document that schools can discharge students as dropouts as readily as students can choose to leave school of their own volition, and also that the production of school dropouts is a social process that can be manipulated for particular policy ends.

A Developmental, Life-Course Perspective on Dropping Out

The current generation of research on school dropouts, and on student engagement more generally, is attempting to join the view of dropping out as an individual process with the view of dropping out as a social and institutional process. This perspective emphasizes how psychosocial development is influenced by school, neighborhood, family, and societal contexts, and views engagement and achievement as the result of the interaction of individual student characteristics with contexts. This orientation to dropouts pays particular attention to the connections among the social institutions of schooling, family, community, and economy, and how institutional arrangements create pathways through the lifecourse that illuminate the antecedents and consequences of dropping out. Longitudinal studies that trace the movement of individuals into and out of the social roles and positions associated with these institutions are a powerful methodological tool for a distinctly sociological perspective on school dropouts.

Ongoing Research Questions

Sociologists are continuing to study the problem of high school dropout, as there are several important unresolved questions about school dropouts that have import for the sociology of education and for educational policy.

Describing and Analyzing the Process of Dropping Out

Although researchers can now describe the characteristics of dropouts and potential dropouts with some precision, the field lacks powerful theories of the process of dropping out. In part, this is because dropping out is often intertwined with other life events, and also because the process of dropping out is often a gradual, invisible process of disengagement that is not captured in the large-scale national panel studies that are the dominant source of information about school dropouts. Future research may need to study potential dropouts over a longer period of time and with much more frequent data collection than the annual or biennial waves

of most large-scale surveys. However, better theories are at least as important as better data in enhancing our understanding of the dropout process.

Understanding the Consequences of Dropping Out

Sociologists are continuing to learn about why dropping out is associated with lowered socioeconomic adult success. There are competing explanations for this association, some of which emphasize the mismatch between individuals and the opportunity structure that is created by dropping out, and others which draw attention to social norms about school enrollment. Studies of the consequences of dropping out may deepen sociologists' understanding of continuities and discontinuities in the life course of individuals.

There also is a need for greater attention to the diverse pathways through high school, and the possibility that different pathways have differing socioeconomic consequences. Of particular interest are what happens when a student "stops out" and later returns to school, and whether the alternative high school credentials that some youth obtain (e.g., the General Educational Development certificate) are commensurate with a traditional high school diploma.

Promoting Effective Dropout Prevention Programs

Finally, there is much to be learned about how to design, implement, and evaluate dropout prevention programs that are successful in keeping young people at risk of school failure in school. Few dropout prevention programs are developed in light of sound theories about the reasons youth drop out of school and about the types of interventions that are likely to be successful in promoting success in school. There are many opportunities for sociologists to contribute to the development of effective programs by incorporating what is already known about the dropout problem into the design and evaluation of programs. Such evaluations can in turn extend our understanding of the dropout process.

REFERENCES

Alexander, Karl L., Gary Natriello, and Aaron M. Pallas. 1985. "For Whom the School Bell Tolls: The Impact of Dropping Out on Cognitive Performance." *American Sociological Review* 50:409–420.

Ayers, Leonard. 1909. *Laggards in our Schools.* New York: Russell Sage Foundation.

Bachman, Jerald G., Green, Swayzer, and Ilona D. Wirtonen. 1971. *Youth in Transition: Vol. 3, Dropping Out: Problem or Symptom?* Ann Arbor, MI: Institute for Social Research.

Barrington, Byron L., and Bryan Hendricks. 1989. "Differentiating Characteristics of High School Graduates, Dropouts, and Nongraduates." *Journal of Educational Research* 82:309–319.

Bryk, Anthony S., and Yeow M. Thum. 1989. "The Effects of High School Organization on Dropping Out: An Exploratory Investigation." *American Educational Research Journal* 26:353–383.

Bryk, Anthony S., Valerie E. Lee, and Peter B. Holland. 1993. *Catholic Schools and the Common Good.* Cambridge, MA: Harvard University Press.

Catterall, James S. 1988. *Dropping Out of School in the North Central Region of the United States: Costs and Consequences.* Elmhurst, IL: North Central Regional Educational Laboratory.

Ensminger, Margaret E., and Anita L. Slusarcick. 1992. "Paths to High School Graduation or Dropout: A Longitudinal Study of a First-Grade Cohort." *Sociology of Education* 65:95–113.

Fine, Michelle. 1991. *Framing Dropouts: Notes on the Politics of an Urban Public High School.* Albany: State University of New York Press.

Frase, Mary. 1989. *Dropout Rates in the United States: 1988.* Washington, DC: U.S. Department of Education, National Center for Education Statistics.

Jarjoura, G. Roger. 1993. "Does Dropping out of School Enhance Delinquent Involvement? Results from a Large-Scale National Probability Sample." *Criminology* 31:149–171.

Lee, Valerie E., Anthony S. Bryk, and Julia B. Smith. 1993. "The Organization of Effective Secondary Schools." In Linda Darling-Hammond (ed.), *Review of Research in Education*, Vol. 19, pp. 171–267. Washington, DC: American Educational Research Association.

Levin, Henry. 1972. *The Costs to the Nation of Inadequate Education.* Report to the Select Committee on Equal Educational Opportunity, U.S. Senate. Washington, DC: U.S. Government Printing Office.

Lichter, Solomon O., Elsie B. Rapien, Frances M. Seibert, and Morris A. Sklansky. 1962. *The Dropouts: A Treatment Study of Intellectually Capable Students who Drop Out of High School.* New York: Free Press.

Lloyd, Dee N. 1978. "Prediction of School Failure from Third Grade Data." *Educational and Psychological Measurement* 38:1193–1200.

McDill, Edward L., Gary Natriello, and Aaron M. Pallas. 1986. "A Population at Risk: The Impact of Raising Standards on Potential Dropouts." *American Journal of Education* 94:135–181.

Morrow, George. 1987. "Standardizing Practice in the Analysis of School Dropouts." In Gary Natriello (ed.), *School Dropouts: Patterns and Policies,* pp. 38–52. New York: Teachers College Press.

National Center for Education Statistics. 1994. *Dropout Rates in the United States: 1993.* Washington, DC: U.S. Government Printing Office.

Pallas, Aaron M. 1986. *The Determinants of High School Dropout.* Report No. 364. Baltimore, MD: Center for the Social Organization of Schools.

———. 1989. "Conceptual and Measurement Issues in the Study of School Dropouts." In Krishnan Namboodiri and Ronald G. Corwin (eds.), *Research in Sociology of Education and Socialization: Selected Methodological Issues,* Vol. 8, pp. 87–116. Greenwich, CT: JAI Press.

Riehl, Carolyn J. 1993. "Determinants of Student Discharge from High School: The Effects of Organizational Environment and Student Performance." Unpublished Ph.D. dissertation, Teachers College, Columbia University.

Roderick, Melissa. 1993. *The Path to Dropping Out: Evidence for Intervention.* Westport, CT: Greenwood.

Rumberger, Russell W. 1995. "Dropping out of Middle School: A Multilevel Analysis of Students and Schools." *American Educational Research Journal* 32:583–625.

Smith, Herbert L. 1986. "Overeducation and Underemployment: An Agnostic Review." *Sociology of Education* 59:85–99.

Stroup, Atlee L., and Lee N. Robins. 1972. "Elementary School Predictors of High School Dropout among Black Males." *Sociology of Education* 45:212–222.

Wehlage, Gary G., Robert A. Rutter, Gregory A. Smith, Nancy Lesko, and Ricardo R. Fernandez. 1989. *Reducing the Risk: Schools as Communities of Support.* London: Falmer.

Yamaguchi, Kazuo, and Denise Kandel. 1987. "Drug Use and Other Determinants of Premarital Pregnancy and Its Outcome: A Dynamic Analysis of Competing Life Events." *Journal of Marriage and the Family* 49:257–270.

HIGHER EDUCATION

Floyd M. Hammack
New York University

The sociological study of higher education is a twentieth-century phenomenon and can be said to have begun with *Higher Learning in America*, by Thorsten Veblen (1918). A vehement attack on the increasing influence of business interests on decision making at U.S. colleges and universities, this book clearly saw the links between educational organizations and other parts of the social order. In criticizing the consequences of the power of business over higher education, and asserting a loss of autonomy experienced by the academy, Veblen began a long debate about whose interests higher education should serve. That debate, of course, continues today. It is in his linking sectors of the society together that makes his analysis, whatever one thinks of its values, sociological. The major growth in interest in higher education comes, however, after World War II, when expansion of enrollments in the United States dramatically increased (Clark, 1973; Kerr, 1991; Baker and Smith, 1997; Rubinson and Hurst, 1997; Dougherty, 1997). Planning for that growth, documenting it, and understanding its consequences have been important sets of tasks. To what degree has this expansion brought this society closer to the goal of equality of educational opportunity?

Although college enrollments grew during the first half of the century, this growth was slow, episodic, and limited by both the number of high school graduates and, in the 1930s and 1940s, by the Depression and World War II. During the first four decades of the century, high school enrollments and graduation rates doubled every 10 years, and the lack of prepared candidates for admission soon ceased to be a barrier to growth in collegiate enrollments. Nevertheless, the poor economy and war combined to keep many high school age students from planning for college and kept many graduates, especially males, from entering college during the 1930s and the first half of the 1940s. After the War, the pressure of those who had been prevented from enrolling in earlier periods became irresistible, and state-supported educational opportunities grew as new colleges were established, community colleges were founded, and enrollments in other colleges and universities increased. Veterans swelled enrollments as they used the support of the federal GI Bill to support their education costs. The growth in enrollments between 1929 and 1939 was 35% (from 1,100,737 to 1,494,203). The next 10 years saw a 78% gain (to 2,659,021). Between 1949 and 1959, the growth slowed, but boomed in periods following, from 3,215,544 in 1959 to 7,136,075 in 1969 (a 122% gain) and 11,569,899 by 1979 (a 62% gain). Among private colleges and universities, enrollments were also expanding and, while their proportion of total enrollments in higher education in relation to public institutions began a steep and enduring decline, their actual enrollments grew as well—today, less than 20% of all college students are enrolled in the private sector compared to 50.7% in 1946. All across the United States, enrollments increased, and state authorities struggled to develop the capacity to provide classrooms and libraries. In many states, that struggle included debates about how the expansion should proceed. Often, as we shall see, an effort was made to limit the expansion at the existing elite university sector, while rapidly expanding former teachers colleges into comprehensive colleges and universities, and establishing community colleges.

The types and number of colleges have increased, the size and diversity of enrollments have dramatically expanded, the content of the curriculum has expanded, and the links between higher education and the country's systems of stratification and its economy have become much stronger. All of these changes have created an educational establishment without precedent and of very recent vintage.

With more and more students attending colleges, the number of ways college degrees were used by graduates and employers also grew. Although a college degree was rare in the nineteenth and early twentieth centuries, and not a necessity for any occupation, the rise in the number of people with college degrees encouraged the creative use of the degree in the labor market. As a result, the educational credentials for many occupations began to rise. This educational upgrading of occupations has created a situation in which a postsecondary degree has become almost a requirement for entering a middle-class occupation. According to recent estimates, between 25 and 30% of the labor force in advanced industrial societies are in the categories of professional, technical, and administrative personnel for whom postsecondary training is appropriate. That 30% level is already exceeded in Japan, the United States, Canada, and Sweden (Kerr, 1987). The variety of occupations for which college degrees are now available is very large, and with so many of the newly entering members of the labor force beginning their careers with college degrees, the educational pressure on older workers has been growing. In fact, the average age of college students has been increasing—at many colleges today it is above 25 years old—as women returning to the labor force after raising children and older workers seeking new educational credentials for greater labor market opportunity begin or return to college.

Sociologists, historians, and others have struggled to keep up with these developments and to chart their consequences (see, for an early example, Jencks and Riesman, 1968). This chapter will review the product of these efforts to date and look briefly into the future to assess whether the trends of the last half of the twentieth century are likely to continue into the twenty-first century. First, we explore the diversity of higher education organizations and their relationship to the system of social stratification in this country. Along the way we review briefly the way enrollments are distributed among the kinds of higher education institutions and among majors. Describing these patterns leads to

a consideration of the research on their consequences for the economic payoff of degrees, for the collegiate curriculum, and for faculty.

Organizational Diversity in Higher Education

With greater demand for higher education, increased opportunities for enrollment—especially in public colleges and universities—have been created. This expansion, however, has been accompanied by greater diversity of higher education settings. Although examples of nineteenth-century-like private, rural, residential liberal arts colleges still exist, schools of this type now enroll only a small proportion of college students (Gilbert, 1995). These early colleges were far from homogeneous, however, as they were founded primarily by religious groups seeking to ensure leadership for their faith's future. Thus although their purposes were similar, their curriculum, students, and sponsors were different. Today, not only are public, large, urban or suburban, commuter, comprehensive colleges and universities far more common, about one-half of all college freshmen are enrolled in 2-year colleges, and explicitly technical and vocational majors dominate undergraduate degree enrollments. The role of these colleges and universities in socialization is now combined with research and service functions that are often supported by state governments as mechanisms of economic growth and development.

A good illustration of this diversification is that created by the "Master Plan" in California, which, in 1960, established a plan for the development of a "system" of higher education, where largely unrelated parts had previously existed (Smelser and Almond, 1974). That plan envisioned a three-tiered system, with the prestigious University of California campuses (Berkeley, Los Angeles, etc.) on the top, offering undergraduate, graduate, and professional degrees to the 12.5% highest achieving high school graduates. The State College and University sector, selecting from the top one-third achieving group of high school graduates and offering undergraduate and Master's degrees, was developed out of the existing teacher's colleges and now includes many new campuses. Finally, for all other high school graduates, admission to a 2-year community college was offered. The curricula in the 2-year sector allowed for transfer to other sectors, as well as free-standing degrees, largely emphasizing career preparation. Thus, the public system in California became highly stratified, according to the student's prior academic achievement. The private sector was not included in the Master Plan, and offers alternatives equal to the most selective parts of the public system (Stanford, Pomona College, etc.) as well as to the less selective parts.

In the Eastern part of the United States, where private colleges and universities had long-established dominance, public higher education developed more slowly, in some states created for the first time during the period following World War II (such as most of the campuses of the State University of New York). In virtually all states, public higher education has been differentiated into sectors based on the mission of the institution, with graduate education and research-oriented universities at the top of the prestige status ladder and having the highest academic criteria for admission. Four-year comprehensive colleges and universities, combining liberal arts with vocationally oriented courses of study, and often offering graduate programs at the Master's degree level, are usually more accessible than the doctoral degree granting university. Two-year community colleges or branch campuses of the large state university available to most with a high school credential fill out the public options. Private alternatives to each of these levels exist as well.

Community colleges, the most recently developed organization form, have expanded dramatically in the past 30 years. Offering the least expensive form of higher education, and frequently with open admissions, their curriculum emphasizes vocational preparation, but affords transfer to 4-year institutions as well. The number of these schools increased from 256 in 1950, enrolling 296,816 students, to 354 schools in 1960, enrolling 712,224 students; in 1970, there were 654 schools, enrolling 2,101,972 students. Today, there are almost 1,000 public 2-year colleges, enrolling over 5,400,000 (Dougherty, 1994:116–117).

Higher Education and Social Stratification

For sociology, the nature of the distribution of scarce and valuable resources (both material, like owning a factory, and symbolic, like esteem) among members of a society is a core question. Whether that distribution is recreated as parents pass on their advantages or disadvantages to their children is central to the description of the nature of social inequalities and their maintenance across generations. The organization of inequalities into vertical layers is called social stratification. It is social because the collective activities and values of a society create and change the amount and kind of inequalities and their distribution present in a society. We do not presume that there is anything "natural" about social inequalities. Their existence is virtually universal, but the variety in the amount and kind of things that are unequally distributed is vast and thus the result of deliberate human action. Just as alternate layers of sediment have produced strata in rock exposed by highway cuts, the layering of social and educational advantage over disadvantage produces social strata. Educational attainment beyond high school, long a valued resource, has until recently been a scarce resource. Its value in the labor market was limited; most occupations, including the professions of law and medicine, did not require degrees. Eligibility and competence were established in other ways, such as "reading for the law" while clerking for a lawyer. Increasingly, however, the formal educational credentials needed to enter occupations have increased as schools and colleges have become the personnel agencies for our society. A college diploma is needed today to enter most law schools, and other professions have moved to graduate level work as a requirement for entry or for continuing employment. A considerable amount of sociological research has centered on the processes associated with the attainment of educational credentials, and how their use by employers and occupational and professional groups has grown (e.g., Collins, 1979; Hammack, 1990).

Yet, it would be incorrect to assert that even in earlier periods, education was not important for the creation and maintenance of social stratification. The adage "knowledge is power" illuminates a critical reality not usually symbolized by the possession of a college degree, which is more often thought of as a link to employment. The control of the means by which what is worth knowing gets defined carries with it considerable power, as does possessing the knowledge itself, symbolized by the degree. In the history of higher education in the United States, this power is clearly seen as group after group has sought to legitimate and secure its attainments by founding colleges for their offspring, and others have sought to have preparation for their occupation take place within the academy. Most of private higher education originated in the impulse of religious groups to arm their sons (and occasionally their daughters) to maintain the faith and to protect their interests in the broader society. Existing colleges, serving other groups interests, could not do the job, and often did not want to do it. Moreover, much of the innovation and change that has taken place in higher education has resulted from the curricular consequences of new groups studying in college (Trow, 1974).

Thus, the higher education system in the United States has become highly stratified, and is stratified in ways that parallel the stratification of the population at large. Although far from perfectly related, student achievement and educational attainment are both strongly correlated with parental position in the social strata (Hurn, 1993). Students from more affluent backgrounds have a higher probability of enrolling in elite public and private 4-year colleges and universities, as full-time, residential students than students from poor families (Karen, 1990; Kingston and Lewis, 1990a; Baker and Velez, 1996; McDonough, 1997). For example, Kingston and Lewis report that the proportion of entering freshmen at highly selective colleges and universities whose parents reported incomes over $100,000 in 1986 was just under 25%, while the figure for all freshmen was 7% (Kingston and Lewis, 1990b:110–111; also see Dougherty, 1994).

Social origins, however, are not the sole predictor of academic achievement and attainment; achievement is itself very strongly related to attainment. Although social origins influence academic achievement, certainly not all privileged students do very well in school and attend elite colleges. Those who do not achieve well are unlikely to have the occupational and income opportunities of less affluent students who do well in school. Nevertheless, the system of higher education is a highly differentiated one that can be seen as paralleling the societal system of social stratification. This parallelism has generated one of the great debates about the function of education in our society.

Some observers, seeing the "correspondence" between social and educational stratification, have asserted that education must be seen as an instrument for the unequal reproduction of social strata in the society (Bowles and Gintis, 1976; Brint and Karabel, 1989).

This view, opposite to one emphasizing the opportunity for social strata mobility offered by educational achievement and attainment, challenges the value this society seems to have placed on education as a means to prevent the development of rigidity in our social strata. Those who emphasize the opportunity afforded by the expansion of educational opportunities see differentiation as a necessary and an efficient way to provide for a variety of educational routes to adulthood and to occupations. Data can be assembled to support both positions, and the debate continues (Dougherty, 1994; Brint and Karabel, 1989; Trow, 1984; Lavin and Hyllegard, 1996). Although one can debate the consequences of a stratified educational system, that it is stratified is an acknowledged fact. Moreover, its stratification has grown as enrollments have increased, and as the links to specific occupational destinations have grown in number and in strength (Educational Testing Service, 1998).

Students and the College Curriculum

Not only are students likely to be distributed along the collegiate hierarchy according to their parental status, personal demographic characteristics are also likely to be associated with their area of studies. One of the most obvious of these differences is in the proportion of females and of Hispanic- and African-American students who major in the sciences and mathematics-based fields of study. Patterns of secondary school attainment in math and science courses show significantly lower level of achievement by these student groups, who are, as a consequence, less well prepared for the rigors of college-level math and science majors. Because many of these majors lead to high-paying occupational opportunities, the preexisting pattern of higher educational achievement and attainment by whites, males, and Asians persists, and disparities in future occupational opportunities and income are affected. The study of how students are distributed among the various sectors in higher education has benefitted from several national longitudinal studies sponsored by the National Center for Educational Statistics, a part of the Department of Education. The National Longitudinal Study (NLS), which began by gathering information from high school sophomores and seniors in 1972 and has periodically returned to the same respondents, has afforded much insight into the educational careers of that cohort of students. More recently, the Beyond High School (BHS) study, which started in 1980, and the National Educational Longitudinal study (NELS), initiated in 1988, are following the development of more recent groups of young people as they progress through the educational system.

The situation of female enrollments and patterns of college majors is particularly interesting. There has been significant change in these patterns, yet inequalities persist. Female students are now the majority of all college students, whether enrolled in 2- or 4-year degree programs. Female enrollment in nontraditional majors has grown considerably in the past decade and a half. In 1994–1995 they earned almost 48% of business administration undergraduate degrees, as compared to 34% in 1980, and 52% of biology and life sciences bachelor degrees, compared to 42% for the same period. However, the movement toward parity with male patterns of majors has essentially stalled in the past few years, and traditionally female fields are still predominantly female in enrollment (e.g., education majors went from 74% female in 1980 to 76% female in 1994–1995). What has contributed to both the growth of parity and its stagnation is a subject of considerable interest. A good example of this research is the work of Jerry Jacobs (1995).

Enrollments of Hispanic- and African-American students have grown as well, though their progress has been slower as compared with that of females. They tend to be concentrated in less selective and 2-year public colleges, even as their enrollments in the private sector have increased (Baker and Velez, 1996; Carter and Wilson, 1996). When they graduate, however, the payoff of their degrees in the labor market may have surpassed that afforded majority students (Pascarella and Terenzini, 1991:522). Nevertheless, the well-paying fields of engineering and computer science require high levels of math accomplishment, an attribute less common among these groups than among white, Asian, and middle-class high school graduates. Second year algebra, for example, was taken by 61.1% of white high school graduates in 1994, by 44% of African-American graduates, 51.1% of Hispanics, and 67% of Asian graduates. Even more striking, 7% of white graduates took a full year course in calculus, 3% of blacks, 6% of Hispanics, and 23% of Asian high school graduates (National Center for Educational Statistics,

1997). Good math preparation in high school is essential for success in college science and math courses, which in turn is essential for entry into engineering and other math- and science-based occupations. The role of higher education in improving the entry of poor and minority students into the highest paid sectors of the labor market is limited by the nature of the preparation such students have at entry. Clearly faculty and departments can do a better job ensuring access to these career opportunities for poor and minority students than they now provide, but the equalizing of this opportunity is the work of the whole educational system, not only higher education. One of the interesting consequences of increased enrollments of women students and those from minority communities is the heightened interest in the curriculum of higher education and how it reflects these racial, religious, and ethnic groups. Demands for black or African-American studies or women's studies departments are not new, of course, but they have been joined now by an increased consciousness of cultural issues in the curriculum among Asian students, gay and lesbian students, etc. Debates over the "canon" in literature or other fields also reflect the curricula ferment now characterizing higher education. To some degree, these debates would probably have occurred anyway as academic fashion evolves. Nevertheless, there can be little doubt that the changing demography of U.S. college students has stimulated the debates and controversies. These students take seriously the notion that knowledge is power, and they seek to embrace that power lent by inclusion in the curriculum in higher education to validate their neglected perspectives (Arthur and Shapiro, 1995).

A related concern of sociologists of higher education has also centered on the composition of the faculty and administrative posts. Studies of disparities among female and male faculty and about the lack of minority faculty in higher education have been frequent. These studies share common ground with other studies of gender and race in the labor market, and concern issues of recruitment, preparation, and rewards (Lomperis, 1990; Bowen and Schuster, 1986). The ability to serve nontraditional student populations is often seen as linked to the presence of faculty from those groups who can help their students achieve. The success of traditionally black colleges and universities has been in part attributed to the shared experiences of students and faculty (Allen, 1992).

Conclusions

The mission of colleges and universities and how it is determined and implemented continue to be important areas of investigation. As enrollments have increased, as the links to occupations and to corporations have become stronger, and as the diversity of enrollment increases, questions about the appropriate curriculum, about the relative balance between research and teaching and service loom large. Whose interests higher education serves, and how those interests are responded to bring us back to the analysis provided by Veblen. How higher education is linked to other aspects of the society is a continuing research question. How higher education should be linked to occupations and to other parts of the economy is an ongoing policy question whose answer depends on the values and political strength of those who ask the question. What does seem clear, however, is that enrollments are likely to continue to rise. The trend in education has been up, to more years of formal schooling for entering the labor force, not fewer. To back off this trend would be a major reversal of a long standing tendency. It may come to be that the costs, economic and social, of education will become too large for it to continue to expand, but we have not yet reached that point, and there is little reason to think that it will be reached anytime soon. There is evidence that the distribution of students among colleges has become less equal, however, as costs have escalated (Educational Testing Service, 1998). Greater opportunity for higher education has certainly been created as the number of institutions has grown and enrollments expand. These opportunities are not equally distributed, however, nor are the benefits afforded by the higher levels of educational attainment. Much remains for policy development and for research around the issues of expanding equality of higher educational opportunity. As with all levels of education, moreover, the controversies and debates over what is taught to whom will continue, providing ample room for further sociological investigation.

REFERENCES

Allen, Walter R. 1992. "The Color of Success: African American College Student Outcomes at Predominantly White and Historically Black Public Colleges and Universities." *Harvard Educational Review* 62 (Spring):26–44.

Arthur, John, and Amy Shapiro, (eds.). 1995. *Culture Wars: Multiculturalism and the Politics of Difference.* Boulder, CO: Westview Press.

Baker, David P., and Thomas Smith. 1997. "Trend 3: A College Education for All?" *Teachers College Record* 99:57–61.

Baker, Theresa, and William Velez. 1996. "Access to and Opportunity in Postsecondary Education in the United States: A Review." *Sociology of Education*, extra issue:82–101.

Bowles, Samuel, and Herbert Gintis. 1976. *Schooling in Capitalist America.* New York: Basic Books.

Carter, Deborah J., and Reginald Wilson. 1996. *Minorities in Higher Education: Fourteenth Annual Status Report.* Washington, DC: American Council on Education.

Clark, Burton R. 1973. "Development of the Sociology of Higher Education." *Sociology of Education* 46(Winter):2–14.

Collins, Randall. 1979. *The Credential Society.* New York: Academic Press.

Dougherty, Kevin J. 1994. *The Contradictory College: The Conflicting Origins, Impacts and Futures of Community Colleges.* Albany, NY: State University of New York Press.

———. 1997. "Mass Higher Education: What Is Its Impetus? What Is Its Impact?" *Teachers College Record* 99:66–72.

Educational Testing Service. 1998. *Toward Inequality: Disturbing Trends in Higher Education.* Princeton, NJ: Author.

Gilbert, Joan. 1995. "The Liberal Arts College—Is It Really an Endangered Species?" *Change* September/October: 37–43.

Hammack, Floyd M. 1990. "The Changing Relationship Between Education and Occupation: The Case of Nursing." In Kevin J. Dougherty and Floyd Hammack (eds.), *Education and Society: A Reader,* pp. 561–573. San Diego: Harcourt, Brace Jovanovich.

Hurn, Christopher J. 1993. *The Limits and Possibilities of Schooling,* 3rd ed. Boston: Allyn & Bacon.

Jacobs, Jerry. 1986. "The Sex Segregation of Fields of Study: Trends During the College Years." *The Journal of Higher Education* 57(2):134–154.

———. 1995. "Gender and Academic Specialties: Trends Among College Degree Recipients During the 1980's." *Sociology of Education* 68(2):81–98.

Jencks, Christopher S., and David Riesman. 1968. *The Academic Revolution.* New York: Doubleday.

Karen, David. 1990. "Access to Higher Education in the United States, 1900 to the Present." In Kevin J. Dougherty and Floyd M. Hammack (eds.), *Education and Society: A Reader,* pp. 264–279. San Diego: Harcourt, Brace Jovanovich.

Kerr, Clark. 1987. "A Critical Age in the University World: Accumulated Heritage Versus Modern Imperatives." *European Journal of Education* 22(2):183–193.

————. 1991. *The Great Transformation in Higher Education, 1960–1980*. Albany, NY: State University of New York Press.

Kingston, Paul William, and Lionel S. Lewis, (eds.). 1990a. *The High-Status Track: Studies of Elite Schools and Stratification*. Albany, NY: State University of New York Press.

————. 1990b. "Undergraduates at Elite Institutions: The Best, the Brightest, and the Richest." In Paul William Kingston and Lionel S. Lewis (eds.), *The High-Status Track: Studies of Elite Schools and Stratification,* pp. 105–120. Albany, NY: State University of New York Press.

Lavin, David E., and David Hyllegard. 1996. *Changing the Odds: Open Admissions and the Life Chances of the Disadvantaged*. New Haven, CT: Yale University Press.

Lomperis, Ana Maria Turner. 1990. "Are Women Changing the Nature of the Academic Profession?" *Journal of Higher Education* 61 (November/December):663–677.

McDonough, Patricia M. 1997. *Choosing Colleges: How Social Class and Schools Structure Opportunity*. Albany, NY: State University of New York Press.

National Center for Educational Statistics. 1993. *The Condition of Education, 1993*. Washington, DC: U.S. Department of Education.

————. 1997. *Digest of Educational Statistics*. Washington, DC: U.S. Department of Education.

Pascarella, Ernest T., and Patrick T. Terenzini. 1991. *How College Affects Students*. San Francisco: Jossey-Bass.

Rubinson, Richard, and David Hurst. 1997. "A College Education for Any and All." *Teachers College Record* 99:62–72.

Smelser, Neil J., and Gabriel Almond, (eds.). 1974. *Public Higher Education in California*. Berkeley: University of California Press.

Trow, Martin. 1974. "Problems in the Transition from Elite to Mass Higher Education." In *Policies for Higher Education. General Report on the Conference on Future Structures of Post-Secondary Education,* pp. 5–101. Paris: OECD.

————. 1984. "The Analysis of Status." In Burton R. Clark (ed.), *Perspectives on Higher Education.* pp. 132–164. Berkeley: University of California Press.

Veblen, Thorsten. 1918. *Higher Learning in America*. St. Louis: B.W. Huebsch.

HIGHER EDUCATION

INTERNATIONAL

James C. Hearn and Jan Sandor
University of Minnesota

In recent decades, worldwide enrollments in higher education have grown dramatically. In keeping with increasing demands for expanded educational opportunity and better educated workforces, the traditional, highly selective, elite-centered university systems of many countries have evolved into more open systems serving greater proportions of the citizenry. Widening postsecondary access has been accompanied by increasing organizational complexity in educational systems around the world, by the emergence of aggressive national policies promoting social and economic development, and by ongoing change in the academic profession. Sociological research on each of these developments will be addressed in this chapter.[1]

Origins of the Research

Several of the earliest sociologists considered higher education a topic worth serious attention. Two merit particular mention here: Émile Durkheim and Max Weber. The French sociologist Émile Durkheim (1858–1917) paid particular attention to the role of education in reflecting and perpetuating the norms and values of the larger society in which it takes place. In stressing this integrative role of education, Durkheim examined the ways educational systems dealt with the possibility of destructive conflict. He suggested that educational systems will tend to differentiate and spe-

cialize because such moves allow potential rivals to operate separately from each other. In this way, direct confrontation and conflict can be avoided and a necessary degree of harmony can be preserved. At the level of universities, Durkheim's proposition translates into significant differentiation among and within institutions, division of labor, and ongoing adaptability to changing circumstances. In a related line of analysis, Durkheim stressed the important interconnections among individualism, reason, and academic autonomy within universities, noting that universities are major beneficiaries of societal ideals of free inquiry.[2]

Like Durkheim, the German sociologist Max Weber (1864–1920) considered higher education within a broad historical and social context. Weber, however, focused more directly on power, interests, status hierarchies, and elites. Because Weber saw educational organizations as elements deeply imbedded in larger social structures and processes, and refused to treat them as relatively closed entities amenable to separable analysis, he is rarely identified as a sociologist of education. His work is nevertheless educationally important in several respects. First, Weber was among the earliest analysts to consider universities from the perspective of the struggle for power within modern societies torn by conflicting values. Whereas Durkheim focused especially on the ways educational institutions help societies avoid social conflicts and alienation, Weber focused on individuals' and groups' efforts to shape social relations and societies to their own advantage, through education as well as through a variety of other means.

---

[1] This chapter considers two types of sociological work: comparative studies of higher education systems around the world, and studies of individual higher-education systems in countries other than the United States and Canada. Because there are separate entries in this volume on several countries outside North America, the second genre is covered more selectively.

[2] For more on the many contributions of Durkheim to the sociological study of higher education, see Clark (1983).

As a consequence, conflict and competition are more frequent themes in Weber's than in Durkheim's work. He, and those who followed in his intellectual tradition, stressed that universities have been important organizational elements in the ongoing struggles of nations to define themselves and establish patterns of legitimated social control. In this work, Weber attended especially to the ways higher education aids in the development of professions and the preservation of their power and status. Second, Weber's thinking on the emergence of the modern bureaucracy, with its focus on expertise, specialization, and careers, has greatly influenced modern theorizing about university organization. Weber's attention to the increasing specialization, departmentalization, and vocationalism of the curriculum is of particular interest in this area. Third, Weber wrote persuasively, in several frequently cited works, on the distinctive place of the social sciences within the older traditions of the natural sciences and the humanities in universities. Finally, Weber provided the field with an enduring model of commitment to systematic comparative (cross-national) study.[3]

In the work of Durkheim and Weber, higher education was considered from the perspective of grand theory, as a central institution in modern societies. Such work was intended to be easily translatable across national boundaries. Individual nations would vary in important ways, of course, but the theories were broad enough to be adjustable to different contexts, and thus applied comparatively. The work of several prominent sociologists of the 1930s through the 1970s (notably, Talcott Parsons) continued this tradition of grand theorizing. In the years after World War II, however, the sociological study of higher education grew in other directions. The emergence of the United Nations and a variety of other international agencies brought greater attention to the challenge of applying broad sociological theories to specific educational contexts. From the 1950s to the 1980s, UNESCO, the World Bank, the Ford Foundation, and other organizations funded sociologically informed analyses of education around the world, with particular attention to the role of universities in economic development and "modernization". Although the funding of such work has slowed in more recent years, the research support was critical to the growth of the field in its time.

Central Concerns within the Sociology of International Higher Education

Contemporary sociologists examining international higher education find publication outlets in book form and in a variety of scholarly journals (notably *Comparative Education*, *Higher Education*, *Sociology of Education*, and the *American Journal of Sociology*). This work may be characterized as having four general thematic concerns: postsecondary education as an element in stratification and attainment processes, the organization of higher education institutions and systems, social policy relating to postsecondary education, and academic careers.

Postsecondary Education as an Element in Stratification and Attainment Processes

Regardless of worldwide trends toward expanded postsecondary access and regardless of the distinctive national and cultural contexts in which they operate, colleges and universities everywhere continue to have clear connections to processes of social stratification and status attainment. That is, those entering postsecondary education are undertaking an activity with profound implications for their eventual social and economic standing in society. Because sociologists have been investigating stratification and status attainment since the earliest years of the field, colleges and universities have been longstanding focuses of sociological research in North America and elsewhere. In the years since World War II, sociologists of education have increasingly addressed questions of who enters postsecondary education, who goes to different kinds of postsecondary institutions, who attains baccalaureate, graduate, and professional degrees, and how levels of educational attainment affect eventual social and economic success. Researchers have addressed these questions at two general levels: at the level of national education systems and at the level of individuals' paths to success within national systems.

At the national level, analysts have often considered the nature of educational selection, sorting, and allocation systems in various countries. Because such stud-

---

ies have focused on the generation of elites within countries, and because elites are virtually always college educated, their work is closely connected to the topic of this chapter. Perhaps the most cited conceptualization in this tradition has been that of Turner (1960), who noted that England and the United States differed in the ways their youth advanced educationally and socially. According to Turner, the United States relied more heavily on "contest" mobility (an open contest for admission into elite educational and occupational status) while the English relied more on "sponsored" mobility (a system of elite-controlled selection and induction into advantaged educational careers).

Turner's original ideas were refined by a number of theorists. Going beyond the sponsorship/contest dimension and beyond Turner's two-country comparison, Hopper (1968) produced a far more detailed typology of national educational systems. Introducing such concepts as centralization, standardization, universalism, and particularism into comparisons of educational systems, Hopper suggested that systems varied on how elite selection occurs, when that selection occurs, who is favored in selection, and why selection occurs. Along similar lines, Martin Trow (1979) delineated three distinctive forms of national postsecondary selection: "elite" systems enrolling less than 15% of the college-age population, "mass" systems enrolling 15–50%, and "universal" systems enrolling more than 50%. Trow suggested that a general international movement from elite toward mass higher education has taken place since the 1950s. These changes in participation rates are paralleled, he notes, by substantial changes in national attitudes, institutional organization and governance, and characteristics of students, faculty, the curriculum, and academic life. Trow cautioned, however, that not all nations have adopted the mass form or moved inexorably toward the universal form, despite the well-known movement of the United States in that direction.

The specific character of higher education's role in the selection of social elites has attracted attention from a number of sociological theorists. John Meyer has suggested that the selection of elites (and, thus, nonelites) is not only a matter of socialization and allocation into a status, but more broadly a process of social legitimation, in which "Education restructures whole populations, creating and expanding elites and redefining the rights and obligations of members" (Meyer, 1977:55). Concentrating on the professions, in partic-

ular, Randall Collins (1979) has argued that the nature of engineering, medical, and legal training in higher education varies substantially by country, as a result of distinctive national historical, social, and economic contexts.

At the level of individuals rather than national systems, researchers have undertaken single-nation and comparative analyses using the attainment theories and causal modeling techniques pioneered in the United States by Blau and Duncan, Sewell, Hauser, and others. For example, Kerckhoff and colleagues (e.g., see Kerckhoff and Everett, 1986) have explored differences between the processes of status attainment in the United States and Great Britain. Comparative and single-nation attainment research in nations other than the United States has tended to find national systems expanding individuals' opportunities for postsecondary education, if not always for "higher" education in the more traditional sense. In other words, although nations' selective colleges and universities have not universally become more open, vocationally oriented institutions have emerged as a popular, less selective alternative. Especially in this more general sense, other nations' patterns of educational attainment are becoming more similar to those in the United States.

The Organization of Higher Education Institutions and Systems

Much of the work in the sociology of higher education around the world has focused on the organization of the enterprise. One of the most substantial contributions along these lines is a widely cited 1962 article by Joseph Ben-David and Abraham Zloczower examining the evolution of university organization in Germany, England, the United States, France, and Russia. Both Durkheim's and Weber's early perspectives on the evolution of educational systems are reflected in this work. Ben-David and Zloczower produced a sociologically informed, theoretically sound analysis of educational reform and innovation by blending analysis of the transnational movement of ideas (like the doctoral degree and the research emphasis) with analysis of the embedding of university systems within distinctive national struggles and status arrangements.

A notable recent trend in research in the field focuses upon the aegis under which higher education is conducted. Studies in this vein have often explored the tensions between public and private interests in higher education. A citizenry's diverse interests cannot be assumed to be fully represented or supported by state or national control of institutions. Higher education systems not only help define who can be educated and thus who can most easily rise to power in societies, but also what will be studied by researchers, which constituencies will be served by institutions, and which interests will be promoted from within educational settings. The public funding of research and the state-supported definition of important knowledge, for example, might be expected to follow the needs of those in power, supporting their desire to remain in power. With this Weberian notion in mind, a number of analysts have examined the conditions leading to the development of large private higher education sectors within different nations. Levy (1986) studied the massive expansion of the private postsecondary sector in Latin America, in the context of a broader consideration of national concerns over freedom, choice, equity, and effectiveness in education. In a similar vein, Geiger (1986) takes a comparative perspective on the emergence of private higher education, with special attention to the connections between church and state that shape the emergence of private higher education around the world.

Burton Clark's 1983 book on academic organization stands out as an intriguing attempt to blend system-level sociological concerns with the unit-level concerns of traditional organization theory. Clark attempts to define the basic organizational elements of higher education systems as they exist in various nations, using evidence from the United States, Japan, Sweden, Italy, Germany, Poland, Mexico, and Thailand. He identifies three basic elements of higher education systems: the division of labor and tasks, the beliefs and values of the players, and the distribution of authority. One particular strength of Clark's analysis is its attention to the varying levels of centralization of academic authority around the world. An advocate of academic autonomy under reasonable conditions, Clark notes the advantages of the relatively weak central bureaucratic control within the U.S. system. Another strength of the analysis is its attention to the dynamics of university change. Observing that campus changes often seem to outsiders to be disjointed and contradictory, Clark notes that such changes can often be clearly understood as a product of interest-group struggle.

Social Policy Relating to Postsecondary Education

Some sociologists have examined the connections between higher education and national policy regarding equality of opportunity, national development, knowledge expansion, and social, political, economic, and cultural change. Arnove (1986), for example, considered the ways in which the Sandinista government in Nicaragua sought to integrate university admissions policies, faculty hiring, and curriculum development with emerging national economic plans, through such devices as the inclusion of a significant work component in all students' programs of study. Other prominent analysts have attended to the problems inherent in meshing societies' sometimes conflicting desires. Recent work in this tradition includes Neave and van Vught's edited volume (1994) exploring the dilemmas facing nations such as Mexico, China, Tanzania, and India as they deal with difficult pressures for efficiency, academic autonomy, organizational control, and improved educational quality.

Academic Careers

Several prominent sociologists have examined the nature of academic life in different national contexts. In 1971, A. H. Halsey and Martin Trow, on the basis of extensive interviews, presented a "sociological portrait of the academic professions" in Great Britain. Reflecting the earlier work of Turner, the authors found academics differing substantially on the question of "elitist" versus "expansionist" visions of higher education. Perhaps the two most often cited recent works in this tradition are volumes edited by Philip Altbach (1977) and Burton Clark (1987). Both works devote chapters to the differing national contexts for faculty careers and to faculty-career issues transcending national boundaries.

Continuing Controversies within the Field

Although one might identify any number of controversies within this active field of inquiry, two seem to merit special attention. The first involves the extent to which analysts see national higher education systems as active agents in reproducing existing elites and suppressing status mobility. Although no one can deny the substantial role of colleges and universities in patterns of stratification and attainment in all countries, some observers see higher education as more directly under the control of privileged groups, and as more clearly serving elite interests. For example, French sociologist Pierre Bourdieu and colleagues (see Bourdieu and Passeron, 1977) have suggested that higher education systems operate under legitimated meritocratic cover (attending to school performance and test scores in admissions standards, for example), but actually select and reward students on the basis of social and cultural characteristics available mainly to those from advantaged backgrounds. That is, personal factors other than subject-area knowledge are critical to advancement within higher education. These social and cultural distinctions affect admission to top universities and, within institutions, affect chances of acceptance into professional fields such as the law and medicine. In this way, higher education systems, although appearing accessible on the surface, actually work to perpetuate existing status orders within societies. Around the world, the "reproduction" reasoning of Bourdieu and others pursuing similar theoretical models has been used in efforts to explain the continuing lag in postsecondary attainment among those from lower socioeconomic and minority backgrounds (this lag has persisted despite increases in student financial aid and despite initiation of many special programs to encourage minorities' attendance). Some analysts have seriously questioned, however, the power of Bourdieu's ideas to explain connections between widened educational access and status attainment among the disadvantaged.[4]

A second area of controversy within the field involves the nature and causes of educational expansion around the world. British sociologist Margaret Archer has produced a series of provocative case analyses of the historical expansion and differentiation of national educational systems, paying particular attention to Britain, France, Russia, and Denmark (Archer, 1984). Largely qualitative essays in this tradition may be contrasted with the sophisticated quantitative work emerging since the 1970s. In complex longitudinal analyses, Meyer et al. (1977) investigated the rapid expansion of primary, secondary, and postsecondary educational enrollments around the world. They concluded that aspects of the larger world system, in concert with local educational conditions—not different nations' levels of economic, political, and social development—have been the primary factors in educational expansion. Often, quantitative work of this kind is done from a perspective that case studies of educational expansion often focus too strongly on limited numbers of settings, usually Western, and attend too little to education as a global cultural phenomenon.

Beyond debating the appropriate scope and methodologies for cross-national analyses, sociologists have also disagreed over whether the expansionist trends in education around the world constitute "convergence" toward a common model of education and over the extent to which these trends represent "progress." For example, Inkeles and Sirowy (1983) see strong evidence for convergence and argue that it portends improving conditions for youth, the poor, minorities, and women around the world, while Archer pointedly argues (1984:209) that recent trends do not necessarily mean that educational systems are becoming "more adaptive, efficient, or legitimate than their antecedents."

Areas for Further Conceptualization and Research

Sociological perspectives can contribute to the understanding of changes in international scholarly communication. The opening of formerly closed national borders, the expansion of the Internet, the improvement of local phone lines for modem and facsimile telecommunications, and the increasing incorporation of telephony, computing, and television have each made scholarly communication across physical boundaries more intensive and extensive. Sociologists have long investigated such topics as academics' divided loyalties to their disciplinary communities and institutional homes, the nature of knowledge growth in the sciences, and the "invisible colleges" built by scholars in academic specialties.[5] Recent political and technological changes demand that these earlier research traditions in sociology develop a more vigorously international perspective.

The remarkable geopolitical developments of the

---

[4] See Morrow and Torres (1995) for a thorough review.

[5] For example, because the community of physicists studying a certain class of subatomic particles may be scattered across several institutions, they may communicate frequently among themselves by mail, phone, and other means.

past decade also raise important issues for sociologists of higher education. In Eastern Europe and Russia, in particular, the fall of the Soviet Union has prompted serious reconsideration of longstanding educational traditions. Those countries seem to be confronting something rare: the opportunity to create substantively different postsecondary systems. The policy and restructuring directions undertaken there will have enduring importance. Organizational, political, social, and cultural analysis of these changes poses a daunting but inviting challenge for the field.

Finally, this field of study unquestionably needs more and better comparative studies of postsecondary education issues. Numerous scholars have made this point before, with only limited results, but the argument still carries convincing weight. Research on a single educational system cannot possibly produce comprehensive understanding of the dominant features of its development, structure, and functioning. With only one national "case" to study, one cannot discern which factor, from a set of factors potentially affecting a process, is most influential. Comparative analysis also brings to the field an awareness of what is distinctive and what is typical in one's own national setting. Much of what appears in U.S. education journals tends to suggest unreflectively that higher education in the United States is normative, in either the ideal or typical sense of that word. That tendency can be countered only through intelligent investigation of social and educational arrangements elsewhere.

REFERENCES

Altbach, Philip G., ed. 1977. *Comparative Perspectives on the Academic Profession.* New York: Praeger.

Archer, Margaret S. 1984. *The Social Origins of Educational Systems.* London: Sage.

Arnove, R. F. 1986. *Education and Revolution in Nicaragua.* New York: Praeger.

Ben-David, Joseph, and Abraham Zloczower. 1962. "Universities and Academic Systems in Modern Societies." *European Journal of Sociology* 3:45–84.

Bourdieu, Pierre, and Jean-Claude Passeron. 1977. *Reproduction in Education, Society, and Culture.* London: Sage.

Clark, Burton R. 1983. *The Higher Education System: Academic Organization in Cross-National Perspective.* Berkeley: University of California Press.

———, ed. 1987. *The Academic Profession: National, Disciplinary, and Institutional Settings.* Berkeley: University of California Press.

Collins, Randall. 1979. *The Credential Society.* New York: Academic Press.

Coser, Lewis A. 1971. *Masters of Sociological Thought.* New York: Harcourt, Brace Jovanovich.

Geiger, Roger L. 1986. *Private Sectors in Higher Education: Structure, Function and Change in Eight Countries.* Ann Arbor: University of Michigan Press.

Halsey, A. H, and Martin Trow. 1971. *The British Academics.* Cambridge, MA: Harvard University Press.

Hopper, Earl I. 1968. "A Typology for the Classification of Educational Systems." *Sociology* 2:29–46.

Inkeles, Alex, and Larry Sirowy. 1983. "Convergent and Divergent Trends in National Educational Systems." *Social Forces* 62:303–333.

Kerckhoff, A. C., and D. D. Everett. 1986. "Sponsored and Contest Education Pathways in Great Britain and the United States." In A. C. Kerckhoff (ed.), *Research in Sociology of Education and Socialization*, Vol. 6, pp. 133–163. Greenwich, CT: JAI Press.

Levy, Daniel C. 1986. *Higher Education and the State in Latin America: Private-Public Patterns.* Chicago: University of Chicago Press.

Meyer, John W. 1977. "The Effects of Education as an Institution." *American Journal of Sociology* 83:55–77.

Meyer, John W., Francisco Ramirez, Richard Rubinson, and John Boli-Bennett. 1977. "The World Educational Revolution, 1950–1970." *Sociology of Education* 50:242–258.

Morrow, R. A., and C. A. Torres. 1995. *Social Theory and Education: A Critique of Theories of Social and Cultural Reproduction.* Albany, NY: State University of New York Press.

Neave, G., and F. van Vught. 1994. *Government and Higher Education Relationships Across Three Continents: The Winds of Change.* New York: Pergamon.

Trow, Martin. 1979. "Elite and Mass Higher Education: American Models and European Realities." In National Bureau of Universities and Colleges [NBUC] (ed.), *Research into Higher Education: Processes and Structures*, pp. 183–219. Stockholm: NBUC.

Turner, Ralph H. 1960. "Sponsored and Contest Mobility and the School System." *American Sociological Review* 25: 855–867.

HIGHER EDUCATION AND SOCIAL EQUALITY

Sophia Catsambis
Queens College, CUNY

Theoretical Interpretations: Two Opposing Traditions

The role of higher education in the stratification of modern society has been an issue of theoretical and empirical investigation since the nineteenth century. It is approached from two main theoretical traditions: structural functionalism and conflict theories.

Structural functionalists, following the work of Talcott Parsons and Emile Durkheim, claim that industrial society, which emerged in the nineteenth and early twentieth century, paves the way for a more democratic and egalitarian social system. This industrialism promotes a new system of equal opportunity where effort and ability determine a person's social status. Therefore, modern society becomes based on "contest mobility"; individuals from all social backgrounds compete for the most desirable social positions (Turner, 1960). Furthermore, due to this contest mobility, educational credentials become the major means by which individuals are allocated into occupational positions and receive social status. Education becomes a key factor in this process because scientific advances and the increasing reliance of capitalist economies on technology require that properly qualified and trained persons are employed in each occupation (Clark, 1962; Kerr et al., 1960).

Structural functionalists also refer to economic needs to explain the expansion of higher education in Western societies. Since World War II, these societies witnessed tremendous increases in scientific and technological innovation, in the growth of the service sector of the economy, and in white-collar jobs. At the same time, higher education also experienced a tremendous expansion: the number of 18 to 24 year olds enrolled in college in the United States more than doubled in the past 40 years. By the early 1990s, half of the college aged population was enrolled in postsecondary institutions (Ballantine, 1993).

The demand for higher education continues to rise; in 1992 about 90% of high school seniors aspired to attend some form of postsecondary education (NCES, 1997a). Individuals from all segments of society have come to consider higher education as the major avenue for social and economic success. Sociologists of the structural functionalist tradition attribute this dramatic rise in the demand for higher education to the increased demands of the American economy for highly skilled technologically trained workers.

Sociologists of the conflict perspective challenged the structural functionalist interpretation of the expansion of higher education. According to Collins (1976), the soaring demand for higher education was not a response to economic needs and did not signify increasing democracy in Western societies. On the contrary, the expansion of higher education was due to educational inflation that rose out of the struggle of different social groups over access to privileged occupational positions. While less privileged groups sought access to these positions by acquiring higher education credentials, power elites constantly increased the educational requirements for these positions in an effort to maintain privileged access to them. Thus, Collins characterizes our society as a credential society where educational credentials do not signify ability or qualifications as much as membership to different social status groups, and where the elites hold the most prestigious degrees.

Similarly, Bowles and Gintis (1976) also contend that schooling in advanced capitalist societies is not an avenue for social mobility. Rather, it is a shorting mechanism that ensures the reproduction of inequalities and social classes. Under the guise of meritocratic ideology and equal educational opportunity, the complex process, which starts in elementary school and continues through all levels of education, ensures that only members of the advantaged classes acquire the highest educational credentials. Therefore, higher education is a means by which social inequalities are reproduced and legitimated.

Empirical evidence concerning the relationship of education to occupational attainment and social mobility has been used to support both structural functionalism and conflict theories. In fact, studies analyzing survey data show that years of education is highly related to occupational achievement (Blau and Duncan, 1967; Sewell and Hauser, 1976). Others, however, claim that careful examination of the data brings into question the role of education in determining social status position. In a synthesis of existing survey data, a team of researchers lead by Jencks attempts to show that schooling is not a strong determinant of adult success (Jencks et al., 1972). Their interpretation of statistical results sparked heated debates during the 1970s. More recently, many scholars agree that although not a cure-all for social inequality, higher education is an avenue for upward social mobility for many members of disadvantaged groups.

This debate over the role of education in social stratification has generated two opposing traditions among sociologists who study higher education. The underlying assumptions and basic arguments of structural functionalist and conflict theories permeated the interpretations of changes in higher education that occurred in recent years, especially in the United States. Supporters of the existing system of higher education interpret these changes on the basis of the structural functionalist belief that modern society is inherently open and meritocratic. Critics of this system develop interpretations that retain the basic arguments of the conflict tradition—that educational institutions are instruments of social control that reproduce and legitimate social inequalities.

Developments in Higher Education: Continuing the Debate

One of the most important developments in higher education has been the expansion of 2-year or community colleges that began in the postwar era and continues today. Enrollments in 2-year colleges more than tripled during the 1960s and 1970s. After World War II, community colleges enrolled only about 10% of all undergraduates in the United States; this percentage rose to about 24% in the 1970s, 41% in the 1980s and about 50% in the 1990s (Ballantine, 1993; Brint and Karabel, 1989; NCES, 1997a).

Proponents of 2-year colleges saw their expansion as paving the way for democracy in higher education. According to Burton Clark (1960), these institutions provide individuals from lower socioeconomic backgrounds, many of whom have been educationally disadvantaged in elementary and secondary schools, an opportunity to enter higher education. If successful, they can transfer to 4-year colleges for a B.A. degree. For individuals with "unrealistic" aspirations, 2-year colleges have a cooling-out function. By attending 2-year colleges, these individuals begin to realize their academic limitations, while at the same time they are offered opportunities for vocational training. This type of college benefits both individuals and society, because it offers a differentiating mechanism that can accommodate individuals of different ability levels and train them in the most needed technical skills (Clark, 1960).

This argument promoted several criticisms by scholars who assert that community colleges, due to their accessibility and low cost, divert many academically competent students away from more selective 4-year institutions. Researchers point out that while white middle class students enter 4-year colleges and universities, working class or disadvantaged students of equal achievement levels enter 2-year colleges. Once enrolled in community colleges, students have limited chances of transferring to 4-year institutions and of realizing their aspirations for a B.A. degree (Brint and Karabel, 1989; Dougherty, 1994; NCES, 1997b).

Moreover, community college degrees provide limited opportunities for occupational success. Among students with equal social background characteristics and achievement levels, community college entrants achieve a lower occupational status than 4-year college entrants. Community colleges tend to have limited occupational and economic advantages over those who begin work after high school graduation (Brint and Karabel, 1989; Dougherty, 1994).

Consequently, from a conflict perspective scholars maintain that 2-year colleges are another form of educational and social stratification. They interpret the expansion of these colleges as a way by which administrators in higher education responded to pressures by disadvantaged groups for equal educational opportunities, while at the same time preserving the more prestigious 4-year colleges and universities as an enclave of the advantaged classes.

In a similar fashion, the policy of open admissions became an issue of intense controversy. During the late 1960s and early 1970s, some colleges and universities adopted a policy of open admissions, under which high school graduates could be admitted regardless of test scores and grades; remedial instruction was provided for those with limited academic preparation. This policy was considered by supporters of the existing higher education system to be an outcome of political pressures by disadvantaged groups. Based on their belief that higher education should be a privilege of the most academically able students, they regarded open admissions as undermining the quality and prestige of academic programs. Others, however, maintained that every high school graduate should have a chance to attend college and that this policy opens the doors of higher education to groups that were severely underrepresented (Lavin and Hyllegard, 1996).

The only study that evaluated the policy of open admissions was conducted on data from the City University of New York (Lavin et al., 1980; Lavin and Hyllegard, 1996). In the early 1970s, when an open admissions policy was in effect at the City University of New York, the proportion of its students from low socioeconomic and minority backgrounds was greatly increased. Despite the high dropout rates, a substantial proportion of students, who would otherwise not have attended college were able to graduate. This policy more than tripled the number of African Americans and doubled the number of Latinos who received a B.A. degree. The educational credentials earned under this open admissions policy translated into substantial socioeconomic benefits as well (Lavin and Hyllegard, 1996). The researchers found no evidence that the policy seriously eroded the academic standards of the university (Lavin et al., 1981).

Open admissions policies became a major means by which disadvantaged groups gained access to higher education and especially to 4-year colleges. The City University of New York eventually abandoned this policy amid budgetary crisis and opposition by some faculty and members of the public. Many public 4-year colleges soon followed; during the 1980s these colleges became more selective, requiring more course work and higher test scores as criteria for admission (Ballantine, 1993).

Overall, while higher education expanded further in the postindustrial era, it also became increasingly differentiated. It is now comprised of institutions with different levels of prestige, ranging from 2-year or community colleges and schools with open admissions, to more selective 4-year colleges, to the most elite ivy-league institutions.

A final controversy centers around the issue of whether graduating from institutions of different selectivity and prestige translates into different opportunities in the job market. Structural functionalists would argue that differences in occupational success associated with graduating from various types of colleges simply reflect differences in individuals' abilities and motivations. Conflict theorists maintain that graduating from a prestigious institution confers occupational advantages that are independent of individuals' abilities and motivations (Collins, 1976).

Although few systematic investigations exist on this subject, some studies confirm the conflict theorists' claim (Dougherty and Hammack, 1990:252). Further research shows that attendance at colleges of different selectivity is dependent not only on individuals' abilities, but on their social and economic background. Given these findings, the debates over the role of higher education in social stratification have shifted to a great extent in recent years toward concerns over equal access to, and success in, higher education.

Higher Education: Access and Success

Most of the existing research on this topic has focused on differences in opportunities for higher education by social class, race/ethnicity, and gender; differences by age and other student characteristics have been examined to a lesser extent.

Social Class Differences
According to structural functionalists, the expansion of higher education in Western societies would increase the socioeconomic opportunities of the lower classes. Further developments, such as open admissions and an expansion of federal student aid in the United States,

would eliminate most of the barriers for upward social mobility of working class individuals. Despite these new opportunities for higher education, family income and social class continue to be highly related to college attendance. High school graduates from low-income families are less likely to attend college than graduates from high-income families (NCES, 1997b). Even among those enrolled in college, working class students attend 2-year colleges more often and are less likely to transfer to 4-year colleges than comparable middle class students (Hurn, 1993). Upper class individuals who graduate from elite private high schools have higher chances of attending selective, prestigious postsecondary institutions than individuals with similar achievement levels who graduate from public high schools (Persell et al., 1992). In fact, social class is a far more important determinant of college attendance than other individual attributes such as gender and race/ethnicity. This is because it is still more difficult for working class students to afford college. In addition, low socioeconomic status is strongly related to other factors that limit access to college, such as low test scores and enrollment in nonacademic programs in high school.

The expansion of opportunities in higher education did not produce dramatic reductions in the relationship between social class and success in higher education. The gains that working class groups have made in higher education are eroded by the continuous devaluation of higher education credentials. The illusion of relative progress may be maintained because the current generation of the working class has more schooling than previous generations. Yet, these individuals are in no more favorable position in social stratification than their forefathers were (Hurn, 1993).

Race and Ethnic Differences

The representation of minority groups in higher education dramatically increased following the Civil Rights Movement in the 1960s and the expansion of federal student aid programs in the early 1970s. The proportion of American college students who are minorities increased from 15.7% in 1976 to 25.3% in 1995 (NCES, 1997a). Despite these increases, many minority groups remain disadvantaged in terms of access to, and success in, higher education. Their patterns of college enrollment also place them at a disadvantage for successfully completing a B.A. degree. Most mi-

nority groups enroll in 2-year colleges and less selective 4-year colleges. Many minority students who aspire to a 4-year degree begin their education at community colleges, and this diminishes their chances of realizing their aspirations. Their chances of attaining a 4-year degree are also hampered by their limited academic preparation and their high probability of enrolling on a part-time basis.

Trends in access to higher education differ by race and ethnic group. African Americans experienced the greatest gains in college enrollments during the 1960s and 1970s. The enrollments of this group nearly doubled between 1970 and 1977. In the 1980s their enrollments begun to decline at all sectors of higher education, although they began to rise again in the 1990s (NCES, 1997a). The decline cannot be explained by students' qualifications, because during the 1980s the proportion of African Americans who graduated from high school increased and so did their average test scores. By 1989 the gap between African-American and white test scores had closed by almost one-third. However, this still leaves substantial differences in test scores between the two groups. Many scholars attribute the decline of African-American college enrollments to the rising costs of higher education and to a shift of federal student aid from grants to student loans.

Latinos and Native Americans have the lowest enrollments in higher education and tend to be concentrated in community colleges. For example, in 1995, 56% of Latino students were enrolled in 2-year rather than 4-year colleges. During the 1980s and early 1990s, the enrollments of Native Americans remained constant, while those of Latinos rose steadily (NCES, 1997a). Despite the Latino gains, both of these groups continue to face great barriers in access to higher education; they are due to inadequacies in their academic preparation and their limited financial resources (Ballantine, 1993; Carnegie Foundation, 1988). Native Americans and Latinos also have high dropout rates in college; their rate of bachelors' degree completion is much lower than that of whites (Koltai, 1993).

Asian Americans are the most successful group of students in higher education. Their enrollments more than doubled between 1976 and 1984. In the mid-1990s, they made up about 5% of the higher education enrollments; this is a very high proportion since they comprise only 2% of the general population (Ballantine, 1993; NCES, 1997a). The question of whether the success of this group will continue remains, as less affluent groups begin to immigrate from East Asia.

The access to, and success in, higher education of some minority groups is hampered by institutional policies and the academic climate of many schools. Scholars suggest that institutions should change their policies by placing less emphasis on test scores for admission and providing educational programs to increase the retention rates of minority students. However, the social climates of many classrooms and campuses make even the most academically prepared minority students feel unwelcome and limit their possibilities for academic success (Ballantine, 1993).

Given these conditions, many minority students opt to enroll in historically black colleges, whose enrollments rose recently. These institutions provide a supportive environment and the academic programs needed by many promising students who are not well prepared for college. Students in these colleges tend to receive better grades and have higher chances of college graduation than comparable students in predominantly white institutions.

Finally, most minority groups are least likely to enroll in educational programs and majors that offer the best opportunities for social mobility. African Americans, Latinos, and Native Americans are severely underrepresented in graduate-level programs and in the professions—law, medicine, science, and engineering (NCES, 1997a).

Demographic data indicate a constant increase in the minority and immigrant populations of the United States. Given these trends, higher education and American society in general face an even more pressing need for programs that promote the academic and adult success of disadvantaged racial and ethnic groups.

Gender Differences

Gender inequalities in higher education are disappearing at a faster pace than race/ethnic inequalities. The representation of women in all sectors of higher education rose dramatically over the past 25 years. For example, between 1974 and 1984 the enrollment of women in higher education increased at a rate that was nine times greater than that of men. Women have also made great strides in completing college and receiving graduate and professional degrees. In 1995 women received 55% of bachelor's degrees, compared to 43% in 1970. In 1995 women received 43% of law degrees,

and more than one-third of the degrees in medicine and business administration. This represents an impressive change, since in 1971 women received less than 10% of all three types of degrees (Landscape, 1994; NCES, 1997a).

Despite their progress in the above professions, women remain overrepresented in community colleges—in 1995 women comprised 58% of all community college students (NCES, 1997a). They are also concentrated in traditionally "female" fields, which include, among others, education, nursing, social work, and English.

Unfortunately, women continue to be underrepresented in disciplines that offer the best opportunities for economic independence and social mobility. These disciplines include professions like business, law, and medicine, as well as mathematics, science, and engineering, where women are most underrepresented. Up to the mid-1990s, twice as many men as women obtained degrees in mathematics and computer sciences, despite the rising demand for workers in these fields. Women are even more underrepresented in engineering, where in 1994 they were outnumbered by men by nearly one to five (Landscape, 1994; NCES, 1997a).

The reasons for the limited participation of women in mathematics and science are not necessarily related to differences in abilities. Gender differences in mathematics achievement have almost disappeared. In high school, female students actually receive better grades in mathematics and science than males. Despite this, strong differences exist in career aspirations that appear at an early age; twice as many eighth-grade boys as girls aspire to a mathematics and science career (Catsambis, 1994).

Although a major reason for women's underrepresentation in mathematics and science is their lack of interest in these careers, institutions of higher education are also responsible. The nature of mathematics and science teaching, and the social environment in mathematics and science departments, creates a "chilly climate" for women. Despite these difficulties, some women decide to pursue these majors and are as successful in their studies and graduation rates as their male classmates (Landscape, 1994). However, a smaller proportion of female than male graduates continues at the doctoral degree level.

Given these difficulties that women face in higher education, single-sex colleges have increased in popularity as safe havens for female students. Those attending women's colleges tend to be quite successful in pursuing mathematics and science-related fields. The graduates of these colleges also enjoy more adult success than female graduates of coeducational colleges (Rice and Hemmings, 1988). It is difficult though to determine whether colleges themselves are responsible for these outcomes. The reason is that these institutions are highly selective and are mostly attended by women from well-to-do families who would be successful anyway. To sustain and increase the social and economic success of all women, all colleges and universities need to develop programs that attract and retain women in nontraditional fields. Institutions should pay particular attention to the needs of older and minority women who are faced with more difficulties in attending and completing higher education.

Nontraditional Students

Perhaps the most dramatic development in higher education over the past 25 years is the changing profile of its student population. A greater percentage of this population now consists of low-income individuals, women, and underrepresented minorities. These students tend to pursue higher education in nonconventional ways, although other, more traditional students begin to change their patterns of college attendance as well. An increasing number of individuals return to college at an older age, pursue studies on a part-time basis, and attend college intermittently (NCES, 1997b).

The number of older students has been rising steadily so that the average age of college students is now over 25 years (Ballantine, 1993). Many individuals return to college in order to improve their employment opportunities; a large proportion of them are women who continue their education after childbearing. Students of nontraditional age are particularly attracted to community colleges due to their accessible locations, low cost, and extended classroom hours (Koltai, 1993). Many attend part time because they hold multiple roles as parents, workers, and students. These nontraditional students are usually enthusiastic and committed to their studies, but they also have special needs. Some institutions, to improve the skills and increase the graduation rates of these students, offer night programs, adult education programs, convenient off-campus locations, child-care facilities, and refresher or remedial courses. In terms of financial assistance, nontraditional students are at a particular disadvantage because few financial aid programs are designed for those who attend college part time.

As the college-going population becomes increasingly diverse, institutions need to restructure educational programs as well as financial aid packages to meet their students' needs. Unfortunately, periodic fiscal crises hamper these developments and even threaten the few programs that already exist. These crises are particularly threatening to public institutions that attract a large proportion of nontraditional students. They threaten the few remaining avenues for upward social mobility of these disadvantaged groups.

Conclusion

Individuals from all segments of society now see higher education as the means to adult success. Sociologists from two opposing theoretical traditions interpret this expanded role of higher education in different ways. Structural functionalists consider higher education as the way Western societies train and allocate individuals into occupations in a meritocratic way. They point to the great number of low-income minority and other disadvantaged groups who attend college and maintain that higher education opens the door of opportunity to all members of society. Theorists from this perspective interpret the differentiation of higher education as a development that is necessary to account for the variation in ability that naturally occurs in the population.

Conflict theorists contend that even though a growing number of disadvantaged individuals attend institutions of higher education, these institutions continue to reproduce social inequalities. Evidence of different types tends to support the propositions of conflict theorists. The expanded system of higher education has become so stratified that low status groups have access mostly to the lower ranking institutions. These groups have limited access to the more prestigious schools and majors that lead to better socioeconomic opportunities. Moreover, the economic returns of education continue to be less for women and minority groups—including Asian Americans—than for whites. Recent developments in American society may further diminish the power of higher education to provide equality of social opportunity. These include increasing unemployment and underemployment rates of college graduates, a decrease in the economic returns of the bachelor's degree, attacks and even retrenchment in affirmative action programs, and budget cuts in higher education. The decline in college enrollments of African Americans in the 1980s is a reminder that gains of disadvantaged groups in higher education are not irreversible. They indicate that increased educational opportunities are not necessarily inherent to Western societies but rather they may be due to the political mobilization of different groups (Karen, 1990).

It is difficult, however, to evaluate the theoretical positions of functionalists and conflict theorists. Both perspectives can account only partially for the developments of higher education in Western societies, and especially in the United States. The functionalist belief in the power of higher education to eliminate socioeconomic disadvantages of low status groups is clearly overstated. Yet, educational opportunities have greatly increased so that higher education is no longer a privilege of the elites. Despite this increase in educational opportunities, low status groups remain in the same relative position for social mobility as in previous decades (Hurn, 1993). A notable exception is that of African Americans, many of whom were able to attain middle class status. The ability of higher education to provide equal opportunities for social and economic success will be further tested, because the population of the United States and of other Western societies is becoming more diverse.

REFERENCES

Ballantine, Jeanne H. 1993. *The Sociology of Education: A Systematic Analysis,* 3rd ed. Englewood Cliffs, NJ: Prentice-Hall.

Blau, Peter, and Otis D. Duncan. 1967. *The American Occupational Structure.* New York: Wiley.

Bowles, Samuel, and Herbert Gintis. 1976. *Schooling in Capitalist America.* New York: Basic Books.

Brint, Steven, and Jerome Karabel. 1989. *The Diverted Dream: Community Colleges and the Promise of Educational Opportunity in America, 1900–1985.* New York: Oxford University Press.

Carnegie Foundation for the Advancement of Teaching. 1988. "Hispanic Students Continue to be Distinctive." *Change* 20:43–47.

Catsambis, Sophia. 1994. "The Path to Math: Gender and Racial-Ethnic Differences in Mathematics Participation from Middle School to High School." *Sociology of Education* 67:199–215.

Clark, Burton. 1962. *Education the Expert Society*. San Francisco: Chandler.

Collins, Randall. 1971. "Functional and Conflict Theories of Educational Stratification." *American Sociological Review* 36:1002–1019.

———. 1979. *The Credential Society*. New York: Academic Press.

Dougherty, Kevin J. 1994. *The Contradictory College: The Conflicting Origins, Impacts, and Futures of the Community College.* Albany, NY: State University of New York Press.

Dougherty, Kevin J., and Floyd M. Hammack. 1990. *Education and Society: A Reader.* New York: Harcourt, Brace Jovanovich.

Hurn, Christopher J. 1993. *The Limits and Possibilities of Schooling: An Introduction to the Sociology of Education.* Boston: Allyn & Bacon.

Jencks, Christopher, et al. 1972. *Inequality: A Reassessment of the Effect of Family and Schooling in America.* New York: Basic Books.

Karen, David. 1990. "Access to Higher Education in the United States, 1900 to the Present." In K. J. Dougherty and F. M. Hammack (eds.), *Education and Society: A Reader.* New York: Harcourt, Brace Jovanovich.

Kerr, Clark, et al. 1960. *Industrialism and Industrial Man.* Cambridge, MA: Harvard University Press.

Koltai, Leslie. 1993. "Community Colleges: Making Winners Out of Ordinary People." In Arthur Levine (ed.), *Higher Learning in America: 1980–2000,* Baltimore, MD: Johns Hopkins University Press.

Landscape. 1994. "Riveters to Rocket Scientists: Exploring the Gender Gap in Quantitative Fields." *Change* November/December:41–44.

Lavin, David E., and David Hyllegard. 1996. *Changing the Odds: Open Admissions and the Life Chances of the Disadvantaged.* New Haven, CT: Yale University Press.

Lavin, David E., Richard D. Alba, and Richard A. Silberstein. 1981. *Right Versus Privilege: The Open Admissions Experiment at the City University of New York.* New York: Free Press.

National Center for Education Statistics. (NCES). 1997a. *Digest of Education Statistics 1997.* Washington DC: U.S. Department of Education, Office of Educational Research and Improvement.

———. 1997b. *The Condition of Education 1997.* Washington DC: U.S. Department of Education, Office of Educational Research and Improvement.

Persell, Caroline Hodges, Sophia Catsambis, and Peter W. Cookson, Jr. 1992. "Family Background, School Type, and College Attendance: A Conjoint System of Cultural Capital Transmission." *Journal of Research on Adolescence* 2:1–23.

Rice, Joy K., and Annette Hemmings. 1988. "Women's Colleges and Women Achievers: An Update." *Signs* 13:546–559.

Sewell, William H., and Robert M. Hauser. 1976. "Causes and Consequences of Higher Education: Models of the

Status Attainment Process." In W. H. Sewell, R. M. Hauser, and D. L. Featherman (eds.), *Schooling and Achievement in American Society*. New York: Academic Press.

Turner, H. Ralf. 1960. "Contest and Sponsored Mobility and the School System." *American Sociological Review* 25:855–865.

HIGHER EDUCATION IN THE UNITED STATES

ACCESS TO BY MINORITIES

*Thomas M. Smith**
Peabody College, Vanderbilt University

Minorities in the United States have long suffered lower economic prosperity and lower social status relative to the white majority. Higher education often serves as the best means of social mobility available to our nation's young people. Graduating from college is associated with more stable patterns of employment and higher earnings. As the gap in earnings between high school and college graduates continues to widen, going to college has become even more important for minorities trying to break into a globally competitive labor market. This chapter reviews the higher education aspirations and preparation, college enrollment rates, college persistence, and completion rates of minorities compared to the majority white population. Trends are emphasized, especially where there appears to be convergence or divergence between white and minority students in higher education access and progress.

For the purpose of this review, the U.S. Office of Management and Budget standard classification scheme is used and the categories of black, Hispanic, Asian/Pacific Islander, and American Indian/Alaskan Native are used to denote racial/ethnic minority groups. These are the most common categories used to collect or aggregate data for different racial/ethnic groups by the federal government. It must be acknowledged from the outset that a large amount of variability exists within these categories. The backgrounds and experiences of Hispanic students with heritage in, for example, Mexico, Cuba and other parts of Latin America, are different and may affect educational access and attainment in different ways. The sample sizes in many national surveys, however, typically do not allow for further breakdowns of these groups into the specific country of origin. Furthermore, in many of the data sets examined for the comparisons reviewed here, the number of Asian/Pacific Islanders and American Indian/Alaskan Natives surveyed are too small to be reported separately. Comparisons across broadly defined racial/ethnic groups mask the relative success of some subgroups, while at the same time understating the educational success of others.

How Do College Aspirations and Plans Differ by Race/Ethnicity?

Planning for college is the first step toward going to college. Although many students decide whether or not to attend college early in their high school career, students' plans as high school seniors are likely to reflect their previous academic performance, their financial means, and their educational and career goals. The type of higher education institution in which students first enroll has a substantial impact on how far they will get in their education. For example, among bachelor's degree seekers who first enrolled in higher education in 1989–1990, only a third of those who started at a community college earned a bachelor's degree or were still enrolled toward one, compared to 73% of their counterparts who started at 4-year institutions (U.S. Department of Education 1996:58). In both 1972 and 1992, similar proportions of black and white seniors planned to attend 4-year colleges and universities. Hispanic seniors were less likely than white seniors to plan to attend a 4-year institution in both 1972 and 1992, although Hispanic plans did increase by 9 percentage

*The views expressed here are the author's own and do not necessarily reflect the views of the National Science Foundation.

points over this time period. In 1992, Asian seniors were more likely than white seniors to plan to attend a 4-year institution immediately after high school graduation.

Although community colleges provide a low-cost opportunity to start higher education, several sociologist have argued that they also serve the function of "cooling out" the educational aspirations of some status groups (Clark, 1960). Among several minority groups, plans to enroll in academic programs in community colleges after high school have increased over the past 20 years. For example, a larger proportion of blacks and Hispanics planned to attend an academic program in a 2-year college in 1992 than in 1972—the proportion of black seniors increased from 5 to 11% while the proportion of Hispanics increased from 11 to 26%. No change occurred among white seniors over this time period. In 1992, Hispanics were more likely than whites to plan to attend a 2-year academic program (Table 1).

Students consider many factors when selecting a college, including financial considerations, such as the cost of attendance and the availability of financial aid. The percentage of black, white, and Hispanic seniors who reported that tuition and expenses were very important in selecting a college declined between 1972 and 1992. There was no significant difference for Asian seniors between the two time periods. Availability of financial aid, however, remained very important over this time period for blacks and Hispanic seniors. In 1992, black and Hispanic seniors were more likely to say that financial aid was a very important consideration in selecting a college (67 and 62%, respectively) than white seniors (40%) (U.S. Department of Education, 1994: Table 3.3a).

How Do Long-Term Educational Expectations Differ from Immediate College Plans?

Students' long-term expectations for education may differ substantially from their short-term plans. Although not all high school seniors plan to attend college immediately after graduation, nearly all students now expect to continue their education eventually. The proportion of seniors expecting to at least finish college

TABLE 1. Percentage of High School Seniors Who Plan to Continue Their Education Next Year at 4-Year Colleges or in 2-Year Academic Programs

RACE/ETHNICITY	4-YEAR COLLEGE PROGRAM		2-YEAR ACADEMIC PROGRAM	
	1972	1992	1972	1992
Total	34	54	11	13
White	35	55	12	12
Black	32	52	5	11
Hispanic	11	20	11	26
Asian/Pacific Islander	47	65	18	12

Source: U.S. Department of Education (1995b:40).

ranged from 62% for Hispanics to 78% for Asian/Pacific Islanders in 1992—an increase of about 20 percentage points since 1972 for whites, blacks, and Hispanics and an increase of 9 percentage points for Asian/Pacific Islanders (U.S. Department of Education, 1995b:Table 4.1). Educational plans and expectations are generally high among white, black, Hispanic, and Asian/Pacific Islander high school seniors (Figure 1).

Generally high levels of educational aspirations were apparent for many of these racial and ethnic subgroups as early as eighth grade. For example, at least 8 out of 10 Asian/Pacific Islander, black, and white eighth graders aspired to at least attend college in 1988 (88, 80, and 79%, respectively). College aspirations among Hispanic and American Indian/Alaskan Native eighth-graders were lower (72 and 61%, respectively) (U.S. Department of Education, 1990:70). Among the eighth-grade class of 1988, however, there was considerable inconsistency between educational expectations and high school program plans. For example, although 55% of Hispanics expect to finish college and/or obtain a graduate or professional degree, only 23% planned to enroll in a college preparatory program in high school. A similar pattern occurred for black and American Indian/Pacific Islanders. Sixty-four percent of black eighth graders indicate that they expect to finish college or obtain a graduate and professional degree, but only 25% plan to enroll in a college preparatory program (U.S. Department of Education, 1990:72). This suggests that while some minority groups may have

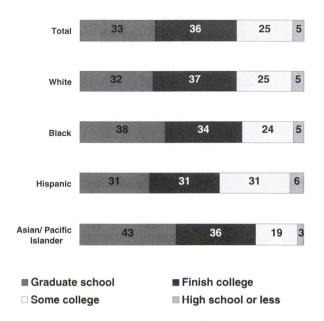

Total 33 | 36 | 25 | 5

White 32 | 37 | 25 | 5

Black 38 | 34 | 24 | 5

Hispanic 31 | 31 | 31 | 6

Asian/ Pacific Islander 43 | 36 | 19 | 3

■ Graduate school　　　■ Finish college
□ Some college　　　　■ High school or less

Figure 1. Percentage of 1992 high school seniors expecting to complete various levels of education.
Source: U.S. Department of Education (1995d:51).

How Has the Preparation for College of Different Racial and Ethnic Groups Changed over Time?

By examining the transcripts of high school graduates, we can see if the academic rigor of the courses they take has changed over time. The average number of academic course units earned by public high school graduates increased between 1982 and 1998 for all racial and ethnic groups, although the range in course-taking patterns remains wide. In 1998, Asian graduates earned the most academic credits (19.1), while American Indian graduates earned the least (17.0). This range is equivalent to four semester courses. White graduates earned 18.4 credits, while Hispanic and black graduates earned 17.8 and 17.6 credits, respectively (U.S. Department of Education, 2000b:153).

This renewed emphasis on academic course taking is also reflected by the increase in the percentage of high school graduates taking the "New Basics" curriculum recommended in *A Nation at Risk*, a core curriculum composed of four units of English and three units each of science, social studies, and mathematics.[1] The proportion of 1998 high school graduates who took this core curriculum ranged from about 40% for Hispanics and American Indians, 55% for blacks and whites, and 66% for Asians. This is a substantial increase from 1982, when only 14% of graduates took this stringent a curriculum (U.S. Department of Education, 2000b: 156) (Table 2).

Students in all racial and ethnic groups are taking more advanced mathematics and science courses, although black, Hispanic, and American Indian graduates still trail their Asian and white counterparts in advanced mathematics and science course taking. For example, the percentage of graduates of the class of 1998 who had taken Algebra II ranged from 47% of American Indian/Alaskan Natives to 70% of Asian/ Pacific Islanders. Percentages for white, black, and Hispanic graduates were 65, 56, and 48%, respectively. Furthermore, Asians were a third more likely than whites to take calculus (18 vs. 12%) and 3 times more likely than blacks, Hispanics, and American Indians (about 6% each). And while 46% of Asian/Pacific Is-

educational aspirations similar to the white majority, they may be less informed about how to make their aspirations come true.

Orfield and Paul (1994) found that counselors may not be presenting the information that students and parents need for making good choices about postsecondary options. Students and parents were uninformed about the influence of curricular tracks, the requirements of selective colleges, or the possibilities for financial aid. Orfield and Paul (1994) speculate that large caseloads and a preference for handling personal problems may prevent counselors from providing the kinds of information that could help students and parents make more realistic decisions about the future. Rosenbaum et al. (1996) also found that counselors do not want to be responsible for discouraging students from making unrealistic plans, that it is an unpleasant task that they have no desire to perform. They argue that counselor's avoidance of the "gatekeeping" role may be preventing students from getting needed information, advice, and preparation for further education. Racial/ethnic differences in this aspirations/ information/preparation gap are revealed when examining high school course-taking patterns.

---

[1] The panel's recommendation of 0.5 units of computer science was not included here, as the use of computers has been integrated into many other courses.

lander graduates took physics in high school, black, Hispanic, and American Indian/Alaskan Natives were less than half as likely to do so (U.S. Department of Education 2000b:156). From a course-taking perspective at least, it appears that all racial and ethnic groups are better prepared for college today than they were in the early 1980s, although blacks, Hispanics, and American Indians are less prepared than their Asian and white peers.

There is strong evidence that both prior achievement and peer influences strongly affect course taking in high school. Although some researchers have found that minority and low socioeconomic status (SES) students are more likely to be assigned to lower curriculum tracks in high school, even after ability is held constant (Rosenbaum, 1976, 1980; Oakes, 1985), others have found that verbal achievement scores and the expectations and guidance of others (parent, teachers, guidance counselor, and peers) are influenced by race and SES and that these mediating variables then influence track placement (Cicourel and Kituse, 1963; Rosenbaum, 1976; Erickson, 1975; Heyns, 1974). Fordham and Ogbu (1986) argue that one major reason black students do poorly in school is that they experience inordinate ambivalence and affective dissonance in regard to academic effort and success. They argue that because of these social pressures, many black students who are academically able do not put forth the necessary effort and perseverance in their schoolwork and, consequently, do poorly in school.

How Is Academic Preparation Reflected in the Achievement of Students near the End of High School?

Course taking is only one component of collegiate preparation; the skills that students take away from those classes constitute another important measure of their readiness to enter college. A student's ability to comprehend and effectively use written language is a skill necessary to master prior to taking on a more advanced college curriculum. There is substantial variation in average reading proficiency among seniors from different racial and ethnic groups in the National Assessment of Educational Progress (NAEP).

Reading proficiency scores for white, black, and Hispanic 17 year olds are available at several points in time

TABLE 2. Percentage of High School Graduates Taking the "New Basics" Curriculum

	1982	1998
Total	14	55
White	16	57
Black	11	56
Hispanic	8	40
Asian/Pacific Islander	20	66
American Indian/Alaskan Native	7	40

Source: U.S. Department of Education (2000:156).

between the early 1970s and 1999. Although the reading gap between whites and their black and Hispanic counterparts remains wide, these gaps have narrowed over time. For example, in 1971, average reading proficiency among 17-year-old blacks was well below that of both 17-year-old and 13-year-old whites (52 and 22 scale points, respectively); although the gap was still large in 1999, the reading proficiency of 17-year-old blacks was closer (31 points) to that of 17-year-old whites and about the same as that of 13-year-old whites (U.S. Department of Education, 2000c:33). There is some evidence, however, that the white-minority gap in reading may be widening again. Since 1988 it has widened somewhat at ages 13 and 17.

Proficiency in mathematics allows students to use higher level thinking skills to solve complex problems. If students do not have a firm grasp of mathematics upon leaving high school they will be at a disadvantage when trying to master that material in college.

Trend data on mathematics achievement are available for white, black, and Hispanic 17 year olds between 1973 and 1999. These data suggest that although a large gap in mathematics proficiency exists at age 17 between whites and their black and Hispanic peers, the gap has narrowed. For example, in 1973, average mathematics proficiency scores for 17-year-old blacks and Hispanics were well below those for 17-year-old whites (40 and 33 scale points respectively). Although the gap was still large in 1999, the mathematics proficiency scores for 17-year-old students increased only 5 scale points between 1973 and 1999, and the scores for 17-year-old blacks and Hispanics increased 13 and 16 scale points, respectively. As with reading, however, the white/black gap in mathematics widened in the 1990s (U.S. Department of Education, 2000c).

Although much of the gap in mathematics achievement between whites and other racial ethnic groups exists before entering high school, there is some evidence that these gaps widen for some groups during high school. In mathematics, the overall differences in eighth- to twelfth-grade gains show that blacks learn less than whites during high school, Hispanics and whites do not significantly differ, and Asians learn more than whites on average. When blacks and whites who complete the same number of math courses are compared, the learning gaps generally are smaller and none are statistically significant. The Asian–white achievement gain differences are also generally reduced among students completing the same number of mathematics courses (U.S. Department of Education 1995a). Data from NAEP suggest, however, that racial/ethnic differences in mathematics persist even among students who have completed similar courses at the time of assessment. For example, among white and black 17 year olds whose highest math course taken at the time of the 1996 assessment was Algebra II, the gap in average scores between these two groups was 21 points, a gap similar to the difference in scores between all 17 year olds whose highest math course was Algebra II and those whose highest course was only geometry (U.S. Department of Education 2000b:144).

To What Extent Do College Entry Rates Vary across Racial and Ethnic Groups?

Since most college students enroll in college immediately after completing high school, the percentage of high school graduates enrolled in college the October following graduation is an indicator of the total proportion who will ever enroll in college. College enrollment rates reflect both the accessibility of higher education to high school graduates, as well as their assessment of the relative value of attending college compared to working, entering the military, or other possible pursuits. Enrollment rates for white high school graduates increased from 50% in the early 1970s to about 60% in the mid-1980s and have fluctuated between 60 and 67% since then. After a period of decline in the late 1970s and early 1980s, the percentage of blacks enrolling in college immediately after high school graduation rose again until the late 1980s, when it appeared to have leveled off at around 50%. Since

1984, college transition rates for black graduates have increased faster than those of whites, closing much of the gap between the two groups. The enrollment rates of Hispanic graduates have been relatively stable over the past 20 years, fluctuating between 45 and 65% between 1972 and 1997 (U.S. Department of Education 2000b:214).

As noted above, the type of institutions that high school graduates first attend can affect their likelihood of completing a bachelor's degree. Students who begin their higher education at a 2-year college are far less likely to earn a bachelor's degree than their counterparts who begin at a 4-year college. In 1994, white graduates were twice as likely to enroll in a 4-year college as a 2-year college after high school, while black graduates were about 1.5 times as likely and Hispanic graduates were equally likely to enroll in a 4-year college (U.S. Department of Education, 1996).

Are Minority Students More Likely Than Their White Counterparts to Enroll in College Part Time?

Students who initially enroll part time in college are less likely to persist toward a bachelor's degree than those who enroll full time (U.S. Department of Education, 1996:204). Hispanic high school graduates aged 18–24 were far more likely to be enrolled in college part time, as opposed to full time, than were their white or black counterparts in 1994.

How Do College Persistence and Completion Rates Vary across Racial and Ethnic Groups?

Students enroll in college with many objectives, only one of which is a bachelor's degree. Among students enrolled towards a qualification (i.e., those that are eligible for student financial aid) in a 2- or 4-year college, about half indicate that their initial degree goal is a bachelor's degree. The most recent "Beginning Postsecondary Survey" from the National Center for Education Statistics is the most comprehensive source of data on persistence towards degrees in postsecondary institutions. Among beginning students seeking bachelor's degrees in 1989–1990, 63% had either completed or were still working toward a bachelor's degree in spring 1994. An additional 8% had earned an associate's degree or a vocational certificate (U.S. Department of Education, 1996:58). Persistence rates were higher for whites and Asians, that is, they were more likely than blacks or Hispanics to have either earned a bachelor's degree or still to be working toward a bachelor's degree in spring 1994 (U.S. Department of Education, 1996:212) (Figure 2).

Among bachelor's degree seekers who were no longer enrolled in spring 1994, whites, blacks, Hispanics, and Asian/Pacific Islanders were equally likely to have earned associate's degrees or vocational certificates, although the latter were less likely to earn vocational certificates. Among non-completers, black students drop out sooner than students from other racial/ethnic groups. As noted above, black and Hispanic students are more likely to enroll in community colleges, as opposed to a 4-year institution, than whites or Asians. Among those who start postsecondary education at a community college, degree attainment in the first institution enrolled is relatively low (less than 25%), although many students transfer and complete degrees or certificates at other institutions. In spring 1994, about 1 in 10 white, black, and Hispanic students who had started in a community college in 1989–1990 had either earned a bachelor's degree or were enrolled in a 4-year college or institution (U.S. Department of Education 1996:205).

White community college students were more likely to earn an associate's degree at their first institution by spring 1994 than their black counterparts (18 and 9%, respectively). Hispanics completed associate's degrees at their first institution at a rate similar to whites, although they were less likely to earn vocational certificates there. Regarding degree attainment, however, Hispanics appear to make more effective use of community colleges than either blacks or whites. Both blacks and whites were more likely to have neither earned an award nor still be enrolled for one by spring 1994 (55 and 50%, respectively) than were Hispanics (40%).

Movement between educational institutions is quite common at the undergraduate level, particularly among students who start their education at community colleges. Four out of 10 first-time, beginning community college students transfer to another institution—half to a 4-year college or university and half to a less than 4-year institution. Transfer rates for whites and blacks were similar, both around 39%. Al-

though transfer rates for Hispanics were higher than for whites in the BPS, these differences were not statistically significant. Hispanics were more likely than whites, however, to transfer to a less than 4-year institution as opposed to a 4-year institution 1994, contributing to lower bachelor's degree attainment rates (U.S. Department of Education, 1996:208).

How Do Racial and Ethnic College Graduation Patterns Vary by Gender?

The ability of colleges and universities to attract and graduate minority students is important to the goal of equal opportunity. Changes in the number of degrees earned by minorities of both sexes, particularly in relation to the number earned by whites, provides a measure of higher education's progress toward this goal. Compared to 1977 levels, the number of bachelor's degrees earned in 1997 was up for males and females in all racial/ethnic groups, with the largest increases occurring for Asian/Pacific Islander and Hispanic males and females (two groups with large immigration rates). Across this 20-year period, the number of bachelor's degrees earned by Asian/Pacific Islanders increased by 480% for men and 320% for women. Among Hispanics, degree growth was more rapid for women than for men, 330% vs. 150%, as was the case for black women and men, 81% vs. 33%. Among whites, the number of degrees earned by women rose 34%, while the number earned by men declined 9% (U.S. Department of Education 2000b:312). (Table 3).

How Does Choice of College Major Vary across Racial and Ethnic Groups?

Career opportunities available to college students are affected by the fields they choose to study. For college graduates, both starting salary and the availability of job opportunities in their chosen career are related to college major. In general, racial/ethnic differences in major selection are much narrower than gender differences, although Asian Asian/Pacific Islanders are far more likely than others to major in some science-related fields, including biological/life sciences, computer and information sciences, and engineering. Black bachelor's degree recipients were more likely than their white counterparts to major in business management or the social sciences and history, but were less likely

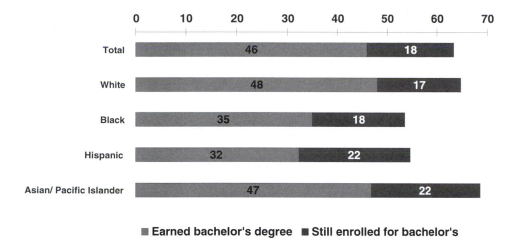

Total   46   18
White   48   17
Black   35   18
Hispanic   32   22
Asian/ Pacific Islander   47   22

■ Earned bachelor's degree ■ Still enrolled for bachelor's

Figure 2. Proportion of 1989–1990 first-time bachelor's degree seekers who had attained or were still enrolled toward a bachelor's degree in spring 1994.
Source: U.S. Department of Education (1996: Table 10–1).

to major in education or engineering. Hispanic bachelor's degree recipients were more likely than whites to major in foreign languages and literatures or the social sciences and history, but were less likely to major in education or health related fields. American Indian/ Alaskan Native bachelor's degree recipients were more likely than whites to major in the humanities, public administration or the social sciences and history, but

were less likely to major in business management or engineering (U.S. Department of Education 2000a: 313). Underrepresentation of blacks, Hispanics and American Indians in science and engineering occupations has more to do with lower college entry rates, and higher dropout rates, than it does with major field selection. Within each racial/ethnic group in 1996, women represented a lower percentage of bachelor's de-

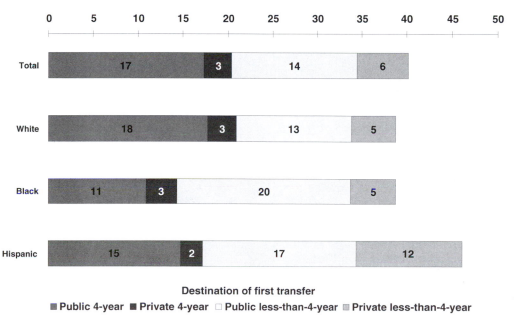

Total   17   3   14   6
White   18   3   13   5
Black   11   3   20   5
Hispanic 15   2   17   12

Destination of first transfer
■ Public 4-year ■ Private 4-year □ Public less-than-4-year ▨ Private less-than-4-year

Figure 3. Proportion of 1989–1990 first-time community college students who transferred to another institution by spring 1994, by destination of first transfer.
Source: U.S. Department of Education (1996: Table 9–2).

TABLE 3. Number of Bachelor's Degrees Conferred (in Thousands)

	MALE			FEMALE		
	1976–77	1996–97	PERCENT CHANGE	1976–77	1996–97	PERCENT CHANGE
Total	494,424	517,901	4.7	423,476	650,122	53.5
White	438,161	401,878	(8.3)	369,527	496,346	34.3
Black	25,147	33,509	33.3	33,489	60,544	80.8
Hispanic	10,318	26,007	152.1	8,425	35,934	326.5
Asian/Pacific Islander	7,638	32,111	320.4	6,155	35,858	482.6
American Indian/Alaskan Native	1,804	2,988	65.6	1,522	4,421	190.5
Non-resident alien	11,356	21,408	88.5	4,358	17,019	290.5

Source: U.S. Department of Education (2000b:312).

grees in science and engineering than in non-science and -engineering. In contrast to white and Asian women, however, black, Hispanic, and American Indian women earned more than half of the bachelor's degrees in science and engineering awarded to their respective racial/ethnic group in 1996 (National Science Foundation 2000: text table 2–4) (Table 4).

Summary

As the gap in earnings between high school and college graduates continues to widen, access to a college education is becoming even more important for minorities wanting to share in the American dream. Almost all high school seniors expect to complete at least some col-

TABLE 4. Percentage Distribution of Bachelor's Degrees Conferred across Fields of Study: 1996–97

MAJOR FIELD OF STUDY	TOTAL	WHITE, non-HISPANIC	BLACK, non-HISPANIC	HISPANIC	ASIAN/ PACIFIC ISLANDER	AMERICAN INDIAN/ ALASKAN NATIVE	NON-RESIDENT ALIEN
All fields, total	100	100	100	100	100	100	100
Biological sciences/life sciences	5	5	4	5	13	5	4
Business	19	19	21	19	21	15	34
Communications and communications technologies	4	4	5	4	2	3	4
Computer and information sciences	2	2	3	2	4	1	5
Construction trades	0	0	0	0	0	0	0
Education	9	10	8	7	2	13	3
Engineering	5	5	3	5	11	4	12
Engineering-related technologies	1	1	1	1	1	1	1
English language and literature/letters	4	5	4	4	3	4	1
Foreign languages and literature	1	1	1	3	1	1	1
Health professions and related sciences	7	8	7	5	7	7	3
Liberal arts and sciences, general studies, and humanities	3	3	4	5	2	5	2
Mathematics	1	1	1	1	1	1	1
Physical sciences and science technologies	2	2	1	1	2	1	2
Psychology	6	6	7	8	6	7	3
Public administration and services	2	2	4	2	1	3	0
Social sciences and history	11	10	12	13	11	12	10
Visual and performing arts	4	4	2	4	4	4	7
Other	12	12	11	13	8	13	7

Source: U.S. Department of Education (2000b:313).

lege, although Hispanic seniors are less likely than their white, black, and Asian/Pacific Islander counterparts to plan to attend college right after high school. High school graduates from all racial and ethnic groups are taking a more rigorous high school curriculum, and mathematics and science test scores are generally up—although blacks, Hispanics, and American Indians/Alaskan Natives continue to trail their white and Asian/Pacific Islander counterparts in critical skill areas. However, black and Hispanic high school graduates are less likely than their white peers to make the immediate transition to college and Hispanics are more likely to enroll in a 2-year college or as part-time students—two conditions that make it less likely they will persist toward a bachelor's degree. Among bachelor's degree seekers, whites and Asian/Pacific Islanders are more likely to persist toward a bachelor's degree than their black and Hispanic counterparts. Of those who earn a bachelor's degree, black and American Indian/Alaskan Native graduates are less likely than their white and Asian/Pacific Islander peers to finish in 4 years or less—a condition that delays their entrance into the full-time labor market.

Several minority groups do tend to major in fields that will help them recoup their college costs. Black, Hispanic, and Asian/Pacific Islander graduates were less likely than whites to major in education. Asian/Pacific Islander graduates were more likely than white graduates to major in computer science and engineering.

REFERENCES

Cicourel, Arron V., and John I. Kituse. 1963. *The Educational Decision-Makers*. New York: Bobbs-Merrill.

Clark, Burton. 1960. "The 'Cooling-Out' Function in Higher Education." In A. H. Halsey, J. Floud, and C. A. Anderson (eds.), *Education, Economy, and Society*. New York: Free Press.

Erickson, Frederick. 1975. "Gatekeeping and the Melting Pot: Interaction in Counseling Encounters." *Harvard Educational Review* 45:44–70.

Fordham, Signithia, and John H. Ogbu. 1986. "Black Students' School Success: Coping with the 'Burden of Acting White.'" *The Urban Review* 18(3):176–205.

Heyns, Barbara. 1974. "Social Selection and Stratification Within Schools." *American Journal of Sociology* 79:89–102.

National Science Foundation. *Women, Minorities and Persons with Disabilities in Science and Engineering: 2000*. NSF 00–327. Arlington, VA: 2000.

Orfield, Gary, and Faith G. Paul. 1994. *High Hopes, Long Odds: A Major Report on Hoosier Teens and the American Dream*. Indianapolis: Indiana Youth Institute.

Rosenbaum, James E. 1976. *Making Inequality*. New York: Wiley.

———. 1980. "Track Misperceptions and Frustrated College Plans: An Analysis of the Effects of Tracks and Track Misperceptions in the National Longitudinal Survey." *Sociology of Education* 53:74–88.

Rosenbaum, James E., Shazia Rafiullah Miller, and Melinda Scott Krei. 1996. "Gatekeeping in an Era of More Open Gates: High School Counselor's Views on Their Influence on Students' College Plans." *American Journal of Education* 104:257–279.

U.S. Department of Education. 1990. National Center for Education Statistics. *A Profile of the American Eighth Grader: NELS: 88 Student Descriptive Summary*. NCES 90–458, by Anne Hafner. Washington, D.C.: U.S. Government Printing Office.

———. 1994. National Center for Education Statistics. *The Condition of Education 1994*, NCES 94–149, by Thomas M. Smith et al. Washington, DC: U.S. Government Printing Office.

———. 1995a. National Center for Education Statistics. *The Condition of Education 1995*, NCES 95–273, by Thomas M. Smith et al. Washington, DC: U.S. Government Printing Office.

———. 1995b. National Center for Education Statistics. *The Digest of Education Statistics 1995*, NCES 95–029, by Thomas D. Snyder. Washington, DC: U.S. Government Printing Office.

———. 1995a. National Center for Education. *Social Background Differences in High School Mathematics and Science Coursetaking and Achievement*, NCES 95–206, by Thomas B. Hoffer, Kennith A. Rasinski, and Witney Moore. Washington, DC: U.S. Government Printing Office.

———. 1995b. National Center for Education Statistics. *Trends Among High School Seniors, 1972–1992*, NCES 95–380, by Patricia Green et al. Washington, DC: U.S. Government Printing Office.

———. 1996. National Center for Education Statistics. *The Condition of Education 1996*, NCES 96–304, by Thomas M. Smith et al. Washington, DC: U.S. Government Printing Office.

———. 2000a. National Center for Education Statistics. *The Condition of Education 2000*, NCES 00–062, by John Wirt et al. Washington, D.C.: U.S. Government Printing Office.

———. 2000b. National Center for Education Statistics. *The Digest of Education Statistics 1999*, NCES 00–031, by Thomas D. Snyder (ed.). Washington, D.C.: U.S. Government Printing Office.

———. 2000c. *National Center for Education Statistics. NAEP 1999 Trends in Academic Progress: Three Decades of Student Performance*, NCES 2000–469, by J.R. Campbell, C.M. Hombo, and J. Mazzeo. Washington, D.C.

Higher Education in the United States: Latinos

Susan Moreno and Chandra Muller
University of Texas at Austin

As the fastest growing, and one of the youngest ethnic groups in the United States, Latinos'[1] participation in education is becoming an especially important concern for educators. In 1992, Latinos numbered 22.3 million, 9% of the United States population, compared to 15.8 million in 1982 (Chapa and Valencia, 1993). Latinos are a relatively young population with a median age of 26.3 years compared to 35.2 years for the non-Latino white population (U.S. Census Bureau, 1992b). These numbers indicate the importance of understanding Latinos' educational needs so that we can ensure their success in our educational system. Thirty-two percent of Latinos between 14 and 34 years old have dropped out of school before high school graduation. In comparison, 12% of African Americans and 8% of whites have dropped out (National Center for Education Statistics, 1995). With attrition so high among Latinos, it is imperative that those who make it to college have a successful experience and earn a college degree. For a more complete view of Latino students' experiences within the U.S. higher educational system, this chapter will discuss the historical and current participation of Latinos in higher education. Not all institutions of higher education provide the same opportunities, thus we will consider participation in 2-year institutions, in 4-year institutions, and in graduate school separately. Finally, the unique experiences of Latinas will be discussed.

Historical Participation in Higher Education

Prior to the late 1950s, the Latino population in the United States was composed of Chicanos[2] in the Southwest and Puerto Ricans in the Northeast, with the majority in the Northeast. With the rise of communism in Cuba in the late 1950s and the political unrest in Central America during the 1980s, the U.S. Latino population grew to include Cuban and Central/South American populations. However, Chicanos and Puerto Ricans still comprise 75% of the Latino population. Unlike the emergence of African-American institutions of higher education in the 1800s and early 1900s, there was no movement by the federal government or religious organizations to establish comparable institutions for Chicanos. Although Chicanos were never legally denied access to institutions of higher education, the maintenance of segregated Chicano elementary and secondary schools, which hindered if not prevented the education of Chicano children, precluded college and university enrollment (Olivas, 1989). Before the 1970s, only a few Chicanos were able to obtain a college education.

Student activism of the Chicano movement during the late 1960s and early 1970s led to significant gains in college enrollment of Chicanos and other Latinos. Concurrent with enrollment increases were the emergence of Chicano studies programs and the first Chicano and Puerto Rican institutions. Still, the Latino

---

[1] In this article, Latino is synonymous with Hispanic and refers to people with an ethnic heritage from Mexico, Puerto Rico, Cuba, Central and South America, and other Spanish origin.

[2] Chicano will be used in this chapter instead of Mexican American although the terms can be used synonymously to identify that part of the Latino population with a Mexican heritage.

college population was overwhelmingly found in predominately white institutions and then mainly in lower status 2-year institutions (Olivas, 1989).

Recent Participation in Higher Education

Although no efforts were made to establish "historically" Latino institutions as was the case for African Americans, Latino-serving institutions have recently developed in the higher education system (de los Santos and Rigual, 1994). Even though they were originally established to serve white students, these institutions now serve a large (at least 25%) Latino population, often because they are in geographic areas with a high Latino concentration. In addition, they tend to be low in cost and therefore more easily accessible. Since they were not originally established to work with Latinos, these institutions are in a period of transition trying to develop programs and classes to serve a predominately Latino population. Therefore, they are redefining their institutional mission statements to meet the needs of their Latino students. The ability of these institutions to do this will have a long lasting effect on the educational attainment of the entire Latino population.

In 1993, 7% of those enrolled in college were Latino compared with 4% in 1976 (National Center for Education Statistics, 1995). Among Latinos in higher education in 1993, 45% were in 2-year institutions, 45% were in 4-year institutions, and 10% were in graduate school, compared with 30, 52, and 18%, respectively, among whites and 34, 54, and 12%, respectively, among African Americans. Although enrollment in higher education is increasing, Latinos are disproportionately enrolled in 2-year institutions.

Diversity among Latinos

Recognizing differences among ethnic groups within the Latino population is the key to understanding trends among them. Importantly, these differences are apparent in educational attainment and later occupation. For example, in 1992, of Latinos aged 25 years or older, only 45% of Chicanos graduated from high school[3]. In comparison, 62% of Cubans, 62% of Cen-

[3] Percentages in this section were calculated from the U.S. Census Bureau Current Population Reports on *The Hispanic Population in the United States: March 1992.*

tral/South Americans, and 61% of Puerto Ricans had graduated from high school. Cubans are the best educated, with 19% of the population having obtained a bachelor's or higher degree, followed by Central/South Americans with 16% of the population with an advanced degree. In contrast, only 6% of Chicanos have earned a bachelor's or higher degree. Puerto Ricans have only a slightly higher level of attainment, with approximately 9% having earned an advanced degree.

One point that must be made is that the various Latino populations immigrate to the United States with different levels of educational attainment. Cubans and Central/South Americans often come with high levels of education which includes professional status occupations. Mexicans often have very low levels of education, less than high school completion, when they immigrate. Their lower levels of education are associated with fewer opportunities for good jobs. It is well known that the level of education and the occupation of one's parents affect one's own education. The different educational levels of Latino immigrants influence the educational opportunities and attainment of the Latino subgroups, thus attainment of this and future generations will, in part, be associated with existing differences. These large differences among Latinos emphasize the importance of identifying which Latino group is being discussed in research articles and policy.

Two-Year Institutions

Community and junior colleges were originally established to provide a bridge between high school and college for average students. Because of their proximity to Latino communities and their relatively low tuition rate, 2-year institutions are an important component of Latinos' access to higher education. Through their vocational programs, 2-year institutions have increasingly become a way of providing the labor market with a skilled, low-level work force. Although sometimes viewed as providing Latinos and other minorities with an equal educational opportunity, 2-year institutions often reinforce and maintain a stratified system that "educates" Latinos to stay at a lower wrung of the economic ladder. Half the undergraduate Latino population was enrolled in a 2-year institution in 1993 compared with only 36% of the white and 39% of the African-American undergraduate population (U.S. Census Bureau, 1994).

With Latinos comprising a larger portion of community college students than might be expected given their numbers in the population, the retention of those enrolled is a priority. McCool (1984) found two factors important in determining who succeeded in community colleges: (1) the student's ability to understand positive and negative reasons that may require them to withdraw from school and (2) the students' perception of their school experiences. McCool also found that Latino students' early success in course work may encourage continued participation in school since this population has a long history of negative self-perception when it comes to ability to do school work.

To provide Latinos with true access to higher education, 2-year institutions must effectively transfer Latinos to 4-year institutions to complete a 4-year degree. Overall, the transfer rate of students from 2-year to 4-year institutions is declining and ranges from 5 to 25%. Latinos, in particular, often have a very low transfer rate of less than 10%. Although most studies indicate that Latinos want to transfer to 4-year institutions, there are several factors that may be preventing their full participation in higher education, including limited contact with faculty outside of class, lack of institutional mechanisms that facilitate transfer, and lack of encouragement from 2-year institutions' faculty (Rendon and Nora, 1987). Without this mentoring and institutional support, Latinos either drop out of school or get tracked into vocational programs.

Four-Year Institutions

A degree from a 4-year institution is becoming increasingly important for access to mid-level and higher prestige careers and, as mentioned previously, Latinos are underrepresented in enrollment in 4-year institutions. Still research conducted on Latinos in higher education focuses on their participation in 4-year institutions and in particular on the largest subgroup, Chicanos. Researchers have typically relied on large education data sets, in which Latinos are oversampled, or on census data for quantitative study because most naturally occurring samples of Latinos in 4-year institutions do not have enough Latinos for reliable analysis. Other researchers have compromised generalizability but gained a deeper understanding of experiences with in-depth interview methods to gather data. Others have simply employed quantitative survey methods with a very small Latino sample.

There are four main areas in which research on Latinos in 4-year institutions has focused.[4] The first area of research provides a global view of Latinos' position within 4-year institutions by addressing their enrollment patterns over time. The second area of research focuses on factors affecting Latinos' participation in higher education, such as policies to increase student success. Another area that has received much attention from researchers is retention and attrition of Latinos. Those who stay in college are more likely to have a sense of social integration while in school, have strong motivation to be in college, and have social support from others. Latinos who felt most alienated and least satisfied with college dropped out more frequently, and were more likely to identify a lack of financial support and counseling from the institution as contributing to their lack of success. Those who withdrew from college expressed feelings of failure and low self-esteem as a result of their college experience.

Finally, a few studies have examined the effect of college life on Latino ethnic identity with seemingly contradictory findings. There appeared to be some conflict over whether identifying with one's Latino ethnicity increased one's adaptation to college life. McCormick's (1994) study of Latino engineering students found that entrance into and retention in engineering might be related to the denial of their Latino culture. Most of the engineering students she interviewed who distanced themselves from the label "Hispanic" felt that opportunities would open for them through this denial. Conversely, a study of Latinos in two Ivy League colleges found that a strong Latino identity led to lower perceptions of threat from other students and thus better adaptation in these schools (Ethier and Deaux, 1990). The conflicting results may be because the Latino engineering students were mainly comprised of Central and South Americans, groups that have high educational attainment levels among Latinos. Since they have higher educational attainment, they can more easily disassociate from the stigma of being Latino in the United States. The students in the Ivy League schools were mostly Chicano and Puerto Rican. With a long history of oppression in the United States, these

---

[4] Aguirre and Martinez (1993) provide a good overview on Chicano research in higher education.

groups may use their identification as Latino as a source of strength.

Graduate School

With the political activism of the 1960s and 1970s, came the hope that Latinos would achieve greater access to educational opportunities demonstrated by more Latinos with advanced degrees. More Latinos with Ph.D.s would mean an increase in the number of Latino role models and mentors for college students. In 1993 (U.S. Census Bureau, 1994), 10% of the Latino college population were enrolled in graduate school, accounting for only 4% of the total graduate school enrollment. A more telling account of Latinos' representation in graduate school, however, is their actual educational attainment numbers at the highest levels. In 1992, only 3% of Latinos 25 years and older had earned a post-baccalaureate degree (U.S. Census Bureau, 1992b). Six percent each of Cuban Americans and Central/South Americans 25 years and older had obtained postbaccalaureate degrees compared with only 2% each for Chicanos and Puerto Ricans. These figures dramatize the plight of Latinos in graduate school even more when one realizes that Chicanos account for 64% of the Latino population.

Unfortunately, few studies focus on the graduate school experiences of Latinos. Most studies analyze the type of graduate degrees Latinos obtained. For example, Solorzano (1995) found that Chicanos with doctorates in social sciences earned their bachelors degree from less prestigious undergraduate institutions and that these small institutions were mostly Latino-serving institutions. This at once highlights the importance of 4-year institutions that are accessible to Latinos and the obstacles faced by many students trying to obtain advanced degrees. Additionally, he found that Chicanos were underrepresented in all academic areas in graduate education.

Latinas

Among women, Latinas have the lowest educational levels. Only 49% of Latinas are high school graduates compared to 77% for white women and 64% for African-American women (U.S. Census Bureau, 1992a). In 1991, Latinas comprised only 3% of those enrolled in college compared to 6% for African-American women and 45% for white women. Latinas' college enrollment is 43% in community colleges, 47% in 4-year institutions, and 11% in graduate school, compared with 32, 50, and 18%, respectively, for white women and 42, 44, and 14%, respectively, for African-American women (U.S. Bureau of the Census, 1993). Using any measure, Latinas have the lowest levels of education.

Although Latinas are underrepresented, especially in comparison to other women, very little research has focused on their specific needs in the higher educational system. What little research has been conducted either combines all the Latina subgroups together or focuses specifically on Chicanas, women of Mexican heritage. Surprisingly, most research has focused on Chicanas in graduate school despite the low levels of participation in 4-year institutions that feed into advanced degree programs.

Thus, the existing research is largely on this successful group and the research questions focus on the positive characteristics of this population that facilitated their academic achievement. Research has also explored the relationship of Latina ethnic identity and adaptation to higher education. Of the studies on Latinas, most have been qualitative in-depth interviews. Only a couple are quantitatively oriented with a fixed choice response method. Of those that were quantitatively oriented the analysis involved a simple descriptive analysis as opposed to a more in-depth analysis using inferential statistics.

One of the most consistent findings in the research is the importance of parental support, especially from the mother, for Latina educational attainment. In almost every study, a mother's strong support, encouragement, and desire for her daughter's economic independence have been influential factors in the daughter's academic success. Another finding across studies is that educationally successful Chicanas attended integrated high schools and felt comfortable in working within the dominant culture and their own ethnic culture. Although successful Chicanas were comfortable in the dominant culture, they were not necessarily highly assimilated. Many maintained close connections with their own cultural heritage.

Some factors appear to work against academic success of Chicanas. Young (1992) found that Chicanas in

As a consequence, conflict and competition are more frequent themes in Weber's than in Durkheim's work. He, and those who followed in his intellectual tradition, stressed that universities have been important organizational elements in the ongoing struggles of nations to define themselves and establish patterns of legitimated social control. In this work, Weber attended especially to the ways higher education aids in the development of professions and the preservation of their power and status. Second, Weber's thinking on the emergence of the modern bureaucracy, with its focus on expertise, specialization, and careers, has greatly influenced modern theorizing about university organization. Weber's attention to the increasing specialization, departmentalization, and vocationalism of the curriculum is of particular interest in this area. Third, Weber wrote persuasively, in several frequently cited works, on the distinctive place of the social sciences within the older traditions of the natural sciences and the humanities in universities. Finally, Weber provided the field with an enduring model of commitment to systematic comparative (cross-national) study.[3]

In the work of Durkheim and Weber, higher education was considered from the perspective of grand theory, as a central institution in modern societies. Such work was intended to be easily translatable across national boundaries. Individual nations would vary in important ways, of course, but the theories were broad enough to be adjustable to different contexts, and thus applied comparatively. The work of several prominent sociologists of the 1930s through the 1970s (notably, Talcott Parsons) continued this tradition of grand theorizing. In the years after World War II, however, the sociological study of higher education grew in other directions. The emergence of the United Nations and a variety of other international agencies brought greater attention to the challenge of applying broad sociological theories to specific educational contexts. From the 1950s to the 1980s, UNESCO, the World Bank, the Ford Foundation, and other organizations funded sociologically informed analyses of education around the world, with particular attention to the role of universities in economic development and "modernization". Although the funding of such work has slowed in more

recent years, the research support was critical to the growth of the field in its time.

Central Concerns within the Sociology of International Higher Education

Contemporary sociologists examining international higher education find publication outlets in book form and in a variety of scholarly journals (notably *Comparative Education*, *Higher Education*, *Sociology of Education*, and the *American Journal of Sociology*). This work may be characterized as having four general thematic concerns: postsecondary education as an element in stratification and attainment processes, the organization of higher education institutions and systems, social policy relating to postsecondary education, and academic careers.

Postsecondary Education as an Element in Stratification and Attainment Processes

Regardless of worldwide trends toward expanded postsecondary access and regardless of the distinctive national and cultural contexts in which they operate, colleges and universities everywhere continue to have clear connections to processes of social stratification and status attainment. That is, those entering postsecondary education are undertaking an activity with profound implications for their eventual social and economic standing in society. Because sociologists have been investigating stratification and status attainment since the earliest years of the field, colleges and universities have been longstanding focuses of sociological research in North America and elsewhere. In the years since World War II, sociologists of education have increasingly addressed questions of who enters postsecondary education, who goes to different kinds of postsecondary institutions, who attains baccalaureate, graduate, and professional degrees, and how levels of educational attainment affect eventual social and economic success. Researchers have addressed these questions at two general levels: at the level of national education systems and at the level of individuals' paths to success within national systems.

At the national level, analysts have often considered the nature of educational selection, sorting, and allocation systems in various countries. Because such stud-

---

[3] Weber's thinking on education is more fully covered in Coser (1971).

less-powerful nations. To more fully understand language of instruction in imperialistic settings, some scholars approach language policy studies eclectically, allowing for the possibility that the use of metropolitan languages in education in less-powerful/developing nations may serve the interests of at least some groups from both nations, though for different reasons.

In considering language of instruction in classical colonial settings, one may think of the establishment of French and English in Africa and Asia by agents of European empires in the nineteenth and twentieth centuries. In these contexts, metropolitan languages served as vehicles for communication between colonial subjects and European masters. As educated, bilingual *indigènes* assumed positions in colonial administrations, the business of colonization—in particular the creation of economic dependencies favoring the metropole—was facilitated.

It would not be accurate to suggest, however, that Europeans were the first to promote their languages in classical colonial contexts. During the Chinese occupation of Vietnam in the first millennium A.D., for example, Vietnamese mandarins were educated in Chinese, and when they themselves occupied Cambodia in the early nineteenth century, the Vietnamese taught their language to Cambodians. Nor would it be accurate to suggest that language of instruction was necessarily—or exclusively—integrated with an economic agenda. Russian, for instance, was purposefully established by Moscow in the republics of the former Soviet Union. While a common language certainly facilitated the economic integration of the republics into the greater Soviet Union, Russian is explicitly associated in Soviet language policy documents with the transmission of socialist ideology. Finally, it should be noted that actors in less-powerful nations responded variously to the promotion of metropolitan languages in classical colonial settings. Although many simply accepted the new linguistic realities—and some benefited personally by brokering their linguistic skills for positions of power and privilege in colonial administrations—others resisted language-in-education innovations, though in so doing they dramatically limited their opportunities for success in the colonial order.

In neocolonial settings, language-in-education policy decisions are made by actors indigenous to the less-developed/powerful nations. Recent studies, however,

have suggested that powerful nations may exert significant influence in such language policymaking through "leveraged" aid—the provision of textbooks, teachers, and opportunities for overseas study tied to a particular metropolitan language or contingent upon the adoption or maintenance of a particular metropolitan language as medium of instruction. Studies have examined language-in-education policymaking in, for example, francophone Africa in relation to France and anglophone Africa in relation to Great Britain and the United States. In these contexts, the provision of assistance tied to the use of French and English, respectively, has been integrated with neocolonial agendas predicated on cultural and economic goals, respectively.

It should be noted, though, that the external promotion of metropolitan languages in nominally independent less-powerful nations does not necessarily signal imperialistic action. In the 1980s, for instance, Vietnam provided educational assistance to Cambodian higher education in Vietnamese. It was argued contemporaneously that this language-in-education policy amounted to cultural hegemony. The fact that language-specific assistance was phased out as Cambodian professors were trained to replace those killed in the 1970s by the Khmer Rouge, however, suggests a rather more humanitarian than imperialistic agenda. The Cambodian case also illustrates the complex response of actors in neocolonial settings to the external promotion of metropolitan languages. Many Cambodian educational policymakers recognized in the use of Vietnamese the potential for cultural imperialism, but nevertheless agreed to enter the educational assistance relationship with Vietnam as the only way, given the national and international constraints under which they were forced to operate, to rebuild the higher education system in the aftermath of the Khmer Rouge regime.

The dynamics of language-in-education policymaking in internal colonial settings more closely resemble those in classical colonial contexts than in neocolonial contexts; decisions about language of instruction for less-powerful "nations" are typically made by representatives of the more-powerful "nation" in a given society. With the 1521 Ordinance of Villers-Cotterêt, for example, French was made the official and educational language throughout France, including peripheral areas containing communities of Basque, Flemish, and Provençal speakers. Scottish-, Welsh-, and Irish-speaking communities in nineteenth-century Great Britain were similarly affected by policies establishing English as the educational medium.

Of course, the use of metropolitan languages in internal colonial settings is not strictly an historical phenomenon. In contemporary Turkey, the substantial Kurdish minority receives education in Turkish rather than Kurdish, while Berber-speaking children in Morocco and Algeria study in Arabic. The English-only movement in the United States provides a final contemporary example; as powerful governmental and nongovernmental groups work to make English the official U.S. language, the future of bilingual education for less-powerful groups grows uncertain.

In both historical and contemporary contexts, the promotion of metropolitan languages in education has had the effect of assimilating less-powerful groups into the dominant society. It is important to recognize, however, that minority populations have both resisted the metropolitan language and adopted it for strategic purposes. In Franco's Spain, for example, Catalan (the language of Catalonia) was repressed in favor of Castilian, though Catalan speakers refused to abandon their native language. In Occitania in southern France, on the other hand, Occitan speakers shifted rapidly to French under pressure from Paris, though the decision appears to have been pragmatic, based upon a positive assessment of the social and economic mobility available in the larger society to French speakers.

It is not accurate to suggest that metropolitan languages are used for instruction in all imperialistic settings. For example, many contemporary bilateral aid agency projects promote indigenous languages as the medium of instruction. This may mean, however, that the imperialistic agenda of the powerful nation is fundamentally concerned with successful transmission of knowledge and ideology.

Knowledge and Curriculum

Curriculum represents the selection of skills, knowledge, values, worldviews, and ideologies to which students are exposed in school. One can distinguish the formal or official curriculum (the messages that are planned for student consumption and transmitted by teachers, textbooks, and other instructional materials) and the hidden curriculum (the "unplanned" messages communicated by the social relations and behavior of teachers, students, etc.). To investigate imperialism in

relation to curriculum conceived in this way necessitates examining what goes on inside the "black box" of schooling. It also means taking seriously the nexus of knowledge and power, whether one adopts a conflict or functionalist perspective. Curriculum can be oppressive or liberating (from a conflict perspective) or it can promote modern or traditional ways of understanding and operating in the world (from a functionalist perspective).

Studies of curriculum in classical colonial settings have been undertaken in Africa, Asia, and Latin America. From these investigations, we know that the school curriculum in French colonies in Africa was modeled after nonelite elementary schools in France. This meant that students would be exposed primarily to lower status knowledge and would likely be presented with ideologies that not only legitimated French colonial rule but also prepared students for subordinate roles within francophone African societies. Moreover, since French administrators and teachers controlled what they learned, students encountered in the hidden curriculum a message of the legitimacy—or at least the normalcy—of French rule. Although English colonial schools in Africa (and other regions) offered both elite, high status knowledge and nonelite, low status knowledge tracks, the (formal and hidden) curricula in both types of schools were designed to train and socialize the student to fit into the existing unequal relations within the colony and between the colony and England.

Nevertheless, more research is needed to examine how curricular experiences led people to become leaders and followers in independence movements. One aspect to consider is that although the lessons taught by missionaries in many regions, including Latin America, contained messages that encouraged acceptance of European colonial power, they also included ideas supportive of human rights and liberties. Furthermore, we know from the struggles during the French colonial period in Vietnam that teachers, students, and communities passively and actively resisted efforts by the colonial administration to impose a curriculum that disparaged the Vietnamese people's capacity for self-rule and thus justified French colonialism.

Within neocolonial relations, dynamics of knowledge/power continued to operate in and through the curriculum. In francophone African societies, there was often considerable continuity between the curriculum implemented by colonial administrators and teachers and their counterparts in newly independent states, and many of the reforms initiated in France continue to be modeled by the "neocolonies." The ideologies transmitted through the formal and hidden curriculum, at least in Togo, reinforce a gendered division of labor; however, at least some female students ignore or reject such messages and aspire to positions of status and responsibility inside as well as outside the home. Similarly, racial/ethnic group divisions that were created or at least reinforced through colonial schooling, for instance in Malaysia, have been promoted after formal independence, both through the formal curriculum and the hidden curriculum (through segregated schools) with the encouragement or at least consent of elites in both core and peripheral nations.

There is also evidence that in neocolonial settings the teaching of ideologies and values in line with capitalist versus socialist conceptions of development tends to mirror the dominant ideology of the nation providing financial and technical assistance. Case studies of Cambodia, Hungary, Nicaragua, and Tanzania demonstrate how the ideology stressed in the curriculum changed as their international (dependency or development assistance) relations shifted. These cases also demonstrate, however, that leaders in each country were able at times to balance off alternative sources of aid, thus providing some space for indigenous ideas—or at least a selective use of "foreign" ideas—to be promoted through the curriculum.

Native Americans in the United States or other countries in the Americas, Blacks in South Africa during the era of Apartheid, non-Russian minorities in Russia and the Soviet Union, and Aborignal groups in Australia and New Zealand are examples of "nations" colonized via conquest but then absorbed unequally into a society. The education to which these groups are exposed under such situations of internal colonialism tends to denigrate their culture, celebrate the dominating group's culture, and legitimate the societal structures through which the unequal relations are maintained. Despite or because of such cultural imperialism, students and others from these subordinated groups have to varying extents ignored or resisted as well as accommodated to the messages in the formal and hidden curriculum they encounter. Although indigenous ideas inspired resistance, its possibilities have been enabled by contradictory messages transmitted in the curriculum—messages that convey critiques of the

current social system or images of alternative social arrangements—as well as by moral and other forms of support by groups within and outside the society.

Conclusion

The contentious nature of the debates about imperialism and education is the result in part of differences in the political/ideological as well as theoretical perspectives of those who contribute. What is intriguing about the debates is the tendency for scholars to adopt a conflict perspective when interpreting the "imperialist" interventions by nations that have political economies with which they disagree (whether capitalist or socialist), while exhibiting a functionalist perspective when explaining similar "development assistance" interventions by nations that have political economies with which they concur (again whether capitalist or socialist). This may suggest that education and other aspects of imperialist policies and practices pursued by leaders of "capitalist" and by "socialist" nations may have negative as well as positive implications at least for some groups both in more and in less-powerful/developed nations.

REFERENCES

Altbach, Philip, and Gail Kelly, eds. 1978. *Education and Colonialism*. New York: David McKay.

Carnoy, Martin. 1974. *Education as Cultural Imperialism*. New York: David McKay.

Cobarrubias, Juan, and Joshua Fishman, eds. 1983. *Progress in Language Planning: International Perspectives*. Berlin: Mouton.

Fägerlind, Ingemar, and Lawrence Saha. 1983. 2nd ed., 1989. *Education and National Development: A Comparative Perspective*. New York: Pergamon.

Feuer, Lewis. 1986. *Imperialism and the Anti-Imperialist Mind*. Buffalo, NY: Prometheus Books.

Ginsburg, Mark, ed. 1991. *Understanding Educational Reform in Global Context: Economy, Ideology, and the State*. New York: Garland.

Hopkins, Terence, Immanuel Wallerstein, Robert Bach, Christopher Chase-Dunn, and Ramkrishna Mukherjee, eds. 1982. *World-Systems Analysis: Theory and Methodology*. Beverly Hills, CA: Sage.

McLean, Martin. 1983. "Educational Dependency: A Critique." *Compare* 13:25–42.

Phillipson, Robert. 1992. *Linguistic Imperialism*. Oxford: Oxford University Press.

Snyder, Louis, ed. 1962. *The Imperialism Reader*. New York: Van Nostrand.

INTERNATIONAL COMPETITION AND EDUCATION CRISES

CROSS-NATIONAL STUDIES OF SCHOOL OUTCOMES

David P. Baker
Pennsylvania State University

Since the early 1960s, when the Soviet Sputnik space flights caused a cold war crisis in the United States precipitating reforms of American science and mathematics education, the political connection between international competition and educational outcomes has been made tighter than ever before. Over the past century, the nations of the world have come to value an educated citizenry as a national resource to be developed, making formal schooling a central concern of national governments and something to be assessed and compared internationally much like a nation's natural or man-made physical resources.

Sociologists of education examining historical trends have shown that national crises, such as major military losses, colonial failures, or sharp economic decline, often result in various educational reforms (e.g., Archer, 1984; Ramirez and Boli, 1987). Historically, most of this reform has been to increase the amount of schooling required of a nation's youth population and increase their access to local schools. In more recent times, with nearly full expansion of basic schooling in developed countries, national crises focus attention on the quality of educational outcomes such as achievement, graduation rates, and transition to more education or the labor market.

One of the chief factors responsible for the intensified politics around educational quality has been the recent frequency of cross-national studies yielding technically sophisticated comparisons of achievement and other outcomes. These studies provide comparable indicators of educational quality across nations. For example, a recent steady flow of international studies of schooling has shaped policy debates in the United States and elsewhere. The International Association for the Evaluation of Educational Achievement (IEA) in just the past decade produced a series of major international studies on science, mathematics, reading, classroom environments, computer learning, and writing. Most recently the IEA released its Third International Mathematics and Science Study (TIMSS), a massive, 40-country, multifaceted investigation of math and science achievement in fourth, eighth, and twelfth grades. Also, there were two recent International Assessments of Educational Progress (IAEP) and in the late 1980s member countries of the Organization for Economic and Cultural Development (OECD) established a system to report cross-national statistical indicators of the quantity and quality of education in each country. This system is on the verge of routinely collecting comparable school achievement data for all OECD countries. More countries and a larger variety of countries than ever before are participating in these international studies.

What Are These Studies?

These studies all share a similar research design. First, an international team develops a standard achievement test on some subject that is then translated into the different languages of the participating countries and made meaningful to students from different cultures. This is then administered to a predetermined, comparable, and representative sample of students in each country, such as fourth graders, ninth graders, or students in the final year of secondary school. Often the tests are constructed to reflect how much students have learned about specific course material that they have received. And in some studies, very sophisticated parallel assessments are made of the curriculum and teaching approaches used in each participating country. Additionally, many studies also gather information about the social–economic background of the students and their families and other pertinent organizational information about the school they attend. This information along with the test scores forms a database for each country, which is then combined for all the countries and analyzed by numerous researchers, government policymakers, and educators around the world.

What Consequences Do These Studies Have?

The results of these studies can have dramatic effects in some countries. For example, the IEA completed a study of mathematics performance of eighth and twelfth graders in 21 countries in the early 1980s. American students, on average, did not perform well in comparison to some other countries, and in particular did poorly compared to the first place Japanese students. And because the Japanese and American economies were in heated competition at the time, with some indication that the latter was losing out, the stage was set for a round of educational reforms in the United States. The international economic crisis and poor mathematics results from the United States made big news in this country and the subsequent in-depth analysis of the data by American sociologists of education and other education researchers added to the public interest (see for example, Baker, 1993; Bracey, 1991; Lerner, 1982; McKnight et al., 1987; Westbury, 1992; Wolfe, 1977). Similarly, the TIMSS study generated another round of debate in the United States about mediocre international performance (e.g., Baker and LeTendre, 1998). Many other countries are holding similar national discussions about their education systems as a result of these international studies.

In the United States, for example, one consequence of the debate is an appeal for educational reform beginning with the publishing of the influential *Nation at Risk* in which results from the 1980s international math and science studies were used to argue for higher quality, national educational standards and curricular reform in American schools (National Commission of Excellence, 1983). This reform movement, along with the 1989 Education Summit of the Nation's Governors and the National Educational Goals Panel in 1992, is among the most significant of the recent political actions taken in education in the United States and is in

large part due to the results of just several international studies. When, as described above, results from international studies coincide with other national events, such as a lagging economy, a chain of crisis and reform can take place. This has happened recently in the United States, but it should also be noted that this process does not necessarily always happen, nor does it happen in every country. Therefore, international studies have had mixed consequences for general educational research and the sociology of education. At times the scientific impact of cross-national studies has been significant, such as in the case of greater research effort toward explaining curricular and course materials in educational research. But at other times the impact of international studies has been limited as sociologists of education and other educational researchers are often preoccupied with schooling in just one nation or location (Baker, 1994).

What Has Caused the Proliferation of International Comparisons?

There are four distinct trends that increase the importance of international assessments of school outcomes creating a political environment in which national crises and educational reform are tied together.

Trend I: National Sponsorship of Education

One fertile area of the sociology of education research reexamines the history of formal schooling as part of the major political development of the modern nation-state. Sociologists have shown that in the past 200 years the movement has moved away from a world organized politically by empires to one in which the entire human population is organized into modern nation-states. The state as a political entity has created a series of institutions that help it to continue, and perhaps the most central of these institutions is state-supported and mandated schooling. The so-called "rise of the modern nation-state" has depended in part on the effects of the widespread use of what sociologists call "mass schooling." Unlike exclusive schooling for elites, such as the Chinese empire's mandarin class or clerics trained in feudal Europe, mass schooling is designed to provide basic education for all children (i.e., masses). With the rise of the nation-state as the primary political organization throughout the world, schooling went from a mostly privately funded institution for very few children to a publicly funded schooling for all children, providing many functions for the state.

A major consequence of this trend is that national governments are held accountable for school quality and availability. Therefore comparing what is happening educationally in one nation with what is happening in other nations takes on new political and public meaning. Like the comparison of military power, economic condition, political structure, and health care, the comparison of national school systems and their output has become part of a world made up of competing nation-states. And this trend is certainly facilitated by numerous international agencies formed by nations interested in comparison and regulation of worldwide competition (e.g., the UN and UNESCO, OECD, APEC).

Trend II: Citizens as National Capital

Related to trend I is the notion that a nation's citizenry is a major economic resource. This is both a relatively recent political and intellectual idea. Developed in the 1960s, human capital theory of economics moves beyond a focus on just physical capital and labor to include the skills of workers as human capital. This theory, and related research, lends scientific credibility to the general idea that a nation's ability to train and educate its future labor force adds directly to its technological productivity and economic welfare. This line of thought places greater emphasis on the functioning of a nation's schools. No longer seen as just basic socialization for children, schooling is considered a national resource. This means that there is a compelling political logic for national governments to evaluate their nation's schools and hence provide important fiscal resources to undertake such studies. Over the past several decades this kind of a political process has won larger governmental support for international studies of schooling, which in earlier years had been primarily done with limited private funds. The elevation of international comparisons as a main education activity of governments yields greater legitimacy and funding for future studies of this type.

Trend III: Learning Theory and Psychometric Testing

With the development in this century of modern learning theory and the corresponding psychometric techniques used to assess learning, particularly school

achievement, educational testing has become extensive and sophisticated. The so-called "standardized test," American examples being the SAT, ACT, and the California Achievement Test, is widely used in many school systems throughout the world. The main breakthrough for international studies from recent psychometric techniques is the promise of reliable, valid, and administratively manageable tests for a wide range of students using different languages of instruction, from different cultures, and with different approaches to schooling. Although some researchers, including some sociologists of education, are not as convinced that standardized tests provide all that they promise (e.g., Jencks, 1980; Powell and Steelman, 1984; Crouse and Trusheim, 1988), this trend in testing has nevertheless enabled large-scale international comparisons of school outcomes to take place. In addition to the usual multiple choice test, recent international studies have experimented with performance-based testing and other nontraditional assessment techniques, which are new approaches from psychometric research.

Trend IV: School Effects Research

Less obvious perhaps, but equally important, has been the influence of "school effects" research on the motivation for international studies of education and their research designs. Probably the largest contribution of sociologists of education, particularly in the United States, to education research and policymaking in general is the analysis of what kinds of effects schools can have on achievement. Motivated by political questions about racial integration, social class stratification, and educational inequality in modern society, reports such as the *Equality of Educational Opportunity* (Coleman et al., 1966) in the United States and *The Plowden Report* (1967) in the United Kingdom, asked for their time a fundamentally new organizational question about schools: Are there ways of organizing schools that enhance achievement and the distribution of achievement across different types of students? School effects research pointed out the importance of including analysis of how schools are organized into the study of student achievement. This line of research also, with some irony given its original intent, pointed out the need to include detailed information about the family life of students in achievement assessments.

This approach has had a significant effect on the way most international assessments of schooling are done.

Both information on school organization and family background are incorporated in the design of many international studies and often become the focal point of subsequent analyses. So the questions motivating many international studies are not just which country's students achieve the most, but often include attempts to answer questions about the underlying causes of cross-national differences in achievement through a basic school effects approach (e.g., Heyneman and Loxley, 1983).

These trends, one political (trend I), one economic (trend II), and two scientific (trends III and IV) have combined to provide a significant increase in international study of schooling and in turn this has increased the impact that these studies have on educational policy and politics.

What Do These Studies Find?

The recent international assessments of mathematics, science, and reading have shown several interesting patterns of results. First, contrary to the often shrill reports in the popular media linking study findings to the image of an international educational Olympiad with clear winners and clear losers, detailed analyses of the data have shown that many countries cluster together in their abilities to educate their youth (U.S. Department of Education, 1992). For example, reanalysis of IEA's Second International Mathematics Study in the early 1980s indicates that there are probably three clusters of countries in terms of achievement outcomes instead of a clear difference among all 21 participating countries. So although the United States does not rank high among all the countries in the study, its performance puts it in the middle range of achievement. Similar clusters of national performance are reported in the 1997 TIMSS (Beaton et al., 1996a, 1996b). Second, there appears to be some variation across curricular domains in national school achievement. The countries that have done well in mathematics and science are not necessarily those that have done well in reading (Elley, 1992). The notion of a singular national performance in school achievement may not be the best way to think of how countries actually compare with one another.

Third, although the basic school effects approach has helped to understand how school organization, including curricular analyses, can explain mathematics and science achievement cross-nationally (e.g., Schaub and

Baker, 1991; McKnight et al., 1987; Schmidt et al., 1997), this model has worked less well in the areas of reading and language acquisition (Elley, 1992). These kinds of conclusions drawn from international results offer new directions for educational research.

What Will Be the Future of Cross-National Studies of Education?

All indications would suggest that the current interest in comparing educational outcomes across nations will continue. The trends that are responsible for the recent explosion in international studies and their political use worldwide represent substantial factors that will continue into the foreseeable future. The politics of nations as economic competitors will certainly continue and consequently governmental interest in comparable education statistics will continue too. There is little reason to believe that the extensive systems of empirical comparison of national economies and health care systems will not also develop for the education sector. The idea of education as a national resource is now clearly embedded into the political fabric of most administrations around the world and there are some much celebrated cases of national development that have relied on extensive human capital deepening (see Baker and Holsinger, 1996, for a discussion of education and development in Pacific-Rim Asian countries). The technical means to undertake large-scale and sophisticated international assessments of educational outcomes are already in place and will continue to grow. And lastly the questions that have occupied policymakers and sociologists of education alike about what organizational factors in schools improve the schooling of children will continue to be asked.

References

Archer, M. S. 1984. *Social Origins of Educational Systems*. Beverly Hills, CA: Sage.

Baker, D. 1993. "Compared to Japan, The U.S. Really Is a Low Achiever . . . Really: New Evidence and Comment on Westbury." *Educational Researcher* 22(3):18–20.

Baker, D., and D. Holsinger. 1996. "Human Capital Formation and School Expansion in Asia: Does a Unique Regional Model Exist?" *International Journal of Comparative Sociology* XXXVII:159–173.

Baker, D., and G. LeTendre. 1998. "International Competitiveness in Science: Don't Blame U.S. Adolescents or Middle Schools for a 'Slump.'" *Education Week* 46–51.

Beaton, A., J. Martin, I. Mullis, E. Gonzalez, T. Smith, and D. Kelly. 1996a. *Science Achievement in the Middle School Years: IEA's Third International Mathematics and Science Study*. Chestnut Hill, MA: TIMSS International Study Center.

———. 1996b. *Mathematics Achievement in the Middle School Years: IEA's Third International Mathematics and Science Study*. Chestnut Hill, MA: TIMSS International Study Center.

Bracey, G. 1991. "Why Can't They Be Like We Were." *Phi Delta Kappan* 106–121.

Coleman, J., C. Campbell, C. Hobson, J. McPartland, F. Weinfeld, and R. York. 1966. *Equality of Educational Opportunity*. Washington, DC: U.S. Government Printing Office.

Crouse, J., and D. Trusheim. 1988. *The Case Against the SAT*. Chicago: The University of Chicago Press.

Elley, W. 1992. *How in the World Do Students Read?* Hamburg, Germany: Grindeldruck GMBH.

Heyneman, S., and W. Loxley. 1983. "The Effect of Primary-School Quality on Academic Achievement Across Twenty-Nine High- and Low-Income Countries." *American Journal of Sociology* 88(2):1162–1194.

Jencks, C. 1980. "Declining Test Scores, An Assessment of Six Alternative Explanations." *Sociological Spectrum* 1:1–16.

Lerner, B. 1982. "American Education: How Are We Doing." *Public Interest* 59–82.

McKnight, C., F. Crosswhite, J. Dossey, E. Kifer, J. Swafford, K. Travers, and T. Cooney. 1987. *The Underachieving Curriculum: Assessing U.S. School Mathematics from an International Perspective*. Champaign, IL: Stripes Publishing.

Powell, B., and L. Steelman. 1984. "Variations in State SAT Performance: Meaningful or Misleading." *Harvard Educational Review* 54(4):389–401.

Ramirez, F., and J. Boli. 1987. "The Political Construction of Mass Schooling: European Origins and Worldwide Institutionalization." *Sociology of Education* 60(1):2–17.

Schaub, M., and D. Baker. 1991. "Solving the Math Problem: Exploring Mathematics Achievement in Japanese and American Middle Grades." *American Journal of Education* 623–642.

Schmidt, W., C. McKnight, and S. Raizen, 1997. *A Splintered Vision: An Investigation of U.S. Science and Mathematics Education*. Dordrecht, Netherlands: Kluwer Academic Publishers.

United States Department of Education. 1992. *International Mathematics and Science Achievement: What Have We Learned?* NCES Publication 92–011. Washington, DC: U.S. Government Printing Office.

Westbury, I. 1992. "Comparing American and Japanese Achievement: Is the United States Really a Low Achiever? *Educational Researcher* 21(5):18–24.

Wolf, R. 1977. *Achievement in America*. New York: Teachers College Press.

IQ

Christopher J. Hurn
University of Massachusetts/Amherst

The commonly used abbreviation "IQ" refers to "intelligence quotient," a number obtained by dividing the subject's score on a test of "mental age" by his or her chronological age. And, as this suggests, the earliest IQ tests were developed to measure children: a 5 year old with a score on the mental age test of 5 was judged to have an IQ of 100, a 5 year old with a mental age of 4, an IQ of 80, and one with a mental age of 6, an IQ of 120. IQ scores thus provided a summary description of how far a child's intellectual development departed from the population average of that age. By the early decades of the twentieth century IQ scores began to be computed for adults as well. After individuals reached their late teens, psychologists found that scores on IQ tests remained relatively stable, at least until late middle age. They also found that the distribution of scores on the tests formed a bell-shaped curve or "normal" distribution. Thus whereas an IQ of 120 in a 5-year-old child means that he or she scored at the level of the average 6 year old, in an adult the score simply means that he or she scored at levels achieved by only (approximately) 10% of the population.

Understanding the controversy over IQ requires a brief consideration of the history of intelligence testing. IQ tests were developed in a cultural and political climate very different from the era after 1960. The psychologists of the 1920s and 1930s, led by Lewis Terman of Stanford University, were convinced—and persuaded many other educated Americans—that they had made a scientific breakthrough of major proportions (Terman and Oden, 1947). The most important intellectual abilities, they believed, could be measured by a short paper and pencil test lasting less than an hour. Those abilities, in turn, underlay performance in a wide variety of tasks, particularly in schools and in highly skilled occupations, for the same reason that athletic ability or muscular coordination predicted performance in baseball as well as football, or in golf as well as tennis (Terman and Oden, 1947). Because the tests measured general intellectual abilities rather than specific skills, and also because test scores were relatively stable over time, they could be used as predictors of future performance or as screening devices to separate those, for example, who might benefit from an advanced curriculum and those who would be more suited for special schools for the mentally retarded. IQ tests appeared to give more accurate predictions than the subjective judgments of teachers who were well acquainted with the individual. And because the tests measured *general* cognitive abilities, they were better indications of future performance than, for example, grades or examination results. They also could "read through" many of the differences between individuals raised in widely different environments to underlying intellectual abilities. Paradoxically, in view of the critique that developed in the decades after 1960, the psychologists of the 1920s and 1930s saw IQ tests as helping to create a *more* meritocratic society: a way of discovering otherwise hidden talents among disadvantaged populations (Herrnstein, 1971).

But there was a darker side to the growing use of IQ tests in the first half of the century. No doubt the new tests discovered talented youngsters who would otherwise have been denied opportunities—in Britain for example, the use of IQ tests as a basis for selection for more academically oriented schools appears to have substantially increased the number of lower class individuals in these schools. At the same time, however, particularly in the United States, the results of IQ testing were used to provide a "scientific" basis for assigning large percentages of minority students to schools for the retarded and excluding black students from white schools (Gould, 1981). The psychologists of that era were convinced, as few are today, that different ethnic groups as well as different social classes differed in native ability (Brigham, 1923).

After the early 1960s educated opinion about the merits of IQ testing shifted dramatically. The first, and still most common criticism, was that the tests were culturally biased. IQ tests, the critics argued, far from reading through the "superficial" cultural differences between individuals raised in different environments, reflected those differences instead of measuring some hypothetical underlying ability. In one version of this argument, critics claimed that although perhaps accurately estimating the abilities of middle class populations, IQ tests systematically understated the abilities of low status and minority populations. The IQ scores of these groups, therefore, were invalid, in part because the tests assume knowledge or vocabulary that individuals in these groups did not possess, but also because they ignored the likelihood that a testing situation that was familiar and only modestly stressful for one group, was both unfamiliar and highly stressful for another.

The test bias argument also came in a more general form. According to these critics, intelligence itself was a concept that had no general validity across cultural or even class barriers (Hirsch, 1975). Intelligence, at least as measured by IQ tests, was not at all analogous to general athletic ability or eye/hand coordination, as the classical position asserted. IQ scores, these critics conceded, predicted success in school. But that successful prediction largely reflected the fact that schools themselves rewarded middle class styles of learning and middle class skills rather than because they measured some general trait, intelligence, which was more generally valid.

Test bias criticisms were closely linked to the best known controversy about IQ: the role of heredity versus environment. If IQ tests provided a valid measure of general intelligence, largely independent of cultural and class differences, it made sense to argue that scores on these tests reflected, at least in part, *constitutional* differences between individuals. But to the extent that IQ tests essentially measured aptitudes and skills that were associated with white middle class individuals, the claim that scores were substantially heritable was

implausible and arrogant (Kamin, 1974). Only within carefully defined and homogeneous groups did the heritability argument make sense, and even then given the complexity of the interaction between heredity and environment, no firm estimate of their relative importance was warranted.

Whatever the merits of these criticisms, and they will be considered in more detail shortly, there is little doubt that the attack on the classical tradition of the 1920s and 1930s had a significant effect on the use of IQ tests and other tests of cognitive ability or aptitude. During the late 1960s and 1970s, IQ tests were phased out or deemphasized in many schools. In 1972 the National Educational Association called for a moratorium on standardized intelligence testing (Jensen 1980:13). Federal judges during the 1970s ruled that even individually administered IQ tests were not to be used in the placement of children in classes for the educationally retarded if the results of that testing were that disproportionate numbers of minorities were placed in those classes. Aptitude tests, whether for jobs or college entry, also fell into some disrepute. On their own initiative, many universities and colleges employed different cut-off scores for students from different ethnic backgrounds, implicitly accepting the criticism that SAT scores systematically understated the real abilities of minority students. Federal judges ruled that tests of aptitude for particular jobs were unconstitutional unless these tests had a manifest relationship to the skills required for the job in question (Griggs versus Duke Power, 1971). Tests measuring specific skills were allowed; tests measuring general aptitudes, despite the fact that many psychologists believed that they were better predictors of job performance, were highly suspect if they produced different mean scores for different groups. Public attitudes toward ability testing and the scientific status of IQ tests had changed dramatically by the mid-1970s.

Although some psychologists trained in the classical condition accepted part of these criticisms, others argued that they were wildly overstated. The publication of the *Bell Curve* in 1994 marked a major effort to rehabilitate the classical tradition. Herrnstein and Murray (1994) argued that the charge of cultural bias was without foundation. If it were true, for example, that IQ scores systematically understate the abilities of culturally different or low status groups, two implications should follow: the school performance of low scoring individuals from these groups should be less predict-able from their IQ scores than the performance of low scoring individuals from more favored groups. If IQ tests understate the "true" ability of culturally different individuals, they should predict their future performance less well than the scores of middle class populations. A second implication of the cultural bias argument was that differences in the scores of ethnic or class groups should reflect the presence of the more obviously culturally loaded items in the tests: perhaps words or problems with which they are less likely to be familiar. Tests that were less culturally saturated, in other words, should result in smaller differences between subpopulations. But there is plausible evidence that neither of these implications is correct (Klitgaard, 1985). IQ tests, or for that matter SAT scores, predict school or college performance about as well for minorities and low status groups as for middle class white populations. Test differences between groups on the more "culture fair" tests are not smaller (and sometimes larger) than test score differences on conventional "culture-loaded" tests (Jensen, 1980). Nor, finally, is there good evidence that test anxiety or unfamiliarity explains a significant proportion of the difference in test results among different groups (Jensen, 1980).

Recent evidence from studies of twins also tends to weaken the argument that heredity plays little role in IQ differences, at least within a given population. Early studies of identical twins separated at birth and reared in different environments were plagued by small numbers of cases, methodological difficulties, and, some critics argue, by fraud on the part of one major investigator (Gould, 1981). Much larger and more recent studies, in both Minnesota and Sweden, however, support the argument that the aptitudes that IQ tests measure (as well as personality traits such as extraversion or introversion) contain a substantial inherited component (Scarr and Weinberg, 1983). Identical twins reared apart, for example, are much more likely to have similar IQs than siblings reared in the same household and, indeed, rather more similar scores than fraternal twins who were not separated at birth. Adoption studies, while clearly indicating the powerful effects of earlier childhood environments, also support the conclusion that heredity is significant. The IQ of most adoptive children falls between the IQ of their biological parents and that of their adoptive parents (Scarr and Weinberg, 1976), with some evidence suggesting

that over time IQ scores increasingly resembled those of their biological parents (Weinberg et al., 1992). Thus while adoption studies and twin studies demonstrate that early childhood environments are crucially important in the development of the abilities that the tests measure, they are clearly inconsistent with the argument that became popular in the 1960s and 1970s: that hereditary or constitutional factors play no significant role (Kamin, 1974).

There is also some evidence that the critics have overstated the degree to which IQ scores can readily be modified after the first few years of life. During the 1960s and 1970s many educators and psychologists were highly optimistic that scores on tests of cognitive ability could be raised by educational intervention, most notably in the form of Head Start educational programs for disadvantaged children. This optimism was also reflected in changing admission policies of many colleges and universities. Special counseling programs and remedial classes could enable students whose test scores fell below the minimum required for conventional admission to compete on equal terms with other students. The evidence is hardly clear-cut on these questions—intensive Head Start programs have raised IQ and school performance significantly, many students who would not have qualified for college admission have now successfully completed college—but it is also apparent that there are dangers of overconfidence in these respects. The long-term studies of Head Start programs do not show that in most cases, IQ scores are substantially raised, in part perhaps because these programs do not change the early home environment, which deeply affects the child's development (Garber, 1988). Research on students admitted under special admission policies to 4-year colleges indicate that the great majority do not graduate within 6 years (Traub, 1994). Scores on IQ tests and other related tests of aptitude and cognitive ability are hardly set in concrete, as psychologists of the 1920s and 1930s believed, but neither are they so readily malleable as many critics, and one might add commercial test preparation firms, assert.

If progress has been made in our understanding of these issues, fundamental questions about IQ remain not only unanswered, but nowhere close to resolution. What exactly do IQ tests measure? Why are they good predictors of success in school, and to a lesser degree, predictors of success in on-the-job performance? Do they predict because they tap a common core of abilities that can be reasonably called "intelligence" among humans? Or is it rather the case that the aptitudes measured by IQ tests are essentially culture bound—highly useful perhaps within modern industrial societies but not particularly significant outside that small proportion of human cultures? Perhaps the greatest disservice of the classical tradition is that from its beginnings it has identified IQ tests not only with abilities needed for school success (which they predict rather well), but with a quality that all humans, and to some degree, other animals possess: intelligence. Finding water in a desert, remembering the names of tribal ancestors, or steering a canoe to a small island across a thousand miles of ocean are all activities that require what most of us would term intelligence. And no doubt there are considerable variations among individuals in their aptitudes for these tests—aptitudes that if measured might well have a normal distribution or bell-shaped curve. Few would argue, however, that IQ tests tap these kinds of ability. In the absence of neurological evidence of differences in brain functioning that can be paralleled by differences in performance on IQ tests, therefore (but see Jensen, 1993), it seems premature to conclude that IQ refers to a common core of abilities that is highly significant in *any* human society, and that, though clearly shaped by early environments, is substantially inherited. Perhaps, someday, such a common core will be identified. But it seems presumptuous, in the present state of our knowledge, to argue that current IQ tests measure it, if it indeed exists. And although this is not an argument for the abolition of IQ tests, which are, by common consent, useful tools in predicting success in schools, it is an argument against the implication of the first word of the phrase "intelligence quotient": that these tests measure not *one* among *many* forms of human ability but general intelligence (Gardner, 1983).

REFERENCES[1]

Brigham, C. C. 1923. *A Study of American Intelligence.* Princeton, NJ: Princeton University Press.

Garber, H. L. 1988. *The Milwaukee Project: Preventing Mental Retardation in Children at Risk.* Washington, DC: American Association on Mental Retardation.

*Gould, S. J. 1981. *The Mismeasure of Man.* New York: W. W. Norton.

Herrnstein, R. J. 1971. "IQ." *Atlantic Monthly* (September): 43–64.

*Herrnstein, Richard J., and Charles Murray. 1994. *The Bell Curve.* New York: Free Press.

*Jensen, A. R. 1980. *Bias in Mental Testing.* New York: Free Press.

———. 1993. "Spearman's Hypothesis Tested with Chronometric Information-Processing Tasks." *Intelligence* 17: 44–77.

*Kamin, L. 1974. *The Science and Politics of IQ.* Hillsdale, NJ: Lawrence Erlbaum Associates.

Klitgaard, R. 1985. *Choosing Elites: Selecting "The Best and the Brightest" at Top Universities and Elsewhere.* New York: Basic Books.

Patterson, P. O. 1989. "Employment Testing and Title VII of the Civil Rights Act of 1964." In B. R. Gifford (ed.), *Test Policy and the Politics of Opportunity Allocation: The Workplace and the Law.* Boston: Kluwer Academic Publishers.

Scarr, S., and R. A. Weinberg. 1976. "IQ Test Performance of Black Children Adopted by White Families." *American Sociological Review* 31:726–739.

*———. 1983. "The Minnesota Adoption Studies: Genetic Differences and Malleability." *Child Development* 54: 260–267.

Terman, L. M., and M. H. Oden. 1947. *The Gifted Child Grows Up: Twenty-Five Years' Follow-up of a Superior Group. Genetic Studies of Genius,* Vol. 4. Stanford, CA: Stanford University Press.

Traub, J. 1994. *City on a Hill.* Reading, MA: Addison-Wesley.

Weinberg, R. A., S. Scarr, and I. D. Waldman. 1992. "The Minnesota Transracial Adoption Study: A Follow-up of IQ Test Performance at Adolescence." *Intelligence* 16: 117–135.

[1] Items marked with an asterisk are recommended for further reading.

LONGITUDINAL STUDIES

AN INTRODUCTION: OPENING THE BLACK BOX

Kathryn S. Schiller
University of Notre Dame

One of the major goals of sociology of education is the understanding of "how schools work." That is to understand what happens to children when they enter the school system that produces learning and socialization. What is the process through which children learn the academic and social skills they will use as adults? What aspects of this process produce the differences between students that lead to social stratification? These questions suggest that schooling is a process. Yet getting a feel for how this process works is often difficult.

One frequent technique used by researchers to explore the schooling process is following students' educational careers over a period of time. In this way, changes in students can be linked to their experiences in schools. These studies are sometimes described as "opening the black box" of schooling. Studies failing to open the black box describe students as entering schools with certain characteristics and exiting with certain skills or knowledge. But what produces those changes is obscured within the black box of the school. Longitudinal studies open this black box and peer inside to watch students as they move through the system.

This chapter provides an introduction to longitudinal studies as they are used in the sociology of education. It briefly describes the characteristics of longitudinal studies before discussing the contributions of a few of these studies to the sociology of education. Insights provided by these studies are vital pieces in our understanding of how the schooling process works.

What Are Longitudinal Studies?

Much of sociological research focuses on relationships between variables at a particular point in time. These "cross-sectional" studies essentially provide a snapshot of the social world at a particular time. Returning to the black box metaphor, cross-sectional studies briefly illuminate the box to provide a static picture of relationships at a particular point in time. Depending on the type of study, this picture may be a very detailed case study or a broad national study.

But, because the data relate to only one point in time, researchers using cross-sectional studies have difficulties establishing that one factor "caused" another. Causality implies one factor or event produced changes in a particular outcome at a later point in time. In scientific research, the strongest causal arguments must show the following three relationships between measures of the cause and effect: (1) *association* or showing the two variables are related to each other; (2) *nonspuriousness* or the relationship is not caused by a third variable; and (3) *direction* or the association is not reciprocal. Cross-sectional analyses can easily show association and nonspuriousness, but often fail to establish direction because of a classic "chicken or egg" dilemma—which came first, the supposed "cause" or "effect"?

One good example of this "chicken or egg" problem might be a study of first grade ability grouping that shows a clear association between ability group level and achievement test scores, with those in higher groups having higher scores. This result might hold even when students' family backgrounds are taken into account, indicating the results are not spurious. But conclusions based on results of cross-sectional studies about whether ability grouping "causes" the difference in test scores are tentative at best. One reason for this is that information on what led up to students being placed in particular groups, including how well they were doing in school, is usually missing from cross-sectional data sets. It could be that achievement level may cause ability group placement rather than the other way around. Without exploring this and other related questions, statements that ability grouping causes differences in achievement are difficult to support.

Longitudinal studies are essentially a series of cross-sectional studies performed at different times that are linked in one of two ways: either by referring to the same population or by using the same participants (see Menard, 1991, for a more detailed review of longitudinal research techniques and analysis). The first are called "trend" studies and show differences in similar populations in different years. These studies show trends or changes in the distribution of particular characteristics of interest over time. For example, analysis of data from the Current Population Surveys (which is collected twice a year) indicates that college enrollment rates for 18- to 24-year-old African Americans dropped sharply between 1977 and 1982 while the rates for whites in the same age group increased steadily (Mare, 1993). This type of analysis is frequently used in demography and economics to describe changes in populations over time. They are not as common in the study of educational systems and the schooling process.

"Panel" studies, the second type of longitudinal studies, are more useful for answering questions about how the schooling process works. These studies consist of a panel of respondents who participate in an initial study (usually called the "base year") and later studies (usually called "follow-ups") at given intervals of time. The base year studies provide a baseline that can be compared to data collected in the follow-ups to see how participants have changed over time and what factors may be related to those changes.

Returning to the example of first grade ability grouping and achievement, information from a panel study can show that students in high-ability groups have greater *growth rates* than those in lower ability

groups. With these data, statistical techniques can be used to compare the expected growth rates of two hypothetical students who start first grade with similar academic skills but are placed in different groups. Results showing that the students' growth rates are different (e.g., the high-ability group student gains or learns more than the low-ability group student) help support the argument that ability grouping "causes" differences in achievement, since the change in achievement occurred after the ability group placements. This is something cross-sectional data usually cannot show.

This is not to say that longitudinal panel studies do not have their own set of problems. Most of these problems arise from the fact that longitudinal studies are usually expensive (just multiply the cost of a cross-sectional study by the number of follow-ups) and time consuming. The researcher must track down and gather information from the same participants several times, often several years apart. In the process, a proportion of the base year sample is lost due to difficulties in locating respondents or respondents who refuse to continue to participate. However, the rich information longitudinal studies provide is invaluable in demonstrating causal relationships and describing the dynamic aspects of the schooling process. Five examples of longitudinal studies are used in this chapter to illustrate the usefulness of these types of studies.

An Early Longitudinal Study: The Wisconsin Status Attainment Models

The first major educational study involving longitudinal data was conducted to illuminate the process through which a father's occupational status is transferred to a son. Earlier cross-sectional studies had shown a clear similarity between what a father and his son earn and the types of jobs they hold. Results from these studies also indicated that one piece of the puzzle is the amount of education a son attains. Sons of higher status fathers achieved higher levels of education, which translates into higher status jobs and incomes. The "Wisconsin Study" was designed to determine the process through which fathers' occupation affected sons' educational attainment by examining factors that influenced sons' educational aspirations (Sewell et al., 1969).

The study began with a sample of Wisconsin high

school seniors in 1957, who were asked about their high school class, their and their friends' educational aspirations, whether their parents and teachers encouraged them to go to college, and their fathers' occupations and earnings. Seven years later, the participants were again surveyed about their educational and their job histories, including salaries, since graduation from high school.

With information gathered from study participants as high school seniors and seven years later, Sewell and his colleagues developed a social-psychological model of socioeconomic achievement (Sewell and Hauser, 1975). The longitudinal data allowed these researchers to measure the son's educational aspirations as seniors and then compare the educational and occupational attainment seven years later of those with higher or lower aspirations. Using the finding that sons of fathers with higher occupational levels had higher aspirations and also attainment, Sewell and his colleagues were able to argue that a son's aspirations mediate between the father's and son's occupations.

Although the Wisconsin studies and other studies similar to it (e.g., Alexander et al., 1975) suggested that students' experiences in school influence their life after graduation, these studies only began to crack the "black box." Their data indicated that how well a son did academically, their friends' aspirations, and encouragement received from teachers were related to a son's aspirations. What they did not explore were the processes through which schools influence students' academic performance and the formation of peer networks. Longitudinal studies conducted in the decades following the Wisconsin studies started to produce answers to those questions.

Estimating the Effects of Schooling and Summer Learning

During the 1970s the number of longitudinal studies concerning education began to increase. Many of these, such as the National Longitudinal Study of 1972 (NLS-72), built off the Wisconsin studies and were designed to trace the effects of schooling on individuals' work careers. One study in particular laid the foundation for using longitudinal studies to explore the schooling process. This study was influenced by results from cross-sectional studies conducted in the 1950s and 1960s indicating that differences in family characteristics

were the main determinant of students' educational achievement. The implication many drew from this finding was that "schools did not matter." Using an innovative longitudinal study design, Barbara Heyns (1978) set out to explore the relative influence of school and family on students' educational achievement.

Heyns' study followed a sample of 3,000 sixth and seventh graders in 42 public schools in Atlanta, Georgia. Students were given achievement tests in the fall and spring of the 1971–1972 school year, and then again in the following fall. This meant that how much students had learned was measured at the beginning and end of a school year, and the beginning and end of a summer. This created a "natural experiment" that allowed comparisons of changes in students' achievement both while they were in school (the academic term) when both family and school factors influence achievement, and while they were out of school (summer) when only family characteristics primarily affect achievement.

The analysis of the longitudinal data showed that (1) students learned more during the school year than the summer, (2) differences in average achievement among socioeconomic and racial groups remained fairly stable across the school year, and (3) differences between socioeconomic and racial groups increased over the summer. From this, Heyns concluded that attending school mitigates against, or helps reduce, differences between students based on their social backgrounds. Thus, she was able to show that "schools matter." Again, though, the black box was only cracked since Heyns' study did not show what happened in schools that reduced differences among students created by their family backgrounds. Studies in the following two decades would widen the crack substantially.

Longitudinal Studies of the 1980s

Concerns about what goes on in school to create or reduce social stratification were one of the major driving forces behind several major longitudinal studies conducted in the 1980s and 1990s. These studies and the resulting publications are too extensive to be discussed in this chapter, so instead three will be used to illustrate how these longitudinal studies have helped to "open the black box" of schooling. These three studies are an analysis of the educational careers of a British birth cohort over 23 years (Kerckhoff, 1993), a comparison of the educational experiences and academic achievement of public and private high school students (Coleman and Hoffer, 1987), and a study of the effect of failing a grade on the educational careers and achievement of a cohort of first graders in Baltimore (Alexander et al., 1994).

Using a British Birth Cohort to Show Institutional Inertia

In contrast with Heyns, Alan Kerckhoff used a study of a British birth cohort to show how schools create differences between students through the consistency over time of students' placements within the educational stratification system (e.g., high and low ability groups for instruction). The tendency for students to follow the "high or low road" through their educational careers is a reflection of "institutional inertia," which results from schools' apparent reliance on students' past placements in making decisions about current or future placements.

Kerckhoff's research uses the National Child Development Study (NCDS) that follows a cohort born in Great Britain during one week in 1958. (The original data were collected to explore factors relating to infant mortality.) Additional data were collected in 1965 when most of the cohort were in their second year of school, in 1969 just before most would be making the transition to high school, in 1974, which was the last year of compulsory schooling for most, in 1978 as 20 year olds, and in 1981 when most were in the workforce for several years. The study began with data on 98.2 percent of the 17,733 children born during the designated week; however, by the final data collection in 1981 information was gathered from only 77.1% of the surviving 15,712 23 year olds.

This illustrates one of the main problems with longitudinal studies: the attrition of cases from the sample due not only to death or leaving the country, but also to the refusal of some respondents to continue to participate and simply losing track of others. In the case of NCDS, the number of survivors from whom data could not be collected rose from 1,392 in 1965 to 3,591 in 1981. Sample attrition is a problem because it raises questions about how representative the sample is of the population from which it is drawn. If the sample is not representative, then erroneous or inaccurate conclusions about the population may be made

from results based on information provided by the nonrepresentative sample. Concerned that participants from low-status or unstable backgrounds were most likely to be lost from the sample, Kerckhoff made efforts to take this trend into account in his analysis. Because doing so did not seem to change his results substantively, it increased confidence that his findings reflect trends in the population.

Although sample attrition is a drawback of longitudinal study, having information from more than one point in time makes up for this problem in most cases. In Kerckhoff's case, having information that spanned individuals' entire educational careers allowed him to study how what happens early in their school careers can affect their lives later in school and beyond. For example, he found a general tendency for those students in low-ability groups in junior school (elementary school in the United States) to be in low-ability groups in high school and to be unlikely to attend postsecondary schools. Conversely, those who were in high-ability groups in junior school had a strong tendency to attend elite high schools or be in high-ability groups in comprehensive high schools, and to attend a university. Kerckhoff ends his analysis by illustrating how the advantages and disadvantages of a students' position and consistent placements within the educational structure result in increasingly divergent outcomes for students. Thus, longitudinal data allowed Kerckhoff to explore the unfolding of students' educational careers and institutional factors that influence them.

The next two studies use longitudinal data spanning shorter periods of time (2 to 8 years) to explore a particular aspect of students' educational careers: attendance at a public or Catholic school, and the effects of failing a grade on students' later self-esteem and success in school. In both cases longitudinal data helped to partially overcome problems with prior research.

Differences between Students' Success in Catholic and Public High Schools

The debate over the benefits of private over public schools became heated in the 1980s as questions were raised about the quality of American public schools. One major contribution to this debate was analysis by James Coleman et al. (1982) using the base year information from High School & Beyond (HS&B), a nationally representative data set of 58,270 high school sophomores and seniors collected in 1980. Using this cross-sectional data, their results were generally favorable for private, especially Catholic, schools. Even taking into account differences in their social backgrounds, students in Catholic schools tended to take more advanced classes, received higher test scores, and were more likely to plan to attend college than students in public high schools. Based on these results, Coleman and his colleagues argued that Catholic schools were more effective at producing higher levels of achievement than public schools.

One of the major criticisms of the study of Coleman et al. was that cross-sectional data did not allow them to adequately account for unmeasured differences in the types of students who would choose to attend a private school rather than a public one. For example, the admissions requirements for private schools may eliminate or discourage low achievers, thus making comparisons to the average public school student inappropriate due to selection bias. After the HS&B first follow-up data were collected for the sophomores as seniors in 1982, Coleman and Hoffer (1987) were able to at least partially address the issue of differences in students' earlier achievement levels due to selection bias related to initial achievement levels. Instead of examining levels of achievement, Coleman and Hoffer compared differences in relative achievement growth between Catholic and public high school students over 2 years (tenth to twelfth grades). Using these data, they could compare two hypothetical students who shared the same sophomore test scores and social backgrounds as an average public school student, but one attended a public high school and the other a Catholic high school. The results from this hypothetical experiment indicated that the Catholic high school senior would be expected to gain the equivalent of almost an additional year of achievement in reading and mathematics (based on the average growth of public school students) over the theoretically identical public high school student. Although Coleman and Hoffer did not silence critics concerned about selection bias, being able to replicate their results from cross-sectional data using longitudinal data strengthened their argument that attending Catholic high schools caused students to learn more than similar students in public high schools.

This analysis along with others concerning differences in dropout and college attendance rates, and the achievement of students who changed school sectors (e.g., moved from a private to a public school), reinforced Coleman's earlier arguments that Catholic schools are more effective at encouraging higher achievement than public schools. Although not based on evidence from longitudinal data, Coleman argues that the type of social community surrounding Catholic schools encourages students to work harder and aspire to postsecondary education.

The Positive and Negative Effects of Repeating a Grade

The last study discussed here also tackles a sensitive topic for many educational researchers, the practice of having students repeat grade levels. Those supporting the practice argue that it is necessary to help students who are struggling academically by giving them a second opportunity to learn the material they failed to master. Those opposing the practice counter that the practice amounts to institutionalized discrimination since socially disadvantaged (i.e., minorities and poor) students are most likely to experience academic difficulties. The concern of these researchers is that retained students are labeled as failures, suffer social and psychological difficulties, and are denied equal access to opportunities for learning. Conflicting and contradictory research on the effects of retention means that each side of the debate has a body of research it uses to support its argument.

Alexander et al. (1994) entered the debate in an effort to clarify the research on the effects of retention. They used the Beginning School Study (BBS), which follows a sample of 470 first graders for 8 years in the Baltimore public schools. As with Kerckhoff's study, sample attrition was a problem with BBS. The base year started with a sample of almost 800 first graders; of these only 60% remained at the end of 8 years. This again illustrates one of the major difficulties with longitudinal studies in that the sample may lose its representativeness as members cannot be located or refuse to continue to participate. Yet the information concerning the school careers of the remaining students provides important insights into the schooling process.

Preliminary analysis of BBS showed that at the end of 8 years, about 36% of students were one or more grades behind the other students in their age cohort (those who were in first grade at the same time). By

408

EDUCATION AND SOCIOLOGY

comparing retained students to those who started school at the same time (year when entered first grade) or who had completed the same grades (e.g., first, second, or third), Alexander and his colleagues were able to describe the patterns of achievement and classroom behavior leading up to students being retained and its effects on their subsequent achievement and school careers. From their results, Alexander and his colleagues describe the severe academic difficulties experienced by students at risk of being held back as the "backdrop of retention." Students with the most serious difficulties are most likely to be held back in the early grades, especially first grade, but those who are retained in higher grades often appeared to be on downward trends that led to their finally failing a grade. Alexander's results pertaining to the effectiveness of retention were mixed, but contained strong indications that the downward trends of students were at least stopped, although retainees rarely caught up with the rest of their age cohort or performed at an average level for their grade. They conclude that "retention calls attention to children's problems, but it neither causes them, nor, as best we can determine, compounds them" (p. 223).

Summary

The purpose of this chapter was to illustrate the usefulness of longitudinal studies for understanding schooling as a process that takes place over time. Longitudinal studies are able to accomplish this because they allow plotting of changes in students as they progress through the school system. Each of the five studies just discussed provides a piece of the puzzle hidden in the "black box." The Wisconsin studies showed how sons' aspirations are the mechanisms through which fathers' education and occupation are translated into similar education levels and occupations for sons. By comparing changes in student achievement during the school year and summer, Heyns' analysis suggested that schools helped to reduce differences between students created by variations in family backgrounds. The last three studies focused on students experiences in schools—consistency of placements in ability groups or institutional inertia, advantages of private over pub-

lic schools, and "the success of failure." What all of these studies suggest is that schooling is a complex process that we are just beginning to understand.

For those readers interested in exploring the power of analyses of longitudinal data, several data sets are publicly available through the United States Department of Education. Two major data sets for plotting trends in education are the National Assessment of Educational Progress (NAEP), which contains information on student achievement nationwide, and the Current Population Survey (CPS), which plots changes in enrollment. In addition to HS&B that Coleman and Hoffer analyzed, the National Education Longitudinal Study of 1988 (NELS:88) is another panel study that started with eighth graders in 1988 and includes follow-ups every 2 years until 1994.

REFERENCES

Alexander, Karl L., Bruce K. Eckland, and Larry J. Griffin. 1975. "The Wisconsin Model of Socioeconomic Achievement: A Replication." *American Journal of Sociology* 81:324–342.

Alexander, Karl L., Doris R. Entwisle, and Susan L. Dauber. 1994. *On The Success of Failure: A Reassessment of the Effects of Retention in the Primary Grades.* New York: Cambridge University Press.

Coleman, James S., and Thomas Hoffer. 1987. *Public and Private High Schools: The Impact of Communities.* New York: Basic Books.

Coleman, James S., Thomas Hoffer, and Sally Kilgore. 1982. *High School Achievement.* New York: Basic Books.

Hauser, Robert M. 1993. "The Decline in College Entry among African Americans: Findings in Search of Explanations." In Sniderman, Tetlock and Carmines (eds.). *Prejudice, Politics, and the American Dilemma.* Stanford, CA: Stanford University Press.

Heyns, Barbara. 1978. *Summer Learning and the Effects of Schooling.* New York: Academic Press.

Kerckhoff, Alan C. 1993. *Diverging Pathways: Social Structure and Career Deflections.* New York: Cambridge University Press.

Menard, Scott. 1991. *Longitudinal Research.* Newbury Park, CA: Sage.

Sewell, W. H., and R. M. Hauser. 1975. *Education, Occupation, and Earnings: Achievement in Early Career.* New York: Academic Press.

Sewell, W. H., A. O. Haller, and A. Portes. 1969. "The Educational and Early Occupational Attainment Process." *American Sociological Review* 34:82–91.

Longitudinal Studies Data Collection Program

Carl Schmidt
The National Center for Education Statistics

During the period 1972 to 1996, the National Center for Education Statistics (NCES) sponsored five national longitudinal studies that have collected data on the educational experiences of the elementary/secondary and postsecondary students in the United States. These studies are described in this chapter with a focus on their utility for sociological analyses.[1] This review includes a discussion of the goals and objectives of the NCES longitudinal studies and an examination of the various data elements collected, an overview of the elementary/secondary and postsecondary longitudinal studies and their sampling designs, some analytic models applicable to the data sets, and a number of cautions the analyst must take into account when using the data.

Overview

The longitudinal data bases, initially collected by the NCES for the administrative purposes of the education community, are obtained from individual students surveyed repeatedly over time.[2] NCES's longitudinal studies program began in 1972 with the National Longitudinal Survey of 1972 (NLS-72), a cohort of high school seniors. This first longitudinal study was followed by the High School and Beyond (HS&B) series in 1980, a survey beginning with both high school sophomores and seniors.[3] The National Education Longitudinal Study of 1988 (NELS:88), the third in the series, began with eighth-grade students. The Beginning Postsecondary Student survey (BPS)[4] and the Baccalaureate and Beyond Survey (B&B),[5] which followed

---

[1] The longitudinal data series at NCES provide the analyst a readily accessible source of nationally relevant data. Although focused on education issues, because of the breadth and scope of the data and the robustness of the samples, the data can readily be used to achieve a variety of analytic objectives. The range of variables included can be extrapolated for the purposes of examining many theoretically relevant issues not limited to education. The work of Emile Durkheim on suicide is a primary example of the use of public data that were collected for administrative purposes for examining complex theoretical issues. C. Wright Mills (1959) in *The Sociological Imagination* also focuses on the question of using information more broadly.

[2] Data collected about the universe of public elementary and secondary schools from schools, districts, and states as well as data collected about the universe of postsecondary institutions also form longitudinal data bases about aggregate analytic units, although they are not part of the NCES longitudinal studies program. Two data sets fall into this category: the census of elementary/secondary schools and districts—the Common Core of Data (CCD) and the census of postsecondary institutions—the Integrated Postsecondary Education Data System (IPEDS).

[3] The high school sophomores and seniors each formed independent longitudinally surveyed cohorts.

[4] The sample of first time students for this study is derived as a subsample from the National Postsecondary Student Aid Study (NPSAS) of 1990, a cross-sectional study of postsecondary students in the United States. The sample was also augmented to maintain robustness. See Burkheimer et al. (1994), Pratt et al. (1996), and Westat Inc. (1992).

[5] This survey was based on a subsample from the 1993 National Postsecondary Student Aid Study of those students who were expected to complete their undergraduate degree (Westat Inc. 1992).

in 1990 and 1993, respectively, were based on post-secondary cohorts. Planning for the sixth in the series, a study beginning with an early childhood kindergarten cohort, began in 1995.[6]

The three longitudinal surveys of elementary/ secondary students (NLS-72, HS&B, and NELS:88) were designed to collect information from students, with supportive and corroborative data from parents, school administrators, and student records.[7] The National Longitudinal Study of the High School Class of 1972 (NLS-72) base year study, together with the five follow-up surveys, attempted to provide data to allow researchers to study how these transitions evolve. NLS-72 was designed to produce representative data at the national level on the cohort of students who were in the twelfth grade in 1972. NCES initiated a second longitudinal study, High School and Beyond (HS&B), to complement the first. HS&B was designed to collect the same types of data gathered in the NLS-72 study, but with added emphases. Declining test scores and minimum competency testing, the dropout rate, the increased opportunities in secondary school vocational education that opened new vistas for youths attentive to their futures, and anxiety over access to postsecondary and vocational education were contemporary issues HS&B studied with the high school students of 1980. The two studies that preceded NELS:88 (the NLS-72 and HS&B) surveyed high school seniors (and sophomores in HS&B) through high school, postsecondary education, and work and family formation experiences. Taken together, this segment of the longitudinal studies provides not only measures of educational attainment but also rich resources in determining the reasons for and consequences of academic success and failure. NELS:88 was designed to expand on this base of knowledge by following young adolescents starting at an earlier age (eighth grade) and by updating information throughout the 1990s. NELS:88 was designed to provide trend data about critical transitions experienced by young people as they develop, attend school, and embark on their careers. It was also designed to complement and strengthen state and local efforts by furnishing new information on how school policies, teacher practices, and family involvement affect student educational outcomes, i.e., academic achievement, persistence in school, and participation in postsecondary education.

Data in the postsecondary series (BPS and B&B) were designed to complement the high school cohort longitudinal studies and to improve data on participants in postsecondary education. Data for these studies were obtained primarily from students, with supportive and corroborative information obtained from student records. The BPS survey was designed to enhance and expand the scope of information available regarding persistence, progress, and attainment from initial time of entry into postsecondary education through leaving and entering the work force. By starting with a cohort that had already entered postsecondary education, BPS could address issues of persistence, progress, and attainment, as well as issues related to transitions between undergraduate and graduate education and transitions between PSE and work. By following a PSE cohort (rather than a single age elementary or secondary school cohort), BPS could determine the extent, if any, students who start PSE later differ in their progress, persistence, and attainment. Because students who delay entry into PSE have different experiences prior to entry than students who enter immediately after high school, their transitions between levels of education and work may also be different. The Baccalaureate and Beyond Longitudinal Study (B&B), the second in the postsecondary series, provides information concerning education and work experiences after completing the bachelor's degree. B&B provides information on entry into, persistence and progress through, and completion of graduate-level education information not available through follow-ups involving high school cohorts or even college entry cohorts, both of which are restricted in the number who actually complete the bachelor's degree and continue their education.

---

[6] Data from this study are expected to be available in 1998/ 99. See West (1996) and NORC (1996) for a discussion of the study design. The early childhood study will make national data available on public and private kindergarten programs and the children who attend them.

[7] Data were also collected from parents in the HS&B and the NELS:88 surveys. For a comprehensive discussion of the timing of data collection, refer to the User's Manuals associated with each of the studies. The User's Manual for the second follow-up of the NELS:88 survey is particularly useful in this regard in that it provides an overview of the preceding longitudinal surveys. It is widely available in libraries and on CD-ROM.

Substantive Focus of the NCES Longitudinal Studies

In 1972, the major goals of the first NCES longitudinal study, NLS-72, were (1) to collect information on education-related issues relevant for different sociohistorical contexts and (2) to fill gaps in information not obtained by "Project Talent."[8] In brief, the longitudinal studies program focuses on areas such as (1) academic progress, (2) cognitive growth, (3) school transition, (4) school effectiveness, (5) dropping out, (6) equity, (7) occupational management, (8) family development, (10) access, and (11) choice,[9] while also making the examination of their relationship possible. In addition, the postsecondary longitudinal studies reflect issues on enrollment, critical transitions between levels of education, persistence, progress, educational attainment, access to graduate and professional schools, and the rate of return on educational investment. Overall, these studies provide a substantial framework of data that readily facilitate the analysis of the critical transitions experienced by young people as they attend school, embark on careers, and develop families. A vast array of noneducation issues can also be addressed using these data sets.

When feasible, demographic information is collected from students, their parents, their teachers, and the school(s) the students attended. The information collected includes "objective" phenomena such as age, race/ethnicity, family income, education, and occupation. Personal and family attributes, influences from peer groups and family members and schools, and student aid are among the many additional factors that can be examined in terms of education outcomes (or achievement in more general terms). Information on attitudes, retrospective behavior based on present evaluation, and estimates about future behavior were used in a limited way because of the unverifiability of such data and the limited survey space and time.

The Foundations of Longitudinal Studies at the National Center for Education Statistics

The underpinnings of the National Education Longitudinal Studies (NELS) program at NCES are imbedded in what has been referred to as the "pluralistic policy research" orientation.[10] According to Coleman, pluralistic policy research is intended to inform a broad range of interests on all sides of policy issues. Data collected with these premises should be broadly accessible and serve diverse parties having an interest in the subject. Therefore, the development of such data requires the incorporation of a broad spectrum of issues and outcomes reflecting the interests of diverse groups.[11]

Accordingly, the NCES longitudinal studies were not designed to examine specific policies, but rather to provide information about many policy areas. These studies were designed in part with a policy focus and also with a more generalized focus on issues pertinent to the process of educating the American population. That is, with these studies, it would be possible to evaluate diverse aspects of policy and also to examine antecedents to various conditions. These studies, thereby, could inform the policy development process about problem areas and also the academic community engaged in research about the education process.

The remainder of this chapter first discusses the elementary/secondary longitudinal studies and then the postsecondary longitudinal studies. These two sections are followed by a separate discussion of some of the analytic designs that could be applied.

Elementary/Secondary Longitudinal Studies: Follow-up Survey Cycles and Sampling Designs

Between 1972 and the present (1996), the National Center for Education Statistics designed and collected data from three surveys that began with cohorts at the elementary/secondary level. The National Longitudinal Study of 1972 (NLS-72), the High School and Beyond

---

[8] Project Talent and the Coleman report on the Equality of Educational Opportunity were one-time surveys. For a discussion of "Project Talent" see Flanagan et al. (1960, 1964, 1966), Shaycoft (1963, 1967). The early work by Coleman, (1966) on the equality of educational opportunity was also a major impetus to the NCES longitudinal studies.

[9] Access and choice are issues on which the postsecondary focused.

[10] Coleman (1974).

[11] For a more comprehensive discussion of types of research, see Coleman (1972), Coleman et al. (1979), and Cronbach and Suppes (1969).

(HS&B) studies, and the NELS:88 are considered to be multipurpose policy studies, addressing issues that are pertinent to policy on students in high school and post-high school, and on the course of life. The NLS-72 survey started in the spring of 1972 with a cohort of high school seniors who were followed up five times until 1986—a span of 14 years. The data are from 1,069 participating base-year schools with twelfth graders, yielding an initial sample of 19,000 students. The sample for the first follow-up survey was augmented to include students from supplemental schools, yielding a total sample of 22,654 students. Students in the fifth follow-up survey were subsampled from the students in the fourth follow-up to maintain statistical viability.[12]

Since this first study, NCES undertook two additional longitudinal studies that also focused on elementary/secondary education cohorts: High School and Beyond (HS&B—High school seniors and sophomores in 1980), and the National Education Longitudinal Study of 1988 (NELS:88—eighth-grade students in 1988).

The survey of the 1980 seniors was designed to elaborate information obtained from the NLS-72 high school seniors. The survey of the 1980 sophomores was designed to capture information about students prior to high school completion and to include those who might drop out prior to completion. Both sophomores and seniors were surveyed four times, biennially, until 1986. The sophomore cohort was surveyed one additional time in 1992, 10 years after scheduled high school graduation. The HS&B[13] data are from a sample of 28,240 senior and 30,030 sophomore students enrolled at the 1,015 participating base-year high schools. Both cohorts were also subsampled in later follow-up surveys.

The NELS:88 survey of the eighth graders followed in the same tradition as the two predecessors with respect to the information gathered. The eighth-grade cohort was surveyed four times biennially, beginning in 1988. The NELS:88 base-year data are from a sample of 24,599 eighth-grade students at 1,052 participating schools. The sample was freshened during the first (1990) and the second follow-up (1992) surveys so that generalization may also be made to the 1990 and the 1992 high school cohorts—not only to the eighth-grade cohort in 1990 and 1992.

Sampling Design of the Elementary/ Secondary Surveys

Overall, the sampling designs for elementary/secondary longitudinal studies are essentially similar in that they are multistaged probability samples. In the base year, students were selected through a two-stage stratified probability sample, with schools as the first units and students within schools as the second-stage units. In NLS-72, all baseline sample members were spring-term 1972 high school seniors. In High School and Beyond, all members of the student sample were spring term 1980 sophomores or seniors,[14] as were all members of the NELS:88 eighth-grader cohort.[15]

Despite the fundamental similarity of the base-year designs, there were some differences in school and subgroup sampling and over sampling strategies across NLS-72, HS&B, and NELS:88.[16] NLS-72 was designed to provide data on one cohort over time—the high school seniors. HS&B, was designed to provide data on two separate cohorts—a representative sample of 1980 sophomores and a representative sample of 1980 seniors. NELS:88 was designed to provide data using a representative sample of 1988 eighth graders, a further

---

[12] See Riccobono et al. (1981:21). See also Tourangeau, et al. (1987).

[13] For a detailed discussion of the High School and Beyond samples see Frankel et al. (1981), Calvin Jones et al. (1993), and Tourangeau et al. (1983).

[14] The HS&B 1980 sophomore and senior samples are fully in-school representative, but the HS&B sophomore 1982 (first follow-up) sample is not, because transfers into the school had no chance of being selected into the sample.

[15] See Spencer et al. (1990), NCES 90–463.

[16] An important difference that may have some consequences for comparability but little effect on analytic strategies involves student sample replacement strategies. NLS-72, unlike HS&B and NELS:88, permitted replacement of non-cooperating students under certain circumstances. Although HS&B and NELS:88 made no attempt to replace students who refused to be part of the survey, HS&B did permit, but NELS:88 did not, replacement of selected students who subsequently died, were discovered to have been listed in error, or who dropped out of school after selection but prior to the survey session. HS&B and NELS:88 also conducted a sample update to accommodate transfers into the baseline schools between the sample selection and data collection phases of the studies.

representative sample of 1990 sophomores, and finally a representative sample of 1992 seniors. In the High School and Beyond first follow-up, students were not added to the original sample (that is, the 1980 sophomore cohort sample was not freshened in 1982 with seniors who had not been sophomores 2 years before and who therefore had no chance of selection into the HS&B baseline). However, in NELS:88, because of the desire to provide sample representatives at three distinct points in time, new students entered the study at tenth grade through two routes: sample freshening (addition of 1990 tenth graders who were not 1988 eighth graders or who were not in the United States in 1988) and change of eligibility status. Furthermore, because NELS:88 began at eighth grade, its follow-ups encompass (like the HS&B sophomore cohort) students, both in the modal grade progression sequence, students out of sequence, and dropouts. Such differences and similarities are documented in detail in the various sampling, technical, and comparative analysis reports associated with each study.

Postsecondary Longitudinal Studies: Follow-up Survey Cycles and Sampling Designs

NCES began the series of postsecondary longitudinal studies in 1993 with the Beginning Postsecondary Student (BPS) survey series and expanded this series in 1995 with the Baccalaureate and Beyond (B&B) study. These studies marked a departure from the elementary/secondary longitudinal studies in several respects. First, they began with a postsecondary cohort. A second difference is that the initial cohort for each was selected from the students in the sample of the cross-sectional survey—the National Postsecondary Student Aid Study (NPSAS).[17] For example, the 1990 NPSAS served as the base year for the first BPS while the 1993 NPSAS cohort served as the basis for selecting the B&B seniors surveyed in 1995. The third departure was the periodicity of the studies. New cohorts are planned to begin every 6 years, while follow-ups are planned to

take place biennially. A fourth departure is that a broad range of "nontraditional" students was included in the surveys.[18] The beginning postsecondary students were included, regardless of the time of completion of secondary school. Those sampled for the B&B survey were included regardless of the amount of academic delay experienced since beginning postsecondary education or since completing the secondary program.

Sampling Design of the Postsecondary Surveys

The sample for the first BPS survey consisted of students beginning their postsecondary education between July 1989 and June 1990. This sample included a subset of interview respondents in the full-scale NPSAS:90 survey and covered all sectors of postsecondary education and all students enrolled in those sectors during the 1989/90 school year. A total of 7,932 full-time beginning students were included in the final BPS sample from 1,092 BPS relevant institutions included in the NPSAS:90 sample.[19] This group of students was first followed up in 1993–1994. Four additional follow-ups are planned. The BPS survey is differentiated in that it provides data generalizable to the college cohort of academic year 1993 in all fields of study throughout the 50 states, the District of Columbia, and Puerto Rico.[20]

The first B&B sample of baccalaureate degree graduates includes those students in the NPSAS:93 sample who were identified by the institution or during the student interview as having completed a bachelor's degree in the 1992–1993 academic year (July 1, 1992 through June 30, 1993). All NPSAS:93 sample persons who satisfied the subsample requirements were included in the B&B sample regardless of whether these persons were

---

[17] One important factor associated with the NPSAS studies is that they are based on student samples drawn throughout the academic year. Hence, students who began their postsecondary education later in the academic year or who were intermittent students could be included if not present at the time of the initial sampling.

[18] Each of the elementary/secondary studies enables an examination of nontraditional postsecondary students, but does not permit generalization to the postsecondary population. They, however, complement the postsecondary studies by providing insights into the antecedent conditions leading to nontraditional student status.

[19] The baseline NPSAS:90 survey was drawn over multiple time segments (a fall and non-fall sample) to capture enrollments throughout the year. For a comprehensive discussion of the NPSAS:90 sample, see Shepherd (1991). For more detailed discussion of the BPS sample structure, see Burkheimer et al. (1994).

[20] See Burkheimer et al. (1994).

respondents in NPSAS:93. A total of approximately 11,000 students from about 1,200 postsecondary institutions were included in the B&B sample.[21]

Analytical Designs and the National Longitudinal Studies Data

The methodology and the foci of the NCES longitudinal data sets and the time cycles in which they were collected enable them to be used for both cross-sectional and longitudinal analyses of the given cohorts. Within the scope of the study designs, various comparative models, including time series and cross-cohort time-lag comparisons and fixed time comparisons, may also be applied for analysis of students and institutions.[22] The section that follows provides a brief overview of these analytic models.

Comparative Analysis of Longitudinal Cohorts

Time Series and Trend Analyses of Cohorts

Because there are continuities in the sample design and in the time points at which the three elementary/secondary surveys were collected, it is possible for the analyst to use the data to compare trends between cohorts in their educational development in terms of changes in access and choice, persistence, and completion.[23] Further, because the data are based on national probability samples, they can be used for making generalizations that apply to specific national cohorts of students at given periods of time.[24] Although the postsecondary series, BPS and the B&B, focus on issues pertinent to postsecondary education, they also include the data elements found in the elementary/secondary data sets. Furthermore, because the sampling designs applied to the postsecondary surveys differ dramatically from those applied to the elementary/secondary surveys, cohort comparisons are at best difficult. Selected subgroups may be compared, but with standard errors[25] that are difficult to estimate.

1. Cohorts can be compared on an intergenerational or cross-cohort time-lag basis. Both cross-sectional and longitudinal time-lag comparisons are possible. For example, NELS:88 1992 data can be examined cross-sectionally (when restricted to sample members who are seniors) and, therefore, can be regarded as the third in a data series pertinent to twelfth graders. Thus, the status of NELS:88 second follow-up seniors in 1992 can be compared to HS&B base-year seniors in 1980, and to NLS-72 seniors in 1972. Additionally, longitudinal change for NELS:88 1990 sophomores 2 years later (that is, in 1992, when the cohort included both students and dropouts) can be compared to changes

---

[21] For a comprehensive discussion of the sampling design and the sample weights, see the methodology report for the B&B survey (Green et al., 1996).

[22] For more detail, consult Ingels et al. (1994, Appendix D).

[23] There are also two major types of differences between NLS-72, HS&B and NELS:88 that must be taken into account. One difference pertains to the sample and research designs; another pertains to differences in questionnaire or cognitive test content that may affect the possibility of drawing valid comparisons. Data users who are familiar with NLS-72 and HS&B will find that despite the considerable similarity between these studies and NELS:88, there are also significant sample definition and statistical design differences. Analysts intending to compare these cohorts should note these differences. Similarly, although some effort has been made to maintain trend items over time, strict test and questionnaire overlap across the three studies is not considerable.

[24] Because the NELS:88 sample was refreshed, estimates obtained may be pertinent to the originally selected cohort and to the cohort reflected in the refreshed sampling. For example, the NELS:88 data set is relevant to the student's eighth-grade cohort of 1988. Because the sample was refreshed in 1990, when the eighth-grade cohort became sophomores, the estimates are also generalizable to the total high school sophomore population, which is likely to differ from the eighth-grade cohort now high school sophomores.

[25] The impact of departures from simple random sampling on the precision of the sample estimates is often measured by the design effect—the ratio of the design-corrected variance to the variance based on the Simple Random Sampling assumptions. The design effect is defined as the ratio of the variance, corrected for the sampling design, to the variance based on a simple random sample. The variance of the estimate is usually larger than the estimate would be if it were based on a simple random sample. To estimate the variance using information about the sample design, it is necessary to use statistical procedures such as Taylor Series approximations, Balanced Repeated Replication, or Jacknife Repeated Replication. Researchers using the longitudinal data are cautioned to use statistical packages such as SUDAAN or OSIRIS to produce design-corrected standard errors, or to adjust the standard errors produced by typical packages by multiplying them by the mean root design effect for that subgroup. See Green et al. (1996).

measured in 1982 from a 1980 HS&B sophomore base-line.

2. Fixed time comparisons, in which groups within each study are compared to each other at different ages though at the same point in time, are also possible. Thus, for example, NLS-72, HS&B senior cohort and HS&B sophomore cohort sample members could all be compared in 1986, some 14, 8, and 6 years after each respective cohort completed high school. Additionally, employment rates in 1986 of the 22-year-old high school graduates of 1980 HS&B seniors, the 24-year-old high school graduates of the 1982 HS&B seniors, and 32-year-old high school graduates of the 1972 NLS-72 seniors can be examined. The only available fixed-time comparison using NELS:88 data, however, involves contrasting HS&B fourth follow-up of 1992 (the 1982 HS&B seniors) and NELS:88 second follow-up 1992 results. Two different cohort generations are compared for the same year on various issues. For example, the analyst might compare the 1992 educational expectations of the two cohorts to explore how 17–18 year olds differ from 27–28 year olds in this respect. Or one might utilize the 1992 life values responses (questions concerning the importance to the respondent of being successful in work, having lots of money, having strong friendships, and so on) to compare HS&B fourth follow-up sophomore cohort members with NELS:88 second follow-up survey participants.

3. Finally, longitudinal comparative analysis of the cohorts can be performed by modeling the history of the age/grade cohorts. NELS:88 trend comparisons need not, however, be strictly limited to NLS-72 and HS&B student responses from surveys. Comparisons are also possible using transcript data collected for high school seniors, not only for HS&B 1982 graduates and NELS:88 1992 graduates, but also for 1987 and 1990 graduates collected as part of the National Assessment of Educational Progress (NAEP) sampled schools.[26] Other national probability samples as well may provide

comparison points.[27] Also, comparisons noted above, involving use of change data in a time-lag comparison, may be viewed as having a longitudinal dimension. Because of the design of these postsecondary surveys, comparison between the postsecondary cohorts is not feasible. Similarly, meaningful comparisons between the postsecondary cohorts and the elementary/secondary cohort members who participated in postsecondary education are, at best, difficult.

Institution-Level Comparisons

Comparisons are not limited to cohorts of individuals; not just the student samples, but also the baseline school samples of NELS:88, HS&B, and NLS-72 are nationally representative, and considerable data have been collected about school-level characteristics. However, the only natural comparison points are of NLS-72 (1972) and HS&B (1980) high schools, since the NELS:88 base-year school sample was limited to the eighth grade.[28]

Individual-Level Comparisons

Comparisons can be made between selected types and categories of students from the respective surveys. With technical adjustments, comparability can be achieved even when age/grade/stage parallels have not been strictly maintained.[29] The HS&B (sophomore cohort)

---

[26] Care has been exercised in designing and implementing the academic transcript study in NELS:88 to maximize the comparability of NELS:88 transcript data with the high school transcript data for 1987 and 1990 graduating seniors. While an independent high school transcript study was not conducted for NLS-72, course-taking summary information was collected from school records for the 1972 seniors.

[27] For example, major national studies of high school seniors, employing test and survey measures, were conducted in 1960 (Project Talent) and 1965 (the Equality of Educational Opportunity Survey) [see Schrader and Hilton in Hilton (1992) for a discussion of comparability issues]; also, the high school graduating classes of 1975–1993 have been surveyed (and followed up as young adults), a key source of trend data on, in particular, drug use and associated factors. (The study added eighth- and tenth-grade cohorts in 1991.) Items that are strictly comparable across such data sets are, however, uncommon.

[28] However, the 1988 NELS:88 school sample might be compared to other data sets, such as the ongoing series of NCES Schools and Staffing Surveys.

[29] See, for example, the account by T. L. Hilton and J. M. Pollack on estimating postsecondary enrollment change over time using NLS-72 fourth follow-up (conducted more than 7 years after graduation) and HS&B third follow-up (conducted just less than 6 years after high school graduation) data, in Hilton (1992).

in 1980 and NELS:88 in 1990 are nationally representative samples of sophomores; NLS-72 in 1972, HS&B (senior cohort) in 1980, and NELS:88 in 1992 comprise nationally representative samples of seniors. The NELS:88 sample was freshened to make it representative of the nation's sophomores (1990) and seniors (1992). Sample freshening was not conducted in HS&B and, therefore, the sophomore cohort does not constitute a valid probability sample of the nation's 1982 seniors. Nevertheless, the 1982 HS&B sophomore cohort and 1992 NELS:88 can be compared, with caveats.[30] HS&B 1982 seniors can also be compared to 1972 NLS-72 and 1992 NELS:88 seniors, though not without some sample and statistical adjustments.[31] Students from the elementary/secondary cohorts cannot be effectively compared with students from the postsecondary cohorts because they each represent different student universes.

The postsecondary longitudinal studies reflect a departure from the models applied to the elementary/secondary surveys. Both BPS and B&B draw their samples from the student universe provided by the 1990 and the 1993 NPSAS surveys.

Need for Caution in Comparing Data across Cohorts

There is substantial content (and format) overlap across the three elementary/secondary studies with respect to the student questionnaire, cognitive test, and transcript data. Although the content area is often parallel or similar, minor variations in format and questionnaire wording need to be evaluated in order to devise techniques for comparing results across surveys.[32] The available questionnaires and supporting information need to be compared to make an effective judgment about the utility of analyzing any area of interest included in the surveys.[33]

Precise trend estimation faces several challenges: sampling and nonsampling error. Sampling error tends to be more complex for intercohort than for intracohort comparisons, since each survey is based on a complex multistage sampling design with different sampling ratios. Differences in two sample means estimated from independent samples will be a function not only of the real differences in means, but also the sampling errors associated with both measurements. Hence small (but not necessarily unimportant) differences may be harder to detect.

In estimating trends based on results from two or more sample surveys, a number of nonsampling errors also may arise. Differences in instrument format and wording, data collection mode or methodology, are potential sources of nonsampling error. Although the requirements of change measurement dictate that the same measures be repeated in the same way, there are also strong disincentives to holding measures and methodologies constant. The goals, the subject, and the technology of education measurement do not remain static. The educational policy agenda changes over time; the manner and matter of education changes as curriculum content and instructional methods are revised; improvements arise—in survey methodologies, data capture technologies, and measurement techniques—that promise large benefits if implemented. Finally, the instrument design process for NLS-72, HS&B, and NELS:88, in which development of instruments had proceeded through broad consensus of the user community at different points in time, militates against a strongly conservative approach to content, format, and methodology, nor is there any correct or simple way to resolve all tensions between improved measurement and comparable measurement.[34]

---

[30] See, for example, the account by T. L. Hilton and J. M. Pollack on estimating postsecondary enrollment change over time using NLS-72 fourth follow-up (conducted more than 7 years after graduation) and HS&B third follow-up (conducted just less than 6 years after high school graduation) data, in Hilton (1992).

[31] Specifically, out-of-sequence students (nonseniors) and nonstudents (such as dropouts and early graduates) must be removed from the HS&B analysis sample, and an adjustment made for the exclusion of students who were seniors in 1982 but were not part of the HS&B base-year sampling frame, that is, 1982 seniors who were not 1980 sophomores in the United States. A simplifying assumption here would be that in results and characteristics, these out-of-sequence 1982 seniors are essentially similar to the HS&B 1980 sophomores who failed to progress in the model grade sequence.

---

[32] For detailed discussions of item comparability issues for the 1980 and 1990 sophomore data, see Rasinski et al. (1993) and, Ingles et al. (1992, Appendix D).

[33] See Rock et al. (1985b), for details.

[34] Indeed, while in the spring 1972 baseline 16,683 seniors in 1,061 schools completed an NLS-72 student questionnaire, 257 schools that could not (because, for example, their

Though the studies were designed to be as comparable as possible, caution must nonetheless be exercised in comparing NLS-72, HS&B, and NELS:88 data. Student response rates differed and the characteristics of the nonrespondents may also differ across the studies. Although nonresponse adjustments in the weights serve to compensate for nonresponse, no adjustment procedure can do so perfectly. Item response rates for questions that appear in both surveys differ as well. Differences in context and question order and form for trend items in the various student questionnaires; differences in test format, content, and context; and other factors such as differences in data collection methodology may also influence the accuracy of intercohort comparisons. In addition, differences in mode and time of survey administration across the cohorts may have an impact on the response.[35]

NLS-72 and HS&B senior cohort sample members were subjected to their first measurement as seniors, HS&B sophomores were administered their second measurement as seniors, and NELS:88 eighth graders their third. Problems associated with repeated measurements (such as remembering past responses to individual items) are likely to be a difficulty, both because of the sheer number of test and questionnaire items asked and the 2-year intervals between data collections. However, participation in a longitudinal study in theory may influence the survey member's subsequent behavior or attitudes. Because most NELS:88 1992 sample members had also been surveyed as eighth and tenth graders, such "panel effects"[36] are in principle

possible with this group (as with HS&B sophomores 2 years later, in 1982). In contrast, 1972 and 1980 seniors (and 1980 sophomores) were new to NLS-72 or HS&B.

Data Availability

Due to the capacity of contemporary computer technology, all of the longitudinal data sets are now analyzable on desktop computers. Data are available, generally on CD-ROM in public use or restricted use formats. Data that are considered for "restricted use" contain confidential information about the respondent. These data, however, can be obtained by applying to the National Center for Education.

REFERENCES

Bradby, D. 1992. *Language Characteristics and Academic Achievement: A Look at Asian and Hispanic Eighth Graders in NELS:88*. Washington, DC: U.S. Department of Education, Office of Educational Research and Improvement, National Center for Education Statistics. NCES 92–479.

Burkheimer, G. J., Jr., B. H. Forsyth, R. W. Whitmore, J. S. Wine, and K. M. Blackwell. 1994. *Beginning Postsecondary Students Longitudinal First Follow-up BPS 90/92: Final Public Technical Report*. Washington, DC: U.S. Department of Education, Office of Educational Research and Improvement, National Center for Education Statistics. NCES 94–369.

Chubb, John E., and Terry M. Moe. 1990. *Politics, Markets, and America's Schools*. Washington, DC: The Brookings Institute.

Coleman, James S. 1966. "Equality of Educational Opportunity Study (EEOS)" [Computer file]. Conducted by Educational Testing Service. Washington, DC: U.S. Department of Health, Education, and Welfare, Office of Education. Distributed by Inter-university Consortium for Political and Social Research, Ann Arbor, MI.

————. 1972. *Policy Research in the Social Sciences*. Morristown, NJ: General Learning Press.

Coleman, James, et al. 1979. Report to the National Center for Education Statistics. October.

Coleman, J. S., T. Hoffer, and S. Kilgore. 1982. *High School Achievement*. New York: Basic Books.

Dowd, K. L., S. J. Ingels, J. M. Pollack, et al. 1991. *NELS:88 Second Follow-Up Field Test Report*. Chicago: NORC. ERIC ED 335–418.

Ekstrom, R. B., M. E. Goertz, and D. A. Rock. 1988. *Edu-*

---

school year ended earlier in the spring) take part in the base year were added, in accordance with the original design — these seniors had now left their schools but they were asked some retrospective (senior year) questions. Such individuals —who redress possible school frame under coverage bias in the NLS-72 base year—do not appear on the NLS-72 base-year files that would typically be employed for comparisons of high school seniors, although the presence of some retrospective data for these individuals permits refinement of comparisons grounded in 1972 data.

[35] For example, NLS-72 and NELS:88 senior questionnaires applied skip patterns more extensively than in the HS&B survey. Also NELS:88 and HS&B questionnaires were more extensive than the NLS-72 survey. The postsecondary surveys applied cati based phone interviews, making interviewer affect more probable.

[36] Discussions of longitudinal conditioning or panel effects (also known as "time in sample bias" or "panel con-

---

ditioning")—for example, whether strong effects potentially exist or could affect data quality—may be found in Kasprzyk et al. (1989). See especially contributions by B. Bailar, D. Cantor, D. Holt, A. Silberstein and C. Jacobs, L. Corder and D. Horvitz, and J. Waterton and D. Lievesley.

cation and American Youth: The Impact of the High School Experience. London: Falmer Press.

Fetters, W. B., Peter Stowe, and Jeffrey A. Owings. 1984a. Quality of Responses of High School Students to Questionnaire Items. Washington, DC: National Center for Education Statistics.

Fetters, W. B., George H. Brown, and Jeffrey A. Owings. 1984b. High School Seniors: A Comparative Study of the Classes of 1972 and 1980. Washington, DC: National Center for Education Statistics.

Flanagan, J. C., T. J. Dailey, Marion Shaycoft, W. A. Gorham, D. B. Orr, and I. Goldberg. 1960. Designing the Study. Technical Report to the U.S. Office of Education, Cooperative Research Project. Project Talent Office, University of Pittsburgh.

Flanagan, J. C., F. Davis, J. T. Dailey, Marion F. Shaycoft, D. B. Orr, I. Goldberg, and C. A. Neyman, Jr. 1964. The American High School Student. Final Report to the U.S. Office of Education, Cooperative Research Project No. 635. Project Talent Office, University of Pittsburgh.

Flanagan, J. C., W. W. Cooley, P. R. Lohnes, L. F. Schoenfeldt, R. W. Holdeman, Janet Combs, and Susan J Becker. 1966. Project Talent One-Year Follow-up Studies. Final Report to the U.S. Office of Education, Cooperative Research Project No. 2333. Project Talent Office, University of Pittsburgh,

Frankel, M. R., L. Kohnke, D. Buonanno, and R. Tourangeau. 1981. HS&B Base Year (1980) Sample Design Report. Chicago: NORC.

Gerst, Arthur, and J. Trent. 1972. An Analytic Review of the Longitudinal and Related Studies as They Apply to the Educational Process: Preliminary Report, Volume I. Center of the Study of Education, UCLA Graduate School of Education, Los Angeles, CA.

Green, P. J. 1993. High School Seniors Look to the Future, 1972 and 1992. Statistics in Brief Series. Washington, DC: National Center for Education Statistics.

Green, P. J., B. L. Dugoni, S. J. Ingels, and E. Camburn. 1994. A Profile of the American High School Senior in 1992. Washington, DC: U.S. Department of Education, National Center for Education Statistics. NCES 94–384.

Green, P. J., Sharon Myers, Pamela Giese, Joan Law, Howard M. Speizer, and Vicki Staebler Tardino. 1996. Baccalaureate and Beyond Longitudinal Study First Followup: Methodology Report. Washington, DC: U.S. Department of Education, National Center for Education Statistics.

Hafner, A., S. J. Ingels, B. Schneider, and D. L. Stevenson. 1990. A Profile of the American Eighth Grader, June. Washington, DC: U.S. Department of Education, National Center for Education Statistics. NCES 90–458.

Haggerty, Catherine, Bernard Dugoni, Laura Reed, Ann Cederlund, and John Taylor. 1996. National Education Longitudinal Study (NELS:88/94) Methodology Report. Washington, DC: U.S. Department of Education, Office of Educational Research and Improvement, National Center for Education Statistics. NCES 96–174.

Hilton, T. L., ed. 1992. Using National Data Bases in Educational Research. Hillsdale, NJ: Erlbaum.

Hoachlander, E. G. 1991. A Profile of Schools Attended by Eighth Graders in 1988. Washington, DC: National Center for Education Statistics. NCES 91–129.

Horn, L., and A. Hafner. 1992. A Profile of American Eighth-Grade Mathematics and Science Instruction. Washington, DC: National Center for Education Statistics. NCES 92–486.

Horn, L., and West, J. 1992. A Profile of Parents of Eighth Graders. Washington, DC: National Center for Education Statistics. NCES 92–488.

Ingels, S. J., and J. B. Baldridge. 1994. Conducting Trend Analyses: NLS-72, HS&B, and NELS:88 Seniors. Washington, DC: National Center for Education Statistics.

Ingels, S. J., and K. L. Dowd. 1994a. Conducting Trend Analyses: HS&B and NELS:88 Sophomore Cohort Dropouts. Washington, DC: National Center for Education Statistics.

———. 1994b. NELS:88 Second Follow-Up Questionnaire Content Areas and Research Issues. Washington, DC: National Center for Education Statistics. NCES 94–497.

Ingels, S. J., and J. B. Taylor. 1994. Conducting Cross-Cohort Comparisons Using HS&B, NAEP, and NELS:88 Academic Transcript Data. Washington, DC: National Center for Education Statistics.

Ingels, S. J., L. Little, S. Lucas, et al. 1987. NELS:88 Base Year Field Test Report. Chicago: NORC. ERIC ED 289–897.

Ingels, S. J., S. Y. Abraham, R. Kara, B. D. Spencer, and M. R. Frankel. 1990a. NELS:88 Base Year Student Component Data File User's Manual. Washington, DC: National Center for Education Statistics.

Ingels, S. J., K. A. Rasinski, M. R. Frankel, B. D. Spencer, and P. Buckley. 1990b. NELS:88 Base Year Final Technical Report. Chicago: NORC.

Ingels, S. J., L. A. Scott, J. T. Lindmark, M. R. Frankel, and D. Myers. 1992. NELS:88 First Follow-Up Student Component Data File User's Manual. Washington, DC: National Center for Education Statistics.

Ingels, S. J., K. L. Dowd, J. L. Stipe, J. D. Baldridge, V. H. Bartot, and M. R. Frankel. 1993. NELS:88 Second Follow-Up: Dropout Component Data File User's Manual. Washington, DC: National Center for Education Statistics. NCES 93–375.

Ingels, S. J., S. B. Plank, B. Schneider, and L. A. Scott. 1994a. A Profile of the American High School Sophomore in 1990. Washington, DC: National Center for Education Statistics.

Ingels, S. J., L. Thalji, P. Pulliam, V. H. Bartot, and M. R. Frankel. 1994b. NELS:88 Second Follow-Up: Teacher Component Data File User's Manual. Washington, DC: National Center for Education Statistics. NCES 94–379.

———. 1994c. NELS:88 Second Follow-Up: Parent Component Data File User's Manual. Washington, DC: National Center for Education Statistics. NCES 94–378.

———. 1994d. NELS:88 Second Follow-Up: School Com-

ponent Data File User's Manual. Washington, DC: National Center for Education Statistics. NCES 94–376.

Ingels, S. J., K. L. Dowd, J. R. Taylor, V. H. Bartot, and M. R. Frankel. 1994e. *NELS:88 Second Follow-Up: Transcript Component Data File User's Manual*. Washington, DC: National Center for Education Statistics. NCES 94–377.

Ingels, S. J., K. L. Dowd, J. D. Baldridge, J. L. Stipe, V. H. Bartot, and M. R. Frankel. 1994f. *NELS:88 Second Follow-Up: Student Component Data File User's Manual*. Washington, DC: National Center for Education Statistics. NCES 93–374.

Ingels, S. J., K. L. Dowd, J. R. Taylor, M. R. Frankel, and V. H. Bartot. 1994g. *NELS:88 Second Follow-Up Academic Transcript Component Data File User's Manual*. Washington, DC: National Center for Education Statistics.

Ingels, S. J., L. A. Scott, D. A. Rock, J. M. Pollack, and K. A. Rasinski. 1994h. *NELS:88 First Follow-Up Final Technical Report*. Washington, DC: National Center for Education Statistics.

Ingels, S. J., S. Abraham, K. A. Rasinski, R. Kara, B. D. Spencer, and M. R. Frankel. *NELS:88 Base Year Data File User's Manual*. Washington, DC: National Center for Education Statistics.

Jones, C., S. Knight, M. Butz, I. Crawford, and B. Stephenson. 1983. *High School and Beyond Transcript Survey (1982): Data File User's Manual*. Chicago: NORC.

Jones, Calvin, et al. 1993. *Sophomore and Senior First Follow-up Data File User's Manual*. Washington, DC: National Center for Education Statistics.

Kasprzyk, D., G. Duncan, G. Kalton, and M. P. Singh, eds. 1989. *Panel Surveys*. New York: Wiley.

Kaufman, P., and D. Bradby. 1992. *Characteristics of At-Risk Students in NELS:88*. Washington, DC: National Center for Education Statistics. NCES 92–042.

Kaufman, P., K. A. Rasinski, R. Lee, and J. West. 1991a. *Quality of Responses of Eighth-Grade Students in NELS:88*. Washington, DC: National Center for Education Statistics.

———. 1991b. *Quality of Responses of Eighth-Grade Students to the NELS:88 Base Year Questionnaire*. Washington, DC: National Center for Education Statistics. NCES 91–487.

Legum, S., N. Caldwell, H. Goksel, J. Haynes, C. Hynson, K. Rust, and N. Blecher. 1992. *The 1990 High School Transcript Study: Final Technical Report*. Rockville, MD: Westat Inc.

Maline, Mindi S. 1993. *The National Longitudinal Study of the High School Class of 1972: Annotated Bibliography*. Washington, DC: U.S. Department of Education, Office of Educational Research and Improvement. OR 93–3156.

Marcus, Alfred C., Ward J. Keesling, Clare Rose, and James Trent. 1972. *An Analytic Review of the Longitudinal and Related Studies as They Apply to the Educational Process: Methodological Foundations for the Study of School Effects,*

Volume III. Center of the Study of Education, UCLA Graduate School of Education, Los Angeles, CA.

McMillen, M. 1992. *Eighth to Tenth Grade Dropouts*. Washington, DC: National Center for Education Statistics. NCES 92–006.

McMillen, M., E. Hausken, P. Kaufman, S. Ingels, K. Dowd, M. Frankel, and J. Qian. 1993. *Dropping Out of School: 1982 and 1992*. Issue Brief Series. Washington, DC: National Center for Education Statistics. NCES 93–901.

Mills, C. Wright. 1959. *The Sociological Imagination*. New York: Oxford University Press.

Mosteller, Fredrick, and Daniel Patrick Moynihan. 1971. *On Equality of Educational Opportunity*. New York: Random House.

Myers, D., and Heiser, N. 1994. *Students' School Transition Patterns between Eighth and Tenth Grades Based on NELS:88*. Washington, DC: National Center for Education Statistics. NCES 94–137.

National Center for Education Statistics. 1984. *High School and Beyond: A National Longitudinal Study for the 1980's: Quality of Response of High School Students to Questionnaire Items*. Washington, DC: GPO # 421 054 4241.

National Center for Education Statistics, Mayflower Conference. 1970. "Technical Background Planning Papers for Longitudinal Studies of Educational Eddicets." Papers from a conference held at the Mayflower Hotel, Washington, D.C. Washington, DC: National Center for Education Statistics.

NORC (National Opinion Research Center). 1996. *Early Childhood Longitudinal Study Design Report*. Washington, DC: National Center for Education Statistics.

Owings, J., and S. Peng. 1992. *Transitions Experienced by 1988 Eighth Graders*. Washington, DC: National Center for Education Statistics. NCES 92–023.

Peng, Samuel S., Celcille E. Stafford, and Robert J. Talbert. 1977. *Review and Annotation of Study Reports,* Washington, DC: U.S. Department of Education, National Center for Education Statistics. NCES 78–238.

Peiper, D., and L. A. Scott. 1993. *User's Guide to the NELS:88 Base Year/First Follow-Up Electronic Codebook*. Chicago: NORC.

Pratt, Daniel J., Roy W. Whitmore, Jennifer S. Wine, Karen M. Blackwell, Barbara H. Forsyth, Thimothy K. Smith, and Elizabeth A. Becker. 1996. *Beginning Postsecondary Students Longitudinal Study Second Follow-up (BPS:90/94): Final Technical Report*. Washington, DC: U.S. Department of Education, Office of Educational Research and Improvement, National Center for Education Statistics. NCES 96–153

Rasinski, K. A. 1994. *The Effect of High School Vocational Education on Academic Achievement Gain and High School Persistence: Evidence from NELS:88*. Report to the Office of Research. Washington, DC: U.S. Department of Education, National Center for Education Statistics.

Rasinski, K. A., and J. West. 1990. *NELS:88: Eighth Graders' Reports of Courses Taken During the 1988 Academic*

Year by Selected Student Characteristics. Washington, DC: National Center for Education Statistics. NCES 90–459.

Rasinski, K. A., S. J. Ingels, D. A. Rock, and J. Pollack. 1993. *America's High School Sophomores: A Ten Year Comparison, 1980–1990*. Washington, DC: National Center for Education Statistics. NCES 93–087.

Riccobono, J., L. B. Henderson, G. J. Burkheimer, C. Place, and J. B. Levinsohn. 1981. *National Longitudinal Study: Base Year (1972) Through Fourth Follow-Up (1979) Data File User's Manual*. Washington, DC: National Center for Education Statistics.

Rock, D. A., and J. M. Pollack. 1991. *Psychometric Report for the NELS:88 Base Year Test Battery*. Washington, DC: National Center for Education Statistics.

Rock, D. A., R. B. Ekstrom, M. E. Goertz, T. L. Hilton, and J. Pollack. 1985a. *Factors Associated with Decline of Test Scores of High School Seniors, 1972 to 1980*. Washington, DC: National Center for Education Statistics.

Rock, D. A., T. L. Hilton, J. M. Pollack, R. B. Ekstrom, and M. E. Goertz. 1985b. *Psychometric Analysis of the NLS-72 and the High School and Beyond Test Batteries*. Washington, DC: National Center for Education Statistics.

Rock, D. A., J. M. Pollack, and A. Hafner. 1991. *The Tested Achievement of the National Education Longitudinal Study of 1988 Eighth-Grade Class*. Washington, DC: National Center for Education Statistics. NCES 91–460.

Rock, D. A., J. A. Owings, and R. Lee. 1994. *Changes in Math Proficiency Between 8th and 10th Grades*. Washington, DC: National Center for Education Statistics. Statistics in Brief series. NCES 93–455.

Rose, Clare, and James Trent. 1972. *An Analytic Review of the Longitudinal and Related Studies as They Apply to the Educational Process: Research in Retrospect: Implications for the Future*, Volume IV. Center of the Study of Education, UCLA Graduate School of Education, Los Angeles, CA.

Rose, Clare, James Trent, Ann Salyard, and Judd Adams. 1972. *An Analytic Review of the Longitudinal and Related Studies as They Apply to the Educational Process: Toward Synthesis*, Volume II. Center of the Study of Education, UCLA Graduate School of Education, Los Angeles, CA.

———. 1973. *An Analytic Review of the Longitudinal and Related Studies as They Apply to the Educational Process: Supplement to the Analytic Review*, Volume I. Center of the Study of Education, UCLA Graduate School of Education, Los Angeles, CA.

Scott, L. A., D. A. Rock, J. M. Pollack, and S. J. Ingels. 1994. *Two Years Later: Cognitive Gains and School Transitions of NELS:88 Eighth Graders*. Washington, DC: National Center for Education Statistics.

Shaycoft, Marion F. 1967. *The High School Years: Growth in Cognitive Skills*. Interim Report 3 to the U.S. Office of Education, Cooperative Research Project No. 3051. Proj-

ect Talent Office, American Institutes for Research and University of Pittsburgh.

Shaycoft, Marion F., J. T. Dailey, D. B. Orr, C. A. Neyman, Jr., and S. E. Sherman. 1963. *Studies of a Complete Age Group—Age 15*. Final Report to the U.S. Office of Education, Cooperative Research Project No. 635. Project Talent Office, University of Pittsburgh.

Shephard, Jane. 1991. *1990 National Postsecondary Student Aid Study: Methodology Report*. Technical Report. Washington, DC: National Center For Education Statistics.

Spencer, Bruce D., Penny Sebring, and Barbara Campbell. 1987. *The National Longitudinal Study of the High School Class of 1972 (NLS-72) Fifth Follow-up (1986) Sample Design Report*. Washington, DC: U.S. Department of Education, Office of Educational Research and Improvement, Center of Educational Statistics. CS 88–403c.

Spencer, B. D., M. R. Frankel, S. J. Ingels, K. A. Rasinski, and R. Tourangeau. 1990. *NELS:88 Base Year Sample Design Report*. Washington, DC: National Center for Education Statistics. NCES 90–463.

Thorne, J., K. Rust, J. Burke, R. Marshall, N. Caldwell, D. Sickles, P. Ha, and B. Hayward. 1989. *1987 High School Transcript Study Technical Report*. Rockville, MD: Westat.

Tourangeau, R. E., H. McWilliams, C. Jones, M. R. Frankel, and F. O'Brien. 1983. *High School and Beyond First Follow-Up (1982) Sample Design Report*. Chicago: NORC.

Tourangeau, R. E., Penny Sebring, Barbara Campbell, Martin Glusberg, Bruce Spencer, and Melody Singleton. 1987. *The National Longitudinal Study of the Class of 1972 (NLS-72) Fifth Follow-up (1986) Data File User's Manual*. Washington, DC: U.S. Department of Education, Office of Educational Research and Improvement, Center For Education Statistics. CS 87–406c.

Trent, James, and Clare Rose. 1973. *An Analytic Review of the Longitudinal and Related Studies as They Apply to the Educational Process: Supplement to the Analytic* Review, Volume V. Center of the Study of Education, UCLA Graduate School of Education, Los Angeles, CA.

Weatat Inc. 1992. *Methodology Report for the 1990 National Postsecondary Student Aid Study*. Washington, DC: U.S. Department of Education, Office of Educational Research and Improvement, National Center for Education Statistics. NCES 92–080.

West, Jerry. 1996. *Early Childhood Longitudinal Study: Kindergarten Class of 1998–1999*. Washington, DC: U.S. Department of Education, National Center for Education Statistics. Unpublished paper.

West, J., L. Diodato, and N. Sandberg. 1984. *A Trend Study of High School Offerings and Enrollments: 1972–73 and 1981–82*. Washington, DC: National Center for Education Statistics.

Williams, S. R., and R. E. Folsom. 1977. *Bias Resulting from School Nonresponse: Methodology and Findings*. Research Triangle Park, NC: RTI.

Magnet Schools in Urban Education[1]

Rolf K. Blank
Council of Chief State School Officers

Magnet schools have become a significant factor in urban education. They offer a means for further desegregating schools, while at the same time enhancing the quality of education. Since magnet schools were initiated, however, there has been growing concern over whether they contribute to inequalities in American education. This chapter examines the development, distribution, and unique characteristics of magnet schools, and discusses research on the role of magnet schools in desegregation, school quality, and equity.

This chapter on magnet schools in urban education draws on results from a national survey of magnet schools conducted in the 1991–1992 school year (Steel and Levine, 1994). The national survey reveals that the number of magnet schools has grown rapidly in large urban school systems since the later 1970s. Magnet schools and programs within schools have unique curricular emphases; a majority have flexibility in staff selection. Other significant findings concern student composition and enrollment. For example, the ethnic composition of magnet schools is the same as that of the districts in which the schools are located. Most magnet schools enroll students by lottery; one-third use some criteria for student selection.

Magnet schools now represent a fundamental shift in how public schools are organized. But the extent to which they offer real choice to parents and learning gains to children depends on magnets' institutional characteristics. For the first time we can now provide a detailed portrait of the magnet school movement and describe its organizational variability.

Evolution of Magnet Schools

Magnet schools have their roots in district wide specialty schools, such as the Bronx High School of Science, the Boston Latin School, Chicago's Lane Tech, and San Francisco's Lowell High School, some of which have been in existence since the turn of the century. Like their forebears, magnet schools offer special curricula, such as mathematics–science or performing arts programs, or special instructional approaches, such as individualized education, open classrooms, or team teaching.

During the 1970s, school districts began to use magnet schools both as an incentive for parents to remain in the public school system and as a means of desegregation. Often magnet school programs were placed in racially isolated schools or neighborhoods to encourage students of other ethnic groups to enroll. If sufficient numbers of white and minority students enrolled in schools outside their neighborhoods, districts could promote school desegregation without resorting to mandatory measures. At the same time, by introducing innovative curricula and instructional approaches, magnet schools could strengthen the educational program in those schools, contributing to overall improvements in educational quality.

With the 1975 court endorsement of magnet schools as a voluntary desegregation strategy, magnet schools expanded to encompass a broad range of programs. Some districts added programs such as humanities, languages, or career exploration to the more traditional program emphases. Other magnet programs provided distinctive instructional approaches, such as alternative education, individualized education, accelerated learning, Montessori, and open classrooms. Typically, stu-

---

[1] The findings presented in this paper do not necessarily reflect the policies or views of the Council of Chief State School Officers.

421

dent and parent input provided the basis for determining the specific programs provided in a community. Many districts carefully monitored interest and enrollment in the various magnet programs, adding, expanding, or dropping programs as necessary to remain consonant with student and parent interests.

Magnet schools have received federal support since 1976, primarily through two programs: the Emergency School Assistance Act (ESAA) and the Magnet Schools Assistance Program (MSAP). ESAA, a federal program designed to provide funds to school districts attempting to desegregate, was amended in 1976 to authorize grants to support the planning and implementing of magnet schools. Between 1976 and 1981, ESAA provided up to $30 million a year to magnet school programs (Blank et al., 1983:8).

The climate of educational reform after the publication of *A Nation at Risk* (National Commission on Excellence in Education, 1983) further stimulated interest in magnet schools as a tool for reform. In particular, attention was directed to the programmatic aspects of magnet schools: What makes them distinctive? Are they more effective in enhancing student learning? In 1984, the federal government resumed support for magnet schools with the enactment of the Magnet Schools Assistance Program. The MSAP explicitly identified both program improvement and desegregation as objectives of magnet schools. Between 1985 and 1991, a total of 117 school districts received federal magnet school grants, totaling $739.5 million. Evidence strongly suggests that MSAP funding has been a significant factor in the development and operation of magnet programs. Districts currently receiving MSAP funds have proportionately more magnet programs than magnet districts that had not received MSAP support (Steel and Levine, 1994). When MSAP funding ended, however, a majority of districts were forced to modify their programs in some way, with one in five indicating they cut back the number of magnet schools and programs offered.

The school choice movement also contributed to a favorable climate for the growth of magnet schools. Magnet schools embody the principles of parental choice as well as competition, school-site autonomy, and deregulation. These same principles are central to the arguments supporting choice as an effective reform (Chubb and Moe, 1990; Raywid, 1989).

National Studies of Magnet Schools

The first national study of magnet schools in the early 1980s found that the number of districts offering magnet programs had increased dramatically since the courts accepted magnets as a strategy for desegregating schools in 1975: from 14 to 138 in 5 years (Blank et al., 1983). By 1983, over 1,000 individual magnet schools and programs schools were being offered in these 138 districts. As magnet schools have become more prevalent, debate over their merits has accelerated commensurately. Several studies have found that magnet schools contribute to school desegregation and to improving educational quality (cf. Archbald, 1988; Blank, 1990; Rossell, 1990; Witte and Walsh, 1990). At the same time, critics express concern over the potential for elitism and inequity that may result (Moore and Davenport, 1989).

A 1991–1992 study assessed the status of magnet schools within public school systems by surveying a nationally representative sample of school districts (Steel and Levine, 1994). A total of 600 multischool districts, representing 6,389 multischool districts nationwide, were randomly selected, and surveys were completed with magnet school administrators in all districts with magnet schools.

The study addressed three main questions:

1. How many magnet schools and programs are there, and how are they distributed across local school systems?
2. What is unique or distinctive about magnet schools?
3. Do magnet schools offer equal opportunities for students to enroll?

Other issues that were examined with the data were trends in magnet school distribution, the characteristics of programs offered, and the participation of ethnic minority and at-risk students in magnet schools.

Growth and Distribution of Magnet Schools

The number of school districts offering magnet schools increased from 138 in 1982 to 230 in 1991–1992. Although these 230 districts represent only 4% of the nation's multischool districts, they serve nearly a quar-

TABLE 1. Percentage of Multischool Districts with Magnet Programs by District Size and Location (*n* = 6,389)

DISTRICT ENROLLMENTS LOCATION (NUMBER OF DISTRICTS)	PERCENT WITH DESEGREGATION PLANS	PERCENT WITH MAGNET PROGRAMS	NUMBER WITH MAGNET PROGRAMS
<5,000 or rural (5105)	6.0	0.6	31
Suburb 5,000–10,000 (317)	17.0	4.7	15
Suburb > 10,000 (237)	21.5	8.9	21
Urban 5,000–10,000 (139)	42.4	21.6	30
Urban > 10,000 (230)	58.7	53.5	12.3
Not reported (301)	18.6	1.9	6

ter of all students nationwide. The number of students enrolled in magnet schools has nearly tripled, from 441,000 to over 1.2 million; the number of individual schools offering such programs has more than doubled, from 1,019 to 2,433 (Blank et al., 1983; Steel and Levine, 1994). In 1991–1992 there were 3,171 magnet schools or distinct programs situated within 2,433 schools.

The 1.2 million students in magnet schools represent nearly one-sixth of the public school population in districts offering magnet schools, indicating the growing popularity of these programs. As of 1992, substantially more students were enrolled in magnet programs than the 681,000 enrolled in nonsectarian private schools [National Center for Education Statistics (NCES), 1993]. Further, the demand for magnet schools is much greater than the current supply. Over three-quarters of the districts with magnet schools cannot accommodate all students who want to enroll; more than 123,000 students are on waiting lists for specific magnet programs. (In the remainder of the chapter, the term magnet program will refer to magnet schools or programs within schools.)

Distribution across School Systems

Because one objective of magnet programs is to promote desegregation, these programs are most likely to be found in districts in which racial imbalance and desegregation are important issues. As of fall 1991, 11% of multischool districts operated under a formal desegregation plan that assigned students to schools in order to attain a specified racial composition; these tended to be the larger districts, serving almost a third of the nation's students. Although magnet programs are

rarely the sole desegregation strategy chosen, by 1991–1992, 29% of these districts offered magnet programs to nearly two-thirds of the more than 10 million students in all districts with current desegregation plans. Other strategies include rezoning, forced busing, controlled choice, and majority-to-minority transfer plans.

Desegregation plans and magnet programs are more commonly found in urban school districts than in rural or suburban areas (see Table 1). A majority of the large urban districts and a significant proportion of the smaller urban districts in the country were operating under desegregation plans in 1991–1992, and almost the same proportion of these districts also offered magnet school programs. In rural and small districts, where desegregation pressures are much lighter than in the large and urban districts, the relative prevalence of magnet schools is low. Only about 10% of suburban districts offer magnet school programs. As of 1992, over 8 of every 10 magnet programs were located in large urban school districts, 7 of 10 programs were in districts with a predominance of minority students, and over half were in districts enrolling mostly low-income students.

Distribution of Magnets by District and Grade Level

Based on 1991–1992 data, the number of magnet programs offered in a district varied widely, from 1 to 175, and the mean number of magnet programs per district was 14. However, half of the districts had 4 or fewer programs, and 20% had only a single magnet program. This number is somewhat dependent on the total number of schools within a district; small districts are clearly limited in the number of magnet programs they

TABLE 2. Percentage of Multischool Districts with Magnet Programs and Other Choice Programs (*n* = 6,389)

TYPE OF PROGRAM OFFERED	NUMBER OF DISTRICTS WITH PROGRAMS	PERCENTAGE OF ALL DISTRICTS	PERCENTAGE OF ALL STUDENTS
Magnet schools/programs	230	4	24
Specialty schools (nonmagnet)	1,057	18	31
Programs of choice (nonmagnet)	1,189	23	26

might offer. Of the remaining districts, 14% had between 11 and 20 magnet programs, 9% had between 21 and 50, 6% had more than 50, and only 1% had more than 100 magnet programs.

Over half of magnet programs were located in elementary schools (while elementary schools comprise 60% of all U.S. public schools; NCES, 1993). One-fifth of magnet programs were at the high school level (high schools comprise 19% of all public schools), and an additional 15% of magnet programs were at the middle level (middle level schools comprise 15% of all public schools). The remaining 11% of magnet programs were found in nongraded or multilevel schools (e.g., K–12, K–8).

Distribution and Growth Compared to Other Public School Choice Programs

Magnet schools largely originated with the desegregation movement in the 1970s. But they become part of the broader debate around school choice. The 1991–1992 national survey also solicited information on the prevalence and location of specialty schools other than magnet schools and on other programs offering voluntary choice. Among multischool districts nationwide, more than one in five offered either magnet or nonmagnet specialty schools, and one district in four offered some form of school choice, through either magnet programs or nonmagnet programs of choice (see Table 2). Unlike magnet programs, however, nonmagnet specialty schools and programs of choice were as likely to be found in small or rural districts as in large urban districts; they were also more likely to be found in districts with predominantly white student populations and less likely than magnet programs to be found in poorer districts.

Although magnet districts comprised a relatively small portion of the districts offering choice, they tend to be those with much larger enrollments. The magnet

programs were also considerably more extensive and diverse than nonmagnet specialty programs. The average number of magnet programs in a magnet district (mean = 14) was over twice the average number of specialty schools in a specialty school district, and the range of options offered by magnet schools was considerably broader. The total number of nonmagnet specialty schools in the nation was 2,217 (compared to 2,433 magnet schools); the curricular themes of nonmagnet specialty schools were predominantly in only three areas: career vocational (41%), instructional approach (33%), and gifted and talented (20%).

What Is Distinctive about Magnet Schools and Programs?

The educational designs developed in magnet schools have become a primary method of innovation and reorganization in urban education. The basic idea of a magnet school is to attract and enroll students based on their interest, not by assignment or ability level. To this end, magnet schools and programs focus on either an instructional approach or a particular academic subject or career path. In theory, all magnet schools and programs are distinctive because of this feature. Magnet schools are also structured differently from traditional schools; some exist as programs within schools, while others are whole schools. And magnet schools may differ from traditional public schools in class size, student–teacher ratio, and selection of teaching staff.

Education Quality

Research on the effects of magnet schools in improving education quality has generally been limited to local district program evaluations that address magnet schools in a single district. Some of the studies are designed to allow determination of the independent role of the magnet school program or curriculum in changing student outcomes. For example, Witte and colleagues (1995) have systematically analyzed and reported on the effects of state-supported vouchers for low-income students to enroll in private schools in Milwaukee. The results show only small improvements in comparison to similar students in other schools. A review of local district studies that used comparison groups and controls for student background showed that some districts and schools do show significant improvement in student achievement with magnet schools (Blank, 1990).

Relatively few data have been available across districts to analyze the effects of magnet schools on education outcomes. The National Education Longitudinal Study of the eighth-grade class of 1988, conducted by the National Center for Education Statistics, provides a reliable source of data for analyses across districts and types of schools. Gamoran (1996) analyzed the effects of attending magnet city high schools as compared to comprehensive city high schools and private city high schools. The analysis showed that city magnet schools enroll students in more higher level math and science courses and that students had higher achievement scores in reading, social studies, and science than comparable students in comprehensive public high schools.

Curricular Emphases

Across the nation, magnet programs provide a wide variety of distinctive curricula, including aerospace technology, travel and tourism, junior ROTC, biotechnology, mathematics, music, fine arts, science, drama, bilingual programs, cosmetology, and small animal care programs. In addition, they offer a variety of instructional approaches, including open classrooms, individualized education, Montessori, and basic skills.

Magnet programs have sometimes been thought to be primarily gifted-and-talented programs, but at the time of the 1991–1992 survey, such programs comprised only one-eighth (12%) of the magnet programs nationwide. Most commonly, magnet programs had specific subject-matter emphases (38%) or provided a distinctive instructional approach (32%). Of the rest, 17% were career vocational and 15% centered on the arts. One-fifth of magnet programs combined different themes and approaches: self-paced instruction in programs together with a computer science or foreign-languages emphasis, for example, or a combination of vocational or subject-matter programs (such as technical training and science).

Program Structures

Magnet programs can be differentiated by whether all students in the school are included in the magnet program (whole-school magnets) or only some of the students in the school participate in the magnet program (program-within-school-magnets). Whole-school magnet schools can be further differentiated by how students enroll: (1) dedicated magnet schools, comprised only of students who apply and are accepted by the magnet program, and (2) attendance-zone magnet schools, comprised of students who apply and enroll from across a district, plus students from a school's regular attendance zone who are automatically enrolled in the magnet program.

In program-within-school magnet schools only a portion of students in the school participate in the magnet program. These programs are often semiautonomous. Students may take some or all of their classes apart from the rest of the school. In the 1992 survey, a total of 38% of the nation's 3,171 magnet programs were classified as programs within schools (62% were classified as whole-school programs). However since programs within schools are, by definition, smaller than schools, about 20% of the population of magnet students were in such magnet schools. A significant proportion (about one-fourth) housed more than one magnet program, with an average of 2.2 programs per school.

Approximately 200 programs within magnet schools, or 16% of the total, were embedded within attendance-zone or dedicated whole-school magnets. The enrollments of program within magnet schools are considerably smaller than regular schools at the same grade level. Whole-school magnets, on the other hand, are slightly larger than average at the middle and high school level, probably due to their predominant location in large urban districts.

Attendance-zone magnet schools, which comprised more than one-quarter (26%) of all programs, emerged in response to parents' concerns about restricted access to the special programs provided by magnets. In programs within magnet schools, participation in the magnet program is governed by racial balance guidelines or goals, thus restricting access of students in the neighborhood. Attendance-zone magnet schools extend access to magnet programs to students in the surrounding neighborhoods, regardless of their ethnicity. In this way, they help alleviate concerns regarding the elitism of magnets.

Do Magnet Schools Offer Equal Opportunities for Students to Enroll?

A common view about magnet schools is that they are oversubscribed and that methods of selecting students produce magnet schools dominated by higher achieving students. Another view is that students (and parents) more familiar with magnet schools and the processes for applying have a major advantage in enrolling. One way to assess opportunities for enrollment in magnet schools is to examine differences in participation by race and student background. The survey data also provide information on the degree of selectivity of magnet school programs, and we can examine the demand and accessibility of magnet schools through data on waiting lists and transportation services to magnet schools.

Participation of Minority versus White Students

From the 1991–1992 survey of magnet schools, we estimate that approximately 1.2 million students were enrolled in magnet programs. Of the total magnet enrollment, 61% of all students were black, Hispanic, or other minority. This percentage is very close to the 62% of all students who were minorities in the districts with magnet programs. However, the enrollment rates differed by type of magnet program structure. In the 1,081 magnet programs within schools, 61% of the magnet students were minorities. However, in the 556 schools in which the programs were located, 71% of the students were minorities. Thus magnet programs within schools do appear to have attracted white students in order to reduce isolation and improve racial balance.

These data are consistent with findings from two analyses of the National Education Longitudinal Study. These studies show that African-Americans and Hispanic students are more likely to enroll in a magnet high school or other public choice high school than are white or Asian-American students (Schneider et al.,

1995; Gamoran, 1996). These results are found when controlling for the availability of magnet schools and choice school (Schneider et al., 1995).

At the time of the 1991–1992 national survey, the ethnic composition of magnet programs varied widely depending on the ethnic composition of the district. In districts where black, Hispanic, or other minority students were the majority, the proportion of minority students enrolled in magnet programs was *lower* than the average proportion of minority students in the districts (68% versus 80%). In districts where a majority of students were white, the opposite was true: The proportion of minority students in magnet schools was *higher* than in the districts overall (46% versus 31%). It thus appears that magnet programs are more likely to attract and enroll students from the nondominant ethnic group.

Participation of At-Risk Students

One criticism frequently leveled at magnet programs is that they are elitist—the population of students served is an advantaged one. To examine this issue, the proportion of students enrolled in magnet programs who were eligible for free or reduced-price lunches, the proportion who were limited or non-English proficient (LEP or NEP), and the proportion who had individualized education plans were compared with overall district characteristics. Students from low-income families comprised nearly half of magnet program enrollments but were still underrepresented in magnet programs relative to their prevalence in the district: Low-income students, on average, comprised 47% of magnet enrollments but 51% of all students in magnet districts. In majority white and more affluent districts, however, low-income students were somewhat overrepresented in magnet programs. Students who were limited or non-English proficient and special education students (i.e., students with learning disabilities) were less likely than other students to be enrolled in magnet programs. On average the proportions of LEP or NEP and special education students in magnet programs were only two-thirds of their overall prevalence in the districts.

Selection Criteria

In 1991–1992, 24% of districts could accommodate all students who wanted to enroll in magnet programs.

For the other 76% of school districts, one or more criteria were used to select students who applied. Over half (58%) of the districts with magnets that use selection procedures used a lottery system (i.e., random selection). Many districts also applied rules or guidelines for magnet student selection, including sibling enrollment, grade-level preference, time on waiting list, and attendance zone (for attendance-zone magnets). More than one-third of the 3,171 magnet schools and programs reported using specific admission criteria in addition to the district procedures and rules. More than half of these programs used standardized test scores (17% of all programs) or teacher recommendations (16%). Grade point average and artistic or creative ability were used in a significant portion of programs. Other commonly used selection criteria were attendance or conduct requirements, specific course requirements, student interest in the focal area or approach, grades in specific courses, interviews, parental involvement, writing samples, recommendations (from other than teachers), and sibling attendance. Specific selection criteria were much more common among secondary-level magnet programs, where 54% had specific criteria compared to only 24% of elementary magnet programs.

Conclusions

Magnet schools have become a major strategy for voluntary choice and desegregation in large urban systems. In the past decade, the number of districts with magnet schools has almost doubled. The number of magnet schools has more than doubled, and the number of students has tripled. More than half the magnet districts and 8 of every 10 magnet schools and programs are located in urban districts with more than 10,000 students. To meet their desegregation goals, magnet schools must vigorously compete for students. The main attractions for students and parents are the special curricular themes and instructional methodologies offered by these programs. To be attractive to students, a diversity of programs that reflect the demands and interests of the community must be offered. The curricular emphasis most frequently found in magnet schools at elementary and middle levels is "subject matter" (e.g., mathematics, science, or foreign language); at the high school level, the most common emphasis is career-vocational.

Magnet schools have often been viewed as havens for high-achieving students within urban school districts. The national survey results present a quite different picture. A majority of districts (5,870) assign students to their magnet schools by lottery. Only one-third of magnet schools and programs reported using specific selection criteria—23% use test scores, 22% use teacher recommendations, and 17% use grade point average. These statistics reveal that while a portion of magnet schools and programs do serve higher achieving students, primarily the gifted-and-talented programs, most magnet programs serve a broad distribution of students in big city school systems.

There is evidence from the national data to suggest that magnet schools and programs may be contributing to desegregation goals. In minority-dominant districts, magnet programs enroll higher-than-average proportions of white students (relative to the overall proportion of white students in the district). In white-dominant districts, the reverse is true.

Magnet programs not only compete for students, they may also improve the quality of schools, recruiting skilled teachers with areas of expertise related to the special focus of the curriculum. Magnet schools recruit in order to attract teachers with the required special skills and interests to teach in magnet programs. Special staffing allowances also characterize magnet programs. As a result, more than one-fourth of magnet programs have smaller class sizes than regular schools at the same grade level.

To understand the effects of magnet schools on urban education, further studies and analyses need to examine the local decisions and context in which magnet schools operate, the extent to which magnet schools actually change the education process, and the extent to which student learning is improved.

REFERENCES

Archbald, D. 1988. "Magnet Schools, Voluntary Desegregation and Public Choice Theory: Limits and Possibilities in a Big City School System." Unpublished Ph.D. dissertation, University of Wisconsin-Madison.

Blank, R. 1990. "Analyzing Educational Effects of Magnet Schools Using Local District Data." *Sociological Practice Review* 1(40):51.1.

Blank, R., R. Dentler, C. Baltzell, and K. Chabotar. 1983. "Survey of Magnet Schools: Analyzing a Model for Quality Integrated Education." Prepared by James H. Lowry and Associates and Abt Associates for U.S. Department of Education, Washington, D.C.

Chubb, J., and T. Moe. 1990. *Politics, Markets, and America's Schools*. Washington, DC: Brookings Institution.

Gamoran, A. 1996. "Student Achievement in Public Magnet, Public Comprehensive, and Private City High Schools." *Educational Evaluation and Policy Analysis* (Spring).

Moore, D. R., and Davenport. 1989. *The New Improved Sorting Machine*. Madison, WI: National Center on Effective Secondary Schools.

National Center for Education Statistics (NCES). 1993. *Public and Private Elementary and Secondary Education Statistics: School Year 1992–93* (NCES Report 93-332). Washington, DC: U.S. Department of Education.

National Commission on Excellence in Education. 1983. *A Nation at Risk: The Imperative for Educational Reform*. Washington, DC: U.S. Department of Education.

Raywid, M. 1989. "The Mounting Case for Schools of Choice." In J. Nathan (ed.), *Public Schools by Choice: Expanding Opportunities for Parents, Students, and Teachers*. Bloomington, IN: Meyer-Stone.

Rossell, C. H. 1990. *The Carrot or the Stick for School Desegregation Policy: Magnet Schools US. Forced Busing*. Philadelphia: Temple University Press.

Schneider, B., K. S. Schiller, and J. S. Coleman. 1995. *Public School Choice: Some Evidence from the National Education Longitudinal Study of 1988*. Chicago: University of Chicago, Center for the Study of the Economy and the State, Working Paper Series No. 113.

Steel, L., and R. Levine. 1994. *Educational Innovation in Multiracial Contexts: The Growth of Magnet Schools in American Education* (Report No. 1 from the Magnet Schools Study). Prepared by American Institutes for Research for U.S. Department of Education, Washington, DC.

Witte, J., and D. Walsh. 1990. "A Systematic Test of the Effective Schools Model." *Educational Evaluation and Policy Analysis* 12(2) (Summer):188–212.

Witte, J. F., A. B. Bailey, and C. A. Thorn. 1993. *Third Year Report: Milwaukee Parental Choice Program*. Madison: University of Wisconsin, Department of Political Science.

MASS SCHOOLING

Francisco O. Ramirez
School of Education, Stanford University

Mass schooling is ubiquitous throughout the world. Moreover the value of mass schooling is taken for granted by peoples of all walks of life. We all believe that children benefit from attending and completing primary or elementary schools. We further believe that there are economic and political benefits to societies from investing in the futures of their children through schooling. Issues of curricular content and teacher training and practices are more likely to be debated. Even in this more contested terrain there is more agreement than is generally recognized. It is precisely this broad frame of consensus that allows us to depict as a crisis the erosion of primary enrollments in Africa (Fuller and Heynemann, 1989), teacher centric pedagogies in parts of Asia and Latin America (UNESCO, 1992; Rust and Dallin, 1990), and low levels of school achievement in science and mathematics in the United States (Stevenson, and Stigler, 1992). Mass schooling issues have become high stakes issues because we assume that everyone should go to school and benefit from learning and that in the aggregate mass schooling contributes to national progress. National progress is often the yardstick against which national governments are evaluated. Thus, a major unintended consequence of so much agreement on the value of mass schooling for individuals and for nation-states is so much conflict over so many different aspects of mass schooling.

But mass schooling has not always been both an ordinary and an important feature of everyday life. The masses did not enter history as a population in need of schooling until the late eighteenth and early nineteenth centuries. Although children today are expected to be exposed to an age-segregated sequentially ordered prescribed curricula for a mandatory period of time (mass schooling), children in earlier times did not face a life course that included an age of schooling. The transition to adult membership in society was more varied, involving initiation ceremonies, apprenticeships, and private tutors. The age of schooling gives rise to the idea of school age children worldwide. To better understand the phenomena of mass schooling the first part of this chapter outlines perspectives on the origins and expansion of mass schooling. Where this institution came from and why it has been so readily adopted throughout the world is an important issue. I examine social order and class imposition functionalist explanations of mass schooling and then consider conflict and institutionalist perspectives.

Next the focus shifts to the more contested terrain of curricula and pedagogy. The content of schooling and in what ways this content is communicated preoccupies many scholars and policymakers alike. I consider both technical/rational and political approaches to these issues. Lastly, the implications of defining mass schooling as a high stakes issue is examined directly. An institutional perspective is brought to bear on this worldwide development of mass schooling as a crucial national policy instrument.

The Origins and Expansion of Mass Schooling

Functionalist Theories

The disruptive forces of industrialization and urbanization have often been cited as the causal factors that gave rise to mass schooling. These forces are imagined to have created problems to which mass schooling was a solution. Some theories have emphasized the systemic need for a better socially integrated population (Dreeben, 1968), while others stress the need for a more disciplined labor force (Bowles and Gintis, 1976). For the former the separation of work from familial and other communal structures results in anomic individuals. Schools emerge and expand to create a new basis for social solidarity and societal integration. For the latter the alienating factory system and other structural features of capitalism lead to a labor force that threatens the dominant elites. Schools emerge and expand to socially control and reorient the working class and other subordinated populations.

The theoretical weaknesses of both the social order and class imposition functionalist theories have been well established (Collins, 1979; Rubinson, 1986). It is simply unconvincing to argue that varying societies or their dominant elites developed common needs, one of which was to establish an elaborate system of compulsory schooling for all. To be sure, these arguments can be persuasive as descriptive accounts of the specific dynamics of particular educational developments. Examples may be found within both social order (Bailyn, 1960) and class imposition (Spring, 1972) accounts of educational developments in the United States. The former were more fashionable in the 1950s and 1960s while the latter gained ascendancy in the 1970s and early 1980s. As more general theoretical explanations these arguments cannot make sense of the inherently progressive vision implied by the call for schooling for all. In country after country opposition to mass schooling came from conservative forces that on class, caste, or gender grounds would have denied schooling to some segments of the population (Furet and Ozouf, 1982; Walters et al. 1990). Moreover, there are too many instances of mass schooling development that preceded industrialization and urbanization. This is true both in the nineteenth and twentieth centuries. Thus, there are both theoretical and empirical grounds for exploring alternative explanations of the origins and expansion of mass schooling.

Conflict Theories

An alternative explanation of mass schooling emphasizes class, ethnic, and religious conflicts as causal factors. Within some perspectives the conflicts stem from the contradictions between democracy and capitalism, with the former emphasizing more egalitarian norms and the latter fostering more hierarchical ones (Carnoy and Levin, 1985). Other perspectives note that condi-

tions of political and educational decentralization generate higher levels of competition and thus conflict among groups seeking to promote their own interests within the school system (Collins, 1971). These perspectives have been used primarily to account for differences in educational structures, for example, differences in access to post-primary schooling, differences in the quality of middle-class versus working-class schools, differences in levels of political control over mass schooling, etc. Varieties of conflict theory gained ground in the 1980s by exposing the more static character of the earlier functionalist explanations. However, these perspectives are less useful in making sense of commonalties in educational aims, organizations, and patterns. In fact the common high value assigned to mass schooling is implicitly presupposed in some of these theories. Why else would schooling be the site of so much competition and conflict? And yet, it is the historical development of the universal value of mass schooling that facilitated the rise of international educational conferences with an optimistic transnational educational discourse. This process manifested itself anew in the World Conference on Education for All (1990), which proclaimed that world progress itself was contingent on the eradication of global illiteracy through schooling.

Institutional Theory

Another alternative to functionalist theories may be found in the institutional theory of mass schooling. From this perspective mass schooling is not a local cultural idea nor an organizational practice attuned to local needs. From its outset mass schooling was part of a broader Western project designed to construct a rational progress-oriented society dependent on the transformative powers of schooling (Boli and Ramirez, 1984; Ramirez and Boli, 1987). Widespread belief in education appears to be due less to local success stories and more to a general secular faith in the powers of schooling to change children into productive citizens. Within this perspective some studies have examined the historical rise of schooling as a national aspiration and the growth of state educational authority via the expansion of national educational ministries and compulsory school legislation (Ramirez and Ventresca, 1992; see Boli, 1989, for a case study of Sweden). These studies show how the establishment of the organizational linkages between mass schooling and the nation-state made mass schooling a project of the nation-state. Research also demonstrates the cross-national pervasiveness of the ideological ties between schooling, individual development, and national progress (Faila and Lanford, 1984).

A second set of studies has analyzed the growth of primary enrollments cross-nationally (Meyer et al., 1977, 1993). These analyses establish that the expansion of enrollments is weakly related to a wide variety of endogenous societal-level variables. These analyses also show that the rate of enrollment growth accelerates after World War II. These studies depict common educational outcomes as a consequence of common national adherence to a transnational model of education for development. From an institutionalist perspective this model is a core component of the Western project. Although many aspects of the Western project have been challenged, mass schooling for national development continues to enjoy worldwide legitimacy.

Institutional theories have been criticized for not paying sufficient attention to internal national factors that may hinder or promote educational development. These factors include issues of curricula and pedagogy that functionalist and conflict theories have earlier addressed. Institutional theories have also been critiqued for not specifying the organizational mechanisms through which transnational models are transmitted. Lastly, the role of power and conflict appears to be neglected within institutional theories of mass schooling. A thoughtful assessment of functionalist, conflict, and institutional perspectives on mass schooling may be found in Rubinson and Browne (1994).

Curricula and Pedagogy

There is a growing interest in cross-national research with respect to curricular and pedagogical issues regarding primary education (see, for example, the papers in Biddle et al., 1996). Many of the debates center on the question of whether curriculum is best conceptualized in technical/rational or in political terms. Those who start from the first premise are mainly concerned with determining which forms of curricular content are more likely to result in higher levels of student achievement. Cross-national studies of student achievement have typically proceeded from this assumption and have investigated the intended as well as the implemented curriculum to gauge the association between variations in curricular emphasis and variations in student achievement (see the papers in Baker et al., 1992). Within this perspective the content of schooling is often conceptualized as an independent variable with attitudinal and cognitive learning outcomes as the dependent variables. However, educational reform initiatives often attempt to match educational governance structures with preferred curricular emphases (e.g., Cohen and Spillane, 1992; Baker and Stevenson, 1991).

From a political perspective studies ask why some forms of knowledge are privileged in schools and why some types of expertise in teachers are more valued. These studies have examined the history of school subjects to show, for example, how the distinction between academic and practical subjects developed and what consequences this dichotomy had on the children of different social classes (Goodson, 1984). Within the same perspective other studies have examined textbooks to ascertain the influence of race, gender, and class in the contents of curricula. All of these studies highlight the importance of problematizing what counts and who counts in curricular studies. They pose a challenge to the more technical approaches to curriculum, questioning their pragmatic assumption that what works will eventually count.

There is a similar dichotomy in research on pedagogy and teacher training. Where teachers should be trained, what the content of their training should involve, what and how should teachers teach—these are questions that have been taken up from both technical and political perspectives. But what the former interprets as matters in the domain of cognitive and educational psychology the latter discusses in a more sociological and political framework.

Most studies of curricula and pedagogy are either historical case studies or cross-national studies employing cross-sectional research designs. The research strategy of the institutionalists is to study simultaneously variation over time and across as many countries as possible. Whereas earlier research focused on the formation of compulsory rules and educational ministries and the expansion of enrollments, more recent studies have examined the curriculum. Much of this later work seeks to identify what subjects are taught in what countries over what time periods. These studies cross-nationally analyze variation in the allocation of official curricular time to these different subjects. They also show that in this century there has been a general trend in the direction of greater cross-national similarity in the kinds of subjects taught in elementary schools and in the ways in which official curricular time is allocated to these subjects (Meyer et al., 1992b). More specific findings document the emergence of science in the national curricula, the decline of geography and the rise of social studies, and the triumph of both national over classical and local languages and English over French as the favored foreign language. These findings are interpreted as evidence of a worldwide official primary curriculum that reflects the influence of world models of knowledge for school children.

With respect to teacher training a general trend is an increase in the years of formal education and its relocation to a university or a post-secondary-level institute (Carnoy et al., 1995). From a technical rational perspective these changes reflect the application of scientific methods to core issues of teaching and learning. The result should be an upgraded and more professional teaching corps (Lockheed and Vespoor, 1991). From a political perspective these changes reflect changes in the distribution of power in society, for example, a decline in the power of teacher unions where principles of seniority and solidarity may have governed the regulation of entry into the world of teachers (for a case study of Mexico, see Bayardo, 1991). Experience and craft, it is feared, are undercut by more scientific and technological models. Mostly positive consequences of more professionalized teacher training are imagined by scholars within the first perspective. Those operating within the latter postulate mostly negative effects, arguing that much of professionalization involves privileging some form of cultural capital, and thus exacerbating social inequality (Popkewitz, 1993). From an institutionalist perspective all educational changes are thought to involve delegitimating some forms of inequality while opening the doors to credential-based ones (Meyer, 1977)

At issue though is why primary teaching is transformed from a practice mostly embedded in unique national history to a transnational object susceptible to scientific discourse and technological manipulation. That earlier and more varying national traditions regarding primary teaching are being challenged is indisputable; note the erosion of status distinctions between primary and secondary teachers (Judge et al., 1994). As the concept of mass schooling extends to include less differentiated systems of secondary educa-

tion, what constitutes quality training for one set of teachers extends to the other as well. Moreover what constitutes quality training is more likely to be discussed in general and abstract ways reflecting the universalistic aspirations of the Western project of education for development. The triumph of the West in this century made possible the globalization of this project. Note however that the egalitarian critiques of scientific and professional models of curricula and pedagogy also have their roots in a Westernized and universalistic world view as well. None of these critiques would tolerate the physical abuse of children by teachers, discrimination against girls by authorities, reduced school services for the "wrong" tribe or caste or class, however much these practices may be locally justified. From an institutionalist perspective the discourse of technical progress and the discourse of human rights are two facets of the same world view promoting the necessity and the significance of mass schooling as an instrument of national policy. Schooling as human capital and schooling as empowerment share a common conviction in the transformative powers of schooling.

Mass Schooling as a High Stakes Issue

Mass media reaction to the publication of *A Nation At Risk* may lead one to believe that this event marked the beginning of mass schooling as a high stakes issue in the United States. But in fact the history of educational reforms all over the world has increasingly presupposed the national importance of mass schooling issues. What happens to children in their early years of schooling is not solely a parental concern or a local issue but rather a vital national one. Moreover the terms of the debates regarding access, curricula, and achievement have become common ones. These typically involve the tensions between commitments to excellence and concerns over equity as well as the conflicts between claims to technical expertise and claims to sound political analysis. Lastly, these debates are not confined within national boundaries but are also increasingly taking place in international conferences and organizations. As noted earlier, the World Conference on Education for All (1990) linked mass schooling to world progress and did so in a forum that included not merely representatives of national governments but also of international nongovernmental organizations and other interested parties. This conference presupposed the necessity of development for all nation-states the value of national development for the world, and the significance of mass schooling for national and world development. This conference also reiterated the principle that access to an elementary education is a basic human right. Thus, mass schooling has become a national and a worldwide high stakes issue.

Education for individual and national development is a world cultural theme that has been diffused through a number of distinctive organization carriers. Both technical and political experts increasingly address transnational audiences. The world, not merely their country, is their domain and their development expertise permeates this domain. Whether armed with psychological theories of self-esteem, economic theories of human capital formation, or political theories of autonomous development, these development experts do not merely provide practical advice for specific countries, but rather they articulate transnational general principles of human learning and national progress. Proliferating development-oriented organizations are influenced by these principles but they generate their own practitioner lore as well. These organizations and the professional societies they create and maintain constitute a network through which the education for development model is also carried. Lastly, the multilateral organizations—UNESCO, UNICEF, and the World Bank—despite their many organizational differences, adhere to an education for development script that is especially influential in less developed countries (Chabbott, 1995).

What we have, therefore, is an expansion of development expertise, development discourse, and development organizations favoring schooling for individual development and national progress. Within this thick cultural framework educational reform failures are but the seeds for new initiatives. With so much consensus on the high stakes character of mass schooling and so little world bureaucracy to shape decision making, what we have is a world that looks very competitive and conflict ridden regarding mass schooling issues. At the national and at the world levels this situation has given rise to theories of competition and conflict that fare well as descriptions of how groups and organizations and countries mobilize but tell us little about the implicit technical and political consensus on the value of mass schooling in promoting individual, national, and world development. Institutional theories have

sought to unpack the taken-for-granted character of mass schooling by examining its historical roots, by describing cross-national similarities in its development across the world, and by starting the much needed task of identifying its organizational carriers.

REFERENCES

Bailyn, Bernard. 1960. *Education In the Forming of American Society.* Chapel Hill: University of North Carolina Press.

Baker, David, and David Stevenson. 1991. "State Control of the Curriculum and Classroom Instruction." *Comparative Education Review* 64:1–10.

Baker, David, C. Ethnington, L. Sosniak, and L. Westbury (eds.). 1992. *In Search of More Effective Mathematics Education: Evidence from the Second International Mathematics Study.* NJ: Ablex.

Bayardo, Barbara. 1991. "The State and the Professional Teacher." Unpublished doctoral dissertation, Stanford University, School of Education.

Biddle, Bruce, Thomas Good, and Ivor Goodson (eds.). 1996. *International Handbook of Teachers and Teaching.* Amsterdam: Kluwer Academic Publishers.

Boli, John. 1989. *New Citizens for a New Society: The Institutional Origins of Mass Schooling in Sweden.* New York: Pergamon Press.

Boli, John, and Francisco O. Ramirez. 1992. "Compulsory Schooling in the Western Cultural Context." In Robert F. Arnove, Philip Altbach, and Gail P. Kelly (eds.), *Emergent Issues in Education: Comparative Perspectives,* pp. 25–38. New York: State University of New York Press.

Bowles, Samuel, and Herbert Gintis. 1976. *Schooling in Capitalist America.* New York: Basic Books.

Carnoy, Martin, and Henry Levin. 1985. *Schooling and Work in the Democratic State.* Stanford, CA: Stanford University Press.

Carnoy, Martin, L. Fendler, Tom Popkewitz, R. Tabachnick, and K. Zeichner. 1995. *The Impact of Structural Adjustment Policies on the Employment and Training of Teachers.* Stanford, CA: Stanford University Press.

Chabbott, Colede. 1995. "Constructing Educational Development: The International Development Field and the World Conference on Education for All." Proceedings of the 1995 NASDEC Conference in Norway on The Role of Aid in the Development of Education for All.

Cohen, David, and James Spillane. 1992. "Policy and Practice: The Relations Between Governance and Instruction." In Gerald Grant (ed.), *Review of Research in Education,* Vol. 18, pp. 3–51. Washington, DC: American Educational Research Association.

Collins, Randall. 1979. *The Credential Society.* Orlando, FL: Academic Press.

Dreeben, Robert. 1968. *On What Is Learned in School.* Reading, MA: Addison-Wesley.

Fiala, Robert, and Audrey Gordon-Lanford. 1987. "Education, Ideology and the World Education Revolution, 1950–1970." *Comparative Education Review* 31(3) (August): 315–332.

Fuller, Bruce, and Stephen Heyneman. 1989. "Third World School Quality: Current Collapse, Future Potential." *Educational Researcher* 18:12–19.

Furet, Francois, and Jacques Ozouf. 1982. *Reading and Writing: Literacy in France from Calvin to Jules Ferry.* Cambridge: Cambridge University Press.

Goodson, Ivar. 1984. "Subjects for Study: Towards a Social History of Curriculum." In I. Goodson, and S. J. Ball (eds.), *Defining the Curriculum: Histories and Ethnographies,* pp. 25–44. London: Falmer Press.

Judge, Henry, M. Lemosee, L. Paine, and M. Sedlak. 1994. *The University and the Teachers: France, the United States, and England.* Oxford: Triangle Books.

Lockheed, Marlaine, and Adrian Verspoor. 1990. *Improving Primary Education in Developing Countries: A Review of Policy Options.* Washington, DC: World Bank Press.

Meyer, John. 1977. "The Effects of Education as an Institution." *American Journal of Sociology* 83(1): pp. 55–77.

Meyer, John, Francisco O. Ramirez, Richard Rubinson, and John Boli. 1977. "The World Educational Revolution, 1950–1970." *Sociology of Education* 50:242–258.

Meyer, John, Francisco O. Ramirez, and Yasemin Soysal. 1992a."World Expansion of Mass Education, 1870–1980." *Sociology of Education* 65:128–149.

Meyer, John, David Kamens, and Aaron Benaovt. 1992b. *School Knowledge for the Masses: World Models and National Primary Curricular Categories in the Twentieth Century.* Washington, DC: Falmer Press.

Popkewitz, Tom. 1991. *A Political Sociology of School Reform: Power/Knowledge in Teaching, Teacher Education, and Research.* New York: Teachers College Press.

Ramirez, Francisco O., and John Boli. 1987. "The Political Construction of Mass Schooling: European Origins and Worldwide Institutionalization." *Sociology of Education* 60(2):2–18.

Ramirez, Francisco O., and Marc Ventresca. 1992. "Building the Institution of Mass Schooling: Isomorphism in the Modem World." In Bruce Fuller and Richard Rubinson (eds.), *The Political Construction of Education: The State, School Expansion, and Economic Change,* pp. 47–60. New York: Praeger.

Rubinson, Richard. 1986. "Class Formation, Politics, and Institutions: Schooling in the U.S." *American Journal of Sociology* 92:519–548.

Rubinson, Richard, and Irene Browne. 1994. "Education and the Economy." In Neil J. Smelser and Richard Swedborg (eds.), *The Handbook of Economic Sociology.* Princeton: Princeton University Press.

Rust, Val, and Per Dalin, eds. 1990. *Teachers and Teaching in the Developing World.* New York: Garland.

Spring, Joel. 1972. *Education and Rise of the Corporate State.* Boston: Beacon Press.

Stevenson, Harold W., and James Stigler. 1992. *The Learning Gap: Why Our Schools Are Failing and What We Can Learn from Japanese and Chinese Education.* New York: Touchstone.

UNESCO Regional Office for Asia and the Pacific. 1992. *Towards Developing New Teacher Competencies in Response to Mega-Trends in Curriculum Reform.* UNESCO.

Walters, Pamela Bamhouse, Holly J. McCammon, and David R. James. 1990. "Schooling or Working: Public Education, Racial Politics, and the Organization of Production in 1910." *Sociology of Education* 63:1–26.

World Conference on Education for All. 1990. *Meeting Basic Learning Needs: A Vision for the 1990s.* New York: Inter-Agency Commission for World Conference on Education for All.

MERITOCRACY

Thomas B. Hoffer
NORC at the University of Chicago

The term meritocracy is usually understood to mean that individuals are selected for educational opportunities and jobs on the basis of demonstrated performance or ostensible predictors thereof. The most widely used meritocratic selection criteria are educational degrees or certificates and examination results. Because examination results are used to screen applicants for educational opportunities, and because opportunities affect later examination results, the relative importance of degrees versus examination results is often difficult to disentangle. Most of the recent efforts by sociologists to assess the degree of meritocratic selection in a given geographic or historical society have framed the issue as one of the relative effects of mental test scores and social background characteristics (especially parental socioeconomic status, but also gender and race or ethnicity) on individual education and occupational outcomes.

Meritocracy first entered the English language through Michael Young's brilliant novel *The Rise of the Meritocracy*, published in 1958. Set in the year 2034, the novel traces the ascendancy of an elite selected by tested competency, and the concomitant declining importance of technically extraneous characteristics such as social class pedigree and seniority. Young was by no means the first to argue that technical competency was becoming more salient in the allocation of individuals to employment and rewards to individuals. Marx and Weber, among others, were at turns tormented and fascinated by the same dialectical processes upon which Young grounded his prophecies. And long before modern social scientists argued over empirical trends, theoreticians from Plato to Rousseau argued for one or another variant of the ideal of "rule by merit" over its main alternative, rule by birthright. As the twentieth century drew to a close, the debates seemed to have only grown in volume.

This chapter addresses the following questions related to the concept of meritocracy: (1) What exactly is meant by meritocracy? (2) What were the social and historical contexts in which meritocracy first emerged as a social issue? (3) What are the contemporary issues surrounding the ideal of meritocracy, and how have sociologists addressed those issues?

The Concept of Meritocracy

Etymologically, meritocracy means "rule by merit," and it is useful to consider the implications of both terms, rule and merit. Meritocracy entails that those with power and authority hold their positions by virtue of their ostensible ability to do the job at least as well as any contenders. As a theoretical model of how positions should be filled, meritocracy is thus applicable to any sphere of life where roles are assigned and controlled by some sort of authority structure. Young used the term to refer to the ruling class: where society was once ruled by a hereditary aristocracy, it would now be ruled by an achieved meritocracy. More commonly, the term is used to characterize a system of allocating people to positions, rather than a distinct class within a society. It is used with reference both to educational opportunities and to the occupational order. Within the institution of education, meritocracy is said to hold when stratified opportunities such as curriculum tracks and college admissions are based on academic performance, rather than family social status or ability to pay. In the occupational sphere, meritocracy means that applicants are selected and promoted strictly on the basis of earned credentials.

Meritocracy is an analytic concept that can be usefully applied to analyses of social structures, but it is also a vigorous ideal that animates the thinking of people in almost all spheres of modern social life. As the connection with authority implies, meritocracy implies the notion of legitimacy. Meritocracy is a system of ruling social life that survives insofar as the people who are ruled believe it is legitimate. How legitimate is meritocratic selection in contemporary society? Consider that in the majority of instances most people would agree that the most effective applicant necessarily deserves the role. Almost everyone believes that meritocracy should carry the day in educational advancement and employment opportunities; perhaps only electoral politics and the family remain safely out of its dominion.

That meritocratic principles enjoy widespread support does not mean that everyone agrees on the content of the principles. Indeed, contemporary American society is fraught with profound disagreements over the meaning of merit and how it is gained. The most common definition of meritocracy conceptualizes merit in terms of tested competency or ability, and most likely as measured by IQ or standardized achievement tests. Most of the relevant quantitative analyses of survey data conceive merit in these terms, and meritocracy in terms of the extent to which the effects of test scores on educational and occupational outcomes overshadow the effects of social background factors.

Despite its popularity, the equation of merit with test scores is surely too narrow, and some have even argued that general intelligence test scores are not essential to meritocracy. The U.S. Supreme Court ruled in 1971 against the use of general intelligence tests for hiring purposes, but affirmed the use of tests of job-specific skills and knowledge. In terms of the principal of meritocracy, test scores are relevant only insofar as they predict actual job performance, for performance is what ultimately matters. As it turns out, though, tests of general ability and broad-based tests of achievement are usually better predictors of job performance than are narrow tests of job skills (see Herrnstein and Murray, 1995, chapter 3 for a discussion of these points). "Prediction" is normally understood in terms of a straightforward statistical association, but that criterion is also frequently disputed. Critics of entrance exams often argue that the skills being tested are sometimes not related to the content of the job. Does it

matter whether a policeman can do algebra? Probably not. Then why might knowledge of algebra predict how a policeman's superior would evaluate the officer? One possibility is that the evaluation system is biased. This could happen if knowledge of algebra were higher among one ethnic group, and members of that ethnic group controlled the system of performance evaluation, and they systematically favored members of their group. In this case, algebra scores are spuriously related with performance ratings. Another possibility is that knowledge of algebra may be associated with a more general problem-solving ability that really does lead to more effective performance as an officer.

On the other hand, a low rate of accurate prediction between tested skills and occupational success does not necessarily mean the tested skills are irrelevant to job performance. Strong analytical skills may be needed to perform competently in certain occupations, and no one with low analytical skills is employed in those jobs. However, many people with strong analytical skills are employed in jobs that do not require those skills. These mismatches can reduce the correlation of tested abilities with occupational status, even while those abilities are crucial to competent job performance.

Even if the test used is a good measure of cognitive abilities needed for or potentially called upon in the job, performance is not strictly a matter of having those cognitive abilities. Effort and a variety of social skills also loom large in one's instrumental effectiveness at work, and these are of course not necessarily measured well at all by tests of IQ and academic achievement. Indeed, the guiding mantra of Young's meritocracy is "merit = IQ + effort." The problem with these other important characteristics is that they are difficult to measure reliably. As a result, statistical analyses typically show much stronger associations between measures of ability and occupational outcomes than between measures of so-called noncognitive variables and occupational success.

If cognitive and noncognitive skills were so well measured that educational and occupational performance were perfectly predicted, would the meritocracy be perfected? Most would probably answer in the negative, for nothing has been said about opportunities to acquire those skills and sensibilities. Historically and very much in the present, opportunities for success in school are strongly dependent upon the accident of birth. Part of the association between parental socioeconomic status and success in school is due to genetic factors, but a large share is due to differences in the parents' socialization practices and the various kinds of educational opportunities that money can buy.

Perhaps the most important educational opportunities in American society that money can buy are represented by the school one attends, "purchased" through the parents' choice of residential location or payment of private school tuition. But most of the differences in student learning outcomes are among students within the same schools, rather than between schools. Since the landmark *Equality of Educational Opportunity* study conducted by James Coleman and his colleagues in 1966, sociologists of education have repeatedly found that only 10 to 20 percent of the variance in student test scores is attributable to average achievement differences among schools. A large part of the differences that are found among schools is further reducible to the social compositions of their student bodies.

At the logical extreme, Michael Young's novel suggests that meritocracy would entail either of two unappealing alternatives. Left unchecked, the meritocracy moves toward an increasingly rigid system of stratification, because of assortative mating patterns. At some point, one's social class becomes almost certainly determined by the social class of the parents, by virtue of both genetic inheritance and of child-rearing advantages usurped by the parents' status group. Alternatively, children could be separated from their parents immediately after birth and raised in strictly controlled conditions designed to maximize intellectual growth. Only this extreme would ensure full equality of opportunity. Of course, both extremes suffer from the drawback of being thoroughly repugnant to most people.

Meritocracy thus seems, like Marx's capitalism, to sow the seeds of its own destruction. The fundamental contradiction, or irony, it contains is that it is propelled by the quest for equal rights, but produces an absolutely unacceptable loss of individual rights when taken to its logical extreme. But logical extremes carry no practical necessity, and there are no indications that parents will be required to forego investing in their children for the sake of more equality of life chances. Much more likely is a movement toward helping families compete more effectively, perhaps coupled with more humane treatment for those who do not fare well in the competition.

What are alternatives to meritocracy? The historical competition is not likely to hold much attraction to most modern citizens. Prior to the industrial revolution, the main alternatives to meritocratic selection was for assignments to be made on the basis of "bloodlines" and patronage. Nepotism, the practice of favoring relatives, was the essential mechanism of allocating individuals to agricultural employment and craft occupations. In the sphere of civil service and administration, the main historical alternative to meritocracy is fealty to the ruler or corporate boss. Political patronage appointments are typically made at least partly on this basis. Due to the ability to concentrate power that patronage systems give rulers, the scope of patronage has steadily declined in multiparty democracies in favor of protected civil service jobs. The contrast between meritocracy and patronage, it should be emphasized, is analytical rather than empirical. Empirically, merit probably had a great influence on many patronage appointments, and many patronage systems probably worked more efficiently than some contemporary bureaucracies where all appointments are based on merit.

In contemporary industrial societies, the main alternative is for classes and status groups to control selection processes. Selections based on race, ethnicity, gender, and status group "life-style" distinctions (e.g., ability to speak "standard" English without an accent) are variants on the same theme. Discrimination against individuals on racial and gender bases is illegal and widely condemned, but statistical underrepresentations of minorities, women, and lower socioeconomic status (SES) persons persist in many spheres of both education and employment. As Daniel Bell (1973) and many others have argued, equality of opportunity is very different from equality of outcome, and underrepresentation does not necessarily mean meritocracy is absent. Nonetheless, democratic regimes are often uneasy with the tendency of even ostensibly meritocratic elites to perpetuate themselves across generations (Husen, 1974). This unease is especially pronounced when the elite is relatively homogeneous in terms of gender and ethnic and racial markers. Most industrial nations have thus developed a variety of control mechanisms to try to reduce the impact of initial advantages on future success. Equalizing opportunities for education is one such mechanism; "affirmative action" programs for groups that are systematically oppressed is another. Affirmative action programs are chronically contested as "reverse discrimination" by those who suspect they have been passed over. Equalizing educational opportunities is thus the route most commonly followed.

As these notes suggest, meritocracy is at once a conservative and a revolutionary ideology. The conservative ideology, favored by those on top and accepted with resignation by many below, claims that the elite have earned their position and privileges by merit, and points to their high test scores, prestigious college degrees, and long hours of work as proof. The counter ideology, favored (though far from unanimously) by those below, claims that the less advantaged have been denied a fair chance for success, and point to either their own humble origins or the advantaged backgrounds of most of those on top. They believe their true merit has either been suppressed or ignored by a system biased in favor of the elite.

The Emergence of Meritocracy as a Social Issue

If it is true that the ideal of meritocracy pervades modern ideologies, can we point to historical contexts where merit was not important? Probably not, at least in general terms. This is because skilled job performances are almost always of some value, even if other criteria for social stratification are more important. Race and gender exclusion rules in American corporations, for example, generally meant that the best qualified white males would compete for the top positions and rewards, not that qualifications did not matter.

Meritocracy as a modern social issue is closely tied to the transformation of economies from agrarian to industrial, and of political orders from hereditary to democratic, particularly multiparty democracies. However they are measured, technical qualifications for employment become particularly salient in bureaucratic organizations, and particularly those competing with other firms in product and service markets. As Weber pointed out, bureaucracies are not unique to industrial societies, but they certainly are the dominant form of employment in those societies. The Chinese developed bureaucratic administrative systems over two thousand years ago, and devised a rather modern-sounding system of formal examinations to screen applicants for higher positions. But societies with most working members employed by bureaucratic organizations coincide with industrialization. Prior to industrialization,

most of the population was employed in agriculture and craft occupations. These positions were filled primarily by family members and itinerant workers. Skill differences were no doubt present and often consequential for the prosperity of the farmer or craftsman. But the importance of skill differences was greatly muted by the simplicity of the main technologies and the division of labor.

As employment shifted from agriculture to industries and services, and as industrial and service corporations became progressively more technically advanced, formal educational credentials have grown in importance. In the United States, the percentage of the male labor force working in agriculture declined from 88% in 1810 to 43% in 1900, to 15% in 1950, to only about 3% in 1990. At the same time, the educational attainments of the population increased rapidly. As employment moved out of the household and into the corporation and government bureau, educational credentials became an important criteria for selecting among applicants for jobs. Predictably enough, the growing importance of education to employment resulted in pressure to make educational opportunities available to all, and to use more objective criteria in deciding who would have access to the more desirable places in the educational system.

The use of examinations to screen entry into jobs in the United States can be traced to World War I, when over two million men were administered mental ability tests. Data are not available on the proportion of jobs that directly use formal examination results as a basis for hiring and promotion, but the number is probably not very high. Some professions, such as law and accounting, require aspirants to pass examinations in order to be eligible for employment. Much more common is the use of educational credentials, or more properly, the résumé of education and experience, as a basis for employment, and performance ratings as the basis for promotion. The reason for these preferences is probably no more complicated than that employers find they can predict job performance better with these devices than with a test.

Test scores for screening college admissions became widespread in the years following World War II, when thousands of new students entered higher education with the help of the GI Bill. The Educational Testing Service piloted the Scholastic Aptitude Test (SAT) in the 1920s, and the Academic Competency Test (ACT) started in the 1940s. Only individuals considering college enrollment take these tests, and proportions of students completing high school and of high school graduates considering college increased greatly in the early and middle decades of the twentieth century.

In the elementary and secondary grades, test scores are widely used as a basis for dividing students into different instructional groups or tracks. This practice also dates from the 1920s, when secondary education transformed from an elite to a mass institution. An objective basis was sought for determining which kind of program a student should follow in high school: a terminal vocational, business or "general," or college preparatory.

That this modern obsession with sorting and selecting individuals according to academic performance and job-related instrumental skills represents a historically unparalleled growth of meritocracy may seem obvious. In one respect, it is obvious and correct: both the absolute and relative number of jobs that have come under the sway of these considerations have certainly grown. This is clear from the simple fact of massive shifts from agriculture to organizational employment. But if only the jobs within the organizational spheres of employment are considered, these may be no more meritocratic today than 50 or 100 years ago. As discussed next, this issue has attracted several important studies and much debate.

Current Debates over Meritocracy

Debates over meritocracy generally concern the extent to which selection criteria are in fact meritocratic as opposed to based on social background distinctions. Thinkers from the full span of the political horizon have weighed in on this issue. The following contemporary issues are of primary concern to social scientists: (1) To what extent can the U.S. educational and occupational systems be characterized as meritocracies? (2) Is there a historical trend toward a growth of meritocracy? and (3) How equal are opportunities for cognitive development?

Is the United States a Meritocracy?

Christopher Jencks has been one of the most active contributors to the debates over meritocracy over the past 25 years. In two landmark studies, *Inequality* (1972)

and *Who Gets Ahead?* (1979), Jencks and his colleagues essentially argue that the United States is far from being a true meritocracy. Social background differences still exert significant effects on educational attainments and occupational success even statistically controlling for individuals' ability. Furthermore, systematic factors like ability and social background account for only at most about half of the variability in occupational outcomes. The remaining, unaccounted for, variability reflects the influence of dumb luck and idiosyncratic factors. Their most recent and comprehensive analyses (1979) show that differences in cognitive ability among U.S. men (women were not included in the studies they examined) account for only about 25% of the variance in years of education completed and occupational status ranking, but only around 5% of the variability in men's earnings. Most of the effects on occupational status and income are associated with higher ability youth attaining higher levels of educational credentials, but independent effects of ability remain when credentials are statistically controlled.

Why is formal education so important as a screening device? The conventional answer is that education imparts the skills and knowledge needed by the modern economic order. But this "technical-rational" model has been vigorously challenged by many observers. Ivar Berg (1971), for example, points out that educational programs are often unrelated to the kinds of jobs filled by graduates, and that students' grades in college do not predict occupational performance very well. Randall Collins (1978) argues that education functions much more as a gatekeeper and sorting mechanism than as a means of recruiting and developing talent. Drawing on Max Weber's insights on competition among status groups, Collins believes the expansion of national educational systems in the twentieth century was primarily driven by competition among occupation-based status groups for better market positions and more power. Occupations try to raise their entrance requirements to make their members appear more distinctive, and to thereby gain more prestige.

Probably the most influential critique of the technical-rational model of educational expansion and selection is Samuel Bowles and Herbert Gintis' *Schooling in Capitalist America* (1976). Drawing on neo-Marxist theories about class structure and conflict, they argue that meritocracy is a fiction perpetrated by the dominant capitalist class in an effort to make an essentially unfair system seem fair. Parents with more money can pass their advantages on to their children by, in effect, purchasing more and better early childhood education, primary and secondary schools (by choosing their place of residence or through private education), summer schooling, home learning resources such as computers and books, and ultimately college and graduate or professional school enrollments. Schools also make special accommodations to higher SES students, placing them in higher tracks than their achievement warrants. As a result of these advantages, the children of more affluent parents almost inevitably score higher on tests of cognitive ability. Bowles and Gintis argue further that the meritocracy is a fraud because test scores are only weakly related to later economic success. The ideology of meritocratic selection is thus very attractive to the ruling class, because it legitimates their advantages over the rest of the population. In its essentials, this argument is still accepted by much of the left intelligentsia in the United States and abroad.

A social class bias in the odds of obtaining a given level of educational or occupational success does not, however, necessarily amount to evidence of organized class control over the system and the school as a breeding ground of false consciousness. The class biases that Bowles and Gintis point to can still be generated by a system that is largely meritocratic and class blind with respect to individual origins per se. Simple differences in the time and resources available to parents and the decisions they make about how to make use of the time and resources can lead to large class biases. This point was first made by Raymond Boudon (1974), and has been the operative assumption of most of the current round of research on the historical issue, discussed next.

Has Meritocracy Increased?

Michael Young's historical thesis, developed in a prelude to his fictional account of the future, is that meritocratic selection has steadily increased in importance, particularly over the past century. His argument is based on an examination of modern British institutions and how they recruit and promote individuals. The British civil service converted in the 1870s from basing appointments on political patronage to a competitive system based on formal educational attainments. At the same time, public-funded education was extended to all with the first compulsory attendance law. Beyond

those watershed events, Young saw a steady erosion of ascribed status in favor of technical expertise in hiring and promotion practices across the full range of the economy.

The question of whether meritocratic selection has grown is at the heart of the status attainment tradition of research on social stratification. Blau and Duncan's original formulation of the status attainment model showed that individuals' educational attainments explained most of the association between status origins and destinations, and exerted a strong independent effect in their own right. To that extent, their findings supported Young's claims that ascribed status had given way to achieved status in the modern economic order. However, their model did not include any measures of cognitive ability or noncognitive factors such as effort and motivation. Thus it was not possible to tell the extent to which formal educational attainments were being earned by the most talented and hardworking youth.

The argument that meritocracy is on the rise is also made by Richard Herrnstein and Charles Murray in *The Bell Curve* (1994). Their basic thesis is that the proportion of the work force employed in "high-IQ" technical and professional occupations has grown rapidly in the twentieth century, and that the occupational order as a whole has become increasingly stratified on the basis of general intelligence. In other words, occupations have become increasingly homogeneous with respect to ability. The evidence they cite in support of this claim is mainly drawn from higher education in the United States. As enrollments in higher education have increased, the brightest youth have become much more likely to go to college after high school, and have also tended to gravitate toward a relatively small number of elite institutions. Focusing on the average IQ and entrance test scores of students attending various types of colleges and universities, they present data documenting the transformation of the status order of colleges and universities from a basis on parental social class and wealth to a basis of student ability or academic achievement.

Herrnstein and Murray present only very limited direct evidence bearing on their key thesis, that occupations have become more homogeneous with respect to ability. In fact, other research studies cast doubt on their claim. Jencks and his colleagues (1979) argue that meritocracy has not significantly increased over the past several decades. The available evidence shows little or no growth in the correlation of tested ability and occupational status or income. David Weakliem and his colleagues (1995) also argue against the Herrnstein and Murray thesis, claiming that, if anything, meritocracy in the United States has declined in recent decades. Their study examines the association of occupational status with vocabulary test scores across several birth cohorts of American adults. Like Jencks, they find no evidence that this association has increased over time. Speculating on why this is the case, they suggest that tested ability is rarely used by employers, who instead tend to select applicants by educational specializations and degrees earned. As firms and bureaus have expanded in size, the demand for and supply of individuals with educational credentials have increased.

With respect to meritocracy within the sphere of education, the Herrnstein and Murray thesis that ability has become more important in determining who continues in school and how far has not been rigorously tested to date with large national samples. The recent international comparison project organized by Yossi Shavit and Hans-Peter Blossfeld (1993) found that the relationship of social class origins with educational attainments has surprisingly not changed over the past several decades in most industrial nations including the United States.

How Equal Are Opportunities for Cognitive Development?

As important as whether merit is justly rewarded by the market is whether the system allows something approaching a fair chance to gain merit to children born to lower SES and minority parents. In general, social class and racial or ethnic differences in achievement test scores are present at the beginning of formal schooling, and the gap grows larger each year (this was first documented in the 1966 *Equality of Educational Opportunity* report by Coleman and his colleagues). This "fan-spread" does not necessarily imply a denial of equal opportunity within school, for the pattern may also be consistent with effects of ability differences and ability grouping or individualized instruction. If, for example, higher ability students learn more quickly, and if they are placed in educational programs that challenge them, then fan-spread would occur even if lower ability

students were also being appropriately challenged. Nonetheless, increasingly large learning gaps are found among students who start at the same level of achievement when they are placed in different ability groups or curriculum tracks. The work of Adam Gamoran and Robert Mare (1989), for example, shows that high school track placements have a large effect on how much students learn in high school, and that SES has a strong effect on track placement even controlling for achievement scores.

Sociologists of education have not had great success in accounting for the large learning differences among students attending the same school. Of the factors they have identified, the most important tend to be parental SES and the ability group or curriculum track placements of the students. Higher SES students are much more likely to be in the higher tracks, but track placements are usually found to have strong independent effects on learning. Some talented children of poor parents who are not especially encouraging of academic success are identified by schools and given the best opportunities. And slow children of upper-middle-class families are sometimes placed in advanced tracks, where their achievement scores improve more than their less-well-connected but equally ungifted peers in the lower tracks. But generally it is true that learning differences are closely aligned with family background differences. Gamoran's (1987) analysis of a large national sample of high school students, for example, shows that about 10 percent of the variability among students' sophomore-to-senior mathematics test score gains is attributable to social background factors like SES, ethnicity, and gender. Adding several measures of the students' curriculum tracks and the numbers and kinds of math courses they completed in high school adds about 5 percent more to the explained variance in test score growth.

Work in the sociology of education on the causes and consequences of early childhood achievement differences is in its infancy, but important studies are beginning to accumulate. But little is understood about the family socialization and organized preschool differences that generate the initial differences. Better understanding of the early elementary years is essential to gaining a more complete view of inequalities and how they might be reduced. The emerging consensus is that differences in the socialization practices of parents in the preschool years have enormous consequences for children's academic abilities. Furthermore, a large part of these socialization differences are due to differences in the economic situations of families (see the paper by Brooks-Gunn et al., forthcoming). In terms of the debate over meritocracy, these differences point to very unequal opportunities to gain the cognitive skills needed for success.

Conclusion

There are many further aspects and ramifications of meritocracy that have not been touched upon here, but that merit more discussion. During 1995 and 1996, Christopher Jencks, Susan Mayer, and Paul Peterson organized a series of seminars on the subject of meritocracy at the University of Chicago and Harvard University, and several new publications will surely emerge from those deliberations. One important issue is that raised first by Michael Young and picked up by Herrnstein and Murray: Does the growth of meritocracy result in an "underclass" of low-ability individuals, few of whom would—quite understandably—accord little legitimacy to the meritocratic system? This of course dovetails with the discussion above on the extent to which meritocracy is in fact operative and to which equality of opportunity is in fact available. Current debates over the future and form of the welfare state will likely be forced at several turns to revisit these issues. Another set of issues relates to connections between school and work, and particularly the kinds of skills and aptitudes that employers try to recruit and promote, and how individuals are matched to jobs. Most of the research reviewed in this chapter focuses on broad correlations among achievement, educational attainment, and occupational outcomes, but ignores actual hiring processes. More work on the decision making of employers and applicants is needed to gain a more concrete understanding of the impact of abilities and backgrounds on outcomes.

REFERENCES

Bell, Daniel. 1973. *The Coming of Post-Industrial Society.* New York: Basic Books.

Berg, Ivar. 1971. *Education and Jobs: The Great Training Robbery.* Boston: Beacon Press.

Boudon, Raymond. 1974. *Education, Opportunity, and Social Inequality.* New York: John Wiley.

Bowles, Samuel, and Herbert Gintis. 1976. *Schooling in Capitalist America: Educational Reform and the Contradictions of Economic Life.*

Brooks-Gunn, Jeanne, Paula Klebanov, and Greg J. Duncan. "Ethnic Differences in Children's Intelligence Test Scores: Role of Economic Deprivation, Home Environment, and Maternal Characteristics." *Child Development* (forthcoming).

Collins, Randall. 1979. *The Credential Society.* New York: Academic Press.

Gamoran, Adam. 1987. "The Stratification of High School Learning Experiences." *Sociology of Education* 60:135–155.

Gamoran, Adam, and Robert Mare. 1989. "Secondary School Tracking and Educational Inequality: Compensation, Reinforcement, or Neutrality?" *American Journal of Sociology* 94:1146–1183.

Herrnstein, Richard J., and Charles Murray. 1994. *The Bell Curve: Intelligence and Class Structure in American Life.* New York: The Free Press.

Husen, Torstein. 1974. *Talent, Equality, and Meritocracy: Availability and Utilization of Talent.* The Hague: Nijhoff.

Jencks, Christopher. 1979. *Who Gets Ahead? The Determinants of Economic Success in America.* New York: Basic Books.

Jencks, Christopher, Marshall Smith, Henry Acland, Mary Jo Bane, David Cohen, Herbert Gintis, Barbara Heyns, and Stephan Michelson. 1972. *Inequality: A Reassessment of the Effect of Family and Schooling in America.* New York: Basic Books.

Shavit, Yossi, and Hans-Peter Blossfeld (eds.). 1993. *Persistent Inequality: Changing Educational Attainment in Thirteen Countries.* Boulder, CO: Westview Press.

Weakliem, David, Julia McQuillan, and Tracy Schauer. 1995. "Toward Meritocracy? Changing Social-Class Differences in Intellectual Ability." *Sociology of Education* 68:271–287.

Young, Michael. 1958. *The Rise of the Meritocracy, 1870–2033: An Essay on Education and Equality.* London: Thames and Hudson.

MULTICULTURALISM

Patricia Gandara
Division of Education, University of California

Nothing is more fundamental to the sociology of the United States than the fact that it is made up of peoples who emanate from all parts of the globe. This central fact has shaped what it means to be American,[1] and yet has also been the source of unresolved conflict in the cultural life of the nation. American attitudes toward its rich ethnic diversity have varied over time, but until the second half of the twentieth century, the predominant mode of dealing with this ethnic pluralism was through the process of cultural assimilation. And the primary vehicle for accomplishing this task has been the public schools.

Anglo Conformity, the "Melting Pot," and Cultural Pluralism

The sociologist Milton Gordon, in his book *Assimilation in American Life, The Role of Race, Religion, and Origins* (1964), posited three theories of assimilation that described the Americanization experience: Anglo conformity, the melting pot, and cultural pluralism. In reality the latter two forms are barely footnotes to the Anglo conformity model, yet represent a lesser reality up until the middle of this century. The classic paradigm of cultural assimilation for European immigrants was the rapid socialization of their children into the American culture. "While this process is only partially completed in the immigrant generation itself, with the second and succeeding generations . . . the impact of

the American acculturation process has been overwhelming" (Gordon, 1954:78). The new immigrants typically did not teach their native language to their children and loss of the native tongue was accompanied by a substantial loss of cultural knowledge as well. Hence the hallmark of successful immigrant families was Americanized children who went to school speaking English and who were culturally indistinguishable from other children in the classroom. Of course, although cultural assimilation, or acculturation, to the Anglo-American norm was encouraged, and to varying degrees enforced for all members of the society, only white Protestant immigrants from Northern and Western Europe were *structurally* assimilated into the broader community.

According to Gordon, the period up until about 1900 was characterized by the Anglo conformity model, in which English-oriented cultural patterns dominated American life, and the value for both the language and culture of Anglo Americans overwhelmed other non-Anglo cultural traits. It was this pattern of assimilation of successive waves of new immigrants that ensured that issues of non-English language and culture would not be raised in the classroom until these children had been fully acculturated to American life.

At the opening of the twentieth century, a new wave of immigrants began arriving on American shores, in greater numbers than ever before, and although most were Europeans, they came from the South and the East of Europe and brought cultural traditions quite distinct from the earlier Anglo-Saxon immigrants. With the increasing variety of ethnic groups came the notion of the "melting pot" society in which all of the newcomers were seen as *blending* into a common American culture. Although the Anglo-American norm had already been

---

[1] The term "American" here is used to refer to citizens of the United States in the way that it is commonly used within the boundaries of the country, while fully acknowledging that "Americans" are, in reality, citizens of any of the nations of the two American continents.

firmly established as the ideal, the melting pot rhetoric, however disingenuous, acknowledged the reality of an increasingly diverse nation. But it also called attention to the fact that "melting" all of these new groups would prove a daunting challenge; one that would require the collaboration of powerful institutions—like the schools. Public schools played a vital role in promoting this model of assimilation in which immigrant groups, with all due speed, would blend themselves into the existing American culture. Public schooling, in fact, was "consciously designed to function as the chief instrument for assimilating the children of immigrants, and . . . more than any other single factor, the public school undermined the capacity of immigrant groups to transmit their native cultures to their American-born children" (Steinberg, 1989:54).

Although many continued to promote the model of the melting pot as the prototype American experience, evidence abounded that not all groups were assimilating with equal ease or success. In particular, Italians and other southern Europeans, as well as African Americans were noted to achieve at much lower levels in school than did Anglo Americans. And although Jews fared better in school than many other groups, like the non-Anglo immigrants, they were not structurally assimilated into American society. High percentages of non-Anglo children dropped out of school as a response to school failure; the situation was especially acute for female students (Olneck and Lazerson, 1974; Perlmann, 1987). Nonetheless, through the first half of the century, until the depression, the economy was largely able to absorb these undereducated youngsters and sociologists continued to observe these differences in adaptation to schooling without sounding any real alarms. Differences in academic achievement were largely blamed on cultural practices in the homes of these children that were in conflict with the aims and the pedagogy of the schools. The children were viewed as being "culturally deprived" and in need of more effective socialization.

The depression years of the 1930s had a marked effect on the way that immigrants, and other non-Anglo Americans were viewed. In most of the states, compulsory education laws were strengthened to keep students in school, and out of the labor force, until the age of 16, and the country began to close its doors to immigration. In the border states of the Southwest, persons of Mexican descent were harassed on the streets

and summarily deported to Mexico, whether they had originated from there or not. People of color were further marginalized and blamed for taking jobs away from "real Americans" as the economy went into crisis. In spite of compulsory education laws, schooling was an unaffordable luxury for many poor children who were consequently left outside of their socializing influence, further contributing to the growth of cultural enclaves and a more pluralistic society.

Milton Gordon had already called attention to the fact of cultural pluralism—the coexistence of multiple cultures within the broader society—in 1954, in spite of the prevailing mythology of the melting pot. Now, other prominent sociologists such as Nathan Glazer and Daniel Patrick Moynihan began to raise their voices on behalf of a cultural pluralism that challenged the melting pot notion of American society. In *Beyond the Melting Pot* (1964), they argued that ethnic differences were powerful forces in shaping the life and schooling experiences of children of non-Anglo groups, particularly in large urban centers like New York where such cultural enclaves flourished. Their views angered people on both sides of the argument as they were seen as giving merit to the idea that other cultures were thriving in competition with the dominant American culture on the one hand. And, on the other hand, they were criticized for their patronizing and sometimes offensive views of non-Anglo culture such as in their contention that urban black culture was devoid of strong institutions and characterized by weak families and social disorganization. This new analysis of the state of intergroup relations in the United States was the harbinger of a series of social policies that would reshape American thinking about cultural assimilation and raise the question of whether schooling for the purpose of cultural assimilation alone could eradicate the consequences that poverty and disadvantage had wrought on disenfranchised people.

World War II and a New Pluralism

World War II marked a turning point in American race relations. In large part due to a fear that the postwar labor market could not accommodate all of the soldiers returning to civilian life, the Congress passed Public Law 346 in 1944, also known as the "GI Bill of Rights." The GI Bill provided funds for returning soldiers to pursue a higher education rather than immediately enter the work force. Many low-income and minority soldiers who would probably never have considered a college education saw this as a viable option and enrolled. As a result, institutions of higher education all over the country began accepting a new kind of student and a generation of college-educated African Americans, Latinos, Asians, and other people of color was created. With increased power and visibility, and a belief that Americans of color had "paid their dues" in the war, minority groups began to press their case for the rights guaranteed to them under the Fourteenth Amendment of the Constitution.

A New Era in Race Relations: *Brown v. the Board of Education*

Several desegregation cases came before the Supreme Court in the years following World War II, but in 1954 the case of *Brown versus the Board of Education of Topeka Kansas* would literally change the face of the nation. In a radical departure from past rulings, the court found that separate schools for black and white children were inherently unequal and therefore unconstitutional. The first major blow against Anglo conformity was struck. Although *Brown* addressed the segregation of black children from white schools, the decision reached far beyond the black/white struggles of the southern United States. In other parts of the country, children of Asian, Native American, and Mexican descent had also been segregated from their Anglo-American peers for purposes of schooling. These children, too, were provided access to an equal education under the new ruling. Of course, schools soon invented intraschool segregation (tracking) to circumvent the intent of the ruling while maintaining the appearance of compliance; nonetheless they were forced to accept the presence of nonwhite, non-Anglo persons in their midst and, as a consequence, neither the schools nor the society would ever again be the same.

The Continuing Struggle for Civil Rights: 1960s and Beyond

The Civil Rights Act of 1964 was the culmination of the post-World War II struggle to advance minority rights and it is symbolic of the era. Yet theory had not kept pace with legislative activity and the country did not have a clear idea of how to pursue its new equity

agenda. Programs such as Headstart, targeting low-income and minority children with enriched preschool experiences, were instituted to help level the playing field in schools, but the norm to which all children were to aspire was still very much an Anglo conformity norm. The curriculum of Headstart had focused on providing these children with experiences similar to those of their middle-class, Anglo-American peers. The belief was that if low-income and ethnic minority children could be removed from their home environments for a portion of the day, and given an "enriched" school-like environment similar to that of their more advantaged peers, the achievement gap between the groups could be closed. Social reformers were dismayed when the first evaluations showed that the Headstart children were unable to sustain their early gains on the IQ test scores. It had not yet occurred to the reformers that the Headstart children might bring unique strengths and abilities to the school, and not just deficiencies.

The attention to civil rights that characterized the 1960s set the stage for increasing emphasis on minority cultures and languages in the United States. By the late 1960s pressure had increased for bilingual education programs and the first ethnic studies departments were being established on university campuses. The melting pot view of American society had given way to cultural pluralism and a new interest in rediscovering the contributions of non-Anglo cultures was increasingly evident, especially on college campuses. Ethnic studies departments became an important element in the new cultural pluralism, as the call for a scholarship on American minorities became an essential prerequisite to teaching about these groups in American classrooms.

Ethnic Studies

Ethnic studies programs were developed to meet a number of perceived needs: to provide a home for research on minority experiences in the United States, to provide a curriculum whereby college students could study about these group experiences, to organize resources within the university and create a community to assist minority students in completing their college educations, and to bring the resources of the university to bear on the problems of these communities. Given the structure and nature of American universities, ethnic studies departments also provided a home for faculty to pursue these scholarly interests in a context in which their research could be evaluated by like-minded peers with similar backgrounds and training.

The history of ethnic studies departments on college campuses, however, has been a difficult one. At campuses across the country, their fortunes have risen and fallen depending on the politics of the time. The 1970s saw an enormous growth in the development of ethnic studies departments in the Vietnam and post-Vietnam political era that was nearly obsessed with self-examination as a nation. However, with the advent of the 1980s, these programs began to fall on hard times as the nation took a turn to the right, and minorities were more and more blamed for their own social and economic plights. Ethnic studies departments became a reminder of unresolved conflicts in American public life and attacks on the "scholarship" of such departments became more frequent. As higher education budgets tightened in the late 1980s, ethnic studies departments were often seen as expendable, or at the least, alterable to the extent that the university could merge them with other departments, thereby reducing both costs and autonomy. Numerous campuses engaged in well-publicized efforts to stave off the downsizing of their ethnic studies programs. Notably, at the midpoint of the 1990s, Harvard University stepped forward with a bold new initiative to strengthen its African-American studies program by bringing in a core of very high-profile and well-published black academics to anchor the program. It remains to be seen if this augurs a resurgence in support for ethnic studies departments at other American universities.

A Changing Demography and a New Call for Pluralism

Changes in the Immigration Act of 1965 that reversed a four-decades-old policy of favoring European immigration, and increasing economic and social pressures in Latin America and Asia created a new wave of immigration to the United States during the 1970s and 1980s to rival that of the early twentieth century. During the 1980s about 84% of the one million new immigrants annually to the United States were from Asia, the Caribbean, or Latin America, and by the year 2010, students of color—mostly Asian and Latino—will represent more than half of the population 18 years and younger in seven of the largest states. Already, in 22 of the 25 largest urban school districts, students of color

are now the majority, and one of every four students in the California public schools speaks a language other than English. The extraordinary speed with which the nation has been diversifying has created a greater urgency to address both the needs and the aspirations of the new Americans. Moreover, with larger critical masses and distinctly different cultural histories, these new immigrants may not concede as easily as earlier immigrants did to the cultural hegemony of Anglo conformity.

Bilingual/Bicultural Education: The 1970s

In 1968, Congress passed Title VII of the Civil Rights Act, which guaranteed equal access to education for limited English proficient students. In much the same way that the Civil Rights Act of 1964 signaled the legitimate right of minority groups to equal opportunity, and by implication, to their ethnic identity as well, Title VII legitimated the use of native languages in the instructional setting. The melting pot notion that in order to receive access to an education, children had to arrive at school already equipped with English language skills, was superseded by an acknowledgment that many children in the United States did not speak English when they went to school, but that this was not an excuse for denying them equal access to an education. The *Lau v. Nichols* Supreme Court decision in 1974 further reinforced this point as the court noted that "students who do not understand English are effectively foreclosed from any meaningful education. Basic skills are at the very core of what these public schools teach. Imposition of a requirement that, before a child can effectively participate in the educational program he must already have acquired those basic skills is to make a mockery of public education" (414 U.S. 563). Henceforth the law of the land dictated that linguistic, as well as ethnic and cultural diversity was to be acknowledged and accommodated by the schools.

Bilingual education was not a new phenomenon in the United States. It, too, had weathered the storms of political fortune. For example, it has been estimated that by 1900, over 200,000 children were being taught in German in public elementary schools, with smaller numbers being taught in Polish, Italian, Norwegian, Spanish, French, Czech, Dutch, and other languages (Nieto, 1993). Spanish, in conjunction with English, was the language of instruction in California during the 1800s, and in New Mexico as late as 1884. However, with the massive immigration of the early part of the twentieth century, and in the aftermath of World War I with its strong anti-German sentiment, laws were passed nationwide that banned instruction in languages other than English. The prevailing viewpoint of the time was recorded in the words of President Theodore Roosevelt: "We have room for but one language here, and that is the English language; for we intend to see that the crucible turns our people out as Americans, of American nationality, and not as dwellers of a polyglot boardinghouse; and we have room for but one sole loyalty, and that loyalty is to the American people" (cited in Brumberg, 1986:7). Hence, where the country had at least tolerated a certain level of language and cultural diversity in the previous century, the twentieth century opened with an ominous repudiation of all languages other than English, and all cultures other than the (Anglo-)American culture. Anything less than full acceptance of this monocultural and monolingual standard was, by implication in Roosevelt's words, evidence of a lack of loyalty to the republic.

By 1923, a Supreme Court challenge to this doctrine of monolingualism in the form of the case of *Meyer v. Nebraska* struck down a Nebraska law prohibiting the instruction of foreign languages (in this case German) to children below the eighth grade. The court ruled in favor of the "right of the individual to contract, to engage in any of the common occupations of life, to acquire useful knowledge" (262 U.S. 390). As a result of the *Nebraska* case, the state could not prevent the teaching of a foreign language in a public or private school classroom, but it also did not require that students with limited English receive any instruction in their primary language. The idea that limited English proficient (LEP) students should receive instruction tailored to their unique linguistic and cultural needs was left to *Lau* and the Lau Remedies that followed in 1975 to establish.

An important development in the research on bilingual education was the increasing awareness that not only the child's language, but also the child's culture, was a critical element in an effective teaching approach. Instructors of foreign languages had long understood that language is the doorway to another culture, for this reason foreign language textbooks always include lessons that place the learner in the cultural context of the language he or she is learning; likewise, it became apparent that if children were to begin their learning through their primary language, it could not be effectively separated from the cultural context that gave meaning to that language. Hence, in both legislation and in practice, comprehensive programs that served LEP students in their native language came to be referred to as bilingual/bicultural or bilingual/multicultural programs, reflecting the fact that many cultures may be incorporated into the instruction for LEP children.

Although the controversy over bilingual education is hardly over, and bilingual/bicultural education remains a highly politicized issue, in many ways this movement laid the groundwork for the multicultural education movement to come, as it established a pedagogically defensible basis for providing instruction in native language and culture as a means of enhancing the achievement of minority group students. The next step, however, was to establish the importance of a multicultural approach to learning for *all* students. This led to the major debates of the 1980s over the historical and literary canon.

The Culture Wars of the 1980s

"Multicultural education, as its major architects have conceived it during the last decade, is not an ethnic- or gender-specific movement. It is a movement designed to empower all students to become knowledgeable, caring, and active citizens in a deeply troubled and ethnically polarized nation and world" (Banks, 1993:23). In attempting to address all students, and not just minority students or members of victimized groups, a view of the fuller picture of the diversity of American society, its history and its literature, needed to be introduced into the curriculum. Exploding onto the national scene during the 1980s, and continuing unabated into the 1990s, what has come to be known as the "culture wars" have surfaced in university faculty committees, at state departments of education, among national standards boards, and in the popular press.

In 1991, *Time* magazine devoted a substantial portion of one issue to the culture wars. With hardly a pretense at evenhandedness, it proclaimed that "the [American] society that evolved and that persists today was modeled on Western examples . . . the influence of the British, who held and ruled the original thirteen colonies is inescapable. The language, the system of representative government, the structure of law and the emphasis on individual liberty were all adopted from . . . what was once known as the mother country. . . . To describe the Western tradition as just one of many equally important contributors to the American identity is to make hash of history" (Gray, 1991:16). As a reflection of the thinking, and the fears, of the American people, *Time* articulated very well the view that multiculturalism is a threat to the nation and a call for disunity. But the other side of this coin is the agenda of inclusion that the multiculturalists have sought.

Since the founding of the first public schools in the United States, there has been widespread consensus that a primary purpose of schooling is the socialization of the young into the norms of the culture. And it has been noted often that there is no better indicator of what we believe as a people, or who we believe we are, than that which we choose to pass on to our children through our schools. Hence, it should not be surprising that few topics would inspire more energetic debate than school curriculum, or that few sites would be more emotion charged than textbook adoption committees. The debate has been no less heated at the university level. When, in 1988, Stanford University undertook to revamp its Western Culture course to include more diverse perspectives, it became a major news story. Near riots broke out on the campus and Stanford humanities faculty were interviewed nightly on the national news. The uproar died down when the university decided to keep the traditional curriculum, augmented by optional readings that reflected other cultural perspectives.

Educating for Multiculturalism: The 1990s

The national standards movement that was kicked off by the Bush administration at the end of the 1980s under the title of the National Education Goals ignited considerable controversy with its expressed intention of establishing national standards for what public school children should learn. As a part of this process, contracts were established with education experts across the country to develop standards in the various subject matter areas. As each set of standards was released, it was met with substantial opposition, often by people who saw a threat to the traditional Anglo-conformist curriculum through the incorporation of new ideas and perspectives that were commonly viewed as "un-American." The recommendation that mathematics students should be organized into small, heterogeneous working groups, rather than individually—a pedagogical tool that grew out of research on culturally diverse styles of learning—was attacked, among other reasons, for failing to inculcate the proper value for individual achievement. History standards were decried as ignoring the important perspectives of traditional American heroes in favor of minority perspectives, and in California, where millions of dollars and several years had been invested in developing new tests aligned with the restructured English curriculum, the governor and the legislature called a halt to the testing, in large part because it included too many nontraditional reading passages. One piece by Alice Walker, the African-American writer, was a particular source of controversy because it was perceived by some to attack "traditional values."

At the close of the twentieth century, the culture wars raged on. Areas that were formerly thought of as culturally neutral, such as mathematics education, have become potent symbols of the deep divisions in the ways people emanating from different backgrounds see the world. It is altogether possible that the national standards movement will be stalled indefinitely because of an inability to gain consensus on core cultural values that should be passed on to our children.

Multicultural Education Theory

The multicultural education movement, however, is not just about the debate over the canon. More fundamentally it has attempted to find ways to include multiple viewpoints on what constitutes a democratic society. In this broader mission it has also been engaged in theory building. Sleeter and Grant (1988) outline five approaches to multicultural education that they contend summarize the various ways that teachers approach the issue. Their typology is drawn from a meta-analysis of the literature on multicultural education and hence is empirically based. The first approach simply focuses on *teaching culturally different children* in a way that promotes their entry into the mainstream of society; it identifies their unique needs and attempts to meet those needs to help them acquire the cognitive skills and knowledge expected of white middle-class children. The second approach is the *human relations* approach. This approach teaches *about* cultural differences in an attempt to build more understanding, and hence better intergroup relations. The third approach is *single group studies* in which the emphasis is on doing in-depth studies of specific groups and encouraging a critical consciousness about their position in society. The *multicultural education* approach is a fourth way that teachers attempt to deal with diversity and this includes total school reform. Students are taught in ways that are culturally appropriate for them, including strategies such as cooperative learning, and instruction that incorporates the full diversity of society whether or not it is represented in the particular school. The fifth approach is a *social reconstructionist* method in which students are helped to actively examine their own life circumstances, to take responsibility for their own education, and to learn skills for effecting social change. The objective of all of these approaches that fall under the general umbrella of multicultural education, according to Grant and Sleeter, is to increase educational equity for all students.

Banks (1989) has also attempted to typologize curricular approaches to multicultural instruction from a more theory-based perspective. He summarizes four approaches that are organized according to levels of integration of ethnic content. At the lowest level is the *contributions* approach, which focuses on discrete cultural elements of a group and simply exposes students to these cultural artifacts. The second level is the *additive* approach, in which concepts and perspectives on multiculturalism are shared with students, but the curriculum remains essentially unchanged. At the next higher level Banks introduces the *transformation* approach, in which the structure of the curriculum is actually changed to enable students to see issues, events, etc. from the perspective of others. The highest level is the *social action* approach in which students make decisions about important social issues and help to solve them.

All of these approaches to multicultural education hold in common the objective of creating a more harmonious society in which prejudice and discrimination are diminished. However, although at one end of the continuum students are simply encouraged to celebrate their differences, at the other end of this continuum educators view a different world, one in which power relations are restructured and Anglo-American cultural hegemony is problematized. It is small wonder that some might consider these views threatening.

As a spokesperson for the Anglo conformist, or traditionalist camp, Arthur Schlesinger, the noted historian and author of *The Disuniting of America: Reflections on a Multicultural Society*, has lamented the fact that with the new immigration of the twentieth century a "cult of ethnicity erupted" whose only result can be "the fragmentation, resegregation and tribalization of American life" (1991:21).

The multiculturalists, however, counter the argument that multicultural education divides the nation by citing what they believe is a false assumption: that the nation is already united. Banks (1993) notes that although we are one nation politically, this is not the case sociologically. He contends that

> multicultural education is designed to help unify a deeply divided nation rather than to divide a highly cohesive one . . . traditionally, the larger U.S. society and schools tried to create unity by assimilating students from diverse racial and ethnic groups into a mythical Anglo American culture that required them to experience a process of self-alienation. However, even when students of color became culturally assimilated, they were often structurally excluded from mainstream institutions. (23–24)

It is notable that both the multiculturalists and the Anglo conformists invoke the notion of *e plurbis unum*—"out of many, one," to make their arguments. On the one side is the fear that the center cannot hold and the *unum* is devolving into a chaotic many; on the other side is the optimism that the *unum* can be negotiated and restructured to reflect the nation's cultural diversity. For demographic reasons alone, it is unlikely that the country will retreat from its increasingly pluralistic character, but the struggle toward a self-acknowledged multiculturalism is far from over. The question remains unresolved whether schools, by shifting their agenda from cultural assimilation to cultural empowerment, can help the next generation of students realize the promise of equity. And as the twentieth century draws to a close, and the politics of ethnicity grow increasingly tense, it is evident that a protracted battle over the American identity is underway.

REFERENCES

Banks, James. 1989. "Multicultural Education: Characteristics and goals." In James Banks and Cherry McGee Banks (eds.), *Multicultural Education, Issues and Perspectives,* pp. 189–207. Boston: Allyn & Bacon.

———. 1993. "Multicultural Education, Development, Dimensions, and Challenges." *Phi Delta Kappan* 75:22–28.

Brumberg, Stephan. 1986. *Going to America, Going to School: The Jewish Immigrant Public School Encounter in Turn of the Century New York City.* New York: Praeger.

Glazer, Nathan, and Daniel P. Moynihan. 1964. *Beyond the Melting Pot, The Negroes, Puerto Ricans, Jews, Italians, and Irish of New York City.* Cambridge, Mass: MIT Press.

Gordon, Milton. 1954. *Assimilation in American Life: The Role of Race, Religion, and National Origins.* New York: Oxford University Press.

Gray, Paul. 1991. "Whose America." *Time* 138:13–17.

Nieto, Sonia. 1993. "Linguistic Diversity in Multicultural Classrooms." In H. Svi Shapiro and David Purpel (eds.), *Critical Social Issues in American Education,* pp. 194–211. New York: Longman.

Olneck, Michael, and Marvin Lazerson. 1974. "The School Achievement of Immigrant Children: 1900–1930." *History of Education Quarterly* Winter:454–482.

Perlmann, Joel. 1987. "A Piece of the Educational Pie: Reflections and New Evidence on Black and Immigrant Schooling since 1880." *Sociology of Education* 60:54–61.

Schlesinger, Arthur. 1991. "The Cult of Ethnicity, Good and Bad." *Time* 138:20.

Sleeter, Christine, and Carl Grant. 1988. *Multicultural Education: Five Approaches to Race, Class, and Gender.* Columbus, OH: Merrill.

Steinberg, Stephen. 1989. *The Ethnic Myth, Race, Ethnicity and Class in America,* 2nd ed. Boston: Beacon Press.

POLITICS OF EDUCATION[1]

Kevin J. Dougherty
Teachers College, Columbia University

Community colleges are one of the most important sectors of U.S. higher education. These public 2-year colleges (excluding branches of state 4-year colleges) comprise over one-quarter of all higher educational institutions in the United States, numbering 949 in 1996 (American Association of Community Colleges, 1997:9).[2] They enroll 38% of all college students (some 5.3 million in fall 1994) and 45% of all first-time freshmen. This enrollment share is even greater for less advantaged students, for whom community colleges are the single widest point of entry into higher education. Community colleges enroll 42% of all minority college students, 44% of all students aged 25 and older, and 54% of all part-time students (American Association of Community Colleges, 1997: 9, 26–35; United States National Center for Education Statistics, 1997a:182, 186, 192, 214).[3] Though some community colleges are largely vocational, most are comprehensive institutions, managing diverse portfolios of programs. Still, in most community colleges, a majority of students are enrolled in occupational education programs, and these programs graduate a large proportion of our nation's nurses, computer operators, and auto mechanics. Though baccalaureate preparation is no longer dominant, baccalaureate aspirants still account for 20 to 30% of community college students, and transfers from community colleges make up a sizable portion of 4-year college students, especially in California and Florida. In addition, community colleges provide remedial education, nonvocational or leisure courses, contract training for employers, advice and assistance to small businesses, and entertainment and other programs for the general community (Cohen and Brawer, 1996:Chapters 8–12).

The governance and finance of community colleges are just as complex as its functions. Depending on the state, community colleges may be governed by local or state boards or a state university. They receive funds from student tuitions, local taxes or appropriations, state appropriations and grants, federal grants, corporate fees and donations, etc. (Cohen and Brawer, 1996:Chapters 4–5).

Despite their educational importance and complex nature, community colleges have received surprisingly little systematic empirical scrutiny. Most research on the community college has tended to have a rather anecdotal, even hortatory quality. However, sociologists have contributed mightily to the small body of systematic research. What I aim to do in this chapter is to demarcate the general boundaries of community college scholarship, describe the sociological intervention, and sketch out where further research is needed. Sociological research on community colleges has focused on how and why they hinder the educational attainment of baccalaureate aspirants. I will summarize this body of research and then identify various holes that merit plugging. At the same time, I also identify other research topics, involving the community college's role in economic development and community services, that deserve much greater attention than they have received so far.

---

[1] I would like to thank the following for comments on this article: Thomas Bailey, Floyd Hammack, Margaret Terry Orr, and Dolores Perin.

[2] In 1985, there were 67 2-year branches of state universities (American Association of Community Colleges, 1997:9; United States National Center for Education Statistics, 1997a:258).

[3] Women enroll at community colleges at a slightly higher rate than do men.

Community College Scholarship Generally

Several journals and many books are devoted exclusively to the community college. But the bulk of this literature is of relatively low analytic scope and rigor. Written largely by community college administrators and teachers and their university mentors, commentary on the community college tends to be anecdotally descriptive and hortatory rather than systematically evaluative and critical. It focuses on describing how the institution operates, what social functions it purportedly meets now and could meet in the future, and the best strategies to advance the community college's position, prestige, and resources. When there is empirical analysis of the community college's social impact and of the forces that gave birth to it and will shape its future, this analysis is often based on single-institution case studies. The implicit analytic framework is an often unconscious functionalism in which the community college is seen as shaped by the consensual needs of "the community," whether for job preparation, educational opportunity, or community building.

Despite the above, there are islands of critical analysis within the main drift of commentary on the community college. Community college officials and scholars such as L. Steven Zwerling (1976), Arthur Cohen and Florence Brawer (1996), and Judith Eaton (1988) have written illuminating analyses of the institution's social role. Nonetheless, these isolated efforts have left a large deficit of critical scholarship that has been substantially filled by a small group of sociologists and other social scientists. In what follows, I will sketch this sociological contribution and note areas needing further research.

The Sociological Intervention

The relatively few sociologists who have studied the community college have had a weighty impact, which community college "locals" have noticed, even if just to criticize. The central concern of this sociological intervention has been whether community colleges inhibit or advance equality of educational opportunity.

Key Early Statements

The sociological analysis of the community college began with Burton Clark's *The Open Door College* (1960),

which astutely analyzed the organizational implications of the community college's open door admissions policy, diffuse social mission, allegiance more to secondary school than the university, and dependence on other educational institutions. Clark posited that the community college is profoundly shaped by its unselective admissions policy, which floods it with students with baccalaureate ambitions but subbaccalaureate prospects. To preserve its academic status, the community college responds by "cooling out" weak but ambitious students by diverting them toward terminal subbaccalaureate degrees. Clark sees this task as a necessary but dirty job: necessary because universities' selectivity must be preserved in order to meet society's need for expertise, but dirty because cooling out must be done behind students' backs in order to be effective (Clark, 1960:162–163).

Clark's attention to the community college's cooling out function and how the college is shaped by its relation to other kinds of educational organizations powerfully shaped subsequent sociological commentary.

In 1972, Jerome Karabel issued a stirring manifesto for subsequent sociology of the community college by picking up Burton Clark's cooling out concept and grounding it in a conflict, rather than functionalist, theory of education. Whereas Clark saw the community college's function as a painful but necessary resolution of the contradiction between the American values of educational opportunity and educational excellence, Karabel (1972) instead saw the community college as a weapon deployed by the capitalist class against the working class in the class struggle over life chances. He argued that those cooled out were largely working class and nonwhite while those upholding the putative value of educational quality were the privileged classes. For Karabel, the community college's emphasis on vocational education arises from a class-stratified capitalist society. In this society, the demand for good jobs outstrips the supply, requiring the elite to find ways of defusing this politically explosive contradiction. In addition, capitalist elites—centered in business, the selective universities, and prestigious foundations—support the vocationalized community college because it provides business with publicly subsidized employee training and selective universities with a covert means of deflecting the enrollment demands of less desirable students. Community college leaders have acquiesced with these capitalist imperatives, according to Karabel

(1972), because vocationalization affords their institution a unique identity: that of a "community" college that is no longer "junior" to the university. However, community college students, particularly minority students, have resisted vocationalization just as workers have resisted capitalist work demands.

Karabel (1972) backed up his argument by citing evidence that community colleges and their vocational programs disproportionately enroll working class students, that very few community college aspirants to a baccalaureate degree ever receive one, and that a key basis of this result is that community college students are pressured to enroll in vocational courses (a process that Karabel termed "cooling out," following Burton Clark). Karabel's argument about the capitalist origins of the community college is more cursory, relying on general comments by business people, foundations, and scholars rather than detailed studies of the founding and later vocationalization of specific community colleges.

Karabel's (1972) arresting argument—which was joined by Fred Pincus (1974)—broke sharply with the celebratory commentary of community college "locals" and Burton Clark's fatalistic belief in the inescapability of social contradictions. As New Left themes diffused through sociological scholarship, Karabel's position set the terms for subsequent sociological research on the community college. This research has strongly buttressed most of Karabel's statements about the community college's *effects*, while calling into question the instrumentalist Marxist analysis of the community college's *origins* that he propounded then (but not in his later work, which will be discussed below).

Later Research on the Effects of Community Colleges

Since Karabel's (1972) ground-breaking article, sociologists of the community college have focused on its impact on students' life chances: namely, college access, eventual educational attainment, and economic attainment. At the same time, other scholars—often not sociologists—have shed light on whether the community college really diverts students away from the universities and effectively meets employers' demand for "middle level" workers.

Student Outcomes. Many different studies converge to impressively validate Karabel's (1972) argument

that the mere fact of entering a community college has a significantly inhibitory impact on students' eventual educational and economic attainment. Primarily using national longitudinal surveys, sociologists David Lavin, William Velez, Kristine Anderson, Elizabeth Monk-Turner, and Fred Pincus, economists David Breneman, Susan Nelson, Charlene Nunley, and W. Norton Grubb, and the higher educational researchers Alexander Astin and Ernest Pascarella have found that even controlling for differences in family background, academic aptitude, high school record, and educational and occupational aspirations, community college entrants on average receive 0.12 to 0.25 fewer years of education, 11 to 19% fewer baccalaureate degrees, and significantly less prestigious and remunerative jobs than similar students entering 4-year colleges and universities (for more on these findings, see Dougherty, 1994:52–61; Pascarella and Terenzini, 1991:372–373, 506–507).

However, a few studies also suggest that defenders of the community college are correct that community colleges are more helpful than 4-year colleges to students with low educational ambitions and disadvantaged backgrounds (Dougherty, 1994:56; Pascarella et al., 1995:90; Pascarella et al., 1995–1996: 38–39; Whitaker and Pascarella, 1994:204). In addition, W. Norton Grubb and Leland Medsker and James Trent have found that areas rich in community colleges have higher college-going rates than areas rich instead in 4-year colleges (see Dougherty, 1994:50–52).

Dougherty (1994:Chapters 3–4) critically synthesizes the evidence on the community college's impact on students and advances a theory of how it produces lower rates of baccalaureate attainment than does the 4-year college. This theory focuses on the *institutional* causes of three critical events for community college entrants: attrition during the first 2 years of college, failure to transfer to 4-year colleges, and attrition after transfer. To explain how community colleges contribute to their students' higher dropout rate, over and above the handicaps students bring with them, Dougherty documents community colleges' lesser ability to socially and academically integrate their students through such influential devices as campus residence and an academically oriented student and faculty culture. To explain why community college students have a low rate of transfer to 4-year colleges, Dougherty examines such institutional factors as inadequate financial aid, weak encouragement of transfer (largely due to community colleges' emphasis on occupational education), and 4-year colleges' preference for freshmen over transfer students. And to explain why community college transfers less often attain a bachelor's degree than do 4-year college juniors, Dougherty shows the impact of loss of academic credits in transfer, difficulty in securing financial aid, poorer preparation for the academic demands of upper-division courses, and inadequate efforts by universities to socially integrate community college transfers.[4]

Diverting Students from the Universities. Various studies document Jerome Karabel's (1972) argument that community colleges do not simply attract students to higher education but also entice them away from universities. W. Norton Grubb, Gary Orfield, and Faith Paul have found that the more extensive a state's community college system the fewer the number going on to 4-year colleges. Moreover, Grubb and others find that the lower tuitions charged by community colleges pull students away from four-year colleges (see Dougherty, 1994:47–49).

Meeting Labor Market Demands. As both critics and defenders of the community college claim, the community college is indeed a central supplier of trained workers for "middle level" or "semiprofessional" occupations. But studies by Fred Pincus (1980) and W. Norton Grubb (1996), among others, find that

---

[4] Pascarella et al. (1995, 1995–1996) question whether community colleges provide inferior academic preparation. They find that with controls for social background and precollege ability and aspirations, community college students perform just as well as 4-year college students on tests of reading comprehension, mathematics, and critical thinking (at the end of the first year) and writing and science reasoning (at the end of the second year). These findings are quite heartening, but three caveats are in order. The community college sample is drawn from only five colleges (yielding 280 students the first year and 147 the second year) and six 4-year colleges. Also, the study controls for the average precollege academic ability of first-year students at each college and whether the students resided on campus or not. This has the effect of controlling for two potent devices by which colleges affect student achievement: exposure to high ability students and provision of campus residence. Finally, it is not clear how well the tests administered measure the skills needed to succeed in a 4-year college (Pascarella et al., 1995:87, 1995–1996:37).

its response to the labor market's call is more clumsy than acknowledged by both its defenders and critics. The community college often under- and overshoots the demands of the labor market: sometimes training far more people than the labor market can absorb and other times producing fewer workers than business would like (see Dougherty, 1994:44–46).

Later Research on the Origins of Community Colleges

Sociologists coming after Karabel (1972) and Pincus (1974) significantly shifted the terms of the debate over why community colleges arose and later moved in a sharply vocational direction. The main element was to recast business influence more in terms of indirect constraint rather than direct intervention and to highlight the important role as well of other actors.

Analyzing national-level data and the history of the community college system in Massachusetts, Steven Brint and Jerome Karabel (1989) substantially reorient Karabel's (1972) analysis of why the community college was vocationalized and bring it closer to Burton Clark's (1960) organizationally oriented argument. In contrast to Karabel (1972), Brint and Karabel (1989) find much less evidence of a direct business role in the rise and vocationalization of the community college; instead business's influence had been mostly indirect, based on its control of jobs that community colleges sought to fill. Moreover, Brint and Karabel argued that the internal dynamics of the field of higher education —particularly entrepreneurial activity by community colleges—played an even greater role than Karabel suggested in 1972. Drawing on institutional theory within organizational sociology, Brint and Karabel portray higher education as an "organizational field" composed of colleges competing for prestige and resources. Within this Darwinian universe, universities are at the top of the food chain, securing the best students, the most revenues, and the greatest prestige. Their chief concern has been to protect their academic and social exclusivity and thus the exchange value of their credentials in the face of the clamor for admissions by less privileged but ambitious students. To avoid throwing their doors open to the teeming masses, the universities supported the expansion of an alternative, the vocationalized community college.

Community colleges, in the meantime, collaborated with this university thrust, according to Brint and Karabel (1989). Seeing that the universities and 4-year colleges had snapped up the best occupational-training markets, community colleges began many years ago to carve out a market of their own, supplying middle level or semiprofessional occupations. Beginning in the 1920s, the American Association of Community Colleges conceived of and then militantly proselytized for a vocationalized community college. And in time, this vision persuaded not only AACC members but also external supporters such as state university heads, government officials, business, and foundations (Brint and Karabel, 1989:16–17, 34–46, 54–66, 77–78, 96–100, 107–108, 124–126, 208–210).

Kevin Dougherty's (1994) examination of the origins and vocationalization of the community college—based on an examination of community college politics at the national level and at the state and local level in five states (California, Washington, Illinois, Indiana, and New York)—both converges with and diverges from Brint and Karabel's. Whereas they advance a largely organizational explanation, Dougherty's analysis is grounded more in political sociology. The crux of Dougherty's argument is that government officials took the lead in establishing and vocationalizing the community college, but they did so within the constraints set by a democratic polity and a capitalist economy. Like Brint and Karabel (1989), Dougherty (1994) concludes that direct student or business demand is insufficient to explain the rise and vocationalization of the community college. However, contrary to Brint and Karabel, Dougherty finds that governmental initiative went well beyond the actions of state university and community college officials. A host of government officials supported the establishment and vocationalization of community colleges in part out of a sincere belief in educational opportunity but also out of more self-interested reasons. At the local level, school superintendents and high school principals instigated local drives to found community colleges in good part because this would bring them prestige as educational innovators and the opportunity to become college presidents. At the state level, governors, state legislators, and state education departments joined state universities in pushing for state aid for community colleges because, among other things, they saw the community college as a cheap way to meet the demand for college access and to stimulate politically popular economic growth through publicly subsidized training for busi-

ness. And at the national level, Presidents and members of Congress supported federal aid for the community college for much the same reasons as their state counterparts.

But if business's direct role in establishing and vocationalizing community colleges was only secondary, Dougherty (1994) finds that its *indirect* role—based on its economic and ideological hegemony—has been quite strong. Dougherty agrees with Brint and Karabel (1989) that one aspect of this indirect influence has been the fact that business controls jobs that community college officials seek to fill. But Dougherty finds that business's power to constrain governmental initiative goes much further. Business also controls capital for investment and thus the pace and distribution of economic growth. Realizing that capital investment is key to economic growth and therefore their own political prospects, public officials have taken the initiative to offer business publicly subsidized vocational education in order to secure business investment in their jurisdictions. Furthermore, business has also ideologically constrained government initiative. Government officials subscribe to values and beliefs—such as the importance of economic growth and that this growth must come through an expansion of jobs in the private rather than public sector—that have made them ready to serve business interests (Dougherty, 1994:125).

For Dougherty (1994), an awareness of the community college's complex origins allows us to see how the community college could powerfully, and yet largely unintentionally, hinder the baccalaureate opportunities of its students. The fact that community colleges lack dormitories contributes to their higher dropout rate, but the reason they lack dormitories is because this made community colleges cheaper to operate, a potent consideration in the minds of the local educators founding them and the state officials financing them. The fact that community colleges are heavily vocational lessens their students' desire to transfer, but they are so strongly vocational not to track students but to meet business's need for trained employees and government officials' desire for an attractive incentive to secure business's political support and economic investment. The fact community colleges are 2-year schools discourages students from pursuing a baccalaureate degree, because they have to transfer to separate 4-year institutions with different academic standards.

But the reason community colleges are 2-year schools is largely because university heads did not want the competition of many more 4-year schools, state officials did not want the financial burden of a myriad of 4-year colleges, and local educators felt it would be easier to establish 2-year rather than 4-year colleges. The precipitate of these varying desires is an institutional structure that unfortunately and largely unintentionally, often subverts to the educational ambitions of baccalaureate aspirants entering community college, even as it opens up opportunities for students with nonbaccalaureate ambitions.

Further Research Needed on the Community College

Although sociologists have powerfully illuminated the community college's effects and origins, there is a need for much more research. Some of this involves refining the findings extant. But there is a need as well for research exploring areas largely neglected by sociologists of the community college, particularly the community college's role in economic development, remedial education, community building, and educating for citizenship and public participation.

Refining the Research on Students' Educational and Occupational Attainment

As noted above, a wide variety of excellent studies show that community college students on average secure less education and poorer jobs than comparable students (in background, high school achievement, and ambitions) entering 4-year colleges. And compared to similar students entering public or private vocational schools, community college entrants do better educationally but, economically, fare no better and sometimes worse (Dougherty, 1994:52–66; Pascarella and Terenzini, 1991:372–373, 506–507).

Despite the strength of this research, there are four areas in which further research is much needed.

More Recent Data. The research extant is based primarily on students who entered college in the 1960s and 1970s, which raises the question of whether the community college's impacts on students have since changed. Because of a heavy reliance on the National Longitudinal Survey of the High School Class of 1972,

most of the best national research on the impact of community colleges has been restricted to analyzing students who entered college in the early 1970s. But in comparison to the early 1970s, community colleges today enroll a much greater number of nontraditional students, provide much more extensive vocational and remedial programs, have sharply raised tuitions in order to make up for sharp cutbacks in government appropriations, etc. These changes raise the question of whether the impact of community colleges on their students' educational and economic attainment has changed considerably.

Luckily, the U.S. National Center for Education Statistics has sponsored three excellent national longitudinal studies examining students who entered college in the 1980s and even 1990s: the High School and Beyond Survey of high school sophomores and seniors in 1980; the National Educational Longitudinal Study of the Eighth Grade in 1988 (some of these students started entering college by 1993); and best yet, the Beginning Postsecondary Student Longitudinal Study (which began with 7,000 respondents in 1989–1990).

Economic Attainment. Sociologists have focused far more on the impact of community colleges on educational attainment (particularly baccalaureate acquisition) than on economic attainment. To be sure, economists such as W. Norton Grubb (1996) have been doing excellent research in this area, but it is still one that sociologists need to pay attention to. There are too few studies that rigorously compare the economic returns to attending a community college to the returns for other 2-year institutions such as proprietary schools, public vocational schools, etc. And there are no studies that I am aware of that compare community colleges with nonschool training providers such as employers, the armed services, distance education services using the Internet, etc.

Variations in Community College Effects. The research extant has focused on main effects, yet there is suggestive evidence that community college effects may vary considerably depending on students' traits and community colleges' characteristics. On the student side, students' aspirations and social background shape what impact community colleges have on their academic, educational, and economic attainment.

White, middle-class, and female students seemingly experience greater cognitive growth and attain more education if they attend 4-year colleges rather than community colleges, but the reverse is true for non-white, working class, and male students (Dougherty, 1994:56; Pascarella et al., 1995:90, 1995–1996:38–39). Similarly, students with high educational or occupational aspirations attain significantly more educationally or occupationally if they enter 4-year colleges rather than community colleges, but those with low aspirations do as well or better attending community colleges (Dougherty, 1994:56; Whitaker and Pascarella, 1994:204). Finally, among community college graduates, men graduating with vocational associates' degrees secure higher status occupations and higher hourly wages than do women, but women get higher hourly wages than men among those graduating with vocational certificates (Dougherty, 1994:75–76). Given this suggestive evidence, we need to examine rigorously how community college effects vary by students' social background (social class, race, sex), age, educational and occupational aspirations, etc. using large national samples with extended followups.

On the institutional side, we know that community colleges vary greatly among themselves in their declared missions, degree of support for college transfer, financial resources, etc. And again we have suggestive evidence that variations in the characteristics of community colleges produce variations in their students' educational and occupational attainment. For example, the more vocational a community college is the lower its transfer rate (Dougherty, 1994:94). Again, this suggests the need to disaggregate community colleges and examine whether different types produce different results for their students.

More Data on How Baccalaureate Aspirants Are Hindered. Though Dougherty (1994:Chapter 4) and others have provided detailed explanations of why baccalaureate aspirants entering community colleges less often acquire bachelor's degrees than their peers entering 4-year colleges, we still could learn more about how this differential effect is produced. The finding that community college entrants suffer higher rates of attrition in the lower division than do comparable 4-year college entrants is based on but a few studies, only two of which control for differences in background, ability,

etc. between the two kinds of students. And both of these studies involve students who entered college in the late 1960s and early 1970s (see Dougherty, 1994:85–92).

Similarly, the finding that community college students have a higher rate of failure to continue on to the upper division than do comparable students who first entered 4-year colleges is based on studies that do not control for a wide range of possible differences between these two kinds of students (see Dougherty, 1994:92–97). Hence, there is a need for careful multivariate studies in order to conclusively establish that there is a significant *institutional* contribution to the lower transfer rate of community college entrants.

Finally, a disagreement has cropped up over whether community college transfers more often drop out of the university than do similar 4-year college juniors. Based on studies done by several states, Dougherty (1994:97–105) argued that community college transfers suffered a higher rate of dropout than did comparable students who started at 4-year colleges. However, based on a multivariate analysis of data from High School and Beyond, Lee et al. (1993) argued that there was no difference in baccalaureate attainment between community college transfers and 4-year college natives. However, there is reason to doubt whether the study by Lee et al. settles the question.[5]

It would be very useful if we could have studies that examine the impacts all at once of all the career contingencies (lower division attrition, failure to transfer, and attrition in the upper division) facing B.A. aspirants. By examining them all within one data set, rather than having to paste together several different studies, we can determine the relative weights of the career contingencies.

Beyond refining our estimates of the impacts of the

---

[5] Lee et al. (1993) do not seem to control for how many credits the students have accumulated; as a result the comparison would become one between the persistence rate of 4-year college natives over 4 years and that for community college transfers only over the years since transfer. As it happens, studies by the states of California, Florida, and Illinois find that 5 years after transfer about 39% of community college transfers have dropped out, but the figure for 4-year native *juniors* (roughly comparable to the transfers in number of credits attained) is only about 24% (Dougherty, 1994:97–99).

career contingencies faced by baccalaureate aspirants, it would help if we better understood *how* precisely these contingencies operated. Here qualitative research would be useful, but sociologists have done it all too rarely. The major exception is the work of Howard London and Kathleen Shaw (London, 1978; Shaw and London, 1998).

Exploring Sociologically Uncharted Dimensions of the Community College

Students' educational and economic attainment are not the only community college impacts of note, but they are the ones that have gotten the lion's share of interest, because they fit nicely with the status-attainment focus of the sociology of education and of social stratification. Yet community colleges have other important goals besides shaping students' life chances, and unfortunately the content and effectiveness of these other goals have been little studied. We need to investigate vast areas of the community college that we have largely left unexplored by sociologists: the community college's role in economic development, remedial education, community building, and education for civic responsibility. Given the community college's complexity of function, governance, and finance, we need to explore its nature as an organization that is quite different from either 4-year colleges or high schools. And as this complex institution comes under massive and conflicting social, economic, and political pressures, we need to forecast its likely and/or desirable future trajectory.

The Community College's Role in Economic Development. In the past two decades, community colleges have taken on a key role as engines for local economic development, but this role is only beginning to be studied in any major way. Community colleges have diversified their economic development role beyond the training of technicians and other "middle-level" workers to include such things as contract training for employers, helping small businesses get started and then prosper, and participating in local economic development planning. Only a few studies of the origins, dimensions, and impacts of this new role have appeared (Brint and Karabel, 1989:192–202; Dougherty and Bakia, 1998; Grubb et al., 1997; Pincus, 1989), and far more are needed. We need to investigate the factors leading to the development of this new economic role,

how that role varies across different kinds of community colleges, how effectively community colleges have discharged this economic development role, and what impact it has had on the community college itself. In studying the community college's effectiveness, we need to examine its contribution not just to meeting the needs of firms but also the larger needs of the community for economic stimulus and economic planning. And on the question of the impact on the community college of its new economic role, we need to analyze how a major commitment to working closely with employers on their training needs affects the community college's willingness and ability to meet its other functions, such as baccalaureate preparation, remedial education, and community building and civic education. Closer connections to employers do appear to benefit community colleges by attracting new funds, enrollments, and political support and spurring useful changes in the curriculum. At the same time, the new economic role may also undermine other functions of the community college by pulling away necessary resources. For example, the organizational energy and imagination necessary to construct and maintain transfer and articulation arrangements with 4-year colleges may instead be poured into forging stronger connections to employers because these promise new funds, enrollments, and political support (Dougherty and Bakia, 1998).

Remedial Education. Because they have long been portals into higher education for students that 4-year colleges would turn away as unprepared for college, community colleges have long provided remedial education (Cohen and Brawer, 1996:Chapter 9). In 1995, 41% of freshmen in public 2-year colleges were enrolled in remedial courses either in reading, writing, or arithmetic, as compared to 29% of college students generally (United States National Center for Education Statistics, 1997b:102). And this role promises to become even larger, as state legislators and 4-year college boards continue to push to have remedial education reduced or even eliminated at 4-year colleges and instead relegated to community colleges (Dougherty, 1998). We need to know more about the forces behind this redefinition of institutional responsibilities for remedial education, what impact it will have on students and their colleges (both 2-year and 4-year), and how well community colleges actually remediate.[6] For example, what proportion of remedial students ever escape from remedial education programs in the community college and go on to graduate? What role does unsuccessful remediation have in the poorer educational attainment of working-class and minority students?

Education for Civic Participation. Under the rubric of general education, the community college has long been committed to the nonvocational education of its students for citizenship and social participation (Cohen and Brawer, 1996:Chapter 12). But we have few rigorous data on how effective it is in this role. We also do not know how the community college's contribution to civic education is affected by its growing role in work force preparation and economic development.

Community Building. Community colleges are an important means of generating a vibrant "civil society," by providing a place for citizens of diverse backgrounds to come together in noncredit evening and weekend classes, public affairs events, arts presentations, etc. (Cohen and Brawer, 1996:Chapter 10). Yet this community-building function, though much described and celebrated by community college observers, has not been systematically studied except in recent research by Kathleen Shaw and Howard London (1998). We need to investigate the degree to which these community-building efforts do enhance civic consciousness and social solidarity in the community and how the community college contribution compares to that of churches, volunteer groups, clubs, etc.

Multicultural Education. The community college has been unique among colleges in its willingness to enroll students of quite different backgrounds. However, we have little information on how successful the community college has been in aiding this diverse clientele to develop mutual understanding and a sense of social solidarity and common civic consciousness.

Analyzing the Community College as an Organization. The preceding remarks about the community

college's multiple roles—baccalaureate preparation, occupational training, economic development, remedial education, civic education, and community building—indicate how complicated its functions are. Add to this its diversity of governance and finance (Cohen and Brawer, 1996:Chapters 4–5) and its multiple linkages to a host of other educational institutions including high schools, postsecondary vocational schools, and public and private 4-year colleges. This complexity makes the community college a unique institution, one quite different from either the 4-year college or the high school. Yet it has received far too little *organizational* analysis except by Burton Clark (1960) and Brint and Karabel (1989). Both the community college and the sociology of educational organizations would benefit greatly from sociological analysis of the structure, culture, internal processes, and external relations and linkages of this complex and unique institution.

Research on the Community College's Future. The community college will not remain static. It will continue to change, perhaps sharply, due to its diffuse institutional mission and high responsiveness to its economic, social, and political environment (Brint and Karabel, 1989; Clark, 1960; Dougherty, 1994). As it is, this environment is changing rapidly and rather chaotically (Dougherty, 1998). Economically, as our economy further globalizes, the occupational composition, class distribution, and employment stability of the U.S. population are being transformed. Semiskilled jobs in factories and offices are being killed or moved abroad, and class inequality is increasing. Hence, community colleges, both out of internal volition and external pressure, are stepping up their efforts at job preparation and economic development. Meanwhile, high immigration is bringing increasing numbers of people who require acculturation and preparation for high-skill jobs. But at the same time, recent changes in immigration law may pull immigrant students out of the community college because they are denied access to social-welfare programs that allow them to afford going to community college. Similarly, the drive to reform welfare by moving people rapidly into jobs is bringing the community college students needing job training but also depriving it of others who have to leave college to take jobs either to make up for the loss of welfare benefits or to meet work requirements in order to retain

---

[6] A notable beginning in this area has been the work of Kathleen Shaw (1997).

them. Finally, the community college faces a more hostile political environment, with government becoming more stingy in its appropriations, demanding greater accountability, and more frequently denouncing remedial education in the community college (Dougherty, 1998).

Beyond affecting the number and kind of students the community college gets, these same external pressures are also affecting its programmatic composition. Occupational and remedial education are rising, but transfer education—despite brave holding efforts—will probably continue to decline. Teaching may change dramatically with the wholesale introduction of distance education designed to keep down instructional costs (Dougherty, 1998).

It is important that sociologists chart how the community college *is* responding to, and being changed by, these environmental pressures. Will the net effect be expansion or contraction of the community college? Will the growth of work force preparation and economic development dangerously undercut the commitment to civic preparation and community building? Because of these dangers, sociologists perhaps should also envisage how the community college *could* respond to environmental changes and yet protect a commitment to equality of opportunity and democratic socialization.

Summary

Sociology of education has given the community college sector far less attention than it deserves, given its large size and key role in education and the economy. Despite this, the small band of sociologists who have studied the institution have made an impressive contribution to understanding its historical origins and its impact on students' educational and economic attainment. But much remains to be done, both in refining the research that has been conducted and in exploring vast areas that have been left untouched. In terms of refining our research on students' educational and economic attainment, we need to update our findings using more recent data sets, further investigate economic attainment, examine how community college effects vary by the characteristics of the students and of the colleges, and further uncover the institutional mechanisms hindering the educational attainment of baccalaureate aspirants. But sociologists need to go beyond plugging holes in existing research. We must also investigate vast areas of the community college that we have largely left unexplored: the community college's role in economic development, remedial education, community building, and education for civic responsibility. We also need studies of the community college as an organization that is highly complex and quite different both from high schools and 4-year colleges. And rounding all this out, we need to investigate the community college's likely and possible future trajectories: how it will be reshaped by the many and conflicting demographic, economic, and political forces now impinging on it.

REFERENCES

American Association of Community Colleges. 1997. *National Profile of Community Colleges: Trends and Statistics, 1997–1998.* Washington, DC: Author.

Brint, Steven G., and Jerome B. Karabel. 1989. *The Diverted Dream.* New York: Oxford University Press.

Clark, Burton. 1960. *The Open Door College.* New York: McGraw-Hill.

Cohen, Arthur C., and Florence B. Brawer. 1996. *The American Community College,* 3rd. ed. San Francisco: Jossey-Bass.

Dougherty, Kevin J. 1994. *The Contradictory College: The Conflicting Origins, Impacts, and Futures of the Community College.* Albany: State University of New York Press.

———. 1998. "Community College Scenarios: Prospects and Perils." New York: Community College Research Center, Teachers College, Columbia University.

Dougherty, Kevin J., and Marianne F. Bakia. 1998. "The New Economic Role of the Community College." New York: Community College Research Center, Teachers College, Columbia University.

Eaton, Judith, ed. 1988. *Colleges of Choice: The Enabling Impact of the Community College.* New York: American Council on Education and Macmillan Publishing.

Grubb, W. Norton. 1996. *Working in the Middle: Strengthening Education and Training for the Mid-Skilled Labor Force.* San Francisco: Jossey-Bass.

Grubb, W. Norton, Norena Badway, Denise Bell, Debra Bragg, and Maxine Russman. 1997. *Workforce, Economic, and Community Development: The Changing Landscape of the 'Entrepreneurial' Community College.* Mission Viejo, CA: League for Innovation in the Community College.

Karabel, Jerome. 1972. "Community Colleges and Social Stratification." *Harvard Educational Review* 42:521–562.

Lee, Valerie E., Christopher Mackie-Lewis, and Helen M. Marks. 1993. "Persistence to the Baccalaureate Degree for Students Who Transfer from Community College." *American Journal of Education* 102 (November):80–114.

London, Howard B. 1978. *The Culture of a Community College.* New York: Praeger.

Pascarella, Ernest T., and Patrick T. Terenzini. 1991. *How College Affects Students.* San Francisco: Jossey-Bass.

Pascarella, Ernest T., Louise Bohr, Amaury Nora, and Patrick Terenzini. 1995. "Cognitive Effects of 2-Year and 4-Year Colleges: New Evidence." *Educational Evaluation and Policy Analysis* 17 (Spring):83–96.

Pascarella, Ernest T., Marcia Edison, Amaury Nora, Linda Hagedorn, and Patrick Terenzini. "Cognitive Effects of Attending Community Colleges." 1995–1996. *Community College Journal* (December–January):35–39.

Pincus, Fred L. 1974. "Tracking in Community Colleges." *Insurgent Sociologist* 4 (Spring):17–35.

———. 1980. "The False Promises of Community Colleges: Class Conflict and Vocational Education." *Harvard Educational Review* 50:332–361.

———. 1989. "Contradictory Effects of Customized Contract Training in Community Colleges." *Critical Sociology* 6:77–93.

Shaw, Kathleen M. 1997. "Remedial Education as Ideological Battleground: Emerging Remedial Education Policies in the Community College." *Educational Evaluation and Policy Analysis* 19 (Fall):284–296.

Shaw, Kathleen M., and Howard B. London. 1998. "The Interplay between Ideology, Culture, and Educational Mobility: A Typology of Urban Community Colleges with High Transfer Rates." AERA presentation. Philadelphia, PA: Temple University, School of Education.

United States National Center for Education Statistics. 1997a. *Digest of Education Statistics, 1997.* NCES 98–015. Washington, DC: U.S. Government Printing Office.

———. 1997b. *The Condition of Education, 1997.* Washington, DC: U.S. Government Printing Office.

Whitaker, David G., and Ernest L. Pascarella. 1994. "Two-Year College Attendance and Socioeconomic Attainment." *Journal of Higher Education* 65(March/April):194–210.

Zwerling, L. Steven. 1976. *Second Best: The Crisis of the Junior College.* New York: McGraw-Hill.

PROGRESSIVE EDUCATION[1]

Susan F. Semel
City College of New York (CUNY)

The beginning of the nineteenth century ushered in the First Industrial Revolution, immigration, and urbanization of unprecedented proportions. Accordingly, the conditions created by these events were met with responses from social reformers whose concerns were far reaching and who attempted to address and redress the evils in American life.

If the beginning of the nineteenth century seemed problematic to Americans, the close of the century must have been even more so. Again, there was a revolution in industry, referred to as the Second Industrial Revolution, this time involving steam-driven and electric-powered machinery. Factories had given way to gigantic corporations, under the control of captains of industry such as Andrew Carnegie, John D. Rockefeller, and Cornelius Vanderbilt. Significantly, immigrant labor played an essential role in this revolution.

At the beginning of the nineteenth century, the largest number of immigrants to the United States came from the northwestern part of Europe, namely Great Britain, Scandinavia, Germany, and the Netherlands. After 1890, an increasingly large number of immigrants came from southern and eastern Europe. These immigrants' languages, customs, and living styles were dramatically different from those of the previous group. They settled in closely crowded substandard living quarters in urban areas and found work in factories. Thus, by the turn of the century, American cities contained enormous concentrations of both wealth and poverty. Indeed, the gap between rich and poor had never been as great as it was at the close of the nineteenth century.

The purpose of education has been seen in a variety of ways: religious, utilitarian, civic, and with Mann, social mobility. The common school was born of an age of reform in this country unprecedented until the period between 1900 and 1914 in which a new reform movement, the Progressive Movement, would sweep the country. Progressive reformers insisted upon government regulation of industry and commerce, as well as government regulation and conservation of the nation's natural resources; moreover, progressive reformers insisted that government at national, state, and local lives be responsive to the welfare of its citizens rather than to the welfare of corporations. Significantly, progressive reforms had a sweeping agenda, ranging from secret ballot to schooling. As reformers such as Horace Mann in the nineteenth century had looked to schools as a means of addressing social problems, so reformers once again looked to schools as a means of preserving and promoting democracy within the new social order.

John Dewey and Progressive Education

An important American philosopher whose influence upon schooling is still very much with us today was John Dewey (1859–1952). Dewey was a contemporary of such reformers as "Fighting Bob La Follette," governor of Wisconsin and architect of the "Wisconsin Idea," which harnessed the expertise of university professors to the mechanics of state government; settlement workers, such as Jane Addams and Lillian Wald; and municipal reformers and labor leaders, such as

[1] Sections of this chapter are adapted from Sadovnik, Alan R., Peter W. Cookson, Jr., and Susan F. Semel. 1994. *Exploring Education: An Introduction to the Foundations of Education*. Needham Heights, MA: Allyn & Bacon; and Semel, Susan F. 1992. *The Dalton School: The Transformation of a Progressive School*. New York: Peter Lang, with permission.

Henry Bruere and John Golden. Thus, progressive education, the movement John Dewey has become associated with, can best be understood, as both historians Lawrence Cremin and Richard Hofstadter remind us, as part of "a broader program of social and political reform called the Progressive Movement" (Cremin, 1961:88).

Just as the schools today are undergoing a transformation due in part to rapidly changing technology, altered life styles, and new, massive waves of immigrants, it could be argued that the schools at the turn of the century were undergoing a similar transformation in their time. In 1909, for example 57.8% of the children in schools in 37 of our largest cities were foreign born (Cremin, 1961:72). Suddenly, teachers were faced with problems of putative uncleanliness (bathing became part of the school curriculum in certain districts), and teachers began to teach basic socialization skills. Just how these socialization skills have come to be interpreted, whether malevolently by radical historians or benevolently by liberal-conservative historians, is not our concern here. What we do need to consider is how Dewey proposed to meet these challenges through education and how his ideas were interpreted by progressive disciples in such a way as to alter the course of schooling in this country.

John Dewey, although born and raised in Vermont, by 1894, had become thoroughly enmeshed in the problems of urbanization as a resident of Chicago and Chair of the Department of Philosophy, Psychology and Pedagogy at the University of Chicago. Distressed with the abrupt dislocation of families from rural to urban environments, concerned with the loss of traditional ways of understanding the maintenance of civilization, and anxious about the effects unleashed individualism and rampant materialism would have upon a democratic society, Dewey sought answers in pedagogic practice (see Westbrook, 1991, for an in-depth biography).

Dewey argued in *My Pedagogic Creed* (1897), *The School and Society* (1899), and *The Child and the Curriculum* (1902) for a restructuring of schools along the lines of "embryonic communities" and for the creation of a curriculum that would allow for the child's interests and developmental level while introducing the child to "the point of departure from which the child can trace and follow the progress of mankind in history, getting an insight also into the materials used and the mechanical principles involved" (Dworkin, 1959:43).

Dewey believed that the end of education was growth, which was firmly posited within a democratic society. Thus, school for Dewey was "that form of community life in which all those agencies are concentrated that will be most effective in bringing the child to share in the inherited resources of the race, and to use his own powers for social ends" (Dworkin, 1959:22).

To implement his ideas, Dewey created the Laboratory School at the University of Chicago. There, children studied basic subjects in an integrated curriculum since, according to Dewey, "the child's life is an integral, a total one" and, therefore, the school should reflect the "completeness" and "unity" of "the child's own world" (Dworkin, 1959:93). Dewey advocated active learning, starting with the needs and interests of the child; he emphasized the role of experience in education and introduced the notion of teacher as facilitator of learning, rather than the font from which all knowledge flows. The school, according to Dewey, was a "miniature community, an embryonic society" (Dworkin, 1959:41) and discipline was a tool that would develop "a spirit of social cooperation and community life" (Dworkin, 1959:40).

Dewey's form of pragmatism, instrumentalism and experimentalism, was founded upon the new psychology, behaviorism, and the philosophy of pragmatism. Additionally, his ideas were influenced by the theory of evolution and by an almost eighteenth-century optimistic belief in progress, but for Dewey, in the attainment of a better society through education. Thus, the school became a place, an "embryonic community," where children could learn skills experientially as well as from books in addition to traditional information, which would enable them to work cooperatively in a democratic society.

Dewey's ideas about education, often referred to as "progressive," proposed that educators start with the needs and interests of the child in the classroom, allow the child to participate in planning his or her course of study, advocated project method or group learning, and depended heavily upon experiential learning.

Dewey's progressive methodology rested upon the notion that children were active, organic beings, growing and changing, and required a course of study that would reflect their particular stage of development. He advocated both freedom and responsibility for students, since those are vital components of democratic living. He believed that the school should reflect the community, to enable students when they graduate to assume societal roles and to maintain the democratic way of life. Democracy was particularly important for Dewey. And he believed that it could be more perfectly realized through education, which would continually reconstruct and reorganize society.

Dewey's vision of schools was rooted in the social order; he did not see ideas as separate from social conditions. He fervently believed that philosophy had a responsibility to society and that ideas required laboratory testing; hence the importance of the school as a place where ideas can be implemented, challenged, restructured, reconstructed with the goal of implementing them to improve the social order. Moreover, he believed that school should provide "conjoint, communicated experience" and that it should function as preparation for life in a democratic society.

In line with the progressive political atmosphere of the turn of the century, Dewey viewed the role of schools within the larger societal conditions of which they were a part. As such, Dewey's vision of schooling must be understood as part of the larger project of social progress and improvement. Although Dewey was certainly concerned with the social dimensions of schooling, he also was acutely aware of the school's effects on the individual. Thus, Dewey's philosophy of education made a conscious attempt to balance the social role of the school with its effects on the social, intellectual, and personal development of individuals. In other words, Dewey believed that the schools should balance the needs of society and community on the one hand, and of the individual on the other. This tension, or what the philosopher of education Maxine Greene (1988) terms the "dialectic of freedom," is central to understanding Dewey's work.

The key to Dewey's vision is his view that the role of the school was to integrate children into a democratic society, not any type of society. Therefore, Dewey's view of integration is premised on the school as an embryonic democratic society where cooperation and community are desired ends. Dewey did not believe, however, that the school's role was to integrate children into a nondemocratic society. Rather, he believed that if schools instilled democratic and cooperative values in children they would be prepared as adults to transform the social order into a more democratic one. Although he located this central function of schools, he never adequately provided a solution to the problem of in-

tegrating diverse groups into a community without sacrificing their unique characteristics. This is a problem still hotly debated.

As the historian of education Diane Ravitch (1983:43–80) notes, Dewey's philosophies of education were often misunderstood and misapplied. It was often misapplied as "life adjustment education" and learning through experience as vocational education; it was often misapplied with regard to freedom, with individual freedom often confused with license and becoming more important than other processes; and it was often totally distorted by providing social class-appropriate education (i.e., vocational education for the poor). Despite these distorted applications, Dewey's philosophy of education, often referred to as progressive education, was central to all subsequent educational theory. For Dewey, the role of the school was to be "a lever of social reform," that is, to be the central institution for societal and personal improvement and to do so by balancing a complex set of processes.

In a progressive setting, the teacher is no longer the authoritarian figure from which all knowledge flows. Rather, the teacher assumes the peripheral position of facilitator. The teacher encourages, offers suggestions, questions, and helps plan and implement courses of study. The teacher also writes curriculum and must have a command of several disciplines in order to create and implement curriculum.

Dewey proposed that children learn both individually and in groups. He believed that children should start their mode of inquiry by posing questions about what they want to know. Today we refer to this method of instruction as problem solving or inquiry method. Books, often written by teachers and students together, were used; field trips and projects, which reconstructed some aspect of the child's course of study, were also an integral part of learning in Dewey's laboratory school. These methods, in turn, became the basis for other progressive schools founded in the Deweyan tradition.

Formal instruction was abandoned and traditional blocks of time for specific discipline instruction were done away with. Furniture, usually nailed to the floor, was discarded in favor of tables and chairs that could be grouped as needed. Children could converse quietly with one another, could stand up and stretch if warranted, could pursue independent study or group work. What at first glance to the visitor used to formal pedagogy might appear as chaotic was a carefully orchestrated classroom with children going about learning in nontraditional, yet natural ways. Lock-step, rote memorization of traditional schools was replaced with individualized study, problem solving, and project method.

Progressive schools generally follow Dewey's notion of a core curriculum, or an integrated curriculum. A particular subject matter under investigation by students, such as whales, would yield problems to be solved using math, science, history, reading, writing, music, art, wood or metal working, cooking, and sewing; all the academic and vocational disciplines in an integrated, interconnected way. Progressive educators support starting with contemporary problems and working from the known to the unknown or what we have come to call in social studies education the curriculum of expanding environments. Progressive educators are not wedded to a fixed curriculum either; rather, curriculum will change as the social order changes, as children's interests and needs change.

There is some controversy over Dewey's ideas about traditional discipline-centered curriculum. Some contemporary scholars (Egan, 1992:402–404) believe that Dewey's emphasis on the need for the curriculum to be related to the needs and interests of the child suggests he was against traditional subject matter and in favor of a child-centered curriculum based on imagination and intuition. Others, including Howard Gardner (1992:410–411), believe that Dewey proposed a balance between traditional disciplines and the needs and interests of the child. I concur with Gardner's reading of Dewey and believe that Dewey thought that an integrated curriculum provided the most effective means to this balance.

Strands of Progressive Education

That John Dewey made important contributions to both the philosophy of education and pedagogic practice is undisputable, especially if we examine what happened to education in the wake of Dewey's early work. And as we do so, we should keep in mind just how rapidly education had expanded in this period. For example, in 1870 about 6.5 million children from ages 5 through 18 attended school; in 1880, about 15.5 million children attended school—a significant increase, indeed. No less than 31 states by 1900 had enacted compulsory education laws. Thus, what occurred

in schools throughout this nation was to influence large numbers of Americans.

Although few can dispute Dewey's influence upon educational reformers, few would take issue with the notion that Dewey was often misread, misunderstood, and misinterpreted. Thus Dewey's emphasis upon the child's impulses, feelings, and interests led to a form of progressive education that often became synonymous with permissiveness, and his emphasis upon vocations ultimately led the way for "life adjustment" curriculum reformers.

Psychologists as well as philosophers became actively involved in educational reform. In fact, two distinctly different approaches to "progressive" educational reforms became apparent: the child-centered pedagogy of G. Stanley Hall and the social efficiency pedagogy of Edward L. Thorndike.

G. Stanley Hall (1844–1924) once referred to as "the Darwin of the mind" (Cremin, 1961:101) believed that children, in their development, reflected the stages of development of civilization. Thus schools, according to Hall, should tailor their curriculums to the stages of child development. Hall argued that traditional schools stifled the child's natural impulses, and suggested that schools individualize instruction and attend to the needs and interests of the children they educate. This strand of progressive reform became known as child-centered reform.

Opposed to child-centered reform was social engineering reform, proposed by Edward L. Thorndike. Thorndike (1874–1949) placed his emphasis upon the organism's response to its environment. Working with animals in the laboratory, he came to the conclusion that human nature could be altered for better or worse, depending upon the education to which it was subjected. Ultimately, Thorndike came to believe that schools could change human beings in a positive way and that the methods and aims of pedagogy to achieve this would be scientifically determined (Cremin, 1961:114).

Thorndike's work, Frederick Winslow Taylor's work in scientific management, and that of other progressive thinkers encouraged educators to be "socially efficient" in the ways they went about educating students. In particular, this thinking led to a belief that schools should be a meaningful experience for students and that schools should prepare students to earn a living. It also suggested that schools might begin to educate students based upon their abilities or talents. In particular, a leading proponent of this view was educational reformer Franklin Bobbitt. An issue of particular importance, although never resolved, was Bobbitt's scientific approach to curriculum design (a curriculum designer was, according to Bobbitt, like a "great engineer"). The purpose of curriculum design was to create a curriculum that would include the full range of human experience and prepare students for life.

Whereas the child-centered schools often emphasized the individualism side of the Deweyan "dialectic of freedom," and the social engineering branch emphasized helping the child adjust to society, a third branch of progressivism, social reconstructionism, emphasized the community side of the equation, especially with regard to the development of a more just, humane, and egalitarian society. Based upon the work of Kenneth Benne (see James, 1995) and George Counts (1932), social reconstructionists viewed schools as the key to building a new social order (James, 1995). Although the child-centered and social reconstructionist strands of progressive education often represented distinctive and separate movements, the child-centered schools that will be discussed in this chapter nonetheless incorporated many of the community-centered aspects of social reconstructionism as they attempted to meet the individual needs of children and simultaneously integrate them into a democratic community. The social engineering strand, however, dominated public education from the 1930s onward, with scientific management and administrative concern with efficiency resulting in such practices as tracking, intelligence testing, and vocational education. The child-centered, and to a lesser extent, the social reconstructionist strand, were more likely to be found in independent, private schools. Although these schools had many of the progressive pedagogic practices advocated by Dewey, their paradox was that they served a primarily affluent population (Semel, 1995; Semel and Sadovnik, 1995).

Progressive Education: 1900–1945

Progressive education has dominated educational thinking for much of the century, so much so that "by the mid-1940s it was no longer referred to as progressive education but as 'modern education' or the 'new educational practice'" (Ravitch, 1983:43). Neverthe-

less, it is an all but impossible task to provide a "capsule definition of progressive education" (Cremin, 1961:X). This is due to its numerous and contradictory strands (Cremin, 1961; Graham, 1967; Ravitch, 1983; Tyack, 1974). It is safe to say, however, that progressive education began as a movement roughly about the same time as Progressivism began as the political reform movement and must be understood against this larger backdrop.

That John Dewey made important contributions to both philosophy of education and pedagogic practice is undisputable. What is particularly important here is his influence upon a group of practitioners who, under his influence, founded independent progressive schools throughout the country that mirrored his Laboratory School, a school that "tried to provide education that balanced the children's interests with the knowledge of adults, that engaged the children in cooperative, active work, and that integrated social and intellectual learning . . . [a school in which] the concepts of growth and active learning imbued the curriculum" (Kaestle, 1990:74).

Although progressive education may be impossible to define, other than to conclude, as does Diane Ravitch, that "it was an attitude, a belief in experimentation, a commitment to the education of all children and to democracy in the schools" (Ravitch, 1983:44), nevertheless there are, as Lawrence A. Cremin suggests, four dominant themes present throughout the movement:

1. a broadening of the school to include a direct concern for health, vocation, and the quality of community life;
2. the application in the classroom of more humane, more active, and more rational pedagogical techniques derived from research in philosophy, psychology, and the social sciences;
3. the tailoring of instruction more directly to the different kinds and classes of children who were being brought within the purview of school . . .;
4. and finally, the use of more systematic and rational approaches to the administration and management of the schools. (Cremin, 1988:229)

Before the 1920s progressive reformers tended to concentrate their efforts in public education, applying scientific management techniques to the administration of schools (Tyack and Hansot, 1982), reforming curriculum, and creating secondary, vocational schools. As Cremin suggests, during the 1920s many progressive educators began to focus "on a select group of pedagogical innovative independent schools catering principally to middle class children" (Cremin, 1988:229). Such a school was the Dalton School, founded by Helen Parkhurst (see Semel, 1992), coincidentally as World War I was drawing to a close and "a great divide in the history of progressive education" (Cremin, 1961:179) was occurring, one in which the thrust toward "social reformism was virtually eclipsed by the rhetoric of child-centered pedagogy" (Cremin, 1961:181).

Dalton was also founded at a time when "progressive private day schools began to emerge in growing numbers" (Kraushaar, 1972:81). These schools, often the creation of parent cooperatives or talented practitioners held the common practice that "each individual has uniquely creative potentialities and that a school in which children are encouraged freely to develop their potential is the best guarantee of a larger society truly devoted to human worth and excellence" (Cremin, 1961:202).

These schools, commonly referred to by educators as "child-centered," were often founded by female practitioners "spurred by the revolt against 'the harsh pedagogy' of the existing schools and by the ferment of change and new thought of the first two decades of the twentieth century" (Kraushaar, 1972:81). Although many historians tend to group these schools together, nevertheless, each has a distinct philosophy and practice according to the particular vision of its founder. For example, City and Country, founded by Caroline Pratt, emphasized the notion of self-expression and growth through play; in particular through play with wooden blocks (Pratt, 1924). Another school, such as The Walden School, founded by Margaret Naumburg, who was heavily influenced by Freudian psychology, emphasized the notion of "individual transformation." Under the leadership of Naumburg's sister, Florence Cane, the school encouraged "children to paint exactly what they felt impelled to paint" (Cremin, 1961:213). Other examples include The Bank Street School founded by Lucy Sprague Mitchell (Antler, 1987), and The Lincoln School, founded by Abraham Flexner, which became a laboratory school for Teachers College, Columbia University (Cremin, 1961:280–286). Outside of New York City, where each of these schools was founded, were other examples of progressive education.

Among these were The Putney School, a boarding school in Putney, Vermont, founded by Carmelita Hinton (Lloyd, 1987), the Francis W. Parker School in Chicago, founded by one of the early pioneers of progressive pedagogy, Colonel Francis W. Parker (Stone, 1976), and The Shady Hill School in Cambridge, Massachusetts (Yoemans, 1979).

Whereas these child-centered progressive schools were almost all independent, private schools, public education was dominated by the social engineering strand of progressivism. From the transformation of the high school from an exclusively academic institution at the turn of the century to one dominated by life adjustment functions by the 1930s, to social class and race-based tracking systems that separated academic and vocational education, public progressive education from the 1930s to the 1960s stressed life adjustment rather than intellectual functions and often helped to reproduce rather than ameliorate social class, race, and gender inequalities.

Progressive Education: 1945–present

During the post-World War II period the patterns that emerged during the Progressive Era were continued. First, the debate about the goals of education (i.e., academic, social, or both) and whether all children should receive the same education remained an important one. Second, the demand for the expansion of educational opportunity became perhaps the most prominent feature of educational reform. Whereas the Common School era opened access to elementary education and the Progressive Era to secondary education, the post-World War II years were concerned with expanding opportunities to the postsecondary level. They were also directed at finding ways to translate these expanded opportunities into more equal educational outcomes at all levels of education. As in the first half of the twentieth century, so too, in the second half, the compatibility of expanded educational opportunity with the maintenance of educational standards would create significant problems. Thus, the tensions between equity and excellence became crucial in the debates of this period.

The post-World War II years witnessed the continuation of the processes that defined the development of the comprehensive high school. The debates over academic issues, begun at the turn of the century, may be defined as the movement between pedagogical progressivism and pedagogical traditionalism. This movement continued a pattern originated at the turn of the century and focused not only on the process of education, but on its goals. At the center of these debates are the questions regarding the type of education children should receive and whether all children should receive the same education. Although many of these debates were over curriculum and method, they ultimately were associated with the question of equity versus excellence.

Perhaps these debates can be best understood by examining reform cycles of the twentieth century, which revolved between progressive and traditional visions of schooling. On the one hand, traditionalists believed in knowledge-centered education, a traditional subject-centered curriculum, teacher-centered education, discipline and authority, and the defense of academic standards in the name of excellence. On the other hand, progressives believed in experiential education, a curriculum that responded to both the needs of students and the times, child-centered education, freedom and individualism, and the relativism of academic standards in the name of equity. Although these poles and educational practices rarely were in only one direction, the conflicts over educational policies and practices seemed to move back and forth between these two extremes. From 1945 to 1955, the progressive education of the previous decades was critically attacked.

These critics, including Mortimer Smith, Robert Hutchins, and Arthur Bestor, assailed progressive education for its sacrificing of intellectual goals to social ones. They argued that the life adjustment education of the period combined with an increasingly antiintellectual curriculum destroyed the traditional academic functions of schooling. Arthur Bestor, a respected historian and a graduate of the Lincoln School, one of the early progressive schools in New York City, argued that it was "regressive education" not progressive education that had eliminated the school's primary role in teaching children to think (Ravitch, 1983:76). Bestor, like the other critics, assailed the schools for destroying the democratic vision that all students should receive an education that was once reserved for the elite. He suggested that the social and vocational emphasis of the schools indicated a belief that all students could not learn academic material. In an ironic sense, many of the conservative critics were agreeing with the radical critique that the Progressive Era distorted the ideals of democratic education by tracking poor and working class children into nonacademic vocational programs.

Throughout the 1950s the debate between progressives who defended the social basis of the curriculum and critics who demanded a more academic curriculum raged on. What was often referred to as "the great debate" (Ravitch, 1983:79) ended with the Soviet launching of the space satellite Sputnik. The idea that the Soviets would win the race for space resulted in a national commitment to improve educational standards in general and to increase mathematical and scientific literacy in particular. From 1957 through the mid-1960s, the emphasis shifted to the pursuit of excellence and curriculum reformers attempted to redesign the curricula in ways that would lead to the return of academic standards (although many doubted that such a romantic age ever existed).

By the mid-1960s, however, the shift in educational priorities moved again toward the progressive side. This occurred in two distinct but overlapping ways. First, the Civil Rights movement led to an emphasis on equity issues. Thus, federal legislation, such as the Elementary and Secondary Education Act of 1965, emphasized the education of disadvantaged children. Second, in the context of the antiwar movement of the times, the general criticism of American society, and the persistent failure of the schools to ameliorate problems of poverty and of racial minorities, a "new progressivism" developed that linked the failure of the schools to the problems in society. Ushered in by the publication of A. S. Neill's *Summerhill* in 1960, a book about an English boarding school with few, if any rules and that was dedicated to the happiness of the child, the new progressivism provided an intellectual and pedagogical assault on the putative sins of traditional education, its authoritarianism, its racism, its misplaced values of intellectualism, and its failure to meet the emotional and psychological needs of children.

Throughout the 1960s and early 1970s a variety of books provided scathing criticisms of American education. These included Jonathon Kozol's *Death at an Early Age* (1967), which assailed the racist practices of the Boston public schools; Herbert Kohl's *36 Children* (1967), which demonstrated the pedagogical possibilities of "open education"; and Charles S. Silberman's *Crisis in the Classroom* (1970), which attacked the bureaucratic, stultifying mindlessness of American education. These books, along with a series of articles by Joseph Featherstone and Beatrice and Ronald Gross on British progressive or open education, resulted in significant experimentation in some American schools. Emphasis on individualism and relevant education, along with the challenge to the unquestioned authority of the teacher, resulted in "alternative," "free," or "open" education: schooling that once again shifted attention away from knowledge (product) to process. Although there is little evidence to suggest that the open classroom was a national phenomena, and as the historian Larry Cuban notes in his history of teaching, *How Teachers Taught* (1984), there has been surprisingly little variation in the twentieth century in teacher methods. (That is, despite the cycles of debate and reform, most secondary teachers still lecture more than they involve students.) Nonetheless, the period from the mid-1960s to the mid-1970s was a time of great turmoil in the educational arena: a time marked by two simultaneous processes: (1) the challenge to traditional schooling and (2) the attempt to provide educational opportunity for the disadvantaged.

By the late 1970s, conservative critics began to react to the educational reforms of the 1960s–1970s. They argued that liberal reforms in pedagogy and curriculum and in the arena of educational opportunity had resulted in the decline of authority and standards. Furthermore, the critics argued that the preoccupation with using the schools to ameliorate social problems, however well intended, not only failed to do this, but was part of an overall process that resulted in mass mediocrity. What was needed was nothing less than a complete overhaul of the American educational system. Although radical critics also pointed to the failure of the schools to ameliorate problems of poverty, they located the problem not so much in the schools, but in the society at large. Liberals defended the reforms of the period by suggesting that social improvement takes a long time, and a decade and a half was scarcely sufficient to turn things around.

In 1983, the National Commission on Excellence, founded by President Reagan's Secretary of Education, Terrel Bell, issued its now famous report, *A Nation at Risk*. This report provided a serious indictment of American education and cited high rates of adult illiteracy, declining SAT scores, and low scores on international comparisons of knowledge by American students as examples of the decline of literacy and

standards. The Committee stated that "the educational foundations of our society are presently being eroded by a rising tide of mediocrity that threatens our very future as a Nation and a people" (1983:5). The report called for increased standards and a return to academic excellence.

The years following this report were characterized by scores of other reports that both supported the criticism and called for reform. During the 1980s and 1990s significant attention was given to the improvement of curriculum, the tightening of standards, and a move towards the setting of academic goals and their assessment.

Contemporary Progressive Educational Reforms

Writing in the 1990s, one is encouraged by the increased interest in progressive education, especially as it relates to attempts to balance individualism and community. After over a decade of conservative domination of educational discourse, and during a period where school choice, tuition vouchers, and widespread loss of faith in public education have been the foundation for Goals 2000, there appears to be a resurgence of interest in progressive practices (Semel and Sadovnik, 1995).

An examination of contemporary progressive educational reform indicates that recent reform efforts echo many of the early concerns of progressive education. For example, the statement of principles of the steering committee of the Network of Progressive Educators drafted on November 10, 1990, reflects contemporary attempts to reintroduce progressive ideas into public school reform. The Network's statement included the following fundamental principles and assumptions:

- Education is best accomplished where relationships are personal and teachers design programs which honor the linguistic and cultural diversity of the local community.
- Teachers, as respected professionals, are crucial sources of knowledge about teaching and learning.
- Curriculum balance is maintained by commitment to children's individual interests and developmental needs, as well as a commitment to community within and beyond the school's walls.

- Schools embrace the home cultures of children and their families. Classroom practices reflect these values and bring multiple cultural perspectives to bear.
- Students are active constructors of knowledge and learn through direct experience and primary sources.
- All disciplines, the arts, sciences, humanities, and physical development, are valued equally in an interdisciplinary curriculum.
- Decision making within schools is inclusive of children, parents, and staff.
- The school is a model of democracy and humane relationships confronting issues of racism, classism, and sexism.
- Schools actively support critical inquiry into the complexities of global issues. Children can thus assume the powerful responsibilities of world citizenship. (Network of Progressive Educators, 1991:3)

These principles can be seen in action at a number of public schools, as progressive educators in the United States have reemphasized the need for progressive education for children from diverse class, race, and ethnic backgrounds (Network of Progressive Educators, 1991:3). One such school, Central Park East Secondary School (CPESS), founded in 1985 by Deborah Meier, is a progressive public school in District 4 in East Harlem in New York City. The school is guided by the principles of the Coalition of Essential Schools, founded by Theodore Sizer. In many respects, it mirrors the pedagogic practices of some of the early independent, progressive schools such as the Dalton School and City and Country School. It has an integrated curriculum, child-centered teaching methods, and an advisory system, and attempts to integrate students into a cohesive community of learners. Although it is not the purpose of this chapter to go into a detailed description and analysis of CPESS, the important point is that unlike most of the historically progressive schools that are independent, private schools, it is a public school with a predominantly working class African-American and Latino student population. The school's success suggests that the type of progressive education that has been the province of the middle and upper middle classes can work effectively with students from lower socioeconomic backgrounds. Thus, it behooves us to examine how lessons from the past can inform present practice.

Central Park East Secondary School is part of the Center for Collaborative Education in New York City. The Center consists of elementary, middle, and high schools and is affiliated with the Coalition for Essential Schools. CPESS subscribes to the Coalition's 12 principles of education:

- Schools that are small and personalized in size.
- A unified course of study for all students.
- A focus on helping young people to use their minds well.
- An in-depth, intradisciplinary curriculum respectful of the diverse heritages that encompass our society.
- Active learning with student-as-worker/student-as-citizen and teacher-as-coach.
- Student evaluation by performance-based assessment methods.
- A school tone of unanxious expectation, trust, and decency.
- Family involvement, trust, and respect.
- Choice.
- Racial, ethnic, economic, and intellectual diversity.
- Budget allocations targeting time for collective planning.

It is interesting to note that there is little if any reference in the literature of Central Park East, the Center for Collaborative Education, or the Coalition of Progressive Schools to progressive education. This is probably due to the continuing contempt for progressive education on the part of mainstream reformers, especially those who control grant funds. Although it is understandable, given pragmatic concerns, that these educational reform groups do not label themselves as progressive, it is also clear that their principles and practices have their historical origin in the Deweyan progressivism of the early twentieth century.

Progressive Education and the Sociology of Education

Although there is a voluminous literature on progressive education, the majority of it has been written by philosophers and historians of education. Some sociologists have written on aspects of progressive education (Labaree, 1900; Sadovnik, 1994); however, there is a dearth of sociological studies, especially on the out-comes of progressive education. What is needed is sociological study of the effects of progressive schools on students, in terms of both cognitive and noncognitive measures. For example, although there is a great deal of attention given to the Coalition of Essential Schools and to Central Park East Secondary School, there have been no comprehensive longitudinal studies of student outcomes and school effects. Additionally, there have been no systematic qualitative case studies of these schools to date. Certainly, these contemporary progressive schools provide fertile ground for sociological research.

Progressive education has been an essential part of the history of education in the twentieth century. Given the heated debates over its efficacy and effects, which are usually ideological and political, sociological research on progressive education can provide important empirical evidence, which to date has been seriously absent from these debates.

REFERENCES

Antler, J. 1987. *Lucy Sprague Mitchell: The Making of a Modern Woman*. New Haven, CT: Yale University Press.

Counts, George. 1932. *Dare the Schools Build a New Social Order?* New York: John Day.

Cremin, L. A. 1961. *The Transformation of the School*. New York: Vintage Books.

————. 1988. *American Education: The Metropolitan Experience*. New York: Harper & Row.

Cuban, Larry. 1984. *How Teachers Taught: Constancy and Change in American Classrooms, 1890–1980*. New York: Longman.

Dewey, J. 1897/1959. "My Pedagogic Creed." In Martin S. Dworkin (ed.), *Dewey on Education*, pp. 19–32. New York: Teachers College Press.

————. 1899/1959. "The School and Society." In Martin S. Dworkin (ed.), *Dewey on Education*, pp. 33–90. New York: Teachers College Press.

————. 1902/1959. "The Child and the Curriculum." In Martin S. Dworkin (ed.), *Dewey on Education*, pp. 91–111. New York: Teachers College Press.

Dworkin, Martin S., ed. 1959. *Dewey on Education*. New York: Teachers College Press.

Egan, Kieran. 1992. "Review of *The Unschooled Mind: How Children Think and How Schools Should Teach*, by Howard Gardner." *Teachers College Record* 94(2):397–406.

Gardner, H. 1992. "A Response." *Teachers College Record* 94(2):407–413.

Graham, Patricia Albjerg. 1967. *Progressive Education: From Arcady to Academe*. New York: Teachers College Press.

Greene, M. 1988. *The Dialectic of Freedom*. New York: Teachers College Press.

James, M., ed. 1995. *Social Reconstruction Through Education: The Philosophy, History, and Curricula of a Radical Ideal*. Norwood, NJ: Ablex.

Kaestle, Carl F. 1990. "The Public Schools and the Public Mood." *American Heritage* (February):66–81.

Kohl, Herbert. 1967. *36 Children*. New York: New American Library.

Kozol, Jonathan. 1967. *Death at an Early Age*. New York: Houghton Mifflin.

Kraushaar, O. F. 1972. *American Nonpublic Schools: Patterns of Diversity*. Baltimore: Johns Hopkins University Press.

Lloyd, S. 1987. *The Putney School: A Progressive Experiment*. New Haven, CT: Yale University Press.

National Commission on Excellence in Education. 1983. *A Nation at Risk*. Washington, DC: U.S. Government Printing Office.

Neill, A. S. 1960. *Summerhill*. New York: Holt.

Network of Progressive Educators. 1991. "Statement of Principles." *Pathways* 7(2):3.

Pratt, C. 1924. *Experimental Practice in the City and Country School*. New York: E. P. Dutton.

Ravitch, D. 1983. *The Troubled Crusade*. New York: Basic Books.

Sadovnik, Alan R. 1994. *Equity and Excellence in Higher Education*. New York: Peter Lang.

————, ed. 1995. *Knowledge and Pedagogy: The Sociology of Basil Bernstein*. Norwood, NJ: Ablex.

Semel, S. F. 1992. *The Dalton School: The Transformation of a Progressive School*. New York: Peter Lang.

————. 1995. "Basil Bernstein's Theory of Pedagogic Practice and the History of American Progressive Education: Three Case Studies." In A. R. Sadovnik (ed.), *Knowledge and Pedagogy: The Sociology of Basil Bernstein*, pp. 337–358. Norwood, NJ: Ablex.

Semel, S. F., and Sadovnik, A. R. 1995. "Lessons from the Past: Individualism and Community in Three Progressive Schools." *Peabody Journal of Education* (Summer):56–84.

Silberman, Charles S. 1970. *Crisis in the Classroom*. New York: Random House.

Stone, M., ed. 1976. *Between Home and Community: Chronicle of the Francis W. Parker School*. Chicago: Francis W. Parker School.

Tyack, David. 1974. *The One Best System*. Cambridge, MA: Harvard University Press.

Tyack, D., and E. Hansot. 1981. *Managers of Virtue: Public School Leadership in America, 1920–1980*. New York: Basic Books.

Westbrook, R. 1991. *John Dewey and American Democracy*. Ithaca, NY: Cornell University Press.

Yeomans, E. 1979. *The Shady Hill School: The First Fifty Years*. Cambridge, MA: Windflower Press.

QUASI-MARKETS IN EDUCATION

Geoff Whitty
Institute of Education, University of London

Public services in many parts of the world have been "privatized" or "marketized" during the 1980s and 1990s. In the United Kingdom, for example, the Thatcher and Major governments have privatized most of the publicly owned "nationalized" industries and utilities. When privatization involves the handing over of a public service to a private monopoly, this does not necessarily stimulate market forces. Conversely, marketization does not necessarily require privatization in strictly economic terms. Recent policy initiatives in relation to education and welfare services often involve introducing a "market" element into the provision of services that continue to be paid for largely out of taxation. This entails making public services behave more like an idealized view of the private sector. It may also involve "privatizing" them in the ideological sense of handing over to individuals and families decisions that were previously a matter of public policy, determined by politicians and bureaucrats. The term "quasi-market" is increasingly being used to characterize such attempts to introduce market forces and private decision making into the provision of welfare.

Levacic (1995) suggests that the distinguishing characteristics of a quasi-market for a public service are "the separation of purchaser from provider and an element of user choice between providers" (p. 167). In other words, provision of a service is separated from its finance and different providers, including sometimes private and voluntary sector bodies, can compete to deliver the service. She adds that a quasi-market often remains highly regulated, with the government controlling "such matters as entry by new providers, investment, the quality of service . . . and price, which is often zero to the user" (p. 167). The lack of a conven-

tional cash nexus and the strength of government intervention distinguish quasi-markets from the idealised view of a "free" market, though few contemporary markets in any field are actually free from government regulation and many of them involve some element of overt or covert subsidy.

In the compulsory phases of education, the introduction of quasi-markets usually involves a combination of parental choice and school autonomy, together with a greater or lesser degree of public accountability and government regulation.[1] Parental choice in this context refers to attempts to enhance opportunities for choice among public schools[2] and sometimes the use of public funds to extend choice into the private sector. School autonomy involves moves to devolve various aspects of decision making from regional and district offices to individual public schools and thus enable their site-based professionals or community-based councils to operate more like those responsible for private schools. Such moves are often justified by reference to the claims of Chubb and Moe (1990) about the reasons for the supposedly superior academic performance of private schools.

Advocates of quasi-market policies argue that they will lead to increased diversity of provision, better and more efficient management of schools, and enhanced professionalism and school effectiveness. Some proponents, such as Moe (1994) and Pollard (1995), have

---

[1] At preschool and postcompulsory level, there is often an element of commercialization as well, which Marginson (1993) distinguishes from both marketization and privatization.

[2] I use the term "public" school here in the North American sense of publicly funded and publicly provided school rather than the English sense of elite private school.

argued that such reforms will bring particular benefits for families from disadvantaged communities, who have been ill-served by more conventional bureaucratic arrangements. However, critics of such reforms suggest that even if they do enhance efficiency, responsiveness, choice, and diversity (and even that they regard as questionable), they will almost certainly increase inequality between schools.

Parental choice and school autonomy are by no means inextricably linked, especially in the United States where the provenance of the two reforms is somewhat different and where, in some respects, they are competing reform strategies. However, although Moe (1994) suggests that choice is a far more potent reform measure than school self-management, school autonomy is seen as necessary to free schools to respond positively to market forces. Similarly, although Domanico (1990) states that "public school choice is not an alternative to school-based management; it is the most effective way of instituting school-based management" (p. 1), he also regards school-based management as "the most promising supply-side educational reform" (p. 2).

This chapter will discuss the development and effects of quasi-markets, drawing particularly on research evidence from England[3] and New Zealand, two of the countries that have adopted such policies with the greatest zeal. It will also refer to relevant policies in the United States that begin to move in that direction. In reviewing the evidence of quasi-markets, I write as a sociologist of education with a particular interest in the relationship between education and social inequality. Foster et al. (1996) have suggested that such concerns often produce a rather one-sided perspective on the part of contemporary British sociologists of education.

However, although not denying that parental choice and school autonomy can bring benefits to individual schools and students and even have their progressive moments, my conclusion from the evidence available to date is that the creation of quasi-markets is likely to exacerbate existing inequalities—especially where the broader political climate and the prevailing approach to government regulation are geared to other priorities.

This is particularly relevant to the cases upon which I focus here, where quasi-markets have become linked to a broader conservative agenda. More particularly, they are often part of a New Right agenda that combines a neoliberal commitment to market forces with a neoconservative reassertion of "traditional" values (Whitty, 1989). Of course, neither enhanced choice nor school autonomy is necessarily linked to this agenda and such measures have, in other circumstances, sometimes been part of a more progressive package of policies (Grace, 1991).

Quasi-Markets in England, New Zealand, and the United States

In England, prior to the 1980s, the vast majority of children were educated in public schools maintained by democratically elected local education authorities (LEAs), which exercised political and bureaucratic control over their schools but also often provided them with considerable professional support. After the Conservative victory at the 1979 election, the Thatcher and Major governments set about trying to break the LEA monopoly of public schooling through the provisions of a series of Education Acts passed in the 1980s and early 1990s.

Although the introduction of the National Curriculum and its associated system of testing in 1988 can be seen as centralizing control, most other measures have sought to enhance parental choice and transfer responsibilities from LEAs to individual schools. In 1980, the Assisted Places Scheme provided public funding to enable academically able children from poor homes to attend some of the country's elite private schools. More recently, the government has created new forms of public school outside the influence of LEAs. City technology colleges (CTCs) are new secondary schools for the inner city, with a curriculum emphasis on science and technology and run by independent trusts with business sponsors. Then in 1988 the Education Reform Act enabled some existing public schools to "opt out" of their LEAs after a parental ballot and run themselves as grant-maintained schools with direct funding from central government. Subsequent legislation has extended the right to opt out to virtually all schools, permitted schools to change their character by varying their enrollment schemes, sought to encour-

---

[3] Different education legislation applies to Scotland and Northern Ireland. There are also some minor differences between England and Wales.

age new types of specialist schools, and made it possible for some private schools to opt in to grant maintained status.

Local management of schools (LMS) has given those schools that remain with their LEAs control over their own budgets and day-to-day management, receiving funds according to a formula that ensures that at least 85% of the LEA's budget is handed down to schools and that 80% of each school's budget is determined directly by the number and ages of its students. Meanwhile, open enrollment allows popular public schools to attract as many students as possible, at least up to their physical capacity, instead of being kept to lower limits or strict catchment areas (or zoning) so that other schools can remain open. This is seen as a necessary corollary of per capita funding in creating a quasi-market in education. In some respects, it is a "virtual voucher" system (Sexton, 1987), designed to make schools more responsive to their clients and either become more effective or close. Prime Minister Major looks forward to the day "when all publicly funded schools will be run as free self-governing schools." He believes in "trusting headmasters [sic], teachers and governing bodies to run their schools and in trusting parents to make the right choice for their children" (*The Times*, 8/24/95, p. 5).

In New Zealand, the initial reforms were introduced by a Labour government, albeit one that had enthusiastically embraced monetarism and "new public management" techniques in the mid-1980s (Wylie, 1995). Based on the government's response to the Picot Report (Picot et al. 1988), the reforms involved a shift in the responsibility for budget allocation, staff employment, and educational outcomes from central government and regional educational boards to individual schools. Schools were given boards of trustees composed of parents (and extended in 1991 to encourage the inclusion of business people) who had to negotiate goals with the local community and agree to a charter with central government.

Boards of trustees also now have effective control over their enrollment schemes, with even lighter regulation than in England. In other respects, the New Zealand reforms "offer a model of school self-management which is more balanced than the English experience." This is because they put "a great emphasis on equity . . . on community involvement . . . on parental in-

volvement [and on] partnership: between parents and professionals" (Wylie, 1994:xv). Furthermore, neither the costs of teacher salaries nor of some central support services were originally devolved to individual school budgets, though there have subsequently been moves in this direction since the election of a conservative administration in 1990. Three percent of New Zealand schools took part in a pilot scheme for "bulk funding" (devolution of 100% of their funding including teachers' salaries) and this option has now been opened up to all schools for a trial period of 3 years. Alongside these reforms, national curriculum guidelines have been introduced but these are far less detailed and prescriptive than the English model and pay some attention to minority Maori interests. The extension of publicly funded choice into the private sector has also begun in 1996 with a New Zealand equivalent of the English Assisted Places Scheme.

In the United States, Newmann (1993) includes parental choice and greater school autonomy among his list of the most popular restructuring reforms. However, it is not easy to generalize about the nature and provenance of such policies. Even in the context of national initiatives, such as America 2000 and Goals 2000, the role of the federal Department of Education has been largely one of exhortation. During the 1980s, President Reagan used it as "a 'bully pulpit' for espousing his beliefs in school choice and local educational autonomy," while George Bush "went further . . . in attempting to reorganise the public school system according to what he believed were sound market principles" (Cookson, 1995:409). This included support for parental choice, self-governing Charter Schools, and for the New American Schools program, which in the original version displayed some parallels with the English CTC initiative. Under Goals 2000, site-based management continues to be seen as contributing to educational improvement, but choice has been much less in evidence in the federal rhetoric under the Clinton administration.

Meanwhile, the more significant decisions continue to be taken at state and district levels. Although a few states, such as Minnesota, have statewide choice plans, many initiatives have been more local. Wells (1993a) demonstrates the huge variety in the nature of the various choice plans that have been mooted or implemented in the United States over the past few years.

Similarly, specialist or "focus" schools have very different origins and purposes, and include schools such as the Boston Latin School and New York's Stuyvesant High School, magnet schools associated with desegregation plans, alternative schools, sometimes based on progressive pedagogic principles, and private Catholic schools (Raywid, 1994). Forms of site-based management also differ significantly from school district to school district (Ogawa and White, 1994; Murphy and Beck, 1995). Even the charter school legislation varies considerably and, in some states, such schools have to negotiate with local school districts for their resources and operate within district enrollment policies (Wohlstetter et al., 1995).

To that extent, little of the current American experience is directly relevant to the claims made by advocates of quasi-markets. Charter schools in some areas are likely to provide their best test to date, but unfortunately there is little research evidence yet available of the sort reported here from England and New Zealand. However, some initial work has been undertaken (Bauman et al., 1994; Becker et al., 1995; Grutzik et al., 1995; Medler and Nathan, 1995; Urahn and Stewart, 1994), while the Pew Charitable Trusts are funding a study by Chester Finn and Louann Bierlein at the Hudson Institute and a major evaluation is planned by the federal Department of Education. In the meantime, advocates of quasi-market policies often cite the success of controlled choice policies in Cambridge, Massachusetts and Montclair, New Jersey, the East Harlem "choice" experiment in New York, and the Milwaukee private school "voucher" experiment and point to active support for them among minority populations.

Insofar as it is possible to generalize, the New Zealand reforms have ushered in a much more thoroughgoing experiment in parental choice than has been tried in England, while both these countries have gone further in this respect than all but a few school districts in the United States. In terms of freedom from local bureaucratic control, New Zealand schools have the most autonomy and those in the United States the least. Within England, grant-maintained schools have the most autonomy, but even LEA schools under LMS have considerably more autonomy than most U.S. schools operating under site-based management. As for freedom in financial management, English schools operating under LMS currently have more resources under their direct control than even New Zealand schools,

apart from those of the latter with "bulk funding." In the United States, financial devolution within school districts has not gone nearly as far as it has in either England or New Zealand, certainly with respect to the funding of teachers' salaries and resources for professional development.

Equity considerations have had different degrees of influence in the three countries. For example, a government minister in England was prepared to dismiss concerns about the potential of choice to produce racial segregation with the statement that her government did not wish "to circumscribe [parental] choice in any way" (quoted in Blackburne, 1988). Race has, however, influenced policies on funding and community influence in New Zealand and on funding and enrollment policies in the United States. On the other hand, concerns about providing opportunities for the single-sex education of girls have been most prominent in England.

Research on Quasi-Markets

Not only have particular concerns within the histories of the three countries influenced the terms in which their policies have been framed, they have also influenced the focus of sociological research on the reforms in the three countries. Issues of class have dominated sociological studies of choice in England, whereas race has been the central concern in the United States. David (1993) points out that gender perspectives are "curiously absent" in most of the research on school choice. Finally, the styles of research adopted have been rather different. Paradoxically, given the scope of the reforms in the different countries, the emphasis in the United States is often on the analysis and reanalysis of large data sets and that in England and New Zealand on indepth ethnographic research in particular communities. Even so, research findings on the effects of quasi-markets in the three countries display more similarities than differences.

In England, a local case study of education within a broader project on quasi-markets in social policy by Le Grand and Bartlett (1993) found that the reforms had been welcomed by many headteachers but less so by other teachers. It points out that although parental choice has been increased by open enrollment, "the door is firmly closed once a school [is full]. And by encouraging an increasingly selective admissions policy in [oversubscribed] schools open enrollment may be having the effect of bringing about increased opportunity for cream-skimming and hence inequality." Furthermore, it found that "the schools which faced financial losses under the formula funding system tended to be schools which drew the greatest proportion of students from the most disadvantaged section of the community" (Bartlett, 1993:149–150). Thus, whatever gains may have emerged from the reforms in terms of efficiency and responsiveness to some clients, there are serious concerns about their implications for equity.

Le Grand and Bartlett regard "cream-skimming" as the biggest threat to equity in the sorts of "quasi markets" created by the Thatcher government. This danger is clearly demonstrated in an important series of studies by Ball and his colleagues on the operation of quasi-markets in London. In an early study, Bowe et al. (1992) concluded that schools are competing to attract greater cultural capital hoping for higher yielding returns. Subsequently, Gewirtz et al. (1995) have found schools seeking students who are "able," "gifted," "motivated" and "committed," and middle class, with girls and children with South Asian backgrounds being seen as particular assets in terms of their potential to enhance test scores. The least desirable clientele include those who are "less able," have special educational needs, especially emotional and behavioral difficulties, as well as children from working class backgrounds and boys, unless they also have some of the more desirable attributes.

Popular schools are thus tempted to become increasingly selective, both academically and socially, through both overt and covert methods of selection. Bartlett and Le Grand (1993) suggest that cream skimming generally involves favoring those clients who will bring the greatest return for the least investment, thus leading to discrimination by providers against the more expensive users. There is certainly evidence of discrimination against children with special educational needs. Bartlett (1993) argues that only if the market price varies with the needs of the client will this not happen. In other words, funding formulas need to be weighted to give schools an incentive to take more expensive children. The current premium paid for children with special educational needs may not be enough, if it makes the school less popular with clients who, although bringing in less money, bring in other desirable attributes.

However, the academically able are the "cream" that most schools seek to attract. Such students stay in the system longer and thus bring in more money, as well as making the school appear successful in terms of its test scores and hence attractive to other desirable clients. Glennerster (1991) suggests that given the opportunity, most schools will want to become more selective because taking children who will bring scores down will affect their overall market position. This is especially so when there is imperfect information about school effectiveness and when only "raw" test scores are made available as they currently are in England. Schools with the highest scores appear best even if other schools enhance achievement more. As long as schools tend to be judged on a unidimensional scale of academic excellence, many commentators have predicted that rather than choice leading to more diverse and responsive forms of provision as claimed by many of its advocates, it will reinforce the existing hierarchy of schools, based on academic test results and social class.

Although parents may choose new types of schools because they are different from the standard local comprehensive school, that does not seem to lead in England to a truly diversified system. Instead, those parents who are in a position to choose are choosing those schools that are closest to the traditional academic model of education that used to be associated with selective grammar schools. Even new types of schools tend to be judged in these terms. For example, parents often choose CTCs not so much for their hi-tech image, but because they are perceived as the next best thing to grammar schools or even elite private schools (Whitty et al., 1993).

In this situation, those *schools* that are in a position to choose often seek to identify their success with an emphasis on traditional academic virtues and thus attract those students most likely to display them. Many of the first schools to opt out and become grant maintained were selective, single sex, and with traditional sixth forms, and this gave the sector an aura of elite status (Fitz et al., 1993). Furthermore, Bush et al. (1993) found that 30% of grant-maintained "comprehensive" schools were now using covert selection. In addition, grant-maintained schools have been identified as among those with the highest rates of exclusion of their existing students and among the least willing to cater to students with special educational needs (Feintuck, 1994). Even some CTCs, which were intended to pioneer a new style of education, may be abandoning that distinctiveness in favor of traditional academic excellence (Walford and Miller, 1992).

More generally, a major empirical study of school parental choice and school response has concluded that there is no evidence to date of choice producing greater diversity in the school system and some evidence of a tendency toward greater uniformity (Glatter et al., 1995). The only exception in that study was where there had been additional government funding to foster the development of specialist technology schools. Thus, it was government intervention rather than market forces that had brought innovation on the supply side. With regard to hierarchy, Glatter et al. found no dramatic movement but certainly no evidence that it had been reduced by the reforms.

There is also little evidence that quasi-markets benefit disadvantaged families. An early study of the Assisted Places Scheme (Edwards et al., 1989) concluded that it had attracted temporarily distressed suburban families rather than those from the inner city. Smith and Noble (1995) conclude from a review of the evidence that English choice policies as a whole are further disadvantaging already disadvantaged groups. Walford (1992b:137) also argues that although choice will lead to better quality schooling for some children, it will "discriminate against working class children and children of Afro-Caribbean descent." Although schools have always been socially and racially segregated to the extent that residential segregation exists, Gewirtz et al. (1995) suggest that choice may well exacerbate this segregation by extending it into previously integrated schools serving mixed localities. Their research indicates that working class children and particularly children with special educational needs are likely to be increasingly "ghetto-ized" in poorly resourced schools. Such trends are particularly evident in inner London, where admissions policies have been relaxed. A recent study (Pennell and West, 1995) has suggested that the new system is serving to reinforce the privilege of "those parents who are able and prepared to negotiate the complexities [of the system] compared with those who are less willing or less able to do so" (p. 14).

The Smithfield Project, a major study of the impact of choice policies in New Zealand, suggests that much the same sort of social polarization is taking place there (Lauder et al., 1994; Waslander and Thrupp, 1995). In another New Zealand study (Fowler, 1993), schools located in low socioeconomic areas were found to be

judged negatively because of factors over which they had no influence, such as type of intake, location, and problems perceived by parents as linked to these. Wylie (1994) too has noted that schools in low-income areas there are more likely to be losing students to other schools. If we could be sure that their poor reputation was deserved, this might be taken as evidence that the market was working well with effective schools reaping their just rewards. But, as in England, judgments of schools tend to be made on social grounds or narrow academic criteria and with little reference to their overall performance or even their academic effectiveness on value-added measures. Gordon (1994b) points out that "schools with a mainly middle class and Pakeha (or, increasingly, Asian) population, tend to achieve better on national examinations because of the high level of 'readiness' and motivation of the pupils, and relatively low levels of social problems that impinge on educational processes" (p. 19). Furthermore, advantaged schools are able to introduce enrollment schemes that "have a tendency to reinforce their social exclusivity" (p. 18). Meanwhile, the current funding regime makes it extremely difficult for schools in disadvantaged areas, usually in the inner city, to break out of the cycle of decline. Wylie's study of the fifth year of self-managing schools in New Zealand (Wylie, 1994) identified schools in low-income areas, and schools with high Maori enrollments, as experiencing greater resource problems than others.

Such research suggests that many of the differences between schools result from factors largely beyond the control of parents and schools, except the power of advantaged parents and advantaged schools to further enhance their advantage and thus increase educational inequalities and social polarization. This is not necessarily an argument against choice, but it is clear that procedures for selection to oversubscribed schools need reconsideration. Significantly, the Smithfield Project found that in only one year, where allocations to oversubscribed schools were based on "balloting" (or drawing lots), did social polarization between popular and unpopular schools decrease.

Wylie (1994, 1995) reports that the combination of choice and accountability measures has led to schools paying more attention to the attractiveness of physical plant and public image than to changes to teaching and learning other than the spread of computers. It has also led to increased attention to the information about school programs and children's progress that reaches parents, changes that "are clearly not without value in themselves." But she also notes that "they do not seem able to counter or outweigh factors affecting school rolls that lie beyond school power, such as local demographics affected by employment, ethnicity, and class" (Wylie 1995:163, citing Gordon, 1994a; Waslander and Thrupp, 1995).

In the United States, the early association of public school choice with racial desegregation may have ensured that equity considerations continue to play a greater part in education reform than in England or even New Zealand. Nevertheless, there are considerable concerns about the equity effects of more recent attempts to enhance choice, especially as there is no clear evidence to date of a positive impact on student achievement (Witte, 1990). What evidence there is about the effects of choice policies on student achievement and equity continues to be at best inconclusive (Plank et al., 1993), despite claims by choice advocates that "the best available evidence" shows that parental choice improves the education of all children, especially low-income and minority students (Domanico, 1990).

Even some of the more positive evidence from controlled choice districts, such as Cambridge (Rossell and Glenn, 1988; Tan, 1990) and Montclair (Clewell and Joy, 1990), which seemed to show gradual overall achievement gains, is now regarded by Henig (1994) as methodologically flawed, making it difficult to attribute improvements to choice per se. Furthermore, although choice has not always led to resegregation as its critics feared, improvements in the racial balance of Montclair and Cambridge schools were most noticeable during periods of strong government intervention. Henig goes on to argue that the much vaunted East Harlem "miracle" (Fliegel, 1990) has "escaped any serious effort at controlled analysis" even though it has had a special role "in countering charges that the benefits of choice programs will not accrue to minorities and the poor" (p. 142). Not only have the apparently impressive gains in achievement now leveled off or even been reversed, it is impossible to be sure that the earlier figures were not merely the effect of schools being able to choose students from higher socioeconomic groups from outside the area or, alternatively, the empowerment of teachers. Overall, both Henig (1994) and Wells (1993a) conclude from exhaustive reviews that the stronger claims of choice advocates cannot be upheld and that choice needs to be carefully regulated if it is not to have damaging equity effects.

It is certainly doubtful whether these policies have brought benefits for minority groups as a whole, even where they have brought benefits for specific communities. As indicated earlier, it is too early to assess with any confidence how charter schools perform in this respect. However, although Medler and Nathan (1995) suggest that charter schools recruit a high proportion of "at-risk" students, Grutzik et al. (1995) and Becker et al. (1995) argue that some of their features, such as the emphasis on parental involvement, may have the effect of excluding students from certain disadvantaged groups. This would certainly be consistent with research in England (Whitty et al., 1993), which suggests that the definitions of "merit" adopted by City Technology Colleges can favor members of some minority ethnic groups over others.

The evidence with regard to private school choice in the United States is also contentious, but relevant to our concerns in view of current demands for an extension of the use of public funds to permit students to attend private schools. Much of the controversy centers around the various interpretations of the data from Coleman's high school studies (Coleman et al., 1982) and, in particular, the work of Chubb and Moe (1990). Although the data show a consistent but relatively small performance advantage for private schools once background has been controlled for, some argue that it is a product of their methodology and that any advantage would disappear with the use of more subtle measures of the cultural differences between low-income families using private and public schools (Henig, 1994:144). Lee and Bryk (1993) accuse Chubb and Moe of a circularity in their argument in support of school choice and suggest that their conclusions concerning the power of choice and school autonomy are not supported by the evidence as presented. Nevertheless, Bryk et al. (1993) claim on the basis of their *own* work that Catholic schools do impact positively on the performance of low-income families, but they attribute this at least as much to an ethos of strong community values antithetical to the marketplace as to the espousal of market forces.

Witte's evaluation of the controversial Milwaukee private school choice experiment, which enables children from poor families to attend private schools at public expense, concludes in its fourth year report that "in terms of achievement scores . . . students perform approximately the same as M[ilwaukee] P[ublic] S[chool] students." However, attendance of choice children is slightly higher and parental satisfaction has been high. For the schools, "the program has generally been positive, has allowed several to survive, several to expand, and contributed to the building of a new school" (Witte at al., 1994:28). Yet some of the stronger claims made both for and against this type of program cannot be sustained by the evidence, as it is a small and narrowly targeted program and certainly not a basis upon which to judge the likely effects of a more thorough-going voucher initiative.

The Milwaukee program overall has not hitherto been oversubscribed and although students are self-selected, the schools involved have not been able to exercise choice. Elsewhere, the combination of oversubscription and self-selection in explaining apparent performance gains through private school choice suggests that cream skimming is a major issue as in England and New Zealand. Smith and Meier (1995) use existing data to test the school choice hypothesis and conclude that competition between public and private schools appears to result in a cream skimming effect. They also argue that there is no reason to expect that such effects will disappear in greater competition among public schools, especially as some schools would begin with competitive advantages, an issue they regard as seriously underplayed by Chubb and Moe and other advocates of choice. Indeed, they predict that choice could lead to a "two tier system," similar to that which is developing in England and New Zealand.

Wells (1993b) argues that the economic metaphor that schools will improve once they behave more like private, profit-driven corporations and respond to the demands of "consumers" "ignores critical sociological issues that make the school consumption process extremely complex." Some of those issues are explored further in an important contribution to the sociology of school choice by Wells and Crain (1992). That paper and Wells' own research suggest that many choice plans are based on false assumptions about how families behave in the educational marketplace. This means that competition will certainly not lead to school improvement "in those schools where students end up because they did not choose to attend a 'better' school." Escape from poor schools will not necessarily result from choice plans because "the lack of power that some families experience is embedded in their social and economic lives" (Wells, 1993b:48).

There does, then, seem to be an accumulation of evidence that combining school autonomy with school choice to create quasi-markets is as likely to exacerbate differences between schools as lead to school improvement across the system as a whole. Although enabling a few schools and families to take advantage of their new found freedoms, there is no evidence that such initiatives alone can overcome system-wide influences on schooling.

Quasi-Markets and Democracy

Although the concept of quasi-market always involves some degree of government regulation, there is disagreement about its nature and extent. In the three countries discussed here, conservative commentators wish to move further toward marketized and even privatized forms of education provision. Indeed, some advocates of devolution and choice have argued that the indifferent performance of the reforms so far is merely evidence that they have not gone far enough. Tooley (1995) favors an even more deregulated system and points out that we cannot necessarily take evidence about quasi-markets—or what he prefers to call "so-called markets"—as constituting an argument against markets in general. However, there is little in the studies reported here to suggest that going further in the direction of marketization would yield major overall improvements in the quality of education and it seems that they would almost certainly have damaging equity effects. Thus, in an inegalitarian society, it seems highly improbable that the sort of "bottom-up" accountability associated with markets, and favored by Chubb and Moe (1992:13), can replace the need for democratic accountability if equity is to remain an important consideration.

Henig (1994) suggests that "the logical coherence, academic legitimacy, and conservative appeal of conventional economic theory results in the market rationale dominating the choice movement in public," but he also observes that "non market rationales account for most of the enthusiasm and support" (p. 194). He points out that "where school choice has appeared most successful—as in some of the many experiments with magnets, magnetised districts, and state-wide open enrollment—it has been at the instigation and under the direction of strong and affirmative government action" (p. 193). Contrary to Chubb and Moe (1990), Smith and Meier (1995) claim that the abolition of neither democratic control nor union power is a prerequisite for tackling the problems of bureaucracy, which are at the heart of many critiques of conventional mass education systems, and their own book is an argument for enhanced democratic control as an alternative to markets.

Whatever gains are to be had from handing decision making to parents and teachers (and they seem to be far fewer than the advocates claim), it seems that key decisions about goals and frameworks still need to be made in the broader political arena, even though the rhetoric accompanying reform often seeks to suggest that education has been taken out of politics as normally understood (Chubb and Moe, 1992). Even Chubb and Moe (1990), who argue that equality is better "protected" by markets than by political institutions, have to concede that choice of school cannot be unlimited and should not be entirely unregulated.

Regulating choice and pursuing equity necessitates the existence of contexts for deciding upon rules and processes for adjudicating between different claims and priorities. This entails the revival or creation of democratic contexts within which such issues can be determined. Unfortunately, though, those public institutions that might act on behalf of the broader interests of the community have been progressively dismantled by New Right governments, which means that creating a new public sphere in which educational matters can even be debated—let alone determined—poses considerable challenges. According to Foucault, new forms of association, such as trade unions and political parties, arose in the nineteenth century as a counterbalance to the prerogative of the state and acted as the seedbed of new ideas (Kritzman, 1988). Modern versions of these collectivist forms of association may now need to emerge to counterbalance not only the prerogative of the state but also the prerogative of the market.

The challenge will be to move away from atomized decision making to the reassertion of collective responsibility without recreating the very bureaucratic systems whose shortcomings have helped to legitimate the current tendency to treat education as a private good rather than a public responsibility. Although quasi-market policies are part of a social text that helps to create new subject positions that undermine traditional

forms of collectivism, those forms of collectivism themselves failed to empower many members of society, including women and minority ethnic groups. Margonis and Parker (1995) point out that the "communitarian metaphors" that are often used to oppose the "laissez-faire metaphors" of the choice proponents fail to take account of institutional racism and the deep structural inequalities in American society that mean that public education has itself never fostered inclusive communities.

We need to consider how the more positive aspects of choice and autonomy might facilitate the development of new forms of community empowerment rather than exacerbating social differentiation. Gordon (1994b:21) argues for "a policy approach that combines the older social democratic goal of educational comparability across class and ethnic boundaries, with real choice for families." But even if the social democratic era looks better in retrospect, or in comparison with current policies, than it did at the time, there is a need to rethink what might be progressive policies for the next century. Given changes in the nature of modern (or "postmodern") societies, we need to develop a conception of citizenship and an education system that creates unity without denying specificity (Mouffe, 1989). As Henig (1994:222) says of the United States, "the sad irony of the current education-reform movement is that, through over identification with school-choice proposals rooted in market-based ideas, the healthy impulse to consider radical reforms to address social problems may be channeled into initiatives that further erode the potential for collective deliberation and collective response."

Wells (1990) argues that equitable choice schemes require clear goal statements, outreach work, information and counseling for parents, a fair, unrestrictive, noncompetitive, and equitable admissions procedure, and provision of adequate transportation for students. Similar safeguards are also recommended in an international study of choice policies in England, Australia, the Netherlands, New Zealand, Sweden, and the United States (OECD, 1994). This concluded that to avoid reinforcing tendencies toward academic and social selection, popular schools may need positive incentives to expand and disadvantaged groups need better information, better transport, and perhaps privileged access to certain schools. Walford (1992a) advocates that entry to oversubscribed schools should be based on random selection, an approach that is still used in some schools in New Zealand.

Yet even the more tightly regulated schemes of devolution and choice need to be subjected to rigorous sociological scrutiny. Atomized decision making in a highly stratified society may appear to give everyone equal opportunities, but transferring responsibility for decision making from the public to the private sphere may actually reduce the possibility of collective action to improve the quality of education for all. This is not necessarily to impute the motives of those who have fostered the current reforms. Although the devolution of decision making can have considerable political utility in crisis contexts (Malen, 1994), this has not been the only or even perhaps the main motivation for devolution. Many people genuinely expected quasi-markets to overcome the lack of responsiveness of bureaucratic systems of mass education, whereas others saw them as a way of giving disadvantaged children the sorts of opportunities hitherto available only to those who could afford to buy them through private schooling or their position in the housing market. Yet these hopes are not being realized and seem unlikely to be realized in the context of broader policies that do nothing to challenge deeper social and cultural inequalities. This is why a sociological perspective ought to have a presence in the ongoing policy debate.

REFERENCES

Bartlett, W. 1993. "Quasi-Markets and Educational Reforms." In J. Le Grand and W. Bartlett (eds.), *Quasi-Markets and Social Policy*. London: Macmillan.

Bauman, P., D. Banks, M. Murphy, and H. Kuczwara. 1994. "The Charter School Movement: Preliminary Findings From the First Three States." Paper presented at the Annual Meeting of the American Educational Research Association, New Orleans, 4–8 April.

Becker, H. J., K. Nakagawa, and R. G. Corwin. 1995. "Parental Involvement Contracts in California's Charter Schools." Paper presented at the Annual Meeting of the American Educational Research Association, San Francisco, 18–22 April.

Blackburne, L. 1988. "Peers Back Policy on Open Enrollment." *The Times Educational Supplement* 13 May:A6.

Bryk, A. S., V. E. Lee, and P. B. Holland. 1993. *Catholic Schools and the Common Good*. Cambridge, MA: Harvard University Press.

Bush, T., M. Coleman, and D. Glover. 1993. *Managing Autonomous Schools*. London, Paul Chapman.

Chubb, J., and T. Moe. 1990. *Politics, Markets and America's Schools*. Washington, DC: Brookings Institution.

———. 1992. *A Lesson in School Reform from Great Britain*. Washington, DC: Brookings Institution.

Clewell, B. C., and M. F. Joy. 1990. *Choice in Montclair, New Jersey*. Princeton, NJ: ETS.

Coleman, J. S., T. Hoffer, and S. Kilgore. 1982. *High School Achievement: Public, Catholic and Private Schools*. New York, Basic Books.

Cookson, P. W. 1995. "Goals 2000: Framework for the New Educational Federalism." *Teachers College Record* 96(3):405–417.

David, M. E. 1993. *Parents, Gender and Education Reform*. Cambridge, Polity Press.

Domanico, R. J. 1990. *Restructuring New York City's Public Schools: The Case for Public School Choice*. Education Policy Paper #3. New York: Manhattan Institute for Policy Research.

Edwards, T., J. Fitz, and G. Whitty. 1989. *The State and Private Education: An Evaluation of the Assisted Places Scheme*. London: Falmer Press.

Feintuck, M. 1994. *Accountability and Choice in Education*. Buckingham, Open University Press.

Fitz, J., D. Halpin, and S. Power. 1993. *Grant Maintained Schools: Education in the Marketplace*. London: Kogan Page.

Fliegel, S., with J. Macguire. 1990. *Miracle in East Harlem: The Fight for Choice in Public Education*. New York: Random House.

Foster, P., R. Gomm, and M. Hammersley. 1996. *Constructing Educational Inequality*. London: Falmer Press.

Fowler, M. 1993. *Factors Influencing Choice of Secondary Schools*. Christchurch, England: University of Canterbury.

Gewirtz, S., J. S. Ball, and R. Bowe, 1995. *Markets, Choice and Equity*. Buckingham, England: Open University Press.

Glatter, R., P. Woods, and C. Bagley. 1995. "Diversity, Differentiation and Hierarchy: School Choice and Parental Preference." Paper presented at the ESRC/CEPAM Invitation Seminar on Research on Parental Choice and School Response, Milton Keynes, 7–8 June.

Glennerster, H. 1991. "Quasi-Markets for Education?" *Economic Journal* 101:1268–1276.

Gordon, L. 1994a. " 'Rich' and 'Poor' Schools in Aotearoa." *New Zealand Journal of Educational Studies* 29(2):113–125.

———. 1994b. "Is School Choice a Sustainable Policy for New Zealand? A Review of Recent Research Findings and a Look to the Future." *New Zealand Annual Review of Education* 4:9–24.

Grace, G. 1991. "Welfare Labourism versus the New Right." *International Studies in the Sociology of Education* 1(1):37–48.

Grutzik, C., D. Bernal, D. Hirschberg, and A. S. Wells. 1995. "Resources and Access in California Charter Schools." Paper presented at the Annual Meeting of the American Educational Research Association, San Francisco, 18–22 April.

Henig, J. R. 1994. *Rethinking School Choice: Limits of the Market Metaphor*. Princeton: Princeton University Press.

Kritzman, L. D. (ed.). 1988. *Foucault: Politics/Philosophy/Culture*. New York: Routledge.

Lauder, H., D. Hughes, S. Waslander, M. Thrupp, J. Mc-Glinn, S. Newton, and A. Dupuis. 1994. *The Creation of Market Competition for Education in New Zealand*. Smithfield Project, Wellington, Victoria: University of Wellington.

Lee, V. E., and A. S. Bryk. 1993. "Science or Policy Argument?" In E. Rassell and R. Rothstein (eds.), *School Choice: Examining the Evidence*. Washington, DC: Economic Policy Institute.

Le Grand, J., and W. Bartlett (eds.). 1993. *Quasi-Markets and Social Policy*. London: Macmillan.

Levacic, R. 1995. *Local Management of Schools: Analysis and Practice*. Milton Keynes: Open University Press.

Malen, B. 1994. "Enacting Site-Based Management: A Political Utilities Analysis." *Educational Evaluation and Policy Analysis* 16(3):249–267.

Marginson, S. 1993. *Education and Public Policy in Australia*. Melbourne: Cambridge University Press.

Margonis, F., and L. Parker. 1995. "Choice, Privatization, and Unspoken Strategies of Containment." *Educational Policy* 9(4):375–403.

Medler, A., and J. Nathan. 1995. *Charter Schools: What Are They Up To?* Denver: Education Commission of the States/Minneapolis, Humphrey Institute of Public Affairs.

Moe, T. 1994. "The British Battle for Choice." In K. L. Billingsley (ed.), *Voices on Choice: The Education Reform Debate*. San Francisco: Pacific Institute for Public Policy.

Mouffe, C. 1989. "Toward a Radical Democratic Citizenship." *Democratic Left* 17(2):6–7.

Murphy, J., and L. G. Beck. 1995. *School-Based Management as School Reform: Taking Stock*. Thousand Oaks, CA: Corwin Press.

Newmann, F. 1993. "Beyond Common Sense in Educational Restructuring: The Issues of Content and Leadership." *Educational Researcher* 22(2):4–13.

OECD. 1994. *School: A Matter of Choice*. Paris: OECD/CERI.

Ogawa, R. T., and P. A. White. 1994. "School-Based Management: An Overview." In S. A. Mohrman, P. Wohlstetter, and Associates (eds.), *School-Based Management: Organizing for High Performance*. San Francisco: Jossey-Bass.

Pennell, H., and A. West. 1995. *Changing Schools: Secondary Schools' Admissions Policies in Inner London in 1995*. Clare Market Papers No. 9. London: London School of Economics and Political Science.

Picot, B., and members of the Taskforce to Review Educational Administration. 1988. *Administering for Excellence* (Picot Report). Wellington: Government Printer.

Plank, S., K. S. Schiller, B. Schneider, and J. S. Coleman. 1993. "Effects of Choice in Education." In E. Rassell, and

R. Rothstein (eds.), *School Choice: Examining the Evidence*. Washington, DC: Economic Policy Institute.

Pollard, S. 1995. *Schools, Selection and the Left*. London: Social Market Foundation.

Raywid, M. A. 1994. "Focus Schools: A Genre to Consider." Urban Diversity Series No. 106, New York: Columbia University, ERIC Clearinghouse on Urban Education.

Rossell, C. H., and C. L. Glenn. 1988. "The Cambridge Controlled Choice Plan." *Urban Review* 20(2):75–94.

Sexton, S. 1987. *My Schools—A Radical Policy*. Warlingham: Institute of Economic Affairs, Education Unit.

Smith, K. B., and K. J. Meier. 1995. *The Case Against School Choice: Politics, Markets and Fools*. Armonk, NY: M. E. Sharpe.

Smith, T., and M. Noble. 1995. *Education Divides: Poverty and Schooling in the 1990s*. London: Child Poverty Action Group.

Tan, N. 1990. *The Cambridge Controlled Choice Program: Improving Educational Equity and Integration*. Education Policy Paper #4. New York: Manhattan Institute for Policy Research.

Tooley, J. 1995. "Markets or Democracy? A Reply to Stewart Ranson." *British Journal of Educational Studies* 43(1):31–34.

Urahn, S., and D. Stewart. 1994. *Minnesota Charter Schools: A Research Report*. St Paul, MN: Research Department, Minnesota House of Representatives.

Walford, G. 1992a. *Selection for Secondary Schooling*. National Commission on Education Briefing Paper 7. London: National Commission on Education.

———. 1992b. "Educational Choice and Equity in Great Britain." *Educational Policy* 6(2):123–138.

Walford, G., and H. Miller. 1991. *City Technology College*. Milton Keynes: Open University Press.

Waslander, S., and M. Thrupp. 1995. "Choice, Competition and Segregation: An Empirical Analysis of a New Zealand Secondary School Market 1990–1993." *Journal of Education Policy* 10(1):1–26.

Wells, A. S. 1990. "Public School Choice: Issues and Concerns for Urban Educators." ERIC/CUE Digest #63. New York: ERIC Clearinghouse on Urban Education.

———. 1993a. *Time to Choose: America at the Crossroads of School Choice Policy*. New York: Hill and Wang.

———. 1993b. "The Sociology of School Choice: Why Some Win and Others Lose in the Educational Marketplace." In E. Rassell and R. Rothstein (eds.), *School Choice: Examining the Evidence*. Washington, DC: Economic Policy Institute.

Wells, A. S., and R. L. Crain. 1992. "Do Parents Choose School Quality or School Status? A Sociological Theory of Free Market Education." In P. W. Cookson (ed.), *The Choice Controversy*. Newbury Park, CA: Corwin Press.

Whitty, G. 1989. "The New Right and the National Curriculum: State Control or Market Forces?" *Journal of Education Policy* 4(4):329–341.

Whitty, G., T. Edwards, and S. Gewirtz. 1993. *Specialisation and Choice in Urban Education: The City Technology College Experiment.* London: Routledge.

Witte, J. F. 1990. "Choice and Control: An Analytical Overview." In W. H. Clune and J. F. Witte (eds.), *Choice and Control in American Education*, Volume 1. New York: Falmer Press.

Witte, J. F., C. A. Thorn, K. M. Pritchard, and M. Claibourn. 1994. *Fourth Year Report: Milwaukee Parental Choice Program.* Madison, WI: Department of Public Instruction.

Wohlstetter, P., R. Wenning, and K. L. Briggs. 1995. "Charter Schools in the United States: The Question of Autonomy." *Educational Policy* 9(4):331–358.

Wylie, C. 1994. *Self Managing Schools in New Zealand: The Fifth Year.* Wellington: New Zealand Council for Educational Research.

———. 1995. "Contrary Currents: The Application of the Public Sector Reform Framework in Education." *New Zealand Journal of Educational Studies* 30(2):149–164.

RACE AND EDUCATION

Roslyn Arlin Mickelson
Department of Sociology, University of North Carolina at Charlotte

The problem of the twentieth century is the problem of the color line.
—W. E. B. Dubois

Dubois' prophetic observation continues to be as applicable to education as it is to most other aspects of American society. Race has shaped the educational experiences of Americans since the birth of the nation. One of the primary ways that unequal political and economic power has been maintained and reproduced is through racially differentiated access to education. During the first four-fifths of the nation's history, formal public education was available or denied based on an individual's racial designation. In fact, during the era of slavery, many southern states formally prohibited the education of youngsters of African descent. Since the middle of this century, the federal government has attempted to enforce laws aimed at ensuring equality of educational opportunity. First, it attacked *de jure*, then *de facto* segregation. Following this, a host of policies including compensatory education, bilingual and multicultural education, and affirmative action were implemented with the aim of eliminating racial disparities in educational opportunities. These policies and programs have met with varying degrees of success. Today, race continues to be as much a part of U.S. education as the chalk board.

What Is Race?

The concept of race is nebulous and ambiguous. The assumption that humans can be divided into biologically discrete human races is a social and political fiction. Social scientists generally agree that the meaning of race is socially constructed in loose relation to perceived phenotypical differences among humans. Broad social, political, and cultural environments create and change racial categories. For example, U.S. southern history demonstrates that who was considered white or black is a matter of politics and history, not biology. A child of one black and one white parent is genetically mixed, but typically that child will be socially constructed as a black person.

Racial formation theory holds that race is always a politically contested construct and the state is the key site for contestation (Omi and Winant, 1994). This process is clearly seen with census racial categories. Categories vary from one enumeration to the next because they are shaped by intensely political processes. For example, recent census distinguish between white and non-white Hispanics, while previous ones did not. Similarly, in the census of 2000, the category of mixed race appeared for the first time. In this chapter, the categories of race used will reflect the five census categories commonly employed by the federal government and most school systems: Asian Americans, blacks, Hispanics, Native Americans, and whites.

What Is Ethnicity?

Race is not the same as ethnicity, but the concepts overlap in part because ethnicity, too, is a question of social construction and political struggle. Ethnicity relates to national ancestry (see King, *Ethnicity*, this volume, p. 247). Among whites, ethnicity typically involves identification with the national origins and culture of one's European ancestors; for Asian Americans, it is the Asian or Pacific Island origins and culture of one's ancestors; and for Native Americans, ethnicity reflects tribal blood quotients. Sociologists stress that a significant part of ethnicity is the belief on the part of people that they descend from common ancestors, share a common culture with coethnics, and choose to identify with that ethnic group (Waters, 1990). This indicates ethnicity, like race, is socially constructed. Many people have ancestors from several ethnic groups, but choose to identify with one. Factors that influence choice of identity include the fluctuating social acceptability of certain ethnicities, which side of a family a person prefers, surnames, generation in the United States, and a host of socioeconomic factors. Waters observes that opportunities to choose and construct ethnic identities are greatest for whites in American society. As members of the dominant social and political racial group, individuals can decide whether or not to identify with a specific ethnic group.

The history of contact with the United States, the conditions of a group's incorporation into American society, and the contemporary politics of an ethnic group's country of origin influence the way an ethnic group is defined, the nature of the education historically provided to its children, and the barriers or bridges to education currently afforded its children. For example, most Cuban-American children until recently were extended unique educational privileges because of their status as political refugees from a communist state. In contrast, because of the presence of undocumented workers in certain states, native-born Americans of Mexican descent face formidable barriers to public education until they can establish their citizenship.

The United States is becoming a more racially and ethnically diverse nation. Table 1 presents the racial and ethnic make up of the American population. Since 1980, the Asian-American population has doubled and Hispanics increased in number by over 50%. Native Americans also are a rapidly increasing population, growing by 40%. During this time, the white population increased by about 10% and the black population has grown by about 14%. Population growth has had the most acute effects on the major metropolitan areas of the United States.

It is impossible to separate the fiscal crisis of urban America from the issues of race and schooling. As the American middle class fled to the suburbs, urban schools lost some of their tax base and public support. At the same time, the population of the urban working poor and underclass has grown both in absolute and relative terms. Because racial and ethnic minorities tend to live in large urban areas, these demographic growth patterns have the largest effects on schools in these areas. Urban areas are experiencing economic and

TABLE 1. Population Estimates of the United States by Major Racial and Ethnic Groups, November 1999 (N = 273,866,000)

RACE/ETHNICITY	U.S. POPULATION (%)
White	82.3
Black	12.8
Native American	0.9
Asian and Pacific Islander	4.0
Hispanic, all races	11.6
White, not Hispanic	71.7
Black, not Hispanic	12.2
Native American, not Hispanic	0.7
Asian and Pacific Islander, not Hispanic	3.8

Source: U.S. Bureau of the Census (1999).

social crises brought about by the restructuring and globalization of the American economy. Large urban city school systems are more likely than suburban systems to serve poor, immigrant, and racial minority communities while their declining resources severely strain their capacity to provide appropriate services for all students. These fiscal and demographic trends are expected to continue into the next century.

Race and Educational Outcomes

One of the key reasons that race continues to have such salience for education is that outcomes are strongly related to race and ethnicity. At the same time, any generalization about racial patterns is fraught with dangers. First, race is highly correlated with class and it is difficult to disentangle their unique and interactive effects on educational processes and outcomes. Second, due to the enormous ethnic and class variations within each racial category, generalizations about a racial group are bound to ignore crucial differences in educational outcomes. Intragroup ethnic variations can be marked. Generation, English language proficiency, nationality, alienage, and social class all contribute to the wide distribution of educational outcomes within racial groups. Gender patterns of achievement vary by racial group as well (see Delamont, *Gender and Education*, Karp, *Gender and Math Education*, and Grant and Rong *Gender Inequality*, this volume, p. 289). Nevertheless, there are identifiable variations in achievement and attainment among racial groups.

Achievement

Table 2 presents math and science achievement by race. National Assessment of Educational Progress (NAEP) scores indicate a long standing pattern that is also reflected in the SAT math and verbal scores that appear in Table 3. Overall, Asian Americans achieve higher than all other racial and ethnic groups. Whites follow and Hispanics and American Indians tend to score alike. Blacks consistently achieve lower than other racial and ethnic groups. During the last few decades, the achievement gap between whites and other groups has been narrowing slightly, especially for blacks and Native Americans. The gap has been narrowing as well in other indicators including enrollment in math and science, and enrollment in college preparatory courses.

Attainment

Attainment differences among racial groups have narrowed markedly in the past 20 years (see Table 2 in Mickelson, *Affirmative Action*, this volume, p. 34). Nevertheless, in higher education, racial differences exist in time to degree, in persistence to degree, in majors, and in enrollment in graduate programs. With the exception of Asian Americans, racial minorities take longer to graduate, are less likely to persist than whites, and are less likely to enroll in graduate programs. The proportion of whites and Asian Americans in graduate programs is greater than their distribution in the population; the proportion of blacks, Native Americans, and Hispanics is less.

Explanations for Racial Variations in Educational Outcomes

Heredity

There is a long tradition of biological determinism in European and American thought. It typically was and still is invoked to legitimize social inequality of some sort. Genetic approaches to explaining racial and ethnic differences in academic achievement continue to be advanced, most recently by Herrnstein and Murray (1994). They argued that racial and class differences in measured IQ are overwhelmingly due to weak genotypes among the cognitively deficient. In so doing, the authors ignore the socially constructed (rather than biological) nature of the phenomena of class, race, and ethnicity; the problematic nature of the twin studies used to calculate the heritability of "intelligence"; the his-

TABLE 2. Average Mathematics and Science Proficiency of Seniors by Racial Groups, 1994

RACE	NAEP MATH	NAEP SCIENCE
American Indian/Alaskan Native	281	286
Asian/Pacific Islander	315	308
Black	275	256
White	305	303
Hispanic	283	273
All	299	294

Source: U.S. Department of Education (1996).

torical legacy of class and ethnic bias in instruments used to measure "intelligence"; research that suggests the nature of human intelligence is multifaceted; and the consensus among scientists that very little is known about how genes influence behavior. Few scholars deny that heredity plays some part in individual differences in intelligence that may be reflected in academic achievement. However, evidence is not sufficient to conclude that observed achievement differences among various racial (or class) groups in the United States are due to group variations in intelligence (see Hurn, *IQ*, this volume, p. 399).

Cultural Values

Another explanation frequently offered to account for racial variations in educational outcomes is that certain racial and ethnic groups have values more conducive to educational success. These values appear in cultures of racial and ethnic groups that excel academically. For

TABLE 3. Average SAT Scores of High School Seniors by Racial and Ethnic Groups, 1997

RACE/ETHNICITY	SAT VERBAL	SAT MATH
American Indian	473	475
Asian American	496	560
Black	434	423
Mexican American	451	458
Puerto Rican	454	447
Other Hispanic	466	468
White	526	526
Other	512	514
All	505	511

Source: Digest of Education Statistics (1998).

example, Caplan et al. (1991) identify a cohesive family and hard work as the "core" values that constitute the bedrock of Southeast Asian refugees' beliefs that have enabled their youth to achieve so well in very few years after arriving in the United States. But it is not clear that the values of ethnic minorities who succeed less well in school, like blacks, are, in fact, essentially different from those of ethnic minorities who do. Steinberg and his colleagues report that U.S. adolescents and parents from Asian-American, Hispanic, black, and white backgrounds did not differ in their beliefs about the value of education; they differ only in their evaluations of the consequences of educational failures (Steinberg et al., 1992).

No cultural values operate in a vacuum; the values that a racial or ethnic group places on education are historically determined and are continually shaped by a group's position in a society. Moreover, the different members of the same cultural groups may have vastly different educational outcomes under diverse societal conditions. For instance, the children of ethnic Burakumin and Koreans who are oppressed minorities in Japan tend to fare poorly in school relative to other Japanese youth. Yet in the United States both groups' children have records of educational success. More recent conceptualizations of minority achievement promise greater explanatory power than simple, static cultural models. These more dynamic approaches share the view that school performance is influenced by youths' perceptions and understandings of the social world in which they live.

Cultural Framework

Ogbu (1991) begins with the proposition that all groups in society, minorities as well as the majority, have a cultural framework or cultural model that serves as a grid for interpreting the world. What distinguishes educationally successful groups from less successful ones is their folk theory of success guiding school behavior. Ogbu makes a key distinction between immigrant or voluntary minorities, like Asian Americans, and involuntary ones, like African Americans. His conception of a cultural model links an ethnic minority group's orientation to education to specific historical conditions of its incorporation into a majority society and group members' experiences once in it.

Cultural models are influenced by two historical forces: (1) the group's initial terms of incorporation and

(2) the nature of their subsequent discriminatory treatment in a society. Because of immigrant minorities' voluntary incorporation into the host society (one can argue that refugees are not truly voluntary immigrants), they possess a dual frame of reference that allows them to develop or maintain an optimistic view of their future possibilities. They compare their current situation with those of kinfolk in their country of origin or with other members of their group in the host society. This leads to the reasonable conclusion that despite real barriers to opportunity, pursuing an education makes sense—at least more sense than not pursuing one.

Involuntary minorities, in contrast, have only the dominant group in their society as a frame of reference. They accurately perceive that relative to the dominant group, they do not receive fair or equitable returns on their educational credentials. For instance, in 1994, white high school dropouts were more likely to be employed than black high school graduates and black males with college degrees were less likely to be employed than white males with similar credentials (U.S. Department of Education, 1996). These realities may lead to disillusionment, perhaps cynicism about schooling, and the reasonable questioning of whether putting time, effort, and hopes for the future into the pursuit of education is necessarily the best use of one's time and efforts. Thus, involuntary minorities' folk theories of success may not necessarily rely upon education.

Another aspect of immigrant minorities' response to discrimination is their interpretation of why they face ethnic barriers. They attribute the barriers to their newness, their language difficulties, and cultural traits that set them apart from the majority. They recognize racism and ethnic prejudice, too. These cultural differences are barriers to be overcome. Acquisition of educational credentials appears to be a suitable response to unequal returns to education because they can continue to believe in the overall societal rules for advancement while they place the onus on themselves to acquire the cultural traits (such as standard English) perceived as necessary to compete in what they still believe to be an essentially meritocratic system. Involuntary minorities like blacks perceive labor market discrimination as a relatively permanent barrier that cannot be scaled through greater education. Consequently, cultural and language differences may become markers of collective identity to be maintained (Ogbu, 1994). This perspective receives expression in an oppositional cultural framework pointedly disdainful of the alleged education/opportunity linkage. Those involuntary minority youth who hold oppositional cultural frameworks resist schooling.

Dual Educational Attitudes

Ogbu's model, however, does not account for the positive attitudes and values toward education that involuntary minorities invariably express. A conceptualization of educational attitudes as multidimensional begins to account for this observed duality. Mickelson (1990) demonstrated that adolescents' educational attitudes are multidimensional. All adolescents hold abstract attitudes that reflect the American Dream's account of the role of education and opportunity as well as a second set of beliefs, concrete attitudes, rooted in the material realities in which educational credentials may or may not be fairly rewarded. Concrete attitudes are the ones that actually shape students' achievement behaviors (see Mickelson, *Educational Attitudes: Abstract and Concrete*, this volume, p. 199). Together, Ogbu's model of oppositional cultural framework and Mickelson's concepts of dual educational attitudes begin to account for both the variations in minority youths' achievement despite their uniform proclamations about the importance of education for their lives.

Opportunities to Learn

Another explanation for racial variations in school outcomes is that students from different racial and ethnic backgrounds have unequal opportunities to learn. Simply put, students in more effective schools, who are in higher tracks, who are exposed to more material, whose teachers expect more of them, and who spend more time on tasks tend to learn more. This conceptualization of opportunity to learn is more than a measure of inputs; it also considers processes (Dougherty, 1996; McPartland and Schneider, 1996). A large body of research has demonstrated that children of different race and class backgrounds have markedly different experiences in segregated minority, integrated, and segregated majority schools. There continues to be evidence that schools attended predominately by racial and ethnic minority youth provide fewer opportunities to learn than do schools attended primarily by whites. Furthermore, schools that are racially integrated are often racially segregated by track within the school, further contributing to the instructional and curricular differences by race (Mickelson and Heath, 1999). The vast literature on tracking captures the process by which race and track interact in ways that can stratify opportunities to learn (see Datnow and Cooper, *Tracking*, this volume, p. 687).

Other Explanations

It is impossible to exhaustively review in this chapter all the social forces that contribute to racial differences in educational outcomes. Two additional ones that should be considered are the concepts of social capital and cultural capital. Both are important because they capture the intersections of racial cultures, social class, and structural forces with school processes (see Madigan, *Cultural Capital* and Schneider, *Social Capital*, this volume, pp. 121, 545).

Race and Ethnic Issues in American Education

Simple categorization of students into a racial group fails to capture the complexity of their social location. Within each racial category are multiple ethnic groups, each with its own history and relationship to the larger American society. Moreover, social class and gender forces influence the ways that an individual's race shapes education. For example, the educational experiences of middle-class black females are vastly different from those of underclass black males, and those of Cuban immigrants in Miami differ from those of Mexican immigrants in South Texas. The following sections review the complexities of educational issues associated with the major racial groups.

Asian Americans

The 9.5 million Asian Americans include people whose ancestry derives from the Indian subcontinent, the Pacific Islands, and the nations of the Pacific Rim. The many successes of Asian-American students have captured the attention and imagination of educators, policymakers, and parents. Often characterized as "model minorities," many have accomplished academic feats that often surpass those of other racial minorities and whites in the United States (Steinberg et al., Brown 1992). Research indicates that Asian Americans are more likely to persist in school, attain more education, and have higher levels of achievement than students from other ethnic and racial groups. In fact, the remarkable educational accomplishments of many Southeast Asian refugee children prompted Caplan and his associates (1992) to proclaim that, indeed, the U.S. educational system actually still works!

While describing the overall patterns of accomplishments among Asian-Americans, it is important to note their tremendous heterogeneity. Asian-American populations vary by country of origin, religion, language, cultural background, generation, and immigration status. These factors all have important implications for school outcomes. Moreover, the "model minority" stereotype masks a more complex reality. The stereotype comes from a popular misconception that all Asian-American students excel and that all Asian-American adults are well educated, prosperous, and law abiding. In fact, not all Asian-American students do well in school. Many struggle to achieve, and certain ethnic groups and recent immigrants have high rates of school failure and dropouts. Asian-American students face many of the same obstacles to school success that other minority students encounter. These may include ethnic hostility from other students and teachers, overcrowded classrooms, and limited English proficiency. For instance, the Supreme Court decision recognizing the right to bilingual education, *Lau v. Nichols*, was brought on behalf of a Chinese-American child. Cultural norms among certain ethnic groups may pose barriers to academic success. For example, Hmong teenage women often drop out in order to have children because of the crucial importance of bearing children to women's status within the group.

Blacks

There are approximately 34 million blacks in the United States. About 2 million were born in the Caribbean, Africa, Latin America, or Western Europe. On average, foreign born blacks tend to perform better and attain more education than native born blacks. In recent decades, the achievement gap between blacks and whites has narrowed, and the attainment gap is closing, too. In 1995, 93% of whites had a high school diploma or its equivalent, compared to 87% of blacks (U.S. Department of Education, 1996). Among high school graduates, 18% of blacks compared to 31% of whites held bachelor degrees or higher.

The history of black education speaks volumes about the racialization of American education. During the era of slavery, it was almost impossible for blacks to gain an education. Those who did tended to live outside the south. Southern blacks who were literate generally were self-taught. Formal schooling was virtually unavailable and in many states it was illegal to educate blacks. The era of Reconstruction brought the opportunity for former slaves to go to school and large numbers of adults and children attended school along with whites. This was the brief period in southern history when mass integrated public schooling was first provided. Following the election of 1876 and the compromise that removed federal troops from the south, schools along with other public accommodations were resegregated as Jim Crow laws of the late nineteenth century codified the breadth and depth of the racial separation that continued for the next 75 years.

After the turn of the century, southern blacks attended segregated black schools. This was a mixed blessing. Typically, these schools were exceedingly crowded, poorly equipped, cold in winter, and sweltering in summer. Their supplies, books, and equipment were either previously used or nonexistent, and many of the teachers were poorly educated themselves. Rural secondary schools were few and far between until after World War I. At the same time, segregated black schools, along with churches, became critical nerve centers for black communities. Many dedicated and excellent teachers and administrators conveyed to their students a healthy sense of human worth and value in addition to educating them. Some blacks lament the loss of control, culture, and community that came with school desegregation following the *Brown v. Board of Education* decision in 1954. Some black educators tie the growth of contemporary oppositional cultural frameworks among black adolescents to the loss of the community control and cultural integrity of segregated black schools.

Until after the first world war, the vast majority of blacks were rural southerners. Today, the majority of blacks are urban residents and growing numbers of middle-class families are moving to suburbs. This development has had a marked effect on urban communities. As the middle class moves to the suburbs, once socioeconomically heterogeneous central city neighborhoods are increasingly becoming concentrated and isolated islands of poverty and despair adjacent to the splendor and wealth of the financial and commercial centers of major cities (Wilson, 1987). As a consequence, many black children attend segregated minority schools in extremely poor neighborhoods. Segregated minority schooling, of course, is not a new phenomenon brought about by recent economic restructure and demographic shifts in metropolitan areas. It was the formal and informal educational policy of the United States through roughly the first three-fourths of this century (see Hochschild, *Brown v. Board of Education*, and Smith, *Desegregation*, this volume, pp. 67, 141).

Hispanics

The Hispanic population of the United States is the fastest growing of any group. Today, there are about 28 million Hispanic Americans of all races. Like Asian Americans, Hispanics are an ethnically diverse population that includes persons whose ancestry traces to Mexico, Puerto Rico, Cuba, and Central and South American countries. Because as a population Hispanics are relatively young and have high fertility rates, children of Hispanic origin will enter the school systems in the future at a faster rate than any other population. Some large city school systems, like the Los Angeles Unified School District, are already majority Hispanic.

Like blacks, the Hispanic population has a growing, well-educated, and moderately affluent middle class. Occupational attainment gaps between whites and Hispanics are narrowing, particularly as more Hispanics enter the professions. But Hispanics remain the least educated major population group in the United States (Gandara, 1995). Due to the poverty that disproportionately characterizes the life of many Hispanics, the limited English proficiency of students and their parents, and the likelihood that they will attend overcrowded and underfunded inner city schools, educational achievement and attainment of Hispanic students are lower than whites and Asians. The attainment gaps between whites and Hispanics did not close between 1971 and 1995. In 1995, 58% of Hispanics had completed high school, and among Hispanic high school graduates, 16% earned a bachelor's degree or higher (U.S. Department of Education, 1996).

Like Asian Americans, generational issues, ethnicity, social class, English-language proficiency, and immigration status complicate Hispanic educational achievement and attainment processes and outcomes (see Zanger, *Bilingual Education*, and Moreno and Muller, *Higher Education in the United States: Latinos*, this volume, pp. 55, 353). Recent research has demonstrated that immigrant Hispanic students, especially those from war-torn areas of Central America, perform better than native-born students. This is particularly true when their achievement is compared to that of Chicano youth who may adopt an oppositional cultural framework.

Native Americans

Native Americans include American Indians and Alaskan Natives (Inuits and Aluets). The Native American population has been growing during the past half century. Today, roughly 2 million people are non-Hispanic American Indians, although over 7 million Americans identify themselves as having some Indian ancestry. Inuits and Aluets, who live primarily in Alaska, number about 100,000 individuals. If language is considered a marker of unique ethnicity, then there are over 200 ethnic groups among Native Americans. More so than language, customs, histories, and traditional modes of production (large and small game hunters, gatherers, farmers) distinguish American Indian, Inuit, and Aluet cultures.

When Europeans first encountered American Indians, communicable diseases decimated about 90% of the indigenous population. Over the next several centuries, survivors of the epidemics were dispossessed of their fertile land through genocidal warfare. Survivors were moved onto largely infertile reservations. Here American Indians were promised education, health care, and other benefits. In the last quarter of the nineteenth century, the federal government took the role of guardian of Indian land. While recognizing each tribe's ownership of the land, the federal government held ultimate authority over American Indian affairs.

Although a small, but growing middle class has emerged recently, most American Indians are likely to have low incomes, high levels of unemployment, and low educational and occupational attainment whether they live on reservations or in urban areas. Reservations are home to about one-fourth of the American Indian population. Reservations have exceedingly high poverty and unemployment rates due to their relative isolation from the U.S. economic mainstream. Farming and, recently, gambling, are major sources of revenue for some tribes. Only a handful of tribes, however, have the resources for the economic development of their reservations. Most tribes suffer from a dearth of fertile land and mineral or other exploitable natural resources, have little venture capital, and have a population that is relatively uneducated, unskilled, and poor. Reservations became islands of desperate poverty and isolation for most Native American people.

Urban American Indians suffer from many of the difficulties other inner city residents endure. Migration to urban areas is difficult for rural people, especially American Indians who tend to have low levels of education and occupational skills. Despite difficulties adjusting to urban life, and a discriminatory labor market, urban American Indians are relatively more prosperous than their counterparts on reservations.

Historically, the education of Indian children was relegated to the Bureau of Indian Affairs (BIA). Indian children were placed in boarding schools where they were taught traditional American curricula. There was a conscious attempt to strip them of their own culture and assimilate Indian children into the dominant white one. Unique among American racial and ethnic groups' educational histories, then, is the fact that for decades Native Americans were segregated on reservations and their children were sent to boarding schools with the explicit purpose of assimilating them (Crow Dog, 1991). By the first quarter of the twentieth century, opposition to this type of schooling led to the transfer of most Indian children into local public schools where the new curricula included more American Indian culture, language, and history.

The problems of Native American education are similar to those of other economically disadvantaged and culturally oppressed children. As with other racial and ethnic minorities, the discontinuities between the culture of native American children and the culture of the school contribute to their educational difficulties (Levine and Havinghurst, 1992). Currently, about 400,000 American Indian students attend a variety of types of schools. Only 8% attend BIA schools on reservations; of the remainder, half attend public schools on or near their reservations. About 50% of American Indian youth attend public schools in urban areas. Today, the federal government's official policy is one of self-determination. Consequently, the education of American Indian children has significantly changed to one that is more sensitive to Native American culture, bilingual educational needs, remediation, special education, and vocational counseling.

Non-Hispanic Whites

White students are the largest group of students in American schools. Like other youth, their educational outcomes are influenced by their social class, ethnicity, and gender. But the privileged position in the American educational system of mainstream white culture and the centrality of European traditions to the core curriculum uniquely position white children to achieve in school. Overall, the cultural capital of middle-class white students is consistent with the curriculum, texts, traditions, and instructional approaches characteristic of most American schools. One reason that middle-class white students tend to have better school outcomes than other groups is that there is strong continuity between their own cultural capital and that of the school (see Madigan, *Cultural Capital*, this volume, p. 121).

White students are more likely to be middle class than are youth from other racial groups. Given the well-established relationship between social class and school performance, it is not surprising that, overall, the performance of white students outranks that of other racial and ethnic groups that have larger proportions of poorer families. However, not all whites enjoy the advantages of social class and cultural capital. This is certainly true of urban working class and poor whites. Moreover, rural students in Appalachia have social and cultural backgrounds that are relatively isolated from the dominant society. Their distinctive language traditions, in combination with their poverty, contribute to poor performance.

Among whites of European descent, ethnicity has become increasingly important for individuals' identity and sense of community (Waters, 1990). Patterns of achievement are less likely to follow ethnic lines than they did in the past, but family background continues to be a fundamental force shaping educational processes and outcomes for white students.

Policy Issues

The previous discussion about race and education raises a number of policy issues that are already subjects of educational debates, especially in urban areas. By the middle of the next century, the population of the United States will be majority nonwhite. Demographic projections suggest that race and ethnicity will continue to be important aspects of urban educational policy. Large city schools are either already majority non-white or will become majority nonwhite within the next decade. Cities along the U.S.–Mexican border and all cities that are major ports of entry will continue to experience growth in non-English-speaking and limited English-speaking students.

The growing diversity of public schools requires curricular and instructional strategies that address the multiple needs of racially and ethnically diverse children. Bilingual and multicultural education will be necessary. Multicultural education raises a number of questions concerning assimilation, acculturation, and separatism. For example, some blacks have begun to advocate not only Afrocentric education, but schools that segregate children by gender and race. This approach directly challenges assumptions that underlie school desegregation (see Smith, *Desegregation*, this volume, p. 141).

At the same time that urban school systems continue to experience increasing demands upon them due to the growth of immigrant, nonwhite, and poor children, their tax bases are dwindling as firms restructure, deindustrialize, and relocate to suburbs where tax breaks provide powerful incentives. Globalization of the American economy has resulted in many large businesses moving abroad. Moreover, federal educational cutbacks have left urban schools strapped for funding. Race, immigration, urbanization, and economic restructuring intersect with current educational policies and are certain to in the future.

Conclusion

Just as the history of the United States is intimately interwoven with race and racism, the fabric of American education is intertwined with them as well. Native Americans faced genocide, blacks were enslaved, Mexicans were invaded and colonized, and Asians faced exclusion and internment in concentration camps (Omi and Winant, 1994). White ethnics, including Jewish, Irish, Italian, German, and Polish Americans, faced less virulent, but genuine forms of ethnic discrimination. It is not surprising, then, that historically the state also provided grossly unequal educational opportunities to children from different racial and ethnic backgrounds. Some commentators today deny the relevance of the legacy of race and ethnic oppression for contemporary educational outcomes. They question the wisdom of

continuing programs like desegregation, compensatory, multicultural, and bilingual education—all of which are designed to overcome the effects of current and past forms of racism, linguistic, or ethnic discrimination. Although the starkest forms of racialized education are gone, there is ample evidence that equality of educational opportunity continues to elude many racial and ethnic minority children. It is indeed ironic that at a time when American schools are becoming increasingly diverse, the capacity of schools to address the complex needs of students is being challenged by economic and political forces beyond the control of educators.

REFERENCES

Caplan, N., M. Choy, and J. Whitmore. 1991. *Children of the Boat People*. Ann Arbor, MI: University of Michigan Press.

College Exam Entrance Board. 1996. *College-bound Seniors*. New York: Author.

Crow Dog, Mary. 1991. *Lakota Woman*. New York: Harper Perennial.

Dougherty, Kevin. 1996. Opportunity to Learn Standards: A Sociological Critique. *Sociology of Education* Extra Issue:40–65.

Gandara, Patricia. 1995. *Over the Ivy Walls. The Educational Mobility of Low Income Chicanos*. Albany, New York: SUNY Press.

Herrnstein, Richard, and Charles Murray. 1994. *The Bell Curve*. New York: The Free Press.

Levine, Daniel U., and Robert J. Havinghurst. 1992. *Society and Education. Eighth Edition*. Boston: Allyn and Bacon.

McPartland, James, and Barbara Schneider. 1996. "Opportunity-to-Learn and Student Diversity: Prospects and Pitfalls of a Common Core Curriculum" *Sociology of Education* Extra Issue:66–81.

Mickelson, Roslyn Arlin. 1990. "The Attitude-Achievement Paradox Among Black Adolescents" *Sociology of Education* 63:44–61.

Mickelson, Roslyn Arlin, and Damien R. Heath. 1999. "The Effects of Segregation and Tracking on African American High School Seniors' Academic Achievement" *Journal of Negro Education* 68:566–586.

Ogbu, John. 1991. Introduction, in *Minority Status and Schooling*. M. A. Gibson and J. Ogbu (eds.), pp. 3–15. New York: Garland.

Omi, Michael, and Howard Winant. 1994. *Racial Formation in the United States*. Second Edition. New York: Routledge.

Rosenbaum, James. 1996. Policy Uses of Research on the High School-to-Work Transition. *Sociology of Education* Extra Issue:102–122.

Steinberg, L., S. Dornbusch, and B. Brown. 1992. Ethnic Differences in Adolescent Achievement: An Ecological Perspective. *American Psychologist*. 47:723–729.

U.S. Bureau of the Census. 1996. Current Population Reports. PPL.-41, U.S. Population Estimates by Age, Sex, Race, and Hispanic Origin. Author.

U.S. Department of Education. 1996. *The Condition of Education 1996*. U.S. Department of Education, Office of Educational Research and Improvement, NCES 96–304. Washington, DC: Government Printing Office.

Waters, Mary C. 1990. *Ethnic Options. Choosing Identities in America*. Berkeley: University of California Press.

Wilson, William J. 1987. *The Truly Disadvantaged*. Chicago, University of Chicago Press.

RESTRUCTURING

Peter M. Hall and Patrick J. W. McGinty
University of Missouri-Columbia

One of sociology's primary assumptions is that the way social contexts, e.g., situations, institutions, and societies, are organized strongly influences the behavior of people within these contexts, all other things being equal. This assumption is clearly manifest in Rosabeth Kanter's (1977) study of a large corporation where distributions of opportunity, power, and social categories (e.g., race, gender) explained employee's behavior. Within the sociology of education (see Ballantine, *Sociology of Education: Open Systems Approach*, this volume) this assumption has been expressed by viewing schools and school systems as organizations to understand the behaviors of administrators, faculties, and students. Some notable contributions toward this analysis have been made by Willard Waller (1932), Charles Bidwell (1965), Ronald Corwin (1973), and Karl Weick (1976). Some key findings on schools stressed the consequences of the multiplicity and ambiguity of goals, the uncertain effects of the primary instructional technology (lecture), the loose connections between administrators and teachers in curriculum and instruction, tensions between bureaucratization in large school districts and school-level, teacher isolation and autonomy, and the practices of tracking and ability grouping on student learning.

When some of these findings (loose coupling, uncertain technology, and goal ambiguity) became linked with other issues in the late 1970s and early 1980s, such as declining SAT scores, violence and drug use in schools, declining interest in teaching as a profession, and American economic problems, the solutions offered in *A Nation at Risk* (National Commission on Education, 1983) were more mandates, and higher requirements (e.g., high school graduation, time on task,

teacher training, evaluation, and certification) that intensified what schools were already doing by focusing on individuals and bureaucratically tightening linkages from the top-down. Although these first wave educational reforms were said to have had some positive effects, they were deemed inadequate to many current and future challenges (Cohen, 1989:40–41).

Consequently, a second wave of reform, begun in the mid to late 1980s and in tune with sociology's structural principle, has advocated a radical transformation of schools. It is not simply an intensification of traditional forms (renewal) or limited change (reform), but a systematic and dramatic alteration that has been characterized as restructuring. Although many of the advocates, policymakers, and researchers in this enterprise are not sociologists, they share the assumption that to improve learner outcomes, alter student and teacher behavior, facilitate family and community involvement, and create collective commitment and collaboration, requires changing the way schools are organized, their internal processes and practices, and linkages to community, district, and state government. Although there are many definitions and forms of restructuring, a composite and rationale are presented to illustrate its holistic and systemic nature.

A Restructuring Framework

Schooling is generally organized around a traditional instructional technology in which the teacher presents information to passive students who represent the facts when requested. However, future societal and individual needs require that all high school graduates possess higher order cognitive skills and critical analytical faculties. Developing these abilities requires changes in student–teacher relationships and the curriculum. Through restructuring students should become engaged by and active in the learning process. They will become problem-finders who participate in collaborative complex tasks that represent processes of intellectual and practical accomplishment. Curriculum then must be changed from a superficial, fragmented series of facts to one that is integrated for depth, coherence, problem orientation, and conceptual grounding.

Teachers accordingly shift their emphases to more indirect learning activities such as creating the conditions for active student learning. They will be more involved in diagnosing students, structuring activities and instructional groupings, and evaluating strategies. Teachers will be coaches, mentors, and tutors more than lecturers, questioners, or testers.

Restructuring suggests that many of the features of schools would have to change to accommodate new curriculum and teacher–student relationships. Time use would be more flexible to allow student progress at more natural rates and completion of larger problem-based projects. Scheduling would reflect an integrated curriculum and problem-oriented topics with larger blocks of time. Student groupings would be altered for interdisciplinary work, cooperative learning, the elimination of tracking, and personalization.

The effective implementation of these arrangements depends upon a common culture, time for teacher collaboration, decentralized decision making, and shared governance. The development of a common culture (vision, goals, expectations) serves to unify, motivate, and mobilize restructuring efforts. Staff must have time to develop, assess, and revise curriculum, team teaching, and student groupings. They require opportunities for professional development, team building, and problem solving. Current knowledge suggests that decision making is most effective when it occurs at the actual practice site and when all stakeholders are empowered to participate. Thus, school level democratic decision making and governance are favored over centralized top-down structures (district level and school principal). Restructuring programs also generally recognize the central roles of family and community in schooling and include those constituencies in shared governance and school programs. Finally, when school populations reflect consequences of poverty and racism, restructured schools have coordinated their programs with social,

health, economic, and community development agencies at the school site.

Under the restructuring emphasis on decentralization, district-level actors would emphasize commitment to comprehensive and diverse change, goal setting, systematic planning, and oversight. They would provide direction, establish accountability mechanisms, allocate and expedite resources equitably, and develop technical assistance processes. State-level priorities shift from regulation and monitoring to stimulating local innovation. This would entail creating public support for change, long-range planning, and the development of congruent state goals and vision. State agencies would be encouraged to develop appropriate accountability systems and performance assessment standards for districts and schools that do not restrict local interests and flexibility to innovate.

Restructuring dramatically alters fundamental assumptions about what schools can do, e.g., expect and facilitate new forms of learning at high levels for all children. It radically transforms the organization of schools because it recognizes the systematic interconnected nature of its components, i.e., only changing parts creates contradictions, conflict, and failure. Restructuring is perceived as an ongoing process with no set end point since schools must continually deal with changing external and internal conditions to which they develop new solutions. They become what has been characterized as "learning organizations." Given the diversity of communities and the inextricable linkage by schools, there is no one standard model of schooling or process of restructuring. Rather restructuring seeks to enable participants to build new forms, roles, and processes that meet collective goals.

Given the previous cited research, restructuring accomplished coupling not by bureaucratic standardization but through the development of a common culture. Commitment and participation are generated by a redistribution of opportunity and resources, not demanded by hierarchical power. Isolation and alienation are overcome through collaboration and community-building processes. Restructuring acknowledges that much of the work of teachers is nonroutine and facilitates professional discretion rather than limiting them with bureaucratic rules. Restructuring overcomes the agricultural school calendar, the factory structure of schools, and the bureaucratic scheduling of time by providing flexibility.

Examples of Restructuring

Since the mid-1980s, four exemplary restructuring programs have emerged, although one of them, the School Development Program, has been working since 1964. The School Development Program (SDP), developed by James P. Comer and by 1994 involved with approximately 400 schools, promotes individual empowerment to create a school community in order to prevent student failure and promote student success in school; at the core of the SDP is the urban high school population that is typically minority and low income. The SDP centralizes its efforts through the establishment of a school planning and management team that serves as the governing body for the school and is charged with annually developing a school plan. Generally, the School Development Program promotes a philosophy based on three assertions: (1) collaboration and respect are required for the school to operate, (2) decision is by consensus, and (3) there is a no-fault approach to problem solving (Haynes and Comer, 1993:175–188).

The Accelerated Schools Project (ASP), developed by Henry M. Levin, involves 700 elementary schools in 34 states. The ASP was developed to target elementary schools whose populations were typically minority and low income. The philosophy of ASP is built on three principles: (1) unity of purpose, (2) empowerment and responsibility, and (3) building on strengths. This vision seeks to bring all students into the educational mainstream by the end of their elementary school careers. Other proposed outcomes of the ASP include improved student achievement, attendance, and self-esteem, as well as increased parental participation, and increased faculty professionalism and work satisfaction (Finnan and Levin, 1994:22–24).

The Coalition of Essential Schools (CES), established in 1984 by Theodore Sizer based on long-term studies of American high schools, is a network of schools working to redesign their curriculum and assessment procedures as well as the organizational structure of the school. A set of nine principals guides these efforts. They include personalization of teaching and learning, demonstration of mastery by exhibition, and a school climate of unanxious anticipation. As of 1994, there were 184 member schools (that had adopted the principles and had an action plan approved by the CES), 115 schools that were preparing action plans, and 470 schools exploring the principles. Schools in the CES network are encouraged to find their own solutions to problems using the principles as a framework rather than being offered a set model for implementation (Sizer, 1992).

Lastly, the Chicago School Reform effort is the result of a grass roots movement that was later realized and adopted as the Chicago School Reform Act in 1988. The Chicago School Reform effort has three components: (1) setting goals that raise the level of student achievement, (2) reallocation of financial resources and responsibility to the school level, and (3) the establishment of local school councils (LSCs)—a type of site-based management. The LSC was charged with adopting a school improvement plan and a spending plan that would facilitate such efforts. The LSC is comprised of parents, teachers, community members, and the school principal. At the high school level a student member was added. All 550 schools in the Chicago Public School system are participants (Hess, 1994:209–210).

Restructuring is not limited to the above programs. Many so-called choice programs or charter school efforts involve restructured organizations. The state of Kentucky has undertaken the support of comprehensive restructuring in conjunction with remedying fiscal inequity among school districts. Many large cities including New York, Miami, Cincinnati, and San Francisco are restructuring their schools. Quite recently, an initiative to spur restructuring in rural schools across the nation has been undertaken by a major foundation. Finally, the emergence of middle schools for young adolescents (12 to 15 years of age) in contrast to junior high schools as miniature senior high schools contains many of the ideas, forms, and processes of restructuring (Carnegie Council, 1989). In fact, the middle school model has served as a stimulation for high school restructuring.

Research on Restructuring

Because restructuring is a relatively recent enterprise, there is little systematic research on its effects, although there are numerous completed and ongoing studies about the transformational process. The most extensive examination of the relationship between school structure and student performance involved more than 11,000 students in 820 high schools nationwide (Lee and Smith, 1994). The authors identified 12 restructuring practices (e.g., interdisciplinary teaching teams, cooperative learning focus, team common planning time, and flexible class time). Of the 820 schools, 46% reported engaging in three or more of them, 42% reported one or two, and 12% reported none. The findings showed that the restructuring schools (three or more practices) produced greater achievement increases from eighth to tenth grade in math, reading, history, and science, as well as greater engagement with school than did the nonrestructuring schools. In addition and perhaps most importantly, the achievement gap between students from high and low socioeconomic backgrounds was smallest for restructuring schools, indicating more equitable consequences from the process. These positive findings will need to be replicated by additional research to establish the relationships with any degree of certainty.

The authors indicate some caveats of note. They do not demonstrate how or why these relationships exist. That requires a different kind of methodology. The practices also are reported and not observed, so it is difficult to know how intensively and pervasively practiced they are in any school. Additionally, the authors state that schools trying more than three of the practices showed less advantage in performance gains or equitable distribution. This suggests some difficulty in implementing restructuring. Finally, they offer the interpretation that their results are due to and would be enhanced nationally by smaller, communal schools (as opposed to larger, bureaucratic ones). Such interpretations are clearly consonant with our previous discussion of the composite.

The best approach to study processes and change in particular involves qualitative methodologies [longitudinal observation and intensive interviewing (see McLaren and Datnow, *Ethnography*, this volume, p. 255)] and multiple cases for comparison. Although there are some good examples of these (Prestine and Bowen, 1993; Muncey and McQuillan, 1993), most of the existing research has focused on single cases and often provides descriptions of the transformation rather than an analysis of the process. It is possible to provide, however, a summary of what is currently believed to facilitate or hinder restructuring.

Schools that are more successful in restructuring efforts are those that have developed the following characteristics.

1. The staff saw themselves as engaged in an overall transformation.
2. They created decision-making teams that worked to involve all interested parties in change discussions.
3. The schools developed vision statements in writing that were developed collectively, creating schoolwide consensus about the goals of schooling.
4. The staff began learning new ways to be responsive to parental input, keep parents informed, and involve more parents in school activities.
5. The schools used district and state curriculum guides as catalysts to develop restructuring efforts.
6. The staff redesigned their schedules to promote more interaction between staff and encourage enhanced teamwork.
7. Principals became facilitators of change and commitment.
8. The schools made professional development of faculty a priority, especially the development of teamwork skills.
9. They were assisted by district offices and officials who encouraged efforts and offered support.
10. The administrators and leaders used frequent public recognition and personal communications to reward school staff and to maintain commitment and participation (Wohlstetter and Mohrman, 1994:3).

Restructuring is an emergent process. It is, by its very nature, not precisely defined nor does it have a clear path or model for its accomplishment. Generally, this process is fraught with conflict and ambiguity and potential resistance to change. Part of the difficulty of change results from the ambiguous nature of restructuring itself. Participants have to define their ends and means. But it is also problematic because many of the involved have vested interests in the status quo. Individuals in schools and districts involved in restructuring then often make sense of the process in terms of their own experiences, which produces responses to restructuring that are less critical of traditional school patterns.

The failure of schools to restructure once a process has begun has been attributed to many factors.

1. There has been omission of or inability to develop a coherent vision. Proceeding into restructuring through a series of fragmented activities does not promote restructuring.

2. Restructuring can easily be derailed by lengthy discussions that do not yield results.

3. The community must be involved in the restructuring effort. Attempts to proceed without community participation further isolates community members from the school and encourages their opposition.

4. Restructuring because of its ambiguous nature can result in a mentality that equates any change with restructuring. This forecloses significant transformation.

5. Viewing governance reform as an end in itself also limits future restructuring possibilities. Active governance reform without a substantive focus and broad participation hampers restructuring efforts (Wohlstetter et al., 1994:282–284).

6. Restructuring is further side-tracked when new learning and teaching activities are measured by old techniques. For restructuring to proceed it is necessary to utilize new ways of assessing learning and achievement (Conley, 1993:316–320; Muncey and McQuillan, 1993a:486–489).

Current Problems and Issues

Research on restructuring has indicated a number of problems and issues. At state and district levels, a critical problem is the development of the capacity to provide technical assistance to restructuring schools. This would require trained staff and other resources to disseminate current information, provide on-site consultation, and conduct evaluation research. Schools need assistance in planning, organizing, problem solving, and conflict resolution as well as substantive knowledge. In addition, schools may also require waivers from state and district offices as incentives to pursue change.

Much restructuring is occurring at separate school sites. Many times only one or several schools in a district are involved, or schools are pursuing different unarticulated or uncoordinated efforts. Districts and states need to "scale up," i.e., expand restructuring to encompass all schools and integrate the multiple efforts in a systematic way. Whether and how this can be accomplished remain unclear.

Time remains a critical issue in restructuring efforts. Restructuring is a long, arduous, uneven process. Therefore outsiders and insiders must give it time to occur and be accepting of its ups and downs. Too often immediate and positive results are demanded. If that persists, restructuring will fail. In addition, many invest so much of themselves in the process over time, that, even while successful, they become exhausted and burnt out. It is important to ensure time for reflection and recommitment as well as the necessity to spread participation. It is also vital that participants experience success over time. Therefore, benchmarks need to be established and timelines reported that demonstrate achievements. It is important that time be arranged to allow educators to plan, rethink, redesign, and restructure their schools. Much of these efforts are deflected by the extraordinarily heavy daily demands on teachers and administrators. The windows of opportunity often appear all too briefly open. Finally, the use of time must be structured in the interests of students and learning rather than for the convenience of educators.

Limited resources represent a major problem for restructuring. Recession-related budget cuts, tax payer resistance to increased taxes, and the threat to roll back government provide the context for this issue. Time for results, "scaling up," provision of technical assistance, and support for planning efforts will require more resources than currently exist. In addition, the necessity for smaller schools, more personalization of students by staff, and increasing equity attention will demand additional resources from federal, state, and local resources, all of which are not currently supportive of those allocations and appropriations.

Finally, a most pervasive problem is the unwillingness by elites, the public, and practitioners to erase their long held assumptions about the distribution of "intelligence" and the incapacity of all children to achieve at levels expected only for college bound and gifted children. This class and race-based belief sustains traditional structures and reinforces unequal results by blaming families and individuals for failure. Changing structures can lead to changed beliefs, so the successes of restructuring require greater publicity, in addition to resources, capacity, and time.

Conclusion

The implications of the research reported here and that are currently in process are fourfold. First, more work is required to establish how student performance outcomes are actually linked to conditions, processes, and practices of restructuring. Second, there is a need for less description of restructuring and more comparative longitudinal analysis of transformational processes. Third, research is necessary to examine processes of scaling up and articulation of change efforts at elementary, middle, and high schools and between diverse restructuring programs. Fourth, it is critically important to determine how to develop a social consensus about the need for restructuring and a commitment to the process that facilitates its success. Otherwise, sociologists of education will have many isolated examples of success that will fade into the broader setting of schooling as usual.

REFERENCES

Bidwell, Charles. 1965. "Schools as Formal Organizations." In James G. March (ed.), *Handbook of Organizations,* pp. 972–1023. Chicago: Rand McNally.

Carnegie Council on Adolescent Development. 1989. *Turning Points: Preparing American Youth for the 21st Century.* Report of the Carnegie Task Force on the Education of Young Adolescents. New York: Carnegie Council.

Center on Organization and Restructuring of Schools. 1995. *Bibliography on School Restructuring.* Madison: University of Wisconsin-Madison, Wisconsin Center for Education Research.

Cohen, Michael. 1989. "Restructuring the System." *Society* 26(May/June):40–48.

Conley, David T. 1993. *Roadmap to Restructuring: Policies, Practices and the Emerging Visions of Schooling.* Eugene: University of Oregon, ERIC Clearinghouse on Educational Management.

Corwin, Ronald G. 1973. *Reform and Organizational Survival.* New York: Wiley.

Finnan, Christine, and Henry M. Levin. 1994. "Using School Organization and Culture to Raise School Effectiveness." Paper presented at the Annual Meetings of the American Educational Research Association, New Orleans.

Haynes, Norris, and James P. Comer. 1993. "The Yale School Development Program: Process, Outcomes, and Policy Implications." *Urban Education* 28:166–199.

Hess, G. Alfred, Jr. 1994. "Introduction: School-Based Management as a Vehicle for School Reform." *Education and Urban Society* 26:203–219.

Kanter, Rosabeth. 1977. *Men and Women of the Corporation.* New York: Basic Books.

Lee, Valerie E., and Julia B. Smith. 1994. "High School Restructuring and Student Achievement." *Issues in Restructuring Schools* 7:1–5, 16. Report of the Center on Organization and Restructuring of Schools.

Lee, Valerie E., Anthony S. Bryk, and Julia B. Smith. 1993. "The Organization of Effective Secondary Schools." In Linda Darling-Hammond (ed.), *Review of Research in Education: Vol. 19,* pp. 171–267. Washington, DC: AERA.

Muncey, Donna E. 1994. "Individual and Schoolwide Change in Eight Coalition Schools: Findings from a Longitudinal Ethnographic Study." Paper presented at the Annual Meetings of the American Educational Research Association, New Orleans.

Muncey, Donna E., and Patrick J. McQuillan. 1993a. "Preliminary Findings from a Five-Year Study of The Coalition of Essential Schools." *Phi Delta Kappan* 74:486–489.

———. 1993b. "Education as Revitalization Movement." *American Journal of Education* 101:393–431.

Murphy, Joseph. 1991. *Restructuring Schools: Capturing and Assessing the Phenomena.* New York: Teachers College Press.

Murphy, Joseph, and Phillip Hallinger. 1993. *Restructuring Schooling: Learning from Ongoing Efforts.* Newbury Park, CA: Corwin.

Murphy, Joseph, and Karen Seashore Louis. 1994. *Reshaping the Principalship: Insights from Transformational Reform Efforts.* Thousand Oaks, CA: Corwin.

National Commission on Education. 1983. *A Nation at Risk.* Washington, DC: Department of Education.

Prestine, Nona A., and Chuck Bowen. 1993. "Benchmarks of Change: Assessing Essential School Restructuring Efforts." *Educational Evaluation and Policy Analysis* 15:298–319.

Sizer, Theodore R. 1992. *Horace's School: Redesigning the American High School.* Boston: Houghton Mifflin.

Waller, Willard. 1932. *The Sociology of Teaching.* NY: Wiley.

Weick, Karl E. 1976. "Educational Organizations as Loosely Coupled Systems." *Administrative Science Quarterly* 21:1–19.

Wohlstetter, Priscilla, and Susan Albers Mohrman. 1994. "School-Based Management: Promise and Process." *CPRE Finance Briefs* 5. A Report of the Consortium for Policy Research in Education, New Brunswick.

Wohlstetter, Priscilla, Roxane Smyer, and Susan Albers Mohrman. 1994. "New Boundaries for School-Based Management: The High Involvement Model." *Educational Evaluation and Policy Analysis* 16:268–286.

School-Based Management

What It Is and Does It Make a Difference

Priscilla Wohlstetter, Kerri L. Briggs, and Amy Van Kirk
School of Education, University of Southern California

School-based management (SBM) is a popular education reform that has been adopted by many states and school districts around the country as a way to improve the performance of the education system. SBM allows people who work in schools to make decisions about how money is spent, who is hired, and how students are taught. Thus, although goals and standards are set by state and local school boards (as in traditionally managed schools), under SBM the processes used to meet those outcomes are made at the school level.

Widespread interest in SBM stems from a belief that the K–12 public education system is not working, partly because decisions are made by a bureaucracy—the district office—that is too large, unwieldy, and distant from students. Proponents of SBM argue that the education system must decentralize decision-making authority in order for school performance to improve. They argue that educators in schools are closest to students, and therefore, are in the best position to assess student needs and to design educational programs to meet those needs. At the same time, teachers and others will gain greater ownership of school improvements, having made the decisions themselves. Proponents of SBM have also argued that decentralized decision making will promote a more effective use of dwindling resources. According to this argument, SBM schools can designate resources, such as funds for staff development and classroom supplies, to meet local needs and priorities rather than relying upon district formulas for resource allocation that may not consider the local context.

In recent years, thousands of districts across the United States have experimented with some form of SBM, and similar efforts have been adopted by Australia, Canada, France, Japan, New Zealand, and the United Kingdom. Decentralized management also has been popular in the private sector as a tool for improving productivity. Since the 1970s, companies faced with increasing competition from other countries (such as Japan) created employee work teams to deal with issues of setting production goals, managing product quality, and determining work methods. Many such companies experienced improvements in employee satisfaction, commitment, and productivity, and saw decreases in employee turnover and absenteeism rates.

This chapter provides an introduction to decentralized management in schools, known as school-based management or site-based decision making. The first sections define SBM and describe the variety of approaches that have been taken in the implementation of SBM. The next several sections focus on impact, asking the question "what difference does SBM make?" The chapter then reviews the key debates surrounding SBM and concludes with a discussion that explores some of the issues remaining for further inquiry.

What Is SBM?

School-based management transfers power from the district office to the school site. Principals, teachers, and often parents and students are given authority to make decisions that affect how the school is managed and what students are taught. In traditionally managed districts, most decisions related to the school budget, staffing, and curriculum are made by administrators in the district office or by local school board members. The district office typically decides how much is spent on every item in the budget, the mix of school staffing positions (e.g., teaching, administrative, clerical), who fills these positions, and how staff are evaluated. Traditionally managed districts also make decisions for schools about what is taught, including the kinds of educational materials that are used, and, sometimes, how students are taught.

In SBM schools, many of these decisions are made at the school level by the principal, teachers, and other constituents at the school site. SBM schools usually receive a lump-sum budget to cover most of their operating expenses. With this budget, individual schools are responsible for deciding how to allocate their own resources and many also have the power to decide who to hire. One school, for example, might decide to give individual teachers a stipend to buy books for their classrooms by eliminating an assistant librarian position, while another school may choose to hire a part-time teacher instead of a custodian. SBM schools also typically have the power to define their own educational mission and how they will achieve it. One SBM high school in Rochester, New York focused its mission on helping students become responsible and effective citizens, and, to accomplish this goal, rescheduled the school day so students could volunteer in the community.

Despite current interest, SBM is not a new phenomenon in the history of education reform and elements of SBM can be traced back to the early 1900s. Some observers have noted that SBM seems to surface in times of crisis or periods of intense stress, such as during a teachers' strike or following a world war. The stress apparently produces a sense of urgency to change the existing system to better meet new demands.

This use of SBM to respond to crisis first surfaced during the Teacher Council Movement (1909–1929), when teacher representatives were elected to serve on teacher councils and empowered to make policy recommendations for individual schools. This movement reflected the labor union movement underway at that time and the strife resulting from that movement led to the realization that teachers needed more say in how schools were run. The Great Depression and World War II prompted the Democratic Administration Movement (1930–1950), during which time SBM recurred and attempts were made to increase teacher, student, parent, and community member participation in school decisions. Impacting many public agencies, this movement tried to improve organizations by making them more democratic in nature. In the mid-1960s,

SBM became popular once again during the Community Control Movement (1965–1975), which stemmed from a concern that the needs of the poor were not being addressed by public agencies. During this movement, a wide range of constituents became involved in making school policy, including leaders of community groups and minority parents. Unlike the previous two movements, which originated within the educational setting, the Community Control Movement started with leaders outside of the schools who demanded to have more voice in school policy decisions (Murphy and Beck, 1995).

All of these attempts at SBM had the unifying feature of a sense of crisis. Once the crisis was perceived to be over, the system centralized once again. Recent interest in SBM is following this pattern—SBM was proposed as a remedy against intense criticism levied at schools during the 1980s.

Variety of Approaches to SBM

Current SBM plans are adopted most often by the local school board and the district superintendent, who oversee the management of all schools in the district. Sometimes the impetus for SBM comes from a teachers' union that is interested in expanding the role and professionalism of teachers. In such cases, provisions governing SBM plans—who has decision-making power and areas of decision-making authority—are usually hammered out through the collective bargaining process, along with the more traditional "bread and butter" issues of salary and tenure. In other instances, local school boards vote to adopt SBM, and plans are implemented under the direction of the district superintendent. In several states, notably Kentucky, Illinois, and Texas, SBM has been mandated at the state level by the legislature. Thus, the decision to adopt SBM is typically made by policymakers outside the school or even the district. Sometimes there is resistance to such mandates by individual schools or local boards and implementation has been slow to start and poorly executed.

At least three different forms of SBM have been implemented throughout the 1980s and 1990s. One approach is principal control, where the school principal is empowered to make decisions and is held accountable for results. Parents and teachers may serve in an advisory capacity to the principal and a site council may or may not exist. A second form of SBM is administrative decentralization or teacher control, where power is shifted down the professional hierarchy to teachers. In this model, a group of teachers usually is elected by the faculty to a site council that serves as the school's policymaking body. Many times parents and administrators also serve on the council. Lastly, power and accountability shift to parents and community members under community control, the third form of SBM. The rationale behind this approach is that these groups are the chief consumers of education: parents care most about what happens to their children and community businesses are concerned about the competencies of future employees. The councils in Chicago public schools follow the community control model. Parents hold a majority of council seats and have the power to hire and fire the principal, among other things.

Regardless of the form of SBM that is adopted, there are some commonalties across SBM schools. First, SBM schools typically have site councils that are composed of some combination of administrators, teachers, parents, community members, and occasionally students (particularly in high schools). Members of councils are elected either by their own constituency or by the school community at large, and serve for fixed terms. In terms of power, the council may only advise the principal or it may be empowered to make all of the major decisions at the school in the areas of budget, staffing, and curriculum. Oftentimes, the principal serves as chair of the council. Another commonalty across SBM schools is the network of subcommittees, work teams, or task forces that is usually created by the school to support the work of the council. Sometimes these groups serve at the discretion of the council and make recommendations to the council for approval; other times the groups have discretion over certain decision areas, such as student assessment or curriculum and instruction. Thus, a key feature of SBM schools is the different forums for discussing ideas that give many school constituents a voice in decision making.

Across districts and states implementing SBM, there is quite a bit of variability in terms of what aspects of SBM plans are centrally prescribed by district offices or state mandates and which are locally designed by individual schools. Although the form of SBM is usually prescribed, the size of the council and who chairs it can be local school decisions. High school councils, for instance, tend to have student representatives and mem-

bers of the community from local businesses while councils at elementary schools often feature high levels of parent involvement. When council meetings are scheduled and how decisions are made (i.e., consensus versus majority vote) are also usually decisions of individual schools. Finally, the extent to which power is transferred to schools varies across SBM plans with budgeting responsibility decentralized most frequently, followed by personnel decisions, and then decisions related to the curriculum.

What Difference Does SBM Make?

The central question of most SBM research has focused on whether SBM is making a difference for schools and students. Consequently, there are two general strands of investigation. One deals with implementation issues, with an emphasis on how SBM affects the ways schools are organized and managed. The second strand of research has focused on outcomes: (1) Does SBM lead to changes for school participants? (2) Does SBM lead to improved school performance, particularly student achievement?

The study methods for this research mainly have taken two forms—qualitative case studies and survey research. The majority of case study research are descriptions of SBM plans from one or a few districts supplemented with examples of how the principal and teachers' roles have changed under SBM. One problem with this line of research is the lack of comparability among the various studies, particularly as SBM plans differ from district to district and the focus of each study often varies. One study, for instance, may document the district's decision to adopt SBM, while another study may examine new governance structures at a sample of schools. Survey research on SBM schools mostly measures the attitudes of school participants about their satisfaction with SBM, whether or not various school groups have the appropriate amount of influence in SBM, the levels of support for SBM among various school constituents, and the extent to which SBM has had an effect on various outcomes, such as teacher morale and the quality of the instructional program. Although such findings are informative, especially when collected over several years, they measure only a few of the intended effects of SBM. Research on SBM has not focused much on looking at outcome data, such as changes in the classroom or in school performance (e.g., graduation rates, attendance, student test scores), even though improving performance is often a rationale for schools adopting SBM. In the following section, we present a summary of findings generated mostly from case studies and surveys regarding the implementation and outcomes of SBM, including some of the more recent findings about school performance.

Implementation Issues

School-based management is most often implemented as a political reform that transfers power from the district office to individual schools. Therefore, research on the implementation of SBM has tended to focus on site councils, the governing body across most SBM sites. This research has been mostly descriptive, with little attention paid to characteristics or conditions that make councils more or less effective in running the school. Instead, the implementation research has explored issues relating to the composition and role of the council, and whether the council has real power in key decision-making areas.

Such research has found that site councils often operate as advisors or endorsers in the decision-making process rather than as policymaking bodies. This is attributed in part to findings that most site councils have little real power. The tendency with most SBM plans is to limit the actual amount of responsibility devolved to schools—after the dust clears from "implementing SBM," school administrators and teachers are given little to manage. Thus, school participants are rarely able to impact issues of curriculum and instruction, and site councils focus instead on peripheral issues, such as building operations (e.g., school schedules, fund raising) and implementing district directives. Another problem is that areas of decision-making power are treated as separate in SBM plans but in reality they are inseparable. For example, a school council that has authority to make curriculum decisions but has little budgetary authority will be severely limited in its ability to purchase instructional materials or train teachers to support new curriculum initiatives. And although schools are now gaining increased decision-making influence over more areas and a wider assortment of people are being empowered, school councils and individuals are not always taking advantage of this authority.

A second set of implementation issues that has been studied concerns changing roles and responsibilities

under SBM at the school site and at the district office. Individuals at the school site—principals, teachers, and parents—experience changes in how they operate with the implementation of SBM. Principals are finding that they must share power and increase the amount of time spent on managerial responsibilities. Some of the new roles for principals include designing participation structures, motivating staff to take on new roles and responsibilities, and acting as a liaison to the outside world to bring in new ideas and funding to the school.

Teachers are changing their work behaviors as well. Involvement among teachers varies widely from advisory roles to decision-making positions. Sometimes the teachers' span of influence is limited to a few issues, while at other schools teachers are rising to become instructional leaders (formerly a principal responsibility) and making decisions that impact many areas of school operations. Across most SBM schools, teachers increasingly are making decisions in noninstruction areas, participating in school management, and helping to establish school policies. This participation in SBM sometimes leads to drawbacks for teachers, including a strain on available time, decreasing levels of participation after a few years, and a general lack of involvement among the majority of teachers while small groups of teachers handle most of the responsibilities.

The final group of school constituents—parents— is also increasing its level of involvement in school operations and enjoying more authority over school operations. Evidence shows, however, that parents are not taking full advantage of their opportunities to participate. Even in districts and states (e.g., Kentucky and Chicago) in which parents have a tremendous opportunity to become involved, only marginal involvement of parents has been found in decision making (e.g., working parents have difficulty attending council meetings) and involvement tends to decline over time as evidenced by decreasing turnout rates for site council elections as SBM reforms age.

Similarly, administrators at the district office also experience changes in how they operate with the implementation of SBM. Schools comment that they need the district office to be helpers, not tellers in the decision-making process. Indeed, studies of district offices that effectively restructured indicate that administrators are becoming more service oriented, responding to needs that schools themselves identify, instead of diagnosing problems and prescribing solutions for the schools. Without this change, schools are unlikely to improve because the district's expectations and controls under centralized management are left intact. District leaders also must make symbolic and public commitments to SBM. Many have found that SBM is more successful when the superintendent encourages risk taking (because risks lead to change), and when the administration creates incentives for reform.

Outcomes of SBM

School-based management has the potential to generate outcomes at three levels—the individual, the classroom, and the school. SBM research tends to focus on individual outcomes, especially teacher professionalism (e.g., leadership, collaborative decision making, commitment) and levels of satisfaction among all school constituents. Many agree that SBM has provided a vehicle for greater parent and community involvement in the schools, and that teacher morale has improved in those districts that have adopted SBM. Individual outcomes have been found to improve when school constituents have multiple opportunities for involvement and decision making. People feel they have a voice in matters that affect them; they have a greater commitment to the school and take greater responsibility for what happens.

One expected outcome of SBM is that the school will use its authority to generate widespread innovations in teaching and learning. Recent findings suggest that when schools couple SBM with efforts to improve classroom practice, there are changes in how teachers teach and what students learn. Other studies suggest that for SBM to make a difference there also needs to be reforms to increase teachers' instructional knowledge, lift regulatory requirements, and allocate additional resources to the school. Thus, if SBM is to produce deep changes in teaching and learning, then more than a change in governance—the creation of a site council, for instance—is required.

Perhaps the most relevant issue is whether SBM will improve school performance, especially student achievement. However, only a few studies have examined the relationship between SBM and student achievement. Based upon these studies, which use only marginally adequate data and fairly poor methods of analysis, Summers and Johnson (1995) conclude that there is little support for the proposition that SBM will improve student achievement. The overall conclusion is that implementing SBM will not automatically lead to improved school outcomes because various factors (such as budget crises, union conflicts, reticence of central offices to share power, and a lack of school and district leadership) keep SBM from impacting school performance.

What Debates Have Emerged about SBM?

The debates surrounding SBM focus on judging its success. Part of the confusion concerns the diversity of goals accompanying various SBM plans. In some instances, the goal of SBM is to infuse democratic values into the schools or to establish legitimacy for the school system in the face of multiple and competing demands. SBM may also be adopted to improve efficiency by allowing schools to make allocation decisions tailored to their own needs. Another reason for implementing SBM is for instrumental reasons, that is, SBM should be implemented so that schools can improve and students can learn more.

These multiple goals reflect the larger debate about how to judge the success of SBM. Is it sufficient that the people closest to the students are making educational decisions? Is SBM successful when schools are allocating limited resources more efficiently? Or should SBM be judged on the quality of those decisions, namely whether they produce higher student achievement? And, if the latter question is most important, why is there scant evidence linking SBM with higher student performance?

A look at decentralized management in the private sector suggests that the success of SBM may be limited because the reform has been only partially implemented. Decentralized management, or high-involvement management as it is sometimes called in the private sector, moves beyond the transfer of power to include a redesign of the whole organization, so that employees not only have the *power* to make decisions, but also receive *training* to carry out their new responsibilities, *information* to make sound decisions, and *rewards* for improved performance (Lawler, 1986). A preliminary test of the high-involvement model in SBM schools differentiated between schools successfully implementing SBM and those struggling. In struggling SBM schools, little real authority had been transferred to the school; the intensive, on-going training needed to make SBM work was largely absent; information, such as budget data and feedback on student performance, was not always available; and there were few rewards for school participants who spent lots of time on shared decision making. Thus, one debate about SBM concerns the definition of the reform. Is SBM merely a governance reform that transfers power, or does SBM require a redesign of the whole school organization that decentralizes power, knowledge and training, information, and rewards? Many districts that have adopted SBM put more energy into deciding who would be on the councils and how they would make decisions than in creating a vision for restructuring schools or in providing schools with the resources they needed to do so.

A second area of debate turns on the issue of equity. Since SBM relies heavily upon the competencies of school-level educators and parents, does it accentuate differences across schools? By placing increased responsibilities on schools that already feel overburdened, will SBM create a few excellent schools while resulting in many other schools that are struggling? Schools do not implement SBM with the same level of resources or competencies, and some critics argue that although SBM is a help to schools that are strong performers, it is a hindrance to schools that have difficulty handling their existing responsibilities.

Conclusion

States and school districts across the United States have adopted SBM to improve the performance of the education system. Despite this goal, most SBM research to date has been descriptive, focusing on who is involved and how, with little attention paid to the conditions and characteristics of SBM that increase effectiveness. As a result, there are still many areas that remain for further inquiry. In particular, there needs to be a better understanding of whether and under what conditions SBM can boost student achievement, including how the political environment and public perception of schools facilitate the reform process, how district offices can best support SBM schools, and what approaches to leadership are most conducive to implementing SBM.

In conclusion, reformers may have overestimated what SBM by itself can accomplish and underestimated the amount of change needed elsewhere in the system to make it work. States and school districts must provide individual schools with the power and resources to assume new responsibilities and schools, in turn, must learn how to make meaningful decisions for their students through a participative process. As a result, SBM should not be treated as merely one of many reform efforts underway, but as a fundamental change in the entire education system that is part of a broader systemic strategy for improving teaching and learning and, ultimately, school performance.

REFERENCES

Bimber, Bruce. 1994. *The Decentralization Mirage: Comparing Decision-Making Arrangements in Four High Schools.* Santa Monica, CA: RAND.

David, Jane L. 1989. "Synthesis of Research on SBM." *Educational Leadership* 46(May):45–53.

Hannaway, Jane, and Martin Carnoy. 1993. *Decentralization and School Improvement: Can We Fulfill the Promise?* San Francisco: Jossey-Bass.

Hill, Paul T., and Josephine Bonan. 1991. *Decentralization and Accountability in Public Education.* Santa Monica, CA: RAND.

Lawler, Edward E. III. 1986. *High Involvement Management: Participative Strategies for Improving Organizational Performance.* San Francisco: Jossey-Bass.

Malen, Betty, Rodney T. Ogawa, and Jennifer Kranz. 1990. "What Do We Know about SBM? A Case Study of the Literature—A Call for Research." In William H. Clune and John F. Witte (eds.), *Choice and Control in American Education, Volume 2: The Practice of Choice, Decentralization, and School Restructuring*, pp. 289–342. Philadelphia: Falmer.

Mohrman, Susan A., and Priscilla Wohlstetter. 1994. *SBM: Organizing for High Performance.* San Francisco: Jossey-Bass.

Murphy, Joseph, and Lynn G. Beck. 1995. *SBM as School Reform: Taking Stock.* Thousand Oaks, CA: Corwin.

Robertson, Peter J., Priscilla Wohlstetter, and Susan A. Mohrman. 1995. "Generating Curriculum and Instructional Innovations through SBM." *Educational Administration Quarterly* 31:375–404.

Summers, Anita A., and Amy W. Johnson. 1995. "Doubts about Decentralized Decisions." *School Administrator* 52:24–32.

Wohlstetter, Priscilla, and Allan R. Odden. 1992. "Rethinking SBM Policy and Research." *Educational Administration Quarterly* 28:529–549.

SCHOOL CHOICE

Amy Stuart Wells
Graduate School of Education and Information Studies, UCLA

Debates over school choice policy in the United States and elsewhere stand at the center of profound ideological disagreements about the role of the state, the market, and civil society in educating future citizens, workers, and consumers. Many advocates of greater parental choice in education favor a smaller state role in the day-to-day operation of schools and argue that the infusion of competitive market forces into the educational system will motivate educators to respond more directly to the demands of civil society. Whereas in the past, school choice policies have relied more upon government intervention than market forces, the current, postmodern age calls for a new paradigm—a market metaphor for educational reform coupled with the demand for greater local, community control of schools.

According to Dale (1994), those who study the politics of education must recognize the increasing importance of the market in educational policy and the related widespread support for devolution of educational decision making and control from the centralized state to individual communities. School choice policies of various shapes and sizes represent the most visible form of this political movement, as choice advocates tout the benefits of school-level competition and parental freedom to choose the best schools for their children.

Sociologists of education have documented the growing emphasis on the market as the metaphor for educational reform, the political attacks on the educational "welfare state," and the outcomes of various school choice policies—those related to this metaphor and those implemented before its popularity—on the educational experiences of students and on civil society in general. Furthermore, sociologists of education have paid particular attention to critical questions such as who gains and who loses under a system of greater choice and local control. This chapter suggests that although market-oriented school choice programs can lead to some impressive but scattered educational innovations, overall, they tend to create more inequality and stratification.

In reviewing the research on parental choice in education, sociologist Geoff Whitty (1996) notes:

> while not denying that parental choice and school autonomy can bring benefits to individual schools and students and even have their progressive moments, my conclusion from the evidence we have to date is that, far from being the best hope for the poor . . . the creation of quasi-markets is likely to exacerbate existing inequalities—especially where the broader political climate and the prevailing approach to government regulation are geared to other priorities.

The Politics of School Choice

School choice policy is located within broader political movements to dismantle the twentieth-century "welfare state"—to get government out of people's lives by reinventing a leaner and less generous state in the likeness of private, competitive corporations. The popularity of this political ideology in the United States and England is traceable to the New Right politics of the Reagan and Thatcher eras. But even beyond these countries, the educational systems of industrialized nations across the globe, including Australia and New Zealand, have been shaped by the powerful rhetoric of devolution, deregulation, and greater parental choice and control (Troyna, 1994).

In his book on the politics of school choice policy in the United States, Henig (1994) notes that the two broadest unifying themes of the Reagan administration—privatization and "New Federalism"—directly fed the demand for a deregulated educational system. These themes relate to neoliberal and neoconservative political movements of the New Right movement described by sociologists of education.

Neoliberal Reformers and the Market Metaphor

Neoliberals or libertarians, for instance, advocate privatization of public institutions and services, reducing the role of the state and increasing reliance on market forces, volunteerism, and individual demands to achieve social ends. The roots of this movement lie in classical political and economic liberalism in the eighteenth and nineteenth century laissez-faire sense, which "sees society as nothing more than a collection of atomistic individuals whose rational self-interested choices lead to optimal social efficiency" (Jonathan, 1990:117–118; also see Cookson, 1994; Wells, 1993a). This neoliberal political movement represents corporate interests by seeking to increase earnings through an extension of markets into the state sector, a reduction of state regulation and taxation, and a "rolling back" of the costly welfare state (Carl, 1994:298).

Critics of neoliberalism and its privatization efforts note that it provides an ideological shift in which democracy is framed in terms of individualism and education is framed in terms of consumerism. According to Kenway et al. (1993:116):

> markets require a shift in focus from the collective and the community to the individual, from public service to private service, and from other people to the self. Clearly, in promoting the marketization of education, policy makers seek to promote and tap into a cult of educational selfishness in the national interest. Educational democracy is redefined as consumer democracy in the educational supermarket.

In a postmodern age in which global markets transcend and dominate political nation-states, the substitution of market forces for government-run services becomes a "natural" evolution. And thus, the educational system is increasingly reified, as social relationships between educators and families become material objects in the sphere of market exchange. Furthermore, the increasing reliance on market forces and the shrinking role of the government in providing educational services naturally lessen the impact of public policy in redistributing resources, such as educational opportunity, to those who most need it. According to Handler (forthcoming) in his book on decentralization, "Privatization shifts power to those who can more readily exercise power in the market" (p. 11).

Neoconservative Reformers and New Federalism

The neoconservative wing of the New Right, on the other hand, represents a coalition of interests—namely the religious right, fractions of disgruntled working- and middle-class whites, and cultural elitists—that see the salvation of Western society from its current decline embedded in "ideal forms of institutions" such as the patriarchal family and religion (Carl, 1994). Neoconservatives in the United States embrace Reagan's notion of "New Federalism" by arguing for a shift of power from the national government to the state and ultimately the local level, thus returning greater control to local governments or individual schools and their constituents while getting "big government" out of their lives (Henig, 1994:84).

In a similar vein, Edsall (1991) argues that Reagan's political popularity was due in large part to his ability to convince white working-class voters that the federal government's welfare state had gone too far in its efforts to redistribute wealth from "hard-working" tax payers to the "undeserving" poor and to protect the rights of racial minorities, women, and gays. According to Carl (1994:300), "Neoconservative rhetoric reserves special disdain for the 1960-era social movements, especially the counterculture, feminism, black power, and gay rights, in part because these movements threaten traditional conceptions of family and nation." Thus, Reagan's symbolic politics of "welfare queens" and useless bureaucrats fanned the flames of a deep resentment toward the federal government and a broader antigovernment rhetoric that is evident today in many political movements—from the call to end affirmative action to the bombing of the Oklahoma City federal building.

Antigovernment neoconservatives resent educational "regulations"—i.e., legislation and court orders—that helped create educational bureaucracies at the federal, state, and local district level and thus a centralization of policymaking over the past 30 years. Many of these regulations and government mandates were designed to address the unequal access that certain students—i.e., racial minorities, handicapped students, and non-English speakers—had to quality educational programs in more locally controlled schools (Lewis and Nakagawa, 1995).

Plank and Boyd (1994) note that historically intervention on the part of federal authorities or courts has been necessary in nearly all instances to overcome indifference or opposition of local communities to the demands of minority members. According to Wise (1982), the centralization of educational policy in the 1960s and 1970s addressed equity issues and overcame problems that the local schools were unwilling or unable to solve, such as segregation. Carl (1994) also notes that both the United States and the United Kingdom have long histories of marginalized groups—especially racial minorities and women—organizing within the state in order to redress grievance, with the schools being one of the most important sites for this organization. This historical perspective on the redistributive and regulatory role of the federal government equity is important to understanding the current political backlash against "big government" and the call for more parental choice and control.

Harmer (1994), a neoconservative who favors deregulated tuition voucher plans, argues that too much education funding is wasted on "narrowly focused categorical programs"—i.e., Title 1, bilingual education, and special education—controlled by "administrators at the top of the top-heavy system." He adds that "These programs take money that should be spent on the academic basics" (Harmer, 1994:44). These categorical programs exemplify the state's efforts to redistribute resources and opportunities to the most vulnerable constituents. Some would argue that in a highly unequal society such as the United States, this is a valid role for the state to play.

According to Jonathan (1990), although the neoconservatives want less state intervention in most areas of their lives, they want the state to be sufficiently strong to maintain property relations and the current unequal distribution of wealth. In education policy, the neoconservatives often demand that the state remain strong in the area of "standards" while at the same time

getting out of the way of parents who want to choose schools for their children and have more say in how these schools are run and whose values are taught.

Carl (1994), for instance, argues that under Chubb and Moe's (1990) tuition voucher or "scholarship" plan in which students receive funding directly from the state, the authority of the state governments who would distribute and monitor the scholarships would be enhanced at the expense of district autonomy. "Bureaucracy disappears and reappears; New Right bureaucrats replace those officials who, to some extent, represent social groupings that struggled, often successfully, for more egalitarian educational policies" (Carl, 1994:303).

Carl (1994:305) writes that "the 'rolling back' of a generic state is not the issue. Rather, the New Right targeted for reorganization structures that had emerged in the New Deal and post-World War II accords . . . as a result, the state is reshaped in ways that eliminate venues where formerly dispossessed groups shared some power."

School Choice and the End of the Welfare State

Thus, the neoliberal market metaphor for privatizing education and the neoconservative demand for local control converge—not necessarily in the complete agreement about the role of the state vis-à-vis the market, but in a call for a reduced "welfare state" and thus less effort on the part of the government to redistribute resources and educational opportunities via strong mandates. "In the 1980s, neoconservative education literature moved beyond criticism and nostalgia of the past to the development of coherent prescriptions for change—usually by hitching the neoconservative cart to the neoliberal horse" (Carl, 1994:300).

Perhaps the most popular policy products of this ideological merger are the numerous deregulated parental choice policies that have come about in the past decade—e.g., open enrollment plans allowing students to transfer from one district to the next and take their state funding with them, charter school (in the United States) and grant-maintained school (in the United Kingdom) policies allowing schools to become autonomous from state and district regulations and enrollment patterns, and private school voucher or "assisted places" plans allowing parents to use public funds to pay private school tuition. Other efforts to turn educational governance over to the private sphere, especially the practice of hiring for-profit firms to manage public schools, are also advocated.

Older school choice policies, which grew out of more and not less government involvement in education—i.e., magnet schools and controlled choice programs—are considered out of sync with the politics of the New Right because they are often the result of court orders to desegregate schools and thus require government regulation to ensure that schools of choice remain racially balanced and accessible to a wide range of students (Wells, 1993b). According to Whitty (1996:16), "far from reflecting the free play of market forces, initiatives such as magnet schools were as much examples of state intervention as the segregated systems they replaced."

Hence, critics of the New Right and its favorite school choice policies are concerned that the current political movement to radically deregulate the educational system, while perhaps provoking some new interesting and progressive reforms at the school level, will eventually lead to greater inequality across schools as some consumers are able to demand more than others from the educational marketplace. Empirical research on the effects of school choice policies—as limited as it is—tends to validate these concerns.

School Choice and Empirical Evidence

Much of the research on the school choice policies and the quasi-markets they create in the educational system is divided into three broad categories:

1. "Supply-side" studies of schools responding to the freer market of school choice.
2. "Demand-side" studies of parents or "consumers" responding to choice policies.
3. "Efficiency" studies that attempt to measure the overall improvement of the educational system in general and student achievement more specifically as a result of school choice policies.

Supply-Side Studies of Schools in Competitive Choice Markets

In his extensive review of research on school choice policies in the United States, England, and New Zealand, Whitty (1996) documents several interesting trends re-

garding schools' responses to these more deregulated systems. For instance, he found that in England, which is about 5 years ahead of the United States in implementing highly deregulated choice policies, the most popular schools tend to become increasingly selective through both overt and covert methods of screening prospective students' prior academic achievement and social status. Rather than expanding to meet the demand of the market, these schools generally capitalize on the "scarcity value of their product" (Whitty, 1996:21). Thus, they engage in what Whitty calls "cream-skimming" those clients who will bring them the greatest return on the least investment. More expensive clients—those who have special needs or those with less-valued cultural capital—are excluded, as popular schools select students who will make them appear successful in terms of test scores and achievement and more desirable in terms of social status.

Pennell and West (1995) examined student access to schools after the breakup of the Inner London Education Authority (ILEA) into 12 London Local Education Authorities (LEAs) with more choice schools. They found that students who are "less able" academically now have fewer choices. They note that as the student admissions and assignment processes have moved from the centralized ILEA to smaller, less diverse LEAs and individual schools of choice that the popular schools gain greater control over who they will and will not accept. Under the old system, the ILEA operated a "banding" system to ensure each comprehensive school enrolled students with a range of achievement levels. Under the new, more decentralized and fragmented system, a growing number of choice schools use "covert selection" processes—i.e., operating their own autonomous admissions policies and employing techniques, such as interviews, to screen out or dissuade applicants from applying. "In these cases there remains the likelihood of more motivated pupils from advantaged family backgrounds being offered places at the expense of those who are from a more deprived background" (Pennell and West, 1995:14).

Meanwhile, the popular and "overchosen" schools often offer the best chance of academic success—in part because their high status ensures their graduates greater access to higher education. The relatively high performance of students in these selective schools—most of whom were high achieving relative to other students anyway—is cited by advocates of greater deregulation.

Still, Whitty (1996:25) notes that even if some students are better served under a choice system, "it is the producer who is empowered and it is the consumer who had to establish fitness for the schools' purposes."

In a powerful study of how competitive school choice policies have shaped the enrollments of 11 secondary schools in New Zealand, Waslander and Thrupp (1995) found that working-class schools entered into a "spiral of decline" while higher socioeconomic status (SES) schools were relatively unaffected as they refused to expand to meet the market's demand. The authors document how the most popular, high-SES schools lobbied the government to lower their enrollment cap so that they would not have to admit additional, potentially lower SES or non-European students: "Ironically, the most advantaged, high SES, schools are not subject to market disciplines and are insulated from competition by virtue of their own popularity" (Waslander and Thrupp, 1995:27).

In the United States where highly deregulated school choice policies, such as state-wide open enrollment plans or charter schools, are relatively new, some researchers have found early signs of the same trends. In state-wide open enrollment plans in which students can transfer from one school and district to the next and take their state funding with them, it is the schools, not the students or parents, who ultimately decide student access by maintaining the right to decide when they have capacity to enroll new students and which students they are able to serve.

For instance, in an article outlining the rights of students with disabilities in school choice programs, Mead (1995) notes that in state-wide open enrollment plans and in tuition voucher plans such as the Milwaukee Parental Choice Program, participating schools frequently deny admission to students with disabilities. She writes that schools often argue they cannot accommodate a disabled child and reject the application. "In essence, the school agrees only to avoid discrimination against those children they deem convenient and inexpensive to serve" (Mead, 1995:482).

In her book on school choice in Minnesota, Judith Pearson (1993) explains how large wealthy school districts actively recruit "desirable" students through the state's open enrollment plan. She highlights in particular how districts use the open enrollment law to recruit high school athletes, especially hockey players (also see Wells, 1993).

As for charter schools, the newest and fastest growing form of deregulated school choice policy in the United States, there appears to be a trend toward greater fragmentation of the educational market, with some schools practicing "niche marketing." For example, there appear to be two fairly distinct groups of charter schools emerging in most states—those targeted toward at-risk students who have dropped out of regular schools and those for more mainstream students whose parents are very involved in their education (Education Commission of the States, 1995a). This first group of charter schools, although often hailed by charter school proponents as proof that this reform effort is not simply an elitist movement serving only white and wealthy students (Finn et al., 1996), is in many ways less interesting and less novel than those in the second group because school districts have been operating or contracting out to educators willing to provide services to at-risk students for many years. Furthermore, these alternative or continuation schools have traditionally been highly autonomous from their local school districts (see Wells, 1993b).

More interestingly, among the second group of charters schools there is a wide variety of themes or foci emerging to target certain niches—e.g., schools with a specialized curriculum such as traditional or back to basics, Montessori, performing arts, or Afro-centricism. This second group is also those schools most likely to employ covert selection processes similar to choice schools in England. Thus, although most of the 20 states with charter school laws forbid schools to maintain formal admissions criteria and require charter schools to enroll students on a first-come, first-served basis, there are covert ways in which certain niches are filled. For example, state department of education officials in one state commented that charter schools have become very sophisticated at dissuading those students they do not want to or feel incapable of serving—particularly special education and bilingual students—from applying while marketing themselves specifically toward those students they most want to serve (Personal Correspondence, 1996).

In a recent survey of charter schools in California, where charter schools are allowed to establish admissions criteria, researchers at the Southwest Regional Laboratory (SWRL, 1995) found that nearly 40% of the charter schools completely controlled their own student admissions processes. The most common form of admissions requirement for charter schools in California is a commitment from the parents to be involved in the school. In fact, many charter schools require parents to sign formal contracts stating that they will be involved a certain number of hours per month or that they will be participating in certain activities, including fund raising, at the school. The SWRL (1995) report noted that although these contracts may provide guidance to parents who want to be involved but are unsure of how to go about it, the contract may also exclude some families, particularly those of at-risk students, from these more selective charter schools.

In an article on the purported benefits of tuition vouchers, Astin (1992) notes that the most likely result of increased competition and deregulation in elementary and secondary education would be a more hierarchical system much like the higher education system in which the most popular and prestigious schools become more selective and difficult to access rather than expanding to meet the growing demand for their services.

Demand-Side Studies of Who Chooses

Research regarding who does and does not choose schools within a more deregulated education system is very complicated and cannot be described using traditional "totalizing" measures of stratification such as race and income. For instance, surveys of public opinion toward school choice policies demonstrate that low-income African Americans and Latinos are very supportive of the idea of choice in the abstract (see Lee et al., 1994; Rove, 1991). But research of actual school choice programs finds that a distinct subgroup of low-income and nonwhite parents is most likely to take advantage of choice plans—those who have been most involved in their children's education in the past, those with more formal education, and those who are more efficacious and self-assured. Meanwhile, as the educational market becomes more fragmented, the schools targeting high school dropouts or other at-risk students will draw many low-income and nonwhite "choosers" who increasingly have no other choice. Thus, the overall race and income demographics of choosers and nonchoosers may be misleading in terms of understanding the more subtle stratification results of deregulated school choice markets.

Witte et al.'s (1993) research on the Milwaukee Pa-rental Choice Program, which is specifically targeted toward students from poor families and allows them to attend private schools at the state's expense, found that although many low-income and African-American parents participated in the choice program, these parents and their families differed in significant ways from nonparticipating low-income African-American families. For instance, the black parents who send their children to the participating private choice schools in Milwaukee tend to have fewer children, more years of education, and higher educational expectations for their children than a comparison group of black parents who are also poor but not participating. Furthermore, the parents sending their children to the private schools are more likely to work at home with their children on education problems and to have participated in their child's prior schools at a higher rate than the average parent.

In a study of the St. Louis voluntary interdistrict school desegregation program, which is a choice plan allowing African-American students from the city to transfer to predominantly white suburban schools, Wells (1993a, 1996) found that the parents of the black students who participated in the program were far more involved in their children's education than were the parents of the students who remained behind in their segregated neighborhood schools. Although the parents who sent their children to suburban schools varied greatly in terms of income, they were similar in their high expectations for their children and their efficacy regarding the role they could play in their children's lives.

Studies of school choice plans that are not specifically targeted toward low-income (as in Milwaukee) or African-American (as in St. Louis) families have also shown that parents' education matters as do race/ethnicity and social class when looking at a wider marketplace of choosers and nonchoosers. For instance, the Rand Corporation's evaluation of the federal government's 1970s voucher demonstration project in Alum Rock, California, found that information levels pertaining to the voucher program were higher among "socially advantaged families," particularly Anglo parents and those parents with some college education (Bridge and Blackman, 1978).

Several additional studies that examined parents' choice of schools—either as part of a school choice plan or in relation to buying a home—demonstrate that low-income, minority, less well-educated and/or less involved parents generally lack information about the various educational programs available or the quality of those programs (see Wells, 1991; Ogawa and Dutton, 1994, for reviews). Still, the sometimes unpredictable interaction of race, class and parents' education or involvement levels do not lead to clear-cut conclusions. For example, in a study of choice and competition in the New Zealand secondary school market, Waslander and Thrupp (1995:9) conclude that "*school choice is primarily dependent on the socio-economic background of students* with the relatively better off families, regardless of ethnicity, sending their children out of local schools" (emphasis in original).

Pennell and West (1995), in their study of school choice in inner London, found that as school application and admission processes were decentralized to the individual school site or the 12 Local Education Authorities they became increasingly fragmented, and parents were forced to make multiple applications rather than completing one application for several schools as had been the case prior to the abolition of the Inner London Education Authority. The authors conclude that this fragmentation has implications for equity, "with those parents who are able and prepared to negotiate the complexities and changes that have taken place being in a more privileged position compared to those who are less willing or less able to do so" (Pennell and West, 1995:14).

Furthermore, various studies of how parents and students choose schools have found that several nonacademic factors play a large role. The location of the school and thus its proximity to the family's home appear again and again as one of the primary reasons why parents choose particular schools. This is generally more true in studies of primary school choice but is also found in studies of choice at the secondary level. These findings also transcend national boundaries and different types of choice plans.

In a review of literature on how parents choose schools in the United Kingdom, West (1994) reports consensus across studies that at the primary school stage, the school's location and thus proximity to home is of prime importance to parents. For instance, in a major study of how parents choose schools in Scotland, Adler et al. (cited in West, 1994) found that the most consistently mentioned factors across geographic regions were the child's happiness, proximity of the

school, and siblings attending the same school. An English study by Hughes et al. (cited in West, 1994) found that the most often-stated reason why parents chose their child's primary school was location or easy accessibility from the child's home. Nearly 80% of the 141 parents interviewed cited this as a key reason while two-thirds mentioned the reputation of the school and about one-third said they had been impressed with the school when they visited.

Studies of parental choice in the United States have also found that the location of schools is important to parents, particularly low-income parents who are often less able to provide private transportation for their children (see Bridge and Blackman, 1978; Maddaus, 1988). For instance, in the Alum Rock voucher experiment, more than 70% of surveyed parents cited location as an important factor in their school choice (Bridge and Blackman, 1978).

In a study of Ohio's open enrollment program allowing students to transfer from one district to the next, Urahn (cited in Lewis, 1995:48) found that the principal reason parents gave for selecting a school in a different district was proximity to their work. Meanwhile, less than 10% of the students said they transferred from one school district to the next because of "greater academic opportunity or a special teacher."

West (1994) notes, however, that in English studies of secondary school choice proximity or location of the school, while remaining an important factor, tends to play a less central role than it does when parents choose primary schools for their children. Meanwhile, their child's desire to go to a particular school is a major factor for many parents of secondary school students, although this appears to play a larger role in the school choice process of working-class as opposed to middle-class and more professional parents. For instance, in one study of parents in inner London, Alson (cited in West, 1994) found that nearly two-thirds of the parents said that one of the most important factors in choosing a secondary school was that their children wanted to go to that particular school; 53% said it was important that the school was close to home. Similarly, Adler et al. (cited in West, 1994) found that when parents considered choosing schools outside their catchment area that a primary factor was their judgment that the students would be happy there, and West and Varlaam (cited in West, 1994) concluded that "where the child wanted to go" was the most important factor for parents in inner London. When students are asked about the schools choice process, those from working-class families were more likely to say that they themselves, as opposed to their parents, decided which school they would attend than were students with middle-class and professional parents (West, 1994).

Similarly, Wells (1993a, 1996) found in her study of the St. Louis choice plan that the parents of the students who remained behind in the all-black city schools said that they allowed their children to choose their own schools and that they could not make them go to a school they did not like. Their children, meanwhile, noted that they chose to remain in their city schools because that was where their friends were and where they best fit in. Both they and their parents noted, however, that the suburban schools were "better" academically than the city schools they attended.

West (1994), in her review of the research in the United Kingdom, notes that parents of certain ethnicities, religions, and social classes, especially Asians, Muslims, and working-class parents, were more likely to mention single-sex enrollments as being important. She concludes that parents—particularly middle-class professional parents and white and Asian parents— are increasingly focusing on "performance" factors, or examination results, as well as what she calls "performance-related" issues, such as a "pleasant school atmosphere or ethos."

David et al. (1994:136) report in their study of families choosing secondary schools in London that the primary reasons parents (particularly mothers, who were most involved in the process) cite for selecting a particular school were the "three P's"—"the academic results of *performance*; the atmosphere/ethos or *pleasant feel*; and the school's location of *proximity to home*" (emphasis in original). The authors note, however, that none of these emerged as the main or central reason for choice of a particular school but rather that these three factors best approximate the "amalgam" of factors that parents presented. Furthermore, David et al. (1994:137) note that significant differences between parents of different racial or ethnic groups did not emerge except for a greater tendency among white and Asian parents to mention the pleasant feel of the school as an important factor. Also, in families where the mother was employed in a professional/managerial/technical or other nonmanual occupation, the pleasant feel or atmosphere factor played an important role.

This finding regarding higher status parents and the "pleasant feel" factor relates to research on parental choice in England by Bowe et al. (1994). Their work examines parents as they participate in school open houses or "open evenings" in which they visit schools to shop for their children. The authors describe the "non-rational" or more emotional way in which parents consume schools—methods of selection related to their existing social relationships. Thus, they argue that parents' comments about the "feel of the place" or their "gut reaction" indicate the emotional moments within the process of consumption. These moments are in turn related to larger social relations and the structural and cultural inequalities in the society. To the extent that well-educated parents are looking for schools that reflect their own highly valued cultural capital, the "feel" of a school may be very important as they attempt to pass on their relative privileged place in society to their children.

"Efficiency" Studies—School Improvement and Student Achievement

Even if empirical evidence suggests that deregulated, quasi-market school choice plans may lead to greater fragmentation and inequality in the educational system, such consequences may be acceptable if the payoff was meaningful school improvement and enhanced student achievement in most, if not all, market-driven schools. The argument that markets are a better supplier of quality educational services than traditional political or democratic forms of school governance was strongly advanced by Chubb and Moe in their 1990 book, *Politics, Markets, and America's Schools*. Based on their analysis of a national longitudinal data base of information from public and private high school students, teachers, and administrators, the authors argue that their constructed "school organization" variable is one of four highly significant variables affecting student achievement between the tenth and twelfth grades. The other three variables affecting student achievement—student's ability at sophomore year, SES of the family, and SES of the student body—are quickly brushed aside. The authors proclaim that quality school organization consists of clear academic goals, strong educational leadership, and ambitious academic programs and is strongly related to institutional autonomy, such as that enjoyed by most private schools. Thus, they conclude that market-driven private schools are better than politically governed public ones and that cutting public schools free of bureaucracy and making them more autonomous, competitive, and thus responsive to the needs of their clients will vastly improve the educational system.

Chubb and Moe's book added to a growing body of research concluding that private schools are better than public ones in educating similar students for several reasons, most notably their enforcement of strong discipline and promotion of positive student behavior, their high degree of "social capital" or parent and community member involvement, and their high expectations for all students. These studies, including the most influential ones by Coleman et al. (1982), Coleman and Hoffer (1987), and Bryk and Lee (1993), have each ignited intense debates over the value of broad general comparisons between public and private schools. Critics of this research claim that comparing private schools in general to public ones is like comparing apples to oranges since most public schools cannot exclude or expel students with low achievement or bad behavior and that private schools enroll a disproportionate number of students with extraordinary parental support and involvement, especially when looking at students from low-income families (see McPartland and McDill, 1982; Alexander and Pallas, 1983; Wells, 1993b).

Despite these criticisms, the research comparing public to private schools has helped fuel the argument for more deregulated school choice plans, especially tuition voucher programs for low-income students. Based on the assertions of this research, voucher programs and deregulated, competitive market-based reforms in general should lead to enhanced student achievement. Thus far, however, research on such choice plans in the United States or elsewhere has not documented such achievement gains.

The Rand study of the Alum Rock "voucher-type" experiment within the public schools concluded that the students experienced no gains in reading test scores (the only achievement data available) as a result of participating in the experiment (see Cookson, 1994). More recently, Witte et al.'s (1993) research on the Milwaukee Parental Choice Program has not shown any steady increase in student achievement as a result of participating in the tuition voucher program. In fact, in the second and third years of the program, choice students

attending private schools at taxpayers expense demonstrated statistically significant declines in reading test scores. In math scores, the choice students showed no change in the first 2 years of the program, and a significant increase in scores in the third year. In their fourth year report, Witte et al. (1994) conclude that in terms of academic achievement scores, the choice students perform approximately the same as a group of comparison students in public schools.

Meanwhile, in the United States, it is the regulated public school choice programs such as those in District Four in New York City and the "controlled choice" plan in Cambridge, Massachusetts, which have produced more positive achievement results than any deregulated and competitive private school choice program. Yet even in these public choice plans, which are heavily monitored and controlled by local district officials to ensure that all students have a seat in a public school of choice, the data on student achievement have not been carefully scrutinized nor have careful controlled analyses been conducted. Furthermore, some of the early achievement gains recorded in these programs have been reversed (see Henig, 1994; Whitty, 1996).

In England, the early assertion by the Grant Maintained Schools Centre that students in the grant-maintained schools were achieving at higher levels is coupled with evidence that many of the first schools to "opt out" of the educational system under this policy were selective, single-sex, and generally more elite schools. Thus, Whitty (1996) notes, citing David Halpin's research, that test results touted by the Centre were almost certainly due to the nature of the "intakes" in the early grant-maintained schools.

Although evidence of student achievement gains are lacking in the research thus far on deregulated school choice programs, advocates still argue that more choice and competition will spur educational innovation and efficiency that will lead to enhanced educational experiences for more students and thus eventually to improved achievement. Evidence supporting this claim is sketchy. It appears that although some interesting educational innovations are occurring in deregulated schools in various countries, it also appears that many of these schools were already considered rather innovative before deregulation occurred. A review of research on parental choice in education by Ogawa and Dutton (1994) concludes that the assumption that educational choice breeds instructional innovation and diversity or that it improves students' academic performance is not supported in the literature.

In a study of English grant-maintained schools, Neill et al. (1995) found that in two-thirds of the schools that responded to the survey, the teachers noted a preoccupation with financial matters at the expense of educational considerations among the educators at the school. This preoccupation with finances, however, appears to be temporary, as respondents in the longer established grant-maintained schools were more likely to state that educational priorities were highest. Furthermore, in those schools in which the head teachers (same as principals) had been the primary instigators in seeking grant-maintained or more autonomous status, the teachers responding to the survey were more likely to be resentful and morale was relatively low. Overall, the conditions for teachers that were most likely to worsen under grant-maintained status were professional isolation, job security, morale, career certainty, contact with support agencies, and class size (Neill et al., 1995).

Other studies on grant-maintained schools have found no indication of significant curricular or pedagogical changes within the schools that opt out of the system (see Whitty, 1996). Furthermore Halpin et al. (1995:2) found that the performance of grant-maintained schools is in many ways no better or worse than that of locally managed LEA schools. Indeed, they note that "a growing number of GM schools are joining the list of those identified as failing to provide an adequate education."

Evidence of the impact of charter school legislation on the actual delivery of educational services or student outcomes is particularly sparse in the United States given the relative newness of the reform effort. Still, an early survey of 110 charter schools in seven states conducted by the Education Commission of the States (1995a) found that educators' most frequently cited reasons for chartering a school were to provide better teaching and learning for all kids, to run their school according to certain principles and philosophy, and to explore new ways to run a school. The extent to which these stated goals will become the reality of charter school reform is not yet known, but given that the survey found that the most frequently cited academic foci of charter schools—"integrated interdisciplinary curriculum," "technology," and "back to basics" (Education Commission of the States, 1995a)—are reforms

that have taken place in many nonchartered public schools, the actual degree of educational innovation directly attributed to becoming a charter school needs to be carefully examined.

The SWRL (1995) study reported that teachers in the California charter schools responding to their surveys had changed their teaching practices. This was especially true for teachers in "new" or start-up charter schools as opposed to those in "converted" schools that had been regular public schools before "going" charter. The most prevalent change appears to be requiring students to build portfolios and directing students in cross-age tutoring and small group instruction. The specific school-level innovations reported were greater teacher and parent involvement in school governance, establishing partnerships with community agencies, and targeting specific populations for instruction. Still, it is not clear how much of this change in instruction or school-wide "innovation" could or could not occur in a regular public school that did not operate under a charter.

An Education Commission of the States' report (1995b:12) on school reform and student achievement noted that although many states are attempting to broaden the reins of governance by including more parents and teachers in school-level decision making, these reforms appear "unlikely" to yield significant improvements in student achievement unless they are coupled with other reforms.

Conclusion

The conceptual and empirical literature examining school choice policies in the United States and other countries to date illustrates the need for much more sociological research on the shifts in the role of the state, the market, and civil society. Critical sociological questions about whose interests are served under a more deregulated and competitive educational system must be asked and answered. Although sociologists of education have already contributed greatly to this debate, they must remain central to the on-going dialogue about the scope of future policies and paradigms that shape school choice policies and thus children's educational opportunities.

Bowe et al. (1994) write that their continued investigation of how parental embeddedness in social contexts informs the school choice and transfer process will lead them to a further assessment of how sociologists employ concepts such as class, race, and gender. Moreover, they write, if sociology of education is to make progress in grasping the nature of social and educational change in these times of massive privatization and deregulation, "it must engage with critical appraisals, theoretical reworkings and new directions in social theory" (Bowe et al., 1994:50).

REFERENCES

Alexander, K., and Pallas, A. 1983. "Private Schools and Public Policy: New Evidence on Cognitive Achievement in Public and Private Schools." *Sociology of Education* 56:170–182.

Astin, A. 1992. "Educational 'Choice': It's Appeal May Be Illusory." *Sociology of Education* 65(October):255–259.

Bowe, R., S. Ball, and S. Gewirtz. 1994. " 'Parental Choice', Consumption and Social Theory: The Operation of Micromarkets in Education." *British Journal of Educational Studies* 42(1):38–52.

Bridge, R. G., and J. Blackman. 1978. *A Study of Alternatives in American Education, Volume IV: Family Choice in Schooling*. Report No. R-2170/4-NIE. Santa Monica, CA: The Rand Corporation.

Bryk, A., and V. Lee. 1993. *Catholic Schools and the Common Good*. Cambridge, MA: Harvard University Press.

Campbell, R. J., D. Halpin, and S. R. Neill. 1995. *Primary Schools and Opting-out: Some Policy Implications*. Report. Warwick, England: University of Warwick.

Carl, J. 1994. "Parental Choice as National Policy in England and the United States." *Comparative Education Review* 38(3):294–322.

Chubb, J., and T. Moe. 1990. *Politics, Markets and America's Schools*. Washington, DC: The Brookings Institution.

Coleman, J., and T. Hoffer. 1987. *Public and Private High Schools: The Impact of Communities*. New York: Basic Books.

Coleman, J., T. Hoffer, and S. Kilgore. 1982. *High School Achievement: Public, Catholic, and Private Schools Compared*. New York: Basic Books.

Cookson, P. W., Jr. 1994. *School Choice: The Struggle for the Soul of American Education*. New Haven, CT: Yale University Press.

Dale, R. 1994. "Applied Education Politics or Political Sociology of Education? Contrasting Approaches to the Study of Recent Education Reform in England and Wales." In D. Halpin and B. Troyna (eds.), *Researching Education Policy: Ethical and Methodological Issues*, pp. 31–42. Washington DC: Falmer Press.

David, M., A. West, and J. Ribbens. 1994. *Mothers Intuition? Choosing Secondary Schools*. London: Falmer Press.

Edsall, T. B. (with Mary Edsall). 1991. *Chain Reaction: The Impact of Race, Rights, and Taxes on American Politics*. New York: Norton.

Educational Commission of the States. 1995a. *Charter Schools: What Are They Up to?* Center for School Change. Denver, CO: Author.

————. 1995b. *Bridging the Gap: School Reform and Student Achievement*. Denver, CO: Author.

Finn, C., Jr., L. Beirline, and B. Manno. 1996. *Charter Schools in Action: A First Look. Report*. Washington, DC: The Hudson Institute.

Halpin, D., J. Campbell, and S. Neil. 1995. *Feeling Good and Bad About Opting Out*. Warwick, England: Institute of Education, University of Warwick.

Harmer, D. 1994. *School Choice: Why You Need It—How You Get It*. Washington DC: CATO Institute.

Henig, J. 1994. *Rethinking School Choice: Limits of the Market Metaphor in Education*. Princeton, NJ: Princeton University Press.

Jonathan, R. 1990. "State Education Service or Prisoner's Dilemma: The 'Hidden Hand' as Source of Education Policy." *British Journal of Educational Studies* 38(2)(May):116–132.

Kenway, J. (with Chris Bigum and Lindsay Fitzclarence). 1993. "Marketing Education in the Postmodern Age." *Journal of Education Policy* 8(2):105–125.

Lee, V. E., R. G. Croninger, and J. B. Smith. 1994. "Parental Choice of Schools and Social Stratification in Education: The Paradox of Detroit." *Educational Evaluation and Policy Analysis* 16(4)(Winter):434–457.

Lewis, D., and K. Nakagawa. 1995. *Race and Educational Reform in the American Metropolis: A Study of School Decentralization*. Albany, NY: SUNY Press.

Lewis, J. F. 1995. "Saying No to Vouchers: What Is the Price of Democracy?" *National Association of Secondary School Principals Bulletin* 79(September):41–51.

Maddaus, J. 1988. "Parents' Perceptions of the Moral Environment in Choosing Their Children's Elementary School." Paper presented at the annual meeting of the Association for Moral Education, Pittsburgh, PA.

McPartland, J., and E. McDill. 1982. "Control and Differentiation in the Structure of American Education." *Sociology of Education* 55(April/July):89–102.

Mead, J. 1995. "Including Students with Disabilities in Parental Choice Programs: The Challenge of Meaningful Choice." *West's Education Law Reporter* (July 27):463–496.

Neill, S., D. Halpin, and R. Campbell. 1955. "Grant-Maintained Schools and the Feel-Good Factor." *Educational Review* 9(1):20–26.

Ogawa, R. T., and J. S. Dutton. 1994. "Parental Choice in Education: Examining the Underlying Assumptions." *Urban Education* 29(3):270–297.

Pearson, J. 1993. *Myths of Educational Choice*. Westport, CT: Praeger.

Pennell, H., and A. West. 1995. "Changing Schools: Secondary Schools' Admissions Policies in Inner London in 1995." Clare Market Papers No. 9. Center for Educational

Research. London: London School of Economics and Political Science.

Personal Correspondence. 1996. "Unidentified State Department Officials in an Anonymous State." (Winter).

Plank, D. N., and W. L. Boyd. 1994. "Antipolitics, Education, and Institutional Choice: The Flight from Democracy." *American Educational Research Journal* 31(2)(Summer):263–281.

Rove, K. 1991. *Public Opinion Survey of Arizona's Minority Communities on Educational Reform: Preliminary Analysis*. Arizona Issue Analysis Report #118. Phoenix, AZ: Goldwater Institute.

Southwest Regional Laboratory. 1995. *Freedom and Innovation in California's Charter Schools*. Los Alamitos, CA: Author.

Troyna, B. 1994. "Reforms, Research and Being Reflexive About Being Reflexive." In D. Halpin and B. Troyna (eds.), *Researching Education Policy: Ethical and Methodological Issues*, pp. 1–15. Washington DC: Falmer Press.

Waslander, S., and M. Thrupp. 1995. "Choice, Competition and Segregation: An Empirical Analysis of a New Zealand Secondary School Market, 1990–93." *Journal of Educational Policy* 10(1)(January–February):1–26.

Wells, A. S. 1991. "Choice in Education: Examining the Evidence on Equity. A Symposium on Politics, Markets, and America's Schools." *Teachers College Record* 93(1):137–155.

———. 1993a. "The Sociology of School Choice: Why Some Win and Others Lose in the Educational Marketplace."

In. E. Rassell and R. Rothstein (eds.), *School Choice: Examining the Evidence*. Washington, DC: The Economic Policy Institute.

———. 1993b. *Time to Choose: America at the Crossroads of School Choice Policy*. New York: Hill and Wang.

———. 1996. "African-American Students' View of School Choice." In B. Fuller, R. Elmore, and G. Orfield (eds.), *School Choice: The Cultural Logic of Families, the Political Rationality of Schools*. New York: Teachers College Press.

West, A. 1994a. "Choosing Schools—The Consumers' Perspective." In M. J. Halstead (ed.), *Parental Choice and Education: Principles, Policy and Practice*. London: Kogan Page.

Whitty, G. 1996. "Creating Quasi-Markets in Education: A Review of Recent Research on Parental Choice and School Autonomy in Three Countries." *Review of Research in Education* 22.

Wise, A. E. 1982. *Legislated Learning: The Bureaucratization of the American Classroom*. 2nd ed. Berkeley, CA: University of California Press.

Witte, J. F., C. A. Thorn, K. A. Pritchard, and M. Claibourn. 1984. *Fourth-Year Report: Milwaukee Parental Choice Program*. Department of Political Science and The Robert La Follette Institute of Public Affairs. Madison, WI: University of Wisconsin-Madison.

Witte, J. F., A. B. Bailey, and C. A. Thorn. 1993. *Third-Year Report: Milwaukee Parental Choice Program*. Department of Political Science and The Robert La Follette Institute of Public Affairs. Madison, WI: University of Wisconsin-Madison.

SCHOOL EFFECTS

Roger C. Shouse
Department of Education Policy Studies, The Pennsylvania State University

Along with the family, the church, and the government, the school is one of the world's most pervasive social institutions. Especially in democratic societies, it is the institution held chiefly responsible as an avenue for social mobility. It is no surprise then, that in nations such as ours, highly sensitive to the impact of social and economic divisions, the issue of school effectiveness should loom so large. Its predominance as a research issue clearly relates to our democracy's enduring quest for equality of opportunity.

This point is evident in the title and research approach of the first, and perhaps most famous, large-scale study of school effects, undertaken 30 years ago. In *Equality of Educational Opportunity*, James S. Coleman and his associates (1966) began with the premise that the key problem of school effectiveness centered on the significant "achievement gap" between racial and socioeconomic groups. Based on this understanding, these researchers used multiple regression analysis to examine how differences in various types of physical, human, and social resources across schools related to school average achievement levels.

The "Coleman Report" (as it soon became known) reached four major conclusions. First, factors related to a student's home environment were the strongest predictors of achievement across all racial groups. Second, student composition variables (e.g., a school's percentage of white students, its students' average economic background) were the next strongest predictor of achievement among *minority* students. Third, teacher characteristics (e.g., education, years of experience) had some impact on achievement, but only among southern black children. Finally, after controlling for the effects above, variables related to school physical resources (e.g., curricular or instructional facilities, per-pupil spending) appeared to have little or no effect on school achievement.

The Coleman Report represented a challenge to educational researchers and policymakers, who no doubt found discomforting the idea that what many believed to be indicators of school instructional quality had little or no influence on student learning. And though it received a good deal of methodological criticism, subsequent investigations have tended to support its general pattern of findings. In fact, the Coleman study continues to serve as an important starting point for those interested in examining how schools influence student achievement. Research over the past 30 years has proven this task to be a daunting one. It persists, however, driven by the belief that schools can improve and that equality of educational opportunity can be increased.

In the remaining sections, we discuss the range of conceptual and methodological approaches, as well as the findings, resulting from this effort. Before starting out, however, two points should be kept in mind. First, when we speak of "school effects," it is understood that schools influence students in a number of different ways. For example, while we expect schools to impart an array of factual, conceptual, and practical knowledge, we also expect them to shape students' attitudes, motivation, work habits, and social skills. Research has nevertheless tended to focus mainly on cognitive outcomes, in particular, scores from standardized tests of mathematics and reading. There are several reasons for this, the foremost being the relative reliability and accessibility of test scores in contrast to the uncertainty and obscurity involved in measuring affective outcomes. In addition, a good case can be made that intellectual growth represents the fundamental purpose of schooling as an institution, the foundation upon which other secondary outcomes emerge. It seems noteworthy, for instance, that public concern over schooling is directed at cognitive (rather than affective) gaps across racial and socioeconomic categories, as well as those apparent in cross-national comparisons. It should be noted, however, that some important studies do consider outcomes, which, though linked to student achievement, are not strictly cognitive (such as attendance, morale, and sense of school attachment and engagement).

A second consideration is the tendency to focus on the *relative effects* of schooling, that is, on those related to variation in policy, organizational, or instructional characteristics. Though the findings of such studies are often weak or inconsistent, it is important not to overlook the powerful *absolute effects* of schooling, that is, the way in which attending (versus not attending) school mitigates inequalities across socioeconomic groups. In other words, without schools, the achievement gaps described here would be much wider (Heynes, 1978).

Production Function Studies

Production function analysis relates educational inputs (per-pupil spending, physical facilities, teachers' experience, etc.) to educational outputs (standardized achievement test scores). Sometimes referred to as "black box analysis," Coleman's work as well as the early wave of subsequent studies exemplify this approach. Though it offers a reasonable first step toward understanding educational influences, production function analysis poses several difficult conceptual and methodological problems. Typifying the latter, researchers challenged Coleman's major "non-finding" (that differences in school fiscal resources had little influence on educational outputs) as resulting from a mixing of levels of analysis.

To appreciate this problem, imagine two different ways of measuring variation in the school output "achievement." First, we could measure it at the student level, recording a separate score for every student. Alternatively, we could aggregate these individual scores into a school average, recording a single mean score for each school. School inputs, such as teacher experience, can be similarly measured; at the student

level (assigning students an individual score based on the total years of experience of all their teachers), or at the school level (assigning schools a score based on the total experience of all their teachers). Now, if we wished to observe the correlation between academic achievement and teacher experience, we could relate outputs to inputs at the student level and the school level, or we could "mix" our levels of analysis by examining the relationship between the school-level measure of teachers' experience and student-level achievement scores.

Working with the data available to them, Coleman and his associates adopted this last strategy. This approach was confounded, however, by what Coleman and other researchers have come to recognize as a fundamental characteristic of students and schools, namely, that for any representative sample, the variation in *individual* achievement *within* schools is generally three to four times greater than the variation in *average* achievement *between* schools. Thus, although the variation in Coleman's "output" was due mainly to differences *within* schools, his school-mean "input" measures could account only for that part of the variation caused by differences *between* schools. This being such a small portion of the overall variance in achievement made it unlikely that any significant school resource effect would be found.

In a further analysis of the Coleman data, Hanushek (1972) addressed the "mixed level" problem by computing school average measures of achievement (for black and white students separately) and using these as the dependent variable. Relating school-average resource inputs to school-average achievement scores in effect "filtered out the noise" caused by the student-level variation. Even after controlling for the powerful educational impact of family background and student attitude, Hanushek found school-average teacher experience to be a significant positive predictor of school-average achievement for both black and white students.

Despite Hanushek's findings, numerous subsequent production function studies have failed to show consistent evidence of a relationship between school resources and educational outcomes. This inconsistency largely results from the fact that these studies cannot detect or account for critical processes occurring inside the school. For instance, schools do not typically distribute their resources evenly or consistently among students. Nor do students share equal access to the library, the computer laboratory, or to the most experienced teachers. In addition, schools generally assign students to different tracks or ability groups, thus exposing them to different types and levels of instruction. Thus, as Barr and Dreeben (1983) suggest, schools are better understood as "switching yards" than as units of instruction.

Effective Schools Research

Although differences in student academic outcomes could not be strongly linked to differences in school average resource levels, researchers and policymakers faced the reality that schools did appear to vary greatly in their effectiveness. Some produced higher achievement levels even after controlling for the powerful influence of family background. Beginning in the early 1970s, a diverse series of studies sought to identify these high achieving schools and the characteristics and processes that seemed to explain their success. In addition, these so-called "effective schools" studies sought to develop a model that could be applied toward improving *ineffective* schools.

A typical method of analysis was the "outlier study" in which samples of both highly effective and unusually ineffective schools were identified, then examined for differences in school characteristics and teacher behaviors. Allan Odden (1995) summarizes the findings of these studies along instructional and organizational dimensions. For example, effective teachers maximize instruction time, are well prepared, and maintain a steady instructional pace, especially during the first few weeks of school. Effective teachers focus on academic learning and emphasize student mastery of material. In short, by "hitting the ground running" on a daily and yearly basis, effective teachers lead their students to higher achievement. With regard to organizational characteristics, Odden identifies seven main research themes: (1) strong instructional leadership, usually provided by the principal; (2) consensus on a set of academically focused school goals; (3) realistic but high expectations for student learning; (4) emphasis on active and engaging classroom instruction; (5) a system for monitoring the school's progress toward academic goals; (6) ongoing staff development; and (7) a safe, orderly environment and a strong and consistently enforced student discipline program.

Notable, too, are the "nonconclusions" of the effective schools studies. For example, no consistent pattern of direct effects was found for such characteristics as length of school day, length of school year, class size, ability grouping, or the retention (or "holding back") of poorly performing students. Though researchers continue to examine these issues, each is quite complex and worthy of an entire chapter's discussion.

The effective schools "movement" was extremely influential, not only among researchers and educators, but also among policymakers at every level of American government, many of its key understandings included in national reports such as *A Nation at Risk* and *Goals 2000*. Equally important, it signified a major shift in our understandings about how schools work, from explanations involving fiscal capital to those centered on human and social capital.

Still, the movement has its critics, and numerous conceptual and methodological questions persist regarding its findings. Most of these, for instance, were based on studies of elementary schools serving low-income, mostly minority, urban youth, and it is unclear how they apply to secondary schools or schools serving more affluent students. In addition, although "effective schools" clearly shared important features, it has never been consistently established that *ineffective* schools could become more effective by adopting them. Thus although effective schools researchers argued that certain characteristics produced higher achieving students, the reverse could also be the case: that schools maintain these characteristics because they happen to have greater numbers of high achieving students. The fact that some schools identified as effective were found not to be so at a later point in time, for example, might support the latter possibility. Addressing such problems clearly would require the use of larger, more representative, and even longitudinal samples of schools and students.

Schools as Small Societies

Besides these concerns, it was evident that changing schooling to become more effective amounted to more than simply changing key *processes*. Beginning over 60 years ago with Waller's *The Sociology of Teaching* (1967), an important body of empirical and theoretical literature indicates that students themselves have considerable power to reshape and redirect those processes. Waller observed, for instance, that although teachers worked to build a strongly academic school culture, students were capable of building their own contrasting culture. Important later studies by Gordon (1957) and Coleman (1961) revealed that by applying its own sanctions and rewards, this student subculture could gradually erode teachers' academic standards.

In what is widely regarded as a classic theoretical study of the school as a social system, Bidwell (1965) links this power of students to their number, their youthful energy, and to their "near-total personal involvement" in school, in contrast to the partial involvement of teachers. Important, too, was what Bidwell saw as a crucial role conflict for teachers. On one hand, as "officers of the bureaucracy," they are expected to carry out institutional tasks in an objective, "universalistic" way. On the other hand, the day-to-day realities of classroom life compel them to establish more affective, "particularistic" relationships with students, and to treat them differently based on individual need. Although this type of student–teacher relationship is often said to encourage student attachment to school, it can also lead to classroom "bargaining" in which teachers lower expectations to accommodate minority, low-ability, or otherwise "problematic" students (Sedlak et al., 1986).

Thus, for critical school processes to change in any significant way, more recent research points to the need to think about schools as small societies driven by their own beliefs, values, and prevailing behavioral norms. Improvements in school effectiveness are thus linked to these deeper, more fundamental qualities of schools, and the way they help shape and establish a school's organizational culture. One of the more fertile concepts in this regard has been that of schools as communities; the idea that schooling will have its most profound influence on students when their day-to-day activities unfold within a supportive and purposive framework. In a key study combining elements of theoretical and empirical analysis, Bryk and Driscoll (1988) argue that "communally organized" schools evidence (1) a consensus over beliefs and values, (2) a "common agenda" of course work, activities, ceremonies, and traditions, and (3) an ethic of caring that pervades the relationships of student and adult school members. Based on analyses of a national sample of schools and students, Bryk and Driscoll's study indicates that schools with higher levels of communality also report higher attendance rates, better morale (among both students and faculty), and higher levels of student achievement.

Of course, as with the effective schools literature, the critical question becomes that of institutional change—that is, can schools become more communal, and if so, how? Some recent studies have examined the concept of "restructuring" (Elmore, 1990), viewing it as a promising avenue toward the development of a more communal and more effective type of schooling. Lee and Smith (1995), for example, found positive achievement effects associated with schools' adoption of various "restructuring practices" said to reflect a greater sense of shared purpose and mutual responsibility among school members. Such practices included site-based decision making, team teaching, cooperative learning, and common academic course work for all students. In contrast, however, other studies indicate that more traditional types of classroom practices and organizational arrangements are associated with higher achievement in schools serving mostly low SES students (Hallinger and Murphy, 1986; Shouse, 1998). Other important questions loom regarding the idea of "schools as communities," raised in part by a number of the studies cited above. For instance, as schools and teachers become more concerned with students' social needs, might they become less concerned with students' academic needs? And if they perceive low-income urban students as having the most obvious social needs, will these students more likely be exposed to socially therapeutic, rather than academically challenging, educational experiences? If so, what effect will this have on equality of educational opportunity across socioeconomic levels?

These questions were recently explored as part of a broader investigation into improving math and science performance of American high school students (Coleman et. al., 1997). Based on data from a national sample of schools, the study separately examined the achievement effects of both "sense of community" [as measured along lines similar to those of Bryk and Driscoll's (1988) earlier cited study] and "academic press" (measured in terms of an assortment of survey items reflecting school academic climate, disciplinary climate, and teachers' instructional behavior and emphasis). Two important findings emerged with respect to student achievement in low-SES schools. First, the most academically effective low-SES schools were those with strong combinations of sense of community and academic press. Average achievement in such schools, in fact, rivaled that of schools serving more affluent students. Second, the least academically effective low-SES schools were those with strong sense of community and weak academic press. These findings reveal the tension that can arise between meeting students' social and academic needs, and also reveal the possibility and tremendous potential of supportive, cohesive, yet academically oriented social networks.

The Persistent Problem of Institutional Change

Though researchers can point to a diverse range of technical, organizational, and social characteristics associated with school academic effectiveness, they have been much less successful in providing any sort of reliable prescription for ineffective schools to follow. Of course, there are numerous anecdotal studies of schools that have turned themselves around; the publicity attached to such cases reveals just how inconsistent and daunting efforts to "fix" our schools have been. On the other hand, our schools may in fact be changing, but very slowly, and more perhaps in response to demands from their external environment. Like other institutions, schools respond in kind to the values and expectations of the community they serve. In truth, a few notable voices notwithstanding (Charles Eliot, Robert Hutchins, Arthur Bestor, etc.), until fairly recently there has been little consistent political, professional, or economic pressure for schools to emphasize or provide high-quality intellectual training for all students.

In the years just prior to his untimely death in the spring of 1995, James Coleman considered the problem of how external incentives might be structured to produce more academically effective schools. His notion of the "output driven school" (Coleman et al., 1997) conveyed the idea that schools would become more effective when academic standards were established outside the boundaries of the institution itself, by employers, colleges, or even by standardized exams. In a real sense, the ability to raise or lower academic standards amounted to a burden from which once freed, teachers could act more as "coaches" or supportive adults than as authoritative distributors of academic reward. Driven more by external demands than by external characteristics, truly engaged in common academic activity, schools might indeed become transformed into meaningful learning communities.

Coleman's idea reminds us that like its larger real-life counterparts, the small society of the school owes much of its power to shape young people to forces beyond its immediate control. Like other key social institutions, schools must therefore often grapple with the tension between setting a course and following one. For example, although the attainment of equal educational opportunities and outcomes has been a primary research and policy interest over the past 30 years, the public is clearly quite willing to tolerate and even demand a fair amount of educational inequality. This is evident in current policy battles over school funding, school choice, "outcome-based education," "detracking," etc. The implication would appear to be that those examining or promoting school change need to consider and be more open about their own ideological preferences and how these jibe with popular notions of "school effectiveness."

A Final Word

Our understanding of school effects continues to rely on thoughtful conceptual and methodological effort. A critical part of this effort involves the construction and conducting of large-scale surveys research at the state and national level. Over the past 25 years, studies such as the Longitudinal Study of American Youth (LSAY), High School and Beyond (HS&B), and the National Educational Longitudinal Study of 1988 (NELS:88) have proven to be invaluable tools for investigating schools and evaluating their effects. Having learned the value of systematic monitoring of student progress from the effective schools movement, the further development of creative national school surveys represents the large-scale application of that lesson.

REFERENCES

Barr, Rebecca, and Robert Dreeben. 1983. *How Schools Work*. Chicago: The University of Chicago Press.

Bidwell, Charles E. 1965. "The School As A Formal Organization." In J. March (ed.), *Handbook of Organizations*, pp. 972–1022. Chicago: Rand McNally.

Bryk, Anthony S., and Mary E. Driscoll. 1988. "The School as Community: Theoretical Foundations, Contextual Influences, and Consequences for Students and Teachers." Madison, WI: University of Wisconsin, Wisconsin Center for School Research, National Center on Effective Secondary Schools.

Coleman, James S. 1961. *The Adolescent Society*. New York: Free Press.

Coleman, James S., Ernest Q. Campbell, Carol J. Hobson,

James McPartland, Alexander M. Mood, Frederic D. Weinfeld, and Robert L. York. 1966. *Equality of Educational Opportunity*. Washington, DC: U.S. Government Printing Office.

Coleman, James S., Barbara Schneider, Stephen Plank, Kathryn Schiller, Roger Shouse, and Hua-Ying Wang. 1997. *Redesigning American Education*. Boulder, CO: Westview Press.

Elmore, Richard F. 1990. *Restructuring Schools: The Next Generation of Reform*. San Francisco: Jossey-Bass.

Gordon, Charles W. 1957. *The Social System of the High School*. Glencoe, IL: The Free Press.

Hallinger, Philip, and Joseph F. Murphy. 1986. "The Social Context of Effective Schools." *American Journal of Education* 94(3):328–355.

Hanushek, Eric. 1972. *Education and Race*. Lexington, MA: Heath.

Heynes, Barbara. 1978. *Summer Learning and the Effects of Schooling*. New York: Academic Press.

Lee, Valerie E., and Julia B. Smith. 1995. "Effects of High School Restructuring and Size on Early Gains in Achievement and Engagement." *Sociology of Education* 68(4):241–270.

Odden, Allan R. 1995. *Educational Leadership for America's Schools*. New York: McGraw-Hill.

Sedlak, Michael W., Christopher W. Wheeler, Diana C. Pullin, and Philip A Cusick. 1986. *Selling Students Short: Classroom Bargains and Academic Reform in the American High School*. New York: Teachers College Press.

Shouse, Roger C. 1998. "Restructuring's Impact on Student Achievement: Contrasts by School Urbanicity." *Education Administration Quarterly* 34(5).

Waller, Willard. 1967. *The Sociology of Teaching*. New York: Wiley.

SCHOOL, FAMILY, AND COMMUNITY PARTNERSHIPS

Joyce L. Epstein
Center on Families, Communities, Schools and Children's Learning,
Johns Hopkins University

Mavis G. Sanders
Center for Research on the Education of Students Placed at Risk, Johns Hopkins University

Overview: A Base on Which to Build

Sociologists' attention to schools, families, and communities has changed dramatically over the past 30 years. In the late 1960s and 1970s, most studies of families, schools, or communities were conducted as if these were separate or competing contexts. Researchers argued heatedly about whether schools or families were more important for students' cognitive and social development. There was clear agreement about the importance of families, disagreement about the effectiveness of schools, cursory attention to communities, and little attention to how these contexts worked together.

At about the same time, the topic of "parent involvement" gained prominence with the implementation of federal Head Start, Follow Through, and Title I programs in preschool and early elementary grades. These programs legislated the involvement of low-income parents in the education of their young children to prepare them for successful entry to school. Also, in the 1960s, more women were graduating from college, entering the work force, and becoming active in decisions about the early care and schooling of their children. There were, then, pressures and opportunities for families with more *and* with less formal education to increase their participation in their children's education.

In the 1970s, the effective schools movement captured the attention of educators and researchers interested in improving schools for traditionally underserved students. Parent involvement was one topic that research and practice suggested would strengthen schools and increase student success. Community involvement also became a central issue in school reform during this period. For example, the New York City community control movement challenged educators, policy leaders, and researchers to test new practices of community participation in decisions about the education of minority and low income.

In the past decade, attention has focused on improving schools to maintain U.S. leadership and competitiveness in a global economy. In addition to concerns about the quality of students' skills for occupations that will determine the nation's success in the twenty-first century, there are concerns about the growing social and economic problems faced by families in this country. There are more families in which both parents are employed during the school day; more young, single parents, many of whom work outside the home; more children in poverty; and more family mobility during the school years. At the same time, there are proportionally fewer federally subsidized social programs for the number of children, families, and communities in need of assistance. These factors increase the importance of good school programs for students and the need to redesign policies and practices that link schools, families, and communities.

The simultaneous influence on children of schools, families, and communities is undeniable, but too often the connections across contexts are ignored in theory, research, policy, and practice. Sociologists who study schools rarely examine how school practices affect family or community influences on children or how families and communities affect the schools. Similarly, sociologists who study families rarely account for school or community characteristics or interactions that affect family life.

New Concepts and Theoretical Perspectives

The first frameworks to explain the concept of parent involvement focused mainly on the roles that *parents* need to play and not the work that *schools* need to do to organize strong programs to involve all families in their children's education. The community was rarely considered in research that examined family conditions or school effects on students.

In the 1980s, studies began to clarify terms, recasting the emphasis from *parent involvement* (activities left up to the parent) to *school and family partnerships* (programs that include school and family responsibilities). Discussions also turned to ways that communities influence the quality of family life and students' futures. It is now generally agreed that *school, family, and community partnerships* are needed to improve the children's chances of success in school. Advances in theory and research have helped to shape the field.

Theory of Overlapping Spheres of Influence

The results of early empirical studies of the effects of parent involvement could not be explained by established sociological theories that stressed that schools or families are most effective if they set separate goals and unique missions. Rather, a social organizational perspective was needed that posited that the most effective families, schools, and communities had common goals and shared missions concerning children's learning and development, and that these contexts are overlapping spheres of influence (Epstein, 1987).

The model of overlapping spheres of influence includes external and internal structures. The *external structure* can, by conditions or design, be pulled together or apart by important forces (i.e., background and practices of families, schools, and communities, developmental characteristics of students, historical and policy contexts). These forces create conditions, opportunities, and incentives for more or fewer shared activities in school, family, and community contexts. The *internal structure* of the model specifies institutional and individual lines of communication, and locates where and how social interactions occur within and across the boundaries of school, home, and community. The theory integrates and extends many ecological, educational, psychological, and sociological theories of

social organizations, interpersonal relationships, and life course development. The overlapping spheres model places concepts of cultural capital, social networks, and social capital in a broader theoretical context, as the areas of overlap and internal structure show where and how networks are formed and cultural and social capital are acquired.

Summary of Research

Research is accumulating that confirms the usefulness of the theory of overlapping spheres of influence. Many surveys and field studies of teachers, parents, and students at the elementary, middle, and high school levels indicate that everyone believes family involvement in education is important, but only some schools and teachers presently conduct positive, comprehensive partnerships with all families. Educators presently do more to involve families in the younger grades, but age-appropriate involvement is found at all grade levels. Although parents express interest in many types of involvement, most want to know more about how to help their own child at home each year. This type of involvement is least well organized by teachers after the earliest grades.

Researchers from many disciplines are using various methodologies to study the implementation and effects of connections of schools and communities with families of various backgrounds and cultures, and with students at different age and grade levels (see numerous authors in Booth and Dunn, 1995; Chavkin, 1993; Christenson and Conoley, 1992; Fagnano and Werber, 1994; Fruchter et al., 1992; Henderson and Berla, 1994; Rioux and Berla, 1993; Ryan et al., 1995; Schneider and Coleman, 1993; Swap, 1993, for studies and practical programs that illustrate the interdisciplinary nature of the field). Four major conclusions from many studies in the United States and other nations provide a foundation for future research:

1. *Teachers, parents, and students presently have little understanding of each others' interests in children and in schools.* Most teachers do not know parents' goals for their children, how parents try to help their children, how they might be involved at school, and what information parents want to be more effective in their interactions with their children about schoolwork. Most parents do not know much about existing or new school

programs, improvement plans, assessments, course offerings, or what teachers require of their children each year in school. Similarly, neither parents nor teachers fully understand what *students* think about family–school partnerships. Many studies in the United States and other nations point to the need to measure and compare teachers', parents', and students' views to identify gaps in knowledge that each has about the other and to identify their common interests in education.

2. *School and classroom practices influence family involvement.* Presently, on average, families with more formal education and higher incomes are more likely to be partners with their children's schools (Lareau, 1989). However, studies show that teachers' practices to involve families are as or more important than family background variables such as race, ethnicity, social class, marital status, or mother's education or work status for determining whether and how parents become involved in their children's education. Also, family practices of involvement are as or more important than family background variables for determining whether and how their children progress and succeed in school. At the elementary, middle, and high school levels, many studies confirm that *if* schools implement good programs, parents respond by conducting those practices, including parents with less formal education or lower incomes who might not have otherwise become involved on their own.

3. *Teachers who involve parents rate them more positively and stereotype families less.* Teachers who frequently involve families in their children's education rate single and married parents, and more and less formally educated parents, equally in helpfulness and follow-through with their children at home. By contrast, teachers who do not frequently involve families give more stereotypic ratings to single parents and to those with less formal education, marking them lower in helpfulness and follow-through than other parents. Importantly, parents and principals give higher ratings to teachers who frequently involve families. By involving families, educators change their attitudes about parents' skills and interests in education.

4. *Specific results or outcomes are linked to different types of involvement.* The results of many studies and activities in schools, districts, and states contributed to the development of a framework of six major types of

involvement that fall within the overlapping spheres of influence models (Epstein, 1995). Briefly, the following six types of involvement are needed in schools' comprehensive programs of partnership:

Type 1—*Parenting:* Assist families with parenting and childrearing skills, family support, understanding child and adolescent development, and setting home conditions to support learning at each age and grade level. Obtain information from families to help schools understand families' backgrounds, cultures, and goals for children.

Type 2—*Communicating:* Communicate with families about school programs and student progress with school-to-home and home-to-school communications. Create two-way communication channels so that families can easily communicate with teachers and administrators.

Type 3—*Volunteering:* Improve recruitment, training, activities, and schedules to involve families as volunteers and audiences at the school or in other locations to support students and school programs.

Type 4—*Learning at Home:* Involve families with their children in academic learning activities at home, including homework, goal setting, and other curricular-linked activities and decisions.

Type 5—*Decision Making:* Include families as participants in school decisions, governance, and advocacy activities through PTA, committees, councils, and other parent organizations. Assist family representatives to obtain information from and give information to those they represent.

Type 6—*Collaborating with Community:* Coordinate the work and resources of community businesses, agencies, cultural and civic organizations, colleges or universities, and other groups to strengthen school programs, family practices, and student learning and development. Enable students, staff, and families to contribute service to the community.

Each type of involvement may be operationalized by hundreds of *practices* that schools may choose to develop their programs. Each of the six types poses specific *challenges* to schools for the successful implementation of activities. Also, different types of involvement lead to different *results* or outcomes for students, parents, and teachers. That is, the most immediate results of involvement will be linked to the design and focus of the practice.

In sum, questions about school, family, and community involvement and effects are being studied with increasing sophistication. Researchers across disciplines employ many methodologies including surveys, case studies, experimental and quasi-experimental designs, longitudinal data collections, field tests, program evaluations, and policy analyses. As research proceeds, researchers must ask clearer questions, employ better samples, collect deeper data, create more fully specified measurement models, and conduct more elegant analyses to more clearly identify the results of school–family–community partnerships.

New Directions: Questions to Address

Four topics have emerged from recent research that set an extensive agenda for new studies of school, family, and community connections: transitions, community connections, students' roles in partnerships, and results.

Transitions

Which practices of school–family–community partnership are effective at important *points of transition*—from one grade level to the next, across school levels, or at other times that students change teachers or schools?

Students and their families change grade levels, classes, and teachers every year. In the overlapping spheres of influence models, time is one of the forces that affects the nature and extent of family–school–community connections. Research is needed on *regular transitions across the grades and to new school levels* to learn how practices of partnership change or remain the same from birth through high school; the challenges for schools, families, and communities at each stage of children's development; and the results of partnerships across the grades. Studies of continuity and change are demanding because they require longitudinal data, retrospective data, or other innovative cohort data and analyses.

Many studies report dramatic declines in family involvement as students move to new levels of schooling. Research is needed on the design and effects of activities to help students and their families make successful

transitions from preschool to elementary, elementary to middle, middle to high schools, and high schools to postsecondary settings. How should families be included in transitional processes to help students adjust, prevent failure, and maximize success in their new schools? Should feeder or receiver schools, or both, conduct these activities? How might teachers collect information from families about their children each year? How do families learn about new teachers' criteria for children's success in their classrooms? What are the results of alternative approaches to help students and families with these regular transitions?

Questions also are emerging about the *annual transitions* that students and their families experience from the summer to the fall of the school year: How can partnerships help prevent the loss of skills that occur for some students over the summer? What are the best designs for summer learning opportunities for students with their families and peers in school, at home, and in the community? How should summer learning activities be organized and by which teachers—as part of the *concluding* school year or as part of the *oncoming* school year? What are the effects in the fall on students of various summer intervention programs and activities?

Other questions should be addressed about various *unscheduled transitions in schooling* due to family moves, migrancy, homelessness, disciplinary suspensions, expulsions, or transfers, and other circumstances that affect children, families, and their connections with schools. Research is needed on the organization and effects of various approaches to partnerships with families in highly mobile schools and communities.

Community Connections

How can we better understand components of "community" in school, family, and community partnerships?

Community is a venerable and vast term in sociology that demands new and focused attention in studies of school, family, and community partnerships. The "community" includes the schools, families, children, and all of the businesses, organizations, neighborhoods, and other groups and individuals who have a stake in the success of children in school, and who serve children and families as a matter of course or in times of trouble.

Beyond Demographic Data. In the past, many sociologists identified and categorized communities using census data on education, income, race, or other descriptors of populations. Although useful, these data do not address the inherent powers *within* all communities. Studies are beginning to identify the human talents and social resources that represent strengths of people, programs, and organizations in any community. More than low or high rankings on demographic characteristics, the qualities within communities may more accurately predict and explain the success of students, the strengths of school programs, and the capacities of families to guide and assist their children. It is important to ask: How might adults in all communities share their varied skills, knowledge, and talents with children, such as making repairs, gardening, butchering, cooking, using transportation, obtaining needed services, public speaking, chess, sports, music, dance, art, science, and others? How might local communities identify, organize, and study the effects of available resources to help students, families, and schools? With what results for the children, adults, schools, and communities?

Participation in Community Organizations and Programs. Questions should be asked about the effects on achievement and behavior of student participation in community activities, including clubs, community service, and religious activities. For example, studies show that African-American students' regular involvement in church activities has positive effects on school-related attitudes and behaviors which affect achievement (Sanders, 1996). Similar results are reported for other groups of students.

Diverse Cultural Communities. Researchers are beginning to explore the strengths of families and communities with various racial, ethnic, and cultural characteristics, with attention to family and community rituals, values, cultural norms, aspirations for children, racial identity development, and formal and informal networks of support. Studies are needed to learn the following: What are the commonalities and contrasts in diverse families' support for children's education? How do schools help all students' families become part of a whole-school community?

Integrated Services. There is widespread interest in *integrating services* of schools, governmental agencies,

and community organizations to support families, provide health, recreation, training, and other services, and to increase student success in school (Dryfoos, 1994). Studies of interagency connections have been mainly anecdotal and focused on conditions for implementation. Research is needed to know the following: What are the effects of alternative approaches of interagency collaborations that include health, recreation, job training, child care, and other services? What structures and processes are required for two, three, or more organizations to integrate their services, and with what effects for students and families?

New directions for studies about community start from the inside out with attention to the traditions, talents, and resources of families and other individuals and groups. Studies are needed on how to identify and harness the strengths that are present in all communities to assist students, engage families, and improve schools.

Students' Roles. How can we better understand the role of students in school, family, and community partnerships?

The theory of overlapping spheres of influence places students at the center of the model. Indeed, the main reason that educators, parents, and students interact is to assist students to succeed in school and in life. Ironically, students often are excluded from family–school communications. Most often, students feel "acted on" rather than actors, or "done to" rather than the doers in their education. Research is needed to define, design, and study students' roles in school, family, and community partnerships across the grades from preschool through high school. A few studies in this and other countries have asked students for their views of and experiences with home–school–community connections. Students express an overwhelming desire to participate in parent–teacher conferences and on school committees, to have their families better informed about and more involved in their education and extracurricular activities, and to communicate more with their families about schoolwork, goals, and decisions.

When they believe that their families are involved in their education, students report that their schools and families are more similar, that their teachers and parents know each other, that they do more homework on weekends, and that they like school better. In high school, students who report that their families are involved have more positive attitudes about school, better attendance, and better grades than other students, even after accounting for their scores on these measures in the middle grades.

Without question, students are responsible for their own education, but they can be helped or hindered in their attainments by their schools, families, and communities and by the connections or lack of connections across contexts. Knowledge gained to date prompts many questions about students' roles in education and in partnerships: How should education be organized to enable students to take appropriate leadership for their learning at all grade levels? What are the results of alternative practices that include students with their families and communities in the six major types of involvement?

Results

What are the effects of particular types of involvement for families, students, and for teaching practice at all levels of schooling?

One of the most persistent misunderstandings of many researchers, policy leaders, and educators is that *any* family involvement activity leads to all good things for students, parents, teachers, and schools. Results are accumulating that show that not all partnership activities lead directly to student learning, better report card grades, or higher standardized test scores. Rather, different outcomes are theoretically linked to each of the six types of involvement. For example, studies conducted in the United States and other nations indicate that subject-specific interactive homework that encourages parent–child discussions at home initially affects students' skills and achievement in the specific subject. By contrast, information about school attendance policies and phone calls about absences are more likely to increase student attendance, whereas information on child development is more likely to boost family confidence about parenting.

Many studies are needed on the effects of specific partnership activities on the attitudes, behaviors, skills, and approaches of students, parents, and educators. Studies of results also are needed on the three topics discussed above, i.e., the effects of alternative programs and practices at times of transition, in connection with the community, and of students' roles in partnerships.

Positive and Negative Results of Involvement. Although positive results of family involvement on various student outcomes have been given the most attention, some studies report negative correlations of some types of involvement with student achievement, behavior, and parental attitudes. For example, teachers more often telephone or have conferences with parents of students who need extra help to improve their academics or behavior. More communications about students' problems are negatively related to parents' ratings of schools; parents are less satisfied when their children are in trouble or failing. Importantly, negative correlations are not found when schools develop comprehensive programs of partnership that include positive phone calls, conferences, and other positive communications with all families, not just those whose children have academic or behavioral problems. We know relatively little about which practices produce positive or negative results, for whom, and under what conditions. Longitudinal studies are needed on whether and how school communications with families help students improve *over time*. That is, which contacts are most successful in helping students with problems return to successful paths?

Conclusion

Research on school–family–community partnerships has become interdisciplinary, international, and central for fully understanding children's learning and development. Studies confirm the following:

- Schools can be assisted by thoughtful federal, state, district, and school leadership and policies to develop strong and responsive programs of partnerships with families and communities.
- More parents become involved when schools establish good programs including six types of partnerships.
- Communities possess resources to promote student social and intellectual development and family strengths.

Students are more positive about and do better in school if their families and communities are involved in various productive ways.

Opportunities for Sociologists

Despite many advances in understanding the nature and results of school, family, and community partnerships, there still is much to learn. In addition to the four topics discussed in this chapter, other inquiries are needed to increase knowledge and improve practice:

- Federal, state, and local policies promote partnerships, but there are few rigorous studies of the separate and combined effects of policies across levels on the design or results of programs. Comparative studies are needed on the effects of varied budgets, staff responsibilities, and other allocations for developing partnerships.

- Courses are increasing that prepare teachers and administrators to involve families in children's education. Studies are needed on the impact of alternative forms and contents of preservice, inservice, and advanced courses on educators' attitudes and practices of partnership.

- Most studies have been conducted with data from mothers, but we need to know more about the nature and effects of the involvement of fathers, siblings, and other family members across the grades.

- Most progress in the past decade in understanding partnerships has been made by researchers, educators, policy leaders, parents, and others working together to define questions that are important for improving practice. Research is needed on the impact of alternative forms of collaborative arrangements such as university-school programs and various action research approaches.

- Partnerships are one item on most school improvement agendas, but studies are needed on the design and effects of connections of school–family–community partnerships with other components of school reform.

Sociologists of education, family, community, occupations, and organizations have important contributions to make to the field of school–family–community partnerships. Opportunities for research are enhanced by the availability of national data (such as the National Education Longitudinal Study or the forthcoming Early Childhood Longitudinal Study) that can be used to address many of the questions raised in this chapter. Researchers' data collected in local, regional, state, and national surveys, case studies, interviews, and field studies also are needed for in-depth analyses of the design and effects of partnerships at all levels of schooling.

The organization, implementation, and results of school, family, and community connections should interest sociologists who study educational environments and outcomes, family structures and processes, intergenerational studies, mobility, cultural diversity, attainment processes, and development over the life course. Researchers with these and related specialties are needed to increase knowledge about partnerships to contribute to more effective educational policy and practice. The topics discussed in this chapter and the application of research on partnerships should interest educators, social workers, school psychologists, and others who work with children, families, schools, and communities. Practitioners are needed to apply research-based practices of partnership in order to increase the opportunities for all families to be productively involved in their children's education.

Acknowledgments

This research was supported by grants from the U.S. Department of Education, Office of Educational Research and Improvement, OERI. The opinions expressed are the authors' and do not represent OERI positions or policies.

This chapter draws from and extends J. L. Epstein. 1995. "Perspectives and Previews on Research and Policy for School, Family, and Community Partnerships," in A. Booth and J. Dunn (eds.), *Family-School Links: How Do They Affect Educational Outcomes?* Mahwah, NJ: Lawrence Erlbaum. See that chapter for other discussion points and a full bibliography, or contact the authors for lists of related publications.

REFERENCES

Booth, Alan, and Judith F. Dunn, eds. 1996. *Family-School Links: How Do They Affect Educational Outcomes.* Mahwah, NJ: Lawrence Erlbaum.

Chavkin, Nancy, ed. 1993. *Families and Schools in a Pluralistic Society.* Albany NY: SUNY Press.

Christenson, Sandra, and Jane Conoley, eds. 1992. *Home and School Collaborations: Enhancing Children's Academic and Social Competence.* Colesville, MD: National Association of School Psychologists (NASP).

Dryfoos, Joy. 1994. *Full-Service Schools.* San Francisco: Jossey-Bass.

Epstein, Joyce. 1987. "Toward a Theory of Family-School Connections: Teacher Practices and Parent Involvement." In Klaus Hurrelmann, Frederick Kaufmann, and Frederick Losel (eds.), *Social Intervention: Potential and Constraints,* pp. 121–136. New York: de Gruyter.

———. 1995. "School/Family/Community Partnerships: Caring for the Children We Share." *Phi Delta Kappan* 76:701–712.

Fagnano, Cheryl L., and Beverly A. Werber, eds. 1994. *School, Family, and Community Interaction: A View from the Firing Lines.* Boulder, CO: Westview.

Fruchter, Norm, Anne Galletta, and J. Lynne White. 1992. *New Directions in Parent Involvement.* Washington, DC: Academy for Educational Development.

Henderson, Anne T., and Nancy Berla, eds. 1994. *A New Generation of Evidence: The Family is Critical to Student Achievement.* Washington, DC: National Committee for Citizens in Education.

Lareau, Annette. 1989. *Home Advantage: Social Class and Parental Intervention in Elementary Education.* Philadelphia: Falmer.

Rioux, J. William, and Nancy Berla, eds. 1993. *Innovations in Parent and Family Involvement.* Princeton Junction, NJ: Eye on Education.

Ryan, Bruce A., Gerald R. Adams, Thomas P. Gullotta, Roger P. Weissberg, and Robert L. Hampton, eds. 1995. *The Family-School Connections: Theory, Research, and Practice.* Thousand Oaks, CA: Sage.

Sanders, Mavis. 1996. "School-Family-Community Partnerships and the Academic Achievement of African-American Urban Adolescents." Center Report. Baltimore: Center for Research on the Education of Students Placed at Risk, Johns Hopkins University.

Schneider, Barbara, and James S. Coleman, eds. 1993. *Parents, Their Children, and Schools.* Boulder, CO: Westview.

Swap, Susan M. 1993. *Developing Home-School Partnerships: From Concepts to Practice.* NY: Teachers College Press.

School Textbooks and Cultural Authority

Sandra L. Wong
Department of Sociology, Wesleyan University

Textbooks are a primary classroom resource in American public schools. As instructional tools textbooks play a key role in imparting knowledge and skills to elementary and high school students. As cultural artifacts they also legitimate particular traditions, events, and ideas as knowledge worth knowing. Because schoolbooks serve both pedagogical and symbolic functions, their content and quality have been the subject of much interest, and often controversy, among parents, activists, and educational reformers. For sociologists, the ideas and images conveyed in textbooks are a central concern, but so too are the processes by which textbook knowledge is produced and chosen. Hence, sociological research has focused not only on the content of textbooks, but also on their production and selection. Whose knowledge is validated as official knowledge? How is school knowledge selected?

Two theoretical perspectives have guided sociological approaches to addressing these questions. Based on Marx's notion of ruling ideas, models of reproduction and cultural hegemony treat educational materials as instruments of social control. School knowledge reflects and reinforces the values and interests of dominant social groups and serves to validate and reproduce the status quo. While alternative perspectives are excluded and delegitimized, meanings and ideas that support the social order are filtered through a process of "selective tradition" (Williams, 1991:414). According to the assumptions of reproduction theories, we would expect school textbooks to support established social norms, traditions, and political and economic ideas, and to provide little, if any, attention to information that counters a conventional view of its heritage and culture.

By contrast, theories of counterhegemony posit a less deterministic relationship between knowledge and power, one that treats the selection of knowledge as a site of social conflict. Whether the object of struggle pertains to issues of race, religion, class, gender, or sexual orientation, textbook struggles are symbolic of broader political contests as social groups treat educational knowledge as a means of gaining recognition, representation, and official legitimation.

These theoretical perspectives raise several important questions for research. Does textbook knowledge teach students to be good citizens and to embrace particular values and beliefs without question, or does it motivate young people to work toward solving social problems and initiating social transformations? Does textbook knowledge present one interpretation of American history, or does it convey multiple perspectives and points of view? To examine what textbooks teach, researchers have used the method of content analysis to identify prominent textbook themes and the ways in which these themes have changed over time.

Studies of textbook content indicate that schoolbooks of the nineteenth century depicted American society in ways consistent with reproduction theories. In her book, *Guardians of Tradition*, Ruth Elson describes how textbooks of this period extolled the virtues of republicanism, patriotism, and social order (Elson, 1964). Likewise, Frances FitzGerald's work *America Revised* argues that "few American educators believed that textbooks—or schooling in general—could or should be an instrument for changing culture" (Fitz-Gerald, 1979:74). At the turn of the century history textbooks began to address the impact of immigration and ethnic diversity on American society. Nonetheless, depictions of immigrants clearly affirmed the values of hard work, achievement, and assimilation, values consistent with the nation's ethos and the aims of common schooling.

Indeed, it was not until the 1960s that the view of American society as a great melting pot began to disappear. Most studies of textbook content document notable changes in themes and tone. FitzGerald (1979:97) writes:

> Only in the nineteen-sixties did the textbooks finally end their rear-guard action on behalf of a Northern European America. The civil-rights movement had shattered the image of a homogeneous American society and, for the first time in the twentieth century, raised profound questions about the national identity. The answer given by that movement and accepted as orthodoxy by most state and big-city school boards was that the United States is a multiracial, multicultural society.

By including more information about women and non-European minorities in their photographs and narratives, schoolbooks attested to the success of progressive social movements and counterhegemonic mobilizations as well as to the growing legitimacy of a more pluralistic view of American society.

But although researchers tend to agree that textbooks have increased their attention to previously excluded social groups, not all agree that these changes represent significant reforms. Though students are more likely to see pictures of politicians, artists, or inventors from diverse groups, textbook critics remain skeptical of the ways in which schoolbooks present different groups and perspectives. Post-1960s textbooks, several studies reveal, either ignore or minimize the importance of social conflict and issues related to social inequality. In her study of the treatment of labor history, Jean Anyon concludes that textbooks give scant coverage of labor struggles and working-class experiences. They provide insufficient information with which to understand the concept of social class and its role in reproducing inequality (Anyon, 1979). Likewise, Sleeter and Grant found that textbooks reinforce values of individualism and achievement. The books project a vision "of harmony and equal opportunity—anyone can do or become whatever he or she wants; problems among people are mainly individual in nature and in the end are resolved" (Sleeter and Grant,

1991:99). Furthermore, although textbook publishers have sought to include more women and nontraditional gender roles in their books, female figures continue to receive tokenistic treatment.

James Loewen's analysis of United States history textbooks, *Lies My Teacher Told Me* (1995), identifies major omissions and distortions in textbook knowledge pertaining to Native American history, slavery, racism, poverty, and the settlement of the United States. Describing textbook discussions of race relations, he observes:

> When textbooks make racism invisible in American history, they obstruct our already poor ability to see it in the present. The closest they come to analysis is to present a vague feeling of optimism: in race relations, as in everything, our society is constantly getting better. We used to have slavery; now we don't. We used to have lynchings; now we don't. Baseball used to be all white; now it isn't. The notion of progress suffuses textbook treatments of black-white relations, implying that race relations have somehow steadily improved on their own (Loewen, 1995:163).

Providing support for theories of cultural reproduction, these interpretations of schoolbook content suggest that textbooks remain oversimplified and superficial. Overall, they convey an optimistic, patriotic tone. According to these findings, schoolbook material is more likely to affirm what has been traditionally taught than to address conflict and controversy or to encourage students to think critically about history, culture, and society.

But although advocates of progressive changes in education wish to see textbooks that include different groups and multiple views, the changes initiated in the 1960s have also encountered stiff resistance from parents, interest groups, and scholars who have challenged the influence of progressive, multicultural aims on school knowledge. In the 1970s textbook disputes in Kanawha County, West Virginia pitted fundamentalist and modernist groups in conflicts that erupted into violent struggle (Nelkin, 1977). Organizations such as the Daughters of the American Revolution and the Eagle Forum have protested against textbooks that, in their view, place too much emphasis on social problems and give too much attention to feminist beliefs and minority group experiences. One scholarly account suggested that textbooks since the 1960s have reflected a "history by quota" approach to selecting knowledge (Lerner et al., 1995).

In sum, textbook knowledge continues to be a source of conflict between groups who expect textbooks, and schools more generally, to preserve traditional values and beliefs across generations, and those who view education as a basis for developing alternative ideas. Protests from multiple groups have pressured state officials and schoolbook publishers to accommodate a range of interests. In fact, some analysts of textbook knowledge have argued that in their effort to avoid controversy, publishers produce books that convey a proliferation of facts without a point of view.

Clearly, analyses of textbook content have yielded important, albeit conflicting, interpretations of the messages students receive in schools. They provide support for both reproduction and counterhegemonist theories. Yet theory and research that focus solely on schoolbook battles leave several sociological questions unresolved. How is knowledge chosen? How do pressures and protests come to bear on decision-making processes? To address these questions, researchers have investigated the perspectives and practices of both schoolbook publishers and textbook selection committees.

School textbooks comprise a significant portion of publishing sales. "Thirty percent of all books sold are purchased by the education system and the elementary school/high school market accounts for approximately 16 percent of total annual sales. While textbooks are not a particularly high profit item (averaging approximately 12 percent net income), they offer a large press-run" (Keith, 1991:45). Though textbook sales provide a valuable source of profit, production requires a substantial investment of resources, and in most cases, publishers must wait several years before their costs can be recouped. Hence, they choose markets selectively, paying close attention to state educational systems and school districts that are scheduled to buy large quantities of new books. The textbook market is comprised of 28 states that adopt textbooks locally, and 22 states that adopt books through centralized systems. The latter are very important to publishers because local school districts can use state funds to purchase only those books that are included on state-approved lists. Due to the high volume of sales and large student enrollments in states such as California and Texas, publishers have

much at stake in meeting their particular needs and interests.

In Texas, for example, preferences are communicated to publishers in several ways. The state issues prescriptions for content, called proclamations, annually; these official requirements delineate what textbooks for each subject must include. The state also invites interested parties to review textbooks submitted for adoption and to voice their concerns in public hearings. Both the curriculum guidelines and demands from pressure groups have been a subject of interest and often controversy because they are believed to influence the selection and presentation of knowledge. Media attention to textbook debates creates the impression that protests significantly influence the decisions of state authorities, adoption committees and publishers.

In actuality, research evidence suggests that the ideological influence of statewide adoptions is mixed. Since the 1960s, decision makers have listened to views from various points of the political spectrum. Participants at state-level hearings have included not only patriotic organizations and Christian fundamentalists, but also liberal women's organizations, professional associations such as the National Council for Social Studies, and progressive advocacy groups such as Broader Perspectives and People for the American Way. Joan DelFattore's work on textbook censorship in America shows that organizations that have portrayed textbooks as "unpatriotic, socialistic, communistic, humanistic, anti-religious, anti-creationist, anti-authoritarian, and anti-family" (DelFattore, 1992:140) have had limited influence on the decisions of state textbook committees and boards of education. Contrary to the arguments of traditionalist groups, state officials have, for example, required that textbooks recognize the struggles of minority groups. They "do not seem to have endorsed requests to exclude named African Americans from textbooks" (DelFattore, 1992:158).

In addition, the state's "1989 and 1990 requirements represent more action on women's issues than Texas has ever seen" (DelFattore, 1992:161). In 1989 the state board "mandated changes from **girls** to **young women** and from **unwed** to **single**. In the 1990 adoption, the publisher of a business book was required to show pictures of a female executive, a female construction worker, and a male child-care worker" (DelFattore, 1992:160–161). These findings might appear to indicate the disproportionate influence of progressive groups; however, persistent criticisms from these groups in Texas and California suggest that state officials and schoolbook publishers have not been entirely responsive to their interests either.

In spite of the controversies created by public protests, research on textbook production and adoption indicates that schoolbook publishers pay more attention to the needs and interests of teachers and other educators than to the claims and objections of activists and textbook critics. In Texas, state textbook committees are commonly composed of classroom teachers, curriculum specialists, administrators, and counselors who review textbooks and recommend a list of approved books to the state board of education. They also hear testimony from individuals and advocacy groups at public hearings. But although these hearings presumably provide an opportunity for citizens, parents, and interest groups to make an impact on the selection of textbooks, textbook committee members do not regard reviewers' criticisms or suggestions as a significant part of their decision-making process (Marshall, 1991a).

Interview data reveal that committees regard public comments as being too general, lengthy, and, in some cases, fanatical to be of use. They question whether laypersons know enough about pedagogical strategies and students' needs to be evaluating textbook quality (Wong, 1991). In contrast to the kinds of ideological concerns raised at hearings, teachers view textbook knowledge in a much different light. Whereas protestors focus on the inclusion or exclusion of particular topics, and on information they perceived to be biased, textbook selection committees focus on the pedagogical and practical aspects of textbooks. "According to data provided by STC members in Texas, their three most prominent textbook evaluation criteria were ranked as 'organization and presentation of content,' 'adherence to the proclamation,' and 'pedagogical strength'" (Marshall, 1991b:122). Observations of selection proceedings indicate that committees judge books mainly by their physical and pedagogical characteristics — readability, versatility, organization, length of chapters, vocabulary skills, quality of graphs, charts, and illustrations, timelines, introductory outlines, end-of-chapter discussions, and test questions (Wong, 1991). For them, textbooks must be suited to the needs and capabilities of both students and teachers within schools and across districts.

The priorities of selection committees have been at-

tributed to a number of factors including the qualifications of committee members and their training in textbook evaluation, predesigned evaluation instruments that often determine the criteria they consider, and procedural constraints in the review process itself. The schedule of adoption practices limits the amount of time available for evaluating volumes of material. More significantly, the emphasis on professionalism minimizes active and thorough discussion of the kinds of concerns that attract interest group and media attention. In fact, educators strive to distance themselves from the political issues that dominate textbook controversies.

What textbook selection committees value, in turn, affects the priorities of schoolbook publishers. Pedagogical, practical, and cosmetic criteria are likely to play a greater role in shaping decisions at the stage of textbook production than do debates about perspectives, values, or traditions. Some critics of textbook quality assert that the "aesthetics of textbooks" have become a primary publishing concern as visual qualities and gloss seem to play a key role in committee choices (Tyson-Bernstein and Woodward, 1991:96–97).

The expectation of selection committees that books contain familiar items and skills tends to discourage publishers from pursuing innovative approaches to presenting knowledge. Constraints on creativity as well as concentration within the publishing industry contribute to a high degree of homogeneity among books in most subject areas. In their study of book publishing, Coser et al. (1982) describe the production of "managed" texts that are conceived and produced by staffs of writers, academic consultants, editors, artists, and designers, as opposed to single authors. The fact that publishing decisions are shaped by economic pressures rather than concerns about substantive merit is one reason some theorists refer to textbooks as commodified culture (Apple, 1991).

Given the relationship between state-level practices, textbook publishing strategies, and the ways in which educators select knowledge, one question that deserves further inquiry is whether statewide centralized adoptions pose an obstacle to textbook reform, or whether they can be a source of curricular transformations. Critics of textbook adoption practices have called for "the dismantling of the state textbook adoption system. . . . Even at its best," Tyson-Bernstein and Woodward (1991:100) argue, "statewide adoption is still a top-down process on the old, authoritarian, industrial model."

However, centralized adoption systems are established institutions that are unlikely to be dismantled soon. In light of their probable endurance, future sociological investigations might focus on the relationships between educational organization, professional expertise, and cultural production. As states and school districts move increasingly toward designing and implementing multicultural curricular policies, textbooks will play a central role in disseminating new knowledge. As such, they will continue to generate the kinds of conflicts and controversies that have characterized previous textbook debates over inclusion and representation. Indeed, in the early 1990s, debates over textbook content shifted to a new source of controversy as the state of California attempted to recognize ethnic diversity in its elementary and secondary school curricula. These efforts prompted one publisher to create a series of books specifically designed to meet the state's multicultural requirements. But although the majority of the state's local school districts adopted the new books, several districts rejected the series, asserting that the books were not inclusive or multicultural enough for their students, more than 90% of whom were nonwhite.

Although the controversies will continue, research on the significance of these political conflicts will be incomplete without further investigation of the kinds of concerns and interests that drive decision makers who have the power and authority to produce and select textbook knowledge. Understanding the perspectives of these key actors and the contexts in which they make choices is crucial to explaining how knowledge and ideas that contradict or challenge the dominant culture are incorporated, rejected, or modified, as well as the factors that contribute to the production of textbooks as encyclopedic collections of facts rather than stimulating historical narratives. These issues require sociological attention to the form of textbooks as well as to their content, and to the institutional processes that mediate cultural struggles.

REFERENCES

Altbach, Philip G., Gail P. Kelly, Hugh G. Petrie, and Lois Weis, eds. 1991. *Textbooks in American Society*. Albany: State University of New York Press.

Anyon, Jean. 1979. "Ideology and United States History Textbooks." *Harvard Educational Review* 49(August): 361–386.

Apple, Michael. 1991. "The Culture and Commerce of Textbooks." In Michael Apple and Linda Christian-Smith (eds.), *The Politics of the Textbook*. New York: Routledge.

———. 1993. *Official Knowledge*. New York: Routledge.

Apple, Michael W., and Linda Christian-Smith, eds. 1991. *The Politics of the Textbook*. New York: Routledge.

Coser, Lewis A., Charles Kadushin, and Walter W. Powell. 1982. *Books: The Culture and Commerce of Publishing*. New York: Basic Books.

DelFattore, Joan. 1992. *What Johnny Shouldn't Read*. New Haven; CT: Yale University Press.

Elson, Ruth. 1964. *Guardians of Traditional American Schoolbooks of the Nineteenth Century*. Lincoln: University of Nebraska Press.

Fitzgerald, Frances. 1979. *America Revised*. Boston: Little, Brown.

Keith, Sherry. 1991. "The Determinants of Textbook Content." In Philip G. Altbach, Gail P. Kelly, Hugh G. Petrie, and Lois Weis (eds.), *Textbooks in American Society*. Albany: State University of New York Press.

Lerner, Robert, Althea K. Nagai, and Stanley Rothman. 1995. *Molding the Good Citizen*. Westport, CT: Praeger.

Loewen, James W. 1995. *Lies My Teacher Told Me*. New York: New Press.

Luke, Alan. 1988. *Literacy, Textbooks, and Ideology*. London: Falmer Press.

Marshall, J. Dan. 1991a. "With a Little Help from Some Friends: Publishers, Protesters, and Texas Textbook Decisions." In Michael Apple and Linda Christian-Smith (eds.), *The Politics of the Textbook*. New York: Routledge.

———. 1991b. "State-Level Textbook Selection Reform: Toward the Recognition of Fundamental Control." In Philip G. Altbach, Gail P. Kelly, Hugh G. Petrie, and Lois Weis (eds.), *Textbooks in American Society*. Albany: State University of New York Press.

Nelkin, Dorothy. 1977. *Science Textbook Controversies and the Politics of Equal Time*. Cambridge, MA: MIT Press.

Sleeter, Christine E., and Carl Grant. 1991. "Race, Class, Gender, and Disability." In Michael Apple and Linda Christian-Smith (eds.), *The Politics of the Textbook*. New York: Routledge.

Tyson-Bernstein, Harriet, and Arthur Woodward. 1991. "Nineteenth Century Policies for Twenty-first Century Practice: The Textbook Reform Dilemma." In Philip G. Altbach, Gail P. Kelly, Hugh G. Petrie, and Lois Weis (eds.), *Textbooks in American Society*. Albany: State University of New York Press.

Williams, Raymond. 1991. "Base and Superstructure in Marxist Cultural Theory." In Chandra Mukerji and Michael Schudson (eds.), *Rethinking Popular Culture*. University of California Press.

Wong, Sandra L. 1991. "Evaluating the Content of Textbooks: Public Interests and Professional Authority." *Sociology of Education* 64:11–18.

Single-Sex Education and Coeducation

Helen M. Marks
The Ohio State University

Single-sex high schools and colleges constitute a very small proportion of the universe of U.S. secondary and postsecondary educational institutions. Because of dwindling enrollments during the 1960s and 1970s, many single-sex institutions either closed or became coeducational. By the late 1980s, just 4.4% of U.S. high schools and 1.5% of U.S. colleges were single sex. Virtually all of these single-sex schools and colleges were private. Internationally, single-sex high schools—both public and private—are quite common in many developing and developed countries.

As single-sex schools declined as an educational option for U.S. students, research interest in their effectiveness compared to coeducational schools began to develop. The earliest research studies focused on the relative effectiveness of single-sex and coeducational colleges. Most of the more recent research has focused on the consequences of school gender organization for high school students. National and international data bases incorporating information on single-sex and coeducational high schools have made such comparative studies possible. Because school gender organizational data are generally lacking for postsecondary students, less research exists on the relative effects of single-sex and coeducational colleges.

High School Gender Organization and Educational Policy

In the 1980s, within the contexts of educational equity and school improvement generally, the question of "what kinds of schools work best for whom" led U.S. researchers to investigate the school experience of boys and girls in culturally and organizationally diverse educational environments, including single-sex and coed-

ucational high schools. Such research had import for gender-related educational policy affecting several areas: (1) the disparity between male and female achievement—particularly in math and science, (2) the continued absence of women in some traditionally male professions and careers, and (3) the differences in opportunity to learn occurring as a function of students' gender, as well as of their race and social class.

Although coeducation has been the uncontested norm for schooling in the public sector in the United States since the expansion of the common school ideal in the mid-nineteenth century, the question of its relative effectiveness for boys and girls has received little attention. Historians have recognized, however, that the almost universal adoption of coeducational schooling occurred on the basis of economic pragmatism with little heed to whether shared or separate classrooms were educationally more appropriate for boys and girls (Tyack and Hansot, 1990). Nonetheless, in some large cities, where the economics of their existence was not problematic, single-sex public high schools persisted until the passage of Title IX in 1972 effectively precluded their continuation. Schooling in the private sector, however, evolved differently.

Single-Sex and Coeducational Private High Schools

Most Catholic and independent high schools developed as single-sex institutions, growing out of ecclesial, social, or educational traditions that antedated the American public school. Catholic schools served a religious clientele; independent schools—that is, elite private schools—educated the children of the upper classes.

In the early 1970s, as society subjected beliefs, practices, and institutions to intense scrutiny, Catholic and independent private schools also evaluated the relevance of their missions—bringing to bear considerations of equity, excellence, fiscal soundness, and long-term viability. Convinced that their educational role had contemporary value, many single-sex schools committed themselves to pursuing their traditional missions with renewed purpose and often substantial adaptation.

Single-sex schools that opted for coeducation generally had one of two rationales: Attuned to the markets upon which they depend for survival, some schools, often reluctantly, chose to reckon with the prospects of rising costs and declining enrollments by enlarging their applicant pool with students of the opposite sex. Others regarded the coeducational environment as desirably egalitarian, conducive to personal development during adolescence, and effective preparation for life in a coed world. Choosing a middle path, a third group of single-sex schools adopted coordinate or coinstitutional status with an opposite sex school. Under such agreements, schools arrived at mutually advantageous arrangements affecting schedules, personnel, transportation, extracurricular activities, and classes.

Evolution of Research on High School Gender Organization

Research on the relative effectiveness of single-sex and coeducational secondary schools began to develop in the late 1960s and early 1970s. Originating outside the United States in Australia, New Zealand, and the United Kingdom, these studies frequently took as their reference point the contention of Coleman (1961): Because the values of the adolescent subculture with its "rating and dating" hold sway over academics in coeducational high schools, coeducation may actually be detrimental to the optimal development of the sexes during adolescence. Largely psychological in orientation, this wave of research compared students in the two school types on their attitudes toward school and peers. Unfortunately, the studies suffered from two limitations: (1) small nonrandom samples of students and schools afforded minimal generalizability; and (2) reliance on bivariate analyses ignored the potentially confounding effect of student background characteristics.

With the availability of several large national data bases, investigators a decade later initiated a second

wave of more rigorous and widely generalizable studies. Decidedly sociological in rationale and method, this research focused primarily on academic achievement, but also extended to students' personal and social values. In the United States, research drew on the *National Longitudinal Study of the High School Class of 1972* (NLS) and the *High School and Beyond* (HS&B) study that began in 1980 with students who were at either sophomore or senior year in high school (Lee and Bryk, 1986; Riordan, 1985). Abroad, the *International Association for the Evaluation of Educational Achievement* (IEA) provided data on students in both developing and developed nations (e.g., Lee and Lockheed, 1990).

Researchers using the national data bases in this country have generally restricted their investigations to Catholic schools, as neither NLS nor HS&B sampled independent schools (i.e., member schools of the National Association of Independent Schools) in numbers adequate for comparative research. Internationally, however, because public schools are often single sex, research populations have included students in state, Catholic, and independent schools. These more recent studies have incorporated multivariate analyses and introduced statistical adjustments for student background differences. In addition, research on single-sex education in the 1980s has attempted to address the issue of selection bias, i.e., the possibility that students who attend single-sex schools have personal and familial characteristics that favor them over their counterparts in coed schools (for example, Lee and Marks, 1990; Lee and Bryk, 1986). Furthermore, because both NLS and HS&B track students beyond high school, the question of whether the effects of the single-sex high school experience are sustained after the graduates finish college and/or have begun their careers has also gained research attention (Lee and Marks, 1990; Riordan, 1990).

Review of the Research on High School Gender Organization

Studies comparing single-sex education and coeducation have typically examined outcomes in four major categories: (1) school-related values and experiences, (2) student perceptions of the school climate, (3) academic behaviors and achievement, and (4) personal and social values. Other more recent studies have investigated selection into single-sex schools and examined the issue of sexism in single-sex and coeducational classrooms.

School-Related Values and Experiences

Qualities admired in peers, social interaction, and attitudes toward schoolwork have constituted the focus of investigations in this category. Primarily involving students in Catholic schools in the United States and Canada, these studies reported that subculture values —being in the leading crowd, having money and good looks—mattered more to students in coed schools, whereas academic values—finding schoolwork interesting and challenging, spending more time on home assignments—characterized students of both sexes in single-sex schools (Lee and Bryk, 1986; Riordan, 1985).

In the U.S. independent school sector, a study focusing on female students found those in single-sex schools reporting more eagerness to learn and a greater investment of time on homework, whereas those in coeducational schools reported greater involvement in extracurricular activities (Trickett et al., 1982).

Perceptions of School Climate

How students look upon their school environments varies according to the school types, but also according to country. Students in coeducational schools in Canada and England have tended to characterize their environments as more pleasure oriented and affiliative, whereas students in single-sex schools in those countries have generally perceived theirs to be more disciplined and controlled (Schneider and Coutts, 1982; Dale, 1971). Among girls in independent schools in the United States, however, students in single-sex schools, although they were more likely to report their environments as controlled, also reported higher levels of affiliation than did their counterparts in coeducational schools (Trickett et al., 1982).

Academic Behaviors and Achievement

Boys in the United States, including minorities, who attend Catholic single-sex schools tend to take more mathematics courses than boys in coed schools, but they are also inclined to have more sexually stereotyping views about math (Lee and Bryk, 1986). These findings departed from an earlier study among students in the United Kingdom that reported attendance at coeducational schools increasing boys' interest and

achievement in math (Dale, 1974). In the developing countries, among somewhat younger boys—eighth grade in Thailand and ninth grade in Nigeria—students in coeducational schools registered higher achievement.

With performance on the Scholastic Aptitude Test in mathematics (SATM) as the outcome measure, the results were once again mixed. Riordan (1985), using NLS-72 data and adjusting for socioeconomic status and region of the country only, reported that although boys in single-sex Catholic schools ranked significantly higher on the SATM than their counterparts in coeducational schools, neither group performed at the level of boys in public schools. Lee and Marks (1990), using HS&B and the identical, elaborate set of control variables as found in the earlier study it replicates (Lee and Bryk, 1986), report no difference in SATM between boys in single-sex and coed schools in the Catholic sector.

For girls the effects in mathematics achievement are generally more consistent. Girls in Catholic single-sex schools take more math, hold less stereotyping views of math (Lee and Bryk, 1986), and achieve at a higher level than girls in coeducational schools (Riordan, 1985). Internationally in mathematics, girls in single-sex schools have outscored their counterparts in coeducational schools (Lee and Lockheed, 1990; Dale, 1974). On the SATM, however, although Riordan (1985) found that girls in Catholic single-sex schools outperformed those in coeducational schools and tested at parity with girls in public schools, Lee and Marks (1990) report no gender organizational effects on girls' SATM scores.

In other academic areas, specifically the scientific and verbal, Lee and Bryk (1986) found that boys in single-sex schools took more physical science courses during high school, and, in tenth grade, outscored boys in coeducational schools in reading and writing. The latter finding was consistent with a study in the United Kingdom that found coeducation associated with a decrease in boys' language and literary abilities (Dale, 1974). On the verbal section of the Scholastic Aptitude Test (SATV), whereas Riordan (1985) found an advantage favoring boys in coeducational schools, Lee and Marks (1990) did not.

For girls, the single-sex school experience appears to have decided benefits in the sciences. An Australian sample of girls attending single-sex and coeducational high schools in the public, Catholic, and independent sectors found the single-sex experience contributing to girls' pursuing a heavily scientific curriculum in twelfth grade. In a study of students in England, girls in single-sex schools in ninth grade achieved at higher levels than boys in biology and chemistry (Finn, 1980). Finn also reported that attitudinal and skill disparities between boys and girls in physics and practical sciences were greater for students in coeducational schools. Furthermore, the cognitive growth in science of girls in single-sex schools did not slow down relative to boys' as it did for girls in coed schools (Finn, 1980). In a recent study using HS&B data but incorporating fewer controls for student differences than provided by Lee and Bryk (1986), separate analyses for white and minority girls found students in single-sex schools in both groups with substantially higher science achievement than those in coeducational schools (Riordan, 1990).

Virtually all the research in the United States and in England has pointed to the superiority in verbal achievement of girls in single-sex schools. The exception is Dale (1974), who associates coeducation with increases in girls' language and literary abilities. To the contrary, however, girls in single-sex schools in the Catholic sector in the United States scored higher in reading achievement in tenth and twelfth grade than did girls in coed schools, and as well, their achievement gain between tenth and twelfth grades was significantly greater. In England, girls in single-sex schools surpassed their male counterparts in reading, whereas girls in coeducational schools did not (Finn, 1980). Similarly, unlike girls in single-sex schools, girls in coeducational schools declined in cognitive growth in reading relative to the boys with whom they attended school (Finn, 1980). In civics, white and minority girls attending single-sex schools achieved significantly beyond their coeducational counterparts (Riordan, 1990). Finally, on the SATV, although Riordan (1985) reported significantly higher scores for girls in single-sex schools, Lee and Marks (1990) did not.

Personal and Social Values

Research involving students in the United States points to the empowering effect of the single-sex school experience for girls. In the Catholic sector, compared with their coeducational school counterparts, girls in single-sex schools at tenth grade have a higher self-concept, and at twelfth grade have a more internalized locus of control (Lee and Bryk, 1986). Sex-role stereotyping was

significantly less characteristic of girls in single-sex schools than of those in coeducational schools at tenth or twelfth grade in the Catholic sector, and, in fact, the girls became significantly less stereotyping over the course of their high school careers (Riordan, 1990; Lee and Bryk, 1986). In a study reporting on the independent school sector, girls in coeducational schools were less likely than those in single-sex schools to be interested in the women's movement (Trickett et al., 1982). Girls in single-sex Catholic schools had higher educational aspirations than those in coeducational schools at both tenth and twelfth grades and they registered a significantly higher gain in educational aspirations over the last 2 years of high school (Lee and Bryk, 1986).

Selection into Single-Sex Schools

Selection into independent single-sex schools has been investigated by Lee and Marks (1990). Although these schools proved to draw students from their traditional clientele, that is, students with a family history of single-sex schooling, they are also attracting first-generation patrons, who may view single-sex education as an opportunity structure. Students who choose single-sex over coeducational schools report a commitment to this educational form. Although single-sex schools may appeal to these students because of their records in college placement or because they are boarding schools, school gender organization is the most important school feature affecting students' enrollment decisions.

Sexism in Single-Sex and Coeducational School Classrooms

The questions of how single-sex and coeducational schools differentially socialize students into gender and the extent to which sexism may be involved in the process of socialization were examined by Lee et al. (1994). Analyzing observational data evenly distributed across 86 classrooms in 21 girls', boys', and coeducational schools (seven of each gender grouping), the authors found 55% of the classrooms free of sexism and close to 50% of them actively promoting gender equity. Although the number of incidents of sexism observed in the three types of schools was roughly equal, the forms that were most characteristic in each type of school were not.

Classrooms in single-sex schools were more likely to reinforce students' gender identities and to evidence embedded discrimination and sex-role stereotyping. Explicitly sexual incidents occurred only in boys' school classrooms. Coeducational independent schools tended to have imbalanced enrollments according to gender (18% more boys than girls) and to employ a comparatively small proportion of female teachers (29%). Both gender domination and active discrimination against girls occurred in coeducational school classroom environments.

Postsecondary Research

Whether the effects of attending a single-sex high school persisted for students during their postsecondary years was investigated by Lee and Marks (1990). A single-sex secondary education, according to these researchers, proved to exert sustained effects on the personal and social values of students, stronger and more extensive for young women than for young men.

Lee and Marks (1990) found four major sets of sustained effects: (1) Single-sex school graduates were more likely to enroll at highly selective colleges than were the coeducational school graduates, with the young men significantly less likely to attend a community college and more likely to attend a private college; (2) young women who attended a single-sex high school surpassed those from coeducational schools in educational aspirations measured 2 years after high school graduation; (3) 4 years out of high school, these young women were significantly more likely to be free of work-role stereotyping and to be politically active; and (4) graduates of single-sex high schools were comparatively more likely to consider graduate or professional school, following upon their interest in the professions, particularly law.

A second and earlier stream of postsecondary education research in the mid-1970s had begun to document positive effects of single-sex colleges, especially for women, in terms of self-image, career choice, and occupational achievement. Examining the educational backgrounds of successful women, researchers found that women's colleges, especially smaller ones (under 500 students) and the Seven Sisters colleges (Barnard, Bryn Mawr, Mount Holyoke, Radcliffe, Smith, Vassar, and Wellesley), produced a disproportionate share of both female leaders and women who had earned the doctoral degree (Oates and Williamson, 1978; Tidball & Kistiakowsky, 1976).

Based on a longitudinal study of 200,000 students from 300 colleges, Astin (1977) documented a pattern of "almost universally positive" effects for single-sex colleges on men and, especially, women. Students' academic involvement, interaction with faculty, intellectual self-esteem, and satisfaction with school (except the social life, for men) were highest among students in single-sex colleges. In a longitudinal study (1972–1986) following women who attended single-sex and mixed-sex colleges, Riordan (1990) found positive effects for womens' colleges on educational and occupational attainment, as well as on social-psychological outcomes, such as self-esteem, locus of control, and happiness in marriage.

The issue of sexism has received attention in postsecondary studies of the effects of school and classroom gender organization on students. Coeducational colleges and universities have warranted criticism for classroom educational practices hostile to women (Sandler, 1986). Researchers have also studied the effects of classroom gender composition and instructor gender on men and women—particularly the extent to which men and women speak up, and the extent of cross-gender, instructor–student interactions. A consistent finding is that men are more vocal in class regardless of the proportion of other males and the gender of the instructor. Findings on the relationship of instructor gender to female participation have been mixed.

What the Research Suggests

Uneven and diffuse, the relatively small body of research on single-sex schools has nonetheless demonstrated considerable consistency. Studies have generally reported effects favorable to single-sex education, particularly for girls and women. Over the course of two decades, across nations, and occasionally cultures, a portrait of single-sex schools has emerged showing them to be ordered and academically oriented environments. High school students in single-sex schools perform at least as well academically as students in coeducational schools, but very often they surpass them.

For girls and young women the single-sex experience appears to have some additional benefits, freeing them from social and academic stereotypes, encouraging higher educational and career aspirations and attainment, and inclining them toward participation in public life.

Research on the gender organization of classrooms at both the secondary and postsecondary level has indicated that males receive more attention from teachers in the coeducational environment and they also tend to dominate classroom activities.

Emerging Issues

Targeting academic and social issues, some public schools have recently begun either to initiate or to explore the possibility of initiating experiments with single-sex classrooms. These schools seek to evaluate the efficacy of the single-sex classroom environment for girls' mathematics achievement, classroom discipline and student academic engagement, and as a setting for providing an Afro-centric curriculum to African-American boys. Because the initiatives are scattered, and most are in their early stages, little research evidence is available to evaluate their effectiveness.

Although these initiatives have generally received considerable public support where they have been introduced, they could incur challenges to their legality under Title IX, which prohibits sexual discrimination in educational programs that receive public funds. State-sponsored single-sex military colleges for men are encountering such challenges on behalf of women who wish to experience the educational and career benefits such schools have to offer.

REFERENCES

Dale, R. R. 1974. *Mixed or Single-Sex School? Vol. 3: Attainment, Attitudes, and Overview.* London: Routledge & Kegan Paul.

Finn, Jeremy D. 1980. "Sex Differences in Educational Outcomes: A Cross-National Study." *Sex Roles* 6:9–25.

Lee, Valerie E., and Anthony S. Bryk. 1986. "Effects of Single-Sex Secondary Schools on Student Achievement and Attitudes." *Journal of Educational Psychology* 78:381–395.

———. "Effects of Single-Sex Schools: Response to Marsh." *Journal of Educational Psychology* 81:70–85.

Lee, Valerie E., and Helen M. Marks. 1990. "Sustained Effects of the Single-Sex Secondary School Experience on Attitudes, Behaviors, and Values in College." *Journal of Educational Psychology* 82:578–592.

———. 1992. "Who Goes Where? Choice of Single-Sex and Coeducational Independent Secondary Schools." *Sociology of Education* 65:226–253.

Lee, Valerie E., Helen M. Marks, and Tina Byrd. 1994. "Sexism in Single-Sex and Coeducational Independent Secondary School Classrooms." *Sociology of Education* 67:92–120.

Oates, M. J., and S. Williamson. 1978. "Women's Colleges and Women Achievers." *Journal of Women in Culture and Society* 3:795–806.

Riordan, Cornelius. 1985. "Public and Catholic Schooling: The Effects of Gender Context Policy." *American Journal of Education* 5:518–540.

———. 1990. *Girls and Boys in School: Together or Separate?* New York: Teachers' College Press.

Sandler, Bernice Resnick. 1987. "The Classroom Climate: Still a Chilly One for Women." In Carol Lasser (ed.), *Educating Men and Women Together.* Urbana: University of Illinois Press.

Tidball, M. E., and V. Kistiakowsky. 1980. "Baccalaureate Origins of American Scientists and Scholars." *Science* 193:646–652.

Trickett, E. J., J. J. Castro, P. K. Trickett, and Shaffner, P. 1982. "The Independent School Experience: Aspects of the Normative Environments of Single-Sex and Coed Secondary Schools." *Journal of Educational Psychology* 74:374–381.

Tyack, David, and Elisabeth Hansot. 1990. *Learning Together: A History of Coeducation in American Public Schools.* New Haven, CT: Yale University Press.

SOCIAL CAPITAL

A UBIQUITOUS EMERGING CONCEPTION

Barbara Schneider
NORC and The University of Chicago

In 1990, James S. Coleman published *Foundations of Social Theory*, perhaps his most comprehensive and major theoretical work in which he set out to describe the changing nature of purposively constructed social organizations. Part II of this massive work, which is titled "Structures of Action," contains the chapter "Social Capital," which is an updated and extensive modification of his *American Journal of Sociology* article (1988), "Social Capital in the Creation of Human Capital." Tracing the conception of social capital to Loury (1977), who introduced the term to describe how individuals use resources that accrue through social relationships in the family and community for their own benefit, Coleman explains how Loury's ideas of social relationships can be used to promote individual and collective interests. Citing Bourdieu (1977) and De Graaf and Flap (1988), who also use the concept of social capital in a similar fashion, Coleman expands on Loury's (1977) definition to identify various types of social capital and the ways in which it can be created.

Coleman's conception of social capital as relational ties that help to establish norms can be traced back to earlier sociological work by Park and Burgess (1921) and Mead (1934). Park, Burgess, and Mead refer to social institutions as communities of mutual interests that form mores and values of social control. Through common understandings that emerge from discourse and activities, such institutions define socially responsible patterns of conduct. Janowitz (1975) argues that the task of empirical social research is to investigate the forms and consequences of social control that enable a social group to regulate itself in terms of a set of legitimate moral principles. [I would like to thank Charles Bidwell for pointing out the sociological roots

of social capital. Sampson and Laub also link social capital with Janowitz's conception of social control in their book *Crime in the Making: Pathways and Turning Points Through Life* (1993, see pp. 17–19).]

Robert Putnam, the noted political scientist, credits Coleman in his book on local governments in Italy (1993), as does Fukuyama (1995) in his book on trust, with developing the theoretical framework for present conceptions of social capital. However, Putnam (1995b) maintains that the current understanding of social capital was first introduced by Jane Jacobs in 1961 in her book on American cities. Both Putnam and Fukuyama, in their interpretations of Coleman's notion of social capital, define it as a set of relationships that enhances the ability of people to work for a common good.

Putnam (1995a, 1995b) perceives social capital not only as a social resource that potentially benefits an individual or a group, but also as a means for enhancing cooperation that serves civic ends. Social capital, from Putnam's perspective, refers to people's connections with the civic life of their communities, not strictly their politics. A grass roots movement, according to Putnam, is a social capital-intensive form of political participation, whereas writing a check to a political candidate is a political act, but does not create social capital.

Fukuyama takes the concept of social capital and uses it to construct a theory of social trust. The strength of social capital in a community depends upon the degree to which associates share norms and values and are able to moderate self-interests for the common good. From these shared values comes trust. Fukuyama argues that trust generated through positive, socially constructed relationships that are based on reciprocal action, moral obligation, and reflection, rather than based on routine and rational calculation, can promote economic prosperity.

What Coleman, Putnam, and Fukuyama share is the belief that social capital is not just relational ties that can effectively transmit information. Rather, social capital is the formation of networks through which norms and trust are created that advance a productive end, be that the intellectual and emotional well-being of children, civic engagement, or economic prosperity.

Defining Social Capital

From Coleman's perspective, social capital can be defined by its function, not its structure. Coleman views social capital as a set of relational ties that facilitates action. In this definition, Coleman expands on Lin's (1982, 1990) conception of social resources, which is intended to explain how individuals negotiate with other individuals to enhance their social standing. Lin views social resources instrumentally from the perspective of the individual. An individual forms ties with others initially to protect and gain resources. This maintenance and protection of resources are driven by emotional forces, whereas gaining resources requires calculated motives and actions (see Lin, 1990:262–264).

Coleman, in contrast, defines social capital as inhering in the structure of relations between persons and among persons. He sees it as a network of relations not lodged in individuals (see Coleman, 1990:302). Even more importantly, the social capital that comes about through relational exchanges helps to generate trust by establishing expectations, and creating and enforcing norms. This normative aspect of social capital is also articulated by Granovetter (1985) in his concept of embeddedness, which explains how personal relations and networks of relations give social systems a history and continuity.

The major distinction between Coleman and other economists and sociologists who use social resources instrumentally from a somewhat rational action perspective is that he develops a concept that can be used to describe social systems, not only economic ones. Social capital exists in social structures, be it the family, school, or community. It facilitates the actions of individuals who are within the structure. Like other forms of capital, such as human and physical capital, it makes possible the achievement of certain ends that would be impossible without its presence. Whereas social capital may help to facilitate some actions, it also may be useless or harmful for others.

For example, in a parent-operated school, parents are expected to actively participate in school activities, including volunteering in the classroom, accompanying the class on different field trips, and assisting the teacher in the classroom with various tasks. This broad commitment on the part of the parents makes it difficult for both parents to hold full-time jobs. For example, a mother who chooses to enroll her child in this private, parent-operated school may be forced to reduce the number of hours she is employed outside the home. This, in turn, creates a financial drain on the family, which makes it difficult to purchase or participate in certain educationally beneficial activities, such as buying a new computer or taking a family vacation. In this example, although the social capital in the school among the parents and the teachers and students is increased, there are real costs to the family for being part of such a social network.

Characteristics of Social Capital

Social capital is created through relational ties; the denser and closer these ties are, the greater the likelihood that information important to providing a basis for action will be communicated. For example, in small, close communities, information about which teachers are the best teachers is often widely discussed. Parents who are privy to this information often will try to move their child to the preferred classrooms.

But exchanging relevant, useful information is only a part of the value of social capital. The more critical component is its ability to foster normative behavior that enhances the productivity of the organization. This is accomplished through the fulfillment of expected obligations that engender trust. From Coleman's perspective, the value of social capital is in its ability to provide a mechanism of social control through the creation of voluntary norms that are based on obligations, expectations, and trustworthiness of the structure.

The presence or absence of social ties helps to establish links between all parents in the network. In communities where these ties have been made across generations, the social capital is even greater, for all individuals within the closed network have some link to another member in the system. Coleman hypothesizes that such intergenerational closure can provide a mechanism not only for maintaining effective norms, but also for creating trustworthiness.

It is trustworthiness that allows the establishment of obligations and expectations. Trustworthiness can provide the same type of sanctions that closure can in structures that are open. From Coleman's perspective, in social structures where individuals have clear expectations of how they are supposed to act and how others are expected to act, this information is shared throughout the system. Obligations of action are a resource unto themselves, and they can be made tangible by their availability to others when needed.

For example, in a school community that values high academic success, teachers can call upon the parents to help them in implementing new policies, such as stricter rules regarding the completion of homework. The more social capital in the system, the greater the number of parents and students who will follow these new rules regarding homework completion. In this example, the teachers assume that parents and students will fulfill their obligations to the principles endorsed by the school. For the parents, this may mean that they have to more carefully monitor their child's time, which requires more of their attention away from other interests. To comply with these rules, the students will also have to forego time they might have spent watching television or visiting with friends. Both parents and their children have to forego spending time on other preferred activities and act in the interests of the collectivity, in this instance the school. A norm of this sort, Coleman argues, reinforced by status, honor, and other rewards, constitutes a powerful source of social capital (see Coleman, 1988:104–105).

This social capital, Coleman maintains, not only facilitates certain actions, but also constrains others. Let us assume that a school encourages students to spend several hours during a given semester doing community service. The social service agencies in the community are aware of the school's aim and make available different types of volunteer work. The school and community work together to place the youngsters at different sites. The stronger the social capital, the less likely students are to "blow off" their community service agreement.

In addition to these broad principles of social capital, Coleman also specifically defines social capital in the family and community. With respect to the family, he sees it as the number of adults in the family and the quality of attention they give to the children in the home for their personal development. With respect to social capital in the community, Coleman defines it as the social relationships that exist among parents in the closure exhibited by the parents' ties with other parents and the institutions in the community. Social capital in the community depends greatly on the stability and strength of the community's social structure.

Coleman maintains that even where the social structure of neighborhoods has deteriorated, social capital can be created through functional communities. These social institutions, which may or may not be neighborhood based, can provide a functional linkage among parents. One social institution that Coleman uses as an example of a functional community that increases the social capital among its members is the religious community surrounding religious schools. He concedes that other institutions may play a similar role for some public schools. Coleman asserts that his analysis using High School and Beyond (HS&B) data, which compare the low dropout rates in religious schools with public and secular private schools, demonstrates the important benefits of social capital created by such functional communities (Coleman, 1991; Coleman and Hoffer, 1987).

Coleman believes that closer connections between parents and their children, for example, schools organized around the parents' workplace, can strengthen social ties between teachers and families more than is currently found with neighborhood schools where most parents work outside their residential neighborhood. Coleman believes that one way to improve schools is to create close ties among parents and their child's school, where parents, teachers, and students share a common set of standards that social norms help to bring about and monitor.

A New Wave of Social Capital Research

Although Coleman may be credited with giving social capital some definitional properties, it has become a term of ubiquitous dimension. Within the past 3 years the number of journal articles and paper presentations on this topic has grown enormously. Some of the more recent works on this topic are reviewed below.

Entwisle and Astone (1994), in an invited paper in

Child Development entitled "Some Practical Guidelines for Measuring Youth's Race/Ethnicity and Socioeconomic Status," define social capital as the resources embodied in social relationships. They recommend using measures of household and family structure in the household, including the number of birth parents in the home, an indicator of whether there is a stepparent in the home, and an indicator of whether there is a grandparent in the home. Although these measures of structure are exceedingly valuable for identification of structure, unless there are some measures of the quality of the relationships these individuals have with the child, Coleman's definition of social capital is only partially addressed. Coleman's perspective on what makes social capital in the family is that the structural ties are linked to behaviors that foster the development and well-being of the child.

Coleman's definition of social capital in the family is expanded in *Parents, Their Children, and Schools* (Schneider and Coleman, 1993), which demonstrates, using data from the base year of the National Education Longitudinal Study of 1988 (NELS:88), how social resources in the family, community, and school serve as capital assets for improving student academic performance and psychological well-being. The work in this volume focuses on the actions parents take with their children at home and in other social systems that promote norms and expectations that positively influence their child's education. The chapters provide empirical analyses that examine the relationship among family composition, parent involvement and student outcomes, effects of maternal employment on family activities and student outcomes, and school-based parent involvement, including school choice and its effect on student performance.

Another more recent work that uses a social capital framework can be found in Furstenberg and Hughes' article, "Social Capital and Successful Development Among At-Risk Youth," in *Journal of Marriage and the Family* (1995). Using a longitudinal sample of 252 at-risk children over a 3-year period, the researchers explored the relationships between measures of social capital and several indicators of successful adulthood. Relying on Coleman's concept of social capital in the family, generated by parents' social investment in their children, such as help with homework, activities with parents, parents' expectations for school performance, mother's encouragement of child, and family links to the community, including religious involvement, social supports for advice and help outside the family, family residential stability, and quality of school and neighborhood, Furstenberg and Hughes estimated what effect these measures had on the likelihood of these at-risk students graduating from high school, enrolling in college, entering and remaining in the labor force, avoiding early family formation and criminal activity, and maintaining robust mental health. They found that most of the measures of social capital were related to markers of socioeconomic success in early adulthood. However, social capital measures showed no effect in predicting early parenthood for girls and problems with the criminal justice system for boys. The authors conclude that distinct aspects of social relationships are important to different youth outcomes. They caution scholars from using a unitary measure of social capital and a unitary measure of success in early adulthood.

One area that is presently receiving more attention is social capital in the schools. For example, Stanton-Salazar and Dornbusch (1995), in a recent article in *Sociology of Education* entitled "Social Capital and the Reproduction of Inequality: Information Networks Among Mexican-Origin High School Students," apply Lin et al.'s (1981) conception of how individuals use social relationships to achieve mobility and status attainment. In their study, the authors selected 205 Mexican-origin students from six high schools in the San Francisco-San Jose area. Conducting semistructured interviews, they determined students' social support networks, their familistic orientations and practices, and their future plans regarding college, work, and marriage. Information was also obtained on student advice networks and friendship networks. Looking specifically at weak ties students have at school and with their families, the authors find that for many minority students and for students from working-class backgrounds, school personnel are frequently the most available source for informed guidance on specific matters. However, the students report having confidence in only one or two adults. Their findings suggest that highly bilingual students may have an advantage over working-class, English-dominant students in gaining access to adult social capital. The authors conclude that social ties network-analytic models offer considerable promise for understanding social mobility and attainment among Mexican-origin and other minority youths.

Several other important studies are currently underway that examine relational ties among teachers in high school subject departments and their relationship to teacher work satisfaction and student achievement (Bidwell and Bryk, 1994; Talbert and McLaughlin, 1994), and adolescent peer network ties in school and their effect on student aspirations and other behaviors (Bidwell et al., 1996). This work uses conceptions of social capital combining the perspectives of Lin et al. (1981), Granovetter (1982), and Coleman (1988, 1990) to demonstrate the impact of networks of relational ties on both the communicative and persuasive elements of social control.

More nested in the Coleman, Putnam, and Fukuyama conception of social capital, new empirical work by Schneider and Bryk (1996) elaborates a theory of social trust for promoting school improvement. Using data from a 3-year longitudinal case study of 12 elementary schools in Chicago and teacher and student surveys from 270 elementary schools, the authors show how relational ties based on mutual expectations and obligations can facilitate collective action.

Furstenberg and Hughes (1995), in the conclusion to their article, raise a cautionary note about social capital. From their perspective, as well as Coleman's, social capital is not a global concept that ensures a successful, universalistic outcome. In fact, as outlined in this entry, social capital, although promoting some effects, may produce negative effects for different aims. As a concept, it potentially has very useful analytic properties for understanding relational ties and how they can promote norms, sanction behaviors, and imbue trust. But sometimes the norms can be socially undesirable and trust blindfully upheld, regardless of whether expectations and obligations are fulfilled. As with any sociological concept, its value will be, as Furstenberg and Hughes demonstrate, as a mechanism for understanding the relational ties and outcomes in some social systems that comprise our technological, postmodern society.

References

Bidwell, C. E., and T. Bryk. 1994. *How Teacher's Work is Organized: The Content and Consequences of the Structure of the High School Workplace* (Report No. 94–1). Chicago: NORC and The University of Chicago, Ogburn-Stouffer Center.

Bidwell, C. E., S. Plank, and C. Muller. 1996. "Peer Social Networks and Adolescent Career Development." In A. C. Kerckhoff, (ed.), *Generating Social Stratification: Toward a New Generation of Research*. Denver, CO: Westview Press.

Bourdieu, P. 1977. "Cultural Reproduction and Social Reproduction." In J. Karabel and A. H. Halsey (eds.), *Power and Ideology in Education,* pp. 487–511. New York: Oxford University Press.

Coleman, J. S. 1988. "Social Capital in the Creation of Human Capital." *American Journal of Sociology* 94:95–120.

———. 1990. *Foundations of Social Theory*. Cambridge, MA: The Belknap Press of Harvard University Press.

———. 1991. "Changes in the Family and Implications for the Common School." *The University of Chicago Legal Forum*.

Coleman, J. S., and T. Hoffer. 1987. *Public and Private High Schools: The Impact of Communities*. New York: Basic Books.

De Graaf, N. D., and H. D. Flap. 1988. "With a Little Help from My Friends: Social Resources as an Explanation of Occupational Status and Income in West Germany, the Netherlands, and the United States." *Social Forces* 67:453–472.

Entwisle, D., and N. M. Astone. 1994. "Some Practical Guidelines for Measuring Youth's Race/Ethnicity and Socioeconomic Status." *Child Development* 65(6):1521–1540.

Fukuyama, F. 1995. *Trust: Social Virtues and the Creation of Prosperity*. New York: The Free Press.

Furstenberg, F., and M. E. Hughes. 1995. "Social Capital and Successful Development Among At-risk Youth." *Journal of Marriage and the Family* 57:580–592.

Granovetter, M. 1982. "The Strength of Weak Ties: A Network Theory Revisited." In P. V. Marsden and N. Lin (eds.), *Social Structure and Network Analysis,* pp. 105–130. Beverly Hills, CA: Sage Publications.

———. 1985. "Economic Action, Social Structure and Embeddedness." *American Journal of Sociology* 91:481–510.

Jacobs, J. 1961. *The Death and Life of Great American Cities*. New York: Random House.

Janowitz, M. 1975. "Sociological Theory and Social Control." *American Journal of Sociology* 81:82–108.

Lin, N. 1982. "Social Resources and Instrumental Action." In P. V. Marsden and N. Lin (eds.), *Social Structure and Network Analysis,* Beverly Hills, CA: Sage.

——— 1990. "Social Resources and Social Mobility: A Structural Theory of Status Attainment." In R. L. Breiger (ed.), *Social Mobility and Social Structure,* pp. 247–271. Cambridge: Cambridge University Press.

Lin, N., J. C. Vaugn, and W. M. Ensel. 1981. "Social Resources and the Strength of Ties: Structural Factors in Occupational Status Attainment." *American Sociological Review* 46:393–405.

Loury, G. 1977. "A Dynamic Theory of Racial Income Differences." In P. A. Wallace and A. Le Mund (eds.), *Women, Minorities and Employment Discrimination*. Lexington, MA: Lexington Books.

Mead, G. H. 1934. "The Social Foundations and Functions

of Thought and Communications, the Community and the Institution." In *Mind, Self, and Society*, pp. 253–273. Chicago: University of Chicago Press.

Park, R. E., and E. W. Burgess. 1921. Social Control and Schools of Thought, Control and the Collective Mind, Social Control Defined, Classification of the Materials." In *Introduction to the Science of Sociology*, pp. 27–42, 783–799. Chicago: University of Chicago Press.

Putnam, R., with Robert Leonardi and Raffaella Y. Nanetti. 1993. *Making Democracy Work: Civic Traditions in Modern Italy*. Princeton, NJ: Princeton University Press.

Putnam, R. 1995a. "Bowling Alone: America's Declining Social Capital." *Journal of Democracy* 6(1):65–78.

———. 1995b. "Tuning In, Tuning Out: The Strange Disappearance of Social Capital in America." *Political Science and Politics* (December):664–683.

Sampson, R. J., and J. H. Laub. 1993. *Crime in the Making: Pathways and Turning Points through Life*. Cambridge, MA: Harvard University Press.

Schneider, B., and A. Bryk. 1996. *Social Trust: A Moral Resource for School Improvement*. Chicago: Center for School Improvement.

Schneider, B., and J. Coleman. 1993. *Parents, Their Children, and Schools*. Boulder, CO: Westview Press.

Stanton-Salazar, R. D., and S. M. Dornbusch. 1995. "Social Capital and the Reproduction of Inequality: Information Networks Among Mexican-Origin High School Students." *Sociology of Education* 68(2):116–135.

Talbert, J. E., and M. W. McLaughlin. 1994. "Teacher Professionalism in Local School Contexts." *American Journal of Education* 102:123–153.

SOCIAL REPRODUCTION

David Swartz
Boston University

Social reproduction theory entered the sociology of education in the late 1960s and early 1970s as a critical reaction to liberal educational reform. Though liberal reformers expected public education to promote individual development, social mobility, and greater political and economic equality, social reproduction theorists contend that schools actually enhance social inequalities rather than attenuate them. Drawing particularly on the work of Karl Marx, but also Max Weber and Emile Durkheim, social reproduction theorists focus on how the social class structure is perpetuated from one generation to the next. Why, they ask, do working-class children tend to end up in working-class jobs whereas youth of privileged origins tend to secure positions of prestige and power? Concern with the effects of social background on educational performance and attainment and the contribution of schooling to occupational achievement have of course been long-standing concerns in the sociology of education (Davies, 1995:1449; Dreeben, 1994:29). But social reproduction theorists see in the class–education nexus an indicator of broader institutional arrangements that reveals a particularly rigid social class structure.

Social reproduction theorists differ, however, in their views on just how the stratification order is constituted and perpetuated. Differences can be observed on the following issues: How tightly coupled are education and the capitalist labor market? How much agency is introduced into a structural analysis? How much micro- as well as macro-levels of observation and analysis are carried out? How much gender, race, and other status factors as well as social class are considered? How much room there is for innovation or change? Although the antecedents and effects of social reproduction theory are many, this presentation is limited to only the few most influential theorists who have also conducted original research in education.

Bowles and Gintis: The Correspondence Principle

The first social reproduction perspective to have a major impact on education theory and research is the neo-Marxist work of Samuel Bowles and Herbert Gintis, *Schooling in Capitalist America* (1976). Central to their approach is the "correspondence principle," which builds from Marx's argument that the various parts of capitalist society fit together so that the exploitative social relations between workers and capitalists are reflected throughout society and perpetuated integenerationally. Education in capitalist society reflects the hierarchical structure of the capitalist firm. The structural similarities between the social relationships that govern personal interaction in the workplace and those in the educational system can be seen in four ways. First, the patterns of power and authority between managers and workers and among administrators, teachers, and students leave little room for workers to control the content of their jobs and for students to control their curriculum. Second, wages, grades, and threat of unemployment and expulsion all impose external rather than internal motivational systems for work and learning. Third, the institutionalized competition and specialization of academic subjects reflect the fragmentation of jobs. And fourth, just as the lowest job levels in the capitalist enterprise emphasize rule following, the middle levels, dependability, and the highest levels of autonomy and self-direction, a similar hierarchy of values can be observed stretching from the lowest levels and tracks of the educational ladder up through the middle and highest levels.

Because of this correspondence between schools and the workplace, schools reproduce capitalist society in three ways: they allocate students into different levels in the capitalist work hierarchy so that workers' children become workers and capitalists' children become capitalists; they socialize students to have the skills and attitudes appropriate to those different levels (self-direction for managers, but obedience for workers); and they legitimate these processes of allocation and socialization in terms of individual merit.

This early work represents a kind of neo-Marxian functionalism where the skills, values, and norms transmitted through education correspond directly to the needs for hierarchy in the capitalist firm and in the social class structure. The same tightly coupled education/capitalist labor market nexus can also be found in the early work of Anyon (1980), Carnoy (1974, 1975), and Carnoy and Levin (1976). Apple's (1979) early work in particular uses the idea of the "hidden curriculum" to stress how school knowledge subtly transmits capitalist values.

This neo-Marxism functionalism soon comes under attack, however, from those who stress the contradictory character of capitalism (Apple, 1982; Katznelson and Weir, 1985; Wexler, 1976). Contradiction as well as correspondence characterize the relationship between education and work. Carnoy and Levin (1985:2–4), for example, repudiate their earlier Marxist functionalist perspective to emphasize the "central paradox" in the relationship between education and work where education both produces the skills, values, and norms that enhance the hierarchy of social relations in the capitalist firm and fosters democratic values that directly conflict with that hierarchy.

Bowles and Gintis do acknowledge that the experience of the universities in the 1960s demonstrates the capacity of education to foster criticism and protest of capitalist social relations. But the clear emphasis in their early work is on how schools reflect and reproduce rather than challenge the capitalist social order. Later, they (Bowles and Gintis, 1981) modify this view giving greater emphasis to how education can occasionally contradict capitalist interests.

The early neo-Marxist versions of social reproduction theory are also sharply criticized for not offering suit-

able insight into the actual processes that perpetuate capitalist social relations (Apple and Weis, 1985; Connell et al., 1982; Giroux, 1983; Willis, 1977). An alternative cultural reproduction perspective emerges offering distinctively different emphases. The curriculum and ideology of schools come to be seen as sources of social inequality. In contrast to the correspondence principle, more emphasis is given to cultural as well as structural features of reproduction. Cultural institutions, including education, are seen as "relatively autonomous" from underlying economic and social constraints. More emphasis is given to agency and new attention is given to sources of potential conflict and resistance as well as to structural determination. Researchers insist on the importance of ethnographic study of actual processes through which structures are reproduced. Pierre Bourdieu, a leading French sociologist, is an early and key architect of this widely influential theory of cultural reproduction.

Pierre Bourdieu: Cultural Capital and Reproduction

Bourdieu (1984, 1988, 1996; Bourdieu and Boltanski 1977; Bourdieu and Passeron 1977, 1979) is centrally concerned with how dominant class groups are able to pass their advantages on to their children so that their inheritance of privilege appears legitimate. Although this recalls Marxism, Bourdieu draws more from Weber and Durkheim to stress the cultural components of social stratification. Central to his argument, and his most important contribution to reproduction theory, is his landmark concept of "cultural capital." [For illustrative uses of this concept in education research, see Cookson and Persell (1985), DiMaggio (1982), DiMaggio and Mohr (1985), and Lareau (1989).] Cultural capital covers a wide variety of resources including general cultural awareness, knowledge, skills, and verbal facility that are acquired in childhood socialization and can be passed on from one generation to the next. Social classes differ in the amounts and types of cultural socialization. Dominant class children inherit substantially more cultural capital than do working-class youth. Children who grow up in families that read books, attend concerts, visit museums, and go to the theater and cinema receive a distinct dominant culture of knowledge, style, and language facility.

Schools reward the inherited cultural capital of the

dominant classes by implicitly requiring it for good academic performance and systematically devalue the culture of the subordinate classes. Some of Bourdieu's most insightful ethnographic observations about French schooling show how French teachers reward good language style, especially in essay and oral examinations, a practice that tends to favor those students with considerable cultural capital. Dominant class groups are able to capitalize on that advantage by translating their inherited cultural resources into high levels of scholastic performance and attainment. Moreover, schools legitimate this process by explaining academic success in terms of individual motivation and talent. Yet, school success, Bourdieu argues, is best explained by the amount and type of cultural capital inherited from the family milieu. Furthermore, dominant classes are able to reconvert their academic success into a competitive edge in the labor market thereby reproducing the stratification order.

This reproductive process, according to Bourdieu, does not presuppose a tight fit between social class, schooling, the labor market, and the state as neo-Marxist theories do. First, Bourdieu (1973) points out that economic capital and cultural capital are not perfectly correlated. The dominant class is internally differentiated into two opposing segments: a dominant segment based on substantial economic capital and a dominated segment based on cultural capital. The dominant segment relies principally on its substantial economic capital to maintain power and privilege, whereas the dominated segment bases its claim to power on the investment and accumulation of cultural capital. Thus, the entire education system is not directly subordinated to the interests of the capitalist class and labor market as Marxists contend. Drawing inspiration from Weber, Bourdieu links higher educational expansion since World War II to conflicts between social classes over the cultural and economic capital and among cultural elites for positions in cultural markets and the state. Indeed, he suggests that the biggest beneficiaries of the expanding educational meritocracy are not the capitalists, as Marxists argue, but those richest in cultural capital, namely, intellectuals, professionals, and government officials.

Second, the education system establishes a "relative autonomy" from outside interests by its capacity to develop a distinct status culture and its own organizational and professional interests. Referring to Durkheim (1977), Bourdieu and Passeron (1977:195–198) point to the educational system's capacity to recruit its leadership from within its own ranks as the reason for its unusual historical continuity and stability, analogous more to the Catholic Church than to business or the state. Education's virtual monopoly over recruitment, training, and promotion of personnel allows the educational system to adapt its programs and activities to its own specific needs for self-perpetuation. The combination of an internally generated body of knowledge and professional and organizational interests forms the basis for the relative autonomy of the educational system from state control and corporate pressure.

Bourdieu further distances himself from neo-Marxist accounts of reproduction by integrating a dynamic of agency into his structural analysis. His concept of "habitus," which is akin to the idea of class subculture, and established initially through childhood socialization, refers to a set of relatively permanent and largely unconscious dispositions about one's chances of success and how society works that is common to members of a social class or status group. The concept of habitus permits Bourdieu to stress that educational choices are dispositional, tacit, informal decisions rather than conscious, rational calculations. Yet, these dispositions lead individuals to act unwittingly in ways that can reproduce the prevailing structure of life chances and status distinctions. Bourdieu believes there is generally a high correlation between subjective hopes and objective chances. A child's ambitions and expectations with regard to education and career are the structurally determined products of parental and other reference-group educational experience and cultural life. Whether students stay in school or drop out, and the course of study they pursue, Bourdieu argues, depend on their practical expectations of the likelihood that people of their social class will succeed academically. Intergenerational reproduction is most likely to occur at the lower and upper reaches of the class structure where education opportunities, cultural capital, and habitus match. If working-class youth do not aspire to high levels of educational attainment, it is because they have internalized and resigned themselves to the limited opportunities for success in schools that devalue their kind of cultural background. By contrast, dominant class youth internalize their social advantages and the school's validation of dominant class culture as expectations for academic success and stay in school. Bourdieu, thus, insightfully demonstrates how much educational selection in fact occurs through self-selection.

Where disjuncture occurs between educational aspirations and actual educational opportunities, social reproduction becomes more precarious and there is potential for crisis as Bourdieu (1988) thinks occurred during the 1968 student revolts. Overall, however, the social reproduction process seems to occur without great difficulty in Bourdieu's analyses. Schooling seems to ensure the privileged of success and the less fortunate of failure. Risks of downward mobility for upper-class individuals are only mentioned, not explored. And the chances for upward mobility for lower-class youth are suggested to be minimal.

Basil Bernstein: Linguistic Codes and Reproduction

The work of Basil Bernstein (1971, 1973, 1975) in Great Britain provides an influential elaboration of the importance of cultural resources and education in social reproduction by focusing on language patterns. Drawing more from Durkheim than from either Marx or Weber, Bernstein identifies an underlying relationship between the social division of labor, language socialization in families, and the education system. Working-class children grow up in families and communities where limited mobility and education and traditional authority roles at work and at home create familiar, taken-for-granted social relations. These children are socialized into "restricted" linguistic codes in which meanings remain implicit and embedded in their social context. By contrast, middle-class children grow up in families where education, mobility, and changing work and family roles create a cultural and social universe where appropriate roles need to be negotiated and specified. Meanings are less tied to local, taken-for-granted sets of social relations. These children are socialized into "elaborate" linguistic codes that oblige speakers to select from a broader array of syntactic and lexical alternatives to make explicit intended meanings. Because schools operate according to elaborated codes, working-class children find themselves at a distinct disadvantage, whereas middle-class children are linguistically equipped to meet school demands. Even progressive pedagogies that stress role negotiation and discovery put those with restricted codes at a disadvantage. Class

relations are this way mediated and reproduced through the way schools deal with restricted and elaborated language patterns.

Reproduction and Resistance

The early stress on social reproduction predictably elicited a critical reaction against the structural determination emphasis by calling for greater attention to actual experience of schooling and to potential forms of protest and agency. By the early 1980s, the reproduction theme fell into disrepute even among some of its original proponents (Apple and Weis, 1983). Critics (Apple, 1982; Giroux, 1983; Wexler, 1987; Willis, 1977) argue that the early work of Bowles and Gintis and Bourdieu was too structural, too determinative, and too mechanical, giving insufficient attention to processes of resistance, contradiction, and contestation. Working-class youth were portrayed as passive victims of the selecting and sorting action of schools. A new orientation emerged to see "reproduction through resistance," where opposition to school by working class youth would be seen as a youthful expression of proletarian culture. The study of reproducing patterns of educational and social inequality becomes mitigated by the search for sources of contradiction, conflict, and resistance.

Foremost among these critics is the British sociologist Paul Willis. Though working within the Marxist tradition, Willis sharply criticizes those versions of social reproduction that stress structural determination, giving little attention to agency. His landmark work, *Learning to Labor* (1977), shifts the research focus from macrostatistical patterns to microethnographic observations. He studies a group of disaffected, white, working-class males in a British secondary school in order to understand how structural forces are mediated through cultural practices.

His study of working-class school boys identifies two distinct informal groups. The majority group, the "ear'oles," conform to school rules and norms and aspire to middle-class occupations much like Bowles and Gintis theorize for working- and middle-class groups. But a small nonconformist "counter-school culture" group of "lads" rejects school authority and ideals and actively seeks out every opportunity to "have a laff" by subverting teacher and administrator authority and mocking the ear'oles. They confront teachers, commit petty delinquency and truancy, smoke, fight, avoid school-work, drink, and swagger their sexual exploits.

Willis interprets these familiar expressions of student nonconformity as a form of class politics. On the one hand, their rejection of the school's achievement ideals shows profound insights, or "penetrations," into their limited upward mobility chances under capitalism. Because the lads understand that low-skilled work is unchallenging and only a few can hope to be upwardly mobile, conformism to school standards holds few rewards. Why sacrifice "a laff" for good behavior in school that will lead nowhere. School rebellion, therefore, embodies a submerged critique of capitalism.

On the other hand, this promising insight, which holds potential for generating class solidarity and collective action, is circumscribed by certain "limitations" in the lads' cultural outlook. The lads scoff at the mental labor of schooling, which they associate with the inferior status of femininity, and affirm manual labor, which they equate with masculinity. This antiintellectual and sexist outlook leads them to understand their entry into the dead-end, low-paying jobs of their fathers and brothers as a free, uncoerced choice rather than a form of class domination. And it cuts them off from the possibility of using critical thought as a tool of social transformation. Thus, the lads' nonconformist resistance to the achievement ideals of schooling ultimately contributes to the reproduction of the class structure by channelling working-class youth into working-class jobs.

McRobbie (1981), Apple and Weis (1985), and Weis (1990) offer a feminized version of the Willis argument by claiming that school opposition by working-class females is less aggressive as their "resistance" finds expression in romantic infatuation and exaggerated femininity. By contesting the model student idea this way, they unwittingly reproduce their class position by becoming housewives and unskilled employees.

These studies illustrate that reproduction occurs through the cultural mediation of agency and that ethnographic observation of the everyday cultural practices of individuals and small groups offers insight into the dynamics of reproduction not captured by macrolevel statistical analysis.

Building on the work of Willis and others, Henry Giroux (1983b) has emerged as an influential voice outlining a research program that would move reproduc-tion theory to resistance theory. Giroux's thinking is informed by critical Marxism. Giroux admits that not all student nonconformity embodies progressive politics, and he calls for researchers to dialectically relate agency and structure in ways that individual behaviors and interpretations are measured against structural constraints and a broader political project of human emancipation. Giroux, himself, however, has not tested his research program in any original research.

A landmark and original study by Jay MacLeod, *Ain't No Makin' It* (1995), insightfully synthesizes contributions from all the above theorists, particularly Bourdieu, to inform his ethnographic and participation observation study of two male teenage peer groups. He sees the reproduction process mediated through occupational aspirations that are shaped by a broad range of social and educational factors. His study testifies to the continued relevance of a social reproduction perspective that links ethnographic observation with structural opportunities, that examines youthful protest by situating actor behavior and interpretations within their broader context, and that takes into account other status factors like race.

More recently several of the key resistance theorists (Apple, 1989; Aronowitz and Giroux, 1991, 1993; Giroux and McLaren, 1989; Weis, 1990; Wexler, 1987)—including Willis (1990) himself—have assumed a "post-Marxist" position that extends the analysis beyond social class to include gender and race. The early social reproduction focus on class has been eclipsed by attention to the new social movements of feminism, environmentalism, antiracism, and gay liberation. Indeed, critical theory in the sociology of education has shifted from a social reproduction perspective in the early 1970s to resistance theory by the late 1970s and now to post-Marxist analysis (Davies, 1995).

Yet both resistance and post-Marxist theories share with the earlier social reproduction perspective a common lineage: the search for a source of agency that embodies the promise and capacity for generating broad-based social transformation. This has been perhaps the most enduring impact of the social reproduction perspective on critical thinking about education since the 1960s.

REFERENCES

Anyon, Jean. 1980. "Social Class and the Hidden Curriculum of Work." *Journal of Education* 162:67–92.

Apple, Michael W. 1979. *Ideology and Curriculum*. Boston: Routledge & Kegan Paul.

———, ed. 1982. *Cultural and Economic Reproduction in Education: Essays on Class, Ideology and the State*. London: Routledge & Kegan Paul.

———. 1989. "The Politics of Common Sense: Schooling, Populism and the New Right." In H. Giroux and P. McLaren (eds.), *Critical Pedagogy, the State, and Cultural Struggle*. Albany: State University of New York Press.

Apple, Michael W., and Lois Weis, eds. 1983. *Ideology and Practice in Schooling*. Philadelphia: Temple University Press.

———. 1985. "Ideology and Schooling: the Relationship Between Class and Culture." *Education and Society* 3:45–63.

Aronowitz, Stanley, and Henry Giroux. 1991. *Postmodern Education*. Minneapolis: University of Minnesota Press.

———. 1993. *Education Still under Siege,* 2nd ed. Toronto: OISE Press.

Bernstein, Basil. 1971. *Class, Codes and Control: Theoretical Studies towards a Sociology of Language*, 3 vols, Vol. 1. London: Routledge & Kegan Paul.

———. 1973. *Class, Codes and Control*, 3 vols, Vol. 2. London: Routledge and Kegan Paul.

———. 1975. *Class, Codes and Control: Towards a Theory of Educational Transmissions*, 3 vols, Vol. 3. London: Routledge & Kegan Paul.

Bourdieu, Pierre. 1973. "Cultural Reproduction and Social Reproduction." In R. Brown (ed.), *Knowledge, Education, and Cultural Change*. London: Tavistock.

———. 1984. *Distinction: A Social Critique of the Judgement of Taste*. Cambridge, MA: Harvard University Press.

———. 1988. *Homo Academicus*. Stanford: Stanford University Press.

———. 1996. *The State Nobility*. Stanford: Stanford University Press.

Bourdieu, Pierre, and Luc Boltanski. 1977. "Changes in Social Structure and Changes in the Demand for Education." In S. Giner and M. Scotford-Archer (eds.), *Contemporary Europe: Social Structures and Cultural Patterns*. London: Routledge and Kegan Paul.

Bourdieu, Pierre, and Jean-Claude Passeron. 1977. *Reproduction in Education, Society and Culture*. London: Sage.

———. 1979. *The Inheritors: French Students and Their Relation to Culture*. Chicago: The University of Chicago Press.

Bowles, Samuel, and Herbert Gintis. 1976. *Schooling in Capitalist America: Educational Reform and the Contradictions of Economic Life*. New York: Basic Books.

———. 1981. "Education as a Site of Contradictions in the Reproduction of the Capital-Labor Relationship: Second Thoughts on the 'Correspondence Principle'." *Economic and Industrial Democracy* 2:223–242.

Carnoy, Martin. 1974. *Education as Cultural Imperialism*. New York: McKay.

———. ed. 1975. *Schooling in a Corporate Society*. New York: McKay.

Carnoy, Martin, and Henry Levin, eds. 1976. *The Limits of Educational Reform*. New York: Longman.

———. 1985. *Schooling and Work in the Democratic State*. Stanford, CA: Stanford University Press.

Connell, Robert D., D. Ashendon, D. Kessler, and G. Dowsett. 1982. *Making the Difference*. Sydney: George Allen & Unwin.

Cookson, Peter W., Jr., and Caroline Hodges Persell. 1985. *Preparing for Power: America's Elite Boarding Schools*. New York: Basic Books.

Davies, Scott. 1995. "Leaps of Faith: Shifting Currents in Critical Sociology of Education." *American Journal of Sociology* 100(6):1448–1478.

DiMaggio, Paul. 1982. "Cultural Capital and School Success: The Impact of Status Culture Participation on the Grades of U.S. High School Students." *American Sociological Review* 47(2):189–201.

DiMaggio, Paul, and John Mohr. 1985. "Cultural Capital, Educational Attainment, and Marital Selection." *American Journal of Sociology* 90(6):1231–1261.

Dreeben, Robert. 1994. "The Sociology of Education: Its Development in the United States." *Research in Sociology of Education and Socialization* 10:7–52.

Durkheim, Emile. 1977. *The Evolution of Educational Thought*. London: Routledge & Kegan Paul.

Giroux, Henri. 1983a. *Theory and Resistance in Education: A Pedagogy for the Opposition*. New York: Bergin and Garvey.

———. 1983b. "Theories of Reproduction and Resistance in the New Sociology of Education." *Harvard Educational Review* 53(August):257–293.

Giroux, Henry, and Peter McLaren, eds. 1989. *Critical Pedagogy, the State, and Cultural Struggle*. Albany: State University of New York Press.

Katznelson, Ira, and Margaret Weir. 1985. *Schooling for All*. New York: Basic Books.

Lareau, Annette. 1989. *Home Advantage: Social Class and Parental Intervention in Elementary Education*. New York: Falmer Press.

MacLeod, Jay. 1995. *Ain't No Makin' It: Aspirations & Attainment in a Low-Income Neighborhood*. Revised and updated ed. Boulder, CO: Westview Press.

McRobbie, Angela. 1981. "Settling Accounts with Subcultures: A Feminist Critique." In T. Bennett, F. Martin, C. Mercer and J. Woollacott (eds.), *Culture, Ideology, and Social Process*. London: Open University Press.

Weis, Lois. 1990. *Working Class without Work: High School Students in a De-Industrializing Economy*. New York: Routledge.

Wexler, Philip. 1976. *The Sociology of Education: Beyond Equality*. Indianapolis, IN: Bobbs-Merrill.

———. 1987. *Social Analysis of Education: After the New Sociology*. London: Routledge & Kegan Paul.

Willis, Paul. 1977. *Learning to Labour: How Working-Class Kids Get Working-Class Jobs*. New York: Columbia University Press.

———. 1990. *Common Culture: Symbolic Work at Play in the Everyday Cultures of the Young*. Boulder, CO: Westview.

SOCIOLOGY OF EDUCATION AS CRITICAL THEORY[1]

Michael Young
University of London

Both social and natural scientists face preshaped worlds, though the forms that the preshaping take are fundamentally different. Whereas for the natural scientist, the preshaping consists of a combination of the conceptualizations of earlier scientists and the intrinsic structures of the physical and natural world itself, for the social scientist the preshaping is what makes reality social—the process by which people give meaning to their lives quite independently of social scientific theories, albeit, in circumstances only partly of their own choosing (to paraphrase Marx and Engels). It follows that though both natural and social sciences involve a dialogue among researchers, the social sciences have also to be a dialogue with the social world of which they are a part. Debates within the social sciences, therefore, are not just expressions of professional differences but of real conflicts in people's lives and purposes, however disconnected they may appear to be. Although often seen as a limitation on the status of social scientific knowledge, this difference between the natural and social sciences can equally be seen as a strength. To the extent that social scientists are engaged, at least in part, in similar sense-making activities to people in their everyday lives, the concepts they develop can, at least potentially, become resources for

practitioners, policymakers, and politicians in resolving conflicts and promoting values. On the other hand, it is never adequate for the social scientist to limit the testing of his or her ideas to the interpretations of colleagues. No less important is whether and in what sense those ideas become part of practice (and therefore of social reality in its wider sense).

It is this inescapable relationship with practice and policy that makes the social sciences critical, whether it is recognized by those who undertake the research or not. Sociology (and sociology of education), despite the various attempts to disguise it through methods and technical terms, and despite the many different senses in which it has claimed to be critical, is no exception to this argument. However, perhaps more than other subfields, the sociology of education has faced difficulties with its relationship to a specific institutional context—schooling; it is these difficulties that have, at least in part, led to its current state of crisis of role and identity. At present it appears torn between a laudable concern to expose the contradictions in the current government's attempts to privatize public education and a more pragmatic involvement in various kinds of policy analysis. The relatively coherent theoretical concerns of the 1970s and 1980s have largely disappeared—except in the fragmenting and ultimately incoherent forces of postmodernism (Green, 1994). Two aspects of the problem of sociology of education's boundedness to a specific institutional context can be distinguished; they might loosely be described as theoretical and practical. The theoretical aspect of boundedness for the sociology of education is expressed in the diversity of models of critique that have been adopted—phenomenological, Marxist, Frankfurt School critical theory, and the more recent feminist and postmodernist approaches. It is not

---

[1] This chapter is primarily a commentary on developments in the sociology of education in the United Kingdom. The sociology of education in the United Kingdom has had a unique history, both in its exponential growth in the late 1960s and 1970s, and its equally sharp demise in the 1980s. The analysis of developments in the United Kingdom might have lessons for other countries where sociology in general is more firmly established and sociology of education never took on the high profile that it had in the United Kingdom in the 1970s.

the intention of this chapter to review these various forms of critique, but to start from a particular view of the history of sociology of education itself.

Sociology of education as a critical theory arose in direct response to the expansion of state schooling and, in the United Kingdom, to its failure to develop as a democratic public system of education for all. Both sociology of education and schooling are aspects of modernization and the concept of critique associated with it is one that arises from a largely supportive view of state schooling as a democratic force, though one that has had and will continue to have contradictory and often antidemocratic outcomes. In developing the concept of reflexive modernization Ulrich Beck et al. (1994) provide a useful way of describing this notion of critique and the need to go beyond it. They make a distinction between two ways, reflection and reflexivity, in which the bases of modernization might be confronted with its consequences.

Whereas reflection describes the "increases in knowledge and scientization (and their impact) on modernization," reflexivity refers to the self-confrontation with the effects of risk society (Beck's description of modern industrial society) and in particular with its "autonomous modernization processes which are blind and deaf to their own effects and threats."

Linking Beck's distinction to the more limited concerns of the sociology of education, reflection is associated with the process of modernization and describes the links that were assumed between sociology of education and the improvement of mass schooling. Reflexivity and reflexive modernization, on the other hand, mean "self confrontation with the effects of risk society that cannot be dealt with and assimilated in the system of industrial society."

From the point of view of sociology of education and mass schooling, it follows that reflexivity as a form of critique has to start by recognizing that the problems with mass schooling cannot, as is assumed, for example, by the "school effectiveness movement," be dealt with by the schools alone. The failure of schools to give a high priority to the conditions for learning can be overcome only in a learning society that privileges learning relationships in sphere and sectors of society.

The practical aspect of the institutional boundedness of sociology of education is expressed in the fact that it has been largely located in the institutional context that has been its topic-formal education. Although ini-

tially and still, in some senses, a strength, this location has also been a weakness. It has been a strength because it has led to detailed knowledge about how educational institutions work and has prevented most sociologists of education from escaping into the more rarefied flights of theoretical and methodological abstraction that have characterized other subdisciplines. It has also been a weakness, because the critique of this boundedness has offered little more than the political polemics (capitalist schools must produce alienation) or the educational polemics (most notably in the deschooling arguments) of the 1970s or the theoretical pessimism of the 1990s. The latter view is exemplified in a recent paper by Moore (1996) who argues that it is important to distinguish between critical sociologies of education "which create knowledge about how education works" and what he calls sociologies for education.

Moore goes on to argue that until we have reformulated the project of a critical sociology of education "it is better for [it] to support schools in doing most effectively the things they can do best" (my italics). There is merit in Moore's argument that critical sociologists of education have tended to overestimate the capacity of schools to contribute to social transformation. However, in the mid-1990s, in a period of accelerating social and economic change in every sphere of life, it is increasingly difficult to be sure what the "things are that the schools can do best," in other words his prescription for the sociology of education appears peculiarly ahistorical and conservative. The disturbing consequence of such a view is that in renouncing any relationship between sociology of education and classroom practice, a free space is left that is quickly filled by highly undesirable and reactionary interventions.[2]

In considering in what sense sociology of education might be a critical theory, I want to develop two lines

---

[2] The two most highly publicized examples of such interventions in the United Kingdom have been the uncritical support for didactic "whole class" teaching by Chris Woodhead, the government-appointed Chief Inspector for schools, and the suggestions by David Hargreaves, Professor of Education at the University of Cambridge, in his address to the Teacher Training Agency (the government body that will, in the future, have responsibility for funding a significant proportion of educational research), that most educational research should be undertaken by classroom teachers, and geared to what he calls evidence-based research on ways of improving classroom teaching.

of argument; the first is to go back to the conditions of the emergence of sociology of education as a critical response to contradictions of mass schooling. I shall suggest that in the late 1990s the crisis in mass schooling has shifted from the problem of selection, which to some extent could be solved (and was solved) by more fundamental questions about the relationships among schools, colleges, and universities as specialized learning organizations and the changing society of which they are a part. It will therefore be around these issues that a critical sociology of education of the future must be established. My second line of argument, in disagreement with Moore, is that a sociology for education, in the sense that it provides concepts for teachers and other educational practitioners that may enable them to transform their practice, must be the basis for developing a theory of education that will produce reliable accounts of "how education works" and not just elaborated versions of educators' problems.

My aim in the remainder of this chapter, therefore, is first to comment briefly on a number of recent trends in educational policy in the United Kingdom that have created a crisis for the sociology of education and the deeper social changes that may underlie them. Second, I want to argue that these new circumstances and the crisis it has generated are both a danger and an opportunity for the sociology of education; I shall attempt to show that responding to the roots of the crisis can be a basis for going beyond the distinction between a sociology of education that claims to explain "how education works" but has no relation to teachers' practice and one that becomes trapped in their day-to-day professional concerns.

Learning beyond School: A Process of Structural Dedifferentiation?

The sociology of education was a response to the process of structural differentiation that led to the massive expansion of specialist educational institutions such as schools and colleges (Halsey, 1958). This process of structural differentiation, and the growth of specialized educational institutions, led to a number of distinct but related tensions, for example, those between sectors within increasingly differentiated education systems, those between the self-generated needs of education systems and their wider social role, and those reflecting

the conflicting educational demands of different social groups. It is in analyzing these tensions that sociology of education as a subdiscipline developed.[3] It formulated a critique of the instrumental and largely reproductive role of educational institutions in industrialized societies, the ideological role of state education, the socially selective and divisive role of many assessment, pedagogic, and curricula strategies and the biases in how schools have responded to the diversity of non-school cultures. However, it has remained a creature of the formal education system and has to a very large extent accepted as inevitable the structural differentiation into more specialist learning organizations that was the condition for its emergence.

However, it is just this process of structural differentiation into specialist educational institutions and the devaluing of the informal learning that goes on outside them that is beginning to be challenged by policy development of the past decade and in some of the recent educational policy debates. The most direct illustration is the way that fears about the costs of the ever increasing proportions of the population involved in postcompulsory education are leading governments to search for ways of shifting those costs; one strategy being adopted in the United Kingdom is to make it easier for people to obtain qualifications other than through formal schooling. This shift toward non-school-based learning is often associated with the claim, illusory or not, that information technology can improve access to learning as well as reduce costs. How-

[3] As my colleague David Guile pointed out to me, in its modernizing tendency and, in particular, its efforts to distance itself from the English Public (in fact they were private, exclusive, and fee paying) School tradition, English state education neglected what might be called the "hidden educational dimension" of the English public school that was so eloquently defended by Matthew Arnold. This refers to Arnold's emphasis on "intellectual apprenticeship" and the commitment to learning that he thought English Public Schools should instill in their pupils. The extent to which this vision was realized, even in the Public Schools, is doubtful; however, the concept of intellectual apprenticeship has a much broader significance in the context of creating conditions for lifelong learning. It was linked, in a way that also has wider significance, to the idea of the teacher-intellectual and the easy exchange that took place between teachers at Public Schools and "dons" at Oxford and Cambridge colleges.

ever, there are deeper changes at work in the global processes of production that point to the limitations of continued expansion of specialized learning and knowledge-producing institutions and to the need to shift opportunities for learning and knowledge production to a much wider range of sites not normally associated with either learning or knowledge production (Gibbons et al., 1994; Young and Guile, 1996).

Evidence of the beginning of what might be called "processes of dedifferentiation" away from specialist educational institutions takes a number of forms; I shall mention two trends. The first is the growing enthusiasm for reducing the distinctiveness of educational institutions by a variety of attempts to either privatize educational provision or force on it some kind of "market" or "business principles." This is found in some strands of the "school effectiveness movement," which accept the normality of accountability-led institutions supported by what gets called the "core technologies of teaching and learning." The contradiction in these developments is apparent when this notion of core technology as a way of expressing how teaching should be done is contrasted with the suggestions that come from those researching practical ways in which new technologies might be used to enhance classroom learning (Wood, 1993). This privatizing trend is also expressed in the succession of educational policies such as the Technical and Vocational Educational Education Initiative, Business Compacts, Education–Business Partnerships, and Enterprise in Higher Education, which have been designed to bring education and employment closer together. It is somewhat ironic that this trend is diametrically opposite to the one that established mass schooling in the nineteenth century with the Factory Acts and the first compulsory school leaving age and their aims of protecting children from commerce and industry. Are we so sure that industry and commerce are so different? In some ways these developments can be seen as examples of the way the United Kingdom is catching up, in its own peculiar way, with developments established long ago in the United States (Callaghan, 1972).

The second trend is the increasing emphasis on lifelong, work-based, and experiential learning, all forms of learning that take place outside institutions of formal education. The most successful private companies are seen to be becoming "learning organizations"; schools and colleges are encouraged to copy them, educational

policy documents stress learner centerdness and lifelong learning, and research programs are publicized as promoting a learning society.

All these developments can be seen as reflecting a shift from a policy of expanding the provision of formal education that began in the nineteenth century and took off as a worldwide phenomenon in many countries after World War II. More recent policies have involved limiting expansion of specialist educational organizations and trying to make existing educational organizations "more efficient" according to outcome-based performance indicators. Linked to the drive to make schools and colleges more efficient has been the promotion of the educational potential of "nonformal" contexts in which learning takes place, at least in theory, at no extra cost to government.

These "dedifferentiation processes" are not unique to formal education. Clear parallels can be seen in the closing of psychiatric hospitals and their replacement by community care policies in the health sector. However, it is not possible in this chapter to pursue these parallels further. One approach might be to challenge the new policies in relation to their claimed outcomes and argue that they need to be reversed and the expansionist approach to schooling continued. However, this would be to accept without question the progressive potential of mass schooling and institutional specialization more generally. In keeping with what I referred to earlier as a reflexively critical approach to modernization and its links with mass schooling, I shall suggest that these trends can be treated as an opportunity to "confront," in Beck's terms, the role of mass schooling and its future link with modernization. This will involve recognizing that specialist educational institutions and the categories associated with them such as curricula, examinations, textbooks, and classroom organization may not be an adequate focus of inquiry for a critical sociology of education in the future. Before taking this point further, I want to refer briefly to another linked trend that is changing the context within which sociology of education is located, the shift toward work-based initial and further teacher education.

The Rise and Fall of Sociology of Education in Educational Studies

The expansion and transformation of educational studies in universities have been critical to the development of the sociology of education, at least in the United Kingdom (Young, 1990). Educational Studies began as a largely prescriptive and philosophical foundation for preparing future teachers. However, in the 1960s there was a period of expansion of education at all levels and a belief that this expansion would be facilitated by an expansion of the role of the social sciences. It followed that a more research-oriented agenda formed the basis for programs of teacher education and the growth of sociology of education in educational studies was part of this diversification. As Karabel and Haley (1977) argued, it was the link with the professional education of teachers that shaped the development of sociology of education and it was this institutional basis in university departments of education (and teacher training colleges) that set sociology of education apart from other subdisciplines of sociology.

If you take the view that sociology is able to develop relatively "objective" knowledge about "how education works" within a disciplinary mode of knowledge production, then this professional location would appear as a limitation and likely to distract rather than support research. If, on the other hand, it is recognized that the perspectives of teachers are a major factor in "how education works" then the relationship between the knowledge generated in the sociology of education and the knowledge and attitudes of teachers becomes critical and the professional context becomes, at least in principle, not merely an advantage but a necessity. The involvement of the sociology of education with practitioners, both within teacher training programs and through teachers bringing their professional experiences to their higher degree studies, meant that sociology had a unique opportunity to relate theory and practice. Of course, in some cases, the sociologists "went native" and identified wholly with the professional and political concerns of teachers; however, it would be a mistake to see this as an inevitable outcome of either the institutional location of sociologists of education or their involvement with practical pedagogic issues.

From the latter half of the 1960s to the early 1980s, sociology of education drew on theoretical traditions that ranged from ethnomethodology and Marxism to Durkheim, Weber, and the various traditions of the sociology of knowledge and could lay some claim to be

a critical theory,[4] at least in the sense of challenging many of the dominant conceptions of education of the time. It certainly succeeded in generating angry responses from political and intellectual conservatives. They thought that it represented a challenge to the whole tradition of Western thought and would induce a kind of moral and intellectual relativism that could only make young teachers vulnerable to the "Trotskyist takeover" (Young, 1986). However, both kinds of conservatives were more naive than the student teachers of the time who invariably distinguished between the words of sociologists and the deeds of practicing teachers (Bartholomew, 1997). The Trotskyists were incapable of taking over anything and English educational traditions, for all their elitism and intellectual weaknesses, had survived far more serious challenges. A retrospective assessment would suggest that at the time with its links with professional practice, conditions for the sociology of education to become a critical theory were promising but that the theories were weak. A failure to grasp the contradiction of a sociology that needed to be both critical and supportive of mass education meant that the moment of critique collapsed into forms of political pessimism, cultural oppositionism, and relativism (depending on the different intellectual roots of the theory), and sociology of education failed to provide the concept of future possibilities that might have been the intellectual basis for any genuine educational transformation (Young, 1998).

From the beginning of the 1980s, opportunities for developing the sociology of education within university education departments declined steadily. This process reflected overt government prejudice ("there is no such thing as society" said Mrs. Thatcher, famously, and therefore, of course, no sociology or sociology of education), more practical and skills-oriented approaches to teacher education, and the increasingly inward looking theoretical approaches of the subdiscipline itself. The consequence has been that sociology of education has virtually disappeared from the initial training and further professional development of teachers. In the 1990s some sociologists of education have kept open the idea of a critical dialogue with government policy, especially that concerned with "marketization," and

---

[4] The criteria for a critical theory are a list developed in a highly preliminary discussion with Professor Richard Winter of Anglia Polytechnic University.

others have either given way to the new technicism of school effectiveness or become trapped in a theoretical pessimism that, as suggested earlier, appears to lead to similar consequences to giving up sociology of education altogether as a critical discipline.

This argument about the sociology of education is parallel to that made earlier in this chapter about the more general process of structural differentiation. The twin conditions of an expanding system of mass education and a confidence in the supportive role of the social sciences no longer exist. I want, therefore, to argue that if sociology of education is to make any claims to be a critical theory for the future, it needs to take as its starting points the new crisis in mass schooling as well as the skepticism about the social sciences and to see them as features of a more general crisis in the process of modernization itself. Before suggesting what this might involve, it is useful to consider a division within the subdiscipline that emerged in the conditions of the 1970s. It was in part a product of the specific location of the sociology of education in the United Kingdom in university education departments and was reflected in the tension between the theoretical demands of the subdiscipline and the practical demands of relating theories and findings to the problems facing teachers in schools and classrooms. The division took the form of differences in theoretical "focus" and in political "stance" and the tendency for "focus" to become separated from "stance," thus weakening the potential role of the sociology of education as critical theory.

The Sociology of Education: Differences of Focus and Differences of Stance

It was the rapid expansion of the social sciences in an education system uniquely dominated by social class relations that provided the conditions for the sociology of education to "take off" in the 1960s and 1970s in the United Kingdom, both as a research agenda and as a formative part of the curriculum of initial and further professional development of teachers. Sociology of education at this time was not just another addition to the teacher education curriculum-like history, psychology, or philosophy, of education. It also developed as a form of critical theory by challenging both the assumption that education needed to be seen as in some sense "a good thing" and that it could, in a capitalist society,

deliver on the claims made for it for more than a minority. However, within a broad concept of critique, the sociologists of education varied widely in their theoretical approach and in the political stance they adopted.

Two broad theoretical foci can be distinguished: a contextual focus on classroom practice that saw teachers as the main agent of educational transformation in what became known as the "new sociology of education" and a societal focus on the role of the state, as in the Marxist analyses of Bowles and Gintis (1976) and others that emphasized the priority of class struggle. With hindsight it is easy to see the theoretical weaknesses that were responsible for this division, for example, the overemphasis on the part of the "new sociologists of education" on the emancipatory role of teachers, as well as their neglect of the powerful intermediary actors (such as advisers, administrators, and head teachers) who might have provided the link between the role of teachers and wider structural forces. The major weakness of the structural Marxists was their failure to analyze how world capitalism was changing and how this was transforming the terms of educational struggles.

The location of most sociologists of education not only shaped their theoretical focus, it also shaped their view of the political role of their work. Two stances can be distinguished according to whether their main reference point was the subdiscipline (of sociology of education) or wider political struggles and social changes. The distinction between "intellectualist" and "politicist" stances used by Horton (1968) to describe the different stances of social anthropologists is also useful in distinguishing between the different stances in the sociology of education. It highlights the fact that in the United Kingdom in the 1970s sociologists tended to adopt an intellectualist rather than a politicist stance to theory. In other words the priority was placed on winning battles within the sociology struggles. It was not surprising, therefore, that there were endless intra-subdisciplinary debates and there is little doubt that such debates, which seemed so important at the time, held back the potential role of sociology of education as a critical theory.

This intellectualist stance that privileged sociological questions was important at the time, especially for those working in the education faculties of universities where the culture was often highly prescriptive and framed by unquestioned assumptions about education as a "good." However, there was an overemphasis on internal debates and a stress on the distinctiveness of a sociological approach that separated it from related disciplinary approaches such as history, economics, and psychology, and may account for why it became so vulnerable to political attack and institutional undermining from the beginning of the 1980s. The question for a critical sociology of education for the future is whether (and how), in the new circumstances of the 1990s, the divided foci and stances can be brought together. In the next section of this chapter, I shall suggest how these new circumstances are expressed in current educational trends away from specialized learning organizations such as schools, colleges, and universities.

A New Crisis in Mass Schooling: Conditions for Reconstructing a Critical Sociology for the Twenty-First Century?

Two current developments in educational policy have been referred to in this chapter: the recent emphasis on boosting nonformal learning contexts as exemplified in the growing popularity of ideas such as "the learning organization," a learning society, and lifelong learning (Young, 1995; Young and Guile, 1996) and the attempts to shift teacher education away from universities and to define it according to competency criteria. In the next two sections I shall consider these trends away from specialist learning organizations, before returning to the changes in teacher education.

Earlier in this chapter, I pointed to the origins of the sociology of education in the process of modernization and in particular its links with the contradictions associated with growth of mass schooling. This link was exemplified in its concern, in the United Kingdom, with the social class basis of selection of students and (later) of curriculum knowledge and how these processes of selection were extended from social class to other sources of inequality such as gender and race. Though these contradictions still remain, the circumstances within which they are located have changed. The role of public education itself is under challenge as is the set of values that has, since the nineteenth century, linked science, modernization, progress, and mass schooling. Under the guise of efficiency, investment and current expenditure on public education are being reduced, and within the rhetoric of

choice, anything above a minimum of provision is seen as something people should be encouraged to buy (or not) as a choice. In other words, expanding public education for all is seen, by those with the resources to purchase private school education for their children, as too expensive—and perhaps even too democratic—another ironic return to the nineteenth century!

Sociology of education, therefore, if it is to play a role as critical theory in the next decade, has to relocate itself in this new crisis facing public education and, more generally, in the crisis facing modernization itself. The trends that I have referred to as "dedifferentiation" could have two outcomes. One possibility is that they could be a basis for new forms of contraction, as those in positions of power and influence ensure the future of their own children through a private or quasi-private provision and educational version of what Hutton (1995) has called the 30:30:40 society. In such a scenario, it is difficult to see other than continuing decline and loss of influence for the sociology of education.

The alternative is to respond to the crisis of mass education at a more fundamental level as a crisis in learning and in the production of knowledge. Before elaborating on the possible implications of this alternative for the sociology of education, I shall, in the next section, deal briefly with both the processes of "dedifferentiation" of learning and knowledge production and the broader trends that underlie them.

Beyond Specialized Learning Organizations

The recent interest in experiential and work-based learning and in the educational role of nonspecialist learning organizations reflects deep changes in industrial societies. In the short term this interest reflects attempts to find ways of reducing the growing costs of public formal education as the proportion of the population participating continues to expand. In the longer term it highlights two problems for the older industrialized societies as they face increasing global economic competition. The first problem is what Muller (1996) refers to as the "increasing saliency of knowledge." This arises from the progressive shift away from natural to human resources as the main determinant of a nation's economic prosperity, and from the increasingly short life of new knowledge as it becomes more and more a part of the process of continuous innovation.

Mass formal education, as it has expanded from its nineteenth-century beginnings, is not well suited to the new "saliency" of knowledge. Its modes of knowledge production, which are based on a separation of the production of knowledge from its use and are symbolized by the academic disciplines, are slow (albeit reliable), exclusive, and not easily related directly to external demands. The "knowledge" issue then is expressed in the future of disciplinarity, which has been the bedrock of the growth of science since the nineteenth century and one of the distinguishing features of both the university and the upper secondary school curriculum in every country in the world.

Gibbons and his colleagues (1995) point to the recent emergence of Mode 2 (or transdisciplinary knowledge) where discipline-based scientists form partnerships with business and community groups to produce knowledge related to specific problems. The demise of the university's monopoly on the production of knowledge that is indicated by the emergency of transdisciplinary knowledge creates a new set of conflicts. For example, there are conflicts between the "conservative" academics who want to preserve the disciplinary mode of knowledge production (Gibbons et al.'s Mode 1) and their autonomy, which they see as depending on it, and governments and business who want to steer knowledge production to commercial or industrial ends (Gibbons et al.'s Mode 2).

Is this a shift in the form that modernization is likely to take in the future or is it a sign of the limits of science as a peer group-dominated activity? Should the move toward Mode 2 knowledge production be resisted or encouraged? It is in addressing these questions that a critical sociology of education could be vital. Instead of joining the industrial modernizers or their opponents, the unlikely groupings of conservative and postmodernist academics, the weakness of both positions needs to be analyzed.

Whereas the first group appears willing to allow all intellectual activity supported by public funds accountable to the demands of commerce and industry, the latter treat disciplinarity, a particular historical mode of knowledge production, as an almost universal condition for the creation of new knowledge. The alternative is to explore new relationships between disciplinary and transdisciplinary knowledge and between theory and practice as well as their implications for the role of public education in the twenty-first century and

its relationships with industry, commerce, and the community.

Just as one of the primary purposes of modern universities is the production of new knowledge, they also, together with schools and colleges, have a key pedagogic function; they are, of course, organizations that specialize in developing systematic learning programs. However, most programs have changed little in their structure in the last century and rely on the assumption that learning is a largely individualized process of transmission; they neglect that learning is fundamentally a social process.

This neglect has led to a number of problems that underlie the crisis in mass education. First, because the social conditions for learning are neglected, more and more educational institutions get trapped in the logic of selection, i.e., trying to choose pupils that they think will succeed. One response to government by the current government is it should have more control over selection and thus avoid responsibility for the lower quartiles of the student population. As Bourdieu has argued so cogently, schools are most successful with those who they do not have to teach how to learn, those who have developed that skill elsewhere, usually in the home. Nonlearners or slow learners are treated in various ways as "ineducable," for instance, by being offered special so-called prevocational courses that, in practice, do not lead anywhere.

The crisis of mass schooling is that schools cannot tackle the problem of learning despite the fact that modern societies need all of their citizens to be learners far more urgently than those of previous eras. The second problem with specialist learning organizations is that though they prepare students with knowledge (and even skills), they rarely develop the skills and motivation to continue to learn after they have left school or college.

Learning has traditionally been neglected by sociologists of education except by those in the symbolic interactionist tradition. However, as a research topic, it is no more or less social than any of the other social practices that have been topics for sociological research and theory; learning is, despite much educational psychology, about social relationships and participating in different types of community. The American social anthropologist, Jean Lave, has developed an approach to learning as participation in a "community of practice" (Lave, 1993). The advantage of starting from such a basic definition drawn from anthropological studies is first that it is not "school-centric" and avoids associating learning with formal teaching, and second, that unlike much recent work in adult education, it does not equate learning with individual access (Young, 1995). It does not preclude the possibility that planned pedagogy and systematically organized curricula can assist learning; it merely points out that there is a prior process at the basis of any successful learning.

Another advantage of such a perspective on learning is that it gives priority to learning as a form of social participation, not as in school-centric approaches, as a form of social selection. Lave employs the concept of "legitimate peripheral participation" to show the way that newcomers need to learn from more experienced members of the community, thus giving priority to a view of learning as a social process, whether it takes place in a school or not.

The danger of a perspective that starts from social participation is that it plays down the importance of what is learned, the question that lies at the heart of the justification of formal schooling. The issue, therefore, is not to polarize formal/informal or school/nonschool centric learning as good or bad, as was a feature of some of the debates in the 1970s inspired by the deschooling literature. It is to explore the diverse forms of "community of practice" both within and external to specialist learning organizations and the extent to which they create or inhibit opportunities for what the Finnish researcher, Engestrom (1991), calls "expanded learning."

Having shown albeit briefly, why knowledge and learning have arisen as the major issues in the current crisis in schooling, the final section of the chapter turns to the question of the role of the university (and therefore of any disciplinary knowledge such as the sociology of education) in teacher education.

The Reprofessionalization of Teachers

The 1960s and the 1970s saw the progressive upgrading and expansion of teacher education in the United Kingdom from 2-year to 3- and 4-year courses. An increasingly graduate profession and the growing number of teachers obtaining Master's degrees in Education were all signs of this trend. Student teachers were encouraged to be critical of educational institutions as well as to become competent practitioners. Why did

this process come to a halt? Two developments, I suggest, were important; first, teachers and university education departments became victims of a more general government attack on the professions as vested interests, and second, there was a growing awareness that student teachers were not developing the knowledge and skills that they needed for the increasingly complex problems that they faced in the classroom. The fusion of these two developments was unfortunate; the politically inspired attack on university-based teacher education meant that a radical reassessment of the relations between theory and practice in teacher education was avoided; teacher training programs followed an increasingly narrow competence route on the basis of a fragmented and mechanical view of learning and a highly oversimplified view of a teacher's core tasks.

At its most extreme, the attack on teacher education was expressed in the view that teachers needed no professional education. It was argued by some on the Political Right that they could learn better on the job and from older teachers, and that the best sites for a teacher's initial education were the schools themselves, unencumbered by "useless" theory, and closely in touch with the real classroom skills that the beginning teachers need to develop. The excesses of the opposition to university-based teacher education seems to be avoided by new Teacher Training Agency; however, its proposals for identifying competence levels at a teacher's different career stages do not appear congruent with the increasingly complex demands made on teachers at all stages of their careers.

The demise of disciplinary knowledge in teacher education was part of a more general demand referred to earlier for more "immediate and relevant knowledge"; in this case the demand related specifically to classroom practice. However, the attempt to replace knowledge with skills failed to recognize that the problem of relevance is not just one of content or about skills versus knowledge; it is a question of the relationships between universities and the schools and between the different kinds of knowledge generated in the two contexts. Universities generate knowledge about education that relates to general principles and trends, but not to specific contexts, even when it arises from research that takes place in classrooms. Educational knowledge generated from professional experience relates to individual pupils and aspects of the curriculum as it is experienced in specific schools, though it may have wider relevance. In the 1980s and the 1990s, the trend was to drop the disciplinary knowledge but to create opportunities for interrogating it from the point of view of teachers' "professional" knowledge and vice versa. Educational research and the professional education of teachers are both dialogues between theory and practice, albeit with different but complementary purposes.

The tendency to place more and more responsibility for decision making onto individual schools and colleges will not be reversed. This means that senior staff are going to need to draw on the expertise of all their staff, even those at the beginning of their careers. These wider demands that are being placed on teachers mean that their initial professional education will need to be broader rather than narrower and schools will have to give more emphasis on the further professional development of their staff. This does not suggest a return of specialist higher degrees in the sociology of education that flourished in the 1970s. However, it is difficult to see programs that respond seriously to the new demands on teachers that do not contain a considerable core of sociology of education.

Conclusion: Sociology of Education for a Learning Society

Sociology of education began as a form of critical theory-raising questions about one of the major institutions of modern societies—mass education, and the extent to which, at least in the United Kingdom, it has been in decline since the 1980s, largely through a changed political climate and the collapse of much of its external support and funding, though its own internal tensions have played a part. I have argued that in the 1990s, in the context of a number of new developments in educational policy that have been oriented to developing learning outside the institutional context of formal schooling, the sociology of education is at a crossroads of opportunity.

Increasing global economic competitiveness has created deep problems in the educational institutions of all industrialized societies, perhaps especially those in a country such as the United Kingdom in which so much depends on tradition and social class divisions. These problems, in particular the failure to extend the motivation and skill to learn and the capacity to produce new knowledge beyond a small elite, are partly

recognized by government whose audits at least bring the urgency of the problem into public debate. Their "solutions" to the problem, however, appear more influenced by political dogma than any kind of educational knowledge and rely on the old "technologies" of school effectiveness and didactic approaches to whole class teaching that completely negate the fact that learning is about social participation. It is in relation to this crisis in public education that I have suggested sociology of education must locate itself as a critical theory for the future.

By conceptualizing education as linking learning to the production of knowledge but not restricting either process to specialist institutional forms, a critical sociology can point to a future for schools and learning-oriented society. Such a perspective includes the main elements of a critical theory in that it has a concept of the future and of education in relation to the whole society, has a political purpose associated with realizing the emancipatory potential of learning for all people throughout their lives, represents a constructive critique of current provision and practice, and is reflexive in the sense of recognizing that the process of modernization, and mass schooling as one of its key institutions, is, to return to Beck, "Blind and deaf to their own effects and threats."

It could, therefore, be a basis for tackling the major educational challenges that the United Kingdom faces if it is to give any reality to the idea of becoming a learning society. There are five challenges:

1. how to reflect on the unintended consequences of the new crisis in schooling and the shift toward nonformal learning and, in particular, the new forms of stratification to which it could give rise;
2. how to incorporate the concept of learning as social participation into the social organization of schools, colleges, and universities;
3. how to maximize the potential of information technology for supporting higher level learning when the findings of research on information technology and learning appear in increasingly stark contrast to the educational policies of both government and opposition;
4. how to respond to the crisis in disciplinarity as the dominant mode not only of the production of new knowledge but of how young learners are initiated into forms of specialization; and

5. how to explore the relationships between institutional and noninstitutional learning and their relationship to links between theory and practice in the context of the emerging learning society (Antikainen et al., 1996).

Acknowledgment

I would like to thank my colleague David Guild for his most helpful and constructive comments on earlier drafts of this chapter.

REFERENCES

Antikainen, A., J. Houtsonen, J. Kauppila, and H. Huotelin. 1996. *Living in a Learning Society*. London: Routledge-Falmer.

Bartholomew, J. 1997. "The Schooling of Teachers: The Myth of the Liberal College." In G. Whitty and M. Young (eds.), *Explorations in the Politics of School Knowledge*. Nafferton Books.

Beck, U., A. Giddens, and S. Lasho. 1994. *Reflexive Modernization: Politics, Tradition and Aesthetics in the Modern Social Order*. Oxford: Polity Press.

Bowles, S., and H. Gintis. 1976. *Schooling in Capitalist America*. New York: Basic Books.

Callahan, R. 1972. *Education and the Cult of Efficiency*. Stanford: Stanford University Press.

Engestrom, Y. 1991. " 'Non Scholae sed Vitae Discimus': Toward Overcoming the Encapsulation of School Learning." *Learning and Instruction* 1(3):243–259.

Gibbons, M., C. Limoges, H. Nowotny, S. Schwartzman, P. Scott, and M. Trow. 1994. *The New Production of Knowledge*. London: Sage.

Green, A. 1994. "Post Modernism and Educational Policy." *Journal of Educational Policy* 9(1):67.

Halsey, A. H. 1958. "Trend Report: Sociology of Education." *Current Sociology* 6.

Horton, R. 1968. *Neo-Tylorianism: Sound Sense or Sinister Prejudice*. Man (NS), 3.

Hutton, W. 1995. *The State We Are In*. London: Vintage Books.

Karabel, J., and A. H. Halsey. 1977. *Power and Ideology in Education*. Oxford: Oxford University Press.

Lave, J. 1993. "The Practice of Learning." In S. Chaiklen, and J. Lave (eds.), *Understanding Practice*. Cambridge, UK: Cambridge University Press.

Moore, R. 1996. "Back to the Future: The Problem of Change and the Possibilities of Advance in the Sociology of Education." *British Sociology of Education* 17(2):145–161.

Muller, J. 1996. "The Making of Knowledge." Paper presented at a conference on the future of higher education in South Africa, Capetown, February. In *Reclaiming Knowledge: Social Theory, Curriculum and Education Policy*. London, UK: RoutledgeFalmer.

Wood, D. 1993. "The Classroom of 2015." National Commission Briefing Paper No. 20.

Young, M. 1986. "Education." In P. Worsley (ed.) *The New Introducing Sociology*. Harmondsworth, UK: Penguin Books.

———. 1990. "Bridging the Theory/Practice Divide: An Old Problem in a New Context." *Educational and Child Psychology* 7(3).

———. 1995. "Post Compulsory Education for Learning Society." *Australian and New Zealand Journal of Vocational Education Research* 3(1).

———. 1998. "The Curriculum and the New Sociology of Education." In M. Young, *The Curriculum of the Future*. London, UK: RoutledgeFalmer.

Young, M., and D. Guile. 1996. "Knowledge and Learning in Specialist and Nonspecialist Learning Organizations." Paper presented to the ECLOS (European Conference of Learning Organizations), Copenhagen, May.

Sociology of Education

FEMINIST PERSPECTIVES: CONTINUITY AND CONTESTATION IN THE FIELD

Jo-Anne Dillabough
University of Toronto

Madeleine Arnot
University of Cambridge, England

Every arena and level of social life is shot through with gender hierarchy and gender struggle. Each therefore requires feminist theorization. Each, however, is also traversed by other intersecting axes of stratification and power, including class, "race"/ethnicity, sexuality, nationality, and age—a fact that vastly complicates the feminist project. Although gender dominance is ubiquitous, in sum, it takes different forms at different junctures and sites, and its character varies for differently situated women. (Nicholson, 1995:159).

Nicholson (1995), in articulating her concerns about "gender dominance" and its link to the feminist project, speaks indirectly to the importance of unification in defining feminist movements. At the same time, her remarks imply that any such "unification" must be interpreted flexibly since perspectives on the cause(s) of women's oppression not only depend upon epistemological positions taken up through academic experience, but on the personal experience of those who, as Butler (1995:49) argues, "make claims in the name of women." Such concerns with theoretical interpretation and the contradictions that manifest themselves in feminist thinking (e.g., unification versus unique standpoint) are not new, yet what makes them interesting is their expression in contrasting feminist forms and their resonance in different disciplines. Our task in the present chapter is to track such feminist expres-

sions and their diverse forms in the sociology of education[1].

Broadly speaking, in this chapter we map diverse feminist theoretical perspectives and their impact on educational analyses within the "sociology of education." We also highlight the contemporary issues that have emerged as a result of such analyses. We are well aware of the unpopularity of, and problems associated with, such "mapping exercises" (see Middleton, 1993).[2] However, it is our belief that readers must have access to the "constructed" histories of a field, in particular, its "contents" and links to the study of education. Capturing the essence of this history and its contemporary representations is essential to the formulation of new perspectives on the study of gender in education. However, in qualifying the nature of our task, it must be said that we treat this account as one story about gender and education that, like all other stories, is open to "further deconstruction" (Norris, 1982).

The Development of Gender in Education as a Field of Study

One of the first sociological attempts in the United Kingdom to view gender as a theoretical construct was the work of Ann Oakley (1972). She argued that if gender, as opposed to sex, was a social category then it could be applied to the study of socialization and society, not just sex differences. Oakley's (1972) work

---

[1] It must be said at the outset that feminism is an international development. Here we draw upon traditions that were developed primarily (although not exclusively) in liberal democratic societies and/or Western European cultures. These traditions are linked to the civil rights movements and liberal democratic developments in the postwar era.

[2] We are aware that in drawing up such a map, theorists may become dislocated from their original intentions. We are also aware, all too acutely, that many theorists shift their positions over time, engage in border crossing, and are not easily located on any sort of map.

therefore set the tone for developing the concept of "gender" as analytically, as well as politically, preferable to the concept of "sex" (i.e., biological distinctions between men and women) in sociological analyses of gender in education.

Two key texts illustrated the direction that such a gendered analysis of education could go. Eileen Byrne's (1978) book, *Women and Education*, was the first to document the myriad ways in which sexual discrimination manifested itself in the U.K. education system. This publication, along with Rosemary Deem's (1978) *Women and Schooling*, set a political agenda that was designed to expose those aspects of schooling that served to perpetuate injustices faced by girls and women in society. This case was supported, in many contexts, by drawing upon an examination of the relationship between "patriarchy" and educational access.

Soon to follow these early initiatives was the work of Michelle Barrett (1980), which described the relationship between girls' education and capitalism, and Dale Spender's (1980[3]) polemical account of the "patriarchal paradigm of education." In these early feminist initiatives, novel political themes such as girls' "oppression," "female exploitation," and "male domination" gained recognition as important sociological issues to be tackled in educational theory. More significantly, they were drawn upon as conceptual tools for examining the "gendered" structure of British schooling. As a consequence, the sociological study of education in the United Kingdom was broadened considerably by feminist initiatives.

A series of texts also set the terrain for the development of diverse feminist traditions in the sociology of education. The first collection was Rosemary Deem's (1980) *Schooling for Women's Work*, which pointed to the importance of examining gender issues within the context of classrooms, curricula, and schools. The second text, entitled *State, Family and Education* (David, 1980), set the tone for feminist policy research by identifying important links among the goals of educational policy, male domination in society, and a capitalist economy. The third text, *Class, Gender and Education* (Barton and Walker, 1980), responded to such concerns within Marxist feminism, emphasizing the relationship between the marginal positioning of working-class

women in society and the interdependence of class and gender relations in education. Each of these texts was crucial in defining the theoretical and empirical parameters of the field. Arguably, then, the most important landmark by 1980 was the notion of gender as an analytical construct and an emphasis on the relationship between the state and the economy in the study of gender in education. The outcome of this work is a body of scholarship now commonly identified as the "sociology of women's education" (Arnot, 1985).

These early feminist pursuits aimed to develop a sociological theory of schooling that formalized how education functioned as a political instrument of the state, governed largely by men. As will be seen, the theoretical frames that emerged from this early work emphasized *continuity* over that of *change* (i.e., the consistency of gender relations, the unchanging nature of male domination rather than its diverse gender formations). The theoretical premises supporting such notions were tied primarily to structural functionalism (i.e., Parsonian theories of socialization), Durkheim's moral perspective on society, or Marxist insights on economic formations (Lovell, 1990).

In drawing upon the "European structuralist tradition" (see Sadovnik, 1995) and the concerns of women in society, feminist sociologists became one of the first academic communities to challenge microlevel thinking in education (i.e., the obsession with individualism), arguing for a broader theoretical frame through which to examine the manifestation of gender in educational environments. For example, much early feminist educational research focused upon the study of individuals with little or no reference to social context (e.g., educational psychology), drawing upon empirical traditions in the natural sciences (e.g., the scientific method). By contrast, feminist sociologists have tended to study gender from a critical perspective (e.g., critical ethnography), drawing upon theoretical concerns that address the relationship between human agency and social structure. This attempt to grapple with the conceptual dilemmas that emerge by confronting the relationship between structure and agency in feminist theory has led to greater understanding of the interdependence of micro- and macrosocial forces in the development of society, and the reproduction of gender inequity in schools (Connell, 1987).

In short, much of the work that followed these early

---

[3] See also Spender (1982, 1987).

feminists was an attempt to establish a new agenda in sociology[4] (MacDonald, 1980; Arnot, 1982). However, it was also an attempt to conquer the very real problems women were confronting as "lived experience" in many national educational contexts (Weiner, 1994). This concern with "lived experience" is particularly important, since unlike feminist theorizing in the humanities, it was directly linked to educational practitioners (teachers, lecturers) and their knowledge about gender. Therefore, a strong dialectical relationship was said to exist between educational policy and academic research, and theory and practice. Nowhere in feminist studies has the principle that feminism is not only *about* women, but *for* women, been more relevant. These dialectical relationships, ethical principles, and lived experiences form the foundation of feminist theorizing in education.[5]

Twenty years ago it was a relatively simple task to outline, in conceptual form, feminist theories of education. We do not wish, however, to suggest that such simplicity always be viewed as positive. Indeed, many feminists did not identify with mainstream feminist thought and argued that this very simplicity failed to radically improve women's status in education and society (e.g., Brah and Minhas, 1985; Ellsworth, 1989). They also argued that early feminist movements were middle class and did not speak for (or about) women on the margins (e.g., culturally oppressed women). As a consequence, feminist debates moved beyond their traditional origins. Today, there are numerous "feminism(s) in education" (Weiner, 1994). Many of these new positions derive from the expression of political identities (e.g., lesbian women) in both society and the academy, and interdisciplinary theoretical work in the social sciences. In contrast to second wave theorizing, these new forms, which we call *relational*,[6] tend to em-

phasize *change* (e.g., shifting gender identities) over that of gender continuities. Each of these research traditions takes divergent yet sometimes overlapping approaches to the question of gender of education. The theoretical and empirical questions that are posed in relational accounts may also overlap in the sense that they may address similar phenomenon while deriving their rationale from often incommensurable theoretical explanations.

The Framework of the Chapter

In an effort to locate feminist thinking within the realm of theory, we draw upon the work of Bob Connell. In a book entitled *Gender and Power*, Connell (1987) argues that positions on gender are more easily understood when sorted on some level, particularly in relation to their explanatory frameworks and use of theoretical concepts. Two such theoretical distinctions made by Connell (1987) that are particularly useful in drawing our own map of feminist sociology in education are *intrinsic* and *extrinsic* theories.

Intrinsic theories are those that explain how *concrete* (rather than shifting) notions of gender in society come into being. Such theoretical formulations tend to focus on instrumental rationality and custom and, for example, the impact of intraindividual factors (e.g., self-esteem, sex differences) on the nature of gender roles in society. Extrinsic theories, on the other hand, focus on the social and/or class-based nature of *power* relations in the polity. State structures, relations of production, and the gendered nature of the public sphere all figure in the ways in which gender is understood in education from an extrinsic perspective.

In our view, both types of theory (intrinsic and extrinsic) reside in a category we identify as *rationalistic*, since they either explain women's oppression on the basis of the authority of reason (e.g., quantitative analyses of women's status in higher education) or on a corresponding theory of rationalism. This type of feminist theorizing, despite popular belief, charts linear relations between women's oppression and what are often described as "rationally" determined and deliberately controlled social structures.

We contrast such rationalistic theories to those that are *relational* (see Luke, 1989). These theoretical positions are most commonly (but not exclusively) accorded

---

[4] This work was located predominantly, but not exclusively, in sociology.

[5] The study of gender is not strictly sociological. Rather, it is an interdisciplinary project in which sociology plays a key role in understanding the social aspects of gender.

[6] Other feminist theorists have used the term relational to refer to, for example, forms of feminine expression (Gilligan, 1986) that are articulated through the use of particular methods (e.g., life history). We do not use relational in this sense. Instead, we use it as an overarching term that, broadly speaking, characterizes the nature of many new feminisms in education. This issue will be addressed later in the chapter.

the term postmodern or poststructural, yet they are not theories in the traditional sense. Rather, they are conceptual frameworks that serve to break down theoretical foundations and map a particular set of power relations that leads to "local" understandings of gender in education. They also attempt to capture the shifting nature of gender (as embedded in the power of language) rather than merely charting universal laws about women's experience in the broadest sense. Each of these theoretical distinctions will be discussed in the following sections.

Rationalistic Epistemologies and the Question of "Gender" in Education

An Intrinsic Approach: Liberal Feminist Theory

Liberal feminist thought in education is perhaps best described through the use of metaphor. The metaphor we draw upon is that of the "sword," which carries with it the marks of both honor and defeat. In the name of honor, liberal feminism has paved the way for the recognition of equality of opportunity issues in schools and forced many national governments to be accountable to women and their educational needs. Unfortunately, however, in the name of defeat, it has taken on the liberation project without assessing its underlying ideological foundation (i.e., political liberalism). Indeed, as many critiques of liberal feminism demonstrate, such a metaphor bears the mark of male thought expressed most deliberately through enlightenment ideals. As such, critics of liberalism have argued that liberal feminism cannot be a true feminist form since it is bound by an eighteenth-century notion of the "self" as masculine (see Pateman, 1992). This aspect of liberal feminist theory can therefore be construed as the dark side of the sword. The complicated part of the metaphor emerges when we consider what has been gained when thinking about what constitutes "honor" in society and its implications for women. We hope that an illustration of this notion will emerge in the following description of liberal feminist theory.

The historical roots of liberal feminism lie in the conception of equal rights for women in the eighteenth century. One of its earliest proponents was Mary Wollstencraft (1992, first published in 1792) who wrote *A Vindication of the Rights of Women*. She argued that women, like men, are capable of reason and therefore possess the right to be educated to their full capacities. Central to such campaigns is the belief that men and women should receive similar, if not, identical forms of education. This notion of *equal* education for boys and girls has formed the foundation of a two-tiered liberal feminist philosophy of education in the broadest sense. The top tier represents a vision of women as rational beings (i.e., honorable women), hence educable. The bottom tier represents a vision of society as equal, as democratic.

The theoretical assumptions that form the foundation of these campaigns in education can be summarized generally as follows: (1) respect for women's rights in education is sacrosanct; (2) individual autonomy, opportunity, and choice in education are central to women's self-improvement (Whelahan, 1995); and (3) political equality in schools must be viewed as equal access to school subjects and representation in democratic institutions. These female entitlements are to be achieved through various procedural forms of competition in an open school environment. Therefore, the long-term goal of feminism here is to empower women to take up their rightful place in this "open" system through the development of female autonomy. The key issue is the support of freedom, of play, of subject, and occupational choice, that is, the removal of barriers as an individual right in a democratic society. Education is therefore seen as essentially neutral, once removed of the forms of prejudice and discrimination that impede women's progress in society.

Examples of educational research that have supported the liberal feminist imperative include, for example, the study of sex roles (Delamont, 1980) and sex differences (MacCoby and Jacklin, 1974), the relationship between teachers' expectations and girls' occupational choice, and the study of girls' self-esteem and gender subject preferences (Kelly, 1982). Much of this early research was guided by rationalistic conceptions of truth seeking and objectivity, drawing upon formal quantitative methods such as self-esteem scales, student response checklists, and questionnaires. However, liberal feminist theory has developed over time, becoming more aware of diverse contextual factors that influence male and female responses to their socialization. As a result, more recent research within the liberal tradition has drawn upon qualitative research methods (see Measor and Sikes, 1992). This more recent work has exposed the many barriers to educational access for women in liberal democratic society. Such work has also contributed to what Connell (1987) describes as "the formidable politics of access" in education and has, rather paradoxically, provided a somewhat radical edge to the study of liberal establishments (of which education was one).

Problems with/Contradictions in Liberal Feminist Theory

Despite the advances made by liberal feminists, its problems are numerous. For example, within a liberal feminist model of education, visions of society are equated with individualism and gendered behavior is not linked to school structure (Middleton, 1993). Instead, it is left to women (as individuals) to take up educational opportunities that are created and then monitored by agents of the state. As a result, the school structures in which such opportunities emerge are not critiqued for masculine bias and their ideological basis remains unexposed (Whelehan, 1995). A whole aspect of education is therefore ignored in determining gender inequity—that being the political and economic structures and forms of *power* that constrain one's agency in struggling for social change in education.

A related problem emerges when the relationship between liberal feminist ideals, human agency, and notions of "opportunity" embodied in liberal capitalist ideology is considered. For example, women's struggle for liberation and equality, thought to be achieved through instrumental action, is, by definition, an activity that ultimately forces women to act politically on behalf of themselves. Not only does this view leave men complicit, but it fails to consider the reality that many women cannot be as vocal (or active) in the struggle for opportunity. More significantly, little is learned about the ways in which such an opportunity structure in education suppresses the diverse life experiences of, for example, ethnic minority girls. Consequently, under liberal feminism, notions of political community (e.g., identity politics) and culturally oppressed women's perspectives are lost.

Such tendencies within sociology are identified as gender "essentialisms" (see Roman, 1992), which focus on issues intrinsic to women such as the improvement of one's self-esteem. Women, in such a context, are thought to be a "category"—and to borrow from But-

ler (1995)—a "subject" about which society speaks. Within such a discourse, gender, as a constructed notion, is incontestable.

Extrinsic Approaches to the Study of Gender and Education

Feminist critiques of liberal theory are seen by many (e.g., Whelahan, 1995) as the starting point for the development of a cluster of sociologically driven feminist theories of education. Because the primary criticism of liberal feminism is the absence of a concept of power, it naturally follows that "oppositional" modernist theories identify power (usually state power) as central to women's oppression in education. What varies among these perspectives, however, is the manner in which power is defined.

Connell (1987) refers to theories that focus primarily on abstract forms of state power, collective notions of power as expressed in symbolic (yet concrete) forms of the civil society (e.g., Durkheimian/Marxist perspectives), or power that resides outside a women's control as *extrinsic*. Under the heading *extrinsic*, we discuss three feminist theories of education: radical, maternal, and socialist feminism.[7]

Radical Feminism

Broadly speaking, radical feminist theorizing has attempted to address the problem that liberal feminism in education has created—that is, "merely adding" women to a masculine schooling agenda that, as Middleton (1993) suggests, is at its very core unjust. Drawing heavily upon the politics of popular feminism and feminist social movements in the 1970s and early 1980s, the goal of radical feminism has been to expose the various forms of male domination in education. The "conceptual device"[8] used to challenge male domination is "patriarchy."

In extending its reach beyond education, popular feminists in both the United Kingdom and America have been influential in determining the coherency and structure of the radical feminist argument. As Kate Millet maintains, patriarchal ideology amplifies any

---

[7] Often maternalist and radical feminism are collapsed into one theory. For the sake of theoretical clarity, we have separated these two positions.

[8] This is a term taken from Basil Bernstein (1977, see also 1995).

differences that are commonly thought to exist between men and women. Thong (1989) describes Millet's use of "patriarchy" as

> particularly powerful because through conditioning, men usually secure the apparent consent of the many women they oppress. They do this through institutions such as the academy, the church and the family, each of which justifies and reinforces women's subordination to men. . . . Should a women refuse to accept patriarchal ideology, and should she manifest her mistrust by casting off her femininity—that is, her submissiveness/subordination—men will use coercion to accomplish what conditioning has failed to achieve. (Thong, 1989:96)

The concept of "patriarchy" has found its way, through various feminist interventions, into the sociology of education. A central concern has been to develop an understanding of the relationship between patriarchy and female sexuality, and their complementary links to the subordination of women in society. Consequently, radical feminists have addressed issues that sociologists have traditionally veered away from such as the study of symbolic forms of male power in school curriculum, texts, and school subjects (Spender, 1980, 1987), the sexual language of youth in schools (Lees, 1986), and the sexual dominance of boys in classrooms (Mahony, 1983, 1985). At the same time, radical feminism encouraged women to embrace the notion of liberation through the collective critique of male domination in education (Thompson, 1983). Such analyses emphasized the experiences of girls in schooling, the suppression of their voices, and the devaluing of women's knowledge. On this basis, they described a politically functional category known as "girl" that relied on radical politics embodied within the feminist movement.

Problems with/Contradictions in Radical Feminism

Radical feminist theorizing has many critics. For example, Wolpe (1976) took exception to the essentialism implied in the term patriarchy (all men oppress—all women suffer). She also argued that formal categories of "male" and "female" merely reaffirm crude gender divisions with little reference to the social com-

plexity underpinning notions of masculinity and femininity. From this perspective, both patriarchal relations and the concept of gender appear unchanging, decontextualized, and ahistorical. Contradictions also emerge when examining the theoretical links between the sociological stance taken within radical feminism (i.e., social constructivism) and the political line taken on issues surrounding male domination in schools (i.e., the idea that all men dominate). These contradictions emerge most powerfully when examining qualitative research that suggests that the social construction of gender is conditioned by complex social forces that cannot be solely restricted to male domination (see Connell, 1987). As such, some radical accounts of feminist theory contradict their own political slogans.

Maternal Feminism

While radical feminism has played a role in transforming democratic schooling in the United Kingdom, a strand of radical feminism known as maternal feminism (cf. Deitz, 1989) has made a greater impact on education in America. The rather subtle distinction between these two forms of feminism, radical and maternalist, is an important one. The radical perspective is primarily concerned with exposing the various strains of male domination in schools. The maternalist position has been more concerned with the values of womanhood rather than the manner in which such values are expressed as a result of male domination. Therefore, radical feminists argue for the elimination of "feminine values" whereas maternal feminists argue for their celebration in public life (see Tong, 1989).

The definitive feature of maternal feminism in education is its interest in women's and girls' development, particularly as it is understood by scholars such as Chodorow (1979). The central premises of this work have developed in mainstream disciplines such as psychology (e.g., Carol Gilligan) and educational philosophy (e.g., Roland Martin).[9] Within these traditions there has been a concern with gender difference; "difference" in this context applies both to biological variations be-

---

[9] For a diverse array of perspectives on these issues, see *The Education Feminism Reader* (1994), edited by Lynda Stone. A broad view of feminist perspectives in education can also be found in *Gender Issues in Education: Equality and Difference* (Blair and Holland, 1995).

tween men and women and the gendered nature of women's "predetermined" roles (e.g., nurturers, mothers) in society.

Empirical work conducted in the United States by Carol Gilligan (1982) and Belenky et al. (1986) suggests that feminine values such as female "connectedness" and "nurturing" be translated into ethical standards for educating children and young adults—what Gilligan (1982) identifies as the "ethics of care." The emphasis in schools is therefore placed upon women-centered courses and programs (primarily in higher education) that focus on self-expression and dialogical teaching. The key to these versions of feminism is the importance of empowering women in schools, drawing upon their personal knowledge and expressed concerns about the "moral society" (see Lyons, 1990; Noddings, 1988; Roland Martin, 1982). The assumption here is that the predominance of male values in education cannot promote a just vision of society since they are not governed by an "ethics of care." Therefore, the process of inclusion in education is not individual but collective, using "women's ways of knowing" (Belenky et al., 1986) as the means by which such liberation is encouraged. As a consequence, the category women not only remains intact, but is celebrated for its antielitist and less hierarchical forms of moral authority (e.g., mother/child bond).

Problems with/Contradictions in Maternal Feminism

While there can be little doubt that a concern with "caring" should be central to education, problems with such an approach still remain. For example, the assumption that replacing male culture (in schools) with female culture will lead to a more just society is problematic. Indeed, such a replacement strategy only rarefies women's experience over that of men's—a strategy that does not serve justice in a representative democracy where diverse and complex views about motherhood, gender, and sexuality deserve representation (Deitz, 1995).

A second concern lies in the notions expressed by maternal feminists about womanhood and an education system governed by female culture. Indeed, such notions are problematic precisely because they essentialize women in unacceptable ways (e.g., "women as mother"). As Butler (1991:15) states: "For surely all

women are not mothers; some cannot be, some are too young or too old to be, some choose not to be, and for some who are mothers, that is not necessarily the rallying point of their politicization in feminism." One could also argue that maternal feminism has failed to address the various ways in which identity groupings reconstruct and thus reconstitute notions of gender difference (sexuality) within a social context, largely because of its reliance on a rationalistic conception[10] of "womanhood" as a collective or shared entity. Therefore, despite its extrinsic focus on male power in society, maternal feminism does maintain, albeit subtle, a certain strand of political liberalism that focuses on identity or role, and sexual codes of conduct.

Socialist Feminism

Like other "feminisms in education," socialist feminism has many different yet interrelated theoretical strands. On one hand, it represents a critique of liberal democratic theories (including its role in the formulation of educational institutions) from a sociological perspective.[11] The socialist feminist can therefore be described, albeit loosely and cautiously, as an early deconstructivist[12] to the extent that a critique of the political processes that are legitimated by illusions of neutrality within the liberal tradition is a key concern.

On the other hand, socialist feminists have also recognized the importance of mapping economic structures onto school structures. This has led to an under-

---

[10] Many of the arguments in favor of maternal feminism are based on data that suggest that women do view the world in ways that are qualitatively different from men. As such, this account is based on the authority of the research (acquired through rational means) to "speak" about women's "ways of knowing."

[11] Arguably, socialist feminism in education is most closely tied to the field of sociology because of its strong links to the study of the state, economic structure, and society as the mechanisms thought to impact most directly on the social positioning of women.

[12] It is often assumed by some "new" theorists (postmodern/poststructural) that a radical critique of liberal schooling did not take place prior to the mid-1980s when postmodernism in education was in its infancy. Such an assumption is clearly problematic since socialist feminism took as one of its primary goals, the critique (and deconstruction) of liberal schooling. This critique served as a radical reassessment of the relationship between masculinity and capitalism, with "patriarchy" being defined in relation to economic power.

standing of education as the site for the preparation (and reproduction) of a hierarchically stratified work force, with women being prepared for positions in the secondary labor market or the "reserve army of labor." This emphasis on the reproduction of the social and economic order through education has led to a feminist articulation, within sociology, of *reproduction theory*.

Early versions of social reproduction theory, informed primarily by Bowles and Gintis (1976), viewed education as an instrument of capitalism that reproduces the subordination of women, and, in particular, the subordination of working-class girls (see Acker, 1989; Anyon, 1983; MacDonald, 1980). Social class, therefore, appears with great regularity as the factor that not only prefigures, but determines girls' educational experiences, identity, and consciousness. In this version of reproduction theory, the importance of school structures is privileged over individual attitudes.

Later versions of reproduction theory took on a somewhat different theoretical profile, and mark a shift in our understanding of social theory generally, and feminist thinking specifically. As Arnot and Whitty (1982:98) state:

> Increasingly, [curriculum theorists] came to recognize that the political economy of schooling as presented by Bowles and Gintis had severe limitations.... It failed to describe and explain classroom life, the conflicts and contradictions within the school and the distance and conflict between the school and the economy.

In an attempt to address such concerns, later versions of socialist feminism drew upon theories of class hegemony (Gramsci, 1971), cultural capital (Bourdieu and Passeron, 1977), and educational codes (Bernstein, 1977). For example, Arnot (1982) and Connell (1987) argued that schools reproduced "gender codes" or "gender regimes," respectively. The structure of gender relations in schools constituted and thus reproduced particular versions of masculinity, femininity, and family life (Gaskell, 1983), the dominant versions of which were associated with the upper middle classes. Such analyses focused attention on the simultaneous production of class (also complex racial) conflict, gendered subjects, and their contingent cultures of resistance (cf. Anyon, 1983 on private/public accommodation and resistance). Of particular significance was the attention

such analyses drew to the role of masculinity and femininity in shaping class relations: often disaffection in school was expressed as a celebration of particular masculinities (Willis, 1977) or a cult of femininity (McRobbie, 1978). Gender relations were therefore represented as central to the dynamics of class and racial inequality in contemporary society (McCarthy and Apple, 1988).

Problems with/Contradictions in Socialist Feminism

Despite its ability to inspire what is now a 30 year debate about difference in education, socialist feminism tended to deny, as Roman (1992) has argued, women's experience and agency in transforming educational practice. A second problem lies in its primary focus on the ideological nature of women's work in the public sphere and the political economy of girls' education, without much analysis of women's actual experience of female labor in education and its potential impact on the reconstitution of gender politics in society.

A final concern emerges when one considers issues around socialist visions of change in education and the democratic schooling movement. For example, despite an emphasis on social reproduction and women's welfare in society, socialist feminism and radical democratic change had little in common. This is largely because most socialist feminists argued that the presence of enlightenment concepts (such as democracy) in everyday language undermined the potential for radical education (see Dietz, 1985). As a consequence, the search for a radical language capable of challenging mainstream control over women's lives has proved difficult.

Relational Epistemologies and the Question of "Gender" in Education

In the early 1980's,[13] a period of critical reassessment in the field of feminist theory took place. Such critical endeavors were seen as a radical response to the inadequacies of modernist theorizing. It was suggested, for

---

[13] Indeed, there is some disagreement about when postmodernism "struck" the field of education. However, a review of the earliest and most regularly cited attempts at "being" postmodern in education seems to suggest its initial proliferation during this period.

example, that the category "woman" was either illusory or could no longer speak for all women. Modern feminist perspectives in education were therefore seen as rationalistic discourse—the "master narratives"—of modernity. These narratives found causal and rational explanations for gender inequity. Such explanations, it seemed, bore little relation to the complexity of women's identities, experiences, cultures, and positioning in society.

Black feminism is one example of alternative theory (Hooks, 1989; Safia-Mirza, 1993; Carby, 1982) that challenged rationalistic theorizing in education. Much of this work analyzed the relationship of black families (Pheonix, 1987) and black women to capitalism and imperialism (Hill-Collins, 1990), and set an agenda for the study of black women's experience and gendered discourses of racism in schools (Blair, 1995). The power and dominance of modern discourses in gender and education were thus exposed as Eurocentric and ethnocentric. This work ignited an interest in more relational and postcolonial accounts of feminism in education (see Brah and Minhas, 1985). Such theoretical separations were also made between mainstream feminist theorizing and, for example, lesbian and gay feminism(s).

Such critical stances have led to the development of a variety of new feminism(s) that can be identified broadly as *relational* theories, many of which reside ambiguously in the postmodern or poststructural camp. We focus here on the most pervasive aspect of relational feminist theorizing—poststructuralism—and then only very briefly touch on related feminist theories.

Poststructural Feminism

Poststructural theorizing within education is now a vast terrain and laying out its distinctions within feminist theory is beyond the scope of this chapter. However, it should be said that what sets poststructuralism apart from rationalistic forms of structuralism is its self-conscious and deliberate reflexivity, its link to deconstruction as political action, and its emphasis on the study of relational forms of power (as studied through language) in education.

Over the past 15 years, many poststructural feminists (e.g., Davies, 1986; Ellsworth, 1989; Kenway, 1995) have argued that in order to challenge the manifestation of power in education, four issues central to

understanding its regulatory functions must be embraced:

1. the false dichotomy between linguistic devices used in education to explain concrete and "incontestable" human experiences (e.g., girls' versus boys' experience);
2. the tenet that women's educational experience can be read as a complex representation of "culture" that highlights the contradictory relations of social and political life;
3. the belief that diverse reading(s) of women's lives as "text" leads to the destabilization of the category "woman" (Butler, 1991); and
4. the notion that subjective and "intersubjective" (see Fraser, 1995) human experience profoundly shapes gender relations in education. Such experiences must be represented formally within an antifoundationalist approach to education, rather than merely accepted as abstract, rational descriptions of existence.

The key terms drawn upon by poststructural feminists are "identity," "difference," "deconstruction," "discourse," "subjectivity," and "meaning" (cf. Scott, 1994). Within theory, each of these terms provides an analytical mechanism for assessing women's relationship to, or embeddedness within, education. The theoretical task of the feminist poststructuralist in education is to determine how these "conceptual devices" can be used to deconstruct schooling as a gendered institution or any totalizing discourse that sets out, intentionally or unintentionally, to essentialize women.

Feminism, Foucault, and Educational Research

Foucault's analysis of modern society has particular relevance to feminists working in education. This is largely due to theoretical work offered by theorists such as Walkerdine (1987, 1990), which demonstrates that education is an institutional apparatus involved in regulating the development of social identities, only one of which might be gender identity. Such regulatory mechanisms in education are configured discursively and subjectively, and are thought, for example, to condition the everyday lives of teachers, pupils, staff, and parents (see Walkerdine, 1987). The challenge for many feminist poststructuralists is therefore to identify how such "identities" (as fictions) are generated and regulated as "truths" about girls and women in schools, and how these regulative functions lead to the reconstitution of gender inequities (Walkerdine, 1990), and/or, for example, the unconscious undermining of equal opportunity policies by male teachers in schools (see Kenway, 1995).

Poststructural feminist theories have also emerged that point to the power of knowledge, language, and state discourses in shaping the multiple subjectivities and gendered discourses expressed in schools (see Davies, 1989; Kenway, 1995; Middleton, 1993), and how such discourses are read and reproduced in curriculum, and by pupils and teachers. These accounts, through the study of the temporal relationship between language and power, represent a major critique of existing understandings of the operation of power relations in education and the relationship among structure, agency, and identity. They also challenge the simplicity of early reproduction theory and the totalizing effect of the capitalist–patriarchy relation.

Feminist Standpoint Theories

In the past decade, other strands of relational feminism have emerged that speak to the importance of representing women's lived experience in educational theory. Such experiences are thought to represent a concrete standpoint expressed by women, yet they should not necessarily be seen as shared experiential terrain, nor as views that do not conflict with other women's perspectives. It must be said, however, that many of these feminisms bear the historical marks of modernism while still maintaining some postmodern inflections. These new theoretical frames are not an abrupt break with the past (i.e., modernist history) but instead represent a kind of feminist dialectic that leads to the formal and informal synthesizing of new theoretical forms (Dillabough and McAlpine, 1996).

One such feminism in education is the brand of *feminist materialism* articulated, for example, by Leslie Roman. Drawing upon the work of Jagger (1983) and Harding (1986), she argues that knowledge about gender that emerges through the study of education must be viewed as a dialectical form resulting from the dynamic relation between women's subjectivity (i.e., standpoint) and material conditions in society. Therefore, on the one hand, Roman (1993), unlike many other theorists drawing upon the importance of voice

and standpoint in education, still remains in the realm of the "political" by maintaining an interest in the material conditions of society.

At the same time, an interest in women's "standpoint" also reflects a concern with subjectivity as expressed through, for example, the discourse of youth cultures and the everyday experience of young women (see Roman, 1993). Unlike most sociologists, however, Roman's (1992) ideas about educational transformation are not only linked to formal schooling contexts, but are also related to the politicization of educational research and the gendered nature of research knowledge. She is therefore most concerned with how research knowledge in education can be expressed in more democratic and feminist forms (Roman, 1992, 1993; see also Lather, 1991).

Related accounts that have a less direct focus on the political but point to the importance of subjectivity and women's standpoint in educational theory have also emerged. For example, the sociological work of Casey (1989), Foster (1993), and Luttrell (1994) focuses on women's discourse as a way of understanding how gender and social change are constructed in relation to educational practice (e.g., women's teaching). Much of this work draws on the voices (autobiographies, oral histories, narrative accounts) of women in education, or expressed by women about education. It also has a distinctively "relational" flavor, but like the work of Roman, it remains connected to the "political" and the possibility of educational change in the name of women's concerns.

Another version of relational feminist theorizing is a brand of *critical pedagogy* articulated in a now classic text entitled *Feminism and Critical Pedagogy* (Luke and Gore, 1989). In this text, a variety of contributions on the critical nature and purpose of pedagogy are offered that, like other feminist theories, accommodate both politics and the tools of deconstruction. In most of these accounts, Foucault (or in some cases, Freire) figures as the luminary capable of educating radical educationalists toward a deconstructive pedagogy—an educational method that empowers students to deconstruct canons of knowledge and their male bias. However, at the same time, this work goes beyond versions of critical pedagogy authored by male sociologists such as Giroux (cf. Luke, 1989) to incorporate an explicit feminist poststructural stance. These feminist theorists argue for a "relational theory of knowledge" (Luke, 1989:47; Weiler, 1994) and pedagogical form that represents diverse women's voices and their political perspectives.

Problems with/Contradictions in New Feminism(s)

Despite advances made by feminist poststructuralists and related theorists, their work presents some conceptual dilemmas for educational theory. For example, many critics of feminist poststructuralism (even poststructuralists themselves, see Kenway, 1996) argue that in focusing almost entirely on the study of women's subjectivities we may be collapsing the original feminist project and the notion of women as a collective into the realm of the unknown (see Young, 1995). After all, most research on gender equality in schools has identified "girls" as the issue, their experience as the "problem," and their needs (as a gendered category) as the purpose of educational reform. Educational critics therefore suggest that it becomes more difficult to understand, within such analyses, how feminist poststructuralism and other relational theories can address the "real" problems of gender inequity in schools (see Kenway, 1996). It must be said, however, that much of the work reviewed above does not prove such a claim, nor does it suggest that relational feminist theories (including poststructuralist accounts) have lost their political edge. Perhaps what still remains problematic then is the desire by relational theorists to take the study of women's subjectivity (through) to its extreme, with less room for a rigorous analysis of the role of the state in women's oppression. As a consequence, the search for "truth" about women's oppression may become highly provisional.

A second problem lies in the tendency in much "new" theorizing to ignore original thought articulated and advanced by contemporary feminist women academics who are in support of a relational approach to feminist scholarship, such as Luce Irigaray, Joan Scott, or Judith Butler. Instead, many feminists in education domesticate the "new male" narrative (e.g., the voice of Foucault, Derrida) into their own theoretical perspectives. It is therefore difficult to say whether all relational theories have conquered the masculine bias that has traditionally manifested itself in rationalistic feminist accounts.

Future Considerations

What sociological history or narrative, if any, can be claimed in this account of feminist theories of education? Perhaps this exercise in theoretical narration has demonstrated that feminist theories cannot be understood merely on the basis of their institutional representation in sociology, their sociological underpinnings, or the functions they assume in education. Instead, this work must be seen as an articulation of perspectives that concern who or what is responsible for women's oppression and how this takes form in education. It must also be seen as evidence of the strength and diversity of the feminist education project and its ability to struggle and join hands with history, structure, and biography within the educational sphere.

What then is the future of a feminist sociology of education? One answer might be found in a reconsideration of the importance of the "political" (see Laslett et al., 1995) in the development of contemporary feminist narratives. The development of theoretical forms that serve to resuscitate the importance of political communities (Dillabough and McAlpine, 1996) and economic issues (see Apple, 1996) in feminist theorizing seems most promising, particularly where the creation of bonds between the educational theorist and society are rendered more highly visible. Such ideas, if dealt with effectively, embody the best of both old and new theoretical forms and serve to reinforce the importance of the contemporary feminist dialectic among structure, political community, and agency.

Because these ideas are not new, what must be different is how one goes about conceptualizing this dialectic in feminist theorizing. A more *rigorous* analysis of the relationship of the gendered "self"[14] to political communities (and their mutual interdependence) and local and broader societal contexts is needed. At the moment, however, feminist sociology seems to be more like a feminist psychology, with a focus on the study of individuals abstracted out of the human condition and society. This abstraction does, a priori, present par-

---

[14] One might, for example, study empirically how the very notion of human agency is gendered in a climate of educational reform, and how such gendered formations (yet social formations) lead to particular educational regimes and structures that serve to reconstitute "powerlessness" in society.

ticular visions of society that resonate with neoliberal and neoconservative philosophy. It also falsely implies, as Thatcher has, that there is "no such thing as society" or a community that could play a significant role in the development of contemporary feminist thought or women's lives.

There is much room still for the development of sociological theory that taps the transformation and restructuring of gender relations in education, particularly in relation to contemporary social forces such as globalization, poverty, new family structures, the feminist movement, and discursive logics of marketization. An examination of the ways in which claims about gender are made in education and the construction of new "gender knowledge" would be important elements in the study of these discursive processes. Such work may demonstrate the potential for mapping social change and its gendered manifestations in contemporary educational institutions (such as schools and teacher education faculties), and the ways in which social change impinges on gender identities and consequent gender relations between male and female youth.

Empirical issues are also of some concern in the development of a contemporary feminist sociology of education. For example, efforts are being made to develop a more diverse feminist analysis of educational policy. The current study of educational policy is, in the main, conducted by male sociologists.[15] A broader feminist understanding of neoconservative educational reforms (see Kenway et al., 1994), particularly as they apply to higher education and its material outcomes for women, is therefore needed.

New insights into the construction of the gendered citizen in education (see Arnot et al., 1996; Gordon, 1992; Lahelma et al., 1996) are also emerging. This work could be further advanced by drawing upon disciplines not currently seen as valuable to the study of education such as political science. Research conducted by, for example, Cynthia Cockburn (1996), Chantel Mouffe (1992), and Iris Young (1995), pointing to the importance of women as active citizens, has implications not only for sociology, but in the training of adolescents and teachers about the importance of feminist political communities and their potential impact on

democratic education. Such work has the potential to challenge the Westernized nature of school knowledge about women and feminism, and may encourage students to reexamine themselves and their practice in light of broader political issues and world politics.

Finally, feminist analyses of the construction of masculinity in schools and the impact of both class and cultural diversity on contemporary male/female relations are currently being developed, particularly in Australia, but also in the United Kingdom. Such work is likely to shed light on the presence of new sexisms and the construction of sexuality in schools, particularly in relation to educational reform and broader social change (see Connell, 1995; Kenway, 1995; Mac an Ghail, 1994, 1996).

Conclusion

Our consideration of feminist theories of education has been limited, as all written texts are. Such considerations do not, in themselves, explain every aspect of feminism, but they do account on some level for the historical periods that preceded the rise of feminist concerns in the sociology of education. They also serve as a kind of storytelling in themselves. Indeed, storytelling can accommodate only a reconstruction of the past and, in many cases, much of the story is lost. However, at the same time, it signals the creativity, diversity, and momentum of the feminist theoretical project in sociology. We hope we have identified the creative potential of such feminist momentum and, at the same time, suggested that all perspectives are heavily nuanced in ways that "may lead through to a tension" (Bernstein, 1995:422), which ultimately facilitates the further development of a feminist sociology of education.

REFERENCES

Acker, S. 1989. "The Problem with Patriarchy." *Sociology* 23(2):235–240.

Anyon, J. 1983. "Intersections of Gender and Class: Accommodation and Resistance by Working Class and Affluent Females to Contradictory Sex Role Ideologies." In L. Barton and S. Walker (eds.), *Gender, Class and Education.* Lewes: Falmer Press.

Apple, M. 1996. "Power, Meaning and Identity: Critical Sociology of Education in the United States." *British Journal of Sociology of Education* 17(2):125–144.

Arnot, M. 1981. "Culture and Political Economy: Dual Per-

---

[15] This current trend stands in opposition to that which occurred during the 1970s and early 1980s (David, 1980) in the domain of critical social policy research.

spectives in the Sociology of Women's Education." *Educational Analysis* 3(1):97–116.

———. 1982. "Male Hegemony, Social Class and Women's Education." *Journal of Education* 164(1):64–89.

———. 1985. "Current Developments in the Sociology of Women's Education." *British Journal of Sociology of Education* 6(1):123–130.

Arnot, M., and G. Whitty. 1982. "From Reproduction to Transformation: Recent Radical Perspectives on the Curriculum from the USA." *British Journal of Sociology of Education* 3(1):93–103.

Arnot, M., H. Araujo, K. Deliyanni-Kouimtzi, G. Rowe, and A. Tome. 1996. "Teachers, Gender and the Discourses of Citizenship." *International Studies in Sociology of Education* 6(1):3–35.

Barrett, M. 1980. *Women's Oppression Today: Problems in Marxist Feminist Analysis*. London: Verso.

Belenky, M. F., N. R. Clinchy, Goldberger, and J. M. Tarule. 1986. *Women's Ways of Knowing*. New York: Basic Books.

Bernstein, B. 1977. *Class Codes and Control*, Vol. 3, 3rd ed. London: Routledge and Kegan Paul.

———. 1995. "A Response." In A. R. Sadovnik (ed.), *Knowledge and Pedagogy: The Sociology of Basil Bernstein*. Norwood, NJ: Ablex.

Blair, M. 1995. "Race, Class and Gender in School Research." In J. Holland, M. Blair, and S. Sheldon (eds.), *Debates and Issues in Feminist Research and Pedagogy*. Clevedon: Open University Press.

Blair, M., and J. Holland. 1995. *Gender Issues in Education: Equality and Difference*. MA in Education Study Guide, Open University Press.

Bourdieu, P., and J. C. Passeron. 1977. *Reproduction in Education, Society and Culture*. London: Sage.

Bowles, S., and H. Gintis. 1976. *Schooling and Capitalist America*. London: Routledge and Kegan Paul.

Brah, A., and R. Minhas. 1985. "Structural Racism or Cultural Difference: Schooling for Asian Girls." In G. Weiner (ed.), *Just a Bunch of Girls: Feminist Approaches to Schooling*. Milton Keynes: Open University.

Butler, J. 1991. "Contingent Foundations: Feminism and the Question of 'Postmodernism.'" In J. Butler and J. W. Scott (eds.), *Feminists Theorize the Political*. London: Routledge.

Byrne, E. 1978. *Women and Education*. London: Tavistock.

Carby, H. 1982. "Schooling in Babylon." In Centre for Contemporary Cultural Studies (ed.), *The Empire Strikes Back: Race and Racism in 70s Britain*. London: Hutchinson.

Casey, K. 1989. *I Answer with My Life*. New York: Routledge.

Chodorow, N. 1979. "Feminism and Difference: Gender, Relation and Differences in Psychoanalytic Perspective." *Socialist Review* 46:51–69.

Cockburn, C. 1996. "Women's Bridge Building: Projects in Areas of Conflict." *Soundings: A Journal of Culture and Politics* Issues 1–4.

Connell, R.W. 1987. *Gender and Power*. Cambridge: Polity Press.

———. 1995. *Masculinities*. London: Polity Press.

Cooper, D. 1995. *Power in Struggle: Feminism, Sexuality and the State*. Buckingham: Open University Press.

David, M. 1980. *Women, Family and Education*. London: Routledge.

Davies, B. 1989. *Frogs and Snails and Feminist Tales: Preschool Children and Gender*. Sydney: Allen & Unwin.

Deem, R. 1978. *Women and Schooling*.

Deem, R., ed., 1980. *Schooling for Women's Work*. London: Routledge and Kegan Paul.

Delamont, S. 1980. *Sex Roles and the School*. London: Methuen.

Dietz, M. 1985. "Citizenship with a Feminist Face: The Problem with Maternal Thinking." *Political Theory* (February):19–37.

Dillabough, J., and L. McAlpine. 1996. "Rethinking Research Processes and Praxis in the Social Studies: The Cultural Politics of Method in Text Evaluation Research." *Theory and Research in Social Education* 24(2):167–203.

Ellsworth, E. 1989. "Why Doesn't This Feel Empowering? Working through the Oppressive Myths of Critical Pedagogy." *Harvard Educational Review* 59:297–324.

Foster, M. 1993. "Othermothers: Exploring the Educational Philosophy of Black American Women Teachers." In M. Arnot and K. Weiler (eds.), *Feminism and Social Justice in Education: International Perspectives*. London, Falmer Press.

Fraser, N. 1995. "False Antithesis." In S. Benahabib, J. Butler, D. Cornell, and N. Fraser (eds.), *Feminist Contentions: A Philosophical Exchange*. New York: Routledge.

Gaskell, J. 1983. "The Reproduction of Family Life: Perspectives of Male and Female Adolescents." *British Journal of Sociology of Education* 4(1):19–38.

Gilligan, C. 1982. *In a Different Voice: Psychological Theory and Women's Development*. Cambridge, MA: Harvard University Press.

Gordon, T. 1992. "Citizens and Others: Gender, Democracy and Education." *International Studies in Sociology of Education* 2(1):43–56.

Gramsci, A. 1971. *Selection from the Prison Notebooks*, Q. Hoare and G. Smith (trans.). New York: International Publishers.

Harding, S. 1986. *The Science Question in Feminism*. Ithaca, NY: Cornell University Press.

Hill-Collins, P. 1990. *Black Feminist Thought: Knowledge, Consciousness, and the Politics of Empowerment*. Boston: Unwin & Hyman.

Hooks, B. 1989. *Talking Back, Thinking Feminism, Thinking Black*. Boston, MA: Southend Press.

Jagger, A. 1983. *Feminist Politics and Human Nature*. Rowman and A. Held: Harvester.

Kelly, A. 1981. "Gender Roles at School and Home." *British Journal of Sociology of Education* 3(3):281–295.

Kenway, J. 1995. "Masculinities in Schools: Under Siege, on

the Defensive and under Reconstruction." *Discourse* 16(1):59–81.

———. 1996. "Having a Postmodernist Turn or Postmodernist Angst: A Disorder Experienced by an Author Who Is Not Yet Dead or Even Close to It." In R. Smith and P. Wexler (eds.), *After Postmodernism: Education, Politics and Identity.* London: Falmer Press.

Kenway, J., S. Willis, J. Blackmore, and L. Rennie. 1994. "Making 'Hope Practical' Rather Than 'Despair Convincing': Feminist Post-structuralism, Gender Reform and Educational Change." *British Journal of Sociology of Education* 15:187–210.

Lahelma, E., T. Gordon, and J. Holland. 1996. "Curricula for Nations: The Construction of Citizenship and Difference in Finnish and British Schools." Paper presented at the European Conference of Educational Research, Seville, Spain.

Laslett, B., J. Brenner, and Y. Arat. (eds.) 1996. *Rethinking the Political: Gender, Resistance and the State.* Chicago: University of Chicago Press.

Lather, P. 1991. *Getting Smart: Feminist Research and Pedagogy within the Postmodern Classroom.* New York: Routledge.

Lees, S. 1986. *Losing Out: Sexuality and Adolescent Girls.* London: Hutchinson.

Lovell, T. 1990. *British Feminist Thought: A Reader.* Oxford: Basil Blackwell.

Luke, C. 1989. "Feminist Politics in Radical Pedagogy." In C. Luke and J. Gore (eds.), *Feminisms and Critical Pedagogy.* New York: Routledge.

Luke, C., and J. Gore (eds.). 1989. *Feminisms and Critical Pedagogy.* New York: Routledge.

Luttrell, W. 1994. "Becoming Somebody: Aspirations, Opportunities and Womenhood." In G. Young and B. Dickerson (eds.), *Colour, Class and Country.* London: Zed Books.

Lyons, N. 1990. "Dilemma's of Knowing: Ethical and Epistemological Dimensions of Teachers' Work and Development." *Harvard Educational Review* 60(2):159–180.

Mac an Ghail, M. 1994. *The Making of Men.* Milton Keynes: Open University Press.

———. (ed.). 1996. *Understanding Masculinities.* Milton Keynes: Open University Press.

MacCoby, E. E., and C. N. Jacklin. 1974. *The Psychology of Sex Differences.* Stanford: Stanford University Press.

MacDonald, M. 1980. "Schooling and the Reproduction of Class and Gender Relations." In L. Barton, R. Meighan, and S. Walker (eds.), *Schooling, Ideology and the Curriculum.* Barcombe: Falmer Press.

Mahoney, P. 1983. "How Alice's Chin Really Came to Be Pressed Against Her Foot: Sexist Processes of Interaction in Mixed Sexed Classrooms." *Women's Studies International Forum* 16(1):107–115.

———. 1985. *Schools for the Boys: Coeducation Reassessed.* London: Hutchinson.

McCarthy, C., and M. W. Apple. 1988. "Race, Class, and Gender in American Educational Research: Toward a Nonsynchronous Parallelist Position." In L. Weis (ed.), *Class, Race, and Gender in American Education,* pp. 9–39. Albany, NY: State University of New York Press.

McRobbie, A. 1978. "Working-Class Girls and the Culture of Femininity." In Centre for Contemporary Cultural Studies (ed.), *Women Take Issue: Aspects of Women's Subordination.* London: Hutchinson Educational.

Measor, L., and P. Sikes. 1992. *Gender and Schooling.* London: Cassell.

Middleton, S. 1987. "The Sociology of Women's Education as a Field of Academic Study." In M. Arnot and G. Weiner (eds.), *Gender and the Politics of Schooling.* London: Open University.

———. 1993. "A Post Modern Pedagogy for the Sociology of Women's Education." In M. Arnot and K. Weiler (eds.), *Feminism and Social Justice in Education.* London, Falmer Press.

Mouffe, C. 1992. "Feminism, Citizenship and Radical Democratic Politics." In J. Butler and J. W. Scott (eds.), *Feminists Theorize the Political.* London: Routledge.

Nicholson, L. 1995. "Pragmatism, Feminism, and the Linguistic Turn." In S. Benhabib, J. Butler, D. Cornell, and N. Fraser (eds.), *Feminist Contentions: A Philosophical Exchange.* New York: Routledge.

Noddings, N. 1988. "An Ethic of Caring and Its Implication for Instructional Arrangements." *American Journal of Education* 96(2):215–230.

Oakley, A. 1972. *Sex, Gender and Society.* London: Temple Smith.

Pateman, C. 1992. "Equality, Difference, Subordination: The Politics of Motherhood and Women's Citizenship." In G. Bock and S. James (eds.), *Beyond Equality and Difference: Citizenship, Feminist Politics, Female Subjectivity.* New York: Routledge.

Pheonix, A. 1987. "Theories of Gender and Black Families." In G. Weiner and M. Arnot (eds.), *Gender Under Scrutiny: New Inquiries in Education.* London: Hutchinson.

Roland, Martin J. 1982. "Excluding Women from the Educational Realm." *Harvard Educational Review* 52(2):133–148.

Roman, L. 1992. "The Political Significance of Other Ways of Narrating Ethnography. A Feminist Materialist Approach." In M. D. Lecompte, W. Milroy, and J. Priessle (eds.), *The Handbook of Qualitative Research in Education.* San Diego, CA: Academic Press.

———. 1993. "Double Exposure: The Politics of Feminist Materialist Ethnography." *Educational Theory* 43:279–308.

Sadovnik, A. R. 1995. "Bernstein's Theory of Pedagogic Practice: A Structuralist Approach." In A. R. Sadovnik (ed.), *Knowledge and Pedagogy: The Sociology of Basil Bernstein.* Norwood, NJ: Ablex.

Safia-Mirza, H. 1993. "The Social Construction of Black Womenhood in British Educational Research: Towards a

New Understanding." In M. Arnot and K. Weiler (eds.), *Feminism and Social Justice in Education: International Perspectives*. London, Falmer Press.

Scott, J. 1994. "Deconstructing Equality-versus-Difference: Or, the Uses of Poststructuralist Theory for Feminism." In S. Seidman (ed.), *The Postmodern Turn: New Perspectives on Social Theory*. Cambridge: Cambridge University Press.

Spender, D. 1980. *Man Made Language*. London: Routledge and Kegan Paul.

———. 1982. *Invisible Women: The Schooling Scandal*. London: Writers' and Readers' Publishing Collective.

———. 1987. "Education: The Patriarchal Paradigm and the Response to Feminism." In M. Arnot and G. Weiner (eds.), *Gender and the Politics of Schooling*. London: Hutchinson.

Stone, L. (ed.). 1994. *The Education Feminism Reader*. New York: Routledge.

Thompson, J. 1983. *Learning Liberation: Women's Response to Men's Education*. London: Croom Helm.

Tong, R. 1989. *Feminist Thought*. Sydney: Unwin & Hyman.

Walker, S., and L. Barton (eds.). 1983. *Gender, Class and Education*. Lewes: Falmer Press.

Walkerdine, V. 1987. "Femininity as Performance." *Oxford Review of Education* 15(3):267–279.

———. 1990. *School Girl Fictions*. London: Verso.

Weiler, K. 1993. "Feminism and the Struggle for Democratic Education: A View from the United States." In M. Arnot and K. Weiler (eds.), *Feminism and Social Justice in Education: International Perspectives*. London: Falmer Press.

———. 1994, first published, 1991. "Freire and a Feminist Pedagogy of Difference." In P. McLaren and C. Lankshear (eds.), *Politics of Liberation: Paths from Freire*. New York: Routledge.

Weiner, G. 1994. *Feminism(s) in Education: An Introduction*. Buckingham: Open University.

Whelehan, I. 1995. *Modern Feminist Thought*. Edinburgh: Edinburgh University Press.

Willis, P. 1977. *Learning to Labour*. Farnborough: Saxon House.

Wollstencraft, M. 1992, first published in 1792. *A Vindication of the Rights of Women*. London: Penguin.

Wolpe, A. M. 1976. "The Official Ideology of Education for Girls." In M. Flude and J. Ahier (eds.), *Educability, Schools and Ideology*. London: Croom Helm.

Young, I. M. 1995. "Gender as Seriality: Thinking about Women as a Social Collective." In L. Nicholson and S. Seidman (eds.), *Social Postmodernism*. Cambridge: Cambridge University Press.

Sociology of Education

Marxist Theories

Fred L. Pincus
University of Maryland Baltimore County

Although only a minority of sociologists of education identify themselves as Marxists, this theoretical perspective has come to be accepted as one legitimate way to analyze educational issues. An increasing number of textbooks include Marxism in their discussions of theory and many literature review sections of papers in professional journals dealing with education cite the work of Marxist scholars.

However, there is no single Marxist approach to the sociology of education. Although class conflict is still a theme that runs through most Marxist analysis, many theorists are trying to integrate race and gender conflict into Marxist theory. Although the relationship between schools and the economy has been at the center of much Marxist analysis, other theorists emphasize the role of culture and politics. Some theorists have moved so far away from traditional Marxism that it is difficult to tell whether they are extending the outer limits of Marxist analysis or whether they have left the tradition altogether. Finally, many nonsociologists including economists, historians, and teacher education professionals have influenced the Marxist approach to the sociology of education.

Debates over structural determinism versus human agency have been central to the Marxist view of education. Until the mid-1980s, most Marxists in the sociology of education could be described as "reproduction theorists" since their writing tended to emphasize the way in which the schools helped to reproduce the inequalities of capitalism. A second group of writers, often called "resistance theorists," argues that students and teachers can often resist the school's attempt to relegate poor, working-class and minority students to the lower levels of society. During the 1990s, Marxist sociologists of education attempted to integrate and

extend these two approaches, which are not incompatible insofar as student–teacher resistance to the reproduction of inequality is a persistent dynamic of mass education.

Reproduction Theory

Most reproduction theorists rely on some version of the traditional base-superstructure version of Marxism. According to this view, the capitalist economy is the "base" of the society and is characterized by a conflict between two main classes. The small but wealthy and powerful capitalist class owns most of the income-producing property (factories, banks, farms, real estate, etc.) and the working class majority must sell their labor to the capitalists in return for wages. This system of the private ownership of property is known as the "capitalist relations of production."

The schools, on the other hand, are part of the "superstructure" along with politics, culture, religion, and all other noneconomic institutions. The nature of the educational system, like other aspects of the superstructure, is largely "determined" by the nature of the economic base and is organized around the economic and political interests of the dominant (i.e, capitalist) class.

According to this view, the capitalist class wants a stratified labor force to exploit in order to run its businesses profitably. Good workers must have the necessary technical skills and work habits to produce the products and services that the capitalists must sell. In addition, the capitalist class wants the working-class majority to *believe* that the political and economic system is reasonably fair and just and serves the interests of the entire population. Lastly, "success" and "failure" in this system are defined as personal matters, dependent upon an individual's ambition and ingenuity, not on a social system that is structured in favor of an affluent minority.

During the twentieth century, reproduction theorists argue, the schools played a major role in socializing the working class to be patriotic, productive workers. In addition, they argue that the schools have been reasonably successful in achieving these goals, which, of course, helps the capitalist class continue in its position of power over the working class. Although the role of the capitalist class in developing educational policy can be direct or indirect, reproduction theorists argue that the schools reproduce the capitalist relations of production.

There are, however, important differences in emphasis among reproduction theorists. Stanley Aronowitz and Henry Giroux (1993) suggest three main categories—economic, cultural, and hegemonic-state.

Economic reproduction theorists emphasize the connection between the schools and the labor market. Drawing on the earlier work of Louis Althusser, Sam Bowles and Herbert Gintis (1976) argue that the stratified educational system is similar to the hierarchical labor market, i.e., there is a correspondence between the schools and the labor market. A "hidden curriculum," based on within-school tracking, helps to sort students and prepare them for jobs that are "appropriate" to their social origin. Although the schools are structured to ensure that most poor and working-class students will be less educated than their more privileged counterparts, the ideology of meritocracy and so-called "objective tests" legitimate this process by making it appear that these less privileged students simply did not have the skills to become anything more than lower level workers.

Between-school curriculum differences also provide different educational experiences for students from different backgrounds with different occupational "destinations." According to Jean Anyon (1980), schools with large poor and working-class populations tend to emphasize basic skills and following the rules, whereas schools with large upper-income populations teach creativity and autonomy in their college preparatory and advanced placement courses. Funding differences between the schools in rich and poor districts further exacerbate the unequal educational outcomes.

Economic reproduction theorists have also argued that the structure of higher education corresponds to the needs of a stratified labor market with community colleges at the bottom and elite research institutions at the top. The universities produce both the new knowledge and the professional, technical, and administrative workers needed by business owners. Community colleges, on the other hand, focus on the vocational training of paraprofessional and lower level technical workers and also divert less skilled students away from 4-year colleges. According to Fred Pincus (1980), race- and class-based differences in enrollment in these different institutions help to reproduce capitalist relations of production.

Of course, economic reproduction theorists argue that although members of the capitalist class tend to have good educations, their ownership and control of vast wealth are largely based on a variety of *noneducational* factors, including inheritance. However, the stratified system of education, theorists argue, helps to prevent other classes from challenging the power of the capitalist class, or even learning about it. Class is made invisible.

Cultural reproduction theorists, on the other hand, emphasize the way in which culture operates in the schools to reproduce capitalist relations of production (Pierre Bourdieu, J. Passeron, and Basil Bernstein). Students from different class (and race) backgrounds are said to have different cultural competencies, languages, and styles. These differences are caused, in part, by economic and racial inequalities of the capitalist economy.

The schools, say cultural reproduction theorists, are structured according to the cultural standards of the dominant group(s). The language patterns, cultural values, and disciplinary practices of middle- and upper-income families are relatively similar to those of the schools, while there is a bigger difference between the culture of working-class families and the schools. This gives students from white, upper-income families a much better chance at being successful in school than students from working-class and minority families.

Michael Apple (1993) has argued that the schools, in general, and textbooks, in particular, tend to legitimate the history, culture, and identity of dominant group students at the same time that they help to construct disempowered identities of students from other groups. This, in turn, would increase the motivations of the more privileged students and decrease the intellectual ambitions of the less privileged. In this way, cultural differences that are partly caused by economic inequality play important roles in the reproduction of capitalism.

The *hegemonic-state reproduction* theorists emphasize the way in which the public schools are part of the larger apparatus of the state, which reflects the interests of the capitalist class. The state, which is "relatively autonomous" from the capitalist class, must actively and continually intervene to make sure that the schools are serving their appropriate role.

Louis Althusser sees the schools as part of the Ideological State Apparatus, which helps reproduce the dominant ideology through the curriculum both explicitly, through the curriculum content, and unconsciously, through the values imbedded in the curriculum. Antonio Gramsci also argues that the schools help to reproduce capitalist class hegemony (cultural domination) through teaching the procapitalist relations of discourse and knowledge making.

Finally, Nicos Poulantzas argues that the state, and therefore the schools, is a contested terrain where different classes struggle for control. Although the capitalist class always attempts to use the schools to further its own interests, the working class can gain concessions during certain historical periods. In addition, educators have their own interests, which are not necessarily consistent with those of the capitalist class. Although Poulantzas is a reproduction theorist, in some ways he is a bridge to resistance theorists.

Resistance Theory

Some Marxists, called resistance theorists, criticize the reproduction theorists for being too overdeterminist in describing the relationship between the economic base and the superstructure, in general, and between the capitalist class and the schools, in particular. It is not correct, they argue, to assume that the students passively internalize the hegemonic messages sent by the schools or that teachers always carry out their reproductive roles. The schools do not always produce the types of workers needed by the capitalist class.

Instead, say resistance theorists, the schools should be seen as a "contested terrain" where political struggles can take place. Culture is not simply a given but is something that is both produced and reproduced inside the school.

The process of reproduction can be interrupted in a variety of ways, according to resistance theorists. First, students are active subjects in the educational process and they bring their own world views into the classroom. Based in their families, peer groups, and communities, these world views are often at odds with the hegemonic views that educators attempt to teach.

Paul Willis' *Learning to Labor* (1991) is a classic account of how a group of English working-class "lads" resist the attempts of the school to resocialize them. They are disrespectful to teachers and their antiintellectual attitudes cause great disruptions in the classroom. Unfortunately for the lads, their resistance is also self-defeating as it precludes any chance of gaining the skills necessary for upward mobility in the labor market. Even more important, they fail to gain the intellectual resources needed for a full understanding of how to transform the larger society. Their antiintellectualism frustrates both the institution and their own autonomy.

Student resistance is not always overt. Many students, who feel ill at ease in a culturally foreign environment or who are simply bored with school, tune out in terms of learning either the skills, standard dialect, or cultural attitudes that the schools are trying to teach. Ira Shor refers to this as a "performance strike."

Second, the curriculum, itself, may have contradictions that would lead to acts of resistance. Apple, for example, argues that not all students accept what textbooks try to teach them. Some students may have a "negotiated" response to texts where they dispute a particular claim but accept the overall interpretation of the text. Others may have an "oppositional" response by rejecting the dominant interpretations made by the text.

In looking at the student rebellions in the United States during the 1960s, resistance theorists have argued that the curricular emphasis on freedom, autonomy, and personal choice was inconsistent with the undemocratic nature of many classrooms in high school and college. In addition, the hegemonic American values of freedom and equality of opportunity proved shallow when mass movements challenged racism, poverty, sexism, and foreign policy. Many liberal students seized on these contradictions and became radicalized, demanding more power in the educational process and fundamental change in the larger society.

Resistance theorists emphasize the ongoing struggles over cultural definitions that are a continuing process in the schools. Although these struggles do not always lead to political change, as is the case with Willis' lads, they provide the seeds for the development of radical political movements.

Critical pedagogy is another strand of resistance theory. In his landmark book *Pedagogy of the Oppressed*, published in English in 1970, Brazilian educator Paulo Freire argued that a critical pedagogy can turn illiterate peasants into literate political actors who can transform society. The key is to gear the literacy program to the lived experiences of the peasants by teaching them words and concepts generated from the inequitable conditions of their lives. In this way, literacy will help them to both understand their present conditions and organize for social change.

Ira Shor (1992), Stanley Aronowitz and Henry Giroux (1993), and others have applied and extended Freire's ideas to teaching poor, working-class, and minority students, including adults, in advanced industrialized societies. They especially focus on the role of teachers and teacher education. To practice critical pedagogy, teachers must become "transformative intellectuals" who understand the role of schools in capitalist society but who also reject their role as cultural reproducers.

The goal of critical pedagogy is to empower teachers and students to understand and transform both the schools and the society. Shor (1992) lists 11 adjectives that describe an empowering curriculum: participatory, affective, problem posing, situated, multicultural, dialogic, desocializing, democratic, researching, interdisciplinary, and activist.

Issues for the 1990s

Since the mid-1980s, Marxist analysis of education has continued to move away from the traditional reproductionist view that schools were part of the superstructure that was dominated by the capitalist class in an attempt to control the working class. In part, political and educational developments simply could not be easily explained by traditional Marxist theory. In addition, theorists were influenced by the earlier writings of the French structuralists and the more contemporary writings of poststructuralists, postmodernists, Marxist-feminists, and black Marxists. As a result, current Marxist theories of education are developing along several different dimensions.

1. *Reassessing the Role of the Capitalist Class.* Few Marxists accept the view that the capitalists have absolute control over the schools and there is much more interest in the concept of schools as contested terrain. Martin Carnoy and Henry M. Levin (1985:50), for example, argue that education "is an arena of conflict over the production of knowledge, ideology and employment, a place where social movements try to meet their needs and business attempts to reproduce its hegemony."

The relatively conservative school reform movement of the 1980s, known as the excellence movement, demonstrated that neither the majority of the capitalist class nor the majority of educators believed that the schools were meeting the labor force or political needs of late twentieth-century capitalism. Of course, the excellence movement blamed educational problems on the egalitarian policies promoted by the radical social movements of the 1960s. Structural causes of educational problems like the deskilling of many jobs, the lack of a strong connection between good grades and occupational success, and the growing unemployment among educated young people were largely ignored.

In addition, there were contradictions within the capitalist class about how to improve the schools. Liberals want to continue the emphasis on a strong federal role in education and on improving public schools. Conservatives opted for a more limited federal presence in educational policy and a greater role for private schools through the development of tuition tax credits or vouchers. Both liberals and conservatives, however, emphasized the need for state governments to lengthen the school day and/or school year and to increase academic standards. Clearly, the superstructure was not acting the way in which traditional Marxists expected it to act and the capitalist class was trying to remold the schools.

Research in higher education also reexamined the actions of the capitalist class. Although some of the early Marxist writing on community colleges asserted that the business community actively promoted these institutions for their own gain, Steven Brint and Jerome Karabel showed how community college leaders had to convince the business community that the expansion of these 2-year institutions was good for business. In pursuing their own goals, community college educators practiced "anticipatory subordination" by molding their schools to meet the needs of the business community. Although Brint and Karabel are not Marxists, they illustrate the complex relationship between community college educators and business leaders.

2. *Race, Class, and Gender.* Traditionally, Marxists have relegated race and gender conflicts to the status of secondary contradictions, with class conflict being primary. In practice, race and gender have either been grafted onto class-based theories or have been omitted altogether. During the 1990s, however, an increasing number of Marxists have rejected class conflict as being the only major dynamic of late twentieth-century capitalism.

Non-Asian people of color can be incorporated into some class-based theories because they, like their white working-class and poor counterparts, do poorly in school and are often alienated from the official school culture. Hence, it is possible for economic reproduction theorists to argue that race-based tracking systems help to reproduce racial divisions in the labor market. Similarly, cultural reproductionists argue that minority culture, like working-class culture, is delegitimated in the schools.

It is more difficult to incorporate gender into class-based theories of education because females often *outperform* their male counterparts at all levels of education even though they are at a *disadvantage* in the labor market. Although the curriculum is still biased in favor of males in spite of some recent improvements, women have surpassed men in earning both bachelors and masters degrees. Yet, women still receive *different* educations than men, especially with regard to their underrepresentation in math and science programs that prepare students for higher paying jobs.

Since the late 1960s, socialist feminists and black Marxists have argued that gender and race are as important as class in understanding late twentieth-century capitalism. Postmodernists and poststructuralists have also argued against the class-reductionist view of traditional Marxism. This issue did not become central to Marxist education theory until the 1980s, however.

The most important work in this area has been the development of the "Nonsynchronist Parallelist" view of education by Cameron McCarthy (1993), Michael Apple and Lois Weis (1983), and Emily Hicks. The parallelist part of McCarthy and Apple's work (1988) is that race, class, and gender are equivalent forms of oppression that are linked to each other but are also semi-autonomous, i.e., none of the three dimensions is reducible to the other. In addition, they argue that each of these dimensions is not a static phenomenon but is a process that is continually being produced, reproduced, and contested.

The nonsynchronist part of their work is that these three oppressions are not necessarily additive and are often in contradiction to each other. Class oppression sometimes reinforces racial and gender oppression, but at other times undermines them.

McCarthy (1993:338) discusses four types of relations that govern nonsynchronous interactions of race, class, and gendered groups in the schools. *Relations of competition* include the struggle for various educational resources such as access, credentials, and financial aid. *Relations of exploitation* refer to the ways in which the school mediates the economy's demands for a stratified labor force. *Relations of domination* refer to the hierarchical structure within the school and the way in which the school "mediates demands for symbolic control and legitimation from a racial and patriarchal state." Finally, *relations of cultural selection* refer to the "cultural strategies or rules of inclusion/exclusion or in-group/out-group that determine whose knowledge gets into the curriculum, and that also determine the pedagogical practices of ability grouping, diagnosing, and marking of school youth. . . . In the school setting, each of these four types of relations interacts with, defines and is defined by the others in an uneven and decentered manner."

Although race, class, and gender are important in all school settings, McCarthy (1993:339) argues that each setting usually has a "dominant character" or "articulating principle" that pulls "the entire ensemble of relations in the school setting into a 'unity' or focus for conflict. Such an articulating principle may be race, class, or gender." The nature of this articulating principle is determined by the mix of capacities and interests that actors bring to the school and the ways which the actors negotiate the relations of competition, exploitation, domination, and cultural selection.

Although still somewhat abstract, this theory provides a framework to understand the ways in which race, class and gender intersect at the school levels and in the larger society. With their criticism of class reductionism, McCarthy and Apple (1988) are pushing Marxist analysis to its outer limits.

3. *The Role of Culture.* During the 1990s, an increasing number of Marxists wrote about the importance of culture in understanding education. The curriculum certainly has been a contested terrain with an explicit struggle over what should be taught, especially with regard to multiculturalism, feminism, and sexual orientation.

Marxist views toward multicultural and feminist critiques of the curriculum have been ambivalent, ranging from tolerance to strong support. Although most Marxists have acknowledged the attempts of these movements to democratize a curriculum that has been dominated by the views of wealthy white males, multiculturalism was also seen as something that could divide the working class. Marxists hoped that multiculturalists and feminists would eventually understand that it is class that really ties them together.

Aronowitz and Giroux (1993), however, take a much more positive view of multiculturalism and see it as a major weapon in the struggle for democracy in a diverse society. However, they also discuss the importance of moving beyond simple "binarisms" or "us vs. them" positions and exploring "unity-in-difference" perspectives among different oppressed groups. This unity could include class, but is not restricted to it.

In addition, they argue that "critical multiculturalism" should have an egalitarian activist component. It should address issues of contemporary struggles for political and economic power outside of the educational context. Finally, a critical multiculturalism should "refigure" the relations among teachers, students, administrators, and the larger community.

4. *Praxis.* Although most Marxists are at least nominally committed to combining theory and practice, many theories of education call for the elimination of capitalism without any explanation of how the educational system might help to accomplish this goal. Aronowitz and Giroux (1993) reject this view and argue that Marxists and other radicals must start developing a "language of possibility" in their educational analyses so that the process of transforming capitalism can begin.

They look to critical pedagogy as the means to empower students by teaching them "really useful knowledge." According to Aronowitz and Giroux (1993:153), "[T]he core of what counts as really useful knowledge is knowledge that draws from popular education, knowledge that challenges and critically appropriates dominant ideologies, and knowledge that points to more human and democratic social relations and cultural forms."

Marxist theories of the sociology of education will continue to mature and proliferate. The coming years will show whether Marxists have a better understanding of the problems of education in the twenty-first century than do traditional sociological theories.

REFERENCES

Anyon, Jean. 1980. "Social Class and the Hidden Curriculum of Work." *Journal of Education* 162:67–92.

Apple, Michael W. 1993. *Official Knowledge: Democratic Education in a Conservative Age.* New York: Routledge.

Apple, Michael W., and Lois Weis, eds. 1983. *Ideology and Practice in Schooling.* Philadelphia: Temple University Press.

Aronowitz, Stanley, and Henry A. Giroux. 1993. *Education Still Under Siege,* 2nd ed. Westport, CT: Bergin and Garvey.

Bowles, Sam, and Herbert Gintis. 1976. *Schooling in Capitalist America.* New York: Basic Books.

Carnoy, Martin, and Henry M. Levin. 1985. *Schooling and Work in the Democratic State.* Stanford: Stanford University Press.

Freire, Paulo. 1970. *Pedagogy of the Oppressed.* New York: Seabury.

McCarthy, Cameron. 1993. "Beyond the Poverty of Theory in Race Relations: Nonsynchrony and Social Difference in Education." In Lois Weis and Michelle Fine (eds.), *Beyond Silenced Voices: Class, Race and Gender in United States Schools,* pp. 325–346. Albany: SUNY Press.

McCarthy, Cameron, and Michael W. Apple. 1988. "Race, Class and Gender in American Educational Research: Toward a Nonsynchronous Parallelist Position." In Lois Weis (ed.), *Class, Race and Gender in American Education,* pp. 9–39. Albany: SUNY Press.

Pincus, Fred L. 1980. "The False Promises of Community Colleges: Class Conflict and Vocational Education." *Harvard Educational Review* 50:332–361.

Shor, Ira. 1992. *Empowering Education: Critical Teaching for Social Change.* Chicago: University of Chicago Press.

Willis, Paul. *Learning to Labor.* 1991. New York. Columbia University Press.

Sociology of Education

New

Philip Wexler
Warner Graduate School of Education and Human Development, University of Rochester

Definitions and History

New sociology of education refers to a particular orientation and writings that are a subset of an academic field of knowledge, sociology of education. Academic fields, and their subsets, like new sociology of education, although they are created by specialists, are created not out of whole cloth or simply individual imaginations and conceptualizations. Rather, these specialized groupings or fields of knowledge are created by social beings, people, who, despite their professional specializations, live within particular cultures and historical times.

Academic specializations like new sociology of education, or sociology of education generally, or even sociology itself, are products of specialists who live in at least two contexts: the context of their specialized professional milieu, the world of their like-minded colleagues and the institutions they work in, ordinarily universities, and the wider context of their culture and historical times. New sociology of education can be understood as a product of both these contexts, the professional context of the university and the broader social context of culture and history.

Generally, this professionally specialized knowledge, produced in a social context, called new sociology of education, has two nationally and historically distinct, but interrelated referents: English and American. First, the term is used in England in the early 1970s (Gorbutt, 1972) to indicate a style of theory and research that was different from the work that preceded it in the general field of sociology of education. Unlike the earlier research (Halsey et al., 1961) that emphasized theoretically the structure and function of society and education (so-called structural functionalism), and that approached research by analyzing the relations among variables—often measuring individual characteristics such as academic achievement or social mobility)—the English new sociology of the late 1960s and early 1970s emphasized understanding or interpreting everyday classroom social interaction and the meaning of knowledge in school. Meaning referred both to understandings of the student and teacher participants and to the view that the curriculum, which began to be called "school knowledge," was also part of a wider cultural or social context. The way that this was stated in the professional language of academic fields was that sociology of education, as a field of knowledge, should be seen as belonging to another sociological subspecialty, the sociology of knowledge (Young, 1971).

Sociology of knowledge represents the view that all knowledge is social, and that instead of seeing knowledge as somehow detached, separated, and outside of social life, and therefore as "objective," knowledge, as we have stated at the outset, should be understood as a product of social beings, living and working in professional, organizational, cultural, and historical contexts that very much influence and shape the character of what and how they think and write. Knowledge in school, both in the everyday meanings interchanged between and among students and teachers, and in the formal curriculum, is a social product, created within social, cultural, and historical processes. This is a very different view from, for example, taking the curriculum as objective content and then measuring how well different individual students achieve in acquiring it, as was, and still is, done in sociology of education generally. The English new sociology of education was both interpretive, in its interest in the meanings of school interaction, and based in sociology of knowledge, contextual in its social view of school curriculum.

In England, this interpretive, contextual knowledge approach had been very much influenced by the work of Basil Bernstein, both in his early research, which brought a cultural, language, and social interactional approach to studying education (Bernstein, 1958, 1975), and by his own teaching influence on advanced professional students in the London Institute of Education. By the end of the 1970s, however, the interpretive, contextual knowledge approach that defined the new sociology of education was modified to include also the more politically oriented and so-called radical views that replaced an early structural–functionalist understanding of the larger organization of society with a more Marxist interest in social class, the state, and a political–economic rather than largely cultural interest (Sharp and Green, 1975; Young and Whitty, 1977; Sharp, 1980). New sociology of education became identified with social criticism, the New Left, and the renaissance of Marxist thought in Europe, which occurred in the wider social context in which new sociology of education was produced.

In America, new sociology of education was only in part influenced by the English developments. One of the most evident influences was in the work of Michael Apple (1978, 1979), who directly represented the English approach. But Apple's work also expressed a particularly American aspect of the new sociology of education, and one that would influence the subsequent course of this academic specialization or subfield. What Apple accomplished, within the narrower context of the professional rather than broader cultural, social shaping of academic knowledge, was to appropriate the term "new sociology" for use by academics located in the educationist and curricular rather than sociology departments. This more local contextual shaping of knowledge in the subfield continued the English interest in a sociology of school knowledge or curriculum, but also gave license to a much more open-ended definition of new sociology of education. Educationists, unlike sociologists, were much less constrained to follow the professional history or paradigms of traditional sociology of education (Wexler, 1976). The result was the emergence of an apparent subfield of sociology of education from outside its ordinary institutional con-

text: from England and from specializations outside of sociology.

New sociology of education was then also a professional claim for the legitimacy of professionals not trained in sociology to speak and write about a sociological approach to education. Only much later would mainstream sociology of education incorporate the concepts and research of a new sociology that had in fact originated largely outside the boundaries of its academic, specialized borders. This institutional history is important, not only because the nonsociological professional location of new sociology of education created intellectual openness, but also because it represented a modern chapter in a long story of rivalry and difference between educationists and sociologists working on the same overall questions of education in society, but with different interests, concepts, and methods of analysis. New sociology of education represented also the resurgence of the educationists' socially critical educational sociology over the sociologists' "scientific" sociology of education.

New sociology of education refers to a specific set of concepts and point of view, but it simultaneously represents cultures of its contexts: the larger social changes of the 1960s (Wexler, 1976) and the professional dynamics of the specialists who created this particular orientation to analyzing education socially (Wexler, 1987).

Concepts and Contributions

Sociology of knowledge is not simply a little-known sociological subspecialty, but an orientation that also represents a more general cultural and political mood. As Mannheim (1936) recognized, seeing knowledge socially occurs when there is a climate of political conflict and sociocultural turmoil—a time like the late 1960s and 1970s in American history. Not only the "early" American new sociology of education (Wexler, 1976; Karabel and Halsey, 1977), but the wider public and academic culture also displayed distrust of claims to "objective knowledge." Somewhat suspiciously, critics and analysts of society saw political and economic interest behind not only school curricula, but university institutionalized departments, fields, and disciplines of knowledge (Blackburn, 1972). Knowledge was seen, both in the wider culture and in the academic specialties, as a partial or distorted representation of specific group interests, and not simply as a mirror-like, "objective" reality.

This sort of knowledge becomes redefined as "ideology." New sociology of education brought this concept of ideology to education, generally, and to sociology of education in particular. The analytical work that follows from this concept is often referred to as "ideology critique," showing how specific group interests get represented as general knowledge or even "facts." Ideology, or partial, group interested knowledge is a key concept in the early work of the new sociologists (Young, 1971; Brown, 1973; Wexler, 1976; Karabel and Halsey, 1977; Apple, 1979; Sharp, 1980; Giroux, 1983). The challenge to the ordinary concept of knowledge that "ideology" presents is supplemented by additional shifts in focus from traditional sociology of education and curriculum studies to the new sociology of education.

A second important shift of concepts is the move away from the ordinary understanding of education as a vehicle of individual advance or social mobility toward the sense that the social effect of education is instead to replicate, "reproduce," or maintain socially structured patterns of inequality. Education not only masks group-interested ideology as objective knowledge or curriculum, it also makes the reproduction of social patterns of inequality appear to be differences of individual success in school.

This understanding—that education is part of a process of reproducing patterned inequality—drew from European general social theory to show how sociocultural reproduction works through an apparently individual merit-rewarding educational system (Bourdieu and Passeron, 1977; Althusser, 1971). The conceptual shift, again seeing education as deeply socially produced or constructed, rather than simply as an individually summed process, was then refined to include the concept of "resistance." Although in its early usage (Willis, 1977), the idea that students resist the operation of school as a mechanism of sociocultural reproduction was meant ironically—that resistance unintentionally feeds into reproduction—the concept became a qualifier of the idea that culture and society simply and automatically reproduce themselves, behind the backs of the individual participants. There is "agency" as well as structure (Giroux, 1983).

"Resistance" was not only an important concept in the new sociology shift to a critical, fully social understanding of education in society, but it also underlined the importance of empirical research in schools and among youth generally. Willis' (1977) English study signaled the beginning of an entire style of research that tried to connect general, critical social concepts about education with specific, detailed studies of everyday life in schools. These empirical studies of schooling emphasized how social inequality and power, as "social class," worked in school practice, and what sorts of implications that might have for educational practice or pedagogy (for a sampling, see Apple and Weis, 1983; for a history, see Weis, 1995). Later, this empirical, qualitative study of schooling, undertaken from the conceptual bases of ideology, reproduction, and resistance, came to be known as "critical ethnography" (Anderson, 1989).

The combined interest (1) in knowledge as a social product; (2) in ideology critique of the partial, but seemingly general and socially neutral appearing character of curriculum and culture; (3) in reproduction of patterned inequality appearing on the surface as differences in individual merit-based social mobility; (4) in recognizing that there might be resistance to education's working as a socially reproductive, status quo-maintaining, process; and (5) in trying to show empirically how these key concepts of ideology, reproduction, and resistance can make better sense of everyday school life, in critical ethnographies—all taken together, are the defining features of the new sociology of education.

By the mid-1980s, this "paradigm" began to be modified in ways that altered the course of the new sociology of education. First, the political climate in the wider social context had become much less sympathetic to critical, "radical" social understandings, both in England and in America, than it had been during the heyday of new sociology in the 1970s. Ironically, and complexly, although these socially critical concepts became more popular in university courses and discussions, the boom years of university hiring were already receding, and the opportunities for professional mobility and political risk taking within the academy were diminishing (Wexler, 1987). Second, the increasingly public voice of feminism and the effort to rectify the relative neglect of race in social educational studies led to what Ladwig (1995) describes as the "decentering of class": greater attention to gender and race as topics for critical ethnographies and social theorizing in education (Luke and Gore, 1992; McCarthy and Crichlow, 1993). Relatedly, the somewhat neglected exploration of the practical implication of the new sociology of education was developed in an emphasis on a politically oriented teaching and curriculum, referred to as "critical pedagogy" (for a critical review, Gore, 1993). Third, new currents in European social thought that moved away from the Marxist and ideology-critique interest, and that emphasized the study of culture as language rather than as political distortion of knowledge, influenced the sociology of education: first as "poststructuralism" and then as "postmodernism" (Wexler, 1987; Aronowitz and Giroux, 1991). All of this occurred at a time when a new wave of business, corporate-oriented reform began to alter the shape of American education (Mickelson, forthcoming).

Directions

Currently, the term "new sociology of education" has faded from use. In part, the contemporary lack of usage testifies to the success of new sociology of education. Concepts and research studies that might once have been so labeled are now a more routine part of academic specialties such as sociology of education and curriculum. At the same time, some of the early, defining interests of the subfield now appear, but in different terms, and also with different directions. For example, the unmasking tendency of ideology critique has become an affirmation of group differences in culture and identity. Class, race, and gender are normal categories in writings and teachings about education and society. Cultural studies, as a cross-disciplinary subfield, affirm these sociocultural differences, and carry the sort of political import once identified with a sociology of knowledge or ideology approach (McLaren, 1995). "Reproduction and resistance" are no longer popular terms, although the view of education as deeply social, which they once signaled, has become embedded in our tacit understandings of education. Educational reform, although it has not fully displaced the term "critical pedagogy," now generally represents the conceptual field where conflicting economic and political interests are expressed. Although there is little use of Bowles and Gintis' (1976) term "correspondence principle," which signified both the centrality of social class effects in

education and the connection between work and education, those themes persist, in different terms, in empirical studies of schooling (Wexler, 1992), and, even "after postmodernism," in social theory and education (Smith and Wexler, 1995).

Sociology of education, perhaps like culture more broadly, has now become "multiple" and diverse. Now there is less of a clear-cut division between an "old" liberal and a "new" radical sociology of education. Not that education, or social thinking about education has become less political. Rather, politics, economics, culture, and individual identity work are less neatly arrayed in a postmodern world of multiplicities, of many simultaneous lines and fields of thought and action (Gergen, 1991). Indeed, in an academic field of multiple sociologies of education (Pink and Noblit, 1995), part of the challenge of the future is in not diffusing the political passion and strong desire for social transformation and liberation of new sociology into a bland, undefined, surface tolerance for difference.

What comes now, after both the new sociology of education and its modifications and translations in a postmodern context, may be the reassertion of those same passions and drives, yet, once again, in a different language, for still a "new," but different, social context and historical time.

REFERENCES

Althusser, Louis. 1971. *Lenin and Philosophy and Other Essays*. London: New Left Books.

Anderson, Gary L. 1989. "Critical Ethnography in Education: Origins, Current Status and New Directions." *Review of Educational Research* 59(3):249–270.

Apple, Michael W. 1978. "The New Sociology of Education: Analyzing Cultural and Economic Reproduction." *Harvard Educational Review* 48(1):495–503.

———. 1979. *Ideology and Curriculum*. Boston and London: Routledge & Kegan Paul.

Apple, Michael W., and Lois Weis, eds. 1983. *Ideology and Practice in Schooling*. Philadelphia: Temple University Press.

Aronowitz, Stanley, and Henry Giroux. 1991. *Postmodern Education: Politics, Culture, and Social Criticism*. Minneapolis: University of Minnesota Press.

Bernstein, Basil. 1958. "Some Sociological Determinants of Perception: An Enquiry into Subcultural Differences." *The British Journal of Sociology* 9(2):159–172.

———. 1975. *Class, Codes, and Control: Towards a Theory of Educational Transmissions*. London: Routledge & Kegan Paul.

Blackburn, Robin, ed. 1972. *Ideology in Social Science: Readings in Critical Social Theory*. New York: Pantheon Books.

Bourdieu, Pierre, and Jean-Claude Passeron. 1977. *Reproduction in Education, Society and Culture*. Beverly Hills, CA: Sage.

Bowles, Samuel, and Herbert Gintis. 1976. *Schooling in Capitalist America*. New York: Basic Books.

Brown, Richard, ed. 1973. *Knowledge, Education, and Cultural Change*. London: Tavistock.

Gergen, Kenneth. 1991. *The Saturated Self: Dilemmas of Identity in Contemporary Life*. New York: Basic Books.

Giroux, Henry. 1983. *Theory and Resistance in Education*. South Hadley, MA: Bergin & Garvey.

Gorbutt, L. 1972. "The New Sociology of Education." *Education for Teaching* 3–11.

Gore, Jennifer. 1993. *The Struggle for Pedagogies: Critical and Feminist Discourses as Regimes of Truth*. New York: Routledge.

Halsey, A. H., Jean Floud, and C. Arnold Anderson, eds. 1961. *Education, Economy, and Society*. New York: Free Press.

Karabel, Jerome, and A. H. Halsey. 1977. *Power and Ideology in Education*. New York: Oxford University Press.

Ladwig, James G. 1995. "The Genesis of Groups in the Sociology of School Knowledge." In William T. Pink and George W. Noblit (eds.), *Continuity and Contradiction*, pp. 209–229. Creskill, NJ: Hampton Press.

Luke, Carmen, and Jennifer Gore, eds. 1992. *Feminisms and Critical Pedagogy*. New York: Routledge.

Mannheim, Karl. 1936. *Ideology and Utopia: An Introduction to the Sociology of Knowledge*. New York: Harcourt, Brace & World.

McCarthy, Cameron, and Warren Crichlow, eds. 1993. *Race, Identity and Representation in Education*. New York: Routledge.

McClaren, Peter. 1995. *Critical Pedagogy and Predatory Culture: Oppositional Politics in a Postmodern Era*. London: Routledge.

Mickelson, Roslyn. 2001. "Opportunity and Danger: Understanding the Business Contribution to Public Education." In Kathryn Borman, Peter Cookson, Alan R. Sadovnik, and Joan Spade (eds.), *Sociological Approaches to Implementing Federal Legislation*. Garland Press.

Pink, William, and George W. Noblit, eds. 1995. *Continuity and Contradiction: The Futures of the Sociology of Education*. Creskill, NJ: Hampton Press.

Sharp, Rachel. 1980. *Knowledge, Ideology and the Politics of Schooling: Towards a Marxist Analysis of Education*. Boston: Routledge & Kegan Paul.

Sharp, Rachel, and Anthony Green. 1975. *Education and Social Control: A Study in Progressive Primary Education*. London: Routledge & Kegan Paul.

Smith, Richard, and Philip Wexler. 1995. *After Postmodernism: Education, Politics, and Identity*. London: Falmer Press.

Weis, Lois. 1995. "Qualitative Research in Sociology of Education: Reflections on the 1970s and Beyond." In William T. Pink and George W. Noblit (eds.), *Continuity and Contradiction*, pp. 157–173. Creskill, NJ: Hampton Press.

Wexler, Philip. 1976. *The Sociology of Education: Beyond Equality*. Indianapolis: Bobbs-Merrill.

———. 1987. *Social Analysis of Education: After the New Sociology*. London: Routledge & Kegan Paul.

———. 1992. *Becoming Somebody: Toward a Social Psychology of School*. London: Falmer Press.

Willis, Paul. 1977. *Learning to Labour: How Working Class Kids Get Working Class Jobs*. Westmead, England: Saxon House.

Young, Michael F. D., ed. 1971. *Knowledge and Control: New Directions for the Sociology of Education*. London: Collier-Macmillan.

Young, Michael F. D., and Geoff Whitty. 1977. *Society, State and Schooling*. Sussex, England: Falmer Press.

SOCIOLOGY OF EDUCATION

OPEN SYSTEMS APPROACH

Jeanne H. Ballantine
Sociology Department, Wright State University

To understand an educational system as a whole, integrated, dynamic entity, social scientists are faced with a problem. Most theories and research studies focus on specific parts of the whole system and how the small pieces fit together. An open systems approach is not a panacea for all the problems faced when trying to get the total picture, but it can help social scientists conceptualize a whole system and understand how the small pieces fit together.

Using the open systems approach provides social scientists with a model making it possible to see the interconnections among system parts, sociological theories, and sociological methods. By using the open systems approach the social scientist can break a complex system and its environment (its relationship to other organizations in society) into its component parts for study. This approach avoids the problems of the closed system approach that focuses primarily on the internal functioning of an organization rather than the organization in its larger social context.

The open systems approach favors no one sociological theory, but it does assist sociologists in understanding the contribution that each major sociological theory can make to organizational systems such as schools. One sociological theory may be more applicable than another for the study of certain parts of educational systems or of educational problems that arise in that system.

Presented as a model (Figure 1), the open systems approach provides a useful way of visualizing the many elements in the educational system; it helps order observations and data, and represents a generalized picture of complex interacting elements and sets of relationships (Griffith, 1965:24). The model shown does not refer to one particular organization or theoretical

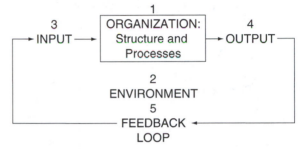

Figure 1. The Open Systems Model. Adapted from Von Bertatantly, L. 1962. "General Systems Theory—A Critical Review." General Systems 7:1–20.

approach, but rather provides a framework to consider the common characteristics of many educational settings. Similar open system models have been used in the areas of organizational studies (Checkland, 1994), cross-cultural education (Cullen, 1994), family therapy (Searland, 1991), health studies (Gustaello, 1992), and group studies (Boer, 1994). Thus, in describing a systems model, note that "it is not a particular kind of social organization. It is an analytical model that can be applied to any instance of the process of social organization, from families to nation .... Nor is [it] a substantive theory—though it is sometimes spoken of as a theory in sociological literature. This model is a highly general, content-free conceptual framework within which any number of different substantive theories of social organization can be constructed" (Olsen, 1978:228).

Thus, although this model indicates the component parts of a total system, it does not imply that one theory is better than another for explaining situations or events in the system. Neither does it suggest which is the best methodology to use in studying any part of the system. It does allow social scientists to visualize the parts they study in relation to the whole system—to see where parts fit in relationship to the whole educational system.

Figure 1 shows the five basic components of an educational open system. An example for each component, or step (Figure 2), is included to help clarify each part of the system.

Step 1: The Organization

The center box, the *organization*, refers to the center of activity and the central concern for many researchers. This box can represent a society (such as the United States), an institution (such as education or family), an organization (such as a particular school or church), or a subsystem (such as a classroom). For purposes of discussion, "the organization" is where the internal activities of the educational organization take place, illustrating that the organization includes action as well as structure, positions, roles, and functions. Within the organizational boundaries is a *structure* consisting of parts and subparts, positions, and roles. Although sociologists speak of the organization as though it were a living entity, they are really referring to the personnel who carry out the activities of the organization and make decisions about the organization's activities. The

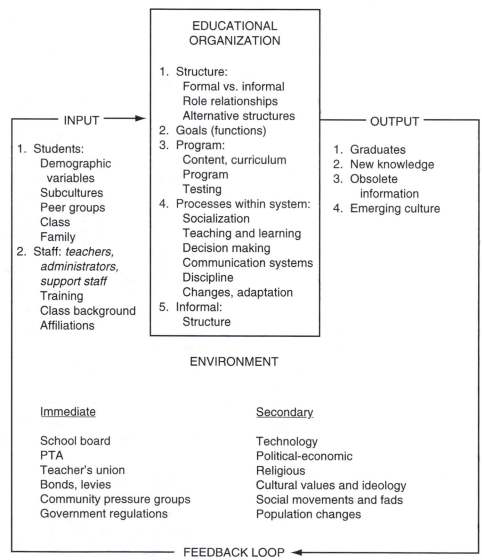

Figure 2. Examples of the Components of an Open System.

processes in the system are the action part, bringing the organization alive. *Decision making* by key personnel, *communication* between members of the educational organization, *socialization* into positions in the organization—these are among the many activities that are constantly taking place.

Some theoretical approaches emphasize only analysis of internal organizational processes, but these processes do not take place in a vacuum. The decision makers holding positions and carrying out roles in the organization are constantly responding to demands from both inside and outside the organization. The boundaries of the organization are not solid, but rather remain flexible and pliable in most organizational systems to allow system needs to be met. Social scientists call this "open boundaries" of an *open system*.

The formal relationships within educational organizations are only part of the picture. Capturing the informal relationships in the school—who eats lunch with whom, who cuts classes, what subtle cues do teachers transmit to students, what is the gossip in the teachers' lounge—can tell as much about the functioning of the school as observing formal roles and structure.

Example: An Open System Organization

"High School" was filmed to show the organization of a real high school. Frederick Wiseman moved his film crew into a high school and shot reels of film. Later, in the editing process, he put together scenes representing life in the high school. The film showed *roles*: teachers were interesting, boring, humiliating, supportive, and threatening when dealing with students. Students were attentive, bored, hostile, compliant. Administrators mediated, scolded, doled out punishments. These represent *manifest processes* of teaching, learning, decision making, communicating, and disciplining, and *latent processes* of rebelling and participating in a peer subculture. Wiseman also looked at the *subparts* or smaller divisions of the high school *structure*. The film contains scenes showing individual classrooms; the principal as he was dealing with parents; the assistant principal's office, where disciplinary matters were being handled; the hallway; the gym; cooking class; the lunchroom.

The film, then, gives an overview of the internal organizational stucture of a school and classrooms, formal and informal roles, and processes or activities taking place in the school.

Step 2: The Environment

An open system implies that there is interaction between the organization and the environment outside the organization. The environment includes other organizational systems that surround the organization and influence it in some way. For a country, the environment would include all other competing or cooperating countries or international organizations. In addition, there is the *technological environment*, with new developments that affect the operation of the systems; the *political environment*, which affects the system through legal controls; the *economic environment*, from which the system gets its financing; the *surrounding community* and its prevailing attitudes; the *values, norms, and changes* in society, which are often reflected in *social movements* or fads; *population changes*; and so forth.

For each organization, the most important environments will differ and can change over time, depending on issues facing the school. The organization depends on the environment for meeting many of its resource requirements and for obtaining information. For instance, each school and school district faces a different set of challenges from the environment. These are necessary and desired interactions with the environment, and may include some that are not desirable. The interaction of the school with the environment takes place in our systems model in the form of inputs and outputs, the next parts of the model.

Example: The Environment

The principal of an elementary school has the responsibility of maintaining a smoothly running school and meeting the goals of educating the children. Some of the factors with which a principal must contend are predictable; others are not. Here are some examples of environmental influences from a week in the life of a principal:

1. A school board meeting is coming up for which the principal must prepare a budget report justifying the expense for a new series of second-grade readers.
2. The Parent-Teachers Association has asked the principal to speak on the counseling program in the school.

3. The principal has received notification from Washington that the school must develop a plan to mainstream some of the community's disabled students and train teachers to deal with them in the classroom with no additional financial allocation.

4. Contract negotiations are coming up with the teachers' union, and the principal must justify the school's needs in several areas, such as in-service training that requires teachers to stay after school.

5. A bond levy will be on the next ballot, asking the voters for funds to buy new playground equipment and library resources. To get the bond passed will require lobbying in the community.

6. A group of citizens is asking for a conference to discuss the Title IX legislation related to sexism in the schools, and what steps are being taken to eliminate sexism at the school.

7. A new reading program has been developed, using sophisticated equipment. The principal must consider whether the expenditure would be worth the potential improvement.

8. Some parents in the community are concerned about Christmas carols being sung in classes and the Christmas tree in the school lobby. A decision must be made as to whether to eliminate these religious symbols.

9. The principal has received the projections for population trends in the community for the next 10 years. They show a likely decline in elementary school enrollment. The principal needs to plan a strategy to deal with the probability.

10. The state legislature passes numerous bills related to education, some of which are directly relevant to the elementary level. The principal must keep up with this information.

Environmental factors influence the internal activities of every school and school district, and cannot be ignored in attempts to understand schools. (Source: Excerpts from interviews with principals conducted by the author.)

Step 3: Input

The organization receives *input* from the environment in forms such as information, raw materials, students, personnel, finances, and new ideas. The persons who are members of an organization all belong to other organizations in the environment and bring into the organization influences from the outside environment.

Some of the environmental inputs are mandatory for the organization's survival; others vary in degree of importance. For most organizations, some inputs are undesirable, but unavoidable—new legal restrictions, competition, or financial pressures. The organization can exert some control over the inputs. For instance, schools have selection processes for new teachers, textbooks, and other curricular materials. Certain positions in the organization are held by personnel who act as *buffers* or liaisons between the organization and its environment. The secretary who answers the phone, for example, has a major protection and controlling function, and the social worker and counselor are links with the environment.

Example: Input

In universities, students are key participants. They fill out forms to enter the system, wait in line or at computer terminals to sign up for classes and pay tuition, come to class to take notes and exams, obtain credits, and are graduated. In systems terms, they are *inputs* into the educational system, and *outputs* upon graduation. And they are "processed" through the system. The process involves waiting in lines to become *inputs*, and suffering humiliation and sometimes defeat in being processed by the system to become *outputs*. Eventually they are rewarded for academic efforts with a diploma.

Students bring to the system their personality, their contributions, their money, *and* their problems. For instance, a number of students attending universities are parents. When the public schools are not in session, they are faced with the problem of child care. At these times, the number of individuals in the university classroom may increase with little persons accompanying their parents, or may decrease because of child-care problems.

The school system includes personnel who act as buffers. For instance, a class is closed. The students really need the class. Instructor's permission is required to let them in, but the instructor is nowhere to be found. The departmental secretary takes student names and assures them that the instructor will be in touch with them *if* they are permitted to enter the class. This is an effective buffer.

Step 4: Output

Output refers to the material items and the nonmaterial ideas that leave the organization: completed products, such as research findings; graduates; waste products from offices and labs; new information; evolving culture; and new technology. There may be personnel in *boundary-spanning* positions, bridging the gap between the educational organization and its environment. Personnel with responsibility for selling the organization's product, whether they work in a manufacturing organization or in a placement office for college graduates, serve this function.

Example: Output

A ceremony with full academic regalia and a sheepskin (or more likely an engraved paper) mark the passage from the school organization to the environment. Graduates are a clear example of a university's *output* or product, which also includes books and articles written by faculty reporting research findings; new ideas and evolving culture that affect our life-style and values; jargon; and major league football and baseball players.

There are "negative" outputs as well—students who drop out or fail, faculty members who do not receive tenure, students who graduate but are unable to find jobs. These can be seen as system failures.

Step 5: Feedback

A key aspect of a systems model is the process of *feedback*. This step implies an organization constantly adapting to changes and demands in the environment as a result of new information it receives. For instance, the organizational personnel compare the current state of affairs with desired goals and environmental feedback to determine new courses of action. The positive or negative feedback requires different responses.

Example: Feedback

The university graduates education majors who obtain teaching jobs in the community. But imagine that the graduates have weak skills in dealing with minority students and their families. Not only are the schools dissatisfied with their new teachers, but the students are frustrated. This message reaches the university and plans are begun to modify the curriculum. Included in the modified curriculum are both course work and practical experience in urban schools and with minority students. The feedback has indicated need for change and decisions have been made within the organization to bring about the needed change.

This represents the full cycle of continuous activity. The processes never cease. Social scientists can only study an organization or some aspect of it at a given moment in time, for new events will bring constant modification to that organization. Most organizations, however, develop sufficient stability and adapt to environmental demand well enough so that change is slow and deliberate. The open systems approach can be used to plan large system change in the interconnected parts, select a starting point for change, and link change events and processes to each other. For instance, a school system may start with the superintendent's team; introduce a pilot project in one school; prepare other schools for the change; provide training, education, and rewards for implementation; and prepare teachers to be ready for the change (Armel, 1997).

The basic open systems model (Figure 1) can serve social scientists in many ways. As conceived by some of its early proponents, it is more inclusive and flexible, and it can help promote interdisciplinary study. Consider, for example, Kenneth Boulding's statement:

an interdisciplinary movement has been abroad for some time. The first signs of this are usually the development of hybrid disciplines. It is one of the main objectives of General Systems Theory to develop these generalized areas and by developing a framework of general theory to enable one specialist to catch relevant communication from other. (Boulding, 1956:197–208)

Sociology of education cannot be discussed within the fields of education and sociology alone, showing the interrelationships between disciplines. Examples of related fields are numerous: economics and school financing; political science, power, and educational policy issues; the family and the school child; church–state separation controversies; health fields and medical care for children; humanities and the arts in school curricula; and the school's role in early childhood training.

Several social scientists have pointed to the value of an open systems approach in organizational analysis, pointing out advantages such as more expansive, more inclusive, and more flexible theoretical structures than are available using any one theory. Both the analysis and planning of change can be facilitated using open systems analysis to consider every aspect of the organization. Changing one subpart cannot bring about system change (Scott, 1963; Armel, 1997). For instance, in the organizational models promoting continuous improvement, all events, processes, problems, and successes are integrally linked to each other. Parts of organizations cannot be taken out like parts of machines, repaired or replaced, and then put back (Armel, 1997). The open systems approach not only serves the functions noted above, but helps give unity to a complex field.

REFERENCES

Armel, Donald. 1997. "Achieving Continuous Improvement: Theories That Support a System Change." ERIC —ED410915. Microfiche Paper, June.

Ballantine, Jeanne. 1997. *The Sociology of Education.* Upper Saddle River, NJ: Prentice-Hall.

Boer, Carla, and Cora Moore. 1994. "Ecosystemic Thinking in Group Therapy." *Group Analysis* 27:105–117.

Boulding, Kenneth E. "GST—the Skeleton of Science." *Management Science* 2:197–208.

Checkland, Peter. 1994. "System Theory and Management Thinking." *American Behavioral Scientist* 38:75–91.

Cullen, Thomas. 1994. "An Open Systems Approach to Cross-Cultural Training." ERIC—ED373696. Microfiche Paper, April.

Griffiths, D. 1965. "Systems Theory and School Districts." *Journal of Educational Research* 8:24.

Gustaello, Stephen J. 1992. *Accidents and Stress-Related Health Disorders among Bus Operators: Forecasting with Catastrophe Theory.* Washington, DC: American Psychological Association.

Olsen, Marvin. 1978. *The Process of Social Organization: Power in Social Systems,* 2nd ed. New York: Holt, Rinehart & Winston.

Scott, W. G. 1963. "Organization Theory: An Overview and an Appraisal." In J. A. Litterer (ed.), *Organization: Structure and Behavior.* New York: Wiley.

Searland, H. Russell. 1991. "Systems Theory and Its Discontents: Clinical and Ethical Issues." *American Journal of Family Therapy* 19: 19–31.

Shachar, Hanna, and Shlomo Sharan. 1995. "Cooperative Learning and the Organization of Secondary Schools." *School Effectiveness and School Improvement* 6:47–66.

SOCIOLOGY OF EDUCATION

POSTMODERNISM*

Alan R. Sadovnik
Rutgers University

Postmodernism developed out of a profound dissatisfaction with the modernist project. Beginning with the poststructural writings of Derrida (1973, 1981, 1982) and Baudrillard (1981, 1984), social theorists, particularly in France, questioned the appropriateness of modernist categories for understanding what they saw as a postmodern world that transcended the economic and social relations of the industrial world that modernists sought to understand. In particular, the work of Lyotard (1982, 1984) rejected the Marxist project and the Enlightenment and modernist assumptions underlying Marxist theory and sought to create a different theory of the late twentieth century. As Rust (1991) points out, although the terms modernism and modernity are sometimes used interchangeably, they are not the same. Modernity refers to the industrial revolution in England, the political revolution in 1789 in France, and the acceptance of scientific and rationalist principles begun during the Enlightenment. Modernism refers to the artistic, literary, and aesthetic movements of the early twentieth century. Much of the postmodern critique is a critique of modernity, rather than modernism, although its use of the term postmodernism may appear to imply the latter.

There is a vast body of literature on the definition of postmodernist theory (Aronowitz and Giroux, 1991; Giroux, 1991; Harvey, 1989; Jameson, 1982, 1992; Jencks, 1987; Lyotard, 1984), as well as a growing body of literature on postmodern approaches to education

(Aronowitz and Giroux, 1991; Cherryholmes, 1988; Doll, 1989; Ellsworth, 1989; Giroux, 1988, 1991; Lather, 1989; McLaren, 1986, 1991; McLaren and Hammer, 1989; Wexler, 1987). Given the scope of this chapter, it is impossible to review all of this work. Therefore, the following sections will draw upon this literature first, to examine postmodernist theory as a critique of modernism (modernity) and second, to examine the major tenets of postmodern theories of education.

Modernist social theory, in both sociology and philosophy, traces its intellectual heritage to the Enlightenment. From the classical sociological theory of Marx (1971), Marx and Engels (1947), Weber (1978), and Durkheim (1947, 1977), to the pragmatist philosophy of Dewey (1916, 1984), and to the social theory of Habermas (1979, 1981, 1982, 1983, 1987), what is usually referred to as modernist theories had a number of things in common. First, they had a belief in progress through science and technology, even if they were skeptical of positivist social science. Second, they emphasized the Enlightenment belief in reason. And third, they stressed Enlightenment principles such as equality, liberty, and justice.

Postmodernist theory developed as a critique of modernist theory, as well as out of a profound dissatisfaction with the failures of modernity to live up to its Enlightenment promise. As Burbules and Rice (1991:397–399) correctly point out, postmodern theories consist of two interrelated types: the first is antimodernist and the second, while providing a critique of modernism, accepts many modernist principles, especially its emphasis on reason, equality, liberty, and justice. On the one hand, Burbules and Rice consider as antimodernist those theories that reject the language

*Adapted from "Postmodernism and the Sociology of Education: Closing the Rift Among Scholarship, Research, and Practice." In George Noblit and William Pink (eds.), *Continuity and Contradiction: The Futures of the Sociology of Education*. Hampton Press, 1995.

of modernism and seek to establish a completely different vocabulary and way of seeing the postmodern world. Elizabeth Ellworth's (1989) critique of Giroux and McLaren falls under this category. On the other hand, they label as postmodernist, those theories that have continuity with modernism and seek to extend modernist visions to the realities of the economic and political crises of the late twentieth century. Aronowitz, Giroux, and McLaren represent this type of postmodern theory. Although these are two distinctive approaches, there is considerable overlap between them, and often antimodern and postmodern writers move back and forth between both positions. Rather than compare and contrast antimodern and postmodern theories, which is not the thrust of this chapter, the following discussion of postmodernism examines the central themes consistent with both approaches.

Although postmodernist thought consists of many interrelated themes, I have chosen to highlight six important ones. First, postmodernism insists on what Lyotard (1984) has labeled the rejection of all metanarratives. By this, Lyotard meant that modernist preoccupation with grand, total, or all encompassing explanations of the world need to be replaced by localized and particular theories. Rejecting the metatheorizing of modernist thought, postmodernism seeks to understand the ways in which particular social conditions give rise to social circumstances. Such a perspective, postmodernists argue, is an antidote to the overly deterministic theories of Marxism and other modernist theories. Postmodernism rejects linear views of historical development and distrusts the Enlightenment belief that science and technology will provide increasingly rational solutions to human dilemmas.

Second, postmodernism stresses the necessary connection between theory and practice as a corrective to the separation of them in much modernist thought. As Anyon (1994) notes, the traditional view that theory and practice are separate phenomena is rejected by postmodern thinkers (Rorty, 1980). Theory needs to affect practice and practice needs to be used as the basis for theory. In this respect, postmodernism rejects the binary oppositions often found in modernist theory, for example, between rational and nonrational, idealism and materialism, modern and traditional, *gemeinschaft* and *gesellschaft*, capitalism and socialism, etc. and seeks a more dialectical analysis of the opposing forces in

society. Such attempts to connect theory to practice and to eliminate binary oppositions are by no means new, but are found in modernist thought as well. For example, the connection between theory and practice was central to Dewey's pragmatism and the dialectical interplay between opposites is a central component of Marxist theory.

Third, postmodernism stresses the democratic response to authoritarianism and totalitarianism. In particular, Aronowitz and Giroux (1991), Giroux (1991), and McLaren and Hammer (1989) call for a democratic, emancipatory, and antitotalitarian theory and practice, with schools seen as sites for democratic transformation. Based upon the rejection of all total or grand theories, postmodernism insists upon the inclusion of the voices of the "other" as central to democratic debate. Again, this theme is by no means new to postmodernism, but as Giroux (1991) points out was central to Dewey's democratic vision of schooling and society. Recent works on democratic theory (Gutmann, 1987), the good society (Bellah et al., 1990), on freedom and education (Greene, 1988), and on Dewey, himself (Westbrook, 1991) all point to the centrality of democratic theory to the core of Dewey's writings. In this respect, this postmodern theme is clearly not a rejection of modernist thought (to the extent that Dewey was a modernist thinker), but rather an attempt to build upon it.

Fourth, postmodernism sees modernist thought as Eurocentric and patriarchal. Giroux (1991), Lather (1991), Ellsworth (1989), and others provide an important critique of the racism and sexism in some modernist writings and the failure of modernism to address the interests of women and people of color. This theme is related to the postmodern concern with the voice of the other as a step toward emancipatory education. Writers such as Giroux (1991) and Greene (1988) are more optimistic about the liberating effects of education; Ellsworth (1989) is skeptical about the empowering effects of postmodern critical theory.

Fifth, postmodernist theorists believe that all social and political discourse is related to structures of power and domination. Although this is an important point, it too is by no means new to postmodernism. The idea that knowledge is related to power and domination is a core concept in both classical sociological theory and the sociology of education. Marx and Engel's (1947) analysis of ideology, Durkheim's (1977) analysis of the history of curriculum in France, Mannheim's (1936) analysis of ideology and utopia, Berger and Luckmann's (1966) phenomenological analysis of the social construction of reality, as well as what is termed critical curriculum theory in the sociology of education (Anyon, 1979, 1981a, 1981b; Apple, 1978, 1979a, 1979b, 1982a, 1982b; Bernstein, 1973a, 1973b, 1977, 1986, 1990, 1996; Sadovnik, 1991; Wexler, 1987; Whitty, 1985) all argue that knowledge is socially constructed and related to structures of power and domination.

Sixth, postmodernism stresses what Burbules and Rice (1991) term "dialogue across differences." Recognizing the particular and local nature of knowledge, postmodern theorists call for an attempt to work through differences, rather than to see them as hopelessly irreconcilable. Thus, postmodern theories of education call for teachers and students to explore the differences between what may seem like inherently contradictory positions in an effort to achieve understanding, respect, and change.

Postmodernist Theories of Education

Although much of postmodern theory developed as a critical theory of society and a critique of modernism, it quickly became incorporated into critical writings on education. Educational theory, which over the past two decades has involved an interdisciplinary mixture of social theory, sociology, and philosophy, has been profoundly affected by postmodernist thought. In particular, critical theories of education, which from the late 1970s attempted to provide an antidote to the overdeterminism of Bowles and Gintis (1976), by the 1980s regularly incorporated postmodern language and concerns. There have been numerous postmodern theories of education or applications of postmodernism to education. From Cherryholmes's (1988) use of poststructural deconstruction to explore the possibilities of schooling, to Ellsworth's (1989) and Lather's (1991) feminist critiques of modernism and their attempt to construct an emancipatory and critical pedagogy, to Miller's (1991) study of teacher empowerment, postmodern theory has produced a rich exploration of the limits and possibilities of schooling.

Of all the postmodern writing in the United States, Henry Giroux's writing represents the most sustained

effort to develop a postmodern theory of education and to connect it to previous critical theories, including neo-Marxism, critical theory, and resistance theory.[1] Although Giroux's work is not representative of all postmodern work in education, it does represent both its limits and possibilities. Therefore, the following section will draw on Giroux's (and Aronowitz's and Giroux's) postmodern theory of education in order to present and critique its contributions to the sociology of education and educational theory.

In *Postmodern Education,* Aronowitz and Giroux (1991:80–81) state that postmodernism, rather than breaking with modernism, builds upon modernist concerns in such a way that it better enables us to understand late twentieth century societies and, more importantly, provides us with the critical tools to change them. Aronowitz and Giroux (1991) and Giroux (1991) provide a detailed and critical analysis of the relationship between modernism and postmodernism and how postmodernist theories of education provide an important vehicle for analyzing and changing schools.

In *Postmodernism, Feminism, and Cultural Politics,* Giroux (1991) provides one of the most in-depth discussions of both postmodernism and postmodern theories of education, linking them to both feminist theory and cultural theory. Further, his chapter "Postmodernism as Border Pedagogy: Redefining the Boundaries of Race and Ethnicity" provides a critical analysis of how postmodern theories of education inform our understanding of the other in curriculum and schooling. Arguing that schools are racist and sexist, Giroux underscores the need for critical pedagogues to understand and embrace the voices of others and to help reshape the dominant language and practice of schooling. Giroux connects postmodernism to his earlier work on resistance theory and teachers as intellectuals and in doing so acknowledges the connection between his agenda and "modernist" theorists such as Marx and Dewey. Although writing about very different eco-

---

[1] Giroux's work since the early 1980s has attempted to develop a critical theory of schooling and culture. Beginning in the early 1980s with a reformulation of neo-Marxism and critical theory into what he termed resistance theory, Giroux developed his critical project by incorporating postmodernist theory. For the development of his theoretical model see Giroux (1981, 1983, 1988, 1991) and Aronowitz and Giroux (1991).

nomic, political, and cultural times, Marx and Dewey argued for the transformation of the social structure; for Marx, it was the capitalist relations of production; for Dewey (and social reconstructionists like Counts), it was the undemocratic schools and political structure. Thus, Giroux's brand of postmodernism clearly is an example of the type of postmodernism Burbules and Rice (1991) suggest is not antimodernist, but rather seeks to incorporate modernist visions of the just and good society into its vision of the postmodern world. Giroux (1991:47–59) outlines nine principles of critical pedagogy, which he states are based on the insights of modernism, postmodernism, and feminism. Thus, he provides a synthesis of three of the important theoretical systems in the twentieth century and from these he develops a critical pedagogy, whose function is to transform teachers, schools, and ultimately society. Most importantly, he acknowledges Habermas's (1979, 1981, 1982, 1983, 1987) critique of postmodernism as antimodernist and inherently conservative and posits a radical, transformative vision of postmodernism.

First, Giroux argues that education must be seen not only as producing knowledge, but political subjects as well (1991:47). Thus, schooling must be linked to a critical pedagogy aimed at the development of democratic education. Based on earlier work on teachers as intellectuals (1988), Giroux's postmodernism calls for the need for teachers, as critical pedagogues, to help transform student consciousness and school organization. He does not, however, leave praxis at the level of schooling alone, but calls for a connection between democratic education and democratic civic and political life, the end being the transformation of an antidemocratic civic culture. Once again, this brand of postmodernism clearly is rooted in a modernist and progressive tradition, with the call for democratic education and civic and political transformation found in the works of earlier progressives such as Dewey (1916, 1984) and social reconstructionists such as Counts (1932).

Second, Giroux indicates that ethics need to be a central concern of postmodern theories of education and critical pedagogy. Modernist conceptions such as reason, social justice, the elimination of inequality, and the reduction of human suffering must be linked to postmodern concerns with difference. Thus, educators must draw upon different conceptions of ethics and help students to construct a critical vision of an ethical

life. Most importantly, such ethical discourse does not remain at an abstract level of philosophical inquiry, but is connected to the particular social, cultural, and historical forces that shape it. From this perspective, students are actively engaged in addressing important ethical issues, particularly those related to questions of human inequality. In some respects similar to Maxine Greene's (1978) concern with wide awakeness and the moral life, Giroux attempts to connect Greene's existential and phenomenological philosophy to a more structural and historical analysis of the social construction of ethics. What is often implicit in Greene's work is made more explicit in Giroux's (i.e., the relationship between structure and agency).

Third, critical pedagogy should focus on postmodern concerns with difference in a politically transformative manner. According to Giroux, students need to understand the social construction of different voices and identities, how these are related to historical and social forces, and how they can be used as the basis for change. The incorporation of different voices into the curriculum and student reflection upon these voices need to be connected to the conception of a democratic community.

Fourth, the concern for difference needs to be translated into a critical language that allows for competing discourses and that rejects any master narratives or curriculum canons. Echoing Cherryholmes's (1988) rejection of any discourse that reduces history to one script or plan, Giroux calls for a pedagogic practice that sees knowledge as socially and historically constructed. Such a view suggests that students can use the knowledge of the past, not merely as subjects to be learned, but rather as something to be reformulated in relation to the present. Critical pedagogy is thus "characterized by the open exchange of ideas, the proliferation of dialogue, and the material conditions for the expression of individual and social freedom" (1991:50).

Fifth, critical pedagogy needs to create new forms of knowledge out of analysis of competing discourses and from voices historically absent from traditional canons and narratives. What constitutes new knowledge, according to Giroux, is not simply an epistemological question, but rather a political and historical one, which must be related to issues of race, class, gender, and ethnicity. Relating critical pedagogy to the struggle for democratic life, Giroux argues that "this is a struggle that deepens the pedagogical meaning of the political and the political meaning of the pedagogical" (1991:50). Thus, pedagogic practice is seen as a political activity, with curriculum development no longer a technocratic exercise concerned with educational goals and objectives, but rather with providing students with new forms of knowledge rooted in a pluralistic and democratic vision of society.

Sixth, the Enlightenment concept of reason, so central to modernist thought, must be reconstituted within a postmodern critical pedagogy. Giroux articulates a notion of reason that is historically and socially constructed and that rejects objective or scientific definitions that would create a totalizing vision of reason. In this respect, critical pedagogy needs to explore the situated nature of reason and its relationship to learning.

Seventh, building upon his earlier work, Giroux suggests that a postmodern critical pedagogy must provide a sense of alternatives through a "language of critique and possibility" (1991:52). Critical pedagogy as critique of what exists and development of what is possible is central to a project of social transformation. Eschewing reified utopian visions of the possible, Giroux suggests that critical pedagogy must explore the dynamics of freedom, and the possibilities of change using a language of "not yet." According to Giroux, "This is the language of 'not yet', one in which the imagination is redeemed and nourished in the effort to construct new relationships fashioned out of strategies of collective resistance based on a critical recognition of both what society is and what it might become" (1991:53).

Eighth, critical pedagogy must be related to a view of teachers as transformative intellectuals. In his work on postmodernism, Giroux develops a theme central to his earlier work and connects it to a view of democratic public life. Giroux calls for teachers to be involved not only within schools, but to connect their voices to democratic politics in their communities and within society, in general. Such a view is not significantly different from the social reconstructionist view of schooling developed by Counts (1932) or from Dewey's progressive view of schooling and democratic life (1916).[2]

Ninth, Giroux argues that critical pedagogy must combine postmodern concerns with difference with feminist emphasis on the political. Such an interplay between a theory of domination and subordination, on the one hand, and a political theory of how to challenge relations of dominance and hierarchy on the other hand, is central to Giroux's analysis of the possibilities of schooling. Critical pedagogy needs to engage students and teachers in the systematic discovery of alternatives to institutional racism, classism, and sexism through the inclusion of the voices of marginalized groups. Such an enterprise should not be, Giroux warns, merely exercises in giving voice to the voiceless, but needs to connect their voices to political strategies aimed at social change.

Through these nine principles, Giroux attempts to synthesize the contributions of modernism, postmodernism, and feminism into a critical pedagogy aimed at both educational and social transformation. Rather than rejecting modernism, Giroux's brand of postmodernism provides a continuation of the insights of progressivism and neo-Marxism. As I pointed out above, his work, although not necessarily representative of postmodern theories of education, does symbolize its limits and possibilities. The following section will outline the strengths and weaknesses of postmodernist work in education in general, and Giroux's work in particular.

The Limits and Possibilities of Postmodern Theories of Education

Postmodern theories of education, particularly those that build upon rather than reject modernism (Aronowitz and Giroux, 1991; Burbules and Rice, 1991; Giroux, 1991), provide an important critique of traditional schooling, as well as a critical pedagogical view of school transformation. As I noted above, although this approach is not significantly different in many respects from the social reconstructionist and progressive tradition on which it builds, nonetheless, it provides some important insights. First, the postmodern emphasis on the rejection of "meta-narratives" reminds us of the potential antidemocratic nature of totalizing theories and the centrality of local and situated meanings. Second, the postmodern emphasis on "dialogues across difference" (Burbules and Rice, 1991) points out the pedagogical importance of finding common ground in

---

[2] For a detailed look at the question of democracy in the work of Dewey, see Robert Westbrook (1991). For a discussion of the political origins of progressive education and their relation to educational philosophy, see James S. Kaminsky (1992).

a world of domination and exploitation.[3] Third, postmodern attempts to develop a critical pedagogy of schooling provides an important opportunity to connect critical and feminist theories to practice.[4] Finally, the postmodern emphasis on the need to build upon modernist theories in light of the profound social, political, and economic changes since the late nineteenth century provides a much needed corrective to social theories often still rooted in a world that no longer exists. Despite these strengths, postmodernist theories of education have significant weaknesses that prevent them from fulfilling their promise.

First, postmodern theories of education often make readers feel as if they are trying to become a member of a group to which they do not belong. Even for those trained in social theory, it is nonetheless difficult to decipher its code, which often seems to be saying that if you do not understand the language then you should not be reading it anyway. Although this is problematic for all academic work, it is more so for a theory that purports to provide an agenda for critique and change in the school.

Second, perhaps because many postmodern theories of education are based on an antipositivist view of science, they usually eschew empirical methods to study schools. Thus, postmodern theories of education often have more to do with philosophy and social theory than with the sociological study of schools. Although this does not question the value of either philosophy or social theory (or what is now termed educational theory), the sociology of education must transcend grand theory and develop what Anyon (1994) terms "useful theory," or a theory that provides the basis for both understanding schools and changing them. This, in part, requires empirical research on schooling—something that postmodernist work in education is short on.

Finally, and most importantly, postmodernist theories of education fail to connect theory to practice in a way that practitioners find meaningful and useful. Although this does not suggest that postmodernists write exclusively for practitioners, if one of the stated aims of theorists such as Giroux is to develop teachers as transformative intellectuals and to provide a critical pedagogy for school transformation, then the problem of language use is of central importance. How can we have dialogues across difference if teachers are excluded from the dialogue?

In conclusion, although postmodernism has made important contributions to educational research, its often impenetrable writing style and its lack of empirical research evidence to support its claims often seriously limit its usefulness for sociologists of education. In the future, the important insights of postmodernism need to be incorporated into a theoretically and empirically grounded sociology of education.

---

[3] For a critical response to Burbules and Rice, see Mary Leach (1992). For their response to Leach, see Nicholas C. Burbules and Suzanne Rice. Leach points out that Burbules and Rice's postmodernism embraces a modernist conception of the liberal humanist self and thus posits individualistic solutions to structural problems. Although their debate is too lengthy and complex to summarize here, my point is that the postmodern project of dialogue, whatever its difficulties, is an important one.

[4] For a critique of critical pedagogy in general and Giroux's work in particular, see Elizabeth Ellsworth (1989). Although many of Ellsworth's points are on target concerning the failure of Giroux's project to provide the tools for emancipatory education, nonetheless, the postmodern concern with critical pedagogy is one of its important features. I will take up its weaknesses in this area below.

REFERENCES

Anyon, J. 1979. "Ideology and United States History Textbooks." *Harvard Educational Review* 49(3):381–386.

———. 1981a. "Social Class and School Knowledge." *Curriculum Inquiry* 11(1):3–42.

———. 1981b. "Elementary Schooling and Distinctions of Social Class." *Interchange* 12:2–3.

———. 1994. "The Retreat of Marxism and Socialist Feminism: Postmodern Theories in Education." *Curriculum Inquiry* 24:115–134.

Apple, M. 1978. "Ideology, Reproduction, and Educational Reform." *Comparative Educational Review* 22(3):367–387.

———. 1979a. *Ideology and Curriculum*. Boston: Routledge & Kegan Paul.

———. 1979b. "The Other Side of the Hidden Curriculum: Correspondence Theories and the Labor Process." *Journal of Education* 162:47–66.

———. 1982a. *Cultural and Economic Reproduction in Education*. Boston: Routledge & Kegan Paul.

———. 1982b. *Education and Power*. Boston: Routledge & Kegan Paul.

Aronowitz, S. 1987/1988. "Postmodernism and Politics." *Social Text* 18:94–114.

Aronowitz, S., and H. Giroux. 1991. *Postmodern Education: Politics, Culture and Social Criticism*. Minneapolis: University of Minnesota Press.

Baudrillard, J. 1981. *For a Critique of the Political Economy of the Sign*. Charles Levin (trans.). St. Louis: Telos Press.

————. 1984. "The Precession of Simulacra." In B. Wallis (ed.), *Art after Modernism: Rethinking Representation*, pp. 213–281. Boston: David Godine.

Bellah, R., R. Madsen, W. Sullivan, A. Swidler, and S. Tipton. 1991. *The Good Society*. New York: Knopf.

Berger, P., and T. Luckmann. 1966. *The Social Construction of Reality*. Garden City, NY: Doubleday.

Bernstein, Basil. 1973a. *Class, Codes and Control, Vol. 1*. London: Palladin.

————. 1973b. *Class, Codes and Control, Vol. 2*. London: Routledge & Kegan Paul.

————. 1977. *Class, Codes and Control, Vol. 3* (revised). London: Routledge & Kegan Paul.

————. 1990. *The Structuring of Pedagogic Discourse: Vol. 4 of Class, Codes and Control*. London: Routledge.

————. 1996. *Pedagogy, Symbolic Control and Identity: Theory, Research, and Critique*. London: Taylor & Francis.

Bowles, S., and H. Gintis. 1976. *Schooling in Capitalist America*. New York: Basic Books.

Burbules, N., and S. Rice. 1991. "Dialogue across Differences: Continuing the Conversation." *Harvard Educational Review* 61(4):393–416.

————. 1992. "Can We Be Heard? A Reply to Leach." *Harvard Educational Review* 62(2):264–271.

Cherryholmes, C. 1988. *Power and Criticism: Poststructural Investigations in Education*. New York: Teachers College Press.

Counts, G. 1932. *Dare the Schools Build a New Social Order?* New York: John Day.

Derrida, J. 1973. *Speech and Phenomenon*. Evanston: Northwestern University Press.

————. 1981. *Positions*. Chicago: University of Chicago Press.

————. 1982. *Of Grammatology*. Baltimore: Johns Hopkins University Press.

Dewey, J. 1916. *Democracy and Education*. New York: Free Press.

————. 1984 (Original published in 1927). *The Public and Its Problems*. In *John Dewey: The Later Works, Vol. 2: 1925–1927*. Carbondale: Southern Illinois University Press.

Durkheim, E. 1947 (Original published in 1893). *The Division of Labor in Society*. Glecoe, IL: Free Press.

————. 1977 (Original published in 1938). *The Evolution of Educational Thought*. London: Routledge & Kegan Paul.

Ellsworth, E. 1989. "Why Doesn't This Feel Empowering? Working Through the Repressive Myths of Critical Pedagogy." *Harvard Educational Review* 59(3):297–324.

Giddens, A. 1982. *Sociology: A Brief But Critical Introduction*. New York: Harcourt, Brace Jovanovich.

Giroux, H. 1981. *Ideology, Culture and the Process of Schooling*. Philadelphia: Temple University Press.

————. 1983. *Theory and Resistance in Education*. South Hadley, MA: Bergin and Garvey.

————. 1988. *Teachers as Intellectuals*. South Hadley, MA: Bergin and Garvey.

————. 1991. *Postmodernism, Feminism, and Cultural Politics: Redrawing Educational Boundaries*. Albany, NY: SUNY Press.

Greene, M. 1978. "Wide Awakeness and the Moral Life." In *Landscapes of Learning*, pp. 42–52. New York: Teachers College Press.

————. 1988. *The Dialectic of Freedom*. New York: Teachers College Press.

Gutmann, A. 1987. *Democratic Education*. Princeton, NJ: Princeton University Press.

Habermas, J. 1979. *Communication and the Evolution of Society*. Boston: Beacon Press.

————. 1981. "Modernity versus Postmodernity." *New German Critique* 8(1):3–18.

————. 1982. "The Entwinement of Myth and Enlightenment." *New German Critique* 9(3):13–30.

————. 1983. "Modernity: An Incomplete Project." In H. Foster (ed.), *The Anti-aesthetic: Essays on Postmodern Culture*, pp. 3–16. Seattle, WA: Bay Press.

————. 1987. *The Philosophical Discourse of Modernity*. F. Lawrence (trans.). Cambridge, MA: MIT Press.

Harvey, D. 1989. *The Condition of Postmodernity: An Inquiry into the Origins of Cultural Change*. Cambridge, MA: Basil Blackwell.

Jameson, F. 1982. "Postmodernism and Consumer Society." In H. Foster (ed.), *The Anti-aesthetic: Essays on Postmodern Culture*, pp. 11–125. Seattle, WA: Bay Press.

Jencks, C. 1987. *What Is Post-modernism*. New York: St. Martin's.

Kaminsky, J. 1992. "A Pre-History of Educational Philosophy in the United States: 1861–1914." *Harvard Educational Review* 62(2):179–198.

Lather, P. 1984. "Critical Theory, Curriculum Transformation, and Feminist Mainstreaming." *Journal of Education* 166(March):49–62.

————. 1989. "Postmodernism and the Politics of Enlightenment." *Educational Foundations*. 3(3):8–9.

————. 1991. *Getting Smart: Feminist Research and Pedagogy within the Postmodern*. New York: Routledge.

Leach, M. 1992. "Can We Talk? A Response to Burbules and Rice." *Harvard Educational Review* 62(2):257–263.

Lyotard, J. F. 1984. *The Postmodern Condition*. G. Bennington and B. Massumi (trans.). Minneapolis: University of Minnesota Press.

Mannheim, K. 1936. *Ideology and Utopia: An Introduction to the Sociology of Knowledge*. New York: Harcourt, Brace and World.

Marx, K. 1971. *The Poverty of Philosophy*. New York: International Publishers.

Marx, K., and F. Engels. 1947 (Originally published 1846). *The German Ideology*. New York: International Publishers.

McLaren, P. 1991. "Schooling and the Postmodern Body:

Critical Pedagogy and the Politics of Enfleshment." In H. Giroux (ed.), *Postmodernism, Feminism, and Cultural Politics: Redrawing Educational Boundaries*, pp. 144–173. Albany, NY: SUNY Press.

McLaren, P., and R. Hammer. 1989. "Critical Pedagogy and the Postmodern Challenge: Toward a Critical Postmodernist Pedagogy of Liberation." *Educational Foundations* 3(3):29–62.

Miller, J. 1990. *Creating Spaces and Finding Voices: Teachers Collaborating for Empowerment*. Albany, NY: SUNY Press.

Rorty, R. 1980. *Philosophy and the Mirror of Nature*. Princeton, NJ: Princeton University Press.

Rust, V. 1991. "Postmodernism and its Comparative Education Implications." *Comparative Education Review* 35(4):610–626.

Sadovnik, A. R. 1989. "Review of H. Giroux, Teachers as Intellectuals." *Contemporary Sociology*. 18(6):951–952.

———. 1991a. "Basil Bernstein's Theory of Pedagogic Practice: A Structuralist Approach." *Sociology of Education*. 64(1):48–63.

———. 1991b. "Connecting the Macro and Micro: Review of Bernstein's The Structure of Pedagogic Discourse." *Contemporary Sociology*. 20(3):471–474.

———, ed. 1995. *Knowledge and Pedagogy: The Sociology of Basil Bernstein*. Norwood, NJ: Ablex Publishing Corporation.

Weber, M. 1978. *Economy and Society, Volumes 1 and 2*. G. Roth and C. Wittich (eds.). Berkeley: University of California Press.

Westbrook, R. 1991. *John Dewey and American Democracy*. Ithaca, NY: Cornell University Press.

Wexler, P. 1987. *Social Analysis: After the New Sociology*. London: Routledge & Kegan Paul.

Whitty, G. 1985. *Sociology and School Knowledge*. London: Metheun.

Sociology of Education

Theoretical Approaches

Jeanne H. Ballantine
Sociology Department, Wright State University

Higher Education

The sociological study of higher education is a twentieth-century phenomenon and can be said to begin with *Higher Learning in America,* by Thorsten Veblen (1918). A vehement attack on the increasing influence of business interests on decision making at U.S. colleges and universities, this book clearly saw the links between educational organizations and other parts of the social order. In criticizing the consequences of the power of business over higher education, and asserting a loss of autonomy experienced by the academy, Veblen began a long debate about whose interests higher education should serve. That debate, of course, continues today. Nevertheless, it is in his linking sectors of the society together that makes his analysis, whatever one thinks of its values, sociological.

The major growth in interest in higher education comes, however, after World War II, when expansion of enrollments in the United States dramatically increased (Clark, 1973). Although college enrollments grew during the first half of the century, this growth was slow, episodic, and limited by both the number of high school graduates, and in the 1930s and 1940s, by the Depression and World War II. During the first four decades of the century high school enrollments and graduation rates doubled every 10 years and the lack of prepared candidates for admission soon ceased to be a barrier to growth. Nevertheless, the poor economy and war combined to keep many high school age students from planning for college and kept many graduates from entering, especially males, during the 1930s and the first half of the 1940s. After the war, the pressure of those who had been prevented from enrolling in earlier periods became irresistible, and state-supported educational opportunities grew as new colleges were established, junior colleges expanded, and enrollments in other colleges and universities increased as veteran's used the federal GI Bill to support their education costs. The growth in enrollments between 1929 and 1939 was 35% (from 1,100,737 to 1,494,203). In the next 10 years there was a 78% gain (to 2,659,021). Between 1949 and 1959, the growth slowed down, but boomed in periods following, from 3,215,544 in 1959 to 7,136,075 in 1969 (a 122% gain) and 11,569,899 by 1979 (a 62% gain). Among private colleges and universities, enrollments were also expanding and, while their proportion of total enrollments in higher education in relation to public institutions began a steep and enduring decline, their actual enrollments grew as well—today, less than 20% of all college students are enrolled in the private sector compared to 50.7% in 1946. All across the United States, enrollments increased, and state authorities struggled to develop the capacity to provide classrooms and libraries. In many states, that struggle included debates about how the expansion should proceed. Often, as we shall see, an effort was made to limit the expansion at the existing elite university sector, while rapidly expanding former teachers colleges into comprehensive colleges and universities, and establishing community colleges.

With more and more students attending colleges, the number of ways college degrees were used by graduates and employers also grew. Although a college degree was rare in the nineteenth and early twentieth centuries, and not necessary for any occupation, the rise in the number of holders of college degrees encouraged the creative use of the degree in the labor market. As a result of the ensuing educational upgrading of occupations, a postsecondary degree has become almost a requirement for entering a middle-class occupation. According to recent estimates, between 25 and 30% of the labor force in advanced industrial societies are in the categories of professional, technical, and administrative personnel for which postsecondary training is appropriate. That 30% level is already exceeded in Japan, the United States, Canada, and Sweden (Kerr, 1987). The variety of occupations for which college degrees are now available is very large, and with so many of the newly entering members of the labor force beginning their careers with college degrees, the educational pressure on older workers has been growing. In fact, the average age of college students has been increasing—at many colleges today it is above 25 years old—as women returning to the labor force after raising children and older workers seeking new educational credentials for greater labor market opportunity begin or return to college.

The types and number of colleges have increased, the size and diversity of enrollments have dramatically expanded, the content of the curriculum has expanded, and the links between higher education and the country's systems of stratification and its economy have become much stronger. All of these changes have created an educational establishment without precedent and of very recent vintage. Sociologists, historians, and others have struggled to keep up with these developments and to chart their consequences. This chapter will review the product of these efforts to date and look briefly into the future to assess whether the trends of the last half of the twentieth century are likely to continue into the twenty-first century. First, we explore higher education's relationship with the system of social stratification and how that link is mediated by the diversity of kinds of higher educational establishments. Along the way we review briefly the way enrollments are distributed among the kinds of higher education institutions and among majors. Describing these patterns leads to a consideration of the research on their consequences for the economic payoff of degrees, for the collegiate curriculum, and for faculty.

Higher Education and Social Stratification

For sociology, the nature of the distribution of scarce and valuable resources (both material, like owning a factory, and symbolic, like esteem) among members of a society is a core question. Whether that distribution is recreated as parents pass on their advantages or disadvantages to their children is central to the description of the nature of social inequalities and their maintenance across generations. The organization of inequalities into vertical layers is called social stratification. It is social because the collective activities and values of society create and change the amount and kind of inequalities present in a society. We do not presume that there is anything "natural" about social inequalities. Their existence is virtually universal, but the variety in the amount and kind of things that are unequally distributed is vast and thus the result of deliberate human action. The layering of advantaged over disadvantaged produces strata, just as alternate layers of sediment have produced strata in rock exposed by highway cuts.

Educational attainment beyond high school, long a valued resource, has until recently been a scarce resource. Its uses in the labor market were limited to only a few advantages; most occupations, including the professions of law and medicine, did not require degrees. Eligibility and competence were established in other ways, such as "reading for the law" while clerking for a lawyer. Increasingly, however, the formal educational credentials needed to enter occupations have increased as schools and colleges have become the personnel agencies for our society. A college diploma is needed today to enter most law schools, and other professions have moved to graduate level work as required for entry or for continuing employment. A considerable amount of sociological research has centered on the processes associated with the attainment of educational credentials, and how their use by employers and occupational and professional groups has grown (Collins, 1979; Hammack, 1990).

Yet, it would be incorrect to assert that even in earlier periods education was not important for the creation and maintenance of social stratification. The adage "knowledge is power" illuminates a critical reality not captured by possessing a college degree. The control of the means by which what is worth knowing is defined carries with it considerable power, as does possessing the knowledge itself, symbolized by the degree. In the history of higher education in the United States, this power is clearly seen as group after group has sought to legitimate and secure its attainments by founding colleges for their offspring. Most of private higher education originated in the impulse of religious groups to arm their sons (and occasionally their daughters) to maintain the faith and to protect their interests in the broader society. Existing colleges could not do the job, and often did not want to do it.

Organizational Diversity in Higher Education

With greater demand for higher education, increased opportunities—especially in public colleges and universities—have been created. This expansion, however, has been accompanied by greater diversity of kinds of places where higher education is offered. Although the nineteenth century of private, rural, residential liberal arts colleges still exists, schools of this type now enroll a small proportion of college students. Not only are large, urban or suburban, commuter, comprehensive colleges and universities far more common, today about one-half of all college freshmen are enrolled in 2-year colleges, and explicitly technical and vocational majors dominated undergraduate degree enrollments.

A good illustration of this diversification is that created by the "Master Plan" in California. By 1960, the state established a "Master Plan" for the development of a "system" of higher education, where largely unrelated parts had previously existed (Smelser and Almond, 1974). This plan provided for the building of several new campuses of the University of California, but much larger expansions in the two other sectors. That plan envisioned a three-tiered system, with the prestigious University of California campuses (Berkeley, Los Angeles, etc.) on the top, offering undergraduate and graduate and professional degrees to the highest achieving high school graduates. The State College and University sector, selecting the next lower achieving group of high school graduates and offering undergraduate and Master's degrees, were developed out of the existing teacher's colleges and now include many new campuses. Finally, for all other high school graduates, admission to a 2-year community college was offered. The curricula in the 2-year sector allowed for transfer to other sectors, as well as free standing degrees, largely emphasizing career preparation. Thus, the public system in California became highly stratified, according to the student's prior academic achievement. Of course, the private sector was not included in the Master Plan, and offers alternatives equal to the

most selective parts of the public system (Stanford, Mills College, etc.) as well as to the less selective parts.

In the eastern part of the United States, where private colleges and universities had long-established dominance, public higher education was developed more slowly, sometimes created for the first time during the period following World War II (such as most of the campuses of the State University of New York). Whether or not a three-tiered system was developed, in virtually all states, public higher education has been differentiated into sectors based on the mission of the institution, with graduate education and research-oriented universities at the top of the prestige status ladder and having the highest academic criteria for admission. Comprehensive colleges and universities, combining liberal arts with vocationally oriented courses of study and with less emphasis on graduate preparation and research, are usually more accessible than the university and come next. Two-year community colleges or branch campuses of the large state university available to most with a high school credential fill out the public options. Private alternatives to each of these levels exist as well.

Thus, the higher education system in the United States has evolved into a highly stratified one, and stratified in ways that parallel the stratification of the population at large. Although far from perfectly related, student achievement and educational attainment are both strongly correlated with parental position in the social strata (Hurn, 1993). Students from more affluent backgrounds have a higher probability of attending elite public and private colleges and universities, to be full-time, residential students attending 4-year schools than students from poor families. Social origins, however, are not the sole predictor of academic achievement and attainment; achievement is itself very strongly related to attainment. Although social origins influence academic achievement, certainly not all privileged students do very well in school and attend elite colleges. Those who do not achieve well are unlikely to go as far as less affluent students who do well in school. Nevertheless, the system of higher education is a highly differentiated one that can be seen as paralleling the societal system of social stratification. This parallelism has generated one of the great debates about the function of education in our society.

Some observers, seeing the "correspondence" between social and educational stratification, have asserted that education must be seen as an instrument for the unequal reproduction of social strata in the society. This view, opposite to one emphasizing the opportunity for social strata mobility offered by educational achievement and attainment, challenges the value this society seems to have placed on education as a means to prevent the development of rigidity in our social strata. Those who emphasize the opportunity afforded by the expansion of educational opportunities, of all kinds, see differentiation as necessary and an efficient way to provide for a variety of educational routes to adulthood and to occupations. Data can be assembled to support both positions, and the debate continues (Dougherty, 1994; Trow, 1984). Although one can debate the consequences of a stratified educational system, that it is stratified is an acknowledged fact. Moreover, its stratification has grown as enrollments increased, and as the links to specific occupational destinations grew in number and in strength. (It is now virtually impossible to become a lawyer without attending law school, which almost always requires graduating from college. Reading for the law, the preparation for entry into the profession, has disappeared in favor of a route mandating formal attainment in higher education.)

Students and the College Curriculum

Not only are students likely to be distributed along the collegiate hierarchy according to their parental status, personal demographic characteristics are also likely to be associated with their area of studies. One of the most obvious of these differences is in the proportion of females and of Hispanic- and African-American students who major in the sciences and mathematics-based subjects. Patterns of secondary school attainment in math and science courses show a significantly lower level of achievement by these student groups, who are thus less well prepared for the rigors of college-level math and science majors. Because many of these majors lead to high-paying occupational opportunities, the preexisting pattern of higher educational achievement and attainment by whites, males, and Asians persists, and disparities in future occupational opportunities and income are affected. The study of how students are distributed among the various sectors in higher education has benefitted from several national longitudinal studies sponsored by the National Center for Educational Statistics, a part of the Department of Education. The

National Longitudinal Study (NLS), which began by gathering information from high school sophomores and seniors in 1972 and has periodically returned to the same respondents, has afforded much insight into the educational careers of that cohort of students. More recently, the Beyond High School study (BHS), which started in 1980, and the National Educational Longitudinal study (NELS), initiated in 1988, are following the development of more recent groups of young people as they progress through the educational system.

The situation of female enrollments and patterns of college majors are particularly interesting. There has been much change in these patterns, yet inequalities persist. Female students are now the majority of all college students, whether enrolled in 2- or 4-year degree programs. Female enrollment in nontraditional majors has grown considerably in the last decade and a half. They now (1990) earn 47% of business administration undergraduate degrees, compared to 34% in 1980, and 51% of life science bachelors degrees, compared to 42% for the same period. However, the movement toward parity with male patterns of majors has essentially stalled in the past few years, and traditionally female fields are still predominantly female in enrollment (e.g., education majors went from 74% female in 1980 to 78% female in 1990). What has contributed to both the growth of parity and its stagnation is a subject of considerable interest. A good example of this research is the study by Jerry Jacobs (1989).

Enrollments of Hispanic- and African-American students have grown as well, though their progress, as compared with that of females, has been slower. They tend to be concentrated in less selective and 2-year public colleges, though their enrollments in the private sector have also increased (Carter and Wilson, 1992).

Although enrollments of minority and poor students have increased, even though not equally at all kinds of colleges or universities, and graduation rates have also increased, the payoff of the degree in the labor market lags behind that afforded majority students. In part, this has to do with the nature of their college majors. For example, engineering and computer science require high levels of math accomplishment, an attribute less common among these groups than among white, Asian, and middle-class high school graduates. Second year algebra, for example, was taken by 52% of white, 39% of black, 38.6% of Hispanic, and 59% of Asian high school graduates in 1990. Even more striking, 7%

of white, 2.8% of black, 3.9% of Hispanic, and 18.6% of Asian high school graduates took a full year course in calculus (National Center of Educational Statistics, 1993:269). Good math preparation in high school is essential for success in college science and math courses, which in turn are essential for entry into engineering and other math- and science-based occupations. The role of higher education in improving the entry of poor and minority students into the highest paid sectors of the labor market is hemmed in by the nature of the preparation such students have at entry. Clearly faculty and departments can do a better job of ensuring access to these career opportunities for poor and minority students than they now provide, but the equalizing of this opportunity is the work of the whole educational system, not only higher education.

One of the interesting consequences of increased enrollments of women students and those from minority communities is the heightened interest in the curriculum of higher education and its reflection upon these racial, religious, and ethnic groups. Calls for black or African-American studies or women's studies departments are not new, of course, but they have been joined now by an increased consciousness of cultural issues in the curriculum among Asian students, gay and lesbian students, etc. Debates over the "canon" in literature or other fields also reflect the curricula ferment now characterizing higher education. To some degree, these debates would probably have occurred anyway as academic fashion evolves. Nevertheless, there can be little doubt that the changing demography of U.S. college students has stimulated the debates and controversies. These students take seriously the notion that knowledge is power, and they seek to embrace that power lent by inclusion in the curriculum in higher education to validate their neglected perspectives (Arthur and Shapiro, 1995).

A related concern of sociologists of higher education has centered on the composition of the faculty and administrative posts. Studies of disparities among female and male faculty and about the lack of minority faculty in higher education have been frequent. These studies share common ground with other studies of gender and race in the labor market, and concern issues of recruitment, preparation, and rewards (Lomperis, 1990; Bowen and Schuster, 1986). The ability to serve nontraditional student populations is often seen as linked to the presence of faculty from those groups who can help their students achieve. The success of traditionally black colleges and universities has been in part attributed to the shared experiences of students and faculty (Allen, 1992).

Conclusions

The mission of colleges and how it is determined and implemented continue to be important areas of investigation. As enrollments have increased, as the links to occupations have become stronger, and as the diversity of enrollment increases, questions about the appropriate curriculum, about the relative balance between and focus of research and teaching and service loom large. Whose interests higher education serves, and how those interests are responded to bring us back to the analysis provided by Veblen. In what ways higher education is becoming linked to other aspects of the society is a continuing research question. In what ways *should* higher education be linked is an ongoing policy question whose answer depends on the values and political strength of those who ask the question.

REFERENCES

Allen, Walter R. 1992. "The Color of Success: African American College Student Outcomes at Predominantly White and Historically Black Public Colleges and Universities." *Harvard Educational Review* 62(Spring):26–44.

Arthur, John, and Amy Shapiro, eds. 1995. *Culture Wars: Multiculturalism and the Politics of Difference.* Boulder, CO: Westview Press.

Carter, Deborah J., and Reginald Wilson. 1992. *Eleventh Annual Status Report on Minorities in Higher Education.* Washington, DC: American Council on Education.

Clark, Burton R. 1973. "Development of the Sociology of Higher Education." *Sociology of Education* 46(Winter):2–14.

Collins, Randall. 1979. *The Credential Society.* New York: Academic Press.

Dougherty, Kevin J. 1994. *The Contradictory College: The Conflicting Origins, Impacts and Futures of Community Colleges.* Albany: State University of New York Press.

Hammack, Floyd M. 1990. "The Changing Relationship between Education and Occupation: The Case of Nursing." In Kevin J. Dougherty and Floyd M. Hammack (eds.), *Education and Society: A Reader,* pp. 561–573. San Diego: Harcourt, Brace Jovanovich.

Hurn, Christopher J. 1993. *The Limits and Possibilities of Schooling,* 3rd ed. Boston: Allyn & Bacon.

Jacobs, Jerry. 1987. *Revolving Doors: Sex, Segregation and Women's Careers.* Stanford, CA: Stanford University Press.

Kerr, Clark. 1987. "A Critical Age in the University World:

Accumulated Heritage Versus Modern Imperatives." *European Journal of Education* 22(2):183–193.

Lomperis, Ana Maria Turner. 1990. "Are Women Changing the Nature of the Academic Profession?" *Journal of Higher Education* 61(November/December):663-677.

National Center of Educational Statistics. 1993. *The Condition of Education, 1993*. Washington, DC: U.S. Department of Education.

Smelser, Neil J., and Gabriel Almond, eds. 1974. *Public Higher Education in California*. Berkeley: University of California Press.

Trow, Martin. 1984. "The Analysis of Status. "In Burton R. Clark (ed.), *Perspectives on Higher Education,* pp. 132–164. Berkeley: University of California Press.

Veblen, Thorsten. 1918. *Higher Learning in America*. St. Louis: B.W. Huebsch.

SPECIAL EDUCATION

Hugh Mehan
University of California, San Diego

Jane R. Mercer
University of California, Riverside

Robert Rueda
University of Southern California

The history of special education has been a contest over the representation of students who are difficult to teach. A moral discourse in which students' educational difficulties are seen as sinful behavior has competed with a social discourse in which school difficulties are attributed to environmental, cultural, socioeconomic, or familial factors and a psychomedical discourse in which school difficulties are attributed to genetic or organic causes. After years of debate, the moral discourse has faded to the periphery, and the psychomedical has dominated, beating back a variety of social explanations for students' school difficulties.

Historical Perspectives on Special Education

What do schools do with children who are difficult to teach and who are troublesome to manage? Such students, no doubt, have always been present in our schools and society. Yet the way we talk about these students, and hence how we act toward them, has changed significantly from the origins of our country to the present time. The shift has been from the "bad," to the "backward," to the "learning disabled."

Students' school difficulties are a type of deviant behavior. Understanding the way in which society represents deviance, therefore, helps us understand how we characterize special students. Deviant acts have been cast in a moral discourse from early colonial times. The childrearing literature of the Puritans assumed a basically evil child for whom adult discipline and Christian guidance were the optimal interventions. From 1875 to 1910, moralistic discourse blamed children's criminal and academic difficulties on cruel and ignorant parents who had recently migrated to the United States. Child savers of the nineteenth century saw educational difficulty as a vice of inferior cultures and classes that needed correction by elevation to an American standard. Their emphasis on parents' cruelty and children's laziness made children's actions seem willful rather than structural. Our sense of what constitutes a deviant act changed from moral lapse or willful recalcitrance to socialization failure caused by family and societal disorganization at the turn of the twentieth century. Social commentators lamented the transformation of the United States from a rural to an urban, industrial society. In presentations that are reminiscent of those generated today, Park et al. (1925) argued that immigrants from Eastern and Southern Europe brought religious beliefs, values, and language that threatened the integration of U.S. society. Urban society lacked the "sociability" and "sympathy" that in earlier, simpler days "naturally" led to social order.

Conceptualizations of special students shifted with this change in thinking about deviance. Turn of the century educators said children who were not adjusting to the academic and social demands of public schools were "backward." This backwardness was the result of "environmental deficits" or "cognitive dysfunctions of uncertain origins" caused by the disorganization of urban life. The poor parenting practices of immigrants from Mediterranean and Catholic counties gave city children too easy access to drugs and gambling. The rise of labor unions also contributed to backwardness. Students who witnessed strikes and the organizational efforts of unions acquired a disrespect for the law, that frequently led to acts of deviance and defiance in the classroom.

This new *social* understanding of deviance facilitated

the extension of social control to educational and medical institutions. Progressive Era reformers believed that agencies of the state were obligated to take responsibility for children who were neglected or difficult to teach. This thinking led to the development of child protection agencies, the construction of child abuse and family violence as social problems (Gordon, 1988), and the sense that public schools should instill self-control in children.

Emergence of Psychomedical Discourse

Medical explanations often compete with moral and social explanations of deviance. The appropriation of a statistical definition of normality and the increased involvement of the medical community in the control of deviance produced a psychomedical discourse that has become the dominant framework for assessing and treating disabilities in the late twentieth century.

From 1850 until the invention of intelligence testing in the early twentieth century, persons labeled as "disabled" were those who had clearly recognizable biological anomalies, such as the feebleminded. Those disabilities ordinarily involved not only behavioral aberrations but organic anomalies that were typically certified and treated by medical practitioners. At the turn of the century, children's "nervous organization," an "underdeveloped brain," a "sense defect," "a slow rate of development," "congenital word blindness," "cellular deficiency," and "streposymbolia" were all proffered as possible organic causes of backwardness despite the lack of any physical defect in children.

Binet (1916) developed a test that purported to measure "natural born" intelligence and yielded a mental age to identify "defective" children for the French government. Binet did more than create an intelligence test. By introducing a statistical sense of normality, he introduced a whole new way of seeing behavior and classifying individuals. Unlike a bipolar medical discourse that defines disabilities in terms of health or sickness, the statistical model defines abnormality in terms of a person's position on an assumed normal distribution relative to others tested in a population. A statistical definition of normal always produces "abnormals." Although a world in which a population did not show symptoms of a particular medical disability

is possible, in the statistical world, a specified percentage of the population will always be disabled. To say that 2.3% of a population is mentally retarded because 2.3% of the population scores more than two standard deviations below the mean is a tautology. There will always be more than 2.3% of any population more than two standard deviations below the mean on any measure, because, by definition, the normal distribution curve places 2.3% of the population more than two standard deviations below the mean.

The amalgamation of the statistical sense of abnormality with the medical sense of organic causes led to increasingly wider definitions of disabilities. Imported by L. M. Termin and John Goddard to the United States, IQ test scores were transformed into a pathological sign carrying all the implications of organic disability but without any evidence that test performance was a direct function of the biological characteristics of the test taker. The analysis of Army Alpha tests administered to draftees during World War I produced the first demonstration that blacks scored lower on IQ tests and that immigrants from Canada, Great Britain, Scandinavia, and Teutonic countries scored higher than immigrants from Latin and Slavic countries. By 1918, paper and pencil tests were developed for the mass measurement of the "intelligence" of public school students. World War I precipitated a flood of black immigrants from the south to urban centers, producing a large population of students who had difficulty managing the standard public school curriculum. Many of these students were diagnosed as "mentally retarded" using IQ tests.

Goddard redefined the previous medical categories of imbecile and idiot using mental age and created a new category of feeblemindedness, "morons," for those who had a mental age between 8 and 12. Few had physical stigmata. Their symptom was invisible, a low "mental age." They could be identified only by a new group of experts using "intelligence tests." Goddard's new diagnostic categories, now based on a statistical distribution of mental age, not an organic measure, were immediately adopted by the American Association on Mental Deficiency. The connection between the statistical and the medical sense of disability was strengthened when Goddard reported that feeblemindedness "runs in families" and when many jailed and impoverished people were identified as "feebleminded."

Psychologists and educators from the early 1930s onward transformed the rather uncertain condition of "backwardness" into a full-fledged neurological impairment, "minimal brain injury." Research by Strauss, Werner, and Orton medicalized the condition of childhood learning difficulties. As a result of their work, the public's way of thinking about and talking about childhood learning problems was reconstituted. What had once been an inexplicable condition with origins that were *perhaps* medical in origin had become a full fledged illness, "brain injury."

The Contemporary Context of Special Education

By 1960, intelligence testing was accepted by the general public and the scientific community as a legitimate scientific procedure. Low test scores were interpreted as clear evidence of "feeblemindedness" or "mental retardation," even when test scores were not accompanied by any biological signs.

Generating New Categories of Disability

Special education categories change. Old categories of disability disappear and new categories emerge to replace them. The new categories are those in which students, typically, do not manifest biological symptoms and diagnoses rest entirely on behavioral manifestations: academic performance, classroom behavior, and standardized test scores.

The "mentally retarded" category was originally divided into the "educable" and the "trainable." The official definition of mental retardation was expanded in the 1950s to include the "borderline retarded." Persons with IQs as high as 85 (which is 16% of the population) could be diagnosed as marginally retarded and be placed in special education programs. Because they were viewed as unqualifiedly beneficial, educators saw no harm in including many children into special classes.

The "learning disability" construct replaced educable mentally retarded (EMR) following litigation over IQ testing. The court order in the *Larry P.* case banned IQ tests in assessments of black students for "mental retardation." Mental retardation referrals have disap-

peared and that category has atrophied even for non-black students, while learning disability has been incorporated in important legislation, including PL 94–142, the Education for All Handicapped Students Act. By 1980, the total number of students in EMR classes in California was reduced from 72% to 2%, while learning disability constituted 63% of placements.

Some special educators have proposed amendments to federal law to create a new category of disability, "Attention Deficit Disorder" (ADD) to cover those students who are impulsive, distractible, and hyperactive. Although advocates of ADD say it is a neurological syndrome, the exact mechanism underlying ADD is unknown. No single lesion of the brain, no single neurotransmitter, no single gene has been identified that triggers ADD. Because there is no way to examine the brain directly, ADD has to be inferred from children's fidgety or inattentive behavior in school or at home. Because virtually all school children exhibit these behaviors at some time, the entire school population is potentially eligible for this new learning disability category.

Challenges to the Psychomedical Discourse of Disability

The discursive shift toward psychomedical explanations of special education students has not gone unchallenged. Researchers who emphasize the social basis of disability have argued that students' special education status is reflexively related to the institutional decision-making machinery of the school. "Normal" students become "special education" students when institutional practices for their recognition and placement are activated. Of 1,234 students referred for special education in Riverside, CA, 865 were tested; of these, 134 scored below the mental retardation (MR) cutoff point. Only 64% were recommended for MR placement; 97% were boys, 75% were low socioeconomic status, 32% were Anglo, 45% were Mexican American, and 22% were black, figures that did not approximate the school population (Mercer, 1973). Students with similar IQ scores were treated differently. Black, male, lower-class students who scored 80 or below were more likely to be transferred to special education than white, female, middle-class students. The disproportionate number of poor, minority, and male students in the MR category, even when they tested as well as their counterparts, suggests that disability is not an inherent characteristic of the student. Instead, disability makes its appearance when the school's sorting machine is turned on.

Concluding that the higher rates of mental retardation among racial and ethnic minorities were due to the cultural loading in intelligence and achievement tests, Mercer (1979) developed an alternative system of assessing students from different cultural groups, one that took socioeconomic and cultural factors into account and used IQ tests as measures of learning potential, not underlying intelligence. Mercer's "System of Multicultural Pluralistic Assessment" (SOMPA) showed that significantly fewer members of minority groups were mentally retarded than predicted by standardized assessment procedures.

Special education is "special" because it presumably identifies a real population based on objective, positive research procedures. If psychologists cannot reliably distinguish between disabled and nondisabled students, however, it is hard to present a rationale for "special" education. Examples of diagnostic anomalies raise questions about the objectivist and positivist assumptions supporting the psychomedical discourse. Shepard (1983a, 1983b) and Yesseldyke et al. (1982, 1983), for example, found they could not clearly differentiate between students diagnosed as "learning disabled" and other low achieving students when their IQ test profiles were compared.

Redefinitions change the learning disabled (LD) population. In response to increasing numbers of LD students, the Houston Independent School District redefined eligibility more stringently. To qualify as LD starting in 1985, a student had to be seriously behind in grade level and had to have a severe discrepancy between academic performance and cognitive ability in at least one domain of school functioning. This redefinition caused the number of students designated as LD to drop by 23% in one year (Singer and Butler, 1987).

Organizational Reasons for Disabled Students

There are organizational reasons for diagnostic anomalies. Educators implementing special education law face economic, legal, and organizational constraints.

Their responses to these constraints construct different students.

PL 94–142 specifies that 12% of students will be in special education. The compulsory thrust of this law provides an incentive to search for, identify, and place students into special education programs in order to meet mandated quotas. The proportion of students receiving special education has leveled off to 11%, but wide variation within special education categories speaks to organizational differences in the interpretation of what counts as special education students.

Disabilities vary from district to district, depending upon their resources, local policies, and the fashionability of disabilities at the moment. In Montgomery County, Maryland's richest school district, about 50% of the children in special education are classified as learning disabled; in Baltimore, the state's poorest district, less than 20% are (Singer and Butler, 1987). One in every eight children in New York's public schools is now classified as handicapped and three quarters of them are classified as learning disabled (Berger, 1991).

Disabilities also vary from state to state. Learning disabilities vary from 2.73% in Georgia to 9.43% in Massachusetts. Mental retardation varies from 0.33% in New Jersey to 3.06% in Alabama. Speech and language handicaps vary from 1.16% in Hawaii to 1.17% in New York to 0.23% in New Jersey (Reschley, 1995).

These variations reflect differences in state and district identification practices, not real differences in student populations. Furthermore, in many wealthy school districts, a learning disability has become a socially acceptable way for parents to get extra help for children having academic difficulty. Shepard (1983) calls learning disability the "middle class disease" because it is so pervasive in wealthy school districts and does not bear the stigma associated with backwardness and mental retardation.

Special education has a different meaning in poor districts. Because minority students are overrepresented in special education programs in financially strapped schools, special education has been accused of becoming a dumping ground for unruly or misbehaving students. Many special education students in poor school districts do in fact come from bleak socioeconomic circumstances. They are more likely to be living with a single mother or their grandparents than in a two-parent family and are more likely to have an unemployed or out of work parent heading the household than one who is working. Such students present regular classroom teachers with challenges they cannot reasonably be expected to handle. Not surprisingly, they call for help with difficult to teach students. Special education is one agency that responds to these calls.

Whether a child actually has a learning disability or is a slow achiever, or is simply slow to mature is a very fuzzy issue. Because the evidence for organic cause is limited and special education definitions are fuzzy, organizational demands prevail. If there are 30 slots for LD students in a school, then there will be 30 kids to fill those slots: often no more or no less (Mehan et al., 1985).

Within psychomedical discourse and special education law, "learning disabled" and "normal" students have certain characteristics distinguished by the discrepancy between IQ tests and achievement. Special education designations are influenced by funding, the calendar, educators' workloads, and available programs, however. These are organizational issues, not individual characteristics, which suggests that disabilities reside in the institutional arrangements of the school, not in the characteristics of individual children.

Response to the Social Construction Discourse

The argument that disability is socially and more specifically *institutionally* constructed, not biologically given, has enjoyed a congenial reception in those anthropology and sociology circles that operate within an interpretive paradigm. Social construction discourse, incorporated into the civil rights movement, contributed to significant legal cases (*Larry P. v. Wilson Riles* and *Diana v. California Board of Education*) in which plaintiffs argued successfully that the cultural bias of IQ tests violates the equal protection provision of the Constitution.

The impact of the social construction discourse on the psychomedical model of disability is much less certain. Attempts to incorporate students' adaptive behavior in assessment (e.g., the SOMPA) have been generally rejected by psychologists. PL 94–142 mandates parental involvement, multiple lines of assessment, shared decision making, and testing in the native language, but school districts simply ignore or circumvent those provisions that do not match their standard operating procedures and well established routines (Mehan et al., 1985; Mercer and Rueda, 1993), which leaves the business of identifying and educating students much the same as it was before the passage of this far ranging law. The psychomedical discourse shapes the entire assessment, placement, and identification process. This way of talking, and the institutionalized practices of the school that flow from it, are so powerful that educators circumvent legal mandates rather than violate its premises.

It is significant that the source of school difficulty has been placed within children—beneath their skin and between their ears. Although the locus has shifted from soul, to heart, to brain, it has always remained inside children, successfully deflecting attempts to redefine disability as social or environmental in nature. A new, socially based construct, "at risk," is emerging to challenge psychomedical representations.

Policy studies written since the 1980s have described the changing conditions of American families. An alarming number of American children live in poverty and within single-parent families. A majority of poor families are recent immigrants and "limited English speakers." These environmental conditions place children "at risk" for school failure. The "at risk" construct, like "backwardness" and "cultural deprivation" before it, alleges that a child suffers from a socially induced deficiency. It will be interesting to see if this new construct will be successful in defeating psychomedical representations, thereby redefining children who are difficult to teach.

Contradictions within the "at-risk" discourse make it vulnerable to absorption by the psychomedical discourse, however. Because the "at-risk" construct focuses on social, economic, and cultural conditions, it presumably stands in contrast to "disability," which indicates a genetic or biological cause. In both cases, however, mothers are blamed for the problems that children experience. Either they passed on a genetic defect or they were a teenage or an unwed mother. Thus, the "at-risk" discourse reduces to the same sense of pathology that has dominated the psychomedical discourse of disability. It deflects attention away from injustices perpetuated and institutionalized by the powerful and once again blames oppressed communities and homes for lacking the cultural and moral resources for advancement (Swadener and Lubeck, 1995).

At this time, the psychomedical discourse is in an ironic position. On the one hand, it is on solid ground in terms of educational practice; on the other hand, it is in a weak position intellectually.

REFERENCES

Berger, J. 1991. "Costly Special Classes Serve Many with Minimal Needs." *New York Times* (April 30), A1, A12.

Binet, Alfred. 1916. *The Development of Intelligence in Children* (The Binet-Simon Scale). Translated from articles in *L'Année Psychologuque* from 1905, 1908, and 1911 by Elizabeth S. Kite. Baltimore: Williams & Wilkins.

Bodine, William. 1905. "The Cause and the Cure." In *Proceedings of the Second National Conference on the Education of Backward, Truant, and Delinquent Children*. Plainfield: Indiana Boys School.

Coles, Gerald. 1987. *The Learning Mystique: A Critical Look at "Learning Disabilities."* New York: Pantheon.

Conrad, Peter, and Joseph W. Schneider. 1992. *Deviance and Medicalization: From Badness to Sickness*. Philadelphia, PA.: Temple University Press.

Franklin, Barry M. 1995. *From Backwardness to "At Risk": Childhood Learning Difficulties and the Contradictions of School Reform*. Albany, NY: SUNY Press.

Gordon, Linda. 1988. *Heroes of Their Own Lives: The Politics and History of Family Violence*. New York: Viking.

Gould, Stephen Jay. 1981. *The Mismeasure of Man*. New York: Norton.

Hallowell, E. M., and J. J. Ratey. 1994. *Driven to Distraction*. New York: Pantheon.

Heber, R. 1959. *A Manual on Terminology and Classification in Mental Retardation. American Journal of Mental Deficiency* 56, Monograph Supplement (rev.).

McDermott, R. P., and Hervé Varenne. 1995. "Culture as Disability." *Anthropology and Education Quarterly* 26(3):324–348.

Mehan, Hugh, Alma Hertweck, and J. Lee Meihls. 1985. *Handicapping the Handicapped: Decision Making in Students' Educational Careeers*. Stanford, CA: Stanford University Press.

Mercer, Jane D. 1973. *Labeling The Mentally Retarded*. Berkeley, CA: University of California Press.

———. 1979. *System of Pluralistic Assessment Technical Manual*. San Antonio, TX: Psychological Corporation.

Office of Special Education. 1987. *Ninth Annual Report to Congress on the Implementation of the EHA*. Washington, DC: U.S. Government Printing Office.

Park, Robert E. 1952. *Human Communities*. Glencoe: The Free Press.

Park, Robert, Earnest W. Burgess, and Robert D. McKenzie, eds. 1925. *The City*. Chicago: University of Chicago Press.

Reschley, Daniel J. 1995. *IQ and Special Education: History, Current Status and Alternatives*. Washington, DC: National Academy of Sciences.

Shepard, L. 1983a. "The Role of Measurement in Educational Policies: Lessons from the Identification of Learning Disabilities." *Educational Measurement* 4–8.

———. 1983b. "Characteristics of Pupils Identified as Learning Disabled." *AERJ* 20(3):309–331.

Singer J., and J. A. Butler. 1987. "The Education for All Handicapped Students Act: Schools as Agents of Social Reform." *Harvard Educational Review* 57:125–152.

Swadener, Beth Blue, and Sally Lubeck. 1995. *Children and Families "At Promise": Deconstructing the Discourse of Risk*. Albany NY: SUNY Press.

Ysselydke, J. E., B. Algozzine, and S. Epps. 1982. "A Logical and Empirical Analysis of Current Practice in Classifying Students as Handicapped." *Exceptional Children* 50:160–166.

Ysseldyke, J. E., B. Algozzine, M. Shinn, and M. McGue. 1983. "Similarities and Differences Between Low Achievers and Students Classified as Learning Disabled." *The Journal of Special Education* 16:73–85.

SPORT AND SCHOOLING

C. Roger Rees

Department of Health Studies, Physical Education and Human Performance Science, Adelphi University

Sport plays a unique role in American education. It is central to the social life of the school, and often to the community within which the school is located. The focus of consolidating rituals (Bernstein, 1975; Rees, 1995) such as the pep rally and the homecoming celebration, it "makes real" the myths of democracy, hard work, competition, and victory, which, paraphrasing historian Eric Hobsbawm (1983), comprise the "invented tradition" of our culture. Supporters of high school athletics see in it a powerful testament to the "open" nature of our society, a reminder that males (and now females) from all socioeconomic backgrounds have the potential to "make it" if they work hard and follow "society's" rules. These rules are literally written on the locker room walls of high schools all across America. Here is the importance of team work ("there is no 'I' in team"), of commitment and dedication ("quitters never win, and winners never quit"), and above all, of victory ("show me a good loser and I'll show you a loser"). Such myths are also part of another "American" tradition, that of individual responsibility for success and failure. Participants in the game of sport (or life) have no one to blame but themselves if they lose. While acting as a unifying force, sport in schools is also an important differentiating ritual, separating the men from the boys (figuratively speaking). Male athletes in particular are usually the elite of the school, at the top of the "pecking order" in the clique structure (Caanan, 1987; Rees, 1995; Foley, 1990a). As such they define acceptable behavior socially as well as educationally. From a pluralistic perspective, participation in sport builds the character of the participants even as it allows them to demonstrate this character to the student body and the community. In many parts of the country, the ritual of interscholastic athletics is the most important source of entertainment. Such competitions often become the social event of the week, the principal source of interaction between town and school, and the basis of community pride. It is no exaggeration to say that for many Americans, high school sports is literally "the only game in town," and that this game constitutes the very core of their community identity (Bissinger, 1990).

This powerful and controversial force has been largely overlooked by sociologists of education. With some notable exceptions (e.g., Coleman, 1961a; Foley, 1990b) the role of sport in the social and educational milieu of youth occurs on the periphery of educational debates, if it occurs at all. As a consequence of this neglect, scholars attempting to build a comprehensive picture of the educational importance of sport in schools (Miracle and Rees, 1994) have drawn on studies from several different academic disciplines (e.g., anthropology, history, and sociology) and a variety of theoretical perspectives. For example, the pluralistic view that participation in interscholastic athletics has a positive effect on the personality and educational skills of adolescents has been challenged by scholars working from a conflict theory perspective (e.g., O'Hanlon, 1980, 1982; Spring, 1974). These scholars have argued that sport in schools replicates the boring and repetitive characteristics of work, and socializes youth to accept the limitations of the capitalist system. More recently, participant observation studies from a critical theory perspective (Foley, 1990b; Grey, 1992) have shown how high school sports can reinforce existing racial, gender, and class inequalities.

This chapter summarizes the current state of knowledge about interscholastic sport as a consensual and differentiating force in school life. Specifically, the relationship between athletics and elements of the formal curriculum such as occupational aspirations, academic attainment, and dropout rates is discussed. This is followed by a review of the research on athletics and the social life of the school, specifically "character" development and gender and racial stereotyping. Finally, theoretical and empirical issues for future research are suggested.

School Sport and Academic Life

Although a detailed description of the origin of school sports is beyond the scope of this chapter (see Miracle and Rees, 1994:Chapters 2 and 3), it can be traced to the "muscular Christian" movement that developed in British education during the nineteenth century (Mangan, 1981). This movement grew up in British private boarding schools (called Public Schools), where the sons and daughters of the elites and the upper-middle class received their education. In these schools, sports such as cricket, rugby, and cross country running became an important (often mandatory) part of the curriculum. Proponents of the movement believed that these sports taught the "manly" characteristics of competitiveness, leadership, courage, fairness, and patriotism, which became the hallmark of the British gentleman (McIntosh, 1968; Redmond, 1978). At about the same time the muscular Christian movement grew in the elite boarding schools of New England, which adopted an athletic curriculum similar to that of the British private schools (Armstrong, 1984; Bundgaard, 1985). The value of sports as a socializing agent became "democratized" in the playground movement (Cavallo, 1981), the Young Men's Christian Association, and the Public School Athletic League (Miracle and Rees, 1994). By the second decade of the twentieth century sport was recognized as an important activity by which schools could instill social values into students (Radar, 1983).

Academic Aspirations and Achievement

The assertion that sport is the panacea for a variety of social and psychological problems confronting youth has been periodically made by teachers, coaches, educational administrators, and politicians since sport became institutionalized in American schools, but it is also true that these statements of support have been increasingly scrutinized by sociologists. Perhaps James

Coleman was the first to question the universal value of sport in schools in his landmark study of high schools in the 1950s (Coleman, 1961a). Although noting its importance as a source of students' identity and community enthusiasm, he felt that athletics could subvert the intellectual aims of the school by becoming too central to the status system of the students (Coleman, 1961b). That "being an athletic star" was considered by students to be a much more important attribute for male popularity than getting high grades or being on the honor role was seen as evidence for this subversion.

Subsequent research using the same methodology as Coleman has confirmed the popularity of male athlete in the high school status hierarchy (Thirer and Wright, 1985), but the implications of this result are subject to a variety of interpretations. That students in Coleman's study were forced to choose among a limited set of alternatives has, according to some critics (e.g., Brown, 1990), led to an overemphasis on the opposition between adolescent cliques and school values. The results of several longitudinal research studies on nationally representative samples of high school students show that participation in high school sports increases the educational and occupational aspirations of participants (Fejgin, 1994; Marsh, 1993; Melnick et al., 1988; Rees et al., 1990), although these general findings are sometimes mediated by combinations of race and gender (Sabo et al., Vanfossen, 1993) and prior academic self-concept (Marsh, 1993). However, none of these studies shows a negative effect of sport on athletes involvement with, or interest in, school culture.

Research that has focused on the issue of academic attainment has also shown no negative relationship with athletic participation. Whereas some studies showed a small positive effect of sport participation on grades (e.g., Hanks, 1979; Fejgin, 1994), others (e.g., Marsh, 1993) found no such effect. Marsh did show that participation in sport favorably affected academic activities such as being in an academic track, school attendance, taking academic courses, taking science courses, and time spent on homework, but he noted that sports participation has little effect on changes in academic achievement over time.

Dropout Rates

Data from longitudinal studies also show that interscholastic athletics plays a role in reducing high school dropout rates. For example, McNeal (1995) showed that participation in athletics and fine arts significantly reduced dropout rates, whereas participation in academic or vocational clubs did not. This relationship held after controlling for race, socioeconomic status, gender, and employment. When all the extracurricular activities were examined simultaneously only athletic participation remained significantly related to dropout reduction.

McNeal conceptualized dropping out more as a voluntary process by students than as a result of preexisting student attributes. He suggested that the importance of athletic status in peer culture, the frequent peer interactions that are part of organized sport, and the great time commitment that interscholastic athletics requires may all contribute to the decisions by athletes to stay in school. However, given the effects of fine arts, he warned against thinking of athletics as the only dropout-reducing activity, and advocated the integration of all students into multiple extracurricular activities.

This warning is somewhat reinforced by the results of an earlier study by Spady (1970) on educational aspiration and achievement. Boys in two high schools were divided into three categories based upon their extracurricular activities (no extracurricular activities, athletics only, multiple extracurricular activities), and tracked through their college careers. Spady found that the males in the "athletics only" extracurricular group had greater difficulty transforming their educational aspirations into achievement than did males in the multiple activities extracurricular group.

Interscholastic Sports and Higher Education

The relationship between high school sport, educational aspirations, and educational achievement takes on great significance when considered in conjunction with another unique aspect of American culture, the college athletic scholarship. Conventional mythology has it that high school athletes (often black and from poor backgrounds) can use sport to fulfill the dream of upward mobility. In this view, participation in sports in high school raises athletes' educational aspirations, allows them access (a "free ride") to a university, and gives them the opportunity to complete their degree. It is a hotly debated issue. Given the quasi-professional nature of some collegiate male basketball and football programs, the ones that give out the most scholarships,

some critics wonder whether it is not the universities that are really getting the "free ride" in their attempts to make money from sport (Sage, 1990:Chapter 8; Sperber, 1990). Despite the Knight Foundation's endorsement of college athletics as "educational in the best sense of the word" (1990:3), it is clear that academic concerns are not foremost in the minds of athletes seeking college scholarships (Doyle and Gaeth, 1990). Data on graduation rates from many "big time" programs show that they too have more important goals than the academic education of their scholarship athletes (Lopresto, 1991).

The limited research on male college athletes (Adler and Adler, 1985; Brede and Camp, 1987; Spady, 1970) shows the problems that confront them in their quest to translate the academic aspirations that have been raised at high school into academic achievement in college. For example, the case study of one elite male basketball program showed that the freshmen athletes entered college with aspirations to balance their academic and athletic roles. However, faced with a grueling physical program, scholastic demands beyond their capabilities, and isolated from the student body in a "jock dorm," they found themselves increasingly alienated from academic life. Falling victim to the "jock trap," they took easy courses to maintain their academic eligibility, which jeopardized their chances of graduation. As seniors they began to see the unrealistic goal of a professional contract in basketball as their only career option (Adler and Adler, 1985). Female college athletes tend to have more academic success, perhaps because they realize that there are fewer opportunities to make money out of professional sport, and therefore are more motivated students, and perhaps because they are placed under less pressure than the males by the college athletic programs (Meyer, 1990).

In summary, the result of these studies show no support for the idea that sports undermines the academic role of the school. In fact there is evidence that it increases educational aspirations and reduces dropout rate. These findings can be generalized since they are based on large representative samples, and the longitudinal designs have allowed researchers to distinguish between selection and change effects. On the other hand, they present a "disembodied" view of high school sports, one that cannot describe the activity as part of the wider culture of the school and community. This topic is the subject of the next section.

School Sports and Values

The tradition that "sport builds character" was the initial reason for the institutionalization of athletics in American education. Exactly which social values (if any) are being instilled into youth via the medium of school sports has been of recent interest to social scientists who have used a number of methodologies to move beyond the usual anecdotal evidence given to support the "sport-builds-character" belief. These include quasi-experiments in which competitive sports are introduced into school groups and the effects recorded (Kleiber and Roberts, 1981), longitudinal studies based on secondary analysis of large data sets (e.g., Best, 1985; Fejgin, 1994; Marsh, 1993; Rees et al., 1990), and studies of the reasoning given by athletes for their behavior in and out of sports (e.g., Bredemeier and Shields, 1986a, 1986b; Bredemeier, et al., 1986; Shields et al., 1995).

The longitudinal research generally supports the view that participation has little effect on prosocial characteristics such as honesty, self-control, or independence, and that high school athletes and nonathletes tend to have similar social values (Best, 1985; Rees et al., 1990). On the other hand, the research of Bredemeier and her associates shows that the higher the level of performance of athletes the lower their moral reasoning, and the greater their tendency to condone aggressive acts (Bredemeier et al., 1986). Interviews of high school and college male and female athletes showed that they often viewed moral issues in sport as irrelevant, or the responsibility of the referee or the coach, or less important than victory (Bredemeier and Shields, 1986a, 1986b). Furthermore, the expectations of peer cheating and aggression among high school and community college baseball and softball players are positively correlated with year in school and years of playing experience (Shields et al., 1995).

School Sports, Masculinity, and Race

Further evidence that the values students identify with sports may be at odds with the ones espoused by the official philosophy of the school comes from studies that examine the importance of sport in the social life of the students, and its function as a form of community entertainment (Bissinger, 1990; Foley 1990a, 1990b; Grey, 1993). The popularity of athletes, par-

ticularly male athletes, means that they are often seen as role models by their peers and consequently have an important effect on defining what is appropriate or acceptable behavior, particularly with regard to masculinity.

The theme of a biologically based male superiority over females is one of the subtexts of sport (Bryson, 1987, 1990) that gets played out in high school athletics. Foley (1990a) provided several instances of this theme at work in the school he studied. Football players prided themselves on being able to give out and take physical punishment, play with pain, and be promiscuous with females. The less physically mature boys were expected to "prove" their manhood by being able to accept pain without wincing, although it was usually the "jock wanabes" rather than the athletes themselves who administered this physical abuse. The "powder puff" football game, in which teams of the most popular senior and junior girls put on football gear and played against each other for the amusement of the male athletes, actually reproduced male power. Ostensibly a role-reversal ritual, this game allowed the males to dress like females and parody traditional female sports roles (cheerleading) in a ridiculous and demeaning manner while belittling the females' attempt at serious "male" sport.

The conventional wisdom of high school sport suggests that it acts in an inclusive manner, cutting across racial and ethnic cliques and assisting the assimilating process. Although research on this subject is limited, the results of two studies call this pluralistic view into question. Foley (1990a) showed that ethnic tensions in the community were replicated in the rituals of high school football. For example, although white and Hispanic football players joked with each other about racial stereotyping, interaction in football did not break down these stereotypes, and decisions over starting roles and homecoming competitions were interpreted as having racial overtones. Foley characterized high school football as reproducing racial inequality.

A similar view was expressed by Grey (1992) in his study of a high school in southwestern Kansas. This school had about 25% Hispanic enrollment, and a 5% Southeastern Asian minority. Many of these minorities were recent arrivals in the community, and consequently had little or no background in "American" sport such as football. Their failure to try out for these sports was interpreted by some community members as evidence that the immigrant children did not want to be assimilated into the mainstream of American culture. In this example school sport acted as a mechanism that perpetuated ethnic differences.

Given the paucity of research on the role of sport in the social life of the school it is impossible to tell the degree to which the participant observation studies described in this section reflect the norms of school and community relations, or are exceptional examples of gender and racial tension. However, the picture of sport in schools that is gained from "reading between the lines" of studies by Foley, Grey, Bredemeier and her colleagues, and Bissinger is one in which the outcome of victory takes precedence over the values of sportsmanship, fair play, and morality usually associated with "character development." The comments of some of the students, athletes, coaches, teachers, and community leaders interviewed in this research support Coleman's concern that an emphasis on athletics as community entertainment can subvert the educational mission of the school. This and other research questions are briefly discussed in the final section.

Areas for Future Research

This chapter has presented a somewhat contradictory picture of the nature of sport and schooling, in part because of the different research methodologies that have been used by scholars interested in this topic. The generally positive (or at least not negative) relationships revealed by longitudinal research has to be set against the often controversial findings of the observation studies. There is a great need for research in diverse school settings that would test the generalizability of the status reproduction findings of Foley and Grey. Female athletic programs would be a particularly interesting focus of this research in order to see what inroads, if any, the recent development of female sport has made into traditional definitions of gender and masculinity.

The relationship between extracurricular activities and high school dropouts is another issue that needs to be set in the social context of the school and the community. For example, coaches and educational administrators may be encouraged by the finding that participation in sports reduces dropout, but if the only reason potential dropouts stay in school is to play sports, then

what has been gained? McNeal (1995) hinted that reducing dropout rates with athletics was a "double-edged sword" when he suggested that potential dropouts need to be encouraged to enter a variety of extracurricular activities including fine arts. He felt that the more "cooperative" atmosphere of fine arts might be more conducive to completing school than the competitive milieu of athletics. In Bourdieu's terminology students are to be encouraged to develop cultural capital in schools in addition to physical capital, since their opportunities to convert physical capital directly into economic capital are limited (Howell et al., 1989), and, as the section on college sport showed, the indirect conversion via higher education can be problematic.

Such research efforts should not treat the school as an isolated institution, but locate it in the context of the community. If members of that community place a higher value on the physical capital of (male) athletes than on developing their cultural capital it is likely that these priorities will be reflected in the social values and the clique structure of the student body. The concept of physical capital (Shilling, 1992, 1993) could prove to be useful in exploring these relationships.

Finally, American schools are unique in the way consolidating rituals in athletics reinforce the symbiosis between education and community entertainment, and encourage the development of physical capital. Comparing American schools with schools in other cultures where interscholastic athletics is either less important or nonexistent (e.g., Rees and Brandl Bredenbeck, 1995) may provide further insights into the importance of sport and schooling in America.

REFERENCES

Adler, Peter, and Patricia A. Adler. 1985. "From Idealism to Pragmatic Detachment: The Academic Performance of College Athletes." *Sociology of Education* 58:241–250.

Armstrong, Christopher F. 1984. "The Lessons of Sport: Class Socialization in British and American Boarding Schools." *Sociology of Sport Journal* 1:314–331.

Bernstein, Basil. 1975. "Ritual in Education." In *Class, Codes and Control: Volume 3,* pp. 54–66. London: Routledge & Kegan Paul.

Best, Clayton. 1985. "Differences in Social Values between Athletes and Non-athletes." *Research Quarterly for Exercise and Sport* 56:366–369.

Bissinger, H. G. 1990. *Friday Night Lights: A Town, a Team, and a Dream.* Reading, MA: Addison-Wesley.

Brede, Richard M., and Henry J. Camp. 1987. "The Education of College Student-Athletes." *Sociology of Sport Journal* 4:245–257.

Bredemeier, Brenda Jo, and David L. Shields. 1986a. "Athletic Aggression: An Issue of Contextual Morality." *Sociology of Sport Journal* 3:15–28.

———. 1986b. "Game Reasoning and Interactional Morality." *Journal of Genetic Psychology* 47:257–275.

Bredemeier, Brenda Jo, Maureen R. Weiss, David L. Shields, and B. Cooper. 1987. "The Relationship between Children's Legitimacy Judgments and Their Moral Reasoning, Aggression Tendencies, and Sport Involvement. *Sociology of Sport Journal* 4:48–60.

Brown, B. Bradford. 1990. "Peer Groups and Peer Culture." In S. Shirley Feldman and Glen R. Elliot (eds.), *At the Threshold: The Developing Adolescent,* pp. 171–196. Cambridge, MA: Harvard University Press.

Bryson, Lois. 1987. "Sport and the Maintenance of Masculine Hegemony." *Women's Studies International Forum* 10:349–360.

———. 1990. "Challenges to Male Hegemony in Sport." In Michael A. Messner and Don F. Sabo (eds.), *Sport, Men, and the Gender Order,* pp. 173–184. Champaign, IL: Human Kinetics.

Bundgaard, Axel. 1985. "Tom Brown Abroad: Athletics in Selected New England Public Schools, 1850–1910. "*Research Quarterly for Exercise and Sport*, Centennial Issue, 56:28–37.

Caanan, Joyce. 1987. "A Comparative Analysis of American Suburban Middle Class Middle School and High School Teenage Cliques." In George Spindler and Louise Spindler (eds.), *Interpretive Ethnography and Education,* pp. 385–406. Hillside, NJ: Erlbaum.

Cavallo, Dominick. 1984. *Muscles and Morals: Organized Playgrounds and Urban Reform, 1880–1920.* Philadelphia: University of Pennsylvania Press.

Coleman, James S. 1961a. *The Adolescent Society: The Social Life of the Teenager and Its Impact on Education.* New York: The Free Press.

———. 1961b. "Athletics in High School." *Annals of the American Academy of Political and Social Sciences* 338:33–43.

Doyle, Carrie A., and Gary J. Gaeth. 1990. "Assessing the Institutional Choice Process of Student-Athletes." *Research Quarterly for Exercise and Sport* 61:85–92.

Fejgin, Naomi. 1994. "Participation in High School Competitive Sports: A Subversion of School Mission or Contribution to Academic Goals?" *Sociology of Sport Journal* 11:211–230.

Foley, Douglas E. 1990a. "The Great American Football Ritual: Reproducing Race, Class, and Gender Inequality." *Sociology of Sport Journal* 7:111–135.

———. 1990b. *Learning Capitalist Culture: Deep in the Heart of Tejas.* Philadelphia: University of Pennsylvania Press.

Grey, Mark A. 1992. "Sport and Immigrant, Minority, and Anglo Relations in Garden City (Kansas) High School." *Sociology of Sport Journal* 9:255–270.

Hanks, Michael P. 1979. "Race, Sexual Status and Athletics in the Process of Educational Achievement." *Social Science Quarterly* 60:482–496.

Hobsbawm, Eric. 1983. "Introduction: Inventing Traditions." In Eric Hobsbawm and Terence O. Ranger (eds.), *The Invention of Tradition,* pp. 1–14. Cambridge: Cambridge University Press.

Howell, Frank M., Andrew W. Miracle, and C. Roger Rees. 1984. "Do High School Athletics Pay? The Effect of Varsity Participation on Socioeconomic Attainment." *Sociology of Sport Journal* 1:15–25.

Kleiber, Douglas A., and Glyn C. Roberts. 1981. "The Effects of Sport Experience in the Development of Social Character: An Exploratory Investigation." *Journal of Sport Psychology* 3:114–122.

Knight Foundation Commission on Intercollegiate Athletics. 1991. *Keeping Faith with the Student-Athlete: A New Model for Intercollegiate Athletics.* Charlotte, NC, March.

Lopresto, Mike. 1991. "Universities Have a Weak Record with Basketball, Football Players." *USA Today* March 27, 6C.

Mangan, James A. 1981. *Athletics in the Victorian and Edwardian Public School.* Cambridge: Cambridge University Press.

Marsh, Herbert W. 1993. "The Effects of Participation in Sport During the Last Two Years of High School." *Sociology of Sport Journal* 10:18–43.

McIntosh, Peter. 1968. *Physical Education in England Since 1800.* London: G. E. Bell.

McNeal, Ralph B., Jr. 1995. "Extracurricular Activities and High School Dropouts." *Sociology of Education* 68:62–81.

Melnick, Merrill J., Donald Sabo, and Beth E. Vanfossen. 1988. "Developmental Effects of Athletic Participation Among High School Girls." *Sociology of Sport Journal* 5:22–36.

Meyer, Barbara B. 1990. "From Idealism to Actualization: The Academic Performance of Female Collegiate Athletes." *Sociology of Sport Journal* 7:44–57.

Miracle, Andrew W., and C. Roger Rees. 1994. *Lessons of the Locker Room: The Myth of School Sports.* Amherst, NY: Prometheus Books.

O'Hanlon, Timothy P. 1980. "Interscholastic Athletics, 1900–1940: Shaping Citizens for Unequal Roles in the Modern Industrial State." *Educational Theory* 30:89–103.

———. 1982. "School Sports as Social Training: The Case of Athletics and the Crisis of World War I." *Journal of Sport History* 9:5–29.

Radar, Benjamin G. 1983. *American Sports: From the Age of Folk Games to the Age of Spectators.* Englewood Cliffs, NJ: Prentice-Hall.

Redmond, Gerald. 1978. "The First Tom Brown's Schooldays: Origins and Evolution of 'Muscular Christianity' in Children's Literature." *Quest* 30:4–18.

Rees, C. Roger. 1995. "What Price Victory? Myth, Rituals, Athletics, and the Dilemma of Schooling. In Alan R. Sadovnik (ed.), *Knowledge and Pedagogy: The Sociology of Basil Bernstein,* 1995, pp. 371–383. Norwood, NJ: Ablex.

Rees, C. Roger, and Hans Peter Brandl-Bredenbeck. 1995. "Body Capital and the Importance of Sport: A Comparison of American and German Adolescents." *Journal of Comparative Physical Education and Sport* 17:50–56.

Rees, C. Roger, Frank M. Howell, and Andrew W. Miracle. 1990. "Do High School Sports Build Character? A Quasi-Experiment on a National Sample." *Social Science Journal* 27:303–315.

Sabo, Donald, Merrill J. Melnick, and Beth E. Vanfossen. 1993. "High School Athletic Participation and Postsecondary Educational and Occupational Mobility: A Focus on Race and Gender." *Sociology of Sport Journal* 10:44–56.

Sage, George H. 1990. *Power and Ideology in American Sport: A Critical Perspective*. Champaign, IL: Human Kinetics.

Shields, David Light, Brenda Jo Light Bredemeier, Douglas E. Gardner, and Alan Bostrom. 1995. "Leadership, Cohesion, and Team Norms Regarding Cheating and Aggression." *Sociology of Sport Journal* 12:324–336.

Shilling, Chris. 1992. "Schooling and the Production of Physical Capital." *Discourse* 13:1–19.

———. 1993. *The Body and Social Theory*. Newbury Park, CA: Sage.

Spady, William G. 1970. "Lament for the Letterman: Effects of Peer Status and Extracurricular Activities on Goals and Achievement." *American Journal of Sociology* 75:680–702.

Sperber, Murray. 1990. "College Sports Inc: The Athletic Department vs. the University." *Phi Delta Kappan* 72:1–10.

Spring, Joel. 1974. "Mass Culture and School Sports." *History of Education Quarterly* 14:483–499.

Thirer, Joel, and Steven D. Wright. 1985. "Sport and the Status of Adolescent Males and Females." *Sociology of Sport Journal* 2:164–171.

STRUCTURALISM

Paul Atkinson
University of Wales, Cardiff

Structuralism is a movement in the social sciences and humanities. French in origin, it proposes a general theoretical perspective that carries with it an analytic method. Its origins go back to the end of the nineteenth century, and its influence on contemporary poststructuralism and postmodernism was strongly felt at the turn of the twentieth century. This chapter explains the historical origins of structuralism, and traces its development in the social sciences. It then explores its uses in the sociology of education in the past 25 years, and briefly mentions poststructuralism and its place in the sociology of education. Structuralism has not produced a single "school" of thinkers in the sociology of education, but a number of major theorists—without characterizing themselves as "structuralists"—have incorporated structuralist insights into their work.

Historical Roots of Structuralism

Structuralism is in origin a French theoretical position, or, more accurately, a francophone (French language) one. The key figures were French, Belgian, and Swiss nationals, whose language was French. The theories and publications were mostly produced in Paris. It drew on intellectual traditions that were characteristically French, and although its key ideas were domesticated by a number of Anglophone scholars, its general flavor remains alien to many of the cherished assumptions of Anglo-American empirical social science. Indeed, Edith Kurzweil (1980:ix) makes the point that structuralism is the perfect example of how "an intellectual movement could be fashionable without being understood." Arguably, its influence lies less in precisely whether it was "understood" and more in how key ideas were used and

interpreted to inspire particular kinds of analysis, and how it suggested particular research problems.

Structuralism has three intellectual roots: one in sociology/social anthropology, another in folklore, and the third in general linguistics. The sociological origins lie with one of the discipline's founding fathers, Emile Durkheim (1858–1917), and his student and colleague Marcel Mauss (1872–1913). Durkheim and Mauss together published a study of thinking in preliterate societies called *Primitive Classification* in 1903 in French, and Mauss followed their line of thought in his essay *The Gift* published in 1925. These books were not well known in the English-speaking world until many years later. Translations appeared in 1963 and 1954, respectively. In *Primitive Classification* Durkheim and Mauss argued that cultures and cosmologies (belief systems) could be analyzed in terms of their basic systems of classification. Such classificatory principles, they argued further, also reflected fundamental social categories and divisions. Cultural categories thus impose particular, culture-specific, patterns and are themselves social in origin. Durkheim's emphasis on cultural classifications implies an important function for *boundaries,* material and symbolic, between different domains (such as that between the "sacred" and the "profane").

The second inspiration derives from Russian formalism, founded by Vladimir Propp's analysis of Russian folklore. Propp analyzed a corpus of Russian folktales and fairy-stories. He suggested that despite all their apparent variety, they could be reduced to a simple set of elements or functions. Some of those functions relate to characters or actors—such as the hero, the true helper, the false helper, the sought-for-person (the princess), and so on. Others relate to actions in the story, or narrative functions—such as the hero being sent on a quest, or the hero acquiring a magical source of help. The surface variety of folktales is reducible to an underlying, stable pattern of functions and relationships (Propp, 1975, first published 1928).

Structuralism's other root is in general linguistics. The Swiss scholar Ferdinand de Saussure (1857–1913) produced a system of linguistic analysis based on a theory of the sign (see Culler, 1976; Saussure, 1959). Saussure's contribution (first published posthumously in 1916) was fundamental: he did more than anyone else to found modern linguistics, and to break with earlier traditions of philology that were concerned primarily with tracing the origins of languages, language change, and classifying languages on the basis of their similarities and common ancestry. Saussure argued that the signs of language are themselves arbitrary, but achieve meaning and significance because they are always part of systems. The elements of language can be used to convey meaning by virtue of their membership of such linguistic systems. Saussure therefore argued that the task of linguistics was not the historical ("diachronic") search for hypothetical origins and the search for regularities in phenomena such as sound change. Rather, the task of a science of linguistics should be the investigation of systems as they operate at any given time ("synchronic" analysis). The principle underlying such linguistic systems is that of opposition or difference. Take the first principle, of the arbitrary nature of the sign. There is nothing inherent in the biological animal we in English call a cat being called "cat": that is an arbitrary label we use for it. (The fact that many European languages use similar words certainly reflects their common origins, but the signs themselves are arbitrary.) But for the word *cat* to be usable as a meaningful term in the language it must be distinguishable from such terms as *pat* or *bat*, *can* or *cap*. Each of those terms has key elements of similarity and contrast with *cat*. Likewise, at a different analytic level, *cat* has meaning because it contrasts with other terms, such as *kitten* or *dog*. The vital thing in Saussure's theory is that things such as sounds and words can be part of a meaningful language from the *system* they are in, not from their essence in themselves. Saussure explained this as follows: "Language is a system of interdependent terms in which the value of each term results solely from the simultaneous presence of the others" (1959:114).

Saussure went on to differentiate between *langue* and *parole* (terms that do not translate into English in any simple way). The possibility of speech (*parole*) exists, for Saussure, only because of the system of relationships (*langue*) that gives the words their meaning. Scholes (1974:14) explains these terms as follows: *Langue* is "language" as we use the word in speaking of the English "language" or the French "language." *Langue* is the language system that each of us uses to generate discourse that is intelligible to others. Our individual utterances are what Saussure calls *parole*.

For Saussure the proper object of study was *langue*, the system underlying the utterances of individuals. This is the key point in Saussure that led to one of the fundamentals of modern structuralism: the search for an underlying system beneath the surface of particular cultural phenomena. Saussure himself saw his linguistics as part of a much more general science of signs, which he referred to as *semiology*.

These two related ideas, the arbitrary nature of the sign and the relationship between *langue* and *parole*, have provided inspiration for structuralism in the social sciences and humanities. The other important analytic technique that derives from Saussure is the separation of the synchronic and the diachronic approaches. As we have seen, Saussure's break with earlier scholarship derived from a rejection of conjectural history in order to concentrate on how particular systems are organized at a particular point in time. This in turn places analytic emphasis on the internal logic of the cultural system and its system of relationships, rather than examination of any one element within it. The other vital insight structuralists draw from Saussure is based on the opposed terms paradigmatic and syntagmatic. Syntagmatic relations express how linguistic items can be put together to construct grammatical utterances; paradigmatic relations construct classes of items that are structurally equivalent within the system. For instance, in the sentence *a pint of milk*, those four words are in syntagmatic relationships to one another, whereas the words *cup, pitcher,* and *liter* occupy paradigmatic relationships with *pint*, and *water, beer,* and *juice* stand in the same paradigmatic relationship to *milk*. Saussure's work was built upon by Roman Jakobson, who had studied language acquisition in children and the loss of language in adults with aphasia. Jakobson stressed polarity and difference as a key to understanding systems such as the phonological system of sounds in any given language. The phonological system can be understood in terms of an elementary set of binary oppositions. For instance, the words *pat* and *bat* differ in only one respect: *p* is what is called "unvoiced" whereas *b* is "voiced," and that is precisely the same difference between, say, *tin* and *din*. Jakobson's emphasis on underlying systems of binary opposition (i.e., systems of difference based on such elementary contrasts) provided a key analytic idea for structuralist analysis.

Structuralism since 1945

The structuralism of the modern era came out of the Saussurian and Durkheimian roots in post-World War II France. A loosely linked group of male intellectuals spread structuralism as a theory and an analytic method through social and cultural anthropology (Levi-Strauss), literary criticism, cultural and media studies (Barthes), sociology (Althusser), psychoanalysis (Lacan), and the history of ideas (Foucault). Their ideas were brought into English-speaking scholarship initially in social anthropology by Edmund Leach and Mary Douglas. Structuralism also became an important approach in literary criticism, popularized by authors such as Culler (1975, 1976) and Hawkes (1977). These scholars developed robustly Anglo-Saxon versions of structuralism in Anglo-American social anthropology and literary criticism. Meanwhile the work of Levi-Strauss, Barthes, Althusser, Lacan, and Foucault was translated into English, published in paperback, and appeared on university reading lists. In the United States the French department at Yale University popularized the work of the structuralists (Scholes, 1974), and in 1966 a large international symposium on structuralism was held at Johns Hopkins University (Macksey and Donato, 1972). This conference included scholars from anthropology, classical studies, comparative literature, linguistics, literary criticism, history, philosophy, psychoanalysis, semiology (the study of signs), and sociology. Education was not included, and in the 1960s the influence of structuralism in educational research was virtually nonexistent. The published papers (Macksey and Donato, 1972) are all by men, and the popularity of structuralism stemmed in part from its exotic Frenchness, and in part from its malestream "scientific" approach to culture via formal linguistic models.

The structuralist program, applied in diverse fields, maintained a number of guiding principles. Among those was the analytic aim of treating and analyzing cultural phenomena as if they were language systems. The aim of structuralist analysis, then, was primarily to "decode" the message systems of culture. By examining the underlying patterns, and their systematic relationships of difference and opposition, the structuralist could uncover the fundamental structures beneath the variety of surface manifestations. These underlying codes in turn could be made to reveal implicit messages about the social and natural world. Ultimately, authors such as Levi-Strauss argued that the models so derived told us important things about human consciousness. Much of the appeal of modern structuralism was its applicability across many disciplines, and the consequent appearance of a general cultural theory. It also appealed to contemporary models of communication and culture based on analogies with information science (such as the importance of binary codings).

One of the best ways to grasp what structuralists are interested in, and therefore what they focus on, is a metaphor put forward by Claude Levi-Strauss (b. 1908), the greatest French anthropologist and the founder of modern structuralism in the social sciences. Levi-Strauss was asked to explain how structuralism differed from the dominant Anglo-Saxon, British, and American mode of analysis popularized by Radcliffe-Brown and Talcott Parsons as *structural functionalism*. Levi-Strauss suggested that we imagine a jigsaw puzzle. A structural functionalist would focus on how to complete the picture, how the 500 pieces (analogous to social institutions) fitted together. She or he would be satisfied when the picture of the Golden Gate was completed on the table. A structuralist would, in contrast, focus on the machinery (the jig) that drove the cutting blade of the saw itself, which shaped the pieces, thereby accounting for the surface pattern in terms of an underlying mechanism. In other words structuralists try to discover what underlying cultural principle generates any social phenomenon, whether it is a myth, an advertising campaign, a novel, a cultural system like *haute culture* fashion, a movie, a psychoanalytic theory, a school ceremony like homecoming or graduation, or a sports event like the Rosebowl. They regard such phenomena as systems of signs, essentially arbitrary in nature, and meaningful by virtue of their mutual relationships.

Structuralism in the Sociology of Education

Structuralism has never been a central part of sociology of education in the English-speaking world. Structuralism has been a minority perspective, and several of the most important structuralists have not even been recognized as such. Equally, however, it must be recognized that some of the most original thinkers in the field have been strongly influenced by structuralist perspectives. Furthermore, there are many issues in the sociology of education that can and should benefit from insights drawn from a broadly structuralist perspective.

In Britain and in the United States the preeminent structuralist is Basil Bernstein. His structuralism derives predominantly from Durkheim rather than Saussure (see Atkinson, 1985, 1995; Davies, 1995; Sadovnik, 1995). His early publications on language and schooling were widely misunderstood, and were not primarily structuralist, despite an early and abiding preoccupation with Durkheimian ideas. Only in the 1970s when Bernstein was associated with the "new" sociology of education, which blended Marxist and phenomenological perspectives and brought several French theorists to the attention of English speakers, did his structuralism become more apparent. The "new" sociology of education (Young, 1971) popularized the French sociologist of education, Pierre Bourdieu, whose ideas can be seen as having structuralism among their inspirations (although Bourdieu himself rejects the label "structuralist").

Bernstein's structuralism is most clearly seen in his early papers on the moral order of the school published in the 1960s (see Atkinson, 1985:Chapter 2), and those on the organization and transmission of school knowledge (e.g., Bernstein, 1971). In fact the writings on language, the family, and education are also an early British attempt at a structuralist analysis of how schooling reproduces class inequalities. Bernstein, in the 1950s and 1960s, lacked a vocabulary to explain what actually concerned him, which was *not* the surface manifestations of talk in the home or the classroom, but the underlying deep structure (the system, the code, or the *langue*) of the British class system and its reproduction.

To understand Bernstein's writings and recognize them for the structuralism they are, it is essential to grasp what he means by *code,* a term Bernstein uses a great deal. A code, in Bernstein's work, is a regulatory principle that operates at a deep level in a culture, beneath the surface manifestations most sociologists of education have studied. The code determines what forms the surface manifestations can take, just as *langue* underlies *parole* (see Atkinson, 1985:Chapter 5). Bernstein posited contrasting codes that generate the distinctive patterns of social relations and cultural forms of working-class and middle-class households. These in turn generate different orientations toward language use, and imply different world views. Faced with rich ethnographic and linguistic detail such as is to be found, say, in Shirely Brice Heath's (1983) work on Trackton and Roadville, Bernstein would be interested in the underlying codes that produce the adult–child talk in the two different communities. What issues of class, power, poverty, employment, gender, and race combine to produce the distinctive cultural codes of Trackton and the Roadville? *Why* are the Trackton children rewarded for fantasy talk (invisible playmates, dragons in the school yard) and the Roadville children punished for them? Bernstein would focus on the underlying speech codes, and their roots in the dynamics of class, race, gender, and power. He would not contrast the speech of the two communities, but would examine how contrasting principles of coding generate different kinds of social identities, different orders of meaning, different subcultures, and different principles of socialization and social control. The work of Cazden (1995) and Hymes (1995) shows how the importance of focusing on the deep structure was only recognized 30 years after Bernstein first tried to develop a structuralist approach to the sociology of language and socialization.

Bernstein's other main structuralist contribution is to be found in his work on school knowledge. He analyzes different types of curriculum, again using the analytic notion of *code.* As in his work on language and socialization, a knowledge code is an underlying principle that generates distinctive kinds of world view, social identities, and kinds of knowledge. Bernstein's most characteristic idea here is derived from Durkheim's emphasis on boundaries, also used by Mary Douglas in her structural anthropology of dirt and pollution. Bernstein analyzes educational curricula in terms of the notion of *classification.* This idea refers to the strength of symbolic boundary between curricular subjects. The kinds of boundaries and the divisions they define are essentially arbitrary classifications that are imposed on the world in order to create what we recognize as "curricula." Boundaries separate subjects from one another; they define the sequence in which topics should be taught and learned; they also create divisions such as those between high-status and mundane knowledge domains. The underlying principles of knowledge codes in turn help to define the organization of educational institutions and the development of students' and teachers' identities within them. The principle of classification is paralleled by that of *framing*, which refers primarily to the organization of pedagogical relationships. The coding of frames regulates the pacing of teaching, the exercise of control over the teaching encounter, and control over the content. The Bernsteinian framework of classification and framing provides a formal model for the description and comparison of different educational institutions and systems.

Parallel to Bernstein in Britain has been the work of Pierre Bourdieu in France. Although not exclusively a structuralist, Bourdieu—especially in some of his early work—undoubtedly incorporated some characteristically structuralist ideas. Bourdieu has been increasingly influential in sociology since his work began to appear in English in the 1970s (Robbins, 1991; Jenkins, 1992). Trained as an anthropologist, and then a colleague of all the central figures in French structuralism, he must be "counted" as a structuralist in the sociology of education, however much he himself rejects the label. Working mostly on higher education, Bourdieu has been concerned with what deep structures in French society preserve success in the high-status universities for students from intellectual upper middle-class homes. Bourdieu's analyses, like Bernstein's, focus on issues of boundaries. Drawing on a Durkheimian idiom, he examines how a society separates what is "thinkable" from what is "unthinkable"; how it distinguishes high-status (almost "sacred") knowledge from everyday, "profane" knowledge. He suggests that such distinctions and discriminations are used as a kind of cultural code. It is a code that reproduces social differences (such as those of social class) implicitly, by reproducing particular kinds of cultural distinction. Thought of from this point of view, educational institutions can be thought of as organizations that encode culture, and where those codes reproduce social categories. They are by no means the only institutions involved in such cultural reproduction; others include the mass media. Because educational codes are

couched in terms of universal values and canons of good taste, they promote social inequalities as reflections of natural, taken-for-granted differences. Bourdieu's work includes empirical research on taste and consumption, on the cultural dispositions of French university academics, on university students' cultural preferences, and on specific cultural domains such as photography.

It is clear that there remains considerable scope for structuralist ideas to inform major research in the sociology of education. Hitherto there have been relatively few empirical studies done in the United States or the United Kingdom using structuralist techniques. In the United Kingdom Walker's (1983) study of social control in teachers' colleges, and Delamont's (1991) analysis of pupil's folklore about transfer from elementary to secondary school are examples. Delamont's monograph on feminism and the social organization of academic elites is an exception to the general neglect (Delamont, 1989). Delamont draws extensively on the ideas of Bernstein and Bourdieu, as well as Douglas and other anthropologists, to examine historical and contemporary issues in the sociology of educational knowledge from a feminist standpoint. Ideas concerning curricular knowledge, discrimination and taste, and the symbolic boundaries that define them, remain fundamental to a sociology of education. Although the "pure" structuralism of scholars such as Levi-Strauss have become much less fashionable in recent years, the general ideas that their theories can inform remain fundamentally important. If we are prepared to look beyond the narrow confines of educational policy and classroom management, and to examine how education (in the broadest sense) reproduces elementary ideas about knowledge, culture, and good taste, then the structuralist program remains vital and valid.

REFERENCES

Atkinson, P. 1985. *Language, Structure and Reproduction: An Introduction to the Sociology of Basil Bernstein.* London: Methuen.

———. 1995. "From Structuralism to Discourse." In A. Sadovnik (ed.), *Knowledge and Pedagogy: The Sociology of Basil Bernstein,* pp. 83–96. Norwood NJ: Ablex.

Bernstein, B. 1971. "On the Classification and Framing of Educational Knowledge." In B. Bernstein (ed.), *Class, Codes and Control,* pp. 85–115. Vol. 2. London: Routledge & Kegan Paul.

Cazden, C. 1995. "Visible and Invisible Pedagogies in Literacy Education." In P. Atkinson, S. Delamont, and B. Davies (eds.), *Discourse and Reproduction: Essays in*

Honor of Basil Bernstein, pp. 159–172. New York: Hampton.

Culler, J. 1975. *Structuralist Poetics: Structuralism, Linguistics and the Study of Literature.* London: Routledge & Kegan Paul.

————. 1976. *Saussure.* London: Fontana.

Davies, B. 1995. "Bernstein, Durkheim and the British Sociology of Education." In A. Sadovnik (ed.), *Knowledge and Pedagogy: The Sociology of Basil Bernstein,* pp. 39–58. Norwood, NJ: Ablex.

Delamont, S. 1989. *Knowledgeable Women.* London: Routledge & Kegan Paul.

————. 1991. "The HIT LIST and Other Horror Stories." *Sociological Review* 39:238–259.

Durkheim, E., and M. Mauss. 1963 (first published 1903). *Primitive Classification.* London: Cohen and West.

Hawkes, T. 1977. *Structuralism and Semiotics.* London: Methuen.

Heath, S. B. 1983. *Ways With Words: Language, Life, and Work in Communities and Classrooms.* Cambridge: Cambridge University Press.

Hymes, D. 1995. "Bernstein and Poetics." In P. Atkinson, S. Delamont, and B. Davies (eds.), *Discourse and Reproduction: Essays in Honor of Basil Bernstein,* pp. 1–24. New York: Hampton.

Jenkins, R. 1992. *Pierre Bourdieu.* London: Routledge.

Kurzweil, E. 1980. *The Age of Structuralism: Levi-Strauss to Foucault.* New York: Columbia University Press.

Macksey, R., and E. Donato, eds. 1972. *The Structuralist Controversy: The Languages of Criticism and the Sciences of Man.* Baltimore: Johns Hopkins University Press.

Mauss, M. 1956 (first published 1925). *The Gift.* New York: Free Press.

Propp, V. 1975 (first published 1928). *Morphology of the Folktale.* Austin, TX: University of Texas Press.

Robbins, D. 1991. *The Work of Pierre Bourdieu.* Buckingham: Open University Press.

Sadovnik, A. 1995. "Basil Bernstein's Theory of Pedagogic Practice: A Structuralist Approach." In A. Sadovnik (ed.), *Knowledge and Pedagogy: The Sociology of Basil Bernstein,* pp. 3–38. Norwood, NJ: Ablex.

Saussure, F. de. 1959. *Course in General Linguistics.* New York: The Philosophical Library.

Scholes, R. 1974. *Structuralism in Literature: An Introduction.* New Haven, CT: Yale University Press.

Walker, M. 1983. "Control and Consciousness in the College." *British Educational Research Journal* 9:129–40.

Young, M. F. D., ed. 1971. *Knowledge and Control.* London: Collier-Macmillan.

STUDENT CULTURES AND ACADEMIC ACHIEVEMENT

Sandra L. Wong
Department of Sociology, Wesleyan University

The relationship between culture and student achievement has been a topic of much interest to sociologists seeking to understand the factors that shape student performance and educational attainment. An examination of literature on this topic over the past 30 years reveals two notable shifts in the thrust of educational research. First, what distinguishes current research is a shift in assumptions about the type of impact cultural differences have on student performance. Whereas cultural differences were once treated as liabilities that needed to be removed, remediated through processes of assimilation, and replaced by majority group norms, language, and meanings, cultural differences are increasingly recognized as an asset to learning, achievement, and identity formation as well as a basis of curricular expansion. Second, sociological theory and research have directed our attention to how students experience schooling, and to the ways in which culture intersects with other forms of capital to shape educational outcomes. Thus sociological investigations have produced more positive interpretations of the effects of cultural differences and moved toward a more precise account of the role of culture in educational achievement.

In the 1960s, research on culture and achievement focused extensively on the relatively low educational attainment and performance of racial minorities; theories of cultural deprivation and cultural assimilation had center stage. Evans and Anderson's study of achievement among Mexican-American students found that despite parental expectations and pressures, students were more fatalistic, and had lower educational aspirations and levels of self-confidence than their Anglo peers. These differences, the authors concluded, were linked to a culture of poverty that resulted from economic deprivation and the marginalized social position of Mexican Americans in the southwest (Evans and Anderson, 1973).

Explanations of educational achievement among African Americans also attributed poor performance to characteristics of their cultural backgrounds. Whether these cultural factors were described as deficits or differences, they were perceived as having negative consequences for achievement in mainstream classrooms. Popular beliefs about cultural deprivation are summarized in Charles Valentine's critical observations:

> On dozens of occasions and in settings ranging from classrooms to counseling sessions to public confrontations with Afro-American parents and children, we have observed white educators expressing highly standardized beliefs and feelings about ghetto children and their families. Key items in this inventory include explicit statements that Afro-Americans are culturally different, that the cultural differences impede or prevent learning, that the school should function to wipe out these differences, but that educators frequently cannot succeed in this aim because the children are psychologically deficient as a result of their cultural difference. (Valentine, 1971)

Theory and research suggested that factors such as family structure, parents' educational and economic attainment, students' English language deficiencies and fatalistic attitudes inhibit success in schools. In short, some students bring liabilities to the classroom and higher achievement can best be attained by providing compensatory programs that help them to adapt to mainstream institutions (Connell, 1994). By contrast, the relatively high level of educational attainment among some groups of Asian Americans has been linked to cultural traits typically described as having positive value. These traits include "a premium on ambition, persistence, and deferred gratification" and "a strong desire for intergenerational social mobility" (Hirschman and Wong, 1991).

Beliefs about the relative success of different groups have been rooted in assumptions about schools as sites of assimilation. Achievement requires not only the acquisition of academic skills and proficiency in English, but the acceptance of mainstream norms, ideologies, and values. Those groups that exhibit attitudes and behaviors consistent with the values and meanings reinforced in schools are praised for their ambition and hard work, whereas those that do not succeed are regarded as impoverished, disabled, at risk, or rebellious. Both theories of cultural deprivation and theories of cultural assimilation explain school performance in terms of whether students strive to meet the expectations of schooling; the schooling process itself is presumed to be neutral, consensual, and fair.

By the early 1970s sociological theory and research began to shift attention away from students' supposed deficiencies to a critical examination of the knowledge, skills, and behaviors valued in schools. In contrast to theories of deprivation, which attribute low achievement to inferior cultural traits, theories of reproduction focus on the power relations that shape what is taught and rewarded in schools. This perspective illuminates the relationship between school knowledge and practices and the values and norms of dominant social classes and status groups. By questioning the objectivity and neutrality of mainstream knowledge and pedagogical styles,[1] reproduction theories offer an alternative explanation of low academic achievement. Minority students are less likely to succeed, not because their cultures are inherently inferior or debilitating to the learning experience, but because what is valued in schools reinforces the knowledge and interests of the most powerful groups.

According to theorist Pierre Bourdieu, working-class students are less likely to succeed because they lack the accumulated cultural capital of their more privileged middle-class peers (Bourdieu and Passeron, 1977). Minority students and new immigrants are also

at a decided disadvantage because they are required to compete in a classroom environment that reinforces the linguistic, intellectual, and social backgrounds of the majority. Hence, reproduction theories suggest that these students are less likely to possess the skills that provide access to what is taught. More significantly, the cultures with which they are familiar receive little or no recognition. Their lack of identification with classroom practices and curriculum not only impairs performance, but also discourages interest in education and further attainment.

Similarly, theories of resistance examine schooling experiences from the vantage point of students. However, in contrast to the reproductive view, they portray students, not as passive individuals who accept the meanings affirmed in schools, but as active agents who seek to maintain distinct racial or ethnic identities. Ogbu has argued that African-American adolescents associate academic achievement with a dominant white society. Rather than internalizing mainstream values of achievement, they develop oppositional identities and norms (Ogbu, 1988). Ogbu attributes these behaviors to the history of African Americans as an involuntary minority group. Unlike European, Asian, and other immigrants who came voluntarily to the United States and have had access to resources and opportunities for upward mobility, African Americans have occupied a caste-like status that affects schooling outcomes across social classes and creates a need for survival strategies. Because minority students who adhere to the norms and practices of schooling may be perceived by their peers as "acting white," some reject educational achievement to maintain a sense of cultural identity as well as the approval of their peers (Ogbu, 1988:177). Resistance to dominant norms may be expressed through low performance, dropping out, or scornful attitudes toward academic work. One study of Chicano students described how students avoided classroom discussion, asking for help, and even carrying books to class (Bianci and Ferdman, 1990). These strategies channel productive and inquisitive energies away from academic diligence and conventional measures of school achievement.

Other researchers suggest that minority students experience a more contradictory process of resistance and accommodation. Group identity may be maintained by selectively participating in the cultural and social life of a school. In his ethnography of an ethnically mixed

---

[1] For a review and critique of reproduction and resistance theories, see Henry A. Giroux (1983).

high school Peshkin found that Mexican students in college preparatory programs pursued academic success even though they regarded their conformity to proper English and particular styles of dress as acting white (Peshkin, 1991:185).

Though studies have produced different, and sometimes contradictory, findings with respect to which activities are valued or shunned by particular groups, the distinction between academic and nonacademic pursuits is a common thread among involuntary minorities. Survival strategies for minorities in a dominant milieu are typically understood to have two negative consequences for academic achievement. First, activities valued by peer groups tend to steer students away from academic pursuits. Second, teachers perceive some forms of resistance, such as facial gestures and body language, as indicative of negative attitudes. These attitudes are expressed through a range of behaviors—group-specific language and slang, disruptive classroom social behavior, alternative music and styles of dress—that runs in opposition to traditionally accepted school norms. Because of their perceived resistance or rebellious attitudes, students may have difficulty gaining the respect of significant authority figures whose support is critical to their success.

Whereas theories of cultural deprivation suggest compensatory programs to remedy cultural deficiencies, and theories of cultural reproduction portray students as passive minorities who will succeed only by assimilating, resistance theories assert that students purposefully reject mainstream expectations and actively construct their own cultural meanings. Yet, because oppositional identities and forms of countercultural expressiveness undermine achievement in a society that values grades and credentials, the gains of resistance and group identity come at a price. Forms of opposition may enhance peer group acceptance, but they contribute to, rather than reverse, low achievement.

In sum, these perspectives posit negative educational outcomes for minority students who do not conform to conventional standards. Even though reproduction and resistance theories move beyond a focus on group deficiencies, they still emphasize the costs of cultural differences. Students' cultural backgrounds do not count toward achievement and the differences students bring to schools must either be checked at the door or asserted in ways that jeopardize their academic success. None of these perspectives suggests the possibility that

change can come from anywhere but the students themselves. In other words, if students are to succeed, it is they who must adapt to the schools they attend. Although cultural differences impede educational achievement, the content and curriculum of schooling are presumed to be given and unalterable.

In contrast to these views, multicultural theories of education have focused more attention on the ways in which cultural differences can facilitate student achievement as well as on the role of schools in accommodating these differences. By affirming and even celebrating cultural diversity, these approaches treat students' backgrounds and experiences as positive components of the learning process. Multicultural and multilingual perspectives emphasize the value of recognizing cultural differences in curricular content and pedagogical practices; they seek to legitimate alternative bodies of knowledge, to validate differences in language, traditions, and values (Perry and Fraser, 1993), and to strengthen the links among schools, families, and communities.

Studies on the effects of integrating cultural differences in educational processes have revealed favorable outcomes in student performance. For example, numerous studies identify a positive relationship between bilingualism and high grades, test scores, and levels of educational attainment. Spanish-speaking students who are bilingual and bicultural are believed to have an advantage over their monolingual peers because they possess the English language skills that are necessary to function effectively in school, but they retain their native language and culture (Rumberger and Larson, 1998). Research on language-minority students suggests that students develop conceptual and linguistic skills most successfully when school programs reinforce their cultural identities, promote and integrate their native language, and include and involve their parents and communities (Cummins, 1993).

Bankston and Zhou's study of Vietnamese youths found that students who maintained close ties with their families and community through language and literacy were able to transfer the cognitive skills from their minority language to academic pursuits in mainstream subjects. These students spent more time on their homework and maintained positive attitudes toward future educational attainment (Bankston and Zhou, 1995). The authors concluded that ethnic language literacy and positive cultural characteristics actually contribute to rather than compete with the goals of traditional schooling. "At the least, educators should view native languages neither as obstructions to be swept out of the way in the rush to assimilation nor as inconveniences to be endured while gradually moving students toward assimilation into an exclusively English-speaking society. Schools should actively promote clubs and activities that are aimed at strengthening the students' skills in their native languages" (Bankston and Zhou, 1995).

Literacy in one's native language also provides a form of social capital that contributes positively to academic achievement. Examining the relationship between social capital and status attainment, Stanton-Salazar and Dornbusch (1995) found that bilingual students were more likely to obtain the necessary forms of institutional support to promote their success in school as well as their chances for future mobility.

Although these findings attest to some of the advantages of maintaining cultural differences, they are also important because they illuminate the complexities of defining cultural groups and the limitations of focusing on cultural explanations alone. As interest in the diverse needs of students has grown, so too has the need to understand how variations in educational achievement are related to particular economic, social, historical, and political circumstances. By focusing on these conditions and contexts sociologists are more likely to avoid the problem of essentialism, or treating social groups "as stable or homogeneous entities" (Stanton-Salazar and Dornbusch, 1995).

Though the achievement of students from particular minority groups may appear to be linked to cultural values or attitudes, they are also related to other factors such as aspirations, social contexts upon arrival, and processes of adaptation (Portes and MacLeod, 1996). These factors require that scholars avoid making generalizations about broadly defined racial and ethnic groups and take care in sorting out the effects of factors that can be differentiated from culture. Current research, for example, links educational achievement to hours spent on homework, modes of incorporation, and community networks, factors that are related to socioeconomic status, contextual advantages, and social capital, respectively (Portes and MacLeod, 1996:256–257).

Identifying variations within as well as between groups is especially important at a time when curriculum developers are paying increasing attention to demographic changes in student populations and the racial and ethnic diversity of public school classrooms. In the 1990s, the concepts of culture and cultural identities are a focus of much interest and debate as curricular reformers consider the positive implications of affirming cultural differences, and are turning to ideas such as multicultural education to address the perceived needs and interests of their students. Sociologists can contribute to this discussion, not by engaging in ideological struggles over pluralism and unity, but by continuing their efforts to explain the significance of cultural differences within and between groups and to identify the ways in which culture intersects with and is shaped by economic resources and forms of social capital. Attention to both the meaning of culture for different groups and the multiple factors that contribute to educational outcomes will enable sociologists to avoid oversimplified and reductive accounts of the relationship between culture and achievement.

REFERENCES

Bankston, Carl L. III, and Min Zhou. 1995. "Effects of Minority-Language Literacy on the Academic Achievement of Vietnamese Youths in New Orleans." *Sociology of Education* 68(January):1–17.

Bianci, Matute, and Bernardo M. Ferdman. 1990. "Literacy and Cultural Identity." *Harvard Educational Review* 60(May):181–204.

Bourdieu, Pierre, and Jean-Claude Passeron. 1977. *Reproduction in Education, Society and Culture*. Beverly Hills, CA: Sage.

Connell, R.W. 1994. "Poverty and Education." *Harvard Educational Review* 64(Summer):125–149.

Cummins, Jim. 1993. "Empowering Minority Students: A Framework for Intervention." In Lois Weis and Michelle Fine (eds.), *Beyond Silenced Voices*, p. 116. Albany: State University of New York Press.

Evans, Francis B., and James G. Anderson. 1973. "The Psychocultural Origins of Achievement and Achievement Motivation: The Mexican-American Family." *Sociology of Education* 46(Fall):404.

Fordham, Signithia. 1996. *Blacked Out*. Chicago: University of Chicago Press.

Giroux, Henry A. 1983. *Theory and Resistance in Education*. New York: Bergin & Garvey.

Hirschman, Charles, and Morrison Wong. 1991. "The Extraordinary Educational Attainment of Asian-Americans: A Search for Historical Evidence and Explanations." In Norman Yetman (ed.), *Majority and Minority*, p. 170. Needham Heights, MA: Allyn & Bacon.

McCarthy, Cameron, and Warren Crichlow. 1993. *Race, Identity and Representation in Education*. New York: Routledge.

Ogbu, John. 1978. *Minority Education and Caste: The American System in Cross-Cultural Perspective*. New York: Academic Press.

Ogbu, John U. 1988. "Class Stratification, Racial Stratification, and Schooling." In Lois Weis (ed.), *Class, Race, and Gender in American Education*, pp. 163–183. Albany: State University of New York Press.

Peshkin, Alan. 1991. *The Color of Strangers, the Color of Friends*. Chicago: University of Chicago Press.

Portes, Alejandro, and Dag MacLeod. 1996. "Educational Progress of Children of Immigrants: The Roles of Class, Ethnicity, and School Context." *Sociology of Education* 69:4 (October):271.

Rumberger, Russell W., and Katherine A. Larson. 1998. "Toward Explaining Differences in Educational Achievement among Mexican American Language-Minority Students." *Sociology of Education* 71(1):69–93.

Stanton-Salazar, Ricardo D., and Stanford M. Dornbusch. 1995. "Social Capital and the Reproduction of Inequality: Information Networks among Mexican-Origin High School Students." *Sociology of Education* 68(April):116–135.

Valentine, Charles A. 1971. "Deficit, Difference, and Bicultural Models of Afro-American Behavior." *Harvard Educational Review* 41(May):137–157.

Weis, Lois, ed. 1988. *Class, Race, and Gender*. Albany: State University of New York Press.

Weis, Lois, and Michelle Fine, eds. 1993. *Beyond Silenced Voices*. Albany: State University of New York Press.

SUMMER LEARNING

Barbara Heyns
New York University

In education, policy debates recur with the regularity of the seasons; the issues and questions about summer learning are no exception. The implications of summer learning for schools are diverse, involving curricula, school calendars, scheduling and timetables, overcrowded classrooms, teachers' salaries, and the efficiency and effectiveness of American public education as a whole. Summer learning has generated interest in policy circles as well as in schools, for an amalgam of diverse reasons. Proponents of year-round schooling argue that increasing the time spent in school will enhance learning for all students and at the same time reduce costs; that it allows the full utilization of school facilities but with greater flexibility; that it can improve educational effectiveness and increase the amount of time American children spend studying academic subjects; and that once parents become used to new schedules they will realize that the September-to-June school year is an obsolete obstacle to educational progress. This mix of educational and administrative concerns has, however, often left parents skeptical and often rather hostile to proposed policies.

Summer learning originated as an effort to conceptualize achievement as a process in time, and as a critique of prevailing notions about the effects of schools. Large-scale studies of educational effects typically collected cross-sectional data about students and cognitive achievement; test scores were then averaged for particular schools or classrooms, usually after individual student background was controlled. The best known studies in this tradition concluded that socioeconomic and ethnic background were far more important for predicting student achievement than any measured characteristic of their school. The methodological strategy common to these studies involved estimating a regression model or an educational production function, associating school "inputs" such as school facilities, teacher qualities, or other resources with achievement as an "output," much as an economist might evaluate the productivity of a factory or firm. The logic was to isolate school factors that were critical in generating achievement, and to compare the strength of their relative contribution. For example, analysts expected that schools with higher per student expenditures or especially talented teachers would produce higher levels of achievement. However, even when variables measuring school or teacher characteristics were significant, they tended to be confounded with individual traits that students brought from home. It proved to be very difficult to prove that any school resource or attribute "added value" to student achievement, independent of family and home environment.

The literature on the effects of schools contributed to a general feeling of pessimism, and to the conviction that education was a very dismal science. Seemingly, research could provide only very limited guidance or scientific support for particular policies, forms of school organization, or educational resources and expenditures. In the aggregate, differences between schools were more strongly related to the average socioeconomic composition of the school than to any other school characteristic. For students from middle-class homes, virtually any combination of educational resources facilitated cognitive growth; in poorer schools with less advantaged students, even the best equipment did not improve average achievement dramatically.

Educational research moved beyond cross-sectional, survey designs rather quickly. Panel studies using longitudinal data became the more common evaluation tool for assessing school effects and achievement gains.

At the microlevel, studies of learning estimated "time-on-task" in the classroom. Educational effects were estimated as a function of the way teachers allocated class time to specific students, assignments, or subject matter. Not surprisingly, the amount of time spent on a given subject strongly influenced how much students learned. Moreover, higher levels of learning were consistently observed in orderly and disciplined classrooms than in somewhat chaotic, inner-city schools.

At the macrolevel, growth in achievement became more important than test scores at a particular point in time. Fall test scores were used as a "pretest" for spring achievement, and as a global control for preexisting differences. Longitudinal data permitted an assessment of learning gains over a year or more, as well as the degree to which cognitive growth varied by time and place; the most appropriate measure of school effectiveness became the gains observed for specific schools or programs. Although most attention naturally focused on differences between the fall and spring, analysts began to look at summer intervals and summer programs as well.

Summer learning was defined as achievement gains observed between the spring and the fall. Even more than representing a period of time, however, summer gains became a variable that could be used to measure "nonschooling," or the effects of family and neighborhood characteristics when schools were closed. The logic was to establish a temporal definition of schooling, rather than a spacial one. If specific school activities influenced learning during the year, other activities must influence learning in the absence of regular programs. Moreover, some students attended summer school and others did not. Family activities or summer compensatory programs could be compared to the effects of programs during the school year. Moreover, learning patterns for children from diverse backgrounds could be compared, both in and out of the school. Families can influence cognitive growth year-round, but school effects are necessarily restricted to achievement gains when schools are open. Defining summer learning in this way, it became possible to conceptualize education as a process mediating, reinforcing, or reversing the effects of families on learning; schooling could either accelerate or retard learning outcomes.

Sociologically, summer learning would be an important educational topic even if very little learning occurred when schools are closed. It is notoriously difficult to separate the effects of schooling from the effects of family or socioeconomic background on achievement, as both influence learning simultaneously. The single, most robust finding in the entire literature on student achievement is that differences in family background consistently predict differences in educational achievement. Virtually every student outcome associated with schooling—including grades, test scores, progress toward degree, attendance, attrition, or extracurricular activities—is related to the social and economic status of families. The more advantaged the home environment, the better a student's achievement.

A voluminous and longstanding literature in education has endeavored to specify and unravel these effects, with limited success. The fact that schools do not—and seemingly cannot—equalize achievement between rich and poor or between black and white children is often interpreted as a devastating indictment of public education. Persistent social inequalities in education challenge the very foundation of American beliefs and faith in equal educational opportunity. Inequalities inherited from one generation to the next seem much less fair than the differences in income and standards of living that accumulate over a lifetime. Hence, inequalities in school achievement related to background are central to national concerns, often more than the growing evidence that American schools have failed to keep pace internationally.

Summer learning offers one of the very few instances in which it is possible to separate analytically the effects of home and family from the effects of classrooms. During the school year, children are presumably influenced by both their home environment and by formal education. But in the summer, when schools close, families assume exclusive control; their impact on learning becomes, therefore, unique, immediate, and unmitigated by education. This formulation assumes that both schools and families produce achievement, independently and in combination. During the school year, the joint or interactive effects of home environment cannot be separated from the influence of schools, but in the summer, unique patterns of learning that depend solely on family background can be discerned.

Modeled in this way, socioeconomic status is assumed to be a constant influence or a fixed effect, while schooling is intermittent. The relative importance of each factor and its respective contribution to achievement can be distinguished. Families promote learning whether or not schools are in session, but their independent influence can be observed only when schools are closed. Seasonal variations in learning provide a measure of experimental control over the influence of families; arguably, the effects of schooling are more properly specified than in studies with only statistical control for home background.

The results for models of learning constructed in this way represent schooling in a manner far closer to conventional ideals than most studies of educational effects. Schools have both an additive and an interactive effect on student achievement. During the school year, the rate of growth in achievement is more rapid than that observed in the absence of schooling, even when the amount of time between testing intervals is taken into account. Moreover, rates of learning are far more equal during the school year than in the summer. During the school year, children from diverse backgrounds tend to learn—that is, to accumulate points on standardized tests—at very similar rates. Although schooling does not equalize differences in achievement in absolute terms, school-year learning is far more equal than the patterns when schools are closed. Advantaged children are still ahead at the end of the school year, but poor, minority children progress almost as quickly. In contrast, the summer is characterized by dramatic increases in social inequality, with learning rates heavily dependent on differences in family background. Precise estimates of the influence of home environment compared to schooling vary, of course, but the general patterns are quite consistent. Approximately 80% of the achievement gap between economically privileged and less advantaged students occurs in the summer months, in the absence of schooling. The general pattern is similar when black and white students are compared, but family economic status seems to play a more important role than race.

As a research tradition, summer learning has contributed a great deal to what is known about cognitive growth, retention, and the measurement of learning over time. Moreover, summer learning supports the conventional image of educators, that schools enhance learning for all children, in spite of persistent socioeconomic inequality. Summer learning conceptualizes schooling not as a particular place or site, but as a time interval; learning is viewed as a process, not a static score. Numerous studies have replicated these original findings, demonstrating that the "summer setback" is a very common occurrence, and that low-income, minority children experience much greater summer loss than children from more advantaged families.

Summer learning has, however, provoked more questions than answers. The first set of issues concerns the specification of achievement gains during specific time periods, and the second concerns the meaning and the magnitude of summer loss. With respect to the first set of issues, the most general conclusion has been that the rate of achievement growth during the winter months—when schools are open—is faster than the month-by-month gains during the summer months for all children. Although this suggests that attending school is more beneficial educationally than the alternatives, it is still difficult to identify exactly what sorts of activities or resources are associated with growth during either the summer or the winter. Some students, particularly those from relatively affluent and educated families, appear to learn at roughly similar rates whether or not schools are in session. Others lose ground, especially in the summer. If schooling accelerates learning, then year-round education should enhance cognitive growth. However, it is very difficult to prove that any particular program benefits children. The actual relationship between time and learning may well be more complex. If the relationship between time and cognitive achievement is not linear, for example, but many students learn in spurts followed by lulls, then a month of time and a given gain in test score might not be equivalent. Moreover, some students seem to learn best in carefully planned, structured sequences, whereas others make the most rapid progress through self-discovery. For the former, schooling might well play a crucial instructional role; but for the latter group, supervision and fixed lesson plans could actually stifle gains. Learning requires a balance of personal motivation and guidance. Schools are charged with providing both formal instruction and encouragement to pursue independent learning. In practice, we know very little about the proper mix, or whether an optimal blend varies by type of student or period of time. One of the reasons given for retaining the 9-month school calendar, in addition to tradition, is the argument that certain students need a prolonged break from normal routine and an opportunity to explore the world in new ways. Although there is little doubt that, on average, students acquire the knowledge measured by standardized achievement tests more quickly during the school year than during the summer, we still do not know much about development and the dynamics of learning. Summer learning poses questions about both what should be learned and how students learn best that cannot be answered at present.

The second issue concerns whether summer achievement loss represents a permanent decline or only a temporary setback. Teachers report that they routinely spend several weeks each fall reviewing material presented the previous year. The reasons they give are relevant to summer learning. Teachers believe that retention during the summer is poor and that students need time to get reaccustomed to school routines in the fall. Either of these reasons could explain the rather mediocre performance on tests in September or October, and we do not know whether fall test scores dip because of poor retention or poor concentration. Achievement tests may drop because students have forgotten material or because they did not learn it adequately initially; if students are more attentive or more motivated at the end of the school year, this could also have an effect on test scores. Each of these interpretations of summer learning is plausible, but each suggests a rather different remedy.

Summer learning involves issues on the frontiers of our knowledge about learning and about the measurement of achievement. Ten or twelve weeks is not a very long time, and changes in achievement tend to be small. Summer gains are usually negligible, but losses are also frequently insignificant. As a result, analysts are not certain whether they should be discussing gains, losses, or test score unreliability. The general findings clearly suggest that a deceleration in cognitive growth occurs during the summer; but standardized tests were not designed to capture small increments—or decrements—of change. We simply do not know enough about cognitive growth and learning, or about retention and relearning, to say for sure whether seasonal variations represent depressed fall scores or inflated spring achievement. Moreover, when one examines specific skills—in math or verbal achievement, for example—there is less consensus on the magnitude of change, or on the question of which skills are more subject to summer loss.

The initial work on summer achievement patterns described the schools and programs in grades five through seven in Atlanta (Heyns, 1978). These results have been replicated in Baltimore for earlier grades (Entwisle and Alexander, 1992, 1994), and in a variety of smaller studies. National achievement data with biannual testing is rare; hence, research on summer learning is generally limited to a single district or school system. Large-scale studies still rely on cross-sectional data, rather than longitudinal follow-up studies. Moreover, when the focus of research is on summer compensatory programs, analysts neglect or avoid inferences based on the seasonal patterns found in annual test scores.

There is an understandable tendency to resist analyzing achievement declines in educational research, because it is difficult to identify the source. Yet in many studies, seasonal patterns potentially confound the interpretation of otherwise exemplary research. If the expected gains during a particular time period are negative, beneficial program effects may be obscured by small changes. Evaluation studies conducted on large, nationally representative samples have frequently reported no significant improvement could be attributed to programs. The Sustaining Effects Study, for example, concluded that summer compensatory programs had little impact on either reading or math scores (Carter, 1984). This conclusion is, however, based on the assumption that gains are expected during the summertime; if the expected change is negative, a summer program that produced little or no loss in relative achievement among participants would be a great success. In the Sustaining Effects Study, learning rates in the winter were substantially greater than in the summer; when minority status and eligibility for a free lunch were introduced as controls, the seasonal patterns are quite similar to those found in many smaller samples. The children assigned to compensatory summer classes were not a random sample of all students, however; the modest and insignificant gains for these students could be interpreted as either an indication that very successful programs prevented the even greater loss that would have occurred in the absence of a summer program, or, following the authors, as indicative of an ineffective program (Heyns, 1987). Without an understanding of seasonal patterns in achievement, however, it is risky to conclude that small or insignificant gains always mean a program has failed. From the point of view of summer learning, a compensatory program that merely arrested declines in learning during the summer months should be viewed as immensely successful.

The implications of summer learning have not been fully incorporated into educational research and evaluation. Advocates of year-round education simply assert the educational advantages of more time in school, without examining the literature carefully. Despite consistent patterns, if rigorous criteria are invoked, studies of summer learning are often as inconclusive as the original studies of school effects. For most children, learning is related to family background much more than to formal schooling; isolating programmatic influences on achievement, in either the winter or the summer, has proved to be extremely difficult. Summer school evaluations are, almost by necessity, nonexperimental or quasi-experimental in design; students do not choose to participate in summer programs at random, and even when these programs are especially targeted to low-income neighborhoods, it is likely that self-selected students who especially enjoy school are more likely to attend. Hence, achievement gains are inevitably subject to confounding and selective bias.

Similar problems afflict studies of year-round schooling. In the "real world" of schools, diverse "natural" experiments exist with varying school calendars, innovative scheduling, and academic requirements. However, most schools have adopted year-round education to reduce crowding, and not to increase the time spent in academic programs. Year-round programs permit the full utilization of school facilities, and enable districts to avoid or defer expensive new buildings. According to the National Association for Year-Round Education (NAYRE), 2,368 schools in 37 states operated some sort of annual program in 1995–1996, a fivefold increase over the previous decade. Most of these schools have rearranged student schedules, however, rather than increased the amount of time spent in school. In 1995, three-fourths of the year-round schools were located in three fast-growing states: California, Texas, and Florida.

In most cases, neither the curriculum nor the time spent on learning has changed with year-round schooling. A common plan consists of establishing multiple tracks and school calendars with shorter, but more frequent vacations. These programs aim to reduce summer achievement loss, but not by extending schooling; supporters argue that losses are the result of long summer vacations, and not the absence of school. A typical program divides the school year into four 9-week terms, separated by four 3-week breaks. Such a schedule retains the 180-day school year that seems sacrosanct in this country; if, however, summer learning is a function of time in class, this is still substantially less time than the 240-day school calendars common in Japan and Germany. Moreover, because it is extremely difficult to assess achievement gains during 9-week or 3-week intervals, year-round schools are unlikely to resolve the truly thorny questions of time and tempo posed by summer learning. Advocates argue that these programs are cost effective, whether or not they increase achievement.

Educational policies designed to address summer learning involve numerous ironies. Year-round schools are often cited as an appropriate policy response, although such programs typically supersede advanced placement and summer enrichment programs for students. Voluntary summer programs are abandoned, in favor of standardized programs with uniform requirements for all. Traditionally, summer programs are much more unstructured and informal than regular programs, whether they stress cognitive learning, remedial education, or enrichment. This means, of course, that the effects of these programs are likely to be diverse as well. Although we cannot predict which programs will foster learning for which students, we endorse and impose rigid schedules that substantially destroy opportunities for creative individual learning, as long as total educational expenditures are lower.

The fundamental issues posed by summer learning concern the pace and tempo of learning and the source of individual or developmental differences. Research on summer learning raises doubts that conventional measures of achievement are adequate for specifying patterns of learning over time, although very few new measures of achievement or alternative outcomes for schooling have been accepted. Standardized achievement tests cannot distinguish forgetting from imperfect learning; effort and concentration improve performance on achievement tests, as well as in other endeavors. Such factors introduce individual and seasonal variations in achievement as measured by standardized tests that defy single explanations. Yet the fact that standardized tests do not measure learning is not a justification for standardized school programs and uniform curricula. Summer could be a very fruitful time for both educational innovation and cognitive growth, but at present few schools have capitalized on the opportunity. Although extending the time spent in school would be costly, such policies have an enormous potential for success.

REFERENCES

Austin, G. R., B. G. Rogers, and H. H. Walbesser. 1972. "The Effectiveness of Summer Compensatory Education: A Review of the Research." *Review of Educational Research* 42:171–181.

Ballinger, C. E., N. Kirschenbaum, and R. P. Poinbeauf. 1987. *The Year-Round School: Where Learning Never Stops*. Bloomington, IN: Phi Delta Kappa.

Carter, L. F. 1984. "The Sustaining Effects Study of Compensatory and Elementary Education." *Educational Researcher* 4–13.

Entwisle, D. R., and K. L. Alexander. 1992. "Summer Setback: Race, Poverty, School Composition, and Mathematics Achievement in the First Two Years of School." *American Sociological Review* 57:72–84.

———. 1994. "Winter Setback: School Racial Composition and Learning to Read." *American Sociological Review* 59:446–460.

Gandara, P., and J. Fish. 1994. "Year-Round Schooling as an Avenue to Major Structural Reform." *Educational Evaluation and Policy Analysis* 16:67–85.

Heyns, B. 1975. "Summer Learning—and Some Are Not." Paper presented to the American Educational Research Association Meetings, Washington, DC, March.

———. 1978. *Summer Learning and the Effects of Schooling*. New York: Academic Press.

———. 1980. "Models and Measurement for the Study of Cognitive Growth." In Robert Dreeben and J. Alan Thomas (eds.), *The Analysis of Educational Productivity Issues in Microanalysis*, Vol. I, Chapter 1. Cambridge, MA: Ballinger.

———. 1985. "Educational Effects: Issues in Conceptualization and Measurement." In J. G. Richardson (ed.), *Handbook of Sociology of Education*, Chapter 12. Westport, CT: Greenwood Press.

———. 1987. "Schooling and Cognitive Development: Is There a Season for Learning?" *Child Development* 58:1151–1160.

Worsnop, R. L. 1996. "Year-Round Schools." *The Congressional Quarterly Researcher* 6(19)(May 17):433–456.

TEACHER ASSESSMENT AND EVALUATION

Richard M. Ingersoll
University of Georgia

Assessment and evaluation of how well elementary and secondary school teachers teach have been recurrent concerns since the initial development of the nation's educational system in the nineteenth century. School officials, education policymakers, researchers, and parents have all had a great deal of interest in both gauging and improving the quality of teachers and the quality of teaching. This is not surprising. Elementary schooling and secondary schooling are mandatory in the United States and it is into the custody of teachers that children are legally placed for a significant portion of their lives. Moreover, the quality of teachers and the quality of teaching are undoubtedly among the most important factors shaping the overall achievement and growth of students.

This concern with the quality of teachers and schools, however, has dramatically increased in the past two decades. Beginning in the 1970s, the number and variety of methods to assess and evaluate teachers—their abilities, preparation, training, and performance—have greatly expanded. As teacher assessment has increased in importance, it has, however, become more controversial. Indeed, research, policy, and practice concerned with teacher assessment are marked by a great deal of disagreement. This disagreement largely surrounds two key questions underlying the assessment and evaluation of teacher quality—what is to be measured and how best to do it (Haertel, 1991; Haney et al., 1987; Millman and Darling-Hammond, 1990).

Teacher quality is a complex phenomenon. It comprises at least two distinctive elements: teacher qualifications and teaching quality. The first refers to the competencies teacher candidates bring to the job and the kinds, amounts, and caliber of training these candidates receive prior to or during their careers. The second refers to the actual caliber of the teaching the teacher does, once on the job. Little consensus exists concerning what constitutes "adequate" teacher qualifications and "good" or "excellent" teaching, and, moreover, what are the best means by which these can be measured.

As discussed below, different approaches to teacher assessment hold very different conceptions of what the process of teaching actually involves, and, hence, what are the key characteristics of the good or effective teacher. Moreover, different approaches turn to different methods for how to best measure these key characteristics.

Conventional Approaches to Assessment

Until recently, the predominant approach to teacher assessment has viewed such evaluation as an issue of employee accountability. A key factor driving this approach is the public perception that school problems are, to an important extent, teacher problems—that is, there are significant inadequacies in the ability, training, motivation, and performance of teachers in the United States. Moreover, there is a widespread perception that schools either cannot or will not correct these inadequacies. In particular, schools do not seem to "weed out" incompetent teachers. The result, over the past two decades, has been a growing demand for and large growth in the use of teacher assessment to enhance the accountability of teachers as public employees. Several methods have been used.

The first and perhaps the most traditional method of teacher assessment is classroom observation of individual teachers, usually conducted by school administrators or supervisors. These are usually referred to as classroom performance assessments. In this method, an evaluator typically spends several class periods observing the teacher at work and grades him or her by utilizing a standard checklist of appropriate teacher practices.

A second method of teacher assessment is the use of written tests or examinations administered to teachers themselves. Unlike classroom observations, these pencil and paper tests do not directly assess teaching performance. Rather, they are designed to measure a teacher's basic literacy and numeracy skills, and subject matter knowledge in particular areas. The most common is the National Teacher Examination, produced by the Educational Testing Service. Their overall use has dramatically increased; as of the late 1980s, more than half of the states used all or part of the National Teacher Examination in teacher assessment.

A final method uses student performance to assess teacher performance. In this case, a teacher's performance is judged by gains in their students' academic achievement, as measured on standardized achievement tests. These have been used to compare the effectiveness of teachers within or between schools or school districts.

In theory, these methods of evaluation are designed to ensure that both the qualifications and performance of teachers are at an adequate level and also to instill a general sense of accountability in the teaching work force, and hence improve teacher quality. As a result, these methods of teacher assessment have gained in popularity and both policymakers and education officials have increasingly instituted their use at the school, district, and state levels. However, despite this widespread acceptance, there has been little, if any, evidence that these testing and classroom observation methods have improved the quality of the teaching force. In fact, all have come under criticism from a number of quarters. Critics have taken issue with both the theory and methods of such programs. Moreover, a number of court and legal challenges to the equity and accuracy of these assessment methods have clouded the legality of school officials' use of them for teachers' employment and promotion decisions (Haertel, 1991).

One set of criticisms surrounds the conception and definition of the teaching processes underlying these methods of assessment. All the above-described

methods—classroom observations, teacher examinations, and student performance measures—have been criticized for subscribing to both a narrow and a shallow view of what the work of teaching entails and, hence, what constitutes effective teaching.

Teacher exams, on the one hand, focus on the "what" of teaching—academic subject knowledge. They usually include only a small number of items devoted to the "how" of teaching—pedagogical knowledge and skills. Although most agree that having basic subject knowledge is an important prerequisite to effective teaching, critics have argued this is certainly not a sufficient indication of the range of knowledge and skills needed to instruct and manage groups of children. Hence, many have concluded that teacher exams do not actually measure a teacher's ability to teach.

The checklists, commonly used in classroom performance assessments, on the other hand, focus almost exclusively on pedagogical skills, as opposed to subject knowledge. These instruments are designed to measure practices and attitudes thought to be associated with effective teaching, such as eye contact, enthusiasm, time on task, and avoidance of negative reinforcement. But, in this case, critics have argued that many of the variables measured on checklists are trivial and superficial. They hold that such checklists do not capture many of the most crucial and sophisticated aspects of teaching, such as the ability to interact with parents, test construction, grading criteria, lesson planning, managing classrooms, ability to communicate, and knowledge of the needs and capacities of different age levels of children. The result, according to the critics, is that classroom performance assessments often focus on teaching style, rather than substance.

Moreover, critics have held that in classroom observations, school administrators typically utilize standardized premade observation forms that, in effect, allow evaluators to bypass the time-consuming, but all important, preliminary task of clarifying what are effective teaching practices in their schools. Critics term this the "law of the instrument"—the criteria of effective teaching are, by default, those underlying the most convenient and available measurement instruments.

The use of student achievement test score gains to assess teachers has also been criticized for the conception of teaching and learning such tests assume. Standardized student achievement tests assess minimum levels of student competence, overlook nonacademic aspects of student learning, and are limited to the kinds of knowledge that can be captured with multiple-choice formats. Critics have pointed out that effective teaching includes a far wider range of skills than simply teaching what is measured on such tests.

Along with the breadth and depth of the conception of teaching underlying conventional forms of assessment, a second set of criticisms surrounds the quality and accuracy of the methods themselves. Numerous analysts have argued that conventional assessment methods suffer from serious problems of accuracy.

For instance, the use of student achievement test score gains to assess teachers has been severely criticized for the inability to separate out the portion of student achievement gains that is actually attributable to specific teachers. There are numerous other factors that could also affect student achievement, such as home background, student personality, attendance, school resources, the peer group, community attitudes, and the socioeconomic status of the students' families. Assessments that do not control for all these other potential factors may hold teachers accountable for things they are unable to influence and, hence, for results not of their own making.

In addition, school administrators charged with evaluating teachers with classroom performance checklists often have no training in evaluation, may know little of the particular subject being taught, and may face a natural conflict of interest between finding fault with a teacher and developing communication with a future colleague. Possibly for these reasons, teachers' performance assessments have been found to lack variability; many administrators simply give most teachers good evaluations.

In sum, as these methods of teacher assessment have become more popular in recent years, they have been subject to an array of serious criticisms on both conceptual and methodological grounds. Critics assert that the most common teacher assessment methods are based on overly simplistic prescriptions for effective teaching; that is, they focus on knowledge and skills that may not be necessary for effective teaching and they omit many of the critical and the most important aspects of teachers' work. Moreover, critics have also charged that many of these instruments do not produce accurate measures; that is, they do not measure what they are supposed to measure with an adequate degree of consistency.

New Approaches to Assessment

Although the above criticisms of conventional teacher assessment methods take a number of forms and come from a number of different quarters, there is a common theme running through much of the debate. Underlying the resistance to the conventional modes of teacher assessment is the notion that the road to improvements in teacher quality will not come through increasing the scrutiny and accountability of teachers. There is a growing consensus among educators, researchers, and policymakers that if teaching is to be improved, an entirely different approach to assessment must be developed. In this view, rather than subjecting teachers to greater control, scrutiny, and accountability, the objective of assessment should be to foster the ongoing personal and professional growth and development of teachers. Moreover, in this view, rather than something imposed on teachers, assessment must be something in which teachers have a hand in creating, administering, and using.

This newer view of teacher assessment is bound up with a larger movement in the realm of education reform that has dramatically grown since the mid-1980s—teacher professionalization. There has been a growing consensus among education reformers, policymakers, and researchers that many of the well-publicized shortcomings of the elementary and secondary education system in the United States are, to an important extent, due to inadequacies in the working conditions, resources, and support afforded to school teachers. Proponents of this view have argued, for example, that teachers are underpaid, have too little say in the operation of schools, have too few opportunities to improve their teaching skills, suffer from a lack of support or assistance, and are not adequately rewarded or recognized for their efforts. The key to improving the quality of schools, these critics hold, lies in upgrading the status, training, and working conditions of teaching, that is, in furthering the professionalization of teachers and teaching. The rationale underlying this view is that upgrading the teaching occupation will lead to improvements in the motivation and efficacy of teachers, which, in turn, will lead to improvements in teachers' performance, which will ultimately lead to improvements in student learning (e.g., Carnegie Forum, 1986).

One of the primary targets of the teacher professionalization movement has been the need for new forms of teacher assessment. In this view, assessment must be built on a more sophisticated conception of what the work of teachers entails and what constitutes effective teaching. In turn, more authentic methods of evaluation must be developed that can accurately assess the complex and sophisticated skills held by effective teachers (Haertel, 1991; Haney et al., 1987; Millman and Darling-Hammond, 1990).

Advocates of new assessment methods argue that conventional approaches subscribe to an outdated model of teaching and learning. To such critics, underlying conventional assessment methods is an overly simplistic conception of the work of teachers. In this conception, the teacher is akin to a trained technician who is responsible for implementing appropriate instructional practices that have been designed by administrators and specialists. In this view, the key objectives of teacher assessment are to ensure that minimum standards concerning ability and training are met and to monitor to what extent teachers do, in fact, enact appropriate practices.

The newer thinking on teacher assessment advocates the use of a fundamentally different conception of what teaching entails and what constitutes effective teaching. In this view, effective teaching is a far more complex, specialized, and broader set of processes than conceived by conventional models and conventional assessment methods. Rather than viewing teaching as a matter of implementing prescribed procedures, critics argue that teaching involves the ongoing use of judgment in the planning, conception, implementation, assessment, and revision of effective teaching practices. Teachers must analyze the needs of their students, assess the resources available, take account of the goals of the school, district, and parents, and then devise appropriate curricular programs. The model of the teacher underlying this view is that of the highly trained, highly skilled professional.

Since the mid-1980s there has been a great deal of research devoted to developing alternative methods of teacher assessment consonant with this new line of thought. The goal of many researchers has been to un-

cover the "true" nature of effective teaching and find the "authentic" means of assessing the characteristics of superior teaching.

Among the most prominent of the new methods of teacher assessment under experimentation is the use of peer and self-evaluations. The latter method, in particular, borrows from the approach to assessment commonly used in higher education. The rationale is that teachers, like other professionals, ought to police their own ranks. In one version, teachers create a portfolio, such as what is used in tenure reviews at colleges and universities, that presents evidence of the teacher's accomplishments and performance. In another version of this approach, a team of peers observes a beginning teacher in the classroom in order to make promotional and other decisions.

A second method under development is the use of assessment laboratories for teacher evaluation. Several prototype centers have been established by the National Board for Professional Teaching Standards, a national organization created by the Carnegie Task Force on Teaching as a Profession to provide leadership in the development of new methods of teacher assessment, licensure, and certification (National Board for Professional Teaching Standards, 1991). The objective of the assessment laboratories is to use a variety of intensive evaluation exercises for the national recognition and certification of outstanding experienced teachers. In this model, senior-level teachers spend from 1 to 3 days undergoing evaluation at a center. Among the evaluation activities that could be used are lesson planning exercises, videotaped teaching performances, exercises in which teachers evaluate and critique textbooks, exercises in which teachers demonstrate the use of curriculum materials, and written examinations requiring extended essay-type answers.

These newer teacher assessment methods are currently under development or are being tested in small numbers of schools and districts. As a result, these newer methods are only beginning to be assessed. In particular, issues of validity and reliability are yet to be addressed. It is becoming clear, however, that these methods may be less amenable to standardization and, hence, more time consuming and expensive to administer than some conventional techniques. Other than acknowledgment of these kinds of concerns, there has, as of yet, been little attempt to explore the strengths and weaknesses of these newer methods of assessment. The following section suggests some of the kinds of limits that these newer methods must overcome.

One of the central problems confronting assessment is how to account for the effect of the social context on teacher performance. That is, the quality and performance of teachers cannot be understood, or evaluated, in isolation from the quality and performance of schools. Laboratory methods of assessment, such as those pioneered by the National Board for Professional Teaching Standards, are designed to clearly scrutinize specific skills and abilities of teachers. In this approach, teachers are removed from the real world of the classroom in schools and assessed in the artificial world of the laboratory. The strength of such experimental methods is that they allow assessors to view how well teachers perform normal activities—conceive lesson plans, use curriculum materials, or present model lessons—in the absence of distractions.

But the distractions screened out of the laboratory setting may, in fact, be very pertinent factors shaping real-life teacher performance. Indeed, some teachers who perform well in the laboratory may not be able to perform well in particular classrooms. Laboratory methods of assessment do not really control, but rather ignore, the effects of social context on teacher quality. As a result, by not viewing teachers under actual classroom conditions, such methods may provide one-sided assessments of actual teacher quality. Moreover, by striving to maximize the professional growth of outstanding teachers, such assessment methods ignore the central objective behind conventional approaches—to ensure the accountability of all those in the nation's classrooms.

On the other hand, the other major example of newer methods—peer and self-evaluations—are better able to account for the effects of social context. In fact, the strength of such methods is that they allow teachers to evaluate themselves in reference to standards that reflect the realities of the school context. The assumption underlying these methods is that those that actually do the job are in the best position to judge how well it could be and actually is done. The standard of comparison and, hence evaluation, is the performance of other teachers in the same or similar schools. Teachers assessed are not expected to perform any better than those who assess them—their peers.

By maximizing teacher involvement in assessment, self-evaluations and peer evaluations may, however, minimize the involvement of others. It is for this reason that peer assessment methods used in higher education have been under attack in recent years. Critics have charged that universities are too research oriented and not concerned enough with teaching or with the needs of students. One common criticism, for example, is that hiring and promotion decisions are dominated by a faculty member's research and publication performance and that teaching performance counts for little. Hence, by placing evaluation in the hands of practitioners, such methods may provide one-sided assessments of actual teacher quality—favoring professional development and neglecting accountability, especially to student clients.

Given these limitations to the newer genre of methods, is the problem of teacher assessment intractable? Are the requirements of accountability methods simply not the same as those of employee development methods? Is it not possible to both hold teachers accountable and also foster their personal and professional growth? Or are these purposes irreconcilable and mutually exclusive?

A Sociological Approach to Teacher Assessment

Although teacher assessment has been an important issue in the realm of education policy and research, it has not been an important topic of research and debate for sociologists. However, the problem of assessing teacher quality is really a subset of the larger issue of evaluation common to all organizations and workplaces. How does one fairly and accurately evaluate and assess employees or members in any setting? This issue has long been a central topic of study for sociologists, especially those in the field of the sociology of work and organizations. The research in this field could make an important contribution to the debate over teacher assessment.

Schools present an especially troublesome and important variant of the employee assessment problem for social scientists. Unlike the productive and technical sectors of the economy, the means and ends of teachers' work are highly ambiguous. In schools, the "production process" involves individuals working not with raw materials or objects, but with other individuals.

Assessment is made difficult because there is no clear definition of what the final "product" is or should be and what is the best "technology" to achieve it. These dilemmas are, however, not unique to schools. Much of the service and public sectors (e.g., hospitals, municipal government, and social work) face the same set of difficulties in employee and organizational assessment. In interactional work of all kinds, evaluation is particularly ambiguous. But, although the degree of difficulty and ambiguity may vary, all settings, organizations, and workplaces must confront similar issues when it comes to employee evaluation and assessment.

Within the field of the sociology of work and organizations all employee and organizational assessment is inherently a normative and social activity, whether those assessed are teachers, social workers, auto plant workers, engineers, or senior managers. The effort to determine what is effective performance is never value free and, whether intended or not, involves a series of highly value-laden choices among numerous possible alternatives. Sociologists of work and organizations have insightfully delineated the range of these decisions and choices that must be confronted in employee assessment and the kinds of values and interests each choice represents. These researchers have effectively shown how different methods of assessment reflect different sets of choices concerning categories such as the purpose of the evaluation, the domain of focus, the level of analysis, the criteria of evaluation, the type of data or information collected and used, and the viewpoint adopted. It is these different sets of choices that distinguish competing methods of assessment. These choices are not usually made explicit or examined, but they are highly consequential. That is, most assessments are influenced substantially by sets of unquestioned premises (Cameron and Whetten, 1983; Kanter, 1981; Goodman et al., 1977).

That decisions concerning what and how to assess are both value laden and consequential is aptly illustrated by comparing the choices adopted by those advocating greater teacher accountability versus those advocating greater teacher professionalization.

To many advocates of increased teacher accountability, school problems are, to an important extent, a result of inadequacies in the classroom performance of teachers. Teachers are held responsible and this is reflected in the kinds of assessment choices made. The target of scrutiny and, ultimately, blame, is typically the ability,

the training, or the motivation of individual teachers. From this viewpoint, there is a need to increase the application and impact of conventional assessment methods, such as classroom observations and the use of student test gains. It logically follows that adherents of this approach look to improving schools by improving teachers, through one of any number of possible prescriptions—more rigorous entry exams, teaching workshops, remediation, merit pay, or termination.

Many advocates of teacher professionalization, on the other hand, begin with a different set of assumptions. To this perspective, school problems are, to an important extent, a result of inadequacies in the school itself and the surrounding environment. In this view, focusing solely on the teacher ignores the social context within which teachers work and unfairly holds teachers responsible for problems not of their making. Inadequacies in teachers' performance may actually be symptoms of a host of other deeper causes such as lack of time to prepare instructional lessons, mismatches between what teachers were trained to teach and what they have been assigned to teach, disruptive conditions related to problems with student misbehavior, lack of adequate teaching and classroom resources, or overly strenuous course load assignments for teachers. Adherents of this approach tend to favor assessments that are either controlled by teachers themselves (e.g., portfolios, peer observations) or that separate assessment from context (e.g., assessment laboratories). Finally, in contrast to the accountability approach, this alternative tends to offer a set of antidotes and prescriptions centered around improving the school and its organization and management.

Although each of these approaches to assessment shares the same overall goal—to improve education—each tends to favor different strategies, different foci, different levels of analysis, and different viewpoints. It is important to identify the choices made, and, hence, the choices not made, by any particular approach to assessment because these choices make a difference. At the heart of assessments are judgments, whether implicit or explicit. These judgments are consequential; they assign responsibility and, ultimately, credit or blame.

Moreover, in truth, both approaches are probably partially correct, but neither is likely sufficient alone. Both employee accountability and employee development are important needs.

The performance of individual teachers and of the schools in which they work are important. Assessments of teachers, schools, districts, and states all require placement in the larger surrounding social context for comparisons to be meaningful. Finally, the viewpoints of individual teachers, faculties, and administrators are all potentially biased, but all are also potentially important sources of information on how well teachers and schools work.

There is a growing consensus among sociologists of work and organizations that the goal of finding the "one best way"—the "authentic objective" measure of quality in any given setting or occupation—is misplaced. In this view, all assessment methods can potentially offer valuable information, but each one is also limited and partial. From a sociological viewpoint, the role of assessors should be, first, to make explicit the underlying, and usually implicit, choices, and, second, to elucidate the strengths and weaknesses inherent in each choice. Armed with some awareness of the limits of each, the role of those charged with employee assessment should be to develop and utilize multiple measures and multiple methods to be used in conjunction with one another.

REFERENCES

Cameron, Kim, and David Whetten. 1983. *Organizational Effectiveness: A Comparison of Multiple Models.* New York: Academic Press.

Carnegie Forum on Education and the Economy. 1986. *A Nation Prepared: Teachers for the 21st Century.* New York: Carnegie Forum.

Goodman, Paul, Johannes Pennings, and associates. 1977. *New Perspectives on Organizational Effectiveness.* San Francisco: Jossey-Bass.

Haertel, Edward. 1991. "New Forms of Teacher Assessment." In *Review of Research in Education*, pp. 3–29. Washington, DC: American Educational Research Association.

Haney, Walter, G. Madaus, and A. Kreitzer. 1987. "Charms Talismanic: Testing Teachers for the Improvement of American Education." In E. Rothkopf (ed.), *Review of Research in Education*, Vol. 14, pp. 169–238. Washington, DC: American Educational Research Association.

Kanter, Rosabeth. 1981. "Organization Performance: Recent Developments in Measurement." *Annual Review of Sociology* 7:321–349.

Millman, Jason, and Linda Darling-Hammond. 1990. *The New Handbook of Teacher Evaluation.* Newbury Park, CA: Sage.

National Board for Professional Teaching Standards. 1991. *Toward High and Rigorous Standards for the Teaching Profession.* Washington, DC: Author.

Teacher Burnout

A. Gary Dworkin
University of Houston

Surveys of school teachers in the United States and other developed nations reveal that between one-third and one-half would not select a career in teaching if they had the opportunity to choose again (Menlo and Poppelton, 1990; National Center for Education Statistics, 1993). Teachers report that they feel alienated from their work, their students, and their colleagues and believe that their efforts are unappreciated by those in their schools, their districts, and by the general public. Job-related stress associated with low salaries, the lack of public confidence in public education, school violence and student discipline problems, declining student test scores, and even school reform and restructuring mandates have combined to depress teacher morale and exacerbate teacher burnout.

Teacher burnout is the product of job-related stress, frequently organizationally and structurally created. Although many cases of burnout can be traced to the absence of collegial support on the part of campus-level administrators or to district-level attempts to deny teachers their professional status and autonomy, teacher burnout over the past decade can also be traced to the implementation of school reform. This is because changes in the conditions of teaching occasioned by school reform add to job stress, even if the reform is intended to increase the degree of decision making accorded to teachers. Such greater decision-making power is accompanied by an expectation of greater accountability for student learning outcomes.

Teacher burnout has principally been the focus of clinical, social, educational, and organizational psychologists. However, there has been some attention paid to the topic by sociologists. Sociologists and psychologists differ in the way they conceptualize and measure burnout, as well as how they prescribe solutions to the burnout problem. The differences have been in terms of the emphasis on structural and organizational causes for burnout compared with individual and personality factors.

Conceptualizations and Assessments of Burnout

Burnout as a Psychological Concept

The term "burnout" was first used by the psychoanalyst Freudenberger in his description of how a human service professional "wears out" and "becomes inoperative to all intents and purposes" (Freudenberger, 1974:160). This psychological view holds that burnout is a personal malady that results from the failure of individuals to cope with stress. Following Freudenberger's definitive essay, other psychologists have attempted to delineate central elements in burnout, including feelings of *exhaustion* or a diminished capacity to work as one had before, *depersonalization* or blaming one's clients, patients, or students for their failures to recover or to learn, and a loss of a sense of *personal accomplishment* or fulfillment from one's work (Maslach and Jackson, 1981). Furthermore, burned out professionals tend to have low moral, are depressed, and frequently withdraw from others.

Most psychological studies of burnout rely upon the three factor model of Maslach and her associates, and utilize the Maslach Burnout Inventory (MBI), which taps the three factors of exhaustion, depersonalization, and personal accomplishment. Another widely used measure is the Burnout Measure (BM), which is based upon the single-factor model of Pines and Aronson (see Pines, 1993). This approach conceptualizes burnout as a single dimension in which emotional and mental exhaustion has resulted from extensive involvement in emotionally demanding situations. Pines (1993) notes that burnout often creates an "existential crisis." As Pines notes, "For most burned-out professionals, work initially provided . . . an answer" (to the question: Who am I?). "They knew why they were put on earth: to do the work for which they had a calling" (1993:39).

The psychological orientation, because it views burnout as a personal malady caused by the inability to cope with stress, offers individualistic strategies for treating burnout. If, as the psychological paradigm holds, burnout is caused by personally maladaptive behaviors and feelings, then the resolution of burnout requires self-help strategies in coping with the stressors linked to burnout. Psychologists have urged the burned out to engage in a variety of clinical solutions from stress management to holistic health practices.

Burnout as a Sociological Concept

The sociological approach to the study of burnout rests with the tradition of studies of worker alienation. Burnout is seen as a form of role-specific alienation, often involving Seeman's (1975) dimensions of powerlessness, meaningless, isolation, normlessness, and estrangement. Burnout, as alienation, has implicit organizational and social structural causes that call for organizational and structural solutions. This is not to diminish the extent to which stress and stressors lead to the experience of burnout, but personality variables, victim blaming, or emphases upon the need to develop coping skills are seen as less essential than structural change in reducing burnout. Another focus of sociologists is to examine the social forces that affect burnout *rates* among groups or in different organizational contexts.

Some work on burnout has examined how public schools and colleges of education create contradictions that constrain the professional expectations and autonomy of public school teachers (Dworkin, 1987; LeCompte and Dworkin, 1991), or how school reform mandates with their accompanying expectations of greater teacher accountability exacerbate burnout levels in a teaching population (Dworkin and Townsend, 1994). This sociological orientation holds that burnout results from contradictions between trained expectations for autonomy and professional standing and organizational and bureaucratic constraints in public education, rather than merely the failure of individuals

to adapt to stressors. Unable to negotiate agreements on role performances or to determine what are the role expectations within the social service bureaucracies, professionals soon acquire a strong sense of powerlessness, which, in turn, soon leads to a strong sense of meaninglessness. Numerous investigators have also reported that burnout is accompanied by withdrawal and isolation as well as feelings of rejection by clients (some of whom are blamed by the burned-out professional for refusing to get better, to learn, or to improve in order "to spite" the professional).

Burnout further incorporates feelings of normlessness, either in the sense that following the rules produces no desired results, or that the rules are vague, ambiguous, unenforceable, or absent. A majority of the urban public school teachers in a series of surveys conducted in Houston between 1977 and 1991 agreed or strongly agreed that "school rules are so rigid and absurd that good teachers have to break them or ignore them" (Dworkin, 1987).

In light of the strong similarity between alienation and burnout, the following conceptual definition of burnout (or alienational burnout) was offered by Dworkin (1985, 1987):

> Burnout is an extreme form of role-specific alienation characterized by a sense that one's work is meaningless and that one is powerless to effect changes which could make the work more meaningful. Further, this sense of meaninglessness and powerlessness is heightened by a belief that the norms associated with the role and the setting are absent, conflicting, or inoperative, and that one is alone and isolated among one's colleagues and clients. (1987:28).

Dworkin (1985, 1987) and LeCompte and Dworkin (1991) noted that organizational changes in schools, especially those involving greater levels of teacher autonomy and greater support and encouragement by principals, effectively reduced burnout levels. Dworkin (1987) held that if burnout is substantially a structural and organizational problem, then psychological approaches to resolve burnout, which focus on teaching individuals to cope, would be less efficient in large urban districts with thousands of teachers than would be organizational changes that taught management skills to a few hundred principals.

How Many Teachers Are Burned Out?

Estimation of the magnitude of the burnout problem has been elusive, in part because of disagreements over its conceptualization and measurement, and the relative absence of large samples from which to derive estimates. More prevalent are estimates of the percentage of teachers who experience significant levels of job-related stress, a precursor of burnout. Litt and Turk (1985) suggested that in comparison with other professionals, teachers are twice as likely to report that their job is a major source of stress in their lives (79% for teachers compared with 38% for other professionals). The Consortium for Cross-Cultural Research in Education (Poppelton, 1990) reported that job stress levels between 80% and 90% characterized teachers from the United Kingdom, Japan, Singapore, and the United States.

Who Is Most Likely to Burn Out?

The psychological literature on burnout suggests those with the malady are most likely to be individuals who have a low tolerance for stress. Individuals who are inflexible and engage in rigid and dogmatic thinking frequently burn out, as do those with "Type A" personalities and those who have an external locus of control (believe that fate, luck, and powerful others control their destinies). The sociological perspective has noted several structural and organizational factors associated with burnout (Dworkin, 1985, 1987; LeCompte and Dworkin, 1991). These include inexperience (burnout is typically highest among new teachers) as well as racial, class, and cultural isolation (where teachers are in schools where they share little in common with the predominant student bodies of the schools). Teachers in highly bureaucratized school settings, especially where the principal treats them as expendable employees, are more likely to burn out. By contrast, teachers who are assigned to principals who treat them as valued colleagues, ask them to become involved in campus planning and decision making, and express concern for them as individuals and professionals, are less likely to experience burnout. This is the case even if stress levels at the schools are as high as they are at schools with unsupportive principals and where burnout levels are high. Principal support is so essential that high levels of co-worker support cannot mitigate burnout if principal support is absent (Dworkin et al., 1990).

Current Issues and Directions in Burnout Research

The Effects of School Reform on Burnout

There have been two relevant waves of school reform in the United States since the publication in 1983 of *A Nation at Risk* by the National Commission on Excellence in Education, and each wave has had marked effects on the rate of teacher burnout in the public schools. The reforms have also affected which groups of teachers are most likely to experience high levels of burnout. The first wave of reform by state legislatures attempted "to introduce uniformity and conformity through standardized curricula, rigorous requirements for student performance, promotion, and graduation, and teacher evaluation" (Smiley and Denny, 1990:235). The second wave emphasized decentralization and shared and local decision making, including a greater policy formation role for teachers, but an increased call for their accountability when student test scores did not rise.

Using data from the Houston metropolitan area, Dworkin and his associates (LeCompte and Dworkin, 1991; Dworkin and Townsend, 1994) found that prior to the school reforms, teacher burnout was most frequently a problem faced by relatively inexperienced teachers. Examining cohorts based on years of teaching experience, we found that levels of burnout (mean burnout score for a cohort) were highest during the first 5 years in the classroom, but then diminished with each cohort through the thirtieth year teaching. First wave reforms involving competency testing of all teachers and on-site evaluations of their teaching ability led to a change in the pattern. Burnout levels were higher for each successive cohort through the fifteenth year in the classroom and then diminished slightly with each cohort through the thirtieth year. During the second wave of reforms, the pattern of the first wave continued, but with somewhat diminished levels of burnout for the experienced cohort. Nevertheless, the magnitude of burnout experienced by teachers, regardless of years in the classroom, was higher than in the years prior to school reform and restructuring. In the first wave, experienced teachers found that their claims to expertise in the classroom were being challenged by the competency testing and site visits, and their burnout levels rose. In the second wave, shared decision making meant that teachers, principals, and community members vied for control, leading to "turf battles." The right to impact policies and introduce new practices also meant the responsibility for the consequences of such policies and practices. Increased accountability heightened stress and resulted in continued high levels of teacher burnout.

Not only did the reforms affect the level of burnout experienced by teachers (the mean burnout scores for cohorts of teachers), they also raised the rate of burnout (the percentage of teachers with at least moderate to high levels of burnout). Prior to the current waves of school reform and school restructuring, approximately one-third of urban public school teachers felt burned out. When first-wave reforms were implemented that included competency testing of teachers, burnout rates rose to 64%. Once newer reforms that involved shared decision making appeared, burnout levels settled to about 51% of the teaching population.

Although school restructuring and decentralized decision making, with their attendant conflicts over domains of influence, contribute to elevated levels of teacher burnout, it is also true that collegiality and professional support mitigate burnout. Evidence suggests that site-based decision making is least stressful in settings in which there has existed a collegium and where principals have been supportive prior to the implementation of restructuring. Future research into the linkages among school reform and restructuring and burnout will be needed to explore the processes that lead to the establishment of support, trust, and collegiality in settings where rules are changing. Such research necessitates longitudinal analysis, with attempts to explore burnout under different organizational climates.

Long-Term Effects of Burnout

Although burnout is strongly related to the desire to quit teaching, the relationship between burnout and actual quitting behavior has been understudied. Most burnout research is cross-sectional in nature and those that have been longitudinal have monitored the process of burnout over a matter of months (Leiter, 1993), or a single year (Jackson et al., 1986), or have relied on small case studies that may limit the generalizability of results (Cherniss, 1992). Generally, the relatively short duration of the longitudinal studies has been a result of the investigator's desire to develop models of the process of burning out early in a career (Leiter,

1993), or because most investigators have assumed that role exits from burnout occur soon after the inception of burnout. Early work sometimes examined individuals who had quit their jobs and attributed burnout, post factum, to the employees' explanations for quitting. However, the difficulties of retrospective histories, where individuals reconstruct past motives in light of present actions (having quit), tend to contaminate such findings.

One-year follow-up interviews of teachers conducted by Jackson et al. (1986) revealed the weak association between burnout and quitting. In fact, although some of the burned-out teachers quit teaching within a year of the initial survey, many of the most burned out did not. Cherniss (1992), in his 10-year longitudinal case study of 25 teachers, observed that burnout early in a career was not linked to turnover. A 5-year follow-up of exit interview data from my sample of 3,444 teachers indicated that in excess of 85% of teachers with moderate to high levels of burnout (and 80% of teachers with the highest levels of burnout) were still teaching in the same district (Dworkin, 1987). An equally large percentage of teachers with high levels of burnout who had stated that they were planning to quit the field of education were also still in the same district as classroom teachers 5 years later. This finding led me to posit that a significant organizational problem for school districts was not teacher turnover, but teacher entrapment, or the condition in which teachers are burned out, want to quit, but cannot find alternative careers. Entrapped teachers in big-city school districts are unlikely to make the needed extra efforts for their students and thereby may contribute to the continued low achievement of children in urban public schools.

Under the aegis of a large-scale research project on demographic forecasting in the metropolitan area, I have examined the turnover of teachers who were in the original burnout study sample from 1977 to 1978, 15 years after the survey. Of the teachers in the initial study who were young enough to not likely have retired by 1992–1993 and on whom full burnout data were available, 39.8% were still teaching in the district after 15 years, 14.2% had quit within the first 5 years of the survey, 44.7% had left between 5 and 15 years of the survey, and 1% had returned between the fifth and fifteenth year. Teachers with low burnout scores were slightly more likely to have remained in the district than those with high burnout scores; it was also true that those with low burnout scores were slightly less likely to have quit within 5 years or to have quit between 5 and 15 years than those with high scores; however, those returning were much more likely to have had high burnout scores than those with low scores. Finally, the youngest cohort (those under age 30 in 1977–1978) were more likely to quit teaching if they were burned out than were any other cohort. This youngest cohort, experiencing burnout, but having made few investments in their teaching careers, had less to lose by quitting than did others. This is clearly consistent with "site-bet" models of commitment that hold that what keeps people working at jobs they dislike are the costs of abandoning career investments, often external to the role itself (including vestment in pension plans, family commitments, inertia, etc.)

Job Stress and Burnout

The relationship between stress and burnout has generally been unquestioned in the research, in part because the long-term consequences of burnout among teachers has rarely been explored. However, recently Dworkin (forthcoming) examined the associations among burnout as a form of alienation, self-reported job stress levels, and the key element in the psychological view of burnout, exhaustion. During the first-wave school reforms, the associations among the three constructs were strong and positive, but with one exception. Among teachers with 16 or more years of classroom experience, there was no significant association between alienational burnout and stress. During the second wave of reforms, stress and exhaustion remained significantly correlated for all cohorts, but for teachers with 6 or more years of experience, alienational burnout was uncorrelated with stress or exhaustion. The implication from the use of the sociologically defined measure of burnout is that burnout as alienation may become a coping mechanism for teachers. That is, under the present conditions of repeated reform and restructuring efforts, burnout may have become an insulator against additional negative personal effects of the reforms. Early in a career there is a direct effect of stress and exhaustion on alienative burnout. The proposition holds that the greater the stress, the greater the exhaustion, and the greater the burnout. However, several years into a career burnout is no longer associated with heightened stress and exhaustion. High burnout is rather indicative of no longer caring enough to feel stressed or exhausted. Organizationally, this relationship raises new problems. Burned out teachers who feel no sense of exhaustion or stress are unlikely to seek ways of changing conditions in their schools. They may be even less willing to make extra efforts for their students than teachers who are burned out and experiencing job stress. In the relative absence of sufficient job stress or exhaustion, they are also less willing to leave teaching. During a period of decentralized decision making, public education can ill afford a teaching force that does not care.

Most of the research in teacher burnout has tended to be static snapshots of teacher attitudes and behaviors taken at different time intervals. Changes in burnout levels across time and within individuals have not been explored. Models need to be developed that can account for the role of burnout on student learning and retention. Although Dworkin (1987) found that teacher burnout adversely affected only the gifted and talented students, the linkages among teacher burnout and student learning, attendance, and dropout behavior are only vaguely understood. What impact does teacher morale have on student learning in settings in which curricula are not teacher proofed and where decision making is shared among teachers, principals, and parents/community actors? What is the interplay among campus, district, and state education agency policies on the dynamics of interpersonal relations in schools and the capacity of teachers and principals to establish collegial relationships? Organizational restructuring of public education ought to consider strategies to improve teacher morale, especially if the attitudes of teachers about their jobs, schools, and students can facilitate or impede the attainment of the academic goals of school reform.

REFERENCES

Cherniss, Cary. 1992. "Long-Term Consequences of Burnout: An Exploratory Study." *Journal of Organizational Behavior* 13:1–11.

Dworkin, Anthony Gary. 1985. *When Teachers Give Up: Teacher Burnout, Teacher Turnover, and Their Impact on Children*. Austin, TX: Hogg Foundation for Mental Health and Texas Press.

——. 1987. *Teacher Burnout in the Public Schools: Structural Causes and Consequences for Children*. Albany: State University of New York Press.

Dworkin, Anthony Gary, and Merric L. Townsend. 1994. "Teacher Burnout in the Face of Reform: Some Caveats in

Breaking the Mold." In Bruce Anthony Jones and Kathryn M. Borman (eds.), *Investing in U.S. Schools: Directions for Educational Policy,* pp. 68–86. Norwood, NJ: Ablex.

Dworkin, Anthony Gary, C. Allen Haney, Rosalind J. Dworkin, and Ruth L. Telschow. 1990. "Stress and Illness Behavior among Urban Public School Teachers." *Educational Administration Quarterly* 26:59–71.

Freudenberger, Herbert J. 1974. "Staff Burn-out." *Journal of Social Issues* 30:159–165.

Jackson, Susan E., Richard L. Schwab, and Randall S. Schuler. 1986. "Toward an Understanding of the Burnout Phenomenon." *Journal of Applied Psychology* 71:630–640.

LeCompte, Margaret D., and Anthony Gary Dworkin. 1991. *Giving Up on School: Student Dropouts and Teacher Burnouts.* Newbury Park, CA: Corwin.

Leiter, Michael P. 1993. "Burnout as a Developmental Process: Consideration of Models." In Wilmar B. Schaufeli, Christina Maslach, and Tadeusz Marek (eds.), *Professional Burnout: Recent Developments in Theory and Research,* pp. 237–250. Washington, DC: Taylor Francis.

Litt, M. D., and D. C. Turk. 1985. "Sources of Stress and Dissatisfaction in Experienced High School Teachers." *Journal of Educational Research* 78:178–185.

Maslach, Christina, and Susan E. Jackson. 1981. "The Measurement of Experienced Burnout." *Journal of Occupational Behaviour* 2:99–113.

Menlo, Allen, and Pam Poppleton. 1990. "A Five-Country Study of the Work Perceptions of Secondary School Teachers in England, the United States, Japan, Singapore, and West Germany (1986–88)." *Comparative Education* 26:173–182.

National Center for Education Statistics. 1993. *America's Teachers: Profile of a Profession.* Washington, DC: U.S. Department of Education.

National Commission on Excellence in Education. 1983. *A Nation at Risk: The Imperative for Educational Reform.* Washington, DC: U.S. Government Printing Office.

Pines, Ayala M. 1993. "Burnout: An Existential Perspective." In Wilmar B. Schaufeli, Christina Maslach, and Tadeusz Marek (eds.), *Professional Burnout: Recent Developments in Theory and Research,* pp. 33–51. Washington, DC: Taylor & Francis.

Seeman, Melvin. 1975. "Alienation Studies." *Annual Review of Sociology* 1:91–123.

Smylie, M. A., and J. W. Denny. 1990. "Teacher Leadership: Tensions and Ambiguities in Organizational Practice." *Educational Administration Quarterly* 26:235–259.

TEACHER UNIONS, OLD AND NEW*

Ronald Henderson
National Education Association

In 1996–1997, members of the National Education Association (NEA) and the American Federation of Teachers (AFT) accounted for nearly 2.5 million of the 2.8 million nonsupervisory professionals employed in U.S. elementary and secondary education (89%).[1] Although both the NEA and AFT organize employees other than K–12 teaching professionals, the two groups are predominantly composed of public school teachers, and in 1996–1997, these K–12 professionals accounted for 91% of the NEA's active membership and 63% of the AFT's.

The NEA remains, as always, the larger of the two organizations. In 1996–1997, excluding retirees, the NEA had 2.0 million active and life members, compared with the AFT's 817,000 members. The NEA accounted for 71% of the membership of both organizations and 80% of the K–12 professional membership.

Both organizations have long histories. The NEA's oldest component—the National Teachers Association—goes back to 1857, and the present organization has existed since 1870. The AFT's oldest component—the Chicago Teacher Federation—goes back to 1897, and the organization has existed in its current form since 1916.

The two teacher groups differ in size and structure in ways that reflect their origins and development. The NEA still exists in its historical form—as an independent federation of state professional associations. In contrast, the AFT is a union affiliated with the AFL–CIO, and although organized in state units, it is fundamentally a federation of large urban locals.

Yet, despite their apparently long histories and some continuities in structure, both organizations are in some vital respects no more than 20 or 30 years old. The basic difference between the organizations as they functioned before and after, say, 1970 has to do with how they are run and how they operate. Today, both organizations claim to represent teachers and are controlled by teachers. Both operate as unions that use collective bargaining and occasionally strikes to advance the interests of their members. Both lobby at the state and national level. Neither organization had all of these characteristics 30 years ago. But beginning in the 1960s, they were transformed by the development of collective bargaining, and they are again undergoing marked changes in the late 1990s, including a trend toward a "new unionism" and intensified discussions of a merger. This chapter highlights the evolution of the groups and presents some of the issues now facing them.

The NEA, 1870–1970

The NEA was not established as a teachers' organization, as such. Rather, the organization was assembled in 1870 as a federation of four organizations representing distinctly different perspectives: the American Normal School Association, the National Association of School Superintendents, the Central College Association, and the National Teachers Association (NTA) (Elsbree, 1939:264–265, 500). Only the last of these groups, the NTA, formed in 1857 from 10 state teachers associations, actually represented teachers, and for roughly the first hundred years of its existence, the

---

*The analysis contained in this article represents the views of the author and does not necessarily reflect the official position of the National Education Association (NEA).

[1] The term *nonsupervisory professionals* includes teachers, librarians, and guidance counselors employed by the public elementary and secondary schools, but it excludes principals, other supervisors, or educational support personnel.

NEA was controlled by administrators rather than teachers, frequently worked against teachers' interests, and opposed collective bargaining. Although the NEA lobbied fairly effectively on the state level on issues such as increasing expenditures on education, consolidating and professionalizing administration of school districts, and establishing certification and standards for teachers, its unwillingness or inability to support candidates for federal elections made it relatively less successful on the national level.

The NEA as the "House of Education"

The National Education Association was set up to advance the interests of the "education profession" as a whole rather than those of teachers in particular. During the late nineteenth and early twentieth centuries, the NEA continued to develop as a federation of state education associations, still representing a variety of administrator groups, teachers, and other professionals. By 1922, such groups had arisen in every state and in Alaska and Hawaii (*NEA Handbook 1956–57*).

Reflecting its national constituency, the central association originally had four main "departments": the National Association of School Superintendents, the American Normal School Association, the Department of Higher Education, and a newly created Department of Elementary Education. These departments functioned as relatively independent organizations; thus, each of the "many mansions" within the House of Education had its own membership, budget, annual meeting, and so on.

In 1917, the NEA established permanent headquarters in Washington, D.C., and in 1919 the organization purchased an actual mansion in the District, the former Guggenheim residence at 1201 Sixteenth Street, N.W., a few blocks north of the White House. Most of the national departments moved to this location (the site is still the NEA's home, although only the mantelpiece remains of the original building). In addition to enlarging the group's office space, the purchase of the facility enabled the national organization to provide centralized publicity for its departments' activities, assistance in producing and marketing their publications, and services to affiliates (Elsbree, 1939:507; Wesley, 1957:276). By 1952, the national organization had grown to some 30 departments (see Appendix 1), including virtually all of the major education organizations (Wesley, 1957:44, 278).

The Dominance of University and School Administrators

The early dominance of the NEA by university presidents, professors of educational administration, and school superintendents was fundamentally the result of their greater participation in the organization (Stinnett, 1968:21; Wesley, 1957:328–329). In 1890, school administrators accounted for 50% of the membership, whereas teachers accounted for only 11% (Murphy, 1990:50). In 1900, only 0.5% of all teachers belonged to the NEA (Elsbree, 1939:505; Wesley, 1957:337).

After World War I, however, administrator dominance of the organization became policy driven as a result of purposive efforts by incumbent leaders. These leaders were reacting to militant urban teachers who began to vie for dominance in the NEA. By the organization's original rules, any member who came to the annual convention could vote on NEA policy. The newly militant urban teachers, most of them also affiliated with the AFT, thus began to pack meetings in an effort to influence policy. NEA administrator-leaders Caroll Pearse and James Crabtree put through a reorganization in 1920 limiting voting at annual meetings to delegates appointed by state associations. Because superintendents dominated the state associations, militant teacher influence at the new representative assembly was effectively quashed (Urban, 1982:126–128).

Although the reorganization drastically limited teacher power in the NEA, it dramatically increased teacher membership. The reason for this apparently paradoxical development was that representation in the national organization was based on the number of state-level members. State-level leaders thus had a strong incentive to increase membership, and local administrators and some school boards put heavy pressure on teachers—or in some cases required them—to become members in the state associations, despite the superintendents' domination of those associations. The percentage of teachers in state teacher associations increased from 34.1% in 1916 to 61.5% in 1923 (Elsbree, 1939:515–517; Murphy, 1990:94). By 1960, state associations included 93% of all school instructional employees (*NEA Handbook 1960–61*:305). The practice of local superintendents "encouraging" teachers to join state associations continued at least through the 1960s (Stinnett, 1968:221–222).

Despite their increasing membership in state affiliates, teachers gained little headway in influencing the national organization between 1920 and 1970 (Tyack et al., 1984:53, 78–79). Symptomatic of this lack of power, the NEA's Department of Classroom Teachers—actually the largest component of the organization—did not have a separate budget, unlike the departments that represented administrators and other groups (Stinnett, 1968:216; Wesley, 1957:275). As late as 1966–1967, classroom teachers remained a minority of the NEA's Board of Directors (Stinnett, 1968:219). Between 1890 and 1970, the NEA facilitated the development of a *factory-type model* of education that eliminated any teacher voice in developing education policy (Tyack, 1974:48, 59, 185, 256–258; Urban, 1982:39–40, 155, 157–158, 161).

The NEA also opposed teachers' participation in unions, partly because the group feared union affiliation would lead to strikes (Murphy, 1990:54, 92, 183, 209–210; Huggett and Stinnett, 1956:371–373; Stinnett, 1968:98–100, 165). At least into the 1960s, even if the right of teachers to strike as such had not been at issue, the old NEA leadership simply could not accept the concept of collective bargaining because it violated their notion of a unified profession.

Lobbying and Political Action

For much of the period before 1970, the NEA lobbied successfully at the state level. The transfer of control over urban school systems from ward bosses to superintendents supported by "independent" school boards was achieved mainly before 1920, as NEA leaders worked with state and local business communities. Improvements in school finance resulted from NEA-supported measures that nearly doubled the state share of school expenditures (Tyack et al., 1984:81) and cut the number of school districts in half (West, 1980:17). State legislation increased the welfare of teachers by providing teachers with tenure, minimum salaries, retirement systems, and group insurance (Huggett and Stinnett, 1956:107–108; Stinnett, 1968:169–171). Finally, the NEA helped improve the quality of the profession by supporting certification laws that in most cases made college graduation with some education credits the minimum requirement for entering the profession (Huggett and Stinnett, 1956:420–424). The NEA's lobbying efforts were conducted by its state affiliates, with the assistance of various NEA committees and commissions that provided the affiliates with a

means to exchange information and share resources (Tyack et al., 1984:72–73, 78–79).

In contrast to its successes at the state level, the NEA's achievements at the federal level were relatively minor before 1970. The NEA's two most consistent goals at the federal level after World War I were to initiate a general program of federal aid to education and to establish a Department of Education with cabinet status. Although the NEA began lobbying toward these ends as early as 1918 (Murphy, 1990:113), substantial federal aid to education did not begin to flow until after the passage of the Elementary and Secondary Education Act in 1965. The cabinet-level Department of Education was established only in 1979, several years after the collective bargaining revolution transformed the NEA.

Although its affiliates were frequently active in state and local elections, the NEA delayed even considering support for candidates in federal elections until 1968. The segregation issue, epitomized by the presence of segregated white Southern affiliates within the NEA, and the political division surrounding federal aid to segregated schools were important factors in this delay. During the 1960s, a series of events—the Civil Rights Act of 1964, the Elementary Secondary Education Act of 1965, bargaining elections in the Northern cities, and the merger with the American Teachers Association in 1966 removed segregation as an issue and made it possible for the NEA to begin exploring the creation of an NEA political action committee (PAC) for federal campaigns (Ethridge, 1984:17–20; Murphy, 1990:205; Stinnett, 1968:77–79, 197; West, 1980:173–174).[2]

The AFT, 1916–1960

The AFT was organized in 1916 by teachers in Chicago and Gary, Indiana. From then until at least the late 1960s, the AFT barely existed beyond the local level (Urban, 1982:135, 148–149, 175). In the mid-1960s, 11 cities accounted for 62% of AFT's nationwide membership and 71% of AFT membership in the states where they were located (Stinnett, 1968:28, 372–373).

---

[2] The American Teachers Association was an organization of black teachers founded in 1904 to promote racial equality in education for both students and teachers. By 1963, the organization had 75,000 members (National Education Association, 1996:32–33).

The AFT's national presence was limited and largely dependent on financial assistance from the American Federation of Labor and its successor organization, the AFL–CIO. Up to 1960, the AFL–CIO paid for the AFT's Washington lobbyist, its field organizers, and its officers' salaries (Murphy, 1990:113–114; Selden, 1985:8–9; Urban, 1985:147–148). The AFT's organizing campaign during the 1960s was also made possible largely through the AFL–CIO's donations of staff and cash (Selden, 1985:60–62, 85, 93–94). As late as 1964, the AFT's headquarters were in Chicago rather than Washington. The entire staff consisted of nine people, including five field organizers (Selden, 1985: 110–111).

From nearly the beginning of its existence in 1917 until the early 1960s, the national AFT maintained an official position that its locals would not strike (Murphy, 1990:109; Urban, 1982:138). Even when the first teacher strikes broke out in the late 1940s, the AFT declined to change its no-strike pledge (Murphy, 1990:183, 210). It was only in 1963 that the AFT recognized the "right of locals to strike in certain circumstances" (Stinnett, 1968:97–98).

Likewise, before 1961, collective bargaining was virtually nonexistent in education circles. When the New York local won its bargaining election in 1961, the union discovered that even AFT locals that had previously struck had not had collective bargaining agreements covering teachers' wages, hours, and working conditions (Selden, 1985:69). Moreover, many of the veteran New York leaders had been prepared to settle with the superintendent on a joint request for funds to the City Council and the legislature, as opposed to a bargaining agreement (Selden, 1985:72). Most locals outside New York felt that their own political climate and perhaps their own members would not accept collective bargaining (Selden, 1985:67).

In addition, the AFT gave school principals the option of organizing in separate locals or joining the teacher locals. Although the original AFT constitution excluded principals and supervisors from membership, by 1921 the union amended its position to permit inclusion (Urban, 1982:140–141). In 1965–1966, a survey of locals representing 85% of AFT members showed that the majority of AFT locals contained department heads and between 15 and 20% contained assistant principals, principals, or other supervisors (Stinnett, 1968:220).

Collective Bargaining Transforms the NEA and AFT

The AFT Takes the Plunge

In 1956 the AFT affiliate in New York decided to make the attainment of collective bargaining its highest priority. At the time, teachers were fragmented into numerous organizations, and the AFT represented less than 5% of the total teaching staff. The organizational fragmentation reflected different and sometimes conflicting interests. High school teachers who had subject-based master's degrees wanted to restore a differential based on degrees in subjects. That differential would not have been available to elementary teachers, who typically had education degrees. Finally, although the teachers were upset about salary and working conditions, they were not necessarily militant or prepared to strike, particularly in the face of antistrike laws affecting public employees that might have cost all of them their tenure or their jobs and required some of them to go to jail (Murphy, 1990:215; Selden, 1985:15, 21–26).

The AFT's victory in New York City led to an enormous growth in AFT membership, from 59,000 in 1960 to 551,359 in 1980 (an 800% increase). Although the combined membership in NEA and AFT nearly tripled in the two decades after 1960, the smaller AFT grew far faster than the NEA, and its share of all organized education employees increased from 7.6% to 24.7% (Murphy, 1990:277; *NEA Handbook 1980–81*:134). This burgeoning membership and militancy led to the legitimization of collective bargaining for teachers in most states. Whereas in 1959 only Wisconsin permitted collective bargaining for public employees, in 1978 some 31 states had bargaining laws on the books (West, 1980:264–265).

The AFT effort succeeded for a number of reasons. A key underlying factor was a dramatic change in the demographics of the teaching force. In the decade after 1954, the instructional labor force became significantly younger, included more men, and was better educated. In 1955–1956, the median age of teachers was 42.9 years. By 1963–1964, it was 39.9 years, with male teachers significantly younger, at 34 years. The percentage of men also increased, from 26% in 1955–1956 to 32% in 1963–1964. Meanwhile, the percentage of teachers with less than a bachelor's degree fell from

22.2% in 1955–1956 to 7% in 1965–1966 (Stinnett, 1968:35).

The young teachers of the late 1950s and early 1960s had markedly higher expectations than their immediate predecessors. Largely from working-class backgrounds, they had attended college with the clear expectation of becoming professionals. Instead they found that they had become "workers in the education industry" (Selden, 1985:228). Younger teachers found themselves reacting against classroom overcrowding resulting from the baby boom and salaries that were often little better than those prevailing in the 1920s. Some 40% of all male teachers, including 75% of all married teachers, were "moonlighting" to approximate what they regarded as a professional income. Teachers also chafed against an educational bureaucracy that denied them any right to participate in shaping educational policy (Stinnett, 1968:35, 80).

A final demographic factor that pressed teachers toward militancy was lack, or perceived lack, of occupational mobility. Although many jobs paid better than teaching in the 1950s, men in particular—most of whom had families—felt that it was too late for them to switch careers (Murphy, 1990:220; Stinnett, 1968: 34, 83). Collective bargaining offered them a chance to fight for improvements.

Teacher anger and frustration very likely would not have led to the success of collective bargaining without the specific, targeted efforts of the AFT in the large cities. In the early 1960s, the AFT, with 59,000 members and a handful of organizers, was attempting to take on the NEA—then administrator dominated and opposed to collective bargaining—with 730,000 members and a large staff. The AFT decided to concentrate its efforts on big cities. Winning bargaining elections and dues check-off in big cities was the fastest way for AFT leaders to increase the organization's membership and income (Selden, 1985:68, 95). In the big union towns, the AFT's connections with the labor movement also were a vital organization-building asset.

The NEA, though much larger than the AFT, had locals in fewer than 20% of the nation's school districts (7,135 locals in 40,420 districts) and carried out political activity mainly at the state and national levels. The NEA's national and state organizations, funded by teacher dues paid directly to them, were not much dependent on the locals. Although the NEA had a presence in most large industrial cities in the early 1960s,

its urban locals were weak. In Chicago and New York, NEA affiliates represented a small fraction of the teachers. In other cities, larger NEA memberships often reflected paper majorities that had been declining for years (Murphy, 1990:224; Stinnett, 1968:43, 73, 75). Many of the NEA's urban locals lacked full-time staff (Stinnett 1968: 48).

The AFT's rapid expansion and pioneering in establishing collective bargaining thus came in the face of an administrator-dominated NEA that was too weak in the cities where the key battles were under way to compete for members or present an alternative strategy. In contrast, the labor movement was willing to fund the AFT, and liberal politicians who might have crushed the rebellion instead came to its aid.

The NEA's Transformation into a Labor Union

The AFT's victory in the 1961 New York bargaining election helped push the NEA leadership into reorganizing the association (West, 1980:56–57). In 1962, the NEA leadership created the Urban Project, which ultimately devoted some $6 million in NEA resources to strengthening locals in the cities. As teachers nationwide increasingly supported proactive collective bargaining, the NEA counterposed the idea of *professional negotiations,* which covered compensation and working conditions, as did collective bargaining, but empowered the superintendent to act as an intermediary between the teachers and the school board. If a school board refused to negotiate or accept what the local and ultimately the state association regarded as reasonable, the NEA rejoinder was not to strike but rather to impose "sanctions" such as advising teachers outside the district not to work for the district.

The professional negotiations approach sought to avoid polarizing NEA's teacher and administrator members and sidestepped the strike issue, thus averting, for the time being, a rift in the organization. Unlike collective bargaining, professional negotiations would keep the superintendents in the organization representing teachers and would prohibit use of outside parties to mediate or impose solutions if the superintendent representing the school board could not reach agreement with other members of the profession (Stinnett, 1968:90, 119, 122).

Ultimately, however, the professional negotiations strategy began to give way to outright bargaining. For one thing, although the NEA did not advocate strikes, it soon refused to take an official no-strike position, and state affiliates were not prohibited from assisting locals that went on strike. Thus, although NEA affiliates were encouraged to seek state legislation to facilitate professional negotiations (West, 1980:67–70), the outcome was actually determined on the ground by teachers and state legislatures. During the 1960s teachers became increasingly assertive, "voting with their feet" on salary and workplace issues, engaging in bargaining elections, strikes, contract negotiations, and pressing for state statutes to establish collective bargaining rights. Many of these teachers were NEA members, and their actions served to transform the NEA into a union from the bottom up.

Of the bargaining elections held between 1963 and 1966, the NEA won most but lost to the AFT in the large industrial cities (Stinnett, 1968:70–72; West, 1980:75). Because most of the teachers were in the cities, the AFT victories there further signaled that the future was moving away from professional negotiations and toward collective bargaining.

Between 1967 and 1969 teacher strikes erupted all over the country, except in the South. In 1968–1969 the NEA and AFT conducted 123 strikes or work stoppages, involving more than 127,000 teachers in 26 states and the District of Columbia. NEA locals accounted for 80% of the strikes and 40% of the employees involved (NEA Research, 1969:4–5). As a result, by 1968–1969, nearly 450,000 teachers were covered by 1,019 collective bargaining agreements. NEA affiliates accounted for 90.5% of the contracts and 61.2% of the teachers (NEA Research, 1974:15).

In addition, between 1966 and 1969, the number of states that had established statutory collective bargaining for teachers increased from 5 to 15 (West, 1980:264–265). Except for prohibiting strikes, most of these public sector bargaining laws tended to follow the private sector legal framework of collective bargaining rather than the alternative of professional negotiations (West, 1980:77–82).

By 1970, states where teachers had statutory collective bargaining rights included nearly one-third of school employees and one-third of the membership of state affiliates. As local associations committed themselves to collective bargaining, increasing numbers of administrators left the NEA. In some cases, their exit was written into the collective bargaining statutes, which typically excluded principals and other supervisors from teacher bargaining units. In other cases, the boards expected the superintendents to operate as the district CEOs and ordered them to resign from the NEA (West, 1980:60).

The widespread participation of NEA members in bargaining and the rapid growth of AFT membership during the 1960s meant that the NEA, to maintain its membership base, had to embrace collective bargaining to keep the bargaining locals in the organization. For this reason, the NEA essentially began to remake itself into a union that limited the influence of administrators, affirmatively supported collective bargaining, and received dues from members at all levels of the organization, including the locals.

The changes that had begun at the grass roots coalesced in 1971, at a constitutional convention to restructure the NEA. The convention decided that administrator representation in the NEA's elected or appointed positions would be no greater than their proportion of the membership. Because teachers constituted 85% of the membership, this decision virtually ensured teacher control (West, 1980:230). In addition, the convention effectively overturned the NEA's historic federation between national teacher and supervisor groups by requiring that NEA affiliates had to have three-fourths of their members in the NEA. Because collective bargaining had pushed many administrators out of local associations, the three major national organizations representing superintendents and principals could not meet this condition. Moreover, having lost control of the NEA, administrators had less reason to stay, and in 1972 the three major national organizations representing administrators—the American Association of School Administrators, the National Association of Elementary School Principals, and the National Association of Secondary School Principals—disaffiliated from the NEA (West, 1980:84).

The exit of administrators from the NEA also required the association to make some important changes in how it conducted its activities. Before collective bargaining, administrators were the NEA's "field organizers"—promoting the organization and pressuring teachers to join (Selden, 1985:183). Now, new field organizers would be required not only to market the organization and help recruitment but to assist elected leaders in various aspects of collective bargaining. In 1970, the NEA and its state affiliates formed a cooperative arrangement called UniServ that provided salaried professional organizers to assist and strengthen NEA locals (West 1980:84, 238).

Toward the Twenty-First Century

Despite disagreements about strategy, both the NEA and AFT have always held goals similar to those expressed in the NEA's current mission statement: "to promote the cause of quality public education, to advance the profession of education," and "to further the interests of educational employees" (*NEA Handbook 1994–95*:389, Wesley, 1957:334). But although they succeeded in expanding public education, they have thus far largely failed to establish public K–12 teaching as a profession on a par with many others in terms of salaries, credentialing, and resources available to accomplish critical tasks. Collective bargaining has been too weak and too narrow in scope to change the basic conditions that prevent teaching from becoming a profession on a par with other vital functions in our society. The NEA's attempt to achieve one-third federal financing for the public schools has failed. As a result, school finance remains largely a state and local function. Finally, demographic, economic, and political changes have put the entire public school system in jeopardy.

Task versus Occupation

Current literature on teaching as an occupation suggests that although the *task* confronting elementary and secondary teachers today is very professional, the *occupation* of public school teaching today is not structured as a profession. Teachers' salaries, roles, career structures, and educations are not treated as fully professional. This problem stems from the way public school teaching was established as an occupation at the turn of the century.

Salaries. Teaching salaries are "professional" only when compared with salaries in other historically underpaid occupations such as nursing, librarianship, and social work that have been largely filled by women. Such discrimination had its roots in the assumption that women were primarily homemakers and were aiming at supplementing a main source of income earned by a male head of household (Carnegie Forum on Education and the Economy, 1986:36; Odden and Kelley, 1997:6). Whether or not this assumption had any validity in the past, it is clear that today an occupation's

pay scale can be seriously considered as professional only if it can attract a work force that is paid on a par with primary income earners, whether they are men or women.

An examination of teacher salaries shows that they are neither "professional" nor competitive. For example, in 1995–1996 male teachers' median earnings ($34,000) were 18% below median earnings for male professionals ($41,639). Although most male teachers had a master's degree, their median earnings ($37,706) were below the median earnings of men with a bachelor's degree ($39,040).

Adding age to the salary comparison does not change the outcome. In 1995–1996 a typical male teacher, 46 years old with a master's degree, earned $38,841—45% less than the earnings of a typical male ($70,602) of similar age (45–49 years) and education. In fact, the typical male teacher (aged 46 years, with a master's degree) earned less than the typical 30- to 34-year-old male nonteacher with a bachelor's degree ($44,844).

For women, who still earn substantially less in the marketplace than men, a comparison of salaries in teaching with those in other occupations yields more ambiguous results. In 1995–1996, the average female teacher aged 44 years with a master's degree earned $34,386, slightly less than the average earnings ($36,918) of all women of similar age and education. The earnings of female teachers fell between the mean earnings reported for similarly aged men who were high school graduates ($33,690) or college dropouts ($39,474; NEA Research, 1997:19, 74, 271–272; U.S. Census Bureau, 1996:Table 7, Table 9).

Teachers' Credentials and Education Are Not Respected. In developing state certification statutes, the NEA originally sought to ensure the professional status of teaching by making certification dependent on graduation from schools of education. Undergraduate programs in education have for years been the main source for training teachers (Choy et al., 1993:48; Gray et al., 1993:8). Yet, such teacher training programs or credentials have been the subject of complaint as far as the turn of the century (Holmes Group, 1986:25). The quality of the students entering education schools is seen as low (Carnegie Forum on Education and the Economy, 1986:28–32, 36, 98; Holmes Group, 1986:6, 35). The training curriculum is seen as intellectually weak and as poor preparation for the classroom (Carnegie Forum on Education and the Economy, 1986:71; Holmes Group, 1986:6, 14–15, 1995:103).

Some recent reviews of teacher education programs have recommended abolishing undergraduate teacher education and making the vocational side of teacher preparation into a fifth-year, graduate-level program (Carnegie Forum on Education and the Economy, 1986:70; Holmes Group, 1986:14, 1995:76). These reports recognize, however, that teacher education reflects the occupational conditions of classroom teaching. Unless the salaries and work roles of teachers change, it seems unlikely that the preparation for them—teacher education—will be improved, as professional education programs seldom *create* a profession and typically *serve* ones that already exist (Carnegie Forum on Education and the Economy, 1986:36; Holmes Group, 1986:8, 26).

Collective Bargaining and Professionalization

Is collective bargaining compatible with professionalization? So far, collective bargaining has not transformed teaching into a profession. In part, this situation reflects the absence of teacher bargaining rights in 16 states. But even where teachers have won extensive bargaining rights, their scope does not extend to negotiating for better learning conditions. In the 1960s and early 1970s, teachers were seeking the basic goals for which industrial workers had fought during the 1930s—improved salaries and benefits, limitations on work load, and due process in transfers and discipline (Selden, 1985:109). In 1975, fewer than a third of teacher collective bargaining agreements contained clauses that limited class size, granted teachers the right to refuse teaching assignments outside their field, or established instructional policy committees. Since 1975, teachers have achieved scant progress in making agreements that enhance learning conditions (Yrchik, 1992:22–23).

In good measure, the failure to enhance learning and professional conditions stems from the fact that teachers have not really challenged the limits on the scope of bargaining. In effect, they have accepted the conventional bargaining system, which supports the existing structure of jobs in education rather than promoting reform and renovation of the education system. Administrators, legislators, courts, and arbitrators have all expected teachers to accept the conventional limits of

bargaining to receive its benefits, and teachers generally have done so. Even today, teacher-negotiators are advised not to bargain over educational restructuring unless more "basic" demands have been met (Yrchik, 1992:34).

In 1975, 30 states had enacted bargaining laws— laws that require school boards to bargain in good faith. Since 1975, however, only 4 more states have been added to the number of bargaining states, bringing the total to 34 (see Appendix 2). Of the 16 remaining nonbargaining states, 12 are right-to-work states, 9 of them from the old Confederacy. Generally hostile to bargaining for any workers, the legislatures of these states are unlikely to enact teacher bargaining laws any time soon (Falzon, 1993:16). Little help is available here at the federal level, as the NEA did not succeed in establishing a federal collective bargaining law for teachers in the late 1960s and early 1970s (West, 1980:24, 82–83).

Failure to Change the School Finance System

In the 1970s, the NEA wanted to secure one-third federal funding for education (*NEA Handbook 1973–74*:64–65). But the highest federal share of education funding achieved was 9.8%, in 1979–1980. By 1990–1991, the level had fallen to 6.2% (U.S. NCES, 1996:151). The failure of the NEA to obtain a significant level of federal support meant that education funding remained dependent on local taxes—primarily property taxes. These have never accounted for less than 43% of education funding, and as recently as 1993–1994, they accounted for 47.8%, the same level as in 1976–1977 (U.S. NCES, 1996:151).

The problem here is that dependence on local property taxes tends to produce gross inequalities between poor and wealthy school districts (Gold, 1994:9). Recent court cases challenging the constitutionality of school finance systems have cited disparities in per pupil expenditures ranging from 20% in Rhode Island to 800% in Texas. Although rural districts are also affected, the most visible effects of the finance system have been in the cities. Beginning in the 1960s, urban tax bases dwindled as wealthier businesses and populations shifted to the suburbs, other states, or overseas. Suburban shopping malls took business from the old urban main streets. The middle class moved to the suburbs, and their place was taken by low-income mi grants and immigrants whose needs greatly increased the cost of all municipal services, including education.

However, urban districts and poor rural districts that are dependent on limited tax bases have been unable to get the resources they need to make substantial improvements. The poorer districts typically tax more to get less. In a recent ruling, *Abbott vs. Burke* (575 A2d. 359), the New Jersey Supreme Court pointed out that the taxation of "overburdened municipalities" is already so severe that substantial tax increases are "almost unthinkable." Voters in wealthy suburban districts do not want their tax dollars taken away or their school expenditures limited to help urban schools. As a result, state legislatures have generally proved unwilling to offer substantial assistance to urban districts (Pipho, 1992:8).

The Current Crisis Develops

Changing economic conditions during the 1970s and 1980s, combined with the failures described above, have created a crisis. In the 1990s, the NEA and AFT face a constant call by conservative politicians for privatizing the public schools.

Beginning in 1973, most Americans' real income went into decline. However, the cost of government increased as a result of rising costs for education, health care, crime, and military expenditures. Taxes increased automatically with inflation. Since the late 1970s, voters and the business community have been seeking to reduce taxes, limit government expenditures, or both.

The public schools increasingly became a target for a number of reasons. Voters especially dislike property taxes that are used to finance the schools. These taxes rose very rapidly during the 1970s inflation but failed to decline proportionally during the subsequent recession (Tyack et al., 1984:203–205). Declining enrollment is another factor. Beginning in the mid-1970s, school expenditures seemed questionable because school enrollment declined without creating a proportional decline in expenditures (Tyack et al., 1984:201). Fewer voters have a stake in the public or urban schools. Since the late 1970s, most households no longer have school-aged children (Rawlings, 1993:vii). Voters with children in private religious schools object to paying for public schools. Affluent voters with children in suburban schools shy away from spending their tax dollars on urban schools (Reich, 1991:269–276).

Finally, the public schools are being increasingly

judged by the low literacy levels of the majority of students who do not go on to college (NCEE, 1990:44–45). These students and the disadvantaged urban schools have become focal points for discussions about the success or failure of public education (Education Week, 1998; Toch, 1991:3–4; Tyack et al., 1984:210–212). The increasing tendency to compare American students' math and science performance unfavorably with that in other developed countries also relies heavily on the performance of disadvantaged students (Biddle, 1997:9). Conservatives maintain that such comparisons show that public schools do not work, and they follow up by arguing that this must be the fault of incompetent teachers and the unions that protect them. The conservatives argue for privatization through vouchers, starting with the urban schools (Chubb and Moe, 1990:65, 152–155, 173, 217–225; Toch, 1991:135, 204).

The Unions' Reaction to the Crisis. During the past two decades, the NEA and AFT have opposed vouchers with considerable success. However, in addition to opposing vouchers, the unions have selectively promoted reforms including site-based decision making, peer review, and charter schools. From the unions' standpoint such reforms have two aspects. On the one hand, they promise to empower teachers, professionalize teaching, and perhaps improve student achievement. Moreover, they tend to appeal to legislators and to teachers, especially those who have recently entered the profession. On the other hand, in certain forms, or beyond a certain point, each of these reforms has the potential to weaken or even destroy collective bargaining and undermine teaching as a career. Hence, both the NEA and AFT have sought to define their own models of these reforms and implement them through a combination of bargaining or lobbying while opposing versions that would be harmful to union interests.

Site-Based Decision Making. Site-Based Decision Making (SBDM) programs start with the premise that substantial improvement in schools will occur only if teachers share in designing the reforms and accept responsibility for making them work. Decision-making authority with regard to curriculum, budget allocation, and staffing is transferred from the school district to individual school sites. Within each school, teachers share decision-making authority with administrators in an attempt to develop an instructional program that best meets the needs of students. In addition, in some of these programs, teachers have become involved in mentoring new teachers and in coaching or evaluating their peers. (David, 1990:227–233; Steinberger, 1990:27; Yrchik, 1991b:7). SBDM requires union leaders and the rank and file members to abandon the premise that management alone is responsible for the failure or success of school programs (Kerchner and Mitchell, 1988:199–201, 237–238).

SBDM tends to transfer the power to determine job security, workload, and even salary from the district to dozens or even hundreds of individual school sites. By splintering the bargaining unit, this decentralization tends to undermine the unions' capacity to function as a bargaining agent. As a result, decentralization is seen as providing an "opportunity" for NEA and AFT locals to transform themselves from bargaining agents to brokers or placement services for teachers who would be contracting individually with specific schools. (Bradley, 1992; Nathan, 1996:91, 95–97, 113).

And yet, in some situations the possible benefits of SBDM and the immediate risks of noninvolvement may outweigh the long-term dangers of decentralization. Typically, a school board or superintendent takes the initiative in developing SBDM in response to public dissatisfaction or pressure for reform. By refusing, the union risks alienating the public and some or even the majority of its members who may want active involvement as professionals in developing curriculums and other school programs. Noninvolvement provides no benefits and may allow administrators to split the union. By participating actively, the union has a chance to preserve or enhance its credibility, minimize the risks, and perhaps help teachers gain some control of their professional lives that would not be possible through conventional bargaining (Yrchik, 1988:221–233, 1992:30–32).

Probably for these reasons both the NEA and AFT have used collective bargaining to establish SBDM projects. Several AFT locals pioneered in developing SBDM, including Dade County, Florida, Hammond, Indiana, and Rochester, New York (Duttweiler and Mutchler, 1990:32; Steinberger, 1990:26–31). However, NEA locals were not far behind. By 1989–1990, a survey showed, approximately 14% of NEA locals were also involved with site-based management programs (Yrchik, 1991b:5).

Peer Evaluation. Peer evaluation means that teachers share responsibility with management for evaluating their peers, providing assistance to those in difficulty, and ultimately recommending dismissal of those who cannot change and cannot be persuaded to leave voluntarily.

The AFT took the initiative in advocating peer evaluation. In 1981, the AFT local in Toledo, Ohio, bargained a peer review provision into its contract. This model was supported by the late Al Shanker beginning in 1985 (Toch, 1991:143). Shanker argued that if the quality of the teaching force is to be improved, teachers can no longer be dictated to and supervised like factory workers (Currence, 1985).

Not surprisingly, peer evaluation is associated with SBDM. If teachers' representatives at a school site take on the responsibility for instructional policy, it becomes their policy, and it can be argued that teachers should be responsible for ensuring that it is properly implemented. In addition, veteran teachers make the best evaluators, because they are most familiar with the limitations and possibilities of a set of teaching conditions (Conley et al., 1988:271).

However, peer evaluation has remained relatively rare, partly because, until very recently, the NEA opposed it (Bradley, 1997; NEA Board of Directors, 1986:309–313). The NEA's opposition was based on a concern that teachers functioning as peer evaluators might lose their bargaining rights or become a source of tension and conflict within the local (NEA General Counsel, 1988:3–4). As of 1997, Columbus, Ohio, was the only cited example of an NEA affiliate with a "peer assistance and review" program (Bradley, 1997).

However, with Bob Chase's arrival as NEA president, the NEA has accepted peer evaluation. In February 1997, Chase told the National Press Club that "we accept our responsibility to assist in removing teachers—that small minority of teachers who are unqualified, incompetent, or burned out" (Chase, 1997). In July 1997, the NEA Representative Assembly adopted a resolution that permits NEA locals to negotiate peer assistance and review and allows the NEA nationally to provide information about successful models (NEA RA, 1997a).

NEA's decision to support peer assistance and review partially reflects a desire to respond to public concerns about inadequate teacher quality and the public's perception that unions make it nearly impossible to fire incompetent teachers (Nathan, 1996:83; Public Agenda, 1994:36, 1997:9, 12). It may also reflect a desire for a more collaborative, less adversarial relationship with management.

Charter Schools. Charter schools are public schools established for a limited period through a "charter" or contract that spells out their objectives. Like most other public schools, charter schools are prohibited from screening students, charging tuition, having a religious affiliation, or discriminating on the basis of race, religion, or disability.

Charter schools exchange greater accountability for greater freedom to innovate and experiment. On the surface, charter schools are accountable in a way that other public schools are not. A charter school must recruit its students; inasmuch as its public funding usually is based on the state and local per pupil expenditure, its existence depends on its success in attracting and maintaining enrollment. In addition, a charter school is not legally permanent. The charter is issued for a term, and the issuing agency may decide not to renew it if the school fails to meet its declared objectives. In return for accepting this accountability, charter schools are typically released from many state and local rules that apply to other schools, including some or all union contract provisions and certification requirements.

Compared with other reforms mentioned here, charter schools are a rapidly growing phenomenon. Minnesota passed its first charter law and approved its first school in 1991. As of July 1997, some 27 states and the District of Columbia had enacted legislation permitting charter schools, and at least 480 schools are in operation (NEA CAPE, 1997; Edgerly, 1997:3). Although the Clinton administration opposed vouchers, it supported providing federal funds for charter school startup costs. The Clinton administration sought to establish 3,000 charter schools by the end of the century.

The rapid growth of charter schools reflects the appeal of this reform to various constituencies with very different agendas. Some groups tend to focus on specific schools. Charter schools attract parents who are either dissatisfied with existing programs or are simply attracted to the new program. Charter schools attract younger teachers and some parents who wish to run their own schools. At the same time, the advocates of private school vouchers may see charter schools as a possible back door or first step to their goal. Investors in Edison and other firms in the "education industry" see charter schools as a possible means of expanding their opportunities (Glassman, 1995; Education Industry, 1997; Lehman Bros., 1996:39). Legislators may see charter schools as an alternative way of satisfying demands for school reform and "choice" without increasing taxes or supporting vouchers.

Under these circumstances, the NEA and AFT have opted for a strategy of defining the kinds of charter schools they support and those they do not. Both organizations favor charters to the extent that their purpose is to *facilitate reform within school districts* by allowing parents and teachers to create alternative schools. In 1988, before nearly everyone else was advocating for charters, Al Shanker proposed charter schools that would be organized by parents and teachers as "schools within schools" or conversion of existing schools with the approval of a joint panel of union and district representatives (Olson, 1988). In 1996, both the NEA and AFT issued detailed guidelines for acceptable charter schools. Under either set of guidelines, charter schools must be approved by local school districts, use certified teachers, and be covered by a collective bargaining agreement—preferably the one covering other district employees (AFT, 1996; NEA CAPE, 1996). The unions are prepared to waive some bargaining union provisions to the extent necessary to permit the implementation of innovative programs. AFT locals in Boston, New York City, and Houston are involved in sponsoring charter schools along these lines (Agreement Between Boston Public Schools and AFT Local 66 1994–97; Jacobson, 1997; Nathan, 1996:114) Likewise, the NEA is sponsoring six charter schools in five states (Arizona, California, Colorado, Connecticut, Georgia, and Hawaii; National Education Association, 1997).

However, the NEA and AFT oppose charter schools if their purpose is seen as *eliminating school districts as employers and operators of schools.* Affiliates of both organizations have opposed state legislation that allows agencies other than local school districts to approve charter schools. Likewise, affiliates of both organizations have sought to limit the number of charter schools (Nathan, 1996:96–105).

In February 1997, Bob Chase, newly elected as NEA president, spoke at the National Press Club about the need to reinvent the NEA as a union. He stated that the public is demanding higher quality public schools and that "we must revitalize our schools from within or they will be dismantled from without." The NEA, Chase argued, must become "the champion of quality teaching and quality public schools in the United States." Hence, rather than sitting on the sidelines of change, the NEA must take the initiative. In place of adversarial bargaining, the NEA would seek to collaborate with management in an agenda of school reform. This agenda would promote higher standards for student achievement, promote comanagement of school districts by teachers and school boards, and accept union responsibility for improving or removing the small minority of teachers who are unqualified or burned out.

Reflecting on this speech, Thomas Toch, an admirer of the late Al Shanker and a strong critic of NEA, noted that "Chase delivered exactly the same message that Albert Shanker had delivered in Niagara Falls 12 years earlier" (Toch, 1997). In sum, beginning with the 1980s, both the NEA and AFT have sought to accommodate rather than to oppose school reform (Kerchner and Mitchell, 1988:160–162; McDonnell and Pascal, 1988:51). Although, as Toch argued, the AFT initially moved faster than NEA, both organizations are now seen as reading from the same page (Bradley and Archer, 1997).

Merger Talks. As their education reform agendas have converged, both organizations have also begun considering a merger seriously for the first time in 20 years.

As early as 1968, David Selden, president of the AFT, had approached the NEA with a proposal to discuss a merger. Selden argued that local money was running dry, and unity was needed to strengthen lobbying efforts at the state and federal levels. In addition, Selden felt that the existence of two unions forced both organizations to dissipate resources on duplicate staff, including organizers whose sole purpose was to fight each other. At that time, the NEA had no official policies either on merger with the AFT or on AFL–CIO affiliation. Hence, the NEA declined the invitation (Selden, 1985:132, 138).

In July 1973, the NEA Representative Assembly adopted a resolution that authorized merger discussions but imposed three conditions for a successful outcome:

- No affiliation with the AFL–CIO
- Guaranteed minority-group participation in the governance and operation of the merged organization
- Use of the secret ballot for the election of officers or the alteration of governing documents.

In early 1974, brief merger talks failed because the parties could not reach agreement on these conditions. Merger talks did not resume until 1993. In the midst of these talks, however, both organizations underwent significant changes in leadership. At the NEA, Bob Chase was elected to replace Keith Geiger as president. At the AFT, Sandra Feldman became president in 1997 following the death of Albert Shanker.

The work of arranging a meaningful and functional merger would require the new leaders to create a framework for resolving some significant structural differences between the two organizations that have been long-term obstacles to unity. Whereas the NEA has quotas guaranteeing minority representation in governance bodies, the AFT has significant minority representation but opposes quotas. The NEA allows any member to run for any office or governance position in the belief that dispersal of power is desirable. The AFT's national executive council is open only to members who hold elective office in their locals. The AFT argues that limiting national decision making to individuals with political power at the local level facilitates the implementation of national policies. Whereas NEA's officers have term limits, the AFT's officers serve indefinitely. The AFT has informal political parties or caucuses that run slates for national office. The NEA does not have caucuses or slate ballots.

By January 1998, the NEA and AFT came to a conceptual agreement on these organizational issues and agreed to submit a merger proposal to their respective membership conventions in July 1998. The conventions voted to accept or reject eight "Principles of Unity" to develop a new "United Organization" (a provisional designation for the still-to-be-named successor organization to both the NEA and AFT). The highlights of the eight unity principles are as follows:

- The United Organization will champion public education by working to eliminate inequities that deny students a safe and supportive learning environment, by promoting practices that enhance student achievement, and by promoting skill development and high standards among education employees.

- Education employees will constitute the core of the United Organization's membership jurisdiction. The education membership will include every category of worker employed either by public education-related agencies, or by private agencies that are funded by public tax dollars. The organization will also include affiliates that represent professional and technical health care employees working in state and local government.

- The United Organization will be governed democratically. A convention of delegates elected by the members will elect the Executive Board and act as the highest policymaking body for the organization. Elections of convention delegates, elections of the Executive Board, and other decisions of the convention will be made by secret ballot.

- State affiliates will be the primary vehicle for providing United Organization programs and services to local affiliates and members. The United Organization will encourage but not require one affiliate in each state, and local. All state and local affiliates will be subject to minimum standards set by the United Organization.

- The United Organization (UO) and state affiliates will jointly finance and administer a UO local staffing program to assist affiliates with advocacy. National dues will be comparable to what dues might be if NEA and AFT remained separate organizations.

- The United Organization will maintain and work to expand minority representation throughout leadership, governance, and staff.

- The United Organization will be a national affiliate of the AFL–CIO and will encourage its state and local affiliates to affiliate at their respective levels.

- The adoption of these principles at the 1998 NEA and AFT conventions will constitute a formal commitment to create a United Organization. In 1999, or by 2000 at the latest, the NEA and AFT conventions will vote on the proposed constitution, bylaws, and unification agreement. By 2003 or 2004, the United Organization will begin operation.

In the late 1960s and in 1973, when the last national merger talks were held, supporters of a merger were a minority in their own organizations. As a result, after a meeting or so, when the obvious obstacles were brought up, the discussion died (Selden, 1985:205, 210–211, 216). State and local mergers continued, but they tended to be one-sided takeovers (Selden 1985:140, 224).

In contrast, the antecedents and the atmosphere surrounding the current talks suggest that even if the national merger does not occur, relationships between the two organizations will never be the same. At the national level, an AFT/NEA Joint Council is working on issues related to school infrastructure, discipline, and teacher quality. At the state level, mergers are imminent in Florida, Montana, and Minnesota. The NEA and AFT have also recently approved local mergers in San Francisco (1989) and Rosemount, Minnesota (1992). Whatever happens, both sides have agreed not to return to the days of counterproductive organizational rivalry (Richardson, 1995:3; NEA RA, 1997b).

Appendix 1: NEA as the House of Education: Departments of the NEA in 1957 and Their Founding Dates[3]

Administration

American Association of School Administrators (1870)

Department of Elementary School Principals (1921)

National Association of Women Deans and Counselors (1918)

National Association of Secondary School Principals (1927)

National Council of Administrative Women in Education (1932)

Curriculum

American Association for Health Physical Education and Recreation (1937)

American Industrial Arts Association (1939)

Association for Supervision and Curriculum Development (1929)

Department of Home Economics (1930)

Department of Vocational Education (1875)

Music Educators National Conference (1940)

National Art Education Association (1933)

---

[3] *Source:* Wesley (1957:278–279).

National Association of Journalism Directors (1939)

National Council for the Social Studies (1925)

National Council of Teachers of Mathematics (1950)

National Science Teachers Association (1895)

Speech Association of America (1939)

United Business Education Association (1892)

Instruction of Specific Groups or Levels

American Association of Colleges for Teacher Education (1948)

Association for Higher Education (1942)

Department of Kindergarten-Primary Education (1884)

Department of Rural Education (1907)

International Council for Exceptional Children (1941)

National Association of Public School Adult Educators (1955)

Services

American Educational Research Association (1930)

Department of Audio Visual Instruction (1923)

Department of Classroom Teachers (1913)

National Association of Educational Secretaries (1946)

National Retired Teachers Association (1951)

National School Public Relations Association (1950)

Appendix 2. The Current Status of Teacher Collective Bargaining Rights[4]

Thirty-four states have laws requiring school districts to bargain in good faith:

Alaska	Nebraska
California	Nevada
Connecticut	New Hampshire
Delaware	New Jersey
Florida	New Mexico[5]
Hawaii	New York
Idaho	North Dakota
Illinois[5]	Ohio[5]
Indiana	Oklahoma
Iowa	Oregon
Kansas	Pennsylvania
Maine	Rhode Island
Maryland	South Dakota

Massachusetts	Tennessee[5]
Michigan	Vermont
Minnesota	Washington
Montana	Wisconsin

In nine states school districts are permitted, but not required, to bargain under meet and confer laws or court rulings:

Meet and Confer Law	Court Ruling
Alabama	Arizona
Missouri	Arkansas
	Colorado
	Kentucky
	Louisiana
	Utah
	Wyoming

In seven states school districts are virtually prohibited from bargaining:

Statute	Court Ruling	Silence
North Carolina	Georgia	South Carolina
Texas	Virginia	Mississippi
North Carolina		

REFERENCES

AFT Charter Schools Research Project. 1996. "Charter School Laws: Do They Measure Up?" Washington, DC: American Federation of Teachers.

Biddle, Bruce J. 1997. "Foolishness, Dangerous Nonsense and Real Correlates of State Differences in Achievement." *Phi Delta Kappan* (September):9–13.

Bradley, Ann. 1992. "School Reforms Bump Up Against Unions' Most Cherished Protections" *Education Week* (December 9).

———. 1997."Fate of Peer Review Rests with NEA Locals." *Education Week* (August 6).

Bradley, Ann, and Jeff Archer. 1997. "NEA Panel Touts Its Union Label." *Education Week* (August 6).

Carnegie Forum on Education and the Economy. 1986. *A Nation Prepared: Teachers for the 21st Century.* New York: Carnegie Corporation.

Chase, Bob. 1997. "The New NEA: Reinventing Teacher Unions for a New Era. Remarks Before the National Press Club." NEA press release, Washington, DC, February, 5.

Choy, Susan, et al. 1993. *America's Teachers: Profile of a Profession.* Washington, DC: U.S. Department of Education, National Center for Education Statistics.

Chubb, John E., and Terry E. Moe. 1990. *Politicos, Markets and America's Schools.* Washington, DC; Brookings Institution.

---

[4] *Sources: Collective Bargaining Quarterly* 9:1 (June 1986); Falzon (1993).

[5] Bargaining law initially enacted after 1975.

Conley, Sharon, et al. 1988. "Teacher Participation in the Management of School Systems." *Teachers College Record* 90:(2):259–280.

Currence, Cindy. 1985. "A.F.T. Head Backs Voucher Proposal for Public Schools." *Education Week* (May 8).

David, Jane L. 1990. "Restructuring in Progress: Lessons from Pioneering Districts." In Richard F. Elmore et al. (eds.), *Restructuring Schools: The Next Generation of Education Reform,* pp. 209–249. San Francisco: Jossey-Bass.

Duttweiler, Patricia C., and Sue E. Mutchler. 1990. "Organizing the Educational System for Excellence: Harnessing the Energy of People." Southwest Educational Development Laboratory paper no. ED 331 121, Austin, TX.

Edgerly, William S. 1997. "The Role of Charter Schools" *Charter School Newsletter* (Summer).

Education Industry. 1997. "The Charter School Management Industry." *Education Industry* 5 (June).

Education Week. 1998. "Quality Counts '98: The Urban Challenge." *1998 Editorial Projects in Education* 27 (January 8).

Elsbree, Willard S. 1939. *The American Teacher: Evolution of a Profession in A Democracy.* New York: The American Book Company.

Ethridge, Samuel B. 1984. *Odyssey in Bargaining and Civil Rights by the National Education Association, 1964 and Beyond.* Unpublished manuscript.

Falzon, Joseph A. 1993. "Collective Bargaining Laws for Education Employees." Unpublished manuscript, NEA Research Division, Washington, DC.

Glassman, James K. 1995. "It's Elementary: Buy Education Stocks Now." *Washington Post* (July 2):H-1.

Gold, Steven D. 1994. "Tax Options for States Needing More School Revenue." National Education Association, Research Division, Washington, DC.

Gray, Lucinda, et al. 1993. *New Teachers in the Job Market, 1991 Update.* Washington, DC: U.S. Department of Education, National Center for Education Statistics.

Holmes Group. 1986. *Tomorrow's Teachers.* East Lansing, MI.

———. 1995. "Tomorrow's Schools of Education." Final draft, East Lansing, MI.

Huggett, Albert J., and T. M. Stinnett. 1956. *Professional Problems of Teachers.* New York: Macmillan.

Jacobson, Linda. 1997. "AFT Elects NYC Leader as New President" *Education Week* (May 14).

Kerchner, Charles T., and Douglas E. Mitchell. 1988. *The Changing Idea of a Teachers' Union.* New York: Falser Press.

Lehman Bros. 1996. "Investment Opportunity in the Education Industry."

McDonnell, Lauren, and Anthony Pascal. 1988. *Teacher Unions and Educational Reform.* Santa Monica, CA: Rand Corporation.

Murphy, Marjoram. 1990. *Blackboard Unions: The AFT and the NEA 1900–1980.* Ithaca, NY: Cornell University Press.

Nathan, Joe. 1996. *Charter Schools.* San Francisco: Jossey-Bass.

NCEE (National Center on Education and the Economy). 1990. *America's Choice: High Skills or Low Wages.* Rochester, NY.

National Education Association. 1996. *NEA Handbook 1996–1997.* Washington, DC: NEA.

———. 1997. "Charter Schools—A Tool for School Reform?" *Hot Topics* (Summer).

NEA Board of Directors. 1986. "Position Statement on Professional Growth and Evaluation." In *Minutes of the NEA Board of Directors and Executive Committee 1985–86.* Washington, DC: National Education Association.

NEA CAPE (Center for the Advancement of Public Education). 1996. "NEA Criteria for Charter Schools," Washington, DC.

———. 1997. "Charter Laws and Proposals," Washington, DC, July.

NEA General Counsel. 1988. "Legal Problems Involved in Education Reform: The Changing Role of Teachers In Educational Decisionmaking," Washington, DC.

NEA RA (Representative Assembly). 1997a. "NEA Annual Meeting Makes History." *NEA RA Online* (July 6).

———. 1997b. "NEA-AFT Merger Discussions Report." *NEA RA Today* (July 7):11.

NEA Research (National Education Association, Research Division). 1969. "Teacher Strikes and Work Stoppages." NEA Research Memo 1969–27, Washington, DC, December.

———. 1974. "Growth of Teacher Contracts: 1966–1973." *Negotiations Research Digest* (January):15–16.

———. 1997. "Status of the American Public School Teacher 1995–96," Washington, DC.

Odden, Allan, and Carolyn Kelley. 1997. *Paying Teachers for What They Know and Do.* Thousand Oaks, CA: Corwin Press.

Olson, Lynn. 1988. "Shanker Argues for a 'New Type' of Teaching Unit." *Education Week* (April 6).

Pipho, Chris. 1992. "Can School Finance Be Reformed?" In *Educational Finance Workshop, Selected Proceedings 1992.* Washington, DC: National Education Association.

Public Agenda Foundation. 1994. *First Things First: What Americans Expect from the Public Schools.*

———. 1997. *Survey of Public Attitudes Toward Public Education.*

Rawlings, Steve W. 1994. "Household and Family Characteristics, March 1993." Current Population Reports, Population Characteristics P20-477. Washington, DC: U.S. Department of Commerce, Bureau of Census.

Reich, Robert B. 1991. *The Work of Nations.* New York: Knopf.

Richardson, Joanna. 1995. "Unions Cling to Differences, Drop Merger Talks." *Education Week* (January 11):3.

Selden, David. 1985. *The Teacher Rebellion.* Washington, DC: Howard University Press.

Steinberger, Elizabeth. 1990. "Teacher Unions Handling

Tricky Turns on the Road to Reform." *The School Administrator* (September):26–31.

Stinnett, T. M. 1968. *Turmoil in Teaching: A History of the Organizational Struggle for America's Teachers*. New York: Macmillan.

Toch, Thomas. 1991. *In the Name of Excellence: The Struggle to Reform the Nation's Schools, Why It's Failing and What Should Be Done*. New York: Oxford University Press.

———. 1997. "Tensions of the Shanker Era: A Speech that Shook the Field." *Education Week* (March 26).

Tyack, David B., et al. 1984. *Public Schools in Hard Times*. Cambridge, MA:: Harvard University Press.

Tyack, David B. 1974. *The One Best System: A History of American Education*. Cambridge, MA: Harvard University Press.

Urban, Wayne. 1982. *Why Teachers Organized*. Detroit: Wayne State University Press.

U.S. Census Bureau (U.S. Department of Commerce, Bureau of Census). 1996. "Money Income in the United States: 1995." Current Population Reports P 60-193, Washington, DC.

U.S. NCES (U.S. Department of Education, National Center for Education and Statistics). 1996. *Digest of Education Statistics 1993*. Washington, DC: U.S. Government Printing Office.

Yrchik, John. 1991a. "Collaborative Bargaining: A Critical Appraisal," National Education Association, Research Division, Washington, DC.

———. 1991b. "Site-Based Decisionmaking: The 1990 NEA Census of Local Associations." National Education Association, Research Division, Washington, DC.

———.1992. "Negotiating Change: Education Reform and Collective Bargaining." National Education Association, Research Division, Washington, DC.

Wesley, Edgar B. 1957. *NEA: The First Hundred Years*. New York: Harper.

West, Alan M. 1980. *The National Education Association: The Power Base for Education*. New York: Free Press.

TEACHERS AND TEACHING

Bruce J. Biddle and Thomas L. Good
University of Missouri

Teachers constitute the largest population of professionals in industrialized nations, numbering more than three million persons in the United States alone. In addition, the activities of teaching constitute a mammoth enterprise, occupying the majority of our waking hours when we are young, and absorbing a large portion of the nation's tax revenues. We expect that our education system will accomplish a good many things, offering high levels of instruction, providing a level playing field for all students, and generating many kinds of citizen services. Thus, the enterprise of education is important to us all, and educators, students, school administrators, parents, citizens, political leaders, and scholars alike have a vital interest in acquiring reliable knowledge about teachers and teaching.

Responding to this need, a great deal of research and scholarship has appeared concerning teachers and teaching. For purposes of analysis, this effort is sorted into several traditions of work.

Traditional Research on Teachers

At least three, long-standing traditions of research and scholarship concerning teachers may be recognized. Some authors have painted pictures of teachers in their official capacities—as employees of formal organizations comprised of social positions that are assigned explicitly stated and agreed-upon rights and responsibilities (see Katz, 1964; Bidwell, 1965; Ballantine, 1989: Chapter Six). In this view, public schools and the systems that embed them are set up by superordinate political entities ("the state" in most industrialized countries, "the community" in America). Such institutions are charged with instructing young persons and with providing other, associated services that comple-

ment instruction, and they are staffed by persons with explicit titles: school board member, superintendent, curriculum specialist, budgetary officer, principal, school nurse, janitor, and the like.

But teachers do most of the real "work" of the school and bear basic responsibility for instructing students who are the primary clients of education. And to structure their activities, teachers are given facilities (such as textbooks and a classroom) and are assigned explicit tasks for reaching curricular and noncurricular goals as well as duties associated with maintaining order, protecting the school environment, meetings with parents, leading extracurricular events, attending outreach activities in the community, and the like.

This first portrayal of teachers tends to undergird a good deal of today's political rhetoric about what might be wrong with education and how to reform it. Such a portrayal presumes that teachers, like "workers" in other types of formal organizations, are mainly motivated by their assigned responsibilities, their salaries, and their loyalties to the entity that employs them. Thus, it tends to ignore such issues as the unique, moral character of education, the needs of students, the professional training and concerns of teachers, the democratic ideals of the society that suggest citizen participation in education and a more egalitarian classroom, the actual, interactive processes involved in instruction, and how educational goals and processes may vary from one context to another.

In contrast, a second, traditional view of teachers has stressed the realities that are faced by teachers who must contend with what actually transpires in classrooms, schools, and school systems (see, for example, Waller, 1932; Lortie, 1975; Sizer, 1985; Bennett and LeCompte, 1990:Chapter 4; Dougherty and Floyd,

1990:Section 4). The latter portrayals focus on dilemmas that are created for teachers by limited budgets, unbending curricula, public disputes about education, structural conditions in the larger society, diffuse goals set for schools, student impulses and needs, and the fact that teachers normally have low status in the bureaucratic organization of the school system.

Central to this second tradition is the idea that such realities not only pose problems for those who choose teaching careers but also that they inhibit accomplishment of the instructional tasks assigned to teachers (see, for example, Coleman, 1961; Bryk and Driscoll, 1988; Oakes, 1990; Bank, in press; Natriello, in press; Spencer, in press). To illustrate, a number of studies have appeared showing how the practice of ability tracking, now widespread in American schools, debases the effects of teaching for many minority students (Oakes, 1985; Hallinan, 1996). Thus, this view honors the idealistic motivations of teachers and accepts as largely legitimate the traditional tasks taken on by the school, but suggests that the realities of school and classroom life may, instead, pose many problems for teachers and govern what they are actually able to accomplish.

One specific stress in this tradition has concerned problems standing in the way of teachers' attaining a true professional status such as that enjoyed by doctors, lawyers, and religious leaders. Persons in these latter professions typically provide services to others, are self-employed, hold advanced academic degrees, set and police requirements for their fields, are presumed to possess "expert" knowledge, and are thought to be motivated by deep, moral commitments. Although good teachers certainly possess expert knowledge (Berliner, 1986), teachers typically do not meet all of these qualifications, hence teaching has sometimes been thought of as a "semiprofession" (Etzioni, 1969). But most teachers are also women, and the other "semiprofessions" identified by Etzioni are also largely staffed by women, so objections have been raised to this characterization. Be that as it may, powerful voices have also been raised recently urging greater professionalization for teachers (see, for example, the Holmes Group, 1986; Carnegie Forum on Education and the Economy, 1986).

Third, an enormous amount of descriptive research appears each year concerning the demographic characteristics of teachers, teacher salaries, and other educational finance issues, societal problems that afflict education, and the morale, plans, and achievements of teachers and students. In the United States, a good deal of this research is published by arms of the federal government such as the Bureau of the Census and the Office of Education, but other bits of it appear regularly from educational consortia, nonprofit research organizations, foundations, teachers' organizations and unions, and mass media sources. Similar government and nongovernment sources generate related information about teachers in other industrialized nations, and additional, related materials appear regularly from international sources such as UNESCO, the OECD, and the International Association for the Evaluation of Educational Achievement (IEA). Sources such as these provide invaluable information about the composition of the teacher corps, the supply of and demand for teachers, the conditions under which teachers work, measured student achievements, and other background details needed for better understanding of teachers and teaching.

Research on Teaching

A newer scholarly tradition reflects the recent, massive outpouring of observationally based research on classroom teaching (see Good and Brophy, 1973, 1997; Dunkin and Biddle, 1974; Anderson, 1995; Good, 1996). As various authors have noted, prior to the early 1960s few researchers had thought to look at the actual events of classrooms, but in subsequent years this picture has certainly been reversed. As a result, a great deal of evidence has now been collected about teacher behavior in classrooms—about teacher initiation, lecturing styles, differential treatment of students, language use, questioning techniques, modes of response to students' questions, strategies for controlling and disciplining students, methods for encouraging student self-directed learning, and a host of other issues concerning teacher classroom conduct—and about the forces that generate differences in teacher behaviors and how those behaviors, in turn, affect student thinking, conduct, and learning.

The bulk of this research has involved quantitative research strategies that employ formal methods of behavioral observation, the coding of classroom events, and the statistical analysis of event records. However, a number of insightful, qualitative studies of teaching have also surfaced (see, for example, Jackson, 1968;

Smith and Geoffrey, 1968; Meehan, 1979; Eder, 1981, in press; Brantlinger, 1993).

One major goal of this research effort, especially prior to the early 1980s, was to explore how variations in teaching behavior might be related to student learning—to study how teaching traits such as "warmth," "clarity," or "enthusiasm," adequate "wait time" for student responses, good classroom managerial skills, or appropriate instructional pace and content coverage might lead to greater student learning. Thus, it is not surprising that recent reviewers have begun to stress the substantial growth in understanding of relations between classroom teaching and measured student achievement (see, for example, Gage, 1991; Weinert and Helmke, 1995; Good and Brophy, 1997).

Another goal of this research effort has involved the desire to document and find ways to combat teacher discriminatory treatment of students depending on the student's race (Rist, 1973), gender (Delamont and Coffey, in press), and assumptions the teacher makes about student ability (Cooper and Good, 1983). And recently, research has begun to appear concerned with student mediation of teaching (see, for example, Pressley and Levine, 1983; McCaslin and Good, 1996). Early work on student mediation (Anderson, 1981; Weinstein, 1983; Rohrkemper and Corno, 1988) stimulated researchers to focus on subject-matter learning, often considered from a cognitive perspective, and this effort has now generated a new conception of instruction often referred to as "teaching for understanding." This conception argues that knowledge is constructed, that social processes are often involved in that construction, and that good teaching involves the gradual transfer of responsibility for managing learning from the teacher to the learner (Blumenfeld et al., in press).

Other Traditions

Although the traditions reviewed above have tended to dominate writings on teachers and teaching to date, other ways of thinking about the topic have also appeared.

One such tradition questions the traditional tasks of schooling. As suggested above, many portrayals of teachers have, in effect, assumed that the effects of education are largely focused on the tasks for which those schools were presumably established. In contrast, a contrarian literature has appeared that challenges this as-

sumption (for illustrations, see Bowles and Gintis, 1976; Wexler, 1992). This literature makes use of neo-Marxist insights and suggests that, whether they realize it or not, schools are often responsible for reproducing social class differences. They do this by encouraging students from working- and lower-class homes to entertain only modest aspirations and to train for laboring jobs, whereas the sons and daughters of affluent parents are encouraged to aspire to and achieve professional careers and positions associated with wealth and power. This literature often blames teachers for such outcomes, although a few authors (e.g., Willis, 1977) have also suggested that students, too, have "agency" and are partly responsible for their willing acceptance of social class differentiations.

Another scholarly vision has focused on role expectations that are held for teachers (see Biddle et al., 1961; Kelsall and Kelsall, 1969; Biddle, 1969, 1985, in press). Works representing this vision note that teachers are affected not only by the rights and responsibilities imposed on them because they are employed in schools, but also by the expectations that they and important others hold for teachers and teaching. Thus, teachers may be influenced not only by what the "rules and regulations" say, but also by their own opinions as well as by what the principal of their school, curriculum specialists, researchers, parents, school board members, union representatives, or other teachers think and say. Within this vision, the lives of teachers are thought to be affected by various sources of influence, and teachers are portrayed as thoughtful actors whose actions in the classroom and school reflect rational choices among alternatives conceived by the teacher and urged by others who are important in the educational scene.

In addition, in the past 15 years a number of valuable studies of the lives and professional work of teachers have been generated based on interviews and biographical materials (see Goodson, 1981, 1992; Spencer, 1986; Goodson and Hargreaves, 1996). This work has provided insights about entry into the teaching profession, stages of the teaching career, and long-term problems that are faced by teachers.

Finally, in the past two decades there has been a substantial flowering of conservative political thought, and this has provoked various attempts to restructure or reduce the scope of public education in Western nations. Many of these attempts have, in effect, scapegoated teachers or attempted to control teachers' activities through "reform" efforts featuring top-down managerial strategies, and this has provoked consternation, disruption, and loss of morale among teachers and other educators. A substantial literature commenting on these events has also begun to appear (see, for example, Aronowitz and Giroux, 1985; Berliner and Biddle, 1995).

Stability and Change

Given the importance of knowledge about teachers and teaching, one would think it highly important to establish which aspects of these phenomena are stable and which tend to shift depending on context and historic changes in the society. Unfortunately, only a few studies have taken on this challenge. Cuban (1984) suggests that the forms of classroom teaching have changed little over the past century, Sirotnik (1983) asserts that they are remarkably similar throughout the United States, and numerous authors have observed that similar classroom forms also tend to occur in other industrialized countries. On the other hand, comparative research suggests that the ways in which schooling is structured, the demographics of the teaching corps, and the tasks assigned to education vary substantially among Western nations (Lindblad, in press). And there can be no doubt that crucial aspects of teachers and teaching are now evolving in response to changes in American society (Darling-Hammond, 1990; Ball, in press). We need a lot more historical and comparative research to answer these crucial questions about teachers and teaching (for discussions of some of these issues, see various studies appearing in Biddle et al., in press).

REFERENCES

Anderson, L. 1981. "Short-Term Student Responses to Classroom Instruction." *Elementary School Journal* 82:97–108.
———. 1995. *International Encyclopedia of Teaching and Teacher Education,* 2nd ed. Oxford: Pergamon.
Aronowitz, S., and H. A. Giroux. 1985. *Education under Siege: The Conservative, Liberal, and Radical Debate over Schooling.* Boston: Bergin and Garvey.
Ball, D. L. In press. "What Do Students Know? Facing Challenges of Distance, Context, and Desire in Trying to Hear Children." In B. J. Biddle, T. L. Good, and I. F. Goodson (eds.), *International Handbook of Teachers and Teaching.* Dordrecht, The Netherlands: Kluwer.
Ballantine, J. H. 1989. *The Sociology of Education: A Systematic Analysis,* 2nd ed. Englewood Cliffs, NJ: Prentice-Hall.
Bank, B. J. In press. "Peer Cultures and Their Challenge for Teaching." In B. J. Biddle, T. L. Good, and I. F. Goodson (eds.), *International Handbook of Teachers and Teaching.* Dordrecht, The Netherlands: Kluwer.
Bennett, K. P., and M. D. LeCompte. 1990. *How Schools Work: A Sociological Analysis of Education.* New York: Longman.
Berliner, D. C. 1986. "In Pursuit of the Expert Pedagogue." *Educational Researcher* 15(7):5–13.
Berliner, D. C., and B. J. Biddle. 1995. *The Manufactured Crisis: Myths, Fraud, and the Attack on America's Public Schools.* New York: Addison-Wesley-Longman.
Biddle, B. J. 1969. "The Role of the Teacher." In R. L. Ebel (ed.), *Encyclopedia of Educational Research,* 4th ed. New York: Macmillan.
———. 1985. "Teacher Roles." In T. Husen and N. Postlethwaite (eds.), *International Encyclopedia of Education: Research and Studies,* pp. 5022–5032. Oxford: Pergamon.
———. In press. "Recent Research on the Role of the Teacher." In B. J. Biddle, T. L. Good, and I. F. Goodson (eds.), *International Handbook of Teachers and Teaching.* Dordrecht, The Netherlands: Kluwer.
Biddle, B. J., H. A. Rosencranz, and E. F. Rankin, Jr. 1961. *Studies in the Role of the Public School Teacher.* Columbia, MO: University of Missouri Press.
Biddle, B. J., T. L. Good, and I. F. Goodson. In press. *International Handbook of Teachers and Teaching.* Dordrecht, The Netherlands: Kluwer.
Bidwell, C. 1965. "The School as a Formal Organization." In J. G. March (ed.), *Handbook of Organizations,* pp. 994–1003. Chicago: Rand McNally.
Blumenfeld, P., R. Marx, H. Patrick, J. Krajcik, and E. Soloway. In press. "Teaching for Understanding." In B. J. Biddle, T. L. Good, and I. F. Goodson (eds.), *International Handbook of Teachers and Teaching.* Dordrecht, The Netherlands: Kluwer.
Bowles, H., and S. Gintis. 1976. *Schooling in Capitalist America.* New York: Basic Books.
Brantlinger, E. 1993. *The Politics of Social Class in Secondary School: Views of Affluent and Impoverished Youth.* New York: Teachers College Press.
Bryk, A. S., and M. E. Driscoll. 1988. *The School as Community: Theoretical Foundations, Contextual Influences, and Consequences for Students and Teachers.* Chicago; The University of Chicago Press.
Carnegie Forum on Education and the Economy. 1986. *A Nation Prepared: Teachers for the 21st Century—The Report of the Task Force on Teaching as a Profession.* New York: Author.
Coleman, J. S. 1961. *The Adolescent Society.* New York: The Free Press.
Cooper, H. M., and T. L. Good. 1983. *Pygmalion Grows Up: Studies in the Expectation Communication Process.* New York: Longman.

Cuban, L. 1984. *How Teachers Taught: Constancy and Change in American Classrooms, 1890–1980.* New York: Longman.

Darling-Hammond, L. 1990. "Teachers and Teaching: Signs of a Changing Profession." In R. Rouston, M. Haberman, and J. Sikula (eds.), *Handbook of Research on Teacher Education,* pp. 267–290. New York: Macmillan.

Delamont, S., and A. Coffey. In press. "Feminism and the Teacher's Work." In B. J. Biddle, T. L. Good, and I. F. Goodson (eds.), *International Handbook of Teachers and Teaching.* Dordrecht, The Netherlands: Kluwer.

Dougherty, K. J., and M. H. Floyd. 1990. *Education and Society: A Reader.* New York: Harcourt, Brace Jovanovich.

Dunkin, M. J., and B. J. Biddle. 1974. *The Study of Teaching.* New York: Holt, Rinehart & Winston.

Eder, D. 1981. "Ability Grouping as a Self-Fulfilling Prophesy: A Microanalysis of Teacher-Student Interaction." *Sociology of Education* 54:151–161.

———. In press. "Sexual Aggression within the School Culture." In B. J. Bank and P. M. Hall (eds.), *Gender Equity and Schooling.* New York: Garland.

Etzioni, A. 1969. *The Semi-Professions and Their Organization: Teachers, Nurses, Social Workers.* New York: The Free Press.

Gage, N. 1991. "The Obviousness of Social and Educational Research Results." *Educational Researcher* 20(1):10–16.

Good, T. L. 1996. "Teaching Effects and Teacher Evaluation." In J. Sikula, T. Buttery, and E. Guyton (eds.), *Handbook of Research on Teacher Education,* 2nd ed., pp. 617–665. New York: Macmillan.

Good, T. L., and J. Brophy. 1973. *Looking in Classrooms.* New York: Harper & Row.

———. 1997. *Looking in Classrooms,* 7th ed. New York: Longman.

Goodson, I. F. 1981. "Life History and the Study of Schooling." *Interchange (Ontario Institute for Studies in Education)* 11(4):62–76.

———. 1992. *Studying Teachers' Lives.* London: Routledge.

Goodson, I. F., and A. Hargreaves, eds. 1996. *Teachers' Professional Lives.* London: Falmer Press.

Hallinan, M. T. 1996. "Race Effects on Students' Track Mobility in High School." *Social Psychology of Education* 1:1–24.

Holmes Group, The. 1986. *Tomorrow's Teachers: A Report of the Holmes Group.* East Lansing, MI: Author.

Jackson, P. W. 1968. *Life in Classrooms.* New York: Holt, Rinehart & Winston.

Katz, F. E. 1964. "The School as a Social Organization." *Harvard Educational Review* 34:428–455.

Kelsall, R. K., and H. M. Kelsall. 1969. *The School Teacher in England and the United States.* Oxford: Pergamon.

Lindblad, S. In press. "Towards a Social Understanding of Teachers: Swedish Positions and Experiences." In B. J. Biddle, T. L. Good, and I. F. Goodson (eds.), *International*

Handbook of Teachers and Teaching. Dordrecht, The Netherlands: Kluwer.

Lortie, D. 1975. *Schoolteacher.* Chicago: University of Chicago Press.

McCaslin, M., and T. L. Good. 1996. *Listening in Classrooms.* New York: Harper Collins.

Mehan, H. 1979. *Learning Lessons: Social Organization in the Classroom.* Cambridge, MA: Harvard University Press.

Natriello, G. In press. "Conditions in American Schools." *Educational Researcher.*

Oakes, J. 1985. *Keeping Track: How Schools Structure Inequality.* New Haven: Yale University Press.

———. 1990. "Opportunities, Achievement and Choice: Women and Minority Students in Science and Mathematics." *Review of Research in Education* 16:153–222.

Pressley, M., and J. Levine, eds. 1983. *Cognitive Strategy Research: Educational Applications.* New York: Springer-Verlag.

Rist, R. C. 1973. *The Urban School: A Factory for Failure.* Cambridge, MA: MIT Press.

Rohrkemper, M., and L. Corno. 1988. "Success and Failure on Classroom Tasks: Adaptive Learning and Classroom Teaching." *Elementary School Journal* 88:297–312.

Sirotnik, K. A. 1983. "What You See Is What You Get: Consistency, Persistency, and Mediocrity in Classrooms." *Harvard Educational Review* 53:15–31.

Sizer, T. 1985. *Horace's Compromise: The Dilemma of the American High School.* Boston: Houghton Mifflin.

Smith, L. M., and W. Geoffrey. 1968. *The Complexities of an Urban Classroom: An Analysis toward a General Theory of Teaching.* New York: Holt, Rinehart & Winston.

Spencer, D. 1986. *Contemporary Women Teachers: Balancing School and Home.* New York: Longman.

———. In press. "Conditions of American Teachers." *Educational Researcher.*

Waller, W. W. 1932. *The Sociology of Teaching.* New York: Russell & Russell.

Weinert, F. E., and A. Helmke. 1995. "Interclassroom Differences in Instructional Quality and Interindividual Differences in Cognitive Development." *Educational Psychologist* 30(1):15–20.

Weinstein, R. 1982. "Students in Classrooms." *Elementary School Journal* 82:397–398.

Weinstein, R., C. Soule, F. Collins, J. Cone, M. Mehorn, and K. Simontacchik. 1991. "Expectations and High School Change: Teacher-Researcher Collaboration to Prevent School Failure." *American Journal of Community Psychology* 19:33–364.

Wexler, P. 1992. *Becoming Somebody: Toward a Social Psychology of School.* London: Falmer.

Willis, P. 1977. *Learning to Labour.* Farnborough: Saxon House.

TRACKING

Amanda Datnow
Ontario Institute for Studies in Education
University of Toronto

Robert Cooper
Johns Hopkins University

Tracking: A Century-Old Tradition

Tracking, almost universal in American schools for the past century, is the practice of sorting students into different programs of study based on their perceived academic ability. The term "tracking" is often used interchangeably with the terms "ability grouping," "homogeneous grouping," and "curriculum differentiation." However, these terms consistently imply some means of grouping students for instruction by ability or achievement so as to create instructional groups that are as homogeneous as possible. In elementary schools, the sorting of students encompasses both "between-class" grouping, in which students are assigned to separate classes based on perceived ability, and "within-class" grouping, in which smaller groups of students at similar performance levels work together in the same classroom. Ability grouping at the elementary level generally leads to tracking at the secondary level. Secondary schools vary in the number, size, and composition of tracks. However, students are generally assigned to a track level: basic, regular, college preparatory, or honors/advanced placement. Some have suggested that in recent years tracking has become more flexible, allowing students to take courses in various tracks (e.g., Hallinan, 1994).

Tracking emerged in response to the expansion of mass secondary schools, which created a school population that was increasingly diverse in social class and ethnic background. Tracking was seen as an efficient means of meeting the needs of all students. The assumption behind tracking was that grouping students with seemingly similar ability in the same classroom would allow schools to best accommodate the students' varying needs and goals. Students demonstrating high ability and goals for college could be separated from those with lower ability who were aspiring to vocational careers. This system was built upon the belief, held also by early sociologists of education, that schools fostered equal opportunity through a meritocratic system based on achievement. Schools were seen as rational sorting devices that ensured that the most important positions in society, which required the most intelligence and education, were filled by the most qualified individuals. Tracking was seen as the logical way to accomplish this sorting.

Many of the assumptions that gave rise to the creation of tracking almost a century ago continue to hold tracking in place today. Despite extensive research suggesting that track placement is influenced by race and social class biases, proponents believe that tracking is meritocratic. Furthermore, many educators strongly believe that students learn better in groups with other students like themselves. Some educators argue that bright students are held back when they are placed in mixed ability classes and the deficiencies of slow students are more easily remedied if they are placed in classes together (Kulik and Kulik, 1982). There is also the assumption that slower students will suffer less emotional distress and failure if they are not in classes with bright students. Additionally, many educators argue that homogeneous grouping reduces teachers' work loads because it allows them to tailor instruction to the common needs of the students in their classes.

In the past decade, the century-old educational practice of tracking has seriously been called into question, and extensive research has been done in this area. Sociologists of education have used both quantitative and qualitative research methods to study the following issues related to tracking: (1) the process of track placement, (2) the differences between tracks, and (3) the consequences of tracking.

Track Placement

Tracking begins as early as kindergarten, when students are placed into reading groups based upon their scores on a school "readiness" test or on the basis of teachers' informal observations of student behavior. What begins as relatively small aptitude differences among students grows gradually wider over time, exacerbated by ability grouping within elementary school classrooms. By middle school, track placement becomes relatively fixed, now legitimated by a student's prior achievement and standardized test scores. The track system then offers little opportunity for mobility. Track placements tend to be stable and long term, and the only movement that occurs is in the downward direction (Oakes, 1985).

The strongest and most disturbing finding about tracking is the consistent correlation among race, social class, and track placement. Studies consistently find that low-income and minority students are disproportionately placed in low-track classes, and advantaged and white students are more often placed in the high track (Braddock and Dawkins, 1993; Oakes, 1985). In high schools, low-income, African-American, and Latino students are underrepresented in college preparatory programs, and they are more frequently enrolled in vocational programs that train for low-paying, dead-end jobs. At all levels, minority students lack representation in programs for gifted and talented students.

The placement of a disproportionate number of low-income and minority students into low tracks is in some cases based on the cumulative effect of early ability grouping, but qualitative studies have shown that counselors and teachers are often biased against these students in track placement. Still others argue that these students "choose" low-track placement based on their own aspirations. Finally, Oakes and Guiton (1995), using case study data collected at three high schools, offer a more complex picture of track placement. They argue that decisions result from the synergy of three powerful factors: differentiated curriculum structures, school cultures alternatively committed to accommodating differences *and* common schooling, and the political actions of efficacious students and

their parents. This dynamic is not neutral, however; advantaged students benefit the most.

Although there are consistent patterns across schools, some studies have suggested that placement of students into tracks is dependent upon the logistical constraints of a school's master schedule, with some schools providing more flexibility across tracks and others less (Hallinan, 1994).

Differences between Tracks

A further outcome of tracking is the differential educational experience across tracks. These differences are most apparent in the areas of curriculum, instruction, teacher expectations, and teacher distribution. Both quantitative and qualitative studies have confirmed that low-track students consistently have lower quality experiences in each of these areas.

Students are exposed to different academic content depending on their track placement. The curriculum in college preparatory tracks is generally demanding and interesting, whereas the curriculum in general or vocational tracks tends to be a watered-down version in terms of scope and content. High-track students are more often presented with traditional academic topics and intellectually challenging skills. Students in high-ability tracks are exposed to a curriculum that surpasses that of the lower tracks in both quality and quantity (Oakes et al., 1992).

Instructional practices in high-track classes are characterized as more effective and students report involvement in positive, active learning interactions. Students in high-track classes report feeling that their teachers are supportive. On the other hand, students in low-track classes feel that their teachers are punitive. There are less active learning activities in the low-track classrooms and there is less student participation. Low-track classes are characterized by passive instruction, consisting largely of rote learning and worksheets. High-track classes typically include more complex material and more thinking and problem-solving tasks (Oakes, 1985). Observational data gathered in classrooms across 25 schools revealed that rates of student participation and discussion are much higher in high-track classes, contributing to the learning gap between groups (Gamoran et al., 1995).

Research shows that teachers have varying goals and expectations for students in different tracks. Teachers expect that high-track students become interested in the subject matter, acquire basic concepts and principles, and learn problem-solving techniques. These goals are typically seen as less important for low-track students, and teachers of low-ability classes tend to place less emphasis on subject-related curriculum goals. Page's (1991) case study of lower track classrooms has confirmed that these classrooms are characterized by discipline and control and chaos and conflict, and that not only are students in low-track classes being exposed to less material, but they are also being socialized to accept their place at the bottom of the social hierarchy.

Most secondary schools track teachers as well as students, although some schools evenly distribute the teaching of low- and high-ability classes from year to year. The more qualified and more experienced teachers are generally found in the high tracks, and the opportunity to teach advanced classes is part of the reward system used by principals. This means that teachers in the lower tracks usually have less experience and are not as well qualified. Low-track students are frequently taught math and science by teachers who are not certified to teach those subjects, and high-track students are more likely to be taught by teachers who are subject certified and hold advanced degrees (Oakes et al., 1992).

The Consequences of Tracking

Tracking has long-term academic, emotional, and social consequences. There is extensive evidence that tracking greatly influences academic achievement, self-esteem, educational aspirations, post-high school options, and peer associations.

The Impact of Tracking on Academic Achievement

The research on the impact of tracking on academic achievement is fairly consistent, showing that tracking has a negative effect on low-track students. However, research on the impact of tracking for high-track students is less consistent. In a meta-analysis of various studies, Kulik and Kulik (1982) found that gifted and talented students benefit from tracking. In contrast, Slavin (1990) argues that the benefits that high-ability track students experience are not related to the fact that they are grouped together; they actually perform just

as well in a heterogeneous setting. In fact, Slavin's meta-analysis of research studies comparing heterogeneous and homogeneous secondary school classes found that no group of students received academic benefits by virtue of being in tracked classes.

Several studies have shown that the impact of tracking on academic achievement varies according to the structural characteristics of individual school tracking systems (Gamoran, 1992; Hallinan, 1994). Using data from High School and Beyond, a national survey of students and schools, Gamoran (1992) found that schools with more mobility in their tracking system had higher math achievement overall and smaller gaps in math and verbal achievement between tracks, when compared to more rigid systems. Using longitudinal survey and achievement data collected in several schools, Hallinan (1994) concluded that track effects on achievement are stronger in some schools than others, but that assignment to a higher track generally increased rate of learning.

The Impact of Tracking on Aspirations and Post-High School Options

Research has shown that tracking is a mediating mechanism in the link between education and career success. Using data from the National Educational Longitudinal Survey of 1988, Braddock and Dawkins (1993) found that across racial groups, students in the high-track math classes were much more likely to express plans for college entrance than those in the low-track math classes. Independent of student background and achievement, tracking affects students' educational aspirations such that low-track students have low aspirations and high-track students have high aspirations.

Even if they do aspire to attend college, the reality is that low-track students seldom graduate from high school with the requirements or skills necessary for college entrance. Using longitudinal survey data, Gamoran (1987) found that college preparatory track students take three to five times as many advanced courses in math and science than non-college preparatory track students. As a result of curriculum differentiation, at the end of high school, high-track students are prepared to attend college, whereas low-track students face much more limited options. Students enrolled in vocational courses seldom acquire the job skills necessary for success in the workplace.

The Emotional Impact of Low Track Placement

In addition to affecting academic achievement and post-high school options, track placement also affects students' self-esteem. Students in low tracks often suffer the stigmatizing consequences of negative labeling. The names or labels given to various groups, classes, or tracks are used to publicly identify the abilities and performances of the students in them. Teachers often quickly identify students in terms of their track labels and treat students accordingly. Students are even defined by their peers in terms of track placement. Not surprisingly, over time, students in the low tracks internalize their labels and level their aspirations accordingly (Oakes, 1985).

The Social Impact of Tracking

Tracking not only leads to inequitable learning opportunities, but it also limits opportunities for cross-cultural social interaction. Tracking creates unequal status realities between groups of students and has a strong negative impact on relationships across ethnic lines. For many children, their first encounter with peers of different racial and ethnic backgrounds is in school. Students tend to choose friends from within their own academic track, suggesting that the classroom is the place that facilitates interactions for the formation of social networks. Even in some of the most racially diverse schools across the country, the vast majority of students "hang out" with students of their same racial or ethnic group, who are also in their same track. The lack of contact between students of diverse backgrounds enables harsh stereotypes and racial tensions to be perpetuated (Hallinan and Williams, 1989).

In sum, research has consistently shown that when schools track, students from different racial groups are not offered equal opportunities to learn (Oakes, 1985; Oakes et al., 1992). African-American and Latino students, who are disproportionately placed in low-track classes, systematically receive fewer resources: teachers are less qualified, expectations are lower, the curriculum is watered down, and there are fewer classroom materials. White students, who are disproportionately placed in the high track, are advantaged by receiving more qualified teachers, greater classroom resources, and an enriched curriculum designed to prepare them to attend college (Oakes et al., 1992). As a result, tracking leads to class- and race-linked differences in op-

portunities to learn and gaps in achievement between white students and their minority peers. Additionally, because tracking in racially mixed schools resegregates students, it constrains intergroup relations and perpetuates stereotypes related to race (Oakes and Wells, 1995).

Overall, the research indicates that "tracking is one of the most divisive and damaging school practices in existence" (Turning Points). Because of tracking practices, educational institutions, like the communities in which they are embedded, sort individuals by race, social class, language, and ability. Tracking serves as the major vehicle to sort and institutionalize the division between the "haves" and "have-nots," resulting in racially identifiable groups of students, with African-American, Latino, and low-income students receiving an unequal distribution of educational access and opportunity.

Detracking: An Issue for Further Sociological Inquiry

Despite robust findings of the negative effects of tracking, it is still widely practiced in American schools. Although it may be easy from reviewing the research to conclude that tracking should be reduced or eliminated, it is much harder to make this a reality. First, there are practical issues involved with reorganizing schools and revamping curriculum and instruction. Second, tracking is held in place by a belief that the American educational system is meritocratic. And finally, there are strong constituencies supporting tracking because they believe gifted and talented students will lose out in a detracked system.

Oakes and Lipton (1992) offer some early lessons from the field about what might make detracking work successfully. First, because tracking coexists with many problematic school practices, detracking must be part of a larger plan to change the curriculum and instructional practices at the school. Although new technologies and organizational arrangements are necessary for detracking, they must make sense to the educators expected to implement them. Creating a culture of detracking is more important than any particular technical alternative a school might attempt. Oakes and Lipton (1992) suggest that teachers must engage in a process of inquiry in which they challenge the norms that surround the firmly embedded practice of tracking. This inquiry process must be voluntary, characterized by open communication, reflection, and experimentation.

Redistributive policies such as detracking are thus likely to make those who benefit from a privileged position in the status quo rather uneasy. Because tracking is often sustained by political interests, detracking will require new political arrangements among educators, community members, and policymakers. Naturally, creating new arrangements may be a source of conflict. The political leadership of educators is essential to forging these new arrangements. Detracking also requires a scaffolding of support from institutions at the state and local level. Without the removal of barriers at these levels, efforts at the school level will be stunted (Oakes and Lipton, 1992).

Although a number of schools have been exploring alternatives to tracking in recent years, few studies of detracking have been completed to date. The studies that have been conducted focus on either *small-scale* untracking programs that do not encompass an entire school, or the *process* of detracking.

Several studies of efforts to "untrack" groups of students in schools have proven these programs to be successful. Blending quantitative outcome data with rich ethnographic description in a study of an untracking program in 17 schools, Mehan and his colleagues (1996) concluded that untracking previously low-achieving minority students by placing them into college preparatory classes led to high college enrollment rates among "untracked" students. Especially important in this program were the institutional "scaffolds" that allowed students to learn the hidden curriculum of school success. Although the findings of such small-scale untracking programs are promising, these programs still exist within the context of a larger tracking system in the school.

We are beginning to learn more about what happens when schools attempt full-scale detracking. Wheelock (1992) offers vignettes, including examples of programs and practices, from schools around the country that are implementing alternatives to tracking. Oakes and Wells (1996) have recently completed a longitudinal case study of 10 racially detracking mixed schools. This study offers the most comprehensive assessment of what happens when schools undertake detracking.

All of the schools in the Oakes and Wells (1996) study undertook efforts to reduce and/or eliminate basic and remedial courses and most provided more students access to high level classes. In numerous cases, the educators in these schools found that detracking enabled them to improve the quality of student work and ameliorate racial tension among students (see also Cooper, 1996). However, none of the schools were able to achieve the degree of detracking that the proponents for reform had initially sought. Detracking reforms were challenged and compromised by powerful norms and politics around race and social class, and to some extent, language and gender. Pressure from powerful, white and wealthy parents forced many schools to maintain some separate, elite classrooms (Oakes et al., 1997). This allowed the hierarchical track structure to persist, leading to continued unequal expectations for students of color and their white counterparts.

Oakes and Wells (1997) conclude that efforts to dismantle tracking will require a deep dialogue about equity at the school-community level as well as at the university level, so as to challenge the norms and politics that hold tracking in place. Technical changes to schools' tracking structures will otherwise prove ineffectual. Given the research findings on the complexity of detracking and the persistent negative effects of tracking, further study on alternatives to tracking is certainly warranted.

REFERENCES

Braddock, Jomills H., and Marvin P. Dawkins. 1993. "Ability Grouping, Aspirations, and Attainments: Evidence from the National Educational Longitudinal Study of 1988." *Journal of Negro Education* 62:324–336.

Cooper, Robert. 1996. "Detracking Reform in an Urban California High School: Improving the Schooling Experiences of African American Students." *Journal of Negro Education* 65:190–208.

Gamoran, Adam. 1987. "The Stratification of High School Learning Opportunities." *Sociology of Education* 60:135–155.

———. 1992. "The Variable Effects of High School Tracking." *American Sociological Review* 57:812–828.

Gamoran, Adam, Martin Nystrand, Mark Berends, and Paul LePore. 1995. "An Organizational Analysis of the Effects of Ability Grouping." *American Educational Research Journal* 32:687–715.

Hallinan, Maureen. 1994. "School Differences in Tracking Effects on Achievement." *Social Forces* 72:799–820.

Hallinan, Maureen, and R. Williams. 1989. "Interracial

Friendship Choices in Secondary Schools." *American Sociological Review* 54:67–78.

Kulik, Chen-Lin C., and James A. Kulik. 1982. "Effects of Ability Grouping on Secondary School Students: A Meta-Analysis of the Evaluation Findings." *American Education Research Journal* 19:415–428.

Mehan, Hugh, Irene Villanueva, Lea Hubbard, and Angela Lintz. 1996. *Constructing School Success: The Consequences of Untracking Low Achieving Students.* Cambridge: Cambridge University Press.

Oakes, Jeannie. 1985. *Keeping Track: How Schools Structure Inequality.* New Haven, CT: Yale University Press.

Oakes, Jeannie, and Gretchen Guiton. 1995. "Matchmaking: The Dynamics of High School Tracking Decisions." *American Educational Research Journal* 32:3–33.

Oakes, Jeannie, and Martin Lipton. 1992. "Detracking Schools: Early Lessons from the Field." *Phi Delta Kappan* 73:448–454.

Oakes, Jeannie, and Amy Stuart Wells. 1996. *Beyond the Technicalities of School Reform: Policy Lessons from Detracking Schools.* Los Angeles: UCLA.

Oakes, Jeannie, Adam Gamoran, and Reba Page. 1992. "Curriculum Differentiation: Opportunities, Outcomes, and Meanings." In Philip W. Jackson (ed.), *Handbook of Research on Curriculum,* pp. 570–608. New York: Macmillan.

Oakes, Jeannie, Amy Stuart Wells, Makeba Jones, and Amanda Datnow. 1997. "Detracking: The Social Construction of Ability, Cultural Politics, and Resistance to Reform." *Teachers College Record* 98:482–510.

Page, Reba N. 1991. *Lower Track Classrooms: A Curricular and Cultural Perspective.* New York: Teachers College Press.

Slavin, Robert E. 1990. "Achievement Effects of Ability Grouping in Secondary Schools: A Best Evidence Synthesis." *Review of Educational Research* 60:471–499.

Wheelock, Anne. 1992. *Crossing the Tracks: How Untracking Can Save America's Schools.* New York: New Press.

Urban Schools

Julia Gwynne
University of Chicago

In 1842 Horace Mann, one of the leading educational reformists of the nineteenth century, wrote in his Fifth Annual Report as Secretary of the Massachusetts Board of Education the following: "Education, then beyond all other devices of human origin, is the great equalizer of the conditions of men—the balance wheel of the social machinery. . . . It does better than to disarm the poor of their hostility toward the rich; it prevents being poor" (Mann in Katz, 1971). Mann had a unique vision regarding the power of schooling. He wrote during a period when the face of America was rapidly changing: the Industrial Revolution had arrived from England and factory systems were springing up throughout the major urban areas. Subsequently, vast numbers of immigrants were arriving daily in search of employment and a better life. Concerned about the growing economic divisions between the rich and poor especially apparent in urban areas, Mann fought for the implementation of a new type of school system: one that would be tax supported, nonsectarian, and available to all children. He saw the common school as a sort of "leveling" mechanism, in which children of diverse backgrounds would come together to be educated and through which equality of opportunity for all would be ensured.

Mann eventually won his struggle and the first publicly funded school was established in Lexington, MA in 1839. Yet more than 150 years after Mann sought to implement a mechanism for ensuring equality of opportunity, it is apparent that Mann's vision has in fact never been fully realized. This is most evident from an analysis of the educational experiences of those students attending inner city urban schools. Increasingly, inner city youth are less likely than their peers attending suburban schools to receive an adequate education.

The most startling difference lies in the number of students quitting school without a high school diploma. A New York City cohort analysis for the class of 1991 revealed that after 4 years of high school, 35.3% of the class had graduated and 3.6% had obtained their High School Equivalency Diploma, 17.2% had dropped out, and 16% had transferred out of the district. Although 27.8% were still enrolled, previous cohort analyses have indicated that typically less than half of those still enrolled will ever graduate (The University of the State of New York/The State Education Department, 1993). Of those students who dropped out of school, an overwhelming percentage are minorities: 22.5% were Hispanic and 17.9% were black. White students comprised 11.6% of the drop outs. Although the rest of the State of New York has not yet initiated such detailed cohort analyses, a comparison of annual dropout rates reveals that students who attend schools in New York City dropout at a rate that is almost three times as great as students in the rest of the state: in 1991 the public school annual dropout rate was 7.1% for New York City and 2.5% for the rest of the state.

Equally as dire are the situations of those students who *do* graduate yet are not adequately prepared by their high school experiences. In his recent book on City College (a school that historically draws its student population from New York City), James Traub recounts some of the deplorable high school educations experienced by current City students, such as that of one student who had completed 4 years of high school in the Bronx without ever reading a book. In a comparison of the college experiences of students graduating from New York City public schools to those of recent immigrants, Traub states, "it was the students who hadn't gone through the public school system, and hadn't grown up in New York, who seemed likeliest to make it" (Traub, 1994).

What happens within the walls of the urban public school that so often results in the "noneducation" of its students? To answer this question, it is necessary first to examine the environment in which urban schools and urban youth exist. Today, perhaps the most defining characteristics of central cities are high rates of poverty, racial/ethnic isolation, and extreme levels of social dislocation (violence, drugs, gangs, teenage pregnancies, etc.). And although urban areas have always exhibited these characteristics in greater percentages than their nonurban counterparts, within the past 20 years the presence of these three factors has become more intensified within the urban setting.

The relationships between racial/ethnic isolation, poverty, and social dislocation are extremely complex. Yet, in an effort to provide insight into the urban school setting, it is perhaps helpful to attempt a simplified relationship framed within an economic context. Historically, cities have always attracted diverse populations. Migrants from other parts of the country as well as immigrants from other parts of the world have flocked to cities in search of greater employment and economic opportunities. At the turn of the century when urban areas were increasingly becoming industrial centers, cities witnessed huge influxes of immigrants from Eastern Europe, and to a lesser degree from Asia as well; later, beginning in the 1920s, blacks from the South also began migrating northward in search of better jobs. However, beginning in the late 1960s and continuing through the 1970s and 1980s, the employment opportunities that cities had historically been able to offer began to change significantly. Industrial and manufacturing jobs left the city in increasing numbers, as corporations and businesses sought locations elsewhere in which labor could be purchased more cheaply. Many middle-class workers, of which the majority were white, concurrently left the city, either following their jobs to other locations or pursuing different employment opportunities elsewhere (Wilson, 1987).

Some of the void created by the departure of industrial and manufacturing businesses was filled by a growth in the service sector industry—government, sales, food service, etc. Yet this change in the employment base of cities has had a profound economic impact on cities, resulting in increasing levels of poverty. The working class, traditionally employed in factories, was not qualified for many of the new service sector positions that required high levels of educational attainment; thus, they were forced either into unemployment or low-skills, low-wage service positions. The combined factors of a shrinking middle class and substantially reduced wages for the working class have resulted in high levels of poverty within the inner city. Although the number of people living in poverty in the United States increased from 24.1 million (12.1% of the population) in 1969 to 34.4 million (15% of the population) in 1982, the bulk of this increase was primarily born by those residing within metropolitan areas and specifically in central cities. The number of poor people residing in metropolitan areas rose from 13.1 million in 1969 (9.5% of the metropolitan population) to 21.2 million in 1982 (13.6% of the metropolitan population). However, upon examining only those residents of central cities, the situation looks even bleaker. From 1969 to 1982 the number of central-city residents living in poverty increased from 8 million (12.7% of the population) to 12.7 million (19.9% of the population) (Wilson, 1987).

Living in poverty has a tremendous psychological impact. To ensure both mental and physical survival, the poor sometimes resort to activities in which under normal circumstances they would not engage. Although crime and involvement in the drug industry are considered socially unacceptable, ultimately they generate a source of income that might not otherwise be available. Furthermore, studies indicate that other socially unacceptable activities such as teenage pregnancies and involvement in gangs can be considered as efforts by the young to achieve status and self-esteem, qualities of which they have been deprived as a result of living in poverty (Anderson, 1990). Certainly, not everyone living under the pressures of poverty engages in such activities; yet it cannot be denied that examples of social dislocation occur at much higher levels within urban areas than within suburban areas.

With this historical context in mind, it is important to take a closer look at how these characteristics are actually represented within an urban student population. In 1992, the racial/ethnic composition of New York City public schools was as follows: black/non-Hispanic (37.3%), Hispanic (35.7%), white/non-Hispanic (18.0%), and American Indian/Alaskan Native/Asian/Pacific Islander (9.0%). This provides a stark contrast to the racial/ethnic composition of public schools on a statewide basis: white/non-Hispanic (59.9%), black/non-Hispanic (19.8%), Hispanic (15.6%), and American Indian/Alaskan Native/Asian/Pacific Islander (4.7%). Students demonstrating limited-English proficiency comprised 14.1% of the New York City public schools and 6% of the public schools on a state-wide level. In terms of poverty levels, approximately 45% of New York City students attended schools in which there was a high concentration of poverty. On a state-wide level, 3% of students in suburban areas and 7% of students in rural areas attended schools with concentrated poverty (The University of the State of New York/The State Education Department, 1993).

Statistics cannot accurately portray the types of experiences lived by inner city students outside of school; however, Samuel Freedman's book *Small Victories* (1991) provides an excellent journalistic account of the lives of students attending Seward Park High School, located on the lower east side of New York City and serving predominantly immigrant and low-income students. Freedman writes poignantly about one student who lives in a welfare motel, of another who lives in a homeless shelter, and of many who live in crowded, dirty, drug-infested public housing apartments. He recounts the experiences of one student who watched all of his friends become consumed by the drug industry and the experiences of another whose friend was brutally murdered by gang members. Freedman clearly portrays the fact that living in the inner city in poverty-ridden neighborhoods has a tremendous impact on the lives and school experiences of these students.

In terms of academic achievement, a comparison between the performance level of New York City (NYC) students on Regents Competency Tests (RCT, state-mandated standardized tests) and the performance level of students in the rest of New York State provides insight into the gap in educational attainment that exists between the two groups. In 1992, 84% of NYC students passed the RCT Reading exam, compared to a pass rate of 95% for the rest of the state. The pass rate for the RCT Writing exam was 75% for NYC students and 91% for the rest of the state. In mathematics, only 57% of NYC students passed, compared to 91% for the rest of New York State (The University of the State of New York/The State Education Department, 1993).

Thus, we see that students who attend inner city schools are more likely to be minorities from low-

socioeconomic backgrounds, living under stressful circumstances, and more "at risk" of experiencing significant academic failure. Yet, what is the actual relationship between one's life experiences and one's academic experiences? Does one's personal background predetermine one's educational achievement or is the relationship more complex? These questions are ones with which educational researchers have struggled over the course of several decades, and the different ways in which they have been answered have had a significant impact not only on students and schools, but also on the attempts to reform schools so that student achievement will be increased.

Explanations of Educational Inequality: Student-Centered Approaches

The early researchers who attempted to explain why poor and minority students perform poorly in school can generally be categorized into two main camps: those who favor student-centered variables as the primary factor determining educational achievement and those who favor school-centered variables as the primary determinants. Advocates of the primacy of student-centered variables essentially believe it is those qualities that students bring with them to school that determines whether they will succeed there. There are several different manifestations of the student-centered explanation, each with its own policy implications. Perhaps the most controversial points to genetic factors as an explanation for unequal educational outcomes between groups. First put forward by Arthur Jensen in the late 1960s and then receiving renewed support from Charles Murray in 1994, genetic explanations basically state that some groups, specifically minorities, do poorly in school because they are genetically less intelligent than other groups, such as whites. Jensen's argument was based primarily on the work of Heber, who, comparing the percentages of black and white children with IQs lower than 75 at various socioeconomic levels, demonstrated that at each level, there was a higher percentage of black children with IQs below 75 than white children. Jensen argued that "an IQ below 75 reflects more than a lack of cultural amenities" and therefore concluded that there must be a significant genetic component to intelligence (Jensen, 1969). Yet Jensen's work has been strongly criticized. Hurn, in a systematic response to the genetic argument, has illustrated that although there may be a genetic component to intelligence, there is also strong evidence indicating that social factors play a significant role in determining intelligence. Furthermore, Hurn as well as others have pointed out that a substantial portion of the difference between IQ scores for black and white children of similar socioeconomic backgrounds can be attributed to the cultural biases inherent in IQ test questions (Hurn, 1993).

Another manifestation of student-centered variables as an explanation for low academic achievement is derived from the cultural deprivation theory. This theory became widely espoused during the 1960s following the research of James Coleman, and it ultimately led to the implementation of various compensatory education programs. In 1966, Coleman published *Equality of Educational Opportunities* in which he demonstrated that the most significant factors contributing to academic achievement were not differences between schools, as previously thought, but differences among students. He noted that peer groups, family backgrounds, cultures, etc. had a very strong correlation with a student's high or low academic achievement. It is important to note, however, that Coleman did not reject outright the possibility that differences between schools might have an affect on student achievement; however, his early work strongly suggested that differences between students were the most important variables (Sadovnik et al., 1994:Chapter 8).

Prior to the publication of Coleman's work, it was widely believed that minorities and poor students exhibited lower levels of achievement than white, middle-class students because the schools they attended were inferior to the schools of white middle-class students. The general policy focus had been to provide additional funding to these inferior schools to bring them up to a level equal to that of schools found in white suburban neighborhoods. The publication of the Coleman report, however, turned the focus away from trying to improve these schools toward trying to determine which qualities of poor and minority students prohibited them from doing well in school. Furthermore, drawing on the work of Oscar Lewis in Mexico, who proposed that there was a specific "culture of poverty," researchers began to espouse the theory that these students lacked the skills to succeed in school because of their cultural backgrounds; the culture of the poor and of minorities was viewed as deprived of those re-

sources, both physical and attitudinal, that would provide them with the necessary tools to do well in school. For example, students from low-income or minority families were less likely to have magazines, books, and newspapers around their homes. Furthermore, these students were less likely to embody the values of hard work and the importance of school, the ability to delay gratification, etc., all of which are necessary to do well in school (Sadovnik et al., 1994:Chapter 9).

The espousal of the "cultural deprivation" theory had two primary impacts on policy initiatives attempting to address the problem of improving academic achievement among historically low achieving students. The first was that it targeted a specific age that would be most appropriate for outside intervention: educational researchers focused on the preschool years as the most critical time for an intervention program aimed at reversing the supposed inadequacies of the child's environment. The second impact was the substantial increase in the number of "compensatory education" programs supported by the federal government and designed to instill typical middle-class values in poor and minority populations. "If the disadvantaged were deprived of a culture, they would be supplied with a middle class one" (Natriello et al., 1990).

Head Start is probably the best known compensatory education program. It was first begun in 1965 and held a wide scope for its mission, seeking to improve and enhance all of the basic areas in a child's life: cognitive skills, physical health, socioemotional development, family involvement in the child's life, etc. The actual success of Head Start programs in achieving their goals has been widely debated, with many of the early program assessments indicating that these programs were not achieving their goals. However, today the general conclusions regarding these programs is that although they have become increasingly effective in preparing preschoolers for the transition into school life, their impact on cognitive as well as affective development is rather limited. Differences between students who have participated in Head Start programs and those who have not tend to disappear by second or third grade, thereby failing to produce any long-term effects on its participants in terms of academic achievement (Natriello et al., 1990). Although there have been other, local versions of Head Start programs, such as the High/Scope Perry Preschool Program and the Bereiter-Englemann Academic Preschool Program, which have produced more impressive immediate results in academic achievement (as compared to Head Start), the participants in these programs also fail to demonstrate long-term gains in cognitive skills after several years of elementary school.

Although early intervention was one of the major goals for designers of compensatory programs, the fact that preschool programs were for the most part unable to produce long-term results pushed policymakers toward increasing funding for similar programs designed for elementary school aged children. Initiated in 1965, Title 1/Chapter 1 has subsequently become the largest compensatory program funded by the federal government. Funds are allocated based on the number of low-income students enrolled in a school district. Similar to Head Start, the goal of Title 1/Chapter 1 is to provide a means of compensating for the educational disadvantages that have been associated with poverty (Natriello et al., 1990). Funding has been used by districts in a variety of ways, such as hiring additional resource staff or developing special curricula to enhance cognitive skills, particularly in the areas of reading, writing, and mathematics.

Title 1/Chapter 1 programs have also received mixed reviews in terms of their ability to raise overall levels of academic achievement among low-income and minority students. Generally speaking, researchers agree that from 1975 on, Title 1/Chapter 1 programs have achieved some short-term results but, as is the case with Head Start, they demonstrate very little impact on academic achievement among "at-risk" students in the long term.

In examining both Head Start and Title 1/Chapter 1 programs, two of the most significant compensatory programs, there is a striking similarity between them: although both have achieved some short-term effects in improving cognitive ability, they offer little or no long-term benefits in terms of academic achievement. There are, of course, substantial differences in the ways in which Head Start programs and Title 1/Chapter 1 programs are administered, thereby making comparisons between the two difficult. Head Start programs are complete programs in and of themselves; on the other hand, Title 1/Chapter 1 programs are frequently either pull-out or add-on programs, and thus students participating in these programs only do so for a limited portion of the day and then return to regular classes for the rest of the day. However, these differences can

also provide an explanation for the lack of long-term gains for participating students and can shed light on the limitations of compensatory programs in general. Researchers have long suggested that a possible explanation for the fade-out phenomenon observed among Head Start students is the inability of elementary schools to fully capitalize on the cognitive gains achieved during the preschool years (Natriello et al., 1990). A similar analysis can be made of Title 1/Chapter 1 programs. With pull-out and add-on programs there is little coordination between the compensatory teacher and the regular teacher and thus regular instruction is not designed to profit from any gains made in specialized instructional programs. Ultimately, the weakness of compensatory programs lies in the fact that they tend to focus on only one-half of the equation: students. Schools are left virtually unchanged, with no consideration as to how their overall structure, organization, and methods might contribute to the lack of school success among low-income and minority students.

School-Centered Explanations

Although compensatory programs, designed to provide low-income and minority students with the requisite skills to succeed in school, were an outgrowth of the original work of Coleman, it is important to recall that although his early work emphasized the importance of student-centered variables over school-centered variables, he did not completely reject the idea that schools can impact student achievement. In fact, Coleman's later work, a study of public and private schools conducted during the 1980s, is somewhat of a reversal of his earlier findings. After closely analyzing schools and their approaches to educating their students, as well as the differences in academic performance between students in the same school, Coleman concluded that there are some very specific school-centered processes that can influence students' academic achievement (Sadovnik et al., 1994:Chapter 9).

Educational research during the 1980s expounded upon Coleman's findings and brought to light several important differences in the typical school experiences of "at-risk" students compared to their white, middle-class counterparts. For example, "at-risk" students are more likely to be "tracked" into less challenging classes such as vocational education or remedial courses, clearly limiting their chances of continuing their education by going on to college. These different course placements also frequently result in lowered teacher expectations for these students, which can have a dramatic impact on their overall academic achievement as well (Sadovnik et al., 1994).

The work of Basil Bernstein highlights another significant difference in the experiences of students from low socioeconomic backgrounds: they are more likely to attend schools that foster an authoritarian approach in which instruction is primarily teacher centered and learning becomes very much of a passive process for students. Middle-class, white students, on the other hand, are much more likely to attend schools in which the classroom environment is more student centered and the teacher actively elicits student participation and contribution to the lesson (Sadovnik et al., 1994).

Perhaps the most visible of these differences in the school experience of "at-risk" students is in the area of school funding. Because many states' school-funding formulas are determined by revenues generated from local property taxes, inner city schools are often subject to lower per-pupil expenditures than their suburban counterparts. In theory, the state attempts to compensate poorer districts by providing them with additional funds to ensure that their per-pupil expenditures are at an acceptable level. However, the result is rarely equivalent per-pupil expenditures between urban and suburban schools as the state typically defines the level of acceptable funding to be at a point well below that of suburban districts. In his book *Savage Inequalities*, Jonathan Kozol writes of the plight of inner city schools subjected to this institutionalized discrimination. Kozol describes how inner city schools are seldom able to attract the best, new teachers because they are often relegated to lower salary ranges. He also paints a vivid picture of the impact that lower per-pupil expenditures have on instructional materials. His book is replete with stories about urban schools that offer science classes but cannot afford laboratory equipment, English classes without enough textbooks for all students to have their own copy, and history classes that use books that cover material only through the 1970s (Kozol, 1991).

Shortages of funds also translate into fewer auxiliary staff, such as counselors, who can be vital resources for inner city youth frequently facing a variety of emotionally trying circumstances as a result of living in low-income, urban neighborhoods. Lack of funds can also result in a school's inability to maintain its physical plant in a desired manner. Whereas broken windows and peeling paint are often a common sight in urban schools, Kozol also describes some of the more extreme consequences due to a shortage of funds. In one school raw sewage periodically floods the halls because of old pipes that have not been adequately maintained over the years (Kozol, 1991).

Clearly, the school experiences of "at-risk" students can be dramatically different from their middle-class counterparts. Perhaps one of the most damaging aspects of the above mentioned school practices is the unspoken message that they send to "at-risk" students. Poor facilities, authoritarian environments, and lowered teacher expectations all give the implicit message that the education of these students is not a top priority. By law, schools are required to provide educational services to all students, but for those who may be the most challenging to educate for a variety of reasons, schools often follow the path of least resistance in order to comply with their responsibilities. Students understand this tactic only too well.

Apart from the psychological message that many of these practices impart, there are basic pedagogical problems as well. Teacher-centered classrooms that invoke little student participation are certainly not atmospheres that promote learning. Tracking has also been shown to have few educational benefits, whereas heterogeneous grouping has many more positive effects for both high and low achievers.

Toward a Synthesis

Upon closely examining the school experiences of "at-risk" students, it becomes clear that there are specific school-centered variables that do contribute to lowered academic achievement among these students. And yet, is the solution simply to reverse these patterns? Could we expect dramatic increases in the levels of achievement demonstrated by "at-risk" students simply as a result of equalizing school funding, creating less authoritarian environments, changing teachers' attitudes? It seems likely that we would witness some improvements occurring as the result of these reform measures, and yet it also seems likely these improvements would be limited in nature, much in the same way that compensatory programs foster improvement but only in a limited and short-term way. The problem is the same: by focusing only on school-centered variables, one-half of the equation has been ignored.

At this point, it seems clear that given the limitations of focusing reform efforts on either students or schools, the answer is found only when both sides are addressed. But how is that most effectively accomplished? In some ways, the cultural difference theory is a step in the right direction. Advocates of the cultural difference theory believe that "at-risk" youth generally have a cultural background that is quite different from the average white middle-class culture. Therefore, "working class and nonwhite students may indeed arrive at school with different cultural dispositions and without the skills and attitudes required by schools" (Sadovnik et al., 1994). However, cultural difference theorists differ from advocates of cultural deprivation in that they recognize the validity of different cultures. Furthermore, they understand that in large part, working class and nonwhite students have had to develop certain dispositions as strategies for survival within their environment where they face poverty, racism, and discrimination on a daily basis. But because schools are often designed to reflect a white, middle-class culture, there is, in essence, a cultural clash between working class, nonwhite students and their schools, which often results in low academic achievement or in their dropping out. The work of John Ogbu suggests that for black students to succeed in school, they must suppress their own cultural identities and take on the dominant culture of their school. Very few are willing to do this for fear of being labeled as "acting white." Ogbu's work has been influential in supporting the move to a more multicultural curriculum and approach, in an attempt to infuse a greater relevance into the studies of "at-risk" students.

Although the cultural difference theory in general, and Ogbu's work in particular, brings us closer to the point of framing the problem in terms of both student- and school-centered variables, it does not quite take us all the way in providing solutions. In his essay "Empowering Minority Students: A Framework for Intervention," Jim Cummins provides us with what may be considered part of the missing link. He writes that

the major reason previous attempts at educational reform have been unsuccessful is that the relationships between teachers and students and be-

tween schools and communities have remained essentially unchanged. The required changes involve personal redefinitions of the way classroom teachers interact with the children and communities they serve. In other words, legislative and policy reforms may be necessary conditions for effective change, but they are not sufficient. Implementation of change is dependent upon the extent to which educators, both collectively and individually, redefine their roles with respect to minority students and communities (Cummins, 1993).

Cummins is arguing that unless change occurs on that most basic of levels, the level on which student and teacher interact, all reforms will eventually prove to be ineffective. He states that schools in general, and teacher–student relationships specifically, represent society at large. In society we see the existence of a dominant group controlling the various institutions as well as the overall reward systems. The dominated group is considered inferior by those in control, and their access to positions of power are consistently blocked. Mirroring the larger society, school becomes a disempowering experience and a process that alters nothing in terms of future life chances for them.

In her poignant book *Framing Dropouts* Michelle Fine provides powerful insight into the power inequities that so often exist between teacher and student. Fascinated by the statistic that many urban public schools have dropout rates that range between 40% and 60%, Fine studied the manner by which an inner-city high school functions to "silence" the voices of many of its students, thereby alienating them from the educational process. In her study of a large comprehensive high school in New York City that predominantly serves students from low-income backgrounds, Fine found that the school systematically refused to address the social and economic inequalities that exist within our society and to which its students were exposed daily. The following classroom discussion exemplifies this process:

White teacher: What's EOE?
African-American male student: Equal over time.
White teacher: Not quite. Anyone else?
African-American female student: Equal Opportunity Employer.

Teacher: That's right.

African-American male student 2: What does that mean?

Teacher: That means that an employer can't discriminate on the basis of sex, age, marital status, or race.

African-American male student 2: But wait, sometimes white people only hire white people.

Teacher: No, they are not supposed to if they say EOE in their ads. Now take out your homework.

Later that day.

MF to teacher: Why don't you discuss racism in your class?

Teacher: It would demoralize the students, they need to feel positive and optimistic—like they have a chance. Racism is just an excuse they use not to try harder. (Fine, 1991)

Effectively, this teacher has refused to allow the realities of his students' lives to enter into the classroom discourse. Although he does solicit some input from students, ultimately he provides his own version of the "truth," one with which he is presumably more comfortable. Yet his actions succeed only in increasing the gap between what these students learn in school and what they experience in their lives, thereby resulting in many students viewing school as meaningless to their lives.

Both Fine and Cummins stress the importance of teachers and schools enabling the empowerment of "at-risk" students. Until they are able to help students find their own voice within the classrooms, as well as within the society at large, lack of school success among these students is guaranteed to continue.

Central Park East: An Example of School- and Student-Centered Reform

The importance of the student–teacher relationship is at the core of the philosophical approach of Central Park East Secondary School (CPESS), an innovative public high school serving predominately low-income Latino and African-American students in New York City's District 4 located in East Harlem. The school was begun in 1985, and in its 10-year history it has successfully demonstrated that traditional modes of schooling can be restructured to ensure academic success for all students, without sacrificing academic rigor. Central Park East Secondary School is part of the Center for Collaborative Education in New York City. The Center consists of elementary, middle, and high schools and is affiliated with the Coalition for Essential Schools. CPESS subscribes to the Coalition's twelve principles of education:

- Schools that are small and personalized in size.
- A unified course of study for all students.
- A focus on helping young people to use their minds well.
- An in-depth, intradisciplinary curriculum respectful of the diverse heritages that encompass our society.
- Active learning with student-as-worker/student-as-citizen and teacher-as-coach.
- Student evaluation by performance-based assessment methods.
- A school tone of unanxious expectation, trust, and decency.
- Family involvement, trust, and respect.
- Choice.
- Racial, ethnic, economic, and intellectual diversity.
- Budget allocations targeting time for collective planning.

CPESS was founded by Deborah Meier, an elementary school teacher, who had been instrumental in starting three elementary schools within District 4 during the 1970s and early 1980s. Meier and her colleagues sought to reverse the district's trend of its students having the lowest average standardized test scores out of 32 districts in the city. Their goal was to create a small school that embodied the concept of "personalized" education. Meier believed that for a teacher to fully facilitate a student's learning process, it was critical for that teacher to know and understand each student as an individual. Once a teacher had a solid understanding of each student's academic needs as well as capabilities, then the teacher could structure each student's learning process in a way that was most appropriate for that individual. Recognizing that student–teacher relationships take time to develop, the decision was made to allow students to remain with the same teacher for 2 years at a time. Additionally, Meier believed that the school structure and organization must facilitate the personalizing of each student's education as much as possible; this often translated into "the less the intrusion of school bureaucracy into the educational process, the better." Central to this commitment was the belief that for teachers to create the most effective learning environment for their students, they needed to be granted a high degree of autonomy, a quality that teachers rarely experience in traditional schools. At Central Park East elementary school it is the teachers who decide what they will teach, how it will be communicated, and which materials will be used to facilitate that process.

The impetus to start a high school came initially from the graduates of the CPE elementary schools. Former students repeatedly complained to Meier about their high school experiences within the walls of large, anonymous, comprehensive high schools. Teachers who were responsible for 150 to 180 students each day hardly had the chance to learn each student's name much less learn about their individual talents and needs. In 1984, armed with the commitment to rethink high school education, Meier and colleagues began the arduous task of assessing the manner by which traditional urban high schools so often fail to educate their students.

Surprisingly, the answers that they uncovered were fairly simple and closely related to the problems that they had sought to remedy within the elementary setting. Learning had increasingly become a passive, mindless, and fragmented activity with little connection to the real world. Meier writes, "Do you change supervisors every 40 minutes in the real world? we asked. Not to mention job tasks or team members? In what real world job is the sequence of tasks (classes) so unconnected to the larger product? What college student attends eight lecture courses a day running back to back with only one breather?" (Meier, 1994).

In 1985 Central Park East Secondary School opened its doors to 80 seventh graders; today it serves a population of 450 students enrolled in grades 7 through 12. Much of what Meier learned from the CPE elementary schools, such as the importance of personalized education and teacher autonomy, were immediately implemented at CPESS. Structurally, the design was made simple so that students and teachers could focus on more important issues, namely learning. The school is organized into three divisions with approximately 150 students and 8 or 9 teachers in each. Division I represents the equivalent of grades 7 and 8, and Division II the equivalent of grades 9 and 10. The third division is the Senior Institute. Most students spend 2 years in each division; yet some will spend longer in the Senior Institute to ensure that they are adequately prepared for life after high school.

As a means of facilitating a deeper understanding of the relationship that exists between different realms of knowledge, classes are taught in an interdisciplinary manner; students spend 2 hours a day in humanities (literature, history, art, and social studies) and 2 hours a day in math/science. An additional hour each day is devoted to advisory, in which each staff member (including administrators) is responsible for meeting with a group of 15 students. The time can be spent in a variety of ways, such as small group tutorials or study hall. Yet often the advisory group meeting is spent discussing issues that touch the lives of the students, such as racism. Furthermore, if a student is experiencing difficulties at school, either academic or personal, the advisor works closely with that student to sort through and resolve the issue. Each advisor is also responsible for acting as a liaison to the parents, keeping them regularly updated on their child's progress at school.

Much of the schooling that occurs today does so in a rapid fire manner in which great emphasis is placed on covering the most amount of material in the shortest amount of time; yet CPESS' organizational structure and pedagogical approaches have effectively slowed down this process, allowing students the time to explore knowledge in a more in-depth manner. Although the organizational structure and pedagogical approaches implemented by the CPESS staff may cast an innovative light on the school, it is important to remember it is what occurs within these frameworks, rather than the frameworks themselves, that makes CPESS a special place. Meier states that schools must become places that inspire "a passion for learning" among students. All students, regardless of their background, need to be able to see a bridge between their own education and the world outside. For students from middle-class backgrounds, this connection may be an obvious one. For others, such as the students attending CPESS whose lives have been filled with the injustices inherent in our society, the connection is less clear. Thus, much of the staff's time is spent creating an educational environment that actively engages students in the learning process. Classes tend to be small and discussions are generated from students' thoughts and ideas. At CPESS teachers believe their role is to act as a sort of coach, guiding students along paths on which they can acquire the skills necessary to explore, penetrate, and ultimately make connections: connections between what is learned in books and what occurs in real life and connections between how knowledge of one can facilitate understanding as well as impacting the other. For example, understanding the role that demonstrations have historically played in ensuring America's democracy is greatly facilitated by being given the opportunity to organize a march on City Hall protesting the treatment of Rodney King.

Knowledge is power, yet so many urban kids are denied access to that power. However, at the Central Park East elementary and secondary schools, the structural changes combined with the staff's unwavering commitment to the belief that all students are intellectuals have created an environment in which kids who might have fallen through the cracks in a traditional setting are succeeding in school. In a city in which the dropout rate approaches 50%, Central Park East Secondary School breaks the mold. As of 1991 less than 5% of the students who start CPESS in ninth grade drop out of school before graduation. Furthermore, 90% of all CPESS graduates continue on to college.

In Central Park East Secondary School we find an extraordinary example of a school that has engaged in a thoughtful assessment of its students as well as their educational needs. Perhaps even more importantly, the staff at CPESS has taken the knowledge gained from that assessment and used it to restructure the manner in which it educates those students. CPESS and its staff have recognized the talent and intellect that each of its students holds, while simultaneously recognizing that school has not always been an environment that fosters the growth and development of these qualities. For many inner city youth, school has become a disempowering experience much like what they experience living in our society. Yet CPESS has purposefully and systematically broken down the barriers within its walls and provided a comfortable yet demanding space in which students can explore and develop to their fullest potential. Effectively, CPESS has addressed both student-related variables and school-related deficiencies and as a result is able to provide a remarkable educational experience.

Yet, it is at this point that we must ask the question:

"What sort of implications do schools such as CPESS have for urban education today?" Does school restructuring provide the means by which urban educators can bridge the educational gap between low-income, minority students and white, middle-class students? Certainly the manner in which the schooling process has been rethought at CPESS has had a significant impact on the educational experiences of its students, as indicated both by the school's low dropout rate as well as its high college attendance rate. Yet even CPESS continues to see the impact of students' background on academic achievement. "Our SAT [Scholastic Aptitude Test] scores came in. Half above 790, half below. Once again they are largely a measure of the social class of our students. Plus race." Of course, convincing arguments can and have been made regarding the fact that the design of the SAT is geared to measure knowledge of the middle-class culture. But although this bias may exist, it seems likely that it would only partially explain the relationship between background and achievement. Thus, it appears that the impact of a school, even a good school, continues to be limited when confronted with the economic and social inequalities inherent within our society. And ultimately the lack of school success typically translates into restricted opportunities after school. As a society, we must recognize the need for systemic change in which issues of growing poverty and increasing racism are addressed. Certainly, this is not a call to abandon the task of improving the schooling experiences of "at-risk" urban students while we wait for societal reform; yet to ensure that each member of our society has an equal chance of establishing a secure and productive life, change must occur not only within schools but across society as well.

REFERENCES

Anderson, Elijah. 1990. *Streetwise: Race, Class and Change in an Urban Community*. Chicago: The University of Chicago Press.

Cummins, Jim. 1993. "Empowering Minority Students: A Framework for Intervention." In Lois Weis and Michelle Fine (eds.), *Beyond Silenced Voices: Class, Race, And Gender in United States Schools,* pp. 101–118. Albany, NY: State University of New York Press.

Fine, Michelle. 1991. *Framing Dropouts: Notes on the Politics of an Urban Public High School*. Albany, NY: State University of New York Press.

Freedman, Samuel. 1991. *Small Victories: The Real World of a Teacher, Her Students, and Their High School*. New York: Harper Perennial.

Hurn, Christopher. 1993. *The Limits and Possibilities of Schooling*. Needham Heights, MA: Allyn & Bacon.

Jensen, Arthur. 1969. "How Much Can We Boost IQ and Scholastic Achievement?" *Harvard Educational Review* 39:1–123.

Katz, Michael B. 1971. *School Reform: Past and Present*. Boston: Little, Brown.

Kozol, Jonathan. 1991. *Savage Inequalities: Children in America's Schools*. New York: Crown.

Meier, Deborah. 1995. *The Power of Their Ideas: Lessons for America from a Small School in Harlem*. Boston: Beacon.

Natriello, Gary, Edward McDill, and Aaron Pallas. 1990. *Schooling Disadvantaged Children: Racing against Catastrophe*. New York: Teachers College Press.

Sadovnik, Alan R., Peter W. Cookson, and Susan F. Semel. 1994. *Exploring Education: An Introduction to the Foundations of Education*. Needham Heights, MA: Allyn & Bacon.

The University of the State of New York/The State Education Department. 1993. *A Report to the Governor and the Legislature on the Educational Status of the State's Schools: Statewide Profile of the Educational System*. Albany, NY: Author.

Traub, James. 1994. *City on a Hill: Testing the American Dream at City College*. Reading, MA: Addison-Wesley.

Wilson, William J. 1987. *The Truly Disadvantaged: The Inner City, the Underclass, and Public Policy*. Chicago: The University of Chicago Press.

Vocational Education

James E. Rosenbaum
Northwestern University

Vocational education describes a variety of programs in high schools and postsecondary schools that aim to equip students with work and life skills by offering instruction tailored to students' occupational interests. Almost 16 million Americans are enrolled in public vocational education programs. Although some programs are disproportionately comprised of one gender, total enrollments are almost evenly divided among males and females. Minority students represent 22.5% of the enrollment in vocational education, which is roughly equal to their proportion in the general population. Of the students enrolled in vocational education, approximately 60% (9.3 million) are enrolled in secondary programs and 40% (6.3 million) are enrolled in postsecondary programs. About 95% of all high school graduates take at least one vocational course in high school, according to a recent Department of Education study.

Unlike other nations that have a clear system for making the school-to-work transition (Rosenbaum et al., 1990), the United States lacks such a system, and sociological research has identified many problems that arise in the high school-to-work transition. American high school graduates face a poorly organized system for labor market entry that fails to offer them ways to attain desirable jobs. Youth have difficulty getting jobs, they have high unemployment, and their jobs generally offer poor pay, poor job security, and few training or advancement opportunities (Borman, 1991). In addition, youth rarely have informal ties to primary labor market employers, rarely get employment help from schools, and rarely see incentives for school efforts (Rosenbaum et al., 1990).

In the absence of a formal system to aid the school-to-work transition, vocational education is the main institution for helping American youth make the transition from school to work. However, by offering a separate curriculum, vocational education is a form of tracking, which raises sociological concerns about whether vocational education creates limits on opportunity.

A great deal of sociological research has been conducted on tracking. Over 50 years ago, sociologists described social aspects of tracking (Hollingshead, 1949), and conceptual analyses have identified many of the issues raised by tracking practices (Rosenbaum, 1976; Sørensen, 1970). Whereas educators have discussed curricular and pedagogical issues about vocational education, sociologists raise questions about the social features of the practice: Does vocational education include students from other programs? Does it deprive students of choice? Does it select students based on their social background? Does it preclude college options? Does it lower students' achievement? and does it improve employment?

The National Assessment of Vocational Education (Wirt, 1989) has done extensive analyses of the effects of vocational education based on national surveys of students (primarily the High School and Beyond survey) and analyses of course enrollments in a national sample. Their findings provide some of the best evidence on the questions of interest.

Inclusiveness

It is widely believed that vocational education separates students, and this is supported by older studies. Few college-bound students took vocational courses in the

1960s and 1970s (Kaufman and Schaefer, 1967). However, vocational programs have become far more inclusive in recent years. Based on a national survey of course enrollments, the National Assessment of Vocational Education (NAVE) (Wirt, 1989) concludes:

> A striking characteristic of secondary vocational education is that student participation is nearly universal.... Surprisingly, college-bound students also take substantial amounts of vocational education, and not just general, introductory, or consumer and homemaking courses, but occupationally specific vocational education as well.... Students planning to work after high school took an average of 6.06 credits of vocational education during high school, ... and students who planned to graduate from college averaged 3.17 credits. (Wirt, 1989:10).

Obviously, vocational classes no longer isolate work-bound students from others as they did in earlier decades.

Of course, even small differences in enrollments may influence friendship choices. Some older research indicates informal social separation of friendships in schools, and some research indicates that these social groupings may be associated with tracking (Rosenbaum, 1976), but recent evidence is lacking on this point. Of course, even if informal separation is shown, it will still be difficult to determine whether vocational tracking is a causal influence.

Choice

Vocational programs generally get high marks for giving students choices. However, free choice is not sufficient. If students are not given full information, then their choices may not reflect their true preferences (Rosenbaum, 1976:Chapter 6). Although there is some evidence that *general tracks* misrepresent their outcomes and allow students to believe mistakenly that they are in college preparatory curricula (Rosenbaum, 1980), there are no reports of vocational programs being unclear about their intended specialty or promising unrealistic outcomes.

Selectivity

Although vocational education has been called a dump-

ing ground for low-income and minority students, this is mostly contradicted by the data. If it were true, it would be an expensive dumping ground, as equipment costs and small classes tend to make vocational courses more expensive than college-track or general-track courses (Wirt, 1989). Furthermore, even tracking critics find that blacks are *not* more likely to be in vocational courses than whites (Oakes, 1985). Oakes' study does suggest that black and white students take different kinds of vocational courses, but this finding is based on small numbers of students.

NAVE's analyses also contradict the idea that vocational programs are a dumping ground for low-income minorities. NAVE concludes that low-income students are somewhat *excluded* from some vocational programs. "Schools with the highest poverty rates and lowest academic achievement are 40 percent *less* likely to offer their students access to an area vocational facility than schools with the lowest poverty rates. Schools with the largest percentage of disadvantaged students offer 40 percent *fewer* vocational courses, [and] a third as many occupational programs ... than schools with the smallest percentage of disadvantaged students" [emphases mine]. Thus, rather than low-income children being channelled into vocational education as a dumping ground, as some critics have suggested, low-income youth are actually deprived of these programs, particularly better and more varied programs. The issue of handicapped students is more complex. NAVE found that academically disadvantaged and handicapped males are proportionately represented in the better vocational programs, but such females are not.

Unfortunately, neither within-school or between-school studies control for individuals' attributes or preferences, so it is difficult to reach clear conclusions. Oakes' and NAVE's findings indicate that the selectivity problem of vocational education is not that it is being used as a dumping ground for low-socioeconomic status (SES) students, but the opposite: fewer vocational schools and courses are available to these students. Although some critics call for abolishing vocational programs (Oakes, 1985:170), the opposite conclusion might easily be reached from these findings—the nation should expand high-quality vocational course offerings for low-SES, minority, and female students to give them as much access as others.

Scope

The primary criticism of vocational education as a distinct track comes from the belief that it prevents students from attending college. Of course, since students may choose vocational education because they do not want to attend college, the college decision may precede the vocational program. Two national surveys found that vocational graduates rarely get 4-year college degrees; fewer than 4% of graduates of the class of 1972 (3.7%) and the class of 1980 (3.4%) obtained a 4-year degree in the 6 years following high school graduation (U.S. Department of Education, 1991:Table 289). In contrast, college-track students were much more likely to get 4-year degrees (43.6% and 37.4% for the two cohorts).

Yet a very different picture emerges for other college programs. Although few vocational graduates attended college in the 1960s, the enormous growth of community colleges in subsequent decades has changed that. "The largest increase in the rate of college attendance in the past decade has been among high school students who majored in vocational education" (Wirt, 1989:xvii). Although only 5.5% of vocational graduates in the class of 1972 obtained a 1- or 2-year degree in the following 6 years, 12.6% of the class of 1980 had done so (U.S. Department of Education, 1991:Table 289). This is a notable gain. Moreover, some vocational programs are more likely to lead to community colleges than others. Although relatively few students in agriculture, home economics, and trades programs attend community colleges, substantial proportions attend from distributive education (25.7%), business (20.6%), and health [22.2%; Rosenbaum, unpublished analyses High School and Beyond (HSB) Sophomore Cohort]. Indeed, these programs also lead to higher rates of attendance in 4-year colleges: 17.8% in distributive education, 11.8% in business, and 15.2% in health.

Of course, these rates may have changed in recent years. Since the mid-1980s, reforms to increase the academic requirements for high school graduation may have increased these college-attendance rates, although concomitant increases in college entrance requirements would work in the other direction for 4-year college attendance (community colleges have not increased requirements). We must await the findings of recent surveys (e.g., the NELS survey) to address the recent era.

Achievement Outcomes

Achievement outcomes are a key concern. Unfortunately, nearly all of the *best* studies on achievement outcomes of tracking (where students were randomly assigned to tracked or untracked classes) have been done in elementary or middle schools, not high school. Reviewing studies of ability grouping in secondary schools, Slavin (1990:484) states that "above ninth grade the evidence is too sparce for firm conclusions."

Because no random assignment studies have been done on high school tracking, and political and ethical considerations make such a prospect unlikely, multivariate analyses appear to provide the best research method available. Although it is not possible to be as confident about inferences from statistical controls as those from random-assignment experiments, multivariate analyses are the best evidence we are likely to get. Despite their limitations, such studies do give an overview of the ways diverse high schools operate across the nation.

Vocational education is sometimes justified as a way of providing a more applied context for teaching academic skills. Cognitive psychology suggests that learning is more effective if done in appropriate contexts. Moreover, motivation may be enhanced if vocational education makes lessons more relevant to students' interests. Analyzing the effects of various vocational courses on students' math achievement, NAVE found that "vocational courses in applied mathematics (e.g., business math, vocational math) and vocational courses that included substantial math content (e.g., electronics, drafting, accounting, agricultural science) were associated with significant gains in math learning" in the last two years of high school, although traditional vocational courses led to no gains (Wirt, 1989:xiv). These gains are particularly striking because the achievement test in the HSB survey probably *understates* the math benefits of these particular courses (p. 83). These results are encouraging. They suggest ways that vocational courses do contribute to academic outcomes. Yet a great deal more research is needed on this topic before firm conclusions can be drawn.

Job Outcomes

Ultimately, the success of vocational education rests on

whether it leads to better employment outcomes. Critics have claimed that vocational programs offer preparation for only low-skill jobs. Indeed, some programs are in low-skill occupations, and the graduates of these programs do tend to get poorly paying jobs.

However, most research shows strong job benefits from vocational courses. Several national studies have been done. Studying the 1983 National Longitudinal Survey on 6,953 youth, Campbell et al. (1986) found that vocational graduates were 8.2% more likely to be in the labor force and their pay was 5.6% higher than academic program graduates, after controlling for test scores and enrollment in higher education. In another sample, the 6,098 youth in the HSB, Campbell et al. (1986) found that vocational graduates were 14.9% more likely to be in the labor force and were paid about 9% more than academic graduates, after controlling for test scores and college attendance. Analyses that focused on HSB seniors who did not attend college full time found similar results, with male vocational graduates getting 8% higher wages, working 10–12% more, and earning 21–35% more in 1981, the first calendar year following graduation. For females, vocational graduates got 8% higher wages, worked 18% more, and earned 40% more during 1981 than academic graduates (Kang and Bishop, 1986).

Research also suggests *how* vocational programs improve employment outcomes: increasing high school graduation rates and allowing youth to get jobs using higher level job skills. After controlling for individual attributes, "taking one vocational course each year during the four years of high school raises the graduation rate of at-risk youth by 6 percentage points, and this raises expected earnings by about 2 percent" (Bishop, 1988).

Vocational programs also allow students to get jobs that use higher job skills. Although the

> economic benefits are zero if a training-related job is not obtained, if a training-related job is obtained, monthly earnings are . . . greater, unemployment is substantially reduced, labor force participation is more consistent, and productivity on the job is increased. . . . Unfortunately, less than one-half of the graduates of high school vocational programs who did not go to college work in occupations that match (very broadly defined) their training. (Bishop, 1988)

NAVE found similar benefits for postsecondary vocational programs, and other recent analyses have confirmed the economic benefits (Lewis et al., 1993). However, job relevance is also an important condition for these benefits. NAVE found that "additional amounts of vocational training that are related to the field of employment result in substantial wage benefits. Students with 'low' amounts of job matched vocational credits earn an average of $6.59 per hour, while similar students with a 'high' number of credits matching their job earn $8.00" (Wirt, 1989:108).

Similarly, when NAVE analyzed the factors affecting the payoff to high school vocational education, it concluded that "the largest single influence [on low payoff] in most analyses was unrelated placements. In the first three years after graduation, unrelated placements . . . accounted for 25–31% of the underutilization for men, and 37–44% for women" (p. 73). Both Bishop and NAVE conclude that high schools should devote more attention to helping students with job placements and to getting employers more involved.

Although surveys have not examined school job referrals in detail, two surveys had a single question on the topic. Holzer's employer survey finds that school referrals are not a common way to get a job, but school referrals are more often used to fill desirable occupations than less desirable ones. Of workers recruited into more desirable occupations (management, sales, clerical, craft) 3–7% come through high school referrals, but only 1–3% of workers recruited to less desirable occupations come via school referrals (operative, labor, service; Holzer, 1996:53).

The High School and Beyond (HSB) national survey of students in the class of 1982 had a question on how students found jobs after graduation. Analyses indicate that less than 10% of seniors report receiving help from high school in getting their first jobs (Rosenbaum and Roy, 1996). Although white males rely heavily on relatives (25.6%), and rarely use school help (4.6%), females and minorities are more likely to rely on school help in getting their jobs; 17% of black women, 12% of Hispanic women, and 9% of black men found their jobs through school help.

In addition, Rosenbaum and Roy (1996) conducted multivariate analyses of the determinants of wages in the year after graduation. Not surprisingly, they found that those who get their jobs through relatives get better wages. Although school job referrals had virtually no wage payoff for college or general track students, school job referrals have a large wage payoff for vocational-track students, as large as the payoff from help from relatives (8.8%). Moreover, following these 1982 graduates 10 years later, analyses find that these students received 25.3% higher wages in 1992 than other students (Rosenbaum and Roy, 1996).

Unfortunately, the Holzer and the HSB surveys each asked only one question about high school job help, and other surveys have asked nothing. If we want to understand how school help works, we are going to need more detailed studies (cf. Rosenbaum and Jones, 1995).

The available research indicates that vocational education works somewhat differently than a tracking critique might imply. Vocational tracks are not generally coercive; they are usually based on free choice. They are also not a dumping ground for disadvantaged students; if anything, the better programs are not sufficiently available to these students.

On other criteria, the evidence is mixed. Although vocational programs lead to some separation (college-bound students take fewer vocational courses than vocational students), college-bound students do take many vocational courses, including occupationally specific ones. Although vocational students have lower rates of 4-year degrees (with causality uncertain), they have only slightly lower rates of 1- and 2-year degrees than college-track students, and rates differ greatly by vocational field. The evidence on achievement effects in high school arrives at mixed results; some kinds of tracking systems and some kinds of vocational courses raise achievement, and others do not. Similarly, vocational programs have varying employment outcomes; sometimes they improve employment and sometimes they do not.

Overall, the findings of research do not support the usual tracking critique as applied to vocational education. The critique is less applicable to vocational programs than to other noncollege tracks, e.g., "general tracks," which reduce academic offerings without any corresponding advantages (Rosenbaum, 1976). The critique is also less applicable to some vocational program areas than to others. Rather than condemning all vocational programs with a single set of critiques, research indicates that some programs suffer from these problems and others do not.

Consequently, for anyone wanting to make a policy

decision about vocational education, an assessment must consider specific features of the program, e.g., whether its particular design separates students, coerces choices, and encourages homogeneity or permanence of placements. Abolishing tracking is one possible policy approach, but that runs the risk of ignoring real differences in the preparation, motivation, interests, and needs of students, particularly in very heterogeneous schools.

Less extreme reforms are also possible. If educators want to offer a variety of course offerings, track mechanisms can be designed so that opportunities are not curtailed. For instance, special summer and after-school programs can allow poorly prepared, but highly motivated, ninth-grade students to catch up to honors classes. One such program greatly increased the number of students in honors classes (doubling the number of minorities in honors classes) without lowering the standards of these classes; it increased electiveness while reducing selectiveness and scope (Rosenbaum, unpublished). Other programs reduce track distinctions by offering academic instruction that stresses vocational applications or by creating career-oriented programs with strong academic components (Stern et al., 1992). Although such programs tend not to include the most and least motivated students (the former tend not to apply and the latter are screened out), they provide ways to increase opportunities and reduce tracking distinctions.

In sum, one must be skeptical about vocational education (or any kind of tracking), but one cannot accept the tracking critique uncritically either. Because so much depends upon the structure imposed by the system in a particular school, this chapter indicates that critics must ask more complex questions to understand tracking program effects and that reform must involve changes on multiple dimensions.

REFERENCES

Bishop, J. 1988. *Vocational Education for At-Risk Youth: How Can It Be Made More Effective?* Working Paper 88–11. Cornell University. Ithaca, NY: New York State School of Industrial and Labor Relations.

Borman, K. M. 1991. *The First "Real" Job: A Study of Young Workers.* Albany: State University of New York Press.

Campbell, P. B., K. S. Basinger, M. B. Dauner, and M. A. Parks. 1986. *Outcomes of Vocational Education for Women, Minorities, the Handicapped and the Poor.* Columbus: The National Center for Research in Vocational Education, The Ohio State University.

Hollingshead, A. B. 1949. *Elmstown's Youth*. New York: Wiley.

Holzer, Harry. 1996. *What Employers Want*. New York: Russell Sage Foundation.

Kang, Suk, and John Bishop. 1986. "The Effect of Curriculum on Labor Market Success." *Journal of Industrial Teacher Education* (Spring):133–148.

Lewis, D. R., J. C. Hearn, and E. E. Zilbert. 1993. "Efficiencies and Equity Effects of Vocationally Focused Postsecondary Education." *Sociology of Education* 66(3):188–205.

Oakes, J. 1985. *Keeping Track*. New Haven, CT: Yale University Press.

Rosenbaum, J. E. 1976. *Making Inequality*. New York: Wiley.

———. 1980. "Social Implications of Educational Grouping." In D. C. Berliner (ed.), *Annual Review of Research in Education*, pp. 361–404. American Educational Research Association.

Rosenbaum, J. E., and S. A. Jones. 1995. "Creating Linkages in the High School-to-Work Transition: Vocational

Teachers' Networks." In M. Hallinan (ed.), *Making Schools Work*. New York: Plenum.

Rosenbaum, J. E., and K. Roy. 1996. "The Short-Term and Long-Term Effects of School Job Referrals on Earnings: Evidence from the High School and Beyond." Paper presented at the Annual Meetings of the American Sociological Association, New York.

Rosenbaum, J. E., T. Kariya, R. Settersten, and T. Maier. 1990. "Market and Network Theories of the Transition from High School to Work." *Annual Review of Sociology* 16:263–299.

Slavin, Robert E. 1990. "The Effects of Ability Grouping in Secondary Schools." *Review of Educational Research* 60(3):471–499.

Sørensen, A. 1970. "Organizational Differentiation of Students and Educational Opportunity." *Sociology of Education* 43:355–376.

Stern, D., J. M. Raby, and C. Dayton. 1992. *Career Academies*. San Fransisco: Jossey-Bass.

U.S. Department of Education. 1991. *Digest of Educational Statistics*. Washington, DC: U.S. Government Printing Office.

Wirt, John. 1989. *National Assessment of Vocational Progress (NAVE)*. Washington, DC: Government Printing Office.

WORKING PARENTS

Chandra Muller
University of Texas at Austin

The dramatic increase in the participation of women in the labor force since the middle 1960s has brought about widespread concern for the well-being of children. The largest increases in labor force participation have been among mothers with preschool and school-aged children. With those changes have come a redefinition of gender roles and family responsibilities that affect family processes and parent–child relationships. Research and public concern have focused on the potentially negative consequences of maternal employment for children, family relationships, and the home environment. This chapter will focus on that research; however, it will also examine the history of parental employment since the Industrial Revolution, other aspects of family life that are affected by maternal employment, and the consequences of paternal employment and unemployment on children and family processes.

Industrialization and Parenting

Although the focus of much public debate about maternal employment is on changes in women's participation in the labor force since the mid-1960s, it is useful to consider the implications of the economic activity for family life and parenting over a longer period of time. In the 200 years since the Industrial Revolution, there have been changes in the way children are viewed and in the dynamics of family life. The Industrial Revolution was accompanied by a demographic transition characterized by increased longevity, lower infant mortality, and lower fertility, which meant that children were more likely to live until adulthood, they were more likely to have both parents alive throughout childhood, and families had fewer children. With the

separation of the spheres of economic production from family life, a consequence of the Industrial Revolution, has come an emphasis on the home as a place for nurturing and a gradual emergence of the gender roles in which women's work, centered in the home, was not economically valuable. Initially, with the onset of industrialization, children's participation in the labor force increased because of the rapid increase in the demand for low-skilled workers. At the turn of the twentieth century child labor laws were enacted that placed restrictions on the age at which children could work and the number of hours they could work. During this period there was also a shift from a view of the child as a source of economic return to one in which economic and other investments should be made in children without an expectation of tangible return. The "common school" emerged as a vehicle to educate children of all social classes together in one school, to provide opportunity for individual social mobility, and to educate the masses to participate responsibly in a democratic society.

These combined forces of the separation of spheres, the decrease in the economic value of the child to the family (because the child would not be contributing directly to the family enterprise), and the shift of the responsibility for education and socialization from family to schools have brought about a greater public interest in the well being of the child. With this shift to increased public interest has come less autonomy for parents regarding how their children are raised and a public opinion that emphasizes the needs of the child independent from the daily operation of family life. Furthermore, consistent with the separation of spheres and the growing public interest in the child is a keen public interest in the extent to which parents are behaving in ways that are consistent with their gendered roles and, in this way, seen as adequately providing for their children.

Maternal Employment

Recently, much of the research on working parents has been on the effects of maternal employment on the child. One policy concern about the effect of maternal employment involves children whose mothers are subject to popular programs that link maternal welfare payments to work and training programs; to qualify for payments mothers are required to engage in these programs, sometimes referred to as "workfare." Interest in the effect of maternal employment on the achievement of children is not limited to researchers in the United States. As Dronkers (1989) points out, however, the political context of the debate is sharply different depending on the country. In the Netherlands, for example, researchers are motivated by government policy that discourages mothers with young children from working, a policy that is challenged by those who believe in a mother's right to work. In the United States there is public controversy over whether middle-class mothers of young children should work outside the home, although there is broad public support for workfare policies requiring mothers in need of public assistance to participate in either job or job training programs.

Effects on Child Outcomes

The findings of research on the effects of maternal employment on the child have been mixed. In a review of research on maternal employment and children's achievement for the National Academy of Sciences, Heyns (1982) concluded that there are no measurable differences in children's achievement based on the employment status of their mothers. Another review, published 2 years earlier, found measurable differences in academic performance and other indicators of the child's well-being depending on maternal employment status, and that girls especially benefit when mothers are employed. (Hoffman, 1980). Each has since maintained and elaborated its position (cf. Heyns and Catsambis, 1986; Hoffman, 1989).

The conditions of the mother's employment and of her decision to work outside the home may influence the effect of maternal employment on the child. Hoffman (1989) concurs about the importance of considering the circumstances under which the mother is employed in evaluating the effect of employment, however, her conclusions are different from those of Heyns and Catsambis (1986). In very-low-income families Hoffman finds employment has a positive effect on children, most likely because of the importance of the increase in available income due to the mother's paid job. Maternal employment has a positive effect on girls' expectations and self-concept, when accompanied by the mother's positive attitudes about self and job, however, there is no evidence that these positive attitudes contribute to higher academic achievement of daughters of women in the labor force. Hoffman finds a negative relationship between full-time maternal employment and achievement of boys. These results are corroborated by others (e.g., Desai et al., 1990). Hoffman stresses that differences in achievement of subgroups of children (boys and girls, middle income and low income) may be explained by differences in the relative need for income and in parent–child relationships.

Effects on Family Processes

Nock and Kingston (1988) find differences in the amount of time parents spend with their child or children depending on maternal employment status, although the differences are most pronounced for parents of preschoolers. They distinguish between child-oriented activities of the parent with the child and other activities in which the child is present but not the center of attention, like homemaking activities. Among parents of preschoolers, they find large differences in the amounts of time parents spend with their child in non-child-centered activity when single earner and dual-earner families are compared, but little difference in child-centered activity, mainly because parents of preschoolers engage in very little child-centered activity. Among mothers of school age children, there are no differences in the amount of time spent on child-centered activity. In contrast, mothers employed outside the home spend much less time with their children while engaging in the routine chores associated with domestic life, like housekeeping, mainly because they spend less time engaging in those activities. They are more likely to use the time with their children on child-oriented activity.

Muller (1995) examined the relationship among mother's employment status, parents' involvement with their child's education, and the academic achievement of adolescents. In general, children whose mothers are employed full-time attain slightly lower test scores than those whose mothers are not in the labor force. The difference, however, can be explained entirely by differences in the amount of time the eighth graders were left unsupervised after school. When the mother is employed full-time, parents are less involved in activities outside the home and particularly in activities that are more likely to require a fixed time for engagement, like volunteering at school, after school supervision, maintaining friendships with other parents, and restricting the amount of weekday television watched. Concerning activities that are more time flexible (and probably conflict less with work schedules), parents do not have different levels of involvement based on whether the mother works full-time or is not in the labor force. This suggests that parents are not less interested in involvement when the mother is employed full-time, but that certain kinds of activity are difficult. Among activities less constrained by external factors, the amount parents talked with their child about current school activities is an especially important predictor of the child's achievement. There were no differences in these levels of interaction depending on whether the mother was employed full-time or was not in the labor force.

Muller (1995) also finds that parents tend to be most involved with their child's education when the mother is employed part-time and that these adolescents achieve higher test scores. Parental involvement does not explain the difference in performance. There may be something about the children, their parents, and families that contributes both to the mother's decision to work part-time and to the ways parents are involved. Families that have more income and education, are two earners, and make their child's education a high priority may be more able and likely to arrange for the mother to work part-time outside the home. This allows parents to balance the needs of children with the needs of the family for the mother to be employed. These findings illustrate Heyns and Catsambis' (1986)

point that the relationship between maternal employment and the outcomes of the child is linked in very important ways to the circumstances of the mother's employment.

Menaghan and Parcel (1995) examined characteristics of the mother's occupation and also find this to be true. They studied the relationship between changes in job status of the mothers and changes in the level of stimulation in the home environment. Occupations that involved more complexity and, independently, higher wages were associated with positive changes in the stimulation of the home environment. The interaction of wages and complexity of the job task had especially strong associations with home environment, particularly in homes of mothers with low paying jobs that were also low in complexity.

Paternal Employment

The father's employment is also an important factor in family life and in the course of childhood. With the Industrial Revolution came the "good provider" role of men, who were expected to maintain gainful employment to fully support the family. A family consisting of an employed father and a homemaker mother gradually came to be considered ideal and a sign of a successful, masculine male (because he could support the entire family). Recently, because of changes in the economy and the decline in real wages, it has been increasingly difficult for families to survive on one income. Most research on paternal employment thus has been focused on the deviation from that ideal, namely on the effects of unemployment or loss of income on children and on family processes. The unemployment of married fathers is closely linked to negative effects on each member of the family and on men's participation in family life (Elder et al., 1985).

In the groundbreaking and controversial book, *The Truly Disadvantaged*, Wilson (1987) linked marriage to the employment status of African-American men. Thus, argued Wilson, there are fewer jobs available to African-American men because industry has moved from central urban areas to suburban areas, but African Americans have for the most part remained in central cities. Couples tend to marry when the male is employed, and with the extraordinarily high rates of unemployment have come low rates of "marriageable" males. Wilson went on to argue that this phenomenon, coupled with continued fertility, created a high rate of female-headed households, because women continued to have children but they did not marry. This is important because there is growing evidence that children who are raised in mother-only families have more academic and behavioral problems, in large part due to lower income (McLanahan and Sandefur, 1994).

The Effects of Family on Work

Most of the research on the relationship between work and family has examined the effects of employment on family process or child outcomes. However, the effect of family on employment, work experiences, and productivity is an area of increasing attention, in part because of the concerns of employers about these issues. Even though the majority of women take very little time off from work after the birth of a child, their work life may change as a consequence of the changing demands of family or the attitudes of their employers about their ability to balance work and having a young child. Women are sometimes placed on the "mommy track" in which they are given fewer career opportunities and promotions. Although less frequent, this type of tracking has also been documented for men. Another way that employed parents deal with the demands of family life is to postpone activities such as marriage, child bearing, or accepting work-related challenges to accommodate demands in other areas of life. Finally, some couples work special shifts such as the night shift so that one member of the couple is home with the children while the other is at work. Many of these "solutions" create additional but sometimes unavoidable stress.

Increasingly, employers are recognizing that employees will be more productive and satisfied and that there will be less turnover with policies designed to support rather than compete with family life. Such policies include flexible work hours, which allow parents to be home after school, onsite child care (or a child care stipend or help finding quality child care), parental leave, and a work at home option. Very little is known about the effect of these policies on a large scale, however, their increasing prevalence suggests that employers have found them cost effective.

Occupational Variation

Occupation is an important factor in determining the effect of work on family life and the effect of family life on work. The timing of completion of education and entrance into career varies in important ways depending on occupation. Typically, individuals will postpone child bearing, and therefore parenting until they have completed their education. Thus, parents with higher levels of education and more prestigious, higher paying jobs generally have fewer children and are older at the birth of their first child. They are also likely to have more income and their income will rise over a longer period of time (because white-collar professional jobs usually have higher and later earnings ceilings), thus there will be differential economic resources available to the children of middle- and upper middle-class families, especially when the children are older.

Furthermore, although the ideal family in the middle of the twentieth century consisting of a male breadwinner and full-time homemaker wife was a dominant norm, many families have never conformed to the ideal, sometimes because it was impossible to live on only one income. In fact, this model applied on a large scale only to middle-class families during a few decades. Rather than considering only one direction of causality between work life and family life, researchers and policymakers must recognize that each affects the other, and that parents and families are usually engaged in balancing the two.

Some Methodological Issues

The ever changing relationship between work life and family life means that the best way to study the cause and effect relationships is with temporally ordered data and variables that can be compared over time. Furthermore, it is important to take an array of factors that measure aspects of opportunity into account. The structure of economic opportunity associated with work plays an important role in the ways that work and family interact. Parents and students have different opportunity, including, importantly, the availability of quality child care and the availability for older children of supervised, quality after-school activities. Parents make judgments that reflect the balance of these and other factors that affect work-related decisions, family processes, and child outcomes. Because of these continual adjustments, it is important to study the process using longitudinal data so that researchers can measure prior conditions and, at a later point in time, the changes in behavior, attitudes, and family and work processes and outcomes.

Within this context of opportunity, differences in family process vary considerably depending on racial, ethnic, and cultural differences. There are cultural variations in the conception of gender roles and attitudes about women's participation in the labor force, and in family processes including the ways family members interact and in the values and priorities placed on various activities and allocation of resources. Families with different traditions engage in different activities. Furthermore, the interface between work and family and school and family will be different depending upon the culture of the family and the culture of the school or workplace. For families with a culture other than the dominant Anglo culture in the United States the interface may imply the need to bridge cultures. Thus, in any study that considers either effects of family on child outcomes or effects of work on family processes, one must be cognizant of the racial, ethnic, and cultural context of the family and the larger social setting.

Future Research and Public Policy

Research suggests that the contextual parameters of the lives of working parents and the characteristics of parents' work shape the ways families provide resources for their children. The work lives of parents have changed over the past few decades, so that now the majority of children are raised by parents who work outside the home. Furthermore, institutions that support and affect the ways families raise children, including child care, community and school-based services, and the work place, may be adapting to the changing labor force participation more slowly than the change in the needs of families. For example, schools may be slow to offer after-school programs sufficient to meet the demand of parents, or they may still schedule meetings with parents during work hours, making it nearly impossible for parents to participate in school activities other than during an emergency. Similarly, although some em-

ployers are offering family-friendly options others are slow to do so.

Future research must investigate how social programs and employer-based programs can best meet the needs of families. What types of programs, in schools, communities, and the work place, most effectively reduce stress associated with balancing family and work? What job characteristics contribute to family processes associated with student success? What needs of children, such as supervised after-school activities or school programs during nonwork hours, are not being met because of parents' work-related demands? Research must focus on narrowing down the kinds of family supports that are most useful to parents and children and that allow them to effectively balance the demands on families that have resulted from the growing participation of women in the labor force.

REFERENCES

Heyns, Barbara. 1982. "The Influence of Parents' Work on Children's School Achievement." In S. B. Kamerman and C. D. Hayes (ed.), *Families that Work: Children in a Changing World*, pp. 229–267. Washington, DC: National Academy Press.

Heyns, Barbara, and Sophia Catsambis. 1986. "Mother's Employment and Children's Achievement: A Critique." *Sociology of Education* 59:140–151.

Hoffman, Lois W. 1980. "The Effects of Maternal Employment on the Academic Attitudes and Performance of School-Age Children." *School Psychology Review* 9:319–336.

———. 1989. "Effects of Maternal Employment in the Two-Parent Family." *American Psychologist* 44:282–292.

McLanahan, Sara, and Gary Sandefur. 1994. *Growing Up with a Single Parent: What Hurts, What Helps*. Cambridge, MA: Harvard University Press.

Menaghan, Elizabeth G., and Toby L. Parcel. 1995. "Social Sources of Change in Children's Home Environments: The Effects of Parental Occupational Experiences and Family Conditions." *Journal of Marriage and the Family* 57:69–84.

Muller, Chandra. 1995. "Maternal Employment, Parent Involvement, and Mathematics Achievement Among Adolescents." *Journal of Marriage and the Family* 57:85–100.

Nock, Steve, and Paul Kingston. 1988. "Time with Children: The Impact of Couples' Work-Time Commitments." *Social Forces* 67:59–85.

Wilson, William J. 1987. *The Truly Disadvantaged*. Chicago, IL: University of Chicago Press.

INDEX

A

Abbott vs. Burke, 673
ability
  measurement components, 243
  and meritocracy, 435
ability groups. *See* tracking
abstract attitudes, educational, 199–201
academic achievement
  attitude/achievement paradox, 201
  and Catholic schools, 76, 77–78, 206,
    406–407
  and cooperative learning, 117–118
  and culture of students, 639–642
  gender differences, 182–183
  and home schooling, 366–367
  and inequality, 242–244
  and school desegregation, 70, 71
  and sports participation, 626
  as status determinant, 85–86
  and teacher expectations, 245
  and tracking, 86, 243–244, 689
  urban schools, 695
  See also educational productivity
Academic Revolution, The (Riesman), 8
Accelerated Schools Project (ASP), 497
acculturation, meaning of, 247
achievement level. *See* academic
    achievement; educational
    productivity; high achievers; low
    achievers
achievement motivation
  African Americans, 8, 43–46
  need for achievement (nAch), 43–44
  research areas of, 44–46
  theoretical basis, 43–44
Achievement Motive, The (McClelland et
    al.), 43
Adams v. Califano, 30–32
Adams v. Richardson, 143, 159, 161–162
Adarand Construction v. Pena, 31
Addams, Jane, 463
Adolescent Society, The (Coleman), 17, 262
adolescents, stereotype of, 17
adolescents and schools, 17–21
  curriculum, 18–21
  research needs, 21
  sociological studies, 17–18

See also secondary schools
adoption studies, of IQ, 401
adult education, 23–28
  growth of, 23–24, 26
  historical view, 23
  learner needs and characteristics, 23–24,
    27
  material functions of, 26
  older college students, 340, 614
  social function of, 26–27
  sociological perspectives, 24–27
  specialization in, 26
  supply and demand for, 27
affirmative action, 29–40
  Bakke decision, 31, 32, 156–157
  court cases related to, 31–33, 156–157
  debate, elements of, 36–38
  faculty employment effect, 29, 35, 36
  history of, 30–33
  opponent views, 37, 39–40, 164–165
  proponent views, 38
  race-based scholarships, 163–164
  and school desegregation, 29–30
  student enrollment effect, 30, 32,
    33–35
  types of practices, 29
African-American discrimination
  and Civil Rights Act, 30, 58, 70
  civil rights movement, 68
  and Civil War amendments, 67
  educational. *See* higher education and
    desegregation; racial/ethnic
    inequality; school desegregation;
    school segregation
  "equal but separate" decision, 67–69
  institutional racism, 45
  Jim Crow laws, 43, 67–68, 490
  and research studies, 43, 46
African-American studies, 154, 325
  Harvard program, 446
African-Americans, 490–491
  achievement motivation, 8, 43–46
  alienation by schools, 20, 346
  cultural framework of, 488
  and Culture of Poverty thesis, 44–45
  employment and marriage of men,
    713–714
  foreign born and achievement, 490

gains and desegregation, 145, 205
higher education. *See* higher education
    and racial/ethnic minorities
as involuntary minority, 488, 640
parental involvement, 512
resistance theory, 640
and school choice, 513–514
secondary school achievement, 346–347
self-concept of, 45–46
U.S. population statistic, 490
Afrocentric education, 72
Ain't No Makin' It (MacLeod), 555
Alexander, Lamar, 238
alienation, burnout as, 660
Allen University, 360
Allen v. Wright, 161
Allen, Walter R., 43, 359
Althusser, Louis, 382–383, 588, 589, 635
Aluets, 491
America Revised (FitzGerald), 533, 534
American Association of Community
    Colleges (AACC), 103, 455
American Dilemma, A (Myrdal), 46
American Educational Research
    Association (AERA), Division L-
    Educational Policy and Politics, 7
American Federation of Teachers (AFT),
    667–669
  and collective bargaining, 668–669
  history of, 667–668
American Normal School Association, 665
American University, The (Parsons and
    Platt), 8
*America's Choice: High School or Low
    Wages!*, 4
Anglo conformity model, assimilation,
    443–444
anomie, Durkheim's view, 267–268
Apple, Michael W., 381, 588–589,
    591–592, 594
Archer, Margaret, 333
Argonauts of the Western Pacific
    (Malinowski), 256
Army Alpha tests, 620
Arnot, Madeleine, 571
Aronowitz, Stanley, 589, 590, 597
Aronson, Elliot, 117
Asian Americans, 489–490

and affirmative action, 33, 34, 36
bilingual education lawsuit, 58–59,
    446, 490
culture and achievement, 641–642
and higher education, 33, 34, 36, 325,
    338–339, 345–350
mathematics achievement, 325
model minority stereotype, 489–490
secondary school achievement, 346–347
U.S. population statistic, 489
Asian/Pacific Islanders, and higher
    education, 344–350
assessment laboratories, teacher
    assessment, 654–655
assimilation
    Anglo conformity model, 443–444
    cultural pluralism, 444
    meaning of, 247
    melting pot model, 444
*Assimilation in American Life: The Role of
    Race, Religion, and Origins*
    (Gordon), 443
Assisted Places Scheme, 478
at-risk students, **49–53**
    charter schools for, 511
    compensatory programs, 696–697
    factors related to, 50–53
    interventions for, 53
    magnet schools, 426
    prevalence of, 53
    social capital and success, 548
    social construction view, 623
    at urban schools, 698–699
    use of term, 49–50
athletics. *See* sports
Atkinson, Paul, 633
Atlanta University, 360
attendance-zone magnet schools, 425–426
attention deficit disorder (ADD)
    features of, 621
    theories of cause, 621
attitudes, educational, **199–202**
authentic assessment, 195–196
    concerns related to, 196
    elements of, 195
authentic questions, of high achievers, 128
authority, role of teacher, 83–84

B

Baccalaureate and Beyond (B&B) study,
    410, 413–414
Bache, Alexander Dallas, 308
back-to-basics movement, 18
Baker, David P., 393
Ballantine, Jeanne H., 599, 613
Bank Street School, 468
Banks, James, 251
Barnard, Henry, 308
Barnett, Ross, 157
Barrett, Michelle, 572
Barry, Mary Francis, 161
Basic Educational Opportunity Grants,
    156
Becker, Gary, 171, 377

Beginning Postsecondary Student (BPS)
    survey, 410, 413–414
behaviorism, of Thorndike, 466
Bell Curve, The (Herrnstein and Murray),
    241, 400–401, 440, 487
Bell, Terrell, 221, 470
Ben-David, Joseph, 331
Benjamin Banneker Scholarship, 163
Benne, Kenneth, 467
Bennett College, 360
Bennett, William, 221, 237
Berends, Mark, 203
Berg, Ivar, 377
Berger, Peter, 248
Bernstein, Basil
    code theory, 89–96, 236, 554
    on curriculum, 91–92, 636–637
    on pedagogic discourse and practice,
        92–95
    and social reproduction theory, 383,
        554, 588, 698
    and structuralism, 636–637
Bestor, Arthur, 469
Beyond the Melting Pot (Glazer and
    Moynihan), 444
Biddle, Bruce J., 681
Bierlein, Louann, 476
biethnicity, meaning of, 251
bilingual education, **55–62**
    debate, elements of, 57, 58–62
    early-exit and late-exit programs, 56
    effectiveness of, 56–57, 62
    goals of, 55
    historical view, 59–60, 446–447
    legal aspects, 446–447
    maintenance model, 55
    research studies, 56–58
    sociolinguistic studies, 57–58
    sociopolitical context, 58–62
    transitional models, 55
    two-way or immersion model, 55, 56,
        62
Bilingual Education Act of 1968, 60
Bilingual Education Act of 1984, 51
Binet intelligence test, 194, 620
biological theory
    gender and mathematics, 283
    race and IQ, 487, 695–696
black box analysis, Coleman Report as,
    520
black colleges, **359–364**
    and acculturation, 360
    and civil rights era, 361–362
    Freedman's education movement,
        359–360
    funding of, 360–361
    future view, 362–364
    goals of, 360
    Hampton/Tuskegee model, 360–361
    listing of schools, 360
    missionary-founded schools, 359–360
    rise in enrollment, 339
    student outcome, 339
    white-controlled schools, 361, 363
    white enrollment in, 165
black feminism, focus of, 579
Blank, Rolf K., 421

Bloom, Alan, 226
Bobbitt, Franklin, 467
Boli, John, 307
Boston Compact, 224
Boston Latin School, 476
Boulding, K., 172
Bourdieu, Pierre
    cultural capital concept, 121, 122, 236,
        333, 552–554, 588, 640
    habitus concept, 553
    and structuralism, 637
Bowles, Samuel
    on meritocracy, 439–440
    social reproduction theory, 172, 236,
        270, 383, 551–552, 578, 588
Bradley, Karen, 295
Brawer, Florence, 452
Briggs, Kerri L., 501
Brint, Steven, 454–455
Broader Perspectives, 535
Brown-Scott, Wendy, 363–364
Brown v. Board of Education, **67–73**
    antecedents of, 67–68, 151–153
    Brown II, 69
    doll studies, 45n
    enforcement of, 69–70, 157–159
    features of decision, 68–69
    multicultural impact of, 445
    public response to, 69–71
    See also higher education and
        desegregation; school desegregation
Bruere, Henry, 464
Bureau of Indian Affairs (BIA), regulation
    of education, 492
burnout. *See* teacher burnout
Burnout Measure (BM), 659
Bush, George, H. W.
    National Education Goals, 448
    New American Schools Program, 475
    voucher program, 237
Bush, George W., goals for education,
    228
Business-Higher Education Forum, 237
busing, 141–142, 146–148
    district-wide reassignment, 142
    inequalities related to, 147–148
    interdistrict busing, 141, 142
    Milliken decision, 142
    Nixon ban on, 142, 157, 159
    pre-desegregation busing, 146
    Swann decision, 141–142, 146–148
Byrne, Eileen, 572

C

California
    affirmative action issue, 32, 33, 40, 164
    language diversity issue, 60
    textbook adoption, 536–537
California Commission on the Teaching
    Profession, 226
Callahan, Raymond, 237
Canady, Charles, 164
Cane, Florence, 468
capitalism
    and hidden curriculum, 126

Marxist theory of, 111–112, 587–588
Cardinal Principals of Secondary Education, 261
care perspective, maternal feminism, 574–575
Carnegie Commission Report (1986), 9
Carnegie Report of the Task Force on Teaching as a Profession, 237
    on teacher education, 226–227
Carter, Jimmy, education policy, 237
Catholic Church, in history of education, 307–308
Catholic schools, **75–80**
    and academic achievement, 76, 77–78, 206, 406–407
    academic values of students, 541
    benefits for female students, 339–340, 542, 543
    demographics of, 75
    dropout rate, 318
    and educational productivity, 206
    features of, 76, 78–80
    future view, 80
    historical view, 75
    longitudinal study, student achievement, 406–407
    mathematics achievement, 541
    compared to public schools, 406–407
    and school desegregation, 77
    science achievement, 541–542
    secondary schools, 18, 75, 78–80
    single-sex education, 540–544
    social justice position of, 77
    sociological study of, 76
    and Vatican Council II, 76–77
    verbal/reading achievement, 542
Catholic Schools and the Common Good (Bryk et al.), 80
Catsambis, Sophia, **335**
Center for Collaborative Education, 471
Center for Multicultural Education, 251
Central College Association, 665
Central Park East Secondary School (CPESS), 471, 700–702
    effectiveness of, 702
    goals of, 700–701
    instructional practices, 701–702
    principles of education of, 700
Central State University, 157
Chamberlain, N., 172
charter schools, 511–512
    parental involvement, 512
    results of research on, 223
    for at-risk students, 511
    specialized curriculum schools, 511
    student admission policies, 511–512
    teacher unions on, 675–676
Chase, Bob, 674, 676
Cheyney State University, 143, 157
Chicago Teacher Federation, 665
child-centered model
    child-centered schools, examples of, 468
    of progressive education, 466–468
Child and the Curriculum, The (Dewey), 464
Chubb, John E., 222, 238, 514
Citadel, female admissions, 143

citizenship, 6–7
    and community college, 107, 459
    definition of, 6
    dimensions of, 6–7
    and educational reform, 6
City and Country, 468
city schools. *See* urban schools
City Technology Colleges, England and Wales, 215–216, 474
City University of New York, open-admissions, 31, 154, 156, 337
Civil Rights Act of 1964
    enforcement of, 69–70, 157–161
    Nixon curtailment of, 157
    racial discrimination ban, 30, 58, 445
    Title IX, sex discrimination ban, 20, 70, 154, 159, 263, 281, 539
Civil Rights Act of 1968, Title VII, rights of limited English proficient students, 446
Civil Rights Act of 1991, on discriminatory hiring practices, 178
civil rights movement
    achievements of, 141
    and multiculturalism, 445
    National Association for the Advancement of Colored People (NAACP), 68
    See also school desegregation
Clark, Burton, 100, 101, 452
Clark, Kenneth, 45n, 69
Clark, Mamie, 45n, 69
Clark University, 360
Class, Codes, and Control, Volume I (Bernstein), 90
Class, Gender and Education (Barton and Walker), 572
classification
    in Bernstein's curriculum theory, 91–92
    in structuralism, 633, 636–637
classroom instruction. *See* curriculum; instructional approaches
classroom observation, teacher assessment, 651–652
classroom processes, **83–87**
    aggressive versus quiet students, 302, 304
    gender differences, 275, 283–284, 301–302
    student friendships, 86–87
    student status hierarchy, 85–86
    teacher's role, 83–85
Clayton, Thomas, 387
Clinton, Bill, educational policy, 221, 228–229
cliques, features of, 86–87
Closing of the American Mind, The (Bloom), 226
Coalition of Essential Schools (CES), 9, 226, 230, 497
    educational principles of, 471, 700
code theory, **89–92**
    development of, 89–91
    roots of, 89, 94–95
    and structuralism, 636–637
coeducation
    and gender inequality, 297

school climate, 541
    and sexism, 542–543
    compared to single-sex schools, 541–543
    transition from single-sex education, 540
cognitive theory, and cooperative learning, 115
Cohen, Arthur, 452
Cohen, Elizabeth G., 83
cohort dropout rate, 316
cohorts
    analysis in longitudinal studies, 414–415
    cohort rate, meaning of, 316
    trend estimation difficulties, 416
Coleman, James S.
    on adolescent society, 17, 262
    functionalist approach of, 269
    on school effects, 519–520, 522, 523
    on social capital, 545, 546–548
Coleman Report (*Equality of Educational Opportunity Study*)
    on African-American achievement, 44–45
    as black box analysis, 520
    criticism of, 407
    major conclusions of, 519, 696
    meritocracy context of, 437
    on school resources and achievement, 206, 238, 241–242
collective bargaining, teacher unions, 668–669, 672, 678
college entrance exams
    Catholic school students, 541
    gender bias, 282, 303
    SAT mathematics scores and gender, 281–283
    SAT score decline, 18
    scores of racial/ethnic minorities, 487
    validity/reliability, 37–38
colleges. *See* higher education
Collins, Randell, 3, 113, 270, 331, 439
colonialism
    classical type of, 387
    and common language, 389
    neocolonialism, 387, 389
    See also imperialism and education
Commission on Reorganization of Secondary Education, 261
Common Countenance, A (Tomkins), 137
common school hypothesis, Catholic schools, 79–80
communally-organized schools, 522
communication, code theory, 89–92
community colleges, **99–108, 449–460**
    admissions method, 452
    citizenship, preparation for, 107, 459
    community-building function, 107, 459
    conflict theory, 337, 452–453
    cooling out concept, 453
    as diversion from 4-year colleges, 102, 105–106, 336, 343, 454, 455–456
    early research, 100–101
    economic role of, 104, 106–107, 108, 458–460

financing of, 99, 459
functionalist theory, 452
funding of, 449
and future and occupations, 336, 454, 456–457
future research needs, 456–460
future view, 107–108
governance of, 440, 459
Hispanics in, 354–355
historical development, 102–104, 454–456
and immigration, 459
and multiculturalism, 459
and occupational attainment, 336
racial/ethnic minorities, 99, 107, 343–344, 348, 352–353
and remedial education, 107, 458–459
and social stratification, 337, 452–453
sociological study of, 452–456
student outcome, 101–102, 104–105, 107, 453–454, 456–458
student population profile, 449
vocational education, 452–453
women in, 339, 457
Community Control Movement, 502
Community Home Education (CHE) model, 368
community and schools
and community college, 107, 459
educational productivity, 208
neighborhood effects, theories of, 208
and at-risk students, 52
and school-based management, 503
school as community view, 522
school-family-community partnerships, 525–531
social capital in community, 546–547
competition theory, of neighborhood effects, 208
competitiveness, gender differences, 301–302
complex instruction, 85
CompuHigh, 368
Comte, Auguste, 6
concrete attitudes, educational, 199–201
conflict theory
of community colleges, 337, 452–453
early sociologists' views, 111–112
compared to functionalist theory, 270
of higher education, 329–330, 335–336
imperialism and education, 388
of Marx, 111–112, 270
mass schooling, 430
of sport in schools, 625
of Weber, 112, 270
conflict theory of education, 111–114
adult education, 25, 27
educational credentials in, 113–114, 270
educational inequality, 3, 112–113
modern, era of, 112
schooling and social class, 270
sociology of education, 3
Connell, Bob, 573, 574
consensus model, adult education, 24–25, 26, 27

conservative agenda, and quasi-markets, 474, 481
contact theory, and intergroup relations, 118
contagion theory, of neighborhood effects, 208
contributions approach, multicultural education, 449
controlled choice programs, 510
positive outcome of, 515
Cookson, Peter W., Jr., 221, 235, 267
cooling out concept, community colleges, 453
Cooper, Robert, 687
Cooperative Integrated Reading and Composition (CIRC), 116–117
cooperative learning, 115–119
and academic achievement, 117–118
and female students, 284
and friendliness, 86–87, 118
Group Investigation method, 117
Jigsaw method, 117
Learning Together model, 117
and low achievers, 118
prerequisites for learning, 115–117
research on, 117–118
and self-esteem, 118
Student Team Learning methods, 115–117
correspondence principle, 551–552
Counts, George, 467
Cousin, Victor, 308
Crabtree, James, 666
Credential Society, The (Collins), 3, 113
credentials. See educational credentials
Cremin, Lawrence, 464, 467–468
Crime in the Making: Pathways and Turning Points Through Life (Janowitz), 545
Crisis in the Classroom (Silberman), 469
criterion-referenced tests, elements of, 192
critical ethnography, aspects of, 258–259
critical pedagogy
feminist theory, 590–591
goal of, 590
Marxist theory, 590, 592
and new sociology of education, 596
and teachers, 590
critical theory
imperialism and education, 387
sociology of education as, 559–569
cross-cultural view
curriculum, 129
curriculum history, 137–138
England and Wales, educational reform, 211–219
high school dropouts, 315
quasi-markets, 474–476
tracking, 244
women's fields of study, 186
See also globalization of education; international higher education
cross-national studies, 393–397
on citizens as human capital, 395
consequences related to, 394
on curricula/pedagogy, 431–432
future view, 396

on nationalization of education, 394–395
pattern of study results, 396
on psychometric testing, 395
purposes of, 393–394
on school effects, 395–396
cross-sectional studies, causation in, 403
Cuban, Larry, 226, 470
cultural bias, IQ tests, 400–401
cultural capital, 121–124
connection to economic capital, 553
criticisms of concept, 123
meaning of, 114, 121, 552
objectification of, 121
profits from, 122
as research concept, 122–123
and social class, 121–123, 552–553
and social reproduction, 552–553
cultural citizenship, aspects of, 6–7
cultural deprivation
and academic achievement, 639–642
impact on public policy, 696
Cultural Literacy (Hirsch), 226
cultural models
historical influences on, 488
of racial/ethnic minorities, 488–489
cultural pluralism, meaning of, 444
cultural reproduction theory, 588–589
cultural values, and racial/ethnic minorities, 487–488
culture
and communication style, 57
and nonverbal communication, 57
study of. See ethnography
culture and achievement, 639–642
culture fair tests, 401, 622
Culture of Poverty, elements of, 44–45
curriculum, 18–21, 125–130
and authentic assessments, 195
back-to-basics movement, 18
Bernstein's theory, 91–92, 636–637
for black students, 154
content coverage and learning, 126
cross-cultural view, 129
empowering curriculum, features of, 590
formal curriculum, 18–19
and globalization of education, 311
goals and educational assessment, 193
hidden curriculum, 19–21, 125–126
and ideology, 381–385
in imperialistic settings, 390–391
limitations, 18–19
of magnet schools, 425
measurement-driven instruction, 193–194
National Curriculum, England and Wales, 213–215
New Basics curriculum, 345
of progressive education, 466, 467
reform movement, 133
sexist, 303
and social class, 588
sociology of education focus, 8–9, 125
and student socialization, 125–126
and tracking, 126–128, 242–244
use of term, 125

curriculum development
    Durkheim on, 128
    functionalist approach, 128
    future view, 129–130
    historicist approach, 128
    revision, suggestions for, 19
    world-system approach, 128–129
curriculum history, **133–138**
    cross-cultural view, 137–138
    gender-centered study, 137
    historical and unhistorical approaches,
        135
    interactionist approach, 133–134
    philosophical studies, 134–135
    social history of subjects, 136–137

D

Dalton School, 468
Darling-Hammond, Linda, 226, 228
Datnow, Amanda, 255, 687
Davis, Kingsley, 169
de facto segregation, 68, 152, 154
de jure segregation, 69, 70, 152, 154, 163
Death at an Early Age (Kozol), 469
Declaration on Christian Education, 76
deconstructive ethnography, 259
Deem, Rosemary, 572
Delamont, Sara, 273
DelFattore, Joan, 535
delinquency, and high school dropouts,
    317
demand-side, and school choice, 512–514
democracy
    and progressive education, 465
    and quasi-markets, 480–481
Democratic Administration Movement,
    502
Dennison, Edward, 172
Department of Education, 237
Department of Health, Education
    enforcement of school segregation,
        158–160
    and Welfare (HEW), 141
desegregation. *See* higher education and
    segregation; school desegregation
detracking, 690–691
    effects of, 243, 691
    pre-detracking considerations, 690–691
Dewey, John, and progressive education,
    463–467
Diana v. California Board of Education,
    623
Dillabough, Jo-Anne, 571
Dillard University, 360
Direct Government Student Loans,
    National Service, and Safe Schools
    Act, 229
discrimination. *See* African-American
    discrimination; inequality; racism
    and discrimination
Distinction (Bourdieu), 122
*Disuniting of America: Reflections on a
    Multicultural Society, The*
    (Schlesinger), 449
Division of Labor (Durkheim), 267

doctoral degrees
    African-Americans, 166
    gender differences, 289
documents, ethnographic study, 257
Dole, Robert, 164
doll studies, 45n
Donly, Brenda, 235
Dougherty, Kevin J., 99, 237, 451, 455,
    457–460
Douglas, Mary, 635
downsizing, educational implications, 173
Dreeben, Robert, 269
dropouts. *See* high school dropouts
dual-labor market
    mechanics of, 291–292
    socialist feminist theory of, 292–293
DuBois, W.E.B., 68, 71, 153, 361
Dunlop, J., 172
Durkheim, Emile
    conflict, view of, 111
    on curriculum, 128
    on education, 6, 9
    functionalist theory, 169, 267–268
    on higher education, 329, 335
    and structuralist theory, 89, 94–95,
        633, 636
Dworkin, A. Gary, 659

E

Eaton, Judith, 452
Eckhaus, R.S., 172
economic costs, and high school dropouts,
    317
economic development
    and community colleges, 104,
        106–107, 108, 458–460
    and human capital theory, 378
economic functions, of schooling, 268
economic reproduction theory, 588
economic theory
    evolution of, 170
    functionalist approach, 169–170
    Keynesian economics, 169
economics of education, **169–179**
    consumption of education, 171
    and educational productivity, 203–204
    human capital theory, 170–173,
        175–176
    income distribution, 176–177
    managed competition, aspects of, 175
    performance-education correlation, 174,
        177–178
    price competition, 176–177
    productivity-education correlation,
        173–174, 178
    sociological focus of, 171, 172, 177
    and women, 172, 176–177
Edmunds, Ron, 225
education
    functionalist theory of, 267–270
    structural differentiation in, 561–562
Education for All Handicapped Students
    Act (PL 94–142), 621, 622
Education Commission of the States, 516

*Education and Jobs: The Great Train
    Robbery* (Berg), 377
*Education-Jobs Gap: Underemployment or
    Economic Democracy* (Livingstone),
    377
Education and Sociology (Durkheim), 268
educational aspirations
    of Mexican Americans, 639
    and single-sex education, 542
    and sports participation, 626
    and tracking, 689
educational assessment, **191–196**
    authentic assessment, 195–196
    and curriculum goals, 193
    performance assessment, 195–196
    purposes of, 191–192
    reform movement, 195–196
    standardized tests, 192–195
educational attainment. *See* educational
    credentials
educational attitudes, **199–202**
    abstract attitudes, 199–201
    attitude/achievement paradox, 201
    concrete attitudes, 199–201
    policy implications, 201–202
    of racial/ethnic minorities, 200–201,
        489
    and wealth/poverty of school, 206
    and women, 200–201
educational credentials
    conflict theory of, 113–114, 270
    correspondence theory, 551–552
    and occupational opportunity,
        113–114, 269–270, 324–325, 336
    parental, effects of, 297
    of racial/ethnic minorities, 487
educational inequality, **241–246**
    Coleman report, 241–242
    and conflict theory, 3
    conflict theory of, 112–113
    England and Wales, 217–218
    and gifted programs, 244
    interpretations of, 241–242
    and meritocracy, 436–442
    and peer interactions, 245–246
    and performance assessment, 196
    and quasi-markets, 474, 477–479,
        481–482
    and race/ethnicity. *See* racial/ethnic
        inequality; school segregation
    remedy for African-Americans. *See*
        school desegregation
    and school choice, 480, 511
    and school climate, 242
    sociology of education focus, 2–3,
        241–242
    and special education, 244
    and teacher behavior, 245–246
    and tracking, 126–128, 194, 207,
        242–244
    versus liberal democratic ideals, 2–3
educational organizations, as open system,
    600–604
educational policymaking
    and power elite, 235–239
    See also educational reform
educational productivity, **203–209**

and Catholic schools, 206
community effects, 208
and economic theory, 203–204
and family, 207–208
meaning of, 203
and racial/ethnic minority gains,
    204–205
and school characteristics, 205
and school resources, 206–207
and school size, 206
and socioeconomic status, 205, 206,
    207
and tracking, 207
See also academic achievement
educational reform, **221–231**
charter schools, 223
and citizenship, 6
curriculum, 133
educational assessment, 195–196
elite influence, 235–239
Goals 2000, 228–229
Great Britain. *See* England and Wales,
    educational reform
of 1980s, 221–222
of 1990s, 222
progressive education, 463–472
school-based management, 225
school-business partnerships, 224
school choice, 222–224
school effectiveness movement,
    225–226
school-to-work programs, 224
sociology of education focus, 8
and teacher burnout, 661–662
teacher education, 226–228
themes of, 222, 229–231
tuition vouchers, 223
educational status
and high-profile occupations, 113–114
maternal, and at-risk children, 51
effective schools
features of, 225
See also school effectiveness movement;
    school effects
Elementary and Secondary Education Act
    of 1965
Clinton reauthorization of, 229
federal aid and school desegregation, 70
elite
and educational policymaking,
    235–239
higher education, cross-cultural view,
    331
influence, theories of, 236–237
and Ivy League education, 270, 615
members of, 235
networks of, 238
on school choice, 238–239
Elmtown's Youth (Hollingshead), 17
Elson, Ruth, 533
Emergency School Assistance Act (ESAA),
    422
employment, and educational credentials,
    270
employment inequality

Griggs decision, 178
rise of, 2
test results and hiring, 178
See also income inequality
encapsulation, ethnic, 251
enculturation, meaning of, 247
England
new sociology of education, 594, 595
pre-1980 schooling, 211–213
quasi-markets in, 474–475, 476–478,
    510–511
England and Wales, educational reform,
    211–219
City Technology Colleges, 215–216,
    474
evaluation of, 218–219
Funding Agency for Schools, 216
grant-maintained schools, 216, 217
local education authorities (LEAs), 213,
    215–217, 474–475, 476
local management of schools (LMS),
    216–217, 475, 476
National Curriculum, 213–215
1988 Educational Reform Act, 211,
    213, 474
1992 Education (Schools) Act, 215
1993 Education Act, 216–218
open enrollment, 475
parental choice of schools, 514
student selection, inequality of,
    217–218, 477, 510
environment, in open system, 601–602
Epstein, Joyce L., 525
Equal Opportunity Act of 1996, 164–165
equal protection clause, 152
Equality of Educational Opportunity Study.
    See Coleman Report
ethnic capital
importance of, 5
meaning of, 379
ethnic identity
influencing factors, 486
meaning of, 247
white students, 492
ethnic studies, 445–446, 617
ethnicity, **247–253**
aspects of, 249–250
biethnicity, 251
definitions of, 247, 485–486
educational issues, 252–253
ethnic enclaves, 248
future inquiry on, 248, 252–253
social construction of, 248–249
terms related to, 247
typology of stages of, 251
See also racial/ethnic minorities
ethnocentrism, meaning of, 247
ethnography, **255–259**
critical ethnography, 258–259
deconstructive ethnography, 259
ethnographic accounts, writing of,
    257–258
ethnographic study, aspects of,
    256–257
features of, 255
impact of studies, 255–256

methods of study, 257
origins of, 256
as process/product, 255
reflexive ethnography, 259
and sociology of education, 255–256
Etzioni, Amatai, 9
event dropout rate, 315–316
Evolution of Educational Thought, The
    (Durkheim), 268
excellence movement, 590
extracurricular activities, **261–264**
gender bias, 293
origins of, 561–562
research topics on, 262–263
extrinsic theories, in feminist theory, 573,
    575–578

F

faculty members. *See* higher education
    faculty
false consciousness, of Marx, 112, 113
family
code theory, 89–92
and educational productivity, 207–208
and gender inequality in education,
    296–297
gender and mathematics achievement,
    284
gender role socialization, 284–285, 289
and high-risk children, 51
and high school dropouts, 316
and home schooling, 365–366
parental educational attainment, effects
    of, 297, 404–405
parental employment, 711–715
as social capital, 547, 548
women's role, traditional, 292–293
See also parental involvement
Farmer v. University and Community
    College System of Nevada, 32, 33
fathers
educational attainment, effect on sons,
    404–405
employment, family effects, 713–714
fear of success, and gender socialization,
    302
Featherstone, Joseph, 470
federal funding
magnet schools, 422
Native American colleges, 32
feedback, in open system, 603–604
Feldman, Sandra, 676
Feminism and Critical Pedagogy (Luke and
    Gore), 590
feminist theory, **571–582**
black feminism, 579
critical pedagogy, 590–591
critical perspective of, 572–573
of dual-labor market, 292–293
of education and gender research, 276,
    571–573
extrinsic theories, 573, 575–578
feminist materialism, 590
future research needs, 581–582

gender in education as topic, 571–574
of gender inequality in education, 293, 299
on ideology and identity, 384–385
intrinsic theories, 573, 574–575
liberal feminist approach, 574–575
maternal feminism, 576–577
poststructural feminism, 579–581
radical feminism, 575–576
rationalistic theories, 573
relational theories, 573–574, 578–581
research topics, 273, 276
resistance theory, 555
socialist feminism, 292–293, 575–576
Fifth Amendment, 67
Fine, Michelle, 699–700
Finn, Chester, 238, 476
Fisk University, 360
Fitcher, Joseph, 76
FitzGerald, Frances, 533
Flexner, Abraham, 468
Florida ex rel. Hawkins v. Board of Control, 153
folktales, and structuralism, 633–634
Follow Through, 525
Ford Foundation, 330
formalism, 633
Foundations of Social Theory (Coleman), 545
Fourteenth Amendment, 67, 152
framing
    in Bernstein's curriculum theory, 91–92
    in structuralism, 637
Framing Dropouts (Fine), 699
Francis W. Parker School, 468
Frasier v. Board of Trustees of the University of North Carolina, 153
Freedman, Samuel, 695
Freedmen's Bureau schools, 359
Freeman v. Pitts, 142
Freire, Paulo, 590
friendships
    among students, 86–87
    and cooperative learning, 87, 118
    cross-race friendships, 245–246
    same sex friends, 87
"Functional and Conflict Theories in Educational Stratification" (Collins), 270
functionalist theory, 267–270
    community colleges, 452
    compared to conflict theory, 270
    curriculum development, 128
    of Durkheim, 169, 267–268
    economic theory, 169–170
    educational applications, 268–269
    evaluation of, 270
    on functions of schooling, 268
    future view for, 270
    of higher education, 329, 335
    imperialism and education, 388
    mass schooling, 429–430
    of Merton, 269
    of Parsons, 268–269
    research applications, 269–270
    structural functionalism, 635

G

Gaines v. Canada, 151
Galbraith, John Kenneth, 236
Gamoran, Adam, 125, 441
Gandara, Patricia, 443
Gardner, Howard, 466
Geiger, Keith, 676
Geire v. Sundquist, 158
gender differences
    academic achievement, 182–183
    age of schooling, 181
    classroom interaction, 275
    competition, 301–302
    fields of study, 185–186
    graduate degrees, 185, 187
    high school transition to college, 185
    labeling as disabled, 181–182
    math and science achievement, 182–183
    parental involvement in education, 184–185
    professional degrees, 289
    speed of response, standardized tests, 282
    teacher behavior, 181, 184
gender and education research, 273–277
    ethical issues, 274
    feminist view. *See* feminist theory
    future view, 276–277
    guidelines for good research, 274–275
    and hidden/privileged realm curriculum, 274
    inconclusive areas, 275–276
    life histories, 274
    narratives, 274
    research methods used, 273–274
    research topics, 275–276
    sexist bias in, 273, 276, 279
    single-sex schools, 276, 339–340, 542, 543
    of women professionals in education, 277
gender equity
    educational access, 295–296, 298–299
    legal prohibition of sex discrimination, 20, 263, 281
    and parental educational attainment, 297
    participation in sports, 263
    and state policies, 296
    textbook content, 535
gender essentialisms, 575
gender inequality, 289–293
    income inequality, 186–188, 281
    and industrial era, 291
    and labor market, 291–293
    prevention of. *See* gender equity
    socialist feminist theory of, 292–293
    sociology of education focus, 8
    See also gender inequality in education; sex discrimination; sexism
gender inequality in education, 295–299
    choice factor, 298, 299
    and coeducation, 297
    and college entrance exams, 282, 303
    community college programs, 339, 457

and curriculum subject areas, 129
educational access issue, 296–298
and family, 296–297
female areas of study, 185–186, 298, 325, 339, 616
feminist view. *See* feminist theory
global view, 296–297
and hidden curriculum, 20, 291
and labor market, 292, 298
manifestations in classroom, 20
Marxist theory, 591
and mathematics. *See* gender and mathematics
professional degrees and gender, 289, 303
in research studies, 273, 276, 289
social reproduction theory, 299, 578
Southern schools, 143
teacher interactions, 181, 184, 245, 275, 277, 283–284, 304
See also gender and education research
gender and mathematics, **281–285**
    achievement differences, 182–183
    attitudes toward math, 183–184
    biological variables, 283
    and career opportunities, 281, 325, 339
    Catholic schools, 541
    confidence gap, 282–283
    and gender role socialization, 284–285
    guidelines for educators, 285
    home variables, 284
    SAT score differences, 281–283
    school variables, 283–284
    in secondary schools, 282
    and standardized tests, 303
Gender and Power (Connell), 573
gender socialization
    emotional/relational aspects and girls, 301
    and family, 284–285, 289
    and gender inequality, 289–290
    and play, 302, 304
gender socialization and education, 291, 292, **301–305**
    aggressive versus quiet students, 302, 304
    and child-rearing, 301
    and college experience, 303
    competitive aspects, 301–302
    and fear of success, 302
    limitations for females, 301–302
    and mathematics achievement, 284–285
    and racial/ethnic minorities, 304
    and same-sex play, 302
    sexist curricula/textbooks, 303
    and social class, 304
    teachers role, 302–303
genetic factors, IQ, 401, 695–696
geography, as aspect of ethnicity, 250
G.I. Bill, 143, 172, 321, 438, 613
    and multiculturalism, 444–445
Gift, The (Mauss), 633
gifted programs
    criticism of, 244
    recent modifications of, 244
Gilligan, Carol, 574–575

Gingrich, Newt, 239
Ginsburg, Mark B., 387
Ginsburg, Ruth Bader, 162
Gintis, Herbert
    on meritocracy, 439–440
    social reproduction theory, 236, 270,
        383, 551–552, 578, 588
Ginzberg, E., 172
Giroux, Henry
    critical pedagogy, 590
    as new sociologist, 595
    on postmodernism, 607–609
    reproduction theory, 236
    resistance theory, 555
Glass Ceiling Commission, 378
Glazer, Nathan, 444
global economy
    competitive factors, 175
    and educated workforce, 4–6
    human capital theory, 378
globalization of education, 307–313
    credentialing standards, 311
    cross-national studies, 393–397
    and curriculum, 311
    educational access and women,
        295–296
    gender equity, 295–296, 311
    gender inequality, 296–297
    intensification, reasons for, 307
    internationalism, 309
    nationalization of education, 307–308,
        311, 394–395
    nineteenth-century, 308–309
    scholarly interest in, 312–313
    and state formation, 309
    and UNESCO, 296, 307, 310–312,
        330
    See also imperialism and education;
        international higher education
Goals 2000, 195, 221, 228–229
    provisions of, 229
    sociological analysis of, 229
Goddard, Henry H., 194
Goddard, John, 620
Golden, John, 464
Good for Business: Making Full Use of the
    Nation's Human Capital, 378–379
Good, Thomas L., 681
Goodlad, John, 227
Goodson, Ivor F., 133, 136
Gordon, Milton, 443–444
grading, inequality related to, 113
graduate degrees
    African-Americans, 166
    gender differences, 185, 187
    Hispanics, 356
Gramsci, Antonio, 382, 589
grand theory
    of higher education, 330
    compared to middle range theory, 269
Grant, Linda, 289
grant-maintained schools
    England and Wales, 216, 217, 509
    financial factors, 516
    student outcome, 515
grass roots movement, meaning of, 545
Gratz et al. v. Bollinger et. al., 40

Gray, Frank, Jr., 158
Great Britain. See England and Wales,
    educational reform
Green v. County School Board, on
    desegregation plan, 1541
Greene, Maxine, 465, 608
Griggs v. Duke Power Co., 178
Gross, Beatrice, 470
Gross, Ronald, 470
Group Investigation method, 117
group learning. See cooperative learning
Grubb, W. Norton, 454, 456
Grutter et al. v. Blolinger et al., 40
Guradians of Tradition (Elson), 533
Gwynne, Julia, 693

H

habitus concept, 553
Hall, G. Stanley, 466
Hall, Peter M., 495
Hallinan, Maureen T., 241
Halsey, A.H., 332
Hammack, Floyd M., 321
Hampton Institute, 360
Handbood of Theory and Research for the
    Sociology of Education
    (Richardson), 9
Head Start
    effectiveness of, 401, 445, 696–697
    parental involvement in, 525
health, and at-risk students, 52
Hearn, James C., 329
hegemonic-state reproduction theory, 589
Henderson, Ronald, 665
Heritage Foundation, 230, 237
Herrnstein, Richard, 241, 400–401, 440,
    487
Heyns, Barbara, 405, 645
Hicks, Emily, 591
hidden curriculum, 19–21, 125–126
    and bilingual students, 57–58
    definition of, 19–20
    and gender-based research, 274
    and gender inequality, 20, 291
    and labor market, 589
    and racial/ethnic inequality, 20–21
    secrets of children's culture, 274
    and social class, 21, 126
high achievers
    and conflict theory, 113–114
    content of classroom discussion, 128
    and cooperative learning, 118
    and magnet schools, 421–426
    teacher treatment of, 245
    tracking effects, 243–244
high school. See Secondary schools
High School and Beyond (HS&B), 77,
    406, 409–413, 540, 708–709
high school dropouts, 315–319
    Catholic schools, 318
    cohort dropout rate, 316
    cross-cultural view, 315
    disadvantages for future, 317
    event dropout rate, 315–316
    and family, 316

    individual attainment process view,
        317–318
    life-course view, 319
    and low achievers, 316–317
    minority students as, 20, 50
    prevention, 318, 319
    regional differences, 316
    research issues, 319
    at-risk children of, 51
    social/institutional process view,
        318–319
    and socioeconomic status, 316
    and sports participation, 627
    status dropout rate, 316
    and urban schools, 316, 318, 693, 699
    versus stopouts, 316, 319
higher education, 321–326, 329–334
    college athletes, 627
    community colleges, 99–108, 336–337
    conflict theory of, 329–330, 335–336
    credentials and occupational attainment,
        113–114, 270, 324–325, 336
    cross-cultural view. See globalization of
        education; international higher
        education
    diversity of settings for, 322–323,
        615–616
    era of growth for, 321–322, 335, 613
    female versus male enrollment, 185,
        298–299, 325, 339, 616
    functionalist theory of, 329, 335
    gender inequality. See gender inequality
        in education
    and gender socialization, 303
    nontraditional students, 340
    older students, 340, 614
    preferential admissions policies, 36–37
    and racial/ethnic minorities. See higher
        education and desegregation; higher
        education and racial/ethnic minorities
    single-sex education, 539–544
    and social class, 240, 324, 337–338
    and social equality, 335–341
    and social stratification, 323–324, 333,
        336, 589, 614–615
    sociological study of, 613–617
    sociology of education focus, 8, 325
    as stratified system, 324
Higher Education Act of 1965, 31, 154
higher education and desegregation,
    151–167
    Adams decision, 143, 159, 161–162
    curriculum issues, 154
    diversity goals, 155–156, 159–160
    faculty/administrator hiring, 160–161,
        165
    and Latino students, 143, 154, 155
    1990 trends, 163–165
    in North, 154–156
    open-admissions policy, 31, 154, 156
    outcome of, 165–166
    post-Brown decision events, 153–163
    social science viewpoint of, 166–167
    in South, 143, 157–163
    students' reaction to, 154–157
    white enrollment in black colleges, 165
    white resistance to, 157–159

See also higher education and racial/
    ethnic minorities
higher education faculty
    affirmative action, 29, 35, 36
    cross-cultural view, 332
    gender-based research, 277
    legacies, 37
    racial/ethnic minority faculty/
        administrators, 160–161, 165, 325,
        362, 448
    selection criteria, 35
    women, 35, 325
higher education and racial/ethnic
        minorities, 343–350
    affirmative action, 29–40
    African-Americans, 325, 337, 338,
        345–350, 616–617
    areas of study, 349–350
    Asian Americans, 33, 34, 36, 325,
        338–339, 345–350
    black colleges, 143, 151, 153, 157,
        165, 339, 359–364
    college counseling, 345
    community college, 99, 107, 343–344,
        348
    completion rate, 347–348
    equal access. See affirmative action;
        higher education and desegregation
    ethnic studies, 154, 155, 325, 353,
        445–446, 617
    faculty/administrative positions,
        160–161, 165, 325
    and financial aid, 344
    graduate-level degrees, 166, 339, 356
    Hispanics, 143, 325, 337, 338, 343,
        353–358, 616–617
    long-term expectations of, 344–345
    math preparation and career
        opportunities, 325, 616–617
    Native American, 338, 345
    and open admissions, 337
    part-time enrollment, 347
    secondary school preparation for,
        345–347
    women, 325, 348, 356–357
Higher Learning in America (Veblen), 8,
    321, 613
Hinton, Carmelita, 468
Hirsch, E.D., 226, 230
Hispanics
    and affirmative action, 33, 34, 36
    in bilingual programs, 59, 60, 61
    in community college, 354–355
    diversity within population, 354
    dropout rate, 20
    educational attainment of, 491
    ethnic identity and college students,
        353–354
    foreign born and achievement, 491
    graduate school attendance, 356
    and higher education, 143, 325, 337,
        338, 344–350, 353–358, 616–617
    Hispanic studies programs, 154, 155,
        353
    Latina educational level, 356–357
    population statistics, 353
    secondary school achievement, 346–347

social capital of, 548
    U.S. population statistic, 491
historicist approach, curriculum
    development, 128
history, as aspect of ethnicity, 249, 251
Hochschild, Jennifer L., 67
Hoffer, Thomas B., 407, 435
Hofstadter, Richard, 464
Holmes Group, on teacher education,
    226–227
Holmes, Hamilton, 157, 226
home schooling, 365–369
    and academic achievement, 366–367
    Community Home Education (CHE)
        model, 368
    and Internet, 368–369
    legal issues, 363–364
    and local schools, 368
    out-of-home activities, 367
    parental motivation for, 365–366
    prevalence of, 365
    school attendance rate, 373
    and social development, 367
homeless children/youth, 371–374
    disabled homeless, 373
    educational problems of, 372–373
    homeless youth, profile of, 371
    McKinney Act provisions, 372
    parental involvement, 374
    population statistics, 371
    at-risk status of, 52
    run-aways, 372
    state policies, scope of, 373–374
homosexual students
    research needs, 276
    school-based difficulties, 20
Hood, James, 157, 158
Hopwood v. Texas, 32, 33, 40, 163–164
Horace's Compromise (Sizer), 19
How Teachers Taught (Cuban), 470
Howard University, 151, 153, 360
Hudson Institute, 476
Hughes, Everett, 256
Human Capital: A Theoretical and
    Empirical Analysis, with Special
    Reference to Education (Becker),
    377
human capital theory, 377–379
    applied to education, 170–173,
        175–176, 377–378
    and cross-national studies, 395
    and economic development, 378
    limitations of, 378–379
human relations approach, multicultural
    education, 449
humanism, on adult education, 27
Hunter, Charlayne, 157
Hunter, Margaret, 43
Hurn, Christopher J., 111, 399
Hutchins, Robert, 469

I

idealogues, and home schooling, 366
identity formation
    and activity participation, 262–263

and ethnicity, 251
ideology
    applied to schooling, 382–385
    conceptions of, 381
    contradictions within, 382
    and curriculum, 381–385
    feminist view of, 384–385
    Marxist view, 381–382
    and new sociology of education, 595
    reproduction studies, 383–384
    and social dynamics, 382
    subjectivity and identity, 384
immersion model, bilingual education, 55,
    56, 62
immigration
    assimilation of groups, 443–444, 488
    and community colleges, 459
    first wave, 463
    new wave, 446
    See also racial/ethnic minorities
Immigration Act of 1965, 446
imperialism and education, 387–391
    conflict theory, 388
    critical theory, 387
    curriculum, 390–391
    functionalist theory, 388
    language of instruction, 388–390
    role of teacher, 388
    world-systems theory, 387–388
    See also racial/ethnic minorities
Improving America's Schools Act of 1993,
    229
income inequality
    and educational inequality, 298
    rise of, 2, 5
    women, 186–188, 281
individualism
    and social mobility, 2
    See also progressive education
individualized instruction, 84
    progressive education, 465–466
industrialization
    Durkheim on, 111
    and gender inequality, 291
    Industrial Revolution, 463
    and mass schooling, 429–430
    and parental employment, 711–712
inequality
    early sociologists' view of, 111–112
    rise in United States, 2
    See also educational inequality; gender
        inequality; income inequality; racial/
        ethnic inequality
Inequality (Jencks), 439
Ingersoll, Richard M., 651
input, in open system, 602–603
institutional racism, and locus of control,
    45
institutional theory, mass schooling,
    430–431
instructional approaches
    cooperative learning, 115–119
    and learning styles, 245
    progressive education, 465–466
    for at-risk children, 53
intelligence
    types of, 244–245

See also IQ
intelligence tests. *See* IQ tests
interactionist approach, curriculum
   history, 133–134
International Association for the
   Evaluation of Educational
   Achievement (IEA), 312–313, 393,
   394, 540
International Baccalaureate, 311
International Bureau of Education, 310
international higher education, 329–334
   academic careers, 332
   class-based enrollments, 331
   educational expansion issue, 333
   future research issues, 333–334
   organizational factors, 331–332
   and power elites, 331
   and social policy, 332
   and social stratification, 330–331,
      333–334
   and sociological theory, 329–330
International Schools Association, 311
internationalism, 309
Internet, on-line schooling, 368–369
interviews, ethnographic method, 257
intrinsic theories, in feminist theory, 573,
   574–575
Inuits, 491
IQ (intelligence quotient)
   adoption studies, 401
   genetic factors, 401, 695–696
   measurement of, 399
   of mentally retarded, 621
   twin studies, 401
IQ tests, **399–402**
   bell curve concept, 241, 400–401, 440,
      487
   cultural bias, 400–401
   culture fair tests, 401, 622
   development of, 194, 399, 620
   function of, 399
   and future performance, 399, 401, 436
   score changes, 401
Ivy League colleges, and elite, 270

J

Jakobson, Roman, 634–635
Jencks, Christopher, 439, 440–441
Jensen, Arthur R., 400, 401, 695
Jentes–Mason, Roberta, 17
Jesuits, 308
Jewell, Joseph O., 359
Jigsaw method, 117
   Jigsaw II, 117
Jim Crow laws, 43, 67–68, 490
jobs and occupations
   and community college degree, 336,
      454, 456–457
   correspondence theory, 551–552
   educational credentials and opportunity,
      113–114, 270, 324–325, 336,
      551–552, 588
   gender inequality, 5, 291–292, 298
   and hidden curriculum, 589
   and mathematical ability, 281, 325

pre-hiring testing ban, 400, 436
   and schooling, 268, 269
   and status attainment, 269
   and vocational education, 707–709
John XXIII, Pope, 76
Johnson, Lyndon
   on racial segregation, 30, 31
   on school segregation, 156

K

Kallikaks, study of, 194
Karabel, Jerome, 100–102, 452–453,
   454–455
Karp, Karen, 281
Katopes, Peter, 23
Katzenback, Nicholas, 157–158
Kearns, David, 231, 237
Kennedy, Robert, 157–158
Kerckhoff, Alan, 406
Keyes v. School District No. 1, Denver,
   district-wide desegregation,
   141–142
Keynesian economics, 169
King, Edith W., 247
Kliebard, H.M., 136–137
Kohl, Herbert, 469
Kozol, Jonathan, 469, 698

L

La Folette, Robert, 463
labeling of students, at-risk students,
   49–50
labor market. *See* jobs and occupations
Laboratory School, 464, 465
language
   as aspect of ethnicity, 250, 251–252
   linguistics, structural theory, 634–635
language of instruction, in imperialistic
   settings, 388–390
Larry P. v. Wilson Riles, 621, 623
Latin School (Boston), school
   desegregation issue, 30
Lau v. Nichols, 58–59, 446, 490
Layton, David, 135
Leach, Edmund, 635
learning disabilities, evolution of category
   of, 620–622
*Learning to Labor: How Working Class
   Kids Get Working Class Jobs*
   (Willis), 17, 18, 554, 589
learning styles
   and instructional approaches, 245
   types of, 245
Learning Together model, 117
legacies, 37
Lesko, Nancy, 17
Levi–Strauss, Claude, and structuralism,
   635
Levinson, David L., 1, 221, 377
Lewis, Oscar, 696
liberal democratic principles, versus
   operation of schools, 2–3
liberal feminist approach

on gender and education, 574–575
   history of, 574
   problems related to, 575
   research topics, 574–575
Lieberman, Anne, 226
Lies My Teacher Told Me (Loewen), 534
life adjustment curriculum, 466
life-course theory, high school dropouts,
   319
life histories, gender and education
   research, 274
limited English proficiency (LEP)
   bilingual education, 55–62
   legal rights of, 446, 447
   meaning of, 51
   and at-risk status, 51–52
   school-based social capital, 548
Lincoln School, 468, 469
Lincoln University, 143
linguistic codes, and social reproduction,
   554
linguistics, and structuralism, 634–635
Livingston College, 360
Livingstone, D.W., 377
local education authorities (LEAs), 213,
   215–217, 474–475, 476, 510
local management of schools (LMS),
   216–217, 475, 476
locus of control
   and African-Americans, 44–46
   elements of, 44
longitudinal data of National Center for
   Educational Statistics (NCES),
   409–417
   Baccalaureate and Beyond (B&B) study,
      410, 413–414
   Beginning Postsecondary Student (BPS)
      survey, 410, 413–414
   data availability, 417
   High School and Beyond (HS&B)
      study, 409–413
   individual-level comparisons, 415–416
   institution-level comparisons, 415
   NELS:88, 409–414, 425
   NLS-72 study, 409–413
   and policymaking, 411
   sampling designs, 411–413
   time series/trend analysis of cohorts,
      414–415
   topics of focus, 409–410, 411
   trend estimation difficulties, 416
longitudinal studies, **403–417**
   disadvantages of, 404, 406
   National Longitudinal Study of 1972,
      405
   panel studies, 404
   of repeating a grade, 407–408
   summer learning, effects of, 405, 648
   tracking effects, 406
   trend studies, 404
   Wisconsin Study, 404–405
low achievers
   and conflict theory, 113
   and cooperative learning, 118
   as high school dropouts, 316–317
   at-risk students, 49–53
   teacher treatment of, 245

tracking effects, 86, 113, 243–244
Lowell High School (San Francisco), school desegregation plan, 30
Luckmann, Thomas, 248
Lucy, Autherine, 157

M

McCarthy, Cameron, 591
McClelland, David, 43
McGinty, Patrick J.W., 495
McLaren, Peter, 255
McLauren v. Oklahoma State Regents, 151–152
MacLeod, Jay, 236, 555
Madigan, Timothy J., 121
magnet schools, 421–427
    attendance-zone magnets, 425–426
    curricula of, 425
    and desegregation plans, 421, 423
    distribution by district, 423–424
    distribution by grade level, 424
    effectiveness of, 222
    evolution of, 421–422
    federal funds to, 422
    growth of, 422–423
    instructional approaches, 425
    national studies of, 422
    opportunities for enrollment, 426
    program-within-school-magnets, 425
    quality of education, 424–425
    racial/ethnic minority students, 423, 426
    at-risk students, 426
    compared to school choice, 424
    selection criteria, 426–427
    specialties of, 245
    in urban areas, 423
    whole-school magnets, 425
Magnet Schools Assistance Program (MSAP), 422
mainstreaming, 244
maintenance model, bilingual education, 55
Malone, Vivian, 157, 158
Manhattan Institute, 237
Mann, Horace, 6, 308, 463, 693
Mare, Robert, 441
Marks, Helen M., 75, 539
Marshall, Thurgood, 68, 69
Marx, Karl. *See* Marxist theory
Marxist theory, 587–597
    capital class, reassessment of, 590–591
    conflict in, 111–112, 270
    and critical pedagogy, 590, 592
    false consciousness in, 112, 113
    gender in, 591
    on ideology, 381–382
    on multiculturalism, 597
    and new sociology of education, 594
    race in, 591
    resistance theory, 587, 589–590
    social class in, 111–112, 587–588
    and social reproduction theory, 351–355, 383–384, 587–589

See also resistance theory; social reproduction theory
masculinity
    masculine behavior and classroom, 302
    and sports participation, 628
Maslach Burnout Inventory (MBI), 659
mass schooling, 429–433
    conflict theory, 430
    curriculum, 431–432
    functionalist theory, 429–430
    institutional theory, 430–431
    issues related to, 429, 432–433, 566
    and teacher training, 432
Master Plan, University of California, 615
maternal employment, 712–713
    and child outcome, 712
    and family activities, 712–713
maternal feminism
    focus of, 574–575
    on gender and education, 576–577
    problems related to, 575
maternal influence, and high-risk children, 51, 52
mathematics achievement
    Catholic school students, 541
    and high level occupations, 281, 325
    importance of, 281
    racial/ethnic minorities, 204–205, 325, 345, 346–347, 487, 616–617
    See also gender and mathematics
Mauss, Marcel, 633
Mayberry, Maralee, 365
measurement-driven instruction, 193–194
    pros/cons of, 193
Mehan, Hugh, 619
Meier, Deborah, 471, 700–701
melting pot model, assimilation, 444
men
    early socialization, 302
    fields of study, 298
    intolerance toward effeminate types, 276
    masculine behavior and athletics, 628
    masculine behavior and classroom, 302
    research needs related to, 276–277
    stigma of good student, 302
    See also gender differences
men students, education and parental decision, 297
mentally retarded
    IQ of, 621
    psychomedical model of, 620–621
    as special education category, 621–622
Mercer, Jane R., 619
Meredith, James, 157
meritocracy, 435–442
    contradiction related to, 437
    fictional work on, 435
    and higher education, 333
    increase in, 440–441
    influence on cognitive development, 441–442
    schools as, 112–113
    as social issue, 438–439
    and United States, 439–440
    use of term, 435

Merton, Robert, functionalist theory of, 269
metropolitan languages, instruction in developing nations, 388–390
Mexican-American studies, 154, 155
Mexican Americans, educational aspirations of, 639
Meyer, John, 236
Meyer v. Nebraska, 447
Mickelson, Roslyn Arlin, 29, 199, 371, 485
micro-macro theory, school desegregation, 145
middle range theory, compared to grand theory, 269
migrant students, at-risk status of, 52
Milkin, Michael, 175
Miller, S.M., 173
Millet, Kate, 575–576
Milliken v. Bradley, 70, 142
Milwaukee Parental Choice Program (MPCP), 223, 476
    African-American students, parent profile, 512
    evaluation of, 479–480, 515
    and students with disabilities, 511
minimal brain injury, 621
minorities. *See* Racial/ethnic minorities; specific minority groups
Missouri v. Jenkins, 142
Mitchell, Lucy Sprague, 468
modernist theory, elements of, 605
Moe, Terry M., 222, 238, 514
Moore, Wilbert, 169
moral aspects, of ethnicity, 250
Moral Education (Durkheim), 268
moral reasoning, and athletes, 628
Morehouse College, 360
Moreno, Jacob, 86
Moreno, Susan, 353
Morrill Act of 1862, 360
Morris Brown College, 360
mothers, employment, effects of, 712–713
motivation. *See* achievement motivation
Moynihan, Daniel Patrick, 444
Muller, Chandra, 353, 711
multiculturalism, 443–450
    anti-multiculturalism events, 448
    bilingual education, 446–447
    and *Brown* decision, 445
    and community college, 107, 459
    criticism of, 448, 449
    ethnic studies, 445–446
    and G.I. Bill, 444–445
    goals of, 447
    limited-English proficiency students, 446
    Marxist theory of, 597
    and new immigrants, 446
    policy issues, 252
    teaching approaches, 448–449
multiple-choice tests, limitations for assessment, 193
Murray, Charles, 241, 400–401, 440, 487, 695
Murray, Henry, 43
muscular Christian movement, 626

My Pedagogic Creed (Dewey), 464
Myrdal, Gunnar, 46

N

narratives, gender and education research, 274
Nation Prepared: Teachers for the 21st Century, The, 226–227
Nation at Risk, A, 7, 18
  cross-national information as impetus, 394
  curriculum recommendations, 345
  focus of, 470
  functionalist perspective of, 269–270
  on mathematics requirements, 182
  and school effectiveness movement, 225
  on world competitors, 204, 237
National Assessment of Educational Progress (NAEP), 182, 204, 346
National Assessment of Vocational Education (NAVE), 705–709
National Association for the Advancement of Colored People (NAACP)
  and *Brown* decision, 68, 142–143, 151–152
  and enforcement of Title IV, 159
National Association for Equal Opportunity in Higher Education, 159
National Association of School Superintendents, 665
National Association for Year-Round Education (NAYRE), 649
National Board for Professional Teaching Standards, 654, 655
National Center for Educational Statistics (NCES). *See* longitudinal data of National Center for Educational Statistics (NCES)
National Center for the Restructuring of Education, Schools, and Teaching, 226, 230
National Child Development Study (NCDS), 406
National Commission on Excellence. *See* *Nation at Risk, A*
National Commission on Excellence in Teacher Education, 226, 228
National Council for Student Studies, 535
National Defense Education Act, 172
National Education Goals, 448
National Education Longitudinal Study of 1988 (NELS:88), 409–414, 425
National Education Organization (NEA), 665–667
  administrator dominance, 666–667
  history of, 665–667, 677–678
  lobbying efforts, 667
  as teacher union, 669–671
National Governors Association, and educational reform, 222, 237
National Longitudinal Study of High School Class of 1972, 405, 540
National Teacher Examination, 657
National Teachers Association (NTA), 665

nationalization of education, 307–308, 311, 394–395
Native Americans, 491–492
  and affirmative action, 34
  alienation by schools, 20–21
  communication style of, 57
  and cultural imperialism, 391, 492
  current school attendance, 492
  federal funds to colleges of, 32
  genocide of, 491
  and higher education, 338, 344–350
  native language, repression of, 59
  reservations, 491, 492
  segregation/regulation of schooling, 492
  socioeconomic status of, 491–492
  U.S. population statistic, 491
Natriello, Gary, 49
Naumburg, Margaret, 468
need for achievement (nAch)
  elements of, 43–44
  limitations of theory, 43–45
  See also Achievement motivation
Neill, A.S., 469
neocolonialism, meaning of, 387
nepotism, 437
Network of Progressive Educators, principles of, 470–471
New Age movement, and home schooling, 366
New Right
  and quasi-markets, 474, 481
  and school choice, 474, 481, 508–509
new sociology of education, 593–596
  and Bernstein's theory, 95, 594
  and critical pedagogy, 596
  in England, 594, 595
  focus of, 564
  and ideology, 595
  and Marxist theory, 594
  and resistance theory, 595
  and social reproduction theory, 595
  in United States, 594
New Zealand, quasi-markets in, 475, 478–479, 511
Nixon, Richard, curtailment of school desegregation, 142, 157, 159
nonconformity
  as class-based politics, 554–555
  in resistance theory, 554–555, 589
"Nonsynchronist Parallelist" (McCarthy, Apple, Weis), 591–592
nonverbal communication, and culture, 57
norm-referenced tests
  elements of, 192
  uses of, 192
North Carolina Agriculture and Technical College, 153
Nozaki, Yoshiko, 381
nutrition, and at-risk students, 52

O

Oakley, Ann, 571–572
Oberlin, 143
occupations. *See* jobs and occupations
Odegaard v. DeFunis, 156

Office of Educational Research and Improvement, 229
On What Is Learned in School (Dreeben), 269
open-admissions policy, 31, 154, 156
  community college, 452
  end of, 337
  England, 475
  results of, 337
open classroom, 84
Open Door College, The (Clark), 100, 452
open systems approach, 599–604
  environment in, 601–602
  feedback in, 603–604
  input in, 602–603
  organization in, 600–601
  output in, 603
  usefulness of, 599
organization, in open system, 600–601
Organization for Economic Development (OECD), 1, 4, 5
organizational analysis, sociology of education focus, 7–8
output, in open system, 603
overidentification phenomenon, special education, 194

P

Pallas, Aaron M., 315
panel studies, longitudinal, 404
Pang, Ooka, 252
parental choice. *See* school choice
parental employment, 711–715
  and industrialization, 711–712
  maternal employment, 712
  occupational variation, 714
  paternal employment, 713–714
parental involvement
  charter schools, 512
  definition of, 526
  and education/social class, 404–405, 512–513, 527
  and educational productivity, 208
  effects of, 208
  of ethnic minorities, 252, 512
  in federal programs, 525
  forms of involvement, 527
  and gender of child, 184–185
  homeless children, 374
  and maternal employment, 713
  and school-based management, 504, 505
  and school choice, 512–513
  school-family-community partnerships, 525–531
  and social capital, 547–548
  and teacher practices, 527
Park, Robert, 256
Parker, Francis W., 468
Parkhurst, Helen, 468
parochial schools, Catholic schools, 75–80
Parsons, Talcott
  on higher education, 335
  structural functionalism of, 268–269, 635

participant observation, ethnographic method, 257
Passeron, Jean-Claude, 236, 588
patriarchy, radical feminist view, 576
Paul, Faith G., 151
Paul Quinn College, 360
Pearse, Caroll, 666
pedagogic discourse, Bernstein's theory, 92–95
pedagogic practice, Bernstein's theory, 93–95
pedagogues, and home schooling, 366
Pedagogy of the Oppressed (Freire), 590
Pedagogy, Symbolic Control and Identity (Bernstein), 89
peer evaluation
    teacher assessment, 654–655
    teacher unions on, 674–675
peers
    and classroom inequality, 245–246
    friendships among students, 86–87, 118
    peer tutoring, 244, 245
    tracking effects, 690
Pell Grants (Basic Education Opportunity Grants), creation of, 31
People for the American Way, 535
performance assessment, 195–196
personal choice
    educational, of women, 298, 299
    high school dropouts, 317–318
    single-sex education, 542
    vocational education, 706
personal growth
    and adult education, 27
    Catholic school students, 542
    elements of, 195
    issues related to, 196
Pew Charitable Trusts, 476
Picot Report, 475
Pincus, Fred L., 454, 587
play
    gender roles in, 304
    same-sex, 302
Plessy v. Ferguson, 67–69, 70, 151, 360, 361
Plowden Report, The, 395
Podoresky v. Maryland, 31, 32–33, 163–164
politics
    as aspect of ethnicity, 250, 252
    and school-based management, 504
    and school choice, 507–509
    and schooling, 268
Politics, Markets and America's Schools (Chubb and Moe), 222, 238, 514
positivism, 6
Postmodern Education (Aronowitz and Giroux), 607
postmodernism, **605–610**
    Giroux's theory, 607–609
    history of, 605–606
    pros/cons of theory, 609–610
    themes in, 606–607
Postmodernism, Feminism, and Cultural Politics (Giroux), 607
poststructural feminism

focus of, 579, 580
Foucalt's influence, 589–590
    problems related to, 581
    standpoint theories, 590
poverty
    Culture of Poverty thesis, 44–45
    emotional effects of, 694
    and hidden curriculum, 21
    and high school dropouts, 316
    and Hispanics, 491
    homeless children/youth, 371–374
    and Native Americans, 491–492
    perpetuation by schools, 21, 194
    and at-risk status, 50–51
    and single-parent families, 51
    and special education classes, 622–623
    and teacher expectations, 85
    and tracking, 194
    urban schools, 694–697
    See also social class; socioeconomic status
Pratt, Caroline, 468
price competition, economics of education, 176–177
Primitive Classification (Durkheim and Mauss), 633
private schools
    child-centered/progressive schools, 468
    effectiveness of, 222, 515
    parochial schools. *See* Catholic schools
    compared to public schools, 515
    school choice, 479–480
production function analysis, of school effects, 520–521
program-within-school-magnet schools, 425
progressive education, **463–472**
    child-centered model of, 466–468
    child-centered private schools, examples of, 468
    contributions to educational philosophy, 466–467
    contributions to pedagogy, 466–467
    criticisms of, 469, 470
    curriculum of, 466, 467
    and democracy, 465
    Dewey's concept of, 463–467
    features of movement, 467
    history of, 463–470
    instructional approach, 465–466
    Network of Progressive Educators, principles of, 470–471
    and open/alternative education, 470
    and public schools, 471
    and secondary schools, 468–469
    and social efficiency model, 466
    and social engineering, 467–468
    and social reconstructionism, 467
    and sociology of education, 471–472
    teacher's role in, 465
Progressive Movement, agenda of, 463
Project Head Start, 252
Project Talent, 411
Proposition 187, 60
Proposition 209 (California Civil Rights Initiative), 32, 33, 40, 164
Propp, Vladimir, 633, 633–634

PSAT (Preliminary Scholastic Aptitude Test), gender differences and scores, 303
psychomedical model, of mental retardation, 620–621
psychometric theory, 192
public schools
    compared to Catholic schools, 406–407
    magnet schools, 421–427
    compared to private schools, 515
Puerto Rico, historical view, 59
Puget Sound Community School, 368
Putnam, Robert, 545
Putney School, 468

Q

qualifications, educational, 113–114
quasi-markets in education, **473–482**
    and democracy, 480–481
    and educational inequality, 474, 477–479, 481–482
    in England, 474–475, 476–478
    meaning of, 473
    and New Right, 474, 481, 508–509
    in New Zealand, 475, 478–479
    parental choice in, 473–474
    proponents/critics of, 473–474
    research studies, 476–480
    school autonomy in, 473–474, 476
    in United States, 475–476, 479–480, 511–512
    See also school choice
Quetelet, Adolphe, 309
Quiroz, Pamela Anne, 261

R

race, meaning of, 485
racial/ethnic inequality
    and hidden curriculum, 20–21
    inequality of opportunity, 489
    and IQ tests, 400–401
    rise of, 5
    and tracking, 194, 243, 346, 489, 688
    and university admissions policies, 36–37
    See also African-American discrimination
racial/ethnic minorities, **485–493**
    affirmative action, 29–40
    age and academic success, 56
    bilingual education, 55–62
    in Catholic schools, 75, 78–79
    cross-race friendships, 245–246
    cultural models of, 488–489
    and cultural values, 487–488
    culture and academic achievement, 639–642
    educational attainment by race, 487
    educational attitudes of, 200–201, 489
    educational productivity gains, 204–205
    gender socialization and education, 304
    groups in the U.S. (1999), 486

and higher education. *See* higher
    education and racial/ethnic minorities
involuntary minorities, cultural
    framework of, 488, 640
IQ issue, 241, 400–401, 440, 487
in magnet schools, 423, 426
in Marxist theory, 591
mathematics achievement, 204–205,
    325, 346–347, 487
parental involvement, 252, 512
perception of inequality, 488–489
at-risk status, 50, 52
SAT scores, 487
and school choice, 513–514
science achievement, 487
special education placement, 194
and sports participation, 628–629
in vocational education, 705, 706
See also multiculturalism; specific
    minority groups
racism and discrimination
    Americans' awareness of, 68
    institutional racism, 45
    as moral aspect of ethnicity, 250
    textbook presentation of, 534
    See also African-American
        discrimination; inequality
radical feminism, 575–576
    patriarchy, view of, 576
    problems related to, 576
    research topics of, 576
Ramirez, Francisco O., 429
rationalistic theories, in feminist theory,
    573
Ravitch, Diane, 269, 465, 467
reading achievement
    Catholic school students, 542
    racial/ethnic minorities, 204–205
reading proficiency, racial/ethnic
    minorities, 346
Reagan, Ronald, education policy, 237,
    470, 475, 508
Reder, M., 172
Rees, C. Roger, 625
Reese, A., 172
reflexive ethnography, 259
reform. *See* educational reform
*Regents of the University of California v.
    Bakke*, 31, 32, 156–157
regional differences, high school dropouts,
    316
Reich, Robert, 231, 236
*Reinventing Education: Entrepreneurship in
    America's Public Schools* (Gerstner),
    7
*Reinventing Public Education: How
    Contracting Can Transform
    America's Schools* (Hill et al.), 7
relational theories, in feminist theory,
    573–574, 578–581
relative deprivation theory, of
    neighborhood effects, 208
religion
    as aspect of ethnicity, 250
    parental, and home schooling, 366, 368
religious schools. *See* Catholic schools

remedial education, and community
    colleges, 107, 458–459
repeating a grade
    and high school dropouts, 316
    longitudinal study of, 407–408
reproduction. *See* social reproduction
    theory
research methods
    causation, criteria for, 403
    cross-sectional studies, 403
    ethnographic research, 257
    longitudinal studies, 403–417
reservations, Native Americans, 491, 492
resistance theory, 554–555, 589–590
    and African-Americans, 640
    feminist theory, 555
    importance of, 595
    and new social movements, 555
    and new sociology of education, 595
    nonconformity in, 554–555, 589
    student resistance, forms of, 589–590,
        640
restructuring, **495–500**
    Accelerated Schools Project (ASP), 497
    Coalition of Essential Schools (CES),
        497
    criteria for implementation of, 496
    and district-level priorities, 496
    facilitation and school characteristics,
        498
    failure and school characteristics, 499
    issues related to, 499
    outcome of, 496, 522
    research on, 497–499
    School Development Program (SDP),
        497
    and state-level priorities, 496
    and student performance, 498
retention. *See* repeating a grade
rewards, in cooperative learning, 115, 117
Rise of the Meritocracy, The (Young), 5,
    435
Rong, Xue Lan, 289
Rosenbaum, James E., 705
Rueda, Robert, 619
run-aways, reasons of, 372
rural schools, restructuring, 497

S

Sadovnik, Alan R., 1, 89, 221, 267, 605
Sanders, Mavis G., 525
Sanders v. Ellington, 158
Sandor, Jan, 329
SAT. *See* College entrance exams
de Saussure, Ferdinand, and structuralism,
    634–635
Savage Inequalities (Kozol), 698
Schiller, Kathryn S., 403
Schlesinger, Arthur, 449
Schmidt, Carl, 409
Schneider, Barbara, 545
scholarships, race-based, 156, 163–164
school autonomy, in quasi-markets,
    473–474, 476
school-based management, 225, **501–506**

effectiveness of, 225, 503–504
history of, 502
implementation issues, 504–505
issues related to, 505–506
operation of, 501–502
outcomes of, 505
and parental involvement, 504, 505
principal control approach, 502–503
site council as policymaker, 503, 504
teacher control approach, 503, 504
School Board of Oklahoma City v. Dowell,
    142
school-business partnerships, 224
    effectiveness of, 224
school choice, 222–224, **507–517**
    charter schools, 223, 509, 511–512
    controlled choice programs, 510, 515
    controversy related to, 222–223
    demand-side studies, 512–514
    and educational inequality, 480, 511
    efficiency studies, 514–516
    grant-maintained schools, 216, 217,
        509
    magnet schools, 421–427, 424, 510
    neoconservative reformers on, 508–509
    neoliberal reformers on, 508
    parental choice of schools, 473–474,
        512–515
    and parental involvement, 512–513
    political aspects, 507–508
    as power elite policy, 238–239
    private schools, 479–480
    and reduction of welfare state, 509–510
    research topics, 223
    and restructuring, 497
    state-wide open enrollment plans, 511
    and student academic outcome,
        514–515
    as student decision, 513–514
    successful programs, 476, 479–480
    supply-side studies, 510–512
    and teaching practices, 516
    tuition vouchers, 223, 509, 512, 515
    See also quasi-markets in education
school climate
    coeducational school, 541
    culture and power studies, 384
    and educational inequality, 242
    measurement of, 242
    single-sex schools, 541
school desegregation, 67–73, **141–148**
    and affirmative action, 29–30
    and African-American achievement, 70,
        71
    African-American views of, 71
    busing, 70, 146–148
    and Catholic schools, 77
    colleges/universities. *See* affirmative
        action; higher education and
        desegregation
    conditions for, 145–146
    Green decision, 141
    Keyes decision, 141–142
    and magnet schools, 421, 423
    micro-macro theory, 145
    Milliken II remedies, 142
    and minority gains, 145, 205

outcomes, 144–145
Plessy decision, 67–69, 70, 151, 363
secondary school level, 30
sociological evaluation of, 71–73
and U.S. regions, 144, 146
and white flight, 71, 72, 144
white resistance to, 30, 69–71
within-school approaches, 146
See also Brown v. Board of Education;
busing
School Development Program (SDP), 497
school districts
choice plans, 475–476
and restructuring, 496
and school-based management,
502–503, 506
school effectiveness movement, 225–226
basic premise of, 562
effective schools, features of, 225, 521
school restructuring approach, 226
school effects, 519–523
absolute effects, 520
Coleman's view, 519–520, 522, 523
effective schools research, 521
implementation of changes, 533
implications for ineffective schools, 521,
523
importance of, 521
production function studies, 520–521
relative effects, 520
and restructuring, 496, 522
and school-family-community
partnerships, 525–531
and school as social system, 521–523
student influence on, 521–523
and summer learning, 646–650
school-family-community partnerships,
525–531
overlapping influences theory, 526
parental involvement, forms of, 528
research study conclusions on, 526–527
research needs, 529–530
sociological inquiry needs, 531
school resources
and educational productivity, 206–207
and restructuring, 499
and at-risk children, 52–53
school segregation
black schools, pre-civil rights, 490
current rise of, 5, 70
de facto segregation, 68, 152, 154
de jure segregation, 69, 70, 152, 154,
163
DHEW enforcement of, 158–160
and dual-system of higher education,
361–363
end of, 8, 45
school size
and educational productivity, 206
and extracurriculum, 262
School and Society, The (Dewey), 464
School Subjects and Curriculum Change
(Goodson), 136
school vouchers, teacher unions on, 673
School-to-Work Opportunities Act of
1994, 224, 229
school-to-work programs, 224

components of, 224
effectiveness of, 224
schooling
definition of, 205
functions of, 268, 308
Schooling in Captialist America (Bowles
and Gintis), 3, 270, 439–440, 551
Schooling for Women's Work (Deem), 572
Schultz, T., 171
Schundler, Bret, 239
science, attitudes toward, gender
differences, 183–184
science achievement
Catholic school students, 541–542
gender differences, 182–183
racial/ethnic minorities, 487
science occupations, women, income
inequality, 179–180
Science for the People (Layton), 135
scientific management, educational
application, 466–467
secondary schools
Catholic schools, 18, 75, 78–80
female math performance, 282
high school dropouts, 315–319
New Basics curriculum, 345
opportunities and minorities, 37, 346
and progressive education, 468–469
racial/ethnic minorities achievement,
346–347
racial/ethnic minorities and college
preparation, 345–347
school desegregation, 30
single-sex schools, 539–544
Selden, David, 676
selection committees, textbook adoptions,
536
self-concept
and achievement motivation, 45–46
of African-Americans, 45–46
self-esteem of students
and cooperative learning, 118
female Catholic school students, 542
and teacher behavior, 245
and tracking, 244, 690
self-evaluation, teacher assessment,
654–655
self-fulfilling prophesy, and labeling,
49–50
Semel, Susan F., 221, 463
separate but equal, *Plessy* decision, 67–69,
70, 151, 361, 363
Seven Sisters colleges, 543
Sewell, William, 318
sex discrimination
dual-labor market theory, 291–293
secondary discrimination, 292
types of jobs, 292
sexism
in coeducation, 542–543
in curriculum, 303
in gender and education research, 273,
276, 279
single-sex schools, 542–543
textbooks, 303
sexual harassment, 20
sexuality, research data, ethical issues, 274

Shady Hill School, 468
Shaffer, H.G., 171
Shankar, Albert, 238, 676
Shape of the River, The (Bowen), 32
Shaw University, 360
Shopping Mall High School (Powell et al.),
18, 225
Shor, Ira, 589, 590
Shouse, Roger C., 519
Silberman, Charles S., 469
single group studies approach,
multicultural education, 449
single-parent family
and high school dropouts, 316
homeless families, 371
and at-risk status, 51
single-sex education, 539–544
academic achievement, 541–542
benefits for female students, 339–340,
542, 543
and educational aspirations, 542
issues related to, 544
research focus, 276, 539, 540–541
research studies on, 540
school climate, student perception of,
541
sexism in, 542–543
as student choice, 542
student involvement in schoolwork, 541
sustained effects of, 543
and Title IX, 539
transition to coeducation, reasons for,
540
Sipuel v. Board of Regents, 151
site-based decision making, and teacher
unions, 673–674
site council, and school-based
management, 503, 504
Sizer, Theodore R., 9, 226, 230, 471
Slaughterhouse Cases, 67
slavery, abolition of, 67
Slavin, Robert E., 115
Small Victories (Freedman), 695
Smith, Adam, 169, 203
Smith, Mortimer, 469
Smith, Stephen Samuel, 141
Smith, Thomas M., 181, 343
Smithfield Project, 478
social action approach, multicultural
education, 449
social capital, 545–549
characteristics of, 546–547
Coleman on, 545, 546–548
and community, 546–547
as constraint, 546, 547
meaning of, 5, 546
and parental involvement, 547–548
and private schools, 515
and at-risk students, 548
school-based, 548–549
and social mobility, 5–6
theoretical conceptions of, 545–546,
548
"Social Capital in the Creation of Human
Capital" (Coleman), 545
social class
as aspect of ethnicity, 250, 252

code theory, 89–92
   and conflict theory of education,
      112–113, 270
   and cultural capital, 121–123, 552–553
   and curriculum, 588
   elite and educational reform, 235–239
   gender socialization and education, 304
   and hidden curriculum, 21, 126, 588
   and higher education, 270, 324,
      337–338, 615
   and linguistic codes, 554
   location factors, 513
   Marxist theory of, 111–112, 587–588
   and nonconformity, 554–555
   and parental choice, 512–513
   and pedagogic practice, 92, 93
   See also elite; poverty; socioeconomic
      status
social efficiency model, and progressive
   education, 466
social efficiency movement, features of,
   261
social-emotional development, and home
   schooling, 367
social engineering, and progressive
   education, 467–468
social justice, and, Catholic schools, 77
social policy, and international higher
   education, 332
social ranking, student hierarchies, 85–86
social reconstructionist approach
   multicultural education, 449
   and progressive education, 467
social reproduction theory, **551–555**
   correspondence principle, 551–552
   criticism of, 552, 554–555
   and cultural capital, 552–553
   cultural reproduction theory, 588–589,
      640
   economic reproduction theory, 588
   gender codes, 578
   gender inequality in education, 299,
      578
   hegemonic-state reproduction theory,
      589
   linguistic codes, 554
   and Marxist theory, 351–355, 383–384
   and new sociology of education, 595
   reproduction studies, 383–384
   and resistance theory, 554–555
   and socialist feminism, 578
   sociological roots of, 551
   and textbooks, 533, 534, 588–589
social status, and tracking, 86, 243
social stratification
   and community colleges, 337, 452–453
   and educational stratification, 616–617
   and higher education, 323–324, 333,
      336, 588, 589, 614–615
   and international higher education,
      330–331, 333–334
   meaning of, 323
social system, school as, 521–523
socialist feminism
   on dual-labor market, 292–293
   focus of, 575–576
   on gender and education, 575–576

problems related to, 578
   social reproduction theory, 578
socialization
   gender socialization, **301–305**
   and hidden curriculum, 125–126
   meaning of, 247, 301
   neighborhood effects, 208
   reproduction theory, 383
   scope of, 125
   societal effects, 268
   See also gender socialization; gender
      socialization and education
society, societal value of schooling, 268,
   269
socioeconomic status
   adult learners, 26–27
   and affirmative action, 39–40
   as aspect of ethnicity, 250
   and educational productivity, 205, 206,
      207
   and hidden curriculum, 21
   and high school dropouts, 316
   low-SES schools, student achievement,
      522–523
   and parental involvement, 404–405,
      512–513, 527
   and teacher expectations, 85
   and tracking, 86, 126, 243, 441, 688
   wealthy schools, advantages of, 206
   See also elite; poverty; social class
sociology of education, **1–10**
   and citizenship, 6–7
   and conflict theory, 3
   as critical theory, 559–569
   and dedifferentiation in education, 562,
      565
   development of field, 9–10, 562–564
   elements of, 3–4
   feminist theory of, 571–582
   functionalist theory, 267–270
   and higher education, 8, 613–617
   importance of, 1–3
   intellectualist stance, 564–565
   learning as topic in, 566–567
   mainline tradition, 269
   Marxist theory, 587–597
   new sociology of education, 564,
      593–596
   open systems approach, 599–604
   organizational analysis in, 7–8
   postmodernism, 605–610
   and structural differentiation in
      education, 561–562
   and structuralism, 636–637
Sociology of Teaching, The (Waller), 112,
   256, 521
sociometry, origin of, 86
sociopolitical context
   affirmative action, 36
   bilingual education, 58–62
Soodak, Leslie C., 191
Southern Regional Education Board, 227
Spade, Joan Z., 301
special education, **619–624**
   and category of disability, 621–622
   history of, 619–620
   homeless disabled students, 373

legal aspects, 621, 622, 623
   mainstreaming, 244
   organizational issues related to,
      622–623
   overidentification phenomenon, 194
   and poor, 622–623
   social construction view of, 623
   testing for placement, 194–195
specialized curriculum schools, 511
Spelman College, 360
Spencer, Herbert, 169
Spender, Dale, 572
sports, **625–629**
   and academic achievement, 626
   American myths related to, 625
   college athletes, 627
   conflict theory of, 625
   dropout rate reduction, 626–627
   and educational aspirations, 626
   female participation in, 263
   future research, 629
   history of, 626
   and masculinity, 628
   and racial/ethnic minorities, 628–629
   and social values, 628
Sputnik, 173, 204
   and U.S. educational reform, 469
standardized tests, 192–195
   criterion-referenced tests, 192
   criticisms of, 192–195
   cross-national studies, 395
   curriculum/instruction concerns,
      192–193
   and gender bias, 282, 303
   norm-referenced tests, 192
   for special education placement,
      194–195
State, Family and Education (David), 572
states and state regulation
   home schools, 367–368
   learning disabilities variations, 622
   state-wide open enrollment plans, 511
   textbook adoption, 536–537
   textbook content, 535–536
   and tuition vouchers, 509
status attainment
   and equality of opportunity, 241–242
   Wisconsin model view of, 318
status dropout rate, 316
status of students
   classroom determinants, 85–86
   and cultural capital, 122–123
   and student-teacher interaction,
      125–126
stepfamily, and high school dropouts, 316
Stewart B. McKinney Homeless Assistance
   Act, 372
stopouts, 316, 319
structuralism, **633–637**
   code theory, 89–92, 636–637
   history of, 633–635
   pedagogic discourse, 92–95
   pedagogic practice, 93–95
   research based on, 637
   and sociology of education, 636–637
   structural functionalism, 635

Struggle for the American Curriculum, The (Kliebard), 137
student performance, as teacher assessment, 652
Student Team Learning methods, 115–117
   Cooperative Integrated Reading and Composition (CIRC), 116–117
   Student Team Learning methods, 551–552
   Student Teams-Achievement Divisions (STAD), 116
   Teams-Games-Tournament (TGT), 116
students
   classroom status hierarchy, 85–86
   friendships of, 86–87
   influence on school standards, 521–522
   sociology of education focus, 9
students with disabilities. *See* special education
Studies in Curriculum History (Goodson), 136
Stuyvesant High School, 476
subjectivity and identity, 384
Suicide (Durkheim), 267
summer learning, **645–650**
   longitudinal study of, 405, 648
   rationale for, 646
   compared to school-year learning, 646–648
   sociological focus on, 646
   year-round education, 649
Summerhill (Neill), 469
Sumner, William Graham, 169
supply-side economics, and school choice, 510–512
Sustaining Effects Study, 648
Swann v. Charlotte-Mecklenburg, on intradistrict busing, 141–142, 146–148
Swartz, David, 551
Sweatt v. Painter, 68, 151
symbolic control, Bernstein's theory, 92–93
System of Multicultural Pluralistic Assessment (SOMPA), 622

T

Taxman v. Board of Education of the Township of Piscataway, 23, 33
Taylor, Frederick W., 466–467
teacher assessment, **651–657**
   assessment laboratories, 654–655
   classroom observation, 651–652
   criticism of, 652–653
   National Teacher Examination, 657
   new view of, 653–654
   peer evaluation, 654–655
   self-evaluation, 654–655
   sociological approach to, 655–656
   student performance as, 652–653
teacher behavior
   bias and gender, 181, 184, 245, 275, 277, 283–284, 304
   bias and race, 245

   bias and student achievement, 85, 113, 245
   teacher evaluations, 84
   teacher expectations, 245
   and tracked students, 125–126, 245
teacher burnout, **659–663**
   adverse effects on students, 663
   high-risk personalities, 661
   long-term effects, 662–663
   measures of, 659–660
   prevalence of, 661
   psychological view of, 659–660
   and school reform, 661–662
   sociological view of, 660
   and stress, 663
Teacher Council Movement, 502
teacher education, 226–228
   concerns related to, 226–227, 671–672
   major reports on, 226–227
   and mass schooling, 432
   recommendations for change, 228, 672
teacher unions, **665–678**
   American Federation of Teachers (AFT), 667–669
   on charter schools, 675–676
   collective bargaining, 668–669, 672, 678
   merger proposal, 676–677
   National Education Organization (NEA), 665–667, 669–671
   on peer evaluation, 674–675
   on school finance system, 672–673
   on school vouchers, 673
   and site-based decision making, 673–674
teachers
   authority position of, 83–84
   change of methods, effects of, 84–85
   and critical pedagogy, 590
   and parental involvement, 527
   reform goals of 1980s-1990s, 229–230
   reprofessionalization of, 567–568
   research on teachers, 679–680, 683–684
   research on teaching, 682–683
   and restructuring, 496
   role in progressive setting, 465
   salaries, 671
   and school-based management, 503, 504
   sociology of education focus, 9
Teachers College, Columbia University, 468
Teachers for Our Nation's Schools, 227
team learning. *See* cooperative learning
Teams-Games-Tournament (TGT), 116
teenage pregnancy
   and high school dropouts, 317
   and at-risk children, 52
Temporary National Economic Committee, 175
Terman, Lewis, 399, 620
test anxiety
   and IQ test studies, 401
   standardized tests, 193
test bias, IQ tests, 400
Texas, textbook adoption, 536–537

textbooks, **533–537**
   content absent from, 534–535
   cost factors, 535
   functions of, 533
   ideological analysis of, 385
   sexist, 303
   and social reproduction theory, 533, 534, 588–589
   and societal changes, 533–534
   state adoption practices, 536–537
   state influence on content, 535–536
   theoretical perspectives related to, 533
Thematic Apperception Test (TAT), 43
Third International Mathematics and Science Study (TIMSS), 393, 396
Third World. *See* imperialism and education
Thirteenth Amendment, 67
36 Children (Kozol), 469
Thomas, Clarence, on affirmative action, 39
Thompson, Charles, 153
Thorndike, Edward L., 466
Time for Results: The Governor's 1991 Report on Education, 238
time series analysis, of cohorts, 414–415
Title I programs, 525
   effectiveness of, 697
Title IX. *See* Civil Rights Act of 1964, Title IX
To Teach as Jesus Did, 76–77
Toch, Thomas, 676
Tomkins, George, 137
Tomorrow's Schools of Education, 227
Tomorrow's Teachers, 227
Tonnies, Ferdinand, 267
tort law, legal basis, 152
tracking, **687–691**
   and academic achievement, 86, 243–244, 689
   basis for, 242–243
   Catholic schools, 78
   cross-cultural view, 244
   and curriculum differentiation, 126–128
   detracking, 243, 690–691
   differential educational practices, 688–689
   and educational aspirations, 689
   and educational productivity, 207
   emotional impact, 244, 690
   history of, 687
   and inequality, 126–128, 194, 207, 242–244, 346
   longitudinal study of, 406
   nonacademic factors, 243
   proponents view of, 243
   and racial/ethnic minorities, 194, 243, 346, 489, 688
   social impact, 690
   and socioeconomic status, 86, 126, 243, 441, 688
   and teacher-student interaction, 125–126, 245
transformation approach, multicultural education, 449

transitional models, bilingual education, 55
Traub, James, 693–694
trend studies
    limitations of, 416
    longitudinal, 404
    trend analysis of cohorts, 414–415
Tribally Controlled Community College Assistance Act, 31
Trow, Martin, 332
Truly Disadvantages, The (Wilson), 713
tuition vouchers, 223
    and state control, 509
    and student outcome, 515
    student selection, 512
Turner, Ralph H., 331
Tuskegee Institute, 360–361
Twentieth Century Fund, 237
twin studies, of IQ, 401
two-way model, bilingual education, 55, 62

U

UNESCO
    Convention against Discrimination in Education, 296
    and globalization of education, 296, 307, 310–312, 330
unions. *See* teacher unions
United Organization, 676
universities. *See* Higher education
University of California, Master Plan, 615
University of North Carolina, enrollment and race, 143, 144
urban schools, **693–702**
    academic achievement, 695
    Central Park East Secondary School (CPESS), 700–702
    high school dropouts, 316, 318, 693, 699
    magnet schools, 423
    and poor, 694–697
    population characteristics, 694–695
    restructuring, 497
    and at-risk students, 698–699
    school-centered research, 697–698
    student-centered research, 695–697
U.S. v. Fordice, 32, 40, 162
U.S. v. Louisiana, 32, 40

V

values
    cultural, 487–488
    and sports participation, 628

Van Kirk, Amy, 501
Vatican Council II, effects on Catholic schools, 76–77
Veblen, Thorsten, 8, 321, 613
verbal achievement, Catholic school students, 542
Vindication of the Rights of Women, A (Wollstencraft), 574
Virginia Military Institute, female admissions, 143
vocational education, **705–709**
    and college attendance, 707
    community colleges, 452–453
    isolation of students, 705–706
    job outcome, 707–709
    racial/ethnic minorities in, 705, 706
    school-to-work programs, 224
    student choices, 706
    student outcome, 707
    student selection, 706

W

Wald, Lillian, 463
Walden School, 468
Wales. *See* England and Wales, educational reform
Walford, Geoffrey, 211
Walker, Alice, 448
Wallace, George, 157–158
Waller, Willard, 112, 262, 521
Warren, Earl, 68
Washington, Booker T., 360–361
Wealth of Nations (Smith), 169, 203
Weber, Max
    conflict theory of, 112, 270
    on higher education, 329–330
    on social status, 236
Weis, Lois, 591
Weisbrod, Burton, 171
welfare state, and school choice, 509–510
Wells, Amy Stuart, 507
Wessman v. Gittens, 32
Westerhof-Shultz, Jolanda, 17
Wexler, Philip, 593
What Do Our Seventeen Year Olds Know? (Ravitch and Finn), 225
white flight, and school desegregation, 71, 72, 144
white students
    and educational attainment, 492
    ethnic identity, 492
Whittle, Chris, 238
Whittle Communications, 238
Whitty, Geoff, 473
Who Gets Ahead? (Jencks), 439
whole-school magnet schools, 425

Wilberforce University, 143
Willis, Paul, 17, 18, 554, 589
Wirth, Louis, 256
Wisconsin Idea, 463
Wisconsin Study, 404–405
    on educational attainment, 318
Wisconsin v. Yoder, 367
Wohlstetter, Priscilla, 501
Wollstencraft, Mary, 574
women
    and adult education, 24
    and affirmative action, 31–32, 33–37
    and economics of education, 172, 176–177
    educational achievements, 181–188
    educational attitudes of, 200–201
    educational inequality. *See* gender inequality in education
    fields of study, 298, 325
    as higher education faculty, 35, 325
    successful, single-sex school graduates, 543
    work and motherwork roles, 292, 714
    See also gender differences; gender inequality; sex discrimination; sexism
Women and Education (Byrne), 572
Women and Schooling (Deem), 572
women's studies, 325
Wong, Sandra L., 533, 639
Wooden v. Board of Regents of the University System of Georgia, 32
workforce, education, importance of, 4–5
workplace. *See* jobs and occupations
World Bank, 5, 330
World Conference on Education for All, 432
World Survey of Education, 312
world-systems approach
    curriculum development, 128–129
    imperialism and education, 387–388
World War II, and G.I. Bill, 143, 172, 321, 438, 444–445, 613
Wrong, Dennis, 236

Y

Yale School Development Program, 7
year-round education, rationale for, 649
Young, Michael, 5, 435, 437, 440

Z

Zanger, Virginia Vogel, 55
Zloczower, Abraham, 331
Zwerling, L. Steven, 452